LOCAL GOVERNMENT LAW

CASES AND MATERIALS

Sixth Edition

■ ■ ■

by

Gerald E. Frug

Louis D. Brandeis Professor of Law,
Harvard University

Richard T. Ford

George E. Osborne Professor of Law,
Stanford University

David J. Barron

Judge,
U.S. Court of Appeals for the First Circuit
Visiting Professor,
Harvard Law School

AMERICAN CASEBOOK SERIES®

Mat #41615922

American Casebook Series is a trademark registered in the U.S. Patent and Trademark Office.

Printed in the United States of America

ISBN: 978-1-62810-028-0

For Charlie, Maddie, and Joseph

—Gerald E. Frug

For Marlene, Cole, and Ella

—Richard T. Ford

For Cecilia, Leo, and Jeremiah

—David J. Barron

ACKNOWLEDGMENTS

We are indebted to the following authors and publishers for their generosity in allowing us to include in this book excerpts from copyrighted materials, all of which are reprinted by permission:

Carl Abbott and the Fannie May Foundation for excerpts from Carl Abbott, The Portland Region: Where City and Suburbs Talk to Each Other—And Often Agree, Housing Policy Debate 8(1):11–51

The American Planning Association for excerpts from THE GROWING SMART LEGISLATIVE GUIDEBOOK, (Chicago: American Planning Association, September 2002)

Michelle Wilde Anderson for excerpts from Michelle Wilde Anderson, Democratic Dissolution: Radical Experimentation in State Takeovers of Local Governments, 39 Fordham L. J. 577 (2012)

Michelle Wilde Anderson and the Yale Law Journal for excerpts from Michelle Wilde Anderson, Dissolving Cities, 121 Yale L. J. 1364 (2012) and for Michelle Wilde Anderson, The New Minimal Cities, 123 Yale L.J. 1118 (2014)

Keith Aoki and The Fordham Urban Law Journal for excerpts from Keith Aoki, Race, Space, and Place: The Relation Between Architectural Modernism, Post–Modernism, Urban Planning, and Gentrification, 20 Fordham Urb. L. J. 699 (1993)

Yale University Press for excerpts from Philippe Aries, The Family and The City in the Old World and the New, contained in V. Tufte and B. Myerhoff, eds., CHANGING IMAGES OF THE FAMILY, copyright © 1979 by Yale University Press

Benjamin Barber and The University of California Press for excerpts from Benjamin Barber, STRONG DEMOCRACY: PARTICIPATORY POLITICS FOR A NEW AGE, copyright © 1984 by The Regents of the University of California

University of Pennsylvania Law Review for excerpts from David Barron, The Promise of Cooley's City: Traces of Local Constitutionalism, 147 U. Pa. L. Rev. 487 (1999)

Rosalyn Baxandall, Elizabeth Ewen and Perseus Books Group for excerpts from PICTURE WINDOWS: HOW THE SUBURBS HAPPENED by Rosalyn Baxandall and Elizabeth Ewen, copyright © 2000 by Rosalyn Baxandall and Elizabeth Ewen, reprinted by permission of Basic Books, a member of Perseus Books, L.L.C.

Derrick Bell and The Washington Law Review for excerpts from Derrick Bell, The Referendum: Democracy's Barrier to Racial Equality, 54 Wash. L. Rev. 1 (1978)

Fred Bosselman, Nancy Stroud, and The Nova Law Journal for excerpts from Fred Bosselman and Nancy Stroud, Mandatory Tithes: The Legality of Land Development Linkage, 9 Nova L.J. 383 (1985)

Farrar, Straus and Giroux for excerpts from "Cities for Sale: Merchandising History at South Street Seaport" by M. Christine Boyer, excerpts from "See You in Disneyland" by Michael Sorkin, and excepts from "Silicon Valley Mystery House" by Langdon Winner from VARIATIONS ON A THEME PARK: THE NEW AMERICAN CITY AND THE END OF PUBLIC SPACE edited by Michael Sorkin. Compilation copyright © 1992 by Michael Sorkin. Copyright © 1992 by M. Christine Boyer. Copyright © 1992 by Langdon Winner. Reprinted by permission of Hill and Wang, a division of Farrar, Straus and Giroux, LLC

Richard Briffault and The Columbia Law Review for excerpts from Richard Briffault, Our Localism: Part I—The Structure of Local Government Law, 90 Col. L. Rev. 1 (1990), and Richard Briffault, Our Localism: Part II—Localism and Legal Theory, 90 Col. L. Rev. 346 (1990)

Public Choice for excerpts from James Buchanan, Principles of Urban Fiscal Strategy, XI Public Choice 1 (1971)

Harcourt Brace Jovanovich, Inc. for excerpts from Italo Calvino, INVISIBLE CITIES, translated from the Italian by William Weaver, copyright © 1972 by Giulio Einaudi s.p.a.; translation copyright © 1974 by Harcourt Brace Jovanovich, Inc.

Sheryll Cashin and the Cornell Law Review for excerpts from Middle-Class Black Suburbs and the State of Integration, 86 Cornell L. Rev. 729 (2001)

Alfred A. Knopf, Inc. and Robert A. Caro for excerpts from Caro, THE POWER BROKER, copyright © 1974 by Robert A. Caro

John Chubb, Terry Moe, and the Brookings Institution Press for excerpts from John Chubb and Terry Moe, POLITICS, MARKETS, AND AMERICA'S SCHOOLS, copyright © 1990 by The Brookings Institution

Wade Crowfoot and David Binder for excerpts from Wade Crowfoot and David Binder, District Elections in San Francisco, February, 2000 SPUR Newsletter

Robert Dahl and Yale University Press for excerpts from Robert A. Dahl, DILEMMAS IN PLURALIST DEMOCRACY, copyright © 1982 by Yale University Press

Richard DeLeon and the University Press of Kansas for excerpts from Left Coast City: Progressive Politics in San Francisco, 1975–1991, by Richard DeLeon, published by the University Press of Kansas © 1992. www.kansaspress.ku.edu

Gregg Easterbrook and the Fannie Mae Foundation for excerpts from Gregg Easterbrook, Comment on Karen A. Danielson, Robert E. Lang, and William Fulton's "Retracting Suburbia: Smart Growth and the Future of Housing," Housing Policy Debate 10(3): 541–547

Peter Eisinger and Sage Publications for excerpts from Peter Eisinger, The Politics of Bread and Circuses, 35 Urb. Affairs Rev. 316 (2000)

Robert Ellickson and University of Pennsylvania Law Review for excerpts from Robert Ellickson, Cities and Homeowners Associations, 130 U.Pa. L.Rev. 1519 (1982)

John Findlay and the University of California Press for excerpts from John Findlay, MAGIC LANDS: WESTERN CITYSCAPES AND AMERICAN CULTURE AFTER 1940, copyright © 1992 The Regents of the University of California

Basic Books, Inc. for excerpts from Robert Fishman, BOURGEOIS UTOPIAS, copyright © 1987 by Basic Books, Inc., a division of HarperCollins Publishers, Inc.

The Harvard Law Review Association for excerpts from Richard Ford, The Boundaries of Race: The Assertion of Political Space in a Critical Jurisprudence, 107 Harv. L. Rev. 1841, copyright © 1994 by The Harvard Law Review Association

Stanford Law Review for excerpts from Richard Ford, Geography and Sovereignty: Jurisdictional Formation and Racial Segregation, 49 Stan. L. Rev. 1365 (1997)

Michigan Law Review for excerpts from Richard Ford, Law's Territory (A History of Jurisdiction), 97 Mich. L. Rev. 843 (1999)

Princeton University Press for excerpts from Gerald Frug, CITY MAKING: BUILDING COMMUNITIES WITHOUT BUILDING WALLS, copyright © 1999 Princeton University Press

Archon Fung and Sage Publications for excerpts from Archon Fung and Erik Olin Wright, Deepening Democracy: Innovations in Empowered Participatory Governance, 29 Politics & Society 5 (2001)

Joel Garreau and the Doubleday Broadway Publishing Group for excerpts from Garreau, EDGE CITY: LIFE ON THE NEW FRONTIER, copyright © 1991 by Joel Garreau, reprinted by permission of Doubleday, a division of Random House, Inc.

John Gaventa and The University of Illinois Press for excerpts from Gaventa, POWER AND POWERLESSNESS: QUIESCENCE AND REBELLION IN AN APPALACHIAN VALLEY, copyright © 1980 by John Gaventa

Lani Guinier and the Virginia Law Review for excerpts from Lani Guinier, No Two Seats: The Elusive Quest for Political Equality, 77 Va. L. Rev. 1413 (1991)

Peter Hall for excerpts from Peter Hall, CITIES OF TOMORROW: AN INTELLECTUAL HISTORY OF URBAN PLANNING AND DESIGN IN THE TWENTIETH CENTURY, copyright © 1988 by Peter Hall

Kenneth Jackson and Oxford University Press for excerpts from Kenneth Jackson, CRABGRASS FRONTIER: THE SUBURBANIZATION OF THE UNITED STATES, copyright © 1985 by Oxford University Press, Inc.

Harvard University Press for excerpts from Rosabeth Kanter, COMMITMENT AND COMMUNITY, copyright © 1972 by The President and Fellows of Harvard College

Gerrit Knaap, Arthur Nelson, and the Lincoln Institute of Land Policy for excerpts from Gerrit Knaap and Arthur Nelson, THE REGULATED LANDSCAPE: LESSONS ON STATE LAND USE PLANNING FROM OREGON, copyright © 1992 Lincoln Institute of Land Policy

Robert Lang and Dawn Dhale for excerpts from RELUCTANT CITIES, Metropolitan Institute of Virginia Tech (2003)

Debra Livingston and the Columbia Law Review for excerpts from Debra Livingston, Police Discretion and the Quality of Life in Public Places: Courts, Communities, and the New Policing, 97 Colum. L. Rev. 551 (1997)

Audrey McFarlane and the Brooklyn Law Review for excerpts from Audrey McFarlane, When Inclusion Leads to Exclusion: The Uncharted Terrain of Community Participation in Economic Development, 66 Brooklyn L. Rev. 861 (2001)

Evan McKenzie and Yale University Press for excerpts from Evan McKenzie, PRIVATOPIA, copyright © 1994 by Yale University

Evan McKenzie for excerpts from Private Gated Communities in the American Urban Fabric: Emerging Trends in Their Production, Practices, and Regulation, http://tigger.uic.edu/~mckenzie/hoa.html

Frank Michelman and The Indiana Law Journal for excerpts from Frank Michelman, Political Markets and Community Self Determination, 53 Ind. L. J. 145 (1977–78)

Gary Miller and the MIT Press for excerpts from Gary Miller, CITIES BY CONTRACT: THE POLITICS OF MUNICIPAL INCORPORATION, copyright © 1981 by The Massachusetts Institute of Technology

Eric Montarti for excerpts from A Brief Lesson in Tax Increment Financing, http://hellskitchen.net/develop/FWS/TIF/IntellectualAmmunition. html

Harcourt, Inc. for excerpts from "Suburbia and Beyond" in THE CITY IN HISTORY: ITS ORIGINS, ITS TRANSFORMATION, AND ITS PROSPECTS by Lewis Mumford, copyright © 1961 and renewed 1989 by Lewis Mumford

Basic Books, Inc. and Robert Nozick for excerpts from Robert Nozick, ANARCHY, STATE AND UTOPIA, copyright © 1974 by Basic Books, Inc., a division of HarperCollins Publishers, Inc.

International Creative Management, Inc. for excerpts from David Osborne and Ted Gaebler, REINVENTING GOVERNMENT, copyright © 1992 by David Osborne and Ted Gaebler, reprinted by permission of International Creative Management, Inc.

Hanna Pitkin and Sara Shumer for excerpts from Pitkin and Shumer, On Participation, 2 democracy 43 (1992)

James Ramsey and The Academy of Political Science for excerpts from James Ramsey, Selling the New York Subway: Wild-eyed Radicalism or the Only Feasible Solution?, contained in Hanke, ed., PROSPECTS FOR PRIVATIZATION, PROCEEDINGS OF THE ACADEMY OF POLITICAL SCIENCE, vol. 36, copyright © 1987 by The Academy of Political Science

Jamin Raskin and University of Pennsylvania Law Review for excerpts from Jamin Raskin, Legal Aliens, Local Citizens: The Historical, Constitutional and Theoretical Meanings of Alien Suffrage, 141 U.Pa.L.Rev. 1391 (1993)

Laurie Reynolds and the Florida Law Review for exerpts from Laurie Reynolds, Taxes, Fees, Assessments, Dues, and the "Get What You Pay For" Model of Local Government, 56 Fla. L. Rev. 373 (2004)

David Rusk and The Johns Hopkins University Press for excerpts from David Rusk, CITIES WITHOUT SUBURBS, copyright © 1993 by The Woodrow Wilson International Center for Scholars

Saskia Sassen and Princeton University Press for excerpts from Saskia Sassen, GLOBAL CITY, copyright © 1991 by Princeton University Press

Richard Schragger and the Michigan Law Review for excerpts from Consuming Government, 101 Mich. L. Rev. 1824 (2003)

Richard Schragger for excerpts from Mobile Capital, Local Economic Regulation, and the Democratic City, 123 Harv. L. Rev. 483 (2009)

Richard Schragger and the University of Chicago Law Review for excerpts from Richard Schragger, Rethinking the Theory and Practice of Local Economic Development, 77 U. Chi. L. Rev. 311 (2010)

Gary Schwartz and the U.C.L.A. Law Review for excerpts from Gary Schwartz, The Logic of Home Rule and the Private Law Exception, 20 U.C.L.A. L. Rev. 670 (1973), copyright © 1999, The Regents of the University of California, All Rights Reserved

Jonathan Schwartz and Southern California Law Review for excerpts from Jonathan Schwartz, Prisons of Proposition 13: Sales Taxes, Property Taxes, and the Fiscalization of Municipal Land Use Decisions, 71 S.C. L. Rev. 183 (1997)

William Simon and the Wisconsin Law Review for excerpts from William Simon, The Community Economic Development Movement, 2002 Wisc. L. Rev. 377

David Sklansky and the U.C.L.A. Law Review for excerpts from David Sklansky, The Private Police, 46 U.C.L.A. L. Rev. 1165, copyright © 1999, The Regents of the University of California, All Rights Reserved

Edward Soja and Verso Books for excerpts from Edward Soja, POSTMODERN GEOGRAPHIES: THE REASSERTION OF SPACE IN CRITICAL SOCIAL THEORY, copyright © 1989 Edward W. Soja

Rick Su for excerpts from A Localist Reading of Local Immigration Regulations, 86 N.C. L. Rev. 1619 (2008) and from Local Fragmentation as Immigration Regulation, 47 Houston L. Rev. 367 (2010)

The University of Chicago Press for excerpts from Charles Tiebout, A Pure Theory of Local Expenditures, 64 J. Pol. Econ. 416 (1956)

Michael Warner and The Free Press for excerpts from THE TROUBLE WITH NORMAL: SEX, POLITICS, AND THE ETHICS OF QUEER LIFE by Michael Warner, copyright © 1999 by Michael Warner, reprinted and edited with the permission of The Free Press, a Division of Simon & Schuster, Inc.

Margaret Weir for excerpts from Coalition Building for Regionalism, from REFLECTIONS ON REGIONALISM by Bruce Katz (copyright © 2000) and for excerpts from Justice for the Poor in the New

Metropolis, from JUSTICE AND THE AMERICAN METROPOLIS, Clarissa Haywood and Todd Swanstrom (eds) 2010

Iris Young and Princeton University Press for excerpts from Iris Young, JUSTICE AND THE POLITICS OF DIFFERENCE, copyright © 1990 by Princeton University Press

Alfred A. Knopf, Inc. and Michael Zuckerman for excerpts from Michael Zuckerman, PEACEABLE KINGDOMS, copyright © 1970 by Michael Zuckerman

INTRODUCTION

Studying local government law requires thinking about the organization of American government: how much decentralization of power is possible—and desirable—in the United States? Given the way that decentralized power is now being exercised by local governments in metropolitan regions throughout the country, one could frame this question in more specific terms: can governmental power be decentralized without creating and perpetuating inequality within and between local jurisdictions? Or, put differently, how can power be decentralized in a way that would overcome existing inequality?

Decentralization has always been a controversial topic in American political life. Many people, both on the right and the left of the American political spectrum, argue that decentralization of power is an essential—and increasingly threatened—ingredient of political freedom. Genuine democratic selfgovernment, they claim, is possible only on a local level because only local government is close enough to its constituents to permit their own participation in the decision making that affects their lives. Moreover, only a local government can tailor its policies to the needs and desires of a particular community. Others, however, defend the long-standing effort in the United States to increase the power of state governments over cities and to increase the power of the federal government over both states and cities. Centralization, they contend, is necessary to regulate the effects of local decision making on outsiders, to minimize conflicts between local policies, to overcome interjurisdictional inequity, and to prevent the invasion of minority rights.

Local government law is one of the ways in which the legal system resolves this debate between proponents of decentralization and centralization. The Constitutional provisions, statutes, and cases reproduced in this casebook not only raise but seek to answer critical questions about the proper organization of governmental power: Should local government law embody a view of society that favors the decentralization of power? If so (or if not), how is the term "decentralization" defined? What specifically can (and should) be done to change the balance of power among federal, state, and local governments?

To examine the answers offered by local government law to these questions, this casebook is organized into four parts. Chapter One introduces the basic arguments for and against the decentralization of power that pervade the cases and materials found in the rest of the casebook. It also introduces the complexities involved in making a public/private distinction when power is decentralized in America—not just to cities, local public authorities, business improvement districts, and charter schools but also to homeowners associations and shopping malls. Chapter Two then addresses the question of the relationships between cities and states, between cities and the federal government, and between cities and international law. Since local governments are subject to the exercise of higher-level governments, the extent of their authority depends in large part on how this centralized power is exercised. Chapter Two thus focuses on important state law concepts, such as home rule, on issues of federal Constitutional law, such as the recent effort by the Supreme Court of the United States to limit federal power over both cities and states, and the emerging connection between cities and international organizations and among the world's cities themselves.

Chapter Three shifts the subject of inquiry to the problem of interlocal relationships. Because American metropolitan areas are divided into dozens (sometimes hundreds) of separate cities, decentralization of power requires an allocation of responsibilities not only between cities and higher levels of government but also among neighboring cities. Chapter Three focuses specifically on the relationships between central cities and suburbs—and among the suburbs—located in the same metropolitan area. It examines critical issues such as race and class segregation, inequalities of wealth, and sprawl. In doing so, it deals not only with the current legal rules that determine the nature of these relationships but also with possible changes in the existing legal structure, such as regional solutions to city-suburb conflict. Finally, Chapter Four investigates the legal relationship between city governments and their constituents. The quality of life of most Americans is significantly affected by the exercise of city power: by the ability of cities to determine the community's character through zoning and economic development policies, by the ways in which cities raise revenue and deliver city services, and by the allocation of the right to vote in local elections. Chapter Four addresses issues such as these and, by doing so, examines such cutting edge urban issues as the privatization of governmental services, crime control mechanisms ranging from community policing to private security guards, school vouchers, the cities' role in establishing immigration policy, and the transformation of areas of major central cities into urban theme parks.

This casebook, in sum, concentrates on three relationships: between cities and higher levels of government, between neighboring cities, and between cities and the people who live within their boundaries. The problems engendered by these three relationships are the basic ingredients of local government law, and the ways in which these ingredients interact helps determine the extent to which current local government law rules generate—or help to overcome—inequality.

An example of what we have in mind when we say this might be helpful. Consider two legal powers discussed below in Chapter Three: the stategranted power given many American local governments to engage in exclusionary zoning and the additional power states grant them to spend the money they raise in property taxes solely on their residents. The first of these powers allows cities to design what their communities look like and, by doing so, has enabled them to determine the types of residents that will inhabit them. The easiest way to achieve such a goal is to specify the kind of housing that will be permitted in the city and to do so in a way that makes it very expensive: limiting housing to single-family residences, requiring large lots on which they can be built, increasing the amount of space between houses, and so forth. If no apartments or houses suitable for the poor are allowed, the poor are not able to move to town. The town can therefore become what is often called an "exclusive" community. This zoning power is then accompanied by the second important legal power just mentioned: the ability of residents to treat the property within their city limits as their own property—as a resource that can be used to support the people who live within city boundaries and no one else. Since local government financing is largely dependent on the property tax in the United States, prosperous communities, once they exclude the poor, can therefore support their services in a much more lavish way than can their poorer neighbors. Indeed, if their property is worth a lot, they can raise a lot of money even with a low tax rate. In cities with low property values, on the other hand, it is impossible to raise much money even if the tax rate is very high.

For many, these two rules create a legal structure that allows people to govern themselves. By delegating these powers to local residents, the states enable them to fund their own governments and create the kind of community in which they would like to live. This perspective has considerable influence; that's why most states have enacted these two rules. From this perspective, an effort to redistribute local taxes to neighboring communities would be seen as an attempt to reallocate the wealth. And an effort to limit the exercise of the zoning power would be viewed as inviting centralized control over the character of one's own community. Besides, advocates of these rules might add, by allowing each community to offer prospective residents a package of services, priced through taxes at a certain level, neighboring cities can compete with one another and thereby enable a mobile citizenry to choose the package they prefer.

For us, however, as for many others, these two legal rules do as much to limit local power as to protect it. Together, they fuel suburban sprawl. They enable the wealthy to move to an area that excludes the poor and then spend the money raised in taxes only on themselves. Indeed, those who can afford to move across city lines can dramatically improve their life simply by leaving other people behind. Some people move to wealthy communities, if they can afford it, simply to save the money that they would have spent on the poor had they remained in a class-integrated jurisdiction. As the wealthy move to their suburbs with this cost-consciousness in mind, taking their resources with them, the cities they abandon begin to decline. As a result, people in the middle class move to their own suburbs and exclude those poorer than they are, and the central cities decline even further. In short, these two legal rules create a sprawl machine—they create a legally-generated incentive to move out of town. By offering this legally-generated incentive, they disempower the cities left behind.

The materials in all four chapters are designed to investigate how this sprawl machine is constructed by legal doctrine and the kinds of changes that could be made in legal rules in order to produce a different, more equitable, metropolitan design. They are also designed to question whether moving to a more equitable metropolitan design requires us to give up on decentralization. Could a change in the design of this sprawl machine promote local power rather than limit it? If so, what would such a change look like?

As this example illustrates, the selection and organization of topics and materials in this casebook—like in any casebook—represent only one of the many possible ways to define the relevant subject matter. Some topics have been omitted that could well have been covered in a local government law course, and others have been included even though no one before us has thought them essential. Although this kind of partiality exists in all casebooks, we want to encourage readers of this casebook to be mindful of our prejudices. Question why the materials are presented in the way they are, and consider what kinds of issues and perspectives have been omitted. We have sought to emphasize the relevance of our partiality in this casebook by including a number of excerpts from our own published work. We believe that this form of presentation alerts readers to the fact that our discussion of an issue is not the only possible way to understand it. We expect these excerpts from our work to be read critically; they are included not only to persuade but also to provoke thinking about the subject.

This casebook also includes a number of excerpts from books and articles dealing with questions of political theory, urban history, urban sociology, urban economics, and geography (as well as a few excerpts from a work of fiction). These excerpts are designed to introduce the reader to non-legal materials that illuminate—and are illuminated by—legal doctrine. We have included relatively substantial excerpts from these works in the belief that local government law can be understood only in the context of the historical development of cities in America and in terms of the variety of non-legal theories that the legal doctrines governing city power have relied on and incorporated. Not only are non-legal materials scattered throughout the casebook but a special section of each chapter of the casebook is devoted entirely to democratic theory. These sections are designed to suggest criticisms of the conceptions of democracy found in local government law and to offer ways of thinking about alternatives to these conceptions. To evaluate the possible ways of decentralizing power in America, it is important to understand not only the versions of democracy that the law has embraced but also the versions that, although possible, the law has rejected.

Finally, we need to make a technical point about the presentation of the materials. Citations and footnotes have been omitted from both the cases and the work of commentators—and concurring and dissenting opinions have been omitted from the cases—without specifically noting these omissions. When footnotes are included in the materials, they retain the original numbering.

GERALD E. FRUG

RICHARD T. FORD

DAVID J. BARRON

July 2014

SUMMARY OF CONTENTS

TABLE OF CONTENTS

TABLE OF CASES

The principal cases are in bold type.

TABLE OF AUTHORITIES

LOCAL GOVERNMENT LAW

CASES AND MATERIALS

Sixth Edition

[T]he strength of free nations resides in the local community. Local institutions are to liberty what primary schools are to science; they bring it within people's reach, they teach people to use and enjoy it. Without local institutions, a nation may establish a free government, but it cannot have the spirit of liberty. Transient passions, momentary interests, the chance of circumstances, may create the external forms of independence; but the despotic tendency which has been repressed into the interior of the social body will, sooner or later, appear on the surface.

Alexis de Tocqueville,

Democracy in America

[In a] pure democracy, by which I mean a society consisting of a small number of citizens, who assemble and administer the government in person, * * * [a] common passion or interest will, in almost every case, be felt by a majority of the whole; a communication and concert results from the form of government itself; and there is nothing to check the inducements to sacrifice the weaker party or an obnoxious individual. Hence it is that such democracies have ever been spectacles of turbulence and contention; have ever been found incompatible with personal security or the rights of property; and have in general been as short in their lives as they have been violent in their deaths.

The Federalist No. 10

(Madison)

CHAPTER 1

INTRODUCTION TO THE PROBLEMS OF DECENTRALIZATION

■ ■ ■

A. DECENTRALIZATION OF POWER TO LOCAL GOVERNMENT: THE PROS AND CONS

Debates about the definition and desirability of decentralizing political power have taken place repeatedly throughout American history. The argument over the ratification of the Constitution of the United States was itself largely an argument over its impact on state and local power. Proponents of the Constitution argued that the Constitution properly strengthened the authority of the national government, while its opponents, the anti-federalists, argued that the Constitution threatened the primacy of the states and, as a consequence, endangered the preservation of individual liberty.[1] Since the adoption of the Constitution, debates about decentralization have recurred frequently, for example in the struggle between the Whigs and the Jacksonians in the 1830s, in the conflict over the extension of slavery in the territories in the 1850s, in the controversy over Progressivism at the beginning of the 20th century, and in the arguments over the enactment of Civil Rights legislation in the 1960s.[2]

---

[1] For the federalists' argument, see The Federalist Papers (Clinton Rossiter ed. 1999); for the anti-federalists' argument, see The Complete Anti-Federalist (Herbert Storing ed. 1981); Herbert Storing, What The Anti Federalists Were For (1981). Selections from both sides of the debate have been conveniently collected in The American Constitution: For and Against (J.R. Pole ed. 1987). For an overview of the historical debate, see Gordon Wood, Federalism from the Bottom Up, 78 U. Chi. L. Rev. 705 (2011); Alison LaCroix, The Ideological Origins of American Federalism (2010); Gordon Wood, The Creation of the American Republic 1776–1787 (1987). For more recent versions of the federalist/anti-federalist argument, see, e.g., Larry Kramer, Putting the Politics Back into The Political Safeguards of Federalism, 100 Colum. L. Rev. 215 (2000); Alan Brinkley et al., New Federalist Papers: Essays in the Defense of the Constitution (1997); Michael McConnell, Federalism: Evaluating the Founders' Design, 54 U.Chi.L.Rev. 1484, 1491–1511 (1987).

[2] For a discussion of these debates, see, e.g., William Novak, The People's Welfare: Law and Regulation in Nineteenth-Century America (1996); John Dittmer, Local People: The Struggle for Civil Rights in Mississippi (1994); Thomas Brown, Politics and Statesmanship: Essays on the American Whig Party (1985); Daniel Walker Howe, The Political Culture of the American Whigs (1979); Social Theories of Jacksonian Democracy: Representative Writings of the Period (J. Blau ed. 1954); Eric Foner, Free Soil, Free Labor, Free Men: The Ideology of the Republican Party Before the Civil War (1970) and Politics and Ideology in the Age of the Civil War (1980); George Mowry, The Era of Theodore Roosevelt 1900–1912 (1958); Arthur Stanley Link, Woodrow Wilson and the Progressive Era (1954); and Gabriel Kolko, The Triumph of Conservatism (1963).

No participant in these recurrent debates about decentralization contended that governmental power in the United States should be fully centralized or fully decentralized. Everyone supported a role both for the national government and for state and local governments. The controversies instead concerned the relative importance of centralized or decentralized authority; it was in the process of articulating the comparative value of concentrating and dispersing power that a number of classic arguments for and against decentralization were developed. These arguments pervade local government law; indeed, local government law is one of the products of, as well as one of the contributors to, this debate. It is important here at the outset, therefore, to become familiar with the arguments about the values and dangers of decentralization.

Two important contributions to the debate over decentralization are excerpted below. The first is an excerpt from Alexis de Tocqueville's Democracy in America, an eloquent defense of decentralization of power to local government. The second is an excerpt from James Madison's Federalist 10, a highly influential (perhaps *the* most influential) argument against decentralization of power. When reading these excerpts, try to identify both the appeal and the fear of decentralization of decisionmaking authority that the authors articulate. How does each side of the argument answer the points made by the other side?

The final excerpt is from the Supreme Court's decision in Romer v. Evans, which confronts this debate in the context of gay rights. Is Justice Scalia just echoing Madison in Federalist 10 when he writes in his *Romer* dissent that voters in Colorado were legitimately seeking to "counter both the geographic concentration and the disproportionate political power of homosexuals by . . . resolving the controversy [over gay rights] at the statewide level . . ."? Or does Justice Kennedy better characterize the situation when he portrays the local adoption of antidiscrimination ordinances as part of the process that helps to "constitute ordinary civic life in a free society"?[3] Should local governments always be permitted to determine the scope of antidiscrimination law, even if the state government would provide more protection? Should local governments never be allowed to determine the scope of anti-discrimination laws, leaving that power solely to the state government? If "never" and "always" are both problematic answers, when should local governments be permitted to make antidiscrimination policy?

Our inclusion in this casebook of works such as Tocqueville's and Madison's assumes a significant relationship between political theory and legal doctrine. The chapter reproduced below from Invisible Cities, a novel by the great Italian writer Italo Calvino, does not directly address the question why studying theory is important to understanding local

---

[3]   For an analysis of the 'localization of sexuality" in the United States, see Yishai Blank, The Geography of Sexuality, 90 N.C. L. Rev. 955 (2012).

government law. But a consideration of the relationship that Calvino suggests between Eudoxia's carpet and the city in which it is housed might be helpful in thinking about the issue.

ITALO CALVINO, INVISIBLE CITIES
Pp. 96–97 (1974).

In Eudoxia, which spreads both upward and down, with winding alleys, steps, dead ends, hovels, a carpet is preserved in which you can observe the city's true form. At first sight nothing seems to resemble Eudoxia less than the design of that carpet, laid out in symmetrical motives whose patterns are repeated along straight and circular lines, interwoven with brilliantly colored spires, in a repetition that can be followed throughout the whole woof. But if you pause and examine it carefully, you become convinced that each place in the carpet corresponds to a place in the city and all the things contained in the city are included in the design, arranged according to their true relationship, which escapes your eye distracted by the bustle, the throngs, the shoving. All of Eudoxia's confusion, the mules' braying, the lampblack stains, the fish smell is what is evident in the incomplete perspective you grasp; but the carpet proves that there is a point from which the city shows its true proportions, the geometrical scheme implicit in its every, tiniest detail.

It is easy to get lost in Eudoxia: but when you concentrate and stare at the carpet, you recognize the street you were seeking in a crimson or indigo or magenta thread which, in a wide loop, brings you to the purple enclosure that is your real destination. Every inhabitant of Eudoxia compares the carpet's immobile order with his own image of the city, an anguish of his own, and each can find, concealed among the arabesques, an answer, the story of his life, the twists of fate.

An oracle was questioned about the mysterious bond between two objects so dissimilar as the carpet and the city. One of the two objects—the oracle replied—has the form the gods gave the starry sky and the orbits in which the worlds revolve; the other is an approximate reflection, like every human creation.

For some time the augurs had been sure that the carpet's harmonious pattern was of divine origin. The oracle was interpreted in this sense, arousing no controversy. But you could, similarly, come to the opposite conclusion: that the true map of the universe is the city of Eudoxia, just as it is, a stain that spreads out shapelessly, with crooked streets, houses that crumble one upon the other amid clouds of dust, fires, screams in the darkness.

ALEXIS DE TOCQUEVILLE, DEMOCRACY IN AMERICA

Volume 1, Pp. 74–76, 112–119, 302–304, 310, 313–332.
(F. Bowen ed., 1863, revised and edited).

It is not by accident that I examine the town first. The town is the only association which is so perfectly natural, that, wherever people come together, it seems to constitute itself.

Communal society, then, exists in all nations, whatever their laws and customs may be: it is man who makes monarchies and establishes republics, but the town seems to come directly from the hand of God. But although towns have existed as long as man, communal freedom is a rare and fragile thing. A nation can always establish great political assemblies, because it generally contains a certain number of individuals fitted by their talents, if not by their habits, for the direction of affairs. The town, on the contrary, is composed of coarser materials, which are less easily fashioned by the legislator. The difficulty of establishing its independence increases rather than diminishes with the increasing intelligence of the people. A highly civilized community can hardly tolerate a town's independence, is disgusted at its numerous blunders, and is apt to despair of success before the experiment is completed. Of all forms of liberty, that of the town, which is established with so much difficulty, is least of all protected against the encroachments of power. The institutions of a local community can hardly struggle against a strong and enterprising government on their own, and they cannot defend themselves with success unless they are identified with the customs of the nation and supported by public opinion. Thus, until local freedom has become part of the culture of a people, it is easily destroyed; and it can become part of the culture only after long existence in law. Communal freedom is not the fruit of human effort; it is rarely created; it somehow gives birth to itself. It develops almost in secret in the midst of a semi-barbarous state of society. The constant action of laws and national habits, peculiar circumstances, and, above all, time, may consolidate it; but there is certainly no nation on the continent of Europe which has experienced its advantages. Yet the strength of free nations resides in the local community. Local institutions are to liberty what primary schools are to science; they bring it within people's reach, they teach people how to use and enjoy it. Without local institutions, a nation may establish a free government, but it cannot have the spirit of liberty. Transient passions, momentary interests, or the chance of circumstances, may create the external forms of independence; but the despotic tendency which has been repressed into the interior of the social body, will, sooner or later, reappear on the surface. * * *

The partisans of centralization in Europe claim that the government can administer the affairs of each locality better than the citizens could for themselves: this may be true, when the central power is enlightened, and the local authorities are ignorant; when it is alert, and they are slow; when it is accustomed to act, and they to obey. Indeed, it is evident that this double tendency must grow with the growth of centralization, and that the readiness of the one and the incapacity of the others must become more and more prominent. But I deny that it is so, when the people are as enlightened, as awake to their interests, and as accustomed to reflect on them, as the Americans are. I am persuaded, on the contrary, that, in this case, the collective strength of the citizens will always more powerfully produce social welfare than the authority of the government. I know it is difficult to point out with certainty the means of arousing a sleeping population, and of giving it passions and knowledge which it does not possess; it is, I am well aware, an arduous task to persuade men to busy themselves about their own affairs. It would frequently be easier to interest them in the details of court etiquette, than in the repairs of their common dwelling. But whenever a central administration tries completely to supersede the persons most interested, I believe that it is either misled, or wants to mislead. However enlightened and skillful a central power may be, it cannot of itself embrace all the details of the life of a great nation. Such an achievement exceeds the powers of man. And when it attempts unaided to create and set in motion so many complicated springs, it must submit to a very imperfect result, or exhaust itself in futile efforts.

Centralization easily succeeds, indeed, in subjecting the external actions of men to a certain uniformity, which we come at last to love for its own sake, independently of the objects to which it is applied, like those devotees who worship the statue, and forget the deity it represents. Centralization imparts without difficulty an admirable regularity to the routine of business; provides skillfully for the details of social control; represses small disorders and petty misdemeanors; maintains society in a *statu quo* alike secure from improvement and decline; and perpetuates a drowsy regularity in the conduct of affairs, which the heads of the administration are apt to call good order and public tranquillity; in short, it excels in prevention, but not in action. Its force deserts it, when society is to be profoundly moved, or accelerated in its course; and if once the co-operation of private citizens is necessary to the furtherance of its measures, the secret of its impotence is disclosed. Sometimes the centralized power, in its despair, invokes the assistance of the citizens; it says to them: "You shall act just as I please, as much as I please, and in the direction which I please. You are to take charge of the details, without aspiring to guide the system; you are to work in darkness; and afterwards you may judge my work by its results." These are not the conditions on which the alliance of the human will is to be obtained; it must be free in its style, and responsible for its acts, or (such is the constitution of man) the citizen had rather remain a passive spectator, than a dependent actor, in schemes with which he is unacquainted. * * *

Granting, for an instant, that the villages and counties of the United States would be more usefully governed by a distant central authority than by functionaries taken from among them,—admitting, for the sake of argument, that there would be more security in America, and the resources of society would be better employed there, if the whole administration centered in a single arm,—still the *political* advantages which the Americans derive from their decentralized system would induce me to prefer it to the contrary plan. It profits me but little, after all, that a vigilant authority always protects the tranquillity of my pleasures, and constantly averts all dangers from my path, without my care or concern, if this same authority is the absolute master of my liberty and my life, and if it so monopolizes movement and life, that when it languishes everything languishes around it, that when it sleeps everything must sleep, and that when it dies the state itself must perish.

There are countries in Europe, where the natives consider themselves as a kind of settlers, indifferent to the fate of the spot which they inhabit. The greatest changes are effected there without their concurrence, and (unless chance may have apprised them of the event) without their knowledge; nay, more, the condition of his village, the policing of his street, the repairs of the church or the parsonage, do not concern him; for he looks upon all these things as unconnected with himself, and as the property of a powerful stranger whom he calls the government. He has only a life-interest in these possessions, without the spirit of ownership or any ideas of improvement. This want of interest in his own affairs goes so far, that if his own safety or that of his children is at last endangered, instead of trying to avert the peril, he will fold his arms, and wait till the whole nation comes to his aid. This man, who has so completely sacrificed his own free will, does not, more than any other person, love obedience; he cowers, it is true, before the pettiest officer; but he braves the law with the spirit of a conquered foe, as soon as its superior force is withdrawn: he perpetually oscillates between servitude and license.

When a nation has arrived at this state, it must either change its customs and its laws, or perish; for the source of public virtues is dried up; and though it may contain subjects, it has no citizens. * * *

It is not the *administrative,* but the *political* effects of decentralization, that I most admire in America. In the United States, the interests of the country are everywhere kept in view; they are an object of solicitude from the village to the entire Union, and every citizen is as warmly attached to them as if they were his own. He takes pride in the glory of his nation; he boasts of its success, to which he conceives himself to have contributed; and he rejoices in the general prosperity by which he profits. The feeling he entertains toward the state is analogous to that which unites him to his family, and it is by a kind of selfishness that he interests himself in the welfare of his country.

To the European, a public official represents a superior force; to an American, he represents right. In America, then, it may be said that no one renders obedience to man, but to justice and to law. If the opinion which the citizen entertains of himself is exaggerated, it is at least salutary; he unhesitatingly confides in his own powers, which appear to him to be all-sufficient. When a private individual considers some enterprise, however directly connected it may be with the welfare of society, he never thinks of soliciting the co-operation of the government; but he publishes his plan, offers to execute it, courts the assistance of other individuals, and struggles mightily against all obstacles. Undoubtedly he is often less successful than the state might have been in his position; but in the end, the sum of these private undertakings far exceeds all that the government could have done.

As the administrative authority is within the reach of the citizens, whom in some degree it represents, it excites neither their jealousy nor hatred: as its resources are limited, every one feels that he must not rely solely on its aid. Thus, when the administration thinks fit to act within its own limits, it is not abandoned to itself, as in Europe; the duties of private citizens are not supposed to have lapsed because the state has come into action; but every one is ready, on the contrary, to guide and support it. This action of individuals, joined to that of the public authorities, frequently accomplishes what the most energetic centralized administration would be unable to do. * * *

Aristocracies are infinitely more expert in the science of legislation than democracies ever can be. They are possessed of a self-control which protects them from the errors of temporary excitement; and they form far-reaching designs, which they know how to nurture until a favorable opportunity arrives. Aristocratic government proceeds with the dexterity of art; it understands how to make the collective force of all its laws converge at the same time to a given point. Such is not the case with democracies, whose laws are almost always ineffective or inopportune. The means of democracy are therefore more imperfect than those of aristocracy, and the measures which it unwittingly adopts are frequently opposed to its own cause; but the object it has in view is more useful.

Let us now imagine a community so organized by nature, or by its constitution, that it can support the transitory action of bad laws, and that it can await, without destruction, the *general tendency* of its legislation: we shall then conceive how a democratic government, notwithstanding its faults, may be best fitted to produce the prosperity of this community. This is precisely what has occurred in the United States; and I repeat, what I have before remarked, that the great advantage of the Americans consists in their being able to commit faults which they may afterwards repair. * * *

At the present time, civic spirit seems to me to be inseparable from the exercise of political rights; and I think that the number of citizens will be found to increase or decrease in Europe in proportion as those rights are extended.

How does it happen that in the United States, where the inhabitants arrived yesterday upon the soil which they now occupy, and brought neither customs nor traditions with them there; where they met each other for the first time with no previous acquaintance; where, in short, the instinctive love of country can scarcely exist;—how does it happen that every one takes as zealous an interest in the affairs of his township, his county, and the whole State, as if they were his own? It is because every one, in his sphere, takes an active part in the government of society.

The common man in the United States understands the influence exercised by the general prosperity upon his own welfare; simple as this observation is, it is too rarely made by the people. Besides, he usually considers this prosperity as his own achievement. The citizen looks upon the fortune of the public as his own, and he labors for the good of the State, not merely from a sense of pride or duty, but from what I dare to call greed. * * *

Democratic government brings the notion of political rights to the level of the humblest citizens, just as the dissemination of wealth brings the notion of property within the reach of all men; to my mind, this is one of its greatest advantages. I do not say it is easy to teach men how to exercise political rights; but I maintain that, when it is possible, the effects which result from it are highly important; and I add, that, if there ever was a time at which such an attempt ought to be made, that time is now. Do you not see that religious belief is shaken, and the divine notion of right is declining?—that morality is debased, and the notion of moral right is therefore fading away? Argument is substituted for faith, and calculation for the impulses of sentiment. If, in the midst of this general disruption, you do not succeed in connecting the notion of right with that of private interest, which is the only immutable point in the human heart, what means will you have of governing the world except by fear? When I am told that the laws are weak and the people are turbulent, that passions are excited and the authority of virtue is paralyzed, and therefore no measures must be taken to increase the rights of the democracy, I reply, that, for these very reasons, some measures of the kind ought to be taken; and I believe that governments are still more interested in taking them than society at large, for governments may perish, but society cannot die. * * *

It is not always feasible to consult the whole people, either directly or indirectly, in the formation of the law; but it cannot be denied that, when this is possible, the authority of the law is greatly increased. This popular origin, which impairs the excellence and the wisdom of legislation, contributes much to increase its power. There is an amazing strength in the expression of the will of a whole people; and when it declares itself, even the imagination of those who would wish to contest it is overawed. The truth of this fact is well known by parties; and they consequently strive to make out a majority whenever they can. If they have not the greater number of voters on their side, they assert that the true majority abstained from voting; and if they are foiled even there, they have recourse to those persons who had no right to vote.

In the United States, except slaves, servants, and paupers supported by the towns, there is no class of persons who do not exercise the elective franchise, and who do not indirectly contribute to make the laws. Those who wish to attack the laws must consequently either change the opinion of the nation, or trample upon its decision.

A second reason, which is still more direct and weighty, may be adduced: in the United States, every one is personally interested in enforcing the obedience of the whole community to the law; for as the minority may shortly rally the majority to its principles, it is interested in professing that respect for the decrees of the legislator which it may soon have occasion to claim for its own. However annoying an enactment may be, the citizen of the United States complies with it, not only because it is the work of the majority, but because it is his own, and he regards it as a contract to which he is himself a party.

In the United States, then, that numerous and turbulent multitude does not exist, who, regarding the law as their natural enemy, look upon it with fear and distrust. It is impossible, on the contrary, not to perceive that all classes display the utmost reliance upon the legislation of their country, and are attached to it by a kind of paternal love.

I am wrong, however, in saying all classes; for as, in America, the European scale of authority is inverted, the wealthy are there placed in a position analogous to that of the poor in the Old World, and it is the rich who frequently look upon the law with suspicion. I have already observed that the advantage of democracy is not, as has been sometimes asserted, that it protects the interests of all, but simply that it protects those of the majority. In the United States, where the poor rule, the rich have always something to fear from the abuse of their power. This natural anxiety of the rich may produce a secret dissatisfaction; but society is not disturbed by it, for the same reason which withholds the confidence of the rich from the legislative authority, makes them obey its mandates: their wealth, which prevents them from making the law, prevents them from withstanding it. In civilized nations, only those who have nothing to lose ever revolt; and if the laws of a democracy are not always worthy of respect, they are always respected; for those who usually infringe the laws cannot fail to obey those which they have themselves made, and by which they are benefited; and the citizens who might be interested in breaking them are induced, by their character and station, to submit to the decisions of the legislature, whatever they may be. Besides, the people in America obey the law, not only because it is their work, but because it may be changed if by any chance it is harmful; a law is observed because, first, it is a self-imposed evil, and, secondly, it is an evil of transient duration. * * *

On passing from a free country into one which is not free, the traveller is struck by the change; in the former, all is bustle and activity; in the latter, everything seems calm and motionless. In the one, amelioration and progress are the only topics; in the other, it seems as if the community wished only to repose in the enjoyment of advantages already acquired. Nevertheless, the country which exerts itself so strenuously to become happy, is generally more wealthy and prosperous than that which appears so contented with its lot; and when we compare them, we can scarcely conceive how so many new wants are daily felt in the former, while so few seem to exist in the latter.

If this remark is applicable to those free countries which have preserved monarchical forms and aristocratic institutions, it is still more so to democratic republics. In these States, it is not a portion only of the people who endeavor to improve the state of society, but the whole community is engaged in the task; and it is not the needs and convenience of a single class for which provision is to be made, but the needs and convenience of all classes at once.

It is not impossible to conceive the surprising liberty which the Americans enjoy; some idea may likewise be formed of their extreme equality; but the political activity which pervades the United States must be seen in order to be understood. No sooner do you set foot upon American ground, than you are stunned by a kind of tumult; a confused clamor is heard on every side; and a thousand simultaneous voices demand the satisfaction of their social wants. Everything is in motion around you; here, the people of one quarter of a town meet to decide upon the building of a church; there, the election of a representative is going on; a little further, the delegates of a district are rushing to the town in order to consult upon some local improvements; in another place, the laborers of a village quit their ploughs to deliberate upon the project of a road or a public school. Meetings are called for the sole purpose of declaring their disapproval of the conduct of the government; while in other assemblies, citizens salute the authorities of the day as the fathers of their country. Societies are formed which regard drunkenness as the principal cause of the evils of the state, and solemnly bind themselves to give an example of temperance.

The great political agitation of American legislative bodies, which is the only one that attracts the attention of foreigners, is a mere episode, or a sort of continuation, of that universal movement which originates in the lowest ranks of the people, and extends successively to all the classes of citizens. It is impossible to spend more effort in the pursuit of happiness.

It is hard to describe the place political concerns occupy in the life of a citizen of the United States; to involve himself in the government of society and to talk about it is his most important business and, so to speak, the only pleasure an American knows. This feeling pervades the most trifling habits of life; even the women frequently attend public meetings, and listen to political harangues as an escape from household troubles. Debating clubs are, to a certain extent, a substitute for theatrical entertainment: an American does not know how to converse, he argues; he does not speak, he holds forth. He speaks to you as if he were addressing a meeting; and if he happens to get excited, he will say "Gentlemen" to the person with whom he is conversing.

In some countries, the inhabitants only accept with a sort of repugnance the political rights which the law gives them; it would seem that they set too high a value upon their time to spend it on the interests of the community; and they shut themselves up in a narrow selfishness, marked out by four ditches topped by hedges. But if an American were condemned to confine his activity to his own affairs, he would be robbed of one half of his existence; he would feel an immense void in the life which he is accustomed to lead, and he would become incredibly unhappy. I am persuaded that, if ever a despotism should be established in America, it will be more difficult to overcome the habits which freedom has formed, than to conquer the love of freedom itself.

This ceaseless agitation which democratic government has introduced into the political world passes into civil society. I am not sure that, upon the whole, this is not the greatest advantage of democracy; and I am less inclined to applaud it for what it does, than for what it causes to be done.

It is incontestable that the people frequently conduct public business very poorly; but it is impossible that the people should take part in public business without extending the circle of their ideas and without their spirit emerging from the rut of ordinary routine. The common man who participates in the government of society acquires a certain degree of self-respect; and as he possesses authority, he can command the services of minds more enlightened than his own. Constant efforts are made to enlist his support, and, in seeking to deceive him in a thousand ways, they really enlighten him. He takes a part in political undertakings which he did not originate, but which give him a taste for undertakings of the kind. New improvements are daily pointed out to him in the common property, and this gives him the desire of improving that property which is his own. He is perhaps neither happier nor better than those who came before him, but he is better informed and more active. I have no doubt that the democratic institutions of the United States, joined to the physical constitution of the country, are the cause (not the direct, as is so often asserted, but the indirect cause) of the prodigious commercial activity of the inhabitants. It is not created by the laws, but the people learn how to promote it by the experience derived from making the laws.

When the opponents of democracy assert that a single man performs what he undertakes better than the government of all, it appears to me that they are right. The government of an individual, supposing an equality of knowledge on either side, is more consistent, more persevering, more uniform, and more accurate in details, than that of a multitude, and it selects with more discrimination the men whom it employs. If any deny this, they have never seen a democratic government, or have judged upon partial evidence. It is true that, even when local circumstances and the dispositions of the people allow democratic institutions to exist, they do not display a regular and methodical system of government. Democratic liberty is far from accomplishing all its projects with the skill of an adroit despotism. It frequently abandons them before they have borne their fruits, or risks them when the consequences may be dangerous; but in the end, it produces more than any absolute government; if it does fewer things well, it does a greater number of things. Under its sway, the grandeur is not in what the public administration does, but in what is done without it or outside of it. Democracy does not give the people the most skillful government, but it produces what the ablest governments are frequently unable to create; namely, an all-pervading and restless activity, a superabundant force, and an energy which is inseparable from it, and which may, however unfavorable circumstances may be, produce wonders. These are the true advantages of democracy. * * *

THE FEDERALIST
Number 10 (Madison).

Among the numerous advantages promised by a well-constructed Union, none deserves to be more accurately developed than its tendency to break and control the violence of faction. The friend of popular governments never finds himself so much alarmed for their character and fate as when he contemplates their propensity to this dangerous vice. He will not fail, therefore, to set a due value on any plan which, without violating the principles to which he is attached, provides a proper cure for it. The instability, injustice, and confusion introduced into the public councils, have, in truth, been the mortal diseases under which popular governments have everywhere perished; as they continue to be the favourite and fruitful topics from which the adversaries to liberty derive their most specious declamations. The valuable improvements made by the American constitutions on the popular models, both ancient and modern, cannot certainly be too much admired; but it would be an unwarrantable partiality, to contend that they have as effectually obviated the danger on this side, as was wished and expected. Complaints are everywhere heard from our most considerate and virtuous citizens, equally the friends of public and private faith, and of public and personal liberty, that our governments are too unstable, that the public good is disregarded in the conflicts of rival parties, and that measures are too often decided, not according to the rules of justice and the rights of the minor party, but by the superior force of an interested and overbearing majority. However anxiously we may wish that these complaints had no foundation, the evidence of known facts will not permit us to deny that they are in some degree true. * * *

By a faction, I understand a number of citizens, whether amounting to a majority or minority of the whole, who are united and actuated by some common impulse of passion, or of interest, adverse to the rights of other citizens, or to the permanent and aggregate interests of the community.

There are two methods of curing the mischiefs of faction: the one, by removing its causes; the other, by controlling its effects.

There are again two methods of removing the causes of faction: the one, by destroying the liberty which is essential to its existence; the other, by giving to every citizen the same opinions, the same passions, and the same interests.

It could never be more truly said than of the first remedy, that it was worse than the disease. Liberty is to faction what air is to fire, an aliment without which it instantly expires. But it could not be less folly to abolish liberty, which is essential to political life, because it nourishes faction, than it would be to wish the annihilation of air, which is essential to animal life, because it imparts to fire its destructive agency.

The second expedient is as impracticable as the first would be unwise. As long as the reason of man continues fallible, and he is at liberty to exercise it, different opinions will be formed. As long as the connection subsists between his reason and his self-love, his opinions and his passions will have a reciprocal influence on each other; and the former will be objects to which the latter will attach themselves. The diversity in the faculties of men, from which the rights of property originate, is not less an insuperable obstacle to a uniformity of interests. The protection of these faculties is the first object of government. From the protection of different and unequal faculties of acquiring property, the possession of different degrees and kinds of property immediately results; and from the influence of these on the sentiments and views of the respective proprietors, ensues a division of the society into different interests and parties.

* * * The regulation of these various and interfering interests forms the principal task of modern legislation, and involves the spirit of party and faction, in the necessary and ordinary operations of the government.

No man is allowed to be a judge in his own cause, because his interest would certainly bias his judgment, and, not improbably, corrupt his integrity. With equal, nay, with greater reason, a body of men are unfit to be both judges and parties at the same time; yet what are many of the most important acts of legislation but so many judicial determinations, not indeed concerning the rights of single persons, but concerning the rights of large bodies of citizens? And what are the different classes of legislators but advocates and parties to the causes which they determine? Is a law proposed concerning private debts? It is a question to which the creditors are parties on one side and the debtors on the other. Justice ought to hold the balance between them. Yet the parties are, and must be, themselves the judges; and the most numerous party, or, in other words, the most powerful faction must be expected to prevail. Shall domestic manufactures be encouraged, and in what degree, by restrictions on foreign manufactures? are questions which would be differently decided by the landed and the manufacturing classes, and probably by neither with a sole regard to justice and the public good. The apportionment of taxes on the various descriptions of property is an act which seems to require the most exact impartiality; yet there is, perhaps, no legislative act in which greater opportunity and temptation are given to a predominant party to trample on the rules of justice. Every shilling with which they overburden the inferior number, is a shilling saved to their own pockets.

It is in vain to say that enlightened statesmen will be able to adjust these clashing interests, and render them all subservient to the public good. Enlightened statesmen will not always be at the helm. Nor, in many cases, can such an adjustment be made at all without taking into view indirect and remote considerations, which will rarely prevail over the immediate interest which one party may find in disregarding the rights of another or the good of the whole.

The inference to which we are brought is, that the *causes* of faction cannot be removed, and that relief is only to be sought in the means of controlling its *effects*.

If a faction consists of less than a majority, relief is supplied by the republican principle, which enables the majority to defeat its sinister

views by regular vote. It may clog the administration, it may convulse the society; but it will be unable to execute and mask its violence under the forms of the Constitution. When a majority is included in a faction, the form of popular government, on the other hand, enables it to sacrifice to its ruling passion or interest both the public good and the rights of other citizens. To secure the public good and private rights against the danger of such a faction, and at the same time to preserve the spirit and the form of popular government, is then the great object to which our inquiries are directed. Let me add that it is the great desideratum by which this form of government can be rescued from the opprobrium under which it has so long laboured, and be recommended to the esteem and adoption of mankind.

By what means is this object obtainable? Evidently by one of two only. Either the existence of the same passion or interest in a majority at the same time must be prevented, or the majority, having such co-existent passion or interest, must be rendered, by their number and local situation, unable to concert and carry into effect schemes of oppression. If the impulse and the opportunity be suffered to coincide, we well know that neither moral nor religious motives can be relied on as an adequate control. They are not found to be such on the injustice and violence of individuals, and lose their efficacy in proportion to the number combined together, that is, in proportion as their efficacy becomes needful.

From this view of the subject it may be concluded that a pure democracy, by which I mean a society consisting of a small number of citizens, who assemble and administer the government in person, can admit of no cure for the mischiefs of faction. A common passion or interest will, in almost every case, be felt by a majority of the whole; a communication and concert results from the form of government itself; and there is nothing to check the inducements to sacrifice the weaker party or an obnoxious individual. Hence it is that such democracies have ever been spectacles of turbulence and contention; have ever been found incompatible with personal security or the rights of property; and have in general been as short in their lives as they have been violent in their deaths. Theoretic politicians, who have patronised this species of government, have erroneously supposed that by reducing mankind to a perfect equality in their political rights, they would, at the same time, be perfectly equalised and assimilated in their possessions, their opinions, and their passions.

A republic, by which I mean a government in which the scheme of representation takes place, opens a different prospect, and promises the cure for which we are seeking. Let us examine the points in which it varies from pure democracy, and we shall comprehend both the nature of the cure and the efficacy which it must derive from the Union.

The two great points of difference between a democracy and a republic are: first, the delegation of the government in the latter, to a small number of citizens elected by the rest; secondly, the greater number of citizens, and greater sphere of country, over which the latter may be extended.

The effect of the first difference is, on the one hand: to refine and enlarge the public views, by passing them through the medium of a chosen body of citizens, whose wisdom may best discern the true interest of their country, and whose patriotism and love of justice will be least likely to sacrifice it to temporary or partial considerations. Under such a regulation, it may well happen that the public voice, pronounced by the representatives of the people, will be more consonant to the public good than if pronounced by the people themselves, convened for the purpose. On the other hand, the effect may be inverted. Men of factious tempers, of local prejudices, or of sinister designs, may, by intrigue, by corruption, or by other means, first obtain the suffrages, and then betray the interests, of the people. The question resulting is, whether small or extensive republics are more favourable to the election of proper guardians of the public weal; and it is clearly decided in favour of the latter by two obvious considerations:

In the first place, it is to be remarked that, however small the republic may be, the representatives must be raised to a certain number, in order to guard against the cabals of a few; and that, however large it may be, they must be limited to a certain number, in order to guard against the confusion of a multitude. Hence the number of representatives in the two cases not being in proportion to that of the two constituents, and being proportionally greater in the small republic, it follows that, if the proportion of fit characters be not less in the large than in the small republic, the former will present a greater option, and consequently a greater probability of a fit choice.

In the next place, as each representative will be chosen by a greater number of citizens in the large than in the small republic, it will be more difficult for unworthy candidates to practise with success the vicious arts by which elections are too often carried; and the suffrages of the people being more free, will be more likely to centre in men who possess the most attractive merit and the most diffusive and established characters.

It must be confessed that in this, as in most other cases, there is a mean, on both sides of which inconveniences will be found to lie. By enlarging too much the number of electors, you render the representative too little acquainted with all their local circumstances and lesser interests; as by reducing it too much, you render him unduly attached to these, and too little fit to comprehend and pursue great and national objects. The federal Constitution forms a happy combination in this respect; the great and aggregate interests being referred to the national, the local and particular to the State legislatures.

The other point of difference is, the greater number of citizens and extent of territory which may be brought within the compass of republican than of democratic government; and it is this circumstance principally which renders factious combinations less to be dreaded in the former than in the latter. The smaller the society, the fewer probably will be the distinct parties and interests composing it; the fewer the distinct parties and interests, the more frequently will a majority be found of the same party; and the smaller the number of individuals composing a majority, and the smaller the compass within which they are placed, the more easily will they concert and execute their plans of oppression. Extend the sphere, and you take in a greater variety of parties and interests; you make it less probable that a majority of the whole will have a common motive to invade the rights of other citizens; or if such a common motive exists, it will be more difficult for all who feel it to discover their own strength, and to act in unison with each other. Besides other impediments, it may be remarked that, where there is a consciousness of unjust or dishonourable purposes, communication is always checked by distrust in proportion to the number whose concurrence is necessary.

Hence, it clearly appears that the same advantage which a republic has over a democracy, in controlling the effects of faction, is enjoyed by a large over a small republic—is enjoyed by the Union over the States composing it. Does the advantage consist in the substitution of representatives whose enlightened views and virtuous sentiments render them superior to local prejudices and to schemes of injustice? It will not be denied that the representation of the Union will be most likely to possess these requisite endowments. Does it consist in the greater security afforded by a greater variety of parties, against the event of any one party being able to outnumber and oppress the rest? In an equal degree does the increased variety of parties comprised within the Union increase this security. Does it, in fine, consist in the greater obstacles opposed to the concert and accomplishment of the secret wishes of an unjust and interested majority? Here, again, the extent of the Union gives it the most palpable advantage.

The influence of factious leaders may kindle a flame within their particular States, but will be unable to spread a general conflagration through the other States. A religious sect may degenerate into a political faction in a part of the Confederacy; but the variety of sects dispersed over the entire face of it must secure the national councils against any danger from that source. A rage for paper money, for an abolition of debts, for an equal division of property or for any other improper or wicked project, will be less apt to pervade the whole body of the Union than a particular member of it; in the same proportion as such a malady is more likely to taint a particular county or district, than an entire State.

In the extent and proper structure of the Union, therefore, we behold a republican remedy for the diseases most incident to republican government. And according to the degree of pleasure and pride we feel in being republicans, ought to be our zeal in cherishing the spirit and supporting the character of Federalists.

ROMER V. EVANS

Supreme Court of the United States, 1996.
517 U.S. 620, 116 S.Ct. 1620, 134 L.Ed.2d 855.

JUSTICE KENNEDY delivered the opinion of the Court. * * *

The enactment challenged in this case is an amendment to the Constitution of the State of Colorado, adopted in a 1992 statewide referendum. The parties and the state courts refer to it as "Amendment 2," its designation when submitted to the voters. The impetus for the amendment and the contentious campaign that preceded its adoption came in large part from ordinances that had been passed in various Colorado municipalities. For example, the cities of Aspen and Boulder, and the city and County of Denver each had enacted ordinances which banned discrimination in many transactions and activities, including housing, employment, education, public accommodations, and health and welfare services. * * * What gave rise to the statewide controversy was the protection the ordinances afforded to persons discriminated against by reason of their sexual orientation. Amendment 2 repeals these ordinances to the extent they prohibit discrimination on the basis of "homosexual, lesbian or bisexual orientation, conduct, practices or relationships." Colo. Const., Art. II, § 30b.

Yet Amendment 2, in explicit terms, does more than repeal or rescind these provisions. It prohibits all legislative, executive or judicial action at any level of state or local government designed to protect the named class, a class we shall refer to as homosexual persons or gays and lesbians. The amendment reads:

> "No Protected Status Based on Homosexual, Lesbian or Bisexual Orientation. Neither the State of Colorado, through any of its branches or departments, nor any of its agencies, political subdivisions, municipalities or school districts, shall enact, adopt or enforce any statute, regulation, ordinance or policy whereby homosexual, lesbian or bisexual orientation, conduct, practices or relationships shall constitute or otherwise be the basis of or entitle any person or class of persons to have or claim any minority status, quota preferences, protected status or claim of

discrimination. This Section of the Constitution shall be in all respects self-executing." * * *

Sweeping and comprehensive is the change in legal status effected by this law. So much is evident from the ordinances the Colorado Supreme Court declared would be void by operation of Amendment 2. Homosexuals, by state decree, are put in a solitary class with respect to transactions and relations in both the private and governmental spheres. The amendment withdraws from homosexuals, but no others, specific legal protection from the injuries caused by discrimination, and it forbids reinstatement of these laws and policies.

The change Amendment 2 works in the legal status of gays and lesbians in the private sphere is far reaching, both on its own terms and when considered in light of the structure and operation of modern anti-discrimination laws. That structure is well illustrated by contemporary statutes and ordinances prohibiting discrimination by providers of public accommodations. "At common law, innkeepers, smiths, and others who 'made profession of a public employment,' were prohibited from refusing, without good reason, to serve a customer." *Hurley v. Irish-American Gay, Lesbian and Bisexual Group of Boston, Inc.*, 515 U.S. 557, 571, 115 S.Ct. 2338, 2346, 132 L.Ed.2d 487 (1995). The duty was a general one and did not specify protection for particular groups. The common-law rules, however, proved insufficient in many instances, and it was settled early that the Fourteenth Amendment did not give Congress a general power to prohibit discrimination in public accommodations, *Civil Rights Cases*, 109 U.S. 3, 25, 3 S.Ct. 18, 31–32, 27 L.Ed. 835 (1883). In consequence, most States have chosen to counter discrimination by enacting detailed statutory schemes.

Colorado's state and municipal laws typify this emerging tradition of statutory protection and follow a consistent pattern. The laws first enumerate the persons or entities subject to a duty not to discriminate. The list goes well beyond the entities covered by the common law. * * * These statutes and ordinances also depart from the common law by enumerating the groups or persons within their ambit of protection. * * * [T]hey set forth an extensive catalog of traits which cannot be the basis for discrimination, including age, military status, marital status, pregnancy, parenthood, custody of a minor child, political affiliation, physical or mental disability of an individual or of his or her associates— and, in recent times, sexual orientation.

Amendment 2 bars homosexuals from securing protection against the injuries that these public-accommodations laws address. That in itself is a severe consequence, but there is more. Amendment 2, in addition, nullifies specific legal protections for this targeted class in all transactions in housing, sale of real estate, insurance, health and welfare services, private education, and employment. * * * Homosexuals are forbidden the safeguards that others enjoy or may seek without constraint. They can obtain specific protection against discrimination only by enlisting the citizenry of Colorado to amend the State Constitution or perhaps, on the State's view, by trying to pass helpful laws of general applicability. This is so no matter how local or discrete the harm, no matter how public and widespread the injury. We find nothing special in the protections Amendment 2 withholds. These are protections taken for granted by most people either because they already have them or do not need them; these are protections against exclusion from an almost limitless number of transactions and endeavors that constitute ordinary civic life in a free society. * * *

The Fourteenth Amendment's promise that no person shall be denied the equal protection of the laws must coexist with the practical necessity that most legislation classifies for one purpose or another, with resulting disadvantage to various groups or persons. We have attempted to reconcile the principle with the reality by stating that, if a law neither burdens a fundamental right nor targets a suspect class, we will uphold the legislative classification so long as it bears a rational relation to some legitimate end. * * *

Amendment 2 confounds this normal process of judicial review. It is at once too narrow and too broad. It identifies persons by a single trait and then denies them protection across the board. The resulting disqualification of a class of persons from the right to seek specific protection from the law is unprecedented in our jurisprudence. * * * It is not within our constitutional tradition to enact laws of this sort. Central both to the idea of the rule of law and to our own Constitution's guarantee of equal protection is the principle that government and each of its parts remain open on impartial terms to all who seek its assistance. * * * A second and related point is that laws of the kind now before us raise the inevitable inference that the disadvantage imposed is born of animosity toward the class of persons affected. * * *

The primary rationale the State offers for Amendment 2 is respect for other citizens' freedom of association, and in particular the liberties of landlords or employers who have personal or religious objections to homosexuality. Colorado also cites its interest in conserving resources to fight discrimination against other groups. The breadth of the amendment is so far removed from these particular justifications that we find it impossible to credit them. We cannot say that Amendment 2 is directed to any identifiable legitimate purpose or discrete objective. It is a status-based enactment divorced from any factual context from which we could discern a relationship to legitimate state interests; it is a classification of persons undertaken for its own sake, something the Equal Protection Clause does not permit. * * * We must conclude that Amendment 2

classifies homosexuals not to further a proper legislative end but to make
them unequal to everyone else. This Colorado cannot do. A State cannot
so deem a class of persons a stranger to its laws. * * *

JUSTICE SCALIA, with whom CHIEF JUSTICE REHNQUIST and JUSTICE
THOMAS join, dissenting.

The Court has mistaken a Kulturkampf for a fit of spite. The
constitutional amendment before us here is not the manifestation of a
" 'bare . . . desire to harm' " homosexuals, but is rather a modest attempt
by seemingly tolerant Coloradans to preserve traditional sexual mores
against the efforts of a politically powerful minority to revise those mores
through use of the laws. * * * Despite all of its hand wringing about the
potential effect of Amendment 2 on general antidiscrimination laws, * * *
[t]he only denial of equal treatment it contends homosexuals have
suffered is this: They may not obtain *preferential* treatment without
amending the State Constitution. That is to say, the principle underlying
the Court's opinion is that one who is accorded equal treatment under the
laws, but cannot as readily as others obtain *preferential* treatment under
the laws, has been denied equal protection of the laws. If merely stating
this alleged "equal protection" violation does not suffice to refute it, our
constitutional jurisprudence has achieved terminal silliness.

The central thesis of the Court's reasoning is that any group is
denied equal protection when, to obtain advantage (or, presumably, to
avoid disadvantage), it must have recourse to a more general and hence
more difficult level of political decisionmaking than others. The world has
never heard of such a principle, which is why the Court's opinion is so
long on emotive utterance and so short on relevant legal citation. And it
seems to me most unlikely that any multilevel democracy can function
under such a principle. For *whenever* a disadvantage is imposed, or
conferral of a benefit is prohibited, at one of the higher levels of
democratic decisionmaking (*i.e.,* by the state legislature rather than local
government, or by the people at large in the state constitution rather
than the legislature), the affected group has (under this theory) been
denied equal protection. To take the simplest of examples, consider a
state law prohibiting the award of municipal contracts to relatives of
mayors or city councilmen. Once such a law is passed, the group
composed of such relatives must, in order to get the benefit of city
contracts, persuade the state legislature—unlike all other citizens, who
need only persuade the municipality. It is ridiculous to consider this a
denial of equal protection, which is why the Court's theory is unheard of.

The Court might reply that the example I have given is *not* a denial
of equal protection only because the same "rational basis" (avoidance of
corruption) which renders constitutional the *substantive discrimination*
against relatives (*i.e.,* the fact that they alone cannot obtain city

contracts) also automatically suffices to sustain what might be called the *electoral-procedural discrimination* against them (*i.e.,* the fact that they must go to the state level to get this changed). This is of course a perfectly reasonable response, and would explain why "electoral-procedural discrimination" has not hitherto been heard of: A law that is valid in its substance is automatically valid in its level of enactment. But the Court cannot afford to make this argument, for as I shall discuss next, there is no doubt of a rational basis for the substance of the prohibition at issue here. * * * The case most relevant to the issue before us today is not even mentioned in the Court's opinion: In *Bowers v. Hardwick*, 478 U.S. 186, 106 S.Ct. 2841, 92 L.Ed.2d 140 (1986), we held that the Constitution does not prohibit what virtually all States had done from the founding of the Republic until very recent years—making homosexual conduct a crime. * * * If it is constitutionally permissible for a State to make homosexual conduct criminal, surely it is constitutionally permissible for a State to enact other laws merely *disfavoring* homosexual conduct.

But assuming that, in Amendment 2, a person of homosexual "orientation" is someone who does not engage in homosexual conduct but merely has a tendency or desire to do so, *Bowers* still suffices to establish a rational basis for the provision. If it is rational to criminalize the conduct, surely it is rational to deny special favor and protection to those with a self-avowed tendency or desire to engage in the conduct. Indeed, where criminal sanctions are not involved, homosexual "orientation" is an acceptable stand-in for homosexual conduct. * * * But though Coloradans are, as I say, *entitled* to be hostile toward homosexual conduct, the fact is that the degree of hostility reflected by Amendment 2 is the smallest conceivable. The Court's portrayal of Coloradans as a society fallen victim to pointless, hate-filled "gay-bashing" is so false as to be comical. Colorado not only is one of the 25 States that have repealed their antisodomy laws, but was among the first to do so. But the society that eliminates criminal punishment for homosexual acts does not necessarily abandon the view that homosexuality is morally wrong and socially harmful; often, abolition simply reflects the view that enforcement of such criminal laws involves unseemly intrusion into the intimate lives of citizens.

There is a problem, however, which arises when criminal sanction of homosexuality is eliminated but moral and social disapprobation of homosexuality is meant to be retained. The Court cannot be unaware of that problem; it is evident in many cities of the country, and occasionally bubbles to the surface of the news, in heated political disputes over such matters as the introduction into local schools of books teaching that homosexuality is an optional and fully acceptable "alternative life style." The problem (a problem, that is, for those who wish to retain social disapprobation of homosexuality) is that, because those who engage in homosexual conduct tend to reside in disproportionate numbers in certain communities, have high disposable income, and, of course, care about homosexual-rights issues much more ardently than the public at large, they possess political power much greater than their numbers, both locally and statewide. Quite understandably, they devote this political power to achieving not merely a grudging social toleration, but full social acceptance, of homosexuality.

By the time Coloradans were asked to vote on Amendment 2, their exposure to homosexuals' quest for social endorsement was not limited to newspaper accounts of happenings in places such as New York, Los Angeles, San Francisco, and Key West. Three Colorado cities—Aspen, Boulder, and Denver—had enacted ordinances that listed "sexual orientation" as an impermissible ground for discrimination, equating the moral disapproval of homosexual conduct with racial and religious bigotry. * * * I do not mean to be critical of these legislative successes; homosexuals are as entitled to use the legal system for reinforcement of their moral sentiments as is the rest of society. But they are subject to being countered by lawful, democratic countermeasures as well.

That is where Amendment 2 came in. It sought to counter both the geographic concentration and the disproportionate political power of homosexuals by (1) resolving the controversy at the statewide level, and (2) making the election a single-issue contest for both sides. It put directly, to all the citizens of the State, the question: Should homosexuality be given special protection? They answered no. The Court today asserts that this most democratic of procedures is unconstitutional. * * *

B. THE CITY AS A PUBLIC OR PRIVATE ENTITY

The preceding materials, by sketching the arguments for and against decentralization of power, introduced one of the basic themes of local government law. This section introduces another basic theme—the question whether cities, when they exercise decentralized power, should be treated as public or private entities. As an initial matter, the answer to this question may seem obvious. Of course, one might say, cities are public entities. Cities are governments, just like states; they are not at all like private entities, such as corporations.

As the doctrines of local government law covered in this book demonstrate, however, the answer to the question of the nature of city power is more complicated than it first appears. Cities can certainly be understood as exercising the coercive power of government. But cities have also traditionally been understood as collective entities organized to pursue not the interests of the state but the interests of the people who live within them. Although cities are partly created by state law, they also are partly created by city residents seeking to exercise their own power independent of national or state control. Throughout our history, cities have been seen not only as governments but also as vehicles for the exercise of self-determination.

As an historical matter, this dual nature of cities can be traced to their ancestral roots in the medieval town. A medieval town was a corporation and, like other corporations (such as universities and the church), it was a device that enabled a group of people to exercise collective power. Moreover, the towns, like corporations generally, wielded both political and economic power; medieval theorists did not classify corporations as political or economic, as public or private. Instead, corporate (and, consequently, the towns') activity was understood in medieval society as raising the general question of the role of groups, as distinguished from the roles of individuals or the nation-state, in social life. Defending the autonomy of medieval towns against national control was a way to maintain individual liberty by securing the entitlements of a group. By ensuring the rights of a corporation, one could protect the group as a whole.[4]

To be sure, since medieval towns and other corporations wielded considerable power, they often were under attack by those who wanted to curb their influence in social life. These critics generally sought to reallocate corporate (and thus the towns') power either to the central government or to individuals. In England, municipal corporations were able to resist this attack because of their economic strength and their status as entities with rights protected against the King. Ultimately, the nature of these rights themselves became the subject of a major controversy between the King and the cities. This controversy led, after the Glorious Revolution of 1688, to even further protection of municipal rights against the King.[5]

In colonial America, the rights of cities were also resolved as part of the question of the relationship between corporations in general and governmental power. Before the nineteenth century, it is important to emphasize, there was no legal distinction in England or in America

---

[4] For further discussion of the medieval town, see, e.g., Cary Nederman, Lineages of European Political Thought (2009); James Lee, Urban Policy and Urban Political Culture: Henry VII and his Towns, 82 Hist. Res. 217, 493–510 (2009); Saskia Sassen, Territory, Authority, Rights: From Medieval to Global Assemblages 31–71 (2006); Norman Pounds, The Medieval City (2005); Gerald Frug, City Making: Building Cities Without Building Walls 27–32 (1999); Otto Friedrich von Gierke, Political Theories of the Middle Ages (Frederic Maitland trans. 1958); Henri Pirenne, Medieval Cities (Frank Halsey trans. 1925); Frederic Maitland, Township and Borough (1898).

[5] For materials on early modern towns, see, e.g., Bert De Munck and Anne Winter (eds.), Gated Communities?: Regulating Migration in Early Modern Cities (2012); David Michael Palliser, Towns and Local Communities in Medieval and Early Modern England (2006); Gerald Frug, City Making: Building Cities Without Building Walls 32–36 (1999); Peter Clark and Paul Slack, English Towns in Transition 1500–1700 (1974); Jennifer Levin, The Charter Controversy in the City of London 1600–1688 and Its Consequences (1969); Fernand Braudel, Towns, in Capitalism and Material Life 1400–1800, at 373 (Miriam Kochan trans. 1967).

between public and private corporations, between businesses and cities. All corporations had the same rights. But, although these corporate rights had been resolved in the corporations' favor against the King, the relationship between corporations and state legislatures remained unsettled. The problem of city power in early America lay in defining that relationship. The excerpt below, taken from Gerald Frug's book, City Making, describes how the nature of the relationship between corporations and legislatures became established. It shows that the law distinguished between public corporations, such as towns and cities, and private corporations, such as businesses.

The six cases that follow the excerpt deal with current problems generated by the public/private dichotomy in local government law. Oregon v. City of Rajneeshpuram holds that a private religious community cannot legitimately become a city; Marsh v. Alabama, by contrast, treats a privately owned company town as a city over its objections. What do these two cases suggest about whether state law, local residents, or some other source determines whether a group of people who live in the same geographical area live in a "city"? The next three cases—International Society for Krishna Consciousness v. Lee, New Jersey Coalition Against War in the Middle East v. J.M.B. Realty, and Mazdabrook Commons Homeowners' Association v. Khan—raise questions about the public/private distinction on a smaller scale. Krishna Consciousness treats a government-owned airport as if it were a private entity, thereby upholding its ability to limit the freedom of speech; New Jersey Coalition provides (at least some) protection for freedom of speech at a private shopping mall; Mazdabrook Commons extends free speech protections (in a limited way) to homeowners associations. Are airport terminals and shopping malls both "public" spaces and, therefore, places that should be open to protestors and solicitation by religious groups? Or are they both more like a private store than a mini-downtown? Are bedroom suburbs and homeowners associations both public communities or both private communities? Of course, these locations might also be considered distinguishable from each other, with one more "public" than the other. If so, how should their "public" nature be determined? The final case, Council of Organizations v. Engler, confronts the hybrid public/private nature of charter schools. What makes a charter school— what makes any school—a "public" school? Is it enough that it receives a state charter? Or must be it be open to all applicants, regardless of their academic ability?

GERALD FRUG, CITY MAKING: BUILDING
COMMUNITIES WITHOUT BUILDING WALLS
Pp. 38–45 (1999).

The question of the appropriate extent of legislative power over the cities was decided as part of the larger issue of the desired extent of legislative power over all corporations, whether cities or other mercantile bodies. In late eighteenth century America, the larger issue was deeply troubling. On the one hand, corporate rights had been protected from the King by the Glorious Revolution; these rights, once recognized, seemed to deserve protection from legislative infringement as well. America had rejected the English notion of legislative supremacy in favor of the Lockean concept of a legislative power limited by natural rights. Legislative denial of these rights could be tolerated no more than could executive denial. On the other hand, corporations exercised power in society that seemed to limit the rights of individuals to earn their livelihood, and this power, wielded by an aristocratic elite to protect their monopolistic privileges, needed to be controlled by popular—that is, legislative—action. Thus while the exercise of legislative power was perceived as a threat to corporate rights, the exercise of corporate rights risked the curtailment of legislative power thought necessary to protect the welfare of the people.

On a deeper level, the corporation represented an anomaly to political thinkers who envisioned the world as sharply divided between individual rightholders and state power, the ruled in conflict with the ruler. The corporation exhibited traits of both poles: it was part ruled and part ruler, both an association of individuals and an entity with state-granted power. * * * Even more troublesome, the corporation was in some aspects a protector of, while in other ways a threat to, both individual rights and the state. In one capacity, the corporation not only protected individual property rights but also served as a useful vehicle for the exercise of state power. Yet, at the same time, the corporation, like the medieval town, restricted the freedom of individual enterprise and operated as a miniature republic, impervious to state power. The dilemma created by the corporation, then, could be solved neither by retention of its present form nor by abolition in favor of individual rights, as urged by Adam Smith, or in favor of the state, as advocated by Hobbes. * * *

To solve the problem created by the intermediate status of the corporation, early-nineteenth-century legal doctrine divided the corporation into two different entities, one assimilated to the role of an individual in society and the other assimilated to the role of the state. The corporation as an entity that was simultaneously a rightholder and a power wielder thus disappeared. In its place emerged the private corporation, which was an individual rightholder, and the public corporation, an entity that was identified with the state. The very purpose of the distinction was to ensure that some corporations, called "private," would be protected against domination by the state and that others, called "public," would be subject to such domination. In this way, the corporate anomaly was resolved so that corporations, like the rest of society, were divided into individuals and the state.

This public/private distinction for corporations was not purely a legal invention. The distinction had been generally emerging since the American Revolution, and both the newly created identities, public and private, were the product of a pervasive attack on the exclusive privileges and oligarchic power wielded by corporations. The attack which established the "private" character of business corporations developed as their number expanded, rising from only eight in 1780 to several hundred by the time of the critical *Dartmouth College* opinion in 1819. Even though these business corporations were public service enterprises, such as canals, bridges, water supply companies, and banking enterprises, their creation raised troubling questions concerning the amount of protection afforded their investors and participants. As the courts gradually developed protections for the investors' property, pressure mounted on the legislature to expand the opportunities for incorporation from a favored few to the more general population. Yet, as the legislature yielded to this drive for more incorporations, the demand for protection of property rights for those involved itself increased. As one commentary noted, "The process which multiplied the institution [of the corporation] and the unfoldment of its private character reacted upon each other in a reciprocal, accumulative fashion. Every new grant strengthened the grounds for considering it private; every new affirmation of privateness strengthened the hands of those who demanded new grants." This process gathered momentum, culminating in the middle of the nineteenth century in the Jacksonian effort to pass general incorporation laws, thus allowing the "privilege" of incorporation to be exercised by all.

The attack on the exclusiveness of city corporations worked in another direction. With the sovereignty of the people as the emerging basis of republican politics, and with population growth fueling a need to add new functions to city corporations, the pressure for state legislation to end aristocratic corporate governance mounted. The most important closed corporation in America, that of Philadelphia, was abolished by radical republican legislators in 1776, and it was replaced several years later with a modified, more broadly based, corporation. This attack on the privileged control of city corporations and the simultaneous expansion of participation in corporate governance made it increasingly difficult to separate the city corporation from the people as a whole, that is, to view city corporate rights as distinct from the rights of the public at large. The movement toward what was then considered universal suffrage, in the 1820s and 1830s, helped confirm the emerging public character of city corporations, thus setting them in contrast to "private" business corporations. * * *

Despite these developments, American courts in the early nineteenth century had great difficulty in establishing the public/private distinction for corporations. All corporations continued to have similar characteristics. Corporations, whether cities or mercantile entities, were chartered only to further public purposes, and many of their functions overlapped. All corporations were in one sense created by individuals and, in another sense, created by the state through the award of the franchise. Many mercantile corporations wielded the same powers as cities, such as eminent domain, while many cities received their income from the same sources as mercantile corporations, primarily commerce and trade. Both cities and mercantile corporations served to protect the private investments of individual founders and allowed those active in their governance a large degree of self-determination. Many cities and mercantile corporations were controlled by an elite, and consequently both were subject to popular attack. Finally, cities and mercantile corporations alike could be viewed as associations of individuals organized to achieve commercial ends. In short, all corporations wielded power and all corporations protected rights. The concepts of power and rights, so fully merged in the medieval town, had not yet been segregated into their public and private identities. In determining where to draw the public/private distinction for corporations, the courts first decided what was important to protect against state power. In *Trustees of Dartmouth College v. Woodward*, decided in 1819, the United States Supreme Court gave its response to this question, an answer that came straight from Locke: what needed protection was property. The scope of property rights divided private from public corporations, private corporations being those founded by individual contributions of property, and public corporations being those founded by the government without such individual contributions.

Having decided the importance of property rights, the Court then sought to determine the status of cities under the public/private distinction. While three major opinions were delivered in the case, Justice Story, who had four years earlier first made the public/private distinction for corporations in a Supreme Court opinion, presented the most complete discussion of the issue:

> Another division of corporations is into public and private. Public corporations are generally esteemed such as exist for public political purposes only, such as towns, cities, parishes, and counties; and in many respects they are so, although they involve some private interests; but strictly speaking, public corporations are such only as are founded by the government for

public purposes, where the whole interests belong also to the
government.

This passage is ambiguous. Justice Story may have been arguing that the
critical distinction between private and public corporations was whether
they were founded by individuals or "founded by the government for
public purposes, where the whole interests belong to the government."
This seems close to the positions taken by both Chief Justice Marshall
and Justice Washington. Only if the corporation were completely a state
creation, Justice Washington argued, would there be a diminished need to
protect property rights from state domination; protection of contract
rights would be unnecessary if there were but one party, the state,
involved in the foundation of the corporation. Yet, if that were the
definition of public corporations, most cities could not be public
corporations: most were not founded by the government, nor did they
belong wholly to the government. Alternatively, Justice Story may have
accepted what was "generally esteemed" at the time, if not "strictly
speaking" true: that all cities were public corporations. He twice referred
to "towns, cities, and counties" as examples of public corporations. Which
of these positions Justice Story held with regard to the place of cities
within the public/private distinction is unclear. Moreover, the notion of
property rights could not, in itself, distinguish cities from other
mercantile corporations. Many cities possessed property contributed by
individual founders, and mercantile corporations could readily be created
by governments for their own purposes. In fact, Justice Story recognized
in *Dartmouth College* that cities possessed certain property rights,
although he did not indicate what, if any, additional legal protection from
legislative interference cities should receive.

Seventeen years later in his *Commentaries on American Law*,
Chancellor Kent offered his own view of the status of cities within the
public/private distinction:

> Public corporations are such as are created by the government
> for political purposes, as counties, cities, towns and villages; they
> are invested with subordinate legislative powers to be exercised
> for local purposes connected with the public good, and such
> powers are subject to the control of the legislature of the state.
> They may also be empowered to take or hold private property for
> municipal uses, and such property is invested with the security
> of other private rights.

In this passage, Chancellor Kent apparently rejected the notion that, in
order for an entity to constitute a public corporation, the "whole interest"
must belong to the government. He simply asserted that cities were
"created by the government," thus denying their actual history both in
England and in America. Having taken that step, Kent then divided city

authority into two parts: legislation for the public good, and the possession of property for municipal uses. Of these, only city property received protection from state control. Just as public and private corporations are distinguished by the need to protect private property, cities themselves became bifurcated by the same need—self-determination was retained only for the protection of their private property. It is this view that became, and remains, the law concerning the status of cities in the United States. * * *

It is by no means self-explanatory why, once corporate property rights were protected, early nineteenth century writers like Chancellor Kent seemed to think it obvious that the other functions of cities would be subordinate to state power. Cities, like other corporations, had never based their resistance to state control simply on the protection of property. Freedom of association and the exercise of self-government had always been values sought to be protected by the defense of the corporation. It did not follow from the need to protect property that property alone needed protection and that these other values could be sacrificed to state domination. Even at the time, these other values were seen as part of the definition of liberty, their importance being most clearly articulated in the defense of state power against federal control encapsulated in the doctrine of federalism. Indeed, the subordination of cities to the state turned the political world as it then existed upside down. New England towns had controlled state legislatures since prior to the Revolution, and the move in other sections of the country to end aristocratic city governance in favor of democracy was not made with the intention of establishing state control over cities. Nor was the subservience of cities to the state inevitable. The proper relationship of city to state was instead a hotly contested political issue. Some argued that the sovereignty of the people required control at the local level, but others feared the power of democratic cities. Aristotle, Montesquieu, and Rousseau could be invoked in favor of power at the local level, while Madison and Hume could be cited to show the danger of local self-government. The fact that legal theorists could classify cities as public corporations and thereby subject them to state control thus requires an explanation.

In seeking to understand why cities became subordinate to state power, I will not seek to isolate some factor as the "cause" of this change in city status. I will suggest instead how an early-nineteenth-century thinker could have conceived of state control of cities as a defense, rather than as a restriction, of freedom. Such a thinker could acknowledge city rights, once the cities became synonymous with the people within them, only if he were willing to recognize the right of association and self-determination for any group of people, however large. This recognition would threaten many other important values. It would limit the nation's ability to establish a unified political system under the federal Constitution, thereby preventing the needed centralization of authority and perpetuating the idea that the nation was merely a loose federation of localities. Moreover, these groups, particularly small groups, could be seen as "factions" dangerous to the individuals within them, inhibiting the individual's free development and threatening his property rights. In other words, recognizing the rights of the city as an exercise of the freedom of association would frustrate both the interests of the state and of individuals. Recognizing the rights of the city as an association would thus bring to the surface what political theorists sought to deny: that corporations were the continuation of the group rights of the medieval town, protecting both the associational and property rights of their members. Recognition of city rights would also bring to the surface the conflict between the values of association and of property rights themselves, a conflict that had been hidden by the fact that both values had traditionally been protected by the corporate form. Prior to the emergence of the public/private distinction, there was no difference between a corporation's property rights and its rights of group self-government. But now group self-government—or popular sovereignty—seemed a threat to property rights, and property rights seemed a necessary limit to popular sovereignty. Any recognition of the rights of the city would therefore require the courts to choose between associational rights and property rights in particular cases, rather than simply protecting property rights against the power of "governmental" collective action. All these problems seemed to disappear, however, if recognition of the rights of cities were avoided.

The amount of emphasis to put on the fear of democratic power in explaining the judicial decision to limit the power of cities is a matter of conjecture. Such fear plainly existed, even in the minds of such champions of local power as Jefferson and Tocqueville. While Jefferson saw towns as the "elementary republics" of the nation that must be preserved so that "the voice of the whole people would be fairly, fully, and peaceably expressed * * * by the common reason" of all citizens, he also saw them as objects to be feared: "The mobs of great cities add just so much to the support of pure government, as sores do to the strength of the human body." For Tocqueville, "the strength of free peoples resides in the local community," giving them both the "spirit of liberty" and the ability to withstand the "tyranny of the majority." But he also thought that the size of American cities and the nature of their inhabitants were so threatening to the future of the republic that they required "an armed force which, while remaining subject to the wishes of the national majority, is independent of the peoples of the towns and capable of suppressing their excesses." This vision of cities as being the home of "mobs," the working class, immigrants, and, finally, racial minorities, is a theme that runs throughout much of nineteenth-and twentieth-century thought. Chancellor Kent's own fears of the democratic cities were certainly no secret.

Yet one need not rely on the assertion that the subordination of cities was the product of the unwillingness to protect the cities' rights of association and the fear of democratic power. Since the issue of city power was decided as part of the issue of corporate power, the threatening ideas associated with the rights of association did not need to be brought to consciousness. It is for this reason that the classification of American cities as corporations mattered. It can be understood as helping to obscure the notion that associational rights were being affected in defining the laws governing city rights. No rights of association needed to be articulated when the rights of "private" corporations were discussed, since property rights were sufficient to protect them against state power. There was also nothing that required rights of association to be imagined when the subordination of "public" corporations was discussed. Yet if no rights of association were recognized, cities, increasingly deprived of their economic character—the basis of their power for hundreds of years—had little defense against the reallocation of their power to the individual and to the state. There was nothing left that seemed to demand protection from state control.

The developments in legal doctrine that led to the public/private distinction for corporations did not immediately alter the allocation of power between American states and cities. In fact, prior to the 1850s, local autonomy remained largely intact. The impetus for the assertion of state political power to curb local autonomy finally came when the desire to restrict city activity in favor of private activity increased. In light of the new conception of public and private activities, the investment by cities in business enterprises no longer seemed an appropriate "public" function, and local regulation of a city's business community seemed to invade the "private sphere." Hence state control over these city activities was invoked. But state control of cities during this period was by no means limited to the assurance of a "laissez-faire" policy designed to prevent both cities and states, as governments, from intervening in the private sector. Much state legislation compelled the cities to raise and spend money for state-supported causes, including the promotion of economic enterprise. Other state legislation—so-called ripper legislation—simply sought to transfer control of the city government to state-appointed officials. For a wide variety of purposes, state power to control cities could now be exercised, and was exercised, as a matter of law. * * *

OREGON V. CITY OF RAJNEESHPURAM

United States District Court, District of Oregon, 1984.
598 F.Supp. 1208.

FRYE, JUDGE.

Defendants have moved the court to dismiss plaintiff's complaint for failure to state a claim upon which relief can be granted. * * * In its complaint, the State of Oregon seeks a declaratory judgment * * * [d]eclaring that the State of Oregon is not required by state law to recognize the municipal status of the City of Rajneeshpuram because to do so would violate the religion clauses of the Oregon and United States Constitutions. * * *

The City of Rajneeshpuram is a municipal corporation located in Wasco County, Oregon. The City was incorporated by a Proclamation of Incorporation on May 26, 1982, following a unanimous vote of 154 electors. Later a city council was elected, a city government organized, and a city charter enacted. The City is comprised of three separate parcels of land and a county road connecting the parcels. An additional parcel was later added by annexation, which is being challenged in other litigation. The City is located entirely within the confines of Rancho Rajneesh, a 64,229 acre parcel controlled by Rajneesh Foundation International (RFI). The only public thoroughfare and the only publicly owned property within Rancho Rajneesh and the City is a county road. RFI is a nonprofit religious corporation organized to advance the teachings of the Bhagwan Shree Rajneesh. The followers of the Bhagwan assert that he is an enlightened religious master. RFI is a part of the organizational structure through which the followers of the Bhagwan practice their religion. The Rajneesh Investment Corporation (RIC) is a for-profit Oregon corporation. RIC was capitalized in December, 1981, by a transfer of the Rancho Rajneesh real property from RFI to RIC in exchange for stock. All of the stock in RIC is owned by RFI. RIC is the sole owner of Rancho Rajneesh, including all of the real property within the City of Rajneeshpuram, except the county road. All of the officers and directors of RIC are followers of the Bhagwan. The Rajneesh Neo-Sannyas International Commune ("the Commune") is a corporation organized under Oregon's Co-operative Corporations Act and does not issue stock. The Commune was incorporated in December, 1981. The purpose of the Commune, according to its articles of incorporation, is "* * * to be a religious community where life is, in every respect, guided by the religious teachings of Bhagwan Shree Rajneesh and whose members live a communal life with a common treasury * * *." The Commune is governed by a Board of Directors, of which the personal secretary to the Bhagwan, Ma Anand Sheela, is an ex officio member. All members of the Commune are followers of the Bhagwan. Applications for membership in the Commune are considered by the Board of Directors, but no one may be admitted as a member without the approval of Ma Anand Sheela. The Commune holds a long-term leasehold on Rancho Rajneesh, including all of the real property within the City of Rajneeshpuram, except the county road. All of the City of Rajneeshpuram's real property and offices are subleased or otherwise made available to the City by the Commune. Ma Anand Sheela is the President of RFI. She is a member of the Board of Directors of RIC. She holds an unlimited general power of attorney from the Bhagwan Shree Rajneesh. She is married to Swami Prem Jayananda, who is the President and a member of the Board of Directors of RIC. He is "senior executive" of the Commune and has served as police commissioner for the City of Rajneeshpuram. Because of the interrelationship of the religious and for profit corporations that own and control all of the real property within the City of Rajneeshpuram, the sovereign power exercised by the City is subject to the actual, direct control of an organized religion and its leaders. RFI, a religious corporation, is the sole owner of RIC, which owns all real property in Rajneeshpuram. Ma Anand Sheela and her husband are a controlling majority of the Board of Directors of RIC. The Commune, lessee of all real property in Rajneeshpuram, is dedicated to creating and maintaining a religious community guided by the teachings of the Bhagwan. Ma Anand Sheela has actual control over admission to and expulsion from the Commune, and by virtue of the Commune's dedication to the Bhagwan and the Bhagwan's delegation of power to Ma Anand Sheela, has the power to exercise actual control over the affairs of the Commune. Because of the Commune's control over all real property in and around the City, no person may reside in Rajneeshpuram without the consent of the Commune and Ma Anand Sheela. All residents of Rajneeshpuram are either members or invitees of the Commune. The Commune possesses and has exercised substantial and direct control over visitor access to Rajneeshpuram. Only a small portion of Rajneeshpuram is accessible by the county road. Most of the City, including City Hall, is accessible only by means of roads controlled by the Commune. Visitors to the City are asked to check in at a visitor's center and have been required to obtain a visitor's pass as a condition to access to facilities (other than City Hall) not located directly on the county road right-of-way. Some visitors have been searched as a condition of entry to the City. By the terms of the leases, RFI has the option to lease back from the Commune and RIC any or all of the Rancho Rajneesh property for religious purposes. The followers of the Bhagwan assert that the development of Rajneeshpuram is the fulfillment of a religious vision. Work of every kind is considered a form of worship. Work stations are called "temples" and various City functions are designated as temples and supervised by the Commune. The primary purpose for establishing the City of Rajneeshpuram was to advance the religion of Rajneeshism. The City was founded to fulfill a religious vision. The City was designed and functions as a spiritual mecca for followers of the Bhagwan worldwide. It serves as a monument to and the residence of the Bhagwan, and as a gathering place for followers at institutions of religious training and at three annual religious festivals. * * *

In *Lemon v. Kurtzman*, 403 U.S. 602, 91 S.Ct. 2105, 29 L.Ed.2d 745 (1971), the Supreme Court laid down a three-part test for use in Establishment Clause cases. * * * First, the statute must have a secular legislative purpose; second, its principal or primary effect must be one that neither advances nor inhibits religion; finally, the statute must not foster "an excessive government entanglement with religion." * * * Defendants' first argument in support of their motion to dismiss is that the State of Oregon cannot prevail because in the present case there is no governmental "act" to which the *Lemon* tests can be applied. Defendants contend that all of the allegations contained in the State's complaint involve merely private acts that, taken individually, are lawful and constitutionally protected, such as forming the defendant corporations and associating for the purpose of practicing a religion. * * * The State of Oregon argues, however, that, taking all of the allegations of its complaint together, recognition of the municipal status of the City of Rajneeshpuram constitutes the establishment of a theocracy—that is, the granting of governmental power to a religion. * * * The court deems that the governmental acts alleged are those of the State of Oregon and Wasco County, through the operation of state law, in imparting sovereign municipal status to the City of Rajneeshpuram and the acts of the City of Rajneeshpuram itself in using those powers. The private defendants' individual corporate and religious activities are not the acts upon which the State's claim is based. However, allegations of the private defendants' individual, corporate, and religious activities are necessary allegations in support of the State of Oregon's claim that granting municipal power and status to the City of Rajneeshpuram gives sovereign governmental power to a religion and its leaders.

Defendants next argue in support of their motion to dismiss the State of Oregon's complaint that governments do not violate the Establishment Clause simply by doing acts that incidentally benefit religion, so long as the acts have a secular purpose and the non-secular benefit to religion is remote, indirect, and incidental. For example, defendants point out that (1) it is not unconstitutional for a government to give police, fire, or other public services to a church in the same manner as it provides such services to other citizens; (2) that the operation of an otherwise lawfully incorporated city does not violate the Establishment Clause simply because the population of the city is composed of members of one religious faith; and (3) that many cities in the United States were established by adherents of one particular religious faith, such as the German Benedictines of Mount Angel, Oregon. * * * The State of Oregon's main argument is that it is unconstitutional to give municipal power and status to a city (1) in which all land is subject to the control of a religious corporation, (2) in which residency is controlled by a religious corporation and limited to followers of that religion or their guests, and (3) whose *raison d'etre* is the practice and advancement of a particular religion. Under such facts, the State of Oregon argues, giving the City of Rajneeshpuram municipal status and power is the same as giving municipal status and power to a religion * * *. Defendants counter that the only alleged factual difference between a city composed entirely of adherents of one religion, such as the German Benedictines of Mount Angel, and the Rajneeshees of the City of Rajneeshpuram, is the form of land ownership and the concomitant restriction on residency in the city. Defendants argue that to find the existence and operation of the City of Rajneeshpuram unconstitutional would be to penalize defendants because they believe in communal rather than private ownership of land. * * *

The existence of the City of Rajneeshpuram gives the appearance of a joint exercise of legislative authority by church and state. Religious organizations control or own all real property within the City of Rajneeshpuram. The potential for religious-secular conflict with respect to actions of the City is inherent. Finally, the nature and extent of potential or actual control by religion over the government of the City raises serious entanglement problems. * * * If the facts alleged in the State of Oregon's complaint are true, the court concludes that the potential injury to the anti-establishment principle of the first amendment by the existence and the operation of the City of Rajneeshpuram clearly outweighs the potential harm to defendants' free exercise of religion rights. To deny defendants the right to operate a city is the only means of achieving a compelling state and federal interest—that of avoiding an establishment of religion. If the City of Rajneeshpuram were to cease to exist, defendants would not be precluded from practicing their religion nor from associating with whom they choose in order to do so. Defendants would not be denied access to public services. Public services would be provided by Wasco County. In short, although defendants' freedom to freely practice their religion would be burdened if the City of Rajneeshpuram were no longer recognized as a city, the burden upon them is small and indirect compared to the harm to be done to the Establishment Clause by allowing the City of Rajneeshpuram to operate as a city.

Furthermore, if the facts alleged in the State of Oregon's complaint are true that (1) there is a close interrelationship between various defendant religious organizations; (2) these organizations control all of the real property within the City of Rajneeshpuram; and (3) these religious organizations control who may and may not reside within the City of Rajneeshpuram, then the court could conclude that the exercise of control over the City of Rajneeshpuram by these religious organizations is different enough from the control exercised by the religious leaders in a city of private landowners of one religion as to allow a constitutional distinction to be made between the two situations.

Similarly, there is a difference between the effect on and benefit to religion of the provision of ordinary municipal services to a city of private landowners of one religion and to the City of Rajneeshpuram, where the land is communally owned and controlled by religious organizations. The provision of services by a municipal government in a city whose residents are private landowners of one religious faith has the direct and primary effect of aiding the individual landowners and residents living in the city. The effect on the religion of those private landowners is remote, indirect, and incidental. In contrast, if, as alleged, all of the real property in the City of Rajneeshpuram is owned or controlled by religious organizations, the provision of municipal services by the City of Rajneeshpuram necessarily has the effect of aiding not only the individual residents of the City of Rajneeshpuram, but also of directly, obviously, and immediately benefitting the religious organizations themselves.

Given the facts as alleged by the State of Oregon, the court could conclude that the acts of the State of Oregon and Wasco County in recognizing the existence and operation of the City of Rajneeshpuram have as a principal and primary effect the advancement of the religion of Rajneeshism. Finally, given the alleged power and control of religious organizations and leaders over all real property and residency within the City of Rajneeshpuram, the court could conclude that the existence and operation of the City of Rajneeshpuram would represent "an excessive government entanglement with religion." *Lemon*, supra, 403 U.S. at 613, 91 S.Ct. at 2111.

MARSH V. ALABAMA

Supreme Court of the United States, 1946.
326 U.S. 501, 66 S.Ct. 276, 90 L.Ed. 265.

MR. JUSTICE BLACK delivered the opinion of the Court.

In this case we are asked to decide whether a State, consistently with the First and Fourteenth Amendments, can impose criminal punishment on a person who undertakes to distribute religious literature on the premises of a company-owned town contrary to the wishes of the town's management. The town, a suburb of Mobile, Alabama, known as Chickasaw, is owned by the Gulf Shipbuilding Corporation. Except for that it has all the characteristics of any other American town. The property consists of residential buildings, streets, a system of sewers, a sewage disposal plant and a "business block" on which business places are situated. A deputy of the Mobile County Sheriff, paid by the company, serves as the town's policeman. Merchants and service establishments have rented the stores and business places on the business block and the United States uses one of the places as a post office from which six carriers deliver mail to the people of Chickasaw and the adjacent area. The town and the surrounding neighborhood, which can not be distinguished from the Gulf property by anyone not familiar with the property lines, are thickly settled, and according to all indications the residents use the business block as their regular shopping center. To do so, they now, as they have for many years, make use of a company-owned paved street and sidewalk located alongside the store fronts in order to enter and leave the stores and the post office. Intersecting company-owned roads at each end of the business block lead into a four-lane public highway which runs parallel to the business block at a distance of thirty feet. There is nothing to stop highway traffic from coming onto the business block and upon arrival a traveler may make free use of the facilities available there. In short the town and its shopping district are accessible to and freely used by the public in general and there is nothing to distinguish them from any other town and shopping center except the fact that the title to the property belongs to a private corporation.

Appellant, a Jehovah's Witness, came onto the sidewalk we have just described, stood near the post-office and undertook to distribute religious literature. In the stores the corporation had posted a notice which read as follows: "This Is Private Property, and Without Written Permission, No Street, or House Vendor, Agent or Solicitation of Any Kind Will Be Permitted." Appellant was warned that she could not distribute the literature without a permit and told that no permit would be issued to her. She protested that the company rule could not be constitutionally applied so as to prohibit her from distributing religious writings. When she was asked to leave the sidewalk and Chickasaw she declined. The deputy sheriff arrested her and she was charged in the state court with violating Title 14, Section 426 of the 1940 Alabama Code which makes it a crime to enter or remain on the premises of another after having been warned not to do so. Appellant contended that to construe the state statute as applicable to her activities would abridge her right to freedom of press and religion contrary to the First and Fourteenth Amendments to the Constitution. This contention was rejected and she was convicted. * * *

Had the title to Chickasaw belonged not to a private but to a municipal corporation and had appellant been arrested for violating a municipal ordinance rather than a ruling by those appointed by the corporation to manage a company-town it would have been clear that appellant's conviction must be reversed. * * * [N]either a state nor a municipality can completely bar the distribution of literature containing religious or political ideas on its streets, sidewalks and public places or make the right to distribute dependent on a flat license tax or permit to be issued by an official who could deny it at will. * * * [H]ad the people of Chickasaw owned all the homes, and all the stores, and all the streets, and all the sidewalks, all those owners together could not have set up a municipal government with sufficient power to pass an ordinance completely barring the distribution of religious literature. Our question then narrows down to this: Can those people who live in or come to Chickasaw be denied freedom of press and religion simply because a single company has legal title to all the town? For it is the state's contention that the mere fact that all the property interests in the town are held by a single company is enough to give that company power, enforceable by a state statute, to abridge these freedoms.

We do not agree that the corporation's property interests settle the question. The State urges in effect that the corporation's right to control the inhabitants of Chickasaw is coextensive with the right of a homeowner to regulate the conduct of his guests. We can not accept that contention. Ownership does not always mean absolute dominion. The more an owner, for his advantage, opens up his property for use by the public in general, the more do his rights become circumscribed by the statutory and constitutional rights of those who use it. Thus, the owners of privately held bridges, ferries, turnpikes and railroads may not operate them as freely as a farmer does his farm. Since these facilities are built and operated primarily to benefit the public and since their operation is essentially a public function, it is subject to state regulation. And, though the issue is not directly analogous to the one before us we do want to point out by way of illustration that such regulation may not result in an operation of these facilities, even by privately owned companies, which unconstitutionally interferes with and discriminates against interstate commerce. Had the corporation here owned the segment of the four-lane highway which runs parallel to the "business block" and operated the same under a State franchise, doubtless no one would have seriously contended that the corporation's property interest in the highway gave it power to obstruct through traffic or to discriminate against interstate commerce. And even had there been no express franchise but mere acquiescence by the State in the corporation's use of its property as a segment of the four-lane highway, operation of all the highway, including the segment owned by the corporation, would still have been performance of a public function and discrimination would certainly have been illegal.

We do not think it makes any significant constitutional difference as to the relationship between the rights of the owner and those of the public that here the State, instead of permitting the corporation to operate a highway, permitted it to use its property as a town, operate a "business block" in the town and a street and sidewalk on that business block. Whether a corporation or a municipality owns or possesses the town the public in either case has an identical interest in the functioning of the community in such manner that the channels of communication remain free. As we have heretofore stated, the town of Chickasaw does not function differently from any other town. The "business block" serves as the community shopping center and is freely accessible and open to the people in the area and those passing through. The managers appointed by the corporation cannot curtail the liberty of press and religion of these people consistently with the purposes of the Constitutional guarantees, and a state statute, as the one here involved, which enforces such action by criminally punishing those who attempt to distribute religious literature clearly violates the First and Fourteenth Amendments to the Constitution.

Many people in the United States live in company-owned towns. These people, just as residents of municipalities, are free citizens of their State and country. Just as all other citizens they must make decisions which affect the welfare of community and nation. To act as good citizens they must be informed. In order to enable them to be properly informed their information must be uncensored. There is no more reason for depriving these people of the liberties guaranteed by the First and Fourteenth Amendments than there is for curtailing these freedoms with respect to any other citizen.

When we balance the Constitutional rights of owners of property against those of the people to enjoy freedom of press and religion, as we must here, we remain mindful of the fact that the latter occupy a preferred position. As we have stated before, the right to exercise the liberties safeguarded by the First Amendment "lies at the foundation of free government by free men" and we must in all cases "weigh the circumstances and appraise * * * the reasons * * * in support of the regulation of [those] rights." *Schneider v. State*, 308 U.S. 147, 161, 60 S.Ct. 146, 151, 84 L.Ed. 155. In our view the circumstance that the property rights to the premises where the deprivation of liberty, here involved, took place, were held by others than the public, is not sufficient to justify the State's permitting a corporation to govern a community of citizens so as to restrict their fundamental liberties and the enforcement of such restraint by the application of a State statute. Insofar as the State has attempted to impose criminal punishment on appellant for undertaking to distribute religious literature in a company town, its action cannot stand. * * *

MR. JUSTICE REED, dissenting. * * *

What the present decision establishes as a principle is that one may remain on private property against the will of the owner and contrary to the law of the state so long as the only objection to his presence is that he is exercising an asserted right to spread there his religious views. This is the first case to extend by law the privilege of religious exercises beyond public places or to private places without the assent of the owner. As the rule now announced permits this intrusion, without possibility of protection of the property by law, and apparently is equally applicable to the freedom of speech and the press, it seems appropriate to express a dissent to this, to us, novel Constitutional doctrine. Of course, such principle may subsequently be restricted by this Court to the precise facts of this case—that is to private property in a company town where the owner for his own advantage has permitted a restricted public use by his licensees and invitees. Such distinctions are of degree and require new arbitrary lines, judicially drawn, instead of those hitherto established by legislation and precedent. While the power of this Court, as the interpreter of the Constitution to determine what use of real property by the owner makes that property subject, at will, to the reasonable practice of religious exercises by strangers, cannot be doubted, we find nothing in the principles of the First Amendment, adopted now into the Fourteenth, which justifies their application to the facts of this case.

Both Federal and Alabama law permit, so far as we are aware, company towns. * * * These communities may be essential to furnish proper and convenient living conditions for employees on isolated operations in lumbering, mining, production of high explosives and large-scale farming. The restrictions imposed by the owners upon the occupants are sometimes galling to the employees and may appear unreasonable to outsiders. Unless they fall under the prohibition of some legal rule, however, they are a matter for adjustment between owner and licensee, or by appropriate legislation. * * *

An owner of property may very well have been willing for the public to use the private passway for business purposes and yet have been unwilling to furnish space for street trades or a location for the practice of religious exhortations by itinerants. The passway here in question was not put to any different use than other private passways that lead to privately owned areas, amusement places, resort hotels or other businesses. There had been no dedication of the sidewalk to the public use, express or implied. Alabama so decided and we understand that this Court accepts that conclusion. * * * A state does have the moral duty of furnishing the opportunity for information, education and religious enlightenment to its inhabitants, including those who live in company towns, but it has not heretofore been adjudged that it must commandeer, without compensation, the private property of other citizens to carry out that obligation. * * * In the area which is covered by the guarantees of the First Amendment, this Court has been careful to point out that the owner of property may protect himself against the intrusion of strangers. * * *

Our Constitution guarantees to every man the right to express his views in an orderly fashion. An essential element of "orderly" is that the man shall also have a right to use the place he chooses for his exposition. The rights of the owner, which the Constitution protects as well as the right of free speech, are not outweighed by the interests of the trespasser, even though he trespasses in behalf of religion or free speech. We cannot say that Jehovah's Witnesses can claim the privilege of a license, which has never been granted, to hold their meetings in other private places, merely because the owner has admitted the public to them for other limited purposes. Even though we have reached the point where this Court is required to force private owners to open their property for the practice there of religious activities or propaganda distasteful to the owner, because of the public interest in freedom of speech and religion, there is no need for the application of such a doctrine here. Appellant * * * was free to engage in such practices on the public highways, without becoming a trespasser on the company's property.

INTERNATIONAL SOCIETY FOR KRISHNA CONSCIOUSNESS, INC. V. LEE

Supreme Court of the United States, 1992.
505 U.S. 672, 112 S.Ct. 2701, 120 L.Ed.2d 541.

JUSTICE REHNQUIST delivered the opinion of the Court. * * *

Petitioner International Society for Krishna Consciousness, Inc. (ISKCON) is a not-for-profit religious corporation whose members perform a ritual known as *sankirtan*. The ritual consists of " 'going into public places, disseminating religious literature and soliciting funds to support the religion.' " The primary purpose of this ritual is raising funds for the movement.

Respondent Walter Lee, now deceased, was the police superintendent of the Port Authority of New York and New Jersey * * *. The Port Authority owns and operates three major airports in the greater New York City area: John F. Kennedy International Airport (Kennedy), La Guardia Airport (La Guardia), and Newark International Airport (Newark). The three airports collectively form one of the world's busiest metropolitan airport complexes. * * *

The airports are funded by user fees and operated to make a regulated profit. Most space at the three airports is leased to commercial airlines, which bear primary responsibility for the leasehold. The Port Authority retains control over unleased portions, including La Guardia's Central Terminal Building, portions of Kennedy's International Arrivals Building, and Newark's North Terminal Building (we refer to these areas collectively as the "terminals"). The terminals are generally accessible to the general public and contain various commercial establishments such as restaurants, snack stands, bars, newsstands, and stores of various types. Virtually all who visit the terminals do so for purposes related to air travel. * * *

The Port Authority has adopted a regulation forbidding within the terminals the repetitive solicitation of money or distribution of literature. * * * The regulation effectively prohibits petitioner from performing *sankirtan* in the terminals. As a result, petitioner brought suit seeking declaratory and injunctive relief under 42 U.S.C. § 1983, alleging that the regulation worked to deprive them of rights guaranteed under the First Amendment. * * *

It is uncontested that the solicitation at issue in this case is a form of speech protected under the First Amendment. But it is also well settled that the government need not permit all forms of speech on property that it owns and controls. Where the government is acting as a proprietor, managing its internal operations, rather than acting as lawmaker with the power to regulate or license, its action will not be subjected to the heightened review to which its actions as a lawmaker may be subject. Thus, we have upheld a ban on political advertisements in city-operated transit vehicles even though the city permitted other types of advertising on those vehicles. Similarly, we have permitted a school district to limit access to an internal mail system used to communicate with teachers employed by the district.

These cases reflect, either implicitly or explicitly, a "forum-based" approach for assessing restrictions that the government seeks to place on the use of its property. Under this approach, regulation of speech on government property that has traditionally been available for public expression is subject to the highest scrutiny. Such regulations survive only if they are narrowly drawn to achieve a compelling state interest. The second category of public property is the designated public forum, whether of a limited or unlimited character—property that the state has opened for expressive activity by part or all of the public. Regulation of such property is subject to the same limitations as that governing a traditional public forum. Finally, there is all remaining public property. Limitations on expressive activity conducted on this last category of property must survive only a much more limited review. The challenged regulation need only be reasonable, as long as the regulation is not an effort to suppress the speaker's activity due to disagreement with the speaker's view. * * *

The suggestion that the government has a high burden in justifying speech restrictions relating to traditional public fora made its first appearance in *Hague v. Committee for Industrial Organization*, 307 U.S. 496, 515, 516, 59 S.Ct. 954, 963, 964, 83 L.Ed. 1423 (1939). Justice Roberts, concluding that individuals have a right to use "streets and parks for communication of views," reasoned that such a right flowed from the fact that "streets and parks * * * have immemorially been held in trust for the use of the public and, time out of mind, have been used for purposes of assembly, communicating thoughts between citizens, and discussing public questions." We confirmed this observation in *Frisby v. Schultz*, 487 U.S. 474, 481, 108 S.Ct. 2495, 2500, 101 L.Ed.2d 420 (1988), where we held that a residential street was a public forum.

Our recent cases provide additional guidance on the characteristics of a public forum. In *Cornelius* [*v. NAACP Legal Defense and Education Fund, Inc.*,] we noted that a traditional public forum is property that has as "a principal purpose * * * the free exchange of ideas." 473 U.S. [788], at 800, 105 S.Ct. [3439], at 3448. Moreover, consistent with the notion that the government—like other property owners—"has power to preserve the property under its control for the use to which it is lawfully dedicated," *Greer* [*v. Spock*], 424 U.S. [828], at 836, 96 S.Ct. [1211], at 1217, the government does not create a public forum by inaction. Nor is a public forum created "whenever members of the public are permitted freely to visit a place owned or operated by the Government." *Ibid.* The decision to create a public forum must instead be made "by intentionally opening a nontraditional forum for public discourse." *Cornelius, supra*, 473 U.S., at 802, 105 S.Ct., at 3449. Finally, we have recognized that the location of property also has bearing because separation from acknowledged public areas may serve to indicate that the separated property is a special enclave, subject to greater restriction.

These precedents foreclose the conclusion that airport terminals are public fora. Reflecting the general growth of the air travel industry, airport terminals have only recently achieved their contemporary size and character. But given the lateness with which the modern air terminal has made its appearance, it hardly qualifies for the description of having "immemorially * * * time out of mind" been held in the public trust and used for purposes of expressive activity. Moreover, even within the rather short history of air transport, it is only "[i]n recent years [that] it has become a common practice for various religious and non-profit organizations to use commercial airports as a forum for the distribution of literature, the solicitation of funds, the proselytizing of new members, and other similar activities." 45 Fed.Reg. 35314 (1980). Thus, the tradition of airport activity does not demonstrate that airports have historically been made available for speech activity. Nor can we say that these particular terminals, or airport terminals generally, have been intentionally opened by their operators to such activity; the frequent and continuing litigation evidencing the operators' objections belies any such claim. In short, there can be no argument that society's time-tested judgment, expressed through acquiescence in a continuing practice, has resolved the issue in petitioner's favor.

Petitioner attempts to circumvent the history and practice governing airport activity by pointing our attention to the variety of speech activity that it claims historically occurred at various "transportation nodes" such as rail stations, bus stations, wharves, and Ellis Island. Even if we were inclined to accept petitioner's historical account describing speech activity at these locations, an account respondent contests, we think that such evidence is of little import for two reasons. First, much of the evidence is irrelevant to *public* fora analysis, because sites such as bus and rail terminals traditionally have had private ownership. The development of privately owned parks that ban speech activity would not change the public fora status of publicly held parks. But the reverse is also true. The practices of privately held transportation centers do not bear on the government's regulatory authority over a publicly owned airport.

Second, the relevant unit for our inquiry is an airport, not "transportation nodes" generally. * * * To blithely equate airports with other transportation centers * * * would be a mistake. * * * As commercial enterprises, airports must provide services attractive to the marketplace. In light of this, it cannot fairly be said that an airport terminal has as a principal purpose "promoting the free exchange of ideas." *Cornelius v. NAACP Legal Defense and Educational Fund, Inc.*, 473 U.S. 788, 105 S.Ct. 3439, 87 L.Ed.2d 567 (1985). To the contrary, the record demonstrates that Port Authority management considers the purpose of the terminals to be the facilitation of passenger air travel, not the promotion of expression. * * * Thus, we think that neither by tradition nor purpose can the terminals be described as satisfying the standards we have previously set out for identifying a public forum.

The restrictions here challenged, therefore, need only satisfy a requirement of reasonableness. * * * We have no doubt that under this standard the prohibition on solicitation passes muster. * * *

JUSTICE O'CONNOR, concurring * * *.

I * * * agree that publicly owned airports are not public fora. * * * There is little doubt that airports are among those publicly owned facilities that could be closed to all except those who have legitimate business there. Public access to airports is thus not "inherent in the open nature of the locations," as it is for most streets and parks, but is rather a "matter of grace by government officials." *United States v. Kokinda*, 497 U.S. 720, 743, 110 S.Ct. 3115, 3128, 111 L.Ed.2d 571 (1990) (Brennan, J., dissenting). * * * The airports house restaurants, cafeterias, snack bars, coffee shops, cocktail lounges, post offices, banks, telegraph offices, clothing shops, drug stores, food stores, nurseries, barber shops, currency exchanges, art exhibits, commercial advertising displays, bookstores, newsstands, dental offices and private clubs. The International Arrivals Building at JFK Airport even has two branches of Bloomingdale's. * * * In my view, the Port Authority is operating a shopping mall as well as an airport. The reasonableness inquiry, therefore, is not whether the restrictions on speech are "consistent with * * * preserving the property" for air travel, *Perry,* 460 U.S. at 50–51, 103 S.Ct., at 958, but whether they are reasonably related to maintaining the multipurpose environment that the Port Authority has deliberately created. * * *

JUSTICE KENNEDY, with whom JUSTICE BLACKMUN, JUSTICE STEVENS, and JUSTICE SOUTER join as to Part I, concurring in the judgment. * * *

I

* * * [T]he Court's analysis * * * leaves the government with almost unlimited authority to restrict speech on its property by doing nothing more than articulating a non-speech-related purpose for the area, and it leaves almost no scope for the development of new public forums absent the rare approval of the government. The Court's error lies in its conclusion that the public-forum status of public property depends on the government's defined purpose for the property, or on an explicit decision by the government to dedicate the property to expressive activity. In my view, the inquiry must be an objective one, based on the actual, physical characteristics and uses of the property.

The First Amendment is a limitation on government, not a grant of power. Its design is to prevent the government from controlling speech. Yet under the Court's view the authority of the government to control speech on its property is paramount, for in almost all cases the critical step in the Court's analysis is a classification of the property that turns on the government's own definition or decision, unconstrained by an independent duty to respect the speech its citizens can voice there. The Court acknowledges as much, by reintroducing today into our First Amendment law a strict doctrinal line between the proprietary and regulatory functions of government which I thought had been abandoned long ago. * * *

The Court's analysis rests on an inaccurate view of history. The notion that traditional public forums are property which have public discourse as their principal purpose is a most doubtful fiction. The types of property that we have recognized as the quintessential public forums are streets, parks, and sidewalks. It would seem apparent that the principal purpose of streets and sidewalks, like airports, is to facilitate transportation, not public discourse, and we have recognized as much. Similarly, the purpose for the creation of public parks may be as much for beauty and open space as for discourse. Thus under the Court's analysis, even the quintessential public forums would appear to lack the necessary elements of what the Court defines as a public forum.

The effect of the Court's narrow view of the first category of public forums is compounded by its description of the second purported category, the so-called "designated" forum. The requirements for such a designation are so stringent that I cannot be certain whether the category has any content left at all. In any event, it seems evident that under the Court's analysis today few if any types of property other than those already recognized as public forums will be accorded that status.

The Court's answer to these objections appears to be a recourse to history as justifying its recognition of streets, parks, and sidewalks, but apparently no other types of government property, as traditional public forums. * * * In my view the policies underlying the doctrine cannot be given effect unless we recognize that open, public spaces and thoroughfares which are suitable for discourse may be public forums, whatever their historical pedigree and without concern for a precise classification of the property. * * * Without this recognition our forum doctrine retains no relevance in times of fast-changing technology and increasing insularity. In a country where most citizens travel by automobile, and parks all too often become locales for crime rather than social intercourse, our failure to recognize the possibility that new types of government property may be appropriate forums for speech will lead to a serious curtailment of our expressive activity.

One of the places left in our mobile society that is suitable for discourse is a metropolitan airport. It is of particular importance to recognize that such spaces are public forums because in these days an airport is one of the few government-owned spaces where many persons have extensive contact with other members of the public. Given that private spaces of similar character are not subject to the dictates of the First Amendment, see *Hudgens v. NLRB*, 424 U.S. 507, 96 S.Ct. 1029, 47 L.Ed.2d 196 (1976), it is critical that we preserve these areas for protected speech. In my view, our public forum doctrine must recognize this reality, and allow the creation of public forums which do not fit within the narrow tradition of streets, sidewalks, and parks. * * * Under the proper circumstances I would accord public forum status to other forms of property, regardless of its ancient or contemporary origins and whether or not it fits within a narrow historic tradition. If the objective, physical characteristics of the property at issue and the actual public access and uses which have been permitted by the government indicate that expressive activity would be appropriate and compatible with those uses, the property is a public forum. The most important considerations in this analysis are whether the property shares physical similarities with more traditional public forums, whether the government has permitted or acquiesced in broad public access to the property, and whether expressive activity would tend to interfere in a significant way with the uses to which the government has as a factual matter dedicated the property. In conducting the last inquiry, courts must consider the consistency of those uses with expressive activities in general, rather than the specific sort of speech at issue in the case before it; otherwise the analysis would be one not of classification but rather of case-by-case balancing, and would provide little guidance to the State regarding its discretion to regulate speech. Courts must also consider the availability of reasonable time, place, and manner restrictions in undertaking this compatibility analysis. The possibility of some theoretical inconsistency between expressive activities and the property's uses should not bar a finding of a public forum, if those inconsistencies can be avoided through simple and permitted regulations. * * *

 Under this analysis, it is evident that the public spaces of the Port Authority's airports are public forums. First, the District Court made detailed findings regarding the physical similarities between the Port Authority's airports and public streets. These findings show that the public spaces in the airports are broad, public thoroughfares full of people and lined with stores and other commercial activities. An airport corridor is of course not a street, but that is not the proper inquiry. The question is one of physical similarities, sufficient to suggest that the airport corridor should be a public forum for the same reasons that streets and sidewalks have been treated as public forums by the people who use them.

Second, the airport areas involved here are open to the public without restriction. * * * [W]hile most people who come to the Port Authority's airports do so for a reason related to air travel, either because they are passengers or because they are picking up or dropping off passengers, this does not distinguish an airport from streets or sidewalks, which most people use for travel. * * *

Third, and perhaps most important, it is apparent from the record, and from the recent history of airports, that when adequate time, place, and manner regulations are in place, expressive activity is quite compatible with the uses of major airports. * * * In fact, the history of the Authority's own airports, as well as other major airports in this country, leaves little doubt that such a solution is quite feasible. The Port Authority has for many years permitted expressive activities by the plaintiffs and others, without any apparent interference with its ability to meet its transportation purposes. * * * [P]roblems have been dealt with in the past, and in other settings, through proper time, place, and manner restrictions; and the Port Authority does not make any showing that similar regulations would not be effective in its airports. * * *

NEW JERSEY COALITION AGAINST WAR IN THE MIDDLE EAST V. J.M.B. REALTY CORPORATION

Supreme Court of New Jersey, 1994.
138 N.J. 326, 650 A.2d 757.

WILENTZ, C.J.

The question in this case is whether the defendant regional and community shopping centers must permit leafletting on societal issues. We hold that they must, subject to reasonable conditions set by them. Our ruling is limited to leafletting at such centers, and it applies nowhere else. It is based on our citizens' right of free speech embodied in our State Constitution. It follows the course we set in our decision in *State v. Schmid*, 84 N.J. 535 (1980).

In *Schmid* we ruled that our State Constitution conferred on our citizens an affirmative right of free speech that was protected not only from governmental restraint—the extent of First Amendment protection—but from the restraint of private property owners as well. We noted that those state constitutional protections are "available against unreasonably restrictive or oppressive conduct on the part of private entities that have otherwise assumed a constitutional obligation not to abridge the individual exercise of such freedoms because of the public use of their property." And we set forth the standard to determine what public use will give rise to that constitutional obligation. The standard takes into account the normal use of the property, the extent and nature of the public's invitation to use it, and the purpose of the expressional activity in relation to both its private and public use. This "multi-faceted" standard determines whether private property owners "may be required to permit, subject to suitable restrictions, the reasonable exercise by individuals of the constitutional freedoms of speech and assembly." That is to say, they determine whether, taken together, the normal uses of the property, the extent of the public's invitation, and the purpose of free speech in relation to the property's use result in a suitability for free speech on the property that on balance, is sufficiently compelling to warrant limiting the private property owner's right to exclude it, a suitability so compelling as to be constitutionally required. * * *

On November 8, [1990] President Bush announced a major increase in the number of troops stationed in Saudi Arabia and the Persian Gulf in order to provide "an adequate offensive military option." Plaintiff—a coalition of numerous groups—opposed military intervention and sought public support for its views. * * * On November 10 plaintiff's members and representatives went to the malls and requested permission to leaflet. Four of the defendant malls granted plaintiff permission to leaflet on their premises, and plaintiff did in fact leaflet at two of those malls. * * * Although the six remaining malls refused permission, one of those malls—Hamilton—ultimately allowed plaintiff to leaflet. * * * As a consequence of defendants' refusal to allow plaintiff access to the malls, and the restrictions imposed on such access where allowed, few of the thousands of people at those malls on November 10 learned of plaintiff's views. * * *

Each of the ten defendant shopping centers is very large. For instance, one defendant mall, Woodbridge Center, serves an area with a population of 1,400,000. On an average day in 1990, approximately 28,750 people shopped there. * * * Nine of the defendant shopping centers are "regional centers." A regional shopping center is defined in the industry as one that provides shopping goods, general merchandise, apparel, furniture and home furnishings in full depth and variety. It is built around the full-line department store, with a minimum GLA [gross leasable area] of 100,000 square feet, as the major drawing power. * * * The regional centers involved in this case have from 93 to 244 tenants, including not only department stores, but also restaurants and other retail and business establishments, such as art galleries, automotive centers and gas stations, banks, brokerage houses and finance companies, leisure and entertainment centers, optical centers, travel agencies, hair salons, shoe repair shops, theaters, ticket agents, insurance agencies, doctors' offices, and a United States postal booth during the holiday seasons. * * * The tenth defendant is a "community" shopping center. A community center is smaller than a regional center and lacks the variety of merchandise available at a regional mall. * * * [A community center] is built around a junior department store, variety store or discount department store although it may have a strong specialty store. The typical size of a community center is 150,000 square feet. In practice a community center can range from 100,000 to 300,000 square feet. The only community center involved in this case, the Mall at Mill Creek, covers twenty-seven acres. It has a discount department store, a supermarket, sixty-two smaller retail stores, and a seven-restaurant food court. * * *

Each of the defendants permits and encourages a variety of non-shopping activities on its premises. Six of the malls provide access to community groups. * * * Some of the non-shopping activities permitted by defendants involved speech, politics, and community issues.* * * Despite the myriad of permitted uses, including many involving the distribution of issue-oriented literature—leaflets—and accompanying speech, despite the explicit permission given to plaintiff to leaflet at four of them, and despite the display of tenants' posters at most of them, posters that were visible from the common areas and expressed support for our armed forces in the Persian Gulf, all of the centers claim to prohibit issue-oriented speech and leafletting. * * *

Before reaching our discussion of the law, we must first examine the background against which this question is raised. * * * Statistical evidence tells the story of the growth of shopping malls. In 1950, privately-owned shopping centers of any size numbered fewer than 100 across the country. * * * By 1992, the number expanded to at least 1,835. * * * The share of retail sales attributable to regional and super-regional malls has demonstrated a similar pattern. Nationally, regional malls' market share of "shopper goods sales" was 13% in 1967 and 31% in 1979. In 1991 retail sales in "shopping centers," a category that includes not only regional malls but other types of urban and suburban retail centers, "accounted for over 56% of total retail sales in the United States, excluding sales by automotive dealers and gasoline service stations." * * * Thus, malls are where the people can be found today. Indeed, 70% of the national adult population shop at regional malls and do so an average of 3.9 times a month, about once a week. Therefore, based on adult population data from the 1990 census, more than four million people on average shop at our regional shopping centers every week, assuming New Jersey follows this national pattern.

The converse story, the decline of downtown business districts, is not so easily documented by statistics. But for the purposes of this case, we do not need statistics. This Court takes judicial notice of the fact that in every major city of this state, over the past twenty years, there has been not only a decline, but in many cases a disastrous decline. This Court further takes judicial notice of the fact that this decline has been accompanied and caused by the combination of the move of residents from the city to the suburbs and the construction of shopping centers in those suburbs. * * * That some downtown business districts have survived, and indeed thrive, is also fact, demonstrated on the record before us. The overriding fact, however, is that the movement from cities to the suburbs has transformed New Jersey, as it has many states. The economic lifeblood once found downtown has moved to suburban shopping centers, which have substantially displaced the downtown business districts as the centers of commercial and social activity.

The defendants in this case cannot rebut this observation. Indeed, the shopping center industry frequently boasts of the achievement. The industry often refers to large malls as " 'the new downtowns.' " It correctly asserts that "the shopping center is an integral part of the economic and social fabric of America." * * * Beyond that, one expert maintains that shopping centers have "evolved beyond the strictly retail stage to become a public square where people gather[ ]; it is often the only large contained place in a suburb and it provides a place for exhibitions that no other space can offer." * * *

The question whether citizens may exercise a right of free speech at privately-owned shopping centers without permission of the owners has been litigated extensively. * * * It is now clear that the Federal Constitution affords no general right to free speech in privately-owned shopping centers, [*Lloyd Corp. v. Tanner*, 407 U.S. 551 (1972)], and most State courts facing the issue have ruled the same way when State constitutional rights have been asserted. * * * California, Oregon, Massachusetts, Colorado, and Washington, however, have held that their citizens have a right to engage in certain types of expressive conduct at privately-owned malls. Of those five, only California has held that its free speech clause protects citizens from private action as well as state action and grants issue-oriented free speech rights at a regional shopping center. *Robins v. Pruneyard Shopping Ctr.*, 592 P.2d 341, 347 (Cal.1979), *aff'd*, 447 U.S. 74, 100 S. Ct. 2035, 64 L. Ed. 2d 741 (1980). Massachusetts and Oregon relied on clauses other than their free speech clauses. *Batchelder v. Allied Stores Int'l*, 445 N.E.2d 590, 593 (Mass.1983) (relying on state constitution's "free-and-equal elections" provision); *Lloyd Corp. v. Whiffen*, 849 P.2d 446, 453–54 (Or.1993) (*Whiffen II*) (relying on state constitution's initiative and referendum provision and declining to address whether free speech clause was also source of right to collect signatures at mall). Colorado relied on its constitution's free speech provision to hold that political activists had a constitutional right to distribute literature at a privately-owned mall. *Bock v. Westminster Mall Company*, 819 P.2d 55 (Colo.1991). The *Bock* court, however, did not dispense with a state action requirement for its free speech provision; rather, the Court found that the mall that sought to prohibit the distribution of literature was a state actor. * * *

In New Jersey, we have once before discussed the application of our State constitutional right of free speech to private conduct. In *State v. Schmid*, * * * we held that Schmid, though lacking permission from Princetown University, had the right to enter the campus, distribute leaflets, and sell political materials. We ruled that the right of free speech could be exercised on the campus subject to the University's reasonable regulations. * * * We find that each of the elements of the standard in *Schmid*, the use, the invitation, and the suitability of free speech at the centers, supports the existence of a constitutional free speech right in the plaintiff and a corresponding obligation in the defendants. "Taken together, these ... relevant considerations" of the "multi-faceted" standard set forth in *Schmid* lead to the conclusion that these regional and community shopping centers must "be required to permit, subject to suitable restrictions, the reasonable exercise by individuals of the constitutional freedoms of speech and assembly," here the leafletting sought by plaintiff. * * *

Our holding today applies to all regional shopping centers. That holding is based on their essential nature. The mammoth size of these regional centers, the proliferation of uses, the all-embracing quality of the implied invitation, and the compatibility of free speech with those uses: the inevitable presence and coexistence of all of those factors more than satisfy the three elements of the *Schmid* standard. Furthermore, these regional shopping centers are, in all significant respects, the functional equivalent of a downtown business district, a fact that provides further support for our holding. These are the essential places for the preservation of the free speech that nourishes society and was found in downtown business districts when they flourished. * * * We are unable, however, to apply that command to community shopping centers with only one such center before us, for while we believe all others share its characteristics, we are not yet sufficiently certain of that fact. * * *

Our holding is limited to leafletting and associated speech in support of, or in opposition to, causes, candidates, and parties—political and societal free speech. We affirmatively rule that our State Constitution does not confer free speech rights at regional and community shopping centers that go beyond such speech. In addition to some doubt—the issue is really not before us—whether our constitutional provision was intended to cover commercial speech in any way at all, we find this limitation the result of our application of the elements and standard in *Schmid*. * * * [T]he commercial free speech could obviously be directly in conflict with the centers' activities, uses, and success, the most obvious example being leafletting seeking to persuade shoppers and non-shoppers to go elsewhere. We will not require these centers to carefully review every application for commercial free speech and put them to the test of justifying its exclusion under some balance. It is obviously a most serious intrusion on the property interests of these owners; it does not satisfy the standard of *Schmid*; it does not have State constitutional protection.

As for the manner of speech, our ruling is confined to leafletting and associated free speech: the speech that normally and necessarily accompanies leafletting. Plaintiff has sought no more. It does not include bullhorns, megaphones, or even a soapbox; it does not include placards, pickets, parades, and demonstrations; it does not include anything other than normal speech and then only such as is necessary to the effectiveness of the leafletting. The free speech associated with leafletting, handbilling, and pamphleteering, as commonly understood, is only that which is needed to attract the attention of passersby—in a normal voice—to the cause and to the fact that leaflets are available, without pressure, harassment, following, pestering, of any kind. Additionally, the sale of literature and the solicitation of funds on the spot (as distinguished from appeals found in the leaflets themselves) are not covered by the protection. * * *

We do not believe our opinion will result in any harm to these centers, to their businesses, nor any less enjoyment for those who visit, shoppers and non-shoppers. The free speech we have permitted * * * is the least intrusive form of free speech and the easiest to control. The experience elsewhere proves the ability of those centers to absorb such speech without harm. The rare instances of disturbance resulted from circumstances most unlikely to occur here. Obviously, we cannot guarantee that disturbances will not occur as a result of our decision. Indeed, we could not guarantee freedom from such disturbances even in the absence of a right to leaflet. However, the slim possibility of disruption is the price we all pay as citizens of this state; the danger that some will abuse their rights is a necessary result of our constitutional commitment to free speech. * * *

GARIBALDI, J., dissenting. * * *

[T]he majority departs from the *Schmid* test and argues that shopping malls are the "functional equivalent" of the traditional downtown business districts or town squares. In support of that theory, the majority relies on "common knowledge" of the Court outside the record, ignoring the factual findings of the trial court and evidence that many of the towns in Essex, Hudson, and Morris Counties around the malls have become more, not less, vibrant. Under the majority's theory, private property becomes municipal land and private-property owners become the government. * * * The inescapable mission of shopping malls is not to be the successor to downtown business districts; rather, it is to provide a comfortable and conducive atmosphere for shopping, a mission into which mall owners have invested large sums and energy.

Common sense also dictates that privately-owned-and-operated shopping malls are not the functional equivalent of downtown business districts. They are not "replicas of the community itself." Shopping malls do not have housing, town halls, libraries, houses of worship, hospitals, or schools. Nor do they contain the small stores, such as the corner grocer, that used to serve as the forum for exchange of ideas. Indeed, most shopping malls do not allow people even to walk their dogs there.

The shopping mall is not a community. There is no "mayor of the mall." Shoppers do not elect a common council. They do not have a say in the day-to-day affairs of the mall, nor do they expect one. They do not visit the mall to be informed or to inform others of social or political causes; they go to shop. Even though the malls sponsor community events, visits from Santa, and orchestral concerts, visitors do not mistake them for grassroots gathering places, Santa's Workshop, or a mecca of the arts or culture. * * *

The majority's opinion ignores the basic commercial purpose of these private malls, ascribes to them the downfall of urban business districts, and delegates to them the responsibility to fulfill the role once, and arguably still, played by town squares. It does all of that without any legitimate or rational justification. Moreover, the Court places burdens on the private malls that they are ill-suited to handle. Ultimately, mall owners will pass those burdens on to the consumer. The private property owner and ultimately the consumer, the forgotten person in the majority opinion, will have to pay the increased costs that result from the expanded security and other expenses associated with the public's free access to the mall for expressional activities. Unlike the municipalities that the majority thinks the malls have supplanted, malls are not exempt from most tort claims under the New Jersey Tort Claims Act.

Plaintiffs cannot claim that they have no means to express their opinion to the public other than by distributing pamphlets in shopping malls. No evidence shows that plaintiffs could not effectively distribute their pamphlets in other areas. Indeed, according to plaintiff's November 9, 1990, press release, they distributed their materials in at least thirty locations, including several downtown areas. They were able to distribute over 85,000 pamphlets in those locations during a three-day period. Plaintiffs do not need to use the malls, save for their own convenience. * * * Were we to adhere to *Schmid* and deny access to the malls, plaintiffs would nevertheless remain able to reach the public outside supermarkets and movie theaters, at train stations and bus stops, in parks and post offices, in the media, and even in the numerous still-vibrant downtown shopping districts. Plaintiffs can voice their opinions today more readily and more accessibly in more places and in more formats than ever before in human history. * * *

MAZDABROOK COMMONS HOMEOWNERS' ASSOCIATION V. KHAN

Supreme Court of New Jersey, 2012.
210 N.J. 482, 46 A.3d 507.

CHIEF JUSTICE RABNER delivered the opinion of the Court.

The question in this appeal is whether a homeowners' association can prohibit residents from posting political signs in the windows of their own homes. Defendant Wasim Khan lives in a planned townhouse community that is managed by plaintiff Mazdabrook Commons, a homeowners' association. In 2005, Khan ran for Parsippany Town Council and posted two signs in support of his candidacy at his private residence—one inside the window of his townhouse and another inside the door. Mazdabrook notified Khan that the signs violated the association's rules and ordered their removal. Mazdabrook's regulations banned all residential signs except "For Sale" signs. * * *

Mazdabrook Commons is a planned community of 194 townhomes in Parsippany-Troy Hills. The development is enclosed, but not gated, and has no public through-streets. The Mazdabrook Commons Homeowner's Association, Inc. * * * is a non-profit corporation that manages the development. Each owner of a townhouse in the development is a member of the Association, which elects a Board of Trustees. The development is a common-interest, interdependent community in which individual owners agree to certain common rules and restrictions for the benefit of the entire group. * * * Unit owners receive various closing documents in connection with the purchase of a townhome * * *. [The documents inform] purchasers that they must comply with the restrictions * * * adopted by the Association. Among other things, * * * [the] documents restrict the posting of signs. * * * [Residents also] may not hang laundry outside, install unshielded floodlights, use exterior loudspeakers, place trailers or boats in common areas, or maintain a dog pen outside. * * * Khan bought a home in Mazdabrook in 2003. He received and reviewed the * * * [documents] when he purchased his unit. * * * A few days after posting the signs, Khan received a letter from the Board, which stated that a political sign was displayed in his window and ordered its immediate removal. The letter cited to the prohibition on signs * * * and assessed a $25 fine for violating that policy. Khan complied and removed the signs. * * *

New Jersey's Constitution guarantees individuals a broad, affirmative right to free speech. Under the Constitution, "[e]very person may freely speak, write and publish his sentiments on all subjects, being responsible for the abuse of that right. No law shall be passed to restrain or abridge the liberty of speech or of the press." *N.J. Const.* art. I, ¶ 6. That provision has been described as "broader than practically all others in the nation." *Green Party v. Hartz Mountain Indus., Inc.,* 164 N.J. 127, 145, 752 A.2d 315 (2000). The affirmative guarantee in the first sentence offers greater protection than the First Amendment, which bars the government from restraining speech. Federal case law requires some form of "state action" to trigger the protections of the First Amendment. State law, interpreting a broader constitutional right, does not. In New Jersey, an individual's affirmative right to speak freely "is protected not only from abridgement by government, but also from unreasonably restrictive and oppressive conduct by private entities" in certain situations. *N.J. Coalition Against War in the Middle East v. J.M.B. Realty Corp.,* 138 N.J. 326, 353, 650 A.2d 757 (1994) (citing *State v. Schmid,* 84 N.J. 535, 563, 423 A.2d 615, 1980). As this Court explained in *Schmid,* the free speech and assembly clauses in the New Jersey Constitution can be invoked against private entities "because of the public use of their property." *Schmid, supra,* 84 N.J. at 560, 423 A.2d 615.

As a result, this Court has previously found that a private university and privately owned shopping malls assumed a constitutional obligation to protect free expression on their premises. At the core of those cases, the Court balanced the legitimate interests of private property owners—to be free "from untoward interference with or confiscatory restrictions upon" the reasonable use of their property—and the individual right to free speech and assembly. The Court considered the reasonableness of restrictions imposed on speech and assembly in light of those competing interests. * * *

Both sides rely heavily on this Court's * * * recent decision in *Committee For A Better Twin Rivers v. Twin Rivers Homeowners' Ass'n,* 192 N.J. 344, 929 A.2d 1060, 2007, which addressed facts similar to the ones * * * now before us: the free speech rights of homeowners who live in a large, planned, residential community managed by a homeowners' association. A group of residents there had formed a committee to try to change how the Twin Rivers association governed the development. The group filed a complaint against the association that sought to invalidate its sign policy. That policy, which existed to "avoid the clutter of signs" and "preserve the aesthetic value of the common areas," limited residents to posting one sign in any window of their home and a second sign in a flower bed no further than three feet from the residence. * * * The *Twin Rivers* Court * * * found that Twin Rivers' private property interest was stronger than the interests asserted in *Schmid* or *Coalition*; unlike those private forums, Twin Rivers had not invited the public onto its property. Also, the association's sign restrictions were relatively "minor"; they limited the number and placement of signs but permitted expressional activities. On balance, the Court found that the restrictions were not unreasonable and did not violate the State Constitution. * * *

Khan is not an outsider or visitor like a leafletter visiting a university campus or a shopping mall. He owns the private property where he wishes to speak. Viewed from his perspective, the primary use of the property—in this case, the townhouse—is * * * residential. * * * [T]he extent of the public's invitation to use the property becomes less relevant when viewed through Khan's eyes because he is the property's owner and not an invited guest. * * * Here, the Association restricted political speech, which lies "at the core" of our constitutional free speech protections. * * * As the United States Supreme Court has recognized, "residential signs have long been an important and distinct medium of expression"—"a venerable means of communication that is both unique and important." *City of Ladue v. Gilleo,* 512 U.S. 43, 54–55, 114 S.Ct. 2038, 2045, 129 L.Ed.2d 36, 47 (1994). In addition * * *, the Court noted that "[r]esidential signs are an unusually cheap and convenient form of communication." Residential signs are important for another reason as well: "[p]recisely because of their location," they connect the message directly to the speaker and thus add to the words on display. * * *

On one hand, we evaluate * * * [this] expressional activity in light of the overall Mazdabrook development—a private, residential community whose members agreed to abide by common rules and regulations when they purchased their units. The reciprocal nature of those rules benefits the entire community. See *Twin Rivers, supra*. The Association's regulations can help preserve the architectural design of the units, promote a uniform, aesthetic look, and maintain property values, which are all legitimate interests. At the same time, the proposed speech should be considered in relation to Khan's use of his own private property, not common property of the Association. He, too, possesses legitimate property rights, and he claims a right to free expression on his own property. A near-complete ban on residential signs, which bars all political signs, cannot be considered a minor restriction as to Khan. For him, it hampers the most basic right to speak about the political process and his own candidacy for office. * * * Yet, here, there is only minimal interference with the Association's property or common areas. Khan did not erect a billboard, put up a soapbox, or use a loudspeaker. He posted two signs in the window and door of his home, which people passing by could choose to view or ignore. * * *

Political signs advancing a resident's candidacy are not by their nature incompatible with a private development. They do not conflict with the purpose of the development—unlike signs that might encourage shoppers to leave a mall and shop elsewhere. See *Coalition, supra*. Rather, * * * a window sign in support of a candidate is a relatively minor interference with private property. The Association, of course, had the power to adopt reasonable time, place, and manner restrictions to serve the community's interests. The homeowners' association in *Twin Rivers* accomplished that by limiting the number and location of residential signs. Reasonable limits could also be placed on the size of signs. * * *

In assessing the reasonableness of a restriction, courts also consider whether convenient, feasible, alternative means exist for individuals "to engage in substantially the same expressional activity." *Twin Rivers, supra*. Mazdabrook suggests that Khan had ample alternatives to posting a sign at his townhouse: he could walk door-to-door, distribute pamphlets, prepare mass mailings, stop and speak to neighbors on the street, speak to them before or after Association meetings, and telephone them. Those options, though, are not substitutes for a more enduring message, identified with the speaker, in the form of a political sign in the window of the speaker's home. * * * On balance, the importance of Khan's right to promote his candidacy for office, and the relatively minor interference his conduct posed to private property, outweighs the interests Mazdabrook asserts here. We find that the Association's sign policy, which prevented Khan from posting a political sign on his home, violates the State Constitution's guarantee of free speech. * * *

[A]t oral argument, the Association claimed that Khan waived his constitutional right to free speech because he bought his unit with full knowledge of the sign restrictions listed in the offering and governing documents. To be valid, waivers must be knowing, intelligent, and voluntary. Under the circumstances of this case, we do not find a valid waiver. * * * Can fundamental constitutional rights be properly waived by including waiver language in the midst of a more than fifty-page, single-spaced document? * * * [I]t is unclear that the approach in this case can result in a *knowing* and *intelligent* waiver of fundamental constitutional rights. * * * We also note that tens if not hundreds of thousands of New Jersey residents live in developed communities like Mazdabrook. The proliferation of residential communities with standard agreements that restrict free speech would violate the fundamental free speech values espoused in our Constitution * * *. [W]e cannot accept that a complete waiver of free speech rights in one's home could be possible in this context. Instead, as discussed earlier, the exercise of those rights can be subject to reasonable time, place, and manner restrictions. * * *

JUDGE WEFING (temporarily assigned), dissenting. * * *

My colleagues rightly note our nation's and our state's commitment to a free and vigorous debate of public questions. I have no quarrel with that commitment; I embrace it. In my judgment, however, individuals are equally entitled to seek shelter from political debate and division. If a group of individuals wish to live in a common-interest community that precludes the posting of signs, political or otherwise, and have agreed freely to do so, and * * * there is no showing of overreaching or coercion, I would adopt the principles enunciated in Judge Miniman's dissent in the Appellate Division, that these mutually-agreed upon covenants ran with the land, were reasonable, and were enforceable. * * *

COUNCIL OF ORGANIZATIONS AND OTHERS FOR EDUCATION ABOUT PAROCHIAID, INC. V. ENGLER

Supreme Court of Michigan, 1997.
455 Mich. 557, 566 N.W.2d 208.

BRICKLEY, JUSTICE.

This case concerns 1993 P.A. 362, the statute commonly known as the charter schools act, which authorized the creation of public school academies. The plaintiffs brought this suit to enjoin the distribution of public funds by challenging the constitutionality of the statute. * * *

Under Act 362, a public school academy is organized as a nonprofit corporation under the Nonprofit Corporation Act. A public school academy is administered under the direction of a board of directors in accordance with Act 362 and the nonprofit corporation bylaws contained in the public school academy's contract. * * * To organize a public school academy, an applicant, either a person or an entity, must submit an application to an authorizing body. * * * Act 362 specifies four types of authorizing bodies: (1) the board of a school district, (2) intermediate school board, (3) the board of a community college, and (4) the governing board of a state public university. An authorizing body is not required to issue any public school academy contracts, but if it does, it must issue the contracts "on a competitive basis taking into consideration the resources available for the proposed public school academy, the population to be served by the proposed public school academy, and the educational goals to be achieved by the proposed public school academy." Before granting a contract to operate a public school academy, an authorizing body is required to adopt a resolution establishing the method of selection, length of term, and number of members of the public school academy's board of directors. The authorizing body for a public school academy is the fiscal agent for the public school academy, and its aid payments are paid to the authorizing body. The authorizing body is responsible for the public school academy's compliance with the contract and all applicable law. Further, the contract may be revoked at any time the public school academy fails to abide by the statute.

Subsection 501(1) states that "[a] public school academy is a public school under section 2 of Article VII of the state constitution of 1963, and is considered to be a school district for the purposes of section 11 of article IX of the state constitution of 1963." Act 362 * * * states that "[a] public school academy shall comply with all applicable law. . . ." Moreover, the act states that a church or other religious organization cannot organize a public school academy and that a public school academy is prohibited from having organizational or contractual affiliations with churches or other religious organizations to the extent such agreements are prohibited by the state or federal constitutions. Furthermore, Act 362 specifically provides that a public school academy is prohibited from charging tuition and is required to abide by the pupil admission policies set forth in the statute. If the public school academy has more applicants than space, it is required to hold a random selection process for the enrollment of its students. * * *

The 1963 Michigan Constitution does not define the term "public schools." However, it does state that the Legislature has the responsibility for "maintain[ing] and support[ing] a system of free public education. . . ." Art. 8, § 2. * * * The appellees assert that the system established by our Legislature violates art. 8, § 2 because public school academies are not public, 1) in that they are not under the ultimate and immediate, or exclusive, control of the state and 2) because the academy's board of directors is not publicly elected or appointed by a public body. * * *

[P]laintiff's first assertion fails because there is no requirement in our constitution that the state must have exclusive control of the school system. While our constitution requires only that the Legislature "maintain and support a system" of public schools, the parties argue and several other states have recognized the need for the state to have some control in order to qualify for public funding. Michigan's public school academies meet this requirement because they are under the ultimate and immediate control of the state and its agents. First, a charter may be revoked any time the authorizing body has a reasonable belief that grounds for revocation exist, such as either the academy's failure to abide by the terms of its charter or its failure to comply with all applicable law. Second, because authorizing bodies are public institutions, the state exercises control over public school academies through the application-approval process. During this process, the authorizing body can reject any application with which it is not completely satisfied in any detail, and through the authorizing body's right to revoke the charter of any public school academy that does not comply with its charter. Third, the state controls the money. The act provides for the funding of public school academies in the manner of other public schools, and public school academies may not charge tuition. * * * Finally, the Legislature intended the other sections of the School Code to apply to the public school academies. There are no specific restrictions in 1993 P.A. 362 that would limit the power of the state. * * *

The plaintiffs further argue that because a public school academy is run by a private board of directors and because the authorizing body has no means for selecting members of the board, the public school academies are not public schools. * * *

Subsection 503(3) of 1993 P.A. 362 provides:

An authorizing body shall adopt a resolution establishing the method of selection, length of term, and number of members of the board of directors of each public school academy subject to its jurisdiction.

Therefore, the Legislature has mandated the board of director's selection process. The Legislature has this control, and it can change this process at any time. Additionally, the board of the authorizing bodies is publicly elected or appointed by public bodies. While the boards of the public school academies may or may not be elected, the public maintains control of the schools through the authorizing bodies.

Further, if we examine the common understanding of what a "public school" is, * * * we find that public school academies are "public schools." Under 78 CJS, Schools and School Districts, § 2, p. 39, a "public school" is

established and maintained at public expense, primarily from moneys raised by general taxation, as contradistinguished from a private or denominational school, or, in other words, a school comprised in the free school system which has been generally adopted in the United States.

It has further been defined as,

> broadly speaking, open and public to all in the locality, which the state undertakes through various boards and officers to direct, manage, and control, and which is subject to and under the control of the qualified voters of the school district in which it is situate. * * *

> [W]e do not have a requirement in our state constitution that mandates that the school be under the control of the voters of the school district. In fact, a review of our constitutional history shows that our forefathers envisioned public education to be under the control of the Legislature, which is under the command of the entire state electorate. * * * [T]here was never a requirement that the local school board had to be appointed by a public body as opined by the Court of Appeals majority in this case. * * *

Article 8, § 2 was amended by the electorate in 1970 by what is commonly known as the parochiaid amendment. This amendment added to § 2 the following language:

> No public monies or property shall be appropriated or paid or any public credit utilized, by the legislature or any other political subdivision or agency of the state directly or indirectly to aid or maintain any private, denominational or other nonpublic, pre-elementary, elementary, or secondary school. No payment, credit, tax benefit, exemption or deductions, tuition voucher, subsidy, grant or loan of public monies or property shall be provided, directly or indirectly, to support the attendance of any student or the employment of any person at any such nonpublic school or at any location or institution where instruction is offered in whole or in part to such nonpublic school students. The legislature may provide for the transportation of students to and from any school. * * *

As far as the voters were concerned in 1970, the result of all the preelection talk and action concerning Proposal C [the parochiaid amendment] was simply this "—Proposal C was an anti-parochiaid amendment—no public monies to run parochial schools—and beyond that all else was utter and complete confusion." *Traverse City School Dist. v. Attorney General*, 384 Mich. 390, 185 N.W.2d 9 (1971). * * * [T]he common understanding of the voters in 1970 was that no monies would be spent to run a parochial school. However, public school academies are not parochial schools. The statute specifically prohibits religious organization from organizing a public school academy and further prohibits any organizational or contractual affiliations with churches or other religious organizations. Additionally, a public school academy is not a parochial school in that the charging of tuition is prohibited, as is any restrictions on admission other than a random selection process if the school is has more applicants than space. * * * We hold that 1993 P.A. 362 does not violate art. 8, § 2 or art. 8, § 3 of the Michigan Constitution of 1963. * * *

BOYLE, JUSTICE (dissenting). * * *

Approximately twenty-five states, including Michigan, and the District of Columbia have enacted charter school legislation. An innovative and creative bid at educational reform, charter schools are public schools that are autonomous, at least in part, from state regulation. * * * The "freedom" deemed necessary by charter school proponents is the flexibility achieved by relieving the schools from state or local regulation. However, because legislation may not circumvent the constitution, freedom from regulation is precisely that element of the charter school concept that brings it into potential conflict with the constitution. Stated otherwise, if 1993 P.A. 362 "privatizes" charter schools, the fundamental constitutional value has been transgressed. Thus, unless art. 8, § 2 is amended, the viability of the charter school initiative will depend on how "public" the system is under successive acts. * * *

Despite the illusion of public control created by the 1993 act, and the conclusion of the lead opinion that "the public maintains control of the schools through the authorizing bodies," public school academies are controlled by privately selected, rather than publicly elected, boards of directors and are subject only to limited oversight by the authorizing bodies and State Board of Education. A careful reading of the 1993 act reveals that neither the authorizing body nor the State Board of Education has the power to appoint individual members to the academy board. In fact, the State Board of Education has no authority whatsoever under the statute to supervise the selection, retention, or removal of academy board members. Moreover, the authorizing body's influence over the academy board of director selection process is constrained under the 1993 act so that the authorizing body only has the authority to establish the "method of selection, length of term, and number of members of the board of directors. . . ." Once this nebulous criteria is established, the public academy has full authority to appoint as a member of its board of directors any individual it deems fit. The academy application must describe "qualifications and method for appointment or election of members of the board," and need not disclose the actual identity of proposed board members. Moreover, under the 1993 act, the authorizing body has limited recourse against the public school academy if it is dissatisfied with an individual member of the academy board. The State Board of Education has even less recourse.

The limited authority of the authorizing body and State Board of Education to oversee academy school operations is further evidenced by the process of contract issuance and revocation as provided under the 1993 act. * * * [T]he authorizing body, as opposed to the State Board of Education, has sole authority to approve and issue a contract. * * * In addition to the power to issue a contract, the authorizing body is given sole, albeit limited, authority to revoke the contract. * * * As was true of contract issuance, despite the fact that the State Board of Education is constitutionally mandated to lead and supervise public education, there is no provision under the 1993 act that grants authority to the State Board of Education to revoke a charter contract.

Lack of public control over the academy school board of directors, and limited control of the authorizing body and State Board of Education over the process of contract issuance and revocation are not the only flaws in the 1993 act. Despite the fact that public school academies must comply with "all applicable law," academy schools are not subject to large portions of the public School Code. As an example, public school academies are not expressly required to use state certified teachers. Although some, including the defendants, argue that public school academies must clearly use state certified teachers, the answer to this issue is less than obvious. What is obvious is that this deficiency was corrected under 1994 P.A. 416 when the Legislature expressly required, in two separate provisions, that academy schools use certified teachers. In addition, there is disagreement over whether public school academies must comply with core curriculum requirements. Clearly, there is no express provision in the 1993 act that requires compliance with any curriculum requirement. Rather, the act authorizes a public school academy to designate in its articles of incorporation "the educational goals of the public school academy and the curriculum to be offered and methods of pupil assessment to be used. . . ." * * *

[W]hile academy schools are bound to comply with some restrictions that are generally applicable to all public schools, such as the Freedom of Information Act, academy schools have significant independence under 1993 P.A. 362 from state or local regulation. When coupled with private boards of directors that have limited obligations to answer to the public, and with authorizing bodies and a State Board of Education that are essentially powerless to supervise academy school organization and operation, the academy schools established by the 1993 act are private schools that have been given selected accoutrements of public schools in the hope that they will be characterized as the functional equivalent of public schools. Simply put, this "innovative" act effectively grants academy schools nearly "total independence to decide what to teach and how to teach it, whom to hire and how to use their resources, what hours to operate and how best to meet students' needs." In my judgment, the 1993 act is facially violative of art. 8, § 2 of the Michigan Constitution.* * *

C. THE FORMS OF LOCAL POWER

This section continues our examination of the decentralization of power and of the public/private distinction by focusing on entities that now exercise decentralized power in the United States other than city governments. The first two excerpts—by Robert Ellickson and Evan McKenzie—present contrasting views of homeowners associations.[6] Homeowners associations are creatures of property law rather than local government law: covenants and servitudes, instead of city ordinances, specify the rules that govern how these residential communities operate. Some homeowners associations have tens of thousands of inhabitants and are thus larger than many cities; many of them control land use decisions and provide services in a manner comparable to city governments. According to the Community Association Institute, a trade association, in 2012 there were more than 25 million units, housing more than 63 million people, in homeowners associations in the United States. Is Professor Ellickson persuasive when he argues that homeowners associations do not present the dangers that Madison identifies with the exercise of power by small, decentralized groups? Is your answer to this question affected by the excerpt by Gary Miller, reproduced below, describing a homeowners association that became a city? What difference does it make—should it make—whether a homeowners association receives a city charter? Should homeowners associations, like the company town in Marsh v. Alabama, simply be treated as if they are cities?

The two cases that follow the readings on homeowners associations— Municipal Building Authority v. Lowder and Ball v. James—introduce another form of decentralized power: special purpose governments.[7]

---

[6] See, e.g., Michael Pollack, Judicial Deference and Institutional Character: Homeowners Associations and the Puzzle of Private Governance, 81 U. Cin. L. Rev. 839 (2013); Steven Siegel, The Public Interest and Private Gated Communities: A Comprehensive Approach to Public Policy That Would Discourage the Establishment of New Gated Communities and Encourage the Removal of Gates from Existing Private Communities, 55 Loy. L. Rev. 805 (2009); Paula A. Franzese, Trust and Community: The Common Interest Community as Metaphor and Paradox, 72 Mo. L. Rev. 1111 (2007); Steven Siegel, The Public Role In Establishing Private Residential Communities: Towards a New Formulation of Local Government Land Use Policies That Eliminates the Legal Requirement to Privatize New Communities in the United States, 38 Urb. Law. 859 (2006); Robert Nelson, Private Neighborhoods and the Transformation of Local Government (2005); Paula A. Franzese, Privatization and its Discontent: Common Interest Communities and the Rise of Government for the "Nice," 37 Urb. Law. 335 (2005); Lee Anne Fennell, Contracting Communities, 2004 U. Ill. L. Rev. 829 (2004); David Callies et al., Ramapo Looking Forward: Gated Communities, Covenants, and Concerns, 35 Urb. Law 177 (2003); Paula Franzese, Does It Take a Village? Privatization, Patterns of Restrictiveness and the Demise of Community, 47 Vill. L. Rev. 553 (2002); Donald Stabile, Community Associations: The Emergence and Acceptance of a Quiet Innovation in Housing (2000); David Kennedy, Residential Associations as State Actors: Regulating the Impact of Gated Communities on Nonmembers, 105 Yale L.J. 761 (1995); Clayton Gillette, Courts, Covenants, and Communities, 61 U. Chi. L. Rev. 1375 (1994); Dilemmas of Group Autonomy: Residential Associations and Community, 75 Cornell L. Rev. 1 (1989); Note: The Rule Of Law In Residential Associations, 99 Harv. L. Rev. 472 (1985).

[7] See, e.g., Nadav Shoked, Quasi-Cities, 93 B.U. L. Rev. 1971 (2013); Megan Mullin, The Conditional Effect of Specialized Governance on Public Policy, 52 Am. J. Pol. Sci. 1, 125–41 (2008); Sara C. Galvan, Wrestling With MUDS To Pin Down the Truth About Special Districts,

Is MTA a special purpose gov't?

Special purpose governments (often denominated as public authorities or special districts) are government-created entities designed to perform a single function or limited range of functions: in *Lowder*, for example, the public authority was designed to construct a new jail facility and in *Ball*, the special district was established to provide water and electricity services. Special purpose governments are often envisioned more as business entities than as governments: they are often run by an appointed board of directors (or by officers elected by a limited class of voters, such as property owners), immunized from restrictions on city governments, and, sometimes, given their own sources of revenue. In fact, as the two cases illustrate, these entities are frequently created to avoid popular democratic decision making. Is it legitimate for public authorities to avoid the restrictions that the state has imposed on city power, as *Lowder* suggests? Is *Ball* persuasive that special districts need not be run pursuant to democratic, one-person one-vote, control? What conception of the public/private distinction animates your answers to these questions?

The final case, Kessler v. Grand Central District Management Association, introduces a final example of decentralized power: business improvement districts (BIDs).[8] Like homeowners associations—and like the special district at issue in *Ball*—BIDs are controlled by property owners, not citizens. And, like public authorities, they provide specialized services comparable to those offered by city governments. Are these new forms of local government organization innovative ways of dealing with local problems that city governments cannot handle? Or are they improper incursions on democratic control of local policy making?

---

75 Fordham L. Rev. 3041 (2007); Laurie Reynolds, Local Governments and Regional Governance, 39 Urb. Law. 483 (2007); Kathryn Foster, The Political Economy of Special-Purpose Government (1997); Nancy Burns, The Formation of American Local Governments: Private Values in Public Institutions (1994); Richard Briffault, Who Rules at Home?: One Person/One Vote and Local Governments, 60 U. Chi. L. Rev. 339 (1993); Donald Axelrod, Shadow Governments: The Hidden World of Public Authorities (1992).

   8   See, e.g., Wayne Batchis, Business Improvement Districts and the Constitution: The Troubling Necessity of Privatized Government for Urban Revitalization, 38 Hastings Const. L.Q. 91 (2010); Symposium: Business Improvement Districts and the Evolution of Urban Governance, 3 Drexel L. Rev. 1 (2010); Goktug Morcol, Lorlene Hoyt, Jack W. Meek, and Ulf Zimmermann, Business Improvement Districts: Research, Theories, and Controversies (2008); Wendell E. Pritchett, Beyond Kelo: Thinking About Urban Development in the 21st Century, 22 Ga. St. U. L. Rev. 895 (2006); Audrey McFarlane, Preserving Community in the City: Special Improvement Districts and the Privatization of Urban Racialized Space, 4 Stan. Agora 5 (2003); Daniel Garodnick, What's the BID Deal? Can the Grand Central Business Improvement District Serve a Special Limited Purpose?, 148 U. Pa. L. Rev. 1733 (2000); Richard Briffault, A Government For Our Time? Business Improvement Districts and Urban Governance, 99 Colum. L. Rev. 365 (1999); Robert Ellickson, New Institutions For Old Neighborhoods, 48 Duke L. J. 75 (1998); Lawrence Houstoun, BIDS: Business Improvement Districts (1997).

ROBERT ELLICKSON, CITIES AND HOMEOWNERS ASSOCIATIONS

130 U.Pa.L.Rev. 1519, 1519–1520, 1521–1523, 1526–1527 (1982).

In his recent article, *The City as a Legal Concept,* Professor Gerald Frug compared the city and the business corporation as possible vehicles for the exercise of decentralized power. In the course of his analysis, Frug asserted that American law is deeply biased against the emergence of powerful cities and, by implication, is less restrictive on corporate power. * * * Frug never directed his attention at a third candidate for the exercise of decentralized power: the private homeowners association. The association, not the business corporation, is the obvious private alternative to the city. Like a city, an association enables households that have clustered their activities in a territorially defined area to enforce rules of conduct, to provide "public goods" (such as open space), and to pursue other common goals they could not achieve without some form of potentially coercive central authority. Although they were relatively exotic as recently as twenty years ago, homeowners associations now outnumber cities. Developers create thousands of new associations each year to govern their subdivisions, condominiums, and planned communities.

American law currently treats the city and the homeowners association dramatically differently. One is "public"; the other, "private." In law, as Frug correctly points out, much now turns on this distinction. * * *

This Article compares the legal status of cities and homeowners associations. In contrast to Professor Frug, I generally rely on empirical methods to identify legal phenomena. Part I of the Article examines the fundamental characteristics of cities and homeowners associations. Although cities are considered "public" and homeowners associations "private," I discern only one important difference between the two forms of organization—the sometimes involuntary nature of membership in a city versus the perfectly voluntary nature of membership in a homeowners association. I assert that this difference explains why cities are more active than associations are in undertaking coercive redistributive programs. * * *

Professor Frank Michelman, unquestionably the preeminent legal mind on community governance, has offered a characteristically useful one-sentence guide for identifying the existence of a "governmental" organization:

> We know perfectly well, granting that there are intermediate hard cases, how to distinguish governmental from non-governmental *powers* and *forms of organization:* governments are distinguished by their acknowledged, lawful authority—not

dependent on property ownership—to coerce a territorially defined and imperfectly voluntary membership by acts of regulation, taxation, and condemnation, the exercise of which authority is determined by majoritarian and representative procedures.

Although this particular quotation was an aside in an article mainly addressed to other issues, a scholar as careful as Michelman no doubt crafted the sentence to encapsulate insights gained through years of puzzling over the essence of governmental organizations.

The homeowners association, although certainly one of Michelman's "intermediate hard cases," is currently viewed by both ordinary and legal observers as a "private" organization, not a "government." In fact, it is sufficiently "private" that it has rarely been granted any intermediate legal status that a hard case might be thought to deserve, but instead has been treated much like any other private organization. This is so even though the modern homeowners association has virtually all of the indicia that Michelman would have us associate with a government. First, a homeowners association rules a "territorially defined" area, and, in the usual case, obtains its power to do so through no form of property ownership. For example, when the members of a condominium association own the common areas as tenants in common, the association itself owns no real property at all.

Nor does Michelman's list of the tell-tale governmental powers do much to distinguish a homeowners association from a city. An association is typically entitled to undertake acts of both regulation and taxation, as those terms are ordinarily used. Associations, for example, may restrict to whom a member may sell his unit, prohibit certain kinds of conduct (not only in common areas but also within the confines of individual homes), and tightly control the physical alteration of a member's unit. An association's "taxation" takes the form of monthly assessments on members. Assessments can be raised without the unanimous consent of the membership. Payment of an assessment is secured by a lien on a member's unit, making the assessment almost as hard to evade as a municipal property tax is. To be sure, association powers are not as extensive as those possessed by "public" bodies. The regulations of a homeowners association in sum are likely to be less intrusive and comprehensive than what one finds in a typical municipal code. Cities have far more ways to raise revenue than associations do. Lastly, it would be highly unusual for an association to have the power to condemn a member's unit—the third governmental power Michelman lists. Some homeowners associations do have the power to expel members for misbehavior—a power that comes close to the power of condemnation. But even if they did not, exercise of eminent domain power by a local government is rare; it would be remarkable if the presence of this power were a necessary condition for the use of the adjective "public" in ordinary or legal language.

Nor does one stretch ordinary language out of shape to describe an association as having "majoritarian and representative procedures." Much as citydwellers choose a city council, association members elect a board of directors to manage association affairs.

Only one part of Michelman's description of a government remains: its "imperfectly voluntary membership." Public entities have involuntary members when they are first formed. For example, the statutory procedures for incorporating a new city invariably authorize a majority (perhaps only concurrent or extraordinary majorities) to coerce involuntary minorities to join their organization. By contrast, membership in a private organization is wholly voluntary. A central thesis of this Article is that the presence of *involuntary members* is both a necessary condition for the use of the adjective "public" in ordinary language, and also a powerful explanation for the different legal treatment currently accorded public and private organizations. * * *

The initial members of a homeowners association, by their voluntary acts of joining, unanimously consent to the provisions in the association's original governing documents. In the language of Buchanan and Tullock, this unanimous ratification elevates those documents to the legal status of a private "constitution." The original documents—which today typically include a declaration of covenants, articles of association (or incorporation), and by-laws—are a true social contract. The feature of unanimous ratification distinguishes these documents from and gives them greater legal robustness than non-unanimously adopted public constitutions, not to mention the hypothetical social contracts of Rousseau or Rawls. * * *

EVAN MCKENZIE, PRIVATOPIA
Pp. 10–11, 126–129, 135, 142–149 (1994).

As late as 1962 there were fewer than five hundred homeowner associations in the United States, and the dominant form of middle-class housing was still the suburban "big-lot" subdivision. But rising land prices and a population boom pressured developers to find ways to squeeze more people onto smaller parcels of land. With the endorsement of the Federal Housing Administration, which provided developers with detailed guidelines on how to create condominiums and PUDs [planned unit developments] that would receive federal mortgage insurance, the real estate industry began in the mid-1960s to promote common-interest housing for the middle class, offering open spaces owned in common in lieu of large private yards. By the 1960s the real estate industry was increasingly dominated by large-scale corporate "community builders."

These builders made housing a mass-produced consumer commodity, and they found CIDs [common-interest developments] enormously profitable. The CIDs allowed them to build more units per acre while satisfying middle-class consumer preferences for such amenities as swimming pools, golf courses, parks, private beaches, recreation rooms, security gates and guards that would be prohibitively expensive for individual middle-class owners.

The CID movement received another boost from the "new town" boom, which began in the 1960s. Dozens of large, heavily planned and relatively self-contained communities were built, including Rancho Bernardo and Irvine, in California; Reston, Virginia; and Columbia, Maryland. Projected populations ranged as high as five hundred thousand. The sponsors of these "instant cities," as Theodore Roszak called them, included such corporate giants as Gulf Oil, Humble Oil, Goodyear Tire and Rubber, Westinghouse, and General Electric. Some developers received federal assistance, but that was withdrawn in the mid-1970s amid a rash of insolvencies. Despite the mixed results of the new town movement, the preference for CID housing among large developers was by then strong. To reduce risk while continuing to reap substantial profits, the industry shifted to construction of smaller developments but applied the same principles it used with the bigger developments. Beginning in the mid-1970s, financially strapped local governments also found CID housing appealing because it had features of private infrastructure, allowing communities to grow and add property-tax payers at reduced public cost.

These private initiatives in housing policy, and their validation by government, brought about astonishing nationwide growth in CID construction. There were fewer than five hundred such homeowner associations in 1964. By 1970 there were 10,000 homeowner associations; by 1975 there were 20,000; by 1980, 55,000; by 1990, 130,000; and by 1992, there were 150,000 associations privately governing an estimated 32 million Americans. In 1990 there were 11.6 million CID housing units constituting more than 11 percent of American housing. Of these, 51 percent were planned-unit developments of single-family homes, 42 percent were condominiums, and 7 percent were housing cooperatives. By 2000 there is expected to be a total of 225,000 homeowner associations in the country. * * *

Although the precise names and legal descriptions vary slightly from state to state, there are four basic types of CIDs: condominiums, planned developments, stock cooperatives, and community apartments. * * * In a CID, everybody who buys a unit automatically becomes a member of the community association. So, although the decision to purchase may be voluntary, membership is mandatory. The association is founded on, and governed by, certain documents that are akin to a state's constitution and set of codes. Typically these include some, or all, of the following: a set of covenants, conditions, and restrictions that run with the land and are legally binding on present and future owners of the property; articles of incorporation, if the association is incorporated; bylaws; and rules and regulations.

The CC & Rs are written by the developer and are normally only subject to modification by supermajority vote of all members, not just of those who choose to vote. For example, a typical provision for amending the CC & Rs would require a two-thirds vote of the entire membership. Amendments are therefore difficult to enact, especially because most CIDs have a number of absentee owners who rent their units and are not present to vote, even if they are interested in the issue. So the developer's idea of how people should live is, to a large extent, cast in concrete. This rigidity was advocated in the 1964 Homes Association Handbook, in which ULI and FHA proposed that changes in the CC & Rs require the two-thirds vote and a three-year waiting period before they would become effective. This permanence was seen as an asset for mortgage insurance purposes because it tended to prevent owners from banding together to relax the developer's property maintenance standards by amending the CC & Rs. * * * The articles of incorporation, similar to those of any other nonprofit corporation, primarily set out the purpose of the corporation, which is to maintain and protect the common areas and to enforce the CC & Rs. The bylaws and rules and regulations are also written by the developer.

These documents are every bit as enforceable as the laws, charters, and constitutions of public governments, though new owners often fail to recognize that fact. Taken together, they give a developer the power to create a distinct lifestyle in a development, which the developer can use as a powerful marketing tool. Moreover, they are the rules of the regime under which, ultimately, the residents will be living. The documents provide for the election of a board of directors of the association from among the membership, so neighbors eventually will be running one another's lives, without any minimum requirements of education, experience, or professional competence. They are not paid for their services. At the outset, however, the developer staffs all board positions with his own employees and customarily retains three votes for every unsold unit, so the developer is effectively in control of the association until nearly the entire project is sold. The developer then presides over a transition period during which elected residents take over all positions on the board of directors and the operation of the development.

Only property owners are eligible to vote in elections, so renters are disenfranchised. This ownership qualification for voting raises constitutional questions, especially considering the large number of rented units in many developments. In California, a median of 20 percent of the CID units are rented; in 14 percent of the developments the majority of units are rented. Additionally, only one vote per unit may be cast, rather than one vote per adult occupant. These elected directors are responsible for seeing that the dictates of the developer's governing documents are carried out. This includes maintenance of the common areas and management of all association assets, which can range from next to nothing to millions of dollars. The funds for maintenance and the association's other functions come from monthly assessments and dues that the owners must pay, as well as special assessments for particular purposes. These payments are the "taxes" of the private government, and they can range from relatively nominal fees to hundreds of dollars each month, depending on how extensive the common areas and facilities are. In addition to caring for the common areas, the association is charged with enforcement of the governing documents over all unit owners and occupants. This power is very real but often underestimated by new purchasers unfamiliar with CIDs, and it is the source of a great deal of acrimony.

The overriding purpose of the association, as defined by its documents, is the protection of property values through maintenance of the property itself and through preservation of the project's character and appearance. In carrying out this purpose the board of directors has all the powers of any nonprofit corporation, including the power to buy and sell property. Beyond these basic requirements there is an enormous range of restrictions that the developer may have created as part of a target-marketing strategy. The association is empowered—and required—to enforce these CC & R provisions by imposing fines. The quasi-adjudication process is typically quite informal, considering how much is at stake. Charges of violation are made and heard by the board. There are no policies that separate the roles of accuser and trier of fact or that call for the empaneling of an independent, impartial jury. In most states, failure to pay the fine authorizes the association to attach a lien interest to the individual unit, and, ultimately, to sell the unit at auction if the fine is not paid.

In addition, the association can impose certain standards of behavior on residents and anyone who visits the property. Taken as a whole, these powers permit the regulation of a wider range of behavior than any within the purview of a public local government. Among other things, the governing documents require the individual owner to maintain certain standards of repair and maintenance in his or her individual unit. Unkempt yards, peeling paint, and other indications of neglect that might affect the neighborhood's property values are subject to censure. Generally there are also restrictions on the uses to which the units can be put, such as the number of occupants permitted, age restrictions for residency, maximum lengths of stay for guests, and whether any sort of business can be conducted from the home. In addition, owners who wish to make physical alterations in the home—painting it a different color or adding a room, a patio, or even an awning—are generally required to submit their plans to the board of directors or to a committee created by the board to review such matters and approve or reject the applications. * * *

The lawful powers and activities of CID boards of directors fit [Sanford] Lakoff's definition of a private government. They are limited-purpose associations; they are ostensibly voluntary in membership; they exist "alongside and subordinate to" public governments; and, most important, they exhibit "fundamental political characteristics." That is, they exercise power over members and even nonmembers in vital areas of concern, in that their decisions govern what individuals do in the privacy of their own home and what they do with the physical structure of the house and its surroundings. Their actions touch on what is perhaps the most basic human drive: the desire to exercise control over our immediate environment. They do this with the force of law, because their edicts are enforceable, and they have more or less well-developed systems for rule making and enforcement. * * *

In CIDs, management companies and other professionals (lawyers, accountants, actuaries, architects, engineers, and so forth) retained by the board of directors carry out many responsibilities, and, of course, the board itself makes the decisions. There is a pronounced tendency toward a lack of involvement among the rank and file, who seem to prefer to turn things over to the board and management company * * *. In this sense, CID residents, in their concern with property values, often behave like the stockholders in any large corporation, who neither know nor care about corporate affairs as long as their stock goes up and they keep receiving dividend checks. This sort of peripheral interest is especially disturbing when the corporate affairs in which people are uninterested are the workings of their own neighborhood. According to the Barton and Silverman study, the corporate management model seems to permeate the thinking of board members as well as residents, so that the CID is thought of as "a type of business, where efficient property management saves money and increases the value of owners' investments," an attitude that conflicts with neighborliness. As Barton and Silverman concluded, "We see a general tendency for both associations and professional managers to emphasize ease of management over member involvement and to regard 'people problems' as simply a complication of property management. This emphasis is misplaced."

A more speculative matter is the long-term social and psychological effect on the American family of having the corporate model imposed on the home and its surroundings. For example, imagine that a family sweltering through a long, hot summer decides to relieve the heat by installing a window air conditioner. The family then receives a command from the board of directors to remove the unit, which allegedly violates a common prohibition on installing anything except drapes in, on, or around the windows. This family will have to obey the command and explain it to the children. The honest explanation would be to say that the family must endure the heat because they are all part of a corporation dedicated to preserving everybody's property values, and this restriction, though it seems ridiculous and unfair, actually aims to prevent people from hanging from their windows such items as wet laundry, signs advertising cars for sale, and other undesirable things—including dripping, rattling air conditioners—all of which would tend to make the development take on a Tobacco Road ambiance and depress property values. This rationale is different from saying "We can't do it because it's a crime" or "We can't do it because we are friends with the Jones family downstairs, and it just makes too much noise for them." The rationale is neither completely authoritarian nor one that rests entirely on cooperation with and respect for the rights of neighbors. It is a corporate, business, and property-oriented rationale. * * *

Some of the most troubling questions arise when we see CIDs as private governments and then attempt to find a legitimate basis for their rule. The classical liberal justifications used to legitimize American government tend to undermine, rather than support, this form of private government. CID regimes are inconsistent not only with political theories of legitimacy but with the normal process by which governments are created. For example, the Puritans who brought European ways to America in the seventeenth century had the advantage of beginning with a community of people who shared basic values—in this case, religious ones—and then proceeding to try to construct a civil society in which people could live in a manner consistent with God's laws. Homeowner associations reverse this order, and in so doing they exalt the status of rules—rules designed first and foremost to protect property values— above the fabric of the community. The creators of CIDs—corporate developers and their lawyers—begin their projects on paper. They design the entire development, including houses, streets, and recreation facilities, complete to the last detail. Using relatively standardized CC & Rs, articles of incorporation, and bylaws, they set up a system of government complete with a set of rules. They obtain permission from the state to subdivide the land, and from local agencies they acquire the necessary building permits. Then they hire numerous contractors to build the houses and the common areas. In short, they build a sort of ghost town, with everything in it but human beings. Finally, they begin selling the project to the people who eventually will live there. The priorities embodied in this process are clear and explicit: first, there is a plan; second, there is property; third, there are rules to protect the property; fourth, there is a physical "city"; and last, there are people to live in the city and to follow the rules that protect the property. In short, a CID is a prefabricated framework for civil society in search of a population. The population may come and go, but the property and the rules will remain, and the population will remain in service to the property.

This is a reversal of the Lockean belief that the right to own property arises in the state of nature, before the social contract is established, and is therefore largely outside the reach of government regulation, except for necessary taxation. * * * In the theories of Hobbes and Locke we see the development of the distinction between private and public that, though often unclear, is with us today. The private sphere, for these theorists, is what we retain from the state of nature, and it remains ours by natural right. For Hobbes, the essential natural right is self-preservation. Locke adds to this the right to possess property. In the public sphere is the state, or government, along with the laws that regulate our behavior and are consistent with the legitimate ends of government—meaning, for Locke, that government would protect property rights and certainly not unduly interfere with them.

This order of events is turned on its head in the CID. At the outset there is nothing—a state of nature devoid of people except for the developer-creator, who begets the "community" and its social order to his liking and makes it unchangeable. After that is done, the people arrive at his invitation and are permitted to live there forever according to his rules, long after he has abandoned them to their own devices. This scenario is closer to Genesis than Locke, resembling the early days of the Garden of Eden more than the Puritans' arrival in the New World. It also deviates significantly from the classical liberal justification for government.

In a variety of ways, CIDs elevate rules and legalisms above the social fabric of the subsociety. In essence, law, instead of serving the community, is elevated above it. There are three ways this priority of rules over community manifests itself, all of which relate to what it means to be a citizen of these subsocieties, and these factors tend to undermine any claim to legitimacy under principles with which Americans are familiar:

1. There is a serious question regarding whether there is any meaningful consent to the rules of these subsocieties.

2. The concept of "rights" is replaced with the idea of "restrictions" as the guiding principle in the relationship of the individual to the community.

3. The concept of responsibility to the community is defined as nothing more than meeting one's economic obligations and conforming to the rules—all of which has the ultimate stated purpose of simply protecting property values. * * *

In what sense can people be said to consent to the laws of the private government when they did not participate in their making and when membership in the association is compulsory? People could certainly participate in changing the rules to the limited extent possible, but in fact they did not even participate in making the rules by which the rules can be changed. Consent is not just a logical issue, because developers routinely require a super-majority vote, such as 80 percent of all eligible voters, for changing the restrictions. Considering the poor turnout for city elections, one can imagine how hard it is to attain such a vote. Some states have passed laws making it possible for fewer residents than the supermajority to go to court to change these requirements, under certain conditions.

Developers and other proponents of CIDs typically argue that people consent to the rules of a CID by buying and living there. If they don't move out, it is assumed that they consent. But this argument, a standard in the industry, runs aground on the facts. First, it is increasingly difficult to find non-CID housing in many parts of the country. Second, as the real estate market consolidates at the large corporate level, the opportunity for real choice among CIDs—that is, for meaningful choices among different lifestyles and regimes of rules—may be diminishing. Any diversity that exists is provided at the discretion of the real estate development industry. * * *

A second way CIDs embody a different kind of citizenship by placing rules ahead of community is in how CIDs have replaced the concept of rights with that of restrictions. These restrictions are legally known as "equitable servitudes," a legal concept that predates the constitution. In essence, equitable servitudes allow somebody to sell land but still control how that land is used. In CIDs, the doctrine has a specific and characteristic application. The developer initially owns all the land in the development, then subdivides it and creates the document of covenants, conditions, and restrictions that goes with each parcel. So all buyers are mutually bound by the same restrictions from the moment of purchase, meaning there was never a time when they buyers were in a "state of nature," because the developer had that to himself. And there was never a time when they created civil government, reserved certain rights to themselves as inalienable, and gave certain rights to government. The developer did all that. Instead, they were bound to enforce the CC & Rs against each other and were restricted in their use of the land by those CC & Rs and the other documents. In essence, they never had rights, natural or otherwise, to begin with. The very essence of their ownership interest is that it was partial ownership, burdened with permanent restrictions on how the property may be used.

Residents in CIDs commonly fail to understand the difference between a regime based formally on rights, such as American civil governments, and the CID regime, which is based on restrictions. This often leads to people becoming angry at board meetings and claiming that their "rights" have been violated—rights that they wrongly believe they have in the CID. This absence of rights has important consequences because the balance of power between individual and private government is reversed. It could be said that, in reality, public governments try to accomplish the same thing, but the point is that in the CID it is not a subversion, or a perversion, of justice for this to occur, but quite legal and proper. There is also an irony here. It is perhaps no coincidence that in the country in which the distinction between private and public is thought to be so clear, and the concomitant preservation of the private sphere so complete, we also find a peculiarly American form of private government in which the property rights of the developer, and later the board of directors, swallow up the rights of the people, and public government is left as a bystander. * * *

3 A third indication of the new citizenship in CIDs is the assumption that a resident's responsibilities to the "community" can be satisfied by meeting one's economic obligations. This consists of making house payments, paying association dues and assessments, and conforming to a set of lifestyle restrictions that have the sole stated purpose of preserving the value of the commonly owned property. It could be said that civil government permits a similarly detached citizenship. Citizens pay taxes, obey the law, do their jobs, vote if they choose, and serve in the military if drafted. Beyond that, any further involvement in community affairs is a matter of choice. But cities, states, and nations have vast networks of private and public threads that tie citizens together and make them interdependent. We are linked via law, religion, the mass media, and bureaucracies in ways that encourage or compel us to be responsible to, and for, each other. These responsibilities extend far beyond maintaining property values and conformity. In CIDs, a different, more restricted model of civic responsibility obtains.

The long-term effects of these departures from liberal assumptions may be significant. Students of politics have long recognized that people learn a great deal about the meaning of citizenship from day-to-day life in their communities. Robert Dahl has written that "what Pericles said of Athens, that the city is in general a school of the Grecians, may be said of every city of moderate size: It is a marvelous school." The spread of common-interest housing means that different lessons are being learned and that generations of children are "going to school" on the streets of a new kind of city. * * *

GARY J. MILLER, CITIES BY CONTRACT
Pp. 88–91 (1981).

* * * [T]he first upper-income housing development on the [Palos Verdes] peninsula [in Los Angeles County], which was to become a synonym for conservativism and wealth, * * * gradually evolved into a private, gated community called Rolling Hills. Restrictions were placed on the property, and in 1936 the Rolling Hills Community Association was established to enforce the restrictions.

As the Guide to Rolling Hills, put out by the Community Association, hints to prospective buyers, "Each property owner has a stake in preserving the simple, quiet, rural atmosphere of Rolling Hills." The homeowners on the peninsula have been ever vigilant against threats to local property values in the form of neighboring tract developments, apartment houses, industry, and commercial development. In the postwar period these threats were embodied in the city of Torrance which lay at the foot of the peninsula's hills. As the city manager of Rolling Hills explained to me, Torrance was one of the largest cities in the county at the time—a diversified city with residential neighborhoods, commercial property, and industry. However, it lacked exclusive residential neighborhoods with high property values. Torrance's vigorous annexation program in the 1950s was designed to bring in that form of property, through annexation of the Rolling Hills community, or of similar developments on the peninsula.

The first community to respond to the threat from Torrance was not Rolling Hills, but its newer neighbor to the north of Palos Verdes Drive, Rolling Hills Estates. Serving as a buffer between Rolling Hills and Torrance, Rolling Hills Estates was a twin to Rolling Hills in most characteristics, although its roads were open to the public and it lacked an effective private homeowners' association to enforce building restrictions. Instead, it had over two dozen property owners' associations for as many tiny neighborhoods. With development less strictly controlled, it had already grown to twice the population of Rolling Hills (about 3,000) in the early 1950s when it felt itself threatened by tract developers. The homeowners of Rolling Hills Estates soon became convinced that the county supervisors were unable or unwilling to restrict development to their satisfaction, a conviction that other residents of exclusive neighborhoods around the county came to share over the years. However, the homeowners found that threatening incorporation was an effective card in bargaining with the county and with the developers. * * *

[T]he proincorporation group formed an incorporation committee, and paid $9,500 for a feasibility study, doing much of the work on the study themselves, to keep the cost low. It took them 18 months to perform the study and proceed with the rest of the stages of incorporation before the election in September of 1957.

By way of comparison, the community of Rolling Hills already had the problem of organization solved, since it had an ongoing active community association which was accustomed to running the private road system and raising money. * * * Despite the fact that their incorporation proceedings were initiated after those in Rolling Hills Estates, they were able to go to election nine months earlier. Both incorporations were successful.

Not only were the incorporations successful, the cities were successful. Rolling Hills Estates, shortly after incorporating, was able to make two strip annexations to the southwest to pick up valuable commercial property. This made it possible, according to the individual who was mayor at that time, to provide ample services for the residential community at a low tax cost. Indeed, after the first few years, Rolling Hills Estates was able to abolish its property tax and subsist on the income of its commercial property and state subventions. * * *

Rolling Hills, too, was successful in its incorporation goals. While it did not annex a commercial tax base as Rolling Hills Estates did, its limited municipal activities, subventions, and contracting kept the tax rate low. And, as assessments increased, the city lowered its tax rate accordingly.

Rolling Hills is a unique example of the private use of public government. The city government is in many ways simply an extension of the private homeowners' association. The Community Association has rigid architectural control over its houses. In fact, one homeowner volunteered, "If there's any single issue that would be the biggest complaint it might be the building restrictions. They even tell you what shades of white paint you can use on your house." (Colors other than white are not allowed.) While the Community Association is responsible for controlling the roads and maintaining the entrances, there is a city ordinance that threatens a $500 fine for outsiders who enter the city limits uninvited. The Community Association even levies a private property tax for maintaining the roads and recreation areas, based on the county assessment less personal property. Recreational facilities are owned by the city of Rolling Hills and leased by the Association. The city of Rolling Hills is responsible for contracting with the county sheriff for fire and police protection. While the Community Association and the city have separate five-person governing boards, the boards share administrative and legal staff. * * *

MUNICIPAL BUILDING AUTHORITY V. LOWDER

Supreme Court of Utah, 1985.
711 P.2d 273.

ZIMMERMAN, JUSTICE:

Defendants, the auditor, treasurer and clerk of Iron County, appeal from a district court decision upholding the Utah Municipal Building Authority Act ("the Act") against a variety of constitutional challenges and finding that the actions proposed by the Iron County Board of Commissioners and the Iron County Municipal Building Authority ("the Authority") to finance construction of a new jail facility under that Act are lawful. * * *

Testimony before the district court indicated that the fifty-year-old Iron County jail has not met even minimum state and federal standards of habitability for some time. * * * Lengthy studies have underscored the need to build an entirely new jail. To finance its construction, the Iron County Commissioners proposed issuing general obligation bonds. Article XIV, section 3 of the Utah Constitution requires that such bonds be approved by the voters because they would be a long-term debt of the county. In December of 1981, a bond election was held and the proposal was defeated, leaving the county in a difficult dilemma. As a practical matter, the new facility had to be built; yet the Iron County taxpayers were unwilling to pay for the facility through the traditional means of financing major capital improvements—general obligation bonds.

The Board of Commissioners devised a plan which would permit a jail to be built without prior voter approval. Article XIV, section 3 requires voter approval of long-term indebtedness only when the indebted entity is a county or a subdivision of a county. The commissioners, acting under the Utah Municipal Building Authority Act, created the Iron County Building Authority, a quasi-municipal governmental entity designed *not* to be a "subdivision" of the county and, therefore, to be free from the voter-approval requirement of article XIV, section 3. As required by the Act, the Authority's board of trustees consists of all of the Iron County commissioners. The Authority is empowered to finance and construct a new jail facility and lease it to the county. Because the Authority, not the county, will borrow money for the construction, voter approval of its bond issue will not be necessary, yet a new jail will be made available to the county.

To implement the plan, the county and the Authority propose to enter into several related agreements. For a nominal consideration, the existing jail facility will be transferred to the Authority in fee; in effect, the present jail will be donated to the Authority. That property, now appraised at $124,000, will be traded by the Authority to a private developer for another site upon which the new jail facility will be constructed. Should there be some legal obstacle to this transfer in fee, the county proposes to lease a project site to the Authority. In either event, once the Authority has secured a site, it will issue revenue bonds with a term of twenty years to finance construction, pledging as security its interest in the project site and the facility to be constructed. As part of the same transaction, the county will lease the new jail facility from the Authority for twenty years, on a year-to-year basis. After the twenty years have passed and the bonds are paid in full, the Authority will transfer title to the new facility to the county. The agreements between the county and the Authority provide that in the event the Authority defaults on the bonds before they are paid off, the bond holders may foreclose upon the new jail facility and whatever interest the Authority has in the site, but they will have no recourse against the county or its taxpayers. * * *

We first address defendants' contention that the Act allows counties to evade the constitution's debt limitations. Some background is necessary. Article XIV, section 3 of the Utah Constitution prohibits, *inter alia,* any county from incurring debt in excess of the current year's tax revenues without prior approval of a majority of the property taxpayers. A companion provision, article XIV, section 4, limits the debt a county can incur even with taxpayer approval to two percent of the assessed valuation. These two provisions demonstrate the drafters' concern in 1895 that absent limits on total debt and a requirement that any debt to be paid from future revenues be approved by taxpayers, local governmental units might be fiscally irresponsible. Members of the constitutional convention expressed strong concern about the tendency of local governments to provide present benefits to voters and to pay for them from future revenues. Sections 3 and 4 of article XIV were a direct response to that concern.

Historically, local governments, often aided and abetted by the state legislature, have tried to find ways to provide facilities needed by an increasingly urbanized society without being hobbled by the strict limitations in sections 3 and 4 of article XIV. This Court has often been receptive to such efforts. For example, the court-created "special fund doctrine" excludes certain bonds from section 3's election requirement if those bonds are repaid from revenues generated by the facilities constructed with the bond proceeds, rather than from general tax revenues. The underlying theory is that the bond holders have no recourse to the general tax revenues and, therefore, the bonds are not "debt" of the governmental entity in question.

Another means of avoiding the debt limitations is the creation of a special district. This Court has held that such a district is exempt from the limitations of sections 3 and 4 of article XIV because it is a quasi-municipal entity rather than a "city, county, town or subdivision thereof."

Despite some attempts by this Court to limit the use of such districts on varying grounds, they have continued to proliferate. In fact, article XIV was amended in 1975 to clarify the status of such districts and to provide for legislative control over them.

There is no question that the Utah Municipal Building Authority Act is yet another attempt to develop a means for financing needed capital improvements without being restricted by the rigid debt ceiling of article XIV, section 4 or by the taxpayer approval requirement of section 3. Defendants contend that the Act must be struck down as inconsistent with article XIV, sections 3 and 4. We find these arguments without merit.

Defendants contend that the Authority's debt is debt of the county, within the meaning of article XIV, section 3. This Court has rejected similar arguments in the past, and we see no reason to depart from those precedents. The express terms of sections 3 and 4 of article XIV apply only to specified entities, including counties and their subdivisions; they do not apply to quasi-municipal entities such as building authorities. Therefore, a debt of the Authority for which the county is not responsible is not subject to the restrictions of article XIV, sections 3 and 4. * * *

Defendants assert that the proposed plan of action works a fraud upon the taxpayers because they expressly disapproved construction of a new jail. This mischaracterizes the election. The voters only expressed an unwillingness to incur a general obligation debt to finance the jail's construction; they were not asked whether the facility should be built if general obligation bonding could be avoided. The difference is significant. Under the constitution, it is only the former proposal that must be put before the voters.

Defendants next argue that there is no real difference between the proposed method of financing and general obligation bonding. This is not true. General obligation bonds would irretrievably obligate future taxpayers to pay off the debt incurred to build the jail; financing construction through the Authority will not. Under the proposed arrangement, the county will lease the jail facility on a year-to-year basis. The county retains the option of terminating the lease at the end of each year. Should this occur, neither the Authority nor the bond holders will have any recourse against the county or the taxpayers for the amount remaining unpaid on the bonded indebtedness.

In addition to the practical differences between a long-term bond indebtedness and a year-to-year obligation, there is a constitutionally significant legal difference: under article XIV, section 3, a contractual obligation that can be discharged within one year is not considered a debt that must be submitted to the voters. Our cases have held that the aggregate amount that may ultimately be paid under a multi-year contract or lease need not be taken into account in determining whether the debt represented by the contract or lease exceeds the current year's revenues so long as the actual amount due under the contract accrues only as the services are provided and the municipality cannot be coerced into paying for services not yet rendered.

In the present case, the county has the right to terminate the contract at the end of any year. The amount due in any one year is only for services provided during that year. Therefore, the proposed lease qualifies for treatment on a year-to-year basis. Of course, as a practical matter the county will renew the lease for the next twenty years. But that does not affect the analysis so long as the county cannot be held legally responsible for other than the services it receives during the current tax year.

We conclude that the proposed arrangement between the county and the Authority does not work a fraud, injustice or inequity upon the bond holders or the taxpayers. * * *

The next contention advanced by defendants in an attempt to bring the transaction before us within the prohibitions of article XIV, sections 3 and 4 is that the Act has an impermissible purpose—it allows municipalities to evade constitutional debt limits and create debt indirectly where it cannot be created directly. Defendants' argument belabors the obvious. Of course the Act is intended to permit avoidance of the constitutional debt limitations. It is the very rigidity of those limitations that has led the courts to narrowly construe them and the legislature to actively assist local government in avoiding them. We reject defendants' argument. If the express terms of an enactment do not offend the constitution, its purpose alone will not render it unconstitutional. And nothing prohibits local governments from lawfully avoiding these constitutional limitations.

Defendants' final argument under article XIV, sections 3 and 4 is that the use of general tax revenues to make the yearly rental payments under the jail lease will have the same economic result as if general obligation bonds had been issued; therefore, the jail lease payments should be considered debt subject to the constitution's restrictions. They reason that the use of general tax revenues to make the annual rental payments will result in a reduction of funds otherwise available to the county and will require the county to raise taxes to compensate for the expenditure on the jail. The net result is that the taxpayers will pay higher taxes just as if they had approved the original bond proposal. Defendants' assumptions may be correct, but their conclusion—that transactions resulting in the same economic burdens must be treated similarly for purposes of article XIV, sections 3 and 4—is not.

It is true that if the county continues with the lease for its full term, the taxpayers will pay as much for the jail facility as if general obligation bonds had been issued. In fact, they almost certainly will pay more, since general obligation bonds probably would have carried a lower interest rate than the somewhat riskier bonds being issued by the Authority. But that fact is not relevant to the legal inquiry—will the technical requirements of the constitution be violated by the proposed transaction?

As noted above, so long as the county's liability is limited to the annual rental installment for the current year, only that payment is considered in determining whether article XIV, section 3's debt limitation is exceeded. The full amount due over the term of the lease is not considered. The question here raised is whether the fact that taxes may have to be raised to cover the annual lease payment invalidates the transaction. Article XIV, sections 3 and 4 limit the indebtedness that can be incurred without a vote to "debt [not] in excess of the taxes for the current year." Under our decisions, compliance with this provision requires that the debt contracted for, taken together with all other debts of the county at the time of contracting, cannot exceed the amount of revenue the county anticipates it will receive during the tax year. So long as the anticipated revenues are sufficient to cover the annual payment, the debt incurred is valid under article XIV, section 3. Thus, the fact that the county will have to raise taxes in order to pay the jail rental does not invalidate the annual rental debt, so long as at the time the county becomes obligated to pay the debt it has sufficient anticipated revenues for that year to pay all of its debts. * * *

BALL v. JAMES

Supreme Court of the United States, 1981.
451 U.S. 355, 101 S.Ct. 1811, 68 L.Ed.2d 150.

JUSTICE STEWART delivered the opinion of the Court.

This appeal concerns the constitutionality of the system for electing the directors of a large water reclamation district in Arizona, a system which, in essence, limits voting eligibility to landowners and apportions voting power according to the amount of land a voter owns. The case requires us to consider whether the peculiarly narrow function of this local governmental body and the special relationship of one class of citizens to that body releases it from the strict demands of the one-person-one-vote principle of the Equal Protection Clause of the Fourteenth Amendment.

The public entity at issue here is the Salt River Project Agricultural Improvement and Power District (District), which stores and delivers untreated water to the owners of land comprising 236,000 acres in Central Arizona. The District, formed as a governmental entity in 1937, subsidizes its water operations by selling electricity, and has become the supplier of electric power for hundreds of thousands of people in an area including a large part of metropolitan Phoenix. Nevertheless, the history of the District began in the efforts of Arizona farmers in the 19th century to irrigate the arid lands of the Salt River Valley, and, as the parties have stipulated, the primary purposes of the District have always been the storage, delivery, and conservation of water.

As early as 1867, farmers in the Salt River Valley attempted to irrigate their lands with water from the Salt River. In 1895, concerned with the erratic and unreliable flow of the river, they formed a "Farmers Protective Association," which helped persuade Congress to pass the Reclamation Act of 1902, 43 U.S.C. § 371 *et seq.* Under that Act, the United States gave interest-free loans to help landowners build reclamation projects. The Salt River Project, from which the District developed, was created in 1903 as a result of this legislation. In 1906, Congress authorized projects created under the Act to generate and sell hydroelectric power, and the Salt River Project has supported its water operations by this means almost since its creation. The 1902 act provided that the water users who benefited from the reclamation project had to agree to repay to the United States the costs of constructing the project, and the Salt River Valley Water Users Association was organized as an Arizona corporation in 1903 to serve as the contracting agent for the landowners. The Association's Articles, drafted in cooperation with the Federal Reclamation Service, gave subscribing landowners the right to reclamation water and the power to vote in Association decisions in proportion to the number of acres the subscribers owned. The Articles also authorize acreage-proportionate stock assessments to raise income for the Association, the assessments becoming a lien on the subscribing owners' land until paid. * * *

The Association faced serious financial difficulties during the Depression as it built new dams and other works for the project, and it sought a means of borrowing money that would not overly encumber the subscribers' lands. The means seemed to be available in Arizona's Agricultural Improvement District Act of 1922, which authorized the creation of special public water districts within federal reclamation projects. Such districts, as political subdivisions of the State, could issue bonds exempt from federal income tax. Nevertheless, many Association members opposed creating a special district for the project, in part because the state statute would have required that voting power in elections for directors of the District be distributed per capita among landowners, and not according to the acreage formula for stock assessments and water rights. In 1936, in response to a request from the Association, the state legislature amended the 1922 statute. Under the new statutory scheme, which is essentially the one at issue in this case, the legislature allowed the District to limit voting for its directors to voters, otherwise regularly qualified under state law, who own land within the District, and to apportion voting power among those landowners according to the number of acres owned. The Salt River Project Agricultural Improvement and Power District was then formed in 1937, its boundaries essentially the same as the Association's. Under the 1937 agreement, the Association made the District its contracting agent, and transferred to the District all its property, and the Association in turn agreed to continue to operate and maintain the Salt River Project. Under the current agreement, the District itself manages the power and water storage work of the project, and the Association, as agent for the District, manages water delivery. As for financing, the statute now permits the special districts to raise money through an acreage-proportionate taxing power that mirrors the Association's stock assessment scheme or through bonds secured by liens on the real property within the District, though the bonds can simultaneously be secured by District revenues.

This lawsuit was brought by a class of registered voters who live within the geographic boundaries of the District, and who own either no land or less than an acre of land within the District. The complaint alleged that the District enjoys such governmental powers as the power to condemn land, to sell tax-exempt bonds, and to levy taxes on real property. It also alleged that because the District sells electricity to virtually half the population of Arizona, and because, through its water operations, it can exercise significant influence on flood control and environmental management within its boundaries, the District's policies and actions have a substantial effect on all people who live within the District, regardless of property ownership. Seeking declaratory and injunctive relief, the respondents claimed that the acreage-based scheme for electing directors of the District violates the Equal Protection Clause of the Fourteenth Amendment. * * *

Reynolds v. Sims held that the Equal Protection Clause requires adherence to the principle of one-person-one-vote in elections of state legislators. *Avery v. Midland County,* 390 U.S. 474, 88 S.Ct. 1114, 20 L.Ed.2d 45, extended the *Reynolds* rule to the election of officials of a county government, holding that the elected officials exercised "general governmental powers over the entire geographic area served by the body." The Court, however, reserved any decision on the application of *Reynolds* to "a special purpose unit of government assigned the performance of functions affecting definable groups of constituents more than other constituents." In *Hadley v. Junior College District,* 397 U.S. 50, 90 S.Ct. 791, 25 L.Ed.2d 45, the Court extended *Reynolds* to the election of trustees of a community college district because those trustees "exercised general governmental powers" and "performed important governmental functions" that had significant effect on all citizens residing within the district. But in that case the Court stated: "It is of course possible that there might be some case in which a State elects certain functionaries whose duties are so far removed from normal governmental activities and so disproportionately affect different groups that a popular election in compliance with *Reynolds* * * * might not be required * * *." *Id.*, at 56, 90 S.Ct., at 795.

The Court found such a case in *Salyer*. The Tulare Lake Basin water district involved there encompassed 193,000 acres, 85% of which were farmed by one or another of four corporations. *Salyer Land Co. v. Tulare Lake Basin Water Storage District*, 410 U.S. [719], at 723, 93 S.Ct. [1224], at 1227. Under California law, public water districts could acquire, store, conserve, and distribute water, and though the Tulare Lake Basin district had never chosen to do so, could generate and sell any form of power it saw fit to support its water operations. The costs of the project were assessed against each landowner according to the water benefits the landowner received. At issue in the case was the constitutionality of the scheme for electing the directors of the district, under which only landowners could vote, and voting power was apportioned according to the assessed valuation of the voting landowner's property. The Court recognized that the Tulare Lake Basin district did exercise "some typical governmental powers," including the power to hire and fire workers, contract for construction of projects, condemn private property, and issue general obligation bonds. Nevertheless, the Court concluded that the district had "relatively limited authority," because "its primary purpose, indeed the reason for its existence, is to provide for the acquisition, storage, and distribution of water for farming in the Tulare Lake Basin." The Court also noted that the financial burdens of the district could not but fall on the landowners, in proportion to the benefits they received from the district, and that the district's actions therefore disproportionately affected the voting landowners. The *Salyer* Court thus held that the strictures of *Reynolds* did not apply to the Tulare district, and proceeded to inquire simply whether the statutory voting scheme based on land valuation at least bore some relevancy to the statute's objectives. The Court concluded that the California legislature could have reasonably assumed that without voting power apportioned according to the value of their land, the landowners might not have been willing to subject their lands to the lien of the very assessments which made the creation of the district possible.

As noted by the Court of Appeals, the services currently provided by the Salt River District are more diverse and affect far more people than those of the Tulare Lake Basin District. Whereas the Tulare district included an area entirely devoted to agriculture and populated by only 77 persons, the Salt River District includes almost half the population of the

State, including large parts of Phoenix and other cities. Moreover, the Salt River District, unlike the Tulare District, has exercised its statutory power to generate and sell electric power, and has become one of the largest suppliers of such power in the State. Further, whereas all the water delivered by the Tulare Lake Basin District went for agriculture, roughly 40% of the water delivered by the Salt River district goes to urban areas or is used for nonagricultural purposes in farming areas. Finally whereas all operating costs of the Tulare District were borne by the voting landowners through assessments apportioned according to land value, most of the capital and operating costs of the Salt River District have been met through the revenues generated by the selling of electric power. Nevertheless, a careful examination of the Salt River District reveals that, under the principles of the *Avery, Hadley,* and *Salyer* cases, these distinctions do not amount to a constitutional difference.

First, the District simply does not exercise the sort of governmental powers that invoke the strict demands of *Reynolds.* The District cannot impose ad valorem property taxes or sales taxes. It cannot enact any laws governing the conduct of citizens, nor does it administer such normal functions of government as the maintenance of streets, the operation of schools, or sanitation, health, or welfare services.

Second, though they were characterized broadly by the Court of Appeals, even the District's water functions, which comprise the primary and originating purpose of the District, are relatively narrow. The District and Association do not own, sell, or buy water, nor do they control the use of any water they have delivered. The District simply stores water behind its dams, conserves it from loss, and delivers it through project canals. It is true, as the Court of Appeals noted, that as much as 40% of the water delivered by the District goes for nonagricultural purposes. But the distinction between agricultural and urban land is of no special constitutional significance in this context. The constitutionally relevant fact is that all water delivered by the Salt River District, like the water delivered by the Tulare Lake Basin district, is distributed according to land ownership, and the District does not and cannot control the use to which the landowners who are entitled to the water choose to put it. As repeatedly recognized by the Arizona courts, though the state legislature has allowed water districts to become nominal public entities in order to obtain inexpensive bond financing, the districts remain essentially business enterprises, created by and chiefly benefiting a specific group of landowners. As in *Salyer,* the nominal public character of such an entity cannot transform it into the type of governmental body for which the Fourteenth Amendment demands a one-person-one-vote system of election.

(3) Finally, neither the existence nor size of the District's power business affects the legality of its property-based voting scheme. As this Court has noted in a different context, the provision of electricity is not a traditional element of governmental sovereignty, *Jackson v. Metropolitan Edison Co.,* 419 U.S. 345, 353, 95 S.Ct. 449, 454, 42 L.Ed.2d 477, and so is not in itself the sort of general or important governmental function that would make the government provider subject to the doctrine of the *Reynolds* case. In any event, since the electric power functions were stipulated to be incidental to the water functions which are the District's primary purpose, they cannot change the character of that enterprise. The Arizona Legislature permitted the District to generate and sell electricity to subsidize the water operations which were the beneficiaries intended by the statute. A key part of the *Salyer* decision was that the voting scheme for a public entity like a water district may constitutionally reflect the narrow primary purpose for which the District is created. In this case, the parties have stipulated that the primary legislative purpose of the District is to store, conserve, and deliver water for use by District landowners, that the sole legislative reason for making water projects public entities was to enable them to raise revenue through interest-free bonds, and that the development and sale of electric power was undertaken not for the primary purpose of providing electricity to the public, but "to support the primary irrigation functions by supplying power for reclamation uses and by providing revenues which could be applied to increase the amount and reduce the cost of water to Association subscribed lands."

The appellees claim, and the Court of Appeals agreed, that the sheer size of the power operations and the great number of people they affect serve to transform the District into an entity of general governmental power. But no matter how great the number of nonvoting residents buying electricity from the District, the relationship between them and the District's power operations is essentially that between consumers and a business enterprise from which they buy. Nothing in the *Avery, Hadley,* or *Salyer* cases suggests that the volume of business or the breadth of economic effect of a venture undertaken by a government entity as an incident of its narrow and primary governmental public function can, of its own weight, subject the entity to the one-person-one-vote requirements of the *Reynolds* case.

The functions of the Salt River District are therefore of the narrow, special sort which justifies a departure from the popular election requirement of the *Reynolds* case. And as in *Salyer,* an aspect of that limited purpose is the disproportionate relationship the District's functions bear to the specific class of people whom the system makes eligible to vote. The voting landowners are the only residents of the District whose lands are subject to liens to secure District bonds. Only these landowners are subject to the acreage-based taxing power of the District, and voting landowners are the only residents who have ever committed capital to the District through stock assessments charged by the Association. The *Salyer* opinion did not say that the selected class of voters for a special public entity must be the only parties at all affected by the operations of the entity, or that their entire economic well-being must depend on that entity. Rather, the question was whether the effect of the entity's operations on them was disproportionately greater than the effect on those seeking the vote.

As in the *Salyer* case, we conclude that the voting scheme for the District is constitutional because it bears a reasonable relationship to its statutory objectives. Here, according to the stipulation of the parties, the subscriptions of land which made the Association and then the District possible might well have never occurred had not the subscribing landowners been assured a special voice in the conduct of the District's business. Therefore, as in *Salyer,* the State could rationally limit the vote to landowners. Moreover, Arizona could rationally make the weight of their vote dependent upon the number of acres they own, since that number reasonably reflects the relative risks they incurred as landowners and the distribution of the benefits and the burdens of the District's water operations. * * *

JUSTICE WHITE, with whom JUSTICE BRENNAN, JUSTICE MARSHALL, and JUSTICE BLACKMUN join, dissenting. * * *

The District involved here clearly exercises substantial governmental powers. The District is a municipal corporation organized under the laws of Arizona and is not, in any sense of the word, a private corporation. Pursuant to the Arizona Constitution, such districts are "political subdivisions of the State, and vested with all the rights, privileges and benefits, and entitled to the immunities and exemptions granted municipalities and political subdivisions under this Constitution or any law of the State or of the United States." Under the relevant statute controlling agricultural improvement districts, the District is "a public, political, taxing subdivision of the state, and a municipal corporation to the extent of the powers and privileges conferred by this chapter or granted generally to municipal corporations by the constitution and statutes of the state, including immunity of its property and bonds from taxation." The District's bonds are tax exempt, and its property is not subject to state or local property taxation. This attribute clearly indicates the governmental nature of the District's function. The District also has the power of eminent domain, a matter of some import. The District has also been given the power to enter into a wide range of contractual arrangements to secure energy sources. Inherent in this authorization is the power to control the use and source of energy generated by the District, including the possible use of nuclear power. Obviously, this broad authorization over the field of energy transcends the limited functions of the agricultural water storage district involved in *Salyer.*

The District here also has authority to allocate water within its service area. It has veto power over all transfers of surface water from one place or type of use to another, and this power extends to any "watershed or drainage area which supplies or contributes water for the irrigation of lands within [the] district. * * *" 45 Ariz.Rev.Stat.Ann. § 172.5 (Supp.1980).

Like most "private" utilities, which are often "natural monopolies," private utilities in Arizona are subject to regulation by public authority. The Arizona Corporation Commission is empowered to prescribe "just and reasonable rates" as well as to regulate other aspects of the business operations of private utilities. The rate structure of the District now before us, however, is not subject to control by another state agency because the District is a municipal corporation and itself purports to perform the public function of protecting the public interest that the Corporation Commission would otherwise perform. Its power to set its own rates and other conditions of service constitutes important attributes of sovereignty. When combined with a consideration of the District's wide-ranging operations which encompass water for agricultural and personal uses, and electrical generation for the needs of hundreds of thousands of customers, it is clear that the District exercises broad governmental power. With respect to energy management and the provision of water and electricity, the District's power is immense and authority complete.

It is not relevant that the District does not do more—what is detailed above is substantially more than that involved in the water storage district in *Salyer,* and certainly enough to trigger application of the strict standard of the Fourteenth Amendment under our prior cases. Previous cases have expressly upheld application of the strict requirements of the Fourteenth Amendment in situations where somewhat limited functions were involved. *Salyer* itself suggested that it would be a different case if a water district like the one involved in that case generated and sold electricity. In concluding that the Tulare District did not exercise normal governmental authority, the court specifically noted that the District provided "no other general public services such as schools, housing, transportation, *utilities,* roads, or anything else of the type ordinarily financed by a municipal body." 410 U.S., at 728–729, 93 S.Ct., at 1230 (emphasis supplied). In *Cipriano,* we held that a bond election which concerned only a city's provision of utilities involved a sufficiently broad governmental function. In *Kramer,* the Court noted that the "need for close judicial examination" did not change "because the district meetings and the school board do not have 'general' legislative powers. Our exacting examination is not necessitated by the subject of the election; rather, it is required because some resident citizens are permitted to

participate and some are not." In *Hadley v. Junior College District,* 397
U.S. 50, 90 S.Ct. 791, 25 L.Ed.2d 45 (1970), the Court applied *Kramer*
despite the fact that the powers exercised by the trustees of a junior
college district were substantially less significant than those exercised in
Avery v. Midland County, 390 U.S. 474, 88 S.Ct. 1114, 20 L.Ed.2d 45
(1968). It was sufficient that the trustees performed important
governmental functions with sufficient impact throughout the District.

I therefore cannot agree that this line of cases is not applicable here.
The authority and power of the District are sufficient to require
application of the strict scrutiny required by our cases. This is not a single
purpose water irrigation district, but a large and vital municipal
corporation exercising a broad range of initiatives across a spectrum of
operations. Moreover, by the nature of the state law, it is presently
exercising that authority without direct regulation by state authorities
charged with supervising privately owned corporations involved in the
same business. The functions and purposes of the Salt River District
represent important governmental responsibilities that distinguish this
case from *Salyer.*

In terms of the relative impact of the Salt River District's operations
on the favored landowner voters and those who may not vote for the
officers of this municipal corporation, the contrast with the water district
in *Salyer* is even more pronounced. * * *

With these facts in mind, it is indeed curious that the Court would
attempt to characterize the District's electrical operations as "incidental"
to its water operations, or would consider the power operations to be
irrelevant to the legality of the voting scheme. The facts are that in *Salyer*
the burdens of the water district fell entirely on the landowners who were
served by the District. Here the landowners could not themselves afford
to finance their own project and turned to a public agency to help them.
That agency now subsidizes the storage and delivery of irrigation water
for agricultural purposes by selling electricity to the public at prices that
neither the voters nor any representative public agency has any right to
control. Unlike the situation in *Salyer,* the financial burden of supplying
irrigation water has been shifted from the landowners to the consumers
of electricity. At the very least, the structure of the District's indebtedness
together with the history of the District's operations compels a finding
that the burdens placed upon the lands within the District are so minimal
that they cannot possibly serve as a basis for limiting the franchise to
property owners.

It is apparent in this case that landowning irrigators are getting a
free ride at the expense of the users of electricity. It would also seem
apparent that except for the subsidy, utility rates would be lower. Of
course, subsidizing agricultural operations may well be in the public

interest in Arizona, but it does not follow that the amount of the subsidy and the manner in which it is provided should be totally in the hands of a selected few.

To conclude that the effect of the District's operations in this case is substantially akin to that in *Salyer* ignores reality. As recognized in *Salyer,* there were "no towns, shops, hospitals, or other facilities designed to improve the quality of life within the district boundaries, and it does not have a fire department, police, buses, or trains." In short, there was nothing in the water storage district for its operations to effect except the land itself. The relationship between the burdens of the District and the land within the District's boundaries was strong. Here, the District encompasses one of the major metropolitan areas in the country. The effects of the provision of water and electricity on the citizens of the city are as major as they are obvious. There is no strong relationship between the District's operation and the land *qua* land. The District's revenues and bonds are tied directly to the electrical operation. Any encumbrance on the land is at best speculative. Certainly, any direct impact on the land is no greater than in *Phoenix* where we rejected the same argument presented today. Simply put, the District is an integral governmental actor providing important governmental services to residents of the District. To conclude otherwise is to ignore the urban reality of the District's operations.

Underlying the Court's conclusion in this case is the view that the provision of electricity and water is essentially a private enterprise and not sufficiently governmental—that the District "simply does not exercise the sort of governmental powers that invoke the strict demands" of the Fourteenth Amendment because it does not administer "such normal functions of government as the maintenance of streets, the operation of schools, or sanitation, health, or welfare services." This is a distinctly odd view of the reach of municipal services in this day and age. Supplying water for domestic and industrial uses is almost everywhere the responsibility of local government, and this function is intimately connected with sanitation and health. Nor is it any more accurate to consider the supplying of electricity as essentially a private function. The United States Government and its agencies generate and sell substantial amounts of power; and in view of the widespread existence of municipal utility systems, it is facetious to suggest that the operation of such utility systems should be considered as an incidental aspect of municipal government. Nor will it do, it seems to me, to return to the proprietary-governmental dichotomy in order to deliver into wholly private hands the control of a major municipal activity which acts to subsidize a limited number of landowners.

In *Indian Towing Co. v. United States,* 350 U.S. 61, 67–68, 76 S.Ct. 122, 125–126, 100 L.Ed. 48 (1955), the Court remarked:

" 'Government is not partly public or partly private, depending upon the governmental pedigree of the type of a particular activity or the manner in which the Government conducts it.' *Federal Crop Insurance Corp. v. Merrill,* 332 U.S. 380, 383–384, 68 S.Ct. 1, 2–3, 92 L.Ed. 10. On the other hand, it is hard to think of any governmental activity on the 'operational level,' our present concern, which is 'uniquely governmental,' in the sense that its kind has not at one time or another been, or could not conceivably be, privately performed."

In *Lafayette v. Louisiana Power & Light Co.,* 435 U.S. 389, 98 S.Ct. 1123, 55 L.Ed.2d 364 (1978), Justice Stewart, after quoting the above passage from *Indian Towing Co.,* described the distinction between "proprietary" and "governmental" activities as a "quagmire" involving a distinction " 'so finespun and capricious as to be almost incapable of being held in the mind for adequate formulation.' " 435 U.S., at 433, 98 S.Ct., at 1147 (Stewart, J., dissenting) (quoting *Indian Towing Co.,* 350 U.S., at 65–68, 76 S.Ct., at 124–126). Justice Stewart went on to conclude that whether proprietary or not, the action of providing electrical utility services "is surely an act of government."

In *Salyer,* the Court nowhere suggested that the provision of water for agricultural purposes was anything but governmental action for a public purpose. The Court expressly recognized that the water district was a public entity. The question presented, in part, was whether its operations and authority were so narrow as not to require application of the *Kramer* rule. In *Cipriano,* the Court necessarily held that the provision of electrical, water, and gas utility services was a sufficiently important governmental service to require application of the Fourteenth Amendment's strict scrutiny safeguards. If the provision of electrical and other utility services by a municipal corporation was so "proprietary" or "private" as not to require application of the stricter standards of the Fourteenth Amendment, *Cipriano* could not have been decided as it was. The Court's facile characterization of the electrical service provided by the municipal corporation in this case as essentially a private function is a misreading of our prior holdings. * * *

KESSLER V. GRAND CENTRAL DISTRICT MANAGEMENT ASSOCIATION, INC.

United States Court of Appeals, Second Circuit, 1998.
158 F.3d 92.

KEARSE, CIRCUIT JUDGE: * * *

To promote commercial development in urban areas, the New York State legislature has authorized municipalities in the State to establish business improvement districts ("BIDs"). In a BID, owners of nonexempt real property pay a periodic assessment to the municipality, over and above their ordinary municipal taxes. That assessment money is used to fund the construction of capital improvements to land in the district and the provision of certain services intended to promote business activity in the district. * * *

The Grand Central BID was established in 1988, and its territory was extended in June 1995, pursuant to the procedures set forth in the Act and the corresponding City ordinances. As extended, the Grand Central BID encompasses 337 properties on sections of 75 blocks in midtown Manhattan, including the Grand Central Terminal railroad station. There are 242 owners of property within the GCBID. That property includes approximately 71 million square feet of commercial space, constituting approximately 19% of the total commercial space in Manhattan. The office space in the GCBID "exceeds the entire space inventory of the Central Business District in such cities as Houston, San Francisco, Dallas, Denver, and Boston." The GCBID also contains approximately 897,000 square feet of residential space, occupied by approximately 930 residents.

The District Plan authorizes the construction of capital improvements (the "Improvements") and the provision of additional services (the "Services") in the GCBID. The Improvements include the renovation of sidewalks and crosswalks; the planting of trees; the installation of new lighting, street signs, bus shelters, news kiosks, and trash receptacles; contributions to the renovation of Grand Central Terminal; and "the creation of a restaurant facility" on 42nd Street. The Services "may include any services required for the enjoyment and protection of the public and the promotion and enhancement of the District," * * * including [security, sanitation, tourist information, social services for homeless persons, special maintenance and repair, public events, and retail improvements.] Pursuant to a contract between the City Department of Business Services and [Grand Central District Management Association, Inc. ("GCDMA")] dated July 30, 1993 (the "Contract"), GCDMA became the Grand Central BID's management association. * * *

To carry out the District Plan, GCDMA, through its operating entity, Grand Central Partnership, Inc., employs approximately 63 security guards, most of whom are unarmed. These guards "patrol the streets and sidewalks of the District" and "attempt[ ] to obtain compliance with City regulations controlling vending, sidewalk obstructions, noise generation, and air pollution." They are "tied into [the New York City Police Department's] communications network" and act "[i]n cooperation with [the New York City Police Department] and the building staffs of private property-owners." GCDMA employs "sanitation" workers, who perform functions such as sweeping sidewalks and streets, as well as removing graffiti, washing sidewalks, caring for trees and plants, "poster removal, cleaning street signs, and repainting street furniture." These workers bag trash, which is in due course collected by the City's Department of Sanitation in the normal course of its refuse removal duties. GCDMA also provides other services to improve the attractiveness of the district, such as giving free assistance to retailers in removing old signs and designing new signs and facades; and it provides assistance in complying with applicable City ordinances. * * * In addition, GCDMA contributes to the funding and operation of a 24-hour "outreach, assessment and referral" facility for homeless persons that provides services such as job training. Other GCDMA Services include operating tourist information booths in the district and sponsoring events, such as an alcohol-free New Year's Eve celebration, in the district's public spaces. GCDMA "retains the flexibility to eliminate or add to" the Services listed in the District Plan. * * *

The primary source of funding for the Grand Central BID is an assessment that the City levies against and collects from all industrial, commercial, and residential property within the district. * * * Any assessment money that the City collects must be "separately accounted for in the books and records" of the City and may not be "used for any purposes other than those set forth in the district plan." * * * GCDMA's proposed annual budgets, along with a detailed account of the previous year's expenditures, were required to be submitted to the Commissioner of the City's Department of Business Services (the "Commissioner"). * * * The performance of the Services is "subject to the review and reasonable direction and control of the Commissioner." * * *

GCDMA's bylaws provide for a Board comprising groups of directors selected by four voting classes:

a) Class A. Owners of record of real property in the [D]istrict * * * [are eligible to] be Class A members of [GCDMA].

b) Class B. Tenants not eligible for Class A membership, who are occupants pursuant to leases of commercial space within the District . . . [are eligible to] be Class B members of [GCDMA].

c) Class C. Tenants not eligible for Class A or Class B membership, who are occupants pursuant to leases of dwelling units within the District . . . [are eligible to] be Class C members of [GCDMA].

d) Class D. The persons serving from time to time as directors of [GCDMA] by virtue of their appointment by [City officials] shall be Class D members of [GCDMA].

GCDMA holds annual elections, in which each class of voters separately elects a specified number of directors. In accordance with N.Y.

Gen. Mun. Law § 980–m(b) and the corresponding N.Y.C. Admin. Code § 25–414(b), GCDMA's bylaws provide that "the number of Class A Directors shall at no time constitute less than a majority of the Board." Currently, in addition to the four Class D directors appointed by the City, GCDMA's Board is composed of 31 directors elected by the members of Class A, 16 directors elected by the members of Class B, and one director elected by the members of Class C. * * *

Plaintiffs are residents of the Grand Central BID. They live in an apartment building at 372 Fifth Avenue, which was added to the GCBID in June 1995. Plaintiffs' building is owned by a cooperative association, in which they hold shares. That cooperative association, as an owner of property within the GCBID, is entitled to Class A membership in GCDMA. As non-property-owning noncommercial residents, plaintiffs individually are entitled only to Class C membership.

Plaintiffs commenced the present action in November 1995 pursuant to 42 U.S.C. § 1983 (1994). * * * They sought, inter alia, a declaration that

> the system of representation on the Board . . . violates the Equal Protection Clause by denying to the plaintiffs, who are residential tenants in the district, representation on the basis of the principle of one person, one vote

and they requested a permanent injunction ensuring plaintiffs equal voting rights. * * *

[T]he general framework established by the Supreme Court is that elective bodies performing governmental functions that "are general enough and have sufficient impact throughout the district," *Board of Estimate v. Morris*, 489 U.S. [688] at 696, 109 S.Ct. 1433 [(1989)], i.e., entities with " 'normal governmental' authority," *Salyer* [*Land Co. v. Tulare Lake Basin Water Storage District*], 410 U.S. [719] at 729, 93 S.Ct. 1224 (1973), are subject to the one-person-one-vote requirement, but that entities with a "special limited purpose and . . . [a] disproportionate effect" on certain constituents, id. at 728, 93 S.Ct. 1224, are exempt from that requirement, and may use voting schemes that need only be reasonably related to their purposes. * * *

With these principles in mind, we consider the purpose of the GCBID, the functions, responsibilities, and powers of GCDMA, and the impacts of GCDMA activities on those owning or residing on property within the district. * * * [T]he purpose of the Grand Central BID is the promotion of business. * * * While *Salyer* involved 193,000 acres of rural land devoted almost exclusively to agricultural use, the GCBID encompasses all or parts of 75 city blocks, in which the businesses are diverse and the premises concentrated. While owners of agricultural land often have no greater concern than their need for adequate water supplies, the problems of property owners in the GCBID, which includes some of the most heavily developed land in the nation, are necessarily more complex, involving the need to maintain a lively, safe, and attractive commercial center through which millions of people pass daily. * * * Yet the complexity of the projects aimed at promoting business in the GCBID should not obscure the fact that the promotion of business is a limited purpose. The GCBID, like the water districts at issue in *Salyer* and *Ball* [*v. James*, 451 U.S. 355, 101 S.Ct. 1811, 68 L.Ed.2d 150 (1981)], is not concerned with the provision of general public services such as schools, housing, hospitals, jails, firefighting, transportation, utilities, or zoning. And although, some of GCDMA's functions are of a public welfare nature, its functions as a matter of law cannot supplant the fundamental obligations of the City. * * *

Not only does the purpose of the Grand Central BID not encompass many traditional governmental functions, the GCDMA lacks the powers normally enjoyed by a governmental body. GCDMA does not have the power, for example, to impose income taxes or sales taxes. Nor, indeed, does GCDMA levy or collect the assessments needed to fund the GCBID. Those functions are performed by the City, which holds the moneys until they are disbursed—either to GCDMA, or perhaps to another entity if the City is displeased with GCDMA's performance and elects to contract with a new manager * * *. Further, GCDMA has no authority to enact or enforce any laws governing the conduct of persons present in the district. It cannot, for example, make or enforce any environmental or other sanitation regulations. * * * And although GCDMA employs security guards, its guards have no authority to perform typical law enforcement functions. The guards are not authorized by the Act or the District Plan to, for example, make arrests, conduct investigations, obtain warrants for searches, or detain suspects. * * * Their tools are communications equipment tying them into the City's police network to enable them to summon law enforcement personnel from the City police department. * * *

As a matter of law GCDMA does not have primary responsibility for providing security, sanitation, or social services within the district. The Act requires that the

> [s]ervices for which district property owners are charged pursuant to the [district] plan must be in addition to or an enhancement of those provided by the municipality prior to the establishment of the district.

Thus, the City itself has—and by law must retain—the primary responsibility for providing security, sanitation, and social services in the GCBID. * * * Moreover, the City retains significant control over the disposition of the money collected. The assessments collected are under "custody and control of, and are directly expend[ed]" by the City, not

GCDMA. * * * In addition, the City has considerable supervisory authority over GCDMA's expenditure of whatever money GCDMA does receive from the City. * * * In sum, in light of (a) the BID's limited goal of improving the area for business, (b) the fact that GCDMA is not the primary provider of the limited security, sanitation, or social services it performs, and (c) the City's control over GCDMA's performance with respect to the functions it performs, we conclude that here, as in *Salyer* and *Ball*, the district's manager has relatively limited authority and does not exercise the sort of governmental powers that normally triggers the one-person-one-vote principle. * * *

We further conclude that the establishment and operation of the GCBID has a substantially greater effect on property owners than on nonowning residents. Most significantly, the principal burden imposed by the GCBID—the mandatory assessment—falls directly on property owners and only property owners. * * * Each property owner's bill for that assessment is based on the number of square feet of district property that he owns. District residents, on the other hand, are not, unless they own property, subject to the assessment. * * * Of course some property owners who lease their property to others may seek to pass all or part of the cost of the assessment to their tenants—whether commercial or residential—by raising rents. * * * Nonetheless, the possibility that part of the cost of an assessment would be passed on to resident nonlandowners existed as well in the water district cases and indeed inheres in any case in which an assessed landowner has a tenant. Whether or not part of the cost is passed on to any tenant, "there is no way that the economic burdens of district operations can fall on residents qua residents." *Salyer*, 410 U.S. at 729, 93 S.Ct. 1224. We conclude that the burdens of the GCBID assessments fall disproportionately on property owners. * * *

With respect to the benefits of GCDMA's activities, we note that since the money raised by the assessments against district property must be used for the specific business "purposes . . . set forth in the [D]istrict [P]lan," that money may not permissibly be used for the general benefit of the residents in the district. Nonetheless, certain GCDMA activities, such as the improvement of security and aesthetics within the district, will provide some benefit to district residents as well as district businesses; but

> [t]he *Salyer* opinion did not say that the selected class of voters for a special public entity must be the only parties at all affected by the operations of the entity. . . . Rather, the question was whether the effect of the entity's operations on them was disproportionately greater than the effect on those seeking the vote.

Ball, 451 U.S. at 371, 101 S.Ct. 1811. * * * The principal economic benefit from GCDMA's activities, however, plainly accrues to the property owners, who will enjoy an increase in the value of their property. * * *

Since the GCBID is a special-purpose district that affects property owners disproportionately, the Constitution requires only that the weighted voting system for electing GCDMA's Board bear a reasonable relationship to the purposes of the GCBID. Plaintiffs have made no attempt to argue that GCDMA's weighted voting system lacks such a reasonable relationship, and we think such a relationship is obvious. The need for cooperative action among property owners is clear. * * * In *Ball*, the Supreme Court found that weighted voting had the requisite reasonable relationship by virtue of the fact that the creation of the district "might well have never occurred had not the subscribing landowners been assured a special voice in the conduct of the District's business." Here too, if a sufficient number of property owners in the district had objected, they could have prevented the establishment of the GCBID. * * * Since only property owners are assessed to fund GCDMA's activities, the State legislature could reasonably have concluded that property owners, unless given principal control over how the money is spent, would not have consented to having their property subject to the assessment. The guarantee that property owners will have majority representation on the Board is thus reasonably related to the goal of promoting commercial activity in the GCBID. * * *

WEINSTEIN, DISTRICT JUDGE, dissenting: * * *

Hadley [v. *Junior College Dist.*, 397 U.S. 50, 53–54, 90 S.Ct. 791, 25 L.Ed.2d 45 (1970)] extended the one person, one vote requirement to local bodies whose scope of activity was much narrower than those in [*Avery v. Midland County*, 390 U.S. 474, 481, 88 S.Ct. 1114, 20 L.Ed.2d 45 (1968)]. At issue in *Hadley* was the election of a board of trustees for a local junior college district. Unlike the commissioners in *Avery*, who were responsible for providing a wide range of governmental services, the board of trustees in *Hadley* provided one specific municipal service—junior college education. The fact that the trustees were responsible for providing a narrowly defined program, nevertheless, did not place them outside the requirements of the one person, one vote principle.

The relevant inquiry for the Court in *Hadley* was not how many services the local body provided but rather the importance of the assistance it provided to the community and the amount of discretion allowed. Education, the Court pointed out, has traditionally been a "vital governmental function." The trustees enjoyed significant discretion in the performance of their public duties. They had the ability to levy and collect taxes, issue bonds (with certain restrictions), hire and fire teachers, make contracts, collect fees, and supervise and discipline students. The impact of these activities on the community as a whole, the Court reasoned, warranted the application of the one person, one vote requirement * * *.

As in both *Hadley* and *Avery*, the GCDMA performs important governmental functions which directly impact the lives of all those who live and work within its jurisdiction. Some of the services, such as security, sanitation, social services, capital improvement, maintenance of public roads, and promotion of tourism, are traditional functions of government. In fact, the GCDMA provides a far broader range of traditional governmental services than that provided by the board of trustees in *Hadley*. * * * The GCDMA impacts the daily lives of the residents of the district in a large variety of ways. * * * Operation of a police force is a sensitive and challenging undertaking which carries with it many potential dangers as well as benefits for the residents and inhabitants of the district. * * * The GCDMA's social services [also] are of great importance to the district's inhabitants who may feel threatened or concerned about the homeless. In a 1995 City Council report, the GCDMA's social services program was cited by the New York City Council as a paradigmatic example of the lack of accountability among New York's BIDs: * * *

> Long before allegations were made in 1995 that GCSSC workers operated as "goon squads," the GCSSC was the subject of two separate $5 million lawsuits stemming from incidents in 1990 and 1992 which alleged that GCSSC workers in the Multi-Service Center used excessive physical force against homeless people. * * *

Appellees contend that the plaintiffs are not "affected" by the GCDMA's activities because they are not property owners and therefore do not "pay" for the services. In all likelihood the tenants of the district do in fact "pay" for the services of the GCDMA in the form of higher rents passed on as a result of higher real property "taxes." *City of Phoenix v. Kolodziejski*, 399 U.S. 204, 90 S.Ct. 1990, 26 L.Ed.2d 523 (1970), recognized that tenants and consumers often end up paying for property tax increases in the form of higher rents or prices. * * * Even if tenants and co-op residents do not absorb BID assessments, appellees' argument is untenable. As already demonstrated, our nation has long since discarded the antiquated and elitist notion that only property owners enjoy a sufficient "stake" in society to deserve the franchise. Furthermore, the Supreme Court has previously addressed and rejected the appellees' payment of taxes argument. See *City of Phoenix v. Kolodziejski*, 399 U.S. 204, 90 S.Ct. 1990, 26 L.Ed.2d 523 (1970); *Cipriano v. City of Houma*, 395 U.S. 701, 89 S.Ct. 1897, 23 L.Ed.2d 647 (1969); *Kramer v. Union Free Sch. Dist.*, 395 U.S. 621, 89 S.Ct. 1886, 23 L.Ed.2d 583 (1969). * * *

All the residents of the Grand Central BID have a right to meaningfully participate in the GCDMA's electoral process because the GCDMA daily substantially impacts the lives of all of them (transient workers and visitors are not entitled to vote under our traditional voting system). There is no justification for allowing the corporate and individual entities who own land within the district to reduce the electoral participation of the district's residents. * * * As in both *Hadley* and *Avery*, the one person, one vote requirement is warranted because the GCDMA has wide discretion and great policy making authority in deciding how New York's public funds will be utilized. * * * The GCDMA decides, for example, such matters as how many security guards will patrol the district, where they will patrol, which kinds of behavior they will monitor, and the manner in which they will conduct themselves on the streets. It decides how to supervise and discipline its security force, and whether to implement procedures or safeguards to help ensure that those who have been charged with protecting the public do not infringe upon the personal rights of individuals. The GCDMA decides which streets within the district will be the cleanest, the most well lit, and the most closely patrolled. It decides who within the district will get "extra" street lights, trash collection, assistance in upgrading and cleaning facades and signs, and graffiti removal. The GCDMA decides whether to operate homeless shelters within the district and, if so, where, how many and what types of services these centers will provide. It decides where tourist information centers will be located and where within the district the taxi stands will located. It also plays the leading role in determining when and where millions of dollars of city money and tax exempt bond proceeds will be used to make capital improvements within the district.

The salaries of the GCDMA's employees and other allocations of resources are issues which affect all those within the district. The current board of the GCDMA has voted to allocate over $100,000 per year to the salary of the president. The district's security and sanitation chiefs have reportedly earned more than the City's Police and Sanitation Commissioners. By contrast, a federal trial court's finding that the current board decided to pay sub-minimum wages to many of its other employees has resulted in a legal verdict against the BID.

In formulating budgets, allocating finite resources, and making important policy decisions regarding the safety, health and welfare of those within the BID, it is imperative that the GCDMA fairly represent the interests of all voters within the district. As it is currently constituted, the GCDMA effectively represents only a select minority of those found within the BID. Much in the same way that the franchise was once delegated in this country to the privileged few who enjoyed status and wealth, the voting scheme of the GCDMA excludes the majority of the residents of the BID from meaningfully participating in the political affairs of their own community. * * *

The "special purpose" exception of *Salyer* and *Ball* to the fundamental constitutional principle of equal suffrage must be applied narrowly to factual circumstances and contexts similar to the ones in those cases. * * * The Grand Central BID provides a far wider range of governmental services than the water districts in *Salyer* and *Ball*. * * * Its activities are far more typical of general local governmental services than of those involved in *Salyer* and *Ball*. In *Ball* the Court reasoned that the water district at issue did not fall within the one person, one vote requirement because the district did not perform normal governmental activities such as "the maintenance of streets, the operation of schools, or sanitation, health, or welfare services." In the instant case, the GCDMA performs at least three of these paradigmatic governmental functions. In addition, the GCDMA provides other "core" governmental functions to the district such as the provision of security. * * * The fact that the Grand Central Business Improvement District does not provide the district with all possible governmental services and functions is not dispositive. * * * Local government may not, by carving up its civic services and functions into a multitude of "specializations," each one subject to privatization, immunize the municipality from the strictures of one person, one vote. * * *

Appellees contend that the application of the one person, one vote principle to the GCDMA is not justified because the City exercises sufficient control over the BID's activities. This argument is mistaken for several reasons. First, the City appears to have neither the authority nor the resources to monitor and control the GCDMA's essential policy-making powers. Second, even if it were true that the City "controlled" the GCDMA in some sense, this fact would not justify the virtual exclusion of the non-property owners from participation in control of their BID. The possibility that the City might occasionally intervene in the GCDMA's affairs is not an adequate substitute for the nonproperty owners' equal electoral participation in the BID's governance. Even when they enjoy an equal vote, those individuals without property struggle to match the political and economic influence wielded by the commercial and non-commercial real estate holders in the City of New York. * * *

If BIDs such as the GCDMA are not held to the one person, one vote requirement of the Fourteenth Amendment, there is a significant risk that a substantial portion of this country's urban population will be effectively prevented from controlling much of local government. Cities today are utilizing BIDs in increasing numbers and experimenting with their use in new and different circumstances. New York City, for example, has considered a BID in a purely residential area in order to place approximately 500 "private" security guards in the Upper East Side of Manhattan. * * * While it is true that the District Plan provides that general municipal services will not be reduced within the district as a result of the GCDMA's presence, there is nothing to prevent the City from reducing the services it provides on a City wide basis as a result of its reliance on the City's growing number of BIDs. BIDs decrease both the need and the incentive for the City to expand or maintain the general municipal services it provides to the City as a whole. * * * When BIDs multiply in number and expand into new and innovative uses, they constitute an ever larger portion of the public sphere. Unless BID boards are elected in a democratic fashion, the result of this trend may be the effective disenfranchisement of a substantial percentage of our urban population.

Appellees argue that this loss of voting power is justified because BIDs provide services which are only "supplemental" to the municipal services provided by the City. Yet, there appears to be no principled way to distinguish services which are "supplemental" from those which are "essential." Virtually every municipal service is "supplemental" in the sense that city residents can survive with a reduction in the service. Trash may be collected several times a day in a BID, but it need not be collected as often in non-BID areas if the only requirement is that the City provide the most "basic" service. As larger and larger numbers of New Yorkers come under the umbrella of BIDs, on what basis shall it be determined that a service is sufficient to constitute the minimum floor for non-BID residents? Today the GCDMA spends some $12 million per year on the provision of services. How high must that figure rise until their services are important enough to qualify for constitutional scrutiny? * * *

D. THE CITY AND DEMOCRATIC THEORY: PART ONE

Five different approaches toward the decentralization of power are excerpted below. The first is from an influential article on economic theory by Charles Tiebout. The second is from an eloquent statement of libertarian political philosophy by Robert Nozick. The third, by James Buchanan, is an example of the "public choice" approach to city power, one that builds on Tiebout's work by suggesting that cities should make public expenditures "strategically" in order to maximize their "per-capita fiscal dividend." The fourth, by Frank Michelman, offers a critique of this public choice model by describing a very different conception of city power, one he labels "the public-interest model." Finally, Iris Young presents a vision of city life that rejects not only the public choice model but also the communitarian ideal of building cities (and neighborhoods) on the basis of a common self-identification or culture. These five excerpts provide very different justifications for the decentralization of power, contrasting views of the public/private distinction, and conflicting normative visions of the relationships between individual cities and their neighbors. Which of these approaches presents the most persuasive argument for city power? Are there other conceptions of city power that are more compelling? What does the first excerpt below, another chapter from Italo Calvino's Invisible Cities, suggest about the value of imagining alternative versions of the cities in which we live?

ITALO CALVINO, INVISIBLE CITIES
Pp. 32–33 (1974).

In the center of Fedora, that gray stone metropolis, stands a metal building with a crystal globe in every room. Looking into each globe, you see a blue city, the model of a different Fedora. These are the forms the city could have taken if, for one reason or another, it had not become what we see today. In every age someone, looking at Fedora as it was, imagined a way of making it the ideal city, but while he constructed his miniature model, Fedora was already no longer the same as before, and what had been until yesterday a possible future became only a toy in a glass globe.

The building with the globes is now Fedora's museum: every inhabitant visits it, chooses the city that corresponds to his desires, contemplates it, imagining his reflection in the medusa pond that would have collected the waters of the canal (if it had not been dried up), the view from the high canopied box along the avenue reserved for elephants (now banished from the city), the fun of sliding down the spiral, twisting minaret (which never found a pedestal from which to rise).

On the map of your empire, O Great Khan, there must be room both for the big, stone Fedora and the little Fedoras in glass globes. Not because they are all equally real, but because all are only assumptions. The one contains what is accepted as necessary when it is not yet so; the others, what is imagined as possible and, a moment later, is possible no longer.

CHARLES TIEBOUT, A PURE THEORY OF LOCAL EXPENDITURES
64 J.Pol.Econ. 416, 418–420 (1956).

Consider for a moment the case of the city resident about to move to the suburbs. What variables will influence his choice of a municipality? If he has children, a high level of expenditures on schools may be important. Another person may prefer a community with a municipal golf course. The availability and quality of such facilities and services as beaches, parks, police protection, roads, and parking facilities will enter into the decision-making process. Of course, non-economic variables will also be considered, but this is of no concern at this point.

The consumer-voter may be viewed as picking that community which best satisfies his preference pattern for public goods. This is a major difference between central and local provision of public goods. At the central level the preferences of the consumer-voter are given, and the government tries to adjust to the pattern of these preferences, whereas at the local level various governments have their revenue and expenditure patterns more or less set. Given these revenue and expenditure patterns, the consumer-voter moves to that community whose local government best satisfies his set of preferences. The greater the number of communities and the greater the variance among them, the closer the consumer will come to fully realizing his preference position.

The implications of the preceding argument may be shown by postulating an extreme model. Here the following assumptions are made:

1.   Consumer-voters are fully mobile and will move to that community where their preference patterns, which are set, are best satisfied.

2.   Consumer-voters are assumed to have full knowledge of differences among revenue and expenditure patterns and to react to these differences.

3.   There are a large number of communities in which the consumer-voters may choose to live.

4.   Restrictions due to employment opportunities are not considered. It may be assumed that all persons are living on dividend income.

5.   The public services supplied exhibit no external economies or diseconomies between communities.

Assumptions 6 and 7 to follow are less familiar and require brief explanations:

6.   For every pattern of community services set by, say, a city manager who follows the preferences of the older residents of the community, there is an optimal community size. This optimum is defined in terms of the number of residents for which this bundle of services can be produced at the lowest average cost. This, of course, is closely analogous to the low point of a firm's average cost curve. Such a cost function implies that some factor or resource is fixed. If this were not so, there would be no logical reason to limit community size, given the preference patterns. In the same sense that the average cost curve has a minimum for one firm but can be reproduced by another there is seemingly no reason why a duplicate community cannot exist. The assumption that some factor is fixed explains why it is not possible for the community in question to double its size by growth. The factor may be the limited land area of a suburban community, combined with a set of zoning

laws against apartment buildings. It may be the local beach, whose capacity is limited. Anything of this nature will provide a restraint.

In order to see how this restraint works, let us consider the beach problem. Suppose the preference patterns of the community are such that the optimum size population is 13,000. Within this set of preferences there is a certain demand per family for beach space. This demand is such that at 13,000 population a 500-yard beach is required. If the actual length of the beach is, say, 600 yards, then it is not possible to realize this preference pattern with twice the optimum population, since there would be too little beach space by 400 yards.

The assumption of a fixed factor is necessary * * * in order to get a determinate number of communities. It also has the advantage of introducing a realistic restraint into the model.

7.   The last assumption is that communities below the optimum size seek to attract new residents to lower average costs. Those above optimum size do just the opposite. Those at an optimum try to keep their populations constant.

This assumption needs to be amplified. Clearly, communities below the optimum size, through chambers of commerce or other agencies, seek to attract new residents. This is best exemplified by the housing developments in some suburban areas, such as Park Forest in the Chicago area and Levittown in the New York area, which need to reach an optimum size. The same is true of communities that try to attract manufacturing industries by setting up certain facilities and getting an optimum number of firms to move into the industrially zoned area.

The case of the city that is too large and tries to get rid of residents is more difficult to imagine. No alderman in his right political mind would ever admit that the city is too big. Nevertheless, economic forces are at work to push people out of it. Every resident who moves to the suburbs to find better schools, more parks, and so forth, is reacting, in part, against the pattern the city has to offer.

The case of the community which is at the optimum size and tries to remain so is not hard to visualize. Again proper zoning laws, implicit agreements among realtors, and the like are sufficient to keep the population stable.

Except when this system is in equilibrium, there will be a subset of consumer-voters who are discontented with the patterns of their community. Another set will be satisfied. Given the assumption about mobility and the other assumptions listed previously, movement will take place out of the communities of greater than optimal size into the communities of less than optimal size. The consumer-voter moves to the community that satisfies his preference pattern.

The act of moving or failing to move is crucial. Moving or failing to move replaces the usual market test of willingness to buy a good and reveals the consumer-voter's demand for public goods. Thus each locality has a revenue and expenditure pattern that reflects the desires of its residents. The next step is to see what this implies for the allocation of public goods at the local level.

Each city manager now has a certain demand for n local public goods. In supplying these goods, he and $m-1$ other city managers may be considered as going to a national market and bidding for the appropriate units of service of each kind: so many units of police for the ith community; twice that number for the jth community; and so on. The demand on the public goods market for each of the n commodities will be the sum of the demands of the m communities. In the limit, as shown in a less realistic model to be developed later, this total demand will approximate the demand that represents the true preferences of the consumer-voters—that is, the demand they would reveal, if they were forced, somehow, to state their true preferences. In this model there is no attempt on the part of local governments to "adapt to" the preferences of consumer-voters. Instead, those local governments that attract the optimum number of residents may be viewed as being "adopted by" the economic system. * * *

ROBERT NOZICK, ANARCHY, STATE AND UTOPIA
Pp. 297, 309–312, 316–317, 320–323, 329–331 (1974).

* * * It would be disconcerting if there were only one argument or connected set of reasons for the adequacy of a particular description of utopia. Utopia is the focus of so many different strands of aspiration that there must be many theoretical paths leading to it. Let us sketch some of these alternate, mutually supporting, theoretical routes.

The first route begins with the fact that people are different. They differ in temperament, interests, intellectual ability, aspirations, natural bent, spiritual quests, and the kind of life they wish to lead. They diverge in the values they have and have different weightings for the values they share. (They wish to live in different climates—some in mountains, plains, deserts, seashores, cities, towns.) There is no reason to think that there is *one* community which will serve as ideal for all people and much reason to think that there is not. * * *

Wittgenstein, Elizabeth Taylor, Bertrand Russell, Thomas Merton, Yogi Berra, Allen Ginsburg, Harry Wolfson, Thoreau, Casey Stengel, The Lubavitcher Rebbe, Picasso, Moses, Einstein, Hugh Heffner, Socrates, Henry Ford, Lenny Bruce, Baba Ram Dass, Gandhi, Sir Edmund Hillary, Raymond Lubitz, Buddha, Frank Sinatra, Columbus, Freud, Norman Mailer, Ayn Rand, Baron Rothschild, Ted Williams, Thomas Edison, H.L.

Mencken, Thomas Jefferson, Ralph Ellison, Bobby Fischer, Emma Goldman, Peter Kropotkin, you, and your parents. Is there really *one* kind of life which is best for each of these people? Imagine all of them living in any utopia you've ever seen described in detail. * * *

No utopian author has everyone in his society leading exactly the same life, allocating exactly the same amount of time to exactly the same activities. *Why not?* Don't the reasons also count against just one kind of community?

The conclusion to draw is that there will not be *one* kind of community existing and one kind of life led in utopia. Utopia will consist of utopias, of many different and divergent communities in which people lead different kinds of lives under different institutions. Some kinds of communities will be more attractive to most than others; communities will wax and wane. People will leave some for others or spend their whole lives in one. Utopia is a framework for utopias, a place where people are at liberty to join together voluntarily to pursue and attempt to realize their own vision of the good life in the ideal community but where no one can *impose* his own utopian vision upon others. The utopian society is the society of utopianism. (Some of course may be content where they are. Not *everyone* will be joining special experimental communities, and many who abstain at first will join the communities later, after it is clear how they actually are working out.) * * *

If the ideas must actually be tried out, there must be many communities trying out different patterns. The filtering process, the process of eliminating communities, that our framework involves is very simple: people try out living in various communities, and they leave or slightly modify the ones they don't like (find defective). Some communities will be abandoned, others will struggle along, others will split, others will flourish, gain members, and be duplicated elsewhere. Each community must win and hold the voluntary adherence of its members. No pattern is *imposed* on everyone, and the result will be one pattern if and only if everyone voluntarily chooses to live in accordance with that pattern of community.

The design device comes in at the stage of generating specific communities to be lived in and tried out. Any group of people may devise a pattern and attempt to persuade others to participate in the adventure of a community in that pattern. Visionaries and crackpots, maniacs and saints, monks and libertines, capitalists and communists and participatory democrats, proponents of phalanxes (Fourier), palaces of labor (Flora Tristan), villages of unity and cooperation (Owen), mutualist communities (Proudhon), time stores (Josiah Warren), Bruderhof, kibbutzim, kundalini yoga ashrams, and so forth, may all have their try at building their vision and setting an alluring example. It should not be thought that every pattern tried will be explicitly designed *de novo*. Some will be planned modifications, however slight, of others already existing (when it is seen where they rub), and the details of many will be built up spontaneously in communities that leave some leeway. As communities become more attractive for their inhabitants, patterns previously adopted as the best available will be rejected. And as the communities which people live in improve (according to their lights), ideas for new communities often will improve as well. * * *

The operation of the framework has many of the virtues, and few of the defects, people find in the libertarian vision. For though there is great liberty to choose among communities, many particular communities internally may have many restrictions unjustifiable on libertarian grounds: that is, restrictions which libertarians would condemn if they were enforced by a central state apparatus. For example, paternalistic intervention into people's lives, restrictions on the range of books which may circulate in the community, limitations on the kinds of sexual behavior, and so on. But this is merely another way of pointing out that in a free society people may contract into various restrictions which the government may not legitimately impose upon them. Though the framework is libertarian and laissez-faire, *individual communities within it need not be,* and perhaps no community within it will choose to be so. Thus, the characteristics of the framework need not pervade the individual communities. In *this* laissez-faire system it could turn out that though they are permitted, there are no actually functioning "capitalist" institutions; or that some communities have them and others don't or some communities have some of them, or what you will.*

In previous chapters, we have spoken of a person's opting out of particular provisions of certain arrangements. Why now do we say that various restrictions may be imposed in a particular community? Mustn't the community allow its members to opt out of these restrictions? No; founders and members of a small communist community may, quite properly, refuse to allow anyone to opt out of equal sharing, even though it would be possible to arrange this. It is not a general principle that every community or group must allow internal opting out when that is feasible. For sometimes such internal opting out would itself change the character of the group from that desired. Herein lies an interesting theoretical problem. A nation or protective agency may not compel redistribution between one community and another, yet a community such as a kibbutz may redistribute within itself (or give to another community or to outside individuals). Such a community needn't offer its members an opportunity to opt out of these arrangements while

---

* It is strange that many young people "in tune with" nature and hoping to "go with the flow" and not force things against their natural bent should be attracted to statist views and socialism, and are antagonistic to equilibrium and invisible-hand processes.

remaining a member of the community. Yet, I have argued, a nation should offer this opportunity; people have a right to so opt out of a nation's requirements. Wherein lies the difference between a community and a nation that makes the difference in the legitimacy of imposing a certain pattern upon all of its members?

A person will swallow the imperfections of a package P (which may be a protective arrangement, a consumer good, a community) that is desirable on the whole rather than purchase a different package (a completely different package, or P with some changes), when no more desirable attainable different package is worth to him its greater costs over P, including the costs of inducing enough others to participate in making the alternative package. One assumes that the cost calculation for nations is such as to permit internal opting out. But this is not the whole story for two reasons. First, it may be feasible in individual communities also to arrange internal opting out at little administrative cost (which he may be willing to pay), yet this needn't always be done. Second, nations differ from other packages in that the individual himself isn't to bear the administrative costs of opting out of some otherwise compulsory provision. The other people must pay for finely designing their compulsory arrangements so that they don't apply to those who wish to opt out. Nor is the difference merely a matter of there being many alternative kinds of communities while there are many fewer nations. Even if almost everyone wished to live in a communist community, so that there weren't any viable noncommunist communities, no particular community need also (though it is to be hoped that one would) allow a resident individual to opt out of their sharing arrangement. The recalcitrant individual has no alternative but to conform. Still, the others do not force him to conform, and his rights are not violated. He has no right that the others cooperate in making his nonconformity feasible.

The difference seems to me to reside in the difference between a face-to-face community and a nation. In a nation, one knows that there are nonconforming individuals, but one need not be directly confronted by these individuals or by the fact of their nonconformity. Even if one finds it offensive that others do not conform, even if the knowledge that there exist nonconformists rankles and makes one very unhappy, this does not constitute being harmed by the others or having one's rights violated. Whereas in a face-to-face community one cannot avoid being directly confronted with what one finds to be offensive. How one lives in one's immediate environment is affected.

This distinction between a face-to-face community and one that is not generally runs parallel to another distinction. A face-to-face community can exist on land jointly owned by its members, whereas the land of a nation is not so held. The community will be entitled then, as a body, to determine what regulations are to be obeyed on its land; whereas the citizens of a nation do not jointly own its land and so cannot in this way regulate its use. If *all* the separate individuals who own land coordinate their actions in imposing a common regulation (for example, no one may reside on this land who does not contribute *n* percent of his income to the poor), the same *effect* will be achieved as if the nation had passed legislation requiring this. But since unanimity is only as strong as its weakest link, even with the use of secondary boycotts (which are perfectly legitimate), it would be impossible to maintain such a unanimous coalition in the face of the blandishments to some to defect.

But some face-to-face communities will not be situated on jointly held land. May the majority of the voters in a small village pass an ordinance against things that they find offensive being done on the *public* streets? May they legislate against nudity or fornication or sadism (on consenting masochists) or hand-holding by racially mixed couples on the streets? Any private owner can regulate his premises as he chooses. But what of the public thoroughfares, where people cannot easily avoid sights they find offensive? Must the vast majority cloister themselves against the offensive minority? If the majority may determine the limits on detectable behavior in public, may they, in addition to requiring that no one appear in public without wearing clothing, also require that no one appear in public without wearing a badge certifying that he has contributed *n* percent of his income to the needy during the year, on the grounds that they find it offensive to look at someone not wearing this badge (not having contributed)? And whence this emergent right of the majority to decide? Or are there to be no "public" place or ways? * * * Since I do not see my way clearly through these issues, I raise them here only to leave them. * * *

Nor do I assume that all problems about the framework are solved. Let us mention a few here. There will be problems about the role, if any, to be played by some central authority (or protective association); how will this authority be selected, and how will it be ensured that the authority does, and does only, what it is supposed to do? The major role, as I see it, would be to enforce the operation of the framework—for example, to prevent some communities from invading and seizing others, their persons or assets. Furthermore, it will adjudicate in some reasonable fashion conflicts between communities which cannot be settled by peaceful means. What the best form of such a central authority is I would not wish to investigate here. It seems desirable that one not be fixed permanently but that room be left for improvements of detail. I ignore here the difficult and important problems of the controls on a central authority powerful enough to perform its appropriate functions, because I have nothing special to add to the standard literature on federations, confederations, decentralization of power, checks and balances, and so on.

One persistent strand in utopian thinking, as we have mentioned, is the feeling that there is some set of principles obvious enough to be accepted by all men of good will, precise enough to give unambiguous guidance in particular situations, clear enough so that all will realize its dictates, and complete enough to cover all problems which actually will arise. Since I do not assume that there are such principles, I do not assume that the political realm will wither away. The messiness of the details of a political apparatus and the details of how *it* is to be controlled and limited do not fit easily into one's hopes for a sleek, simple utopian scheme.

Apart from the conflict between communities, there will be other tasks for a central apparatus or agency, for example, enforcing an individual's right to leave a community. But problems arise if an individual can plausibly be viewed as *owing* something to the other members of a community he wishes to leave: for example, he has been educated at their expense on the explicit agreement that he would use his acquired skills and knowledge in the home community. Or, he has acquired certain family obligations that he will abandon by shifting communities. Or, without such ties, he wishes to leave. What may he take out with him? Or, he wishes to leave after he's committed some punishable offense for which the community wishes to punish him. Clearly the principles will be complicated ones. Children present yet more difficult problems. In some way it must be ensured that they are *informed* of the range of alternatives in the world. But the home community might view it as important that their youngsters not be exposed to the knowledge that one hundred miles away is a community of great sexual freedom. And so on. I mention these problems to indicate a fraction of the thinking that needs to be done on the details of a framework and to make clear that I do not think its nature can be settled finally now either.

Even though the details of the framework aren't settled, won't there be some rigid limits about it, some things inalterably fixed? Will it be possible to shift to a nonvoluntary framework permitting the forced exclusion of various styles of life? If a framework could be devised that could not be transformed into a nonvoluntary one, would we wish to institute it? If we institute such a permanently voluntary general framework, are we not, to some extent, ruling out certain possible choices? Are we not saying in advance that people cannot choose to live in a certain way; are we setting a rigid range in which people can move and thus committing the usual fault of the static utopians? The comparable question about an individual is whether a free system will allow him to sell himself into slavery. I believe that it would. (Other writers disagree.) It also would allow him permanently to commit himself never to enter into such a transaction. But some things individuals may choose for themselves, no one may choose for another. So long as it is realized at what a *general* level the rigidity lies, and what diversity of particular lives and communities it allows, the answer is, "Yes, the framework should be fixed as voluntary." But remember that any individual may contract into any particular constraints over himself and so may use the voluntary framework to contract himself out of it. (If all individuals do so, the voluntary framework will not operate until the next generation, when others come of age.) * * *

JAMES M. BUCHANAN, PRINCIPLES OF URBAN FISCAL STRATEGY

XI Public Choice 1, 13–16 (1971).

The fiscal incapacity of central cities is a characteristic feature in almost all discussions of urban ills. The demands for expanded public outlays have increased and will continue to increase relative to past and anticipated increases in taxable capacities. Both sides of the urban fiscal account have been adversely affected by the flight of persons and firms to the independently-organized suburbs. With this as diagnosis, there seem to be only two directions for reform. The first is the provision of financial relief from external sources, presumably in the form of federal grants. The second a widening of the local fiscal base, presumably through the consolidation of central city and suburban governmental units.

In this paper, I shall not examine either the prospects for or consequences of expanded external financial support, whether from the federal government or from the states. Nor shall I discuss specifically the problems or the effects of incorporation and annexation of suburbs. Indeed one implication of that analysis is that attempts to resolve the fiscal plight of cities in this way may be unsuccessful. If the city widens its fiscal base without recognizing the strategic aspects of the fiscal problems that it faces, the result may be more rather than less inefficiency in economic and locational patterns.

I shall show how a city governmental unit may prevent its fiscal dilemma from arising in the first place. I introduce the term "strategy" deliberately in its game-theoretic meaning. The decision-makers for the cities must recognize the effects of their own fiscal actions on the behavior of taxpaying and benefits-receiving citizens. Fiscal decisions must be made strategically rather than reactively. Translated into practical policy terms this means that potentially-mobile central-city taxpayers who contribute to net fiscal surplus must be deliberately induced to remain in the sharing community by appropriate fiscal adjustments. This simple principle has long been recognized by politicians and by community leaders. It has not, to my knowledge, been explained or interpreted analytically. An essential step in the process is the discarding of familiar cliches concerning the application of standard equity norms. * * *

The objective for rational urban fiscal strategy is the maximization of per capita fiscal dividend or surplus. This translates directly into the requirement that all persons who contribute positively to the generation of fiscal surplus be kept within the club. To the extent that persons or groups who do make net contributions are observed to migrate to the suburbs, urban fiscal strategy has failed. Those who contribute most are those who pay the largest share of costs, and these are presumably those whose demands are highest. I have made the standard assumption that the good produced by municipal governments are characterized by positive income elasticities. If this is accepted, the relative emphasis on retaining the high-income, high-wealth residents becomes obvious.* * * Regardless of just who makes up the dominant political coalition, rational strategy suggests that consideration be given to the suburban migration of those who receive relatively higher incomes and who own relatively higher-valued assets. This arises solely from the self-interests of those citizens who remain in the city. It has nothing to do with the "deservingness" of the high-income or the low-income groups, or with "justice" or "equity" as an abstract ethical norm. * * *

We may identify several features that determine the sort of adjustments that will be made under an optimally preferred strategy. These are: (1) the "publicness" of the budgetary bundle that is offered by the municipality; (2) the elasticity of demand for this bundle by the group considered; (3) the costs of outmigration and the formation of alternative purchase-provisions arrangements. These factors are controllable to some extent by the municipal decision-makers. An inclusive strategy should, therefore, be directed toward *increasing* the "publicness" of the budgetary items, toward *decreasing* the high-income recipients' elasticity of demand for this bundle, and toward *increasing* the costs of making alternative arrangements.

Since municipalities normally provide a whole set of goods and services, budgetary adjustments should place relatively greater emphasis on those components that exhibit relatively large sharing efficiencies at the group-size margin. Goods and services that exhibit little or no gains from joint consumption or which exhibit gains which are exhausted before the effective city size is reached should be relatively reduced or eliminated from the city budget. Financing these by direct user charges rather than by taxation may be indicated. Such changes in budgetary composition may seem harmful to low-income consumers. In the larger strategic context, however, these policies, by preserving the fiscal base of the community, may benefit the very groups that seem initially to be harmed. * * *

[R]elatively greater attention should be given to the municipal supply of those goods and services that potential suburbanites might find difficult or very costly to secure independently. To offer practical examples, municipalities should listen more carefully to those who recommend fiscal support for art museums, symphony orchestras, theaters, and parks. Once such services as these are provided, however, appropriate exclusion arrangements, through charges or otherwise, must be introduced to insure that suburbanites who are nonresidents cannot enjoy the "publicness" benefits without making their own contribution to internal fiscal surplus. * * *

One means of increasing the "publicness" of the budgetary bundle may involve differential adjustments on the consumption services side. This is observed to occur in special police details in high-income areas of cities, in better parks in some areas than in others, in better-equipped and better-staffed schools, etc. As with tax-side adjustments designed to accomplish the same purposes, such differentials in public service standards among differing income groups in the municipality may seem to violate traditional equity norms. When strategic considerations are recognized, however, the existence of such differentials may provide evidence that the decision-makers are, in fact, behaving in the interest of the low and middle income constituents. * * *

Municipal governments from which outmigration has taken place should insure that all sales of goods and services to newly-formed suburbs or to private individuals and groups are made on an explicit recognition of the monopolistic powers of the parent unit. If prospective suburbanites are aware of the costs of making repurchase and tie-in agreements with the central city, they may be inhibited from making suburban migrations in the first place. More importantly, even if suburbs are formed beyond city boundaries, suburbanites can be forced to contribute toward the fiscal surplus of city residents by appropriate pricing policies. This aspect of urban strategy has several direct applications, for example in water-line and sewer-line extensions, extended fire protection and police coverage. * * *

Differing environments will indicate differing strategies; no generally applicable rules can be laid down for municipalities to follow. The analysis raises critical questions about the appropriateness of any *general* norm for fiscal organization. Differences in migration potential among subgroups must be taken into account, and intraclass as well as interclass adjustments may be required. Optimal strategies may dictate that economic units which seem comparable in many respects be treated differently by municipal fiscal systems. The familiar practice of allegedly favored treatment accorded high-income residential property owners in assessments may be "explained" as one part of an optimal strategy. If such an explanation is at all accurate, the interests of city residents who are assessed unfavorably may dictate continuation rather than elimination of the favoritism. * * *

FRANK I. MICHELMAN, POLITICAL MARKETS AND COMMUNITY SELF-DETERMINATION: COMPETING JUDICIAL MODELS OF LOCAL GOVERNMENT LEGITIMACY

53 Ind. L. J. 145, 148–156 (1978).

[This essay considers] * * * the coexistence in the judicial mentality of two different, and contradictory, modes of local-government legitimacy * * *—an economic or "public choice" model and a non-economic "public interest" or "community self-determination" model. * * *

In the economic or public choice model, all substantive values or ends are regarded as strictly private and subjective. The legislature is conceived as a market-like arena in which votes instead of money are the medium of exchange. The rule of majority rule arises strictly in the guise of a technical device for prudently controlling the transaction costs of individualistic exchanges. Legislative intercourse is not public-spirited but self-interested. Legislators do not deliberate towards goals, they dicker towards terms. There is no right answer, there are only struck bargains. There is no public or general or social interest, there are only concatenations of particular interests or private preferences. There is no reason, only strategy; no persuasion, only temptation and threat. There are no good legislators, only shrewd ones; no statesmen, only messengers, no entrusted representatives, only tethered agents.

Madison

The opposed, public-interest model depends at bottom on a belief in the reality—or at least the possibility—of public or objective values and ends for human action. In this public-interest model the legislature is regarded as a forum for identifying or defining, and acting towards those ends. The process is one of mutual search through joint deliberation, relying on the use of reason supposed to have persuasive force. Majority rule is experienced as the natural way of taking action as and for a group—or as a device for filtering the reasonable from the unreasonable, the persuasive from the unpersuasive, the right from the wrong and the good from the bad. Moral insight, sociological understanding, and goodwill are all legislative virtues. Representatives are chosen in part for their supposed excellence in such virtues. This model, no doubt, is as sentimental as the public-choice model is unlovely; but though public interest may in that sense be a less "realistic" way of looking at the world than public choice, I doubt that it is less real as a description of our actual way of experiencing and interpreting our political life; nor is it less real— and here is a major thesis of this essay—as a description of the way judges perceive that life.

Coexistence of the two opposed models of legitimacy may be connected with a deep controversy in our philosophical tradition between opposed notions of human freedom and value. On the one hand there is a tradition deeply entrenched in Western thought * * * that conceives individual freedom in such a way that its attainment depends on the possibility of values that are communal and objective—jointly recognized by members of a group and determinable through reasoned interchange among them. In this conception advanced by Rousseau and Kant, freedom is the state of giving law to oneself. This conception is, to put it a bit crudely, one of self-regulation as opposed to self-indulgence. It implies that unfettered trade in a perfectly free, competitive market cannot by itself constitute a person's freedom: for by itself free trade can be taken as a reflection of perfect enslavement to wants or appetites that are not chosen but just impinge on one inexplicably and uncontrollably. Freedom in the Kantian view means *choosing* one's ends by an activity of reason. * * * Reasoning in such a constitutive mode seems to involve constraint of choice by some principle or set of principles other than the principle of maximizing the satisfaction—even the long range satisfaction—of one's present wants.

There may be grounds for thinking that, for many if not all individuals, the possibility of such a reasoned choice of ends will depend upon the individual's functioning—by participation and commitment—as a member of a group of persons engaged in making choices by which all members are bound. If so, then it is the case not only that freedom for individuals depends upon the possibility of objective ends to which one can commit oneself on principle; but also that for individuals in secular society such ends or values will encompass matters of interpersonal relationship, obligation, and respect and, for the freedom-seeking socialized individual, political process will be both a medium for reasoning towards the ends (and acting towards their attainment) and, at the same time, itself one of the ends. * * *

On the other hand there is a strictly individualist and subjectivist conception of human experience, a conception which serves as a foundation for modern economic analysis. * * * The general idea is that values, so-called, are taken to be nothing but individually held, arbitrary and inexplicable preferences (the subjectivist element) having no objective significance apart from what individuals are actually found choosing to do under the conditions that confront them (the behaviorist element); from which it seems to follow that there can be no objective good apart from allowing for the maximum feasible satisfaction of private preference as revealed through actual choice—or, in other words, through "willingness to pay." The resulting allocation of resources to the highest-paying employments is the state known to economists as efficiency. * * * The normative economic theory of governmental institutions can be seen as proceeding at two levels. At the first level is what has been variously called the "protective," or the "minimal," or the "night-watchman" state: Every individual's basic entitlements will just obviously be worth more to the several individuals * * * if enforcement is guaranteed by an impartial institutional enforcer rather than left to self-help. But the protective state as thus explained will be limited to articulating and enforcing obvious rules against assault, trespass, fraud, theft, promise-breaking and the like. * * *

[I]t is possible to give an individualistic-economic rational for the welfare state, too. In fact, at least two accounts are available—what I shall call the "big-bribe" and the "market-failure" accounts. * * * Suppose we say the problem is to justify continued acceptance by the relatively well-endowed—those who would be the best-off if everyone were left unmolested in an ungoverned state of nature—of governmental authority to tax and regulate for welfarish, redistributive or productive purposes. Then the answer is that such acceptance is a price (or call it a bribe) those better-endowed should find worth paying, in exchange for peaceful acceptance by the naturally worse-endowed of the government's protective police authority. * * *

The market-failure account * * * may have more influence in contemporary interpretations of our prevailing governmental institutions. * * * Where large numbers of persons are involved, getting them organized will itself be a costly operation. The difficulties are aggravated by the likelihood of strategic concealment by freeloaders and hold-outs. Each person, hoping or expecting that others will choose to pay for a good which once produced will necessarily be available to the entire neighborhood or community, will have some motivation to understate his true demand for the good; and each will realize that all the others are subject to the same temptation. For such reasons a largish group of neighbors might well fail to provide themselves with something like a jointly financed police patrol—and fail even to make the attempt—even though, were the truth known, a bargain could be struck which each would regard as privately advantageous.

Taught to appreciate this sort of problem, members of a residential community might unanimously agree to organize themselves into a political unit within which decisions about investment in public goods and programs would thenceforth be made collectively, typically by majority rule and very likely by elected representatives. * * * Each member would realize that virtually every public decision would depart in some measure from his or her true individual preferences, and that on occasion such departures might be quite seriously harmful to him or her. Public choice theorists have called such departures "political externalities," in recognition that they are costs that some persons are enabled to impose on others by majority rule. Yet each member, by subscribing to the arrangement, would signify an expectation that his or her political-externality costs will over the long run be more than offset by gains derived from coordination that only a political, essentially majoritarian mechanism can achieve at feasible transaction costs. * * *

IRIS YOUNG, JUSTICE AND THE POLITICS OF DIFFERENCE
Pp. 234–241 (1990).

Undesirable Political Consequences of the Ideal of Community

* * * In ordinary speech in the United States, the term community refers to the people with whom one identifies in a specific locale. It refers to neighborhood, church, schools. It also carries connotations of ethnicity, race, and other group identifications. For most people, insofar as they consider themselves members of communities at all, a community is a group that shares a specific heritage, a common self-identification, a common culture and set of norms. * * * [S]elf-identification as a member of such a community also often occurs as an oppositional differentiation from other groups, who are feared, despised, or at best devalued. Persons feel a sense of mutual identification only with some persons, feel in community only with those, and fear the difference others confront them with because they identify with a different culture, history, and point of view on the world. The ideal of community, I suggest, validates and reinforces the fear and aversion some social groups exhibit toward others. If community is a positive norm, that is, if existing together with others in relations of mutual understanding and reciprocity is the goal, then it is understandable that we exclude and avoid those with whom we do not or cannot identify.

Richard Sennett discusses how a "myth of community" operates perpetually in American society to produce and implicitly legitimate racist and classist behavior and policy. In many towns, suburbs, and neighborhoods people do have an image of their locale as one in which people all know one another, have the same values and life style, and relate with feelings of mutuality and love. In modern American society such an image is almost always false; while there may be a dominant group with a distinct set of values and life style, within any locale one can usually find deviant individuals and groups. Yet the myth of community operates strongly to produce defensive exclusionary behavior: pressuring the Black family that buys a house on the block to leave, beating up the Black youths who come into "our" neighborhood, zoning against the construction of multiunit dwellings.

The exclusionary consequences of valuing community, moreover, are not restricted to bigots and conservatives. Many radical political organizations founder on the desire for community. Too often people in groups working for social change take mutual friendship to be a goal of the group, and thus judge themselves wanting as a group when they do not achieve such commonality. Such a desire for community often channels energy away from the political goals of the group, and also produces a clique atmosphere which keeps groups small and turns potential members away. Mutual identification as an implicit group ideal can reproduce a homogeneity that usually conflicts with the organization's stated commitment to diversity. In recent years most socialist and feminist organizations, for example, have taken racial, class, age, and sexual diversity as an important criterion according to which the success of political organizations should be evaluated. To the degree that they take mutual understanding and identification as a goal, they may be deflected from this goal of diversity.

The exclusionary implications of a desire for face-to-face relations of mutual identification and sharing present a problem for movements asserting positive group difference * * *. [T]he effort of oppressed groups to reclaim their group identity, and to form with one another bonds of positive cultural affirmation around their group specificity, constitutes an important resistance to the oppression of cultural imperialism. It shifts the meaning of difference from otherness and exclusion to variation and specificity, and forces dominant groups to acknowledge their own group specificity. But does not such affirmation of group identity itself express an ideal of community, and is it not subject to exclusionary impulses?

Some social movements asserting positive group difference have found through painful confrontation that an urge to unity and mutual identification does indeed have exclusionary implications. Feminist efforts to create women's spaces and women's culture, for example, have often assumed the perspective of only a particular subgroup of women— white, or middle class, or lesbian, or straight—thus implicitly excluding or rendering invisible those women among them with differing identifications and experiences. Similar problems arise for any movement of group identification, because in our society most people have multiple group identifications, and thus group differences cut across every social group.

These arguments against community are not arguments against the political project of constructing and affirming a positive group identity and relations of group solidarity, as a means of confronting cultural imperialism and discovering things about oneself and others with whom one feels affinity. Critique of the ideal of community, however, reveals that even in such group-specific contexts affinity cannot mean the transparency of selves to one another. If in their zeal to affirm a positive meaning of group specificity people seek or try to enforce a strong sense of mutual identification, they are likely to reproduce exclusions similar to those they confront. Those affirming the specificity of a group affinity should at the same time recognize and affirm the group and individual differences within the group.

City Life as a Normative Ideal

Appeals to community are usually antiurban. Much sociological literature diagnoses modern history as a movement to the dangerous bureaucratized *Gesellschaft* from the manageable and safe *Gemeinschaft*, nostalgically reconstructed as a world of lost origins. Many others follow Rousseau in romanticizing the ancient *polis* and the medieval Swiss *Bürger* deploring the commerce, disorder, and unmanageable mass character of the modern city. Throughout the modern period, the city has often been decried as embodying immorality, artificiality, disorder, and danger—as the site of treasonous conspiracies, illicit sex, crime, deviance, and disease. The typical image of the modern city finds it expressing all the disvalues that a reinstantiation of community would eliminate.

Yet urbanity is the horizon of the modern, not to mention the postmodern, condition. Contemporary political theory must accept urbanity as a material given for those who live in advanced industrial societies. Urban relations define the lives not only of those who live in the huge metropolises, but also of those who live in suburbs and large towns. Our social life is structured by vast networks of temporal and spatial mediation among persons, so that nearly everyone depends on the activities of seen and unseen strangers who mediate between oneself and one's associates, between oneself and one's objects of desire. Urbanites find themselves relating geographically to increasingly large regions, thinking little of traveling seventy miles to work or an hour's drive for an evening's entertainment. Most people frequently and casually encounter strangers in their daily activities. The material surroundings and structures available to us define and presuppose urban relationships. The very size of populations in our society and most other nations of the world, coupled with a continuing sense of national or ethnic identity with millions of other people, supports the conclusion that a vision of dismantling the city is hopelessly utopian.

Starting from the given of modern urban life is not simply necessary, moreover; it is desirable. Even for many of those who decry the alienation, bureaucratization, and mass character of capitalist patriarchal society, city life exerts a powerful attraction. Modern literature, art, and film have celebrated city life, its energy, cultural diversity, technological complexity, and the multiplicity of its activities. Even many of the most staunch proponents of decentralized community love to show visiting friends around the Boston or San Francisco or New York in or near which they live, climbing up towers to see the glitter of lights and sampling the fare at the best ethnic restaurants.

I propose to construct a normative ideal of city life as an alternative to both the ideal of community and the liberal individualism it criticizes as asocial. By "city life" I mean a form of social relations which I define as the being together of strangers. In the city persons and groups interact within spaces and institutions they all experience themselves as belonging to, but without those interactions dissolving into unity or commonness. City life is composed of clusters of people with affinities— families, social group networks, voluntary associations, neighborhood networks, a vast array of small "communities." City dwellers frequently venture beyond such familiar enclaves, however, to the more open public of politics, commerce, and festival, where strangers meet and interact. City dwelling situates one's own identity and activity in relation to a horizon of a vast variety of other activity, and the awareness that this unknown, unfamiliar activity affects the conditions of one's own.

City life is a vast, even infinite, economic network of production, distribution, transportation, exchange, communication, service provision, and amusement. City dwellers depend on the mediation of thousands of other people and vast organizational resources in order to accomplish their individual ends. City dwellers are thus together, bound to one another, in what should be and sometimes is a single polity. Their being together entails some common problems and common interests, but they do not create a community of shared final ends, of mutual identification and reciprocity.

A normative ideal of city life must begin with our given experience of cities, and look there for the virtues of this form of social relations. Defining an ideal as unrealized possibilities of the actual, I extrapolate from that experience four such virtues.

(1) *Social differentiation without exclusion.* City life in urban mass society is not inconsistent with supportive social networks and subcultural communities. Indeed, for many it is their necessary condition. In the city social group differences flourish. Modernization theory predicted a decline in local, ethnic, and other group affiliations as universalist state institutions touch people's lives more directly and as people encounter many others with identifications and life styles different from their own. There is considerable evidence, however, that group differences are often reinforced by city life, and that the city even encourages the formation of new social group affinities. Deviant or minority groups find in the city both a cover of anonymity and a critical mass unavailable in the smaller town. It is hard to imagine the formation of gay or lesbian group affinities, for example, without the conditions of the modern city. While city dwelling as opposed to rural life has changed the lives and self-concepts of Chicanos, to take another example, city life encourages group identification and a desire for cultural nationalism at the same time that it may dissolve some traditional practices or promote assimilation to Anglo language and values. In actual cities many people express violent aversions to members of groups with which they do not identify. More than those who live in small towns, however, they tend to

recognize social group difference as a given, something they must live with.

In the ideal of city life freedom leads to group differentiation, to the formation of affinity groups, but this social and spatial differentiation of groups is without exclusion. The urban ideal expresses difference * * *, a side-by-side particularity neither reducible to identity nor completely other. In this ideal groups do not stand in relations of inclusion and exclusion, but overlap and intermingle without becoming homogeneous. Though city life as we now experience it has many borders and exclusions, even our actual experience of the city also gives hints of what differentiation without exclusion can be. Many city neighborhoods have a distinct ethnic identity, but members of other groups also dwell in them. In the good city one crosses from one distinct neighborhood to another without knowing precisely where one ended and the other began. In the normative ideal of city life, borders are open and undecidable.

(2) *Variety*. The interfusion of groups in the city occurs partly because of the multiuse differentiation of social space. What makes urban spaces interesting, draws people out in public to them, gives people pleasure and excitement, is the diversity of activities they support. When stores, restaurants, bars, clubs, parks, and offices are sprinkled among residences, people have a neighborly feeling about their neighborhood, they go out and encounter one another on the streets and chat. They have a sense of their neighborhood as a "spot" or "place," because of that bar's distinctive clientele, or the citywide reputation of the pizza at that restaurant. Both business people and residents tend to have more commitment to and care for such neighborhoods than they do for single-use neighborhoods. Multifunctional streets, parks, and neighborhoods are also much safer than single-use functional spaces because people are out on the streets during most hours, and have commitment to the place.

(3) *Eroticism*. City life also instantiates difference as the erotic, in the wide sense of an attraction to the other, the pleasure and excitement of being drawn out of one's secure routine to encounter the novel, strange, and surprising. The erotic dimension of the city has always been an aspect of its fearfulness, for it holds out the possibility that one will lose one's identity, will fall. But we also take pleasure in being open to and interested in people we experience as different. We spend a Sunday afternoon walking through Chinatown, or checking out this week's eccentric players in the park. We look for restaurants, stores, and clubs with something new for us, a new ethnic food, a different atmosphere, a different crowd of people. We walk through sections of the city that we experience as having unique characters which are not ours, where people from diverse places mingle and then go home.

The erotic attraction here is precisely the obverse of community. In the ideal of community people feel affirmed because those with whom they share experiences, perceptions, and goals recognize and are recognized by them; one sees oneself reflected in the others. There is another kind of pleasure, however, in coming to encounter a subjectivity, a set of meanings, that is different, unfamiliar. One takes pleasure in being drawn out of oneself to understand that there are other meanings, practices, perspectives on the city, and that one could learn or experience something more and different by interacting with them.

The city's eroticism also derives from the aesthetics of its material being: the bright and colored lights, the grandeur of its buildings, the juxtaposition of architecture of different times, styles, and purposes. City space offers delights and surprises. Walk around the corner, or over a few blocks, and you encounter a different spatial mood, a new play of sight and sound, and new interactive movement. The erotic meaning of the city arises from its social and spatial inexhaustibility. A place of many places, the city folds over on itself in so many layers and relationships that it is incomprehensible. One cannot "take it in," one never feels as though there is nothing new and interesting to explore, no new and interesting people to meet.

(4) *Publicity.* Political theorists who extol the value of community often construe the public as a realm of unity and mutual understanding, but this does not cohere with our actual experience of public spaces. Because by definition a public space is a place accessible to anyone, where anyone can participate and witness, in entering the public one always risks encounter with those who are different, those who identify with different groups and have different opinions or different forms of life. The group diversity of the city is most often apparent in public spaces. This helps account for their vitality and excitement. Cities provide important public spaces—streets, parks, and plazas—where people stand and sit together, interact and mingle, or simply witness one another, without becoming unified in a community of "shared final ends."

Politics, the critical activity of raising issues and deciding how institutional and social relations should be organized, crucially depends on the existence of spaces and forums to which everyone has access. In such public spaces people encounter other people, meanings, expressions, issues, which they may not understand or with which they do not identify. The force of public demonstrations, for example, often consists in bringing to people who pass through public spaces those issues, demands, and people they might otherwise avoid. As a normative ideal city life provides public places and forums where anyone can speak and anyone can listen.

Because city life is a being together of strangers, diverse and overlapping neighbors, social justice cannot issue from the institution of an Enlightenment universal public. On the contrary, social justice in the city requires the realization of a politics of difference. This politics lays down institutional and ideological means for recognizing and affirming diverse social groups by giving political representation to these groups, and celebrating their distinctive characteristics and cultures. In the unoppressive city people open to unassimilated otherness. We all have our familiar relations and affinities, the people to whom we feel close and with whom we share daily life. These familial and social groups open onto a public in which all participate, and that public must be open and accessible to all. Contrary to the communitarian tradition, however, that public cannot be conceived as a unity transcending group differences, nor as entailing complete mutual understanding. In public life the differences remain unassimilated, but each participating group acknowledges and is open to listening to the others. The public is heterogeneous, plural, and playful, a place where people witness and appreciate diverse cultural expressions that they do not share and do not fully understand. * * *

CHAPTER 2

THE RELATIONSHIP BETWEEN CITIES AND STATES, BETWEEN CITIES AND THE FEDERAL GOVERNMENT, AND BETWEEN CITIES AND THE WORLD

■ ■ ■

A. THE RELATIONSHIP BETWEEN CITIES AND STATES

The heart of local government law has traditionally been an analysis of the relationship between cities and states. In the nineteenth century, there was an important debate over the nature of this relationship between those who viewed cities as creatures of the state and those who believed that cities should have a right to self-government. Advocates who sought to portray cities as creatures of the state embraced this conception as a way to limit the dangers posed by local majorities—for example, the threat of faction that Madison articulated in Federalist 10. The way to curb the potential abuse of power, they thought, was to restrict city power to matters delegated under state law. John Dillon's treatise on Municipal Corporations, which we examine below, is the most important articulation and defense of this position. Advocates of the right of local self-government, on the other hand, often defended city power on the ground that it enabled citizens to engage in an essential ingredient of democratic government: participation in local decision making. From this perspective, limiting city power to state delegated authority would be an infringement on an important aspect of human freedom.

As we shall see, these conflicting perspectives animated the debate over the enactment—and currently animate the debate over the meaning—of state constitutional protections for home rule, as well as state constitutional limitations on a state's power to pass "local" or "special" legislation. They are also of relevance in thinking about the legal status of local governments as a matter of federal constitutional law. The competing positions about the proper state-city relationship are explored below, but they should be related as well to the materials on the public/private distinction presented above in Chapter One. What is the source of city power? Is city power properly understood as derived from state law or from the actions of the city's own citizens?

127

In reflecting on these questions, it is important to remember that debates over decentralization do not occur in a vacuum. As the readings below emphasize, they are powerfully informed by the social and political context of the time. Are battles over the scope of local power really just battles over how a policy should be substantively decided? If not, what is the relationship between the substance of policymaking and the level at which the policy should be resolved?

1. THE CITY-STATE RELATIONSHIP AS A MATTER OF FEDERAL CONSTITUTIONAL LAW

According to the first case reproduced below, Hunter v. Pittsburgh, states can exercise virtually limitless power over cities as a matter of federal constitutional law. In reading the case, consider how the Supreme Court envisions the city-state relationship. What distinction does the Court suggest between cities and, for example, administrative departments of the state government (such as the state Department of Education)? The second case, City of New York v. State of New York, was decided nearly a century later and considers whether a city can sue the state of which it is a part.[1] A positive answer to this question suggests that cities have interests that are independent of those of the state; a negative answer suggests, like *Hunter*, that a dispute between a city and its "parent" should be viewed as a controversy between the state government and one of its administrative subdivisions and thus unsuitable for judicial resolution. Does the majority opinion in *City of New York* follow from the Supreme Court's analysis in *Hunter*?

The next case—Equality Foundation of Greater Cincinnati Inc. v. Cincinnati—addresses whether the local political process has a unique federal constitutional status in protecting minorities. In *Equality Foundation*, an amendment to the Cincinnati city charter prohibiting the establishment of "protected status" on the basis of sexual orientation was upheld against a constitutional challenge. The court distinguished Romer v. Evans—the Supreme Court case invalidating a similar statewide initiative in Colorado excerpted in Chapter One—on the ground that the local political process was more deserving of judicial deference than that of the state. Read together these two arguments might suggest a principle: minority friendly local decisions should receive judicial protection from statewide (but not from locally initiated) interference. Is such a principle defensible? Is it necessarily inconsistent with the Court's opinion in *Hunter*? The selection from David Barron's article, *The Promise of Cooley's City*, provides an historical, legal and normative argument for deference to local decision making as a matter of federal constitutional law. What implications does Barron's argument have for *Equality*

[handwritten margin note: distinguishes from Romer]

---

[1]   See Brian Keenan, Subdivisions, Standing and the Supremacy Clause: Can A Political Subdivision Sue Its Parent State under Federal Law?, 103 Mich. L. Rev. 1899 (2005).

Foundation? Is your view on the issue affected by the fact that Cincinnati voters reversed course in 2004, repealing the prohibition upheld in *Equality Foundation* and thus enabling the enactment, in 2006, of a local gay rights ordinance?

HUNTER V. CITY OF PITTSBURGH

Supreme Court of the United States, 1907.
207 U.S. 161, 28 S.Ct. 40, 52 L.Ed. 151.

MR. JUSTICE MOODY * * * delivered the opinion of the court:

The plaintiffs in error seek a reversal of the judgment of the supreme court of Pennsylvania, which affirmed a decree of a lower court, directing the consolidation of the cities of Pittsburgh and Allegheny. This decree was entered by authority of an act of the general assembly of that state, after proceedings taken in conformity with its requirements. The act authorized the consolidation of two cities, situated with reference to each other as Pittsburgh and Allegheny are, if, upon an election, the majority of the votes cast in the territory comprised within the limits of both cities favor the consolidation, even though, as happened in this instance, a majority of the votes cast in one of the cities oppose it. The procedure prescribed by the act is that after a petition filed by one of the cities in the court of quarter sessions, and a hearing upon that petition, that court, if the petition and proceedings are found to be regular and in conformity with the act, shall order an election. If the election shows a majority of the votes cast to be in favor of the consolidation, the court "shall enter a decree annexing and consolidating the lesser city * * * with the greater city." The act provides, in considerable detail, for the effect of the consolidation upon the debts, obligations, claims, and property of the constituent cities; grants rights of citizenship to the citizens of those cities in the consolidated city; enacts that "except as herein otherwise provided, all the property * * * and rights and privileges * * * vested in or belonging to either of said cities * * * prior to and at the time of the annexation shall be vested in and owned by the consolidated or united city," and establishes the form of government of the new city. This procedure was followed by the filing of a petition by the city of Pittsburgh; by an election, in which the majority of all the votes cast were in the affirmative, although the majority of all the votes cast by the voters of Allegheny were in the negative; and by a decree of the court, uniting the two cities.

Prior to the hearing upon the petition the plaintiffs in error, who were citizens, voters, owners of property, and taxpayers in Allegheny, filed twenty-two exceptions to the petition. These exceptions were disposed of adversely to the exceptants by the court of quarter sessions, and the action of that court was successively affirmed by the superior and supreme courts of the state. The case is here upon writ of error. * * *

Briefly stated, the assertion in the fourth assignment of error is that the act of assembly deprives the plaintiffs in error of their property without due process of law, by subjecting it to the burden of the additional taxation which would result from the consolidation. The manner in which the right of due process of law has been violated, as set forth in the first assignment of error and insisted upon in argument, is that the method of voting on the consolidation prescribed in the act has permitted the voters of the larger city to overpower the voters of the smaller city, and compel the union without their consent and against their protest. The precise question thus presented has not been determined by this court. It is important, and, as we have said, not so devoid of merit as to be denied consideration, although its solution by principles long settled and constantly acted upon is not difficult. This court has many times had occasion to consider and decide the nature of municipal corporations, their rights and duties, and the rights of their citizens and creditors. It would be unnecessary and unprofitable to analyze these decisions, or quote from the opinions rendered. We think the following principles have been established by them and have become settled doctrines of this court, to be acted upon wherever they are applicable. Municipal corporations are political subdivisions of the state, created as convenient agencies for exercising such of the governmental powers of the state as may be intrusted to them. For the purpose of executing these powers properly and efficiently they usually are given the power to acquire, hold, and manage personal and real property. The number, nature, and duration of the powers conferred upon these corporations and the territory over which they shall be exercised rests in the absolute discretion of the state. Neither their charters, nor any law conferring governmental powers, or vesting in them property to be used for governmental purposes, or authorizing them to hold or manage such property, or exempting them from taxation upon it, constitutes a contract with the state within the meaning of the Federal Constitution. The state, therefore, at its pleasure, may modify or withdraw all such powers, may take without compensation such property, hold it itself, or vest it in other agencies, expand or contract the territorial area, unite the whole or a part of it with another municipality, repeal the charter and destroy the corporation. All this may be done, conditionally or unconditionally, with or without the consent of the citizens, or even against their protest. In all these respects the state is supreme, and its legislative body, conforming its action to the state Constitution, may do as it will, unrestrained by any provision of the Constitution of the United States. Although the inhabitants and property owners may, by such changes, suffer inconvenience, and their property may be lessened in value by the burden of increased taxation, or for any other reason, they have no right, by contract or otherwise, in the unaltered or continued existence of the corporation or its powers, and there is nothing in the Federal Constitution which protects them from these injurious consequences. The power is in the state, and those who legislate for the state are alone responsible for any unjust or oppressive exercise of it.

Applying these principles to the case at bar, it follows irresistibly that this assignment of error, so far as it relates to the citizens who are plaintiffs in error, must be overruled.

It will be observed that, in describing the absolute power of the state over the property of municipal corporations, we have not extended it beyond the property held and used for governmental purposes. Such corporations are sometimes authorized to hold and do hold property for the same purposes that property is held by private corporations or individuals. The distinction between property owned by municipal corporations in their public and governmental capacity and that owned by them in their private capacity, though difficult to define, has been approved by many of the state courts (Dill.Mun.Corp. 4th ed. §§ 66 to 66a inclusive), and it has been held that, as to the latter class of property, the legislature is not omnipotent. If the distinction is recognized it suggests the question whether property of a municipal corporation owned in its private and proprietary capacity may be taken from it against its will and without compensation. Mr. Dillon says truly that the question has never arisen directly for adjudication in this court. But it and the distinction upon which it is based have several times been noticed. Counsel for plaintiffs in error assert that the city of Allegheny was the owner of property held in its private and proprietary capacity, and insist that the effect of the proceedings under this act was to take its property without compensation and vest it in another corporation, and that thereby the city was deprived of its property without due process of law, in violation of the 14th Amendment. But no such question is presented by the record, and there is but a vague suggestion of facts upon which it might have been founded. In the sixth exception there is a recital of facts with a purpose of showing how the taxes of the citizens of Allegheny would be increased by annexation to Pittsburgh. In that connection it is alleged that while Pittsburgh intends to spend large sums of money in the purchase of the water plant of a private company and for the construction of an electric light plant, Allegheny "has improved its streets, established its own system of electric lighting, and established a satisfactory water supply." This is the only reference in the record to the property rights of Allegheny, and it falls far short of a statement that that city holds any property in its private and proprietary capacity. Nor was there any allegation that Allegheny had been deprived of its property without due process of law. The only allegation of this kind is that the taxpayers, plaintiffs in error, were deprived of their property without due process of law because of the increased taxation which would result from the annexation, an entirely different proposition. * * * [N]o question of the

[margin note: ← depriv. of property w/o due proc. — 14]

effect of the act upon private property rights of the city of Allegheny was considered in the opinions in the state courts or suggested by assignment of errors in this court. The question is entirely outside of the record and has no connection with any question which is raised in the record. For these reasons we are without jurisdiction to consider it, and neither express nor intimate any opinion upon it.

CITY OF NEW YORK V. STATE OF NEW YORK

Court of Appeals of New York, 1995.
86 N.Y.2d 286, 631 N.Y.S.2d 553, 655 N.E.2d 649.

LEVINE, J.

The City of New York, Board of Education of the City, its Mayor and Chancellor of the City School District (hereinafter the municipal plaintiffs) have brought this action against the State and various State officials seeking declaratory and injunctive relief. They allege three causes of action in their amended complaint: (1) that the present State statutory scheme for funding public education denies the school children of New York City their educational rights guaranteed by the Education Article of the State Constitution; (2) that the State's funding of public schools provides separate and unequal treatment for the public schools of New York City in violation of the Equal Protection Clauses of the Federal and State Constitutions; and (3) that the disparate impact of the State's funding scheme for public education on members of racial and ethnic minority groups in New York City violates title VI of the Federal Civil Rights Act of 1964 as amended and its implementing regulations.

We agree with the courts below that the municipal plaintiffs lack the legal capacity to bring this suit against the State. Despite their contrary claims, the traditional principle throughout the United States has been that municipalities and other local governmental corporate entities and their officers lack capacity to mount constitutional challenges to acts of the State and State legislation. This general incapacity to sue flows from judicial recognition of the juridical as well as political relationship between those entities and the State. Constitutionally as well as a matter of historical fact, municipal corporate bodies—counties, towns and school districts—are merely subdivisions of the State, created by the State for the convenient carrying out of the State's governmental powers and responsibilities as its agents. Viewed, therefore, by the courts as purely creatures or agents of the State, it followed that municipal corporate bodies cannot have the right to contest the actions of their principal or creator affecting them in their governmental capacity or as representatives of their inhabitants. Thus, the United States Supreme Court has held:

" 'A municipal corporation is simply a political subdivision of the State, and exists by virtue of the exercise of the power of the State through its legislative department. The legislature could at any time terminate the existence of the corporation itself, and provide other and different means for the government of the district comprised within the limits of the former city. The city is the creature of the State.' " (*Trenton v. New Jersey*, 262 US 182, 189–190.) * * *

New York has long followed the Federal rationale for finding that municipalities lack the capacity to bring suit to invalidate State legislation. * * * The only exceptions to the general rule barring local governmental challenges to State legislation which have been identified in the case law are: (1) an express statutory authorization to bring such a suit; (2) where the State legislation adversely affects a municipality's proprietary interest in a specific fund of moneys; (3) where the State statute impinges upon "Home Rule" powers of a municipality constitutionally guaranteed under article IX of the State Constitution; and (4) where "the municipal challengers assert that if they are obliged to comply with the State statute they will by that very compliance be forced to violate a constitutional proscription." * * *

The municipal plaintiffs have not pointed to any express statutory language or legislative history which would necessarily imply that the Legislature intended to confer upon them the capacity to bring a suit challenging State legislation. * * * Moreover, in view of the manifest improbability that the Legislature would have intended to authorize the municipal plaintiffs to challenge the constitutionality of its own public school funding allocation formula, the evidence from "necessary implication" would have to be particularly strong to support capacity to sue here, and it certainly is not. * * *

Although not a point advanced by the municipal plaintiffs on this appeal, the dissent seeks to bring this case within the already noted exception to the lack of capacity to sue rule, where municipal officials contend that " 'if they are obliged to comply with the State statute they will by that very compliance be forced to violate a constitutional proscription.' " The dissent fails to cite to any specific constitutional proscription, that is, prohibition, that the State school funding formula forces the municipal officials to violate. Surely, it cannot be persuasively argued that the City officials in question should be held accountable either under the Equal Protection Clause or the State Constitution's public Education Article by reason of the alleged State underfunding of the New York City school system over which they have absolutely no control.

Thus, the municipal plaintiffs have failed to bring their claims within any recognized exception to the general rule that municipalities lack capacity to sue the State and their action must be dismissed. We decline the invitation to erode that general rule. Our adherence to that rule is not, as suggested by the dissent "a regression into formalism and rigidity." The lack of capacity of municipalities to sue the State is a necessary outgrowth of separation of powers doctrine: it expresses the extreme reluctance of courts to intrude in the political relationships between the Legislature, the State and its governmental subdivisions. * * *

CIPARICK, J. (dissenting). * * *

We first address the capacity of the school plaintiffs. * * * [S]chool plaintiffs are not attempting to augment their powers, but instead seek a determination in the form of a declaratory judgment that the State is not in compliance with its constitutional obligations. School plaintiffs complain that the statutory scheme for funding public education fails to provide them with sufficient resources to enable them to discharge their obligations under the Education Article of the State Constitution. This case thus falls squarely within a well-defined exception to the general rule of lack of capacity to sue which arises where "municipal challengers assert that if they are obliged to comply with the State statute they will by that very compliance be forced to violate a constitutional proscription." * * *

In our view, the majority's extremely limited application of the general rule of lack of capacity is inappropriate here because it undermines the power and autonomy of local Boards of Education. Public education in New York is a complex, collaborative enterprise between a decentralized State authority and autonomous local districts endowed with broad powers and responsibilities for the management and control of day-to-day educational affairs. * * * The right to sue logically and necessarily derives from this statutory state of affairs. Indeed, how are local school districts to discharge their many duties if they are powerless to hold the State responsible where, as here, it is claimed that the State is failing to carry out its own constitutional mandate with respect to funding public education? For our system of education to work, there must be accountability.

Otherwise powerless to hold State responsible

Contrary to the majority's view, local school districts and Boards of Education are not mere "artificial creatures of statute;" rather, they are substantially autonomous entities entrusted with carrying out a State purpose, and they possess broad powers and duties delegated to them by the State * * *. The City Board of Education is charged with the general administration and control of all aspects of educational affairs. Among other powers, duties, and responsibilities, it is empowered to create, abolish, and maintain positions, divisions, boards, bureaus, etc.; appoint superintendents, examiners, directors, principals, teachers, nurses, etc.; take care, custody, control and safekeeping of all school property and dispose of and sell all property; lease property for school accommodations; purchase and furnish equipment, books, textbooks, furniture, and other supplies as may be necessary for the use of children; establish, maintain and equip libraries and playgrounds; and, authorize the general courses of study in schools and approve the content of such courses. * * *

The majority's reliance on several older United States Supreme Court decisions which merely state the general rule that municipal corporations are but agents of the State have little persuasive value in the specific context of this modern-day challenge to the constitutionality of the State's public school financing scheme. The cases cited by the majority fail to reflect the Supreme Court's more recently expressed view that local school districts are not mere arms of the State, but actually possess a significant degree of independence and autonomy which must be recognized and respected.

In *Milliken v. Bradley* (418 US 717), the Supreme Court rejected interdistrict busing as a remedy for unconstitutional segregation in the Detroit, Michigan, public school system. The District Court in Milliken, as does the majority here, took a narrow view of local school districts as mere political subdivisions established for administrative convenience. The Supreme Court soundly rejected this analytical approach as "contrary to the history of public education in our country." The Supreme Court noted that in Michigan, as in this State, school districts are formally considered "instrumentalities of the State and subordinate to its State Board of Education and its legislature." Nonetheless, while Michigan school districts were instrumentalities of the State in theory, in practice the Michigan educational structure actually endowed them with "a large measure of local control" over day-to-day educational affairs, as evidenced by their statutory powers to acquire real and personal property, hire and contract with personnel, borrow money, determine the length of school terms, determine courses of study, make rules and regulations for operating schools, and so on. Thus, although school districts are, in theory, creatures of the State, the State's theoretical supremacy must sometimes give way to the realities of local control and autonomy, most especially in the area of education. * * *

In *Washington v. Seattle School Dist. No. 1* (458 U.S. 457), the Supreme Court permitted a local school district to assert the Fourteenth Amendment to invalidate a State initiative aimed at banning the use of mandatory busing as a means of promoting integration in Washington's public schools. The Court acknowledged the State's formal authority over local school districts, but found it highly significant that "Washington has chosen to meet its educational responsibilities primarily through 'state and local officials, boards, and committees,' . . . and the responsibility to devise and tailor educational programs to suit local needs has emphatically been vested in the local school boards."

The Supreme Court of Kentucky has addressed the precise issue before us today, holding that local school districts have capacity to sue the legislature in the context of a constitutional challenge to the public school financing scheme (see, *Rose v. Council for Better Education*, 790 S.W.2d 186, 201, n. 16). Notably, the court rejected the same "sterile logic" the majority resurrects today—that local Boards of Education are creatures of the State who cannot sue the State. We agree with the Kentucky court's reasoning that such a rule would be illogical in light of the many broad and specific powers conferred upon school districts by the legislature and the absence of any statutory restriction on the right of local boards to sue. * * * As the Kentucky Supreme Court stated, "a lawsuit to declare an education system unconstitutional falls within the authority, if not the duty, of local school boards to fulfill their statutory responsibilities, no matter who the defendants are." * * *

Finally, we address the city plaintiffs' capacity to sue. The New York City Charter expressly authorizes the City to sue and be sued * * *. Thus, New York City, through its Corporation Counsel, may bring suit to protect and vindicate the rights, property, and revenues of the City and its citizens. The city plaintiffs are responsible for the maintenance and support of public schools in the City School District and have distinct functional responsibilities within the zone of interest to be protected. The City is under a statutory obligation to provide substantial financial support for its school children, and if the educational financing system is constitutionally infirm, as is alleged here, the City is obviously affected, as it is saddled with, among other things, an increased financial burden. Moreover, the New York City Charter imposes significant responsibilities on the City with respect to education. The city plaintiffs' capacity to bring this suit in order to protect the rights, property and revenue of the City must be inferred from these responsibilities and from its financial obligations. * * *

EQUALITY FOUNDATION OF GREATER CINCINNATI, INC. v. CITY OF CINCINNATI

United States Court of Appeals, Sixth Circuit, 1997.
128 F.3d 289, cert. denied, 525 U.S. 943, 119 S.Ct. 365, 142 L.Ed.2d 302 (1998).

KRUPANSKY, CIRCUIT JUDGE. * * *

[D]efendant/appellant the City of Cincinnati ("the City"), and intervening defendants/appellants Equal Rights Not Special Rights ("ERNSR"), challenged the lower court's invalidation of an amendment to the City Charter of Cincinnati ("the Charter") for purported constitutional infirmities, and its permanent injunction restraining implementation of that measure. As a result of an initiative petition, the subject amendment had appeared on the November 2, 1993 local ballot as "Issue 3" and was enacted by 62% of the ballots cast, thereby becoming Article XII of the Charter (hereinafter "the Cincinnati Charter Amendment" or "Article XII"). Article XII read:

NO SPECIAL CLASS STATUS MAY BE GRANTED BASED UPON SEXUAL ORIENTATION, CONDUCT OR RELATIONSHIPS.

The City of Cincinnati and its various Boards and Commissions may not enact, adopt, enforce or administer any ordinance, regulation, rule or policy which provides that homosexual, lesbian, or bisexual orientation, status, conduct, or relationship constitutes, entitles, or otherwise provides a person with the basis to have any claim of minority or protected status, quota preference or other preferential treatment. This provision of the City Charter shall in all respects be self-executing. Any ordinance, regulation, rule or policy enacted before this amendment is adopted that violates the foregoing prohibition shall be null and void and of no force or effect.

Defendant ERNSR had drafted and initiated Issue 3 in response to the prior adoption by the Cincinnati City Council ("Council") of two city ordinances. On March 13, 1991, Council enacted Ordinance No. 79–1991, commonly known as the "Equal Employment Opportunity Ordinance," which mandated that the City could not discriminate in its own hiring practices on the basis of * * * sexual orientation * * *. Subsequently, Council on November 25, 1992 adopted Ordinance No. 490–1992 (commonly referred to as the "Human Rights Ordinance") which prohibited private discrimination in employment, housing, or public accommodation for reasons of sexual orientation. * * *

On May 12, 1995, this reviewing court * * * [concluded] that the Cincinnati Charter Amendment offended neither the First nor the Fourteenth Amendments to the United States Constitution and accordingly could stand as enacted by the Cincinnati voters. *Equality Foundation I*, 54 F.3d 261 (6th Cir.1995). * * * On May 20, 1996, the United States Supreme Court decided *Romer v. Evans*, 517 U.S. 620, 116 S.Ct. 1620, 134 L.Ed.2d 855 (1996). In that decision, the Court invalidated an amendment to the Colorado constitution ("Colorado Amendment 2") enacted by a statewide plebiscite as an infringement of the Equal Protection Clause of the Fourteenth Amendment to the United States Constitution. * * * [T]he *Romer* Court invalidated Colorado Amendment 2 because it was deemed invidiously discriminatory and not rationally connected to the advancement of any legitimate state objective.

Subsequently, on June 17, 1996, the Supreme Court granted the plaintiffs' petition for a writ of certiorari in the case sub judice, vacated this court's judgment in *Equality Foundation I*, and remanded the cause to this forum "for further consideration in light of *Romer v. Evans*." *Equality Foundation of Greater Cincinnati v. City of Cincinnati*, 518 U.S. 1001, 116 S.Ct. 2519, 135 L.Ed.2d 1044 (1996). * * *

The more restricted reach of the Cincinnati Charter Amendment, as compared to the actual and potential sweep of Colorado Amendment 2, is noteworthy. Colorado's Amendment 2 provided:

> No Protected Status Based on Homosexual, Lesbian, or Bisexual Orientation. Neither the State of Colorado, through any of its branches or departments, nor any of its agencies, political subdivisions, municipalities or school districts, shall enact, adopt or enforce any statute, regulation, ordinance or policy whereby homosexual, lesbian or bisexual orientation, conduct, practices or relationships shall constitute or otherwise be the basis of or entitle any person or class of persons to have or claim any minority status, quota preferences, protected status or claim of discrimination. This Section of the Constitution shall be in all respects self-executing. * * *

[T]he language of the Cincinnati Charter Amendment, read in its full context, merely prevented homosexuals, as homosexuals, from obtaining special privileges and preferences (such as affirmative action preferences or the legally sanctioned power to force employers, landlords, and merchants to transact business with them) from the City. In stark contrast, Colorado Amendment 2's far broader language could be construed to exclude homosexuals from the protection of every Colorado state law, including laws generally applicable to all other Coloradans, thus rendering gay people without recourse to any state authority at any level of government for any type of victimization or abuse which they might suffer by either private or public actors. Whereas Colorado Amendment 2 ominously threatened to reduce an entire segment of the state's population to the status of virtual non-citizens (or even non-persons) without legal rights under any and every type of state law,[7] the Cincinnati Charter Amendment had no such sweeping and conscience-shocking effect, because (1) it applied only at the lowest (municipal) level of government and thus could not dispossess gay Cincinnatians of any rights derived from any higher level of state law and enforced by a superior apparatus of state government, and (2) its narrow, restrictive language could not be construed to deprive homosexuals of all legal protections even under municipal law, but instead eliminated only

[Handwritten margin note: city v. state / Cincin. v. Colorado ordinance]

---

7   The *Romer* Court opined: "We must conclude that Amendment 2 classifies homosexuals not to further a proper legislative end but to make them unequal to everyone else. This Colorado cannot do. A State cannot deem a class of persons a stranger to its laws."

"special class status" and "preferential treatment" for gays as gays under Cincinnati ordinances and policies, leaving untouched the application, to gay citizens, of any and all legal rights generally accorded by the municipal government to all persons as persons.

At bottom, the Supreme Court in *Romer* found that a state constitutional proviso which deprived a politically unpopular minority, but no others, of the political ability to obtain special legislation at every level of state government, including within local jurisdictions having pro-gay rights majorities, with the only possible recourse available through surmounting the formidable political obstacle of securing a rescinding amendment to the state constitution, was simply so obviously and fundamentally inequitable, arbitrary, and oppressive that it literally violated basic equal protection values. Thus, the Supreme Court directed that the ordinary three-part equal protection query was rendered irrelevant.

This "extra-conventional" application of equal protection principles can have no pertinence to the case sub judice. The low level of government at which Article XII becomes operative is significant because the opponents of that strictly local enactment need not undertake the *[differentiates Romer from present]* monumental political task of procuring an amendment to the Ohio Constitution as a precondition to achievement of a desired change in the local law, but instead may either seek local repeal of the subject amendment through ordinary municipal political processes, or pursue relief from every higher level of Ohio government, including but not limited to Hamilton County, state agencies, the Ohio legislature, or the voters themselves via a statewide initiative.

Moreover, unlike Colorado Amendment 2, which interfered with the expression of local community preferences in that state, the Cincinnati Charter Amendment constituted a direct expression of the local community will on a subject of direct consequences to the voters. Patently, a local measure adopted by direct franchise, designed in part to preserve community values and character, which does not impinge upon any fundamental right or the interests of any suspect or quasi-suspect class, carries a formidable presumption of legitimacy and is thus entitled to the highest degree of deference from the courts. * * * As the product of direct legislation by the people, a popularly enacted initiative or referendum occupies a special posture in this nation's constitutional tradition and jurisprudence. An expression of the popular will expressed by majority plebiscite, especially at the lowest level of government (which is the level of government closest to the people), must not be cavalierly disregarded. See, e.g., *City of Eastlake v. Forest City Enterprises, Inc.*, 426 U.S. 668, 679, 96 S.Ct. 2358, 2364–65, 49 L.Ed.2d 132 (1976) (explaining that the referendum process is "a basic instrument of democratic government") * * *.

In any event, *Romer* should not be construed to forbid local electorates the authority, via initiative, to instruct their elected city council representatives, or their elected or appointed municipal officers, to withhold special rights, privileges, and protections from homosexuals, or to prospectively remove the authority of such public representatives and officers to accord special rights, privileges, and protections to any non-suspect and non-quasi-suspect group. Such a reading would disenfranchise the voters of their most fundamental right which is the very foundation of the democratic form of government, even through the lowest (and most populist) organs and avenues of state government, to vote to override or preempt any policy or practice implemented or contemplated by their subordinate civil servants to bestow special rights, protections, and/or privileges upon a group of people who do not comprise a suspect or a quasi-suspect class and hence are not constitutionally entitled to any special favorable legal status. * * *

[T]he *Romer* majority's rejection of rational relationship assessment hinged upon the wide breadth of Colorado Amendment 2, which deprived a politically unpopular minority of the opportunity to secure special rights at every level of state law. * * * In essence, the high Court resolved that a state constitutional amendment * * * could not be justified by the proffered public interests purportedly advanced by that state enactment, namely enhancement of the associational liberty of the state's residents and the conservation of public resources, because the citizens of the affected subordinate bodies politic had elected, or otherwise would elect, to forgo those identified public interests in favor of guaranteeing, through local governmental instrumentalities, nondiscriminatory treatment of the gay citizens of their local governmental units. A state law which prevents local voters or their representatives, against their will, from granting special rights to gays, cannot be rationally justified by cost savings and associational liberties which the majority of citizens in those communities do not want. Clearly, the financial interests and associational liberties of the citizens of the state as a whole are not implicated if a municipality creates special legal protections for homosexuals applicable only within that jurisdiction and implements those protections solely via local governmental apparatuses. For this reason, the justifications proffered by Colorado for Colorado Amendment 2 insufficiently supported that provision, and implied that no reason other than a bare desire to harm homosexuals, rather than to advance the individual and collective interests of the majority of Colorado's citizens, motivated the state's voters to adopt Colorado Amendment 2.

In contradistinction, as evolved herein, the Cincinnati Charter Amendment constituted local legislation of purely local scope. As such, the City's voters had clear, actual, and direct individual and collective interests in that measure, and in the potential cost savings and other contingent benefits which could result from that local law. Beyond contradiction, passage of the Cincinnati Charter Amendment was not facially animated solely by an impermissible naked desire of a majority of the City's residents to injure an unpopular group of citizens, rather than to legally actualize their individual and collective interests and preferences. Clearly, the Cincinnati Charter Amendment implicated at least one issue of direct, actual, and practical importance to those who voted it into law, namely whether those voters would be legally compelled by municipal ordinances to expend their own public and private resources to guarantee and enforce nondiscrimination against gays in local commercial transactions and social intercourse.

Unquestionably, the Cincinnati Charter Amendment's removal of homosexuals from the ranks of persons protected by municipal antidiscrimination ordinances, and its preclusion of restoring that group to protected status, would eliminate and forestall the substantial public costs that accrue from the investigation and adjudication of sexual orientation discrimination complaints, which costs the City alone would otherwise bear because no coextensive protection exists under federal or state law. Moreover, the elimination of actionable special rights extended by city ordinances, and prevention of the reinstatement of such ordinances, would effectively advance the legitimate governmental interest of reducing the exposure of the City's residents to protracted and costly litigation by eliminating a municipally-created class of legal claims and charges, thus necessarily saving the City and its citizens, including property owners and employers, the costs of defending against such actions. Although the *Romer* Court never rejected associational liberty and the expression of community moral disapproval of homosexuality as rational bases supporting an enactment denying privileged treatment to homosexuals, it concluded that under the facts and circumstances of *Romer*, the state's argument in support of Colorado Amendment 2 was not credible. Because the valid interests of the Cincinnati electorate in conserving public and private financial resources is, standing alone, of sufficient weight to justify the City's Charter Amendment under a rational basis analysis, discussion of equally justifiable community interests, including the application of associational liberty and community moral disapproval of homosexuality, is unnecessary to sustain the Charter Amendment's viability. * * *

DAVID J. BARRON, THE PROMISE OF COOLEY'S CITY: TRACES OF LOCAL CONSTITUTIONALISM

147 U.Pa.L.Rev. 487, 490–491, 562–564, 568–571, 577–578, 586–591, 603, 612 (1999).

The unique public function that local governments perform in fashioning communal political life calls into question their current treatment as institutions that are no different from state environmental agencies on the one hand, or private homeowner associations on the other. Towns and cities are often the institutions that are most directly responsible for structuring political struggles over the most contentious of public questions, whether they concern the proper means of overcoming racial stratification, securing quality public education, or protecting disfavored groups from private discrimination. For that reason, local governments are often uniquely well positioned to give content to the substantive constitutional principles that should inform the consideration of such public questions—better positioned in some instances, that is, than either federal or state institutions.

It is necessary to inquire, therefore, whether the Federal Constitution may be understood to protect local governments from state attempts to prevent local governments from bringing their special institutional capacities to bear in these constitutional contexts. Such an understanding would not relieve local governments of their obligations to enforce the Constitution. It would instead free local governments from state law constraints that preclude them from exercising their discretion in fulfilling those constitutional obligations. * * *

[I]t is important to lay a bit of groundwork in order to dispose of a looming objection that will no doubt occur to many readers. To the extent that Supreme Court doctrine has addressed the federal constitutional status of local governments, it has often described them as mere creatures of the states that have created them. A federal constitutional claim for local governmental independence from state control would therefore appear to be in direct tension with settled doctrine that establishes state law to be the sole determinant of the permissible scope of local political power. * * * Although the cases are legion that assert that state law defines the scope of local governmental power, none has done so more forcefully, or more famously, than *Hunter v. City of Pittsburgh.* * * * *Hunter*'s seemingly unlimited holding is, however, more confined than it appears. The *Hunter* Court considered a particular type of federal constitutional claim to local governmental independence, one that invited the majority to speak more broadly in describing the subordinate legal status of towns and cities than the federal constitutional structure warranted. The federal constitutional claim before the Court arose from an annexation dispute. The plaintiffs asserted a vested contractual right in a municipal charter. They contended that a state annexation law violated the Contract Clause of the Federal Constitution because it purported to alter retrospectively the terms of the charter. The contention threatened to make the Contract Clause a provision that would transform the several states into the powerless overseers of constitutionally inviolable mini-republics, each free to enjoin any state attempt at supervision that could be termed an alteration of the foundational local charter.

Faced with such a dangerous claim, the Court went to great lengths to make clear that the Federal Constitution did not apply to a state's regulation of its municipal charters in the same manner that the Constitution applied to a state's regulation of its contracts with private parties. To that end, the Court seized upon the image of local governments as creatures of state law and emphasized that, implicit in the state's act of creation, was the reservation of the unlimited future power to alter or modify the creature. The *Hunter* Court employed sweeping descriptions of local governmental subordination to state control, therefore, to refute a particular kind of federal constitutional claim for local governmental independence—one that rested on a notion of vested state law property rights that would have dramatically limited a state's basic supervisory authority.

As a result, while *Hunter*'s positivist description of local governmental power was necessary to reject the Contract Clause claim in question, it was also necessarily incomplete. It ignored the degree to which local communities may provide the vital institutional context within which people live their public lives in a constitutional democracy. A local community is not simply a type of state administrative agency to be shaped at will to serve the need of the central state. It is, in a fundamental sense, the locus for those human interactions that comprise what we conceive to be democratic life in a constitutional system committed to self-government. So understood, local governments are necessarily something more than the mere creatures of state law, a point that the *Hunter* Court did not acknowledge.

If *Hunter* ignored a more social conception of local government, the modern Court clearly embraced it in several Warren Court-era decisions. For as much as *Hunter*'s sweeping contentions retain a hold on the legal imagination, the limits of that extreme, positivist conception of localism are evident in a set of cases in which the Court has expressly declined to give broad sanction to the state creature metaphor. * * * [These] cases demonstrate the Court's unwillingness to insulate from judicial review state laws respecting local affairs when such laws trench on the federal constitutional rights of local residents. * * * These cases do not * * * support the further proposition that local governments are entitled to a degree of constitutional protection from an exercise of state power that would not interfere with a judicially enforceable individual constitutional right. * * * Yet it is precisely this latter class of constitutional claims— claims by local governments against their states for the authority to provide extra-judicial constitutional protection to their residents—for which [more recent cases such as *Washington v. Seattle School District No. 1* and *Romer v. Evans* provide support.] * * *

[I]n *Milliken v. Bradley*, the Supreme Court invoked localist principles to reverse a federal district court decree that had been designed to remedy racially segregative policies in the Detroit school system. The decree required interdistrict busing and compelled the participation of numerous surrounding suburbs. The Court explained that, in providing interdistrict relief for an intradistrict violation, the district court erred in assuming that "school district lines are no more than arbitrary lines on a map drawn for political convenience." In fact, the Court explained, "no single tradition in public education is more deeply rooted than local control over the operation of schools. . . ."

Because Michigan provided "for a large measure of local control," the Court concluded that the district court's remedy would "alter the structure of public education in Michigan." Critical questions regarding financing, school assignment, the political authority of local boards, and the authority to impose taxes, all of which the state had left to its local school districts, would suddenly be removed from local control.

> [T]he District Court will become first, a de facto "legislative authority" to resolve these complex questions, and then the "school superintendent" for the entire area. This is a task which few, if any, judges are qualified to perform and one which would deprive the people of control of schools through their elected representatives.

The Court therefore held that an interdistrict school desegregation remedy could be ordered only if there had been a "constitutional violation within one district that produces a significant segregative effect in another district."

There would be reason to question whether *Milliken*'s professed respect for local control contained a public constitutional dimension if it served merely to constrict the power of federal courts to remedy constitutional wrongs. If *Milliken* is read in conjunction with the Court's subsequent decision in *Washington v. Seattle School District No. 1*, however, the localist notes that *Milliken* sounded may be read to have a constitutionally generative force. For if the Court's recognition of localism in *Milliken* served to sanction suburban segregation, then the Court's recognition of localism in *Seattle School District* served to constrain a state's attempt to preclude urban efforts to foster integration. * * *

In *Seattle School District*, several State of Washington school districts challenged Initiative 350, a statewide measure that precluded local school districts from effecting race-based school assignment plans intended to achieve racial balance. The school districts claimed that the state law violated the Equal Protection Clause, even though they acknowledged that the plans they wished to adopt were designed to remedy de facto, as opposed to de jure, segregation and thus could not have been ordered by a federal court. The Court upheld the school districts' challenge[.] * * *

Seattle School District may be understood to rest on a defense of local constitutionalism. The case suggests that, as a matter of federal constitutional structure, states may not preclude their local political institutions from promoting a norm of constitutional equality that lies beyond direct judicial enforcement. Such a reading takes *Milliken's* respect for localism seriously. It reads that respect to rest on the premise that broad, local remedial discretion is a precondition for federal judicial restraint in the area of school desegregation. * * * *Seattle School District* noted that *Milliken* had constricted federal court remedial power out of respect for a long-standing tradition of local governmental control over public education. The logic of *Milliken,* the Court explained, strongly supported the school boards' claims. "If local school boards operating under a similar statutory structure are considered separate entities for purposes of constitutional adjudication when they make segregative assignment decisions, it is difficult to see why a different analysis should apply when a local board's desegregative policy is at issue." School boards, the Court implied, must have at least as much authority to fulfill *Brown's* mandate as they did to resist it. By interpreting *Milliken* in this manner, the Court may be read to suggest that there is a distinction of constitutional significance between states and their local governments.
* * *

The Supreme Court's recent decision in *Romer v. Evans* reveals that the connection between localism and an affirmative constitutionalism is not a relic of a bygone era in constitutional law. The decision concerned an equal protection challenge to Amendment 2, a Colorado constitutional referendum that prevented the State's municipalities (and the state legislature) from enacting measures designed to protect gays and lesbians from private discrimination. *Romer* may be read to suggest * * * that there is a deep connection between localism and positive constitutional enforcement. Federal courts are necessarily poorly positioned to assess the degree of affirmative "protection" that citizens are owed from private power. Federal courts could directly enforce a broad constitutional norm that prohibited private discrimination only by intruding deeply into the practices and functions of local self-government, and thereby calling their own legitimacy into substantial doubt. Such a declaration would obliterate the line between the public and private and threaten to make any private action subject to constitutional challenge. * * *

Given this background, Colorado's blanket action to bar all of its local political institutions from determining that a certain class of persons needed statutory protection appeared to upset the careful structure of the federal constitutional framework. Such state action, as Justice Blackmun had noted in *Crawford v. Board of Education,* " 'curtail[s] the operation of those political processes ordinarily to be relied upon to protect minorities.' " As the *Romer* Court explained, "[t]he change Amendment 2 works in the legal status of gays and lesbians in the private sphere is far reaching, both on its own terms and when considered in light of the structure and operation of modern antidiscrimination laws." The State had chosen to reserve to itself the power to determine the statutory protection that should be afforded homosexuals. "This is so no matter how local or discrete the harm, no matter how public and widespread the injury." Precisely because the State had purported to preclude all localities from providing protection against private discrimination against gays and lesbians, there was "nothing special in the protections Amendment 2 withholds."

The breadth of the state's prohibition ensured that it would preclude the adoption of those "protections taken for granted by most people either because they already have them or do not need them; these are protections against exclusion from an almost limitless number of transactions and endeavors that constitute ordinary civic life in a free society." It ensured, in other words, that private discrimination would persist no matter how "public" the resulting injuries. Such a broad-based state prohibition against the excesses of local action to provide protection for a group of residents is itself a "denial of equal protection of the laws in the most literal sense." * * *

[T]he defense of local governmental independence offered here differs markedly from the now-ascendant formalist defense of state independence from federal control. The defense offered here would not prohibit states from "commandeering" their local governments, even though the modern defense of federalism holds that Congress may not conscript a state. Nor would a defense of local constitutionalism preclude states, as a general matter, from attempting to coerce their political subdivisions into complying with a statewide rule. This is true even though the principles of modern federalism may justify judicially enforceable constraints upon the federal government's exercise of coercive power over the states. A defense of local constitutionalism also does not seek to define any category of traditionally local governmental functions—such as police protection—that, as the Supreme Court once suggested in its federalist doctrine, are immune from centralized control.

The local constitutionalist defense offered here is simply not predicated on a formalist notion that there is some residual core of local governmental sovereignty, written silently into the Federal Constitution, that must be protected from central intrusion for its own sake. This defense proceeds instead from a structural conclusion that substantive constitutional rights sometimes presuppose the existence of a local decision-making process capable of ensuring the protection of those rights. That conclusion in turn supports the determination that it is appropriate for courts to protect the local decision-making process from state interference incident to the enforcement of the underlying substantive constitutional right even though that right would not be susceptible to more direct judicial protection. The defense proceeds, in other words, from a conception of individual constitutional rights as partially dependent upon local political action. * * *

Too much of our daily experience with self-government occurs at the local level for us to dismiss localism as an embarrassing feature of constitutional democracy. Local governments are too central to the lives of too many people to serve as passive administrative agents of state majorities without an independent interest in enforcing constitutional norms. Local governments are also too intimately involved in resolving the central public questions of our time to be protected arenas for the aggregation of private preferences, free from constitutional obligations to resist central or private power.

True, the constitutional text does not mention the special role that local governments play in giving life to constitutional principles. As Thomas Cooley, [the Michigan State Supreme Court Justice and constitutional treatise writer] concluded more than a century ago, however, "[s]ome things are too plain to be written." Local governments, the political structures that govern our lives on a daily basis, may be the means through which we discover our constitutional rights. That, at least, is the promise of Cooley's City. It is a promise that constitutional doctrine would do well to fulfill. * * *

2. DILLON'S RULE

This subsection continues our examination of an issue of fundamental importance in local government law: the source of city power. Given the materials on the public/private distinction presented in Chapter One, and the materials on the dominance of the state creature idea in federal constitutional law presented in Subsection One of this chapter, cities might appear to have two possible sources of power: authorization for their actions could come from their own citizens or it could come from the state government. To appreciate the significance of the difference between these alternative sources of power, consider how other entities in our society, such as corporations, unions, or churches, obtain authorization for their actions. Is their power limited to express or implied grants of authority by the states or do they have general authority, derived from their members, to do what they want to do unless prohibited by state law? What would be the impact on the power and freedom of these entities if they could only take actions authorized by state government? What would be the impact on your own power and freedom if you were able to engage in only those activities authorized by state law?

The reason for asking these questions will become apparent once you turn to the first reading in this subsection, an excerpt from an influential treatise on local government law written by John Dillon and published in 1872. The excerpt contains what is known in local government law as "Dillon's Rule," a rule that specifies the extent to which local government power is restricted to actions authorized by enabling legislation enacted by the state legislature. This subsection is devoted to an examination of the emphasis on enabling legislation found in Dillon's Rule.

Dillon's Rule is a very important aspect of local government law; it has been cited in hundreds and hundreds of cases.[2] It is one manifestation of the dominant view that cities (the lower level of government) are mere delegates of the state (the higher level of government). On this view, local governments do not possess reserved powers in the way that states or nations do; they are dependent on state law delegations for any powers that they may exercise. It is important to emphasize, however, that Dillon's Rule does not merely require that cities be able to trace their power to a state legislative delegation. The rule also instructs judges to construe narrowly those state laws that might be interpreted as delegating power to cities. In this way, Dillon's Rule permits cities to act only when they can identify a relatively clear state law delegation of power.

Not all local governments are subject to Dillon's Rule. Indeed, many states have expressly rejected it for their cities. But even in those states that have done so, Dillon's Rule is often still relevant. For example, a state that does not apply Dillon's Rule to its cities may apply the rule to

---

[2] For a general discussion of the principles found in Dillon's Rule, see John Martinez, Local Government Law, Chapter 3 (2nd ed. 2012–13); Jesse Richardson, Dillon's Rule is From Mars, Home Rule is From Venus: Local Government Autonomy and the Rules of Statutory Construction, 41 Publius J. Federalism 4, 662–85 (2011); Kenneth A. Stahl, The Suburb as a Legal Concept: The Problem of Organization and the Fate of Municipalities in American Law, 29 Cardozo L. Rev. 1193 (2008); Louis V. Csoka, The Dream of Greater Municipal Autonomy: Should the Legislature or the Courts Modify Dillon's Rule, a Common Law Restraint on Municipal Autonomy, 29 N. C. Cent. L. J. 194 (2007); Nestor M. Davidson, Cooperative Localism: Federal-Local Collaboration in an Era of State Sovereignty, 93 Va. L. Rev. 959 (2007); Gordon Clark, Judges and the Cities: Interpreting Local Autonomy (1985). See also George W. Liebman, The New American Local Government, 34 Urb. Law. 93 (2002); Clayton Gillette, In Partial Praise of Dillon's Rule, or, Can Public Choice Theory Justify Local Government Law, 67 Chi.-Kent L. Rev. 959 (1991); Richard Briffault, Home Rule, Majority Rule, and Dillon's Rule, 67 Chi.-Kent L. Rev. 1011 (1991); Gary Schwartz, Reviewing and Revising Dillon's Rule, 67 Chi.-Kent L. Rev. 1025 (1991); Comment: Redefining The Scope of Local Regulatory Power, State v. Hutchinson, 1981 Utah L. Rev. 617; Harold Bruff, Judicial Review in Local Government Law: A Reappraisal, 60 Minn. L. Rev. 669 (1976); Comment: The Dillon Rule: A Limit on Local Government Powers, 41 Mo. L. Rev. 546 (1976). For more specific discussions of how Dillon's Rule operates in particular contexts, see, e.g., Elijah Swiney, John Forrest Dillon Goes to School, 79 Tenn. L. Rev. 103 (2011); Michael A. Woods, The Propriety of Local Government Protections of Gays and Lesbians from Discriminatory Employment Practices, 52 Emory L.J. 515 (2003); David Owens, Local Government Authority to Implement Smart Growth Programs: Dillon's Rule, Legislative Reform, and the Current State of Affairs in North Carolina, 35 Wake Forest L. Rev. 671 (2000); Manuela Albequerque, California and Dillon: The Times They Are A-Changing, 25 Hastings Const. L. Rev. 187 (1998).

counties or school districts and even to some kinds of municipalities. Because of its continuing importance, some historical background about the rule, taken from Gerald Frug's City Making, follows the excerpt from Dillon's treatise reproduced below.[3] Three cases then raise questions about the rule. The first case, Olesen v. Town (City) of Hurley, shows just how limiting Dillon's Rule can be: the majority construes it to prevent a city from deciding to expand its food service at a city-owned bar. The second case, Arlington County v. White, involves a county's attempt to extend employee health benefits to the domestic partners of its employees. A strict application of Dillon's Rule results in the invalidation of the county's health care plan. The final case, State v. Hutchinson, contains a full-scale debate about the desirability of Dillon's Rule.

In reading these materials, consider the relevance of the arguments about centralization and decentralization and about the public/private distinction discussed above in Chapter One. What is the impact of Dillon's Rule on the possibility of decentralization of power in America? How are the courts' (and your own) views of the wisdom of Dillon's Rule affected by different attitudes toward the exercise of decentralized power by public and private entities? Consider as well whether the substance of the local policy at issue is really driving the courts' analysis. Would the *White* Court, which ruled against the local power to provide benefits to same-sex partners, be equally hostile to local power if confronted with the same issue presented in *Olesen*, which concerned whether a city bar could also be a restaurant?

JOHN DILLON, MUNICIPAL CORPORATIONS
Vol. 1, pp. 448–455 (5th ed. 1911).

§ 237(89). **Extent of Power; Limitations; Canons of Construction.**—It is a general and undisputed proposition of law that *a municipal corporation possesses and can exercise the following powers, and no others:* First, those granted in *express words;* second, those *necessarily or fairly implied* in or *incident* to the powers expressly granted; third, those *essential* to the accomplishment of the declared objects and purposes of the corporation,—not simply convenient, but indispensable. Any fair, reasonable, substantial doubt concerning the existence of power is resolved by the courts against the corporation, and the power is denied. Of every municipal corporation the charter or statute by which it is created is its organic act. Neither the corporation nor its

[handwritten note in right margin: expressio unius]

---

[3] For alternative interpretations of this history, see, e.g., Kenneth A. Stahl, The Suburb as a Legal Concept: The Problem of Organization and the Fate of Municipalities in American Law, 29 Cardozo L. Rev. 1193 (2008); David Barron, The Promise of Cooley's City: Traces of Local Constitutionalism, 147 U. Pa. L. Rev. 487, 515–523 (1999); Joan Williams, The Constitutional Vulnerability of American Local Government: The Politics of City Status in American Law, 1986 Wis. L. Rev. 83, 90–100. See also Hendrik Hartog, Public Property and Private Power: The Corporation of the City of New York in American Law 1730–1870, 220–24, 262–63 (1983).

officers can do any act, or make any contract, or incur any liability, not authorized thereby, or by some legislative act applicable thereto. All acts beyond the scope of the powers granted are void. Much less can any power be exercised, or any act done, which is forbidden by charter or statute. *These principles are of transcendent importance, and lie at the foundation of the law of municipal corporations.* Their reasonableness, their necessity, and their salutary character have been often vindicated, but never more forcibly than by the learned Chief Justice Shaw, who, speaking of municipal and public corporations, says: *"They can exercise no powers* but those which are conferred upon them by the act by which they are constituted, or such as are necessary to the exercise of their corporate powers, the performance of their corporate duties, and the accomplishment of the purposes of their association. This principle is derived from the nature of corporations, the mode in which they are organized, and in which their affairs must be conducted."

§ 238(90). **Same Subject.**—"In aggregate corporations, as a general rule," continues Chief Justice Shaw, "the act and will of a majority is deemed in law the act and will of the whole,—as the act of the corporate body. The consequence is that a minority must be bound not only without, but against, their consent. Such an obligation may extend to every onerous duty,—to pay money to an unlimited amount, to perform services, to surrender lands, and the like. It is obvious, therefore, that if this liability were to extend to unlimited and indefinite objects, the citizen, by being a member of a corporation, might be deprived of his most valuable personal rights and liberties. The security against this danger is in a steady adherence to the principle stated, viz., *that corporations can only exercise their powers over their respective members, for the accomplishment of limited and defined objects.* And if this principle is important, as a general rule of social right and municipal law, it is of the highest importance in these States, where corporations have been extended and multiplied so as to embrace almost every object of human concern." The language of another learned judge on this subject is well chosen, and fittingly supplements that which we have quoted in the preceding section. "In this country," says Church, J., "all corporations, whether public or private, derive their powers from legislative grant, and can do no act for which authority is not expressly given, or may not be reasonably inferred. But if we were to say that they can do nothing for which a warrant could not be found in the language of their charters, we should deny them, in some cases, the power of self-preservation, as well as many of the means necessary to effect the essential objects of their incorporation. And therefore it has long been an established principle in the law of corporations, that they *may exercise all the powers within the fair intent and purpose of their creation which are reasonably proper to give effect to powers expressly granted.* In doing this, they must [unless restricted in this respect] have a choice of means adapted to ends, and are not to be confined to any one mode of operation."

§ 239(91). **Same Subject; Principles of Construction.**—The *extent of the powers of municipalities,* whether express, implied, or indispensable, is one of construction. And here the fundamental and universal rule, which is as reasonable as it is necessary, is, that while the construction is to be just, seeking first of all for the legislative intent in order to give it fair effect, yet any ambiguity or fair, reasonable, substantial doubt as to the extent of the power is to be determined in favor of the State or general public, and against the State's grantee. The rule of strict construction of corporate powers is not so directly applicable to the ordinary clauses in the charter or incorporating acts of municipalities as it is to the charters of private corporations; but it is equally applicable to grants of powers to municipal and public bodies which are out of the usual range, or which grant franchises, or rights of that nature, or which may result in public burdens, or which, in their exercise, touch the right to liberty or property, or, as it may be compendiously expressed, any common-law right of the citizen or inhabitant. * * * The rule of strict construction does not apply to the *mode adopted* by the municipality *to carry into effect powers expressly or plainly granted,* where the mode is not limited or prescribed by the legislature, and is left to the discretion of the municipal authorities. In such a case the usual test of the validity of the act of a municipal body is, Whether it is reasonable? and there is no presumption against the municipal action in such cases.

The general principles of law, stated in this and in the preceding sections, are indisputably settled, but difficulty is often experienced in their application, on account of the complex character of municipal duties, and the various, miscellaneous, and frequently indefinite purposes or objects which municipalities are authorized to execute or carry into operation.

GERALD FRUG, CITY MAKING: BUILDING COMMUNITIES WITHOUT BUILDING WALLS
Pp. 45–50 (1999).

The legal doctrine that cities were subject to state authority was enthusiastically endorsed by John Dillon, who in 1872 wrote the first and most important American treatise on municipal corporations. Dillon did not seek to disguise the values he thought important in framing the law for municipal corporations. In speeches, law review articles, and books, Dillon eloquently defended the need to protect private property from attack and indicated his reservations about the kind of democracy then practiced in the cities. It would be a mistake, however, to read Dillon's defense of strict state control of cities as simply a crude effort to advance the interests of the rich or of private corporations at the expense of the poor inhabitants of cities. Instead, it is more plausible to interpret Dillon as a forerunner of the Progressive tradition: he sought to protect private property not only against abuse by democracy but also against abuse by private economic power. To do so, he advocated an objective, rational government, staffed by the nation's elite—a government strong enough to curb the excesses of corporate power and at the same time help those who deserved help. It is important to understand how Dillon could consider state control of cities as a major ingredient in accomplishing these objectives.

According to Dillon, a critical impediment to the development of a government dedicated to the public good was the intermingling of the public and the private sectors. Strict enforcement of a public/private distinction was essential both to protect government from the threat of domination by private interests and to protect the activities of the private economy from being unfairly influenced by government intervention. Moreover, to ensure its fully "public" nature, government had to be organized so that it could attract to power those in the community best able to govern. Class legislation in favor of either the rich or the poor had to be avoided—neither a government of private greed nor one of mass ignorance could be tolerated. Instead, it was the role of the best people to assume responsibility by recognizing and fulfilling their communal obligations: "It is a duty of perpetual obligation on the part of the strong to take care of the weak, of the rich to take care of the poor." This vision pervades Dillon's work on municipal corporations. From his perspective, cities presented problems that seemed almost "inherent" in their nature. By merging the public and private spheres, cities had extravagantly invested in private businesses, performing functions "better left to private enterprise." As both a state and federal judge, Dillon saw firsthand the problems engendered by municipal financing of railroads. He therefore advocated constitutional limitations and restriction of the franchise to taxpayers to prevent such an expenditure of money.

At the same time, Dillon believed that all of the functions properly undertaken by cities should be considered "public." He therefore criticized the courts for contributing to the division of city activities into public and private spheres. For half a century, courts had distinguished the city's governmental functions, which were subject to absolute state power, from its proprietary functions, which received the constitutional protection afforded to rights of private property. While conceding that such a distinction was "highly important" in municipal corporation law, Dillon found a city's retention of any private identity "difficult exactly to comprehend." Since a city was by definition created by the state, "which breathed into it the breath of life," there seemed nothing private about them at all. Most troubling of all, according to Dillon, cities were not managed by those "*best fitted* by their intelligence, business experience, capacity and moral character." Their management was "too often both *unwise* and *extravagant.*" A major change in city government was therefore needed to achieve a fully public city government dedicated to the common good.

But how could this be achieved? To Dillon, the answer seemed to lie in state control of cities and in judicial supervision of that control. State control, though political, was purely public, and the "best fitted" could more likely be attracted to its government. Moreover, enforcement of the rule of law could play a role, since law was "the beneficence of civil society acting by rule, in its nature * * * opposed to all that [was] fitful, capricious, unjust, partial or destructive." The state and the law working together could thus curb municipal abuse by rigorously enforcing the public/private distinction. In his treatise, Dillon could not have more broadly phrased the extent of state power over city functions. State power "is supreme and transcendent: it may erect, change, divide, and even abolish, at pleasure, as it deems the public good to require." In addition to legislative control, he argued for a major role for the courts:

> The courts, too, have duties, the most important of which is to require these corporations, in all cases, to show a plain and clear grant for the authority they assume to exercise; to *lean against constructive powers,* and, with firm hands, to hold them and their officers within chartered limits.

Once all these steps were taken, Dillon argued, the cities' governance could properly be left to democratic control.

These days, it is hard fully to comprehend Dillon's confidence in noblesse oblige and in the expectation that state and judicial control would help ensure the attainment by cities of an unselfish public good. The late-nineteenth-century legislature now seems as unwise and extravagant as the late-nineteenth-century city, and the contemporary definition of law is somewhat more restrained than Dillon's. The important point, however, is that the legal doctrines emphasized by Dillon—state control of cities, restriction of cities to "public" functions, and strict construction of city powers—are not necessarily tied to his vision of society. While for Dillon the law of cities and the goals of public policy formed a coherent whole, he stated the law so broadly and categorically that it could simply be extracted from its context and applied generally. Dillon's vision of society may be gone forever, but his statement of the law of municipal corporations, stripped of its ideological underpinnings, largely remains intact today. For example, in the current edition of his treatise, Professor Antieau's articulation of the subservience of cities to state power (absent specific state constitutional protection for cities) is no less emphatic than Dillon's in 1872. His emphasis upon the strict construction required of grants of power is simply a paraphrase of the so-called Dillon's Rule. He too criticizes the public/private distinction within municipal corporation law as "difficult to draw," although, like Dillon, he has no difficulty with the distinction between public and private corporations themselves. Only his statement of the law of what are now called public utilities seems more accepting than Dillon's. * * *

Dillon's thesis did not go unchallenged at the time. The major challenge was launched by Judge Thomas M. Cooley, only three years after publishing his celebrated *Treatise on Constitutional Limitations*. In a concurring opinion in *People ex rel. Le Roy v. Hurlbut,* Cooley denied the existence of absolute state supremacy over cities. Relying on American colonial history and on the importance of political liberty in the definition of freedom, he argued that local government was a matter of "absolute right," a right protected by an implied restriction on the powers of the legislature under the state constitution.[36] Amasa Eaton advanced the same thesis in a series of articles entitled "The Right to Local Self-Government." Eaton canvassed English and American history to demonstrate that this "right to local self-government" existed prior to state incorporations and could not be subjected to state restriction.

The most extensive rebuttal to Dillon was published in 1911 by Eugene McQuillin in his multivolume treatise, *The Law of Municipal Corporations*. In an exhaustive survey, McQuillin traced the historical development of municipal corporations and found the essential theme to be a right to local self-government. He rejected the suggestion that cities were created by the state, arguing that "[s]uch [a] position ignores well-established, historical facts easily ascertainable." McQuillin strongly criticized courts that failed to uphold the right of local self-government:

> The judicial decisions denying the right of local self-government without express constitutional guaranty, reject the rule of construction that all grants of power are to be interpreted in the light of the maxims of Magna Carta, or rather the development of English rights and governmental powers prior to that time; that is, the common law transmuted into our constitutions and laws. They ignore in toto the fact that local self-government does not owe its origin to constitutions and laws. * * * They disregard the fact that it is a part of the liberty of a community, an expression of community freedom, the heart of our political institutions. They refuse to concede, therefore, that it is a right in any just sense beyond unlimited state control, but rather it is nothing more than a privilege, to be refused or granted in such

---

[36] People ex rel. LeRoy v. Hurlbut, 24 Mich. 44, 93 (1871) (Cooley, J., concurring).

measure as the legislative agents of the people for the time being determine.

McQuillin sought to buttress his argument by inventing a new rationale for the public/private distinction within municipal corporation law, the distinction that had so confused other writers. There was a general consensus, McQuillin noted, that absolute state power could only be exerted over a city's "public functions." Those functions, he argued, were those that in fact had been given the city by the state. Since the justification for state supremacy depends on the idea of state creation, state control must be limited to those things so created. Powers not derived from legislative action must therefore be "private" and subject to the same constitutional protection as other private rights. The power of the locality that historically was exercised prior to a state charter—the right to local self-government—is, then, a "private" right and could not be subject to state supremacy.

History has not been kind to the Cooley-Eaton-McQuillin thesis. In a later edition of his treatise, Dillon specifically denied the theory's usefulness and noted its lack of judicial acceptance. In a similar vein, Howard Lee McBain, a noted municipal law authority of the time, argued that most courts had properly rejected the right of self-government. In discounting the thesis, McBain seized upon the weak links in the way the proponents framed the right. He denounced the idea of an "implied limitation" on legislative power as dangerous and unworkable. He argued that even if the right to local self-government were a common law right, it would not therefore be beyond the legislative power to change the common law. He also denied that there was in fact an historical right to self-government, at least if interpreted as the right to democratic, popular control of local officials. McBain's arguments were cleverly aimed at the phrasing, and not the substance, of the Cooley-Eaton-McQuillin thesis. The proponents of the thesis could have responded that the power of public corporations was a "liberty" interest expressly protected by the Due Process Clause in the same way that the "property" interests of private corporations were protected. They could also have explained that this liberty interest was not the democratic control of corporations as understood in the nineteenth century but the kind of local autonomy all corporations had exercised before the ideas of property and sovereignty were separated in the late eighteenth and the nineteenth centuries. They did not make these arguments. But it would not have mattered if they had. By the time of McBain's attack, courts were not willing to eliminate the distinction between public and private corporations—even Cooley, Eaton and McQuillin did not challenge that distinction. The idea that state power over cities was different from state power over corporations had become an automatically accepted part of legal thought.

In 1923, William Munro, in his classic work, *The Government of American Cities,* stated that Dillon's position on state control of cities was "so well recognized that it is not nowadays open to question." McQuillin's thesis, on the other hand, has been substantially revised even in his own treatise by its current editor:

> [U]nless granted by the state constitution, the general rule is that a municipal corporation has no inherent right of self-government that is independent of legislative control. * * * Distinction should be made between the right of local self-government as inherent in the people, and the right as inherent in a municipal corporation; while as to the people, the right has quite commonly been assumed to exist, but as to the municipal corporation the right must be derived, either from the people through the constitution or from the legislature.

No other serious academic challenge to the Dillon thesis has ever been made. * * *

OLESEN V. TOWN (CITY) OF HURLEY

Supreme Court of South Dakota, 2004.
2004 S.D. 136, 691 N.W.2d 324.

EKRICH, CIRCUIT JUDGE.

* * * [The] Olesens operated Little Philly's Café in Hurley, South Dakota from the mid-1980s until 1998. From 1995 until this lawsuit commenced in 1998, the City sold food within the confines of the Hurley Municipal Bar. Little Philly's and the bar were the only two competing food service establishments in Hurley. City's restaurant served alcohol; whereas Olesens' did not.* * * The parties co-existed peacefully together until 1995 when City expanded its food preparation and service facilities. The expansion allowed City to offer full course meals. City's menu included lunch and supper—offered six days a week—featuring steaks, salads, potatoes, a variety of hot sandwiches, various appetizers, and other hot food. The expansion of City's menu was a substantial departure from its past offerings of potato chips, chislic, and snack food. * * *

* * * Municipalities "possess only those powers conferred upon them by the Legislature . . . [but] a grant of authority includes those incidental or implied powers that are necessary to enable a municipality to perform the function authorized." *City of Rapid City v. Rensch,* 77 S.D. 242, 90 N.W.2d 380, 383 (S.D. 1958). This is a fundamental rule of statutory construction known as "Dillon's Rule." It is a rule of strict construction. * * * City's express authority to operate a bar is found in SDCL 9–29–6. That statute provides: "Every municipality shall have powers to engage in retailing alcoholic beverages as provided in Title 35." SDCL 9–29–6. * * * Here, City, under the guise of a municipal bar, offered full-course lunch

and supper meals six days a week. City's expanded restaurant operation was only made possible because of its decision to upgrade, renovate, and expand commercial kitchen facilities. Additionally, in 1998 when this lawsuit was commenced, City's revenue from food was nearly $67,000. City's revenue from on-sale beer was $46,742. City's revenue from on-sale liquor was $7,923. These figures do not suggest that City's restaurant business was merely incidental to its bar business. City has an on-sale liquor license granted to it by express statutory authority. This license clearly gives City the power to sell alcohol upon the premises. However, City's express power to sell alcohol by the glass does not, in these circumstances, imply a necessary power to operate a restaurant. * * *

GILBERTSON, J. (dissenting).

* * * The record indicates City began serving a limited food menu in 1979 in conjunction with its bar operation. City's municipal bar food service was not advertised to the general public, or to patrons inside the bar. The menu was made available to bar patrons only while on site. Menu items such as hamburgers, french fries, chislic, and other grill items were added to the bar menu over time. A modern grill was installed in 1995 as part of a capital project designed to bring the bar into compliance with health and safety codes. When soup was added to the menu, Olesens complained to City and soup service was immediately discontinued. No complaint about the grill service was ever offered by Olesens prior to the commencement of their law suit. A full service, sit down restaurant menu was never offered by City. City offered testimony at trial that bar revenues from on-sale beer and liquor and off-sale beer and liquor were insufficient in and of themselves to keep the bar in operation. The bar was not financially viable without the food service revenue. Additionally, City noted that the consumption of food with alcohol slows the absorption rate of alcohol into the blood stream as support for its efforts to provide bar patrons with limited food service while consuming alcohol.

The effect of this Court's decision is devastating to the numerous small towns in this state that have only a municipal bar as a source of food as well as liquor. Prior to 1998, the town of Hurley had two eating establishments, the one owned by Olesens and the other run by the City. Olesens shut down in 1998 and this decision effectively shuts down the City's food service. In light of this decision, what other small town will dare to offer food to the public at its municipal liquor establishment and open up its public treasury in the process? I doubt the legislature intended such a result when it contemplated the authority it would grant to municipalities.[1] * * * The Court's assertion that City's express power to sell alcohol by the glass does not imply a *necessary power* to sell food by

---

[1]   As to larger municipalities, what of the fate of municipal swimming pools, baseball and soccer complexes, and municipal golf courses that sell food?

Dissent's Core Argument [handwritten margin note]

the plateful is not a correct statement of the law or the facts of this case. City's express power to sell alcohol by the glass confers upon it the implied and incidental powers to do what is necessary to operate the municipal bar within reasonable limits, and those explicitly imposed by the legislature and the state constitution. City's limited food service operation was an exercise of incidental powers that was not in conflict with any state statute or the state Constitution itself. As such, the food service operation was not an ultra vires act.[2]

ARLINGTON COUNTY V. WHITE

Supreme Court of Virginia, 2000.
259 Va. 708, 528 S.E.2d 706.

KOONTZ, JUSTICE. * * *

On March 12, 1998, Andrew White, Diana White, and Wendell Brown, residents and taxpayers of Arlington County (the Taxpayers), filed a bill of complaint in the trial court against Arlington County and its County Board (collectively, the County). The Taxpayers sought a declaration that the County lacked the authority to extend coverage to the newly defined category of domestic partners under its self-funded health insurance benefits plan. * * * The record shows that in an Employee Relations Benefits Newsletter, issued in May 1997, the County * * * listed eight criteria in defining an "adult dependent" as "[t]he domestic partner . . . who" * * * has resided with the employee for a 1 year period; * * * shares with the employee the common necessities of life and basic living expenses; * * * is financially interdependent with the employee; * * * is involved with the employee in a mutually exclusive relationship of support and commitment; * * * is not related by blood to the employee; * * * is not married to anyone; * * * was mentally competent at time of consent to relationship; * * * is 18 years of age or older. A stipulation entered into by the parties states that "[a] 'domestic partner' eligible for coverage as an adult dependent of a County employee under the County's health benefits plan may be either a same-sex or opposite-sex domestic partner of a County employee" * * *.

domestic partner extended to under self-funded insurance benefits plan [handwritten margin note]

Citing Code §§ 15.2–1517(A) and 51.1–801, the County correctly points out that "[t]he General Assembly specifically authorizes a local government to provide self-funded health benefit programs for its employees and their dependents." The County notes that neither statute defines the term "dependent" or refers to other statutory provisions that define the term for different purposes. Continuing, the County further notes that no express statutory provision specifies which employee

---

[2] Mrs. Olesen acknowledged the Hurley Bar should be permitted to serve "bar food," a term she defined to mean "munchies and chislic and things." Are significant issues such as * * * legislative grants of authority to municipal corporations to be hinged on whether a frozen pizza constitutes a "munchie?"

dependents are eligible to participate in a locality's self-funded health benefits plan or by what method their eligibility is to be determined. Under these circumstances, the County correctly maintains, "[t]he power to determine who is an employee's dependent . . . is fairly and necessarily implied." Furthermore, the County asserts, "the locality must make [the] determination itself"; indeed, it "could not carry out its authority without exercising its discretion." In the process, the County submits, the term "dependent" should be given its plain and ordinary meaning as one "[r]elying on . . . the aid of another for support." The American Heritage Dictionary 501 (2nd College Ed.1985).

In the end, the County opines, the "appropriate inquiry is whether [its] decision to include domestic partners as dependents in its plan is a reasonable method of implementing its authority." This inquiry, the County concludes, must be answered in the affirmative.

> Under Dillon's Rule, [local governing bodies] have only those powers which are expressly granted by the state legislature, those powers fairly or necessarily implied from expressly granted powers, and those powers which are essential and indispensable. Where the state legislature grants a local government the power to do something but does not specifically direct the method of implementing that power, the choice made by the local government as to how to implement the conferred power will be upheld as long as the method selected is reasonable. Any doubt in the reasonableness of the method selected is resolved in favor of the locality.

City of Virginia Beach v. Hay, 258 Va. 217, 221, 518 S.E.2d 314, 316 (1999).

In light of these principles, we must decide whether the County's inclusion of domestic partners as defined by the County is a reasonable implementation of the County's authority to define an employee's dependent for purposes of coverage in the County's self-funded health benefits plan. For the reasons that follow and giving the County the benefit of any doubt, we conclude that the County's definition of dependent is not reasonable and, therefore, violates the Dillon Rule.

In 1997, responding to an inquiry from a member of the General Assembly, the Attorney General * * * concluded that "[i]n the absence of any statutory authority indicating an intent to permit a local governing body to extend health insurance coverage provided employees to persons other than the spouse, children or dependents of the employee . . . a county lacks the power to provide such coverage." In reaching this conclusion, the Attorney General expressly noted that the requirement that the employee be "financially interdependent" with the "domestic partner" was contrary to the established definition of a "dependent" as one who "must receive from the taxpayer over half of his or her support for the calendar year."

The County's benefit plan extends coverage to a County employee and one other adult, who may be the employee's spouse, another adult who is properly claimed as a dependent on the employee's federal tax return, or the employee's "domestic partner." The County's definition of "domestic partner" includes eight criteria. Only two of these criteria address financial dependency—sharing expenses and being "financially interdependent." Neither of these criteria is synonymous with "financially dependent." The inclusion of a spouse as a dependent for the purpose of coverage under the County's benefit plan does not eliminate the significance of this distinction. It is a matter of common knowledge and experience that a spouse may or may not be financially dependent on the employee-spouse. However, including a spouse as a dependent for coverage such as this is of such long standing that, even in the absence of financial dependence, there can be no dispute that the General Assembly contemplated that a spouse would be included for coverage under local benefit plans.

It is, nevertheless, equally clear that the General Assembly in leaving the definition of dependent to the local governing bodies which adopt self-funded health insurance benefit plans did not contemplate adoption of a definition that does not require some aspect of financial dependence rather than mere financial interdependence. This is the essential position of the Attorney General's opinion cited above and, in our view, it is sound. * * * [T]he expanded definition of dependents eligible to receive coverage under the self-funded health insurance benefits plan adopted by the County is not a reasonable method of implementing its implied authority under those statutes and is, therefore, an ultra vires act. * * *

HASSELL, JUSTICE, with whom CHIEF JUSTICE CARRICO and SENIOR JUSTICE COMPTON join, dissenting in part, and concurring in judgment. * * *

The County's expanded definition of the word "dependents" clearly and unequivocally violates the Dillon Rule. * * * The County's expanded definition of eligible dependents is nothing more than a disguised effort to confer health benefits upon persons who are involved in either common law marriages or "same-sex unions," which are not recognized in this Commonwealth and are violative of the public policy of this Commonwealth. The General Assembly, by enacting Code § 20–45.2, expressly prohibited marriage between persons of the same sex. * * * Furthermore, and just as important, the County's expanded definition of dependents is inappropriate because it permits the County to legislate in the area of domestic relations, a prerogative that lies within the exclusive domain of the General Assembly of this Commonwealth. The General Assembly, not a county, is entrusted with the responsibility of recognizing and defining marital relationships. * * *

STATE V. HUTCHINSON

Supreme Court of Utah, 1980.
624 P.2d 1116.

STEWART, JUSTICE.

Defendant, a candidate for the office of Salt Lake County Commissioner, was charged with having violated § 1–10–4, Revised Ordinances of Salt Lake County, which requires the filing of campaign statements and the disclosure of campaign contributions. * * * Defendant contends that because the Legislature has not specifically authorized counties to enact ordinances requiring disclosure of campaign contributions in county elections, Salt Lake County had no power to enact the ordinance in question. * * *

Concededly, * * * the Legislature has not expressly authorized enactment of an ordinance requiring disclosure of campaign contributions in county elections. However, the Legislature has conferred upon cities and counties the authority to enact all necessary measures to promote the general health, safety, morals, and welfare of their citizens. Section 17–5–77, U.C.A. (1953) * * *. The specific issue in this case is whether § 17–5–77 by itself provides Salt Lake County legal authority to enact the ordinance for disclosure of campaign contributions, or whether there must be a specific grant of authority for counties to enact measures dealing with disclosures of campaign financing to sustain the ordinance in question. Defendant claims that the powers of municipalities must be strictly construed and that because Salt Lake County did not have specific, delegated authority to enact the ordinance in issue, the ordinance is invalid.

The rule requiring strict construction of the powers delegated by the Legislature to counties and municipalities is a rule which is archaic, unrealistic, and unresponsive to the current needs of both state and local governments and effectively nullifies the legislative grant of general police power to the counties. * * * Dillon's Rule, which requires strict construction of delegated powers to local governments, was first enunciated in 1868. The rule was widely adopted during a period of great mistrust of municipal governments * * *. The courts, in applying the Dillon Rule to general welfare clauses, have not viewed the latter as an independent source of power, but rather as limited by specific, enumerated grants of authority. More recently, however, reasoned opinion regarding the validity of the rule has changed. One authority has noted the harmful effects that the rule of strict construction has had upon the effective exercise of appropriate municipal authority:

> This rule was formulated in an era when farm-dominated legislatures were jealous of their power and when city scandals were notorious. * * * This rule sends local government to State legislatures seeking grants of additional powers; it causes local officials to doubt their power, and it stops local governmental programs from developing fully. * * *6

As pointed out in Frug, *The City As A Legal Concept,* 93 Harvard L.Rev. 1059, 1111 (1980):

> Most troubling of all to Dillon, cities were not managed by those "*best fitted* by their intelligence, business experience, capacity and moral character." Their management was "too often both *unwise* and *extravagant.*" A major change in city government was therefore needed to achieve a fully public city government dedicated to the common good. [Emphasis in original.]

If there were once valid policy reasons supporting the rule, we think they have largely lost their force and that effective local self-government, as an important constituent part of our system of government, must have sufficient power to deal effectively with the problems with which it must deal. * * * The fear of local governments abusing their delegated powers as a justification for strict construction of those powers is a slur on the right and the ability of people to govern themselves. Adequate protection against abuse of power or interference with legitimate statewide interests is provided by the electorate, state supervisory control, and judicial review. Strict construction, particularly in the face of a general welfare grant of power to local governments, simply eviscerates the plain language of the statute, nullifies the intent of the Legislature, and seriously cripples effective local government.

There are ample safeguards against any abuse of power at the local level. Local governments, as subdivisions of the State, exercise those powers granted to them by the State Legislature, and the exercise of a delegated power is subject to the limitations imposed by state statutes and state and federal constitutions. * * * In addition, local governments are without authority to pass any ordinance prohibited by, or in conflict with, state statutory law. Also, an ordinance is invalid if it intrudes into an area which the Legislature has preempted by comprehensive legislation intended to blanket a particular field.

In view of all these restraints and corrective measures, it is not appropriate for this Court to enfeeble local governments on the

---

6 Advisory Commission on Intergovernmental Relations, State Constitutional and Statutory Restrictions Upon the Structural, Functional, and Personnel Powers of Local Government, 24 (1962).

unjustified assumption that strict construction of delegated powers is necessary to prevent abuse. * * * This view is shared by the Advisory Commission on Intergovernmental Relations which has urged that local governments be given broad powers. The Commission's Report states: * * *

> The abuse by local government of broad powers troubles the Commission minimally. It is not currently wide-spread in any serious way. The fact that abuse conceivably might occur is no more reason to deny broad delegations of power than it is to deny a Boy Scout a knife because he might cut himself. Additionally, we are of the opinion that if a broad functional delegation of power is a part of the total power residing in the local governing body it will be more responsive to popular control. * * *

Nothing in § 17–5–77 * * * suggests that the general welfare clause should be narrowly or strictly construed. Its breadth of language demands the opposite conclusion. * * * When the State has granted general welfare power to local governments, those governments have independent authority apart from, and in addition to, specific grants of authority to pass ordinances which are reasonably and appropriately related to the objectives of that power, i.e., providing for the <u>public safety, health, morals, and welfare</u>. And the courts will not interfere with the legislative choice of the means selected unless it is arbitrary, or is directly prohibited by, or is inconsistent with the policy of, the state or federal laws or the constitution of this State or of the United States. * * *

Broad construction of the powers of counties and cities is consistent with the current needs of local governments. The Dillon Rule of strict construction is antithetical to effective and efficient local and state government. The complexities confronting local governments, and the degree to which the nature of those problems varies from county to county and city to city, has changed since the Dillon Rule was formulated. Several counties in this State, for example, currently confront large and serious problems caused by accelerated urban growth. * * * The problems that must be solved by these counties are to some extent unique to them. According a plain meaning to the legislative grant of general welfare power to local governmental units allows each local government to be responsive to the particular problems facing it.

Local power should not be paralyzed and critical problems should not remain unsolved while officials await a biennial session of the Legislature in the hope of obtaining passage of a special grant of authority. Furthermore, passage of legislation needed or appropriate for some counties may fail because of the press of other legislative business or the disinterest of legislators from other parts of the State whose constituencies experience other, and to them more pressing, problems. In granting cities and counties the power to enact ordinances to further the general welfare, the Legislature no doubt took such political realities into consideration.

We therefore hold that a county has the power to preserve the purity of its electoral process. The county was entitled to conclude that financial disclosure by candidates would directly serve the legitimate purpose of achieving the goal that special interests should not be able to exercise undue influence in local elections without their influence being brought to light. * * *

MAUGHAN, JUSTICE (dissenting): * * *

The majority * * * interprets Section 17–5–77 as a carte blanche delegation of the state police power to local government, unless there be a specific and direct conflict between state and local law. This interpretation is inconsistent with the multiple statutes, wherein the legislature confers specific powers and duties on local government, and distorts the nature of the police power. The State is the sole and exclusive repository of the police power, neither the federal nor local government has any such inherent power. The police power is awesome, for it confers the right to declare an act a crime and to deprive an individual of his liberty or property in order to protect or advance the public health, safety, morals, and welfare. The decision of whether a problem should be deemed one of local concern and should be regulated under the police power should initially be decided by the legislature representing all the citizens of this state. The legislature may then elect to delegate the power to local government to deal with the specific area of concern. It is equally a legislative judgment to deny delegating this power to local government. * * * All exercise of the police power by local government is derivative, none is inherent, and it is the exclusive prerogative of the State to establish the conditions under which it will be exercised. If local government discerns a condition which merits control through the police power, this matter should be submitted to the legislature so that representatives of the entire state may resolve whether the problem should be addressed on a local level.

It is within the context of the foregoing principles that the specific delegation of the police power in Section 17–5–77 should be interpreted in this case. * * * The County advocates the view that the general welfare clause of Section 17–5–77 constitutes a broad, general grant of the state's police power to counties. * * * [But] the question * * * [is] whether the challenged ordinances are *substantially and reasonably* related to the promotion of the prosperity and improvement of the morals, peace and good order, comfort and convenience of the county and its inhabitants. The circumstances of this case compel a negative answer; there is neither a substantial nor reasonable relationship between the aforecited purposes and the campaign disclosures of elected county officials. This matter is best illustrated by three cases: *Bohn v. Salt Lake City*,[14] *Salt Lake City v. Revene*,[15] and *Nance v. Mayflower Tavern, Inc.*[16]

In *Bohn* the issue concerned the authority of the city to include certain special provisions in a contract to construct storm sewers. These provisions were included solely for the purpose of alleviating the unemployment situation * * *. This Court particularly concentrated on the provision in the contract concerning minimum wage. The power to fix a minimum wage and to prescribe the hours which constitute a day's labor are generally regarded as an exercise of the police power. The Court explained * * *

> There is in this state no express or implied power conferred upon a municipality which directly or by implication authorizes a city to dictate to a contractor the wages that he shall pay his employees * * *. In this jurisdiction, inasmuch as municipalities have none of the elements of sovereignty in exerting their given powers, we think the provision in the proposed contracts with respect to the minimum wage must be ruled out.

In the *Revene* case, the city urged, an ordinance, setting the closing hours of barbershops, was a valid exercise of the police power delegated by the Legislature to the city to regulate for the safety and preservation of health in the community. This Court characterized the issue as whether the fixing of the closing hours was a reasonable regulation within the scope of the *delegated* police power, i.e., did it have a reasonable relationship to the protection of the health of the public. * * * The opinion then recited and relied on the principle that any fair, reasonable, substantial doubt concerning the existence of the power is resolved by the courts against the corporation, and the power denied. * * *

In the *Nance* case the challenged ordinance provided for civil rights concerning restaurants. The Court said cities had no inherent or original legislative power. * * * The Court held:

> * * * The power to enact civil rights legislation is not granted in express words either by constitution or by statute, nor is it necessarily or fairly implied in or incident to the powers expressly granted. Likewise it cannot be held to be essential to the accomplishment of the declared objects and purposes of the corporation, or as Dillon states, "indispensable" to the accomplishment of the declared objects. We therefore hold that cities have no power to enact such civil rights legislation * * *.

---

[14] 79 Utah 121, 8 P.2d 591 (1932).

[15] 101 Utah 504, 124 P.2d 537 (1942).

[16] 106 Utah 517, 150 P.2d 773 (1944).

In the matter at hand, there is no express grant conferring authority on Salt Lake County to enact a corrupt practices act concerning local elected officials. Such authority cannot be implied from the general welfare clause of Section 17–5–77 since it does not have a sufficiently direct, substantial, immediate effect on the specific general welfare interests set forth therein. * * *

3. CONSTITUTIONAL PROHIBITIONS AGAINST LOCAL OR SPECIAL LEGISLATION

Even at the time of the publication of Dillon's treatise, political efforts were already underway to restructure the legal relationship between states and cities. The most important of these political efforts, known as the home rule movement, is the subject of the next subsection. But an earlier effort—aimed at prohibiting so-called special legislation—was significant in its own right. The effort to prohibit special legislation was in part a direct consequence of the dominance of the state creature idea. That approach to the state-local relationship was intended to ensure that local power would not run amok. It ensured that cities would be supervised by their states. But it had another important consequence. It encouraged state legislators to intervene in the affairs of municipalities, not only as a class, but also individually. As urban centers began to grow in the nineteenth century, legislators increasingly began to enact special laws that targeted particular cities. Sometimes these laws prohibited the targeted city from exercising power, but often they authorized or required the city to act. In either event, the growth of special legislation became a source of great concern among municipal reformers and the public at large. Some objected that special legislation made it too easy for the state legislature to control local affairs. Others argued that special legislation facilitated corruption. As the municipal law expert Howard Lee McBain explained in 1916, "The large rewards which lay in cities' offices, their contracts, and the franchises in their streets, became the mark of the political spoilsman in the state legislature."[4]

Concerns like these underlay state constitutional prohibitions against targeted legislative control of local affairs, and most state constitutions now include a specific provision prohibiting the enactment of "local" or "special" legislation. Despite the wide variety of forms these constitutional restrictions on local or special legislation have taken, all of them are based on the belief that if the legislature acts through general legislation, rather than legislation aimed at specific cities, there will be less state intervention into city affairs. Clearly, however, states have a legitimate interest in enacting legislation designed to solve problems found only in particular areas of the state; not every state law can appropriately be applied state-wide. The courts, therefore, have

---

[4] Howard Lee McBain, The Law and Practice of Municipal Home Rule (1916).

repeatedly had to determine when, in light of the constitutional prohibitions against special legislation, legislation limited to a specific category of cities is reasonable. The cases included in this section explore the difficulty of making this determination. Both Chicago National League Ball Club v. Thompson and Empire State Chapter v. Smith concern state legislation that affected a limited number of cities (in *Chicago National League* only one city) in the state. In both cases, the legislation was upheld as constitutional under the relevant "special legislation" provision. What is the meaning of the constitutional protection against local and special legislation under these cases? When is legislation that creates a "class of one" problematic?[5] Is prohibiting special legislation an effective means of protecting local power?

[handwritten margin note: Issue in cases re special legislation]

CHICAGO NATIONAL LEAGUE BALL CLUB, INC.
V. THOMPSON

Supreme Court of Illinois, 1985.
108 Ill.2d 357, 91 Ill.Dec. 610, 483 N.E.2d 1245.

WARD, JUSTICE.

The Chicago National League Ball Club, Inc., is a corporation which owns and operates the Chicago Cubs, the major league baseball team, and the Cubs' home ball park, Wrigley Field. On December 19, 1984, the corporation (the Cubs) filed a complaint in the circuit court of Cook County seeking a declaratory judgment that a 1982 amendment to the Environmental Protection Act and a Chicago city ordinance violate the * * * equal protection and special-legislation clause[s] * * * of the Constitution of Illinois. * * * The statute, which amends title VI, section 25, of the Environmental Protection Act, provides:

> "The [Pollution Control] Board shall, by regulations under this Section, categorize the types and sources of noise emissions that unreasonably interfere with the enjoyment of life, or with any lawful business, or activity, and shall prescribe for each such category the maximum permissible limits on such noise emissions. * * *

> No Board standards for monitoring noise or regulations prescribing limitations on noise emissions shall apply to any organized amateur or professional sporting activity except as

---

[5] For an analysis of constitutional restrictions on special legislation, see, e.g., John Martinez, Local Government Law, Chapter 3 (2nd ed. 2012–13); Maggie Cox, Up in Smoke, 88 Neb. L. Rev. 612 (2010); Christopher Thompson, Special Legislation Analysis in Missouri and the Need for Constitutional Flexibility, 61 Mo. L. Rev. 185 (1996); Thomas Palisi, Comment: Town of Secaucus v. Hudson County Board of Taxation: An Analysis of the Special Legislation and Tax Uniformity Clauses of the New Jersey Constitution, 47 Rutgers L. Rev. 1229 (1995); Clayton Gillette, Expropriation and Institutional Design in State and Local Government Law, 80 Va. L. Rev. 625, 642–657 (1994); John Winters, Classification of Municipalities, 57 Nw. U. L. Rev. 279 (1962).

otherwise provided in this Section. Baseball, football or soccer sporting events played during nighttime hours, by professional athletes, in a city with more than 1,000,000 inhabitants, in a stadium at which such nighttime events were not played prior to July 1, 1982, shall be subject to nighttime noise emission regulations promulgated by the Illinois Pollution Control Board."

The provisions of the Chicago ordinance are:

"It shall be unlawful for any * * * person * * * to * * * present any athletic contest * * * if any part of such athletic contest * * * takes place between the hours of 8:00 p.m. and 8:00 a.m., and is presented in a stadium or playing field which is not totally enclosed and contains more than 15,000 seats where any such seats are located within 500 feet of 100 or more dwelling units."

The Cubs challenge the constitutionality of the statute, apparently considering that night baseball games at Wrigley Field would violate the nighttime-noise-emission regulations of the Pollution Control Board. * * * The parties * * * are agreed that the ordinance would have the effect of prohibiting night games at Wrigley Field. Wrigley Field is located on the north side of Chicago in the Lake View area. * * * It is an open-air ball park with a seating capacity of slightly over 37,000, and it is the only park in the major leagues that, because it does not have lights, does not have night games. * * * The area surrounding Wrigley Field is predominately residential, with some light industry to the south and west of the ball park. Most of the buildings in the area are multi-unit dwellings, which gives Lake View a highly concentrated population. There are no expressways in close proximity to Wrigley Field to accommodate the influx of spectators on days when games are played at the field, and there are few off-street parking facilities in the area. In general, only the neighborhood streets are available for parking. * * *

The provision in the Constitution of Illinois prohibiting special legislation states: "The General Assembly shall pass no special or local law when a general law is or can be made applicable. Whether a general law is or can be made applicable shall be a matter of judicial determination." * * * Legislation which confers a benefit on one class and denies the same to another may be attacked both as special legislation and as a denial of equal protection, but under either ground for challenge it is the duty of courts to decide whether classifications are unreasonable. Though the constitutional protections involved are not identical, a claim that the special-legislation provision has been violated is generally judged by the same standard that is used in considering a claim that equal protection has been denied. Unless legislation operates to the disadvantage of a suspect classification or infringes upon a fundamental right, the legislation, to be upheld as constitutional, must simply bear a rational relationship to a legitimate governmental interest. * * * There is a presumption in favor of the validity of any legislation, including of course a legislative act enacted under the police power. The burden of showing legislation to be an unreasonable exercise of the police power is on the party challenging it. When a classification under a statute is called into question, if any state of facts can reasonably be conceived to sustain the classification, the existence of that state of facts at the time the statute was enacted must be assumed.

The declared purpose of title VI of the Environmental Protection Act is "to prevent noise which creates a public nuisance." * * * The purpose of * * * [the] amendment to the Act was to protect, within the comprehensive regulatory scheme, the property and other rights of residents who live near stadia by making the nighttime use of the stadia subject to the regulations of the Pollution Control Board. * * * Only stadia in cities with more than one million inhabitants are subject to the regulations. Chicago is the only city in our State that has a population of more than one million. * * * Considering the terms of this amendment, there is a rationally founded difference between a less populous city and a city with a greater population. It might be reasonably anticipated that in a typical urban setting more people would be affected in the larger city by the noise from spectators in a stadium for a nighttime event. The problems attending a densely populated area would be exacerbated: limited areas for parking would become overburdened; neighborhood streets would become busier and thus potentially more dangerous to residents of the area and their children; and thoroughfares to and from the area would become more congested. Too, a rational basis may be found in the concern that there would be less open space in an area with a highly concentrated population that could serve as a buffer zone against the noise generated.

The same considerations serve as a proper basis for the distinction made by the legislature between nighttime and daytime sporting events. The General Assembly well might have concluded that the evening hours are traditionally spent in restful and quieter pursuits and should be protected by closer regulation. More residents would be at home during the evening hours, and there are variations in traffic patterns and in police patrol deployment between night and day hours which might have served as reasonable considerations by the legislature in enacting the statute.

The amendment distinguishes between professional and amateur sporting events. Amateur sports generally have shorter seasons than their professional counterparts and often attract fewer spectators. There also is a widely entertained opinion that amateur athletics benefit the public, and the legislature may therefore have decided to limit the applicability of the statute to professional sports, which are profit-oriented enterprises. Finally, a provision exempts stadia where nighttime events were held prior to July 1, 1982. A legislature may, if it finds remedial measures necessary, address problems one step at a time. "The legislature may select one phase of one field and apply a remedy there, neglecting the others." (*Williamson v. Lee Optical of Oklahoma, Inc.* (1955), 348 U.S. 483, 489, 75 S.Ct. 461, 465, 99 L.Ed. 563, 573.) We are unwilling to strike down as constitutionally infirm a classification because the legislature may have chosen to regulate expectant interests and not established interests.

An ordinance adopted by the governing body of a city must satisfy the same requirement of reasonableness that is applicable to statutes enacted by the General Assembly. Here the ordinance distinguishes between the hours of use, whether the stadia are open-air or enclosed, the seating capacity of the stadia and the proximity to dwelling units. As we observed earlier in discussing the statute, a regulatory scheme intended to abate public nuisances may reasonably distinguish between the hours of permissible use of land when that use may operate to interfere with property and other rights of the community. The distinction between open-air stadia and enclosed stadia may be rationally based on the different volumes of decibels of noise coming from open and enclosed stadia. The noise from an enclosed stadium is muted and less intrusive on area residents.

The city council established 500 feet as the required distance between a stadium and the nearest dwelling unit. There is, of course, a reasonable relationship between the distance from the source of noise and the effect that the noise will have on the surrounding community. The city council also decided to restrict the ordinance's reach to stadia with seating capacities in excess of 15,000. The noise from smaller stadia with fewer spectators would not have the same intrusive effect on a neighborhood as the noise from larger stadia. The discretion of the council to create legislative classifications includes the authority to set permissible boundaries. The creation of classifications is for the judgment of the legislature, and its amending or modifying is not for courts to decide. * * *

EMPIRE STATE CHAPTER OF ASSOCIATED BUILDERS AND CONTRACTORS, INC. V. SMITH

Court of Appeals of New York, 2013.
21 N.Y.3d 309, 992 N.E.2d 1067, 970 N.Y.S.2d 724.

SMITH, J. * * *

The Wicks Law, originally enacted in 1912, requires public entities seeking bids on construction contracts to obtain "separate specifications" for three "subdivisions of the work to be performed"—generally, plumbing, electrical and HVAC (heating, ventilating and air conditioning) work (L. 1912, ch. 514, § 50). The law has long been controversial; public entities have complained that it makes contracting more burdensome and expensive. Until 2008, the Wicks Law applied everywhere in the state to contracts whose cost exceeded $50,000. This case concerns amendments to the Wicks Law enacted in 2008 that raised the $50,000 threshold, imposed so-called "apprenticeship requirements" on some public contracting, and made other changes not relevant here (L. 2008, ch. 57, part MM). The new, higher thresholds, unlike the old one, are not uniform throughout the state. They are $3 million in the five counties located in New York City; $1.5 million in Nassau, Suffolk and Westchester Counties; and $500,000 in the other 54 counties.

Plaintiffs' main claim, asserted in their first cause of action, is that the 2008 legislation violates article IX, § 2 of the State Constitution (the Home Rule section) by unjustifiably favoring the eight counties with higher thresholds—i.e., by loosening Wicks Law restrictions to a greater extent for them than for the other counties. * * * The Home Rule section of the State Constitution says:

"(b) Subject to the bill of rights of local governments and other applicable provisions of this constitution, the legislature: . . .

"(2) Shall have the power to act in relation to the property, affairs or government of any local government only by general law, or by special law only (a) on request of two-thirds of the total membership of its legislative body or on request of its chief executive officer concurred in by a majority of such membership, or (b) except in the case of the city of New York, on certificate of necessity from the governor reciting facts which in the judgment of the governor constitute an emergency requiring enactment of such law and, in such latter case, with the concurrence of two-thirds of the members elected to each house of the legislature."

It is undisputed that neither of the prerequisites described in subdivisions (a) and (b) of section 2(b)(2)—a so-called "home rule message" or a certificate of necessity from the governor—was met in this case. And we assume, without deciding, that the distinctions drawn between counties in the 2008 legislation make that legislation a "special law," defined in article DC, § 3(d)(4), as relevant here, to be "[a] law which in terms and in effect applies to one or more, but not all, counties." Nevertheless, we conclude that the legislation was not forbidden by the Home Rule section.

The language of article DC, § 2(b)(2) seems broadly to prohibit, where the specified prerequisites are not met, the enactment of any special law "in relation to the property, affairs or government of any local government." Another subdivision of the same section, section 2(c)(i), uses similar language in granting power to local governments: "every local government shall have power to adopt and amend local laws not inconsistent with the provisions of this constitution or any general law relating to its property, affairs or government."

These two provisions might be read to mean that, in the absence of a home rule message or certificate of necessity, a local government's "property, affairs or government" is an area in which local governments are free to act, but from which the state legislature is excluded unless it legislates by general law. It was long ago recognized, however, that such a reading of the Constitution would not make sense—that there must be an area of overlap, indeed a very sizeable one, in which the state legislature acting by special law and local governments have concurrent powers. As Chief Judge Cardozo put it in his concurring opinion in *Adler v. Deegan*, 251 N.Y. 467, 489, 167 N.E. 705 (1929) * * *: "The Constitution . . . will not be read as enjoining an impossible dichotomy." He added: "The test is . . . that if the subject be in a substantial degree a matter of State concern, the Legislature may act, though intermingled with it are concerns of the locality . . . I do not say that an affair must be one of city concern exclusively to bring it within the scope of the powers conferred upon the municipality . . . I assume that if the affair is partly State and partly local, the city is free to act until the State has intervened. As to concerns of this class there is thus concurrent jurisdiction for each in default of action by the other."

We have adopted in later cases the test as Chief Judge Cardozo formulated it. And we have found support in the Constitution's text for the view that the permitted spheres of the state legislature and localities overlap. We relied * * * on article IX, § 3(a)(3) of the Constitution, which says: "Except as expressly provided, nothing in this article shall restrict or impair any power of the legislature in relation to . . . [m]atters other than the property, affairs or government of a local government." This language is not a mere redundancy—a statement that article IX, § 2(b)(2) does not prohibit what it does not prohibit. A great deal of legislation relates both to "the property, affairs or government of a local government" and to "[m]atters other than the property, affairs or government of a local government"—i.e., to matters of substantial state concern. Where that is true, section 3(a)(3), as we interpreted it * * *, establishes that section 2(b)(2) does not prevent the State from acting by special law.

This principle controls this case. It can hardly be disputed, and plaintiffs here do not dispute, that the manner of bidding on public construction contracts is a matter of substantial state concern. The existence of the Wicks Law itself for the last century, and of much other legislation governing public contracting attests to this. The very amendments of which plaintiffs complain, though they do not treat all counties alike, unquestionably affect the state as a whole. Plaintiffs argue, however, that a finding that the legislation addresses a substantial state concern is not the end of the analysis. Relying on *City of New York v. Patrolmen's Benevolent Assn. of City of N.Y.*, 89 N.Y.2d 380, 654 N.Y.S.2d 85, 676 N.E.2d 847 (1996) (*PBA I*), they say that the Home Rule section also imposes a separate reasonableness test on "special" legislation. Plaintiffs read too much into the *PBA I* decision.

PBA I involved an intervention by the state legislature in a dispute between New York City and one of its employee unions. The City and the PBA had failed to negotiate a collective bargaining agreement, and the City had requested its local Board of Collective Bargaining (BCB) to appoint an impasse arbitration panel. "[A]t that time," the legislature, acting without a home rule message, passed a bill "which purported to give . . . exclusive jurisdiction over negotiation impasses between the City and the New York City police" to the BCB's state counterpart, the Public Employment Rotations Board (PERB). The legislature thus sought to create an exception, applicable only to negotiations between New York City and the police, to the statewide rule that local governments could "completely opt out of PERB's jurisdiction over impasse procedures."

We held the legislation invalid under the Home Rule section, finding that it "cannot be upheld under any substantial State interest." To the assertion that the expressed purposes of the legislation—"to create State-wide uniformity with respect to impasse procedures" and to "provide a fairer forum for the New York City police"—were of statewide import, we responded that the legislation "bears no reasonable relationship to those goals." Uniformity could hardly be advanced by legislation applicable to one jurisdiction only, and the "fairness" rationale was shown to be pretextual, because of the "unchallenged substantial equivalency" between PERB's impasse arbitration procedures and those of local bodies. In short, we found in *PBA I* that the challenged legislation was the sort of state meddling in purely local affairs that the Home Rule section was enacted to prohibit. By contrast, five years later in a second PBA case, *Patrolmen's Benevolent Assn. of City of N.Y. v. City of New York*, 97 N.Y.2d 378, 387, 740 N.Y.S.2d 659, 767 N.E.2d 116 (2001), we upheld legislation providing "that all collective bargaining impasses reached between local governments and their police and fire unions are resolved by PERB". This new statute, we said, "was enacted in furtherance of and bears a reasonable relationship to a substantial State-wide concern."

The legislation here is nothing like the legislation at issue in *PBA I*; its relationship to matters of substantial state concern is obvious and undisputed. Plaintiffs claim that the relationship is not "reasonable" in that nothing in the legislative history, or in the arguments now made by the State, provides a reasonable explanation for the disparity that the 2008 legislation introduced into the Wicks Law thresholds—which are now six times as high in New York City, and three times as high in certain surrounding counties, as in the rest of the state. But *PBA I* did not use "reasonable relationship" in this sense; that case is not an invitation to subject every geographical disparity in statewide legislation to a freestanding reasonableness analysis. The absence of a "reasonable relationship" in *PBA I* established that the challenged legislation was purely parochial, and of no real statewide importance; it could not reasonably be said to advance a substantial state interest. No such claim can be made in this case.

To subject legislation like the 2008 amendments to the Wicks Law to Home Rule analysis would lead us into a wilderness of anomalies. If statewide legislation like this is subject to Home Rule restrictions, how are the restrictions to be implemented? From where must a home rule message come? Plaintiffs' logic leads to the conclusion that there should have been such a message from every one of the 62 counties affected. And if the law was passed in violation of the Home Rule provisions, what is the remedy? Are we to cure the disparity between counties by raising the Wicks Law threshold in 54 counties, or by reducing it in eight counties to the level established elsewhere? Or should we hold the 2008 legislation wholly invalid—so that the Wicks Law threshold remains at $50,000 throughout this state, a result that surely would not please plaintiffs? We conclude that the Home Rule provisions of the Constitution were never intended to apply to legislation like this. They were intended to prevent unjustifiable state interference in matters of purely local concern. No one contends such interference has occurred here. * * *

4. HOME RULE INITIATIVE

The prohibition against special legislation attacks one problematic consequence of the state creature idea, but it does not challenge its basic conception of the state-local relationship. The home rule movement, by contrast, represented a far more fundamental attempt to rethink the legal status of cities. Begun in the late nineteenth century, the movement's first objective was to give cities a power of initiative in city affairs, allowing them to operate under a general grant of authority from the state (at least with respect to "local" or "municipal" affairs) instead of requiring them to rely on individualized delegations for particular purposes. The second objective was to give cities an area of autonomy immune from state control, even by general legislation. These two objectives, it should be recognized, are not necessarily connected: cities could be given a broad power to initiate actions on their own ("Home Rule Initiative") without giving them immunity from the state's power to overrule these actions if the state chooses to do so ("Home Rule

Immunity"). The first of these objectives is covered in this subsection of the book; the second is covered immediately below.[6]

Missouri became the first state in the nation to include a home rule provision in its state constitution in 1875; since that time, most state constitutions have been amended to provide for municipal home rule. In some states, however, home rule is conferred by general statute and thus has no state constitutional status. Moreover, even states that recognize home rule often do not grant it to smaller municipalities, counties, and other important local institutions, such as school boards. Nevertheless, the home rule movement was largely successful. Almost all states recognize some form of home rule.

Despite the differing premises about decentralization that seem to animate Dillon's Rule and Home Rule, it would be wrong to view home rule as simply the antithesis of Dillon's Rule. Dillon's Rule does not purport to identify a set of powers that are of distinct local concern. Dillon's Rule instead sets forth an interpretive presumption that the state legislature is free to override. In this respect, Dillon's Rule might actually permit cities to exercise a great deal of power, at least in those states in which the legislature is inclined to delegate significant power to cities. There is some evidence to suggest that throughout much of the nineteenth century, state legislatures were quite responsive to city requests for state law authorizations to act. Indeed, that was in part why

---

[6] For general analyses of the concept of home rule, see, e.g., John Martinez, Local Government Law, Chapter 4 (2nd ed. 2012–13); Paul Diller, The City and the Private Right of Action, 64 Stan. L. Rev. 1109 (2012); Symposium: Home Rule, 86 Denv. U. L. Rev. 1241 (2008); Richard Briffault, Home Rule and Local Political Innovation, 22 J.L. & Pol. 1 (2006); Chester Antieau, Municipal Corporation Law, Chapter 3 (1980); Richard Briffault, Home Rule for the Twenty-First Century, 36 Urb. Law. 253 (2004); Daniel Rodriguez, Localism and Lawmaking, 32 Rutgers L.J. 627 (2001); George Vaubel, Toward Principles of State Restraint Upon the Exercise of Municipal Power in Home Rule, 22 Stet. L. Rev.643 (1993); 20 Stet. L. Rev. 845 (1991); 20 Stet. L. Rev. 5 (1990); Michael Libonati, Home Rule: An Essay on Pluralism, 64 Wash. L. Rev. 51 (1989); Michael Sebree, One Century of Constitutional Home Rule: A Progress Report?, 64 Wash. L. Rev. 155 (1989); William Andersen, Resolving State/Local Governmental Conflict: A Tale of Three Cities, 18 Urban Law Annual 129 (1980); Kenneth Vanlandingham, Constitutional Home Rule Since the AMA (NLC) Model, 17 Wm. & Mary L. Rev. 1 (1975); Kenneth Vanlandingham, Municipal Home Rule in the United States, 10 Wm. & Mary L. Rev. 269 (1968); Jefferson Fordham and Joe Asher, Home Rule Powers in Theory and Practice, 9 Ohio St. L. J. 18 (1948); Joseph McGoldrick, Law and Practice of Municipal Home Rule, 1916–1930 (1933); Howard McBain, The Law and Practice of Municipal Home Rule (1916). For analyses of home rule in specific states, see, e.g., Pierce MacLennan, A Long Way From Home: Slow Progress Toward "Home Rule" In South Carolina and a Path to Full Implementation, 64 S.C. L. Rev. 781 (2013); James Macdonald and Jacqueline Papez, Over 100 Years Without True "Home Rule" in Idaho, 46 Idaho L. Rev. 587 (2010); Paul Diller, The Partly Fulfilled Promise of Home Rule in Oregon, 87 Or. L. Rev. 939 (2008); Kerry A. Burchill, Madison's Minimum Wage Ordinance, Section 104.001, and the Future of Home Rule in Wisconsin, 2007 Wis. L. Rev. 151 (2007); Frayda S. Bluestein, Do North Carolina Local Governments Need Home Rule?, 84 N.C. L. Rev. 1983 (2006); Jill Welch, The Iowa Supreme Court Resurrects Dillon's Rule and Blurs the Line Between Implied Preemption and Inconsistency, 30 Rutgers L. J. 1548 (1999); Thomas Smith, Survey of Wyoming Law: No Home On the Range for Home Rule, 31 Land & Water L. Rev. 791 (1996); Steven Cianca, Home Rule in Ohio Counties: Legal and Constitutional Perspectives, 19 U. Dayton L. Rev. 533 (1994); George Vaubel, Municipal Home Rule in Ohio, 3 Ohio North. L. Rev. 1, 355 (1975).

special legislation was prohibited. By contrast, home rule usually seeks to identify, as a constitutional matter, a distinct sphere of local authority. The legal demarcation of such a sphere clearly enhances city power in the sense that it permits cities to act on their own initiative within that sphere. However, the legal demarcation of such a sphere may limit independent action to those actions that are thought to be within the legally demarcated sphere of power. The significance of home rule as a source of city power, therefore, depends in many cases on the particular terms of the home rule grant or on judicial determinations concerning the kinds of actions that are properly understood to concern "local" or "municipal" affairs. In this respect, home rule may prove to be just as much a limitation on city power in practice as is Dillon's Rule.

Home rule provisions can be written to make clear that the scope of local power is intended to be quite broad. For example, a draft Model Constitutional Provision for Municipal Home Rule proposed that a home rule municipality be permitted to "exercise any power or perform any function which the legislature has the power to devolve upon a non-home rule" municipality. The sixth edition of the National Municipal League's Model State Constitution arguably went even further in permitting a home rule municipality to "exercise any legislative power or perform any function * * *." These proposed home rule measures reflect a skepticism about the capacity to divide the world into spheres of local and state concern, and a belief that judges are particularly ill-suited to determine what powers local governments are capable of exercising. The very breadth of these proposals makes judicial intervention unlikely and leaves the regulation of local power to the legislature through the enactment of preemptive legislation.

Such broad home rule proposals have been challenged in an important article by Terrence Sandalow.[7] He argues that "the area of municipal action is so broad, the range of potential experimentation so great, that the ability of the legislature to foresee all of the problems which may arise is highly improbable. Nor can reliance be placed upon legislative action after the exercise of municipal initiative. The relatively narrow impact of many local measures may not arouse sufficient general interest to overcome legislative inertia." Instead, he contends, state constitutional provisions that limit home rule power to matters of "local" or "municipal" concern strike an appropriate balance. They permit judges to construe the provisions broadly to permit local governments to exercise many important powers. At the same time, they permit judges to invalidate "[a] use of governmental power which threatens fundamental values or established state policies" on the ground that such an exercise of power is not a "local" or "municipal" affair.

---

[7] Terrance Sandalow, The Limits of Municipal Power Under Home Rule: A Role for the Courts, 48 Minn. L. Rev. 643 (1964).

Other commentators disagree. In *Reclaiming Home Rule,* David Barron points out that many home rule grants contain significant express limitations—from restrictions on the local power to tax to express limits on the local authority to regulate business—which courts are free to construe broadly. In addition, he argues that the requirement that local powers concern "local" or "municipal" affairs may itself be unduly limiting:

> The texts of home rule grants contain a variety of ambiguities that state courts are free to interpret. The resulting interpretations may reflect judges' particular political ideologies and their hostility to certain forms of governmental regulation of private property. Alternatively, they might reflect a more general judicial uneasiness with creative local actions and a corresponding preference for uniformity. Whatever the explanation, it is clear that, in the hands of many judges, home rule grants turn out to be anything but general grants of local initiatory authority. * * * That home rule provisions sometimes expressly confine home rule initiatory power to matters of "local" concern * * * leaves courts free to denominate matters of pressing societal interest—such as efforts to counteract housing or employment discrimination that may foster intralocal homogeneity—beyond the scope of home rule initiative, precisely because they seem to be of greater-than-local concern. In addition, in some states, the grant of home rule over "local" matters leads courts to construe the scope of initiative narrowly, to avoid engendering a conflict with a state statute that arguably occupies the field.* * * In short, home rule provisions themselves frustrate local efforts to address the very kinds of problems—sprawl, interlocal inequity, a narrowly privatist conception of local politics that promotes exclusionary policymaking—that usually underlie calls for limiting the scope of legal power that cities and suburbs now enjoy. * * * [C]ourts have construed home rule initiative in a way that gives local actors little confidence that the law will be on their side if they undertake controversial and novel regulatory action in the first instance. As a result, a legal regime that is thought to confer a great deal of local power through home rule provisions often encourages local governments to be cautious and unimaginative.[8]

The first reading excerpted below, also from *Reclaiming Home Rule,* provides a brief history of the early home rule movement. It reveals the connection between social and political forces and ideas about decentralization. It also shows how proposals for home rule were early on

---

[8] David J. Barron, Reclaiming Home Rule, 116 Harv. L. Rev. 2255, 2347, 2349–2350 (2003).

defined as much by the limits they sought to place on cities as by the powers they proposed to confer. The first case, McCrory Corporation v. Fowler, then offers a restrictive interpretation of home rule authority. Following the case, an excerpt from Gary Schwartz's article introduces another restriction: the private law exception. The two cases that follow— Marshal House, Inc. v. Rent Review and Grievance Board of Brookline and New Mexicans for Free Enterprise v. City of Santa Fe—offer contrasting interpretation of the private law exception. Can the different results in the two cases be explained by differences in the language of the two state constitutions or the difference between rent control and living wage ordinances? Or are the different results a consequence of the same controversy about the desirability of city authority evident in the Dillon's Rule cases considered earlier? Given its view of the private law exception, do you think that the *New Mexicans for Free Enterprise* court would decide *McCrory* the same way?

DAVID J. BARRON, RECLAIMING HOME RULE
116 Harv. L. Rev. 2255, 2280–2281, 2291–2295, 2300–2301,
2306–2308, 2309–2311, 2325–2328, 2347–2351 (2003).

The early proponents of home rule presented their arguments against a legal background that generally treated all municipalities as, at least formally, creatures of the state. * * * It was this "state creature" understanding of local power that the home rulers sought to dislodge. * * * [T] here was a widespread sense that the rise of the great cities severely challenged a well-accepted view regarding the kind of regulatory activity that cities could properly pursue. Some urban reformers welcomed this challenge as an opportunity to cast off what they considered an unjustifiably restrictive understanding of local regulatory authority. Others feared that this challenge would pressure cities to take on social service and regulatory tasks that they should resist. But significantly, the disputants in this debate agreed that the then-dominant legal conception of cities as mere creatures of the state was problematic. Thus, substantive battles over the proper scope of city power played out among the home rulers themselves and not simply between those who favored the state creature idea and those who did not. For this reason, the late-nineteenth-century push for home rule was not the unified effort that modern legal scholarship often holds it out to be. Home rulers did not singlemindedly seek to remove formal limits on local power that the state creature idea of local power imposed. Indeed, the very opposite impulse motivated the push for home rule by many urban reformers. Those urban reformers who did seek to remove such limits, moreover, often defended the imposition of new limits of their own that they believed would further their preferred substantive vision of urban authority. The story of the home rule movement set forth below, therefore, is one of conflict over competing substantive visions of local power, rather than one of consensus on the need to decentralize governmental processes generally. As such, it is a story about the plasticity of the home rule idea of local power and its intimate relation to substantive visions of governmental authority. * * *

The call for home rule did not point ineluctably toward greater local freedom from state power. The home rule idea proved popular among urban reformers precisely because it served as a placeholder for an array of conflicting concrete proposals. As one commentator close to the movement observed, the early home rulers were, as a group, ultimately more interested in promoting "good government"—a phrase meant to capture the general reformist aspirations of those alarmed by the urban crisis—than in promoting the exercise of local power for its own sake. * * * In practice, they argued, that goal could be achieved in many instances by augmenting the powers of these municipalities or, more precisely, by altering the mix of powers and disabilities that had formerly defined their roles. But in proposing their own version of home rule, the early urban reformers also were more than willing to call for new limits on local power. These constraints, they contended, could be just as critical to home rule as new grants. Together, the grants and limits could reinforce one another and set local power on the path that the reformers' own respective substantive governmental visions favored.

The resulting debates over the substantive content of urban power generated what, in retrospect, appear to be three distinct (and even contradictory) visions of home rule during this period * * *—the old conservative, administrative, and social variants of home rule * * *.

1. Home Rule and the Old Conservative City.—Beginning in the 1870s, an influential set of urban reformers drew on the privatist idea of the proper bounds of city power to challenge the very state creature idea of local power that Dillon's Rule had sought to protect. Under this new approach, a state constitution would provide a city with the authority to adopt "a charter for its own government" or a "home rule charter" or, as some measures put it, to exercise power over "local" or "municipal" affairs. State constitutions often would provide that such power was subject to limitations set forth in "general" laws. The greater latitude for local adaptation afforded by this new structure promised to make it easier to adhere to the prohibition against special legislation, as the need for state legislative tinkering with local charters presumably would subside.

The close connection between this plea for home rule and the earlier effort to ban special legislation reflected the roots of both reform movements in the substantive premises of the "old conservative" philosophy of the 1850s, 1860s, and 1870s. Old conservatives believed that "decentralized economic and political institutions—a 'self-regulating, competitive market economy presided over by a neutral, impartial, and decentralized "night-watchman" state'—were the fundamental conditions of American freedom." On this view, law's great aim was to protect the public sphere from governmental favoritism in the form of special privileges to favored private actors. This position's underlying logic suggested that a public subsidy to a private corporate actor was just as problematic and indicative of corruption as a redistributive tax. The position therefore put great emphasis on rooting out instances in which special favors were conferred through law, of which special legislation targeting particular localities was a particularly odious species.

For urban reformers of the old conservative disposition, the great cities appeared particularly threatening. These new urban agglomerations seemed to be engaging in unprecedented levels of taxing and spending. Of even greater concern, those taxing and spending decisions often were redolent with the whiff of favoritism for certain private residents. Moreover, the sheer scale of such places seemed at odds with the picture of the private city that the old conservative tradition idealized. What to do about such places, however, was not at all obvious. Staunch advocates of local self-government though they were, the old conservatives had no intention of turning over the reins of power to the political machines that then controlled city centers and that so often drew their ire. At the same time, the old conservative reformers did not believe that one could solve the problems of the cities simply by empowering the state legislature and diminishing opportunities for local self-government. Indeed, the old conservatives were quite suspicious of the corruption that state legislative politics could engender, as their hostility to special legislation reflected. * * *

Finding neither local autonomy nor its opposite attractive, the old conservatives pursued a middle path. They sought to rejigger the city-state legal relationship in a way that would restore the idealized small-scale, low-tax, low-debt, highly privatized (and thus incorruptibly public) ideal of local government that seemed on the verge of being lost forever. It was this aim that underlay their plea for what they called home rule. In this regard, it is not too much to say that "home rule initially developed as a negative response to rising taxes" rather than as a concern that cities were too constrained by a state law regime that construed their sovereign powers narrowly.

So understood, the home rule idea served a purpose—and took a form—nearly the opposite of the one that legal scholars often attribute to it. The standard formulation maintains that the home rule movement overcame the shackles that Dillon's Rule placed on local government initiative—as though that movement's aim was to liberate local governmental autonomy that had been bounded. For the old conservative home rulers, however, Dillon had been right, as a substantive matter, to keep the aims of local power circumscribed. Home rule promised to confine local power to a quasi-private sphere even more effectively than Dillon's rule of strict statutory construction. The purpose of home rule, however, would not simply be to limit local authority. The purpose of home rule would be to enable the city itself to pursue the old conservative governmental vision that state legislative domination had threatened.

To that end, home rule would confer the charter-making power on the city and, in that way, would make it less necessary to enforce strictly the prohibitions against special legislation. At the same time, under the old conservative ideal of home rule, city charters would encompass only those powers that fell within what Dillon had once termed the "usual range." That limit on their scope was rooted in state constitutional provisions that granted home rule only over matters of traditionally "local" concern. Judges could police that boundary in the course of their constructions of the home rule grant. Moreover, state legislators would be barred from taking control of those same powers, on the one hand, or expanding them, on the other. That is because the constitutional provisions that conferred home rule usually required state legislative delegations and preemptions of authority to be "general," and even then some "local" matters likely would be entirely beyond state legislative reach. In addition, state constitutional prohibitions against local taxing and borrowing—prohibitions that old conservative home rulers themselves supported—would confine local action aimed at taxing and spending. * * *

2. Home Rule and the Administrative City.—Other reformers conceived of the urban crisis differently—a view that led them, by century's end, to offer new reasons to find promise in the old analogy between cities and private corporations. These urban reformers also were hostile to the state creature idea and eager for legal reform that would emphasize the responsibility that cities had for their own conditions. In making their case for home rule, however, this set of reformers deployed the corporate analogy that had once pointed back to an image of the incorruptible, segmented private city—run in a fashion designed to serve property owners—to promote an urban future in which expertise and efficiency would shape municipal governance. If the great cities of the day were like private businesses, it was only because they, like modern corporations, should be run by principles of expertise and efficiency rather than by the crass practices of partisan politics. Portraying the city as a kind of private corporation usefully dramatized the apolitical and administrative character of local matters—properly understood—even as it began to challenge some of the privatist premises that had long dominated thinking about the purposes cities were intended to serve.

Here, the home rule idea begins to look more familiar. The defense of home rule points less toward keeping city regulatory power confined, and more toward legitimizing the exercise of the "novel" police powers that Dillon had cast in doubt. This strain of the home rule movement was powerfully influenced by the rise of a new conception of society, and urban life in particular, that broke with many old conservative premises. The conviction that there was a larger social realm beyond one's private life—a realm the teeming city seemed to exemplify—cast doubt on arguments that government in general, and urban government in particular, should be understood as little more than a facilitator of private action.

There was more to this variant of home rule, however, than a simple plea for local freedom from state constraint. New premises about the virtues of administrative forms of governance at all levels informed this "administrative" idea of home rule. The sophisticated argument for home rule that emerged, therefore, once again reflected a complex approach to the effort to "protect" local power. Reformers in search of the administrative city—and a new era of expert, bureaucratic decisionmaking at all levels of government—argued that home rule could be achieved only through a complex mix of state law reforms that would grant local governments some new powers but take away some old ones. This time, the package of grants and limits was not aimed at restoring an idealized remembrance of the frugal private city. Rather, it was aimed at fashioning an as-yet-unrealized administrative city, and a broader program of bureaucratic governance, that could respond—efficiently, expertly, and without corruption—to a fast-changing urban world. * * *

No single city's experience embodies this administrative vision of home rule, but one can grasp its basic premises and underlying logic from the work of Columbia professor Frank Goodnow. * * * Goodnow's somewhat tortured efforts to define local power * * * comprised only half of his argument for the substantive content of his vision of home rule. The other half emphasized the importance of subjecting the local exercise of what he deemed general powers to state administrative (rather than state legislative) oversight. This shift, Goodnow argued, would free the exercise of city powers from state legislative interference. In support of this defense of increased state administrative oversight, Goodnow contended that state legislators lacked the capacity to oversee local action effectively. At most, they would intervene sporadically and without knowing what they should be attempting to accomplish. A regime of special administration, Goodnow therefore concluded, should replace one of special legislation—at least with respect to those matters that were general rather than local. * * *

Importantly, Goodnow and other like-minded urban reformers understood this plea for state administrative oversight—in the form of various administrative boards charged with specialized functions—to be a vital component of, rather than a counterpoint to, their defense of a home rule vision in which cities would assume a range of new responsibilities for improving social life. Such a change would upend a tradition of state legislative tinkering with the exercise of powers by cities and replace it with effective, expert administrative oversight that would, as one representative of this school of urban reform put it, permit "the people of each city to work out their own salvation" and offer "to each the invaluable assistance and advantage of trustworthy knowledge." Subject to administrative rather than legislative oversight, local powers would have a newfound legitimacy. * * *

In this way, Goodnow and urban reformers of a similar mindset broke most directly with the laissez-faire premises of old conservative home rulers. They sought what they called home rule neither to limit governmental power nor to curtail rising taxes, but rather to promote the expansion of governmental power by subjecting it to semi-scientific bureaucratic control. On this idea of home rule, state delegations of general powers to local actors would no longer open the city to all manner of state legislative intervention. Instead, they would bring about expert, state administrative oversight of those particular functions. As a result, urban reformers, fearful of corrupt local machines, would welcome those delegations. For many, home rule and state administrative control went hand in hand, notwithstanding the seeming control that the latter wrested from local actors. As Woodrow Wilson explained: "In urging a perfect organization of public administration I have said not a word in favor of making all administration centered in Washington. I have spoken of giving new life to local organisms, of reorganizing decentralization." * * *

3.   Home Rule and the Social City.—A still more politically radical group of municipal reformers was not content to treat the city as if it were a private corporation properly managed by its stockholders. Nor were these reformers interested, as Goodnow was, in reconceiving the city as an essentially administrative, apolitical unit to be overseen by equally expert state administrative actors. Instead, they saw home rule as a way to challenge more directly the culture of privatism that long had defined urban ambitions and the understanding of legitimate governmental power embedded within it. They reached out for the social city toward which Goodnow only gestured, a place marked by collective action and the ineluctable interdependencies of living cheek by jowl in a growing community.

These reformers predicated their defense of home rule on a description of city power as public and political, rather than as quasi-private or administrative. The benefits of home rule were to be found in the political effect of arousing a public realm too long dominated by private power, rather than in the promotion of administrative or businesslike efficiency. This new vision resulted in proposals to include the power to establish tax policy and to bring about the municipalization of formerly private activities—from the provision of transportation to the design and planning of land uses—within the domain of legitimate local action.

The advocates of the social city agreed that the task at hand was just as Goodnow had identified it—to rethink the city's position within a broader state law structure so that local power could be directed toward useful, rather than destructive, ends—and they were not above praising his efforts to redefine state-local relations. Their underlying urban vision, however, contained crucial distinctions, even if only in their points of emphasis. They sought to defend the novel uses to which local power would have to be put if the social city were to be realized—and to emphasize the public, political element of city power to achieve that end. And they gave less weight to Goodnow's concerns that such expansions of local power would blend "administration" and "politics" in dangerous ways. For these reasons, advocates of the social city felt obliged to answer a charge that earlier variants of home rule were less likely to engender. That charge was socialism.

Bold as this new call for home rule was, it too contemplated significant limits on local power: home rule referred to a substantive proposal regarding city power rather than a deep commitment to local autonomy. Like their predecessors, these reformers did not subscribe to the conventional present-day conception of home rule. They opposed an idea of home rule that would empower private actors to control local utilities or to promote the creation of suburban enclaves, the very point of which was to keep taxes low and public works projects minimal. Insofar as state law operated to promote such a privatized vision of local power, they sought to change it, even if such changes took the form of what might seem to the modern observer to be little more than limits on home rule. Within this home rule program, such limits were better understood as necessary preconditions for the city's realization of its full potential as a social institution. Simply put, these home rulers did not seek to design a system that would promote local choice for its own sake. Indeed, to a significant extent, their outlook was frankly national in scope. Through creation of a "city sense," they aimed to overcome a national bias in favor of laissez-faire policy and thus to promote a more social outlook at all levels of the governmental structure. * * *

McCRORY CORPORATION V. FOWLER

Court of Appeals of Maryland, 1990.
319 Md. 12, 570 A.2d 834.

ELDRIDGE, JUDGE.

Pursuant to the Maryland Uniform Certification of Questions of Law Act, the United States District Court for the District of Maryland has certified to this Court the following * * * [question] concerning a Montgomery County ordinance:

> "(1) Did enactment of Section 27–20(a) of the Montgomery County Code, which creates a private cause of action for employment discrimination entitling a claimant to sue for damages, injunctive or other civil relief, exceed the authority delegated to chartered home rule counties * * *?"

* * * Robert Fowler, a white male, managed a store for McCrory Corporation. Fowler alleged that one of McCrory's managers told him not to hire any more black persons or persons under thirty-five years of age, and that when Fowler requested McCrory executives to repudiate this directive, they refused to do so. Thereafter, Fowler claimed, he was harassed and eventually constructively discharged in retaliation for his protest. Fowler brought an action for money damages against McCrory in the Circuit Court for Montgomery County * * *. At McCrory's request, the case was removed to the United States District Court for the District of Maryland. Fowler filed an amended complaint in the United States District Court, * * * adding a count under § 27–20(a) of the Montgomery County Code * * *. Section 27–20(a) * * * [provides]:

> "Any person who has been subjected to any act of discrimination prohibited under this division shall be deemed to have been denied a civil right and shall be entitled to sue for damages, injunction or other civil relief, including reasonable attorney's fees * * *."

Montgomery County has chartered home rule under Article XI–A of the Maryland Constitution. Article XI–A * * * known as the Home Rule Amendment, enabled counties, which chose to adopt a home rule charter, to achieve a significant degree of political self-determination. * * * Section 3 of Article XI–A provides (emphasis supplied):

> "From and after the adoption of a charter by the City of Baltimore, or any County of this State, as hereinbefore provided, the Mayor of Baltimore and City Council of the City of Baltimore or the County Council of said County, subject to the Constitution and Public General Laws of this State, shall have full power to enact *local laws* of said city, or county * * * upon all matters covered by the express powers granted as above provided * * *."

Article XI–A "does not constitute a grant of absolute autonomy to local governments." *Ritchmount Partnership v. Board*, 283 Md. 48, 56, 388 A.2d 523, 529 (1978). This Court's decisions and the above-quoted passage make it clear that the Home Rule Amendment limits the Montgomery County Council to enacting "local laws" * * *.

Thus, it is first necessary to determine whether § 27–20(a) of the Montgomery County Code is a "local law." * * * In *Steimel v. Board*, 278 Md. 1, 5, 357 A.2d 386, 388 (1976), we stated that a local law "in subject matter and substance" is "confined in its operation to prescribed territorial limits * * *." A general law, on the other hand, " 'deals with the general public welfare, a subject which is of significant interest not just to any one county, but rather to more than one geographical subdivision, or even to the entire state.' " * * *

Section 27–20(a) of the Montgomery County Code authorizes a private citizen to seek redress for another private citizen's violation of a county anti-employment discrimination ordinance by instituting a judicial action in the courts of the State for, *inter alia*, unlimited money damages. Fowler, for example, is seeking over $1.8 million. * * * In creating a new judicial cause of action between private individuals, § 27–20(a) encroaches upon an area which heretofore had been the province of state agencies. In Maryland, the creation of new causes of action in the courts has traditionally been done either by the General Assembly or by this Court under its authority to modify the common law of this State. Furthermore, the creation of new judicial remedies has traditionally been done on a statewide basis.

Abusive employment practices constitute a statewide problem which has been addressed by the General Assembly in Article 49B of the Maryland Code * * *. It is true that the field has not been preempted by the State, and that home rule counties have concurrent authority to provide administrative remedies not in conflict with state law. Nevertheless, creating a remedy which has traditionally been the sole province of the General Assembly and the Court of Appeals, to combat a statewide problem such as employment discrimination, goes beyond a "matter[ ] of purely local concern." [T]he Montgomery County Code affects "matters of significant interest to the entire state" and cannot qualify as a "local law" under Article XI–A.

A contrary holding would open the door for counties to enact a variety of laws in areas which have heretofore been viewed as the exclusive province of the General Assembly and the Court of Appeals. For example, could a county ordinance authorize in the circuit court and the District Court negligence actions in which contributory negligence would not be a bar? Could a county ordinance provide for breach of contract suits upon "contracts" not supported by consideration, or where the parol evidence rule is inapplicable? We believe that the answer is "no." These, and many other legal doctrines, are matters of significant interest to the entire State, calling for uniform application in state courts. They are not proper subject matters for "local laws."

Chief Judge Cardozo recognized that certain areas of the law are matters of statewide concern when he wrote about a city home rule provision in New York's Constitution (*Adler v. Deegan*, 251 N.Y. 467, 167 N.E. 705, 713 (1929) (Cardozo, C.J., concurring)):

Cardozo on Home Rule

> "In every case, 'it is necessary to inquire whether a proposed subject of legislation is a matter of State concern or of local concern.' * * * There are * * * affairs exclusively those of the state, such as the law of domestic relations, of wills, of inheritance, of contracts, of crimes not essentially local * * *, the organization of courts, the procedure therein. None of these things can be said to touch the affairs that a city is organized to regulate, whether we have reference to history or to tradition or to existing forms of charters." * * *

Our holding today is in accord with the position taken in 6 McQuillin, *Municipal Corporations* (3rd Ed.Rev.), § 22.01:

> "The well-established general rule is that a municipal corporation cannot create by ordinance a right of action between third persons or enlarge the common law or statutory duty or liability of citizens among themselves. Under the rule, an ordinance cannot directly create a civil liability of one citizen to another or relieve one citizen from liability by imposing it on another." * * *

We hold, therefore, that an ordinance attempting to combat employment discrimination by creating a new private judicial cause of action is not a "local law" under Article XI–A of the Maryland Constitution, and thus is not within the power of Montgomery County to enact. * * *

GARY SCHWARTZ, THE LOGIC OF HOME RULE AND THE PRIVATE LAW EXCEPTION

20 U.C.L.A. L. Rev. 670, 687–690, 750–756 (1973).

While "private law" is a term employed by lawyers in several very different senses, the suggested home rule private law exception clearly is intended to refer to private law in the rough sense that contracts, property, and torts are private law. With these as examples of private law, we can formulate the following working definition: Private law consists of the substantive law which establishes legal rights and duties between and among private entities, law that takes effect in lawsuits brought by one private entity against another. The complement of private law is thus "public law"—the substantive law defining the legal obligations of private individuals or entities to the government, and also establishing their liberties and opportunities in relation to the government. * * *

While the definition here advanced is understood as conforming to what lawyers generally mean by "private law," it appears that at least some lawyers, somewhat contrary to the definition, may be inclined to block off entire subject matter areas—for example, corporations law, sales law—as innately "private law." * * * [O]ne need only consult the first and still the foremost book-length treatment of home rule, Professor McBain's *The Law and Practice of Home Rule,* published in 1916. In this volume, after 672 pages influenced by a general sympathy for a generous interpretation of home rule, the following passage rather abruptly appears:

> By common understanding such general subjects as * * * domestic relations, wills and administration, mortgages, trusts, contracts, real and personal property, insurance, banking, corporations, and many others have never been regarded by any one, least of all by the cities themselves, as appropriate subjects of local control. No city has been so foolhardy as to venture generally into any one of these fields of law. It has simply been universally accepted that these matters are strictly of "state concern."

A leading contemporary law review assessment of home rule authority, published almost half a century after McBain, includes an affirmation of this "common understanding." Since its "many others" element can presumably be supplied with meaning only if a content common to the specifically enumerated elements can be clarified, this Article will speak of the "McBain nine," those nine legal subjects preceding the "many others" finale. * * *

The home rule literature has noted the useful if obvious point that cities are subject to * * * [the Commerce] clause in the sense that if a state statute is invalid as an "undue burden" on interstate commerce, a city ordinance containing the same requirements would be equally invalid. What has not so far received scholarly attention is the intriguing possibility that a burden on interstate commerce which is constitutionally "due" if imposed by a state can become "undue" if its source is a city, by virtue of the fact that the greater number and proximity of cities (as compared to states) signifies that the burden in the latter situation will be far more onerous. * * * To look back at the McBain nine * * *, it can now be said that certain city enactments covered by the nine might well be precluded in their application to intercity entities by federal commerce clause principles or their state counterparts. * * * Granted, home rule must generally be willing to live with substantial non-uniformity. Nevertheless * * * a home rule authority exception is appropriate and even necessary if there are serious disadvantages to home rule in application and if these disadvantages are convincingly shown to be in excess of the relevant home rule benefits; and there is ultimately no satisfying reason why extreme inefficiency should not be treated like any other functional disadvantage of city lawmaking for exception purposes. * * *

If the conclusion thus is that undue burden and extreme inefficiency do function as predicates for home rule exceptions, it is important to note that the private law component of a city ordinance will often significantly add to the overall magnitude of its burden or the extent of its inefficiency. The reason for this goes back to the fact noted earlier that because of the poor accessibility of city legal documents, the chances of inadvertent and excusable error in the ascertainment of city law are quite high. This fact standing alone applies, of course, to city public and private law alike; but the additional point is that with private law, far more than with public law, the consequences of accidental and minor violations can be enormous. Assume a major private arrangement on which many parties have heavily relied. It is bad enough if one party's innocent misperception of city law leads to a modest public fine; it is something else if this innocent misperception causes the entire arrangement to disastrously collapse. Under a system of city private law, a testator's intentions in disposing of his wealth could be negated by his lawyer's excusable city law mistake, a lender could find that all his mortgages are worthless because of an inadvertent and technical violation of a city ordinance, and so on. * * *

Courts are well suited, and legislatures rather poorly suited, to render low-level determinations that address themselves to the local interests involved in and the inefficiencies produced by particular local ordinances * * *. But if we desire generic determinations which concern themselves with entire legal subjects (for example, the law of contracts), the legislature would be the more appropriate institution to turn to. * * * As a way of testing out the generic approach, we can briefly look back upon the McBain nine. Inevitably, the extent of statutory suppression within the nine renders the home rule authority issues so hypothetical that meaningful comment, while not impossible, is difficult. Especially in these circumstances, it would be unduly ambitious to deal with each of the nine, but I will venture to comment on at least a few; even these comments will concededly be somewhat sketchy and summary. "Corporations" law seems generally lacking in characterization difficulties, and one can imagine relatively few city corporations ordinances that would advance legitimate city interests without entailing unacceptable inefficiencies; therefore, the legislature—or a court, if a proper case arises—should declare corporations law beyond home rule authority. Similar thinking suggests the appropriateness of "wills" and "trusts" exceptions; that these subjects almost always entail private law magnifies, for reasons indicated above, the potential inefficiency of city lawmaking. On the other hand, "contract" law and "real property" law

except to home rule

exceptions would lead to significant characterization problems, and as home rule exceptions they would be significantly over-inclusive. One does not know, for example, whether landlord-tenant law sounds in "contract" or in "real property" or in both; whichever, it does not seem that the local interests furthered by city landlord-tenant lawmaking are plainly inferior to the resulting inefficiencies. Therefore a tentative judgment is that neither a categorical "contracts" exception nor a categorical "real property" exception would be a good idea; however, in light of the convincingly strong public interest against uncertainties ("clouds") in real property title, an exception limited to the law of title is warranted. For similar reasons, a full "domestic relations" exception would be inappropriate, but at least a "marital status" exception is probably justifiable. * * * As for the fair housing, cooling-off-period, landlord-tenant, rental-car liability, and comparative negligence ordinances, it is hardly clear that their inefficiencies exceed the benefits of local lawmaking, and therefore a particular approach would not place them within the extreme inefficiency exception. * * *

MARSHAL HOUSE, INC. V. RENT REVIEW AND GRIEVANCE BOARD OF BROOKLINE

Supreme Judicial Court of Massachusetts, 1970.
357 Mass. 709, 260 N.E.2d 200.

CUTTER, JUSTICE.

The plaintiff (Marshal House) owns more than ten units of housing accommodations in Brookline. It seeks declaratory relief against the board and the town concerning art. XXV (the by-law) of the Brookline by-laws, entitled "Unfair and Unreasonable Rental Practices in Housing Accommodations." * * * The * * * by-law * * * recites "that a serious public emergency exists with respect to the housing of * * * citizens of the town due to a substantial shortage of low and moderate income rental accommodations * * * [and that unless the town] is empowered to * * * order that the landlord not * * * receive rent * * * in excess of an amount which * * * [a rent review and grievance board] shall determine to be fair and reasonable under the circumstances, such emergency * * * will produce serious threats to the public health, safety and general welfare of the citizens of the town." * * *

The principal contentions of the town and the board are (a) that the town has been given by art. 89, § 6, of the Amendments to the Constitution of the Commonwealth very broad legislative power, subject only to the Legislature's power to supersede local legislation by general laws; (b) that these powers under § 6 include the power to adopt a rent control by-law without further authorization (by the Legislature or otherwise) than is found in § 6; and (c) that nothing in art. 89, § 7, so limits the power granted to the town by § 6 as to preclude the adoption of the by-law or to impair its validity. * * *

We quote (emphasis supplied) pertinent portions of art. 89. Section 1 provides, in part, "It is the intention of this article to reaffirm the * * * traditional liberties of the people with respect to the *conduct of their local government,* and to grant and confirm to the people of every * * * town the right of self-government *in local matters,* subject to the provisions of this article and to such standards and requirements as the general court may establish by law in accordance with the provisions of this article." Section 6 contains a broad grant of powers to cities and towns, "Any * * * town may, by the adoption * * * of local * * * by-laws, exercise any power * * * which the general court has power to confer upon it, *which is not inconsistent with the constitution* or laws enacted by the general court in conformity with powers reserved to the general court by section eight, and which is not denied * * * to the * * * town by its charter * * *." The powers, which at first glance seem to be granted by § 6, are limited substantially by § 7, which reads "Nothing in this article [89] shall be deemed to grant to any * * * town the power to (1) regulate elections * * *; (2) to levy * * * taxes; (3) to borrow money or pledge the credit of the * * * town; (4) to dispose of park land; (5) *to enact private or civil law governing civil relationships except as an incident to an exercise of an independent municipal power;* or (6) to define and provide for the punishment of a felony or to impose imprisonment as a punishment for any violation of law; provided, however, that the *foregoing enumerated powers may be granted by the general court* in conformity with the constitution and with the powers reserved to the general court by section eight * * *." * * * No contention appears to be made that there is any basis of authority other than art. 89, § 6, for the town's action in enacting the by-law.

Ambiguity exists concerning the meaning of the italicized language in § 7(5). * * * This court * * * is faced with interpreting novel and very general language concerning which there exist only inconclusive indications concerning the intentions of the draftsmen. * * * We recognized in *Answer of the Justices,* 250 N.E.2d 450, 452–453, that the language of "§ 6 * * * standing by itself, is broad enough to authorize a * * * [town] to enact a rent control * * * by-law. The limitation in § 7(5) simultaneously withholds part of the authority prima facie conferred by § 6 * * *." So far as § 7 removes specified subjects from the scope of municipal legislative action, the several exclusions must be interpreted broadly enough to accomplish their purposes. * * * The term "private or civil law governing civil relationships" is broad enough to include law controlling ordinary and usual relationships between landlords and tenants. The language is not so confined as clearly to apply only to general legislation like the Uniform Commercial Code, or the laws governing marriage or intestate succession to property.

The town contends that the "by-law is a public law governing the economic relationship between landlords and tenants, not a private [or civil] law governing civil relationships." It also is argued that it is "in substance a temporary substitute for market forces * * * distorted by unusual conditions," rendering unreliable the usual process of determining "the amount of rent for an apartment * * * by bargaining between the landlord and [the] tenant." * * * [A]lthough we assume the purpose of thus affecting the landlord-tenant relationship to be public, the method adopted is primarily civil in that it affords to the board power in effect to remake, in important respects, the parties' contract creating a tenancy. * * * The question for decision is a relatively narrow one of applying art. 89, § 7(5), in a particular situation. Does the by-law so directly affect the landlord-tenant relationship, otherwise than "as an incident to an exercise of an independent municipal power," as to come within § 7(5)? * * *

It is suggested that rent control is, in its nature, a purely local function and that, therefore, a town by-law, even though it directly affects a principal aspect of the landlord-tenant relationship, is incident to an exercise of an independent municipal power. Doubtless, under art. 89, § 6, a town possesses (subject to applicable constitutional provisions and legislation) broad powers to adopt by-laws for the protection of the public health, morals, safety, and general welfare, of a type often referred to as the "police" power. We assume that these broad powers would permit adopting a by-law requiring landlords (so far as legislation does not control the matter) to take particular precautions to protect tenants against injury from fire, badly lighted common passageways, and similar hazards. Such by-laws, although affecting the circumstances of a tenancy, would do so (more clearly than in the case of the present by-law) as an incident to the exercising of a particular aspect of the police power.

Rent control, in a general sense, is for the purpose of providing shelter at reasonable cost for members of the public, a matter comprised within the broad concept of the public welfare. Rent control, however, is also an objective in itself designed to keep rents at reasonable levels. Is the attempt to achieve this objective to be viewed as merely incident to the exercise of the whole range of the police power, or does art. 89, § 7(5), imply that the separate components of the police power are to be considered individually in determining whether the exercise of one of them enacts "civil law governing civil relationships except as an incident to an exercise of an independent municipal power"? The quoted vague language points, in our opinion, to viewing separately the various component powers making up the broad police power, with the consequence that a municipal civil law regulating a civil relationship is permissible (without prior legislative authorization) only as an incident to the exercise of some independent, individual component of the municipal police power. To construe § 7(5) otherwise might give it a very narrow range of application.

We conclude that it would be, in effect, a contradiction (or circuitous) to say that a by-law, the principal objective and consequence of which is to control rent payments, is also merely incidental to the exercise of an independent municipal power to control rents. We perceive no component of the general municipal police power, other than the regulation of rents itself, to which such regulation fairly could be said to be incidental. * * * [W]e hold that § 7(5) prevents the adoption of local rent control by-laws in the absence of an explicit delegation to municipalities by the Legislature of power to engage in such regulation of the landlord-tenant relationship. * * *

NEW MEXICANS FOR FREE ENTERPRISE V. CITY OF SANTA FE

Court of Appeals of New Mexico, 2005.
138 N.M. 785, 126 P.3d 1149.

FRY, JUDGE.

Plaintiffs New Mexicans for Free Enterprise, the Santa Fe Chamber of Commerce, and several local business owners challenge an ordinance enacted by the City of Santa Fe mandating certain city-based businesses to pay a minimum wage higher than the current state and federal minimum hourly wage. Plaintiffs contend that the ordinance is beyond the power of a home rule municipality to enact and that the state minimum wage law preempts local policymaking in this area. * * * We conclude that a home rule municipality may set a minimum wage higher than that required by the state Minimum Wage Act because of the independent powers possessed by municipalities in New Mexico and the absence of any conflict with state law. * * *

The ordinance as amended requires for-profit businesses or non-profit entities that are registered or licensed in Santa Fe and that employ twenty-five or more workers (either full-time or part-time) to pay a minimum hourly wage of $8.50. This wage increases to $9.50 in 2006 and to $10.50 in 2008; thereafter, the hourly wage is to be increased in tandem with increases in the Consumer Price Index. * * * In passing the amendments to the ordinance, the council issued legislative findings, including a finding that many workers in Santa Fe earn wages insufficient to support themselves and their families and that the community bore the burden when workers could not meet basic needs such as housing, food, shelter, and health care. The council also found that the cost of living in Santa Fe is 18 percent higher than the national average, while average earnings in Santa Fe are 23 percent below the national average. * * * The City, which is a home rule municipality, recited two bases for the authority to pass the ordinance: (1) the powers given to home rule municipalities by the section of our constitution which we will refer to as the "home rule amendment," N.M. Const. art. X, § 6; and (2) the police and general welfare powers delegated by the legislature to all municipalities by NMSA 1978. * * *

[W]e turn * * * to a more detailed examination of the authority granted by the home rule amendment and the limitations on that authority. * * *

The home rule amendment, in pertinent part, states:

> D.   A municipality which adopts a charter may exercise all legislative powers and perform all functions not expressly denied by general law or charter. This grant of powers shall not include the power to enact private or civil laws governing civil relationships except as incident to the exercise of an independent municipal power.

> E.   The purpose of this section is to provide for maximum local self-government. A liberal construction shall be given to the powers of municipalities.

N.M. Const. art. X, § 6(D), (E) * * *

Plaintiffs contend that the ordinance is a private or civil law governing the civil relationship of employer and employee because it "seeks to establish legal duties between private businesses and their private employees, and it establishes a new cause of action against private businesses that do not pay the wage." We agree. While there are no bright-line divisions between public law and private law, private law has been defined as consisting "of the substantive law which establishes legal rights and duties between and among private entities, law that takes effect in lawsuits brought by one private entity against another." Gary T. Schwartz, *The Logic of Home Rule and the Private Law Exception*, 20 UCLA L. Rev. 671, 688. That definition certainly applies to the ordinance, which sets a mandatory minimum wage term for labor contracts between private parties that the employee may enforce by bringing a civil action against the employer. The fact that the city administrator may punish violation of the ordinance as a misdemeanor does not convert the ordinance into "public law" nor does it alter the basic nature of the ordinance, which is to set and enforce a key contract term between private parties. *See Marshal House, Inc. v. Rent Review & Grievance Bd. of Brookline, 357 Mass. 709, 260 N.E.2d 200, 206 (Mass. 1970)* (noting that public enforcement is not dispositive of the private law nature of an ordinance). The relationship between private employer and employee has been described as a civil relationship because it is governed by the civil law of contracts. We conclude that the ordinance is a private or civil law governing civil relationships within the meaning of the home rule amendment. * * *

Although the ordinance is a private law, nonetheless the home rule amendment permits a municipality to enact such a law if it is "incident to the exercise of an independent municipal power." N.M. Const. art. X, § 6(D). Both commentators and courts have noted the ambiguity of this independent power exemption. * * * [T]he Massachusetts Supreme Judicial Court held in *Marshal House, Inc.* that for an ordinance to fall within the independent power exemption, a municipality must point to an "individual component of the municipal police power" that provides it authority to act; otherwise, the private law exception might have "a very narrow range of application." * * * Plaintiffs urge us to follow *Marshal House, Inc.* by requiring that the City point to an "individual component" of its police power providing the power to pass the ordinance. We decline to adopt the reasoning in *Marshal House, Inc.* for two reasons. First, the court in that case provided a specious answer to the question "What is the object of the regulation?" by concluding the object was "to control rent payments." There, the stated "principal objective" of the municipality was not to control rent payments as an end itself, but to provide for the general health and welfare of residents by providing sufficient affordable housing. Second, because New Mexico municipalities have been delegated a generic police and general welfare power, we think that forcing a municipality to point to an "individual component" of its police power puts an unduly restrictive gloss on the exemption and reads words into the home rule amendment that are not there.

The exemption refers to an "independent municipal power," which we conclude means any power other than home rule. There is no indication in the phrase "independent municipal power" that such a power must be in some way particularized or tailored; as long as there is a power granted by the legislature that is independent from home rule power, that is enough. We take the view that as long as a municipality can point to a power that the legislature has delegated to it, and the regulation of the civil relationship is reasonably incident to, and clearly authorized by that power, the exemption can apply.

The only additional limitation on a municipality's power, which we have gleaned from the commentators, is the need for uniformity that informs any consideration of the private law exception and independent powers exemption. *See* Howard McBain, *The Law and the Practice of Municipal Home Rule* (1916) 673; Schwartz, *supra*, at 720–47. Given this concern for uniformity, we conclude there are two prerequisites to a municipality's regulation of a civil relationship. Where a municipality has been given powers by the legislature to deal with the challenges it faces, those may be sufficiently independent municipal powers to allow regulation of a civil relationship as long as (1) the regulation of the civil relationship is reasonably "incident to" a public purpose that is clearly within the delegated power, and (2) the law in question does not implicate serious concerns about non-uniformity in the law. This rule allows a home rule municipality to regulate a civil relationship as far as necessary within its delegated powers to address local public concerns, while preventing the harm at which the private law exception is primarily aimed. This rule is also sufficiently flexible to allow a fact-intensive evaluation of any given municipal action by balancing the municipality's pursuit of the public interest to address local issues against the need for stability and uniformity in the law across the state. * * *

In light of this holding, we apply the rule and evaluate (1) whether the ordinance's regulation of the civil relationship is reasonably "incident to" a public purpose that is clearly within the legislature's delegation of specific, independent powers, and (2) whether the ordinance implicates serious concerns about non-uniformity in the law. With respect to public purpose within a municipality's delegated powers, the legislature has given all municipalities the power to provide for the general welfare of their residents by the general welfare clause in Section 3–17–1(B). * * * The connection between wages and the general welfare of workers is well established in American jurisprudence and is clearly within the police power of a state to regulate. * * * Given this authority, we conclude that setting a minimum wage is unquestionably a public purpose and that such legislation is within the police and general welfare power of a New Mexico municipality. * * *

The object of this legislation is not to regulate private wages as an end in itself or to set comprehensive "reasonable wages" in the City, but rather to provide for the general welfare of workers and taxpayers in the City. * * * The ordinance is analogous to many types of other health and safety ordinances that may impact private and civil relationships, but which are aimed at the health, welfare, or safety of renters, workers, or consumers. *See, e.g.,* Santa Fe, N.M., Environmental Regulations: Prohibition of Smoking ID Places of Employment ch. X, § 6.6 (1999) (mandating that private employers in the city provide a smoke-free workplace); Santa Fe, N.M., Fair Housing: Discrimination in Sales or Rental of Housing ch. VII, § 14.8 (1999) (prohibiting discrimination in the sale or rental of private housing within the city); Santa Fe, N.M., Environmental Regulations: Premises to be Free from Litter and Refuse ch. X, § 1.14 (requiring private property owners to keep their premises free of litter and refuse).

We now turn to the second prong of the rule permitting regulation of a civil relationship and consider whether the ordinance seriously implicates concerns about non-uniformity. * * * The nature of the ordinance is central in determining whether it implicates serious concerns about non-uniformity. For example, substantial disorder and confusion would result if the City rejected the Uniform Commercial Code, adopted a contributory negligence regime, or if it imposed heightened burdens on corporate boards of directors for companies doing business in the City. Leaving aside potential conflicts with state law (which will often bar such local laws), these types of private or civil law changes would frustrate and confuse even the most diligent consumer, businessperson, or lawyer. Those contracting with city parties, corporations doing business there, or those injured by tortfeasors in the City would have little reason to know of these special rules and each would cause notice, compliance, and choice of law issues. Our task is to determine whether such issues are so pervasive that the ordinance disrupts or confuses New Mexico law.

Here, the ordinance does not raise serious concerns about non-uniformity in the way that any of the prior examples would. Any concerns about inefficiency in terms of high notice and compliance costs are allayed by the limited application of the ordinance—it applies only to employers who are registered or licensed in the City. * * * [T]he burden on a regional or national business of discovering and applying a higher wage for city workers is modest at most. * * * Thus, the ordinance does not implicate any serious concerns about generating non-uniformity in New Mexico law. * * *

Deciding that the City has the authority to enact a minimum wage regulation under the home rule amendment is not the end of the inquiry; we must finally determine whether the ordinance is inconsistent with state law. * * * The Minimum Wage Act sets a minimum hourly wage, prohibiting the payment of wages below $5.15 per hour. The Minimum Wage Act does not "permit" only its rate, and it does not establish any type of comprehensive wage scheme or express any need for uniformity. The City's ordinance does not allow an employer to pay less than this minimum but requires wages to be higher than this minimum. We view the Minimum Wage Act as setting only a wage floor that does not bar higher local minimum wage rates. Thus, the ordinance is merely complementary to the Minimum Wage Act and is not antagonistic toward the Minimum Wage Act's policy of ensuring that all workers are paid a minimum of $5.15 per hour. Because we find that the ordinance is not in conflict with the Minimum Wage Act, under Section 3–17–1, the ordinance is not inconsistent with state law and is permitted. The legislature remains the ultimate check on home rule municipal policymaking when a subject is one of statewide concern. The legislature clearly knows how to preempt local lawmaking when it wants to do so. Minimum wage policymaking is within the scope of municipal power unless the legislature clearly intends to remove it or when there is a conflict between an ordinance and general state law. * * *

5. HOME RULE AS A PROTECTION AGAINST STATE POWER

Given the plenary nature of state power over cities as described in Hunter v. Pittsburgh, the autonomy of cities from states, to the extent it exists at all, depends on state law.[9] There are, in fact, a wide variety of state law provisions designed to create some degree of protection from state control for city decision making. In this book, we examine only two such provisions: prohibitions against special legislation, which we covered in subsection 2, and protection of home rule immunity, which we cover in this section.

As the following materials demonstrate, before cities can be given home rule immunity, a way has to be found to distinguish those city actions that are subject to state regulation from those that can be allocated to a sphere of local autonomy. States plainly have power to bar *some* kinds of city activity. A variety of ways of dividing decision making power between centralized and decentralized governments have been adopted by state courts. Notice that the discussion of the problem in the cases below is bound up with questions of institutional role. Aside from the question of which activities should be reserved to exclusive local control, there is the question of who should decide (the courts or the legislature, the city or the state) which activities are of exclusive local concern and which are not.

The first two cases—New Orleans Campaign for a Living Wage v. City of New Orleans and Town of Telluride v. Lot 34 Venture—address the scope of home rule immunity that cities enjoy in the face of state legislative acts that divest them of powers that it is not clear the cities would possess pursuant to their home rule initiatory power. *New Orleans Campaign for a Living Wage* revisits the issue addressed in *New Mexicans for Free Enterprise*: the extent of city authority to pass living wage laws. There is a debate between the two cases (and within the *New Orleans* case) over the city's power of initiative. But do they disagree on whether the city has home rule autonomy over the issue? The next case also raises questions about cities' power of home rule initiative. Do cities with home rule power have the authority, even in the absence of preemptive legislation, to adopt local ordinances that attach conditions to residential real estate development in order to promote affordable housing (as in *Telluride*)? How important are the doubts about the

---

[9] It should be noted that some federal constitutional restraints have been imposed on states' ability to control cities notwithstanding Hunter v. Pittsburgh. For example, the states' ability to draw city boundaries has been limited by the Fifteenth Amendment's prohibition on discrimination against voting on the basis of race. Gomillion v. Lightfoot, 364 U.S. 339, 81 S.Ct. 125, 5 L.Ed.2d 110 (1960). Other federal constitutional restrictions on state power, based on the Fourteenth Amendment, are covered below in Chapter 4. None of these federal constitutional restrictions on state power, however, enable cities to engage in self-government in a manner immune from state control.

existence of home rule initiatory power to the outcome of these cases concerning home rule immunity?

The final two cases, Webb v. City of Black Hawk and City of Tucson v. State of Arizona, consider the scope of home rule immunity in the face of state legislative acts that divest them of authority they do possess pursuant to their home rule initiatory power. What are the differences in the approach to the problem that the opinions take? What is the relationship between the effort to specify the scope of home rule autonomy for cities and the attempt to find an area of individual autonomy not subject to state control in the right of property (as in Lochner v. New York, 198 U.S. 45, 25 S.Ct. 539, 49 L.Ed. 937 (1905))[10] or the right of privacy (as in Roe v. Wade, 410 U.S. 113, 93 S.Ct. 705, 35 L.Ed.2d 147 (1973))? More fundamentally, how should one define the area of city autonomy that should be immune from state control? Should there be *any* such area of autonomy? The cases excerpted below concern local efforts to regulate employers and land use, and to control local traffic and local elections. Is it possible to distinguish among these powers in defining the scope of home rule immunity? If so, what distinction would you draw?[11]

NEW ORLEANS CAMPAIGN FOR A LIVING WAGE V. CITY OF NEW ORLEANS

Supreme Court of Louisiana, 2002.
825 So.2d 1098.

JUSTICE KIMBALL. * * *

Effective August 15, 1997, Act 317 of 1997 prohibits local governmental subdivisions from establishing a minimum wage rate which a private employer would be required to pay employees. In passing this Act, which became *La. R.S. 23:642*, the [state] legislature found that in order for Louisiana businesses to remain competitive and to attract and retain the highest caliber of employees, and thereby to remain sound, a

---

[10] In State Building and Construction Trades Council of California v. City of Vista, 279 P.3d 1022 (2012), the Supreme Court of California held that a home rule city's decision not to require its contractors to pay the state's prevailing wage was a "municipal affair," rather than a matter of state-wide concern and, therefore, exempt from the state's requirement that prevailing wages be paid to employees of city contractors. "Autonomy with regard to the expenditures of public funds," the court said, "lies at the heart of what it means to be an independent governmental entity." The dissent likened this position to the *Lochner* decision, "in which the high court extolled the virtues of the freedom to contract over nearly all other freedoms." "Every government * * * has an interest in conserving public funds," the dissent continued. If this desire were sufficient, "no state law could ever prevail over local desires, for all conflicting state laws have the potential to increase a city's costs."

[11] For an extended analysis of this issue, see Gordon Clark, Judges and the Cities (1985). See also John Martinez, Local Government Law, Chapter 4 (2nd ed. 2012–13); Michael Libonati, Reconstructing Local Government, 19 The Urban Lawyer 645 (1987); Michael Libonati, Do Local Governments Have Rights?, 10 Urban, State and Local Law Newsletter 1 (1987); and the references cited in Chapter Two, Section A 3, above.

business must work in an environment of uniform minimum wage rates. The legislature further found that local variation in mandated minimum wages would lead to economic instability and decline and to a decrease in the standard of living for Louisiana's citizens.

In September 2001, the New Orleans City Council passed Ordinance No. 20376, an ordinance placing on the ballot for vote by the electorate of New Orleans a proposal to add a new Chapter 5 to Article IX of the home rule charter of the City of New Orleans (the "City"). The proposed Charter Amendment (the "minimum wage law") establishes a minimum wage to be paid to employees performing work in the City of New Orleans of $6.15 per hour, or $1.00 above the prevailing federal minimum wage, whichever is greater. * * * On Saturday, February 2, 2002, New Orleans voters approved the proposed Charter Amendment. The following day, Sunday, February 3, 2002, the New Orleans Campaign for a Living Wage, joined by two individuals, Jean Matthews and Philomenia Johnson (collectively the "Proponents"), instituted a declaratory judgment proceeding against the City, its mayor and City Council, and the State of Louisiana, seeking a declaration of the validity of the City's new minimum wage law. In addition, petitioners sought a declaration that *La. R.S. 23:642*, the state law that prohibits local governmental subdivisions from establishing a minimum wage, is unconstitutional as applied to the City of New Orleans, a pre 1974 home rule charter city. * * *

Local governmental autonomy or home rule exists only to the extent that the state constitution endows a local governmental entity with two interactive powers: the power to initiate local legislation and the power of immunity from control by the state legislature. *City of New Orleans v. Board of Comm'rs of Orleans Levee Dist.*, 640 So.2d 237, 242 [1994]. * * * *Article VI, § 4 of the 1974 Louisiana Constitution* grants the City both the power of initiation and the power of immunity. * * * Thus, although "home rule" does not entail complete autonomy, "in affairs of local concern, a home rule charter government possesses 'powers which within its jurisdiction are as broad as that of the state, except when limited by the constitution, laws permitted by the constitution, or its own home rule charter.'" *Smith & Wesson Corp.* 785 So.2d at 14. *Article VI* also serves to foster local self-government by allowing home rule entities to utilize their powers and functions on the local level without revocation, change, or affect by law unless it is necessary to prevent an abridgement of the reasonable exercise of the state's police power. Thus, Article VI protects home rule governments from unwarranted interference by the state in their internal affairs.

Article VI, however, also contains a provision in *Section 9(B)* that ensures the powers granted to home rule governments will not be used to deprive the state government of its inherent powers. This section, entitled "Limitations of Local Government Subdivisions," provides:

Notwithstanding any provision of this Article, the police power of the state shall never be abridged.

This provision was adopted "as a principle of harmonizing the replete home rule powers granted local governments with a basic residuum of the state's power to initiate legislation and regulation necessary to protect and promote the vital interests of its people as a whole." *City of New Orleans v. Board of Com'rs of Orleans Levee Dist.*, 640 So.2d at 249. * * *

If we determine that this statute was passed pursuant to a reasonable exercise of the police power of the state, and that the local minimum wage law conflicts with this statute, then the minimum wage law must fall. * * * Section (A) of *La. R.S. 23:642* indicates that the prohibition against local governmental subdivisions establishing minimum wage rates for private employers was passed to promote economic stability and growth for all the citizens of the state. * * * In enacting *La. R.S. 23:642*, the legislature determined the policy of the State of Louisiana with respect to minimum wage requirements. It prescribed that minimum wage policy decisions should be made by the state to preserve consistency in the wage market. It is the role of the legislature to make such policy decisions for our state. In making this policy determination, the legislative history reveals that the legislature relied on the expert opinion of a local economist and the opinions of citizens and local businesses. These are precisely the types of opinions the legislature should consider in setting statewide policy and, based on the opinions presented, we find the legislature's policy choice is a reasonable one.

At the trial before the district court, the Proponents presented the testimony of two expert economists who voiced disagreement with the findings of the legislature regarding the need for statewide consistency in regulation of minimum wage rates in *La. R.S. 23:642*. * * * We recognize these expert opinions, but conclude they represent a disagreement among experts regarding the necessity of statewide regulation of minimum wage policy. Both sides of the issue appear to be backed by legitimate concerns and it is the legislature's function to fashion policy from these competing viewpoints. The legislature chose to require statewide regulation of minimum wage laws to maintain consistency in the wage market, and we find this policy choice to be reasonable in light of the evidence presented. * * * Clearly, the legislature's determination regarding the exercise of police power must be given great weight and the judicial branch should not substitute its opinion for the choice made by the legislature. Rather, the judicial branch should analyze the legislature's choice to determine whether there is support for the legislative determination that a measure constitutes a reasonable exercise of the police power. * * * [W]e find the provisions of *La. R.S. 23:642* are necessary to protect the vital interest of the state as a whole and do not constitute such an interference with the

City's constitutional rights that the statute must be held unenforceable against the City. Consequently, we conclude that *La. R.S. 23:642* constitutes a reasonable exercise of the state's police power, is constitutional, and is applicable to the City. Because we find *La. R.S. 23:642*, prohibiting local governmental subdivisions from establishing a minimum wage rate which a private employer would be required to pay employees, is a legitimate exercise of the state's police power, we conclude the City's minimum wage law, which sets a minimum wage rate private employers are required to pay their employees, abridges the police power of the state. Therefore, we find the minimum wage law invalid. * * *

CHIEF JUSTICE CALOGERO concurs in the decree but dissents from the majority's reasons; and assigns reasons. * * *

I agree with the majority that Ordinance No. 20376, which establishes a minimum wage that a private employer would be required to pay its employees working in the City of New Orleans, violates the Louisiana Constitution; however, I cannot join in the majority's reasons, with which I disagree. I believe this case is resolved by an examination of the ordinance's effects on private and civil relationships under La. Const. art. VI, § 9(A), rather than its effects relative to the state's police power under La. Const. art. VI, § 9(B). * * *

I believe the opponents in this matter have not sufficiently proven that Ordinance No. 20376 abridges the state's police power in violation of La. Const. art. VI, § 9(B). It is not axiomatic that, simply because the state enacts general legislation in an area under its police powers, a local governmental subdivision is automatically precluded from acting in that same area. To say otherwise would be to hold pre-1974 home rule charter cities hostage to the whim and caprice of the legislature, a consequence that was surely not the intention of the drafters of our 1974 Constitution. Similarly, the judiciary in deciding whether a local government's legislation abridges the state's police power must do more than merely rely on the legislature's pronouncement that a matter is of true "statewide" concern, found here in the preamble to *La.Rev.Stat. 23:642*. * * * Applying the "careful scrutiny" required of us by our prior jurisprudence, I do not view the evidence produced by the opponents as showing that *Rev. Stat. 23:642*, which prohibits a local government from establishing a minimum wage, is reasonably necessary to protect the vital interest of the state as a whole. * * *

WEIMER, J., concurring in the result. * * *

In my view, it is not necessary to reach the issue of whether the state's police power trumps that of the City of New Orleans, a pre-1974 home rule charter entity, because the Constitution, in *Article VI, § 9(A)*, denies to any local governmental subdivision the power to enact legislation governing private or civil relationships unless the legislature by general law confers upon the local governmental unit the express authority to act. Because Ordinance No. 20376, which establishes a minimum wage that a private employer would be required to pay its employees working in the City of New Orleans, is an ordinance that governs a private and civil relationship, and because the State, through the enactment of *LSA R.S. 23:642*, has expressly denied to the City the authority to legislate with respect to the minimum wage paid by private employers, Ordinance No. 20376 cannot withstand constitutional scrutiny and must be stricken as an unlawful attempt by the City to legislate in an arena expressly reserved to the State by the 1974 Constitution. * * *

[T]he employment relationship is both a private relationship and a civil relationship. It is a private relationship because the parties to the relationship, particularly those the City's minimum wage ordinance seeks to affect, are private individuals. It is a civil relationship because it is a relationship established by the civil law: the employment agreement is a species of lease governed by Title IX of the Civil Code. * * * While the relationship between an employer and his or her employees is thus a private and civil relationship within the meaning of *Section 9(A)(2)*, virtually all public regulation infringes upon private relationships to some extent. In acknowledgment of this fact, the constitutional prohibition of *Section 9(A)(2)* extends only to those ordinances that seek to "govern," or regulate, such relationships. * * * The City's ordinance impermissibly seeks to "govern" the private employment relationship because it modifies existing rights and obligations between the parties to the relationship, directly and unavoidably affecting the ability of the parties to negotiate price.

The fact that the avowed purpose of the ordinance is public—"to make it reasonably possible for [employees who work in the City of New Orleans] to earn a sufficient income to afford the basis necessities of food and shelter"—and that its violation is punishable as a crime, does not relieve the ordinance of its constitutional infirmity. The civil, private, public and criminal aspects of the ordinance may "overlap" to some extent. Nevertheless, the methods of carrying out the public objective contained in the ordinance are predominantly civil in character and directly govern a private and civil relationship. Just as the City could not regulate the civil relationship of marriage by criminalizing divorce, it cannot regulate the private employment relationship by criminalizing the failure of a private employer to pay a specified minimum wage. * * *

JOHNSON, J., dissenting. * * *

There is no empirical evidence to support the State's conclusion that a variation in the minimum wage would be detrimental to the State's interests. In fact, there is overwhelming evidence to the contrary. In my mind, the State has failed to show that *LSA-R.S. 23:642* is "necessary" to protect the vital interest of the state as a whole. The City's effort to insure that a working family has the ability to live above the poverty line, without relying on government subsidies (food stamps, etc.), is a legitimate exercise of its authority under the Home Rule Charter. * * *

TOWN OF TELLURIDE V. LOT THIRTY-FOUR VENTURE
Supreme Court of Colorado, 2000.
3 P.3d 30.

JUSTICE KOURLIS delivered the Opinion of the Court. * * *

In June 1994, respondent, Thirty-Four Venture, acquired title to Lots 34 and 34B in the Accommodations Two (AC–2) zoning district within the Town of Telluride. The AC–2 district permits visitor-oriented accommodations and recreation facilities to serve visitors and residents in limited commercial uses. In September 1994, the Town Council of the Town of Telluride (Town Council) adopted Ordinance 1011, which amends the Telluride Land Use Code to add "affordable housing" mitigation requirements. The Town Council enacted the ordinance to address concerns generated by the pressures of new development in the area. The ordinance requires owners engaging in new development to mitigate the effects of that development by generating affordable housing units for forty percent of the new employees created by the development. A developer must provide 350 square feet of housing space for forty percent of the number of employees a proposed development generates. The mitigation requirement is imposed uniformly in the majority of zoning district classifications within the Town, including the AC–2 district.

Ordinance 1011 provides developers with four general options, or a combination thereof, to satisfy the affordable housing requirement. They may (1) construct new units and deed-restrict them as affordable housing; (2) deed restrict "existing free market units" as affordable housing; (3) pay fees in lieu of deed restricted housing; or (4) convey land to the Town of Telluride with a fair market value equivalent to the fee paid under option three.

Approximately two weeks after adopting the ordinance, the Town Council also adopted the Telluride Affordable Housing Guidelines (Guidelines). The Guidelines, working in conjunction with Ordinance 1011, establish the price guidelines and regulations for rental units, and the conditions for tenant eligibility. If the developer chooses either of the deed restriction options, then the Guidelines set maximum rental rates per square foot for the property. A unit's maximum rent is determined by multiplying a constant monetary amount, such as $1.42 for a single bedroom apartment, with the square footage of the unit. The Guidelines cap rental rate increases for units designated as affordable housing at no more than 2.5% per annum, unless the Telluride Housing Authority allows a higher increase. The sale of deed restricted properties is similarly limited. Properties may be sold only to qualified residents, or to a qualified owner who will rent to qualified residents, for a maximum sale price per square foot with the annual growth of the sale price capped. The Guidelines also set a base price for the payment-in-lieu of construction option. The Town will use the payments for the production of additional affordable housing.

Thirty-Four Venture sought to enjoin the Town from enforcing the ordinance, arguing that it constitutes rent control, and therefore, violates section 38–12–301, 10 C.R.S. (1999), which precludes municipalities from "enact[ing] any ordinance . . . which would control rents on private residential property." * * * We granted certiorari to consider whether Ordinance 1011 is a form of "rent control" within the purview of section 38–12–301, and if so, whether section 38–12–301, enacted by the General Assembly in 1981, constitutionally supercedes Ordinance 1011.

The first issue on appeal requires us to determine whether Telluride's affordable housing scheme falls within section 38–12–301's prohibition of "rent control." The statute is titled "Local Control of Rents Prohibited" and states,

> The general assembly finds and declares that the imposition of rent control on private residential housing units is a matter of statewide concern; therefore, no county or municipality may enact any ordinance or resolution which would control rents on private residential property. This section is not intended to impair the right of any state agency, county, or municipality to manage and control any property in which it has an interest through a housing authority or similar agency.

The General Assembly did not define "rent control." * * * Thus, we first must interpret the meaning of the phrase "rent control." * * * We find the term "rent control" to be clear on its face. Rent control is commonly understood to mean allowable rent capped at a fixed rate with only limited increases. Because Ordinance 1011 sets a base rental rate per square foot and then strictly limits the growth of the rental rate, the ordinance constitutes rent control. The scheme as a whole operates to suppress rental values below their market values. Therefore, the court of appeals correctly concluded that the ordinance restricts the property owner's ability to develop his land as he sees fit.

Although the ordinance has the laudable purpose of increasing affordable housing within the communities where lower income employees work, the ordinance nevertheless violates the plain language of the state prohibition on rent control. * * * Because we have determined that the statute is clear on its face, we need not consider the legislative history, including the historic conditions that triggered the General

Assembly's decision to ban rent controls. * * * Ordinance 1011 cannot be saved on the grounds that it applies only to new construction while existing housing units are not subject to the controls. * * * [T]he statutory ban on rent control makes no distinction between existing units and those subsequently developed. * * * The fact that the ordinance offers developers several options for satisfying the "affordable housing requirement" does not change the character of, or redeem, the rent control provisions. Either the provisions constitute rent control and cannot be enforced, or they do not. * * * Because Ordinance 1011 imposes a base price for rental and sale values, and thereafter limits the rate growth, we conclude that the ordinance constitutes rent control within the plain meaning of section 38–12–301.

Because we hold that Ordinance 1011 is a form of rent control, we must address the second question presented for review: whether Telluride may nonetheless impose rent control because it is a home rule municipality. * * * Home rule cities are granted plenary authority by the constitution to regulate issues of local concern. See Colo. Const. art. XX, § 6. If a home rule city takes action on a matter of local concern, and that ordinance conflicts with a state statute, the home rule provision takes precedence over the state statute. See id; see also City & County of Denver v. State, 788 P.2d 764, 767 (Colo.1990) (finding a state statute unconstitutional because it conflicted with a local initiative on a matter of local concern). If the matter is one of statewide concern, however, home rule cities may legislate in that area only if the constitution or a statute authorizes the legislation. Otherwise, state statutes take precedence over home rule actions. If the matter is one of mixed local and statewide concern, a home rule provision and a state statute may coexist, as long as the measures can be harmonized. If the home rule action conflicts with the state legislature's action, however, the state statute supercedes the home rule authority. * * *

In determining whether the state interest is sufficient to justify preemption of home rule authority, this Court has articulated various factors that drive the analysis. These include: (1) the need for statewide uniformity of regulation; (2) the impact of the measure on individuals living outside the municipality; (3) historical considerations concerning whether the subject matter is one traditionally governed by state or local government; and (4) whether the Colorado Constitution specifically commits the particular matter to state or local regulation. * * *

We begin with two general propositions. First, courts must avoid making decisions that are intrinsically legislative. * * * Second, we note that the General Assembly here did announce that the preclusion of rent control is a matter of statewide concern. * * * [T]his pronouncement is not dispositive, but it is instructive. * * * We turn then to the specific factors. The first consideration is whether the state has a pervading interest in statewide uniform regulation. * * * Here, both the municipality and the state have significant interests in maintaining the quality and quantity of affordable housing in the state. Ordinances like Telluride's can change the dynamics of supply and demand in an important sector of the economy—the housing market. A consistent prohibition on rent control encourages investment in the rental market and the maintenance of high quality rental units. Although economic conditions may vary in housing markets across the state, the legislature has seen fit to enact a uniform ban on rent control as a matter of public policy. In addition, the rent control statute is part of the state statutory scheme regulating landlord and tenant relations. Landlord-tenant relations are an area in which state residents have an expectation of consistency throughout the state. Uniformity in landlord-tenant relations fosters informed and realistic expectations by the parties to a lease, which in turn increases the quality and reliability of rental housing, promotes fair treatment of tenants, and could reduce litigation.

The second factor is the closely related question of whether the home rule municipality's action will have any extraterritorial impact. An extraterritorial impact is one involving state residents outside the municipality. * * * The findings in Telluride's ordinance itself recite that the issue is one that impacts other communities: "Maintaining permanent and long-term housing in proximity to the source of employment generation serves to maintain the community, reduce regional traffic congestion, and minimize impacts on adjacent communities." See Ordinance 1011, § 3–710.A. Managing population and development growth is among the most pressing problems currently facing communities throughout the state. Restricting the operation of the free market with respect to housing in one area may well cause housing investment and population to migrate to other communities already facing their own growth problems. * * *[9]

Where does this analysis lead us, then, in assessing and measuring the various interests at stake? The state's interests include consistent application of statewide laws in a manner that avoids a patchwork approach to problems. Further, the state has a legitimate interest in preserving investment capital in the rental market, ensuring stable quantity and quality of housing, maintaining tax revenues generated by rental properties, and protecting the state's overall economic health. Telluride, on the other hand, has a valid interest in controlling land use, reducing regional traffic congestion and air pollution, containing sprawl,

---

[9]   Telluride argues that Ordinance 1011 is an exercise of the municipality's police power to regulate land use, an area traditionally regulated by local government. We reject this contention. Even though the measure amended the Telluride Land Use Code, the ordinance does not dictate permissible uses of real property; rather, it dictates the rate at which the property may be used for a permissible purpose. It is, therefore, properly characterized as economic legislation.

preserving a sense of community, and improving the quality of life of the Town's employees.

On the whole, we cannot conclude that this matter is so discretely local that all state interests are superceded. Given the legitimacy of both the state interests and Telluride's interests, we conclude that rent control represents an area of mixed state and local concern. * * * Because the two measures conflict, the local ordinance must yield to the state statute. Therefore, Ordinance 1011 is invalid. The corollary to this determination is the question of whether sections 38–12–301 and–302 are constitutional. Because the issue of rent control is one of mixed concern, the state may regulate in the area. Therefore, the rent control statute is constitutional, and does not violate the home rule amendment. * * *

CHIEF JUSTICE MULLARKEY, dissenting.

The majority interprets the anti-rent-control statute * * * very broadly. * * * [T]he statute, its legislative history, and other legislative enactments support the conclusion that the legislature intended to prohibit enactment of a specific type of ordinance, and the Telluride ordinance is not within that category. * * * Rent control ordinances evolved as a means to address rapidly rising residential housing rates caused by an inadequate supply of new housing stock. * * * While identifying a need to control rental rate increases, * * * [it was] also recognized that rate restrictions would deter future investment, thereby exacerbating the housing stock shortage. Thus, * * * "[r]ent control" as it was understood when the legislature acted had several common characteristics: the scope of rent control encompassed only existing units by exempting new development; hotels and other "transient" units were exempted; qualifying owners were not given choices with respect to non-rent controlling alternatives; the rental rate restrictions applied to all qualifying units based upon the characteristics or classification of a unit. * * *

Ordinance 1011 arose from very dissimilar, if not opposite, economic conditions. A shortage of affordable housing exists in Telluride because of a high degree of capital investment in development projects, rather than the stagnant investment that motivated rent control. Thus, the economic condition precipitating the creation of Ordinance 1011, and consequently, the intended effect of that ordinance—to mitigate the deleterious effects of high levels of economic development—are not within the scope of "rent control" as the General Assembly understood it. * * * [Moreover,] unlike the concept of rent control which applied only to existing units by exempting new developments from the rate restrictions, section 3–740.A of the ordinance applies the affordable housing requirements only to new development. Thus, not one single housing unit that is subject to Ordinance 1011 would fall within any of the rent control laws considered by the legislature, and conversely, not one single housing unit subject to rent control legislation would have fallen within Ordinance 1011. This difference does not reflect a mere implementation choice but represents a fundamental distinction between the rent control model and the mitigation measures of today. * * *

Ordinance 1011's incorporation of alternatives to rental rate restrictions in its mitigation model also differs substantially from rent control ordinances. By allowing developers a choice as to mitigation measures, including some alternatives that do not impose restrictions on the rental rates, the applicability of Ordinance 1011 is not a function solely of the classification of a unit; instead, the applicability can be a function of the choice elected by the developer. * * * These are fundamental structural differences that place the Telluride ordinance outside of the construct of the rent control model contemplated by the legislature. * * *

[T]he broad interpretation accorded to the concept of "rent control" by the majority impermissibly creates a conflict with other statutory provisions. * * * Section 38–12–301 declares rent control on private residential housing units to be a matter of statewide concern. On the other hand, section 31–23–207 * * * contains a finding and declaration of the General Assembly that "the rapid growth and development of the state and the resulting demands on its land resources make new and innovative measures necessary to encourage planned and orderly land use development" and "to provide for the needs of . . . residential communities."

The majority creates rather than avoids a constitutional infirmity. It does this by according the General Assembly's rent control statute an extremely broad reading and local land use regulation an extremely narrow scope. * * * The majority finds Ordinance 1011 to be economic legislation * * *. To the contrary, I contend that Ordinance 1011 is fundamentally a land use regulation, an area that the General Assembly and this court have consistently recognized to be a matter of local concern. * * * The majority's finding of a * * * need for uniformity is contrary to the General Assembly's consistent refusal to consider land use regulations as requiring statewide legislation. * * * [T]he majority's extraterritoriality analysis [also] strikes at the fundamental premise of land use planning, zoning, and development regulations by exalting free operation of the housing market over the police power of local government to shape the design of a community. The majority's rationale ignores the fact that the General Assembly, when considering the role of local government in land use control, has consistently decided in favor of local prerogative to employ market restrictions to manage growth. * * * [T]he majority characterizes Telluride's effort to reasonably mitigate the impacts of new development on its community as if it were imposing a burden on other communities. Yet, Telluride's ordinance is aimed directly at mitigating the effects on other localities of an ever-increasing public problem in mountain resorts. Workers cannot afford to live where they work because the housing market left to itself prices out the laborers in favor of tourists and second home owners. Enabling people to live where they work is a key concept in reducing pollution, congestion, and demand on transportation infrastructure, such as new or expanded roads or transit to carry workers from their overnight abodes to where they earn their wages.

The majority misanalyzes the extraterritorial impact of Telluride's ordinance. It has precisely the opposite impact: it attempts to contain the effects of growth within Telluride. The ordinance assists the livability of people and communities in the areas surrounding the city of Telluride by addressing the particular concerns that its geography and demographics present. This positive effect is of a different character than the negative effects previously recognized by this court to support a state concern determination. * * *

Because Telluride's interests so significantly outweigh those of the state, I would hold that Ordinance 1011 constitutes legislation of a matter of local concern. Therefore, to the extent that section 38–12–301 conflicts with the ordinance, the statutory provision is unconstitutional in violation of article XX, section 6. Telluride validly exercised its powers as a home rule city in enacting and enforcing Ordinance 1011. * * *

WEBB V. CITY OF BLACK HAWK

Supreme Court of Colorado, 2013.
295 P.3d 480.

JUSTICE HOBBS delivered the Opinion of the Court.

This appeal from the district court of Gilpin County concerns whether a home-rule municipality has the authority under article XX of the Colorado Constitution to ban bicycles on local streets absent a suitable alternative bike route as provided by state statute. * * * Black Hawk is a home-rule municipality under article XX of the Colorado Constitution. As such, it has plenary authority to regulate matters of local concern, but it has limited authority when its regulations conflict with state statutes implicating matters of statewide concern. In July 2009, the Black Hawk City Council passed Ordinance 2009–20, granting authority to ban bicycles and other nonmotorized vehicles from any city street where it found their use to be incompatible with safety and the normal movement of traffic. The ordinance pointed to the heavy use by commercial traffic on the city's narrow roads—specifically by over-the-road coaches and delivery vehicles—as a basis for the safety concern. * * * In January 2010, Black Hawk enacted Ordinance 2010–3, prohibiting

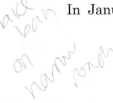

bicycles on virtually all of Black Hawk's streets. The ordinance also ordered the city manager to promulgate rules that would continue to allow bicycle traffic that originated within the Black Hawk city limits— the ordinance only prohibited cyclists passing through Black Hawk, not those beginning their rides there * * *. We conclude that Black Hawk's bicycling ban is not a matter of purely local concern, * * * that Black Hawk's current ordinance conflicts with state law, and [that it] is preempted.

The Black Hawk area sprang up in spring 1859 following the discovery of gold * * *. Situated at the confluence of Gregory Gulch and the North Fork of Clear Creek, Black Hawk sits at an elevation just over 8,000 feet, in Gilpin County. At its height, Gilpin County * * * held a population of 6,690 residents around 1900. By 1925, the population waned and Black Hawk had only one operational mill and the population fell to 200 persons. Black Hawk's population remains small, 118 in the 2010 Census * * *. Today, in keeping with the town's tradition, a new class of hopeful prospectors regularly descends upon Black Hawk seeking fortune—casino gamers. In 1990 * * * Black Hawk retrofitted existing historical structures into casinos and built new, large, modern casinos on the broad, flat locations that once housed ore mills. On October 1, 1991, casinos opened for business, immediately attracting new investments and attention to Black Hawk reminiscent of the previous century. * * * Black Hawk now hosts nearly twenty separate casinos—more than Atlantic City, New Jersey. Due to its primary location for those traveling from the Denver area and its accommodation of over-the-road coaches, Black Hawk has maintained the lion's share of the state gaming proceeds. * * *

On June 5, 2010, [Jamie] Webb, [Jeffrey] Hermanson, and [Michaleen] Jeronimus were completing a long-distance bicycle ride. * * * While riding through Black Hawk along Gregory Street, the only street connecting Central City to the Peak-to-Peak Highway, the Bicyclists were pulled over and ticketed for violating section 8–111 of the Black Hawk Municipal Code, the provision prohibiting bicycling on several streets, including Gregory Street, in the City of Black Hawk. * * * The question we address in this appeal is whether the ordinance Black Hawk enacted * * * is solely a matter of local concern so as not to be preempted by a conflicting state statute that requires a suitable alternative route. To answer this question, we must determine whether the ordinance is a matter of local, state, or mixed local and statewide concern. *City of Commerce City v. State*, 40 P.3d 1273, 1279 (Colo.2002). If a local ordinance conflicts with state statute in a matter of purely local concern, the ordinance validly supersedes state law. If the ordinance conflicts in a matter of statewide or mixed concern, however, the state statute supersedes the local ordinance. Whether a particular matter is one of state, local, or mixed concern is a legal issue, requiring a court to consider the totality of the circumstances in reaching its conclusion. *Town of Telluride v. Lot Thirty-Four Venture, L.L.C.,* 3 P.3d 30, 37 (Colo.2000). * * *

Practically, it is rare that regulatory matters fit neatly within one of these three categories. Regulations that are of local, mixed, or statewide concern often imperceptibly merge or overlap. Because the categories do not reflect factually perfect descriptions of the relevant interests of the state and local governments, categorizing a particular matter constitutes a legal conclusion involving considerations of both fact and policy. A number of relevant factors help guide our inquiry, including (1) the need for statewide uniformity of regulation; (2) the extraterritorial impact of local regulation; (3) whether the matter has traditionally been regulated at the state or local level; and (4) whether the Colorado Constitution specifically commits the matter to state or local regulation. Although not conclusive in itself, a determination by the General Assembly that a matter is of statewide concern is relevant. * * *

Before we * * * apply these principles * * *, it is helpful to outline the progression of Colorado bicycle law to understand the issue here. * * * Our legislature has * * * recognized bicycle traffic within a broad regulatory framework, owing to the fact that bicycles share automobile roadways and require additional safeguards to ensure bicyclist and motorist safety. * * * As the statutes clearly express, bicycles are required to abide by local rules when off state highways. Local authorities, such as home-rule cities, have expressly maintained the authority to regulate certain aspects of traffic behavior within their local jurisdictions, * * * including parking, traffic direction, intersection protocol, and speed. In 1965, the General Assembly delineated additional powers of local authorities, including the power to regulate bicycles. * * * As a part of the 1973 bicycle amendment, the legislature enacted language allowing local authorities, based on an engineering and traffic study, to prohibit bicycles on "heavily traveled streets," provided that suitable bike paths or other trails have been established within one-quarter mile of the street's right-of-way. * * * In the case before us, the Bicyclists argue that Black Hawk did not comply with the statutory conditions in prohibiting bicycles. We agree. * * *

First, we look at whether a statewide interest in the uniform regulation of bicycles and vehicles exists. * * * In *Commerce City*, we found that Colorado's interest in uniform traffic regulation was strengthened by the "reality of Colorado's complex system of roads and highways." "Without uniform state legislation," we continued, "Colorado drivers may be subject to a significant variety of conflicting local legislation, further increasing the potential for confusion and substantially affecting their expectations." * * * Colorado is a state with a lengthy history of bicycling, * * * and the state clearly has an interest in uniform bicycle regulations as it continues to develop its bicycle infrastructure and promote bicycling within the state. At the same time, state statutes and our decisions construing them support local control over traffic regulations in purely local matters, such as traffic at street intersections or parking. * * *

We have defined extraterritorial impacts as those involving the expectations of state residents, as well as those that create a ripple effect impacting state residents outside the municipality. * * * The city fails to demonstrate * * * how the ordinance lacks an extraterritorial impact. The record in this case clearly shows that Black Hawk's ordinance affects the expectations of residents outside of the municipality. The Bicyclists are not Black Hawk residents, demonstrating the effect of the ordinance on Colorado residents in general. * * * There is a "ripple effect" presented by the ordinance affecting communities beyond Black Hawk. Bicyclists migrate to our state roadways and mountain towns in the summer and autumn months in search of recreation and scenery. The ordinance effectively closes off the neighboring town of Central City from receiving bicycle traffic on connected routing of long-distance bicycle rides and may also affect a bicyclist's decision to visit other mountain towns * * * that benefit from recreational tourism. * * * Because of Black Hawk's ordinance and the strong negative public perception of the bicycle ban, especially by bicyclists, the ordinance will likely cause future bicycle tours to bypass the area entirely, resulting in a "ripple effect" harming nearby communities that rely on additional tourism. Black Hawk's ordinance may lead to other municipal bicycle bans by local communities which, like Black Hawk, would like to favor large transportation coaches over bicycles. Such an occurrence may dramatically affect recreational bicycling, creating a patchwork of local and state rules contrary to the state legislation's wording and intent. We conclude the Black Hawk ordinance has an extraterritorial impact. * * *

The next factor we address is whether the regulation of bicycle traffic is a matter traditionally governed by state or local governments. * * * While we have determined local regulation to be proper in a handful of circumstances, we have simultaneously determined that the regulation of vehicle traffic is not distinctly either a local or statewide matter. * * * The final factor relevant to our examination is whether the Colorado Constitution specifically commits the regulation of bicycles to either the city or the state. * * * [W]e conclude that both the state and Black Hawk have important interests in this matter * * * [and] that the regulation of bicycles on city streets is a matter of mixed state and local concern. * * * Black Hawk does not have authority, in a matter of mixed state and local concern, to negate a specific provision the General Assembly has enacted in the interest of uniformity. A staple of our home-rule jurisprudence articulates that a municipality is free to adopt regulations conflicting with state law only when the matter is of purely local concern. * * *

CITY OF TUCSON V. STATE OF ARIZONA

Supreme Court of Arizona, 2012.
229 Ariz. 172.

BALES, JUSTICE.

Since statehood, Arizona's Constitution has included a "home rule" provision authorizing eligible cities to adopt charters. Ariz. Const. art. 13, § 2. A charter city has the power to frame its own organic law, including the power to determine "who shall be its governing officers and how they shall be selected." *Strode v. Sullivan*, 72 Ariz. 360, 368, 236 P.2d 48, 54 (1951). * * * Tucson city council members are nominated in ward-based primary elections but elected in at-large (city-wide) general elections. These elections are partisan: the primary selects nominees for particular political parties and the general election ballot identifies candidates by party affiliation. * * * In 2009, the Arizona Legislature amended A.R.S. § 9–821.01 to * * * [bar] a city from electing its city council in partisan elections or in ward-based primaries combined with at-large general elections. The City of Tucson filed this case against the State, claiming that the amendments to § 9–821.01 do not apply to it as a charter city. * * *

Nineteenth century case law and legal commentary generally viewed cities and towns as entirely subordinate to and dependent on the state's legislature for any governmental authority. The framers of Arizona's Constitution, however, rejected that view, valuing local autonomy. * * * [O]ur Constitution * * * permits any city of more than 3500 people to "frame a charter for its own government consistent with, and subject to, the Constitution and the laws of the state. The purpose of the home rule charter provision of the Constitution was to render the cities adopting such charter provisions as nearly independent of state legislation as was possible." *City of Tucson v. Walker*, 60 Ariz. 232, 239, 135 P.2d 223, 226 (1943). * * * "[A] home rule city deriving its powers from the Constitution is independent of the state Legislature as to all subjects of strictly local municipal concern." *City of Tucson v. Tucson Sunshine Climate Club*, 64 Ariz. 1, 8–9, 164 P.2d 598, 602 (1945). * * *

[The] nineteen "charter cities" in Arizona * * * differ significantly in how they elect their city councils. Before statehood, cities generally selected council members—then referred to as aldermen—by wards, that is, each was elected from a particular district within the city. * * * Groups such as the National Municipal League (now the National Civic League) advocated for the election of city councils in at-large, nonpartisan elections, contending that ward-based election systems resulted in city governments susceptible to control by "political bosses," corruption, and parochial neighborhood interests. Many of Arizona's charter cities adopted at-large elections for their city councils, and twelve currently use this method. Over time, however, there has been renewed support for district-based council elections. Proponents contend that at-large elections may be used to deny representation to particular groups, such as concentrated populations of minority or low-income residents, or may result in the neglect of neighborhood interests. * * * Six of Arizona's charter cities now elect their city councils on a district or ward basis.

Arizona's Constitution and statutes regarding municipalities do not express a preference between at-large or district-based council elections. This flexibility recognizes that each form of election has possible advantages and disadvantages; for example, although at-large members are responsible to electors in the entire city, this may diminish attention to the interests of particular neighborhoods or groups; district-based elections, in contrast, assure representation from different geographic areas but may elevate particular interests over citywide ones.

Tucson is unique among Arizona's charter cities in its method for selecting council members. * * * Council members are nominated by ward, so that the council includes members from different geographic regions of the city, but they are elected by all the city's voters in the general election. In November 1991, Tucson voters rejected a proposal to replace at-large general elections with district-based elections. Two years later, they rejected a proposal to change from partisan to non-partisan elections.

More than sixty years ago, this Court considered a charter city's authority to structure its own government in *Strode*, which involved the non-partisan election system that Phoenix adopted in 1912. State statutes then generally entitled political parties to be represented on ballots for state, county, and city offices. The Court, however, held that these statutes did not displace the Phoenix charter. * * * *Strode* recognized that Article 13, Section 2 requires city charters to be "consistent with, and subject to, the Constitution and the laws of the state." This provision, the Court held, does not subject charter cities to the legislature's plenary power. Instead, the phrase "laws of the state" refers to laws addressing matters of "statewide interest" rather than "local concern."

Consistent with earlier decisions, the Court in *Strode* applied a formalistic analysis: whether general state laws displace charter provisions depends on whether the subject matter is characterized as of statewide or purely local interest. This approach can be problematic in application. The concepts of "local" versus "statewide" interest do not have self-evident definitions. Many municipal issues will be of both local and state concern, and distinguishing between matters that are properly subject to local versus state control often involves case-specific line drawing. *Strode* recognized as much * * *. But whatever the general difficulties in identifying matters of local concern, *Strode* is absolutely clear that charter city governments enjoy autonomy with respect to structuring their own governments. * * * Underscoring this point, the Court said: "We therefore specifically hold that the method and manner of conducting elections in the city of Phoenix is peculiarly the subject of local interest and is not a matter of statewide concern." * * *

Under *Strode*, Tucson's manner of electing its city council members supersedes the conflicting provisions of A.R.S. § 9–821.01(B) and (C). * * * If the local autonomy granted by Article 13, Section 2 allows a city to opt not to use partisan elections, the converse must also be true: a city may choose to use partisan elections. *Strode's* rationale also extends to Tucson's decision to use ward-based primaries and at-large general council elections. In characterizing the method of electing city officers as a "purely municipal concern," *Strode* noted that * * * [it] could "conceive of no essentials more inherently of local interest or concern to the electors of a city than who shall be its governing officers and how they shall be selected." If the "home rule" provisions of Article 13, Section 2 are to have effect, they must at the least afford charter cities autonomy in choosing how to elect their governing officers. * * *

The State argues that we should defer to the legislature's finding in A.R.S. § 9–821.01(A) that "the conduct of elections described in this section is a matter of statewide concern." * * * Although we respect findings by the legislature, whether state law prevails over conflicting charter provisions under Article 13, Section 2 is a question of constitutional interpretation. * * * We do not question that some aspects of the conduct of local elections may be of statewide concern. See, e.g., *City of Tucson v. State,* 191 Ariz. 436, 439, 957 P.2d 341, 344 (App.1997) (finding statewide interest in specifying uniform dates for municipal elections). But election dates, other administrative aspects of elections, and the various examples listed in § 9–821.01(A) all involve matters qualitatively different from determining how a city will constitute its governing council.

The State also contends that the federal Voting Rights Act ("VRA"), 42 U.S.C. § 1973 (2006), creates a statewide interest in barring Tucson's use of at-large council elections. Since the 1975 amendments to the VRA, Arizona has been a "covered jurisdiction": the state and its political subdivisions must seek federal approval (preclearance) under section 5 of the VRA before implementing any change affecting voting. To be relieved of the preclearance requirement, Arizona must show that * * * it and "all governmental units within its territory . . . have eliminated voting procedures and methods of election which inhibit or dilute equal access to the electoral process." The State argues that Tucson's continued use of at-large elections might jeopardize Arizona's ability to be relieved from the preclearance requirements because at-large council elections have sometimes been found to violate the VRA. The VRA, however, does not alter *Strode's* analysis of the relative power of the state legislature and charter cities regarding the structure of city government. Tucson undeniably must comply with applicable federal law. But at-large elections do not necessarily violate either the federal constitution or the VRA. The State does not claim, nor is there any evidence in the record suggesting, that Tucson's method of selecting its city council violates the VRA. Indeed, Tucson has elected minority council members for decades and two of its current council members are Hispanic. * * *

Independent of the VRA, the State contends that § 9–821.01 involves matters of statewide concern because it promotes "equality in the democratic process." * * * Some state courts have held that legislatures may require home-rule cities to adopt district-based elections for city councils. See, e.g., *Jacobberger v. Terry*, 211 Neb. 878, 320 N.W.2d 903 (1982); *Casuse v. City of Gallup*, 106 N.M. 571, 746 P.2d 1103 (1987). Other state court decisions, like *Strode*, have recognized that aspects of municipal elections are of local concern, although some of these decisions concern constitutional provisions that specifically empower cities to regulate municipal elections. See, e.g., *Johnson v. Bradley*, 4 Cal.4th 389, 14 Cal.Rptr.2d 470, 841 P.2d 990 (1992) (holding that city charter authorizing partial public financing of campaigns for elective city office superseded state statute * * *); *State v. Callahan*, 96 Okla. 276, 221 P. 718 (1923) (holding that state law did not displace charter provisions for non-partisan municipal primary); *Ex parte Boalt*, 123 Or. 1, 260 P. 1004 (1927) (stating that election of municipal judge was of purely local concern). We are not persuaded by the out-of-state cases cited by the State. * * *

The State finally observes that Tucson's method of electing council members has resulted in candidates winning in the general election who did not receive the most votes in the ward from which they were nominated. * * * But Tucson council members, although nominated by ward, represent the entire city, just as do council members elected at large in other cities. An at-large council election by its nature allows candidates to win who may not receive a majority of votes in particular areas of the city. (District based elections, in contrast, allow council members to vote on matters affecting the entire city even though they are not elected, and might not be preferred, by a majority of the city's voters.) The provisions in Arizona's Constitution regarding voting rights * * * do not require cities generally to adopt district-based elections. * * * Given Article 13, Section 2, the intent of Arizona's framers, and the history of municipal government in our state, we hold that electors in charter cities may determine under their charters whether to constitute their councils on an at-large or district basis and whether to conduct their elections on a partisan basis. * * *

6. STATE LEGISLATIVE PREEMPTION

In the absence of state constitutional provisions to the contrary (such as the grant of home rule or the prohibition against special legislation), states have the power to modify or reverse any city decision. In any particular case, however, it is necessary to decide whether a state has exercised this power. According to the doctrine of preemption, state law prevails if there is a direct conflict between state law and a local law. But as the *Telluride* case presented in the Home Rule section demonstrates, even when a state law clearly prohibits certain types of local legislation, preemption doctrine requires courts to make a determination about the nature of both the state law and the local law in question. The *Telluride* court found that the town's housing ordinance was a form of preempted rent control. But, as the dissent argues, perhaps the Telluride ordinance should not have been preempted because the ordinance—although it did provide for controlled rents—was not the "rent control" that the legislature meant to forbid.

A conflict between state law and a local ordinance need not be based on the kind of express preemption clause at issue in *Telluride*. A conflict can be found, in the absence of such a clause, simply on the basis that the local ordinance is inconsistent with the state law or frustrates its purpose. Moreover, even if there is no *direct* conflict between a state and local law, a state law may still preempt a local law if state policy is interpreted to forbid local legislation of any kind (in the language of the preemption doctrine, the issue is whether the state government intended "to occupy the field"). Silence on an issue can itself be interpreted to mean that no local legislation of any kind is permitted. In many cases, however, the state's intent is not clear. Even though the state and a city have adopted different policies to deal with the same problem, it doesn't necessarily follow that the state has forbidden local decisionmaking on the issue. Both state and local policies might be able to be pursued simultaneously. Determining whether they can be is one task of the doctrine of preemption.[12]

---

[12] For an analysis of preemption, see, e.g., Annie Decker, Preemption Conflation: Dividing the Local from the State in Congressional Decision Making, 30 Yale L. & Pol'y Rev. 32 (2012); Paul Diller, Intrastate Preemption, 87 B.U. L. Rev 1113 (2007); Paul Weiland, Preemption of Local Efforts to Protect the Environment: Implications for Local Government Officials, 18 Va. Envtl. L.J. 467 (1999); Stephen Gardbaum, The Nature of Preemption, 79 Cornell L. Rev. 767 (1994); Preemption in the Age of Local Regulatory Innovation: Fitting the Formula to a Different Kind of Conflict, 70 Tex. L. Rev. 1831 (1992); S. Candice Hoke, Preemption Pathologies and Civic Republican Values, 71 B.U. L. Rev. 685 (1991); Note, A Framework for Preemption Analysis, 88 Yale L. J. 363 (1978); Note, Conflict Between State Statutes and Municipal Ordinances, 72 Harv. L. Rev. 737 (1959).

The first three cases below explore these different forms of preemption. *Telluride* interprets an express preemption clause; Holt's Cigar Company, Inc. v. City of Philadelphia finds preemption based on the inconsistency between state and local law; and American Financial Services Association v. City of Oakland is based on field preemption. Each of these cases has a vigorous dissent, demonstrating how controversial the application of preemption doctrine is. The reading that follows these cases, from a study of home rule in the Boston metropolitan area, describes the effect that the resulting uncertainty about the application of state preemption law may have on the confidence of local officials exercising their lawmaking powers. The final case, Cincinnati Bell Telephone Company v. City of Cincinnati, is a response to this uncertainty: it requires an "express statutory provision" for state preemption of local laws. Should a clear statement be required before state preemption is found?[13] Would such a limitation be practical given the way legislation is enacted and interpreted? Would it be consistent with the state-city relationship envisioned by cases like *Hunter* or Dillon's Rule? On the other hand, is the absence of a clear statement requirement consistent with the grant of home rule?

TOWN OF TELLURIDE V. LOT THIRTY-FOUR VENTURE

[See Chapter 2, Section A–5, supra.]

HOLT'S CIGAR COMPANY, INC. V. CITY OF PHILADELPHIA

Supreme Court of Pennsylvania, 2011.
10 A.3d 902.

JUSTICE MCCAFFERY. * * *

On January 23, 2007, the Philadelphia City Council enacted an ordinance * * * designed "to correct and control a[ ] growing trend among Philadelphia youth and others to purchase cigars, empty the tobacco from those cigars, and substitute marijuana and/or stronger illegal drugs into the cigar wrapping." To this end, the ordinance banned the sale of flavored cigars and other tobacco products that are preferred by illicit drug users as vehicles for smoking marijuana and other illegal drugs, and also banned the sale of cigars and other tobacco products in quantities of less than three. No mens rea provision was included in the above ordinance; hence, the mere sale of the listed items constituted a violation, without regard to the seller's intent or knowledge. In addition, the ordinance prohibited the sale of single or flavored tobacco products or of drug paraphernalia within 500 feet of a school, recreation center, day care center, church, or community center, "regardless of the intent as to use of

---

[13] For a draft of a statute requiring a clear statement of the intent of Congress as a prerequisite to federal preemption, see Robert Freilich, A Proposed Congressional "Statute of Federalism," 19 The Urban Lawyer 539, 545–46 (1987).

the item." Philadelphia Code §§ 9–622(5)(a) and 9–629(2). Violators of the ordinance were subject to a fine of up to $2,000, and to revocation of their business privilege license.

On January 30, 2007, Holt's Cigar Company and other tobacco retailers, manufacturers, and trade associations * * * sought * * * a preliminary injunction against enforcement of the ordinance and a declaratory judgment that the ordinance was preempted by the drug paraphernalia provisions of the Controlled Substance, Drug, Device and Cosmetic Act (hereinafter the "Act")[, a state law that] * * * bars the delivery of drug paraphernalia under circumstances where the offender knew or reasonably should have known that the paraphernalia would be used to introduce a controlled substance into the human body in violation of the Act. * * *

[W]e have recently explained that there are three closely related forms of state preemption of local lawmaking authority. In express preemption, "a statute specifically declares it has planted the flag of preemption in a field." In field preemption, a "statute is silent on supersession, but proclaims a course of regulation and control which brooks no municipal intervention." Finally, pursuant to the doctrine of conflict preemption, which is the only form of preemption at issue in the instant case, a local ordinance that contradicts, contravenes, or is inconsistent with a state statute is invalid. For conflict preemption to be applicable, the conflict between the statute and the ordinance must be irreconcilable. Further, the ordinance in question must be considered in light of the objectives of the General Assembly and the purposes of the relevant statute. A local ordinance may not stand as an obstacle to the execution of the full purposes and objectives of the Legislature. But "it has long been the established general rule, in determining whether a conflict exists between a general and local law, that where the legislature has assumed to regulate a given course of conduct by prohibitory enactments, a municipal corporation with subordinate power to act in the matter may make such additional regulations in aid and furtherance of the purpose of the general law as may seem appropriate to the necessities of the particular locality and which are not in themselves unreasonable." *Mars Emergency Medical Services, Inc. v. Township of Adams*, 559 Pa. 309, 740 A.2d 193, 195 (1999). * * *

The Act recognizes that some drug paraphernalia have legitimate as well as illegitimate uses, and, in contrast to the ordinance, one of the Act's implicit objectives is to not penalize those who sell dual-use items for legitimate uses. * * * The question before us is whether the challenged ordinance is consistent or irreconcilably conflicts with the Act. A seller of a dual-use item violates the Act only if he or she knows or reasonably should know that the dual-use item is to be used for an illegal, drug-related purpose. In contrast, a seller of certain dual-use items violates the ordinance by merely engaging in the sale, with no consideration as to whether the item was sold for a legitimate use or for an illegal, drug-related purpose, and no consideration of the seller's state of mind or intent. The presence of a mens rea element in the statute and the absence of a mens rea element in the ordinance, for the same proscribed conduct, i.e., selling certain dual-use items, constitute an irreconcilable conflict between the two enactments. Although the ordinance does not stand as an obstacle to the primary purpose of the Act, i.e., to decrease the unauthorized use of controlled substances, the ordinance does contradict an implied objective of the Act to protect those who sell dual-use items for legitimate purposes. * * * [T]he ordinance is thus preempted.

The City argues that there is no conflict between the Act and the ordinance because the former provides for criminal penalties and the latter is a civil statute. We do not agree. [Our focus is directed toward the particular conduct proscribed by the Act] and by the ordinance; the nature or severity of the penalties imposed is not determinative and does not eliminate the conflict arising from the discrepancy with respect to mens rea for a particular course of proscribed conduct.

The City further suggests that the General Assembly was simply silent as to the possible imposition of per se liability for the delivery of dual-use items. The City argues that * * * such silence should not be interpreted as a legislative intent to prohibit local regulation of the sale of dual-use items in a manner free of a scienter requirement. * * * Again, we cannot agree with the City * * *. With regard to offenses involving delivery of drug paraphernalia, the General Assembly was far from silent as to the mens rea element. The Act expressly requires that an offender know or reasonably should know that the drug paraphernalia would be used in conjunction with a controlled substance in violation of the Act; thus, a seller of a dual-use item for legitimate purposes is protected from any penalty under the Act. * * *

CHIEF JUSTICE CASTILLE, dissenting. * * *

The Majority * * * concludes that the Ordinance * * * contradicts what it discerns to be some "implied objective" of the Act to supposedly "protect" those who sell dual-use items for "legitimate" purposes. * * * The proper questions before the Court are whether the Act and the Ordinance are irreconcilable, and whether the Ordinance stands as an obstacle to the execution of the full purposes and objectives of the General Assembly. * * * Generally, an irreconcilable conflict exists where simultaneous compliance with both the local and state enactments is impossible. Conversely, an ordinance that collaterally touches upon a given course of conduct regulated by a state statute, but does not confront affected persons with a choice of obeying one enactment over the other, is not directly in conflict with a state enactment. * * * The caselaw * * * disfavors the simple, mechanical comparison of the local and state enactments and the automatic rejection of local regulatory schemes that are not identical to statewide statutes. Indeed, such an approach leaves little room for legislating to account for local variations. * * * The essential question in the analysis of an alleged direct conflict is the practical one of whether it is possible for affected persons to comply with both the state and local regulations. If the answer is no, then the local enactment is preempted and invalid. If the answer is yes, then the next inquiry is whether the ordinance stands as an obstacle to fulfilling the purposes of the state law. * * *

With respect to the Act and the Ordinance in the case sub judice, the answer to the question above plainly is yes, for the following reasons. * * * Of course, the course of conduct targeted by the provisions entails the same physical act—the sale of a dual-use item—and, thus, they are related. But, the targeted conduct manifestly is different, for purposes of a principled conflict preemption analysis, because the Act criminally punishes the sale of drug paraphernalia (i.e., the sale of a dual-use item with knowledge that it will be used to propagate use of illegal drugs), while the Ordinance burdens, and thereby discourages, the sale of dual-use items via civil penalties. To answer the Majority simply, the conduct criminally proscribed by the Act is the sale of drug paraphernalia, while the conduct burdened and penalized by the Ordinance is the sale of dual-use items. Moreover, the state and local enactments act in parallel, as the fines and business license consequences of violating the Ordinance are in addition to, not in lieu of, the Act's criminal penalties; they are civil consequences of behavior that, in circumstances described by the Act, may also be punished criminally. The Ordinance does not purport to remove—and does not even address—the mens rea or actus reus requirements for criminal conviction under the Act; it merely describes what amounts to a violation of a local Ordinance, with attendant civil consequences.

It is not impossible for an individual to comply with both the state and the local regulation. * * * Simply because the Act criminalizes only knowing delivery of drug paraphernalia dual-use items, it is not logical to conclude that, as a corollary, the Act affirmatively "protects" all commercial interests of retailers in sales of dual-use items—whether those retailers are wholly innocent or strategically blind to the uses. And, notably, given that the statute specifically describes in no uncertain terms that "[n]othing in this act relating to drug paraphernalia shall be deemed to supersede or invalidate any consistent local ordinance . . . relating to the possession, sale or use of drug paraphernalia," 35 P.S. § 780–141.1, the Majority's reliance on the Act's silence as conveying a fixed and global intention to affirmatively shield the commercial conduct of all dual-use purveyors is misplaced. Indeed, if the General Assembly truly had intended to provide the non-nuanced commercial protection described by appellants, it could easily have said so explicitly rather than implicitly embedding such an important shield against local regulation into a criminal statute. * * *

As I would find that no direct conflict exists between the Ordinance and the Act, I now address the second consideration in conflict preemption analysis: whether the local enactment stands "as an obstacle to the execution of the full purposes and objectives of the [General Assembly]." * * * Here, the goal of the Philadelphia Ordinance is fully congruent with the Act's purpose. The Ordinance targets dual-use items often used locally as drug paraphernalia, and seeks to provide disincentives for their distribution in the form of civil penalties. The items identified by the City as being closely related to drug use name a broad array of dual-use items, and include loosies and flavored tobacco in addition to the items specifically listed by the Act. The more expansive and locally-tailored reach of the Ordinance, however, is not a basis upon which to conclude that the municipality acted contrary to the General Assembly's intent. * * * According to the City, the local Ordinance addresses the peculiar local problems of (1) criminal enforcement of the Act when retail establishments that sell dual-use items are pervasive in a large city with an overburdened police force; and (2) readily available, cheap, loose and flavored tobacco products being used to ingest a controlled substance. In this sense, the Ordinance provisions regarding loosies and flavored tobacco further the Act's purpose by making it more difficult to obtain those specific items and discouraging a specific kind of illicit drug use. * * * In my view, the Ordinance * * * [is] not preempted by the Act. * * *

AMERICAN FINANCIAL SERVICES V. CITY OF OAKLAND

Supreme Court of California, 2005.
34 Cal.4th 1239, 23 Cal.Rptr.3d 453, 104 P.3d 813.

JUSTICE BROWN.

"Predatory lending" is a term generally used to characterize a range of abusive and aggressive lending practices, including deception or fraud, charging excessive fees and interest rates, making loans without regard to a borrower's ability to repay, or refinancing loans repeatedly over a short period of time to incur additional fees without any economic gain to the borrower. Predatory lending is most likely to occur in the rapidly growing "subprime" mortgage market, which is a market generally providing access to borrowers with impaired credit, limited income, or high debt relative to their income. Mortgages in this market tend to be in smaller amounts, and with faster prepayments and significantly higher interest rates and fees, than "prime" mortgages.

In 2001, California enacted legislation to combat predatory lending practices that typically occur in the subprime home mortgage market. Eight days before Division 1.6 was signed into law by the Governor, the City of Oakland adopted an ordinance regulating predatory lending practices in the Oakland home mortgage market. * * * We conclude that the Ordinance is preempted by Division 1.6, and therefore reverse the judgment of the Court of Appeal. * * *

Division 1.6 and the Ordinance are similar in that they regulate the same subject matter, i.e., predatory lending practices in home mortgages. However, Division 1.6 and the Ordinance differ in significant respects with regard to how they regulate these predatory practices. * * * We now turn to the question of whether these similarities and differences may coexist or, if instead, the Ordinance is preempted by Division 1.6. * * * Division 1.6 comprehensively regulates predatory lending practices in home mortgages. It delineates at length what mortgages are covered, what lending acts are prohibited, who can be held liable for violations of Division 1.6, the various enforcement mechanisms available, who may invoke such enforcement mechanisms, and defenses to such violations. The provisions of Division 1.6 "are so extensive in their scope that they clearly show an intention by the Legislature to adopt a general scheme for the regulation of" predatory lending tactics in home mortgages. (*In re Lane* [1962] 58 Cal.2d [99,] at p. 103, 22 Cal.Rptr. 857, 372 P.2d 897.)

Moreover, in regulating such lending tactics in home mortgages, the Legislature was not suddenly entering an area previously governed by municipalities and unexplored at a statewide level. To the contrary, as the City acknowledges, regulation of mortgage lenders has historically occurred at the state, not the municipal, level. In determining whether the Legislature intended to occupy the field of regulation of predatory home mortgage lending, we consider this historical role, and view Division 1.6 not in isolation, but as part of an overall legislative scheme addressing mortgage lending. * * * Indeed, when asked at oral argument, the City could point to no other instance in over 150 years of state history where a municipality had attempted to regulate mortgage lending. Thus, state activity in the area of regulation of mortgage lending was not only historically dominant, it was exclusive. * * *.

Moreover, it is beyond peradventure that effective regulation of mortgage lending, and in particular here abusive practices in such lending, "requires uniform treatment throughout the state." (*Chavez [v. Sargent,]* [1959] 52 Cal. 2d. [162,] at p. 177, 339 P.2d. 801.) California's housing market is one of its most critical, and securities based on home loans in this market are sold not only on a statewide, but on a national level. Commercial reality today would confound any effective regulation of mortgage lending based on potentially hundreds of competing and inconsistent measures at the local level. Rather, centralized command over such mortgage lending practices provides an essential "regulatory lever." * * * We therefore conclude that through the enactment of Division 1.6, the Legislature has fully occupied the field of regulation of predatory tactics in home mortgages. While in other cases the determination of whether the state and local laws occupy the same "field" may be somewhat nuanced, little is left to the imagination of even the most casual reader here. Both Division 1.6 and the Ordinance regulate predatory lending tactics in home mortgages, and do so in parallel fashion. * * * [I]t is undisputed the Ordinance applies to at least all home loans covered by Division 1.6. Moreover, the Ordinance regulates many of the same predatory practices addressed by Division 1.6, and prevalent in subprime lending, such as excessive prepayment fees, making loans without any reasonable expectation they can be repaid, refinancing with no benefit to the borrower, encouraging default on an existing loan in connection with refinancing that loan, financing unnecessary products such as credit insurance, unfairly accelerating indebtedness, and financing excessive points and fees. Thus, the Ordinance is not supplementary legislation that in other contexts might be allowed, but a line item veto of those policy decisions by the Legislature with which the City disagrees. In revisiting this area fully occupied by state law, the Ordinance undermines the considered judgments and choices of the Legislature, and is therefore preempted.

In drafting Division 1.6, the Legislature balanced two compelling and competing considerations, i.e., the need to protect particularly vulnerable consumers from predatory lending practices and the concern homeowners not be unduly hindered in accessing the equity in their own homes. * * * While destructive lending practices occur most often in connection with subprime lending, such lending is not inherently abusive, and has enabled an entire class of individuals with impaired credit to enter the housing market or access the equity in their homes. Severe regulation of subprime lending might cause lenders to cease making such loans in California, or preclude borrowers from obtaining a loan based on equity in their home even though such loans can serve a legitimate need. Moreover, increased regulation generally entails additional cost, decreasing further the availability of loan funds to subprime borrowers. Thus, the Legislature was aware regulation of certain predatory practices in mortgage lending, practices which occur most often in the subprime market, could have the unintended consequence of hurting those the legislation was intended to help, and sought to balance these competing concerns. The Ordinance, and the possibility of other divergent and competing local measures throughout California, upsets that balance. * * *

Taking just one example, Division 1.6 expressly does "not impose liability on an assignee that is a holder in due course" and the provisions of the division do not apply to "persons chartered by Congress to engage in secondary mortgage market transactions." (Fin. Code, § 4979.8.) The Ordinance expressly imposes such liability. (Oak.Mun.Code, § 5.33.070.) Such an extension of liability to "[a]ny person who purchases or is otherwise assigned a home loan" (§ 5.33.070) may result in secondary purchasers being hesitant or unwilling to purchase mortgages originating in Oakland. Should other cities adopt a similar extension of liability, subprime lending could conceivably be sharply curtailed in the state, despite the Legislature's efforts to avoid such an event. As AFSA observes, the Ordinance "not only contradicts a careful legislative choice, [it] threatens to disrupt secondary market transactions, interrupting the flow of loan capital to this state," and "divide the state's economy into tiny geographic markets."

For the reasons cited above, it is difficult to imagine how the state could maintain a centralized and uniform command in regulating predatory tactics in home mortgages if municipalities were free to regulate the area with respect to loans in amounts in excess of the state statutory ceiling. * * *

CHIEF JUSTICE GEORGE (dissenting).

* * * Under normal circumstances, the mere absence of express preemption language would not be dispositive. But here the party arguing in support of preemption explicitly has admitted that there were insufficient votes in the Legislature to enact the bill with an express preemption provision. * * * This is not a situation where the preemption issue was abstract or peripheral. Indeed, the issue of preemption was arguably at the forefront of the debate * * *. For instance, the members of the Senate Banking Committee that forged the legislative compromise that led to passage of the bill heard testimony from Oakland City Councilman Ignacio de la Fuente regarding the imminent passage of the Ordinance. In response to this testimony, a committee member expressed concern that without express preemption language, there would be a host of different lending policies from community to community. In response, the bill's co-author, Assemblywoman Migden, stated * * *: "We're trying to make sure that everyone can live with the bill, industry and consumers alike and . . . we've decided . . . to be silent on [preemption], which does lend different interpretations." * * * At the same hearing, the committee also heard from numerous financial industry representatives who urged the committee to include preemption language. * * * This effort by the financial industry to include express preemption language in the statute further establishes that silence on the preemption issue was not inadvertent but deliberate, part of a legislative compromise "to make sure that everyone can live with this bill, industry and consumers alike." * * *

Nonetheless, it can be argued * * * that the stalemate on the preemption issue neither supports nor undermines a conclusion as to preemption, and that the court should resort to certain default rules about preemption that it has developed over the years. But one of those rules, indeed the principal rule, is that legislative intent be clearly indicated. * * * The need for such a "clear indication" is especially acute when the extrinsic evidence and the concession of the parties demonstrate that the Legislature declined to adopt an express preemption provision because such a provision would not command a majority of the Legislature. A legislative stalemate on preemption is not an indication of a clear intent to preempt local legislation. * * *

The majority's emphasis on state uniformity and historical regulation patterns also fails to acknowledge properly the respect this court traditionally has accorded to localities regarding issues that have a unique local impact. * * * The regulation of predatory lending undoubtedly is an area of statewide concern. Nevertheless, I am not persuaded that the field is *exclusively* so, thus leaving no room for local regulation. * * * [A]lthough the need for state uniformity is an important consideration in resolving preemption questions, the interests of the locality also are entitled to considerable weight. * * * The record in this case establishes that Oakland's Ordinance was adopted because many low-income homeowners in the City of Oakland were targeted by unethical mortgage lenders using predatory lending practices. Many low- and moderate-income homeowners in Oakland were unable to obtain conventional legitimate financing. Local conditions allowed predatory lenders to thrive, and their practices unfairly stripped homes of equity value and resulted in a number of unjust home foreclosures. Often, through fraudulent means, homeowners were charged exorbitant fees and interest rates and unfairly were persuaded to incur mortgage debt in excess of their needs or ability to pay. The record reflects that the Oakland City Council, in passing the ordinance in question, found that the predatory lending problem in Oakland was particularly aggravated "because of the high number of minority and low income homeowners in Oakland, and the pressures of gentrification in certain neighborhoods" that increase property values and home equity," which have led to a situation in which "Oakland residents in low income areas have been perceived to be 'the house rich and the cash poor' and thus are prime targets for predatory lending practices." * * *

Oakland's particular interest in regulating subprime loans goes beyond merely protecting its particularly vulnerable citizens. As one amicus curiae points out, "predatory lending is not just a consumer protection issue; it is a *community development* issue, because it threatens the stability of lower income homeowning neighborhoods. * * * Predatory home mortgage lending has enormous impacts on targeted neighborhoods. Predatory lending practices, particularly the phenomenon of 'asset based lending,' contribute to an increase in the number of foreclosures. This can result in abandoned houses and blighted neighborhoods and contribute to the physical and economic deterioration of lower-income, minority, and inner city communities. 'Foreclosures, especially in low-and moderate-income neighborhoods turn what might be typically viewed as a consumer protection problem . . . into a community development problem, in which increased foreclosures lead to property abandonment and blight.' "

In view of the community degradation caused by predatory lending, Oakland reasonably could have concluded that it was important to include holders in due course within the Ordinance's purview. The bulk sale of mortgage loans on the secondary market is the primary profit incentive for subprime mortgage lenders. The innovation of selling mortgage loans in bulk is, in fact, what fueled the enormous growth of the subprime mortgage industry. As the City of Oakland points out, "sales of subprime loans by predatory lenders is the inducement and profit-basis for their business practice of encouraging ever higher and larger loans to subprime borrowers, i.e. larger 'inventory' of loans for sale to others—all to the detriment of the consumer public." Thus, Oakland reasonably could have concluded that because the bulk of subprime loans are sold on the secondary market, the Ordinance would have significantly greater deterrence effect if borrowers were able to invoke the defense of predatory lending in a foreclosure or other enforcement action against the secondary buyers who otherwise might be immune from liability. Otherwise, as one amicus curiae points out, "[s]ince most subprime loans are sold on the secondary market, the lack of assignee liability provides little incentive to the industry to clean up its practices." * * *

In view of the documented evidence that predatory lending is especially pervasive in low-income and minority neighborhoods, it is beyond dispute that Oakland and other similarly situated localities have a more significant interest in regulating subprime lending than localities that, because of demographics and composition, are not targeted in similar ways. Local regulation thus is not only constitutionally valid, but practically vital to the affected communities. Although predatory lending certainly is a matter of statewide concern, the specific interests of the communities most affected by the banned practices make the regulation of this field particularly amenable to local variations. Oakland's own interest in preventing predatory lending provides ample justification for that locality's enactment of stricter and more protective regulations designed to ensure that its residents receive adequate information before saddling themselves with financial obligations that could prove devastating. * * *

DAVID J. BARRON, GERALD E. FRUG, & RICK T. SU,
DISPELLING THE MYTH OF HOME RULE: LOCAL
POWER IN GREATER BOSTON
Pp. 9–12 (2004).

* * * Municipalities often want to pass local laws that may or may not conflict with state statutes. They might want to impose sanctions on a particular activity stricter than the state imposes or regulate a subject matter in a different way. That was the case when one town unsuccessfully sought to regulate the use of pesticides when not used for agricultural or domestic purposes. Even though the town bylaw would not have permitted a use of pesticides contrary to the Massachusetts Pesticide Control Act, the question remained whether localities were impliedly barred from prohibiting the use of pesticides allowed by the state act. In this instance, the town went ahead and enacted the bylaw, but the Supreme Judicial Court concluded that the Pesticide Control Act preempted the local action, albeit only by implication. Given this kind of judicial decision and the fact that the state has extensive regulations dealing with almost all aspects of local governance, it is difficult for municipalities to enact anything without questioning whether they are infringing on state policies. Court decisions dealing with preemption generate further confusion because they often rely on judicial interpretations of what the state intended to do in enacting the legislation in question—an interpretation that is hard to predict in advance.

An official from Duxbury commented on the general confusion regarding home rule authority: "I don't think most people totally understand what that authority is or what that power may be, real or perceived." Town officials of Foxborough named state preemption as one of the dominant roadblocks inhibiting their ability to take action because it is so difficult to determine beforehand what has not been preempted by state statute. When one town counsel was asked whether she ever advised town administrators to abandon a course of action because it contravened a state statute, she answered that it "was not at all uncommon" for her to do so. "Whatever the particular issues is, [the town has] to understand that although there is home rule, [it only exists] within this framework. It really isn't true home rule." She added: "You can almost always trace back a connection to state statutes. If the city council asks my office, we want to pass this ordinance on x, is that all right? We have to look and see if there's state law on that that precludes us from doing anything, certain things, or are we left on our own. They trumpet the home rule idea and you would think that means you can do whatever you like. Far from it. The first inquiry has to be, what's already there and how much does it confine us."

To emphasize the degree to which state presence is pervasive, a Gloucester official said: "pooper-scooper laws are also big—that's an area where municipalities have complete authority. But how important is that?" Comments from a town official from Sherborn cast doubt on the notion that even this area is free of state interference. She suggested that it was difficult for the town to address local issues such as "dog complaints" without consulting with the state because penalties and hearings are heavily regulated by the state. Even town officials who felt home rule established a presumption in favor of local power noted the prevalence and malleability of state preemption. A Sherborn official defended the importance of home rule but commented on how difficult it is to use those powers confidently because of the prevalence of state preemption.

As a result of this ambiguity, localities, whether or not they think they may have power to take a particular action, often file a home rule petition seeking state legislative permission to act—unless, that is, they abandon their intended course of action altogether. An example comes from the town of Arlington. The town wanted to establish a bylaw that would protect certain historic buildings by placing them into a "special places" category. But Arlington did not want to rely on the specific statutes that might have given them the power to do so. It did not want to establish a separate historic district pursuant to its powers delegated by chapter 40C because that would require establishing several districts, each of which would encompass only one building. For the same reason it did not want to establish special zones pursuant to its zoning powers under chapter 40A. Although neither of these statutes expressly prevented the town from acting on its own in the manner it envisioned, fears that a court would hold that its bylaw frustrated these existing state statutes led the town to file a home rule petition seeking legislative authorization of its action rather than going ahead with confidence in its home rule authority. By offering an alternate, but safer, path, the ability to obtain enabling legislation from the state thus discourages municipalities from using their home rule authority.

One legal counsel for towns in the Boston area offered another example of the practice. He noted that towns routinely seek special legislative permission whenever they enter into a long-term lease because "there's some reference to time limits in the statutes," even though, in his view, most long-term leases would not be covered by those statutes. Some of the impetus for this caution, he and other respondents noted, may come from the private parties with whom the municipality is dealing. They may be fearful of entering into a loan agreement or a land deal with a municipality without complete assurance about the locality's authority— assurance that can best be secured through special state legislation.

The internalization of this kind of cautiousness structures the second category of municipal response to the grant of home rule power: communities come to believe that the grant of home rule authority in fact did not turn over any real power to them. To some extent, this sentiment is unwarranted as a legal matter. The legal counsel for two municipalities in the region explained that "there's still a great tendency on the part of municipalities to assume that they need legislative authority to do things that they probably have the right to do. [There is a] huge number of home rule petitions filed in the legislature, most of which are unnecessary." Nevertheless, the sense that localities lack legal authority clearly shapes how municipal officials conceive of their legal options. One town administrator told us that towns "do not have home rule powers, the state controls everything that we do." Another felt that municipalities have home rule in name only. From his own experience and his comparison with other home rule states, he found the traditional concept of home rule flipped in Massachusetts: "If it doesn't specifically say that you can do it, you can't." * * *

It is important to note that a number of respondents had the opposite view of local home rule authority. They described their home rule experience according to its traditional definition—as a municipality's power to act whenever the state has not specifically prohibited it from doing so. However, the frequency of this answer was low—even among the majority of respondents who concluded that home rule was, as an overall matter, strong in the state. The officials that expressed this more positive view of their home rule powers seemed confident that the general grant of home rule authority enabled them to proceed as they saw fit. For example, an official from Bedford noted that, even though there are instances where the state intruded, for the most part a town could proceed "without worrying about what the state says." A respondent from Littleton stated that home rule was very important because it allowed the town to adopt bylaws, and not just zoning bylaws, to address specific problems rather than relying on the state. An official from Boxborough agreed, calling the authority to adopt by-laws part of what "allows us to avoid a cookie-cutter approach to problems." An administrator from Nahant further supported municipal independence by stating: "We don't usually go to the state for anything." According to him, Nahant's town meetings and its home rule powers are capable of handling most local issues. As a town official from Hamilton explained: "We have found the basic structure of local government created by the underlying provisions of the Massachusetts General Laws to work well without frequent forays to the legislature to seek additional power. It may be that our Board of Selectmen interprets things so that they can solve local problems with the power they have."

Some of the municipalities that felt they were able to act independently of state supervision said so, however, not out of confidence in their home rule authority but almost in defiance of state power. One municipal administrator, who wished to remain anonymous, stated that he was able to accomplish all of his municipal objectives not by invoking home rule authority but by taking no notice of potential state interference. Another said that most of the time they "ignore the state and try to maximize the interest of the community." It is, then, not the home rule authority that instills these officials with the feeling that they can act. On most issues, they feel the state will never check and never know. * * *

CINCINNATI BELL TELEPHONE COMPANY V. CITY OF CINCINNATI

Supreme Court of Ohio, 1998.
81 Ohio St.3d 599, 693 N.E.2d 212.

MOYER, CHIEF JUSTICE. * * *

Municipal taxing power in Ohio is derived from the Ohio Constitution. Section 3, Article XVIII of the Constitution, the Home Rule Amendment, confers sovereignty upon municipalities to "exercise all powers of local self-government." As this court stated in *State ex rel. Zielonka v. Carrel* (1919), 99 Ohio St. 220, 227, 124 N.E. 134, 136, "[t]here can be no doubt that the grant of authority to exercise all powers of local government includes the power of taxation." However, the Constitution also gives to the General Assembly the power to limit municipal taxing authority. Section 6, Article XIII provides that "[t]he General Assembly shall provide for the organization of cities, and incorporated villages, by general laws, and restrict their power of taxation * * * so as to prevent the abuse of such power." Section 13, Article XVIII provides that "[l]aws may be passed to limit the power of municipalities to levy taxes and incur debts for local purposes * * *."

Appellants [Cincinnati and other cities] assert that their local net profits taxes are valid because the General Assembly has not, pursuant to these constitutional powers, expressly preempted such a tax from local imposition. * * * [They] suggest that the doctrine of implied preemption, upon which appellees rely, be abrogated. Implied preemption of taxation, these appellants and amicus argue, is an anachronistic doctrine, which is rooted in public policy considerations and derives no support from the Constitution. For the reasons that follow, we agree. * * *

This court * * * established the doctrine of implied preemption in *Cincinnati v. Am. Tel. & Tel. Co.* (1925), 112 Ohio St. 493, 147 N.E. 806. There, the city of Cincinnati attempted to levy an excise tax, at an annual flat rate, on all railroads, telegraph companies, and telephone companies operating or doing business within the city limits. At the same time, the state levied excise taxes, on income measured by gross receipts, upon the same companies. This court concluded that the municipal taxes were preempted by the state excise taxes, reasoning that "[t]he power granted to the municipality by Section 3, Article XVIII, of the Constitution * * * does not extend to fields within such municipality which have already been occupied by the state." * * *

That the court has struggled to apply the doctrine it created in *Cincinnati v. AT & T* is reflected by subsequent attempts to define what it meant in its holding that municipal taxing power "does not extend to fields within such municipality which have already been occupied by the state." In one case, we implied that "field" might be defined by the types of taxes involved, i.e., excise as opposed to income taxes. * * * In contrast, this court has at other times taken a broader view of what constitutes the "field" of taxation. In *Haefner* [*v. Youngstown* (1946), 147 Ohio St. 58, 33 O.O. 247, 68 N.E.2d 64], the court premised its application of implied preemption on an analysis of the entire taxing scheme imposed upon utilities by the General Assembly. Similarly, Chief Justice O'Neill, concurring in *Cleveland* [*v. Kosydar* (1973), 36 Ohio St.2d 183, 65 O.O.2d 401, 305 N.E.2d 803], stated that "if the General Assembly has levied a tax on a particular subject matter, it will be presumed that the General Assembly has impliedly exercised its power to prohibit a local tax on the same subject matter." The difficulty encountered by this court in applying the doctrine of implied preemption is perhaps best illustrated by our statement in *East Ohio Gas* [*v. Akron* (1966), 7 Ohio St.2d 73, 36 O.O.2d 56, 218 N.E.2d 608,] that "[a] reading of the cases cited above will demonstrate that the language of this court, in asserting or denying the doctrine of pre-emption by implication, has sometimes been obscure, ambiguous, inconsistent and on occasion, almost contradictory to previous cases in stating the grounds upon which the court's judgment was based."

Today we end that confusion by analyzing municipal taxing power within the context of the source of that power—the Ohio Constitution. Prior to the passage of the Home Rule Amendment, the source and extent of municipal power was derived from the enactments of the General Assembly. Passage of the Home Rule Amendment provided municipalities with "full and complete political power in all matters of local self government." * * * By the grant of this authority, the intention of the Home Rule Amendment was to eliminate statutory control over municipalities by the General Assembly. Its passage granted " 'municipalities sovereignty in matters of local self-government, limited only by other constitutional provisions.' " *Canton v. Whitman* (1975), 44 Ohio St.2d 62, 65, 73 O.O.2d 285, 289, 337 N.E.2d 766, 769. Given this general, broad grant of power that municipalities enjoy under Article XVIII, the Constitution requires that the provisions allowing the General Assembly to limit municipal taxing power be interpreted in a manner consistent with the purpose of home rule.

The clauses from which the General Assembly derives power to limit the exercise of municipal taxing power * * * clearly delegate power to the

General Assembly to limit exercise of the municipal taxing power. When these provisions are interpreted in relation to the purpose and scope of the Home Rule Amendment, it is evident that a proper exercise of this limiting power requires an express act of restriction by the General Assembly. The mere enactment of state legislation that results in an occupation of a field of taxation is not sufficient to constitute an exercise of the General Assembly's constitutional power to limit municipal taxation. To construe the enactment of such legislation to impliedly preempt municipal taxing powers would contravene the principle underlying Article XVIII—that municipal powers are derived from the Constitution and not from the General Assembly. * * * Accordingly, given the delegation, by the people of the state, of power to levy taxes for municipal purposes, the exercise of that power is to be considered in all respects valid, unless the General Assembly has acted affirmatively by exercising its constitutional prerogative. In the absence of an express statutory limitation demonstrating the exercise, by the General Assembly, of its constitutional power, acts of municipal taxation are valid. * * *

Very clearly, there is no provision in the Ohio Constitution that contains words preventing a municipality from exercising its taxing power simply because the General Assembly has enacted tax legislation of its own. Rather, the foregoing analysis indicates a balanced delegation of power, by the people, to municipalities and the General Assembly with respect to municipal taxing power. This balance is best maintained by interpreting the specific limiting power of the General Assembly such that it does not engulf the general power of taxation delegated to municipalities. * * * There is no constitutional provision that directly prohibits both the state and municipalities from occupying the same area of taxation at the same time. Rather, the Constitution presumes that both the state and municipalities may exercise full taxing powers, unless the General Assembly has acted expressly to preempt municipal taxation, pursuant to its constitutional authority to do so. Our interpretation of that authority today is consistent with the constitutional powers granted to municipalities under Article XVIII, and our law that Article XVIII powers may be limited only by other constitutional provisions.

Having determined that there is no constitutional basis that supports the continued application of the doctrine of implied preemption, we are compelled, by virtue of the foregoing analysis, to overrule *Cincinnati v. Am. Tel. & Tel. Co.*, *East Ohio Gas v. Akron*, and paragraph four and the portion of paragraph three of the syllabus in *Haefner v. Youngstown* that is inconsistent with our holding today. The power to restrict municipal taxing power as granted by Section 13, Article XVIII and Section 6, Article XIII of the Ohio Constitution requires the General Assembly to preempt municipal taxing power by express statutory provision. * * *

B. THE RELATIONSHIP BETWEEN CITIES AND THE FEDERAL GOVERNMENT

The ability of cities to exercise independent power requires independence not only from the states but also from the federal government. Of course, the task of establishing the proper relationship between the federal government and state and local governments is a major political issue in the United States. It is also, as this section reveals, a hotly debated issue of federal law.[14]

The name usually given for this set of issues is "federalism," a name that suggests that the relative power of the national government and the states is at stake. But, in fact, federalism is also important for cities. The national government often attempts to regulate what cities can and cannot do. Appeals to federalism-based limits on national power, therefore, provide cities with a potentially critical line of defense against central power.

The label "federalism" can be misleading for another reason. It may suggest there is a single way to protect state and local governments from federal power. But, in fact, there are many different approaches available, and each represents a version of "federalism." The first three cases excerpted below—*National League of Cities v. Usery, Garcia v. San Antonio Metropolitan Transit Authority*, and *Printz v. United States*—provide some examples of how the Supreme Court has treated federalism over the last few decades. In each one, a local government or local governmental official appeals to federalism to prevent enforcement of a federal statute. The fourth case excerpted below, *National Federation of Independent Business (NFIB) v. Sebelius*, involves yet another treatment of federalism. It enforces a limitation on the federal government's ability

---

[14] There is an extensive literature on this debate. See, e.g., Heather Gerkin, Our Federalism(s), 53 Wm. & Mary L. Rev. 1549 (2012); Laurie Reynolds, A Role for Local Government Law in Federal-State-Local Disputes, 43 Urb. Law. 977 (2011); Yishai Blank, Federalism, Subsidiarity, and the Role of Local Governments in an Age of Global Multilevel Governance, 37 Fordham Urb. L. J. 509 (2010); Heather Gerken, Foreword: Federalism All the Way Down, 124 Harv. L. Rev. 4 (2010); David J. Barron, Fighting Federalism with Federalism: If It's Not Just a Battle Between Federalists and Nationalists, What is It?, 74 Fordham L. Rev. 2081 (2006); Robert A. Schapiro, From Dualist Federalism to Interactive Federalism, 56 Emory L.J. 1 (2006); Ernest A. Young, The Rehnquist Court's Two Federalisms, 83 Tex. L. Rev. 1 (2004); Richard H. Fallon, Jr., The "Conservative" Paths of the Rehnquist Court's Federalism Decisions, 69 U.Chi. L. Rev. 429 (2002); Larry Kramer, Putting the Politics Back into the Political Safeguards of Federalism, 100 Colum. L. Rev. 215 (2000); Laurence Tribe, American Constitutional Law 795–961 (3d ed. 2000); Roderick Hills, Dissecting the State: The Use of Federal Law to Free State and Local Officials from State Legislatures' Control, 97 U. Mich. L. Rev. 1201 (1999); Roderick Hills, The Political Economy of Cooperative Federalism: Why State Autonomy Makes Sense and "Dual Sovereignty" Doesn't, 96 U. Mich. L. Rev. 813 (1998); Martha Field, Garcia v. San Antonio Metropolitan Transit Authority: The Demise of a Misguided Doctrine, 99 Harv. L. Rev. 84 (1985); Frank Michelman, States' Rights and States' Roles: Permutations of "Sovereignty" in National League of Cities v. Usery, 86 Yale L. J. 1165 (1977); Herbert Wechsler, The Political Safeguards of Federalism: The Role of the States in the Composition and Selection of the National Government, 54 Colum. L. Rev. 543 (1954).

to use its spending power to condition what states and local governments must do in order to receive federal funds. How can the federal government's offer to pay for something ever infringe the rights of a state or city? Alternatively, if an offer to pay can't infringe their rights, couldn't the federal government use its spending power to get cities and states to do just about anything?

As these cases indicate, the Court has not followed a consistent path in placing federalism-based limits on national power. In *National League of Cities*, the Court struck down a federal statute that imposed a minimum wage for municipal employees. In *Garcia*, the Court overruled *National League of Cities* and held that the Tenth Amendment of the United States Constitution imposed few if any judicially enforceable limits on Congress. *Printz* is one of a number of post-*Garcia* Supreme Court decisions that, notwithstanding the holding of *Garcia*, impose significant federalism restrictions on the national government's power. *NFIB* is another: it enforced a federalism-based limit on the federal government's spending power for the first time in more than half a century.[15]

---

[15] For ease of analysis, it is useful to group the recent federalism cases into five categories. First, there are cases, like *Printz* itself, that bar the federal government from commandeering state and local governments. *See also* New York v. United States, 505 U.S. 144, 112 S.Ct. 2408, 120 L.Ed.2d 120 (1992) (invalidating federal statute governing state siting of hazardous waste facilities). Second, there are cases that limit the federal government's power to regulate interstate commerce. See National Federation of Independent Business v. Sebelius, 567 U.S. ___ (2012) (ruling Congress lacks the power under the Commerce Clause and the Necessary and Proper Clause to require individuals to purchase health insurance, although Congress may rely on its taxing power to require individuals to make a monetary payment for failing to purchase such insurance); United States v. Morrison, 529 U.S. 598, 120 S.Ct. 1740, 146 L.Ed.2d 658 (2000) (holding Congress lacked the power under the Commerce Clause to provide a civil remedy to the victims of gender-motivated violence); United States v. Lopez, 514 U.S. 549, 115 S.Ct. 1624, 131 L.Ed.2d 626 (1995) (holding Congress lacked affirmative power under the Commerce Clause to enact the Gun-Free School Zones Act of 1990, which made it a federal offense to knowingly possess a firearm in a school zone). The third line of cases sets limits on Congress's power to "enforce" the rights guaranteed by the Reconstruction Amendments, such as the Fourteenth and Fifteenth Amendments. See, e.g., Shelby County v. Holder, 570 U.S. ___ (2013) (holding Congress exceeded its power to enforce the Fifteenth Amendment in establishing the formula for determining which state and local jurisdictions were covered by the Voting Rights Act's requirement that they pre-clear changes in voting procedures with the United States Department of Justice); Board of Trustees of the University of Alabama v. Garrett, 531 U.S. 356, 121 S.Ct. 955, 148 L.Ed.2d 866 (2001), (invalidating the provision of Title I of the American With Disabilities Act that authorized private parties to sue States for damages if they failed to make special accommodations in employment of the disabled); Kimel v. Florida Board of Regents, 528 U.S. 62, 120 S.Ct. 631, 145 L.Ed.2d 522 (2000) (invalidating the provision of the Age Discrimination in Employment Act that permitted private individuals to sue states for violating that statute); *Morrison, supra* (holding not only that Congress lacks power under the Commerce Clause to enact the civil remedy provided by the Violence Against Women Act, but also that Congress lacks the power under Section 5 to enact such a measure); City of Boerne v. Flores, 521 U.S. 507, 117 S.Ct. 2157, 138 L.Ed.2d 624 (1997) (holding Congress lacked power under Section 5 to enact the Religious Freedom Restoration Act (RFRA), which barred state and local governments from "substantially burdening" the exercise of religion except upon a showing that the burden served a compelling governmental interest by the least restrictive means). The fourth line of cases has its roots in the Eleventh Amendment's limitation on the amenability of a state to a suit by a private party in federal court. See Seminole Tribe v. Florida, 517 U.S. 44, 116 S.Ct.

The full import of the recent federalism cases—sometimes called the federalism revival or the new federalism—remains to be seen. Many of them have been decided by a 5–4 margin, and the dissenting justices have not indicated an intention to abide by them in the future. But while there were some signs early on that the federalism revival might be running out of steam,[16] the Court's recent decisions invalidating a portion of the Affordable Care Act and a portion of the Voting Rights Act shows that the new federalism jurisprudence remains very much a force.[17] Collectively, then, the new federalism cases demonstrate that a majority of the Court is committed to enforcing meaningful federalism constraints in a way that the majority of the Court that decided *Garcia* was not.

For a course in local government law, a critical question in evaluating this shift concerns whether cities would be better off if the Court returned to the more hands-off approach that *Garcia* seemed to endorse. David Barron explores the complex relationship between limiting central power and promoting local power in *A Localist Critique of the New Federalism*, excerpted below. The United States Conference of Mayors filed a brief defending the federal statute at issue in *Printz*. How does Barron's analysis help explain why it might have done so?

The fact that cities and states often have divergent interests also raises the intriguing possibility that the national government might ally itself with cities to protect them from their states. Should the national government have the power to forge such an alliance? The next two decisions, *Lawrence County v. Lead-Deadwood School District* and *Nixon*

1114, 134 L.Ed.2d 252 (1996) (holding Congress may not exercise its Article I powers to authorize private individuals to sue states in federal court); see also Alden v. Maine, 527 U.S. 706, 119 S.Ct. 2240, 144 L.Ed.2d 636 (1999) (holding that the federal government impermissibly intrudes on state sovereignty when it authorizes a private individual to sue an unconsenting State in its own state court system). The fifth line of cases is, at this time, just a single point, National Federation of Independent Business v. Sebelius, but it may prove to be the most consequential. As the excerpt below shows, a portion of the Court's decision in that case bars the federal government from pressuring states and localities by conditioning the federal funds they may receive in certain circumstances; in that case, the federal government was threatening to terminate funding for existing state Medicaid programs unless states were willing to expand the persons covered by then. Cf. South Dakota v. Dole, 483 U.S. 203 (1987) (upholding federal law conditioning states' receipt of federal highway funds on states adopting a federally-prescribed age-limit for drinking alcohol).

[16] In the wake of *Lopez* and *Morrison*, the Court rejected federalism-based challenges under the Commerce Clause in Gonzales v. Raich, 545 U.S. 1, 125 S.Ct. 2195, 162 L.Ed.2d 1 (2005), and Section Five of the Fourteenth Amendment in Tennessee v. Lane, 541 U.S. 509, 124 S.Ct. 1978, 158 L.Ed.2d 820 (2004) (upholding Title II of the Americans With Disability Act insofar as it permits states to be sued by private parties for denying access to the courts), and Nevada Dep't of Human Resources v. Hibbs, 538 U.S. 721, 123 S.Ct. 1972, 155 L.Ed.2d 953 (upholding Congress's Section 5 authority to permit private suits against states to enforce the Family Medical Leave Act). It also has turned back the only commandeering challenge brought since *Printz*. See Reno v. Condon, 528 U.S. 141, 120 S.Ct. 666, 145 L.Ed.2d 587 (2000) (rejecting South Carolina's contention that the Driver's Privacy Protection Act (DPPA) impermissibly commandeered state officials).

[17] See National Federation of Independent Business v. Sebelius, 567 U.S. ___ (2012); Shelby County v. Holder, 570 U.S. ___ (2013).

v. Missouri Municipal League, present this question in the context of interpreting ambiguous federal statutes. Are the holdings consistent with each other? Is the Court's position in *Lead-Deadwood* consistent with the state/local relationship articulated in *Hunter*? Conversely, is the Court's position in *Nixon* consistent with the widespread recognition of home rule? More generally, is federal power likely to be a promising source for city protection against state power?

Consider too how the uncertain legal status of cities complicates the federal-city relationship. On the one hand, under *Hunter*, local governments are subdivisions of the state; therefore cities, like states, would seem to be entitled to assert federalism-based constitutional protections. On the other hand, there is a long tradition of treating cities as different from their states, either because they have power in their own right or because they are more like private businesses than governments. The Note on the Federal-City Relationship addresses these conflicting understandings of the nature of cities as they arise in constitutional and statutory contexts.

Finally, there is the more strategic, but no less important, question: what should those who believe in decentralization want the federal government to do (particularly if the federal policies are ones they embrace)? An excerpt from an article by David Barron raises concerns that progressive people might have about the continuing role of cities when a federal administration they support takes office. Similar issues, of course, face conservatives when their candidates are in power.

NATIONAL LEAGUE OF CITIES V. USERY

Supreme Court of the United States, 1976.
426 U.S. 833, 96 S.Ct. 2465, 49 L.Ed.2d 245.

MR. JUSTICE REHNQUIST delivered the opinion of the Court.

Nearly 40 years ago Congress enacted the Fair Labor Standards Act, and required employers covered by the Act to pay their employees a minimum hourly wage and to pay them at one and one-half times their regular rate of pay for hours worked in excess of 40 during a workweek. * * * The original Fair Labor Standards Act passed in 1938 specifically excluded the States and their political subdivisions from its coverage. In 1974, however, * * * Congress * * * extended the minimum wage and maximum hour provisions to almost all public employees employed by the States and by their various political subdivisions. Appellants in these cases include individual cities and States, the National League of Cities, and the National Governors' Conference; they brought an action in the District Court for the District of Columbia which challenged the validity of the 1974 amendments. They asserted in effect that when Congress sought to apply the Fair Labor Standards Act provisions virtually across the board to employees of state and municipal governments it "infringed a constitutional prohibition" running in favor of the States *as States.* * * *

We have repeatedly recognized that there are attributes of sovereignty attaching to every state government which may not be impaired by Congress, not because Congress may lack an affirmative grant of legislative authority to reach the matter, but because the Constitution prohibits it from exercising the authority in that manner. * * * One undoubted attribute of state sovereignty is the States' power to determine the wages which shall be paid to those whom they employ in order to carry out their governmental functions, what hours those persons will work, and what compensation will be provided where these employees may be called upon to work overtime. The question we must resolve here, then, is whether these determinations are 'functions essential to separate and independent existence,' [of States, *Coyle v. Oklahoma,* 221 U.S. 55, at 580], so that Congress may not abrogate the States' otherwise plenary authority to make them. * * *

Judged solely in terms of increased costs in dollars, these allegations show a significant impact on the functioning of the governmental bodies involved. * * * Quite apart from the[se] substantial costs * * *, the Act displaces state policies regarding the manner in which they will structure delivery of those governmental services which their citizens require. The Act, speaking directly to the States *qua* States, requires that they shall pay all but an extremely limited minority of their employees the minimum wage rates currently chosen by Congress. It * * * cannot be gainsaid that the federal requirement directly supplants the considered policy choices of the States' elected officials and administrators as to how they wish to structure pay scales in state employment. The State might wish to employ persons with little or no training, or those who wish to work on a casual basis, or those who for some other reason do not possess minimum employment requirements, and pay them less than the federally prescribed minimum wage. It may wish to offer part-time or summer employment to teenagers at a figure less than the minimum wage, and if unable to do so may decline to offer such employment at all. But the Act would forbid such choices by the States. * * *

This congressionally imposed displacement of state decisions may substantially restructure traditional ways in which the local governments have arranged their affairs.* * * The requirement imposing premium rates upon any employment in excess of what Congress has decided is appropriate for a governmental employee's workweek, for example, appears likely to have the effect of coercing the States to structure work periods in some employment areas, such as police and fire protection, in a manner substantially different from practices which have long been commonly accepted among local governments of this Nation. * * * Another example of congressional choices displacing those of the States in the area of what are without doubt essential governmental decisions may be found in the practice of using volunteer firemen, a source of manpower crucial to many of our smaller towns' existence. * * *

Our examination of the effect of the 1974 amendments, as sought to be extended to the States and their political subdivisions, satisfies us that both the minimum wage and the maximum hour provisions will impermissibly interfere with the integral governmental functions of these bodies. * * * [E]ven if we accept appellee's assessments concerning the impact of the amendments, their application will nonetheless significantly alter or displace the States' abilities to structure employer-employee relationships in such areas as fire prevention, police protection, sanitation, public health, and parks and recreation. These activities are typical of those performed by state and local governments in discharging their dual functions of administering the public law and furnishing public services. Indeed, it is functions such as these which governments are created to provide, services such as these which the States have traditionally afforded their citizens. If Congress may withdraw from the States the authority to make those fundamental employment decisions upon which their systems for performance of these functions must rest, we think there would be little left of the States' " 'separate and independent existence.' " *Coyle*, 221 U.S., at 580, 31 S.Ct., at 695. * * * This exercise of congressional authority does not comport with the federal system of government embodied in the Constitution. We hold that insofar as the challenged amendments operate to directly displace the States' freedom to structure integral operations in areas of traditional governmental functions, they are not within the authority granted Congress by Art. I, § 8, cl. 3. * * * The fire and police departments affected here * * * provide[ ] an integral portion of those governmental services which the States and their political subdivisions have traditionally afforded their citizens.[20] * * *

MR. JUSTICE BLACKMUN, concurring.

The Court's opinion and the dissents indicate the importance and significance of this litigation as it bears upon the relationship between the Federal Government and our States. Although I am not untroubled by certain possible implications of the Court's opinion—some of them suggested by the dissents—I do not read the opinion so despairingly as does my Brother Brennan. * * * I may misinterpret the Court's opinion, but it seems to me that it adopts a balancing approach, and does not outlaw federal power in areas such as environmental protection, where

---

[20] As the denomination "political subdivision" implies, the local governmental units which Congress sought to bring within the Act derive their authority and power from their respective States. Interference with integral governmental services provided by such subordinate arms of a state government is therefore beyond the reach of congressional power under the Commerce Clause just as if such services were provided by the State itself.

the federal interest is demonstrably greater and where state facility compliance with imposed federal standards would be essential. With this understanding on my part of the Court's opinion, I join it.

MR. JUSTICE BRENNAN, with whom MR. JUSTICE WHITE and MR. JUSTICE MARSHALL join, dissenting. * * *

The reliance of my Brethren upon the Tenth Amendment as "an express declaration of [a state sovereignty] limitation" not only suggests that they overrule governing decisions of this Court that address this question but must astound scholars of the Constitution. * * * Certainly the paradigm of sovereign action action *qua* State is in the enactment and enforcement of state laws. Is it possible that my Brethren are signaling abandonment of the heretofore unchallenged principle that Congress "can, if it chooses, entirely displace the States to the full extent of the far-reaching Commerce Clause"? *Bethlehem Steel Co. v. New York State Board,* 330 U.S. 767, 780, 67 S.Ct. 1026, 1033, 91 L.Ed. 1234 (1947) (opinion of Frankfurter, J.). * * * [T]he ouster of state laws obviously curtails or prohibits the States' prerogatives to make policy choices respecting subjects clearly of greater significance to the "State *qua* State" than the minimum wage paid to state employees. The Supremacy Clause dictates this result under "the federal system of government embodied in the Constitution."

My Brethren do more than turn aside longstanding constitutional jurisprudence that emphatically rejects today's conclusion. More alarming is the startling restructuring of our federal system, and the role they create therein for the federal judiciary. * * * It is unacceptable that the judicial process should be thought superior to the political process in this area. Under the Constitution the Judiciary has no role to play beyond finding that Congress has not made an unreasonable legislative judgment respecting what is "commerce." For not only early decisions, *Gibbons v. Ogden,* 9 Wheat., at 196; *McCulloch v. Maryland,* 4 Wheat., at 404–407; and *Martin v. Hunter's Lessee,* 1 Wheat. 304, 324–325, 4 L.Ed. 97 (1816), hold that nothing in the Tenth Amendment constitutes a limitation on congressional exercise of powers delegated by the Constitution to Congress. * * *

Judicial restraint in this area merely recognizes that the political branches of our Government are structured to protect the interests of the States, as well as the Nation as a whole, and that the States are fully able to protect their own interests in the premises. Congress is constituted of representatives in both the Senate and House *elected from the States.* * * * Judicial redistribution of powers granted the National Government by the terms of the Constitution violates the fundamental tenet of our federalism that the extent of federal intervention into the States' affairs in the exercise of delegated powers shall be determined by the States' exercise of political power through their representatives in Congress. * * *

MR. JUSTICE STEVENS, dissenting.

The Court holds that the Federal Government may not interfere with a sovereign State's inherent right to pay a substandard wage to the janitor at the state capitol. The principle on which the holding rests is difficult to perceive.

The Federal Government may, I believe, require the State to act impartially when it hires or fires the janitor, to withhold taxes from his paycheck, to observe safety regulations when he is performing his job, to forbid him from burning too much soft coal in the capitol furnace, from dumping untreated refuse in an adjacent waterway, from overloading a state-owned garbage truck, or from driving either the truck or the Governor's limousine over 55 miles an hour. Even though these and many other activities of the capitol janitor are activities of the State *qua* State, I have no doubt that they are subject to federal regulation. * * * Since I am unable to identify a limitation on that federal power that would not also invalidate federal regulation of state activities that I consider unquestionably permissible, I am persuaded that this statute is valid. Accordingly, with respect and a great deal of sympathy for the views expressed by the Court, I dissent from its constitutional holding.

GARCIA V. SAN ANTONIO METROPOLITAN TRANSIT AUTHORITY

Supreme Court of the United States, 1985.
469 U.S. 528, 105 S.Ct. 1005, 83 L.Ed.2d 1016.

JUSTICE BLACKMUN delivered the opinion of the Court.

We revisit in these cases an issue raised in *National League of Cities v. Usery,* 426 U.S. 833, 96 S.Ct. 2465, 49 L.Ed.2d 245 (1976). In that litigation, this Court, by a sharply divided vote, ruled that the Commerce Clause does not empower Congress to enforce the minimum-wage and overtime provisions of the Fair Labor Standards Act (FLSA) against the States "in areas of traditional governmental functions." * * * In the present cases, a Federal District Court concluded that municipal ownership and operation of a mass-transit system is a traditional governmental function and thus, under *National League of Cities,* is exempt from the obligations imposed by the FLSA. * * * Our examination of this "function" standard [as] applied * * * over the last eight years now persuades us that the attempt to draw the boundaries of state regulatory immunity in terms of "traditional governmental function" is not only unworkable but is inconsistent with established principles of federalism and, indeed, with those very federalism principles on which *National*

League of Cities purported to rest. That case, accordingly, is overruled.
* * *

[A]ppellee San Antonio Metropolitan Transit Authority (SAMTA), a public mass-transit authority organized on a countywide basis, * * * currently is the major provider of transportation in the San Antonio metropolitan area * * *. On November 2[, 1979] * * *, SAMTA filed this action against the Secretary of Labor in the United States District Court for the Western District of Texas. It sought a declaratory judgment that * * * *National League of Cities* precluded the application of the FLSA's overtime requirements to SAMTA's operations. * * *

The controversy in the present cases has focused on the * * * requirement * * * that the challenged federal statute trench on "traditional governmental functions." * * * Just how troublesome the task has been is revealed by the results reached in other federal cases. Thus, courts have held that regulating ambulance services, operating a municipal airport, performing solid waste disposal, and operating a highway authority, are functions *protected* under *National League of Cities*. At the same time, courts have held that issuance of industrial development bonds, regulation of intrastate natural gas sales, regulation of traffic on public roads, regulation of air transportation, operation of a telephone system, leasing and sale of natural gas, operation of a mental health facility, and provision of in-house domestic services for the aged and handicapped are *not* entitled to immunity. We find it difficult, if not impossible, to identify an organizing principle that places each of the cases in the first group on one side of a line and each of the cases in the second group on the other side. The constitutional distinction between licensing drivers and regulating traffic, for example, or between operating a highway authority and operating a mental health facility, is elusive at best. * * *

A further cautionary note is sounded * * * by the Court's experience in the related field of state immunity from federal taxation. In *South Carolina v. United States,* 199 U.S. 437, 26 S.Ct. 110, 50 L.Ed. 261 (1905), the Court held for the first time that the state tax immunity recognized in *Collector v. Day,* 11 Wall. 113, 20 L.Ed. 122 (1870), extended only to the "ordinary" and "strictly governmental" instrumentalities of state governments and not to instrumentalities "used by the State in the carrying on of an ordinary private business." While the Court applied the distinction outlined in *South Carolina* for the following 40 years, at no time during that period did the Court develop a consistent formulation of the kinds of governmental functions that were entitled to immunity. * * *

In 1911, for example, the Court declared that the provision of a municipal water supply "is no part of the essential governmental functions of a State." *Flint v. Stone Tracy Co.,* 220 U.S. 107, 172, 31 S.Ct.

342, 357, 55 L.Ed. 389. Twenty-six years later, without any intervening change in the applicable legal standards, the Court simply rejected its earlier position and decided that the provision of a municipal water supply *was* immune from federal taxation as an essential governmental function, even though municipal water works long had been operated for profit by private industry. At the same time that the Court was holding a municipal water supply to be immune from federal taxes, it had held that a state-run commuter rail system was *not* immune. * * * It was this uncertainty and instability that led the Court shortly thereafter, in *New York v. United States,* 326 U.S. 572, 66 S.Ct. 310, 90 L.Ed. 326 (1946), unanimously to conclude that the distinction between "governmental" and "proprietary" functions was "untenable" and must be abandoned. * * *

The distinction the Court discarded as unworkable in the field of tax immunity has proved no more fruitful in the field of regulatory immunity under the Commerce Clause. Neither do any of the alternative standards that might be employed to distinguish between protected and unprotected governmental functions appear manageable. We rejected the possibility of making immunity turn on a purely historical standard of "tradition" in *[Transportation Union v.] Long Island [R. Co.,* 455 U.S. 678, 102 S.Ct. 1349, 71 L.E.2d 547 (1982)] and properly so. The most obvious defect of a historical approach to state immunity is that it prevents a court from accommodating changes in the historical functions of States, changes that have resulted in a number of once-private functions like education being assumed by the States and their subdivisions. At the same time, the only apparent virtue of a rigorous historical standard, namely, its promise of a reasonably objective measure for state immunity, is illusory. Reliance on history as an organizing principle results in linedrawing of the most arbitrary sort; the genesis of state governmental functions stretches over a historical continuum from before the Revolution to the present, and courts would have to decide by fiat precisely how longstanding a pattern of state involvement had to be for federal regulatory authority to be defeated.

A nonhistorical standard for selecting immune governmental functions is likely to be just as unworkable as is a historical standard. The goal of identifying "uniquely" governmental functions, for example, has been rejected by the Court in the field of governmental tort liability in part because the notion of a "uniquely" governmental function is unmanageable. Another possibility would be to confine immunity to "necessary" governmental services, that is, services that would be provided inadequately or not at all unless the government provided them. The set of services that fits into this category, however, may well be negligible. The fact that an unregulated market produces less of some service than a State deems desirable does not mean that the State itself must provide the service; in most if not all cases, the State can "contract out" by hiring private firms to provide the service or simply by providing subsidies to existing suppliers. It also is open to question how well equipped courts are to make this kind of determination about the workings of economic markets.

We believe, however, that there is a more fundamental problem at work here, a problem that explains why the Court was never able to provide a basis for the governmental/proprietary distinction in the intergovernmental tax immunity cases and why an attempt to draw similar distinctions with respect to federal regulatory authority under *National League of Cities* is unlikely to succeed regardless of how the distinctions are phrased. The problem is that neither the governmental/proprietary distinction nor any other that purports to separate out important governmental functions can be faithful to the role of federalism in a democratic society. The essence of our federal system is that within the realm of authority left open to them under the Constitution, the States must be equally free to engage in any activity that their citizens choose for the common weal, no matter how unorthodox or unnecessary anyone else—including the judiciary—deems state involvement to be. Any rule of state immunity that looks to the "traditional," "integral," or "necessary" nature of governmental functions inevitably invites an unelected federal judiciary to make decisions about which state policies it favors and which ones it dislikes. * * * We therefore now reject, as unsound in principle and unworkable in practice, a rule of state immunity from federal regulation that turns on a judicial appraisal of whether a particular governmental function is "integral" or "traditional." Any such rule leads to inconsistent results at the same time that it disserves principles of democratic self-governance, and it breeds inconsistency precisely because it is divorced from those principles. If there are to be limits on the Federal Government's power to interfere with state functions—as undoubtedly there are—we must look elsewhere to find them. * * *

[T]he principal means chosen by the Framers to ensure the role of the States in the federal system lies in the structure of the Federal Government itself. It is no novelty to observe that the composition of the Federal Government was designed in large part to protect the States from overreaching by Congress. The Framers thus gave the States a role in the selection both of the Executive and the Legislative Branches of the Federal Government. The States were vested with indirect influence over the House of Representatives and the Presidency by their control of electoral qualifications and their role in presidential elections. U.S. Const., Art. I, § 2, and Art. II, § 1. They were given more direct influence in the Senate, where each State received equal representation and each Senator was to be selected by the legislature of his State. Art. I, § 3. The significance attached to the States' equal representation in the Senate is underscored by the prohibition of any constitutional amendment divesting a State of equal representation without the State's consent. Art. V. * * * State sovereign interests, then, are more properly protected by procedural safeguards inherent in the structure of the federal system than by judicially created limitations on federal power. * * *

We * * * are convinced that the fundamental limitation that the constitutional scheme imposes on the Commerce Clause to protect the "States as States" is one of process rather than one of result. Any substantive restraint on the exercise of Commerce Clause powers must find its justification in the procedural nature of this basic limitation, and it must be tailored to compensate for possible failings in the national political process rather than to dictate a "sacred province of state autonomy." *EEOC v. Wyoming,* 460 U.S., at 236, 103 S.Ct., at 1060.

Insofar as the present cases are concerned, then, we need go no further than to state that we perceive nothing in the overtime and minimum-wage requirements of the FLSA, as applied to SAMTA, that is destructive of state sovereignty or violative of any constitutional provision. SAMTA faces nothing more than the same minimum-wage and overtime obligations that hundreds of thousands of other employers, public as well as private, have to meet. * * * This analysis makes clear that Congress' action in affording SAMTA employees the protections of the wage and hour provisions of the FLSA contravened no affirmative limit on Congress' power under the Commerce Clause. * * *

JUSTICE POWELL, with whom THE CHIEF JUSTICE, JUSTICE REHNQUIST, and JUSTICE O'CONNOR join, dissenting. * * *

Much of the Court's opinion is devoted to arguing that it is difficult to define *a priori* "traditional governmental functions." *National League of Cities* neither engaged in, nor required, such a task. * * * But nowhere does it mention that *National League of Cities* adopted a familiar type of balancing test for determining whether Commerce Clause enactments transgress constitutional limitations imposed by the federal nature of our system of government. * * *

Today's opinion does not explain how the States' role in the electoral process guarantees that particular exercises of the Commerce Clause power will not infringe on residual State sovereignty. * * * The States' role in our system of government is a matter of constitutional law, not of legislative grace. * * * [T]he harm to the States that results from federal overreaching under the Commerce Clause is not simply a matter of dollars and cents. Nor is it a matter of the wisdom or folly of certain policy choices. Rather, by usurping functions traditionally performed by the States, federal overreaching under the Commerce Clause undermines the constitutionally mandated balance of power between the States and the federal government, a balance designed to protect our fundamental liberties. * * *

The question presented in this case is whether the extension of the FLSA to the wages and hours of employees of a city-owned transit system unconstitutionally impinges on fundamental state sovereignty. * * * The Court does not find in this case that the "federal interest is demonstrably greater." 426 U.S., at 856, 96 S.Ct., at 2476 (Blackmun, J., concurring). No such finding could have been made, for the state interest is compelling. The financial impact on States and localities of displacing their control over wages, hours, overtime regulations, pensions, and labor relations with their employees could have serious, as well as unanticipated, effects on state and local planning, budgeting, and the levying of taxes. As we said in *National League of Cities,* federal control of the terms and conditions of employment of State employees also inevitably "displaces state policies regarding the manner in which [States] will structure delivery of those governmental services that citizens require."

The Court emphasizes that municipal operation of an intracity mass transit system is relatively new in the life of our country. It nevertheless is a classic example of the type of service traditionally provided by local government. It is *local* by definition. It is indistinguishable in principle from the traditional services of providing and maintaining streets, public lighting, traffic control, water, and sewerage systems. Services of this kind are precisely those "with which citizens are more 'familiarly and minutely conversant.'" The Federalist, No. 46, p. 316. State and local officials of course must be intimately familiar with these services and sensitive to their quality as well as cost. Such officials also know that their constituents and the press respond to the adequacy, fair distribution, and cost of these services. It is this kind of state and local control and accountability that the Framers understood would insure the vitality and preservation of the federal system that the Constitution explicitly requires. * * *

PRINTZ V. UNITED STATES

Supreme Court of the United States, 1997.
521 U.S. 898, 117 S.Ct. 2365, 138 L.Ed.2d 914.

JUSTICE SCALIA delivered the opinion of the Court. * * *

The Gun Control Act of 1968 (GCA), 18 U.S.C. § 921 et seq., establishes a detailed federal scheme governing the distribution of firearms. * * * In 1993, Congress amended the GCA by enacting the Brady Act. The Act requires the Attorney General to establish a national instant background check system by November 30, 1998, and immediately puts in place certain interim provisions until that system becomes operative. Under the interim provisions, a firearms dealer who proposes to transfer a handgun must first: (1) receive from the transferee a statement (the Brady Form), containing the name, address and date of birth of the proposed transferee along with a sworn statement that the transferee is not among any of the classes of prohibited purchasers, (2) verify the identity of the transferee by examining an identification document, and (3) provide the "chief law enforcement officer" (CLEO) of the transferee's residence with notice of the contents (and a copy) of the Brady Form. With some exceptions, the dealer must then wait five business days before consummating the sale, unless the CLEO earlier notifies the dealer that he has no reason to believe the transfer would be illegal. * * *

Petitioners Jay Printz and Richard Mack, the CLEOs for Ravalli County, Montana, and Graham County, Arizona, respectively, filed separate actions challenging the constitutionality of the Brady Act's interim provisions. * * * From the description set forth above, it is apparent that the Brady Act purports to direct state law enforcement officers to participate, albeit only temporarily, in the administration of a federally enacted regulatory scheme. * * * The petitioners here object to being pressed into federal service, and contend that congressional action compelling state officers to execute federal laws is unconstitutional. * * *

It is incontestible that the Constitution established a system of "dual sovereignty." *Gregory v. Ashcroft*, 501 U.S. 452, 457, 115 L.Ed.2d 410, 111 S.Ct. 2395 (1991). * * * The power of the Federal Government would be augmented immeasurably if it were able to impress into its service—and at no cost to itself—the police officers of the 50 States. * * * It is an essential attribute of the States' retained sovereignty that they remain independent and autonomous within their proper sphere of authority. It is no more compatible with this independence and autonomy that their officers be "dragooned" (as Judge Fernandez put it in his dissent below) into administering federal law, than it would be compatible with the independence and autonomy of the United States that its officers be impressed into service for the execution of state laws. * * *

[T]he Government puts forward a cluster of arguments that can be grouped under the heading: "The Brady Act serves very important purposes, is most efficiently administered by CLEOs during the interim period, and places a minimal and only temporary burden upon state officers." There is considerable disagreement over the extent of the burden, but we need not pause over that detail. Assuming all the mentioned factors were true, they might be relevant if we were evaluating whether the incidental application to the States of a federal law of general applicability excessively interfered with the functioning of state governments. See, e.g., *National League of Cities v. Usery*, 426 U.S. 833, 853, 49 L.Ed.2d 245, 96 S.Ct. 2465 (1976) (overruled by *Garcia v. San*

Antonio Metropolitan Transit Authority, 469 U.S. 528, 83 L.Ed.2d 1016, 105 S.Ct. 1005 (1985)). But where, as here, it is the whole object of the law to direct the functioning of the state executive, and hence to compromise the structural framework of dual sovereignty, such a "balancing" analysis is inappropriate. It is the very principle of separate state sovereignty that such a law offends, and no comparative assessment of the various interests can overcome that fundamental defect. * * *

We * * * conclude categorically, as we concluded categorically in *New York* [*v. United States*]: "The Federal Government may not compel the States to enact or administer a federal regulatory program." The mandatory obligation imposed on CLEOs to perform background checks on prospective handgun purchasers plainly runs afoul of that rule. * * * The Federal Government may neither issue directives requiring the States to address particular problems, nor command the States' officers, or those of their political subdivisions, to administer or enforce a federal regulatory program. It matters not whether policymaking is involved, and no case-by-case weighing of the burdens or benefits is necessary; such commands are fundamentally incompatible with our constitutional system of dual sovereignty. * * *

JUSTICE STEVENS, with whom JUSTICE SOUTER, JUSTICE GINSBURG, and JUSTICE BREYER join, dissenting. * * *

There is not a clause, sentence, or paragraph in the entire text of the Constitution of the United States that supports the proposition that a local police officer can ignore a command contained in a statute enacted by Congress pursuant to an express delegation of power enumerated in Article I. * * * Absent even a modicum of textual foundation for its judicially crafted constitutional rule, there should be a presumption that if the Framers had actually intended such a rule, at least one of them would have mentioned it. The Court's "structural" arguments are not sufficient to rebut that presumption. The fact that the Framers intended to preserve the sovereignty of the several States simply does not speak to the question whether individual state employees may be required to perform federal obligations, such as registering young adults for the draft, creating state emergency response commissions designed to manage the release of hazardous substances, collecting and reporting data on underground storage tanks that may pose an environmental hazard, and reporting traffic fatalities and missing children to a federal agency.

As we explained in *Garcia v. San Antonio Metropolitan Transit Authority*: "The principal means chosen by the Framers to ensure the role of the States in the federal system lies in the structure of the Federal Government itself. It is no novelty to observe that the composition of the Federal Government was designed in large part to protect the States from overreaching by Congress." * * * The majority points to nothing suggesting that the political safeguards of federalism identified in *Garcia* need be supplemented by a rule, grounded in neither constitutional history nor text, flatly prohibiting the National Government from enlisting state and local officials in the implementation of federal law. * * *

Perversely, the majority's rule seems more likely to damage than to preserve the safeguards against tyranny provided by the existence of vital state governments. By limiting the ability of the Federal Government to enlist state officials in the implementation of its programs, the Court creates incentives for the National Government to aggrandize itself. In the name of State's rights, the majority would have the Federal Government create vast national bureaucracies to implement its policies. This is exactly the sort of thing that the early Federalists promised would not occur, in part as a result of the National Government's ability to rely on the magistracy of the states. * * *

These cases do not involve any mandate to state legislatures to enact new rules. When legislative action, or even administrative rule-making, is at issue, it may be appropriate for Congress either to pre-empt the State's lawmaking power and fashion the federal rule itself, or to respect the State's power to fashion its own rules. But this case, unlike any precedent in which the Court has held that Congress exceeded its powers, merely involves the imposition of modest duties on individual officers. The Court seems to accept the fact that Congress could require private persons, such as hospital executives or school administrators, to provide arms merchants with relevant information about a prospective purchaser's fitness to own a weapon; indeed, the Court does not disturb the conclusion that flows directly from our prior holdings that the burden on police officers would be permissible if a similar burden were also imposed on private parties with access to relevant data. See *New York*, 505 U.S. at 160; *Garcia v. San Antonio Metropolitan Transit Authority*. A structural problem that vanishes when the statute affects private individuals as well as public officials is not much of a structural problem.

Far more important than the concerns that the Court musters in support of its new rule is the fact that the Framers entrusted Congress with the task of creating a working structure of intergovernmental relationships around the framework that the Constitution authorized. Neither explicitly nor implicitly did the Framers issue any command that forbids Congress from imposing federal duties on private citizens or on local officials. As a general matter, Congress has followed the sound policy of authorizing federal agencies and federal agents to administer federal programs. That general practice, however, does not negate the existence of power to rely on state officials in occasional situations in which such reliance is in the national interest. * * *

JUSTICE BREYER, with whom JUSTICE STEVENS joins, dissenting. * * *

At least some other countries, facing the same basic problem, have found that local control is better maintained through application of a principle that is the direct opposite of the principle the majority derives from the silence of our Constitution. The federal systems of Switzerland, Germany, and the European Union, for example, all provide that constituent states, not federal bureaucracies, will themselves implement many of the laws, rules, regulations, or decrees enacted by the central "federal" body. They do so in part because they believe that such a system interferes less, not more, with the independent authority of the "state," member nation, or other subsidiary government, and helps to safeguard individual liberty as well. * * * As comparative experience suggests, there is no need to interpret the Constitution as containing an absolute principle—forbidding the assignment of virtually any federal duty to any state official. Nor is there a need to read the Brady Act as permitting the Federal Government to overwhelm a state civil service. The statute uses the words "reasonable effort," 18 U.S.C. § 922(s)(2)—words that easily can encompass the considerations of, say, time or cost, necessary to avoid any such result. * * *

NATIONAL FEDERATION OF INDEPENDENT BUSINESS V. SEBELIUS

Supreme Court of the United States, 2012.
567 U.S. ___, 132 S.Ct. 2566.

[In 2010, Congress enacted the Patient Protection and Affordable Care Act. One provision of the Act, known as the "individual mandate," requires most Americans to maintain "minimum essential" health insurance coverage or to pay a penalty. Another provision of the Act is the Medicaid expansion. Twenty-six States, several individuals, and the National Federation of Independent Business brought suit in Federal District Court, challenging the constitutionality of the individual mandate and the Medicaid expansion. The Supreme Court upheld the penalty for failing to maintain "minimum essential" health coverage as a valid exercise of Congress's power under the Taxing Clause in a 5–4 opinion, even though a different majority concluded that it was not a valid exercise of Congress's power under the Commerce Clause and the Necessary and Proper Clause. The following excerpt focuses only on the Medicaid expansion. Chief Justice Roberts' opinion was joined by six other members of the Court, with Justices Ginsburg and Sotamayor dissenting.]

* * * The Spending Clause grants Congress the power "to pay the Debts and provide for the * * * general Welfare of the United States." U. S. Const., Art. I, §8, cl. 1. We have long recognized that Congress may use this power to grant federal funds to the States, and may condition

such a grant upon the States' "taking certain actions that Congress could not require them to take." *College Savings Bank* [*v. Florida Prepaid Postsecondary Ed. Expense Bd.*, 527 U. S. 666,] at 686 (1999). Such measures "encourage a State to regulate in a particular way, [and] influenc[e] a State's policy choices." *New York* [*v. United States*, 505 U.S. 144,] at 166 (1992). The conditions imposed by Congress ensure that the funds are used by the States to "provide for the * * * general Welfare" in the manner Congress intended. * * *

But when "pressure turns into compulsion," [*Steward Machine Co. v. Davis*, 301 U.S. 548, 590 (1937)], the legislation runs contrary to our system of federalism * * *. Spending Clause programs do not pose this danger when a State has a legitimate choice whether to accept the federal conditions in exchange for federal funds. In such a situation, state officials can fairly be held politically accountable for choosing to accept or refuse the federal offer. But when the State has no choice, the Federal Government can achieve its objectives without accountability, just as in *New York* and *Printz*. Indeed, this danger is heightened when Congress acts under the Spending Clause, because Congress can use that power to implement federal policy it could not impose directly under its enumerated powers. * * *

In the typical case we look to the States to defend their prerogatives by adopting "the simple expedient of not yielding" to federal blandishments when they do not want to embrace the federal policies as their own. *Massachusetts v. Mellon*, 262 U.S. 447, 482 (1923). The States are separate and independent sovereigns. Sometimes they have to act like it. The States, however, argue that the Medicaid expansion is far from the typical case. They object that Congress has "crossed the line distinguishing encouragement from coercion," *New York*, *supra*, in the way it has structured the funding: Instead of simply refusing to grant the new funds to States that will not accept the new conditions, Congress has also threatened to withhold those States' existing Medicaid funds. The States claim that this threat serves no purpose other than to force unwilling States to sign up for the dramatic expansion in health care coverage effected by the Act. Given the nature of the threat and the programs at issue here, we must agree. * * * When, for example, such conditions take the form of threats to terminate other significant independent grants, the conditions are properly viewed as a means of pressuring the States to accept policy changes.

In *South Dakota v. Dole*, [483 U.S. 203 (1987)], we considered a challenge to a federal law that threatened to withhold five percent of a State's federal highway funds if the State did not raise its drinking age to 21 * * *. [T]he condition was not a restriction on how the highway funds— set aside for specific highway improvement and maintenance efforts— were to be used. We accordingly asked whether "the financial inducement offered by Congress" was "so coercive as to pass the point at which 'pressure turns into compulsion.'" By "financial inducement" the Court meant the threat of losing five percent of highway funds; no new money was offered to the States to raise their drinking ages. We found that the inducement was not impermissibly coercive, because Congress was offering only "relatively mild encouragement to the States." * * * In fact, the federal funds at stake constituted less than half of one percent of South Dakota's budget at the time * * *.

In this case, the financial "inducement" Congress has chosen is much more than "relatively mild encouragement"—it is a gun to the head. Section 1396c of the Medicaid Act provides that if a State's Medicaid plan does not comply with the Act's requirements, the Secretary of Health and Human Services may declare that "further payments will not be made to the State." 42 U.S.C. §1396c. * * * Medicaid spending accounts for over 20 percent of the average State's total budget, with federal funds covering 50 to 83 percent of those costs. The Federal Government estimates that it will pay out approximately $3.3 trillion between 2010 and 2019 in order to cover the costs of pre-expansion Medicaid. In addition, the States have developed intricate statutory and administrative regimes over the course of many decades to implement their objectives under existing Medicaid. It is easy to see how the *Dole* Court could conclude that the threatened loss of less than half of one percent of South Dakota's budget left that State with a "prerogative" to reject Congress's desired policy, "not merely in theory but in fact." The threatened loss of over 10 percent of a State's overall budget, in contrast, is economic dragooning that leaves the States with no real option but to acquiesce in the Medicaid expansion. * * *

Here, the Government claims that the Medicaid expansion is properly viewed merely as a modification of the existing program because the States agreed that Congress could change the terms of Medicaid when they signed on in the first place. * * * But "if Congress intends to impose a condition on the grant of federal moneys, it must do so unambiguously." *Pennhurst* [*State School and Hospital v. Halderman*, 451 U. S. 1,] at 17 (1981). A State confronted with statutory language reserving the right to "alter" or "amend" the pertinent provisions of the Social Security Act might reasonably assume that Congress was entitled to make adjustments to the Medicaid program as it developed * * *. The Medicaid expansion, however, accomplishes a shift in kind, not merely degree. The original program was designed to cover medical services for four particular categories of the needy: the disabled, the blind, the elderly, and needy families with dependent children. Previous amendments to Medicaid eligibility merely altered and expanded the boundaries of these categories. Under the Affordable Care Act, Medicaid is transformed into a program to meet the health care needs of the entire nonelderly population with income below 133 percent of the poverty level. It is no longer a program to care for the neediest among us, but rather an element of a comprehensive national plan to provide universal health insurance coverage. * * *

Nothing in our opinion precludes Congress from offering funds under the Affordable Care Act to expand the availability of health care, and requiring that States accepting such funds comply with the conditions on their use. What Congress is not free to do is to penalize States that choose not to participate in that new program by taking away their existing Medicaid funding. * * * [T]he Secretary cannot apply § 1396c to withdraw existing Medicaid funds for failure to comply with the requirements set out in the expansion.

JUSTICE GINSBURG, with whom JUSTICE SOTOMAYOR joins, * * * dissenting in part. * * *

Expansion has been characteristic of the Medicaid program. * * * Since 1965, Congress has amended the Medicaid program on more than 50 occasions, sometimes quite sizably. Most relevant here, between 1988 and 1990, Congress required participating States to include among their beneficiaries pregnant women with family incomes up to 133% of the federal poverty level, children up to age 6 at the same income levels, and children ages 6 to 18 with family incomes up to 100% of the poverty level. These amendments added millions to the Medicaid-eligible population. * * * Enlargement of the population and services covered by Medicaid, in short, has been the trend.

Compared to past alterations, the ACA is notable for the extent to which the Federal Government will pick up the tab. Medicaid's 2010 expansion is financed largely by federal outlays. In 2014, federal funds will cover 100% of the costs for newly eligible beneficiaries; that rate will gradually decrease before settling at 90% in 2020. By comparison, federal contributions toward the care of beneficiaries eligible pre-ACA range from 50% to 83%, and averaged 57% between 2005 and 2008. * * * The Congressional Budget Office * * * projects that States will spend 0.8% more than they would have, absent the ACA. Whatever the increase in state obligations after the ACA, it will pale in comparison to the increase in federal funding. * * *

This case does not present the concerns that led the Court in *Dole* even to consider the prospect of coercion. In *Dole*, the condition—set 21 as the minimum drinking age—did not tell the States how to use funds Congress provided for highway construction. Further, in view of the Twenty-First Amendment, it was an open question whether Congress could directly impose a national minimum drinking age. The ACA, in contrast, relates solely to the federally funded Medicaid program; if States choose not to comply, Congress has not threatened to withhold funds earmarked for any other program. Nor does the ACA use Medicaid funding to induce States to take action Congress itself could not undertake. The Federal Government undoubtedly could operate its own health-care program for poor persons, just as it operates Medicare for seniors' health care. That is what makes this such a simple case, and the Court's decision so unsettling. Congress, aiming to assist the needy, has appropriated federal money to subsidize state health-insurance programs that meet federal standards. * * *

DAVID J. BARRON, A LOCALIST CRITIQUE OF THE NEW FEDERALISM
51 Duke L. J. 377, 378–381, 385–390 (2001).

The current federalism revival's invocation of local autonomy * * * appears to vindicate the values associated with decentralization that make a localist orientation attractive. And it thus would seem that challenges to the federalism revival must rest on appeals to the ways that centralized power can overcome the pathologies of local decisionmaking. In this way, the current federalism revival draws strength from the current skepticism towards centralization—with the specter of big government and the constraints that it raises—and the current ascendancy of decentralization, with the prospect of self-government and freedom that it offers.

But local autonomy is a more complex concept than we often acknowledge. Before we accept the suggestion that protecting local autonomy from central power promotes localist values, it is important to attend to the absence of a clear baseline in defining what local autonomy means. The baseline problem arises because no city or state is an island jurisdiction. The ability of each locality to make effective decisions on its own is inevitably shaped by its relation to other cities and states, by its relation to broader, private market forces, and, most importantly, by the way the central power structures these relations, even when central governmental power appears to be dormant. Because the local sphere is part and parcel of a larger coordinated system of local jurisdictions that is structured by less visible background central-law rules, central power is often deeply (if not visibly) implicated in what we understand local autonomy to mean. Once one attends to this point, it becomes clear that a single-minded desire to protect local autonomy by limiting central power actually may do little to promote the values normally associated with local autonomy.

To the extent the Court's current attempt to protect local autonomy is intended to promote the values associated with decentralized decisionmaking, it errs in overlooking the baseline problem. It too often takes the current amount of discretion that central law affords local governments to be the baseline against which claimed central governmental infringements of local autonomy are measured. By viewing the existing, centrally established structure as a "neutral" baseline that protects local autonomy, the Court fails to consider how that structure itself acts as a constraint on local autonomy. As a consequence, it does not consider the possibility that changes in central law actually may be shifting the relative autonomy of localities, vis-à-vis each other, rather than limiting local autonomy across the board. Nor does the Court consider that the allegedly infringing central law, by altering the background framework within which local power is exercised, may be creating new opportunities for exercising local power that were not available under the old centrally established framework. So, for example, the Court recently has held that, in the name of protecting local autonomy, the federal government is prohibited from commandeering a local government. The Court does not contemplate, however, that such commands may promote local autonomy by altering the background legal structure in a way that protects local governments from the costs that the current, centrally established legal framework permits local governments to impose upon their neighbors. In other words, the Court ignores— wrongly, I argue—both the ways the preexisting centrally created legal regime may be limiting local autonomy and the ways a new, seemingly less protective centrally established legal regime actually might enhance it.

Inattention to the baseline problem also occurs outside the sphere of constitutional doctrine. The force of the intuitive claim that central law is a constraint on, rather than a component of, local autonomy threatens to tag many important recent reform proposals with a "big government" label they do not deserve. Because such proposals call for the significant exercise of central power, they are seen as a threat to local autonomy, implicating the familiar clash between the benefits of decentralized decisionmaking on the one hand, and the benefits of centralized decisionmaking on the other. Once one acknowledges the more complicated relationship between local autonomy and central power, however, these proposals are better understood as efforts to alter the central frameworks within which local discretion is inevitably exercised, rather than as attempts to substitute centralized command for local control. From this perspective, such proposals are no more threats to local control than the less visible, centrally imposed frameworks they would replace. * * *

Consider * * * [a] case concerning state preemption in which the localist argument for central lawmaking is quite easy to articulate. Local governments are not, in the absence of state intervention, free to determine the amount of resources they allocate to improving air quality. Local decisionmaking is constrained by the approaches to improving air quality that are adopted in neighboring jurisdictions. A neighboring jurisdiction that is lax in policing air quality, or that encourages its industry to locate at the perimeter, may powerfully affect its neighbor's choices about the resources that should be devoted to combating air pollution. The state legislature is considering a law to preempt lax air pollution policies. Does this state legislation infringe local autonomy? The localist defense of the statute is easily offered. The preemptive statute clearly would limit local autonomy in some respects. It would frustrate the policy choices of those jurisdictions with lax air pollution laws, and it would prohibit all local jurisdictions from enjoying the freedom to adopt the now-barred policy. But it also would enhance the decisionmaking discretion of those local jurisdictions now subjected to extralocal costs by the absence of central preemption of lax air pollution policies. These jurisdictions could allocate more resources to other policies they wished to pursue if they no longer had to respond to the negative externalities imposed upon them by their neighbors—negative externalities that the prior rules of central law required them to accept.

There is, in a case of this type, no clear baseline from which an argument for local autonomy can proceed. There are localist arguments both for and against the central law at issue. Local autonomy is in one sense limited by the preemptive central command that directly seeks to constrain the exercise of local power. Viewed from a different baseline, however, local autonomy already is limited by background, centrally established, legal rules that define the horizontal relations between localities and permit some localities to avoid costs that others are then required to bear. From this perspective, the absence of a central law that attempts to alter these preexisting, centrally established, horizontal legal relations itself limits local autonomy. Thus, a case of this sort requires the central government to make a policy judgment about the type of local autonomy that it wishes to promote rather than a choice about whether to trump local autonomy in the name of some greater central governmental interest.

The state government's choice to adopt the preemptive law might depend on an independent assessment of the state's interest in combating air pollution—say, a judgment that requiring the costs of pollution to be internalized will promote cleaner air statewide. But it also might depend upon an assessment of whether state intervention would free more local jurisdictions from extralocal pressures than it would constrain, or upon whether it would relieve local jurisdictions of qualitatively or quantitatively greater constraints on their autonomy than they would confront in the absence of the central law. In making that assessment, one would have to count the likelihood that state air quality would improve as a benefit of the potential state intervention. But one also would have to count as a benefit the likelihood that many local jurisdictions would have more resources to devote to other governmental projects at the local level—resources that otherwise would be devoted to attending to the costs imposed upon them by their neighbors. * * *

The pollution hypothetical highlights a broader point about the autonomy of local jurisdictions in the absence of visible central intervention. A locality's autonomy may in fact be constrained in a number of ways by background rules of central law that too often are taken to be natural. The ways central law requires local jurisdictions to accept the costs of direct negative externalities—like pollution—furnishes only one example. Local autonomy also may be constrained * * * by the competitive pressures that central law permits local jurisdictions to impose upon one another. Local autonomy also may be limited by broader forces in the private market that no local jurisdiction is equipped to address on its own, given the way central law defines local power. Finally, a local entity's autonomy may be constrained by still other, less visible provisions of central law that impose burdens that would be left in place even if the supposedly infringing central governmental statute were invalidated or repealed. The effects of these extralocal constraints may be just as burdensome on local autonomy, as a practical matter, as would the effects of the new, preemptive central law that may be challenged by a particular locality. Each of these constraints would remain in place, however, even if that challenged central intervention were prohibited.

As a result, the effort to protect local autonomy may be incomplete, and perhaps counterproductive, unless one considers how the particular central intervention that is the object of localist ire interacts with these less visible centrally imposed constraints. * * * To be sure, the contention that preemptive central lawmaking may promote local autonomy relies on arguments for central power that are in some respects familiar. It is hardly novel to contend, for example, that central lawmaking may be needed to respond to interlocal externalities or to effectuate interlocal redistribution. However, these classic arguments for central power often are understood as centralist arguments for the promotion of some value— such as efficiency or equal treatment—that can be realized only by acknowledging and overcoming the pathologies that attend smaller-scale decisionmaking. This way of understanding the function of central power is a partial one that has important and unfortunate consequences. If the successful defense of each central intervention depends upon emphasizing the costs of respecting local decisionmaking authority, then an argument for central power inevitably invites the counterargument that central power threatens the values protected by local autonomy. Once one sees the localist dimension in these classic arguments for central intervention, however, the calculus changes. The conventional rejoinder to such exercises of central power becomes weaker when the central law can be understood to promote the values associated with the preservation of local autonomy. Moreover, the argument for central power no longer points inevitably towards ever-increasing centralization. To be defended credibly on localist grounds, the central law must be shown to promote local discretion even as it also limits it. It is not enough to show that it promotes some value of worth to the central government as a whole.

One final point should be emphasized. The mere fact that a preemptive state law sets forth a state policy that may be preferred by the residents of some localities does not mean that it thereby vindicates localism. A state law that limits pollution is not localist just because residents in a majority of local jurisdictions prefer clean air. For the central intervention to be localist in the way I intend, the state law would have to promote the capacity of the local government to adopt policies that current central law frustrates. Preference matching alone, therefore, does not suffice to promote the values associated with localism. Those values are promoted only when central law changes the background legal rules in a way that expands—even as it also may contract—the opportunities for local governments to achieve preferred policies for themselves. Thus, a state law against pollution is localist only because it frees localities from extralocally imposed costs that limit the kinds of policy choices they can make.

With this background in place, it * * * will be possible for those attracted to a localist orientation to see some of the problems with the United States Supreme Court's recent federalism decisions. * * *

LAWRENCE COUNTY V. LEAD-DEADWOOD
SCHOOL DISTRICT

Supreme Court of the United States, 1985.
469 U.S. 256, 105 S.Ct. 695, 83 L.Ed.2d 635.

JUSTICE WHITE delivered the opinion of the Court. * * *

The Payment in Lieu of Taxes Act compensates local governments for the loss of tax revenues resulting from the tax-immune status of federal lands located in their jurisdictions, and for the cost of providing services related to these lands. These "entitlement lands" include wilderness areas, national parks, and lands administered by the Bureau of Land Management. * * * [T]he Secretary of the Interior is required to make annual payments "to each unit of general local government in which entitlement land is located." The local unit "may use the payment for any governmental purpose." 31 U.S.C. § 6902(a). Appellant Lawrence County has received in excess of $400,000 under the Act.

In 1979, South Dakota enacted a statute requiring local governments to distribute federal payments in lieu of taxes in the same way they distribute general tax revenues. Since the county allocates approximately 60% of its general tax revenues to its school districts, the state statute would require the county to give the school districts 60% of the § 6902 payments it receives. The county, however, declined to distribute the funds in accordance with the state statute, claiming that the Payment in Lieu of Taxes Act gave it the discretion to spend the funds for any governmental purpose it chose. * * * Appellee, Lead-Deadwood School District No. 40–1, * * * filed a complaint in state court, seeking a writ of mandamus to compel the county to distribute the federal funds in accordance with the state statute. * * *

Even if Congress has not expressly pre-empted state law in a given area, a state statute may nevertheless be invalid under the Supremacy Clause if it conflicts with federal law or "stands as an obstacle to the accomplishment of the full purposes and objectives of Congress." *Silkwood v. Kerr-McGee Corp.,* 464 U.S. 238, 104 S.Ct. 615, 78 L.Ed.2d 443 (1984). In determining whether the state statute at issue here impeded the operation of the federal Act, the South Dakota Supreme Court limited its inquiry to whether the funding of school districts was a "governmental purpose." Concluding that it was, the court found no inconsistency between the state and federal provisions. This plain language analysis, however, is seriously flawed.

The Act provides that "each unit of general local government"—in this case, the county—"may" use the moneys for "any" governmental purpose. This language appears to endow local governments with the discretion to spend in-lieu payments for any governmental purpose. It seems to say that if the local unit chooses to spend all of the money on roads, for example, it could do so. Under the state statute, however, that is forbidden: the funds must be allocated among the various services in the same manner as other revenues. The State insists that since money used as the law directs would be spent on proper governmental services, there is no inconsistency with § 6902. Under this interpretation, the word "may" confers no discretion on local governments that is immune from state control. The last sentence of § 6902(a) is drained of almost all meaning, since had it been omitted, the legal position of local governments would be precisely as described by the South Dakota Supreme Court. The sentence would become a mere admonition not to embezzle and to spend federal money on proper purposes. At the very least, § 6902 is ambiguous with respect to the degree of discretion it confers on local governments. Contrary to the views expressed in the court below, it does not of its own force dispose of the county's case. Resort to other indicia of the meaning of the statutory language is therefore appropriate. * * *

The Payment in Lieu of Taxes Act was passed in response to a comprehensive review of the policies applicable to the use, management, and disposition of federal lands. The Federal Government had for many years been providing payments to partially compensate state and local governments for revenues lost as a result of the presence of tax-exempt federal lands within their borders. But the Public Land Law Review Commission and Congress identified a number of flaws in the existing programs. Prominent among congressional concerns was that, under systems of direct payment to the States, local governments often received funds that were insufficient to cover the full cost of maintaining the federal lands within their jurisdictions. Where these lands consisted of wilderness or park areas, they attracted thousands of visitors each year. State governments might benefit from this federally inspired tourism through the collection of income or sales taxes, but these revenues would not accrue to local governments, who were often restricted to raising revenue from property taxes. Yet it was the local governments that bore the brunt of the expenses associated with federal lands, such as law enforcement, road maintenance, and the provision of public health services. * * *

The School District acknowledges that this legislative history evidences a clear intent to distribute funds directly to units of local government, bypassing the State. But it argues that the South Dakota statute poses no impediment to the accomplishment of this goal: federal money still flows directly to the county; none of it is thereafter "parcelled out" to other counties that have no federal lands within their borders; and the federal statute merely defines the "point of distribution" of funds, the State having authority to prescribe the "plan of distribution."

As we see it, however, Congress was not merely concerned that local governments receive adequate amounts of money, and that they receive these amounts directly. Equally as important was the objective of ensuring local governments the freedom and flexibility to spend the federal money as they saw fit. * * * The South Dakota statute, mandating that local governments spend these funds according to a specific formula, runs directly counter to this objective. If the State may dictate a "plan" of distribution, as the School District contends, it may impose exactly the kinds of restrictions on the use of funds that Congress intended to prohibit. * * *

Congress also recognized that the costs associated with maintaining and serving federal lands were varied and unpredictable, and that local governments needed the flexibility to allocate in-lieu payments to these needs as they arose. * * * The picture that emerges from the hearings on the Act is that there are many counties in which much of the land is owned by the Federal Government, and whose populations are markedly increased by tourists and hunters in the summer, in deer season, or on the weekends. These transients suffer accidents requiring emergency services or hospitalization for which they cannot always pay; commit crimes that call for police protection, prosecution, and incarceration; create waste that necessitates the construction of sewage treatment plants; use roads that must be paved and maintained; and generally impose a strain on a county's limited resources without providing much in the way of compensating revenues. One cost unlikely to increase with the presence of this largely uninhabited federal land, however, is that of education. * * *

Against this background, we have little trouble in concluding that Congress intended to prohibit the kind of state-imposed limitation on the use of in-lieu payments represented by the South Dakota statute challenged in this case. * * * [T]he allocation of federal payments in the same proportion as local revenue would most likely result in a windfall for school districts and other entities that are already fully funded by local revenues. The federal money would not serve its intended purpose of compensating local governments for extraordinary or additional expenditures associated with federal lands. A county conceivably could avoid this result, but the strong congressional concern that local governments have maximum flexibility in this area indicates that counties should not encounter substantial interference from the State in allocating funds to the area of greatest need.

The School District and the State also argue that because of concerns of federalism, the Federal Government may not intrude lightly into the State's efforts to provide fiscal guidance to its subdivisions. The Federal Government, however, has not presumed to dictate the manner in which the counties may spend *state* in-lieu-of-tax payments. Rather, it has merely imposed a condition on its disbursement of federal funds. The condition in this instance is that the counties should not be denied the discretion to spend § 6902 funds for any governmental purpose, including expenditures that are linked to federal lands within their borders. It is far from a novel proposition that pursuant to its powers under the Spending Clause, Congress may impose conditions on the receipt of federal funds, absent some independent constitutional bar. In our view, Congress was sufficiently clear in its intention to funnel § 6902 moneys directly to local governments, so that they might spend them for governmental purposes without substantial interference. * * * The attempt of the South Dakota legislation to limit the manner in which counties or other qualified local governmental units may spend federal in-lieu-of-tax payments obstructs this congressional purpose and runs afoul of the Supremacy Clause. Congress intended the affected units of local government, such as Lawrence County, to be the managers of these funds, not merely the State's cashiers. * * *

JUSTICE REHNQUIST, with whom JUSTICE STEVENS joins, dissenting.

In *Hunter v. Pittsburgh*, 207 U.S. 161, 28 S.Ct. 40, 52 L.Ed. 151 (1907), this Court unanimously described the "settled doctrines of this Court" with respect to States, on the one hand, and counties and other municipal corporations within them, on the other:

"Municipal corporations are political subdivisions of the State, created as convenient agencies for exercising such of the governmental powers of the State as may be entrusted to them. For the purpose of executing these powers properly and efficiently they usually are given the power to acquire, hold, and manage personal and real property. The number, nature and duration of the powers conferred upon these corporations and the territory over which they shall be exercised rests in the absolute discretion of the State."

Flying in the face of this settled doctrine, the Court today holds that Congress, by providing for payments of federal funds in lieu of taxes to counties in South Dakota, implicitly prohibited the State of South Dakota from regulating in any way the manner in which its counties might spend those funds. * * *

[The] two-sentence statutory provision enacted by Congress certainly does not proclaim by its language any single meaning, but one would be hard pressed to derive a more tortured meaning from it than that chosen by the Court. It may be that Congress, by providing that payments be made directly to the counties rather than to the States, implied a desire to have the money spent in the counties. But nothing in the South Dakota statute requires any contrary result; all the South Dakota statute requires is that the counties allocate a part of the money to school districts within the county, just as general tax revenues and state in-lieu payments are allocated. The Court's collection of reasons why Congress intended to prohibit this result is simply not convincing in the light of the long history of treatment of counties as being by law totally subordinate to the States which have created them. * * *

NIXON V. MISSOURI MUNICIPAL LEAGUE

Supreme Court of the United States, 2004.
541 U.S. 125, 124 S.Ct. 1555, 158 L.Ed.2d 291.

JUSTICE SOUTER delivered the opinion of the Court. * * *

In 1997, the General Assembly of Missouri enacted the statute codified as § 392.410(7) of the State's Revised Statutes:

"No political subdivision of this state shall provide or offer for sale, either to the public or to a telecommunications provider, a telecommunications service or telecommunications facility used to provide a telecommunications service for which a certificate of service authority is required pursuant to this section."

On July 8, 1998, the municipal respondents, including municipalities, municipal organizations, and municipally owned utilities, petitioned the Federal Communications Commission (FCC or Commission) for an order declaring the state statute unlawful and preempted under 47 U.S.C. § 253:

> "No State or local statute or regulation, or other State or local legal requirement, may prohibit or have the effect of prohibiting the ability of any entity to provide any interstate or intrastate telecommunications service." * * *

After notice and comment, the FCC refused to declare the Missouri statute preempted, * * *. The agency concluded that "the term 'any entity' in section 253(a) . . . was not intended to include political subdivisions of the state, but rather appears to prohibit restrictions on market entry that apply to independent entities subject to state regulation."[2] * * * But at the same time the Commission rejected preemption, it also denounced the policy behind the Missouri statute * * *.

At the outset, it is well to put aside two considerations that appear in this litigation but fall short of supporting the municipal respondents' hopes for prevailing on their generous conception of preemption under § 253. The first is public policy, on which the respondents have at the least a respectable position, that fencing governmental entities out of the telecommunications business flouts the public interest. * * * [T]he issue here does not turn on the merits of municipal telecommunications services. The second consideration that fails to answer the question posed in this litigation is the portion of the text that has received great emphasis. The Eighth Circuit trained its analysis on the words "any entity," left undefined by the statute, with much weight being placed on the modifier "any." But concentration on the writing on the page does not produce a persuasive answer here. * * * We think that the strange and indeterminate results of using federal preemption to free public entities from state or local limitations is the key to understanding that Congress used "any entity" with a limited reference to any private entity when it cast the preemption net.

In familiar instances of regulatory preemption under the Supremacy Clause, a federal measure preempting state regulation in some precinct of economic conduct carried on by a private person or corporation simply leaves the private party free to do anything it chooses consistent with the prevailing federal law. * * * But no such simple result would follow from federal preemption meant to unshackle local governments from entrepreneurial limitations. The trouble is that a local government's capacity to enter an economic market turns not only on the effect of

---

[2] The line between "political subdivision" and "independent entity" the FCC located by reference to state law. By its terms, the FCC order declined to preempt the statute as it applied to municipally owned utilities not chartered as independent corporations, on the theory that under controlling Missouri law, they were subdivisions of the State. The Commission implied an opposite view, however, regarding the status, under § 253, of municipal utilities that had been separately chartered. The question whether § 253 preempts state and municipal regulation of these types of entities is not before us, and we express no view as to its proper resolution.

straightforward economic regulation below the national level (including outright bans), but on the authority and potential will of governments at the state or local level to support entry into the market. Preemption of the state advertising restriction freed a seller who otherwise had the legal authority to advertise and the money to do it if that made economic sense. But preempting a ban on government utilities would not accomplish much if the government could not point to some law authorizing it to run a utility in the first place. And preemption would make no difference to anyone if the state regulator were left with control over funding needed for any utility operation and declined to pay for it. In other words, when a government regulates itself (or the subdivision through which it acts) there is no clear distinction between the regulator and the entity regulated. Legal limits on what may be done by the government itself (including its subdivisions) will often be indistinguishable from choices that express what the government wishes to do with the authority and resources it can command. That is why preempting state or local governmental self-regulation (or regulation of political inferiors) would work so differently from preempting regulation of private players that we think it highly unlikely that Congress intended to set off on such uncertain adventures. A few hypotheticals may bring the point home.

* * *

[C]onsider how preemption would apply to a state statute authorizing municipalities to operate specified utilities, to provide water and electricity but nothing else. The enumeration would certainly have the effect of prohibiting a municipally owned and operated electric utility from entering the telecommunications business (as Congress clearly meant private electric companies to be able to do) and its implicit prohibition would thus be open to FCC preemption. But what if the FCC did preempt the restriction? The municipality would be free of the statute, but freedom is not authority, and in the absence of some further, authorizing legislation the municipality would still be powerless to enter the telecommunications business. There is, after all, no argument that the Telecommunications Act of 1996 is itself a source of federal authority granting municipalities local power that state law does not.

Now assume that § 253 has the narrower construction (preempting only laws that restrict authority derived from a different legal source). Consider a State with plenary authority itself, under its constitution, to operate any variety of utility. Assume that its statutes authorized a state-run utility to deliver electric and water services, but drew the line at telecommunications. The restrictive element of that limited authorization would run afoul of § 253 as respondents would construe it. But if, owing to preemption, the state operating utility authority were suddenly free to provide telecommunications and its administrators were raring to enter this new field, where would the necessary capital come from? Surely there is no contention that the Telecommunications Act of 1996 by its own force entails a state agency's entitlement to unappropriated funds from the state treasury, or to the exercise of state bonding authority.

Or take the application of § 253 preemption to municipalities empowered by state law to furnish services generally, but forbidden by a special statute to exercise that power for the purpose of providing telecommunications services. If the special statute were preempted, a municipality in that State would have a real option to enter the telecommunications business if its own legislative arm so chose and funded the venture. But in a State next door where municipalities lacked such general authority, a local authority would not be able to, and the result would be a national crazy quilt. We will presumably get a crazy quilt, of course, as a consequence of state and local political choices arrived at in the absence of any preemption under § 253, but the crazy quilt of this hypothetical would result not from free political choices but from the fortuitous interaction of a federal preemption law with the forms of municipal authorization law.

Finally, consider the result if a State that previously authorized municipalities to operate a number of utilities including telecommunications changed its law by narrowing the range of authorization. Assume that a State once authorized municipalities to furnish water, electric, and communications services, but sometime after the passage of § 253 narrowed the authorization so as to leave municipalities authorized to enter only the water business. The repealing statute would have a prohibitory effect on the prior ability to deliver telecommunications service and would be subject to preemption. But that would mean that a State that once chose to provide broad municipal authority could not reverse course. A State next door, however, starting with a legal system devoid of any authorization for municipal utility operation, would at the least be free to change its own course by authorizing its municipalities to venture forth. The result, in other words, would be the federal creation of a one-way ratchet. A State or municipality could give the power, but it could not take it away later. Private counterparts could come and go from the market at will, for after any federal preemption they would have a free choice to compete or not to compete in telecommunications; governmental providers could never leave (or, at least, could not leave by a forthright choice to change policy), for the law expressing the government's decision to get out would be preempted. * * *

In sum, § 253 would not work like a normal preemptive statute if it applied to a governmental unit. It would often accomplish nothing, it would treat States differently depending on the formal structures of their laws authorizing municipalities to function, and it would hold out no promise of a national consistency. We think it farfetched that Congress meant § 253 to start down such a road in the absence of any clearer signal than the phrase "ability of any entity." * * *

The municipal respondents' position holds sufficient promise of futility and uncertainty to keep us from accepting it, but a complementary principle would bring us to the same conclusion even on the assumption that preemption could operate straightforwardly to provide local choice, as in some instances it might. Preemption would, for example, leave a municipality with a genuine choice to enter the telecommunications business when state law provided general authority and a newly unfettered municipality wished to fund the effort. But the liberating preemption would come only by interposing federal authority between a State and its municipal subdivisions, which our precedents teach, "are created as convenient agencies for exercising such of the governmental powers of the State as may be entrusted to them in its absolute discretion." *Wisconsin Public Intervenor v. Mortier*, 501 U.S. 597, 607–608, 111 S.Ct. 2476, 115 L.Ed.2d 532 (1991). Hence the need to invoke our working assumption that federal legislation threatening to trench on the States' arrangements for conducting their own governments should be treated with great skepticism, and read in a way that preserves a State's chosen disposition of its own power, in the absence of the plain statement *Gregory v. Ashcroft*, 501 U.S. 452, 115 L. Ed. 2d 410, 111 S. Ct. 2395 (1991), requires. What we have said already is enough to show that § 253(a) is hardly forthright enough to pass *Gregory*: "ability of any entity" is not limited to one reading, and neither statutory structure nor legislative history points unequivocally to a commitment by Congress to treat governmental telecommunications providers on par with private firms. The want of any "unmistakably clear" statement to that effect would be fatal to respondents' reading. * * *

JUSTICE STEVENS dissenting. * * *

The Court begins its analysis by asking us to imagine how § 253 might apply to "a state statute authorizing municipalities to operate specified utilities, to provide water and electricity but nothing else," or to a State's failure to provide the necessary capital to a state-run utility "raring" to enter the telecommunications market. Certainly one might plausibly interpret § 253, as the Court does, to forbid States' refusals to provide broader authorization or to provide necessary capital as impermissible prohibitions on entry. And as the Court observes, such an interpretation would undeniably produce absurd results; it would leave covered entities in a kind of legal limbo, armed with a federal-law freedom to enter the market but lacking the state-law power to do so. But we need not—and in my opinion, should not—interpret § 253 in this fashion. We should instead read the statute's reference to state and local laws that "prohibit or have the effect of prohibiting the ability of any entity" to enter the telecommunications business to embody an implicit understanding that the only "entities" covered by § 253 are entities otherwise able to enter the business—i.e., entities both authorized to provide telecommunications services and capable of providing such services without the State's direct assistance. In other words, § 253 prohibits States from withdrawing municipalities' pre-existing authority to enter the telecommunications business, but does not command that States affirmatively grant either that authority or the means with which to carry it out.

Of course, the Court asserts that still other absurd results would follow from application of § 253 pre-emption to state laws that withdraw a municipality's pre-existing authority to enter the telecommunications business. But these results are, on closer examination, perhaps not so absurd after all. The Court first contends that reading § 253 in this manner will produce a "national crazy quilt" of public telecommunications authority, where the possibility of municipal participation in the telecommunications market turns on the scope of the authority each State has already granted to its subdivisions. But as the Court acknowledges, permitting States such as Missouri to prohibit municipalities from providing telecommunications services hardly will help the cause of national consistency. That the "crazy quilt" the Court describes is the product of political choices made by Congress rather than state legislatures renders it no more absurd than the "crazy quilt" that will result from leaving the matter of municipal entry entirely to individual States' discretion.

The Court also contends that applying § 253 pre-emption to bar withdrawal of authority to enter the telecommunications market will result in "the federal creation of a one-way ratchet": "A State or municipality could give the power, but it could not take it away later." But nothing in § 253 prohibits States from scaling back municipalities' authority in a general way. A State may withdraw comprehensive authorization in favor of enumerating specific municipal powers, or even abolish municipalities altogether. Such general withdrawals of authority may very well "have the effect of prohibiting" municipalities' ability to enter the telecommunications market, just as enforcement of corporate governance and tax laws might "have the effect of prohibiting" other entities' ability to enter. But § 253 clearly does not pre-empt every state law that "has the effect" of restraining entry. It pre-empts only those that constitute nonneutral restraints on entry. A general redefinition of municipal authority no more constitutes a prohibited nonneutral restraint on entry than enforcement of other laws of general applicability that, practically speaking, may make it more difficult for certain entities to enter the telecommunications business.

As I read the statute, the one thing a State may not do is enact a statute or regulation specifically aimed at preventing municipalities or other entities from providing telecommunications services. This prohibition would certainly apply to a law like Missouri's, which "advertise[s][its] prohibitory agenda on [its] fac[e]." But it would also apply to a law that accomplished a similar result by other means—for example, a law that permitted only private telecommunications carriers to receive federal universal service support or access to unbundled network elements. * * *

NOTE ON THE FEDERAL-CITY RELATIONSHIP

The Supreme Court's federalism doctrine reveals the difficulty of classifying cities for legal purposes. Sometimes the Court equates them with states and sometimes it does not. That cities are sometimes entitled to federalism-based protections is obvious from *National League of Cities* and *Printz*. But cities do not always fare so well when it comes to federalism. For example, cities do not enjoy Eleventh Amendment immunity from private suits even though states do. This holding dates back to a case from the nineteenth century, Lincoln County v. Luning, 133 U.S. 529, 530, 10 S.Ct. 363, 33 L.Ed. 766 (1890), and has regularly been re-affirmed.[18]

If cities do not enjoy Eleventh Amendment immunity, why should they receive other federalism-based protections from national power? Justice Stevens raised this issue in his dissent in *Printz*:

> [T]hese cases do not involve the enlistment of *state* officials at all, but only an effort to have federal policy implemented by officials of local government. Both Sheriffs Printz and Mack are county officials. Given that the Brady Act places its interim obligations on chief law enforcement officers (CLEO's), who are defined as "the chief of police, the sheriff, or an equivalent officer," 18 U.S.C. 922(s)(8), it seems likely that most cases would similarly involve local government officials. This Court has not had cause in its recent federalism jurisprudence to address the constitutional implications of enlisting nonstate officials for federal purposes. (We did pass briefly on the issue in a footnote in *National League of Cities* * * * but that case was overruled in its entirety by *Garcia* * * *. The question was not called to our attention in *Garcia* itself.) It is therefore worth noting that the majority's decision is in considerable tension with our Eleventh Amendment sovereign immunity cases. Those decisions were designed to "accor[d] the States the respect owed them as members of the federation." *Puerto Rico Aqueduct and Sewer Authority v. Metcalf & Eddy, Inc.*, 506 U.S. 139, 146, 113 S.Ct. 684, 689, 121 L.Ed.2d 605 (1993). But despite the fact that "political subdivisions exist solely at the whim and behest of their State," *Port Authority Trans-Hudson Corp v. Feeney*, 495 U.S. 299, 313, 110 S.Ct. 1868, 1877, 109 L.Ed.2d 264

---

[18] See Melvyn Durchslag, Should Political Subdivisions Be Accorded Eleventh Amendment Immunity? 43 DePaul L. Rev. 577 (1994).

(1990) (Brennan, J., concurring in part and concurring in judgment), we have "consistently refused to construe the Amendment to afford protection to political subdivisions such as counties and municipalities." *Lake Country Estates, Inc. v. Tahoe Regional Planning Agency*, 440 U.S. 391, 401, 99 S.Ct. 1171, 1177, 59 L.Ed.2d 401 (1979). Even if the protections that the majority describes as rooted in the Tenth Amendment ought to benefit state officials, it is difficult to reconcile the decision to extend these principles to local officials with our refusal to do so in the Eleventh Amendment context. If the federal judicial power may be exercised over local government officials, it is hard to see why they are not subject to the legislative power as well.

Justice Scalia, writing for the Court, responded this way: "Contrary to the dissent's suggestion, * * *, the distinction in our Eleventh Amendment jurisprudence between States and municipalities is of no relevance here. We long ago made clear that the distinction is peculiar to the question of whether a governmental entity is entitled to Eleventh Amendment sovereign immunity; we have refused to apply it to the question of whether a governmental entity is protected by the Constitution's guarantees of federalism, including the Tenth Amendment."

In a case decided after *Printz*, Alden v. Maine, 527 U.S. 706, 119 S.Ct. 2240, 144 L.Ed.2d 636 (1999), the Court held that states enjoy sovereign immunity from federal attempts to make them suable not only in federal court but also in their own state courts. The Court based this conclusion not on the Eleventh Amendment, which refers only to states' amenability to suit in federal court, but on basic principles of federalism rooted in the Tenth Amendment. Nevertheless, *Alden* made clear that cities, unlike states, did not enjoy any such immunity. If the state/city distinction is no longer "peculiar to the question of whether a governmental entity is entitled to Eleventh Amendment sovereign immunity," why should cities not be distinguished from states with respect to federalism protections more generally?

The uncertain legal status of cities has also been a source of controversy in the Court's decisions concerning Section 5 of the Fourteenth Amendment. Even though the Eleventh Amendment bars Congress from using its Article 1 powers to permit private actors to sue states (but not cities), Congress may permit such suits pursuant to its Section 5 power to "enforce" the Fourteenth Amendment. In order to act under Section 5, however, Congress must demonstrate that its legislation constitutes a congruent and proportionate response to past unconstitutional state conduct. *City of Boerne v. Flores*, 521 U.S. 507, 117 S.Ct. 2157, 138 L.Ed.2d 624 (1997). A pattern and practice of constitutional violations, in other words, can justify Congressional legislation that is prophylactic. Can evidence of past unconstitutional conduct by cities form the evidentiary basis for Section 5 legislation that would make *states* liable to private parties? In *Board of Trustees of the University of Alabama v.*

Garrett, 531 U.S. 356, 121 S.Ct. 955, 148 L.Ed.2d 866 (2001), the Court held that it could not:

> Respondents contend that the inquiry as to unconstitutional discrimination should extend not only to States themselves, but to units of local governments, such as cities and counties. All of these, they say, are "state actors' for purposes of the Fourteenth Amendment. This is quite true, but the Eleventh Amendment does not extend its immunity to units of local government. These entities are subject to private claims for damages under the ADA without Congress' ever having to rely on Section 5 of the Fourteenth Amendment to render them so. It would make no sense to consider constitutional violations on their part, as well as by the States themselves, when only the States are the beneficiaries of the Eleventh Amendment." *Garrett*, 531 U.S. at 368–369.

Justice Breyer's dissent responded as follows:

> The powerful evidence of discriminatory treatment throughout society in general, including discrimination by private persons and local governments, implicates state governments as well, for state agencies form part of that same larger society. There is no particular reason to believe that they are immune from the "stereotypic assumptions" and pattern of "purposeful unequal treatment" that Congress found prevalent. The Court claims that it "make[s] no sense" to take into consideration constitutional violations committed by local governments. But the substantive obligation that the Equal Protection Clause creates applies to state and local governmental entities alike. Local governments often work closely with, and under the supervision of, state officials, and in general, state and local government employers are similarly situated. Nor is determining whether an apparently "local" entity is entitled to Eleventh Amendment immunity as simple as the majority suggests—it often requires a " 'detailed examination of the relevant provisions of [state] law.' " *Id.* at 378–379.

In the Court's most recent Section 5 case, *Tennessee v. Lane*, 541 U.S. 509, 124 S.Ct. 1978, 158 L.Ed.2d 820 (2004), the Court seemed to reverse course. It held that evidence of past violations by cities could, in some circumstances, provide the basis for congressional legislation aimed at states:

> The Chief Justice dismisses as "irrelevant" the portions of this evidence that concern the conduct of nonstate governments. This argument rests on the mistaken premise that a valid exercise of Congress' § 5 power must always be predicated solely on evidence of constitutional violations by the States themselves. To operate on that premise in this case would be particularly inappropriate because this case concerns the provision of judicial services, an area in which local governments are typically treated as "arm[s] of the State" for Eleventh Amendment purposes, *Mt. Healthy City Bd. of*

Ed. v. Doyle, 429 U.S. 274, 280, 97 S.Ct. 568, 50 L.Ed.2d 471 (1977), and thus enjoy precisely the same immunity from unconsented suit as the States. In any event, our cases have recognized that evidence of constitutional violations on the part of nonstate governmental actors is relevant to the § 5 inquiry. To be sure, evidence of constitutional violations by the States themselves is particularly important when * * * the sole purpose of reliance on § 5 is to place the States on equal footing with private actors with respect to their amenability to suit. But much of the evidence in *South Carolina v. Katzenbach*, 383 U.S., at 312–315, 86 S.Ct. 803, to which the Chief Justice favorably refers, involved the conduct of county and city officials, rather than the States. Moreover, what the Chief Justice calls an "extensive legislative record documenting States' gender discrimination in employment leave policies" in *Nevada Dept. of Human Resources v. Hibbs*, 538 U.S. 721, 123 S.Ct. 1972, 155 L.Ed.2d 953 (2003), in fact contained little specific evidence of a pattern of unconstitutional discrimination on the part of the States. Indeed, the evidence before the Congress that enacted the [Family Medical Leave Act] related primarily to the practices of private-sector employers and the Federal Government. *Id.* at 527 n16.

The Court's difficulty in classifying cities is also evident in its interpretation of federal statutes, as the *Lead-Deadwood* and *Nixon* decisions, reproduced above, reveal. Federal antitrust law provides another important example. The Supreme Court held in *Parker v. Brown*, 317 U.S. 341, 63 S.Ct. 307, 87 L.Ed. 315 (1943), that the Sherman Act implicitly exempts states from anti-trust liability. Do cities enjoy a similar exemption? In *Community Communications Co. v. Boulder*, 455 U.S. 40, 102 S.Ct. 835, 70 L.Ed.2d 810 (1982), the Court held that they did not, at least when their action derived from their home rule powers rather than a specific authorizing statute. On that basis, it held that the City of Boulder could be liable for anti-competitive conduct arising from an ordinance prohibiting a cable company from expanding its service. Since that time, however, the Court has severely limited the risk that municipalities will be held liable for antitrust violations. It has done so by emphasizing that cities are creatures of their states and are thus protected by the *Parker* "state action" exemption even when acting pursuant to relatively general state enabling legislation, *Town of Hallie v. City of Eau Claire*, 471 U.S. 34, 105 S.Ct. 1713, 85 L.Ed.2d 24 (1985), and by describing them as independent sovereigns that are fundamentally distinct from the private companies that are Congress's primary concern. See *City of Columbia v. Omni Outdoor Advertising*, 499 U.S. 365, 111 S.Ct. 1344, 113 L.Ed.2d 382 (1991); *Fisher v. City of Berkeley*, 475 U.S. 260, 106 S.Ct. 1045, 89 L.Ed.2d 206 (1986). As to the latter point, Justice Scalia, writing for the Court in *City of Columbia*, rejected the notion that otherwise legitimate city action is invalid when it is taken pursuant to a "conspiracy" with private parties.

Few governmental actions are immune from the charge that they are "not in the public interest" or in some sense "corrupt." * * * The fact is that virtually all regulation benefits some segments of the society and harms others; and that it is not universally considered contrary to the public good if the net economic loss to the losers exceeds the net economic gain to the winners. *Parker* was not written in ignorance of the reality that determination of "the public interest" in the manifold areas of government regulation entails not merely economic and mathematical analysis but value judgment, and it was not meant to shift that judgment from elected officials to judges and juries. If the City of Columbia's decision to regulate what one local newspaper called "billboard jungles" is made subject to *ex post facto* judicial assessment of "the public interest," with personal liability of city officials a possible consequence, we will have gone far to "compromise the States' ability to regulate their domestic commerce". * * * For these reasons, we reaffirm our rejection of any interpretation of the Sherman Act that would allow plaintiffs to look behind the actions of state sovereigns to base their claims on "perceived conspiracies to restrain trade," *Hoover [v. Ronwin]*, 466 U.S., at 580, 104 S.Ct., at 2001. We reiterate that, with the possible market participant exception, *any* action that qualifies as state action is *"ipso facto* * * * exempt from the operation of the antitrust laws," *id.,* at 568, 104 S.Ct., at 1995.

Justice Stevens, in a dissent in which Justices White and Marshall joined, disagreed:

The Court's assumption that an agreement between private parties and public officials is an "inevitable" precondition for official action * * * is simply wrong. Indeed, I am persuaded that such agreements are the exception rather than the rule, and that they are, and should be, disfavored. The mere fact that an official body adopts a position that is advocated by a private lobbyist is plainly not sufficient to establish an agreement to do so. See *Fisher v. Berkeley.* Nevertheless, in many circumstances, it would seem reasonable to infer—as the jury did in this case—that the official action is the product of an agreement intended to elevate particular private interests over the general good. * * * *Id.* at 394–395.

Is it possible to reject Justice Scalia's view of how local governments make decisions and still conclude that they should be immune from liability for antitrust liability, just as states are? Is it possible to reconcile the multiple positions about the nature of cities adopted by the Supreme Court in the cases discussed in this note?

DAVID J. BARRON, FOREWORD: BLUE STATE
FEDERALISM AT THE CROSSROADS

3 Harv.L. & Policy Rev. 1, 4–6 (2009).

[T]here's no underestimating the depth of the challenge that advocates of progressive decentralization face now that red state dominance of the national political scene has come to an end. Two concerns in particular seem worth highlighting: "crowding out" and "easing off." "Crowding out" refers to the fact that success at the national level can make it difficult to remember the value of active state and local participation in policymaking. It's all too easy to think that, once you've won, you get to make the decisions. And what's more, it's easy to think that, once you've won, you must be the best decision maker there is. The temptation will be particularly great for national officials in the current environment. The critique of national governance for the last eight years has focused so much on its deregulatory bias that it will be hard to resist the idea that the solution inheres in more vigorous national governmental action. There's nothing wrong with that judgment as a general proposition, but once this logic gains momentum, it can easily take on a life of its own.

What exactly should the role be for state and local governments under the incoming administration if the problem during the past eight years was that the feds weren't doing enough? We may have cheered states and cities on when they were fighting for better regulatory frameworks that the feds resisted, but perhaps that just suggests the feds should now implement those frameworks as national policy. After all, climate change can't be solved locally, can it? Inadequate health care coverage is a national problem, isn't it? And the financial system is too integrated globally to be properly regulated in a decentralized manner, right?

The arguments for centralization are as easy to produce as they are familiar. But because they have the ring of truth around them, they threaten to crowd out the reasons for thinking there is value in making space for state and local regulatory action and input. It will be easy enough for the newly ascendant Democrats to understand the crowding-out problem in the abstract, but that also means it may be easy enough for them to sweep objections under the rug with vague statements about the virtues of something as elusive as better "cooperation" between central and local levels of government. * * *

To see just how serious the concern about crowding out is, it is useful to think about how it might play out in the real world. Imagine how a debate over national health care reform or climate change legislation might proceed. At some point in the legislative negotiations, the question will surely arise as to whether the federal legislation should be made exclusive of state and local efforts to augment or supplement it. It will be tempting at that moment for health care advocates or environmental supporters to surrender the preemption issue in order to secure support for federal standards that are marginally tougher than they might otherwise be. But there are real costs to doing so—costs that take the form of cutting off future outlets for social learning, reducing institutional mechanisms that pressure the government to remain dedicated to tackling underlying problems too fundamental to be solved in one fell national swoop, or shrinking the public space for the kinds of citizen participation and mobilization that are always the preconditions to meaningful social change.

"Easing off" presents the flip-side concern to "crowding out." There has been a tremendous surge of progressive energy at the state and local levels in recent years. * * * What's more, a whole new generation has come of age with an unusually strong affinity for community-based political action. * * * It was in the cities and towns, the state capitols and state houses, that real change seemed to be happening. It was there that the tired partisan debates so dominant in national political discourse seemed to give way to a more robust and innovative discourse focused on solving real problems.

Now, of course, particularly for millions of young people, there's nothing cooler than national politics. And that means there is a risk that many of the very same people who were beginning to see the value in becoming active locally may soon come to think of federalism as the dirty word in the progressive political vocabulary that it was for so long—a word that symbolizes the problem the nation needs to overcome rather than the means by which solutions to national problems might be discovered. In other words, even if the federal government does not go out of its way to preempt state and local initiatives, there still needs to be the energy from below to generate them. Decentralization, it must be remembered, is a two way street. Central governments have to give states and localities the room to run, but states and localities must take the initiative and exploit their opportunities. One worries that the creative local activism of recent years may give way to passivity or the uncreative instinct to resort to lobbying for little more than increased federal funding. * * *

C. THE RELATIONSHIP BETWEEN CITIES AND THE WORLD

Traditionally, as this Chapter has demonstrated, the content of local government law in the United States has been determined by state law. In other parts of the world (for example, in the United Kingdom and South Africa), national governments have defined local governmental power. Both of these familiar ways of creating local government law are changing. Parties negotiating international trade agreements, international tribunals arbitrating commercial disputes, United Nations rapporteurs investigating compliance with human rights obligations, and international financial institutions formulating development policy have all begun to express interest in the legal relationship between cities and their national governments. Indeed, cities themselves are beginning to use international institutions to redefine the scope of their domestic powers.[19] The two articles below—one by Yishai Blank and the other co-written by Gerald Frug and David Barron—investigate this new international dimension of city power. The articles were written separately, without knowledge of each other. Yet they describe similar phenomena; indeed, they overlap much more than the edited versions reproduced below suggest. Although both articles are analyzing only an emerging trend, they raise fundamental questions about who should determine the legal framework within which the cities both in the United States and in the rest of the world operate and what that framework should be. Is the emergence of this international dimension for city power something that should be embraced or resisted? How should its impact be evaluated? For example, is the question whether these new developments enable cities to gain or lose power? Or would the more important question be to determine the kind of cities that these international legal interventions are fostering? Do the articles suggest that the cumulative effect of international local government law so far has been fostering a more privatized city—or a more democratic one? What role do cities themselves have in influencing which of these directions—or which other direction—international law will promote?

YISHAI BLANK, THE CITY AND THE WORLD
44 Colum. J. Transnat'l L. 875, 892–906, 915–917, 922–936 (2006).

[L]ocal governments have no legal personality in formal international law. Classic documents of international law—the so-called uncontested sources of international law—do not recognize localities as possessing legal person. No international treaty or convention of the UN, and almost no decision of the International Court of Justice mentions the existence of localities or recognizes them as legal entities under international law. Furthermore, only states can be members of the UN. And, strange as it may sound, the seemingly clear legal principle that denies localities' legal person in international law, is hardly ever mentioned in international covenants, treaties, textbooks, or other documents. * * *

---

[19] For an ambitious re-imagining of the relationship between cities and the world, see Benjamin Barber, If Mayors Ruled the World: Dysfunctional Nations, Rising Cities (2013).

[T]here are several reasons for this tradition that lies at the heart of international law, some theoretical, others more pragmatic. The first, and perhaps the most obvious one is the traditional linkage between international law and the principle of sovereignty. The founding principle of international law is that states are sovereign within their territory and that international law is a self-imposed legal system to which states have to consent. Hence, only states should be the full subjects of international law, and they should be given the liberty to internally organize themselves, and be treated by external powers as unitary. Classic international law was not supposed to curb or diminish the unrestrained sovereignty of states within their territory, to regulate their internal affairs, or to contravene in any way the integrity of states. According to this view, the absence of localities from international law is no more unique than the absence of individuals, groups, associations, or corporations.

Second, the establishment of an efficient international regime depends on a limited and finite number of legally recognized international persons. One commentator explained most lucidly: "To admit [to the UN] all the bits and pieces of former empires as independent states would not only debase the coinage of membership but would surely be more than U.N. structure could bear." And even though this fear was mostly invoked by the demands of various regions and states within former federal and imperial regimes and not by demands of localities to become sovereign, the same logic applies even more strongly as regards local governments, and international law's hostility towards granting them legal person was probably a result of such fear. Indeed, under this view, granting some localities full legal person would not only destabilize the UN structure and unbearably complicate international relations, but it would also encourage many localities to secede from their states in an attempt to acquire full international legal person.

Third, and not unrelated to the previous point, is post-WWII hesitation to grant cities international status following what are seen to be failed experiments with free cities such as Krakow, Shanghai, Danzig, and Fiume, and internationalized cities/territories such as Tangiers and Jerusalem. Some of these experiments were targeted at solving problems of ethnic and national minorities that, following the emergence of the homogeneous nation-states, found themselves oppressed and in need of international protection. Cities where such minorities existed were thus freed from the grip of the state and put under international supervision; others were aimed at mediating between countries competing over resources and territories.

Fourth, local governments are simply seen as integral parts of their states and it would therefore seem odd to even mention them as separate entities. Much like it would be redundant to mention explicitly the existence of the legislature, the executive, or any other state organ—let alone discuss the absurd idea of granting these state actors international legal personality—there is no need to mention localities, or debate their candidacy for an independent international personality. Indeed, localities can actually be understood precisely as those sub-national divisions not recognized in any way by international law, standing in contrast to sub-national units such as states and cantons in federal systems, which international law accommodates in various ways.

It is therefore clear that the international legal order is based not only on the abstract understanding of the relations between sovereign states but also on a normative conception of a desirable hierarchy between various sub-national political divisions. In this regard, localities should not acquire any international legal status regardless of the exact division of powers between the state and its localities, even in cases where localities enjoy a high degree of independence and autonomy vis-a-vis their state. Not only is international law not currently built to fully incorporate a separate local entity, but such incorporation would also seem incompatible with the current understanding of the role of localities in the state. * * *

[I]f the attitude of international law towards local governments is so clearly biased and dismissive, how is it that localities have become, de facto, such important actors in world politics, culture, and economics? What are the legal changes that accompanied the emergence of local governments as world actors? Indeed, despite its explicit refusal to directly acknowledge localities as legal persons, during the past fifty years (and especially during the past three decades), international law began accommodating localities in various manners that are in clear opposition to the doctrinal lack of legal personality. International law burdened localities with duties. Localities became objects of global, international, and transnational regulation. Local governments have assumed the role of enforcers of international norms and standards, and they gained influence as political entities in the world political stage. These quite distinct characterizations of localities in the emerging global order add up to a picture in which localities are the active agents of globalization or internationalization. * * * This role of localities is a result of their unique position as active agents with legally defined powers, mediating between the world and the state, between individuals and their state, and between communities and the world. Localities' functioning as normative mediators in the new world is an outcome of a combination between their domestic legal powers and the emerging global schemes of decentralization * * *.

Thus, localities have become, and will become more so, nodal points for radically distinct governance projects that have as their common goal to transform cities from mere subdivisions of sovereign states into legally empowered entities, able to advance goals and values that are different from their states'. In this process, localities become partners in the evolving new global order in which non-state actors are increasingly more dominant. This change is brought about by four modalities, through which localities become prominent actors on the world stage. First, localities become bearers of international rights, duties, and powers. Second, localities become important objects of international and transnational regulation. Third, localities increasingly enforce international norms and standards. Fourth, localities form global networks. * * *

Though still short of becoming full international legal entities, localities are gradually acquiring a wide range of international duties and authority. As state agents, localities are obligated to comply with duties states have assumed as signatories to international charters and covenants. Indeed, states are often required to take necessary measures to ensure such local compliance with their international obligations. In other cases, localities have been given domestic authority based either on their state's international obligations or on customary international law. Hence, while not yet conferring upon localities the status of full international legal person, many international documents affect the duties of and authorities of localities. These duties cannot always be translated into international disputes in international tribunals, but they can actually impact the rights of individuals and other legal entities in various national settings. This is happening not because there is anything new about localities complying with their states' international responsibilities, but due to changes in the legal context in which localities operate. First, the growing number of international agreements and the fast evolution of customary international law mean that localities now exist in a legal surrounding in which state's monopoly over the determination of localities' rights, duties, and powers is broken and international rules now also apply. Second, many legal systems are decentralizing, particularly in economic terms, making localities economically responsible for international obligations taken by their states, thus creating growing economic tensions between localities and states. * * *

Due to the dual nature of local governments, according to which they are state organs on the one hand and autonomous (or at least independent) legal entities on the other hand, they can be sued in domestic courts for violating obligations that the state took upon itself in international covenants. This structure has some problematic aspects that stem from the fact that in many jurisdictions states have delegated many of their authorities—mainly the provision of various public services—to localities. These decentralizing measures, in themselves encouraged by various international entities, were often accompanied by a transformation of the funding schemes of localities from central funding to self funding. Thus, localities are expected to fund and provide services that the state took upon itself, but has devolved to localities.

And indeed, local governments have been sued by private individuals and by other domestic legal entities in domestic courts, based on international duties and obligations of their states as a result of the localities' status as state agents. And the more states across the globe are delegating various authorities and duties to localities, the more pressure is mounting on local governments to abide by the standards set out in such international documents.

A recent Israeli case demonstrates this point. In *Adalah v. Tel-Aviv*, two civil rights groups challenged the common practice of Israeli localities to post names on street signs in Hebrew and English only, rather than in Arabic as well. There was no doubt that domestic law mandated localities to place names on street signs within their jurisdiction. The plaintiffs argued that according to the United Nations International Covenant on Civil and Political Rights—ratified by the State of Israel in 1991—the state had to respect and protect the language of minorities, and since localities were state organs, they were bound by this duty. The reason localities fought the petition was that it would cost them a lot of money, money they would not receive from the state due to their incorporation as independent public corporations vested with exclusive authority over street signs. The Court rejected the claim that the Covenant established a positive duty upon the state and the city, yet accepted the petition nonetheless, based on the grounds that failing to use Arabic amounted to discrimination. However, had the Court ordered localities to use Arabic because the ICCPR included a positive duty to use minority language on street signs, it would mean that localities would fund with local taxes duties that the state assumed in the first place.

In another recent Israeli case, some of the tensions arising from the duties placed upon local governments—also according to UN covenants—were adjudicated. As a part of the structural shift from state funding of various public services to local funding, the government has cut the budget for public libraries operated by local governments throughout the country, and refused to continue to fund them in equal shares with localities. The Union of Local Authorities petitioned the Israeli Supreme Court and argued that the state is required to continue funding public libraries also based on its obligations according to the International Convention on Economic, Social and Cultural Rights. While accepting the general claim regarding the domestic applicability of international norms (and, apparently, their specific potential applicability to state-local government relationship), the Court rejected the petition in light of various amendments that were adopted into the specifically domestic law. Thus, regardless of the outcome of this dispute, it is evident that international norms have the potential to alter the domestic duties and authority of localities, as well as those of states towards localities.

The Canadian case of the *Town of Hudson* exemplifies another way in which international covenants can become not only a source of duties, but also an authorizing source for localities. In *Hudson*, licensed lawn care companies sought a declaration of invalidity of a by-law passed by the city of Hudson, prohibiting the use of pesticides within its territory, except for specified purposes and locations. Among other arguments, the plaintiffs maintained that the city was not authorized to enact the said by-laws. Dismissing the petition, the Court interpreted the authorizing act—the Canadian Cities and Towns Act that provided for regulation by municipalities "to protect the health and well-being of resident"—as authorizing the city to enact a by-law that protects the environment. The Canadian Supreme Court ruled that giving the town the right to enact the debated by-law was "consistent with principles of international law and policy," and was thus a plausible reading of the authorizing statute, among other reasons. The relevance of international law and policy, explained the Court, is derived from the interpretative principle that was set in *Baker v. Canada*, that "the values reflected in international human rights law may help inform the contextual approach to statutory interpretation and judicial review." The Court further found that environmental protection (and especially the "precautionary principle") was a well-accepted international law principle, and the town's authorization should be construed in a way that will allow it to promote this international principle.

These cases demonstrate the ways in which international duties, standards, and norms are increasingly imposed upon localities. On the one hand, because localities are state agents and as such must comply with their state's expanding international obligations, they are becoming even more dependent on their states' behavior. On the other hand, international law empowers localities since it creates direct authorization that might conflict with the state's policies and interests. Coupled with fiscal decentralization schemes, these developments cause different types of conflicts among localities and between states and local governments. * * *

Targeting localities as objects of regulation means that the physical planning, economic structure, urban development, housing schemes, and poverty management become the business of international and global institutions and not solely of the locality and national governments. * * * For the World Bank, one the major actors in contemporary global governance, the focus on localities is part and parcel of its new development strategy, augmenting the traditional goal of furthering economic growth with advancing participatory democracy and other "social" goals. The Bank's policies concerning localities are also intertwined with its assessment that the world is moving towards urbanization, and the prediction that "within a generation the majority of the developing world's population will live in urban areas and the number of urban residents in developing countries will double, increasing by over two billion inhabitants." The attention given to localities, and particularly to urban areas, is an outcome of the fact that more and more people live in urban settings that need to become more livable, but it is also a result of an idea that decentralization is a necessary condition for economic growth. Thus the Bank targets local governments, imbuing them with a new meaning. In regimes where localities exist as mere administrative subdivisions of their states, the Bank aims to strengthen them, delegate authority to them, burden them with duties such as the provision of public services, and armor them with immunities vis-a-vis the state.

According to these suggested reforms, where local governments are mere administrative conveniences, subject to the state's sovereign will, they ought to gain fiscal independence and political autonomy, changing what it means to be a locality. In fact, though the Bank advocates decentralization, it actually sees itself as merely piggybacking decentralization processes that have already been taking place across the globe. Its main objective, therefore, is to direct decentralization in a specific way, one that will advance economic growth and fit within the Bank's general ideology of efficiency, small government, and a reduction in state subsidies.

The Bank's most explicit goal is fiscal decentralization, the creation of a fiscal structure in which localities mostly fund themselves and provide public services based on their economic abilities. Such fiscal decentralization is closely linked with political decentralization and expanded authorities so that a locality will be able to "tax and spend" as it wills, except for activities designated nationally where the central government can and should intervene. Such decentralization comes with a diminished role of the central state. Interestingly, the Bank's objective to assist localities to become independent of their states and to be able to access the global capital market has another side to it, assisting states to become independent of their localities, and to be able to gradually stop supporting them financially. * * *

These are profound structural reforms and they are closely linked with the reconfiguration of the concept of locality itself. Though the local government remains a public corporation in the visions of the World Bank, it is pushed in the direction of becoming more private. Indeed, the World Bank's ideal city, and ideal locality in general, should have these four features: livability, competitiveness, good government, and bankability. Thus, the logic of a self-funding closed market, of efficiency and privatization of various public services is prevalent in the Bank's rhetoric and policies. Localities are encouraged to engage in public-private partnerships. In other words, in the historical debate concerning the nature of localities, the Bank takes the position of approximating localities to private corporations. In this respect, it fits within the new governance system that sees private actors, as well as private law as vehicles for advancing the Bank's political and economic policies.

The World Bank advances its policies through voluntary agreements in which localities agree to make structural reforms in return for loans and financial assistance. Even though these agreements do not count as international law, they are a crucial element in what contemporary scholarship sees as the new transnational legal order. Currently, the World Bank is involved in contractual relationships with hundreds of localities throughout the world. The Bank's "Urban Development" project is central to the Bank's activities and it has gained the cooperation of UN-Habitat. * * *

Another crucial aspect of the emergence of localities as central actors on the global stage is their participation in enforcing international legal standards. Until recently, it seemed that this role had been imposed on localities from above, by central governments, central legislatures, and courts. However, in recent years localities are no longer mere state agents that simply implement their state's international obligations. * * * Internalization of global norms and standards demonstrates a phenomenon related to globalization that manifests itself particularly in localities and is called "glocalization." This phenomenon is the local appearance of global forces resulting in a unique hybrid arising from the local interpretation, adaptation, or translation of global influences. An example of glocalization is the way global chain-stores adapt themselves to local tastes and preferences. Another example is the way localities interpret global imperatives and development schemes and implement them according to their own unique local culture. In law, such glocalization takes place when national courts adapt international norms and global standards to local legal "tastes" and local legal culture. It also happens when local actors, NGOs, activists, private individuals, and associations try to use international and transnational norms and standards to achieve various goals, or promote their internal agenda.

The processes that I described have been entwined with the emergence of local governments as political actors on the world political stage. The regulation and imposition of international duties on localities are thus accompanied by a growing representation of localities in international entities and by the creation of various associations whose primary goal is to facilitate cooperation among local governments in the face of the challenge posed to them by the new global regime.

A plethora of institutions, associations, networks, and ad hoc activities that comprise localities and that are aimed at turning them into principal global actors have appeared throughout the world in recent years. Some of the associations are global and some are regional, but they all see themselves responding to the growing importance of localities and to the emerging understanding that local governments are among the basic political building blocks of the new global order. Such organizations, associations, and ad-hoc entities include: The World Organization of United Cities and Local Governments (UCLG); International Union of Local Authorities (IULA); Mayors' Organizations; World Federation of United Cities (WFUC); World Urban Forum; The International Council for Local Environmental Initiatives (ICLEI); Global Metro City; and the Glocal Forum.

The meaning of the burgeoning global associations of localities is threefold. First, it denotes a growing awareness of localities to their importance. Second, it implies a current deficit in localities' effective participation in global governance projects, a deficit that induces local governments to cooperate in order to obtain a higher degree of influence. Finally, it marks a break from the competitive order of the nation-states, as localities from all over the world manage to cooperate. The rise in power of localities brings with it institutional changes whose impact we are only beginning to witness and understand. These transnational local networks demonstrate that globalization indeed works hand in hand with localization: As states share their power with localities, the latter group aims to increase its powers further and become full partners in the global order. And while traditional international law is reluctant to acknowledge local governments as full subjects, they manage to utilize civil society mechanisms in order to better their position. * * *

Proponents of local empowerment justify their position through the virtues of localism: economic efficiency and development, more direct and accountable democracy, and the unique ability of local governments to serves as normative mediators between communities and governments, and between local groups and national majorities. In particular, public choice theory has generated great distrust in central governments due to their susceptibility for capture by rent-seeking interest groups, and combined with the Tieboutian model of local expenditures, created a default rule in favor of delegation of power to local governments. In addition, scholars tried to show why democracy is also better served by strengthening local governments. First, the small scale of most localities allows people to exchange ideas and deliberate on a daily basis. Second, public officials cannot hide away from their constituents, hence they are reasonably more accountable and responsive to their constituent's needs. Third, since popular involvement in politics is a function of how much they feel their involvement really matters, positive feedback increases participation. Fourth, the substance of local politics is often more intuitively understood by lay people and it is therefore easier to overcome voter apathy. Lastly, the relative homogeneity of the local populace makes it easier to reach consensus and allow people to deliberate even politically charged matters.

But these justifications are somewhat anachronistic and inaccurate. The variance among localities is so enormous that looking at all of them as if they were all small towns ignores the reality of mega-cities, sometimes bigger in size and population than many countries. And it is overly optimistic in that it trusts formal democracy to naturally produce public deliberation and participation. As the experience in the United States suggests, making democracy work and inducing weak populations to participate in politics requires an active and positive effort on behalf of the ruling regime and a transformation of the political systems that exceeds the oft empty slogan "decentralization." Indeed, power sharing is not a natural outcome of smallness, proximity, or technology.

However, the material conditions that often exist in localities, including smallness, proximity, sharing the same physical and political space with fellow citizens, might be conducive to the fulfillment of the promise of the city. The city can serve as an ideal. Its unique legal structure, the inability and unwillingness to "solve" the ambivalences of localities as democratic yet bureaucratic, public yet private, state agents yet autonomous, is what enables these spatial conditions to facilitate their transformation into being, again, what stands at the forefront of human civilization. Even if big, pluralistic, and multicultural, they suggest a possibility to imagine a community in a more concrete and real way than the imagination of the national community (or, for that matter, the entirely abstract community of mankind). If every group is always somewhat imaginary, what singles out the city as a figure and the locality as the general legal concept that captures its essence is that it is still grounded in daily experiences, even if it clearly also imagined. On the other hand, unlike other "real" group or communitarian identifications, belonging to a city is usually not based on race, religion, gender, ethnicity, or other "immutable" or inherited traits. * * *

GERALD E. FRUG AND DAVID J. BARRON, INTERNATIONAL LOCAL GOVERNMENT LAW
38 Urb. Law 1, 1–5, 23–44, 57–59 (2006).

Anne-Marie Slaughter's *A New World Order*[92] is devoted to a discussion of the emergence of sub-state networks as an important part of the international legal order. * * * [C]ities are involved in the very kinds of networks that Slaughter describes. * * * Among the objectives of the newly created United Cities and Local Governments are promoting "democratic local self-government throughout the world," "political

---

[92] Anne-Marie Slaughter, A New World Order (2004).

representation of local governments" in the work of international organizations, the development of principles of good urban governance, and the "strengthening of free and autonomous local governments" through learning, exchange, and capacity-building. To accomplish these objectives, the organization intends to engage in lobbying in the international arena, information sharing, the establishment of extensive inter-city networks, and the formulation of common policy positions. By design, if it is successful, this kind of activity would strengthen city power. In fact, as an earlier joint statement makes explicit, the cities are seeking the support of nation-states as they try to increase their domestic responsibility and their role in international institutions.

United Cities and Local Governments is the culmination of a history of efforts to create a world-wide inter-city organization. But there are many other kinds of inter-city activities and connections as well, including Sister Cities International (linking 2,500 cities in 125 countries), the International City/County Management Association (providing technical and management assistance to its 8,000 members), and a variety of regional inter-city networks that cross national boundaries. One particularly noteworthy organization is Cities Alliance, launched in 1999 by the World Bank and the United Nations Human Settlements Programme (UN-Habitat). Cities Alliance is designed to foster new ways to develop better slum-upgrading programs for the urban poor and to build a consensus for development strategies and investment. * * *

[B]oth Cities Alliance and United Cities and Local Governments illustrate the complexities of finding the proper vehicle for representing the views of the world's cities. The Board of Directors of Cities Alliance, called the Consultative Group, is co-chaired by officials of the World Bank and UN-Habitat, and has members from financial organizations, international organizations of cities (including United Cities and Local Governments), and national governments. But it includes no representatives from individual cities. The United Cities and Local Governments leadership, by contrast, is made up of city officials. But its top officers include not only the mayors of Paris and Istanbul but also of South Bay, Florida (population: 3,859). (United Cities and Local Governments does have a metropolitan section, called Metropolis, which is the world organization of major metropolises. But its representativeness is itself open to question: at the moment, for example, its membership does not include any cities in the United States.)

United Cities and Local Governments is in the process of becoming the voice of the world's cities in the international arena. In 2003, the Secretary General of the United Nations established a Panel of Eminent Persons, chaired by Fernando Enrique Cardoso, the former President of Brazil, to review the relationship between the United Nations and civil society. The Cardoso report recommended that the United Nations "regard United Cities and Local Governments as an advisory body on governance matters." It also recommended that the UN agencies work closely with local authorities and that the General Assembly debate a resolution "affirming and respecting local autonomy as a universal principle." In 2004, United Cities and Local Governments entered into an Agreement of Cooperation with UN-Habitat to work together on a global campaign on urban governance, a global observatory that will monitor progress on the strengthening of local authorities, the promotion of an international dialogue on the decentralization of power, and similar objectives. In 2005, United Cities and Local Governments called upon national governments at their Millennium +5 Summit in September, 2005, to "formally recognize the role of local government as an essential and unique partner in implementing the United Nation's Millennium Goals." The United Cities and Local Governments website helpfully provided a draft letter, to be signed by individual mayors, which concluded with this sentence: "The role of local governments will become all the more effective if it is recognised at the world level and if UN advisory body status is granted to our organisation United Cities and Local Governments."

Local Agenda 21 is another illustration how local governments have begun to integrate themselves into international decision making. Agenda 21 is a global environmental and development program adopted by the United Nations Conference on Environment and Development held in Rio de Janeiro in 1992. It establishes a "global partnership" to work together on policies ranging from combating poverty to the protection of the atmosphere. This partnership includes not only a Commission on Sustainable Development, made up of nation-states, but also the participation of what are called "major groups." The somewhat-Borgesian list of these major groups includes women, indigenous groups, nongovernmental organizations, business and industry—and local governments. For cities, this recognition of a role in international decision making—a role independent of their nation states—is significant. Chapter 28 of Agenda 21 notes:

> Because so many of the problems and solutions being addressed by Agenda 21 have their roots in local activities, the participation and cooperation of local authorities will be a determining factor in fulfilling its objectives. Local authorities construct, operate and maintain economic, social and environmental infrastructure, oversee planning processes, establish local environmental policies and regulations, and assist in implementing national and subnational environmental policies. As the level of governance closest to the people, they

play a vital role in educating, mobilizing and responding to the public to promote sustainable development.

Agenda 21 called upon local governments to come up with their own "Local Agenda 21" programs. According to a survey published by the Commission on Sustainable Development, more than 6,000 local governments in 113 countries were participating in Local Agenda 21 initiatives by 2001. Local governments' major complaint about their participation, according to the survey, was their lack of adequate authority under domestic law to implement environmental policy. In its conclusion, the survey recommended that national policies affecting local power—in particular, taxation policy and funding mechanisms—be re-evaluated. * * *

Local Agenda 21 engages local governments on international issues through the auspices of international organizations. But local governments are also engaging these issues on their own, an effort that is collectively called "the municipal foreign policy movement." In the movement's early years, local city councils in the United States passed resolutions supporting a nuclear freeze, urging divestment from firms doing business in South Africa, and demanding cuts in the Pentagon's budget. More recently, more than 165 cities have passed resolutions opposing the Iraq War, and more than 180—including New York City—have passed resolutions opposing the Patriot Act.

But the municipal foreign policy movement is not limited to local efforts to take positions with respect to the foreign policies of their host nations. In its contemporary variant, it also involves the local effort to internalize aspects of international law itself. San Francisco and Los Angeles, for example, have adopted the United Nations Convention on the Elimination of all Forms of Discrimination Against Women—a convention that has not been adopted by the United States. Salt Lake City and Seattle have pledged to follow the Kyoto Protocol dealing with global warning, despite the lack of federal support for the Protocol.

The Supreme Court's decision in *Crosby v. National Foreign Trade*, holding that Massachusetts's effort to bar state entities from buying goods from Burma was preempted by a federal statute, is likely to limit these kinds of initiatives. And it may have foreshadowed the future when it cited the interests of an international legal institution—the World Trade Organization—in determining the proper scope of the domestic legal powers of cities. But the fact that the *Crosby* decision was based on statutory interpretation rather than on making the federal government the exclusive foreign policy voice as a constitutional matter means that it is not likely to end the local incorporation of international law. Moreover, *Crosby* does not affect many of the kinds of initiatives cities are undertaking. Cities, like states, have many interests abroad, ranging from trade to tourism, and their active pursuit of these interests is not likely to diminish. Seattle, for example, has a regional public/private partnership that seeks to link city officials and business organizations in an effort to promote domestic and international trade. And the City of Seattle itself, like Atlanta, Göteburg (Sweden), Kyoto (Japan), and other cities, has an office of international relations. The more cities assert themselves internationally in this way, the more likely it is that they will enmesh themselves in international city networks of the kind described above. * * *

We are still at the beginning of these kinds of city efforts to empower themselves domestically by intervening in the international arena. The culmination of these efforts could well be something like The World Charter of Local Self-Government. At the moment, the World Charter is just an idea—a discussion draft that might ultimately be presented to the United Nations General Assembly. But the draft is an important indicator of the current state of thinking about international local government law because it contains language that would revise local government law around the world.

A few excerpts suggest the scope of its ambitions:

Article 2. The principle of local self-government shall be recognized in national legislation, and where practicable guaranteed in the constitution.

Article 3. Local self-government denotes the right and the ability of local authorities, within the limits of the law, to regulate and manage a substantial share of public affairs under their own responsibility and in the interests of the local population.

Article 9(1). Local authorities shall be entitled to adequate financial resources of their own, of which they may dispose freely within the framework of their powers.

Like many of the other initiatives described above, the World Charter is a product of efforts by UN-Habitat and international organizations of city governments. But these organizations did not invent the provisions just quoted. They—and other aspects of the World Charter—derive from an already existing international agreement: the European Charter of Local Self-Government, which was proposed by the Council of Europe in 1985 and came into force in 1993. * * *

It seems uncontroversial to categorize the activities just mentioned as city initiatives. The status of the next two topics—the role of urban governance in international development and international human rights law—is much more ambiguous. Progress on international development policy and human rights is often linked with city empowerment. Cities, it is said, are themselves the best vehicles to improve the quality of urban management and to foster the rights of their citizens. But these aspects of international local government law can just as easily be seen as restrictions on city power rather than as efforts to enable it. As we shall see, urban governance reform has become part of the agenda of international financial institutions as they make development policy, and human rights protections are the product of agreements entered into by national governments, not by the cities themselves. Indeed, these international interventions into city affairs stem from long-standing concerns about local corruption and local disregard for minority rights, concerns that underlie other international attempts to regulate city powers as well. * * *

In recent years, international organizations have increasingly stressed the importance of good governance to effective economic development. Often, this emphasis is presented as just common sense: if governments are not organized to make proper use of development funds, the money is not likely to serve its purpose. Indeed, the language of good governance is increasingly framed in terms of a world-wide consensus, a consensus embraced by international organizations, by international financial institutions as an aspect of their development policies, and by national governments, including those who are recipients of funds from these financial institutions. * * *

UN-Habitat's Global Campaign on Urban Governance makes clear the role of cities in this effort. Cities, the Campaign's concept paper argues, are the engines of economic and social development, and good urban governance is the key ingredient in its success. Cities themselves, the concept paper suggests, understand this and want to embrace good governance. As a result, UN-Habitat adopts an "enabling approach" to progress in this area: it seeks "to increase the capacity of cities and other stakeholders to practice good urban governance." The concept paper also makes clear, however, that the achievement of the campaign's goals—sustainability, subsidiarity, equity, efficiency, transparency and accountability, civic engagement, and citizenship and security—will often require new national legislation. Moreover, as another UN-Habitat paper documents, good urban governance is not just a worthwhile goal that nations should adopt. Important aspects of its goals are a binding obligation of international law—"a legally binding human right."

Good urban governance, then, is three things simultaneously: an international legal obligation, a matter for national legislation, and a method of empowering cities. * * * However it is implemented, UN-Habitat's definition of good urban governance would substantially change local government law around the world. The goal of sustainability would affect both the process of environmental planning and its focus: it involves establishing a consultative process for decision making and includes poverty reduction, as well as historical preservation, in its goals.

Subsidiary envisions developing "clear constitutional frameworks for assigning and delegating responsibilities and commensurate power and resources from the nation to the city level and/or from the city level to the neighborhood level." Equality envisions quotas for women as members of local authorities as well as the revision of regulatory frameworks. Efficiency is designed to promote public-private partnerships, management contracts for delivering public goods, and "equitable user-pay principles" for municipal services. ("[G]overnance is not government," the report makes clear. "[G]overnance includes government, the private sector, and civil society.") Transparency and accountability includes matters as detailed as the reduction of administrative discretion in permit processing and codes of conduct for public officials. Civic engagement refers not only to promoting elections of municipal officials but also to holding referenda on important development issues. Finally, security covers matters ranging from ensuring the poor's access to employment and credit to developing a metropolitan-wide system of policing.

Domestic local government law now controls the resolution of every one of these issues. Given the current ambiguities, it is not clear which of these topics—and they are only illustrative of the list UN-Habitat has prepared—would be discretionary with city officials, required as conditions for receiving funds from international financial organizations, determined by national legislation, or a mandate of international law. Indeed, it might be hard to distinguish among these possibilities: the World Bank, for example, seems likely to support cities that have signed on to the good governance agenda over those that have not. What is clear is that good urban governance has the potential of becoming a substantive agenda that will make international local government law an important vehicle for defining local power. Already, according to UN-Habitat, efforts to implement the agenda are "underway or are planned in Nigeria, Tanzania, Burkina Faso, Senegal, India, The Philippines, Nicaragua, Jamaica, Brazil, Cuba, Peru and the Balkans." * * *

The current international emphasis on human rights could become an equally important transformative vehicle for local government law. The campaign for human rights shares many of the ambiguities—and ambitions—of the focus on good urban governance. Indeed, the two efforts can be seen as part of a common agenda. The goal of the Global Campaign for Urban Governance, according to the concept paper, is an "inclusive city, a place where everyone, regardless of wealth, gender, age, race or religion, is enabled to participate productively and positively in the opportunities cities have to offer." One way to make this possible is the international effort to secure economic, social, and cultural rights—specifically, the rights to education, housing, and health care.

Much has been written about the complexities involved in the attempt to secure these rights. We seek here * * * to focus on an aspect that the literature largely overlooks: the role of cities in this effort. In many parts of the world, education, housing, and health care are local matters. Local governments (or local public authorities) often run schools, provide and regulate housing, and offer health care services. If internationally recognized human rights are implicated in the provision of these local services, important city activities, along with city finances, will have to be organized to take them into account.

As was the case with good governance, many people see the furthering of human rights and city empowerment as going hand-in-hand. By this they mean both that the decentralization of power will promote greater access to education, housing, and health care and also the reverse: that cities' promotion of these human rights will further the prospect of local self-government. The Founding Declaration of United Cities and Local Governments emphasizes the first point. Cities' "responsibilities in housing, health and education allow us to develop responses adapted to the needs of our communities," the Founding Declaration asserts, and it adds: "[w]ell aware of the needs of our communities, local governments propose the creation of a legal framework favorable to increasing the fundamental rights of all citizens, including the right to education, health care, [and] access to housing. . . ." *Local Rule: Decentralization and Human Rights*, a report issued by the International Council on Human Rights, emphasizes the second point: "[w]ere decentralization explicitly linked to human rights, the case for its legal foundation would be strengthened." Yet, as everyone knows, international human rights are the product of efforts of international organizations and of covenants signed by nation-states, not the world's cities. They, not cities, are responsible for the creation of the "framework" that the Founding Declaration calls for. Thus they, not cities, will articulate what these rights mean.

Whoever ultimately defines economic, social, and cultural rights, their implementation, like that of the campaign for good urban governance, will inescapably have an impact on local government law. Consider only a few examples. According to the United Nations Economic and Social Council, the right to education includes the right of all children, regardless of their nationality or legal status, to attend public schools. The right to adequate housing covers matters such as reducing racial segregation, providing basic infrastructure, and limiting forced evictions. The right to health extends "to the underlying determinants of health, such as access to safe and potable water and adequate sanitation." In many parts of the world, responsibility for these issues has been delegated by national or subnational governments to cities. As a result, local government law now determines school admission policies, rules about racial segregation and evictions, and the provision of water and sanitation. Enforcement of economic, social, and cultural rights would thus do more than enhance individual well-being. It would affect the allocation of power to cities, making international local government law one of the ways that city services would be designed. Even now, among other projects, UN-Habitat is working with the governments of Brazil, Burkina Faso, Morocco, and Senegal to secure tenure for people living in informal settlements and slums, and with the governments of Kenya, Tanzania, and Uganda to improve water and sanitation in more than a dozen cities near Lake Victoria. * * *

The campaigns for urban governance and human rights are works-in-progress. They are just beginning to have an impact on city governments. The cases decided by international arbitration tribunals dealing with local land use decisions, to which we now turn, leave this world of "progressive realization." City land use decisions are being intensively reviewed—and sometimes overturned—by tribunals acting pursuant to international trade and investment agreements. This kind of international legal regulation of local land use power is potentially of great significance to the world's cities. No aspect of municipal legal power more visibly shapes city life than the regulation of real estate development. Cities throughout the world have significant authority in this area, even though national and sub-national governments impose many limitations on its exercise. Now, the international legal system is imposing its own limitations on city authority, and, in doing so, transforming the traditional domestic legal relationship between cities and higher levels of government. * * *

Because the cases that we examine are representative of the kinds of international disputes that will likely arise in the next several decades, certain of their common features deserve special emphasis. The agreements they interpret usually guarantee foreign investors a minimum level of treatment and provide them with protections against expropriation—protections that often exceed the level that domestic law would provide. A foreign company can thus enjoy more rights than domestic competitors operating in the same country. Indeed, the conferral of such extra protection is a key goal of such agreements given concerns about the legal systems in some countries. Some of the agreements permit only states to bring claims, but many confer rights directly on private actors. Consistent with the traditional conception of international law, these agreements typically do not make cities directly liable to these private actors and do not directly preempt local laws. The international legal obligation runs only against the nation-state and the remedy for breach is typically compensation rather than injunctive relief.

Still, in order to ensure a favorable climate for foreign investment worldwide, provisions of international trade agreements are increasingly targeting the exercise of ordinary local governmental powers. Moreover, even if the risk of cities' international legal liability remains low, international agreements often prompt states to exert strict regulatory control over their local governments. Some states have suggested that international agreements enable national governments to justify greater supervision of local policymaking than domestic politics alone would permit. At the very least, many nation-states, such as Canada, seem to be taking local compliance quite seriously.

While international agreements are giving national governments new reasons to police their cities, they also encourage cities to assert themselves in reaction. In 2000, the California state senate established a select committee on international trade policy in response to the fact that the state and its cities have become "increasingly obligated under trade rules and policies," and several California cities have passed resolutions opposing the adoption of the Free Trade Agreement of the Americas. The National League of Cities has begun to place these issues on its agenda, lobbying the U.S. Trade Representative to ensure that cities are heard as new agreements are forged and old ones are implemented. * * *

If one case symbolizes the influence of international trade and investment agreements, it is *Metalclad v. United Mexican States*.[183] The case concerned a U.S. company, Metalclad, which had purchased a landfill in the Mexican municipality of Guadalcazar. After the company failed to secure permission to operate the landfill either through the Mexican judicial system or the nation's regulatory authorities, it brought a claim under the North American Free Trade Agreement. The arbitration panel determined that Mexico breached its obligations to provide "fair and equitable treatment" and to refrain from taking action "tantamount to an expropriation." This was one of the first decisions under NAFTA to find for a private investor, and the arbitration panel's multi-million dollar award against Mexico attracted fierce criticism. * * * [I]mportant aspects of the opinion were ultimately reversed. Nevertheless, the panel's decision in *Metalclad* remains important. For many, it reveals international law's potential to preempt policy decisions that had long been thought to be primarily of domestic concern.

The ruling was particularly striking because the government action was hardly the kind that ordinarily requires compensation. Mexico had simply prohibited a landfill from continuing to operate. A similar action would not entitle a company to receive compensation under the Due Process or Takings Clauses of the U.S. Constitution. *Metalclad* thus suggested that NAFTA imposed broad new restrictions on governmental efforts to protect the environment or ensure the health and safety of citizens.

---

[183] 40 I.L.M. 36 (2001).

Our interest in *Metalclad*, however, lies elsewhere: its relationship to the development of international local government law. Often overlooked in the criticism of *Metalclad*'s expansive view of expropriation is the fact that the outcome of the case turned on a dispute over the scope of city power in Mexico. Metalclad ran into trouble when Guadalcazar asserted the power to prohibit the construction and operation of the landfill. The company responded that Guadalcazar lacked power under Mexican law to do so and that higher-levels of the Mexican government had assured it of that fact. The company further argued that, even if the city had some permitting authority, it could only deny a permit for defects in the manner of construction, not on the basis of a determination about where landfills should be sited. The siting issue was for the central government to decide. In other words, the opposition of the local community to the waste treatment site, like that of nearly a dozen neighboring cities, was simply beside the point.

Domestic legal proceedings failed to determine the extent of Guadalcazar's permitting authority prior to the NAFTA tribunal's ruling. But, rather than barring the company's NAFTA claim, the company argued the NAFTA violation inhered in the fact that the scope of the city's authority was unclear. NAFTA's investor protections, it contended, included what amounted to a duty of regulatory transparency, and Mexico breached that duty because of its opaque rules and regulations regarding local authority over landfills. The lack of clarity, Metalclad argued, facilitated what amounted to a bait and switch: the company was induced by Mexican officials to invest, but then had the rug pulled out from under it after its costs were sunk and local opposition grew.

The NAFTA arbitration panel agreed. It ruled that Mexico breached its duty to "ensure a transparent and predictable framework for Metalclad's business planning and investment"—and thus its obligation, under NAFTA Article 1105, to provide "fair and equitable treatment." According to the panel, the breach resulted from the central government's failure to stop the municipality from asserting its expansive view of its domestic legal authority. The panel further determined that Mexico's "permitting or tolerating the conduct of the municipality in relation to Metalclad" constituted a "measure tantamount to expropriation in violation of NAFTA Article 1110(1)," especially given the representations of Mexican officials that local approval was not needed.

This is the aspect of *Metalclad*'s analysis that bears directly on the legal power of cities. In defending itself before the NAFTA tribunal, the Mexican government explained that there was a substantial central/ local conflict within Mexico as to which level of government should control the location of waste treatment facilities. Cities have obvious reasons for resisting landfills, although they also have legitimate interests in influencing decisions to site them in their midst. The Mexican government argued that Metalclad had tried to bypass this domestic dispute. It had pursued what the Mexican government called a "top-down strategy" by seeking support and commitments from central government officials so that it could ignore Guadalcazar's assertion of local power. Thus, the Mexican government argued, a determination that Metalclad had been denied fair and equitable treatment would penalize the country for not having conclusively determined which level of government should have the final say on this issue.

Of course, nations could ensure regulatory transparency by making it clear that cities either possess or do not possess extensive local land use powers. Yet, it is difficult to allocate authority in a way that is transparent and empowering of cities at the same time. Delegations of authority to cities cannot be unlimited because they threaten both central authority and private autonomy. For that reason, in the United States, the interpretive canon known as Dillon's Rule empowers the central government to determine the legitimacy of a city's attempt to subject private actors to novel regulations of their conduct. It instructs courts to construe local powers narrowly in the absence of a clear and express legislative delegation of power. Because of its limits on local power, Dillon's Rule has been very controversial. Many of those who pressed for home rule as an alternative sought to allow cities more leeway to make decisions without express legislative authorization.

In key respects, the NAFTA tribunal's decision in *Metalclad* mirrors Dillon's Rule. Faced with an emerging grass-roots environmental movement, Guadalcazar re-interpreted its existing permitting authority to close down a landfill site. It contended that it could deny a permit not only on the basis of defects in construction but also on the basis of concerns about the location of the site itself. Like a court applying Dillon's Rule, the *Metalclad* panel portrayed this novel assertion of local power as a threatening intrusion on the private sphere that the central government had not clearly authorized. For that reason, it found the government had acted unlawfully. *Metalclad* crafted a rule that limited the ability of cities to make their own interpretations of local regulatory authority, thus taking a position on a central issue of Mexican local government law.

On appeal, the Supreme Court of British Columbia disagreed with the panel's finding that Article 1105 imposes a duty of transparency, and it questioned the breadth of the panel's approach to expropriation. That approach, it noted, could encompass "a legitimate rezoning of property by a municipality or other zoning authority." The Supreme Court, however, did not reverse the panel's alternative Article 1110 finding that Mexico was ultimately liable for imposing an "ecological decree" that would have prevented the siting of any treatment facility at any time. Still, by limiting liability to the issuance of ecological decree, the Supreme Court did reverse the panel's key impact on local government law: the aspect of its decision that found that Mexico had unlawfully acquiesced in Guadalcazar's attempt to block the landfill.

While the Supreme Court's decision should be a welcome development to those concerned by a potential international imposition of Dillon's Rule for the world's cities, the panel decision remains a significant legal development. Those concerned that international trade and investment agreements can reach down and preempt seemingly "local" regulatory actions legitimately cite the *Metalclad* panel's decision as evidence that international economic law can effect major changes in existing legal understandings. But the concerns raised by the *Metalclad* panel's decision should not be limited to the international legal system's capacity to extend the scope of private immunities from governmental regulation. They should also focus on the way in which the international legal system can, in the course of expanding private property rights, re-structure the legal relationship between cities and higher levels of government within a nation-state. After all, Dillon's Rule was itself very much bound up with a late nineteenth century effort to expand private property rights through judicial action. *Metalclad* thus reveals international law's potential to perform a function strikingly similar to one that domestic local government law has performed. * * *

D. THE CITY AND DEMOCRATIC THEORY: PART TWO

The materials in this chapter have raised in a variety of different ways one fundamental question: how can cities in America wield significant power given their susceptibility to control by the state and federal governments? What chance do cities have if (in the image of the Calvino story, printed below) they are "bound to the(se) two crests with ropes and chains and catwalks"? The principal hope for the possibility of city power offered by the cases in this chapter has been the creation of an area of city autonomy not subject to control by higher governments, an area that might be defined, for example, in terms of home rule or (in National League of Cities v. Usery) in terms of "integral operations in areas of traditional governmental functions."

The books and articles excerpted in this section are designed to encourage reflection about this strategy of basing city power on judicial protection of a sphere of city autonomy invulnerable to encroachment by the state or federal government. The first excerpt by Robert Dahl relates the difficulty of identifying such an area of local autonomy to classic dilemmas of liberal democratic theory. The second excerpt, by Michael Zuckerman, introduces an alternative notion of city-state or city-federal relations, one that seeks to protect decentralized power by reversing the flow of power between central governments and cities. This alternative version of city-state relations—one that enabled cities to control the state rather than the other way around—is presented in terms of the history of the early New England town. Could this alternative structure be put into practice in America today? The section concludes with an excerpt by Richard Ford that challenges the very idea of local autonomy. Ford argues that the conception of the "local" which underlies autonomy claims may be a tool of centralized control rather than a form of resistance to it. What is the relationship between Ford's analysis of Equality Foundation v. City of Cincinnati and David Barron's argument for local constitutionalism at the beginning of this chapter? Does Barron's argument for deference to local decision making depend on a defense of the notion of autonomy that Ford criticizes? Does Zuckerman's alternative model of the state-city relationship adequately address Ford's concerns about localism?

ITALO CALVINO, INVISIBLE CITIES
P. 75 (1974).

If you choose to believe me, good. Now I will tell how Octavia, the spider-web city, is made. There is a precipice between two steep mountains: the city is over the void, bound to the two crests with ropes and chains and catwalks. You walk on the little wooden ties, careful not to set your foot in the open spaces, or you cling to the hempen strands. Below there is nothing for hundreds and hundreds of feet: a few clouds glide past; farther down you can glimpse the chasm's bed.

This is the foundation of the city: a net which serves as passage and as support. All the rest, instead of rising up, is hung below: rope ladders, hammocks, houses made like sacks, clothes hangers, terraces like gondolas, skins of water, gas jets, spits, baskets on strings, dumb-waiters, showers, trapezes and rings for children's games, cable cars, chandeliers, pots with trailing plants.

Suspended over the abyss, the life of Octavia's inhabitants is less uncertain than in other cities. They know the net will last only so long.

ROBERT DAHL, DILEMMAS OF PLURALIST DEMOCRACY
Pp. 96–107 (1982).

Democratic Dilemmas

We seem to be trapped in a maze where, having reached the end, we discover ourselves at the beginning. Does this not hint at the possibility that large-scale democracy—indeed democracy on any scale—poses some fundamental dilemmas?

First dilemma: rights versus utility. This dilemma runs like a bright thread through all designs for dealing with the problem of democratic pluralism. Are solutions to be judged exclusively on utilitarian grounds, for their contributions to human well-being, welfare, happiness, satisfaction of wants, preferences, volitions, and so on? Are there not also questions of *rights* that are ultimately independent of utilitarian considerations, or at least cannot be finally settled on purely utilitarian grounds? Do not all human beings, for example, possess the fundamental moral *right* to have their interests taken equally into account? Even a utilitarian would acknowledge the validity of the claim to a certain basic moral equality, in insisting that utility to person A counts precisely the same as utility to person B. Thus Bentham's "Each person counts as one and no more than one."

But beyond this fundamental right there are others that might conflict with a utilitarian judgment. Does a people have a fundamental right to govern itself? If so, does not this fundamental right require all the subsidiary rights implied by the right of self-government? Are rights like these justified on other grounds? Must not utilitarian considerations therefore sometimes yield to considerations of rights?

Tested by mental experiments in the realm of hypothetical cases, it appears impossible to discover any right that can reasonably be justified in utter disregard for its consequences for the well-being of persons affected by the exercise of that right—including the possessor. Yet it is equally unreasonable to contend that rights must *always* give way to utilitarian considerations. Can we justify executing innocent prisoners in order to set an example to others? Is this not a violation of a human right so fundamental that it cannot be justified on utilitarian grounds?

Moral philosophers have struggled endlessly with this dilemma. Utilitarians remain convinced that they have successfully disposed of their critics' arguments. But they have failed to convince a substantial body of other philosophers. What is true of moral philosophy is a fortiori true of political life, as we are now about to see.

Second dilemma: a more exclusive versus a more inclusive demos. In practice, every demos is exclusive; no demos, no matter how large, has ever included all human beings. There simply is not and never has been an association of all human beings governed by the democratic process— or, for that matter, any single government.

The question arises: Why this demos rather than another? Might it not properly be more inclusive—or more exclusive? The question seems to admit of no definitive answer. That answers can be reached at all is the half-concealed mystery of democratic ideas and practices. The question is, in fact, an embarrassment to all normative theories of democracy, or would be were it not ignored. In practice, solutions call not upon theoretical reason, which is baffled by the question, but, as with Lincoln, on primordial attachments to tribe, town, city, subculture, nation, country. Though it is sometimes held that a more inclusive demos is always preferable to a less inclusive one, the argument is patently defective. For the argument logically implies that the only proper demos is all of humanity. But even those who defend an inclusive demos invariably accept, and without serious questioning, the limits on the demos imposed by primordial or historical boundaries—which nowadays are those of nation or country. But why draw the boundaries of the demos at the borders of a country? On the other hand, why not? Suppose we agree that maximum inclusion today really means the largest demos within the historically (and often arbitrarily) given boundaries of a country. There is still the second embarrassment: No demos has ever included children, and those who contend that a more inclusive demos is better than a less inclusive one have no intention of demanding that children be included.

That no one seriously insists that the demos be *completely* inclusive suggests hidden premises at work. One kind of hidden premise often turns out to be utilitarian or expediential: demos X is better than Y because it leads to greater well-being, utility, satisfaction of preferences, welfare, happiness. An assumption of this kind is heir to all the usual defects of utilitarian moral reasoning. However elegant the efforts to quantify the relative utilities, or whatnot, the comparison never in practice leads to anything like an uncontestable conclusion. The quantities, even if precise, are fictitious; in fact, the greater their precision, the greater the fiction. There are also the usual problems of intensity and quality: *is* pushpin as good as poetry, *is* the satisfied fool better than Socrates dissatisfied? And there is the eternal challenge of nonutilitarian moral standards: rights, duties, personal integrity.

Both utilitarian and nonutilitarian arguments can be readily used either way: to justify a more inclusive demos or a more exclusive one. In the end, no solution to the problem can be better than the solution to the conflict between utilitarian and nonutilitarian moral standards.

Third dilemma: equality among individuals versus equality among organizations. The principle of equality in voting, which is central to the idea of democracy, refers to human beings, persons, individuals. Except under certain rare and all but irrelevant circumstances, the principle of voting equality is necessarily violated whenever units, associations, organizations, states, provinces, or countries, rather than individual persons, are granted equal votes. For, as we saw, unless the number of citizens is identical in all the units, then voting equality among units means inequality of votes among citizens. Except in rare cases, the number of citizens is not the same in all the units; if it were, there would be no reason to reject the principle of voting equality for the principle of organizational equality.

Should the principle of voting equality among citizens never be modified in order to allow for greater political equality among organizations (and so less among citizens)? Should a national legislature be designed to represent only citizens, or only provinces or states, or both? The American constitutional solution was, of course, to do both. Ought there to be functional representation? If so, should votes in a functional body be allocated according to the number of citizens in each functional group, in which case the body would not be all that different from one based on territorial constituencies; or should they be allocated equally among certain types of organizations, thereby violating the criterion of voting equality among citizens? Proponents of functional representations have never met this dilemma satisfactorily. Either their solution violates the principle of voting equality on grounds they are unable to justify; or else it does not, and if not, then functional representation offers few advantages over territorial representation.

The question remains: Is it ever justified to permit equality among organizations at the expense of equality among individual citizens? Arguments for doing so rest on considerations both of utility—indeed, often of expediency—and of rights. Systems of democratic corporatism, like the corporate pluralism of the Scandinavian countries, are thought to be justified because they are useful. Is there a better way to arrive at decisions involving the great nationwide interest organizations? Unless the government acts with the consent of the organizations, it is impotent. It cannot *impose* a solution. As is well known, cabinet officers and troops cannot mine coal. But if parliament *is* to act with the consent of the interest organizations, then some system of corporate pluralism seems necessary. But corporate pluralism means * * * that votes count but organizational resources decide. Likewise, consociational democracies may permit any one of several groups to veto policies its leaders think harmful. In effect, consociational democracy requires unanimity among certain major social aggregates and their organizations. These arrangements are held to be justified, not only because of their utility in gaining widespread consent in a segmented society, but also because they guarantee the *right* of each group to have its fundamental interests taken into account. Do Catholics and Calvinists, socialists and liberals, all have an equal right to their own subculture and community life? Do Francophone Walloons and Dutch-speaking Flemish have an equal right to their language and traditions? Should members of the small Italian-speaking minority in Switzerland have the same rights to cultural autonomy as members of the larger French-and German-speaking minorities? In the United Nations General Assembly, all countries are given equal votes. Is this justified only out of expediency, or is it also a matter of right? Would any foreseeable world government, even one much more nearly ideal than the U.N., operate exclusively under a system of majority rule where the demos consists simply of the human species? I do not say that satisfactory answers can never be found. But clearly there is a conflict of fundamental principles.

Fourth dilemma: uniformity versus diversity. As these examples suggest, diversity is precious, not only to groups that prize their own ways, religion, language, place, customs, traditions, history, and values, but also to everyone who holds that human diversity is good in itself or in its results. The protection of diversities can be justified on utilitarian grounds: It yields more satisfaction (or whatever) than uniformity— especially when one adds the costs of suppressing differences valued by their possessors. Protecting diversity can also be justified because one has a right to one's own identity, personhood, personality, culture. Am I to be punished because I insist on speaking my mother tongue? Do I not have a *right* to be different in that way from the majority of my fellow citizens?

In the modern world it is an easy and congenial task to defend diversity. If the idea of uniformity is superficially less attractive, uniformity is nonetheless desirable because not all differences among human beings are matters of right or have good consequences. Do we not advocate uniformity in the protection of fundamental rights? Oppose differences in the right of citizens to vote, to have a fair trial? When differences infringe on basic rights, one's appreciation of diversity crumbles. Should neighborhoods that want to preserve their special character be allowed to exclude anyone who does not fit in? There is also the question of the level at which differences ought to be permitted or protected: at the level of the individuals or the level of the group? If at the group level, what kind of group? With respect to what kinds of differences? To be sure, sometimes protection at the individual level necessarily requires protection at the group level. Religion is ordinarily not only a personal activity: It is social and organizational as well. Consequently, a government cannot protect the right of individuals to their religious beliefs without protecting their right to adhere to diverse religious organizations, to practice their rites in the presence of their coreligionists, and to exclude from membership those who reject the sect's beliefs. Applied to racial differences the same reasoning would require us to tolerate racial segregation in a neighborhood, school, university, workplace, trade union.

Equality means, precisely, identity. If A and B are to be treated as equal with respect to a thing of value, a right, opportunity, duty, or share in some social allocation, then the thing must be identical for A and B. If A and B have an equal right to vote, A's right to vote is identical with B's: the rights of A and B are theoretically interchangeable. Obviously, equality conflicts with diversity. In the steady march of the idea of equality throughout history that Tocqueville believed he discerned at work as a fundamental force in the world, many kinds of differences once widely thought acceptable are no longer. What might from an earlier perspective be justified as a proper difference, a desirable or ineradicable diversity, becomes an unjustified inequality, discrimination, unfairness, inequity. If equality is often desirable, then so is uniformity.

Fifth dilemma: centralization versus decentralization. Uniformity and diversity: centralization and decentralization. Although the two sets of terms are not symmetrical, uniformity often requires some centralization, and diversity often presupposes some decentralization. Let me now specify more precisely what I mean by centralization and decentralization. Suppose that subsystems exist within a more inclusive system of controls. Then the inclusive system—for the moment let me refer to it simply as the organization—is decentralized to the extent that the subsystems are autonomous in relation to other subsystems in the organization. If one subsystem controls all the others with respect to x, then with respect to x it is a center and the organization is centralized with respect to x. Sometimes one subsystem controls all the others over a large range of crucial actions. A subsystem of this kind might be designated *the* Center of the organization. Starting from any given situation, then, to decentralize means to increase the autonomy of subsystems in relation to *the* Center or *a* center. By definition, decentralization also means a decrease in control over the subsystems by a center, and in particular *the* Center. To centralize means exactly the reverse: when a center's control over subsystems increases, subsystem autonomy decreases. Since an organization may be centralized with respect to some matters and decentralized with respect to others, it is obvious that patterns of organization can be extraordinarily complex—a fact painfully familiar to all experienced students of organizations.

For example, every subsystem in the organization might be highly controlled by *a* center; in this sense the organization is highly centralized and might well appear so from the viewpoint of a member of any of the subsystems. But each of the centers might be relatively autonomous in relation to the others: in this sense, each center is also a somewhat independent subsystem. Thus the organization, though centralized, would be collegial rather than monocratic. To describe it in a different way: Control would be centralized in the joint leadership of the centers, but not among the leaders.

If organizations were the mechanisms of pure rationality they were often pictured to be in early theories of organization, and if centralization and decentralization had no other significant consequences than those immediately entailed in shifting control over certain matters toward or away from the Center, then a choice between centralization or decentralization would doubtless be simpler than it usually is. However, organizations are rarely if ever mechanisms of pure rationality; they are not constituted merely of rational actors striving only to maximize the efficient attainment of the organization's official goals. In practice, organizations depart from a model of pure rationality in several ways. For one thing, centralization and decentralization have consequences for communication, and thus for control. Centralized control requires a flow of accurate communications toward the Center. Centralized communication systems are not only in danger of jamming up from overload; they are highly susceptible to distortion. After the king executes the first messenger who brings bad tidings, the word quickly gets around. By decentralizing decisions to autonomous units, lengthy lines of communication can be shortened and the jam-up at the center can be reduced. But the big picture, the synoptic overview, may be destroyed; each unit makes its decisions without much awareness of what is happening elsewhere.

Centralization and decentralization also have consequences for power beyond those described in models of pure rationality. To centralize control is not merely to allocate resources for influencing others to a perfectly neutral incumbent of some central office. Centralization puts resources in the hands of specific human beings at the Center, persons with goals of their own. To decentralize is to allocate resources of influence away from the Center, and thus to convey them to other specific human beings. The problem is, of course, that these actors may very well not devote their resources simply to the ostensible purpose of the exercise, to see that the prescribed goals of the organization are attained more efficiently. They may also use their resources for their own particular purposes. They usually do. It is not going too far to say that leaders almost always use some of the resources available to them for self-aggrandizement. This is the essence of Acton's famous aphorism that power tends to corrupt, and absolute power corrupts absolutely. Is it reasonable to expect that any human beings, any team, group, sect, party, or stratum will long refrain from using the resources available to them in order to enhance their own distinct interests? Even where democratic forms remain, to allocate large resources to the Center may lead to a loss of control by citizens. Conversely, to shift resources away from the Center to more autonomous subsystems may prevent domination by the Center, but * * * decentralization may also allow domination *within* each subsystem.

In political life, at least, to centralize or decentralize is never simply a problem in engineering, where the strengths and tolerances can be nicely determined. It is a problem in political dynamics, where the consequences can only be guessed at. To increase the authority of the Presidency always increases the power of a person, or a group of people, in the White House. Decentralization to local communities increases the power of certain people more or less resident in certain localities.

Although it is always uncertain how these various persons will use their power, human experience supports the hunch that they will use some of it to advance their own interests. And these interests may prove to be sharply adverse to the interests of others.

Sixth dilemma: concentration versus dispersion of power and political resources. Uniformity, centralization, concentration of power and resources; diversity, decentralization, dispersion of power and resources. If the last triad is the program of classical liberalism, what is the first? Liberalism, and in particular liberal ideas about democracy, were formulated in opposition to concentrated power. Liberal democracy represented a movement away from the uniformity of centralized regulation imposed by means of power concentrated in the crown, the royal ministers, and an unrepresentative parliament. By Tocqueville's time the liberal strategy had been so successful in the United States that it was necessary to sound a new liberal warning: By concentrating all power in the people, or rather in majorities, democracy also posed grave risks to liberty, most of all in a country where the citizens were more nearly equal in their conditions than had ever been true before among any numerous body of people.

The hostility of liberalism to concentration of power runs deep; as has often been observed, it may run deepest in that country where liberal ideas have always confronted the weakest challenge. Yet even in the United States, liberalism in the twentieth century yielded up a great deal of its earlier commitment to dispersion. Progressive liberalism, reform liberalism, the liberalism of Woodrow Wilson's New Freedom and Franklin Roosevelt's New Deal, all demanded that certain national policies be enforced uniformly throughout the United States. As a direct consequence, the new liberalism sought greater centralization of control over policies and decisions in federal agencies and a greater concentration of political resources at centers in Washington. Even more important, reform liberals quickly discovered that without strong presidential leadership no reform program could fight its way past the elaborate combination of checkpoints built into the American political process. These, of course, gave great advantages to defenders of the status quo. Liberal reform therefore required that political resources be concentrated in the hands of the president. Richard Nixon did not create the Imperial Presidency; he inherited it. In point of fact it was mainly liberals, not their conservative opponents, who designed, encouraged, supported, and brought about the shift of resources to the White House that finally facilitated the creation of an Imperial Presidency.

If this change took place in a country where hostility to concentrated power was stronger than elsewhere, the same process was bound to occur in other countries where the political traditions were far less monolithically liberal. It is a commonplace, but a valid one, to say that in all democratic countries concentration of power in the executive branch and the central bureaucracies has vastly increased in this century. Although the institutions of polyarchy have not collapsed under this new weight, it would be wrong to say that anxieties about the consequences of concentration have thereby been shown to be irrational. For one thing, the flourishing of dictatorships, sometimes in the extreme form of totalitarian rule, has once again demonstrated that democracy depends on a dispersion of power and resources.

Is this antinomy—concentration versus dispersion of power and resources—rather more lopsided than the others? Are we all really in favor of dispersion? Not necessarily. Once we accept the premise that there must be definite even if not perfectly clear limits to concentration in a polyarchy, then within these limits the dilemma becomes perfectly real.

For whenever (a) uniform enforcement of a policy is desirable, (b) uniformity cannot be attained without centralization, and (c) centralization requires a concentration of power and resources, then either one must forego a desirable uniformity or else accept concentration. Everyone who is not an anarchist is likely to agree that the risks of concentration are sometimes offset by the advantages of a uniform policy. The conflict between the advantages and risks of concentration is genuine, and citizens and leaders cannot escape the force of this dilemma in any democratic country. * * *

MICHAEL ZUCKERMAN, PEACEABLE KINGDOMS
Pp. 10–28, 35–38, 43–45 (1970).

The Context of Community: The Towns and the Province

The pre-eminence of the local community in provincial Massachusetts was, curiously, a new thing under the New England sun. The first Puritans who settled at the Bay had been congregationalists in ecclesiastical polity. They had set sail across the ocean only after decades of denunciation of bishops and synods as dead historical husks of Christianity to be peeled away before the churches could regain their primitive vitality, only after decades of disagreement with the Established Church, and the Presbyterian dissenters, over the scope of central surveillance of the churches of the realm. As the *Arbella* headed out from England, its passengers could hardly have conceived that they would flee the control of Canterbury and of London only to create a comparable one in Boston.

And yet, that was what they did. Under the necessity of governing and the temptation of power, availing themselves of the ambiguities of congregational theory and ignoring inconvenient aspects of its clarities, the magistrates and ministers established a degree of direction from the center that would have been unthinkable a hundred years later. It was only with the passage of decades that power passed to the communities; in the colonial era the assemblies and the synods exercised a close care over all that occurred in the communities and congregations. Throughout the first generation, and in the very teeth of the principles of congregational autonomy which had guided the conception of the colony, the government at Boston practiced an ecclesiastical authority which spanned the settlement. Its control ranged from trifles, such as determination of closing times for services in a single church, to matters of real moment, such as the General Court's 1635 ruling that churches could not be organized at all unless they did "first acquainte the magistrates * * * & have their approbacon herein." * * *

In secular affairs the central government exercised an equally extensive authority. * * * Thus it was the Court, not the communities, which first made education a public obligation; and it did not do so until the 1640's. Thus, as late as 1647, more than a decade after their grant of local self-government, the legislators were still passing "minute provisions" for such minute matters as the ringing of swine and the fencing of common cornfields in particular communities, and before that their economic regulation had been even more extensive, touching trades, standards, and prices, and calling out the citizens to work on public projects such as roads and fortifications. * * * In 1661 the magistrates went so far as to order an Ipswich man's land sold "because the distance of his home from the meetinghouse had caused him to absent himself from its service, 'in order that living nearer the meeting house he might more conveniently attend public worship.' " Such actions were apparently accepted in the seventeenth century. In the eighteenth, they were not even attempted.

Similarly in the matter of settlement policy, the Court often asserted an authority which unmistakably subordinated community to colony even in the years after the colony ceased to be thought of *as* a community. The affirmation of that authority began as early as 1630, when the Court ordered that "no person should plant in any place within the limits of the patent, without leave from the Governor and assistants, or the major part of them." * * * And in 1639 the magistrates enunciated a still more sweeping form of interference with local settlement policy, declaring that they could "dispose of all onsettled p'sons into such towns as they shall judge to bee most fitt for the maintenance of such p'sons and families." * * * In all these matters and in others less important, then, authority was not diffused at the outset. Its later localization was the essential institutional development of the era between settlement and the American Revolution. * * * The localization of authority was not an impulse altogether peculiar to the provincial era, of course. The process began with the very beginnings of settlement, as the American wilderness imposed its own imperatives, and a little later the dispersion of settlement added others. But deliberate effort and the traditional shape of thought held the tendency to decentralization in some degree of control so long as the colony continued under its original charter.

For almost sixty years from its establishment, the Massachusetts Bay Colony acknowledged no more than the merest shadow of colonial dependence on the mother country. * * * The result was an unprecedented era of independence for the infant colony, and where the synods and the central government were the inhabitants' own, men saw little reason to license change. * * * But when the clouds of the Glorious Revolution cleared, William and Mary moved to reassert the authority of England. Massachusetts' original charter was repealed and a new one issued, reducing the almost autonomous colony to a royal province. Under the new instrument of government the settlers at the Bay were permitted to retain full control only over the lower house of their General Court. The Council was now merely nominated by the lower house, subject to the approval of the governor, and the governor himself was now to be appointed by the Crown rather than chosen by the colonists. By that considerable alteration the upper reaches of sovereignty in the province, the control of the executive, were removed from Massachusetts to the mother country. * * *

As long as the largest purposes of the central government had coincided with those of the communities and congregations around the colony, and as long as the colonial governors had been committed to the Puritan mission, the wide powers of the central government had posed no insoluble problems. But the case was not the same after the arrival of the provincial charter. * * * Central authority, growing gradually more distant in any case as settlement spread increasingly beyond the possibility of close surveillance from the center, grew very remote indeed when the separation between governors and governed became psychological as well as geographical. And as it did, an underlying tendency to the local communities as repositories of effective authority became manifest. Thus, what was reluctantly admitted in the seventeenth century came to be openly acknowledged in the eighteenth: the public peace could not be entrusted to Boston, but would have to be separately secured in each town in the province. With the arrival of the new charter, a long-running drift toward devolution was licensed and legitimized. From that time forward to the era of the American Revolution, the locus of power and influence over the lives of the people lay primarily in the towns, not in the province. * * * Local institutions, interposed between Boston and the people, became the prime political institutions of the new provincial society, and as the stakes of political play declined in the capital after 1691, they rose rapidly in the communities themselves.

One element of the new relationship between town and province was established at once and almost automatically. The removal of the executive from the election of the people eliminated the only elections which had ever called out the entire colony, those for the governor, deputy-governor, and assistants. With the governor appointed in England and the councillors chosen by the governor from the nominees of the lower legislative house, there remained not a single occasion which was shared by the whole political citizenry. * * * From the arrival of the new charter to the time of the Revolution, and with the exception only of a couple of insignificant county officials, no town chose any but its own officers or its own deputy to the General Court. The confinement of the towns to the election of their own inhabitants, which was indeliberate with regard to the executive and his council, was quite conscious in the case of the legislative power, and the altered relationship of local to central authority that it presaged was even more profound. The early legislation which settled the structure of the new House of Representatives—the one branch of the legislature left unequivocally to the colonists—continued that body largely as it had been before, but it provided for one fundamental amendment which was a dramatic response to the imperatives of the new balance of power: a residence requirement was instituted for the representatives.

That requirement transformed the very character of the lower house. * * * In the political theory and practice the colonists had carried across the Atlantic, a representative did not need to reside among the constituents of his own electoral district—and often had not done so—because his true constituency was considered to be the whole society. He was to speak for the general welfare. The denial of that premise—a denial implicit in the residential qualification—appeared revolutionary to the * * * dissenters, and it was. Eighty years later it was still sufficiently revolutionary to constitute a prime point of contention between England and her rebellious colonies, which makes it all the more significant that the substitution of actual for virtual representation in Massachusetts was not an accident but a deliberate creation of policy, instituted over articulate opposition. The new residence requirement curtailed the tendency of the general assembly toward autonomy, reducing the House of Representatives to a virtual congress of communities, a body much more likely than its predecessor to be a creature of the towns to which its members thereby became bound. * * *

The most striking institutional expression of the conviction that the representative must be bound in to his own local constituents was the town mandate. The mandate was an instruction or a set of instructions to the representative, drawn up by a committee of the town and then debated and voted upon in town meeting. * * * Under its injunction the deputy became a mere agent of the town, an embodiment of the conception of the attorneyship of representation. Attorneyship of representation was * * * an assertion of town sovereignty against invasion by the assembly. * * * The assertion of *legislative* supremacy in the eighteenth century thus became, at least in Massachusetts, fundamentally an expression of *local* supremacy. As Samuel Eliot Morison has explained, "it was only natural to wish to entrust power to a body, every member of which was elected in town meeting and subject to its instructions."

Direct instruction was by no means the only manner in which towns sought to secure the subordination of their representatives to the wishes of the community. * * * Throughout the early eighteenth century, representatives were customarily required to render an account of the session's proceedings to the town meeting. Later in the provincial period some towns maintained an active correspondence with their agents while the assembly was in session. At least one town even sent a guardian to accompany its deputies to the General Court to be certain that they observed the town's wishes. * * * Several other structural devices also curbed the autonomy of the delegates and helped assure their subjection to their own local communities. One of them was the printing and public distribution of the journals of the House of Representatives, a practice which began in Massachusetts in 1715, half a century before any other colony. * * * [T]wo copies of the journal were printed for each representative each year—one for himself, one for his town—a pattern which clearly emphasized the attachment of the representative to his community since distribution was wholly confined to those towns with representatives actually in attendance rather than to the full complement of towns in the province. No wider publication was provided because no wider audience was intended; the printed journal was simply an instrument of surveillance, by which the towns might see that their representatives were faithful.

Another instrument in the same strategy of subordination was the annual election of representatives. * * * For in the uncommon case of a delegate's disregard of his community's wishes, a remedy was thereby rendered simple: reprisal at the polls. From the perspective of the prerogative that remedy, or at least the threat of its employment, was much more powerful and pervasive than the constraint of an occasional mandate * * *. [B]y 1776 the importance of annual elections was so well established that John Adams could claim that there was not "in the whole circle of the sciences a maxim more infallible than this, 'where annual elections end, there slavery begins.'"

Yet another instrument for the prevention of such "slavery" emerged late in the provincial period. In 1766, upon the urging of a deputy from Cambridge who was himself acting under instruction from his fellow townsmen, the House of Representatives erected a public gallery for visitors. In so doing, the House still further publicized that "special relationship that had always been understood to exist between the representative and his constituents." Displaying its proceedings thus to the public, the lower house gave tangible expression to its situation as an agent of public opinion; and where public opinion in the mother country was something discovered in Parliament, in Massachusetts that public opinion was something out in the country.

All the ties that bound representatives to their constituencies were significant, but it was equally significant that their constituencies were towns. In every colony outside New England the county was the unit of representation; east of the Hudson that unit was the town. * * * Towns were more than merely the constituent elements in the structure of the House. They were also the foundation of financial support for its members, because the basic legislation of 1692 left responsibility for the payment of representatives almost totally to the towns. It reserved to the Court only the residual power to set the delegates' pay scale, and even that was often ignored in the towns, some of them paying as the province required but others giving more than the amount allotted, or less, or nothing at all. * * * Such a situation meant that the assembly was not master even in its own lower house. It meant that representation depended on the situation of the towns, not of the province. Towns that considered themselves in sore circumstances might simply decline to send a delegate rather than bear the expense of his salary. * * *

In the face of such adamant insularity, the central government soon became, in practice, the creature of its constituents. The business that the deputies brought before the Court was basically the business of their fellow townsmen, and, in the absence of any initiative from the governor beyond his opening address and an occasional proposal, the legislative agenda was substantially set by petitions from the towns and their inhabitants. * * * Moreover, the Court's acquiescence in those local desires was quite regular, and in some of them it was unfailing. Administrative appointments were vested formally in higher authorities but actually left totally to the towns to settle for themselves. Appointments of commissioned officers in the militia, issued from Boston, were based in every case upon nominations made by a town committee of militia. Local judicial officers, placed in their seats of judgment by the higher tribunal agencies of the province, really owed their places to presentment to those authorities by their own towns. * * *

Local wishes were likewise the province's commands in matters of policy, almost as consistently as in matters of personnel. Petitioners seeking to be sent off to another town nearly always had their pleas granted if they could show the approval of both their present and prospective communities. So too did applicants for a separate precinct, district, or town who were able to show a favorable vote of the town from which they sought separation. Inhabitants of the towns were aware of the Court's disposition upon the appearance of local unanimity, and they acted accordingly. * * * Court and community alike subordinated provincial considerations to the particularistic demands of local unity. Towns quite commonly set the law aside, without ever a word that went beyond the town boundaries, when the law proved inconvenient for local purposes; and they did so without ever displaying any fundamental animus against the law as such. * * * Indeed, though few towns intended to flaunt the central government and fewer still foresaw open confrontation with it when they did deviate, there was scarcely a law on the books which a town could not safely have neglected. Virtually all of them were, in practice, affairs of local option * * *.

According to Samuel Eliot Morison, the towns had become "in fact the several sovereigns of Massachusetts-Bay. Their relation to the General Court closely approximated that of the states to the Congress of the Confederation, with the important difference that there were not thirteen but almost three hundred of them." This sovereignty once established visibly to all, the towns went on about their business as they had come to see that business. They wrought a revolution. * * *

RICHARD T. FORD, LAW'S TERRITORY (A HISTORY OF JURISDICTION)
97 Mich. L. Rev. 843, 906–911, 914, 922–928 (1999).

This section will explore the relationship between jurisdiction, political subjectivity and the assertion of local particularity. Specifically, it will respond * * * to the belief that centralized power is exercised primarily by repressing local differences in favor of homogeneity and uniformity. It will argue that territorial power is exercised not only through repression or exclusion of difference and centralization, not only through homogenization or assimilation to a mean, but also through the *production* of difference.

The argument of this section parallels that of Michel Foucault in the classic *The History of Sexuality: An Introduction.* Foucault argued against the common understanding that the institutions of bourgeois society from the Victorian era to the present have operated to repress the natural and authentic sexuality of individuals (the "repressive hypothesis"). Instead, Foucault argued, the Victorians were obsessed with sexuality, they saw it everywhere, they constantly discussed it, insisted on its relevance and deployed it as a description of many forms of human behavior. They *produced* sexuality by defining human behavior in terms of sexuality, defining individuals as sexed in various ways, and cataloguing and constructing sexual typologies. Far from repression, this *production* of sexuality was, according to Foucault, what defined the Victorian attitude toward sex, and this *production* of sexuality was a means of control. It was a technology that defined the self according to its sexuality, and thereby kept individuals under a type of sexual surveillance. Further, if anything repressed authentic eroticism—a term whose ontological status is, for Foucault, questionable at best—it was the incessant production of sexuality that limited the possibilities of erotic expression by imposing upon individual eroticism a narrow universe of sexual types.

Now let us turn to jurisdiction. Contemporary discussions of ethnic and cultural diversity characteristically involve a struggle between "universalism" or "common values" on the one hand and "cultural diversity" or "respect for difference" on the other. In the national context, those who favor "universalism"—actually nationalism—lament the fracturing of the nation into antagonistic factions, ethnic enclaves and oppositional subcultures. They advocate a "return" to a common identity, a common purpose and a common culture. By contrast, those who fear cultural homogeneity insist that cultural differences reflect the true and authentic expressions of organic social groups and that failure to respect these differences is a form of tyranny. They advocate a strategy of resistance to cultural hegemony through the assertion of difference.

When the question of political territoriality is introduced into this debate, the consequences are predictable. Those in favor of solidarity seek to prevent the formation of culturally defined jurisdictional subdivisions, wrongly imagining that such divisions would be new and unprecedented and fearing that such divisions would hasten the fracturing of the nation. Those who favor difference embrace jurisdictional "autonomy" as a means of protecting minority cultures from hegemonic oppression and compulsory assimilation.

In this conversation, the "repressive hypothesis" is that Power is exercised exclusively by those who would censor and repress cultural difference and impose a unitary and repressive common culture. But the analytic mistake that underlies this repressive hypothesis is shared by both sides of the debate. Both sides assume that there is an inevitable opposition between common identity and the assertion of difference. The universalists argue that the myopic assertion of difference stands between "us" and meaningful solidarity. Meanwhile, the champions of difference insist that the repressive project of solidarity must yield to respect for authentic cultural difference. * * *

[But the] institution of jurisdiction does its most important work, not by repressing local difference, but by producing it, by dividing society into distinctive local units that are imposed on individuals and groups. The discourse of the organic jurisdiction encourages minority groups to seek out territorial autonomy as a means to resist the power of an often hostile government and the hegemony of the majority culture. But separate territorial status rarely delivers on its promise of autonomy. Often, the subordinate group unwittingly conspires in its own continued subordination and participates in its own quarantine. A subordinate group may insist that it only wishes to attain the type of "autonomy" that members of the majority enjoy. But the position of security that the dominant group enjoys requires the subjugation of a subordinate group. No group can entirely control its own fate without also controlling other groups around it. The coveted position in question is not autonomy, but *hegemony*—a position that, by definition, everyone cannot occupy. Autonomy is a false promise because it promises access to a *space outside of power*, a safe haven from the threat of subjugation, control or influence by outsiders. Such a space does not exist. * * *

It is often said that the history of modernity, the ideological history of something called "liberalism," is the history of centralization. According to this account, the modernist project was the project of rationalization, universalism, uniformity, order. Neighborhood businesses and artisans' guilds gave way to national and international conglomerates. Cottage industry gave way to economies of scale and the Fordist division of labor. The clan yielded place to the province, which in turn was supplanted by the nation-state. Landscapes and communities that were once varied and opaque became regimented and transparent to the eye of power: the Norman Conquest unified the tribes of England, Baron Haussmann forced the labyrinth of medieval Paris to yield to the Grand Avenues of the modern city of light.

This account holds that the modern state struck out against local culture and particularity in every possible respect. It imposed national languages governed by uniform grammatical rules to smother local dialects and idioms. It routinized the collection of taxes to crush local fiefdoms and supplant provincial clientelism. It eliminated local territories in order to facilitate the smooth application of justice and the free alienation of land. It prohibited the variegated customs of dispute resolution in favor of uniform justice and universal rights. Each of these projects required centralization: a single sovereign, a uniform standard of measure, a common tongue, a common law. So the history of the modern era is the history of the centralization of authority, of economy and of culture. It is the story of the birth of the universal everyman and the suppression of the particular personality. It is the narrative of uniformity, homogeneity, the celebration of the one and the censorship of difference.

This, anyway, has become the standard account of things in disciplines as varied as human geography, ethnic studies and the history of law. It is an easy story to tell, if only because it coincides so well with such a variety of ideological precommitments. For the right, the death of localism is a product of the tyranny of intermeddling government, a Frankenstein's creation of liberal social engineering that defined the New

Deal, the Warren Court and the Great Society. For the old left, the destruction of local particularity is nothing other than a symptom of industrial capitalism: the centralization of political authority serves the centralization of the means of production; a uniform and fungible political subjectivity follows the reduction of human labor to fungible capital and the reduction of human needs to fungible commodities. Meanwhile, the social movements of the new left lament an inexorable centralization of power as the active repression of (counter) cultural difference and subversive identities; Washington, D.C. represents the repressive injunction to adopt the voice of "middle America" and the establishment, to accept the disciplinary image of the "reasonable man," the men in gray suits, or simply, "the man." * * *

[But] centralization tells only part of the story. Always buried within these narratives of inexorable, unmediated, unmodified centralization, one finds a glimpse of its opposite: an explosion of differentiation, the production of ever new categories that are represented as "merely descriptive" mappings. No doubt, there was a trend toward centralization that characterized a significant program of modern government; universalism was imposed, difference was punished and censored. But there was also, and to a significant extent, the opposite phenomena: typology, sorting, differentiation to an ever more "precise" and infinitesimal degree, a carving up into distinct parts. This too is the legacy of modernity and of liberal democracy.

This paradoxical differentiation cannot be fully understood as "resistance." The point is not that the members of organic social groups managed, by their tenacity, to cling to local customs despite the imposition of the common law and central courts, it is not that villages and provinces stubbornly continued to speak dialect in the face of sanctions for failure to speak the language of the state, it is not that villages and townships retained their unique character in the face of urban consolidation. Alongside these well acknowledged acts of resistance, but hidden in the shadows, was the active production of localism, the creation of territorially structured differentiation through the institutions of modern government: the state, the corporation, the university and the jurisdiction.

Thus it may be said that localism itself, localism in all of its particularity and difference, was the child, rather than the enemy, of the modern state. Alongside the well chronicled attempt to stamp out local particularity, we also have the production, creation, definition and interrogation of the local in its territorially located specificity. "The local" as a concept, as a category, as a significant object of concern, is the product of a governmental discourse whose goal was to catalogue, define and manage a territory by dividing it into knowable and distinct parts. * * *

The most notorious example of the oppressive production of difference is the apartheid of mid-to late-twentieth century South Africa (what I will call "late apartheid," to separate it from the cruder policies of the earlier twentieth-century regime). What separates late apartheid from the Jim Crow laws of the American South is the intricacy of the former in both the architecture of the physical separation and its legitimation. In both its material and its ideological aspects, the separatist regime of South Africa was as marked an advance over American Jim Crow as the gas chamber is over the hangman's noose. These "advances" were primarily the result of jurisdictional production. In both its material and ideological effects, late apartheid marked a conspicuous expansion of jurisdictional strategies. * * *

Jurisdictional boundaries help to promote and legitimate social injustice, illegitimate hierarchy and economic inequality. This is not to argue that jurisdictional borders are the sole cause of social injustice such that a different jurisdictional system would eliminate illegitimate hierarchy or the evils of poverty. Nor is it to argue that promoting and legitimating inequality and social injustice are the primary purposes or practical effects of territorial jurisdiction in general, or of any jurisdiction in particular. It is to argue that jurisdiction plays an important role in shaping our social and political world and our social and political selves.

Group territorial identification must be understood as part of the status quo. The concentration of social groups in formally defined jurisdictions is a discipline that creates a predictable and easily manageable social order. Territorial identification encourages particular types of political and interpersonal subjectivity while discouraging others. Therefore, we should consciously weigh the pros and cons of territorial identification. We should ask: what aspects of human flourishing are discouraged or excluded and, more importantly, what identities and subjectivities are produced, encouraged, sanctioned or imposed?

The recent Supreme Court decision in *Romer v. Evans* is instructive. In *Romer*, the Court found that a Colorado ballot initiative that forbade the state or its subdivisions from enacting civil rights protections for homosexuals was constitutionally invalid. But the Court did not find that homosexuality was a constitutionally protected classification. Nor did it overturn its earlier decision in *Bowers v. Hardwick*, which upheld the criminalization of homosexual sodomy against a due process challenge. Therefore, the paradoxical effect of *Romer* would seem to be that a state can outlaw homosexual conduct under *Bowers* but must allow its localities to protect such conduct with antidiscrimination ordinances.

Romer is subject to several interpretations, but none entirely resolve this conceptual paradox. * * * [But suppose] the principle established in *Romer* is that the state may not attempt to selectively disempower *localities*, in which homosexuals or any other statewide minority may enjoy a majority of political support, through an initiative passed at the *state* level where those locally favored minorities are overwhelmed by a hostile majority. This principle acknowledges that the state can, by selectively extending the jurisdictional sphere, effectively deny certain minority groups the ability to influence government even at the local level where they may have majority support. On this interpretation, * * * *Romer* protects minority groups, but only when they concentrate in "discrete and insular" jurisdictions. This rationale turns James Madison's argument for the extended sphere on its head. It, in effect, holds that any state-wide minority group has a right to its victory in a local political process free of interference from a hostile majority in the extended sphere of state politics.

Of course, it follows that the minority group has no protection from a hostile local majority. So held the Sixth Circuit in *Equality Foundation of Greater Cincinnati v. City of Cincinnati*. In *Equality Foundation*, a decision upholding a Cincinnati city charter amendment that forbids "special rights" for homosexuals was remanded by the Supreme Court for reconsideration in light of *Romer*. The Cincinnati charter amendment was substantially identical to the amendment at issue in *Romer*. Both forbade civil rights protections for homosexuals. Both were enacted by voter initiative. Both amended the foundational document of the jurisdiction— the state constitution in *Romer*, the city charter in *Equality Foundation*— and were for that reason especially difficult to reverse through the normal political process. The primary difference between the cases was that *Romer* involved a law of statewide applicability while *Equality Foundation* involved an initiative of local applicability. On remand, the Sixth Circuit held that *Romer* did not apply * * *. In order to distinguish the anti-gay legislation at issue in *Romer* and the nearly identical Cincinnati charter amendment, the Sixth Circuit offered a paradigmatic defense of the organic local jurisdiction: "Unlike a state government, which is composed of discrete and quasi-independent levels and entities such as cities, counties, and the general state government, a municipality is a unitary local political subdivision or unit comprised, fundamentally, of the territory and residents within its geographical boundaries." * * *

The jurisdictional architecture at issue in *Romer* and *Equality Foundation* illustrates several points. One point is fairly obvious but often overlooked: territorial identification cuts both ways. Local autonomy may protect gay rights ordinances in Aspen and Denver, but it would also allow antigay laws in more conservative jurisdictions such as Cincinnati. At best, we have a normative principle of compulsory provincialism: minority sub groups can expect favorable treatment only when they accept social isolation and only within the boundaries of "their" jurisdiction. In the broader public culture, social assimilation is required (don't ask, don't tell). * * *

This is the best we can expect from territorial autonomy. But even this impoverished autonomy is far from certain. For what counts as respect for local difference from one perspective is the disproportionate power of a faction from another. For instance, in *Romer* Justice Scalia puts Madison back on his feet, complaining in dissent:

> [B]ecause those who engage in homosexual conduct tend to reside in disproportionate numbers in certain communities, have high disposable income, and, of course, care about homosexual-rights issues much more ardently than the public at large, *they possess political power much greater than their numbers*, both locally and statewide. . . . [Amendment 2] sought to counter both the geographic concentration and the *disproportionate political power of homosexuals*. . . . It put directly, to all the citizens of the State, the question: Should homosexuality be given special protection? They answered no.

Local difference is easily recast as factionalism and the courts toggle back and forth between the two perspectives. Sometimes local decisions are lauded because they supposedly reflect an organic lifestyle deserving of respect. At other times local decisions are denigrated as the result of the disproportionate and concentrated influence of a faction. Territorial identification * * * provides no guarantee of autonomy, no safe haven from outside influence. It can just as easily facilitate stereotyping and targeting an unpopular group. * * *

[J]urisdiction is not a neutral slate on which a preexisting and authentic identity can be inscribed. The choice to adopt a territorial self definition necessarily alters the nature of the self that is so defined. Scalia understands homosexual identity as an urban and elite identity, a sort of decadent, sybaritic indulgence of the effete upper classes. My suggestion is that many homosexuals are pushed into—and are complicit in—such an identification by the compulsory provincialism that the *majority* in *Romer* offers. Justice Scalia may play the harp but Justice Kennedy, the author of the majority opinion, called the tune. The problem here is not simply that homosexuals who don't fit the model are denied protection of any kind. What about rural homosexuals or those in smaller suburbs? The problem is also that those urban, well-to-do homosexuals whom *Romer* ostensibly protects are forced into a fairly narrow range of identities. This is not to say that their authentic selves are being repressed but instead that their authentic selves—at any rate the only selves they're going to get—are being *built* in part by this process of concentration and territorial identification.

We should ask whether the identities and territories produced through compulsory territorialism are the type of identities that can contribute to a healthy and just society. We should also ask whether such identities contribute to the human flourishing of those who, however freely or unwillingly, adopt them. Finally, we should ask, along with Anthony Appiah, whether these are identities that we will want to live with in the long run. * * *

CHAPTER 3

THE RELATIONSHIP AMONG NEIGHBORING CITIES

■ ■ ■

In Chapter Two, we explored the relationship between cities and the larger groups of which they are a part—the states, the nation and the world. This chapter shifts our attention to the connections that cities have with each other. In examining these inter-city relationships, it would be a mistake simply to assume that every city is a separate, autonomous entity able to deal with other municipalities as it pleases. As the materials covered in Chapter Two suggest, states have considerable power to structure and control how cities deal with one another. Indeed, states even have the power to control the location and meaning of the geographic lines that separate cities from each other—the very lines that enable us to distinguish one city from another. To examine inter-city relationships, therefore, we need to recognize at the outset the complexities involved in any effort of citizens in one place to say to those outside its boundaries, "we want to choose our own way of life, to select our own leaders, and to use our resources for our own benefit." Who, for example, decides who is included in the term "we"? To respond that the citizens of each city can answer this question for themselves is circular. Who decides in the first instance who a community's citizens are?

This chapter investigates the complexities of inter-city relationships by concentrating on the most important contemporary location for inter-city conflict in America: metropolitan areas that include both a central city and its suburbs. To this point, we have largely treated "cities" and "local governments" as synonymous terms. As this chapter makes clear, however, this treatment obscures the important ways in which American local government law contributes to the distinction between a central city and its surrounding suburbs that is such a noticeable feature of contemporary life.

The first third of the chapter considers some of the differences between central cities and suburbs, how the city/suburb distinction arose, the consequences that follow from it, and how the distinction is maintained. The second third examines city-suburb and suburb-suburb conflict, focusing specifically on racial and class segregation and on the impact of sprawl on metropolitan life. The final third of the chapter changes the focus from questions about current relationships between central cities and suburbs to contemporary attempts to find regional solutions to conflicts between them. Are there ways of organizing our metropolitan areas better than we do now? If so, what are they? Here, the chapter considers a variety of approaches: voluntary inter-local agreements; the establishment of specialized, state-created bureaucratic agencies; the imposition of more thoroughgoing regional planning requirements; and the formation of full-fledged regional governments. This canvassing of contemporary attempts to overcome metropolitan fragmentation concludes with an excerpt that directly raises a key question that underlies all of the materials in the chapter: is it possible to maintain decentralized forms of democratic life and overcome metropolitan fragmentation? The chapter ends with readings from democratic theory that address the values and pathologies that the legal recognition of geographic boundaries between local communities may promote or breed.

A. THE CITY-SUBURB RELATIONSHIP

Once mere satellites to the nations' great cities, suburbs are now the predominant place in which we live. This demographic fact has important consequences not only for the residents of the suburbs themselves, but also for the residents of the central cities that are near them. This section explores the complex relationship between suburbs and their central cities from a variety of perspectives.[1]

The first subsection presents an introduction to the history and meaning of the city/suburb distinction in America. It explores how state and federal law, as well as broader shifts in social life, helped to bring about the distinction between urban and suburban spaces within a single metropolitan area. The second subsection focuses on how state law rules concerning city formation—namely the rules that permit municipal incorporation and that define the responsibilities that attend municipal incorporation—contributed to the divide between central cities and suburbs. The third and fourth subsections examine the ways in which residency within local boundaries now defines and maintains the crucial

---

[1] The literature on suburbanization is vast. In addition to the works reproduced in this section, see, e.g., Peter Dreier, John Mollenkopf, and Todd Swanstrom, Place Matters: Metropolitics for the Twenty-first Century (2014); Barry Bergdoll and Reinhold Martin, Foreclosed: Rehousing the American Dream (2012); Becky Nicolaides and Andrew Wiese (eds.), The Suburban Reader (2006); Robert Beauregard, When America Became Suburban (2006); Lizabeth Cohen, A Consumers' Republic: The Politics of Mass Consumption in Postwar America (2003); Dolores Hayden, Building Suburbia: Green Fields and Urban Growth 1820–2000 (2003); J. Eric Oliver, Democracy in Suburbia (2001); Lisa McGirr, Suburban Warriors: The Origins of the New American Right (2001); William Lucy and David Phillips, Confronting Suburban Decline: Strategic Planning for Metropolitan Renewal (2000); Andres Duany, Elizabeth Plater-Zyberk, and Jeff Speck, Suburban Nation: The Rise of Sprawl and the Decline of the American Dream (2000); Peter Calthorpe, The Next American Metropolis: Ecology, Community, and the American Dream (1993); Sam B. Warner, Streetcar Suburbs: The Process of Growth in Boston 1870–1900 (1962).

dividing line between central cities and suburbs. To what extent can nonresidents be excluded from—or included in—the definition of those who can participate in local decision making? To what extent does residency determine who can use publicly-owned facilities? To what extent can a locality favor its own residents over outsiders? After the importance of residency has been delineated, the next two subsections address possible changes in the composition of a local government's residents. To what extent can a locality protect itself from such changes? Can it, for example, resist annexation by others or prevent sub-groups from seceding and forming new municipalities?

1. AN INTRODUCTION TO THE RELATIONSHIP BETWEEN CITIES AND SUBURBS

What explains the vast expansion of suburbanization in the United States in the twentieth century? The first seven readings that follow offer a number of contrasting explanations: government policy; class and ethnic conflict; crime and other "city problems"; racial segregation; conceptions of work, family and gender; desires for local control; the search for a sense of community; changes in the national housing market. The final reading offers a contemporary interpretation of the city/suburb divide.

Of course, one cannot explain suburbanization without having some idea of what makes a particular place suburban. There is no single, agreed upon definition of suburbia. The United States Census, for example, does not classify any particular places as "suburbs." The census may nonetheless be of some help in getting a handle on what is meant by suburbanization. The census classifies some places as "metropolitan areas"—namely places with a large population nucleus and adjacent communities that have a high degree of economic or social integration with that nucleus. In addition, the census classifies some places as "urbanized areas" in order to distinguish between rural and non-rural places. Finally, the census classifies some places as "central cities" in order to distinguish between types of urbanized areas. Working from these classifications, one might conclude that the portions of metropolitan areas that do not include either rural areas or central cities make up suburbia.

One might still ask whether our definition of suburbia should be entirely a function of census data. Perhaps there is more to it. Is suburbia defined at least in part by the separation of where one lives from where one works? Is it defined in part by the racial and/or class homogeneity of the place? Is it a consequence of urban form? Is it a state of mind that is attributable to certain residents but that defies a more concrete definition? What idea of the suburb implicitly underlies, and informs, each of the readings excerpted below?

While reading these excerpts, it is important to avoid a stylized picture of suburbs as prosperous and central cities as in decline. There are wealthy suburbs and poor suburbs in the United States, just as there are prosperous central cities and declining central cities. As Margaret Weir emphasizes in the final excerpt, more poor people now live in American suburbs than in central cities. Indeed, as Alan Ehrenhalt argues in his book The Great Inversion and the Future of the American City (2012), there is at least a beginning in many parts of the country of what he calls a "demographic inversion": the rearrangement of living patterns across entire metropolitan areas. Some of this rearrangement involves poor people moving out of central cities while more affluent residents are moving in. No doubt, some central cities are continuing to lose population, and some of these are facing serious fiscal problems. But a number of suburbs are also at risk: older suburbs, overbuilt low-density suburbs at the edge of the metropolitan area, segregated suburbs.[2] It would be a mistake to think that the historic patterns of suburbanization described in some of the following excerpts are reliable predictors of the future.

PETER HALL, CITIES OF TOMORROW
Pp. 291–294 (1988).

There were four main foundations for the suburban boom. They were new roads to open up land outside the reach of the old trolley and commuter rail routes; land uses, to produce uniform essential tracts with stable property values; government-guaranteed mortgages, to make possible long-repayment low-interest mortgages that were affordable by families of modest incomes; and a baby boom, to produce a sudden surge in demand for family homes where young children could be raised. The first three of these were already in place, though sometimes only in embryonic form, a decade before the boom began. The fourth triggered it.

The first part, the roads, were embryonic. * * * [T]hey were there in one or two places: New York from the 1920s, Los Angeles from the 1940s. But, remarkably, developers do not seem to have appreciated their potential for a decade or more after they were in place. Still, in the 1930s, a majority of New Yorkers did not own cars. And many of those who did happen to work in Manhattan, to which car commuting was almost impossible; suburbanization must await the outward movement of jobs to places where the car was more convenient than the subway—which began to happen on any scale only in the 1950s. And in any event, generally the roads were not there. The Depression and the wartime years had brought a halt to the rise in car ownership; not until 1949 did registrations again exceed the level of 1929. And road-building, too, had stagnated.

---

[2] Myron Orfield, American Metropolitics: The New Suburban Reality (2002).

It was the 1956 Federal-Aid Highway Act that marked the real beginning of freeway suburbanization. But at the beginning, it does not seem to have been meant that way at all. True, * * * an Inter-Regional Highways Committee * * * called for a 32,000-mile Interstate system, and Congress duly passed the Federal-Aid Highway Act of 1944. But that was to be a strictly inter-urban system, bypassing the cities; and, before it could be built, political splits emerged: between engineers who just wanted to pour concrete and city planners * * * who wanted to use new roads to cure urban blight, between those who wanted self-financing toll roads and those who wanted federal subsidy. Truman in 1949, Eisenhower in 1954, signed Urban Renewal Acts, but kept highways out of them.

Finally, Eisenhower—who believed that he had won the war on the German *Autobahnen*—accepted the argument that new roads were not only vital for national defense in an era of Cold War, but could also generate an economic boom. He called on a retired General, Lucius Clay, to head a committee of inquiry; most of the evidence came from the pro-roads side—including Robert Moses, who used the roads-fight-blight argument. But the fight over paying for them, which was essentially between fiscal conservatives and the highways lobby, almost killed the resulting bill. Finally, a compromise version, providing for the new roads to be built by a special fund through a tax on gasoline, oil, buses and trucks, was passed in June 1956; in the House of Representatives it went through without dissent, in the Senate one solitary vote was recorded against it. The greatest public-works programme in the history of the world—$41 billion for 41,000 miles of new roads—was under way.

The critical question, still, was what sort of road system it should be. Congress in 1944 had endorsed the principle that it should bypass the cities. Planners like Bartholomew and Moses argued on the contrary that it should penetrate into their hearts, thus removing blighted areas and improving accessibility from the suburbs to downtown offices and shops. In practice, given the strength of the urban renewal lobby in the 1950s and 1960s, there was little doubt about the outcome: the system would be used to create new corridors of accessibility from city centres to potential suburbs, as Moses had tried to do thirty years earlier. When the programme began in earnest, its chief Bertram D. Tallamy said that the new highways were built on principles that Moses had taught him as long ago as 1926; at that time and for long after, Moses was, after all, the only really experienced urban-highway builder in the United States.

The second requirement, zoning, had originated as early as 1880 in Modesto, California, where it had been used to remove Chinese laundries: a particularly apt beginning, since thereafter one of its principal functions was to safeguard property values by excluding undesirable land uses and undesirable neighbors. And * * * the city that took the lead in the zoning movement from 1913 on, New York City, was impelled to do so by the complaints of Manhattan retailers who, complaining that industrial incursions were threatening their profits, appealed loudly to "every man who owns a home or rents an apartment"; the city's Commission on Building Heights accepted their argument that zoning secured "greater safety and security in investment." And the historic 1926 Supreme Court decision, *Euclid v. Ambler,* which confirmed the general validity of zoning seems to have accepted Alfred Bettman's argument that its point was to enhance property values. The point at issue, significantly, was whether land should be zoned industrial or residential.

Because it was meticulously designed as part of a general police power to safeguard "public welfare" and "public health, safety, morals and convenience," thus to avoid all suggestion of compulsory purchase with claims for compensation, New York's comprehensive zoning resolution of 1916 deliberately avoided long-term plans; Edward Bassett, the attorney in change, proudly declared "We have gone at it block by block," invariably confirming the status quo. And most of America followed suit. Thus arose a paradox: land use control in the United States, in sharp contrast to much of Europe, came to be divorced from any kind of land-use planning; it could not be used to raise the level of design * * *.

The third precondition for the suburban boom was cheap long-term housing finance. In this regard, * * * America lagged strangely behind Britain. There, the permanent building societies had developed from the turn of the century, offering twenty-or twenty-five-year mortgages with low down payments, and powerfully fuelling the great suburban spread around London in the 1920s and 1930s. In contrast, until the 1930s, the typical American mortgage was only for five or ten years at 6 or 7 per cent interest: a ruinously high burden for the average family. It was an early New Deal experiment—the Home Owners Loan Corporation (HOLC), introduced as an emergency measure of April 1933 to stem farm foreclosures—that introduced into America the long-term, self-amortizing mortgage. The next year, the National Housing Act established the Federal Housing Authority (FHA) with powers to insure longer-term mortgage loans by private lenders for home construction and sale, with a down payment as low as 10 per cent and a period of twenty-five or thirty years at only 2 or 3 per cent. Between 1938 and 1941, it was insuring some 35 per cent of all home loans in the United States.

From 1934, then, the most powerful constraint to suburban homebuilding had been removed. For the FHA took over from the HOLC the notion of appraising whole neighborhoods, and thereby redlining those deemed to be undesirable; in practice, this meant the whole of America's inner cities. Further, the "FHA exhorted racial segregation and endorsed it as a public policy"; as late as 1966, it had not insured a single mortgage in Paterson or Camden in New Jersey, two predominantly black cities. The central objective of the FHA was identical with that of zoning: it was to guarantee the security of residential real-estate values. And both worked through exclusion, to divert investment massively into new suburban house building at the expense of the central city.

Some of the consequences could already be glimpsed later in that decade. The National Resources Committee's report *Our Cities*, published in 1937 * * *, drew attention to the fact that even between 1920 and 1930, suburbs had grown twice as fast as central cities: "the urbanite is rapidly becoming the suburbanite," as families fulfilled "the urge to escape the obnoxious aspects of urban life without at the same time losing access to its economic and cultural advantages." During that decade, some suburbs had grown at dizzy speed: Beverly Hills by 2,500 per cent; Shaker Heights outside Cleveland by 1,000 per cent. But then, the depression drastically cut new housing starts—by as much as 95 per cent between 1928 and 1933—and brought a huge crop of mortgage foreclosures. Not until after World War Two did the industry completely recover.

Given an almost complete moratorium on new construction—save for essential war-related building—between 1941 and 1945, the result at war's end was a huge accumulated shortage: an estimated 2.75–4.4 million families sharing, and another half-million in non-family quarters. On top of that came the baby boom, as the servicemen returned and the delayed crop of wartime babies coincided with the regular cohorts. The industry spectacularly responded: as against a mere 515,000 starts in 1939, there were 1,466,000 by 1949, 1,554,000 by 1959. And in the 1949 Housing Act—as well as initiating the urban renewal process * * *— Congress massively increased FHA's lending powers. As before, this money went into the suburbs. By 1950, the suburbs were found to be growing at ten times the rate of the central cities; by 1954, it was estimated that in the previous decade 9 million people had moved into the suburbs. The 1950s, as the 1960 Census showed, was the decade of the greatest suburban growth in American history: while the central cities grew by 6 million or 11.6 per cent, the suburbs grew by a dizzy 19 million, or by 45.9 per cent. And ominously, for the first time, some of the nation's greatest cities recorded actual population decline: Boston and St. Louis each lost 13 per cent of their population. * * *

KENNETH T. JACKSON, SUBURBS INTO NEIGHBORHOODS

From Kenneth Jackson, Crabgrass Frontier: The Suburbanization
of the United States 138, 140–142, 144–148, 150–153 (1985).

As new developments in home construction and in urban transportation encouraged American families to move away from their old neighborhoods to new residences on the periphery, the most basic of questions involved the provision of schools, sewers, utilities, and police and fire departments. Four different approaches were possible: (1) cities could simply expand their boundaries by annexing newer sections into the municipal corporation, (2) new municipalities could be created within the suburban ring, (3) special taxing districts could be established to provide for one or more important functions, and (4) county governments could expand their powers by becoming more like cities themselves.

Throughout the nineteenth century, the first alternative was predominant as American cities annexed adjacent land and grew steadily larger in area and in population. Of course, there were always a few small communities here and there that lost population, but most—and certainly all the larger ones—added residents between each decennial census. Historically, city fathers tended to be concerned with the rate of growth and with the relative standing of their community and rival cities. * * * [T]hey expanded outward as well as in density. If the earlier pattern had continued, Boston would probably encompass the entire area circumscribed by Route 128, New York City would reach to White Plains in Westchester County and at least to the Suffolk County line on Long Island, and Chicago would stretch half the distance to Milwaukee. Those who find such assertions fantastic are reminded that dozens of American cities, including all those that boast high population growth rates since World War II, have expanded their boundaries in just such a fashion. * * * Without exception, the adjustment of local boundaries has been the dominant method of population growth in every American city of consequence. If annexation (the addition of unincorporated land to the city) or consolidation (the absorption of one municipal government by another, usually adjacent) had not taken place, there would now be no great cities in the United States in the political sense of the term. Only New York City would have grown as large as one million people, and it would have remained confined to the island of Manhattan. * * *

If we consider the dozen largest American cities that lost population between 1950 and 1980, we find that they had a very different experience in the nineteenth century. Taken as a group, they expanded their boundaries by more than 500 percent through the addition of more than 800 square miles of land between 1850 and 1910. In percentage terms, the decade of greatest gain was the 1850s; in absolute terms, the premier decades were the 1890s and the 1880s. At no time between 1850 and 1930, however, did these dozen cities in the aggregate annex less than an average of 100 square miles in a decade. * * * Appropriately, the most significant annexations in the nineteenth century involved the nation's three largest cities: New York, Chicago, and Philadelphia. * * * The most important municipal boundary adjustment in American history occurred in 1898, when Andrew Haswell Green's lifelong dream of a Greater New York City was realized. Brooklyn, which at the time was the fourth largest city in the United States, joined Manhattan, as did Queens (with a portion withheld as the soon-to-be-created Nassau County), Staten

Island, and additional parts of Westchester County, which came to be known as the Bronx. * * *

[A]nnexing populous suburbs was a perfectly respectable method of fueling the municipal booster spirit. Brooklyn gloried in its rise to third place among the nation's cities when it absorbed Bushwick and Williamsburg in 1855, and Chicago took pride in its second-place status after its massive annexation of 1889. In fact, it was partly the fear that Chicago would become the nation's largest city in 1900 or 1910 that prompted various factions in New York to agree to the consolidation of 1898. * * * The desire to annex was inspired not only by the booster spirit, but also by the business idea that a large organization was more efficient than a small one and that substantial economies would accrue from a consolidation of municipal governments. According to this view, even when suburbs were honestly governed, their management was inefficient; large cities, on the other hand, could be run by highly paid experts. * * *

In many cases, the cry for efficiency was a mask for the desire to exploit and to control; it might be termed the local or downtown brand of urban imperialism. Often the large merchants and businessmen of the central business districts sought to eliminate neighborhood governments that in their view inhibited progress. In Philadelphia, where wharfage taxes, railway rights, and water prices were among the issues of contention between the city and its suburbs, the supporters of consolidation were overwhelmingly middle- and upper-income residents of the core. Suburban supporters of the proposal tended to be well-heeled commuters to the central business district. Neither group was representative of the laboring and farming constituency of the outlying areas to be added. * * *

The desire to regularize the economy was further buttressed by the felt need for greater social control. In New Orleans the so-called "Spanish riot" of 1851 made clear to the city fathers the difficulty of police operations when law enforcement authority was divided among three separate communities. In Philadelphia business leaders thought that a unified police force would eliminate undesirable conditions in districts then beyond the city limits. Riots in 1838, 1844, and 1849 had reduced city and suburbs to a garrison, and a group of prominent Philadelphians proposed consolidation so that "the peace of our community will be preserved and the prosperity of its citizens protected without the unpleasant necessity of a resort to armed force." * * *

Land speculators also supported annexation, but they usually worked behind the scenes, and their precise role is difficult to measure. In a pattern familiar enough over the last century, real-estate promoters purchased large tracts of rural land in the expectation that the advancing horsecarts, steam railroads, and trolleys would make the area attractive to urban families. In the absence of decent sewerage, water, and educational systems, land speculators looked to annexation as a sort of guarantee to potential buyers that the suburb would eventually possess the comforts of the city. * * *

[T]he early nineteenth-century residents of outlying areas were more likely to be poor than affluent, and their residential areas normally could not offer a level of public services comparable to that of the core. Such considerations were apt to be important, particularly to newcomers who might have bought a house without water intakes or sewer outlets, on land that was overrun by snakes and rabbits, on a street that was neither paved nor served by storm drains nor watched over by the police. In Detroit the Fairview Village annexation of 1907 was precipitated because Fairview badly needed a sewer system which the villagers could not afford. Similarly, Roxbury joined Boston partly to gain relief from an intolerable sewerage situation; Hyde Parkers looked to Chicago for better fire protection and cheaper gas rates; and residents of Kensington, Spring Garden, and Germantown were able to share more fully, and at a better price, in a Philadelphia water system that was rated among the best in the world.

As the centrifugal movement of the middle class gathered force after 1865, suburbia gradually shook off its reputation for vice and squalor. Slowly, many peripheral residents came to believe that local autonomy could mean better public services. * * * As suburban services and self-consciousness became stronger, the desire for absorption into the metropolis waned, and fewer annexations were unopposed; some took place over the objections of 90 percent of those concerned. But in the nineteenth century, success depended much less on public than on legislative approval. Legally, of course, a city is a corporation that receives from the state government special powers of regulation over the residents of a precisely defined geographic area. Thus it normally remains within the power of the state to change the boundaries of governmental units under its jurisdiction. In the nineteenth century, states tended to exercise this power without the advice of those who would be affected; that is, rarely were public referendums held on the issue. And when a vote was taken, it was often ignored if it was negative. The predominant view in the nineteenth century was the doctrine of forcible annexation. No small territory could be allowed to retard the development of the metropolitan community; the most important consideration was simply the greatest good for the greatest number. * * * Some annexations did meet with popular approval, but it was in the legislative halls that the annexationists won their most important nineteenth-century victories. * * *

For various reasons, then, the addition of peripheral land to cities was a normal process of urban growth in the nineteenth century. To most people, it seemed entirely logical and even inevitable that cities would add to their boundaries to accommodate a spreading and increasing population, even if the affected families were themselves resistant to the idea. * * * But something has happened—or more precisely has failed to happen—in the twentieth century. For many cities, and particularly for the older ones in the East and Middle West now losing population, metropolitan government is a phenomenon of the past. Quite simply, these cities are no longer able to annex or to consolidate in order to keep pace with the overflow of population beyond established boundaries. * * *

There are basically three reasons why America's older cities are now ringed by incorporated suburbs that emphasize their distinctiveness from rather than their relationship with the metropolis: (1) sharper racial, ethnic, and class distinctions, (2) new laws that made incorporation easy and annexation unworkable, and (3) improved suburban services. Most important was the changing reality and image of the periphery and the center, particularly with regard to demographic characteristics. With the vast increase in immigration in the late nineteenth century, the core city increasingly became the home of penniless immigrants from Southern and Eastern Europe. And of course, in the early years of the twentieth century, increasing numbers of Southern blacks forsook their miserable tenant farms for a place where, they hoped, "a man was a man." In the view of most middle-class, white suburbanites, these newcomers were associated with and were often regarded as the cause of intemperance, vice, urban bossism, crime, and radicalism of all kinds. And as the central city increasingly became the home of the disadvantaged, the number of white commuters rose markedly. These recent escapees from the central city were anxious to insulate their neighborhoods from the "liquor power" and other pernicious urban influences. An independent community offered the exciting promise of moral control. As the Morgan Park Post, a suburban Chicago weekly, remarked in an antiannexationist editorial on March 9, 1907: "The real issue is not taxes, nor water, nor street cars—it is a much greater question than either. It is the moral control of our village. . . . Under local government we can absolutely control every objectionable thing that may try to enter our limits—but once annexed we are at the mercy of the city hall." * * * "What influence would Oak Park have as the tail end of the 35th Ward?" asked one man at a suburban Chicago meeting. "About as much as the hair on a dog's tail," shouted a citizen in the audiences.

Middle- and upper-income suburbs like Oak Park had a much better chance of preserving their independence than did the low-status peripheral communities of the nineteenth century because of changes in incorporation and annexation laws. Although each state conformed to a slightly different pattern, pre-Civil War villages were typically chartered in the same way that cities were chartered, and by about 1820 the village had become a recognized step in the development of a city. A certain area of a township that wished to become a city in the future would incorporate as a village to secure the advantages of individual local services and improvements that might not be of interest in the township as a whole but that might improve the possibility of a community's development into a city. Chartering by state legislatures slowly became a more simple process.

After the Civil War, however, the traditional role of the village as a prelude to the formation of a city began to shift. Small areas that had little hope and less interest in growing to become large cities began to incorporate under the easily met provisions of state incorporation laws. Rather than a first step towards becoming a city, the new wave of village incorporations was essentially a protective action, an attempt to save certain communities from annexation by larger urban units. * * *

In addition to easier incorporation, or "villagification," affluent suburbs like Brookline, Newton, Evanston, Beverly Hills, and Shaker Heights, in cooperation with rural areas, were able to move state legislatures away from the doctrine of forcible annexation. With some notable exceptions in the South and West, where cities can sometimes annex without a popular referendum, it is now commonly held that annexation should be a voluntary affair that must gain the approval of the residents of an affected area. Even so, rigorous procedural and substantive requirements block the way, and special acts calling for annexation have been defeated by antiurban state legislatures. Where annexation is provided for in a state constitution, as in the case of San Francisco, the relevant provision seems intended to thwart rather than to promote the process. Conversely, some states even require that central city services must be provided to newly incorporated communities at central city rates.

A third factor causing the breakdown of annexation as a process has been the improvement of suburban services. Since World War II especially, county governments have grown out of their old rural orientation and have begun to offer municipal-type services. This method has been publicly associated with Nashville, Indianapolis, and Miami, but the trend has been almost everywhere apparent. Even more important in upgrading suburban lifestyles has been the increased use of special service districts. This type of governmental structure was first used as an alternative to annexation in Philadelphia, where after 1790 special districts were established to administer prisons, schools, public health, and port administration. Nineteenth-century examples were the New York Metropolitan Police Board (1857), the New York Metropolitan Board of Health (1866), the Massachusetts District Commission (sewerage, 1889; parks, 1893; water, 1895), and the Chicago Sanitary District (1889). To a man such as Andrew Haswell Green, these regional institutions emphasized the logic of complete consolidations. But to most suburbanites, special-service districts were an alternative rather than an avenue to metropolitan government. By bringing together suburbs that individually lacked the resources to provide high-quality sewerage, water, educational or law-enforcement services, the special-service district enabled suburbanites to have their urban amenities without the urban problems. * * *

LEWIS MUMFORD, THE CITY IN HISTORY
Pp. 494, 495–496, 500, 503, 511–513 (1961).

As an attempt to recover what was missing in the city, the suburban exodus could be amply justified, for it was concerned with primary human needs. But there was another side: the temptation to retreat from unpleasant realities, to shirk public duties, and to find the whole meaning of life in the most elemental social group, the family, or even in the still more isolated and self-centered individual. What was properly a beginning was treated as an end. * * *

But too soon, in breaking away from the city, the part became a substitute for the whole, even as a single phase of life, that of childhood, became the pattern for all the seven ages of man. As leisure generally increased, play became the serious business of life; and the golf course, the country club, the swimming pool, and the cocktail party became the frivolous counterfeits of a more varied and significant life. Thus in reacting against the disadvantages of the crowded city, the suburb itself became an over-specialized community, more and more committed to relaxation and play as ends in themselves. Compulsive play fast became the acceptable alternative to compulsive work: with small gain either in freedom or vital stimulus. Accordingly, the two modes of life blend into each other; for both in suburb and in metropolis, mass production, mass consumption, and mass recreation produce the same kind of standardized and denatured environment. * * *

Both childhood and the suburb are transitional stages * * *. Politically the suburb might be described as an attempt to reduce the functional urban community to a size small enough for an individual family to cope with. The suburb superficially restored the dream of Jeffersonian democracy, almost effaced by the oligarchic proclivities of capitalism, and provided the conditions essential for its success: the small face-to-face community of identifiable people, participating in the common life as equals. Gardening and politics were both "do-it-yourself" activities in the suburb. And just as long as the community retained its natural limitation of area and numbers, it continued to foster this neighborly life. * * *

What began as a flight from the city by families has become a more general retreat, which has produced, not so much individual suburbs as a spreading suburban belt. While the big organizations of the metropolis have become more highly organized, by large-scale bureaucratic supervision, mechanized accountancy, and centralized financial control, they have scattered their fragments—department stores, hotels, insurance offices, laboratories, banks—over the whole metropolitan landscape: some times, confessedly, to shorten the distance to work for the owners and managers. This in itself is an admission that the tedious metropolitan journey to work had become not merely intolerable but unnecessary. Unfortunately, the sum of all these dispersals does not produce a new urban constellation. Though potentially they provided the elements for a new kind of multi-centered city, operated on a regional scale, their effect has so far been to corrode and undermine the old centers, without forming a pattern coherent enough to carry on their essential cultural functions on anything like the old level. * * *

[M]ass Suburbia has done away with most of the freedoms and delights that the original disciples of Rousseau sought to find through their exodus from the city. Instead of centering attention on the child in the garden, we now have the image of "Families in Space." For the wider the scattering of the population, the greater the isolation of the individual household, and the more effort it takes to do privately, even with the aid of many machines and automatic devices, what used to be done in company often with conversation, song, and the enjoyment of the physical presence of others.

The town housewife who half a century ago knew her butcher, her grocer, her dairyman, her various other local tradesmen, as individual persons, with histories and biographies that impinged on her own, in a daily interchange, now has the benefit of a single weekly expedition to an impersonal supermarket, where only by accident is she to encounter a neighbor. If she is well-to-do, she is surrounded with electronic devices that take the place of flesh and blood companions: her real companions, her friends, her mentors, lovers, her fillers-up of unlived life, are shadows on the television screen, or even less embodied voices. She may answer them, but she cannot make herself heard: as it works out, this is a one-way system. * * *

On the fringe of mass Suburbia, even the advantages of the primary neighborhood group disappear. The cost of this detachment in space from other men is out of all proportion to its supposed benefits. The end product is an encapsulated life, spent more and more either in a motor car or within the cabin of darkness before a television set: soon, with a little more automation of traffic, mostly in a motor car, travelling even greater distances, under remote control, so that the one-time driver may occupy himself with a television set, having lost even the freedom of the steering wheel. Every part of this life, indeed, will come through official channels and be under supervision. Untouched by human hand at one end: untouched by human spirit at the other. Those who accept this existence might as well be encased in a rocket hurtling through space, so narrow are their choices, so limited and deficient their permitted responses. Here indeed we find "The Lonely Crowd."

The organizers of the ancient city had something to learn from the new rulers of our society. The former massed their subjects within a walled enclosure, under the surveillance of armed guardians within the smaller citadel, the better to keep them under control. That method is now obsolete. With the present means of long-distance mass communication, sprawling isolation has proved an even more effective method of keeping a population under control. With direct contact and face-to-face association inhibited as far as possible, all knowledge and direction can be monopolized by central agents and conveyed through guarded channels, too costly to be utilized by small groups or private individuals. To exercise free speech in such a scattered, dissociated community one must "buy time" on the air or "buy space" in the newspaper. Each member of Suburbia becomes imprisoned by the very separation that he has prized: he is fed through a narrow opening: a telephone line, a radio band, a television circuit. This is not, it goes without saying, the result of a conscious conspiracy by a cunning minority: it is an organic by-product of an economy that sacrifices human development to mechanical processing. In a well-organized community, all these technological improvements might admirably widen the scope of social life: in the disorganized communities of today, they narrow the effective range of the person. Under such conditions, nothing can happen spontaneously or autonomously—not without a great deal of mechanical assistance. Does this not explain in some degree the passiveness and docility that has crept into our existence? * * *

KENNETH JACKSON, THE FEDERAL HOUSING ADMINISTRATION

From Kenneth Jackson, Crabgrass Frontier: The Suburbanization
of the United States 203–209, 213–218 (1985).

No agency of the United States government has had a more pervasive and powerful impact on the American people over the past half-century than the Federal Housing Administration (FHA). It dates from the adoption of the National Housing Act on June 27, 1934. * * * [I]t was intended "to encourage improvement in housing standards and conditions, to facilitate sound home financing on reasonable terms, and to exert a stabilizing influence on the mortgage market." The primary purpose of the legislation, however, was the alleviation of unemployment, which stood at about a quarter of the total work force in 1934 and which was particularly high in the construction industry. * * * The FHA effort was later supplemented by the Servicemen's Readjustment Act of 1944 (more familiarly known as the GI Bill), which created a Veterans Administration (VA) program to help the sixteen million soldiers and sailors of World War II purchase a home after the defeat of Germany and Japan. * * *

Between 1934 and 1968, and to a lesser extent until the present day, both the FHA and the VA (since 1944) have had a remarkable record of accomplishment. Essentially, they insure long-term mortgage loans made by private lenders for home construction and sale. To this end, they collect premiums, set up reserves for losses, and in the event of a default on a mortgage, indemnify the lender. They do not build houses or lend money. Instead, they induce lenders who have money to invest it in residential mortgages by insuring them against loss on such instruments, with the full weight of the United States Treasury behind the contract. And they have revolutionized the home finance industry in the following ways:

Before the FHA began operation, first mortgages were limited to one-half or two-thirds of the appraised value of the property. * * * By contrast, the fraction of the collateral that the lender was able to lend for an FHA-secured loan was about 93 percent. Thus, down payments of more than 10 percent were unnecessary.

Continuing a trend begun by the Home Owners Loan Corporation, FHA extended the repayment period for its guaranteed mortgages to twenty-five or thirty years and insisted that all loans be fully amortized. * * *

FHA established minimum standards for home construction that became almost standard in the industry. * * *

In the 1920s, the interest rate for first mortgages averaged between 6 and 8 percent. * * * Under the FHA (and later Veterans Administration) program, by contrast, there was very little risk to the banker if a loan turned sour. Reflecting this government guarantee, interest rates fell by two or three percentage points.

These four changes substantially increased the number of American families who could reasonably expect to purchase homes. Builders went back to work, and housing starts and sales began to accelerate rapidly in 1936. * * * Quite simply, it often became cheaper to buy than to rent. * * * Long Island builder Martin Winter recalled that in the early 1950s families living in the Kew Gardens section of Queens were paying about ninety dollars per month for small two-bedroom apartments. For less money, they could and often did, move to the new Levittown-type developments springing up along the highways from Manhattan. * * * Not surprisingly, the middle-class suburban family with the new house and the long-term, fixed-rate, FHA-insured mortgage became a symbol, and perhaps a stereotype, of the American way of life.

Unfortunately, the corollary to this achievement was the fact that FHA programs hastened the decay of inner-city neighborhoods by stripping them of much of their middle-class constituency. In practice, FHA insurance went to new residential developments on the edges of metropolitan areas, to the neglect of core cities. This occurred for three reasons. First, although the legislation nowhere mentioned an antiurban bias, it favored the construction of single-family projects and discouraged construction of multi-family projects through unpopular terms. Historically, single-family housing programs have been the heart of FHA's insured loan activities. * * *

Second, loans for the repair of existing structures were small and for short duration, which meant that a family could more easily purchase a new home than modernize an old one. * * *

The third and most important variety of suburban, middle-class favoritism had to do with the "unbiased professional estimate" that was a prerequisite to any loan guarantee. Required because maximum mortgage amounts were related to "appraised value," this mandatory judgment included a rating of the property itself, a rating of the mortgagor or borrower, and a rating of the neighborhood. The aim was to guarantee that at any time during the term of the mortgage the market value of the dwelling would exceed the outstanding debt. The lower the valuation placed on properties, the less government risk and the less generous the aid to the potential buyers (and sellers). The purpose of the neighborhood evaluation was "to determine the degree of mortgage risk introduced in a mortgage insurance transaction because of the location of the property at a specific site." And unlike the Home Owners Loan Corporation, which used a similar procedure, the Federal Housing Administration allowed personal and agency bias in favor of all-white subdivisions in the suburbs to affect the kinds of loans it guaranteed—or, equally important, refused to guarantee. In this way, the bureaucracy influenced the character of housing at least as much as the 1934 enabling legislation did.

The Federal Housing Administration was quite precise in teaching its underwriters how to measure quality in residential areas. Eight criteria were established (the numbers in parentheses reflect the percentage weight given to each):

Relative economic stability (40 percent)

Protection from adverse influences (20 percent)

Freedom from special hazards (5 percent)

Adequacy of civic, social, and commercial centers (5 percent)

Adequacy of transportation (10 percent)

Sufficiency of utilities and conveniences (5 percent)

Level of taxes and special assessments (5 percent)

Appeal (10 percent)

Although FHA directives insisted that no project should be insured that involved a high degree of risk with regard to any of the eight categories, "economic stability" and "protection from adverse influences" together counted for more than the other six combined. Both were interpreted in ways that were prejudicial against heterogeneous environments. The 1939 *Underwriting Manual* taught that "crowded neighborhoods lessen desirability," and "older properties in a neighborhood have a tendency to accelerate the transition to lower class occupancy." Smoke and odor were considered "adverse influences," and appraisers were told to look carefully for any "inferior and non-productive characteristics of the areas surrounding the site." The agency endorsed restrictive zoning and insisted that any single-family residence it insured could not have facilities that allowed the dwelling to be used as a store, an office, or a rental unit.

Obviously, prospective buyers could avoid many of these so-called undesirable features by locating in suburban sections. In 1939 FHA asked each of its fifty regional offices to send in plans for six "typical American houses." The photographs and dimensions were then used for a National Archives exhibit. Virtually all of the entries were bungalows or colonials on ample lots with driveways and garages.

In an attempt to standardize such ideal homes, the Federal Housing Administration set up minimum requirements for lot size, setback from the street, separation from adjacent structures, and even for the width of the house itself. While such requirements did provide light and air for new structures, they effectively eliminated whole categories of dwellings, such as the traditional 16-foot-wide row houses of Baltimore, from eligibility for loan guarantees. Even apartment-house owners were encouraged to look to suburbia: "Under the best of conditions a rental development under the FHA program is a project set in what amounts to a privately owned and privately controlled park area."

Reflecting the racist tradition of the United States, the Federal Housing Administration was extraordinarily concerned with "inharmonious racial or nationality groups." It feared that an entire area could lose its investment value if rigid white-black separation was not maintained. Bluntly warning, "If a neighborhood is to retain stability, it is necessary that properties shall continue to be occupied by the same social and racial classes," the *Underwriting Manual* openly recommended "subdivision regulations and suitable restrictive covenants" that would be "superior to any mortgage." Such covenants, which were legal provisions written into property deeds, were a common method of prohibiting black occupancy until the United States Supreme Court ruling in 1948 *(Shelley v. Kraemer)* that they were "unenforceable as law and contrary to public policy." Even then, it was not until 1949 that FHA announced that as of February 15, 1950, it would not insure mortgages on real estate subject to covenants. Although the press treated the FHA announcement as a major advancement in the field of racial justice, former housing administrator Nathan Straus noted that "the new policy in fact served only to warn speculative builders who had not filed covenants of their right to do so, and it gave them a convenient respite in which to file."

In addition to recommending covenants, FHA compiled detailed reports and maps charting the present and most likely future residential locations of black families. In a March 1939 map of Brooklyn, for example, the presence of a single, non-white family on any block was sufficient to mark that entire block black. Similarly, very extensive maps of the District of Columbia depicted the spread of the black population and the percentage of dwelling units occupied by persons other than white. As late as November 19, 1948, Assistant FHA Commissioner W. J. Lockwood could write that FHA "has never insured a housing project of mixed occupancy" because of the expectation that "such projects would probably in a short period of time become all-Negro or all-white." * * *

The precise extent to which the agency discriminated against blacks and other minority groups is difficult to determine. Although FHA has always collected reams of data regarding the price, floor area, lot size, number of bathrooms, type of roof, and structural characteristics of the single-family homes it has insured, it has been quite secretive about the location of these loans. * * * Such data as are available indicate that the neighborhood appraisals were very influential in determining "where it would be reasonably safe to insure mortgages." * * * The result was a degree of suburban favoritism even greater than the documentary analysis would have suggested. * * *

For its part, the Federal Housing Administration usually responded that it was not created to help cities, but to revive home building, to stimulate homeownership, and to reduce unemployment. And it concentrated on convincing both the Congress and the public that it was, as its first Administrator, James Moffett, remarked, "a conservative business operation." The agency emphasized its concern over sound loans no higher than the value of the assets and the repayment ability of the borrower would support. And FHA was unusual in the vast array of Washington programs because of its record of earning a small profit for the federal government.

But FHA also helped to turn the building industry against the minority and inner-city housing market, and its policies supported the income and racial segregation of suburbia. For perhaps the first time, the federal government embraced the discriminatory attitudes of the marketplace. Previously, prejudices were personalized and individualized; FHA exhorted segregation and enshrined it as public policy. Whole areas of cities were declared ineligible for loan guarantees; as late as 1966, for example, FHA did not have a mortgage on a single home in Camden or Paterson, New Jersey, both declining industrial cities. This withdrawal of financing often resulted in an inability to sell houses in a neighborhood, so that vacant units often stood empty for months, producing a steep decline in value.

Despite the fact that the government's leading housing agency openly exhorted segregation throughout the first thirty years of its operation, very few voices were raised against FHA red-lining practices. * * * Not until the civil-rights movement of the 1960s did community groups realize that red lining and disinvestment were a major cause of community decline and that home-improvement loans were the "lifeblood of housing." In * * * [1968] Senator Paul Douglas of Illinois reported for the National Commission on Urban Problems on the role of the federal government in home finance:

> The poor and those on the fringes of poverty have been almost completely excluded. These and the lower middle class, together constituting the 40 percent of the population whose housing needs are greatest, received only 11 percent of the FHA mortgages * * *. Even middle-class residential districts in the central cities were suspect, since there was always the prospect that they, too, might turn as Negroes and poor whites continued to pour into the cities, and as middle and upper-middle-income whites continued to move out.

Moreover, as urban analyst Jane Jacobs has said, "Credit blacklisting maps are accurate prophecies because they are self-fulfilling prophecies."

In 1966, FHA drastically shifted its policies with a view toward making much more mortgage insurance available for inner-city neighborhoods. Ironically, the primary effect of the change was to make it easier for white families to finance their escape from areas experiencing racial change. At the same time, the relaxed credit standards for black applicants meant that home improvement companies could buy properties at low cost, make cosmetic improvements, and sell the renovated home at inflated prices approved by FHA. Many of the minority purchasers could not afford the cost of maintenance, and FHA had to repossess thousands of homes. The final result was to increase the speed with which areas went through racial transformation and to victimize those it was designed to help. The only people to benefit were contractors and white, middle-class homeowners who were assisted in escaping from a distress position. * * *

Any serious indictment of federal lawmakers and federal officials for the miserable state of many American cities must take cognizance of two important points. First, and most obviously, it is hazardous to condemn a government for adopting policies in accord with the preference of a majority of its citizens. As novelist Anthony Trollope put it in 1867: "It is a very comfortable thing to stand on your own ground. Land is about the only thing that can't fly away." FHA helped to build houses, and where they were put was less important than that they were built. For more than a century, Americans have had a strong affinity for a detached home on a private lot. Obviously, some popular measures, such as gun control, are not adopted because of special-interest lobbies. But suburbanization was not willed on an innocent peasantry. Without a substantial amount of encouragement from the mainstream of public opinion, the bureaucrats would never have been able to push their projects as far as they did. The single-family house responded to the psychic value of privacy or castlehood. In fact, suburbanization was an ideal government policy because it met the needs of both citizens and business interests and because it earned the politicians' votes. It is a simple fact that homeownership introduced equity into the estates of over 35 million families between 1933 and 1978. The tract houses they often bought may have been dismissed as hopeless by highbrow architectural purists, but they were a lot less dreary to the people who raised families there and then sold to new families at a profit.

Federal housing policies were also not the *sine qua non* in the mushrooming of the suburbs. Mortgage insurance obviously made it easier for families to secure their dream houses, but the dominant residential drift in American cities had been toward the periphery for at least a century before the New Deal, and there is no reason to assume that the suburban trend would not have continued in the absence of direct federal assistance.

The lasting damage done by the national government was that it put its seal of approval on ethnic and racial discrimination and developed policies which had the result of the practical abandonment of large sections of older, industrial cities. More seriously, Washington actions were later picked up by private interests, so that banks and savings-and-loan institutions institutionalized the practice of denying mortgages "solely because of the geographical location of the property." The financial community saw blighted neighborhoods as physical evidence of the melting-pot mistake. To them, cities were risky because of their heterogeneity, because of their attempt to bring various people together harmoniously. Such mixing, they believed, had but two consequences—

the decline of both the human race and of property values. As Mark Gelfand has observed, "Given the chance, bankers would do for their business what they had already done for themselves—leave the city." * * *

[T]he * * * broad patterns of downtown decline, inner-city deterioration, and exurban development * * * are * * * typical of the large population centers of the United States. This same result might have been achieved in the absence of all federal intervention, but the simple fact is that the various government policies toward housing have had substantially the same result from Los Angeles to Boston. The poor in America have not shared in the postwar real-estate boom, in most of the major highway improvements, in property and income-tax write-offs, and in mortgage insurance programs. Public housing projects were intended to redress the imbalance. Unfortunately, * * * it did not work out that way. * * *

RICHARD T. FORD, THE PERPETUATION OF RACIALLY IDENTIFIED SPACES: AN ECONOMIC/STRUCTURAL ANALYSIS

From Richard Ford, The Boundaries of Race: Political Geography in Legal Analysis, 107 Harv. L. Rev. 1841, 1849–1857 (1994).

Much traditional social and legal theory imagines that the elimination of public policies designed to promote segregation will eliminate segregation, or will at least eliminate any segregation that can be attributed to public policy and leave only the aggregate effects of individual biases (which are beyond the authority of government to remedy). This view fails, however, to acknowledge that racial segregation is embedded in and perpetuated by the social construction of racially identified political space.

Trouble in Paradise: An Economic Model

Imagine a society with only two groups, blacks and whites, differentiated only by morphology (visible physical differences). Blacks, as a result of historical discrimination, tend, on average, to earn significantly less than whites. Imagine also that this society has recently (during the past twenty or thirty years) come to see the error of its discriminatory ways. It has enacted a program of reform that has totally eliminated any legal support for racial discrimination and, through a concentrated program of public education, has also succeeded in eliminating any vestige of racism from its citizenry. In short, the society has become color-blind. Such a society may feel itself well on its way to the ideal of racial justice and equality, if not already there.

Imagine also that, in our hypothetical society, small, decentralized and geographically defined governments exercise significant power to tax citizens, and use the tax revenues to provide certain public services (such as police and fire protection), public utilities (such as sewage, water and garbage collection), infrastructure development, and public education.

Finally, imagine that, before the period of racial reform, our society had in place a policy of fairly strict segregation of the races, such that every municipality consisted of two enclaves, one almost entirely white and one almost entirely black. In some cases, whites even re-incorporated their enclaves as separate municipalities to ensure the separation of the races. Thus, the now-color-blind society confronts a situation of almost complete segregation of the races—a segregation that also fairly neatly tracks a class segregation (because blacks earn, on average, far less than whites, in part because of their historical isolation from resources and job opportunities available in the wealthier and socially privileged white communities.)

We can assume that all members of this society are indifferent to the race of their neighbors, co-workers, social acquaintances, and so forth. However, we must also assume that most members of this society care a great deal about their economic well-being and are unlikely to make decisions that will adversely affect their financial situation.

Our (hypothetical) society may feel that, over time, racial segregation will dissipate in the absence of de jure discrimination and racial prejudice. But let us examine the likely outcome under these circumstances. Higher incomes in the white neighborhoods would result in larger homes and more privately financed amenities, although public expenditures would be equally distributed among white and black neighborhoods within a single municipality. However, in those municipalities that incorporated along racial lines, white cities would have substantially superior public services (or lower taxes and the same level of services) than the "mixed" cities, due to a higher average tax base. The all-black cities would, it follows, have substantially inferior public services or higher taxes as compared to the mixed cities. Consequently, the wealthier white citizens of mixed cities would have a real economic incentive to depart, or even secede, from the mixed cities, and whites in unincorporated areas would be spurred to form their own jurisdictions and resist consolidation with the larger mixed cities or all-black cities. Note that this pattern can be explained without reference to "racism": whites might be color-blind and yet prefer predominantly white or all-white neighborhoods on purely economic grounds, as long as the condition of substantial income differentiation obtains.

Of course, simply because municipalities begin as racially segregated enclaves does not mean that they will remain segregated. Presumably blacks would also prefer the higher public service amenities or lower tax burdens of white neighborhoods, and those with sufficient wealth would move in; remember, in this world there is no racism and there are no cultural differences between the races—people behave as purely rational economic actors. One might imagine that, over time, income levels will even out between the races, and blacks would move into the wealthier neighborhoods, while less fortunate whites would be outbid and would move to the formerly all-black neighborhoods. Hence racial segregation might eventually be transformed into a purely economic segregation.

This conclusion rests, however, on the assumption that residential segregation would not itself affect employment opportunities and economic status. But because the educational system is financed through local taxes, segregated localities would offer significantly different levels of educational opportunity: the poor, black cities would have poorer educational facilities than the wealthy, white cities. Thus, whites would, on average, be better equipped to obtain high-income employment than will blacks. Moreover, residential segregation would result in a pattern of segregated informal social networks; neighbors would work and play together in community organizations such as schools, PTAs, Little Leagues, Rotary Clubs, neighborhood-watch groups, cultural associations, and religious organizations. These social networks would form the basis of ties and communities of trust that open the doors of opportunity in the business world. All other things being equal, employers would hire people they know and like over people of whom they have no personal knowledge, good or bad. They would hire someone who comes with a personal recommendation from a close friend over someone without such a recommendation. Residential segregation substantially decreases the likelihood that such connections would be formed between members of different races. Finally, and more concretely, economic segregation would mean that the market value of black homes would be significantly lower than that of white homes; thus, blacks attempting to move into white neighborhoods would, on average, have less collateral with which to obtain new mortgages, or less equity to convert into cash.

Inequalities in both educational opportunity and the networking dynamic would result in fewer and less remunerative employment opportunities, and hence lower incomes, for blacks. Poorer blacks, unable to move into the more privileged neighborhoods and cities, would remain segregated; and few, if any, whites would forgo the benefits of their white neighborhoods to move into poorer black neighborhoods, which will be burdened by higher taxes or provided with inferior public services. This does not necessarily mean that income polarization and segregation would constantly increase (although at times they would), but only that they would not level out over time through a process of osmosis. Instead, every successive generation of blacks and whites would find itself in much the same situation as the previous generation, and in the absence of some intervening factor, the cycle would likely perpetuate itself. At some point an equilibrium might be achieved: generally better-connected and better-educated whites would secure the better, higher-income jobs and disadvantaged blacks would occupy the lower status and lower-wage jobs.

Thus, even in the absence of racism, race-neutral policy could be expected to entrench segregation and socio-economic stratification in a society with a history of racism. Political space plays a central role in this process. Spatially and racially defined communities perform the "work" of segregation silently. There is no racist actor or racist policy in this model, and yet a racially stratified society is the inevitable result. Although political space seems to be the inert context in which individuals make rational choices, it is in fact a controlling structure in which seemingly innocuous actions lead to racially detrimental consequences.

Strangers in Paradise: A Complicated Model

* * * If we now introduce a few real-world complications into our model, we can see just how potent this race/space dynamic is. Suppose that (only) half of all whites in our society are in some measure racist or harbor some racial fear or concern, ranging from the open-minded liberal, who remains somewhat resistant, if only for pragmatic reasons, to mixed-race relations (Spencer Tracy's character in *Guess Who's Coming to Dinner*) to the avowed racial separatist and member of the Ku Klux Klan. Further suppose that the existence of racism produces a degree of racial fear and animosity in blacks, such that (only) half of blacks fear or distrust whites to some degree, ranging from a pragmatic belief that blacks need to "keep to their own kind," if only to avoid unnecessary confrontation and strife (Sidney Poitier's father in *Guess Who's Coming to Dinner*), to strident nationalist separatism. Let us also assume that significant cultural differences generally exist between whites and blacks.

In this model, cultural difference and socialization further entrench racial segregation. Even assuming that a few blacks would be able to attain the income necessary to move into white neighborhoods, it is less likely that they would wish to do so. Many blacks would fear and distrust whites and would be reluctant to live among them, especially in the absence of a significant number of other blacks. Likewise, many whites would resent the presence of black neighbors and would try to discourage them from entering white neighborhoods in ways both subtle and overt. The result is an effective "tax" on integration. The additional amenities and lower taxes of the white neighborhood would often be outweighed by the intangible but real costs of living as an isolated minority in an alien and sometimes hostile environment. Many blacks would undoubtedly choose to remain in black neighborhoods.

But importantly for our purposes, this dynamic would produce racially *identified* spaces. Because our hypothetical society is now somewhat racist, segregated neighborhoods would become identified by the race of their inhabitants; race would be seen as intimately related to the economic and social condition of political space. The creation of racially identified political spaces would make possible a number of regulatory activities and private practices that further entrench the segregation of the races. For example, because some whites would resent the introduction of blacks into their neighborhoods, real estate brokers would be unlikely to show property in white neighborhoods to blacks for fear that disgruntled white homeowners would boycott them.

Even within mixed cities, localities might decline to provide adequate services in black neighborhoods, and might divert funds to white neighborhoods to encourage whites with higher incomes to enter or remain in the jurisdiction. Thus, although our discussion has focused primarily on racially homogeneous jurisdictions with autonomous taxing power, the existence of such jurisdictions might affect the policy of racially heterogeneous jurisdictions, which would have to compete with the low-tax/superior-service homogeneous cities for wealthier residents. This outcome would be especially likely if the mixed jurisdictions were characterized by governmental structures resistant to participation by grassroots community groups or that are otherwise unresponsive to the citizenry as a whole. A dynamic similar to what I have posited for the homogeneous jurisdictions would occur *within* such racially mixed jurisdictions, with neighborhoods taking the place of separate jurisdictions.

Each of these phenomena would exacerbate the others, in a vicious circle of causation. The lack of public services would create a general negative image of poor, black neighborhoods; the inadequate police protection would lead to a perception of the neighborhoods as unsafe; uncollected trash would lead to a perception of the neighborhood as dirty, and so forth. Financial institutions would redline black neighborhoods—refuse to lend to property owners in these areas—because they would likely perceive them as financially risky. As a result, both real estate improvement and sale would often become unfeasible.

Strangers in a Strange Land

One might object that our model has ignored the existence of private developers who would find it profitable to build affordable housing in the white jurisdictions. These developers would be able to sell or to lease housing to blacks who would then reap the benefits of the higher tax base of their new jurisdiction. Developers would find such a venture profitable because blacks would be willing to pay a "premium" for such housing because of the lower taxes or superior public services that would come with it. Developers would have access to sufficient funds to purchase property in white neighborhoods although the individual blacks to whom they would eventually sell or lease may not. The developers would indirectly pool the resources of many blacks, thereby taking advantage of an economy of scale.

This mechanism might succeed in integrating localities and neighborhoods but for one additional real-world complication: the zoning power. Localities with the power to regulate land uses might limit the construction of multi-family housing and moderately priced detached units to certain areas of town, or might even exclude such development altogether. Localities would have a strong incentive to exclude such uses to keep lower-income individuals from diluting the municipal tax base. Again, a purely economic motivation would result in the exclusion of blacks from the municipality.

Conclusion: The Implications for Racial Harmony

* * * The foregoing economic model demonstrates that race and class are inextricably linked in American society, and that both are linked to segregation and to the creation of racially identified political spaces. Even if racism could be magically eliminated, racial segregation would be likely to continue as long as we begin with significant income polarization and segregation of the races. Furthermore, even a relatively slight, residual racism severely complicates any effort to eliminate racial segregation that does not directly address political space and class-based segregation.

One might imagine that racism could be overcome by education and rational persuasion alone: because racism is irrational, it seems to follow that, over time, one can argue or educate it away. The model shows that even if such a project were entirely successful, in the absence of any further interventions, racial segregation would remain indefinitely.

Contemporary society imposes significant economic costs on non-segregated living arrangements. In the absence of a conscious effort to eliminate it, segregation will persist in this atmosphere (although it may appear to be the product of individual choices). The structure of racially identified space is more than the mere vestigial effect of historical racism; it is a structure that continues to exist today with nearly as much force as when policies of segregation were explicitly backed by the force of law. This structure will not gradually atrophy because it is constantly used and constantly reinforced. * * *

ROBERT FISHMAN, BOURGEOIS UTOPIAS: THE RISE AND FALL OF SUBURBIA
Pp. 3–4, 15–16 (1987).

Every civilization gets the monuments it deserves. The triumph of bourgeois capitalism seems most apparent in the massive constructions of iron and steel that celebrate the union of technology and profit: the railroad terminals, exposition halls, suspension bridges, and skyscrapers.

* * * But if * * * we are seeking the architecture that best reveals "the spirit and character of modern civilization," then suburbia might tell us more about the culture that built the factories and skyscrapers than these edifices themselves can. For suburbia too was an archetypal middle-class invention, perhaps the most radical rethinking of the relation between residence and the city in the history of domestic architecture. It was founded on that primacy of the family and domestic life which was the equivalent in bourgeois society of the intense civic life celebrated by the public architecture of the ancient city. However modest each suburban house might be, suburbia represents a collective assertion of class wealth and privilege as impressive as any medieval castle. Most importantly, suburbia embodies a new ideal of family life, an ideal so emotionally charged that it made the home more sacred to the bourgeoisie than any place of worship. * * * [T]he true center of any bourgeois society is the middle-class house. If you seek the monuments of the bourgeoisie, go to the suburbs and look around.

Suburbia is more than a collection of residential buildings; it expresses values so deeply embedded in bourgeois culture that it might also be called the bourgeois utopia. Yet this "utopia" was always at most a partial paradise, a refuge not only from threatening elements in the city but also from discordant elements in bourgeois society itself. From its origins, the suburban world of leisure, family life, and union with nature was based on the principle of exclusion. Work was excluded from the family residence; middle-class villas were segregated from working-class housing; the greenery of suburbia stood in contrast to a gray, polluted urban environment. Middle-class women were especially affected by the new suburban dichotomy of work and family life. The new environment supposedly exalted their role in the family, but it also segregated them from the world of power and productivity. This self-segregation soon enveloped all aspects of bourgeois culture. Suburbia, therefore, represents more than the bourgeois utopia, the triumphant assertion of middle-class values. It also reflects the alienation of the middle classes from the urban-industrial world they themselves were creating. * * *

If there is a single theme that differentiates the history of twentieth century suburbia from its nineteenth century antecedents, it is the attempt to secure for the whole middle class (and even for the working class as well) the benefits of suburbia, which in the classic nineteenth century suburb had been restricted to the bourgeois elite alone. Inevitably, this attempt was to change the basic nature both of suburbia and of the larger city. For how can a form based on the principle of exclusion include everyone?

This paradox is exemplified in the history of Los Angeles, the suburban metropolis of the twentieth century. From its first building boom in the late nineteenth century, Los Angeles has been shaped by the promise of a suburban home for all. The automobile and the highway when they came were no more than new tools to achieve a suburban vision that had its origins in the streetcar era. But as population spread along the streetcar lines and the highways, the "suburbs" of Los Angeles began to lose contact with the central city, which so diminished in importance that even the new highways bypassed it. In the 1920s, a new urban form evolved in which the industries, specialized shopping, and offices once concentrated in the urban core spread over the whole region. By the 1930s Los Angeles had become a sprawling metropolitan region, the basic unit of which was the decentralized suburb.

This creation of a suburban metropolis signaled a fundamental shift in the relationship of the urban core and its periphery, with implications extending far beyond Los Angeles. As we have seen, the suburb emerged during the era of urban concentration, when the limitations of communications and transportation combined to draw people and production into the crowded core. By the 1920s an interrelated technology of decentralization—of which the automobile was only one element—had begun to operate, which inexorably loosened the ties that once bound the urban functions of society to tightly defined cores. As the most important urban institutions spread out over the landscape, the suburb became part of a complex "outer city," which now included jobs as well as residences.

Increasingly independent of the urban core, the suburb since 1945 has lost its traditional meaning and function as a satellite of the central city. Where peripheral communities had once excluded industry and large scale commerce, the suburb now becomes the heartland of the most rapidly expanding elements of the late twentieth century economy. The basic concept of the suburb as a privileged zone between city and country no longer fits the realities of a posturban era in which high tech research centers sit in the midst of farmland and grass grows on abandoned factory sites in the core. As both core and periphery are swallowed up in seemingly endless multicentered regions, where can one find suburbia?
* * *

ROSALYN BAXANDALL AND ELIZABETH EWEN, PICTURE WINDOWS (HOW THE SUBURBS HAPPENED)
Pp. xviii–xxii (2000).

* * * [The] intellectual disdain for the humdrum typical Main Street middle-class life had its roots in the twenties, the first decade of suburban expansion. The city—especially New York—was considered cosmopolitan, and the countryside was seen as a slice of nature's paradise, but suburbia was suspended somewhere in the blah middle. In 1921 Lewis Mumford one of modern America's most important social critics, warned that the suburbs were becoming a new wasteland:

The 19th century American town, with none of the cultural resources that cities like Oxford and Paris had inherited from the middle ages and the renaissance, was the negation of the city—and suburbia was the negation of that negation. The result was not a new synthesis, but a further deterioration.

Some of Mumford's contemporaries echoed his critique of suburbia. Popular writer and historian Frederick Lewis Allen derisively commented on what he called the "suburban nightmare":

The groves where we now look for anemones in spring will be sliced through with orderly little streets down which orderly little commuters will hurry to catch the seven-forty-dash eight train for town while their wives look into each others back windows and tell each other that you never would believe, my dear, what's going on at Mrs. So and So's right in plain sight of everybody.

Christine Frederick, a well-known proponent of scientific management and the standardization of home life, believed that what people looked for in suburbs—modern conveniences, the automobile, privacy, access to the country, and a healthy life— was in fact best found in the city. In her words, "I have enjoyed myself like Thoreau in the privacy of his forest retreat while living in a New York apartment, but in the suburb I have never felt like anything but a worm trying to crawl over a much be-travelled roadway." Suburbia, she believed, was socially and aesthetically empty. Frederick was particularly dismayed by what she viewed as the connection between architectural and behavioral conformity:

These suburban houses for instance, I suppose architects get pleasure out of the neat little toy houses on their neat little patches of lawn and their neat colonial lives, to say nothing of the neat little housewife and their neat little children—all set in neat rows—for all the world like children's blocks . . . the very aspect of it offends me deeply. It is so sugary and commonplace and pathetic in its pretense of an individualism which doesn't exist.

Why did city folk display such malice and venom in their depictions of suburban dwellers? Why did modernists like Frederick Allen, and Mumford, proponents of mass production and garden cities, stick their noses up at the suburban exodus? Why was such a profound socially conscious critic like Mumford so culturally condescending? Why was the suburb and suburbanite seen as the epitome of crass commercial culture and the death of sophisticated, highbrow civilized living?

Suburbs do reflect certain aspects of a conformist culture, such as homogeneity of stage of life, commonality of class, and keeping up with the Joneses. Suburbs have neither the beauty and wildness of the country nor the urbanity and vibrant clashes of the city. Yet there are different kinds of suburbs. In the 1920s such critical attacks were launched at upper-middle-class suburbs. By the 1950s, working-and middle-class suburbs became the focus of the antisuburb barrage.

Suburbia—especially the Levittowns—rarely have generated an active intellectual life. Most intellectuals born in suburbs and small towns flee, only to spend their lives in a vain attempt to rid themselves of their backgrounds. Suburban phobia remains an intellectual cliché, the mantra of the urban refugee against the commercial culture of H. L. Mencken's "booboisie." In the mass exodus of the late 1940s and 1950s this theme gathered steam, even though the class composition of those moving changed. Urban intellectuals such as Mumford, academics such as David Reisman and William Whyte, novelists such as John Keats, Vance Packard, and John Cheever, and feminists such as Betty Friedan all blamed the suburbs for the cultural ills of society: 1950s conformity, the highest levels of mass consumption in history, "low-brow" new media like television, and the problem that had no name, the so-called boredom of the overeducated housewife.

Everything about suburbia, exteriors and interiors alike, was magnified and dissected. Even though homes and apartments everywhere contained a mixture of labor-saving devices and ordinary household objects, the accumulation of these things in the suburbs took on a sinister air. John Seeley, Alexander Sim, and E. W Loosley in their book *Crestwood Heights* claimed that the suburban house had become nothing more than an odd and chilling repository of an exceedingly wide range of artifacts, from freezers and furnaces to mousetraps and mix masters. John Keats in his novel *Crack in the Picture Window* chimed in, claiming that the suburbs resembled George Orwell's *1984*. Combining sexism and anticommunism, Keats created a suburb, Rolling Knolls, where people lived, "in vast communistic, female barracks. This communism . . . began with the obliteration of the individualistic house and self-sufficient neighborhood, and from there on, the creation of mass-produced human beings as the night follows the day." Keats's depictions of suburban life were so exaggerated that he even proclaimed that new suburban houses were "doll houses which out slum the slummiest of our prewar slums."

These virulent denouncements were based on class and ethnicity as well as sex. The 1950s critics attacked not only the suburbs but the new residents themselves. The opening of home ownership to a new class of people represented a changing relationship between the propertied and the propertyless. While this new class believed that it finally was being allowed a piece of the dream, urban tastemakers feared this dream would turn into its opposite, a suburban ghetto. At issue here was whether the new suburbs would bring to fruition a world in which workers would work less, would be better educated, and live in standardized but well-built homes. Or would suburbia turn into a cultural wasteland of conformity as Mumford and others feared?

Even though the suburbs have grown more vital and the majority of Americans choose to live there, the snobbery continues unabated, articulated by a variety of intellectuals. To James Howard Kunstler, author of *The Geography of Nowhere*, and Marc Auge, author of *Non Places*, the suburbs have become synonymous with an empty, anticivic, spiritually dead, dysfunctional society that is slowly enveloping the world. Even cities are becoming suburbanized. As Kunstler puts it, suburbia is "deleterious, insalubrious; it is damaging to our culture, to our aspirations, to our humanity . . . It may get so bad that suburbia will collapse before people are ready or willing to reinvent civic life." This theme is echoed by "neotraditionalist" architects and planners, such as Andres Duany and Elizabeth Plater-Zyberk. For them "The suburb is the last word in privatization and spells the end of authentic civil life."

There is even a zinelike book from the hiphop generation entitled *Bomb the Suburbs* by William Upski Wimsatt. Upski (as he prefers to be called) argues, "It's the American state of mind, founded on fear, conformity, shallowness of character, and dullness of imagination." He feels the suburbs are bad for America. "Socially, they intensify segregation and mistrust. Culturally, they erode the sense of history, narrow the outlook. . . . [Suburbanites] run around in a comfort warp, taking everything for granted and misusing what they have."

None of these books reflects the voices of our students and the myriad Americans—white, black, immigrant, gay, straight, old, young, married, divorced, and single—who have selected to live in suburbia and have inscribed their signatures on its landscape. Moreover, none of these books has bothered to uncover the changing contours of suburban history.

Once we rejected antisuburban snobbery and began compiling oral histories and examining archival records, we found a suburban history that spanned the twentieth century. Indeed, the history of suburbia is at the heart of twentieth-century American history; over the years many believe that the fate of the nation is inextricably bound to the fate of suburbia. At every critical juncture the history of suburbia collides with that of housing and its pivotal role in the evolution of American society. The idea of suburbia was central to visionaries, planners, and socially conscious architects who began to imagine a new America. In their vision suburbia meant a place where ordinary people, not just the elite, would have access to affordable, attractive modern housing in communities with parks, gardens, recreation, stores, and cooperative town meeting places. These ideas were not just pipe dreams.

Towns like these were built in the 1920s and 1930s, first by nonprofit organizations and later by the federal government. The idea that every citizen deserved decent housing captured the public imagination. After the second world war the demand for public affordable housing was so strong that Senator Joseph McCarthy had to hold open hearings for five months to move public sentiment away from the idea of government-sponsored housing and in favor of private real estate interests building mass housing.* * *

[S]uburban life has both shaped and been shaped by some of the most important issues of the past century. * * * [T]he ongoing struggle between ideas about private versus public responsibility for instance, the belief that government should take care of Americans versus faith in private enterprise[,] * * * the relationship of ideas and images to real buildings and places: how battles between aesthetic ideas and differing cultural, political, and economic forces forged suburban developments, [and] * * * the continuing attempt to claim the dream of inclusive democracy and prosperity, and create the kind of American community where people's ideas can be heard, fought over, and realized.

The suburban migration—like the settlement of the West, mass immigration to America, and the black migration from the rural South to northern cities—changed the face of America. * * *

MARGARET WEIR, JUSTICE FOR THE POOR IN THE NEW METROPOLIS

From Clarissa Hayward and Todd Swanstrom (Eds.),
Justice and the American Metropolis 237–256 (2011).

Poverty—never the sole province of the inner city—has spread beyond urban boundaries so that by 2005, 53 percent of the poor in large metropolitan areas lived in the suburbs, not the central city. Among this diverse group are African Americans pushed out of the city by gentrification and public housing reforms; immigrants seeking to settle near employment centers; and white suburban residents buffeted by economic change. To be sure, concentrations of racially and ethnically identified urban poverty persist in cities across the country but the challenges confronting the urban poor have also shifted as cash assistance becomes ever more rare and ongoing economic change moves opportunities further from centers of urban poverty. * * *

The growing immigrant presence in the suburbs has begun to attract wide attention. By the beginning of the twenty-first century, the majority of immigrants lived in suburbs, not cities. Many of these immigrants were new arrivals who had broken the pattern of a century earlier in bypassing the city. Instead, they migrated directly to the suburbs following job growth. Yet, greater proximity to jobs does not by itself guarantee an escape from poverty. Given their lower education levels and greater presence among the working poor, the influx of immigrants has been a significant factor in the growth of suburban poverty. In 2007, 40 percent of poor immigrants lived in suburbs, not cities; 19.2 percent of the suburban poor were foreign born.

The second force remaking metropolitan areas is what Alan Ehrenhalt has called "demographic inversion." In his view, the influx of high-income whites back into cities and the movement of low-income African American residents to suburbs is reconfiguring the basic demographic pattern that has characterized metropolitan areas during the postwar era. The movement of upper-income residents into the city reverses a more basic pattern established in American and British cities during the dawn of the industrial age. Among the drivers of this change are rising traffic congestion, which reduces the quality of life in suburbs; high energy costs, which made suburban life more expensive, and a heavily-marketed cultural shift that has given "downtown living" an attractive, sophisticated patina. For low-income African Americans and some Latinos, these trends have caused displacement, one of the central causes for moving to the suburbs. The shift is a real, but as Ehrenhalt notes, it is an emerging trend that has only begun to alter the older pattern demographic pattern.

The third factor reshaping metropolitan areas is ongoing "job sprawl." The exodus of jobs to suburban areas began in earnest during the 1970s. Since that time, analysts have studied the impact of "spatial mismatch" on the job prospects of African Americans stuck in cities as jobs moved outward. In subsequent decades, that pattern has become even more pronounced and more complex as more jobs have relocated to higher-income suburbs and more lower-income people have moved to suburbs. * * *

As these three forces reshape economic and demographic patterns, they are rendering obsolete the older lens through which the challenges associated with poverty in metropolitan America have been interpreted. Established assumptions about the characteristics of particular places, such as cities and suburbs, no longer hold. Yet the older models are not easily replaced by new labels since *the relationship* among places is central in shaping access to opportunity. Moreover, because the characteristics of place interact with the resources and connections of the people in them and because they vary in light of their history, places that are similar in some respects may, in fact, operate very differently when it comes to connecting residents to opportunity or providing safety nets to them.

These considerations suggest a two-dimensional model by which to characterize subsections of metropolitan areas. The first dimension measures the locational advantage of particular places. The literature on spatial mismatch and concentrated poverty indicates that two features of location are especially salient for low-income residents: the proximity of jobs and the proportion of residents in poverty. A related salient feature of location is fiscal capacity of the jurisdiction. * * * The second dimension characterizes the organizational-political endowment of particular places. The organizational endowment encompasses the myriad non-profit and public institutions that serve as a social safety net and springboard to opportunity for people in low-income communities. The political endowment refers to the capacity within the area to articulate the interests of low-income residents and effectively represent those interests in the arenas where their concerns can be addressed.

A closer look at each dimension, illustrated with examples from the Chicago metropolitan area, suggests how and why these locational advantages and organizational-political endowments vary across subregions within metropolitan areas. * * * Whether suburban residence translates into opportunity for low-income people depends heavily on the locational advantage of the suburban area. This may vary sharply by race and ethnicity. For example, * * * Latinos—who are disproportionately likely to be poor—have moved in the general direction of job growth over the past four decades, while African Americans—also more likely to be poor—have moved in the opposite direction. * * *

For low-income African Americans and Latinos who remain in the city, the locational disadvantages are less extreme than for those in the poor southern suburbs but the ongoing movement of jobs further north and west has increased the challenge they face in connecting to opportunity. African Americans in the poor south suburbs of Chicago are very likely to settle in areas with high levels of poverty and in political jurisdictions with extremely low fiscal capacity. For those who do, the disadvantages of location are extreme. Not only are they far from jobs, they suffer from the attendant ills of concentrated poverty with meager local public resources available for remedying their situation. For immigrants, the story is more complex. Although they are more likely to live closer to job centers, many low-income immigrants are clustered in declining industrial cities (Elgin, Aurora, and Joliet) that have been engulfed by the expansion of the Chicago metropolitan area. Their locational advantage is thus tempered by the dangers of creating new concentrations of poverty and by the limited fiscal capacity of these suburban jurisdictions. When low-income residents are concentrated in separate suburban jurisdictions, meager local fiscal resources make it impossible to reproduce one of the key economic ladders available in affluent suburbs, good schools.

The organizational/political endowments of places may help compensate for or they may exacerbate locational advantages and disadvantages. In many cities, earlier waves of European immigration and/or the more recent innovations of the War on Poverty in the 1960s left (an extremely varied) legacy of organizations dedicated to serving the poor. Indeed many vital institutions that serve low-income communities, such as social service agencies, hospitals, clinics, parks, and recreation centers were the hard-won fruit of community struggles of the 1960s. These institutions—both public and non-profit—have long played a vital role in providing services for the poor; since the 1996 welfare reform shifted policy away from cash assistance, they have been become critical elements of the safety net. These institutions have also played important roles in providing opportunity. Recent research on New York City shows how second generation immigrants can use these institutions to obtain a foothold on the economic ladder. The organizational endowment of these places is strengthened by the presence of local philanthropy. Cities also were (and in many cases remain) the sites of enormous wealth creation, reflected today in the presence of community and national foundations that have invested in the social infrastructure for the poor.

In most suburbs, created as places of private middle-class and working-class life, access to services and community institutions is more difficult for low-income residents. Suburbs have no comparable history that bequeathed a set of institutions designed to serve low-income residents. The network of nonprofit organizations that has developed in cities since the 1960s has no counterpart in the suburbs. Even when region-wide institutions, such as the United Way, try to expand their reach into the suburbs, they often can find no counterparts with which to connect. Likewise, suburbs do not have the philanthropic infrastructure to help support organizations that provide services to the poor. Moreover, the suburban public sector—apart from schools—is generally weak. In the Chicago metropolitan area, for example, this is evident in the absence of a public hospital in the suburban counties.

A similar contrast is evident when it comes to political voice for the poor. Cities, especially those in the North and Midwest, are likely to retain elements of machine politics that make voting more likely. But the poor are not especially powerful in urban politics: the greater advantage in cities stems from the presence of organizations dedicated to serving the poor, which supplies some political influence on their behalf. In some cities, nonprofits forge ties with politicians, creating a machine-like system of political patronage. Such arrangements can funnel dollars to poor neighborhoods even as they restrict the scope of political voice. In other cases, nonprofits can serve as a springboard for more independent advocacy. Public bureaucracies, for which service to the poor is a central mission, may also serve as influential advocates for the poor. In defending their own interests, for example, public hospitals and their employees can offer significant muscle to support institutions that serve the poor. Cities are also more likely to be home to organizing networks, such as ACORN and the Industrial Areas Foundation, and progressive labor unions seeking to mobilize more broadly.

By contrast, the weak organizational infrastructure of the suburbs makes it much more difficult to advocate on behalf of low-income residents. Lacking the residue of machine politics, suburbs typically offer few handholds for mobilizing new voters. Mayors and other politicians in very poor towns may be attentive to the needs of their residents but have little power to address them. In other suburban settings, politicians often devote more effort to discouraging the poor from settling there than to addressing their needs; this may be especially true when the low-income residents are immigrants or African Americans. The private and nonprofit institutions that do provide services in the suburbs, such as health care, are geared to more affluent clients and may be poorly equipped to serve those with less income. These agencies may also seek to avoid the costs associated with serving low-income clients.

I have presented these differences in organizational and political endowments as features that distinguish cities and suburbs but it is important to note that not all cities share these characteristics. Many cities, particularly the sunbelt cities that grew dramatically in the second half of the twentieth century, such as Houston and Phoenix, have no organizational legacy comparable to that of cities in the Northeast and Midwest. With distinct histories and political systems, these cities were late to develop a nonprofit sector and often lack a strong philanthropic community. And, as Amy Bridges has pointed out, the political systems of these cities are more akin to those of reform suburbs, where rule by a narrow set of elites was the norm and political institutions were designed to discourage political participation. * * *

2. CITY FORMATION

The idea that the law should make it easy for a group of people to join together to start their own community resonates with important aspects of our legal, political, and philosophical tradition. Perhaps it is not surprising, therefore, that most states make it relatively easy for the residents in a given area to join together to become an incorporated municipality. In most states, as Professor Richard Briffault explains in the excerpt that follows, "the principal criterion for deciding whether a municipality will be incorporated is whether the local people want it. There are few limits on local discretion." State law generally affords little basis for meaningful judicial review of decisions to incorporate and imposes few requirements that the views of residents of surrounding jurisdictions be considered in the incorporation decision.

Joining together to start a city, however, is not the same thing as joining together to start a business, or a club, or a civic association. The differences between these means of associating may suggest that state law should respond to municipal incorporation efforts with far less deference to the voice of "local" residents than Professor Briffault suggests that it currently does. We saw in Chapter I, in the case concerning the constitutionality of incorporating the City of Rajneeshpuram, a ground for incorporation that the law identifies as suspect. Gary Miller's excerpt considers another reason for municipal incorporation that state law might, but generally does not, deem suspect. Does it make sense for the law to question religiously-motivated municipal incorporation efforts more strictly than financially-motivated ones?

Some communities have the characteristics of cities but choose not to incorporate. Robert Lang and Dawn Dhavale consider such "reluctant cities" and explore why they prefer to remain unincorporated. They suggest that in some cases local government is irrelevant—communities obtain traditionally city-provided services privately or through larger governmental entities such as counties or state agencies. But for poor neighborhoods this status may be a cause for concern; the lines drawn for newly incorporated cities, together with the lines drawn by annexation decisions, often leave the poor in unincorporated areas to their disadvantage.[3]

If we are concerned about municipalities incorporating (or not incorporating) for the wrong reasons, our focus could be on reforming the legal rules that directly govern the process of incorporation. Alternatively, our focus could lie elsewhere. After all, state law regulates municipal incorporation not only directly but also indirectly through the legal consequences that it attaches to the act of incorporation and through the background rules that structure local incentives generally. For example, incorporation confers the right of local residents to impose taxes on property in the locality and to keep the tax revenues for themselves. Incorporation also permits the locality to exercise the zoning power. In this regard, consider whether a stricter approach to incorporation is likely to address the concerns that Gary Miller raises. Is there some other legal change that would address his concerns even better?

The subsection concludes with two cases, Board of Supervisors of Sacramento County v. Local Agency Formation Commission and City of Tucson v. Pima County. These cases examine the constitutionality of two very different incorporation processes. They raise the question: Should communities be allowed to incorporate at their own discretion, or should

---

[3]   Michelle Wilde Anderson, Mapped Out of Local Democracy, 62 Stan. L. Rev. 931 (2010); Michelle Wilde Anderson, Cities Inside Out: Race, Poverty, and Exclusion at the Urban Fringe, 55 U.C.L.A. L. Rev 1095 (2008).

affected neighboring communities be allowed to weigh in? They thus raise an issue that is central to the chapter as a whole: who determines who constitutes the local community? That question, while always difficult, is particularly acute in the context of analyzing the rules that govern the process of municipal incorporation. Prior to a municipality's incorporation, one cannot rely upon existing municipal boundary lines to define the local sphere and thereby evade the force of the question. Given this fundamental problem, it is important to pay attention to who decides, and to consider who should decide, how many separate jurisdictions should be created in America.

Professor Briffault explains that in most states decisions to incorporate are made by "insiders"—those who would be municipal residents if the incorporation effort were to succeed. The two cases excerpted below consider efforts to develop an alternative approach, in which "outsiders"—persons who would not fall within the local boundary if the incorporation effort were to succeed—have an important input into the incorporation decision. Even if we agree on who should decide whether a community may incorporate, there remains the question of what process should be used in making the decision. Professor Briffault explains that state law usually requires residents to incorporate through a referendum. In California, however, the state subjects the local referendum to further review by an expert, unelected agency, and Arizona requires the consent of the neighboring city government. Does it make sense to have municipal incorporation determinations made through popular voting rather than some other means? Notice that the question of who decides whether an incorporation request should be granted is related to the question of the process by which such incorporation decisions are made. California permitted "insiders" to vote democratically to incorporate but permitted "outsiders" to provide input into the incorporation decision only bureaucratically. An alternative approach would be to make incorporation decisions subject to regional referenda— these determinations would be democratic (like most incorporation decisions now are) but regional (like most incorporation decisions now are not). Would it be practical to subject municipal incorporation decisions to regional referenda? Would it be more "democratic" to have appointed regional bodies review local incorporation referenda than to permit such referenda to be determinative in the absence of regional, bureaucratic review?

RICHARD BRIFFAULT, OUR LOCALISM: PART I— THE STRUCTURE OF LOCAL GOVERNMENT LAW
90 Colum. L. Rev. 1, 73–77 (1990).

The law of local government formation is primarily about municipal incorporation. * * * In most states, general enabling legislation places municipal incorporation in the hands of local residents or landowners. State laws provide for the initiation of the process by petitions signed by some number or percentage of local residents or landowners. Thereafter, an election is held in which local residents or landowners participate, and if a requisite percentage of the local electorate approves the incorporation goes forward.[311] Neighboring localities, regional entities and residents outside of the boundaries of the territory proposed to be incorporated generally have no role. Judicial or administrative review is usually ministerial and limited to a determination of whether the signature, voting and other formal requirements have been met.

The principal criterion for deciding whether a municipality will be incorporated is whether the local people want it. There are few limits on local discretion. In many states, the principal requirement is that the incorporators provide a map describing an area of contiguous, unincorporated land containing a population greater than the statutorily prescribed minimum. The statutory minima are often quite small: in some states as few as seventy-five people may suffice for an incorporation. Thus, if a relatively small number of people living on unincorporated land want to create their own municipality, and they can persuade a majority of their neighbors to agree, then they are likely to be able to form that government.

Some states go further and require that the local population be concentrated; that the land be "urban" or suitable for urban development; that the proposed municipality have the need and ability to pay for governmental services; or that the people share a "community of interest." These standards appear to go beyond the subjective local desire for incorporation and suggest an inquiry into whether there is an objective need for a new government. They also indicate a concern for the burden of government on local residents, especially landowners. These requirements, however, do not address the effect of the formation of a new government on the surrounding area, the region or the state.

These additional criteria often prove to be without bite. Courts have treated the local desire for municipal government, as revealed by the incorporation request, as dispositive of the question of local benefit from incorporation. Similarly, the courts have been disinclined to use the "community of interest" requirement as a substantive standard. Courts

---

[311] * * * Many states limit the right to petition for an incorporation or an annexation to landowners in the area proposed to be incorporated or annexed. In re Char, 59 Ohio App. 2d 146, 149–50, 392 N.E.2d 1312, 1314–15 (1978) (construing Ohio law making "good of territory" principal criterion for annexation approval to mean best interests of area landowners since statute limits right to petition for annexation to owners of real estate). It is generally assumed that such a limitation raises no constitutional question since the petition is not itself an election triggering the one person, one vote principle. See, e.g., Berry v. Bourne, 588 F.2d 422, 425 (4th Cir.1978); Township of Jefferson v. City of West Carrollton, 517 F.Supp. 417, 420–21 (S.D.Ohio 1981), aff'd mem., 718 F.2d 1099 (6th Cir.1983) * * *.

have sustained proposed incorporations of areas lacking common stores, businesses, schools or social and cultural amenities, in the face of contentions that the lack of such common facilities negated the presence of a "community of interest." In these cases, "community" was often supplied by the common demand for municipal services, as evidenced by the petition for incorporation.

Similarly, courts have found a "community of interest" even when the area proposed for incorporation was only a small piece of a larger area that arguably comprised a true "community" of common economic and social interactions. There is nothing in the incorporation criteria in most states to preclude incorporators from drawing lines that bring in high-tax or elite residential properties and fence out tax-exempt lands or poor or black people. As a general rule, the impact of the incorporation on the well-being and development of the broader "community" outside the proposed municipal borders is not a factor in judicial review of the incorporation or the proposed boundaries.

Local incorporations may be based on the desires of ethnic or economic groups to separate themselves politically from their neighbors, to wield planning and zoning authority, to control the pace of growth and to restrict local taxable wealth for their immediate uses. Local governments may be created, and usually are, without any regard to differences in wealth among localities or to the fact that incorporation may aggravate those differences or interfere with regional approaches to economic and social problems. Incorporation subtracts land and revenues from the surrounding jurisdiction and denies it to other localities in the area. Incorporation on the urban fringe precludes the extension of central city boundaries to recapture middle-class residents who have moved to outlying areas. In most states, none of this provides a legal basis for challenging or denying an incorporation. Instead, these factors often constitute practical incentives to incorporate.

Despite the lack of a right to local self-government, courts often treat the formation of a local government as a healthy development, reflecting an area's growth and the democratic desires of its residents. This combination of liberal incorporation laws and indulgent judicial attitudes has resulted in a multitude of municipalities—more than 19,000 of them. Many of these municipalities are quite small. More than three-quarters of all municipalities have fewer than 5,000 inhabitants, and fewer than 500 municipalities have populations greater than 50,000. In most metropolitan areas, there are dozens of independent municipalities. * * *

GARY J. MILLER, THE POLITICAL ORIGINS
OF THE LAKEWOOD PLAN

From Gary Miller, Cities By Contract 17, 20–22, 34–35, 37, 81–83, 85 (1981).

North of Long Beach City College and the Douglas Aircraft plant [in Los Angels County] was a small group of houses, among the bean fields and hog farms, called Lakewood Village. In 1949, one of the inhabitants of Lakewood Village was a young lawyer named John Todd. He was a member of the Lakewood Taxpayers' Association, a group which, in Todd's words, "had a strong feeling that Lakewood Village should remain unincorporated. They professed some fear of the city of Long Beach, but expressed a much greater fear of incorporation of the area as the city of Lakewood. To even mention or suggest the same was worse than slurring motherhood." * * * In response, Todd suggested that Lakewood could afford to incorporate if it could contract with the county for the performance of municipal services, in order to avoid costly investments in buildings and equipment. * * * "This, then, was the beginning of the Lakewood Plan."

By mid-1953, with South Lakewood lost to Long Beach, sentiment for incorporation on the basis of county contracting was growing. An incorporation committee was formed, and the businessmen who backed Todd hired a contracting firm called Boyle Engineering to study the possibility. In December, 1953, the Boyle Report was issued, and became the "Bible for the incorporation movement."

The Boyle Report recommended that the city contract with Los Angeles County for road maintenance, health services, law enforcement, a building department, and planning services. The city could remain in the Lakewood sewer maintenance district, the county library district, and the local recreation and park district, and it could contract with a private firm for garbage collection.

Having carefully developed public sentiment for incorporation, the incorporation committee set out to obtain signatures for an incorporation petition. * * * An election was held in March, and the people of Lakewood voted for incorporation by a 60 percent majority. Said Todd, "no one in the city of Long Beach had given the Lakewood incorporation movement a ghost of a chance." * * *

Thus, a new option was presented to the residents of unincorporated urban areas in Los Angeles County. Previously, the options had been basically three in number: (1) remaining under county jurisdiction, without local control over local services and without the power to zone and determine land-use patterns; (2) being annexed and effectively swallowed up by an older neighboring city with large municipal tax rates and perhaps a large population of individuals with different life-styles; or (3) incorporating, and trying to support a police force, fire department, and other urban services with a small tax base. Under pressure from an intense annexation campaign, the first alternative seemed to disappear. The new option, which came to be called the Lakewood Plan, provided the advantages of local autonomy that went with incorporation, but without the expense of creating new bureaucracies to provide necessary services. Tax rates could be kept low by relying on services provided cheaply by the county.

This plan became even more attractive in 1956 with the passage of the Bradley-Burns sales tax, which allowed both cities and counties to participate in a uniform sales tax program at the fixed rate of 1 percent. By thus encouraging a uniform local sales tax, it provided a source of revenue for cities that had previously feared that a local sales tax would force shoppers to other cities. The revenue from the sales tax suggested the possibility of paying for county contracts with sales tax revenue, thus avoiding a municipal property tax altogether.

The popularity of this new option was immediate. In 1956 four new cities incorporated; in 1957, ten; in 1958, two; in 1959, four; in 1960, five. Twenty-six new cities had been created in seven years. Over 580,000 people lived in these cities. By 1970, six more cities had been created, and the population of the combined 32 new cities was over 870,000. All but one of the new cities (Downey) relied primarily on contracting rather than the creation of new bureaucracies for the delivery of urban services. * * *

[W]hy were so many urban communities determined to resist annexation to established cities? Why was incorporation under the Lakewood Plan the preferred option? Most proponents of incorporation explain this preference as springing from a desire to "preserve a local identity" or to "gain local control"; but neither of these responses is entirely satisfactory. For instance, many incorporations did not preserve an identifiable local community. On the contrary, incorporations like those of Bradbury and Irwindale were secessions from long-established unincorporated communities. Others represented agglomerations of several communities, like Pico Rivera and La Canada-Flintridge. Still others, like Commerce and Cerritos, were completely artificial constructs, unrelated to any traditional community. Some clearly identifiable communities like Lancaster voted down incorporation repeatedly, while Centinela, East Whittier, and other established localities quietly let themselves be annexed. Those cities that did incorporate around traditional community boundaries, Downey and Lakewood, for example, often immediately sought annexation of territory far beyond the boundaries of the original community. So "preservation of local identity" is related in no systematic or satisfactory way to municipal incorporation.

The motive of "gaining local control" is also too vague to be satisfactory. Certainly, the creation of an autonomous, authoritative local government is undertaken in order to ensure that local rather than nonlocal interests control decisions—but which decisions? What aspects of municipal government are so crucial that some people will devote hundreds of hours a year, for as many as ten years, to ensure that the local community be incorporated rather than annexed? * * * The explanation for municipal incorporations * * * lies in the basic similarity of individuals summarized by the economic notions of price and income elasticity of demand. Incorporating around a considerable revenue resource allows inhabitants to procure services at a low tax price. Even incorporations around a small tax base can be explained in terms of the centrality of the revenue function and the relative redistributional advantage of incorporating as opposed to being annexed to another community. * * * While other motivations for incorporation (like stricter regulation of land use) influenced at least the leaders in some incorporation movements, the most basic and pervasive common denominator for incorporation was the avoidance of high property taxation. It was explicitly used as the central theme in most incorporation campaigns * * *. Where the leaders of an incorporation campaign were unable to convince the electorate that the city would not require a high property tax, the incorporation failed at the polls. This is true in the case of wealthy communities like Malibu in 1976, and in the case of the east Los Angeles ghetto in 1973. * * *

The only economic explanation for over half of the incorporations in Los Angeles County since 1954 is that there was a sizeable group of individuals who did not want to belong to local governments that would tax them in order to provide local services. So far as these individuals were concerned, Long Beach, Whittier, El Monte, and other old-line cities were supplying something they didn't want to buy. The issue was redistributional; since municipal services are essentially private goods, there is no reason for an individual taxpayer to purchase them from local governments unless it is cheaper to do so, that is, the market price is subsidized at someone else's expense through collective provision. But the middle-class and upper-class taxpayers knew that collective provision of public goods in these old-line, property-taxing cities would be at their expense. Incorporation into non-property-taxing cities was the alternative.

Lacking a redistributional advantage, there is no reason for essentially private goods to be supplied collectively. Police protection can be partially replaced by means of dogs, automatic alarms, fences, guns, and maintenance of a high-income neighborhood. Fire protection can be provided voluntarily (as it is in the most recent Lakewood Plan city, La Habra Heights) even if it means the lowest possible fire insurance rating (as it does in La Habra Heights). Parks and recreation can be provided by means of backyard tennis courts and swimming pools. Books can be purchased rather than taken from the library. The cities of Rolling Hills and Bradbury even rely on privately maintained roads, which incidentally help keep out the criminal element. The Lakewood Plan cities were created and are operated as "minimal cities," not for reasons of efficiency, but as a way out for property owners who didn't want to pay for the municipal provision of private or redistributional services. * * *

The advantages of the Lakewood Plan for middle-class and upper-class home owners are obvious. First, the bureaucratic pressures for governmental expansion are cleanly eliminated by contracting. Contracting for services guarantees that there will never be a homegrown bureaucracy pushing for new services and the expansion of old ones. Secondly, by gaining control of the zoning function, Lakewood Plan cities can direct the makeup of the population to exclude service-demanding, low-income, or renting populations. Most importantly, permanent walls around local property can be erected to guarantee that high-tax-rate cities will not use local homes as a resource for governmental expansion. * * *

ROBERT E. LANG AND DAWN DHAVALE, RELUCTANT CITIES? EXPLORING BIG UNINCORPORATED CENSUS DESIGNATED PLACES

Metropolitan Institute at Virginia Tech, Census Note 03:01, pp. 1–4 (July 2003).

Census Designated Places (CDPs) are the Rodney Dangerfields of urban geography—they get no respect. The public does not understand them and researchers often overlook CDPs because they are seen as census-derived statistical artifacts as opposed to "real" places. Yet a CDP is a residential concentration whose population sees itself as belonging to a specific place, even if the place is not an official city. In that sense, a CDP is a real place and their formation and growth warrant some analysis. The census devised the CDP category to capture urban development that falls outside cities. CDPs range in size from less than 100 to over 100,000 residents. The term dates to 1980, replacing the even less evocative label "unincorporated places." Most large population clusters in the US are officially defined as cities, especially those with more than 50,000 residents. But 1 in 10 places (or 61 of 601) that rise above this threshold is a CDP. Forty one of these big CDPs are unincorporated, while the remaining 20 are incorporated as places other than cities such as "townships." We focus on the 41 big unincorporated CDPs and consider why they remain unincorporated—or in our description "reluctant cities." * * *

Unincorporated CDPs and incorporated places differ in that the latter have legal powers and responsibilities, while CDPs can function as de facto cities without official designation. State and county governments recognize CDPs, but the unincorporated ones have no municipal government of their own. This census note provides a window into why some large urban places never undergo the formal process of becoming incorporated cities. It is especially interesting to consider situations where it appears that no need exists for municipal-level government. We believe that in some cases, local conditions render "cities" all but irrelevant. We look at CDPs above 50,000 because such places are big enough to constitute midsized cities. The 50,000 mark is also used by the census as the minimum size for a city to serve as the primary central city in a metropolitan area. As a group, big CDPs are perhaps the least studied urban phenomena in America. We offer this preliminary descriptive analysis as an exploratory read of these places. While we examine places above 50,000, most CDPs are far smaller. Modest-sized CDPs can make up a big share of metropolitan areas. Consider, for example, that the majority of residents in Washington's metropolitan area live in CDPs below 50,000 in the large Maryland and Virginia suburban counties surrounding the District of Columbia. In the past, many modest-sized CDPs might have formed incorporated local governments below the level of cities. Perhaps, in a future analysis we might find that modest-sized unincorporated CDPs are essentially "reluctant townships." * * *

Only five big unincorporated CDPs top 100,000 residents. Three of these places are in suburban Las Vegas, NV. The Los Angeles and New Orleans metropolitan areas are home to the other 100,000-plus big CDPs. Six big CDPs have from 75,000 to 100,000 residents. There are 30 big CDPs that range between 50,000 to 75,000 people. These places scatter around the nation, but are typically found in the most populous states. Finally, many of the big unincorporated CDP names strike us as a bit contrived—as in probably picked by market research consultants hired by developers. Consider such places as Town 'n' Country, The Woodlands, Casas Adobes, Fountainbleau and Rancho Cordova. Any list of places that starts with Paradise as its biggest example is likely to include lots of market-driven names. * * * The demographic data * * * indicates that, as a group, big unincorporated CDPs are similar to the US as a whole. Big CDPs are slightly more diverse than the nation, with a 64 percent non-Hispanic white population as opposed to 69 percent for the US. But recall that many big CDPs are in large urban states such as California and Florida so their diversity is not surprising. The most diverse big unincorporated CDPs are Florence-Graham and East Los Angeles CDPs in the Los Angeles metropolitan area, which are one and two percent non-Hispanic white respectively. Palm Harbor, FL and Levittown, PA CDPs are the least diverse places, with populations that are over 93 percent non-Hispanic white. * * * [B]ig unincorporated CDPs * * * exceed 40 percent of households married with children, which greatly surpasses the figure for the US. Two of these places—Highlands Ranch, CO and The Woodlands, TX—are large master planned communities that also have a mostly white population of affluent homeowners. By contrast, Florence-Graham, CA, the other big CDP with 40 plus percent of married households with kids, has an almost entirely minority population, and has a very low percentage of homeowners. The vast majority of big unincorporated CDPs lie in major metropolitan areas, including Los Angeles, Washington-Baltimore, Atlanta, Miami, Houston and Denver. We find that despite their relatively large size, most of our big CDPs are not heavily urban places. Most are dominated by residences rather than business. There are few real satellite cities in the list, although Bethesda, MD does contain a large downtown complete with office towers and a subway line. Perhaps the most urban big unincorporated CDP is Paradise, NV, which contains most of the enormous hotels along the Las Vegas Strip. Paradise also has a low percentage of single family detached homes, and contains a far lower percentage of homeowners and households with children than the US as a whole. * * *

Why do some places that reach the population of mid-sized cities not bother to incorporate? We believe that two main conditions explain the rise of big unincorporated CDPs as reluctant cities. There are instances where strong county-level government assumes the role of municipal services and therefore negates the need or incentive to incorporate. There are also places where large private governments emerged in the form of homeowners' associations that provide essentially the same services as municipalities. Because the homeowners' association fees in these places are often high (and not tax deductible), residents may resist an additional layer of what they see as redundant and expensive government. In reluctant cities, governance falls to private organizations, or to larger public structures such as the county. Some places exhibit both these trends, such as Miami and Las Vegas. We consider both these conditions below. The key unifying force we believe is that some alternate form of government fills the service vacuum in the absence of incorporation. Behind the reluctance to form a city is not some strident anti-government ethos, but rather a strategic call that municipal government is unnecessary. * * *

BOARD OF SUPERVISORS OF SACRAMENTO COUNTY v. LOCAL AGENCY FORMATION COMMISSION

Supreme Court of California, 1992.
3 Cal.4th 903, 13 Cal.Rptr.2d 245, 838 P.2d 1198,
cert. denied, 507 U.S. 988, 113 S.Ct. 1588, 123 L.Ed.2d 154 (1993).

MOSK, JUSTICE.

Residents of an unincorporated area of Sacramento County seek to incorporate into a city. Government Code section 57103 provides that only the voters residing in the territory to be incorporated may vote to confirm the incorporation. The Court of Appeal found this law unconstitutional as applied, holding that it violates the guaranty of equal protection of the laws. We conclude that the law is constitutional, both on its face and as applied to the incorporation at issue.

The case before us illustrates the tension between California's financially beleaguered counties and the desire of residents of unincorporated areas to form cities and draw local government closer to home. With the fall in tax rates following the adoption of Proposition 13 in 1978, and a concomitant population-driven rise in demand for services, this tension has grown in recent years: at least one California county has considered bankruptcy and, like the state itself, all counties have had to make painful spending decisions. The counties fear that if tax-rich districts form cities, the counties will be deprived of revenue and their financial position further weakened. On the other hand, community residents and landowners often prefer to govern their local affairs insofar as possible, and cityhood provides them with greater opportunities for self-determination than does residence or ownership in a more amorphous unincorporated area. The evolution of cities is a natural process when population grows and communities begin to form their own identities.

Acknowledging the tension between fiscal concerns and the desire for self-government, the Legislature enacted the Cortese-Knox Local Government Reorganization Act of 1985. * * * The * * * Act requires that every unconsolidated county have a local agency formation commission, appointed by local lawmaking bodies, to "review and approve or disapprove with or without amendment, wholly, partially, or conditionally, proposals for changes of organization or reorganization * * *." The commission cannot act on an incorporation petition unless signed by not less than 25 percent of the registered voters residing in the territory of the proposed city or by not less than 25 percent of the landowners, which latter group must also own not less than 25 percent of the assessed land value. * * * [T]he commission * * * [has] the power to approve or disapprove an incorporation in whole or in part. But the Cortese-Knox Act does not give the commission carte blanche to approve incorporations. Its discretion is limited by [the] requirement[ ], among others, * * * that the proposed city likely will be fiscally sound for three fiscal years following its incorporation. * * * In reviewing an incorporation proposal, the commission is required to consider a multitude of factors.[7]

---

[7]   These include but are not limited to:

"(a) Population, population density; land area and land use; per capita assessed valuation; topography [and] natural boundaries * * *; proximity to other populated areas; the likelihood of significant growth in the area, and in adjacent incorporated and unincorporated areas, during the next 10 years.

(b) * * * [T]he present cost and adequacy of governmental services * * *; probable future needs for those services. * * *

(c) The effect of the proposed action * * * on adjacent areas, on mutual social and economic interests, and on the local governmental structure of the county. * * *"

* * * The commission may make its approval conditional on a virtually limitless array of factors, which are set forth in detail in * * * [the Act].[8] * * * After the commission has completed its inquiry and issued a resolution approving or disapproving the proposal, a county, or others affected by the decision, may request reconsideration. * * * Once the commission has issued its final resolution, the matter is in the hands of the "conducting authority," which in this case is the Sacramento County Board of Supervisors. The board must conduct a public hearing on the proposal. If more than 50 percent of the voters in the territory to be incorporated protest the incorporation, the board must end the proceedings. Otherwise it must order the incorporation, subject to the voters' "confirmation."

As the foregoing recitation reveals, the voters' role under the Cortese-Knox Act in confirming an incorporation is rather like that of the masons who place a keystone at the apex of a high and intricate arch. The voters' approval is an essential piece, but as we have shown, by the time the question reaches the electorate the incorporation proposal will already have undergone a labyrinthine process containing elaborate safeguards designed to protect the political and economic interests of affected local governments, residents, and landowners. * * *

In 1986 persons in the unincorporated Sacramento County community of Citrus Heights, containing a population of approximately 69,000, collected enough valid signatures to qualify an incorporation petition to the Sacramento County Local Agency Formation Commission (commission), which * * * [under the Cortese-Knox Act] supervises municipal incorporations in the county. Following an environmental review and other proceedings, the commission * * * approved a resolution * * * [which] contained a provision designed to mitigate the financial impact on the county: the proposed city limits were relocated to exclude a sales-tax-rich shopping center. Requests for reconsideration of that resolution followed, in part on the ground that the boundaries still unfairly impacted the county's tax base. The commission adopted a new resolution that moved another shopping center outside the proposed city limits, and then, to further mitigate the county's financial loss, amended that resolution to require that the new city's receipt of property taxes be phased in more slowly. In accordance with section 57103, the commission ordered a confirming election to be held only within the territory of the proposed city.

---

[8] These include reimbursement for the acquisition or use of public property, apportionment of bond obligations between the county and the proposed city, the incurring of new debt, property transfers, employee discharges and modification or termination of employment contracts, and the transfer of authority and responsibility among any affected cities and counties for the administration of special tax and special assessment districts.

This lawsuit followed. Plaintiffs include the Sacramento County Board of Supervisors, the Sacramento County Deputy Sheriffs' Association, and Sacramentans to Save our Services. * * * Displeased, among other things, with the law's limitation of the confirming election to the voters in the territory to be incorporated, plaintiffs challenged the limitation's constitutionality on the ground that section 57103 denies them equal protection of the laws. (U.S. Const., Amend. XIV, § 1; Cal. Const., art. 1, § 7.) * * * The question we confront * * * is whether section 57103 impinges on the right to vote in a manner that requires the application of strict scrutiny. As will appear, the statute does not compel that standard of review.

We agree that section 57103 touches on the right to vote. As it happens, the right to vote does not include a right to compel the state to provide any electoral mechanism whatever for changes of municipal organization. Such line-drawing is a function that the Legislature may reserve to itself. But when the state has provided for the voters' direct input, the equal protection clause requires that those similarly situated not be treated differently unless the disparity is justified. * * * [F]ederal precedent requires that we view all Sacramento County residents as similarly situated, for all are affected to some degree by the proposed incorporation.

The mere fact, however, that a state law touches on the right to vote does not necessarily require the application of strict scrutiny. Rather, "the 'compelling interest' measure must be applied if a classification has a 'real and appreciable impact' upon the equality, fairness and integrity of the electoral process." (*Choudhry v. Free* (1976) 17 Cal.3d 660, 664, 131 Cal.Rptr. 654, 552 P.2d 438.) * * * [S]ection 57103's impact in the case before us falls well short of the "real and appreciable," for individual interests in voting are much attenuated by the state's plenary power to oversee and regulate the formation of its political subdivisions, and the same power entitles the state to identify as differing in degree the interests of those who may vote under section 57103 and those who may not.

In our federal system the states are sovereign but cities and counties are not; in California as elsewhere they are mere creatures of the state and exist only at the state's sufferance. Accordingly, the United States Supreme Court has long recognized the states' plenary power to create and dissolve their political subdivisions. In *Hunter v. Pittsburgh* (1907) 207 U.S. 161, 28 S.Ct. 40, 52 L.Ed. 151, * * * [t]he federal high court, noting that "[m]unicipal corporations are political subdivisions of the State," concluded, "The number, nature and duration of the powers conferred upon these corporations and the territory over which they shall be exercised rests in the absolute discretion of the State. * * *" The foregoing language is, of course, immediately noteworthy for the breadth of its scope, and to a certain extent it bespeaks the judicial confidence of a simpler era. But *Hunter's* fundamental holding survives. * * * Thus, though the right to vote is perforce implicated whenever the state specifies that certain people may vote and others may not, we conclude that the essence of this case is not the fundamental right to vote, but the state's plenary power to set the conditions under which its political subdivisions are created. For that reason, the impairment of the right to vote is insufficiently implicated to demand the application of strict scrutiny.

We reach the foregoing conclusion notwithstanding our prior decisions in this area. *Fullerton* [*Joint Union High School Dist. v. State Bd. of Education* (1982) 32 Cal.3d 779, 805, 187 Cal.Rptr. 398, 654 P.2d 168 (*Fullerton*)], considered the constitutionality of a State Board of Education * * * decision to carve a new school district in Yorba Linda from its Fullerton parent. The education board ordered an election to be held on the secession, and ordered the question submitted to the Yorba Linda electorate only. *Fullerton* overturned the education board's decision. * * *

The issue in *Citizens* [*Against Forced Annexation v. Local Agency Formation Com.* (1982) 32 Cal.3d 816, 826, 187 Cal.Rptr. 423, 654 P.2d 193 (*Citizens*)] was whether the Municipal Organization Act of 1977 constitutionally entitled the state to limit an election to confirm an annexation to residents of the territory to be annexed. The city in question had about 40,000 voters, while the territory to be annexed had about a quarter as many. The Legislature had provided that although under certain circumstances, applicable in *Citizens*, the territory's voters must confirm the annexation, the annexing city's voters could also vote to confirm the joinder only if, as relevant to the analysis in *Citizens*, the number of registered voters in the territory was 50 percent or more of those in the city. * * *

We decided that "the establishment of the legal relationship contemplated in this case, like the dissolution of a legal relationship involved in *Fullerton*, has a substantial effect upon the residents of both territories involved. We therefore conclude that the relevant geographic confines, for the purpose of constitutional analysis, include[ ] both the affected territory and the affected city. We must therefore inquire whether the restrictions * * * serve a compelling state interest and are necessary to further that purpose."

Applying strict scrutiny, we noted that the government may have a compelling interest to limit the vote to those "specially interested in the matter at issue." * * * [W]e decided that the state has a compelling interest in permitting unincorporated areas to join cities "even if the city's residents oppose annexation," because the state's interest in "promoting orderly and logical community development, and of providing municipal services to newly urbanized regions" was "of compelling importance," and the state's interest would be thwarted if city residents could veto the annexation.

Because *Citizens* commanded a majority of this court, it requires our considered reexamination. As we now explain, we conclude in hindsight that the reasoning in that case was questionable. * * *

To the extent that *Citizens* is inconsistent with the constitutional principles set forth in this opinion, it is not to be followed. * * * If we were to follow *Citizens*, and apply strict scrutiny, we would now be compelled to declare section 57103 invalid on constitutional grounds. Such a holding would greatly unbalance the Legislature's careful accommodation of competing local governmental and private interests in the subsequently enacted Cortese-Knox Act and would undermine the lawmakers' power over the existence of cities and counties. In such circumstances stare decisis carries less weight. * * *

We conclude that under applicable precedent we should apply a deferential standard in evaluating the classification set forth on the face of section 57103. The Legislature's traditional power to regulate the formation of political subdivisions allows it to decide that the county residents living outside the territory to be incorporated have a lesser degree of interest in the proposed incorporation than those within, in which case the classification must be denied effect only if it lacks a rational basis. * * *

In section 56001 [of the Cortese-Knox Act] the Legislature announced a policy "to encourage orderly growth and development * * * essential to the social, fiscal, and economic well-being of the state," and stated that "the logical formation and determination of local agency boundaries is an important factor in promoting orderly development * * *. [T]he Legislature further finds and declares that this policy should be effected by the logical formation and modification of the boundaries of local agencies."

The foregoing sufficiently shows a legitimate purpose in enacting section 57103. And we conclude that section 57103 is fairly related to the Legislature's declared purpose, for, if large, relatively disinterested majorities could veto incorporations decided through the Cortese-Knox Act's elaborate process, the result might well hinder orderly growth and development. * * * Unlike in *Fullerton*, which involved a discretionary agency decision to hold an election, the Cortese-Knox Act was constructed with a mighty bulwark against the exercise of arbitrary discretion. The act accommodates competing local governmental and private interests, narrowly channeling the commission's ultimate determination before the territory's voters consider the decision. The election merely asks the affected residents to confirm that they desire self-government. To deny the Legislature the authority to let the potentially incorporating territory's voters have the final say in the matter would be to lessen political participation, not increase it. We do not believe that result is required by our federal and state Constitutions. * * *

CITY OF TUCSON v. PIMA COUNTY
Court of Appeals of Arizona, 2001.
199 Ariz. 509, 19 P.3d 650.

EHRLICH, JUDGE.

The ultimate issue presented by this case is whether it is constitutional for the Arizona state legislature to require the consent of a proximate municipality before an area may incorporate. We conclude that the statute requiring such permission as a predicate to municipal incorporation, Ariz. Rev. Stat. § 9–101.01(B)(1) (1996), is constitutional, and we therefore affirm the superior court's judgment dismissing the appellants' contrary contentions. * * *

A.R.S. section 9–101.01 * * * states, in relevant part:

A.   Notwithstanding any other provision of law to the contrary, all territory within six miles of an incorporated city or town, as the same now exists or may hereafter be established, having a population of five thousand or more as shown by the most recent federal census, and all territory within three miles of any incorporated city or town, as the same now exists or may hereafter be established, having a population of less than five thousand as shown by the most recent federal census is declared to be an urbanized area.

B.   No territory within an urbanized area shall hereafter be incorporated as a city or town, and the board of supervisors shall have no jurisdiction to take any action upon a petition to incorporate a city or town within such area, unless:

1.   There is submitted with the petition for incorporation a resolution adopted by the city or town causing the urbanized area to exist approving the proposed incorporation; or

2.   There is filed with the board of supervisors an affidavit stating that a proper and legal petition has been presented to the city or town causing the urbanized area to exist requesting annexation of the area proposed for incorporation and such petition has not been approved by a valid ordinance of annexation within one hundred twenty days of its presentation.

In April 1997, * * * proponents of incorporating the areas known as Tortolita and Casas Adobes to file incorporation petitions with the Pima

County Division of Elections. Both Tortolita and Casas Adobes are within the relevant distance of the City of Tucson and the Towns of Marana and Oro Valley to qualify as "urbanized areas." * * * [T]he superior court held that A.R.S. section 9–101.01(B)(1) is constitutional * * * The appellants contend that A.R.S. section 9–101.01(B) violates the voting-rights doctrine of the Equal Protection Clause of the Fourteenth Amendment of the United States Constitution. The specific argument is that the petition process of A.R.S. section 9–101 triggers a fundamental right to vote and that the consent requirement in section 9–101.01(B) unconstitutionally burdens this right by giving a veto to the city or town that caused the urbanized area to exist. * * *

There is no constitutional right to vote for municipal incorporation. *Hussey v. City of Portland*, 64 F.3d 1260, 1263 (9th Cir.1995) ("There is no federal constitutional right to vote on municipal annexations."); *Hunter v. City of Pittsburgh*, 207 U.S. 161, 28 S.Ct. 40, 52 L.Ed. 151 (1907). * * * The appellants * * * argue that the Equal Protection Clause is violated because only those within the "urbanized area" need to acquire a city's consent. * * * The Equal Protection Clause does not preclude the establishment of distinct classes within a geographic area if the classifications are reasonably related to a legitimate state interest and all persons within the class are treated equally. * * * The state * * * has the power to shape municipalities and to protect the interests of those within existing cities and towns concerning the formation of new political subdivisions. As the superior court concluded * * *:

> It is obvious from the reading of [section] 9–101.01 that the intent of the legislature in enacting it was to grant some control to existing cities and towns with regard to proposed incorporations of areas close to their boundaries. The result of [appellants'] construction would be a proliferation of small towns within a short distance of large cities and the attendant inefficient and uneconomical provision of government services. That does not appear to have been the intent of the legislature. * * *

See also Holt, 439 U.S. at 70–75, 99 S.Ct. 383 (protecting a municipality's interests is a rational basis and city's "governance without the franchise" over outlying area did not violate equal protection); *Town of Lockport v. Citizens for Community Action*, 430 U.S. 259, 268–69, 97 S.Ct. 1047, 51 L.Ed.2d 313 (1977) (state could require county charter approval by both a majority of voters within cities and a separate majority of voters outside of cities because each area had distinct interests in outcome); *Hunter*, 207 U.S. at 178–79, 28 S.Ct. 40.

In this case, given the obvious political and economic implications of consolidation, the incorporation of areas such as Tortolita and Casas

Adobes was made subject to the consent of those in contiguous areas of Pima County: the Towns of Marana and Oro Valley, and the City of Tucson. The policy embodied by A.R.S. section 9–101.01 bears a rational relationship to a legitimate state interest and so does not violate the Equal Protection Clause. * * *

3. THE DISTINCTION BETWEEN RESIDENTS AND NON-RESIDENTS

The materials in the last subsection suggest an important distinction between insiders and outsiders. This subsection begins a more detailed consideration of the relationship between city residents and outsiders. The following three cases provide the federal constitutional background within which states may establish rules regarding the formal political authority of residents and non-residents with respect to one another.

The case of Holt Civic Club v. City of Tuscaloosa involves a city's exercise of regulatory power on people who live outside its borders and who have no formal voice in electing city officials or determining city policy. This kind of exercise of extraterritorial power over neighboring areas is very common in the United States.[4] Yet, as Justice Brennan argues in his dissenting opinion, such a practice of extraterritorial regulation raises fundamental questions about "our basic conception of a 'political community.'" How can an exercise of extraterritorial power be justified? Should formal jurisdiction (police or otherwise) matter given the extra-territorial impacts that all jurisdictions have upon one another, and the interest that those living outside a jurisdiction may have in the policies of that jurisdiction? What impact does the *Holt Civic Club* case have on the ability of central cities to regulate suburban residents?

The decision can also be considered from a different perspective. The majority and the dissent each focus on the rights of those living outside the municipal boundary line to be free from regulation by a government in which they have no say. The case also implicitly addresses, however, the rights of persons to have a say in a government that has no formal jurisdiction over them. Interestingly, while the majority and the dissent disagree as to proper answer to the first question, they seem to agree as to the proper answer to the second question: Holt residents have no right to vote in Tuscaloosa elections if Tuscaloosa has no police jurisdiction over Holt. Would it help or hurt central cities to permit non-residents (such as suburbanites) to vote in central city elections? Would your view change if,

---

[4] See generally, Richard Briffault, The Local Government Boundary Problem in Metropolitan Areas, 48 Stan. L. Rev. 1115 (1996); Comment, The Constitutionality of the Exercise of Extraterritorial Powers by Municipalities, 45 Chi. L. Rev. 151 (1977); David Becker, Municipal Boundaries and Zoning: Controlling Regional Land Development, 1966 Wash. U. L. Q. 1; Frank Sengstock, Extraterritorial Powers in the Metropolitan Area (1962); Russell Maddox, The Extraterritorial Powers of Municipalities in the United States (1955).

in return, central city residents were permitted to vote in suburban elections?

The next two cases, May v. Town of Mountain Village and Wit v. Berman, bring this question more directly to the fore. The *May* case addresses whether non-resident landowners may vote in municipal elections. It upholds the inclusion of such voters against a constitutional challenge. Is there something about land ownership that should privilege this class of non-residents over others with important ties to a city, such as commuters, consumers of city services, or residents of neighboring jurisdictions? Is it that landowners pay property taxes? What then of non-resident consumers who pay sales taxes, employees who pay income taxes, or tourists who pay parking fees? Assuming we can identify a distinction between landowners and other non-residents, it is not clear that we can justify it in light of the cases discussed in *Holt Civic Club* striking down attempts to limit the right to vote to property owners. Is there a constitutional way to include as voters some (but not all) outsiders affected by city policy? If a city were to include outsiders as voters, would city residents have a constitutional claim that their right to self-government was being diluted by the votes of people less affected by city policy than they are? And what of "dual residence" at issue in Wit v. Berman? If we were to open local elections to "interested" parties, is there any reason not to allow people to vote in more than one city?

HOLT CIVIC CLUB V. CITY OF TUSCALOOSA

Supreme Court of the United States, 1978.
439 U.S. 60, 99 S.Ct. 383, 58 L.Ed.2d 292.

MR. JUSTICE REHNQUIST delivered the opinion of the Court.

Holt is a small, largely rural, unincorporated community located on the northeastern outskirts of Tuscaloosa, the fifth largest city in Alabama. Because the community is within the three-mile police jurisdiction circumscribing Tuscaloosa's corporate limits, its residents are subject to the city's "police and sanitary regulations." Ala.Code § 11–40–10 (1975). Holt residents are also subject to the criminal jurisdiction of the city's court, and to the city's power to license businesses, trades, and professions. Tuscaloosa, however, may collect from businesses in the police jurisdiction only one-half of the license fee chargeable to similar businesses conducted within the corporate limits.

In 1973 appellants, an unincorporated civic association and seven individual residents of Holt, brought this statewide class action in the United States District Court for the Northern District of Alabama, challenging the constitutionality of these Alabama statutes. They claimed that the city's extraterritorial exercise of police powers over Holt residents, without a concomitant extension of the franchise on an equal footing with those residing within the corporate limits, denies residents of the police jurisdiction rights secured by the Due Process and Equal Protection Clauses of the Fourteenth Amendment. * * *

The unconstitutional predicament in which appellants assertedly found themselves could be remedied in only two ways: (1) the city's extraterritorial power could be negated by invalidating the State's authorizing statutes or (2) the right to vote in municipal elections could be extended to residents of the police jurisdiction. * * *

Appellants focus their equal protection attack on § 11–40–10, the statute fixing the limits of municipal police jurisdiction and giving extraterritorial effect to municipal police and sanitary ordinances. Citing *Kramer v. Union Free School Dist.*, 395 U.S. 621, 89 S.Ct. 1886, 23 L.Ed.2d 583 (1969), and cases following in its wake, appellants argue that the section creates a classification infringing on their right to participate in municipal elections. The State's denial of the franchise to police jurisdiction residents, appellants urge, can stand only if justified by a compelling state interest.

At issue in *Kramer* was a New York voter qualification statute that limited the vote in school district elections to otherwise qualified district residents who (1) either owned or leased taxable real property located within the district, (2) were married to persons owning or leasing qualifying property, or (3) were parents or guardians of children enrolled in a local district school for a specified time during the preceding year. Without deciding whether or not a State may in some circumstances limit the franchise to residents primarily interested or primarily affected by the activities of a given governmental unit, the court held that the statute was not sufficiently tailored to meet that state interest since its classifications excluded many bona fide residents of the school district who had distinct and direct interests in school board decisions and included many residents whose interests in school affairs were, at best, remote and indirect.

On the same day, in *Cipriano v. City of Houma*, 395 U.S. 701, 89 S.Ct. 1897, 23 L.Ed.2d 647 (1969), the Court upheld an equal protection challenge to a Louisiana law providing that only "property taxpayers" could vote in elections called to approve the issuance of revenue bonds by a municipal utility system. Operation of the utility system affected virtually every resident of the city, not just property owners, and the bonds were in no way financed by property tax revenue. Thus, since the benefits and burdens of the bond issue fell indiscriminately on property owner and nonproperty owner alike, the challenged classification impermissibly excluded otherwise qualified residents who were substantially affected and directly interested in the matter put to a referendum. The rationale of *Cipriano* was subsequently called upon to invalidate an Arizona law restricting the franchise to property taxpayers in elections to approve the issuance of general obligation municipal bonds. *Phoenix v. Kolodziejski,* 399 U.S. 204, 90 S.Ct. 1990, 26 L.Ed.2d 523 (1970).

Appellants also place heavy reliance on *Evans v. Cornman,* 398 U.S. 419, 90 S.Ct. 1752, 26 L.Ed.2d 370 (1970). In *Evans* the Permanent Board of Registry of Montgomery County, Maryland, ruled that persons living on the grounds of the National Institute of Health (NIH), a federal enclave located within the geographical boundaries of the State, did not meet the residency requirement of the Maryland Constitution. Accordingly, NIH residents were denied the right to vote in Maryland elections. This Court rejected the notion that persons living on NIH grounds were not residents of Maryland:

> "Appellees clearly live within the geographical boundaries of the State of Maryland, and they are treated as State residents in the census and in determining congressional apportionment. They are not residents of Maryland only if the NIH grounds ceased to be a part of Maryland when the enclave was created. However, that 'fiction of a state within a state' was specifically rejected by this Court in *Howard v. Commissioners of Louisville,* 344 U.S. 624, 627, 73 S.Ct. 465, 467, 97 L.Ed. 617 (1953), and it cannot be resurrected here to deny appellees the right to vote."

Thus, because inhabitants of the NIH enclave were residents of Maryland and were "just as interested in and connected with electoral decisions as they were prior to 1953 when the area came under federal jurisdiction and as their neighbors who live off the enclave," the State could not deny them the equal right to vote in Maryland elections.

From these and our other voting qualifications cases a common characteristic emerges: the challenged statute in each case denied the franchise to individuals who were physically resident within the geographic boundaries of the governmental entity concerned. * * *

No decision of this Court has extended the "one man, one vote" principle to individuals residing beyond the geographic confines of the governmental entity concerned, be it the State or its political subdivisions. On the contrary, our cases have uniformly recognized that a government unit may legitimately restrict the right to participate in its political processes to those who reside within its borders.

Appellants' argument that extraterritorial extension of municipal powers requires concomitant extraterritorial extension of the franchise proves too much. The imaginary line defining a city's corporate limits cannot corral the influence of municipal actions. A city's decisions inescapably affect individuals living immediately outside its borders. The granting of building permits for highrise apartments, industrial plants, and the like on the city's fringe unavoidably contributes to problems of traffic congestion, school districting, and law enforcement immediately outside the city. A rate change in the city's sales or ad valorem tax could well have a significant impact on retailers and property values in areas bordering the city. The condemnation of real property on the city's edge for construction of a municipal garbage dump or waste treatment plant would have obvious implications for neighboring nonresidents. Indeed, the indirect extraterritorial effects of many purely internal municipal actions could conceivably have a heavier impact on surrounding environs than the direct regulation contemplated by Alabama's police jurisdiction statutes. Yet no one would suggest that nonresidents likely to be affected by this sort of municipal action have a constitutional right to participate in the political processes bringing it about. And unless one adopts the idea that the Austinian notion of sovereignty, which is presumably embodied to some extent in the authority of a city over a police jurisdiction, distinguishes the direct effects of limited municipal powers over police jurisdiction residents from the indirect though equally dramatic extraterritorial effects of purely internal municipal actions, it makes little sense to say that one requires extension of the franchise while the other does not.

Given this country's tradition of popular sovereignty, appellants' claimed right to vote in Tuscaloosa elections is not without some logical appeal. We are mindful, however, of Justice Holmes' observation in *Hudson Water Co. v. McCarter,* 209 U.S. 349, 355, 28 S.Ct. 529, 531, 52 L.Ed. 828 (1908):

> "All rights tend to declare themselves absolute to their logical extreme. Yet all in fact are limited by the neighborhood of principles of policy which are other than those on which the particular right is founded, and which become strong enough to hold their own when a certain point is reached. * * * The boundary at which the conflicting interests balance cannot be determined by any general formula in advance, but points in the line, or helping to establish it, are fixed by decisions that this or that concrete case falls on the nearer or farther side."

The line heretofore marked by this Court's voting qualifications decisions coincides with the geographical boundary of the governmental unit at issue, and we hold that appellants' case, like their homes, falls on the farther side.

Thus stripped of its voting rights attire, the equal protection issue presented by appellants becomes whether the Alabama statutes giving extraterritorial force to certain municipal ordinances and powers bear some rational relationship to a legitimate state purpose. *San Antonio School Dist. v. Rodriguez,* 411 U.S. 1, 93 S.Ct. 1278, 36 L.Ed.2d 16 (1973).

"The Fourteenth Amendment does not prohibit legislation merely because it is special, or limited in its application to a particular geographical or political subdivision of the state." *Fort Smith Light Co. v. Paving Dist.,* 274 U.S. 387, 391, 47 S.Ct. 595, 597, 71 L.Ed. 1112 (1927). Rather, the Equal Protection Clause is offended only if the statute's classification "rests on grounds wholly irrelevant to the achievement of the State's objective." *McGowan v. Maryland,* 366 U.S. 420, 425, 81 S.Ct. 1101, 1104, 6 L.Ed.2d 393 (1961).

Government, observed Mr. Justice Johnson, "is the science of experiment," *Anderson v. Dunn,* 6 Wheat. 204, 226, 5 L.Ed. 242, 247 (1821), and a State is afforded wide leeway when experimenting with the appropriate allocation of state legislative power. This Court has often recognized that political subdivisions such as cities and counties are created by the State "as convenient agencies for exercising such of the governmental powers of the state as may be entrusted to them." *E.g., Sailors v. Board of Education,* 387 U.S. at 108, 87 S.Ct. at 1552; *Reynolds v. Sims,* 377 U.S. 533, 575, 84 S.Ct. 1362, 12 L.Ed.2d 506 (1964); *Hunter v. City of Pittsburgh,* 207 U.S. 161, 178, 28 S.Ct. 40, 46, 52 L.Ed. 151 (1907). In *Hunter v. City of Pittsburgh,* the Court discussed at length the relationship between a State and its political subdivisions, remarking: "The number, nature and duration of the powers conferred upon [municipal] corporations and the territory over which they shall be exercised rests in the absolute discretion of the state." While the broad statements as to state control over municipal corporations contained in *Hunter v. City of Pittsburgh,* have undoubtedly been qualified by the holdings of later cases such as *Kramer v. Union Free School Dist.,* we think that the case continues to have substantial constitutional significance in emphasizing the extraordinarily wide latitude that states have in creating various types of political subdivisions and conferring authority upon them.[7]

The extraterritorial exercise of municipal powers is a governmental technique neither recent in origin nor unique to the State of Alabama. See R. Maddox, Extraterritorial Powers of Municipalities in the United States (1955). In this country 35 States authorize their municipal subdivisions to exercise governmental powers beyond their corporate limits. Comment, The Constitutionality of the Exercise of Extraterritorial Powers by

---

[7] In this case residents of the police jurisdiction are excluded only from participation in municipal elections since they reside outside of Tuscaloosa's corporate limits. This "denial of the franchise," as appellants put it, does not have anything like the far-reaching consequences of the denial of the franchise in Evans v. Cornman, 398 U.S. 419, 90 S.Ct. 1752, 26 L.Ed.2d 370 (1970). There the Court pointed out that "[i]n nearly every election, federal, state, and local, for offices from the Presidency to the school board, and on the entire variety of other ballot propositions, appellees have a stake equal to that of other Maryland residents." Treatment of the plaintiffs in Evans as nonresidents of Maryland had repercussions not merely with respect to their right to vote in city elections, but with respect to their right to vote in national, state, school board, and referendum elections.

Municipalities, 45 Chi.L.Rev. 151 (1977). Although the extraterritorial municipal powers granted by these States vary widely, several States grant their cities more extensive or intrusive powers over bordering areas than those granted under the Alabama statutes.[8]

In support of their equal protection claim, appellants suggest a number of "constitutionally preferable" governmental alternatives to Alabama's system of municipal police jurisdictions. For example, exclusive management of the police jurisdiction by county officials, appellants maintain, would be more "practical." From a political science standpoint, appellants' suggestions may be sound, but this Court does not sit to determine whether Alabama has chosen the soundest or most practical form of internal government possible. Authority to make those judgments resides in the state legislature, and Alabama citizens are free to urge their proposals to that body. See, *e.g., Hunter v. City of Pittsburgh, supra.* Our inquiry is limited to the question whether "any state of facts reasonably may be conceived to justify" Alabama's system of police jurisdictions, *Salyer Land Co. v. Tulare Water Dist.,* 410 U.S., at 732, 93 S.Ct., at 1231 (1973), and in this case it takes but momentary reflection to arrive at an affirmative answer.

The Alabama Legislature could have decided that municipal corporations should have some measure of control over activities carried on just beyond their "city limit" signs, particularly since today's police jurisdiction may be tomorrow's annexation to the city proper. Nor need the city's interests have been the only concern of the legislature when it enacted the police jurisdiction statutes. Urbanization of any area brings with it a number of individuals who long both for the quiet of suburban or country living and for the career opportunities offered by the city's working environment. Unincorporated communities like Holt dot the rim of most major population centers in Alabama and elsewhere, and state legislatures have a legitimate interest in seeing that this substantial

---

[8]   Municipalities in some States have most almost unrestricted governmental powers over surrounding unincorporated territories. * * * [W]e do not mean to imply that every * * * [state law] would pass constitutional muster. We do not have before us, of course, a situation in which a city has annexed outlying territory in all but name, and is exercising precisely the same governmental powers over residents of surrounding unincorporated territory as it does over those residing within its corporate limits. Nor do we have here a case like Evans v. Cornman, supra, where NIH residents were subject to such "important aspects of state powers" as Maryland's authority "to levy and collect [its] income, gasoline, sales, and use taxes" and were "just as interested in and connected with electoral decisions as * * * their neighbors who live[d] off the enclave."

Appellants have made neither an allegation nor a showing that the authority exercised by the city of Tuscaloosa within the police jurisdiction is no less than that exercised by the city within its corporate limits. The minute catalog of ordinances of the city of Tuscaloosa which have extraterritorial effect set forth by our dissenting Brethren is as notable for what it does not include as for what it does. While the burden was on appellants to establish a difference in treatment violative of the Equal Protection Clause, we are bound to observe that among the powers *not* included in the "addendum" to appellants' brief referred to by the dissent are the vital and traditional authorities of cities and towns to levy ad valorem taxes, invoke the power of eminent domain, and zone property for various types of uses.

segment of the population does not go without basic municipal services such as police, fire, and health protection. Established cities are experienced in the delivery of such services, and the incremental cost of extending the city's responsibility in these areas to surrounding environs may be substantially less than the expense of establishing wholly new service organizations in each community.

Nor was it unreasonable for the Alabama Legislature to require police jurisdiction residents to contribute through license fees to the expense of services provided them by the city. The statutory limitation on license fees to half the amount exacted within the city assures that police jurisdiction residents will not be victimized by the city government.

"Viable local governments may need many innovations, numerous combinations of old and new devices, great flexibility in municipal arrangements to meet changing urban conditions." *Sailors v. Board of Education, supra.* This observation in *Sailors* was doubtless as true at the turn of this century, when urban areas throughout the country were temporally closer to the effects of the industrial revolution. Alabama's police jurisdiction statute, enacted in 1907, was a rational legislative response to the problems faced by the State's burgeoning cities. Alabama is apparently content with the results of its experiment, and nothing in the Equal Protection Clause of the Fourteenth Amendment requires that it try something new.

Appellants also argue that "government without franchise is a fundamental violation of the due process clause." * * * Appellants' argument proceeds from the assumption, earlier shown to be erroneous, that they have a right to vote in Tuscaloosa elections. Their conclusion falls with their premise.

In sum, we conclude that Alabama's police jurisdiction statutes violate neither the Equal Protection Clause nor the Due Process Clause of the Fourteenth Amendment. * * *

MR. JUSTICE BRENNAN, with whom MR. JUSTICE WHITE and MR. JUSTICE MARSHALL join, dissenting. * * *

Because "statutes distributing the franchise constitute the foundation of our representative society," *Kramer v. Union School Dist.,* 395 U.S. 621, 626, 89 S.Ct. 1886, 1889, 23 L.Ed.2d 583 (1969), we have subjected such statutes to "exacting judicial scrutiny." *Id.,* at 628, 89 S.Ct., at 1890. Indeed, "if a challenged statute grants the right to vote to some citizens and denies the franchise to others, 'the Court must determine whether the exclusions are *necessary* to promote a *compelling* state interest.' *Kramer v. Union Free School District,* 395 U.S., at 627, 89 S.Ct., at 1890 (emphasis added) * * *." *Dunn v. Blumstein,* 405 U.S. 330, 337, 92 S.Ct. 995, 1000, 31 L.Ed.2d 274 (1972). * * *

Our decisions before today have held that bona fide residency requirements are an acceptable means of distinguishing qualified from unqualified voters. *Dunn v. Blumstein,* 405 U.S. at 343, 92 S.Ct. at 1003. * * * [But] *Dunn v. Blumstein* was careful to exempt from strict judicial scrutiny only bona fide residency requirements that were "appropriately defined and uniformly applied." The touchstone for determining whether a residency requirement is "appropriately defined" derives from the purpose of such requirements, which, as stated in *Dunn,* is "to preserve the basic conception of a political community." At the heart of our basic conception of a "political community," however, is the notion of a reciprocal relationship between the process of government and those who subject themselves to that process by choosing to live within the area of its authoritative application. Statutes such as those challenged in this case, which fracture this relationship by severing the connection between the process of government and those who are governed in the places of their residency, thus undermine the very purposes which have led this Court in the past to approve the application of bona fide residency requirements.

There is no question but that the residents of Tuscaloosa's police jurisdiction are governed by the city.[10] Under Alabama law, a

---

[10] Appellants have included in their brief an unchallenged addendum listing the ordinances of the city of Tuscaloosa, Code of Tuscaloosa (1962, Supplemented, 1975), that have application in its police jurisdiction:

"Licenses:

4–1 ambulance

9–4, 9–18, 9–33 bottle dealers

19–1 junk dealers

20–5 general business license ordinance

20–67 florists

20–102 hotels, motels, etc.

20–163 industry

"Buildings:

10–1 inspection service enforces codes

10–10 regulation of dams

10–21 Southern Standard Building Code adopted

10–25 building permits

13–3 National Electrical Code adopted

14–23 Fire Prevention Code adopted

14–65 regulation of incinerators

14–81 discharge of cinders

Chapter 21A mobile home parks

25–1 Southern Standard Plumbing Code adopted

33–79 disposal of human waste

33–114, 118 regulation of wells

"Public Health:

5–4 certain birds protected

5–4C, 42, 55 dogs running at large and bitches in heat prohibited

14–4 no smoking on buses

municipality exercises "governing" and "law-making" power over its police jurisdiction. Residents of Tuscaloosa's police jurisdiction are subject to license fees exacted by the city, as well as to the city's police and sanitary regulations, which can be enforced through penal sanctions effective in the city's municipal court. The Court seems to imply, however, that

14–15 no self-service gas stations

15–2 regulation of sale of produce from trucks

15–4 food establishments to use public water supply

15–16 food, meat, milk inspectors

15–37 thru 40 regulates boardinghouses

15–52 milk code adopted

17–5 mosquito control

"Traffic Regulations:

22–2 stop & yield signs may be erected by chief of police

22–3 mufflers required

22–4 brakes required

22–5 inspection of vehicle by police

22–6 operation of vehicle

22–9 hitchhiking in roadway prohibited

22–9.1 permit to solicit funds on roadway

22–11 impounding cars

22–14 load limit on bridges

22–15 police damage stickers required after accident

22–25 driving while intoxicated

22–26 reckless driving

22–27 driving without consent of owner

22–33 stop sign

22–34 yield sign

22–38 driving across median

22–40 yield to emergency vehicle

22–42 cutting across private property

22–54 general speed limit

22–72 thru 78 truck routes

"Criminal Ordinances:

23–1 adopts all state misdemeanors

23–7.1 no wrecked cars on premises

23–15 nuisances

23–17 obscene literature

23–20 destruction of plants

23–37 swimming in nude

23–38 trespass to boats

26–51 no shooting galleries in the police jurisdiction or outside fire limits (downtown area)

28–31 thru 39 obscene films

"Miscellaneous:

20–120 thru 122 cigarette tax

24–31 public parks and recreation

26–18 admission tax

Chapter 29 regulates public streets

30–23 taxis must have meters."

residents of the police jurisdiction are not governed enough to be included within the political community of Tuscaloosa, since they are not subject to Tuscaloosa's powers of eminent domain, zoning, or ad valorem taxation. *Ante* n. 8. But this position is sharply contrary to our previous holdings. In *Kramer v. Union Free School Dist.*, for example, we held that residents of a school district who neither owned nor leased taxable real property located within the district, or were not married to someone who did, or were not parents or guardians of children enrolled in a local district school, nevertheless were sufficiently affected by the decisions of the local school board to make the denial of their franchise and local school board elections a violation of the Equal Protection Clause. Similarly, we held in *Cipriano v. City of Houma* that a Louisiana statute limiting the franchise in municipal utility system revenue bond referenda to those who were "property taxpayers" was unconstitutional because all residents of the municipality were affected by the operation of the utility system.

The residents of Tuscaloosa's police jurisdiction are vastly more affected by Tuscaloosa's decisionmaking processes than were the plaintiffs in either *Kramer* or *Cipriano* affected by the decisionmaking processes from which they had been unconstitutionally excluded. * * * The Court today does not explain why being subjected to the authority to exercise such extensive power does not suffice to bring the residents of Tuscaloosa's police jurisdiction within the political community of the city. Nor does the Court in fact provide any standards for determining when those subjected to extraterritorial municipal legislation will have been "governed enough" to trigger the protections of the Equal Protection Clause.

The criterion of geographical residency relied upon by the Court is of no assistance in this analysis. Just as the State may not fracture the integrity of a political community by restricting the franchise to property taxpayers, so it may not use geographical restrictions on the franchise to accomplish the same end. This is the teaching of *Evans v. Cornman*. *Evans* held, contrary to the conclusion of the Maryland Court of Appeals, that those who lived on the grounds of the National Institutes of Health (NIH) enclave within Montgomery County were residents of Maryland for purposes of the franchise. Our decision rested on the grounds that inhabitants of the enclave were "treated as state residents in the census and in determining congressional apportionment," and that "residents of the NIH grounds are just as interested in and connected with electoral decisions as they were prior to 1953 when the area came under federal jurisdiction and as are their neighbors who live off the enclave." Residents of Tuscaloosa's police jurisdiction are assuredly as "interested in and connected with" the electoral decisions of the city as were the inhabitants of the NIH enclave in the electoral decisions of Maryland. True, inhabitants of the enclave lived "within the geographical boundaries of the State of Maryland," but appellants in this case similarly reside within the geographical boundaries of Tuscaloosa's police jurisdiction. They live within the perimeters of the city's "legislative powers."

The criterion of geographical residency is thus entirely arbitrary when applied to this case. It fails to explain why, consistently with the Equal Protection Clause, the "government unit" which may exclude from the franchise those who reside outside of its geographical boundaries should be composed of the city of Tuscaloosa rather than of the city together with its police jurisdiction. It irrationally distinguishes between two classes of citizens, each with equal claim to residency (insofar as that can be determined by domicile or intention or other similar criteria), and each governed by the city of Tuscaloosa in the place of their residency.

The Court argues, however, that if the franchise were extended to residents of the city's police jurisdiction, the franchise must similarly be extended to all those indirectly affected by the city's actions. This is a simple non sequitur. There is a crystal-clear distinction between those who reside in Tuscaloosa's police jurisdiction, and who are therefore subject to that city's police and sanitary ordinances, licensing fees, and the jurisdiction of its municipal court, and those who reside in neither the city nor its police jurisdiction, and who are thus merely affected by the indirect impact of the city's decisions. This distinction is recognized in Alabama law and is consistent with, if not mandated by, the very conception of a political community underlying constitutional recognition of bona fide residency requirements.

Appellants' equal protection claim can be simply expressed: The State cannot extend the franchise to some citizens who are governed by municipal government in the places of their residency, and withhold the franchise from others similarly situated, unless this distinction is necessary to promote a compelling state interest. No such interest has been articulated in this case. Neither Tuscaloosa's interest in regulating "activities carried on just beyond [its] 'city limit' signs" nor Alabama's interest in providing municipal services to the unincorporated communities surrounding its cities are in any way inconsistent with the extension of the franchise to residents of Tuscaloosa's police jurisdiction. Although a great many States may presently authorize the exercise of extraterritorial lawmaking powers by a municipality, and although the Alabama statutes involved in this case may be of venerable age, neither of these factors, as *Reynolds v. Sims,* 377 U.S. 533, 84 S.Ct. 1362, 12 L.Ed.2d 506 (1964), made clear, can serve to justify practices otherwise impermissible under the Equal Protection Clause of the Fourteenth Amendment. * * *

MAY V. TOWN OF MOUNTAIN VILLAGE

United States Court of Appeals, Tenth Circuit, 1997.
132 F.3d 576.

WESLEY E. BROWN, SENIOR DISTRICT JUDGE.

In this civil rights case the plaintiffs, all residents of the Town of Mountain Village, Colorado, initiated a class action against the Town and its governing officers to contest provisions of the Town Charter which allow nonresident landowners to vote in municipal elections. * * * The only question presented in this appeal is whether [these provisions] violate[ ] the 14th Amendment to the federal constitution by diluting the vote of the residents of that Town. * * *

The Town of Mountain Village is located in San Miguel County in the San Juan Range of the Rocky Mountains in southwest Colorado. As of July 1993, San Miguel County had approximately 4,300 permanent residents. The Town, which consists of about 2,049 acres of land, is situated in the mountains above and on the opposite side of a ski mountain from the Town of Telluride, Colorado. * * * In 1984, the Telluride Company began development of the area that was later incorporated as the Town under a development plan first approved by San Miguel County in 1981. The center of the Town is located at the base of the Telluride Ski Area and contains the terminal of the main gondola, which reaches the Town from Telluride. The Town also contains single family and duplex residential units, residential condominium units, hotel rooms, commercial space and facilities for recreational activities such as golf, tennis, swimming and other outdoor activities. * * * At an election on January 17, 1995, the Town received voter approval to incorporate under Colorado law. There were 268 registered voters entitled to vote in this election, all of whom were residents of the Town. * * * On March 7, 1995, a Town election was held on whether to approve a proposed home rule charter for the Town * * *. Only registered voters who were residents of the Town were entitled to vote in this election. Fifty-three residents voted; 40 voted to approve the Charter, 13 voted against doing so. * * *

Section 2.4(a) of the Charter granted the right to vote to all residents of the Town, so long as they had been legal residents for at least 180 consecutive days immediately prior to the election, and were at least 18 years old on the date of the election. Section 2.4(b) of the Charter granted the right to vote to owners of real property located within the Town, who are not legal residents of the Town, so long as they: (a) have been owners of record for at least 180 consecutive days immediately prior to the date of the election; (b) during that 180 days owned a minimum of 50% of the fee title interest in certain real property; (c) are at least 18 years old on the date of the election; and (d) are natural persons. Ownership of both residential and commercial real property entitles the owner to vote, but ownership of parking spaces, hotel units, roads or common areas does not qualify voters. Section 2.4(d) of the Charter further provides that there may only be one vote cast per person, regardless of whether or not he or she may be a qualified Legal Resident and/or own one or more parcels of qualified real property.

Section 1.4(b) of the Charter sets out the reasons for extending the vote to nonresidents:

(b) Provision for Non-resident Voting Rights. Certain non-resident property owners have been extended voting rights concerning municipal and local affairs based upon the following reasons:

1.   Like many resorts, the nature of the economy and the life-style of the people of the Town are, and will in the future remain, unusual. Furthermore, the fact that many of the Town's present and future residential and commercial property owners maintain their primary residences outside of the Town, making them part-time second-home non-residents, is also unusual. Although these facts are not substantially different from most resort towns, they are very unusual for conventional small as well as large towns.

2.   The framers of this Charter took cognizance of the above-mentioned singular state of affairs, most especially the fact that a large number of the property owners of the Town are, and will continue to be, only part-time residents of their Town by granting to them the right to vote on those issues that are strictly limited in nature to Town matters. * * *

As of January 2, 1996, a Town census disclosed that in addition to approximately 505 eligible resident voters in the Town, there were approximately 541 nonresident property owners eligible to vote pursuant to the Charter.

Nonresidents entitled to vote currently own over 34% of the assessed value of real property in the Town, while residents own only about 5%. About 61% of the assessed value of real property in the Town is owned by nonresident corporations and trusts, which are not entitled to vote in Town elections. Nonresidents pay over eight times more in property taxes than the residents do, and it is fair to state that in the future such nonresident property owners will continue to contribute significant revenues to the Town. * * * Under its Charter, the Town has the right to establish land use standards, community services, [and] municipal ordinances, to adopt capital improvement programs, establish property and other taxes, borrow money, issue bonds, create special improvement districts, to control public utilities and to condemn property. By granting nonresident property owners the right to vote on issues limited to Town matters, the Charter gives those nonresidents a voice in the affairs of the Town, including taxes to be paid and how tax dollars will be spent. * * *

Of critical importance to any decision here is the fact that Section 2.4(b) of the Town Charter does not restrict the right to vote—it expands it to include nonresidents owning real property in the Town. As pointed out by the District Court, "[w]here a law expands the right to vote causing voting dilution, the rational basis test has been applied by the vast majority of courts." *May v. Town of Mountain Village*, 944 F.Supp. 821, 824. Among such cases and most factually similar to the case before us are *Spahos v. Mayor & Councilmen of Savannah Beach, Tybee Island, Ga.*, 207 F.Supp. 688 (S.D.Ga.), aff'd per curiam, 371 U.S. 206, 83 S.Ct. 304, 9 L.Ed.2d 269 (1962), and *Glisson v. Mayor and Councilmen of Town of Savannah Beach*, 346 F.2d 135 (1965). Under the facts of these two cases it appears that Savannah Beach was a resort town in Chatham County, Georgia, with a population of 1,385 persons, which was increased by an additional 2,500 persons during the summer. Under state law, non-residents of the town, who resided in the county, who owned real property in Savannah Beach were permitted to vote in Savannah Beach elections. In finding that this election scheme did not violate the equal protection clause of the 14th Amendment, the courts considered that the assessed value of property in the town was $4,414,295, of which $2,852,040 was returned by nonresidents, and that as of December, 1961, there were 549 persons registered to vote as permanent residents, and 443 were registered as non-residents, owning property in the town. A substantial majority of the nonresidents resided in Savannah Beach for periods of one to four months during the summer. * * *

In the case before us, the uncontroverted evidence discussed above supports the District Court's conclusion that:

> Plaintiffs have failed to show that the Defendants' reason for allowing nonresident landowners to vote in the Town ... is either irrational or arbitrary. I find credible Defendants' contentions that the Town ... is a unique resort community where nonresident landowners own the majority of property and pay more than eight times the amount of property tax. Defendants further assert that without the significant revenues the nonresident landowners have contributed to the Town, the Town might never have come into existence. Moreover, the nonresidents continue to bear the weight of the financial burden for the Town. Defendants argue that providing the nonresident landowners the right to vote gives them a voice in the Town's future, including the taxes they will have to pay and how those taxes should be spent ... These factors demonstrate that the Town had a rational basis for enacting the Charter provision granting nonresident landowners the right to vote.

Simply stated, the issue in this case must turn upon the uncontroverted fact that the Town of Mountain Village was incorporated pursuant to the overwhelming vote of registered voters, all of whom were residents of the Town. Following that incorporation, registered voters, again all residents of the Town, approved by an overwhelming majority the Home Rule Charter at issue in this case. Under Article XX of the Colorado constitution Home Rule Towns have the power to "legislate upon, provide, regulate, conduct and control . . . all matters pertaining to municipal elections". Section 1.4(b) of the Charter specifically sets out the reasons for extending the vote to nonresidents of the Town, in particular recognizing the special nature of the resort community. There is no evidence in this case of any suspect classification of voters and equal weight is to be given to the votes of residents and nonresidents. * * * [I]t is clear that the nonresident property owners have a sufficient interest in Town affairs to make it rational for the Town to include them in the political process. * * *

WIT V. BERMAN
United States Court of Appeals, Second Circuit, 2002.
306 F.3d 1256.

WINTER, CIRCUIT JUDGE.

Harold M. Wit and Donald C. Ebel appeal from the dismissal of their complaint by Judge Hellerstein for failure to state a claim. * * * Each appellant has maintained a home in New York City for over forty years. Each pays income and property taxes in the City, owns real property there, is listed in the New York City telephone directory, uses his New York City residence for personal financial statements, and spends a considerable portion of every year living there. In addition, each appellant meets other qualifications—age and citizenship—to register to vote in New York City.

Appellants were once registered to vote in New York City and voted there. However, for some years, both have also lived, and have been registered voters in, the towns of East Hampton and Southampton, respectively. Appellants are currently barred from voting in New York City because they are also registered to vote in the Hamptons. Each alleges that, if they were not registered to vote in the Hamptons, they would be allowed to register in New York City.

Under New York law, one must be a resident of an electoral district to register as a voter in that district. "Residence" is defined in the Election Law as "*that place* where a person maintains a fixed, permanent and principal home and to which he, wherever temporarily located, always intends to return." N.Y. Elec. Law § 1–104(22) (emphasis added). Section 17–104 of the Election Law provides that any person who "[r]egisters or attempts to register as an elector in more than one election district for the same election" is guilty of a felony. * * *

In June 2000, appellants filed the present complaint challenging the constitutionality of the pertinent provisions of the Election Law and seeking declaratory and injunctive relief permitting them to register to vote in local elections in New York City while maintaining the right to vote in the Hamptons. * * * [A]ppellants are not allowed to vote in New York City solely because they are registered in the Hamptons. * * * Therefore, they argue, they are being treated differently than others qualified to vote in the City. Because there is in their view no permissible governmental interest justifying this differential treatment, they conclude that they have been denied their rights under the Equal Protection Clause. We disagree. * * *

The Election Law states that no person may vote unless a "resident" of the particular election district. Residence and the legal concept of domicile are synonymous under the Election Law. * * * For purposes of voting in New York, domicile is defined as "that place" where one has the fixed, permanent, and principal home to which, even with extended periods of living elsewhere, one intends to return. * * * Particularly in modern times, domicile is very often a poor proxy for a voter's stake in electoral outcomes because many of an individual voter's varied interests are affected by outcomes in elections in which they do not vote. Some, or even many, voters may reasonably perceive that their primary political concerns are affected more by outcomes in elections in which they do not vote than by outcomes in elections in which they do vote. There are endless examples of the bad fit between domicile and a voter's interest in electoral outcomes. For example, a person who works in a factory, or owns one, located in a municipality other than where the person lives, has interests in that municipality's tax, traffic, law enforcement, and other policies. To take an interstate example, many voters in New England believe that their lives are directly affected by environmental policies in the mid-west industrial states. * * *

However, while one may mount ethereal arguments against the single-domicile-registration rule, the administrative problems that interests-based rules would cause for thousands of registrars of voters render those rules virtually unthinkable. * * * Honoring the desires of voters to vote in other districts based on their expression of subjective interests in the political decisions of those other districts would essentially lead to a "vote-in-however-many-districts-you-please" rule. Such a rule would be truly chaotic, save for the small measure of order that corruption would bring to it. An objective test of voter interests is equally unworkable. At the very least, it would involve an ever-changing analysis by registrars of the merits of political issues—e.g., does an employee of a firm in one city who lives in another have a sufficient interest in the traffic and tax policies of the former to vote there, or is there sufficiently harmful acid rain in Vermont as a result of loose environmental standards in Ohio to justify a Vermonter voting in Ohio— and would also be chaotic.

Domicile as a rule may have its philosophical defects, therefore, but it has enormous practical advantages over the alternatives. It almost always insures that a voter has *some* stake in the electoral outcome in the domiciliary district and almost always does not involve large numbers of disputes over where one may vote. The domicile rule informs would-be voters where they may vote, a vital function that encourages registration and voting. * * * To be sure, domicile as a test entails administrative difficulties at the margins. The domicile of students is an example. So too is the registration of the homeless. However, these difficulties are slight compared to those that abandonment of the domicile rule and its one domicile/one electoral district restriction might entail. * * *

New York courts have held that, rather than compel persons in appellants' circumstances to establish to the satisfaction of a registrar of voters or a court that one home or the other is their principal, permanent residence, they can choose between them. * * * Moreover, even if appellants were right, the proper remedy for a federal court to order would not be to compel New York to allow appellants to vote in two places. Rather, we would have to order New York to choose between enforcing a strict, single domicile rule, which we believe to be clearly constitutional, or a version of appellants' suggested multiple homes/multiple votes rule.

In any event, we see no infirmity in the one-or-the-other rule because a multiple-vote rule would open the door to a host of administrative problems and potential abuses. * * * The potential difficulties should not be underestimated. Registrars would be called upon to determine, according to criteria not found in appellants' papers, whether a would-be registrant has spent "enough" overnights—or perhaps enough workdays or vacation days—in a district to register. These decisions, moreover, would often have to be made in a very short time frame. Finally, this is no imaginary horrible, because some political organizations might well find it in their interests to attempt to register large numbers of persons with only marginal connections to the electoral district.

The need to avoid these problems, which can grow from a tangle to a morass to outright chaos, is probably the reason that domicile remains the dominant American method of determining where persons may vote. * * * The one-or-the-other rule does not in any sensible use of the word "discriminate" against appellants. Indeed, the Election Law's permissive approach allows appellants to align their strongest, personal political interests with the appropriate voting location. In light of this enhancement of appellants' voting power, the fact that the Election Law does not go further by multiplying appellants' voting power in light of their claimed multiple local interests is not a compelling ground for a claim of discriminatory treatment. * * *

4.   THE ABILITY OF CITIES TO FAVOR THEIR RESIDENTS OVER OUTSIDERS

This subsection examines the extent to which cities can distribute public resources or exercise regulatory power in a way that favors their own residents over outsiders.[5] A similar issue could, of course, be posed for a group of any kind: to what extent can *any* group favor its members over non-members? If a group is not entitled to limit at least *some* of its benefits to members, what would be the difference between membership and non-membership? These questions reintroduce a subject raised in Chapter One—the application of the public/private distinction to cities. How does the legitimacy of cities' favoring insiders over outsiders relate to similar action by private entities (such as private property owners, religious communities, or group health plans)?[6] What is the relationship between a city's preference for its own citizens and comparable action by the United States government with respect to foreign citizens? In reflecting on these questions, it is important see their relationship to the material just covered. There, we saw that the law generally permits cities to exclude non-resident voters, and that it might even limit their ability to include non-resident voters. Is a city's effort to favor residents in its distribution of resources or exercise of regulatory powers consistent or inconsistent with the conception of "political community" that underlies the law of non-resident voting?

---

[5]   For a general analysis of this issue, see Richard C. Schragger, Cities, Economic Development, and the Free Trade Constitution, 94 Va. L. Rev. 1091 (2008); Georgette Chapman Phillips, Boundaries of Exclusion, 72 Mo. L. Rev 1287 (2007); Gerald Neuman, Territorial Discrimination, Equal Protection and Self-Determination, 135 U. Pa. L.Rev. 261 (1987). See also Keaton Norquist, Local Preferences in Affordable Housing: Special Treatment for Those who Live or Work in a Municipality?, 36 B.C. Envtl. Aff. L. Rev. 207 (2009); Richard Schragger, The Limits of Localism, 100 Mich. L. Rev. 371 (2001); Roderick Hills, Poverty, Residency, and Federalism: States' Duty of Impartiality Toward Newcomers, 1999 Sup. Ct. Rev. 277; Patrick Sullivan, Comment, In Defense of Resident Hiring Preferences: A Public Spending Exception to the Privileges and Immunities Clause, 86 Cal. L. Rev. 1335 (1998); Clayton Gillette, Business Incentives, Interstate Competition, and the Commerce Clause, 82 Minn. L. Rev. 447 (1997); Mark Gerger, The Selfish State and the Market, 66 Tex. L. Rev. 1097 (1988); John Varat, State "Citizenship" and Interstate Equality, 48 U. Chi. L. Rev. 487 (1981); Chester Antieau, Paul's Perverted Privileges or the True Meaning of the Privileges and Immunities Clause of Article Four, 9 Wm. & Mary L. Rev. 1 (1967).

[6]   See generally, Lior Jacob Strahilevitz, Exclusionary Amenities in Residential Communities, 92 Va. L. Rev. 437 (2006); Carol Rose, The Comedy of the Commons: Custom, Commerce and Inherently Public Property, 53 U. Chi. L. Rev. 711 (1986). See also Joseph Singer, No Right to Exclude: Public Accommodations and Private Property, 90 N.W. L. Rev. 1283 (1996); Aviam Soifer, Law and the Company We Keep (1995); William Marshall, Discrimination and the Right of Association, 81 N.W. U. L. Rev. 68 (1986); Robert Cover, Nomos and Narrative, 97 Harv. L. Rev. 4 (1983).

The cases below explore cities' attempts to favor their own residents in a variety of contexts: the exclusion of outsiders from city schools and a city park and a requirement that a city's contractors hire a minimum percentage of city residents. In reading the cases, consider how the courts use the public/private distinction in interpreting the variety of federal constitutional provisions (the Equal Protection Clause, the Commerce Clause, the Privileges and Immunities Clause, and the First Amendment) that potentially limit local parochialism. Consider as well whether the cases set forth a consistent policy regarding the propriety of a locality's effort to prefer its own residents to outsiders. Why should a city be allowed to exclude non-residents from its schools but not its beaches? Why should a city be allowed to exclude foreign students but not foreign waste? Exactly *when* should a city be permitted to advance their residents' interests over those of outsiders? Are cities entitled to exclude non-residents from parking on city streets?[7] From using (or selling goods in) public hospitals?

---

[7]   In County Board of Arlington County, Virginia v. Richards, 434 U.S. 5, 98 S.Ct. 24, 54 L.Ed.2d 4 (1977), the United States Supreme Court held that a local ordinance limiting parking in a residential area to local residents did not violate the Equal Protection Clause of the Fourteenth Amendment. The Court reasoned:

> To reduce air pollution and other environmental effects of automobile commuting, a community reasonably may restrict on-street parking available to commuters, thus encouraging reliance on car pools and mass transit. The same goal is served by assuring convenient parking to residents who leave their cars home during the day. A community may also decide that restrictions on the flow of outside traffic into particular residential areas would enhance the quality of life there by reducing noise, traffic hazards, and litter. By definition, discrimination against nonresidents would inhere in such a restriction. * * * The Equal Protection Clause requires only that the distinction drawn by an ordinance like Arlington's rationally promotes the regulation's objectives. On its face, the Arlington ordinance meets this test.

Even if local favoritism of this kind is permissible under the federal constitution, state law may bar it. In New York State Public Employees Federation v. City of Albany, 72 N.Y.2d 96, 531 N.Y.S.2d 770, 527 N.E.2d 253 (1988), the New York Court of Appeals held invalid, as preempted, the City's policy of limiting nonresident parking in designated areas to 90 minutes while allowing residents unlimited parking privileges. Sections 1600 and 1604 of the state's Vehicle and Traffic Law, the court said,

> prohibit localities from excluding persons from free use of the highways except to the extent such limitations are expressly authorized by statute. * * * [R]estrictions on highway use based upon residency—such as that found in the contested ordinance—are [thereby] prohibited. * * * [T]he City maintains that the * * * rule should only be construed as prohibiting distinctions between residents and nonresidents for matters involving travel; that distinction may be drawn for parking matters. * * * [But the] general rule is clear: residents of a community have no greater right to use the highways abutting their land—whether it be for travel or parking—than other members of the public * * *. The Legislature is free to create exceptions to the general rule or delegate the power to do so to localities, but we conclude that it did neither here. * * *

Accord: New York State Public Employees Federation v. City of Albany, 269 A.D.2d 707, 703 N.Y.S.2d 573 (App.Div.2000) (holding that the City of Albany had not been delegated the power to discriminate between residents and non-residents in a pre-paid parking permit plan, which offered permits to residents for $15 and permits to non-residents for $785); People v. Speakerkits, Inc., 83 N.Y.2d 814, 611 N.Y.S.2d 488, 633 N.E.2d 1092 (N.Y.1994) (invalidating, as preempted by a conflicting state statute, an ordinance prohibiting parking in the residential area of a village without a "residential" parking permit).

MARTINEZ V. BYNUM

Supreme Court of the United States, 1983.
461 U.S. 321, 103 S.Ct. 1838, 75 L.Ed.2d 879.

JUSTICE POWELL delivered the opinion of the Court. * * *

Roberto Morales was born in 1969 in McAllen, Texas, and is thus a United States citizen by birth. His parents are Mexican citizens who reside in Reynosa, Mexico. He left Reynosa in 1977 and returned to McAllen to live with his sister, petitioner Oralia Martinez, for the primary purpose of attending school in the McAllen Independent School District. Although Martinez is now his custodian, she is not—and does not desire to become—his guardian. As a result, Morales is not entitled to tuition-free admission to the McAllen schools. Sections 21.031(b) and (c) of the Texas Education Code would require the local school authorities to admit him if he or "his parent, guardian, or the person having lawful control of him" resided in the school district, Tex. Educ. Code Ann. § 21.031(b) and (c) (Supp.1982), but § 21.031(d) denies tuition-free admission for a minor who lives apart from a "parent, guardian, or other person having lawful control of him under an order of a court" if his presence in the school district is "for the primary purpose of attending the public free schools." Respondent McAllen Independent School District therefore denied Morales' application for admission in the fall of 1977.

In December 1977 Martinez, as next friend of Morales, and four other adult custodians of school-age children instituted the present action * * * [alleging] that § 21.031(d) violated * * * the Equal Protection Clause, the Due Process Clause, and the Privileges and Immunities Clause. * * *

This Court frequently has considered constitutional challenges to residence requirements. On several occasions the Court has invalidated requirements that condition receipt of a benefit on a minimum period of residence within a jurisdiction, but it always has been careful to distinguish such durational residence requirements from bona fide residence requirements. * * * A bona fide residence requirement, appropriately defined and uniformly applied, furthers the substantial state interest in assuring that services provided for its residents are enjoyed only by residents. Such a requirement with respect to attendance in public free schools does not violate the Equal Protection Clause of the Fourteenth Amendment.[7] It does not burden or penalize the

---

[7] A bona fide residence requirement implicates no "suspect" classification, and therefore is not subject to strict scrutiny. Indeed, there is nothing invidiously discriminatory about a bona fide residence requirement if it is uniformly applied. Thus the question is simply whether there is a rational basis for it.

This view assumes, of course, that the "service" that the State would deny to nonresidents is not a fundamental right protected by the Constitution. A State, for example, may not refuse to provide counsel to an indigent nonresident defendant at a criminal trial where a deprivation of liberty occurs. As we previously have recognized, however, "[public] education is not a 'right' granted to individuals by the Constitution." Plyler v. Doe, 457 U.S. 202, 221, 102 S.Ct. 2382,

constitutional right of interstate travel, for any person is free to move to a State and to establish residence there. A bona fide residence requirement simply requires that the person *does* establish residence before demanding the services that are restricted to residents.

There is a further, independent justification for local residence requirements in the public-school context. As we explained in *Milliken v. Bradley*, 418 U.S. 717, 94 S.Ct. 3112, 41 L.Ed.2d 1069 (1974):

> "No single tradition in public education is more deeply rooted than local control over the operation of schools; local autonomy has long been thought essential both to the maintenance of community concern and support for public schools and to quality of the educational process. * * * [Local] control over the educational process affords citizens an opportunity to participate in decision-making, permits the structuring of school programs to fit local needs, and encourages 'experimentation, innovation, and a healthy competition for educational excellence.'" 418 U.S., at 741–742, 94 S.Ct., at 3126.

The provision of primary and secondary education, of course, is one of the most important functions of local government. Absent residence requirements, there can be little doubt that the proper planning and operation of the schools would suffer significantly.[9] The State thus has a substantial interest in imposing bona fide residence requirements to maintain the quality of local public schools. * * *

Section 21.031 * * * compels a school district to permit a child such as Morales to attend school without paying tuition if he has a bona fide intention to remain in the school district indefinitely, for he then would have a reason for being there other than his desire to attend school: his intention to make his home in the district. Thus § 21.031 grants the benefits of residency to all who satisfy the traditional requirements. The statute goes further and extends these benefits to many children even if

---

2397, 72 L.Ed.2d 786 (1982) (citing San Antonio Independent School District v. Rodriguez, 411 U.S. 1, 35, 93 S.Ct. 1278, 1297, 36 L.Ed.2d 16 (1973)).

[9]   The Court of Appeals accepted the District Court's findings on the adverse impact that invalidating § 21.031(d) would have on the quality of education in Texas. The District Court explicitly found:

> "28. Declaring the statute unconstitutional would cause substantial numbers of [inter-district] transfers, which would * * * cause school populations to fluctuate. * * *
>
> "29. Fluctuating school populations would make it impossible to predict enrollment figures—even on a semester-by-semester basis, causing over-or-under-estimates on teachers, supplies, materials, etc.
>
> "30. The increased enrollment of students would cause overcrowded classrooms and related facilities; over-large teacher-pupil ratios; expansion of bilingual programs; the purchase of books, equipment, supplies and other customary items of support; all of which would require a substantial increase in the budget of the school districts."

We do not suggest that findings of this degree of specificity are necessary in every case. But they do illustrate the problems that prompt States to adopt regulations such as § 21.031.

they (or their families) do not intend to remain in the district indefinitely. As long as the child is not living in the district for the sole purpose of attending school, he satisfies the statutory test. * * * In short, § 21.031 grants the benefits of residency to everyone who satisfies the traditional residence definition and to some who legitimately could be classified as nonresidents. Since there is no indication that this extension of the traditional definition has any impermissible basis, we certainly cannot say that § 21.031(d) violates the Constitution. * * *

FORT GRATIOT SANITARY LANDFILL, INC. V. MICHIGAN DEPARTMENT OF NATURAL RESOURCES

Supreme Court of the United States, 1992.
504 U.S. 353, 112 S.Ct. 2019, 119 L.Ed.2d 139.

JUSTICE STEVENS delivered the opinion of the Court.

In *Philadelphia v. New Jersey*, 437 U.S. 617, 618, 98 S.Ct. 2531, 2532, 57 L.Ed.2d 475 (1978), we held that a New Jersey law prohibiting the importation of most " 'solid or liquid waste which originated or was collected outside the territorial limits of the State' " violated the Commerce Clause of the United States Constitution. In this case petitioner challenges a Michigan law that prohibits private landfill operators from accepting solid waste that originates outside the county in which their facilities are located. Adhering to our holding in the *New Jersey* case, we conclude that this Michigan statute is also unconstitutional.

In 1978 Michigan enacted its Solid Waste Management Act (SWMA). That Act required every Michigan county to estimate the amount of solid waste that would be generated in the county in the next 20 years and to adopt a plan providing for its disposal at facilities that comply with state health standards. * * * On December 28, 1988, the Michigan Legislature amended the SWMA by adopting two provisions concerning the "acceptance of waste or ash generated outside the county of disposal area." Those amendments (Waste Import Restrictions) * * * provide:

"A person shall not accept for disposal solid waste * * * that is not generated in the county in which the disposal area is located unless the acceptance of solid waste * * * that is not generated in the county is explicitly authorized in the approved county solid waste management plan." * * *

In February, 1989, petitioner submitted an application to the St. Clair County Solid Waste Planning Committee for authority to accept up to 1,750 tons per day of out-of-state waste at its landfill. * * * In view of the fact that the county's management plan does not authorize the acceptance of any out-of-county waste, the Waste Import Restrictions in the 1988 statute effectively prevent petitioner from receiving any solid waste that does not originate in St. Clair County. * * * Petitioner therefore commenced this action seeking a judgment declaring the Waste Import Restrictions unconstitutional and enjoining their enforcement. * * *

Philadelphia v. New Jersey provides the framework for our analysis of this case. Solid waste, even if it has no value, is an article of commerce * * * [and] the commercial transactions unquestionably have an interstate character. The Commerce Clause thus imposes some constraints on Michigan's ability to regulate these transactions. As we have long recognized, the "negative" or "dormant" aspect of the Commerce Clause prohibits States from "advancing their own commercial interests by curtailing the movement of articles of commerce, either into or out of the state." *H.P. Hood & Sons, Inc. v. Du Mond*, 336 U.S. 525, 535, 69 S.Ct. 657, 663, 93 L.Ed. 865 (1949). A state statute that clearly discriminates against interstate commerce is therefore unconstitutional "unless the discrimination is demonstrably justified by a valid factor unrelated to economic protectionism." *New Energy Co. of Indiana v. Limbach*, 486 U.S. 269, 274, 108 S.Ct. 1803, 1808, 100 L.Ed.2d 302 (1988).

New Jersey's prohibition on the importation of solid waste failed this test:

> "* * * [I]t does not matter whether the ultimate aim of ch. 363 is to reduce the waste disposal costs of New Jersey residents or to save remaining open lands from pollution, for we assume New Jersey has every right to protect its residents' pocketbooks as well as their environment. And it may be assumed as well that New Jersey may pursue those ends by slowing the flow of *all* waste into the State's remaining landfills, even though interstate commerce may incidentally be affected. But whatever New Jersey's ultimate purpose, it may not be accompanied by discriminating against articles of commerce coming from outside the State unless there is some reason, apart from their origin, to treat them differently. Both on its face and in its plain effect, ch. 363 violates this principle of nondiscrimination.

> "The Court has consistently found parochial legislation of this kind to be constitutionally invalid, whether the ultimate aim of the legislation was to assure a steady supply of milk by erecting barriers to allegedly ruinous outside competition; or to create jobs by keeping industry within the State; or to preserve the State's financial resources from depletion by fencing out indigent immigrants. In each of these cases, a presumably legitimate goal was sought to be achieved by the illegitimate means of isolating the State from the national economy."

The Waste Import Restrictions enacted by Michigan authorize each of its 83 counties to isolate itself from the national economy. * * * In view of the fact that Michigan has not identified any reason, apart from its origin, why solid waste coming from outside the county should be treated differently from solid waste within the county, the foregoing reasoning would appear to control the disposition of this case. Respondents Michigan and St. Clair County argue, however, that the Waste Import Restrictions—unlike the New Jersey prohibition on the importation of solid waste—do not discriminate against interstate commerce on their face or in effect because they treat waste from other Michigan counties no differently than waste from other States. Instead, respondents maintain, the statute regulates evenhandedly to effectuate local interests and should be upheld because the burden on interstate commerce is not clearly excessive in relation to the local benefits. We disagree, for our prior cases teach that a State (or one of its political subdivisions) may not avoid the strictures of the Commerce Clause by curtailing the movement of articles of commerce through subdivisions of the State, rather than through the State itself. * * *

Michigan and St. Clair County also argue that this case is different from *Philadelphia v. New Jersey* because the SWMA constitutes a comprehensive health and safety regulation rather than "economic protectionism" of the State's limited landfill capacity. * * * We may assume that all of the provisions of Michigan's SWMA prior to the 1988 amendments adding the Waste Import Restrictions could fairly be characterized as health and safety regulations with no protectionist purpose, but we cannot make that same assumption with respect to the Waste Import Restrictions themselves. Because those provisions unambiguously discriminate against interstate commerce, the State bears the burden of proving that they further health and safety concerns that cannot be adequately served by nondiscriminatory alternatives. Michigan and St. Clair County have not met this burden.

Michigan and St. Clair County assert that the Waste Import Restrictions are necessary because they enable individual counties to make adequate plans for the safe disposal of future waste. * * * Michigan could attain that objective without discriminating between in-and out-of-state waste. Michigan could, for example, limit the amount of waste that landfill operators may accept each year. There is, however, no valid health and safety reason for limiting the amount of waste that a landfill operator may accept from outside the State, but not the amount that the operator may accept from inside the State. * * *

CHIEF JUSTICE REHNQUIST, with whom JUSTICE BLACKMUN joins, dissenting. * * *

[W]hile many are willing to generate waste—indeed, it is a practical impossibility to solve the waste problem by banning waste production—few are willing to help dispose of it. Those locales that do provide disposal capacity to serve foreign waste effectively are affording reduced environmental and safety risks to the States that will not take charge of their own waste. The State of Michigan has stepped into this quagmire in order to address waste problems generated by its own populace. It has done so by adopting a comprehensive approach to the disposal of solid wastes generated within its borders. * * * In adopting this legislation, the Michigan Legislature also appears to have concluded that, like the State, counties should reap as they have sown—hardly a novel proposition. It has required counties within the State to be responsible for the waste created within the county. It has accomplished this by prohibiting waste facilities from accepting waste generated from outside the county, unless special permits are obtained. In the process, of course, this facially neutral restriction (i.e. it applies equally to both interstate and intrastate waste) also works to ban disposal from out-of-state sources unless appropriate permits are procured. But I cannot agree that such a requirement, when imposed as one part of a comprehensive approach to regulating in this difficult field, is the stuff of which economic protectionism is made.

If anything, the challenged regulation seems likely to work to Michigan's economic disadvantage. This is because, by limiting potential disposal volumes for any particular site, various fixed costs will have to be recovered across smaller volumes, increasing disposal costs per unit for Michigan consumers. The regulation also will require some Michigan counties—those that until now have been exporting their waste to other locations in the State—to confront environmental and other risks that they previously have avoided. Commerce Clause concerns are at their nadir when a state act works in this fashion—raising prices for all the State's consumers, and working to the substantial disadvantage of other segments of the State's population—because in these circumstances " 'a State's own political processes will serve as a check against unduly burdensome regulations.' " *Kassel v. Consolidated Freightways Corp. of Delaware*, 450 U.S. 662, 675, 101 S.Ct. 1309, 1318–1319, 67 L.Ed.2d 580 (1981). In sum, the law simply incorporates the commonsense notion that those responsible for a problem should be responsible for its solution *to the degree they are responsible for the problem but not further*. At a minimum, I think the facts just outlined suggest the State must be allowed to present evidence on the economic, environmental and other effects of its legislation. * * *

WHITE V. MASSACHUSETTS COUNCIL OF
CONSTRUCTION EMPLOYERS, INC.

Supreme Court of the United States, 1983.
460 U.S. 204, 103 S.Ct. 1042, 75 L.Ed.2d 1.

JUSTICE REHNQUIST delivered the opinion of the Court.

In 1979 the mayor of Boston, Massachusetts, issued an executive order which required that all construction projects funded in whole or in part by city funds, or funds which the city had the authority to administer, should be performed by a work force consisting of at least half *bona fide* residents of Boston. The Supreme Judicial Court of Massachusetts decided that the order was unconstitutional, observing that the Commerce Clause "presents a clear obstacle to the city's order." We granted certiorari to decide whether the Commerce Clause of the United States Constitution, Art. I, § 8, cl. 3, prevents the city from giving effect to the mayor's order. * * *

We were first asked in *Hughes v. Alexandria Scrap Corp.,* 426 U.S. 794, 96 S.Ct. 2488, 49 L.Ed.2d 220 (1976), to decide whether state and local governments are restrained by the Commerce Clause when they seek to affect commercial transactions not as "regulators" but as "market participants." In that case, the Maryland legislature, in an attempt to encourage the recycling of abandoned automobiles, offered a bounty for every Maryland-titled automobile converted into scrap if the scrap processor supplied documentation of ownership. An amendment to the Maryland statute imposed more exacting documentation requirements on out-of-state than in-state processors * * *. In upholding the Maryland statute in the face of a Commerce Clause challenge, we said that "[n]othing in the purpose animating the Commerce Clause prohibits a State, in the absence of congressional action, from participating in the market and exercising the right to favor its own citizens over others." Because Maryland was participating in the market, rather than acting as a market regulator, we concluded that the Commerce Clause was not "intended to require independent justification" for the statutory bounty.

We faced the question again in *Reeves, Inc. v. Stake,* 447 U.S. 429, 100 S.Ct. 2271, 65 L.Ed.2d 244 (1980), when confronted with a South Dakota policy to confine the sale of cement by a state operated cement plant to residents of South Dakota. We underscored the holding of *Hughes v. Alexandria Scrap Corp.,* saying: * * * "[T]he Commerce Clause responds principally to state taxes and regulatory measures impeding free private trade in the national marketplace. There is no indication of a constitutional plan to limit the ability of the States themselves to operate freely in the free market." * * *

The Supreme Judicial Court of Massachusetts expressed reservations as to the application of the "market participation" principle to the city here, reasoning that "the implementation of the mayor's order will have a significant impact on those firms which engage in specialized areas of construction and employ permanent works crews composed of out-of-State residents." Even if this conclusion is factually correct, it is not relevant to the inquiry of whether the city is participating in the marketplace when it provides city funds for building construction. If the city is a market participant, then the Commerce Clause establishes no barrier to conditions such as these which the city demands for its participation. * * * The same may be said of the Massachusetts court's finding that the executive order sweeps too broadly, creating more burden than is necessary to accomplish its stated objectives. * * * [W]e note that on the record before us the application of the mayor's executive order to contracts involving only city funds does not represent the sort of "attempt to force virtually all businesses that benefit in some way from the economic ripple effect" of the city's decision to enter into contracts for construction projects "to bias their employment practices in favor of the [city's] residents."[7] * * *

We hold that on the record before us the application of the mayor's executive order to the contracts in question did not violate the Commerce Clause of the United States Constitution. Insofar as the city expended only its own funds in entering into construction contracts for public projects, it was a market participant and entitled to be treated as such under the rule of *Hughes v. Alexandria Scrap Corp.* * * *

JUSTICE BLACKMUN, with whom JUSTICE WHITE joins, concurring in part and dissenting in part. * * *

Neither *Reeves* nor *Alexandria Scrap* * * * went beyond ensuring that the States enjoy " 'the long recognized right of trader or manufacturer, engaged in an entirely private business, freely to exercise his own independent discretion as to parties with whom he will deal.' " *Reeves*, 447 U.S., at 438–439, 100 S.Ct., at 2278. * * * Boston's executive order goes much further. The city has not attempted merely to choose the "parties with whom [it] will deal."[2] Instead, it has imposed as a condition of obtaining a public construction contract the requirement that *private*

---

[7]   Justice Blackmun's opinion dissenting in part argues that the mayor's order goes beyond market participation because it regulates employment contracts between public contractors and their employees. We agree with Justice Blackmun that there are some limits on a state or local government's ability to impose restrictions that reach beyond the immediate parties with which the government transacts business. We find it unnecessary in this case to define those limits with precision, except to say that we think the Commerce Clause does not require the city to stop at the boundary of formal privity of contract. In this case, the mayor's executive order covers a discrete, identifiable class of economic activity in which the city is a major participant. Everyone affected by the order is, in a substantial if informal sense, "working for the city." Wherever the limits of the market participation exception may lie, we conclude that the executive order in this case falls well within the scope of Alexandria Scrap and Reeves.

[2]   Had the city decided to limit its own hiring to Boston residents, its decision would almost certainly have been permissible under McCarthy v. Philadelphia Civil Service Comm'n, 424 U.S. 645, 96 S.Ct. 1154, 47 L.Ed.2d 366 (1976), as well as Reeves and Alexandria Scrap.

firms hire only Boston residents for 50% of specified jobs. Thus, the order directly restricts the ability of private employers to hire nonresidents, and thereby curtails nonresidents' access to jobs with private employers. * * *

The legitimacy of a claim to the market participant exemption * * * should turn primarily on whether a particular state action more closely resembles an attempt to impede trade among private parties, or an attempt, analogous to the accustomed right of merchants in the private sector, to govern the State's own economic conduct and to determine the parties with whom it will deal. The simple unilateral refusals to deal the Court encountered in *Reeves* and *Alexandria Scrap* were relatively pure examples of a seller's or purchaser's simply choosing its bargaining partners, "long recognized" as the right of traders in our free enterprise system. The executive order in this case, in notable contrast, by its terms is a direct attempt to govern private economic relationships. The power to dictate to another those with whom *he* may deal is viewed with suspicion and closely limited in the context of purely private economic relations. When exercised by government, such a power is the essence of regulation. * * *

The Court indicates that it upholds the executive order on the understanding that, with the exception of the federal grant programs, it is applied solely to construction projects funded entirely by the city. * * * This unique aspect of employment in the construction industry—and of public works construction projects—must also underlie the Court's related justification that "[e]veryone affected by the order is, in a substantial if informal sense, 'working for the city.'" I am not persuaded, however, that even the comparatively limited terms of the executive order constitute "market participation" rather than "market regulation." The "sense" in which those affected by the mayor's order "work for the city" is so "informal," in my view, as to lack substance altogether. The city does not hire them, fire them, negotiate with them or their representative about the terms of their employment, or pay their wages. In the case of the employees of subcontractors regulated by the order, the city does not even pay, or contract directly with, their employers. In short, the economic choices the city restricts in favor of its residents are the choices of private entities engaged in interstate commerce. Thus, the executive order directly impedes "free private trade in the national marketplace," and for that reason I would not hold it immune from Commerce Clause scrutiny. * * *

UNITED BUILDING & CONSTRUCTION TRADES COUNCIL OF CAMDEN COUNTY V. CAMDEN

Supreme Court of the United States, 1984.
465 U.S. 208, 104 S.Ct. 1020, 79 L.Ed.2d 249.

JUSTICE REHNQUIST delivered the opinion of the Court.

A municipal ordinance of the city of Camden, New Jersey, requires that at least 40% of the employees of contractors and subcontractors working on city construction projects be Camden residents. Appellant, the United Building and Construction Trades Council of Camden County and Vicinity (Council), challenges that ordinance as a violation of the Privileges and Immunities Clause, Art. IV, § 2, cl. 1, of the United States Constitution.[1] * * *

We first address the argument, accepted by the Supreme Court of New Jersey, that the Clause does not even apply to a *municipal* ordinance such as this. Two separate contentions are advanced in support of this position: first, that the Clause only applies to laws passed by a *State* and, second, that the Clause only applies to laws that discriminate on the basis of *state* citizenship. The first argument can be quickly rejected. * * * [A] municipality is merely a political subdivision of the State from which its authority derives. It is as true of the Privileges and Immunities Clause as of the Equal Protection Clause that what would be unconstitutional if done directly by the State can no more readily be accomplished by a city deriving its authority from the State. * * *

The second argument merits more consideration. The New Jersey Supreme Court concluded that the Privileges and Immunities Clause does not apply to an ordinance that discriminates solely on the basis of *municipal* residency. * * * We cannot accept this argument. * * * Given the Camden ordinance, an out-of-state citizen who ventures into New Jersey will not enjoy the same privileges as the New Jersey citizen residing in Camden. It is true that New Jersey citizens not residing in Camden will be affected by the ordinance as well as out-of-state citizens. And it is true that the disadvantaged New Jersey residents have no claim under the Privileges and Immunities Clause. But New Jersey residents at least have a chance to remedy at the polls any discrimination against them. Out-of-state citizens have no similar opportunity * * *. We conclude that Camden's ordinance is not immune from constitutional review at the behest of out-of-state residents merely because some in-state residents are similarly disadvantaged.

Application of the Privileges and Immunities Clause to a particular instance of discrimination against out-of-state residents entails a two-step inquiry. As an initial matter, the Court must decide whether the

---

[1]   "The Citizens of each State shall be entitled to all Privileges and Immunities of Citizens in the several States."

ordinance burdens one of those privileges and immunities protected by the Clause. *Baldwin v. Montana Fish and Game Comm'n,* 436 U.S. 371, 383, 98 S.Ct. 1852, 1860, 56 L.Ed.2d 354 (1978). Not all forms of discrimination against citizens of other States are constitutionally suspect.

"Some distinctions between residents and nonresidents merely reflect the fact that this is a Nation composed of individual States, and are permitted; other distinctions are prohibited because they hinder the formation, the purpose, or the development of a single Union of those States. Only with respect to those 'privileges' and 'immunities' bearing upon the vitality of the Nation as a single entity must the State treat all citizens, resident and nonresident, equally."

As a threshold matter, then, we must determine whether an out-of-state resident's interest in employment on public works contracts in another State is sufficiently "fundamental" to the promotion of interstate harmony so as to "fall within the purview of the Privileges and Immunities Clause." *Id.,* at 388, 98 S.Ct., at 1862.

Certainly, the pursuit of a common calling is one of the most fundamental of those privileges protected by the Clause. *Baldwin v. Montana Fish and Game Comm'n.* * * * Public employment, however, is qualitatively different from employment in the private sector; it is a subspecies of the broader opportunity to pursue a common calling. We have held that there is no fundamental right to government employment for purposes of the Equal Protection Clause. *Massachusetts v. Murgia,* 427 U.S. 307, 313, 96 S.Ct. 2562, 2566, 49 L.Ed.2d 520 (1976). And in *White* [*v. Massachusetts Council of Const. Employers,*] we held that for purposes of the Commerce Clause everyone employed on a city public works project is, "in a substantial if informal sense, 'working for the city.' "

It can certainly be argued that for purposes of the Privileges and Immunities Clause everyone affected by the Camden ordinance is also "working for the city" and, therefore, has no grounds for complaint when the city favors its own residents. But we decline to transfer mechanically into this context an analysis fashioned to fit the Commerce Clause. Our decision in *White* turned on a distinction between the city acting as a market participant and the city acting as a market regulator. * * * But the distinction * * * relied upon in *White* to dispose of the Commerce Clause challenge is not dispositive in this context. The two Clauses have different aims and set different standards for state conduct.

The Commerce Clause acts as an implied restraint upon state regulatory powers. Such powers must give way before the superior authority of Congress to legislate on (or leave unregulated) matters involving interstate commerce. When the State acts solely as a market participant, no conflict between state *regulation* and federal regulatory authority can arise. The Privileges and Immunities Clause, on the other hand, imposes a direct restraint on state action in the interests of interstate harmony. This concern with comity cuts across the market regulator-market participant distinction that is crucial under the Commerce Clause. It is discrimination against out-of-state residents on matters of fundamental concern which triggers the Clause, not regulation affecting interstate commerce. * * *

In sum, Camden may, without fear of violating the Commerce Clause, pressure private employers engaged in public works projects funded in whole or in part by the city to hire city residents. But that same exercise of power to bias the employment decisions of private contractors and subcontractors against out-of-state residents may be called to account under the Privileges and Immunities Clause. * * * The opportunity to seek employment with such private employers is "sufficiently basic to the livelihood of the Nation," *Baldwin v. Montana Fish and Game Comm'n,* as to fall within the purview of the Privileges and Immunities Clause even though the contractors and subcontractors are themselves engaged in projects funded in whole or part by the city. The conclusion that Camden's ordinance discriminates against a protected privilege does not, of course, end the inquiry. * * * It does not preclude discrimination against citizens of other States where there is a "substantial reason" for the difference in treatment. * * * The city of Camden contends that its ordinance is necessary to counteract grave economic and social ills. Spiraling unemployment, a sharp decline in population, and a dramatic reduction in the number of businesses located in the city have eroded property values and depleted the city's tax base. The resident hiring preference is designed, the city contends, to increase the number of employed persons living in Camden and to arrest the "middle class flight" currently plaguing the city. The city also argues that all non-Camden residents employed on city public works projects, whether they reside in New Jersey or Pennsylvania, * * * "live off" Camden without "living in" Camden. * * *

Every inquiry under the Privileges and Immunities Clause "must * * * be conducted with due regard for the principle that the states should have considerable leeway in analyzing local evils and in prescribing appropriate cures." *Toomer v. Witsell,* 334 U.S. 385, 396, 68 S.Ct. 1156, 1162, 92 L.Ed. 1460 (1948). This caution is particularly appropriate when a government body is merely setting conditions on the expenditure of funds it controls. * * * [T]he Camden ordinance * * * is limited in scope to employees working directly on city public works projects. Nonetheless, we find it impossible to evaluate Camden's justification on the record as it now stands. No trial has ever been held in the case. No findings of fact have been made. The Supreme Court of New Jersey certified the case for direct appeal after the brief administrative proceedings * * *. It would not be appropriate for this Court either to make factual determinations as an initial matter or to take judicial notice of Camden's decay. We, therefore, deem it wise to remand the case to the New Jersey Supreme Court. That court may decide, consistent with state procedures, on the best method for making the necessary findings. * * *

JUSTICE BLACKMUN, dissenting.

For over a century the underlying meaning of the Privileges and Immunities Clause of the Constitution's Article IV has been regarded as settled: at least absent some substantial, noninvidious justification, a State may not discriminate between its own residents and residents of other States on the basis of state citizenship. * * * Today, however, the Court casually extends the scope of the Clause by holding that it applies to laws that discriminate *among* state residents on the basis of *municipal* residence, simply because discrimination on the basis of municipal residence disadvantages citizens of other States "*ipso facto.*" This novel interpretation arrives accompanied by little practical justification and no historical or textual support whatsoever. * * *

Contrary to the Court's tacit assumption, discrimination on the basis of municipal residence is substantially different in this regard from discrimination on the basis of state citizenship. The distinction is simple but fundamental: discrimination on the basis of municipal residence penalizes persons within the State's political community as well as those without. The Court itself points out that while New Jersey citizens who reside outside Camden are not protected by the Privileges and Immunities Clause, they may resort to the State's political processes to protect themselves. What the Court fails to appreciate is that this avenue of relief for New Jersey residents works to protect residents of other States as well; disadvantaged state residents who turn to the state legislature to displace ordinances like Camden's further the interests of nonresidents as well as their own. Nor is this mechanism for relief merely a theoretical one; in the past decade several States, including California and Georgia, have repealed or forbidden protectionist ordinances like the one at issue here. * * *

LEYDON V. TOWN OF GREENWICH

Supreme Court of Connecticut, 2001.
257 Conn. 318, 777 A.2d 552.

PALMER, J. * * *

The plaintiff, Brenden P. Leydon, commenced this action against the named defendant, the town of Greenwich (town), seeking declaratory and injunctive relief to prohibit the enforcement of a town ordinance limiting access to Greenwich Point Park (Greenwich Point), a town park with a beachfront on the Long Island Sound, to residents of the town and their guests. * * * Greenwich Point is a town owned, 147 acre park facility that * * * contains a number of ponds, a marina, a parking lot, open fields, a nature preserve, shelters, walkways and trails, and picnic areas with picnic tables. There also is a library book drop located on the beach. The only land access to Greenwich Point is over a narrow, broccoli stem shaped piece of land known as Tod's Driftway (driftway), which is owned by * * * [defendant Lucas Point Association, Inc.], a private association of landowners who reside in the residential area adjacent to Greenwich Point. The town holds an easement over a private road on the driftway that provides the only means by which a person seeking to enter Greenwich Point by land may do so. * * *

On August 15, 1994, * * * the plaintiff, a resident of Stamford, attempted to enter Greenwich Point at its main gate. He was refused admission * * *. The plaintiff then filed this action for declaratory and injunctive relief against the town, claiming, inter alia, that the ordinance violates: (1) the first amendment to the United States constitution * * *.[13]

The scope of the government's power to limit speech or other first amendment activity on public property depends on the type of forum involved. * * * "In places which by long tradition or by government fiat have been devoted to assembly and debate, the rights of the State to limit expressive activity are sharply circumscribed. . . . [Such locations include] streets and parks which have immemorially been held in trust for the use of the public and, time out of mind, have been used for purposes of assembly, communicating thoughts between citizens, and discussing public questions. In these quintessential public forums, the government may . . . enforce regulations of the time, place, and manner of expression which are content-neutral, are narrowly tailored to serve a significant government interest, and leave open ample alternative channels of communication. Such close scrutiny is appropriate in these forums because such properties possess long-standing traditions of public usage." *State v. Linares*, 232 Conn. [345,] 366–67, 655 A.2d 737 [1995]. * * * "Because restrictions on speech in public forums receive the highest level of scrutiny and those in nonpublic forums are subject to the lowest . . . a court's initial categorization of property, as a practical matter, necessarily

---

[13] There is nothing in the record to refute the plaintiff's wholly unremarkable assertion that, upon his admission to Greenwich Point, he intended to express himself by conversing with others "on topics of social and political importance." Indeed, the record fully supports the plaintiff's assertion. For example, the plaintiff testified, without contradiction, that, if permitted to enter Greenwich Point, he intended to use the park both for recreational activities *and* to discuss issues of importance to him and to the public, including the use of beach property by members of the general public. The plaintiff also testified that, on one occasion when he sought and was denied admission to Greenwich Point, he was to be interviewed, on the beach, by a reporter from the New York Times, regarding the issue of public access to parks.

determines whether a particular restriction on speech will be invalidated." *State v. Linares, supra.*

Upon application of these principles, we conclude that Greenwich Point is a traditional public forum because it has the characteristics of a public park. * * * In view of the fact that Greenwich Point contains shelters, ponds, a marina, a parking lot, open fields, a nature preserve, walkways, trails, picnic areas with picnic tables, a library book drop and a beach, it is clear that Greenwich Point qualifies as a park for purposes of first amendment analysis. The fact that Greenwich Point has a boundary on the Long Island Sound that serves as a beach for swimming, sun bathing and other activities in no way alters its character as a park. As such, it is a traditional public forum. * * *

In the present case, the town has failed to explain why the ordinance's virtual ban on nonresidents is a reasonable time, place or manner restriction on the use of the park by such nonresidents. Moreover, even if we assume that the town has a compelling interest in restricting nonresident access to the park—an assumption that finds no support in the record—the ordinance is not narrowly tailored to accomplish that end. Consequently, the ordinance does not pass federal constitutional muster. It is apparent, moreover, that the ordinance violates the first amendment both as applied to the plaintiff and for substantial overbreadth. With respect to the former ground for finding the ordinance unconstitutional, the town lawfully cannot bar the plaintiff from Greenwich Point due solely to the fact that he is a nonresident because the park is a *public* forum. Furthermore, the ordinance bars a large class of nonresidents, namely, all nonresidents who cannot find a resident host, from engaging in a multitude of expressive and associational activities at Greenwich Point. Because the town's restriction on the use of Greenwich Point by nonresidents cannot be justified on the ground that it is narrowly tailored to meet a compelling need, the ordinance is facially overbroad. The ordinance, therefore, cannot withstand scrutiny under the first amendment, either as applied to the plaintiff or as applied to other nonresidents who might wish to enter Greenwich Point. * * *

In light of our conclusion that the town cannot restrict access to Greenwich Point on the basis of residency, we also must address: (1) the plaintiff's claim that any agreement between the town and the association to restrict access to Greenwich Point is unenforceable; (2) the association's claim that the use of the easement over its property is restricted to town residents and their guests; and (3) the plaintiff's claim that he is entitled to injunctive relief against the association. We conclude that any agreement between the town and the association is unenforceable and, furthermore, that the plaintiff is entitled to a judgment against the association declaring as much. For the reasons that follow, we also reject the association's contention that, on the basis of its 1945 agreement with the town, the easement over its property may be used only by town residents and their guests. We conclude, however, that the plaintiff is not entitled to any other relief affecting the property rights of the association. * * *

The plaintiff asks us to affirm, inter alia, that part of the judgment of the Appellate Court directing the trial court to grant the plaintiff injunctive relief against the association. The plaintiff's sole basis for such a request, however, is his contention that the Appellate Court was correct in its reasoning that the public trust doctrine required that he be granted access to Greenwich Point over the association's driftway. * * * [T]he public trust doctrine does not extend that far. Furthermore, neither the federal constitution nor the state constitution governs private, as opposed to governmental, conduct in this realm. On this record, therefore, the plaintiff has presented no persuasive reason why the Appellate Court's reasoning vis-a-vis the association should be sustained.

It may be that, under applicable property law or other legal doctrines, the plaintiff and other nonresidents have a right to use the easement created over the driftway in 1892 to gain access to Greenwich Point, the dominant estate, from the property of the association, the servient estate. To the contrary, however, it may be that, if the easement were opened to all persons, it would become overburdened; or that other applicable property law or other legal doctrines would allow the association to limit the use of the easement, or that, failing such limitation, the easement would revert to the association and cease to exist. These issues were not fully explored or litigated at trial and certainly were not fully determined by the trial court. The resolution of these issues will have to await the outcome of what the parties do or do not do in the wake of this decision and will depend on what further remedies any of them may seek. Insofar as the plaintiff's claims against the association are concerned, the issue in this case is limited to whether the association has a right to enforcement of the ordinance's residency requirement. Consequently, the plaintiff is not entitled to a judgment that purports to settle the *property rights* of the association. * * *

5.   THE ABILITY OF CITIES TO ANNEX OUTSIDERS

This subsection raises a critical issue about inter-city relationships both as a matter of history and a matter of theory: who needs to agree before one city can annex another?[8] As between the annexing city and the city to be annexed, at least four answers seem possible:

---

[8]   For a history of annexation, see, e.g., Jon Teaford, City and Suburb: The Political Fragmentation of Metropolitan America, 1850–1970, pp. 32–63 (1979); see also Sam Bass Warner, Jr., Streetcar Suburbs: The Process of Growth in Boston, 1870–1900 (1962). For a consideration of the legal issues raised by annexation, see, e.g., Christopher Tyson, Localism and

1.   Citizens of both the annexing and annexed city could vote, with all ballots counted together according to the principle of one person, one vote.

2.   Only citizens of the annexing city could vote; no one in the annexed city would be entitled to vote.

3.   Only citizens of the annexed city could vote; no one in the annexing city would be entitled to vote.

4.   Citizens of both the annexing and annexed city could vote, but the ballots would be counted separately. Annexation would require both a majority of the vote of the annexing city and a majority of the vote of the annexed city.

All four of these answers have been upheld as constitutional. See Hunter v. Pittsburgh, supra (#1); Murphy v. Kansas City, Missouri, 347 F.Supp. 837 (W.D.Mo.1972) (#2); Moorman v. Wood, 504 F.Supp. 467 (E.D.Ky.1980) (#3); Town of Lockport v. Citizens for Community Action, infra (#4).

In many cases, annexation disputes pit communities of differing sizes against one another. What would justify giving a small city a veto on being annexed by a larger city (as in positions 3 and 4, above)? What would justify letting a large city annex a smaller city when a majority of the smaller city opposes the annexation (as in positions 1 and 2 above)?

Annexation disputes arise for myriad reasons and the particular facts of any such dispute may bear on the method one may choose for resolving it. The federal district court judge in *Moorman* nicely describes some of the forces that underlie annexation disputes:

Although the plaintiffs here claim that the annexations are the result of the efforts of two "affluent subdivisions" to attempt to avoid their fair share of urban problems, this is not always, nor even usually the case in local annexation controversies. The

Involuntary Annexation: Reconsidering Approaches to New Regionalism, 87 Tul. L. Rev. 297 (2012); Christopher Tyson, Annexation and the Mid-size Metropolis: New Insights in the Age of Mobile Capital, 73 U. Pitt. L. Rev. 505 (2012); Judith Wegner, North Carolina's Annexation Wars: Whys, Wherefores, and What Next, 91 N.C. L. Rev. 165 (2012); Amanda K. Baumle, Mark Fossett, Warren Waren, Strategic Annexation Under the Voting Rights Act: Racial Dimensions of Annexation Practices, 24 Harv. BlackLetter L. J. 81 (2008); Robert D. Zeinemann, Overlooked Linkages Between Municipal Incorporation and Annexation Laws: An In-Depth Look at Wisconsin's Experience, 39 Urb. Law. 257 (2007); Clayton Gillette, Voting With Your Hands: Direct Democracy in Annexation, 78 S. Cal. L. Rev. 835 (2005); Nicholas Cooper, Annexation in Iowa and the "Textbook Example" of a Voluntary Annexation that Hardly Seems Voluntary, 9 Drake J. Agric. L. 103 (2004); Clayton Gillette, Expropriation and Institutional Design in State and Local Government Law, 80 Va. L. Rev. 625 (1994); Laurie Reynolds, Rethinking Municipal Annexation Powers, 24 The Urban Lawyer 247 (1992); Daren Waite, Annexation and the Voting Rights Act, 28 How. L. J. 565 (1985); Ethan Lipsig, Annexation Elections and the Right to Vote, 20 U.C.L.A. L.Rev. 1093 (1973); M.G. Woodrooff, Systems and Standards of Municipal Annexation Review: A Comparative Analysis, 58 Geo. L. Rev. 743 (1970); National League of Cities, Adjusting Municipal Boundaries (1962).

court has known citizens of an unincorporated area with no municipal services whatever and a blue collar population to resist annexation to an affluent city of 15,000 and, in another case, a ferocious court battle to be waged to resist annexation to a city with a population of 3,000 or less, where neither the annexors nor the annexees could be described as affluent.

Although, of course, there may be some desire to escape higher taxes and urban problems, in many instances, the motivation for resisting annexation in this vicinity is that many of the people like to live in their small towns where they can know the mayor, city council members and other officials personally, and where they can live their lives, as they see it, relatively free from regulation and have a direct voice in such municipal matters as zoning or the granting of a liquor license.

Where financial considerations are a primary motive in opposing annexations, frequently they involve a conscious desire to accept fewer municipal services as a trade off for lower taxes. For example, many of the smaller communities, both incorporated and unincorporated, keep taxes rather low by utilizing volunteer fire departments, part-time police forces, septic tanks instead of sewers, no city manager or engineer, etc. From this point of view, the prevention of annexation enables those with limited financial resources better to own their own homes. To such people terms like "metro government" and "annexation" are calls to a holy war of resistance.

The annexing cities, on the other hand, are often motivated by a desire to expand their tax base and a perceived need to end the confusion and inefficiency which they contend result from the profusion of small government entities. The court expresses no opinion as to the wisdom of either of these positions. They are described here solely to explain the emotionally charged dilemma with which the legislature was presented.

The three readings that follow—two federal Supreme Court cases and a book excerpt—provide some background for considering the possible ways one might go about deciding annexation issues. The first case, Hunter v. Pittsburgh, is best known for its strong dicta that the federal Constitution places few, if any, constraints on the power of states to create or destroy "their" local governments. We considered that aspect of the decision in Chapter Two; we return to the decision here because the case itself arose out of an annexation dispute between a large city and a smaller one. The Court's decision made it clear that the state had no federal constitutional obligation to treat the residents of the annexing community and the residents of the community to be annexed as if they formed two separate communities. It therefore held that it was constitutional for the larger city to annex the smaller one over the objection of its residents. Indeed, according to the Court, the state could simply impose a new boundary without obtaining the consent of the residents of either the annexing or the annexed city. The next case, Town of Lockport v. Citizens for Community Action, is not strictly speaking a case about annexation. It nevertheless addresses a question related to the one that underlies *Hunter*. In the course of its reasoning, it concludes that the state may, if it chooses, refuse to allow a city's residents to annex a neighboring city without the consent of the voters of the neighboring city.

The book excerpt provides some perspective on how one might resolve the policy questions that federal constitutional law leaves open with respect to annexation disputes. David Rusk, a former mayor of Albuquerque, a city that enjoyed broad annexation authority, suggests that it is important to permit central cities to annex surrounding communities with relative ease. He argues that cities that can easily annex surrounding territory are elastic and therefore can "capture" suburban growth, while cities that cannot are "inelastic" and therefore "contribute to" suburban growth. Note that Rusk seems to assume that something called "suburban growth" is inevitable and that the sole question is whether central cities will be able to capture the benefits of this growth. Moreover, as the *Moorman* case suggests, annexation arises not just from a central city's desire for growth but from land disputes between smaller communities. Expanding urban annexation power may encourage smaller, unincorporated communities to seek incorporation, thereby triggering an annexation war over the dividing line between neighboring communities. If so, the annexation question must be considered together with the other state law rules that distribute power between local communities of varying sizes and wealth.

HUNTER V. PITTSBURGH

[See Chapter 2, Section A–1, supra.]

TOWN OF LOCKPORT V. CITIZENS FOR COMMUNITY ACTION

Supreme Court of the United States, 1977.
430 U.S. 259, 97 S.Ct. 1047, 51 L.Ed.2d 313.

MR. JUSTICE STEWART delivered the opinion of the Court. * * *

County government in New York has traditionally taken the form of a single-branch legislature, exercising general governmental powers. General governmental powers are also exercised by the county's constituent cities, villages, and towns. The allocation of powers among these subdivisions can be changed, and a new form of county government adopted, pursuant to referendum procedures specified in Art. IX of the

New York Constitution and implemented by § 33 of the Municipal Home Rule Law. Under those procedures a county board of supervisors may submit a proposed charter to the voters for approval. If a majority of the voting city dwellers and a majority of the voting noncity dwellers both approve, the charter is adopted.

In November 1972, a proposed charter for the county of Niagara was put to referendum. The charter created the new offices of County Executive and County Comptroller, and continued the county's existing power to establish tax rates, equalize assessments, issue bonds, maintain roads, and administer health and public welfare services. No explicit provision for redistribution of governmental powers from the cities or towns to the county government was made. The city voters approved the charter by a vote of 18,220 to 14,914. The noncity voters disapproved the charter by a vote of 11,594 to 10,665. A majority of those voting in the entire county thus favored the charter. * * *

[E]ver since the seminal case of *Reynolds v. Sims,* 377 U.S. 533, 84 S.Ct. 1362, 12 L.Ed.2d 506, it has been established that the Equal Protection Clause cannot tolerate the disparity in individual voting strength that results when elected officials represent districts of unequal population * * * [I]n voting for their legislators, all citizens have an equal interest in representative democracy, and that the concept of equal protection therefore requires that their votes be given equal weight. The equal protection principles applicable in gauging the fairness of an election involving the choice of legislative representatives are of limited relevance, however, in analyzing the propriety of recognizing distinctive voter interests in a "single-shot" referendum. In a referendum, the expression of voter will is direct, and there is no need to assure that the voters' views will be adequately represented through their representatives in the legislature. The policy impact of a referendum is also different in kind from the impact of choosing representatives— instead of sending legislators off to the state capitol to vote on a multitude of issues, the referendum puts one discrete issue to the voters. That issue is capable, at least, of being analyzed to determine whether its adoption or rejection will have a disproportionate impact on an identifiable group of voters. If it is found to have such a disproportionate impact, the question then is whether a State can recognize that impact either by limiting the franchise to those voters specially affected or by giving their votes a special weight. This question has been confronted by the Court in two types of cases: those dealing with elections involving "special-interest" governmental bodies of limited jurisdiction, and those dealing with bond referenda.

The Court has held that the electorate of a special purpose unit of government, such as a water storage district, may be apportioned to give greater influence to the constituent groups found to be most affected by the governmental unit's functions. *Salyer Land Co. v. Tulare Lake Basin Water Storage District,* 410 U.S. 719, 93 S.Ct. 1224, 35 L.Ed.2d 659. But the classification of voters into "interested" and "non-interested" groups must still be reasonably precise * * *. In the bond referenda cases, the local government had either limited the electoral franchise to property owners, or weighted property owners' votes more heavily than those of nonproperty owners by using a "dual box" separate majority approval system quite similar to the one at issue in the present case. *Cipriano v. City of Houma,* 395 U.S. 701, 89 S.Ct. 1897, 23 L.Ed.2d 647; *Phoenix v. Kolodziejski,* 399 U.S. 204, 90 S.Ct. 1990, 26 L.Ed.2d 523; *Hill v. Stone,* 421 U.S. 289, 95 S.Ct. 1637, 44 L.Ed.2d 172. * * * In support of the classifications, it was argued that property owners have a more substantial stake in the adoption of obligation bonds than do nonproperty owners, because the taxes of the former directly and substantially fund the bond obligation. The Court rejected that argument for limiting the electoral franchise, however, noting that nonproperty owners also share in the tax burden when the tax on rental property or commercial businesses is passed on in the form of higher prices. Although the interests of the two groups are concededly not identical, the Court held that they are sufficiently similar to prevent a state government from distinguishing between them by artificially narrowing or weighting the electoral franchise in favor of the property taxpayers.

These decisions do not resolve the issues in the present case. Taken together, however, they can be said to focus attention on two inquiries: whether there is a genuine difference in the relevant interests of the groups that the state electoral classification has created; and if so, whether any resulting enhancement of minority voting strength nonetheless amounts to invidious discrimination in violation of the Equal Protection Clause. * * *

[I]f * * * it were clear that all voters in Niagara County have substantially identical interests in the adoption of a new county charter, regardless of where they reside within the county[,] the District Court's judgment would have to be affirmed under our prior cases. * * * [But] it appears that the challenged provisions of New York law rest on the State's identification of the distinctive interests of the residents of the cities and towns within a county rather than their interests as residents of the county as a homogeneous unit. This identification is based in the realities of the distribution of governmental powers in New York, and is consistent with our cases that recognize both the wide discretion the States have in forming and allocating governmental tasks to local subdivisions, and the discrete interests that such local governmental units may have *qua* units.

General purpose local government in New York is entrusted to four different units: counties, cities, towns and villages. The State is divided into 62 counties; each of the 57 counties outside of New York City is divided into towns, or towns and one or more cities. Villages, once formed, are still part of the towns in which they are located. The New York Legislature has conferred home rule, and general governmental powers on all of these subdivisions, and their governmental activities may on occasion substantially overlap. The cities often perform functions within their jurisdiction that the county may perform for noncity residents; similarly villages perform some functions for their residents that the town provides for the rest of the town's inhabitants. Historically towns provided their areas with major social services that more recently have been transferred to counties; towns exercise more regulatory power than counties; and both towns and counties can create special taxing and improvement districts to administer services.

Acting within a fairly loose state apportionment of political power, the relative energy and organization of these various subdivisions will often determine which one of them in a given area carries out the major tasks of local government. Since the cities have the greatest autonomy within this scheme, changes serving to strengthen the county structure may have the most immediate impact on the functions of the towns as deliverers of government services. * * * [T]he executive-legislative form of government * * * would significantly enhance the county's organizational and service delivery capacity, for the purpose of "greater efficiency and responsibility in county government." The creation of the offices of County Executive and County Comptroller clearly reflect this purpose. Such anticipated organizational changes * * * could effectively shift any pre-existing balance of power between town and county governments towards county predominance. In terms of efficient delivery of government services such a shift might be all to the good, but it may still be viewed as carrying a cost quite different for town voters and their existing town governments from that incurred by city voters and their existing city governments.

The ultimate question then is whether, given the differing interests of city and noncity voters in the adoption of a new county charter in New York, those differences are sufficient under the Equal Protection Clause to justify the classifications made by New York law. If that question were posed in the context of annexation proceedings, the fact that the residents of the annexing city and the residents of the area to be annexed formed sufficiently different constituencies with sufficiently different interests could be readily perceived. The fact of impending union alone would not so merge them into one community of interest as constitutionally to require that their votes be aggregated in any referendum to approve annexation. Cf. *Hunter v. City of Pittsburgh,* 207 U.S. 161, 28 S.Ct. 40, 52 L.Ed. 151. Similarly a proposal that several school districts join to form a consolidated unit could surely be subject to voter approval in each constituent school district.

Yet in terms of recognizing constituencies with separate and potentially opposing interests, the structural decision to annex or consolidate is similar in impact to the decision to restructure county government in New York. In each case, separate voter approval requirements are based on the perception that the real and long-term impact of a restructuring of local government is felt quite differently by the different county constituent units that in a sense compete to provide similar governmental services. Voters in these constituent units are directly and differentially affected by the restructuring of county government, which may make the provider of public services more remote and less subject to the voters' individual influence.

The provisions of New York law here in question no more than recognize the realities of these substantially differing electoral interests.[18] Granting to these provisions the presumption of constitutionality to which every duly enacted state and federal law is entitled, we are unable to conclude that they violate the Equal Protection Clause of the Fourteenth Amendment. * * *

DAVID RUSK, LESSONS FROM URBAN AMERICA
From David Rusk, Cities Without Suburbs.
Pp. 5, 7, 9–10, 20–23, 26–27, 31–34, 41, 47 (2d ed. 1995).

What lessons can be drawn from a broad look at what has been happening in urban America over the last forty years?

Lesson 1: The real city is the total metropolitan area—city and suburb. * * *

Lesson 2: Most of America's Blacks, Hispanics, and Asians live in urban areas. * * *

Lesson 3: Since World War II all urban growth has been low-density, suburban style. * * *

Lesson 4: For a city's population to grow, the city must be "elastic."

Think of a city as a map drawn on a rubber sheet. If there is a great deal of vacant land within existing city limits, that city's population density is low. The city has room for new population growth by filling in undeveloped land. In effect, the rubber sheet map is slack. Facing growth opportunities, the city is still elastic within its boundaries because of its

---

[18] There is no indication that the classifications created by New York law work to favor city to town voter, or town to city voter. In some New York counties, city voters outnumber town voters; in other counties, the reverse is true. * * * The constitutional and statutory provisions in this case also do not appear to be the sustained product of either an entrenched minority or a willful majority. Instead they have been subject historically to fairly frequent revision. * * *

low population density. It can stretch upward to accommodate new growth.

On the other hand, what if the city is already densely populated? There is little or no vacant land to develop. Its rubber sheet map is stretched taut within its existing boundaries. That high-density city cannot become more dense. (That is not a lifestyle that most postwar, middle-class families "buy.") The high-density city's only path to growth is to expand its boundaries. It must stretch the edges of its rubber sheet map to take in new territory. It must become more elastic outward rather than upward.

The most common method by which a city acquires new territory is annexation. Sometimes, a city annexes undeveloped land. More often, an annexation brings in an existing community. Stretching the edges of the municipal map often creates tension—outside resistance from those to be annexed and inside resistance from a city's current residents. Annexation is not always easy.

How much did cities utilize each mechanism—filling in vacant land and annexing additional territory? Only about 20 percent of all cities actually increased their densities. For many other cities, however, in-fill development was combined with boundary expansion (which often tended to mask the degree of in-fill development).

Boundary expansion contributed most to municipal elasticity. Between 1950 and 1990 more than four-fifths of the 522 central cities expanded their boundaries by 10 percent or more. The municipal expansion champion was Anchorage, Alaska. By absorbing its entire surrounding borough, the city of Anchorage grew from 12.5 square miles to 1,697.7 square miles (13,482 percent)! Overall, the 522 central cities expanded from 10,513 square miles to 27,728 square miles (164 percent, or 149 percent if Anchorage's massive land grab is discounted).

On the threshold of the era of the suburban lifestyle, the cities with the greatest elasticity had vacant city land to develop *and* the political and legal tools to annex new land. These I will call "elastic cities." At the other end of the spectrum were the "inelastic cities"—typically, older cities already built out at higher than average densities and, for a variety of reasons, unable or unwilling to expand their city limits.

This pattern of urban development is sufficiently universal (at least, in America) to embolden me to state the first law of urban dynamics: *only elastic cities grow.*

This concept of a city's elasticity is the central idea of this book. Why have some cities been elastic and others have not? What are the demographic, economic, and social consequences of inelasticity? If being an elastic city is essential to economic, social, and fiscal health, what can be done to make inelastic cities elastic again or, at least, to benefit as if they were elastic? * * *

Lesson 10: Elastic cities "capture" suburban growth; inelastic cities "contribute" to suburban growth.

As I have shown, all postwar growth has been suburban style—low-density development emphasizing detached, single-family homes. Elastic cities * * * captured much of this suburban-style growth within their own municipal boundaries. Inelastic cities could not grow either through in-fill or annexation. * * * Incapable of capturing a share of suburban-type development, inelastic cities actually contributed White, middle-class families to the new suburbs. In recent years in areas such as Washington, D.C., and Atlanta, a rapidly growing Black middle class has moved to the suburbs as well. * * *

Lesson 11: Bad state laws can hobble cities.

State laws differ concerning the power they give municipalities to expand. In New England, for example, the political map has long been set—in some cases since colonial times. New England state laws do not even provide for municipal annexation. In other regions state laws attach conditions that can severely limit a municipality's practical ability to annex additional territory. Annexation may be allowed only upon voluntary petition by property owners. Often an affirmative vote of affected land owners is required (or even approval by voters in the annexing municipality). Such restrictions on annexation authority are found most often in the Northeast and Midwest. * * *

Lesson 12: Neighbors can trap cities.

In some states a municipality cannot expand beyond its home county. By 1950 a few inelastic cities in America had largely filled up small home counties. Other inelastic cities had been transformed into their own counties or into "independent cities" with boundaries that could not expand. By contrast, most elastic cities are located in counties that are geographically much larger; small central cities have room to grow very large.

In all states, however, one municipality cannot annex property within another municipality, regardless of the disparity in size. This can be the most insurmountable barrier to annexation.

A central city's expansion can be blocked by competing municipalities. Many older cities became gradually surrounded by smaller cities, towns, and villages. Newer central cities often faced only farmland, swamp, or sagebrush. * * *

*Lesson 14: Racial prejudice has shaped growth patterns: * * ***

*Lesson 15: Inelastic cities are more segregated than elastic areas. * * ***

Lesson 16: Inelastic areas that segregate Blacks segregate Hispanics.
* * *

Lesson 17: City-suburb income gaps are more critical a problem than overall income levels in metro areas.

The city-suburb per capita income ratio is the single most important indicator of an urban area's social health. Income levels in inelastic cities fall well below suburban levels (Detroit and Cleveland, 53 percent). Elastic cities, however, keep pace with suburban levels (Houston, 89 percent; Nashville, 98 percent) or even exceed suburban levels (Raleigh, 103 percent; Albuquerque, 118 percent). * * *

The crux of the issue is the sharp disparities within the metro area. Inelastic cities had per capita incomes ($11,102) only 68 per cent of suburban levels, while income levels *within* elastic cities ($14,634) were equal (96 percent) to suburban levels. As a result, income levels for elastic cities were 32 percent above income levels of inelastic cities, even though both sets of cities are located in areas of nominally equal wealth.

Many mayors of inelastic cities * * * are trapped between having an ever smaller slice of the metro tax base and an ever growing share of metro social burdens. * * * Mayors of elastic cities, by contrast, find many of their "suburbs" within their own city limits. Their city revenue bases have expanded dramatically. Often city governments of elastic cities are better financed than are outlying jurisdictions. Poor minorities are not heavily concentrated within the central city. For cities that are expanding very aggressively, the "suburbs" outside the city limits are often poor rural and semirural areas. Under such conditions mayors usually choose to handle local problems with local revenues rather than seek federal urban aid.

Lesson 18: Fragmented local government fosters segregation; unified local government promotes integration.

The fragmentation of metro areas into multiple local governments is associated with the degree of residential segregation.

For most Americans, smaller is better and home rule is an unassailable democratic good. But the sad reality is that the smaller the local jurisdiction or school district, the more narrow and exclusive the population served. In general, the more highly fragmented a metro area is, the more segregated it is racially and economically. Smaller jurisdictions are typically organized to promote and protect uniformity rather than diversity. Conversely, areas characterized by geographically large, multi-powered governments and more unified school systems tend to promote more racial and economic integration and achieve greater social mobility.

The critical issue is the number of different governments that control planning and zoning decisions. The key measures are the proportion of the metro area under the central city's control and the number of suburban jurisdictions with planning and zoning powers. * * *

The way a metro area is governed is not the only factor affecting integration. Another factor is age. Old cities generally have more decaying neighborhoods in which poor Blacks and Hispanics are concentrated. Younger cities have emerged in an era of somewhat more enlightened racial attitudes (and some effective civil rights laws). In addition, regional racial patterns and overall economic trends affect the degree of integration.

Does greater socioeconomic integration automatically flow from greater governmental unity? Probably not. What is clear is that, absent federal or state mandates, a metro area in which local government is highly fragmented is usually incapable of adopting broad, integrating strategies. Conversely, a metro area in which key planning and zoning powers are concentrated under a dominant local government has the potential to implement policies to promote greater racial and economic integration if that government has the courage and vision to do so. * * *

Lesson 22: Poverty is more concentrated in inelastic cites than in elastic cities. * * *

Conclusion

* * * An inelastic area has a central city frozen within its city limits and surrounded by growing suburbs. It may have a strong downtown business district as a regional employment center, but its city neighborhoods are increasingly catch basins for poor Blacks and Hispanics. With the flight of middle-class families, the city's population has dropped steadily (typically by 20 percent or more). The income gap between city residents and suburbanites steadily widens. City government is squeezed between rising service needs and eroding incomes. Unable to tap the areas of greater economic growth (its suburbs), the city becomes increasingly reliant on federal and state aid. The suburbs are typically fragmented into multiple towns and small cities and mini school systems. This very fragmentation of local government reinforces racial and economic segregation. Rivalry among jurisdictions often inhibits the whole area's ability to respond to economic challenges.

In an elastic area suburban subdivisions expand around the central city, but the central city is able to expand as well and capture much of that suburban growth within its municipal boundaries. Although no community is free of racial inequities, minorities are more evenly spread throughout the area. Segregation by race and income class is reduced. City incomes are typically equal to or higher than suburban incomes. Tapping a broader tax base, an elastic city government is better financed and more inclined to rely on local resources to address local problems. In fact, local public institutions, in general, tend to be more unified and promote more united and effective responses to economic challenges.

6.   SECESSION AND DISSOLUTION

The commentator, Robert Brooks, writing early in the twentieth century, believed that the great metropolises of his time could reach their full potential only if they seceded from their states. Not satisfied with the grant of home rule authority, he argued:

> [T]he emancipation of metropolitan cities from the controlling influence of state governments must be much more thorough and far-reaching. Completing the evolutionary process * * *, such an emancipation must remove radically the possibility of the many gross abuses and petty irritations of the present system of state control. Why should we not look forward to the entire separation of metropolitan cities such as New York, Chicago, and Philadelphia from state ties, and their erection into free city commonwealths within our federal system? * * * Critics may * * * urge that the proposed solution involves the advocacy of political disintegration, of "secession." But a division of territory that removes forever the cause of a host of old abuses, that separates unlike social units and permits each to develop freely in its own way, is not disintegration but reconstruction. As for "secession," while the new free cities would indeed be separated from their former state affiliations, on the other hand they would become members in full sovereignty of the Union.[9]

The secessionist impulse continues to be felt among city residents, but now the predominant impulse is to break free from the very metropolitan cities that Brooks championed. In 1986, the residents of an area of Boston that includes the city's principal African-American neighborhoods voted in a nonbinding referendum on a proposal that they incorporate themselves as a new city, to be called Mandela. The referendum failed by a 3–1 margin.[10] What is the relationship between the effort of members of Boston's African-American community to secede from Boston and the decision in 1873 by the residents of Brookline, a wealthy neighborhood surrounded by the city of Boston, to remain separate from the city?[11] What does it say about the path of local government law that the impulse to secede in our time is often an impulse to flee the very cities that Brooks wanted to make free?

---

[9]   See Robert Brooks, Metropolitan Free Cities, 30 Pol. Sci. Q. 222, 230–231 (1915).

[10]   See Boston Globe, November 5, 1986, pp. 1, 23.

[11]   See Sam Bass Warner, Streetcar Suburbs: The Process of Growth in Boston, 1870–1900, p. 163 (2d ed. 1978).

A related set of questions concerns who should be entitled to vote on secession efforts. Should it be only the residents of "Mandela" (or Brookline) or all the residents of Boston as a whole? Is there a difference between separating from a city and remaining separate from it—that is, between secession and resistance to annexation? Should the difference in the relative wealth and power of the two communities affect the decision about the proper franchise? The question of the appropriate electorate for secession is addressed in the first case, City of Herriman v. Bell. Is the court convincing in reading the precedents—cases in previous sections of this chapter—to mean that limiting the vote to the area seeking secession is constitutional? Even if it is constitutional, should state law permit the question to be decided without the participation of those left behind? A note that follows the *Herriman* case explores these issues in the context of Staten Island's effort to secede from the City of New York.[12]

Following the note on Staten Island, Gerald Frug's article discusses the more recent attempted secession of the San Fernando Valley, Hollywood, and the Harbor communities from the City of Los Angeles. (Only the San Fernando Valley and Hollywood secession efforts got on the ballot. The applicable legal rule was that secession required a majority both of the area attempting to secede and of the city as a whole. On November 5, 2002, both secession votes lost city-wide by a 2–1 margin, and the effort within Hollywood lost as well. But secession was narrowly approved—by 50.7% of the vote—in the San Fernando Valley.) The proponents of secession in Los Angeles complained that the city was simply too big. They offered this image[13] to illustrate the point:

---

[12] For an analysis of the issues involved in the Staten Island secession, see, e.g., Richard Briffault, Voting Rights, Home Rule, and Metropolitan Government: The Secession of Staten Island as a Case Study in the Dilemmas of Local Self-Determination, 92 Colum. L. Rev. 775 (1992); Florence Cavanna, Home Rule and the Secession of Staten Island: City of New York v. State of New York, 8 Touro L. Rev. 795 (1992). For an analysis of the effort to establish Mandela as a city distinct from Boston, see Ankur Goel, Willie Lovett, Robert Patten, and Robert Wilkins, Comment, Black Neighborhoods Becoming Black Cities: Group Empowerment, Local Control and the Implication of Being Darker Than *Brown*, 23 Harv. C.R.-C.L. L. Rev. 45 (1988). For a discussion of other municipal secession efforts, see Joseph Viteritti, Municipal Home Rule, and the Conditions of Justifiable Secession, 23 Ford. Urb. L. J. 1 (1995); Roni Bruskin, Secession as a Connecticut Story: The Feasibility of an Intramunicipal Secession in New Haven, 14 Q. L. R. 781 (1994). On secession generally, see Cass Sunstein, Constitutionalism and Secession, 58 U. Chi. L. Rev. 633 (1991); Eric Jensen, American Indian Tribes and Secession, 29 Tulsa L. J. 385 (1993).

[13] http://valleyvote.org/. For an analysis of this secession effort, see Michan Connor, "These Communities Have the Most to Gain from Valley Cityhood": Color-Blind Rhetoric of Urban Secession in Los Angeles, 1996 –2002, 40 J. Urb. Hist. 1, 48–64 (2014).

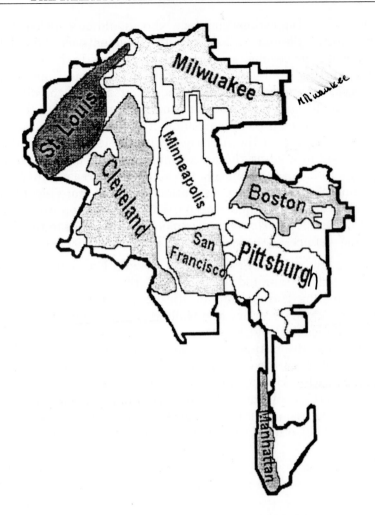

If several major American cities could fit within the corporate jurisdiction of Los Angeles, should Los Angeles be broken up into several cities? Moreover, New York City isn't just as big as several cities put together— it is several cities put together. The Big Apple is the result of the consolidation in 1898 of several municipalities including the largest and third largest cities in the United States at the time—New York (Manhattan) and Brooklyn. Is Staten Island's bid for secession an attempt to go back to the future?

Finally, an article by Michelle Wilde Anderson examines a tactic that seeks the opposite result sought by secession—not an exit from an existing municipality but a decision by a municipality to give up its separate identity by dissolving itself into the surrounding county. What would be the appropriate electorate to decide on this course of action? Does it matter that dissolution expands the relevant borders rather than, as in secession, contracting them? Should it be easier or harder for cities to dissolve than to secede? Should it be easier or harder for cities to dissolve than to incorporate?

CITY OF HERRIMAN V. BELL

United States Court of Appeals, Tenth Circuit, 2010.
590 F.3d 1176.

TYMKOVICH, CIRCUIT JUDGE. * * *

Utah law provides three ways to initiate the process of creating a new school district: (1) through a citizen initiative petition; (2) at the request of the board of the existing or future districts; or (3) at the request of a city or group of cities within the boundaries of an existing school district. Initiating the creation of a new school district under either of the first two methods—citizen initiative or school board action—puts the issue before all legal voters in the existing school district. But initiating the creation of a new school district under the third method puts the issue before only residents within the proposed new school district's boundaries.

In 2007, several cities within the Jordan School District entered into an interlocal agreement to detach from the district. At the time, the Jordan School District was one of the forty largest in the country and served a substantial portion of Salt Lake County. The proposed new district, which would contain approximately forty-three percent of the then-existing Jordan School District's student population, would encompass the cities predominately in the eastern part of the Jordan School District as well as a small portion of a neighboring school district. The * * * [cities] initiated the detachment process using the third method Utah law provides. Thus, only residents in the proposed new district would vote in the election. Shortly before the scheduled election, a number of voters residing within the Jordan School District, but outside of the proposed new district, sought injunctive relief in federal court * * *. They claimed this exclusion from voting violated equal protection principles. Herriman City, also located in the Jordan School District, but outside the proposed new district, joined the suit as well. The district court denied the injunction request * * *. The election occurred as scheduled in November 2007, and residents of the proposed new school district voted to create the district. * * * On appeal, the excluded voters make two equal protection arguments: (1) the district court erred in applying rational basis review to the detachment statute instead of strict scrutiny, and (2) even if rational basis review was appropriate, the detachment statute would nevertheless fail to pass constitutional muster.

The crux of the voters' equal protection argument is that while a state may limit local voting rights to residents in a particular electoral district, strict scrutiny review applies when the state defines that particular district so as to exclude voters who are "substantially interested in and affected by" the election at issue. Utah's detachment statute, they assert, excludes voters in precisely this way. * * * [T]he voters marshal evidence detailing the detachment's impact—most notably the financial consequences they will experience because of the split. These include both short and long-term property tax increases, an abiding property tax disparity with the detaching school district, debt servicing obligations, and approximately $40.5 million in division costs (as opposed to $25.8 million for the new district). On top of these financial costs lie significant logistical and administrative burdens, including appointing a transition team, allocating property between the districts, and transferring educators and personnel. Finally, the detachment affects the Jordan School District's self-governance in the short term—the district must hold elections for its new school board as a result of the separation, as well as in the long term. * * *

[T]he district court correctly held Herriman City may not challenge the constitutionality of a state statute under the Fourteenth Amendment. See *Rural Water Dist. No. 1 v. City of Wilson*, 243 F.3d 1263, 1274 (10th Cir.2001) (noting that because they are creatures of the state, political subdivisions "possess no rights independent of those expressly provided to them by the state"). * * * We * * * turn to the excluded voters' equal protection challenge to the Utah school district detachment statute. * * * Applying the rational basis standard, we conclude the detachment statute furthers reasonable government interests and comports with the requirements of equal protection. * * *

[T]he Supreme Court * * * has consistently upheld laws that give different constituencies different voices in elections, especially those involving the annexation or adjustment of political boundaries. The Supreme Court first considered challenges to state laws defining qualified voters in local annexation elections in *Hunter v. City of Pittsburgh*, 207 U.S. 161, 28 S.Ct. 40, 52 L.Ed. 151 (1907). * * * The *Hunter* Court affirmed that the "state is supreme" in constructing municipalities' boundaries * * *. [But when] a state law discriminates among eligible voters within the same electoral district, strict scrutiny review applies, and compelling government interests must justify restrictions of the franchise. For example, strict scrutiny is appropriate where states differentiate among voters in a particular district on the basis of personal characteristics such as wealth, property ownership, or taxpayer status. *City of Phoenix v. Kolodziejski*, 399 U.S. 204, 90 S.Ct. 1990, 26 L.Ed.2d 523 (1970) (considering law restricting vote in a general obligation bond election to real property taxpayers); *Kramer v. Union Free Sch. Dist. No. 15*, 395 U.S. 621, 89 S.Ct. 1886, 23 L.Ed.2d 583 (1969) (addressing law restricting voting in a school district election to those owning or leasing taxable property or having children enrolled in that school district). * * *

While these holdings shed light on the appropriate equal protection framework, none squarely addresses the constitutionality of a statute restricting the franchise in a school district detachment election like the one presented here. Two cases from the late 1970s, however, support the conclusion that the voting limitations in Utah's school detachment statute are subject to rational basis review. * * * The first case, *Town of Lockport v. Citizens for Community Action at the Local Level, Inc.*, 430 U.S. 259, 97 S.Ct. 1047, 51 L.Ed.2d 313 (1977), concerned a New York voting law that allowed voters from different parts of a county to have a greater voice in strengthening county government. * * * In finding that New York's law accommodated the distinctive interests of the cities and unincorporated parts of a county—as opposed to their interests as a homogeneous unit— the Court recognized "both the wide discretion the States have in forming and allocating governmental tasks to local subdivisions, and the discrete interests that such local governmental units may have qua units." Given the differing interests of city and non-city voters in adopting a new county charter, the absence of invidious discrimination, and the presumption of constitutionality entitled to every duly enacted state law, the Supreme Court held equal protection did not invalidate the voting law. * * *

In a second case, the Supreme Court again emphasized the leeway states have in treating voters residing in separate governmental units or electoral districts differently. * * * In *Holt Civic Club v. City of Tuscaloosa*, 439 U.S. 60, 99 S.Ct. 383, 58 L.Ed.2d 292 (1978), * * * [the Court] distinguished the earlier voting limitation cases such as *Kramer* and *City of Phoenix*. * * * Because Holt's residents were not within the boundary of the governmental unit at issue (Tuscaloosa), the case did not fall within the constrictions of the Supreme Court's previous voting rights cases. * * * In light of the "extraordinarily wide latitude [that States have] in creating various types of political subdivisions and conferring authority upon them," the Alabama law was reasonably related to legitimate governmental interests and thus did not violate equal protection. * * *

Other courts addressing annexation and secession statutes have also deferred to state laws restricting the franchise in local boundary elections. * * * [A] secession case, *City of New York v. State*, 158 A.D.2d 169, *aff'd*, 76 N.Y.2d 479 (1990), involved a New York statute that created a procedure allowing residents of Staten Island to decide whether the borough should detach from the rest of New York City. The procedure involved two referenda in which the residents of Staten Island would vote on detachment, but did not give other voters in New York City an opportunity to vote on the matter. The City challenged the state procedures on equal protection grounds, but the state court declined to apply strict scrutiny. Instead, the court held that *Hunter, Lockport, Holt,* and the Supreme Court's other voting rights decisions provided that "the State can legitimately adopt a geographic classification based upon the boundaries of a proposed new political subdivision to be created if approved by the electorate of the smaller, but significant, separating community." The special interests of Staten Island residents justified limiting the vote to them. * * * [N]umerous other authorities addressing analogous legal issues support our conclusion that the deferential standard of scrutiny is required. See, e.g., *Bd. of Supervisors v. Local Agency Formation Comm'n,* 3 Cal.4th 903, 13 Cal.Rptr.2d 245, 838 P.2d 1198 (1992) (holding that restricting voter participation in a municipal incorporation referendum to county residents of area proposed to be incorporated did not violate the Equal Protection Clause); *Givorns v. City of Valley,* 598 So.2d 1338 (Ala.1992) (upholding under the rational basis test a statute limiting the franchise to qualified voters living within the boundaries of the area to be annexed). * * *

Applying these principles to the Utah school district detachment statute, we find that rational basis review is the appropriate level of scrutiny. First, rational basis review accords with *Hunter's* holding that states have wide discretion in structuring political subdivisions and conferring authority upon them. * * * Second, there is no allegation that the Jordan School District detachment discriminates on an invidious basis—e.g., along racial lines—in a manner that would merit strict scrutiny review. Third, the single-shot nature of the referendum supports applying rational basis review. The detachment elections permitted under the Utah statute serve a limited purpose—the alteration of school district boundaries—and leave other governmental decisions to be made at recurring general elections. For this reason, the equal protection principles involved are calibrated less stringently. See *Lockport.* * * * Finally, because the Utah school district detachment statute distinguishes among voters having genuinely different relevant interests, rational basis review is appropriate.

The Jordan School District voters strongly contest this final point, arguing they do reside in the same governmental unit as those residents allowed to vote, and are equally interested in the detachment issue. They concede a state may limit voting rights to a particular governmental unit, but argue a relevant boundary cannot be drawn where it excludes voters who are as "substantially interested and affected" as those residents who can vote. * * * But no major decision has adopted a substantial interest test for elections involving different governmental units or electoral districts. * * * When read together, *Holt* and *Lockport* * * * indicate courts should defer to the voting restrictions states employ when addressing boundary changes. * * * As in *Lockport,* * * * the detachment law here rests on Utah's identification of the distinctive interests within particular school districts.

The excluded voters emphasize that the split will substantially affect them. That may be true. But in the eyes of the state, their interest is still genuinely different from those seeking to form the new district—in the long term, for example, divergent issues may include tax burdens, the use of tax revenues, local control over education, school district size, and allocation of resources. * * * The statutory scheme challenged in this case is a residency restriction based on relevant electoral criteria. Utah made a determination that the geographical areas that would comprise the new school district would be most directly affected, and thus provided them with the franchise. All the residents of that political entity were allowed to vote. While it may have been better for the legislature to expand the electoral district to include all residents of the existing district, this is a question best left to the legislature, not a federal court. * * *

We need not wrestle long with whether the Utah detachment statute satisfies rational basis review. The detaching cities provide a litany of justifications for the law, including, among many others, supporting the creation of community-based school districts, encouraging the creation of smaller school districts more responsive to the needs of students and parents, and promoting the localized use of tax revenues so that taxes collected within a local area are used for education in the same area. These justifications attest to the statute's constitutionality. The excluded voters seize on this last justification, and assert that localized use of tax revenues among the wealthier eastern cities is the actual reason for detaching from the Jordan School District. Even if this were the only rational basis for the detachment statute, though, the goal of localizing property tax revenues is sufficiently rational to uphold the constitutionality of legislation. See *San Antonio Indep. Sch. Dist. v. Rodriguez*, 411 U.S. 1, 40, 49–50, 93 S.Ct. 1278, 36 L.Ed.2d 16 (1973). * * * [W]hen a subset of cities initiates the creation of a new school district via interlocal agreement, the cities are seeking to create a new, smaller district that is co-extensive with their political boundaries. Limiting the franchise to those in the initiating cities allows the citizens to review the action of their elected officials and confirm their agreement and dedication to the new district. States do not act irrationally in concluding that voters outside the new district should not have a veto power over the election. * * *

NOTE ON THE STATEN ISLAND SECESSION ATTEMPT

One case *Herriman* relied on that is not in the preceding materials is City of New York v. State of New York, 76 N.Y.2d 479 (1990). The *Herriman* opinion might have left the impression that the *New York* case held that Staten Island was allowed to decide on its own whether to secede from the

City of New York. That, however, is not what the case held. The issue before the court was whether state legislation launching a possible Staten Island secession effort was a violation of the home rule immunity that the state constitution gives the City of New York (see Chapter Two). The state legislation at issue authorized a Staten Island-only vote to establish a charter commission to draft a proposal for a separate city and to submit the proposal only to Staten Island voters for approval. No secession would take place, however, without further approval by the state legislature. Moreover, while the court decided that exclusion of the City of New York from the initial stage of a secession effort was not an invasion of the City's home rule immunity, it specifically postponed the issue whether a secession itself would require New York City's consent, labeling that issue "premature."

In November, 1993, Staten Islanders voted in favor of secession by more than a 2–1 margin.[14] Although the court in City of New York v. State of New York approved the initial plebiscite to explore secession, the state legislature later decided, because of home rule, that secession itself required the consent of New York City.[15] The state appellate court eventually rejected a legal challenge to that legislative determination. The legislative determination had been made by the Speaker of the Assembly of the State of New York, on the advice of the Assembly's Home Rule Counsel. The appellate court concluded that the judgment was an internal legislative judgment immune from judicial scrutiny under the Speech and Debate Clause of the New York Constitution.[16] Part of the reason for the legislature's decision may have been the fear that a successful secession of Staten Island would encourage secession movements in New York's other boroughs: Staten Island's secessionists had already inspired a secession movement in Queens.[17]

A brief review of the factors that motivated the secession drive in Staten Island, and the concerns that were engendered by that drive, provides some important context for considering how the law should generally respond to the impulse to secede. Staten Island's bid for secession was motivated by several factors: geographic isolation, ideological and cultural differences from the other four boroughs of New York, and a widespread perception among Staten Islanders of powerlessness in city politics. Perhaps due in part to its geographic isolation, Staten Island has a pace, lifestyle, and political culture quite distinct from the rest of New York City. While all of the other boroughs in New York are majority Democratic, a majority of Staten Islanders are Republicans. In contrast to much of New York City, Staten Island's built environment seems almost suburban in nature: the borough is an island of detached single family homes in a city of townhouses and highrise apartment complexes. Most importantly, Staten Island has long felt powerless and mistreated in New York City's politics. Many Staten Islanders feel that they

---

[14] New York Times, November 8, 1993, Page 1, col. 5.

[15] New York Times, March 5, 1994, Section 1, page 27, col. 4.

[16] Matter of Straniere v. Silver, 218 A.D.2d 80, 637 N.Y.S.2d 982 (App.Div.), affirmed, 89 N.Y.2d 825, 653 N.Y.S.2d 270, 675 N.E.2d 1222 (1996).

[17] The Record, February 5, 1992.

are treated with contempt by their more cosmopolitan neighbors in the other boroughs—especially Manhattan.[18] For example, Borough residents point to Staten Island's Fresh Kills landfill, in which virtually all of New York City's solid waste had historically been disposed,[19] as the ultimate symbol of the borough's subordinate position in city politics.

The greatest impetus for secession may have been the court-ordered demise of one of New York City's two important legislative bodies, the Board of Estimate.[20] The Board of Estimate provided equal representation for each of the city's five boroughs: each borough president served on the body along with three members elected by the city as large. Therefore, despite Staten Island's relatively small population—352,000 as compared to Manhattan's 1,427,000, Queens' 1,891,000, the Bronx's 1,169,000 and Brooklyn's 2,300,000—the borough had a powerful voice in local politics. This arrangement was found unconstitutional by the United States Supreme Court in Board of Estimate v. Morris, 489 U.S. 688, 109 S.Ct. 1433, 103 L.Ed.2d 717 (1989). The Court in *Morris* held that the Board of Estimate's selection process failed to provide New York's voters with equal protection because it effectively allowed the vote of each resident of the smaller boroughs (such as Staten Island) to weigh more heavily in the composition of the Board than the vote of each resident of the more populous boroughs (such as Brooklyn.) After the *Morris* decision, the city's only remaining legislative body—the City Council—continued to be elected according to the one-person, one-vote principle.

GERALD FRUG, IS SECESSION FROM THE CITY OF LOS ANGELES A GOOD IDEA?
49 U.C.L.A. Law Review 1783, 1783–1790 (2002).

Three major efforts are now underway by parts of the City of Los Angeles—the San Fernando Valley, the Harbor Area (San Pedro, Wilmington, and Harbor City), and Hollywood—to secede from the City. All three have been evaluated by the Local Agency Formation Commission for Los Angeles County (LAFCO), the agency that manages the secession process under state law. * * *

Are these attempts to secede from the City of Los Angeles a good idea? What is the idea? Is secession a form of privatization—an effort to isolate some parts of the City of Los Angeles from the problems found in others? Or is it the opposite, an example of what one might call publicazation—an attempt to reinvigorate local democracy by bringing government closer to its constituents? * * *

---

[18] New York Times, August 9, 1993, Section A, page 1, col. 2.

[19] See Richard Briffault, Voting Rights, Home Rule and Metropolitan Governance: The Secession of Staten Island as a Case Study in the Dilemmas of Local Self Determination, 92 Colum. L. Rev. 775 (1992).

[20] The New York Times, March 24, 1989, Section B, page 4, col. 1.

The City of Los Angeles is one of 88 cities in Los Angeles County. These cities range in population from Vernon—a metropolis of 91 residents—to Los Angeles itself (current population: 3.8 million). Altogether, these 88 cities contain 8.7 million of the County's 9.8 million residents. A number of these cities are islands surrounded on at least three sides by the geographical space of the City of Los Angeles: places like Beverly Hills, Inglewood, Santa Monica, West Hollywood, Culver City, and Glendale. The largest city in the County after Los Angeles is Long Beach, with 460,000 people. But there are only 14 other cities with 100,000 people or more. Most of the cities in Los Angeles County are thus very small: There are 21 cities with a population under 20,000. The rest of the County's population—about one million people—lives in its unincorporated territory. This unincorporated territory encompasses two-thirds of the County's land area. According to the County's web site, there are more than 125 separately designated areas within this unincorporated territory. These separately designated areas, being unincorporated, do not have the legal status of cities. But that does not mean that they aren't meaningful. Neighborhoods within the City of Los Angeles do not have legal status either, but people nevertheless find it very meaningful that they live in "Westwood" or "Bel Air" or "Holmsby Hills" rather than somewhere else.

In addition to this fragmentation of the County into separate cities and unincorporated areas, the government of Los Angeles County, one of the largest public bureaucracies in the nation, has very fragmented responsibilities. Like other counties in California, Los Angeles County provides criminal justice, health, and welfare services (among others) countywide, including in the incorporated cities. When performing these functions, the County is acting as a subdivision of the state government. It is implementing state and federal law. Almost two-thirds of the County's expenditures are devoted to its responsibilities as an agent of the state and federal government. The County also contracts with some but not all of the eighty-eight incorporated cities to provide fire and police services (among others). This contracting process (called "the Lakewood plan") has enabled small cities to gain the benefits of incorporation without having to organize and support their own city services. As Gary Miller's brilliant book Cities by Contract demonstrates, the invention of this form of city-county contracting has been a major ingredient in stimulating the incorporation of so many small cities and, thereby, so much fragmentation within Los Angeles County. Finally, the County governs the people who live in its unincorporated territory in the same way that the incorporated cities govern their citizens. The County government's responsibilities are thus very different in different parts of the County. Nevertheless, the County is run by five supervisors elected through one person, one vote elections, with the whole County divided into five equally populated districts. The supervisors' districts contain both incorporated cities and parts of the unincorporated area. In fact, they split the City of Los Angeles into five parts, so that all five supervisors represent a different part of the City.

Los Angeles County, in sum, is a local government law nightmare. No one starting from scratch would organize this kind of government structure for the County. Incorporating eighty-eight separate cities (one with 3.8 million people and eleven with fewer than 10,000 people), having powerful County officials mostly responsible for a portion of the population but elected by all of them—who would think that this is a good way to govern a metropolitan area? And I have not even mentioned the fact that the County has more than two hundred independent special districts and public authorities providing governmental services like sanitation, water, fire, and the library, and eighty-one separate school districts. What the secessionists want to do, critics might say, is to add to this crazy complexity by reducing the size of the City of Los Angeles (by almost half) and bringing the total of separately incorporated cities within the County to ninety-one. This is heading in the wrong direction. It is increasing fragmentation in an already much-too-fragmented metropolitan area.

There is, however, another way to look at the issue. Los Angeles County is not only too fragmented but it is also too centralized. One ingredient of this centralization is the power of Los Angeles County itself. The County's Board of Supervisors exercises substantial authority, and although it is democratically elected, it constitutes a peculiar form of democracy. There are only five supervisors, and this small group combines executive and legislative power in a way that defies traditional notions of the separation of powers. Even more oddly, most of their functions involve the implementation of decisions made by the state— decisions, in other words, that cannot be attributed to the collective will of the people who elect them.

Another aspect of this overcentralization, secessionists argue, is the government of the City of Los Angeles. As the Harbor Vote web site puts it:

> With 3.6 million residents, ... [the City] is three times the population of the second largest city in California which is San Diego with only 1.1 million residents. ... As a "state" the City of Los Angeles would rank larger than 25 other states. The City is so large that the cities of St. Louis, Milwaukee, Cleveland, Minneapolis, Boston, San Francisco, Pittsburgh and Manhattan [sic] could all fit within the city boundaries, and still not cover all of LA! The citizens of these cities, which cover a smaller geographic area than LA, are represented by a combined total of 123 council members. In contrast, the City Council of Los Angeles includes only 15 members, each representing 240,000

citizens, while in most major cities the average council seat represents 20 to 40,000!

The very size of the City of Los Angeles is thus seen as inhibiting democratic accountability. * * *

Besides, as we have already seen, creating new cities in Los Angeles County would not be an innovation. Indeed, all three proposed new cities seem to make more sense than most of the existing cities in the County. A new Valley city would be the County's second largest city, with a potential population of 1.4 million. Hollywood and the Harbor area would be big too: Hollywood would have over 265,000 people, and the Harbor Area would be a city of 140,000. If there are going to be different cities in the County, one might want to support these cities rather than, say, Rolling Hills Estates with 7676 inhabitants or Rolling Hills with 1871 inhabitants, not to mention Vernon with 91. Of course, one could also argue that some of the new cities—especially the Valley—are too big for meaningful decentralization of power. If a new Valley city were established, one might therefore support secession from it as well.

Still, the defense of the proposed new cities is not simply a matter of size. It also depends on whether it would be better, if Los Angeles County is going to have a number of different cities, to create cities that are diverse, like the population of both the County of Los Angeles and the City of Los Angeles, rather than relatively homogeneous. Los Angeles County is 45 percent Latino, 12 percent Asian, 10 percent Black, and 30 percent Anglo. The City of Los Angeles is not much different. Beverly Hills, by contrast, is 85 percent Anglo (and 7 percent Asian, 5 percent Latino, and 1 percent Black); West Hollywood is 81 percent Anglo (and 9 percent Latino, 4 percent Asian, and 3 percent Black); and Santa Monica is 71 percent Anglo (and 13 percent Latino, 7 percent Asian, and 4 percent Black). Compton is 56 percent Latino and 40 percent Black—and 1 percent Anglo. Although it is hard to get exact data on the proposed new cities, all of them are likely to be more diverse than these existing cities (but not as diverse as either the City of Los Angeles or the County). * * * [T]he secession movements cannot—unlike most of the thirty new cities incorporated in the Los Angeles region in the last twenty-five years—be dismissed as an expression of white flight. A recent poll in the Valley shows that Latinos support secession more than Anglos do.

Finally, one should recognize that there is nothing sacred about the boundaries of the City of Los Angeles as they now exist. One reason I have already noted is the presence of separately incorporated cities surrounded by the City. Another is the fact that the City's current boundaries—like the boundaries of every major city in the country—are the product of annexation. Among the places that were annexed were the areas now seeking to secede. San Pedro, Wilmington, and Hollywood, once incorporated cities, were consolidated with the City of Los Angeles in 1909 and 1910. The San Fernando Valley was an unincorporated area when it was annexed in 1915, an annexation that more than doubled the size of the City. In America, annexations frequently take place simply because the central city decides to expand its territory; the consent of the annexed territory is not necessary under American law. In Los Angeles, by contrast, the annexations and consolidations required the affirmative vote of both the City and the area added to the City. Nevertheless, there was enormous pressure—above all, the pressure to get access to water— to agree to the annexations and consolidations. Moreover, the number of people voting in these elections was very small, and the elections were a long time ago. * * *

MICHELLE WILDE ANDERSON, DISSOLVING CITIES
121 Yale L.J. 1364, 1366–1367, 1373–1380, 1400–1401, 1404,
1047–1408, 1419, 1425–1427 (2012).

If the incorporation of a legal city expresses an upward arc of development and growth, the legal disincorporation of a city marks decline. The shutting down of municipal government signals that a community can no longer sustain the cost and institutional responsibility of cityhood. Population, finances, or faith in civic institutions has simply lost too much ground. * * * [If] ever there has been a wave of * * * [dissolutions], we are in one now. More than half of the dissolutions ever recorded took place in the past fifteen years. At least 130 cities have dissolved since 2000—nearly as many as incorporated during that same period. * * *

This Article opens the graves of our departed cities and visits the deathbed towns following closely behind. * * * To get started, a definition: municipal dissolution, also known as disincorporation, is the termination of the political unit of an incorporated municipality, whether city, village, or incorporated town. A municipality can dissolve in order to disincorporate permanently or to reorganize incorporated territory, such as by merging two cities into one. Dissolution into a county and dissolution into another city (merger) can have important similarities, such as origins in economic decline and the loss of a city population's separate legal identity and political autonomy. * * * This Article * * * focuses on the subset of dissolutions that indefinitely remove a layer of municipal government and return a population to unincorporated county or township jurisdiction. * * * Instead of municipal government and county government (or a county and a county subdivisions), the area reverts to unincorporated county rule alone. * * *

The City of Miami held an election to consider dissolution into Dade County in 1996. Miami's city government was awash in crisis: a corruption scandal, a crushing deficit and plummeting bond rating, a state declaration of fiscal emergency, and property tax rates nearly double the rates of neighboring incorporated suburbs and more than four times those of the unincorporated areas of Dade County. A grassroots organization called the Citizens for Lower Taxes launched a successful petition drive to qualify a dissolution referendum for the ballot. * * * The proposal in Miami looked like a preference for county government, and to some extent, it was. But the dissolution campaign was also a breakaway attempt by wealthier neighborhoods within Miami that wanted their own legal cities. Miami's Citizens for Lower Taxes was led by an attorney who had successfully championed the incorporation of several wealthy unincorporated enclaves and a "neighborhood incorporation movement" in Dade County. He and his supporters saw dissolution as a stepping-stone to city formation. Postdissolution, once back in the undifferentiated county, wealthy enclaves could form their own cities without obtaining approval from Miami's electorate. * * * As it happened, the Miami electorate gave * * * [an] answer to the * * * breakaway * * *: no. Recognition of the breakaway intentions of dissolution leaders undermined the group's claims that dissolution would improve the tax and service profile for all Miami. * * *

The power to dissolve a local government (like the power to create one or change its borders) comes from a state constitution and state laws. * * * Forty states have dissolution codes of some kind * * *. Structurally, dissolution is not possible in states that have no unincorporated territory to which a city can revert, including Pennsylvania, New Jersey, Hawaii, and the states of New England (excluding Maine and New Hampshire). In those states, reorganizing a local government tier (e.g., through merger) may be possible, but eliminating one is not. * * * [D]issolutions and dissolution law [in other states] should be classified into three categories: passive, involuntary, and voluntary. The first two lie solely in the power of the state; the third requires formal local initiation or consent. Passive dissolutions occur by operation of law for inactivity (a classic ghost town scenario), usually defined as the failure to elect or appoint municipal officers, levy and collect taxes, provide services, or undertake other basic activities. * * * Involuntary dissolutions are also state-initiated, but they are applied to populated municipalities and may override a local preference against dissolution. * * * Involuntary dissolutions are quite rare and confrontational, and research for this Article indicates that they arise only in cases of corruption or chronic mismanagement. * * *

Voluntary dissolutions originate from the city itself—either its residents or its leaders. Dissolution is overwhelmingly conceived of in this way, i.e., as a locally initiated, locally approved process. Thirty-seven states have voluntary dissolution laws on their books. * * * At the level of individual resident empowerment to effectuate dissolution, most state laws permit residents to trigger the start of dissolution proceedings (such as an election on the question, or a study on the impacts of dissolution). Once initiated, who approves dissolution? In a few states, a dissolution petition itself is the mechanism of approval. If a state permits dissolution of a city via petition without a confirming election or legislative decision, it usually requires higher signature thresholds * * *. More commonly, voters must approve dissolution via a general or special election, regardless of whether it has been initiated by a petition or a vote of the governing body. In a handful of states, dissolution must be approved by a state board or local-regional boundary commission before heading to an election * * *. Alternately, dissolution may remain the province only of the state legislature, a rule likely based on the assumption that dissolutions are too rare to require delegation to local governments. * * *

Dissolution has important consequences for the county or county subdivision into which a city is dissolving. It expands the unincorporated territory of the county, thus affecting counties' budgets (both revenue and costs); bringing new territory and residents into the administrative and land-use planning responsibility of county staff; potentially expanding the territory of county service providers like law enforcement and street maintenance; bringing new properties, assets, and records under county management; and more. If the dissolving city is considerably more populous than the county's other unincorporated territory, the significance is even greater * * *. Yet reading the law governing how to dissolve a city, one might not guess that these impacts on counties were of any significance. Very few states give counties a right to notice regarding a pending dissolution; even fewer states give counties any rights to influence the outcome of a proposed dissolution. * * *

In many states, population is a significant determinant of eligibility for dissolution. Several states permit only municipalities under a certain population threshold to dissolve voluntarily, and these caps tend to be quite low (for instance, 1,000 residents), or they permit only smaller municipalities to dissolve. * * * [T]he thresholds are so low that these states have effectively limited dissolution to ghost towns or rural enclaves. Perhaps states impose these population limits on dissolution as a proxy for burdens on county government; i.e., states limit dissolution of larger cities as a form of protection for counties. * * * Furthermore, such limits convey that dissolution would never be in the public interest for cities above a certain size. * * *

[W]hy do dissolutions happen? * * * Five themes repeatedly arise in these histories: (1) decline (i.e., budgetary crisis and depopulation due to industrial or rural abandonment), (2) taxes, or more specifically, the rebellion against them, (3) reform to address corruption and mismanagement, (4) race, in settings ranging from banishment to autonomy to desegregation, and (5) community, or the desire to preserve neighborly bonds and history. If there is one theme at the heart of the dissolutions * * *, it is economic decline and budgetary collapse. * * * Dissolution is seen as a way to cut costs quickly and dramatically by laying off employees and politicians, consolidating and restructuring services and administration with the county, selling or transferring assets, and the like. * * *

While most of these calls for reducing the layers and costs of local government evoke antigovernment animus, dissolution is not the exclusive province of the political right. From the political left, it has been framed as a means of progressive-style modernization of the state. * * * [T]he leadership from the left has more in common with modern city-county consolidation advocacy and early twentieth-century progressive municipal reform movements—sounding themes of "government performance," "technical efficiency" (meaning creation of economies of scale and professional accountability structures, and the reduction of government duplication), and a reduction in the confusion (and thus shelter for corruption) caused by fragmentation. * * *

[D]issolution * * * creates the potential for counties and townships to serve goals associated with regional government, such as land-use coordination, reduced interlocal conflict, and service consolidation. Dissolution's potential service to defragmentation and regional governance is surprising, because proponents claim to be reducing the scale of local government, not pursuing regionalist—let alone redistributive—ends. Indeed, these proponents are right that dissolution means less government, but it paradoxically also means bigger government. By cutting out the most proximate tier of government, voters and leaders in dissolving cities are opting to rely instead on more distant county or township governments with accountability to larger territories. Perhaps it is for this reason that dissolution cuts across the familiar divides in the debate over regionalism. It can align antigovernment animus with regional government advocacy, poor with middle class voters, and residents of cities with residents of suburbs. * * * [A]s a general matter, it is noticeable that the law also substantively favors the upwards arc, i.e., makes it easier to incorporate than to dissolve. The substantive restrictions on what types of cities are eligible for dissolution are quite severe, for instance, when it comes to population and city size. * * * In short, land and its occupants can leave an unincorporated jurisdiction with greater ease than they can return to it, and counties enjoy little influence over either change. * * *

B. CONFLICTS AMONG CITIES

At best, cities and suburbs work together for the good of the metropolitan region and all of its residents, just as a happy family works together for the good of the entire household. At worst the relationship is more like that of King Lear's daughters—each competing for advantage at the expense of its metropolitan siblings. This section explores two sources of inter-local conflict—race and class segregation and competition for wealth. The materials on segregation examine the extent of segregation and the law and institutions that create and foster it. Wealthier cities have powerful economic incentives to become and remain segregated. They also have the means to do so. Should the law allow such practices, or should it reverse them? The materials on wealth then explore the extent of economic inequality among cities. Again, the main question is whether such inequality should be authorized or be confronted and reversed through public policy. Finally, the section concludes by examining one result of conflict among cities: sprawl. The uncoordinated decisions and policies of numerous cities has produced a sprawling metropolitan area made up of insular local enclaves. The cost of conflict can be measured in long commutes, bad traffic, air pollution, and frazzled nerves. Given the incentives for creating and maintaining segregated enclaves and difficulty of cooperating with neighboring cities, it's not surprising that most American metropolitan areas are sprawling larger and larger with each passing year. The materials that conclude this section examine whether something can—and should—be done about this trend.

1. EXCLUSION: RACE AND CLASS SEGREGATION

So far in this chapter, we have examined the relationship between city residents and outsiders. In this subsection, we consider a city's power to prevent outsiders from *becoming* city residents. In local government law, this issue is rarely confronted directly. Citizens of a city (unlike, say, residents of many condominiums) do not have a formal veto power over who can live in the city. Nevertheless, a wide variety of zoning restrictions—mandating a minimum lot size, prohibiting multi-family housing, or excluding mobile homes, for example—can have the effect of controlling the kind of people able to move into a city (creating what is often called an "exclusive" community). This practice of exclusionary zoning has spawned an enormous literature.[21]

---

[21] See, e.g., Roderick Hills, Saving Mount Laurel?, 40 Fordham Urb. L.J. 1611 (2013); Wayne Batchis, Suburbanization and Constitutional Interpretation: Exclusionary Zoning and the Supreme Court Legacy of Enabling Sprawl, 8 Stan. J. Civ. Rts. & Civ. Liberties 1 (2012); David Kinsey, The Growth Share Approach to Mount Laurel Housing Obligations: Origins, Hijacking, and Future, 63 Rutgers L. Rev. 867 (2011); David Papke, Keeping the Underclass in its Place: Zoning, The Poor, and Residential Segregation, 41 Urb. Law. 787 (2009); Peter W. Salsich, Jr., Toward a Policy of Heterogeneity: Overcoming a Long History of Socioeconomic Segregation in Housing, 42 Wake Forest L. Rev. 459 (2007); Myron Orfield, Land Use and Housing Policies to Reduce Concentrated Poverty and Racial Segregation, 33 Fordham Urb. L.J. 877 (2006); Lisa C. Young, Breaking the Color Line: Zoning and Opportunity in America's Metropolitan Areas, 8 J. Gender Race & Just. 667 (2005); Henry A. Span, How the Courts Should Fight Exclusionary Zoning, 32 Seton Hall L. Rev. 1 (2001); Paul Boudreaux, An Individual Preference Approach to Suburban Racial Desegregation, 27 Ford. Urb. L. J. 533 (1999); Mark Seittles, The Perpetuation of Residential Racial Segregation in America: Historical Discrimination, Modern Forms of Exclusion, and Inclusionary Remedies, 14 J. Land Use &

The first two cases included below offer two different legal responses to exclusionary zoning, one articulated by the United States Supreme Court interpreting the United States Constitution (Village of Arlington Heights v. Metropolitan Housing Development Corporation) and the other articulated by the Supreme Court of New Jersey interpreting the New Jersey Constitution (Southern Burlington County N.A.A.C.P. v. Township of Mt. Laurel (*Mt. Laurel I*)). These two responses suggest alternative visions of inter-city relations. Moreover, they suggest that the legitimacy of exclusionary zoning practices is predicated on a particular conception of cities. Remember that one of the traditional ingredients of the (private) property right is the right to exclude others[22] and that the United States has immigration laws. Do (and should) the cases treat cities like private property associations, like the nation as a whole, or like some other entity? Should all forms of city exclusion be considered identical? For example, should cities' ability to control the *character* of their population be treated in the same way as the ability to control the *size* of their population? In reading the following cases, consider as well the role of the courts in dealing with subjects like exclusionary zoning. Can the New Jersey decisions be defended on the ground that judicial intervention to force legislative action is necessary because suburban representatives can effectively block any legislative proposal to curb exclusionary practices? Is there an alternative solution to the problems generated by exclusionary zoning other than state or federal control of zoning decisions?

The Note on Developments After *Mt. Laurel I* considers the subsequent history of the New Jersey Supreme Court's effort at reform. It explains that the decision spawned a variety of different institutional responses. These responses included increased judicial assertiveness, significant local resistance, and state legislative intervention. The state

---

Envtl. Law 89 (1998); J. Peter Byrne, Are Suburbs Unconstitutional?, 85 Geo. L. J. 2265 (1997); Charles Haar, Suburbs Under Siege: Race, Space, and Audacious Judges (1996); David Kirp et al., Our Town: Race, Housing, and the Soul of Suburbia (1995); James Hartnett, Note, Affordable Housing, Exclusionary Zoning, and American Apartheid: Using Title VIII to Foster Statewide Racial Integration, 68 N.Y.U. L. Rev. 89 (1993); Michael Schill, Deconcentrating the Inner City Poor, 67 Chi.-Kent L. Rev. 795 (1992); Paul Stockman, Note, Anti-Snob Zoning in Massachusetts: Assessing One Attempt at Opening the Suburbs to Affordable Housing, 78 Va. L. Rev. 535 (1992); Douglas Kmiec, Exclusionary Zoning and Purposeful Racial Segregation in Housing: Two Wrongs Deserving Separate Remedies, 18 The Urban Lawyer 393 (1986); M.A. Huls, Exclusionary and Inclusionary Zoning: A Bibliography (1985); M. David Gelfand, Federal Constitutional Law and American Local Government 281–312 (1984); Peter Salsich, Displacement and Urban Reinvestment: A Mt. Laurel Perspective, 53 U. Cinn. L. Rev. 333 (1984); Daniel Mandelker, Racial Discrimination and Exclusionary Zoning: A Perspective on Arlington Heights, 55 Tex. L. Rev. 1217 (1977); John Payne, Delegation Doctrine in the Reform of Local Government Law: The Case of Exclusionary Zoning, 29 Rutgers L. Rev. 803 (1976).

[22] See, e.g., Felix Cohen, Dialogue on Private Property, 9 Rutgers L.Rev. 357, 374 (1954). On the relationship between the history of zoning and the evolving image of private property, see Nadav Shoked, The Reinvention of Ownership: The Embrace of Residential Zoning and the Modern Populist Reading of Property, 28 Yale J. on Reg. 91 (2011). For an analysis of the impact of the involuntary divestment of land on racial minorities, particularly Black Americans, see Audrey McFarlane, The Properties of Instability, Markets, Predation, Racialized Geography, and Property Law, 2011 Wis. L. Rev. 855 (2011).

legislative intervention took the form of a new state statute aimed at promoting fair housing. The statute established a new agency for handling *Mt. Laurel* disputes. The Note also shows, however, that the decisions in *Mt. Laurel* led some local governments to adopt their own innovative responses to the problem of exclusionary zoning. These measures—such as the imposition of development fees and requirements to set aside affordable housing units in new developments—were aimed at promoting a more inclusionary form of zoning and were upheld against legal challenge in part because of the *Mt. Laurel* doctrine. Local governments in New Jersey have power to adopt inclusionary zoning ordinances, while local governments in states that are not subject to the *Mt. Laurel* doctrine sometimes don't. The Supreme Court of Virginia, for example, in Board of Supervisors of Fairfax County v. DeGroff Enterprises, Inc., 198 S.E.2d 600 (1973), held a local inclusionary zoning ordinance invalid on the grounds that it was unauthorized socio-economic zoning. What does this difference between jurisdictions say about how we should understand the value of protecting local autonomy from state interference in decisions about affordable housing?

The materials in this subsection can leave the common misimpression that minority communities are inevitably poor and located in inner cities, while suburbia is the exclusive domain of middle class and wealthier whites. Sheryll Cashin discusses the growth of middle class black suburbs. Most metropolitan areas are home to significant middle class black suburban neighborhoods and cities. As Cashin points out, these communities complicate the typical image of the chocolate city/vanilla suburb and present a normatively ambiguous chapter in the story of racial and class segregation. Black suburbanites often say they prefer racially homogenous communities but that they are also pushed into them by racism and racially biased practices in housing markets. Yet Black suburbs are often as intent on screening out the (often Black) poor as white suburbs are. They are less successful than white suburbs in doing so despite their middle class status; they thus bear a disproportionate amount of the social costs of metropolitan poverty.

The legitimacy of exclusionary zoning practices (wherever exercised) might usefully be compared with the legitimacy of local policies to prevent gentrification—that is, to prevent affluent people from taking over neighborhoods and thereby displacing those not able to keep up with the higher prices.[23] One way to prevent gentrification, for example, is to

---

[23] See generally, Rachel Godsil, The Gentrification Trigger: Autonomy, Mobility, and Affirmatively Furthering Fair Housing, 78 Brook. L. Rev. 319 (2013); Jorge O. Elorza, Absentee Landlords, Rent Control, and Healthy Gentrification: A Policy Proposal to Deconcentrate the Poor in Urban America, 17 Cornell J.L. & Pub Pol'y 1 (2007); Loretta Lees, Tom Slater, and Elvin K. Wyly, Gentrification (2007); Audrey G. McFarlane, The New Inner City: Class Transformation, Concentrated Affluence, and the Obligations of the Police Power, 8 U. Penn. J. Const. L. 1 (2006); J. Peter Byrne, Two Cheers for Gentrification, 46 How. L. J. 405 (2003); John Powell and Marguerite Spencer, Giving Them the Old "One-Two": Gentrification and the K.O. of

regulate condominium conversions. Should the legal rules dealing with exclusionary zoning and the prevention of gentrification be the same? If not, how can these two forms of exclusion be distinguished?

The next-to-last reading in this subsection, an article by Richard Ford, describes racially segregated local governments as a state policy. Is Ford correct to argue that the incorporation of racially or religiously segregated localities is racially discriminatory state action or the establishment of religion? State laws often allow groups of citizens to incorporate with little substantive oversight, but they also sometimes provide for agencies such as California's LAFCO to review proposed incorporations. Is the intent of the citizens who petition for incorporation attributable to the state? The Court in *Hunter* held that there is no constitutional right to local government and the Court in *Holt* opined that local government was an "administrative technique" used by the state. If so, is Ford right that the predictable exclusionary consequences of local incorporation are state policy? Consider in this respect the excerpt from Kenneth Jackson on the Federal Housing Administration reproduced at the outset of this chapter. That excerpt shows the historic role that the government played in promoting housing segregation along racial lines. How does it influence your view of the appropriateness of government action—whether legislative or judicial, local or central, private or public— to eliminate segregation? The Note on Milliken v. Bradley raises these issues and provides a transition to the discussion of school segregation and the Distribution of Local Wealth—the topic of the next subsection.

VILLAGE OF ARLINGTON HEIGHTS V. METROPOLITAN HOUSING DEVELOPMENT CORPORATION

Supreme Court of the United States, 1977.
429 U.S. 252, 97 S.Ct. 555, 50 L.Ed.2d 450.

MR. JUSTICE POWELL delivered the opinion of the Court. * * *

Arlington Heights is a suburb of Chicago, located about 26 miles northwest of the downtown Loop area. Most of the land in Arlington Heights is zoned for detached single-family homes, and this is in fact the prevailing land use. The Village experienced substantial growth during

---

Impoverished Urban Dwellers of Colors, 46 How. L. J. 433 (2003); Symposium, Can Gentrification Save Detroit? 4 Wayne State J. L. Soc'y 1 (2002); David Troutt, Ghettoes Made Easy: The Metamarket/Antimarket Dichotomy and the Legal Challenges of Inner-City Economic Development, 35 Harv. C.R.-C.L. L. Rev. 427 (2000); Jeff Minton, Rent Control: Can and Should It Be Used to Combat Gentrification?, 23 Ohio N. U. L. Rev. 823 (1997); Jon Dubin, From Junkyards to Gentrification: Explicating a Right to Protective Zoning in Low-Income Communities of Color, 77 Minn. L. Rev. 739 (1993); Kathryn Nelson, Gentrification and Distressed Cities: An Assessment of Trends in Intrametropolitan Migration (1988); Neil Smith & Peter Williams (eds.), Gentrification of the City (1986); J. John Palen and Bruce London (eds.), Gentrification, Displacement and Neighborhood Revitalization (1984); Donald Bryant and Henry McGee, Gentrification and the Law: Combatting Urban Displacement, 25 Wash. Univ. J. Urb. & Contemp. L. 43 (1983).

the 1960's, but, like other communities in northwest Cook County, its population of racial minority groups remained quite low. According to the 1970 census, only 27 of the Village's 64,000 residents were black.

The Clerics of St. Viator, a religious order (Order), own an 80-acre parcel just east of the center of Arlington Heights. Part of the site is occupied by the Viatorian high school, and part by the Order's three-story novitiate building, which houses dormitories and a Montessori school. Much of the site, however, remains vacant. Since 1959, when the Village first adopted a zoning ordinance, all the land surrounding the Viatorian property has been zoned R–3, a single-family specification with relatively small minimum lot-size requirements. On three sides of the Viatorian land there are single-family homes just across a street; to the east the Viatorian property directly adjoins the backyards of other single-family homes.

The Order decided in 1970 to devote some of its land to low-and moderate-income housing. Investigation revealed that the most expeditious way to build such housing was to work through a nonprofit developer experienced in the use of federal housing subsidies under § 236 of the National Housing Act.

MHDC is such a developer. It was organized in 1968 by several prominent Chicago citizens for the purpose of building low-and moderate-income housing throughout the Chicago area. * * * After some negotiation, MHDC and the Order entered into a 99-year lease and an accompanying agreement of sale covering a 15-acre site in the southeast corner of the Viatorian property. * * * MHDC engaged an architect and proceeded with the project, to be known as Lincoln Green. The plans called for 20 two-story buildings with a total of 190 units, each unit having its own private entrance from outside. One hundred of the units would have a single bedroom, thought likely to attract elderly citizens. The remainder would have two, three, or four bedrooms. A large portion of the site would remain open, with shrubs and trees to screen the homes abutting the property to the east.

The planned development did not conform to the Village's zoning ordinance and could not be built unless Arlington Heights rezoned the parcel to R–5, its multiple-family housing classification. Accordingly, MHDC filed with the Village Plan Commission a petition for rezoning, accompanied by supporting materials describing the development and specifying that it would be subsidized under § 236. The materials made clear that one requirement under § 236 is an affirmative marketing plan designed to assure that a subsidized development is racially integrated. MHDC also submitted studies demonstrating the need for housing of this type and analyzing the probable impact of the development. * * *

During the spring of 1971, the Plan Commission considered the proposal at a series of three public meetings, which drew large crowds. Although many of those attending were quite vocal and demonstrative in opposition to Lincoln Green, a number of individuals and representatives of community groups spoke in support of rezoning. Some of the comments, both from opponents and supporters, addressed what was referred to as the "social issue"—the desirability or undesirability of introducing at this location in Arlington Heights low-and moderate-income housing, housing that would probably be racially integrated.

Many of the opponents, however, focused on the zoning aspects of the petition, stressing two arguments. First, the area always had been zoned single-family, and the neighboring citizens had built or purchased there in reliance on that classification. Rezoning threatened to cause a measurable drop in property value for neighboring sites. Second, the Village's apartment policy, adopted by the Village Board in 1962 and amended in 1970, called for R–5 zoning primarily to serve as a buffer between single-family development and land uses thought incompatible, such as commercial or manufacturing districts. Lincoln Green did not meet this requirement, as it adjoined no commercial or manufacturing district.

At the close of the third meeting, the Plan Commission adopted a motion to recommend to the Village's Board of Trustees that it deny the request. * * * Two members voted against the motion and submitted a minority report, stressing that in their view the change to accommodate Lincoln Green represented "good zoning." The Village Board met on September 28, 1971, to consider MHDC's request and the recommendation of the Plan Commission. After a public hearing, the Board denied the rezoning by a 6–1 vote.

The following June MHDC and three Negro individuals filed this lawsuit against the Village, seeking declaratory and injunctive relief. * * *

Respondent Ransom, a Negro, works at the Honeywell factory in Arlington Heights and lives approximately 20 miles away in Evanston in a 5-room house with his mother and his son. The complaint alleged that he seeks and would qualify for the housing MHDC wants to build in Arlington Heights. Ransom testified at trial that if Lincoln Green were built he would probably move there, since it is closer to his job.

The injury Ransom asserts is that his quest for housing nearer his employment has been thwarted by official action that is racially discriminatory. If a court grants the relief he seeks, there is at least a "substantial probability," *Warth v. Seldin,* 422 U.S., at 504, 95 S.Ct., at 2208, that the Lincoln Green project will materialize, affording Ransom the housing opportunity he desires in Arlington Heights. His is not a generalized grievance. Instead, as we suggested in *Warth,* it focuses on a particular project and is not dependent on speculation about the possible actions of third parties not before the court. Unlike the individual plaintiffs in *Warth,* Ransom has adequately averred an "actionable causal relationship" between Arlington Heights' zoning practices and his asserted injury. We therefore proceed to the merits.

Our decision last Term in *Washington v. Davis,* 426 U.S. 229, 96 S.Ct. 2040, 48 L.Ed.2d 597 (1976), made it clear that official action will not be held unconstitutional solely because it results in a racially disproportionate impact. "Disproportionate impact is not irrelevant, but it is not the sole touchstone of an invidious racial discrimination." *Id.,* at 242, 96 S.Ct., at 2049. Proof of racially discriminatory intent or purpose is required to show a violation of the Equal Protection Clause. Although some contrary indications may be drawn from some of our cases, the holding in *Davis* reaffirmed a principle well established in a variety of contexts.

Davis does not require a plaintiff to prove that the challenged action rested solely on racially discriminatory purposes. Rarely can it be said that a legislature or administrative body operating under a broad mandate made a decision motivated solely by a single concern, or even that a particular purpose was the "dominant" or "primary" one. In fact, it is because legislators and administrators are properly concerned with balancing numerous competing considerations that courts refrain from reviewing the merits of their decisions, absent a showing of arbitrariness or irrationality. But racial discrimination is not just another competing consideration. When there is a proof that a discriminatory purpose has been a motivating factor in the decision, this judicial deference is no longer justified. * * *

We have reviewed the evidence. The impact of the Village's decision does arguably bear more heavily on racial minorities. Minorities constitute 18% of the Chicago area population, and 40% of the income groups said to be eligible for Lincoln Green. But there is little about the sequence of events leading up to the decision that would spark suspicion. *wow...* The area around the Viatorian property has been zoned R–3 since 1959, the year when Arlington Heights first adopted a zoning map. Single-family homes surround the 80-acre site, and the Village is undeniably committed to single-family homes as its dominant residential land use. The rezoning request progressed according to the usual procedures. The Plan Commission even scheduled two additional hearings, at least in part to accommodate MHDC and permit it to supplement its presentation with answers to questions generated at the first hearing.

The statements by the Plan Commission and Village Board members, as reflected in the official minutes, focused almost exclusively on the zoning aspects of the MHDC petition, and the zoning factors on which they relied are not novel criteria in the Village's rezoning decisions. There is no reason to doubt that there has been reliance by some neighboring property owners on the maintenance of single-family zoning in the vicinity. The Village originally adopted its buffer policy long before MHDC entered the picture and has applied the policy too consistently for us to infer discriminatory purpose from its application in this case. Finally, MHDC called one member of the Village Board to the stand at trial. Nothing in her testimony supports an inference of invidious purpose.

In sum, the evidence does not warrant overturning the concurrent findings of both courts below. Respondents simply failed to carry their burden of proving that discriminatory purpose was a motivating factor in the Village's decision.[21] This conclusion ends the constitutional inquiry. * * *

SOUTHERN BURLINGTON COUNTY N.A.A.C.P. v. TOWNSHIP OF MT. LAUREL

Supreme Court of New Jersey, 1975.
67 N.J. 151, 336 A.2d 713.

HALL, J.

This case attacks the system of land use regulation by defendant Township of Mount Laurel on the ground that low and moderate income families are thereby unlawfully excluded from the municipality. * * * The implications of the issue presented are indeed broad and far-reaching, extending much beyond these particular plaintiffs and the boundaries of this particular municipality.

There is not the slightest doubt that New Jersey has been, and continues to be, faced with a desperate need for housing, especially of decent living accommodations economically suitable for low and moderate income families. The situation was characterized as a "crisis" and fully explored and documented by Governor Cahill in two special messages to the Legislature * * *.

Plaintiffs represent the minority group poor (black and Hispanic) seeking such quarters. But they are not the only category of persons barred from so many municipalities by reason of restrictive land use regulations. We have reference to young and elderly couples, single

---

[21] Proof that the decision by the Village was motivated in part by a racially discriminatory purpose would not necessarily have required invalidation of the challenged decision. Such proof would, however, have shifted to the Village the burden of establishing that the same decision would have resulted even had the impermissible purpose not been considered. If this were established, the complaining party in a case of this kind no longer fairly could attribute the injury complained of to improper consideration of a discriminatory purpose. In such circumstances, there would be no justification for judicial interference with the challenged decision. But in this case respondents failed to make the required threshold showing.

persons and large, growing families not in the poverty class, but who still cannot afford the only kinds of housing realistically permitted in most places—relatively high-priced, single-family detached dwellings on sizeable lots and, in some municipalities, expensive apartments. We will, therefore, consider the case from the wider viewpoint that the effect of Mount Laurel's land use regulation has been to prevent various categories of persons from living in the township because of the limited extent of their income and resources. In this connection, we accept the representation of the municipality's counsel at oral argument that the regulatory scheme was not adopted with any desire or intent to exclude prospective residents on the obviously illegal bases of race, origin or believed social incompatibility.

As already intimated, the issue here is not confined to Mount Laurel. The same question arises with respect to any number of other municipalities of sizeable land area outside the central cities and older built-up suburbs of our North and South Jersey metropolitan areas (and surrounding some of the smaller cities outside those areas as well) which, like Mount Laurel, have substantially shed rural characteristics and have undergone great population increase since World War II, or are now in the process of doing so, but still are not completely developed and remain in the path of inevitable future residential, commercial and industrial demand and growth. Most such municipalities, with but relatively insignificant variation in details, present generally comparable physical situations, courses of municipal policies, practices, enactments and results and human, governmental and legal problems arising therefrom. It is in the context of communities now of this type or which become so in the future, rather than with central cities or older built-up suburbs or areas still rural and likely to continue to be for some time yet, that we deal with the question raised.* * *

Mount Laurel is a flat, sprawling township, 22 square miles, or about 14,000 acres, in area, on the west central edge of Burlington County. * * * [I]ts southerly side * * * is about seven miles from the boundary line of the city of Camden and not more than 10 miles from the Benjamin Franklin Bridge crossing the river to Philadelphia. * * * In 1950, the township had a population of 2817, only about 600 more people than it had in 1940. It was then, as it had been for decades, primarily a rural agricultural area with no sizeable settlements or commercial or industrial enterprises. * * * After 1950, as in so many other municipalities similarly situated, residential development and some commerce and industry began to come in. By 1960 the population had almost doubled to 5249 and by 1970 had more than doubled again to 11,221. * * * The township is now definitely a part of the outer ring of the South Jersey metropolitan area * * *. The growth of the township has been spurred by the construction or improvement of main highways through or near it. * * *

This highway network gives the township a most strategic location from the standpoint of transport of goods and people by truck and private car. There is no other means of transportation.

The location and nature of development has been, as usual, controlled by the local zoning enactments. * * * Under the present ordinance, 29.2% of all the land in the township, or 4,121 acres, is zoned for industry. * * * At the time of trial no more than 100 acres * * * were actually occupied by industrial uses. * * * The amount of land zoned for retail business use under the general ordinance is relatively small—169 acres, or 1.2% of the total. * * * The balance of the land area, almost 10,000 acres, has been developed until recently in the conventional form of major subdivisions. * * * All permit only single-family, detached dwellings, one house per lot—the usual form of grid development. Attached townhouses, apartments (except on farms for agricultural workers) and mobile homes are not allowed anywhere in the township under the general ordinance. * * * The result has been quite intensive development of * * * [some] sections, but at a low density. * * * The general ordinance requirements * * * realistically allow only homes within the financial reach of persons of at least middle income. * * *

There cannot be the slightest doubt that the reason for this course of conduct has been to keep down local taxes on *property* (Mount Laurel is not a high tax municipality) and that the policy was carried out without regard for non-fiscal considerations with respect to *people*, either within or without its boundaries. * * * This policy of land use regulation for a fiscal end derives from New Jersey's tax structure, which has imposed on local real estate most of the cost of municipal and county government and of the primary and secondary education of the municipality's children. The latter expense is much the largest, so, basically, the fewer the school children, the lower the tax rate. Sizeable industrial and commercial ratables are eagerly sought and homes and the lots on which they are situate are required to be large enough, through minimum lot sizes and minimum floor areas, to have substantial value in order to produce greater tax revenues to meet school costs. Large families who cannot afford to buy large houses and must live in cheaper rental accommodations are definitely not wanted, so we find drastic bedroom restrictions for, or complete prohibition of, multi-family or other feasible housing for those of lesser income.

This pattern of land use regulation has been adopted for the same purpose in developing municipality after developing municipality. Almost every one acts solely in its own selfish and parochial interest and in effect builds a wall around itself to keep out those people or entities not adding favorably to the tax base, despite the location of the municipality or the demand for varied kinds of housing. There has been no effective intermunicipal or area planning or land use regulation. * * * One incongruous result is the picture of developing municipalities rendering it impossible for lower paid employees of industries they have eagerly sought and welcomed with open arms (and, in Mount Laurel's case, even some of its own lower paid municipal employees) to live in the community where they work.

The other end of the spectrum should also be mentioned because it shows the source of some of the demand for cheaper housing than the developing municipalities have permitted. Core cities were originally the location of most commerce and industry. * * * The situation has become exactly the opposite since the end of World War II. Much industry and retail business, and even the professions, have left the cities. Camden is a typical example. The testimonial and documentary evidence in this case as to what has happened to that city is depressing indeed. For various reasons, it lost thousands of jobs between 1950 and 1970, including more than half of its manufacturing jobs (a reduction from 43,267 to 20,671, while all jobs in the entire area labor market increased from 94,507 to 197,037). A large segment of retail business faded away with the erection of large suburban shopping centers. * * * There has been a consequent critical erosion of the city tax base and inability to provide the amount and quality of those governmental services—education, health, police, fire, housing and the like—so necessary to the very existence of safe and decent city life. * * *

The legal question before us * * * is whether a developing municipality like Mount Laurel may validly, by a system of land use regulation, make it physically and economically impossible to provide low and moderate income housing in the municipality for the various categories of persons who need and want it and thereby, as Mount Laurel has, exclude such people from living within its confines because of the limited extent of their income and resources. Necessarily implicated are the broader questions of the right of such municipalities to limit the kinds of available housing and of any obligation to make possible a variety and choice of types of living accommodations.

We conclude that every such municipality must, by its land use regulations, presumptively make realistically possible an appropriate variety and choice of housing. More specifically, presumptively it cannot foreclose the opportunity of the classes of people mentioned for low and moderate income housing and in its regulations must affirmatively afford that opportunity, at least to the extent of the municipality's fair share of the present and prospective regional need therefor. These obligations must be met unless the particular municipality can sustain the heavy burden of demonstrating peculiar circumstances which dictate that it should not be required so to do.[10]

We reach this conclusion under state law and so do not find it necessary to consider federal constitutional grounds urged by plaintiffs. * * * This court has * * * plainly warned, even in cases decided some years ago sanctioning a broad measure of restrictive municipal decisions, of the inevitability of change in judicial approach and view as mandated by change in the world around us. * * * The warning implicates the matter of *whose* general welfare must be served or not violated in the field of land use regulation. Frequently the decisions in this state * * * have spoken only in terms of the interest of the enacting municipality, so that it has been thought, at least in some quarters, that such was the only welfare requiring consideration. It is, of course, true that many cases have dealt only with regulations having little, if any, outside impact where the local decision is ordinarily entitled to prevail. However, it is fundamental and not to be forgotten that the zoning power is a police power of the state and the local authority is acting only as a delegate of that power and is restricted in the same manner as is the state. So, when regulation does have a substantial external impact, the welfare of the state's citizens beyond the borders of the particular municipality cannot be disregarded and must be recognized and served. * * *

It is plain beyond dispute that proper provision for adequate housing of all categories of people is certainly an absolute essential in promotion of the general welfare required in all local land use regulation. Further the universal and constant need for such housing is so important and of such broad public interest that the general welfare which developing municipalities like Mount Laurel must consider extends beyond their boundaries and cannot be parochially confined to the claimed good of the particular municipality. It has to follow that, broadly speaking, the presumptive obligation arises for each such municipality affirmatively to plan and provide, by its land use regulations, the reasonable opportunity for an appropriate variety and choice of housing, including, of course, low and moderate cost housing, to meet the needs, desires and resources of all categories of people who may desire to live within its boundaries. Negatively, it may not adopt regulations or policies which thwart or preclude that opportunity. * * *

We have spoken of this obligation of such municipalities as "presumptive." The term has two aspects, procedural and substantive. Procedurally, we think the basic importance of appropriate housing for all dictates that, when it is shown that a developing municipality in its land use regulations has not made realistically possible a variety and choice of

---

[10] While, as the trial court found, Mount Laurel's actions were deliberate, we are of the view that the identical conclusion follows even when municipal conduct is not shown to be intentional, but the effect is substantially the same as if it were.

housing, including adequate provision to afford the opportunity for low and moderate income housing, or has expressly prescribed requirements or restrictions which preclude or substantially hinder it, a facial showing of violation of substantive due process or equal protection under the state constitution has been made out and the burden, and it is a heavy one, shifts to the municipality to establish a valid basis for its action or non-action. The substantive aspect of "presumptive" relates to the specifics, on the one hand, of what municipal land use regulation provisions, or the absence thereof, will evidence invalidity and shift the burden of proof and, on the other hand, of what bases and considerations will carry the municipality's burden and sustain what it has done or failed to do. Both kinds of specifics may well vary between municipalities according to peculiar circumstances. * * *

Without further elaboration at this point, our opinion is that Mount Laurel's zoning ordinance is presumptively contrary to the general welfare and outside the intended scope of the zoning power in the particulars mentioned. A facial showing of invalidity is thus established, shifting to the municipality the burden of establishing valid superseding reasons for its action and non-action. We now examine the reasons it advances.

The township's principal reason in support of its zoning plan and ordinance housing provisions, advanced especially strongly at oral argument, is the fiscal one previously adverted to, *i.e.,* that by reason of New Jersey's tax structure which substantially finances municipal governmental and educational costs from taxes on local real property, every municipality may, by the exercise of the zoning power, allow only such uses and to such extent as will be beneficial to the local tax rate. * * * We have no hesitancy in now saying, and do so emphatically, that, considering the basic importance of the opportunity for appropriate housing for all classes of our citizenry, no municipality may exclude or limit categories of housing for that reason or purpose. While we fully recognize the increasingly heavy burden of local taxes for municipal governmental and school costs on homeowners, relief from the consequences of this tax system will have to be furnished by other branches of government. It cannot legitimately be accomplished by restricting types of housing through the zoning process in developing municipalities. * * *

By way of summary, what we have said comes down to this. As a developing municipality, Mount Laurel must, by its land use regulations, make realistically possible the opportunity for an appropriate variety and choice of housing for all categories of people who may desire to live there, of course including those of low and moderate income. It must permit multi-family housing, without bedroom or similar restrictions, as well as small dwellings on very small lots, low cost housing of other types and, in general, high density zoning, without artificial and unjustifiable minimum requirements as to lot size, building size and the like, to meet the full panoply of these needs. Certainly when a municipality zones for industry and commerce for local tax benefit purposes, it without question must zone to permit adequate housing within the means of the employees involved in such uses. * * * The amount of land removed from residential use by allocation to industrial and commercial purposes must be reasonably related to the present and future potential for such purposes. In other words, such municipalities must zone primarily for the living welfare of people and not for the benefit of the local tax rate.

We have earlier stated that a developing municipality's obligation to afford the opportunity for decent and adequate low and moderate income housing extends at least to "* * * the municipality's fair share of the present and prospective regional need therefor." Some comment on that conclusion is in order at this point. Frequently it might be sounder to have more of such housing, like some specialized land uses, in one municipality in a region than in another, because of greater availability of suitable land, location of employment, accessibility of public transportation or some other significant reason. But, under present New Jersey legislation, zoning must be on an individual municipal basis, rather than regionally. So long as that situation persists under the present tax structure, or in the absence of some kind of binding agreement among all the municipalities of a region, we feel that every municipality therein must bear its fair share of the regional burden. * * *

There is no reason why developing municipalities like Mount Laurel, required by this opinion to afford the opportunity for all types of housing to meet the needs of various categories of people, may not become and remain attractive, viable communities providing good living and adequate services for all their residents in the kind of atmosphere which a democracy and free institutions demand. They can have industrial sections, commercial sections and sections for every kind of housing from low cost and multi-family to lots of more than an acre with very expensive homes. Proper planning and governmental cooperation can prevent over-intensive and too sudden development, insure against future suburban sprawl and slums and assure the preservation of open space and local beauty. We do not intend that developing municipalities shall be overwhelmed by voracious land speculators and developers if they use the powers which they have intelligently and in the broad public interest. Under our holdings today, they can be better communities for all than they previously have been. * * *

It is the local function and responsibility, in the first instance at least, rather than the court's, to decide on the details of * * * [corrective legislation] within the guidelines we have laid down. * * * Courts do not build housing nor do municipalities. That function is performed by private builders, various kinds of associations, or, for public housing, by special agencies created for that purpose at various levels of government. The municipal function is initially to provide the opportunity through appropriate land use regulations and we have spelled out what Mount Laurel must do in that regard. It is not appropriate at this time, particularly in view of the advanced view of zoning law as applied to housing laid down by this opinion, to deal with the matter of the further extent of judicial power in the field or to exercise any such power. The municipality should first have full opportunity to itself act without judicial supervision. We trust it will do so in the spirit we have suggested, both by appropriate zoning ordinance amendments and whatever additional action encouraging the fulfillment of its fair share of the regional need for low and moderate income housing may be indicated as necessary and advisable. (We have in mind that there is at least a moral obligation in a municipality to establish a local housing agency pursuant to state law to provide housing for its resident poor now living in dilapidated, unhealthy quarters.) * * * Should Mount Laurel not perform as we expect, further judicial action may be sought by supplemental pleading in this cause. * * *

NOTE ON DEVELOPMENTS AFTER MT. LAUREL I

The New Jersey Supreme Court's decision in Southern Burlington County N.A.A.C.P. v. Township of Mt. Laurel, known as *Mt. Laurel I,* did not end exclusionary zoning in that state. Many municipalities responded to the judgment by resisting its broader implications and emphasizing its limitations.

Resistance took various forms. For example, *Mt. Laurel I* applied only to the zoning practices of "developing" municipalities, a term that the court did not clearly define. Numerous, time-consuming courtroom clashes followed over whether a particular municipality was or was not "developing." More importantly, the decision did not identify affirmative measures that municipalities should take to meet their state constitutional obligation to zone in a manner that served the general welfare. Nor did it suggest that state judges possessed the authority to require municipalities to take affirmative measures. The court explained instead that "[t]he municipality should first have full opportunity to itself act without judicial supervision. We trust that it will do so in the spirit we have suggested, both by appropriate zoning ordinance amendments and whatever additional action encouraging the fulfillment of its fair share of the regional need for local and moderate income housing may be indicated as necessary and advisable." Such trust proved to be misplaced. The Town of Mount Laurel, for example, responded to the decision by rezoning a very small portion of land that was not particularly suited to the construction of affordable housing. Other localities responded similarly.

Concerned by such municipal inaction, the New Jersey Supreme Court revisited the problem in Southern Burlington County N.A.A.C.P. v. Township of Mount Laurel, 92 N.J. 158, 456 A.2d 390 (1983) (*Mt. Laurel II*). The New Jersey Supreme Court in *Mt. Laurel II* acknowledged that its eight-year-old judgment had proved to be far from effective. "Mount Laurel remains afflicted with a blatantly exclusionary ordinance * * *. Mount Laurel is not alone; we believe that there is widespread non-compliance with the constitutional mandate of our original opinion in the case." Declaring that it remained "more firmly committed to the original *Mount Laurel* doctrine than ever," the court considerably expanded its initial holding.

Mt. Laurel II made clear that all municipalities, not just developing ones, must ensure "a realistic opportunity for decent housing for at least some part of its resident poor who now occupy dilapidated housing." The only exceptions would be for communities in which the resident poor represented a disproportionately large segment of the community. The decision went on to define more concretely which localities were "developing" within the meaning of *Mt. Laurel I*. It held that the term encompassed all localities within the state's "growth" areas, as such areas had been designated in the State Development Guide Plan. The Division of State and Regional Planning in the Department of Community Affairs had issued that plan, after *Mt. Laurel I,* as part of its independent effort to control suburban sprawl. *Mt. Laurel II* also made clear that "a good faith attempt" to provide low and moderate income housing would not constitute compliance with the requirement to provide a fair share of the region's affordable housing; "[t]he housing opportunity created must, in fact, be the substantial equivalent of the fair share."

As a procedural matter, *Mount Laurel II* responded to the widespread municipal recalcitrance by adopting a new system for handling future cases. The court declared that all "future *Mount Laurel* litigation" would be assigned only to judges selected by the Chief Justice with the approval of the state supreme court. Initially, the court assigned such cases to three judges, with each judge responsible for all *Mt. Laurel* cases arising in that judge's region. To further streamline the process, the court circumscribed municipal appeal rights in *Mt. Laurel* cases.

Finally, the court concluded that the invalidation of restrictive municipal zoning practices alone would not bring about the constitutionally mandated housing opportunities identified in *Mt. Laurel I*. The court held for the first time, therefore, that "affirmative governmental devices" must be used, and could be ordered. Such affirmative measures included the local adoption of inclusionary zoning measures, such as low-income density bonuses for developers, and imposition of mandatory set-aside requirements to make sure that some affordable housing units would be constructed in new developments. Perhaps most significantly, the court provided that builder's remedies should be granted to developers who had made good faith, but unsuccessful, attempts to secure the municipal authority to construct housing that included an "appropriate portion" of low-and moderate-income units. Notwithstanding the breadth of the new decision, the court took care to emphasize that the constitutionally required changes in land use policy were not intended to be "drastic or destructive." As the court put it, "[o]ur scenic and rural areas will remain essentially scenic and rural, and our suburban communities will retain their basic suburban character."

Aware of the expansive nature of its new decree, and skeptical that the judiciary could bring about the necessary changes on its own, the court frankly appealed for state legislative intervention. The legislature responded by adopting the Fair Housing Act of 1985, N. J. Stat. Ann. §§ 52:27D–301 to 52:27D–329. The Act established the Council on Affordable Housing, (COAH), an administrative agency that took jurisdiction over *Mount Laurel* cases. COAH was responsible for approving the affordable housing plans of localities subject to the *Mount Laurel* obligation. The Act also put a halt to the imposition of builder's remedies.

The state supreme court upheld the constitutionality of the new act in Hills Development Co. v. Bernards Township, 103 N.J. 1, 510 A.2d 621 (1986) (*Mt. Laurel III*). In doing so, *Hills* described the Act's provision that permitted localities, in effect, to sell their fair share obligation to other localities through regional contribution agreements:

> The Act * * * allows municipalities to share *Mount Laurel* obligations by entering into regional contribution agreements. This device requires either Council or court approval to be effective. Under this provision, one municipality can transfer to another, if that other agrees, a portion, under 50% of its fair share obligation, the receiving municipality adding that to its own. The Act contemplates that the first municipality will contribute to the other, presumably to make the housing construction possible and to eliminate any financial burden resulting from the added fair share. The provision seems intended to allow suburban municipalities to transfer a portion of the obligations to urban areas * * *, thereby aiding in the construction of decent lower income housing in the areas where most low income households are found, provided, however, that such areas are "within convenient access to employment opportunities," and conform to "sound comprehensive regional planning." * * *

This provision, always controversial, was repealed by state legislation in 2008. The 2008 legislation also established other ways to increase the amount of affordable housing in New Jersey. It levied at 2.5% tax on non-residential developers to build affordable housing and provided that a portion of the units be affordable by very low-income families (those earning less than 30% of the median income).

Interestingly, a new round of litigation had already ensued when municipalities began to implement some of the affirmative measures identified in *Mt. Laurel II*. Where before builders had challenged exclusionary municipal zoning ordinances that limited construction opportunities, now developers challenged the legality of the inclusionary zoning measures that towns began to adopt. The challenged measures included ones imposing impact fees on new developments that would then be dedicated to an affordable housing fund or ones requiring builders to set aside low-and moderate-income units in new developments. Builders contended that such measures exceeded the local police and zoning authority and amounted to an unauthorized local exercise of the state taxing power. The New Jersey Supreme Court upheld most such measures in Holmdel Builders Association v. Township of Holmdel, 121 N.J. 550, 583 A.2d 277 (N.J.1990).

The most recent New Jersey Supreme Court case dealing with the *Mt. Laurel* doctrine is In the Matter of the Adoption of N.J.A.C. 5:96 and 5.97 by the New Jersey Council on Affordable Housing, 74 A.3d 893 (2013). The court held invalid the adoption by the COAH of a "growth share methodology" to calculate cities' *Mount Laurel* obligations. Under this methodology, a city's obligation would be a share of the *actual* residential and nonresidential growth within its borders. No effort would have to be made to project what that growth should be and, under the formula, there was no reference to regional needs. The court held, over a vigorous dissent, that the growth share methodology was inconsistent with the framework established by the state legislation that created the COAH. That framework emphasized regional needs as the overriding perspective in fashioning a remedy. The court emphasized at great length, however, that the remedies established by *Mt. Laurel II* thirty years earlier were not constitutionally required. On the contrary, it invited the legislature to reconsider, in light of the intervening experience, what remedies might be most effective. The controversy over the *Mt. Laurel* doctrine in New Jersey is thus likely to continue, and not simply because, in 2011, the state's governor tried (unsuccessfully) to abolish the COAH altogether.

There has been considerable debate in the country as a whole over the legacy of the *Mt. Laurel* doctrine. *Mt. Laurel* is hailed by many as a courageous judicial response to a system of zoning that effectively segregated minorities and the poor, unfairly benefitted wealthy suburbs, and contributed to urban decay. Others see the doctrine as the consequence of unwarranted judicial activism that did little to help those it sought to help. It does appear that the judicial and legislative intervention stimulated the construction of a substantial amount of low and moderate income housing. Evidence suggests, however, that much of this construction has been for elderly housing. It is also not at all clear that the decision has served to alter in any significant way the racial makeup of suburban communities in New Jersey. Of course, one might question whether the spatial deconcentration of African-Americans is even a worthy pursuit, given the limit that such a goal may place on the provision of housing and the possibility that it will severely disrupt the social and political integrity of African-American communities. *See* John Calmore, Fair Housing v. Fair Housing: The Problems of Providing Increased Housing Opportunities Through Spacial Deconcentration, 14 Clearinghouse Rev. 7 (1980).

Whatever the doctrine's merits or demerits, it is clear that *Mt. Laurel* remains an outlier. No other state supreme court has followed a path comparable to the one on which the New Jersey Supreme Court embarked. Some state supreme courts have struck down certain local zoning practices as impermissible efforts to exclude low income-residents, as either a matter of state constitutional law or an interpretation of state zoning enabling acts. *See, e.g.*, Surrick v. Zoning Hearing Bd. of Upper Providence Township, 476 Pa. 182, 382 A.2d 105 (1977) (relying on *Mt. Laurel* and invalidating zoning ordinance that limited multi-family housing). In addition, some states have adopted legislation to limit exclusionary zoning practices. For example, Massachusetts adopted the Massachusetts Low and Moderate Income Housing Act, known as the Anti-Snob Zoning Act, in 1969. The Act established an administrative board with the power to override local exclusionary zoning practices. California and Oregon have similar laws. Cal. Gov't Code §§ 6580 to 65589.8 (West 1983 & Supp. 1987); Or. Rev. Stat. §§ 197.005 to 197.850 (1987).

In reflecting upon *Mt. Laurel* and its aftermath, consider whether the legal shift that it brought about in New Jersey promoted or undermined the possibility of decentralized democratic governance. Were New Jersey's localities more or less "free" from state control before or after *Mt. Laurel*? What understanding of decentralization would one need to articulate in order to answer such a question?

Consider as well the various institutions that one might call upon to redress the problem of exclusionary zoning—the federal judiciary or legislature, the state judiciary or legislature, municipalities themselves, community organizations, private market actors such as homebuyers or developers. Are some of these entities better suited than others to bring about such a shift? Does an answer to this question depend on whether one is committed to decentralization? If so, how?

In addition to considering *who* should be called upon to respond to the problem of exclusionary zoning, it is important to consider *how* such a problem could be addressed. For example, the zoning power is only one possible target of reform. Perhaps energy would be better directed at reforming the system of municipal finance or the public educational system or some other feature of state or municipal law. In this regard, consider as well the various forms that legal remedies might take.

SHERYLL CASHIN, MIDDLE-CLASS BLACK SUBURBS AND THE STATE OF INTEGRATION: A POST-INTEGRATIONIST VISION FOR METROPOLITAN AMERICA
86 Cornell L. Rev. 729, 731–752, 756 (2001).

Although racial segregation in housing has been decreasing incrementally in the United States since the 1960s, segregation of African Americans persists at surprisingly high levels. And economic segregation—the geographic separation of persons by income level—has been increasing. Despite the modest successes of fair housing laws in expanding housing choices for African Americans, * * * a growing segment of middle-class blacks is opting to live in all-black suburban havens. On one level, their motivations seem largely the same as those of other suburbanites: "an affordable and attractive house in a safe neighborhood with low taxes, good public schools and close-to-home retail services." In addition to these common consumer preferences, the middle-class black suburbanite who opts to live in an all-black enclave frequently is acting on a desire to live in a community that creates a " 'we' feeling." * * *

[T]he suburban ideal is largely a chimera for African Americans living in exclusive all-black suburbs. * * * While middle-class black enclaves may be premised on a confident separatism, the rightfully proud residents of these communities must face a painful reality. Try as they might, they cannot completely control their own destiny simply by gaining political control of a suburban locality. Externalities beyond their control are inevitable—a chief external factor being the race-laden private decisions of people and institutions not to invest in, locate in, or cooperate with all-black communities. Try as they might, residents of these black enclaves also cannot completely escape their lower-income brethren or the social distress associated with low-income minority communities.

This reflects a larger conundrum most affluent or middle-class blacks in America face. They cannot live the American suburban dream if that dream means replicating exclusive white suburbs—that is, an enclave of "one's own" with high-quality schools, low property taxes, and desired amenities. * * * Thus, African-American economic or fiscal self-interest lies with integration * * * [even though] for many black suburbanites the psychic benefits of "being with one's own" may be worth the costs of segregation. * * *

While blacks have consistently stated a preference for living in an integrated neighborhood, their conception of integration no longer appears to mean "half-black, half-white." Instead, blacks, like whites, now appear to prefer an integrated neighborhood in which their own group is in the majority. * * * The same surveys * * * revealed that the tolerance of whites toward black neighbors increased between 1976 and 1992. During this time the level of black presence in a neighborhood that would likely produce an exodus of whites increased from 30% to 40%. However, the majority of whites clearly preferred not to live in a neighborhood in which blacks outnumbered them. Indeed, according to some economists, whites are typically willing to pay a 13% premium in order to live in an all-white neighborhood. Furthermore, the economists argue, this premium explains the persistence of de facto segregation after the elimination of de jure segregation. * * *

In 1980, black segregation was nearly as high for affluent and middle-class blacks as it is was for poor blacks, and it was higher for this group than it was for any other racial group, regardless of income. For example, in 1980, affluent blacks in the Los Angeles region were more segregated than poor Hispanics, with a segregation index of 78.9 and 64 respectively. Similarly, an analysis of 1990 Census data in nine of the largest metropolitan regions in the United States found that the majority of middle-class blacks who live in these areas live in neighborhoods where blacks comprise the majority. Thus, racial residential integration of African Americans is much more of an illusion than a reality in the United States. While the all-black, middle-class suburb does not reflect a general trend among suburbanizing African Americans, the segregation that results from such communities is not an aberration. A high degree of residential segregation persists for African Americans in all income brackets. * * *

While black suburbanization has moved incrementally toward integration, predominately black suburbs have emerged and expanded rapidly in most American metropolitan regions. "In 1990, there were 40 U.S. metropolitan areas with at least 50,000 black suburbanites, defined as blacks living outside the central city." By far, the largest black suburban population in the United States is in the Washington, D.C. area. By some estimates, over 480,000 black suburbanites currently live in Prince George's County, Maryland, alone—this exceeds the number of blacks who live in the District of Columbia. The second largest market for black suburbs is the Atlanta region, where new black suburbanites tend to cluster in neighborhoods to the southeast of the city in DeKalb County. * * *

It is difficult to quantify the precise extent to which affluent or middle-class African Americans have formed their own all-black suburban enclaves. Clear examples of these communities, however, exist in Prince George's County, Maryland; DeKalb County, Georgia; Dade County, Florida; and suburbs to the south of Chicago and to the northeast of St. Louis. Notably, the number of affluent black suburbs is quite small. One researcher contends, however, that most metropolitan regions with a large black population have a "Black Belt," created by the black middle class's attempt to escape from poor neighborhoods, that stretches from core, impoverished areas in the central city to periphery areas in the first rung of older suburbs. Consequently, sociologist Mary Pattillo-McCoy argues that the typical middle-class black enclave sits as a buffer between core black poverty areas and suburban white areas. * * *

Beyond notions of racial pride, competence, or even superiority, the most consistent strain in the testimonies of residents of black suburban enclaves is their profound disillusionment with what they perceive as the failed promises of integration. In several books by black journalists and writers like Ellis Cose, Sam Fulwood, and Lawrence Otis Graham, the black middle class attests both to their frustrations with their lack of full advancement or acceptance in "integrated" America and to the balm from this pain found in the all-black neighborhoods where they choose to live. Ironically, the relatively privileged black middle class consistently reports more encounters with racial prejudice and voices stronger reservations about our nation's success in achieving equality than do blacks with lower education and income levels. * * *

It is a quiet truth, spoken of in private conversations but not widely or publicly admitted, that many middle-class black people are uncomfortable living in close proximity to black persons of lower economic or social status. Like their white suburban counterparts, they are attempting to escape the social distress, particularly crime, associated with many urban neighborhoods. In many ways they can be just as hostile to the urban poor as their white counterparts.

An infamous example of this occurred in the summer of 1996 in the Prince George's community of Perrywood. When black kids from neighborhoods of D.C. began traveling out to Perrywood to play basketball with their middle-income brethren, neighbors got upset with the noise and occasional vandalism. They hired a private security company to screen nonresidents from the neighborhood. The irony of black people hiring private police to stop and check the identification of all black male youth in the neighborhood was not lost on many residents. Some expressed misgivings and anger, but not surprisingly the consensus was that the community needed to do what was necessary to protect their homes and property. * * *

Hence the classist premise or defense of middle-class black suburbs is exactly the same as that of affluent white suburbs. Residents of these communities are saying: "I want to escape the ills of the central city, with its crime and high redistributive taxes." The rational way to create a haven of low taxes, low crime, stable property values, and comfortable suburban surroundings is to exclude or distance oneself from populations that bring increased social service demands and the type of antimainstream social behaviors that are frequently cultivated in isolated, poverty-ridden communities. Those suburban localities that do not adopt exclusionary strategies or that do not attempt to attract high-end homes and taxpayers frequently find themselves overwhelmed with the demands of servicing low-and moderate-income families on a small and shrinking tax base. This exclusionary incentive is exacerbated by the fact that localities typically must rely heavily on property taxes to raise revenue for most of the government services they provide. * * *

[R]esidents of Prince George's County and other middle-class black enclaves are not realizing the suburban ideal that they are seeking.

Instead, these suburban middle-class black enclaves, like all black middle-class neighborhoods, tend to be "characterized by more poverty, higher crime, worse schools, and fewer services than white middle-class neighborhoods." One of the primary reasons for these differences between white and black middle-class communities is that black middle-class neighborhoods tend to be located closer to poor black neighborhoods—a contiguous "Black Belt" of poor neighborhoods buffered by middle-class neighborhoods, encouraged and facilitated by real estate agents and other market actors. As a result, African-American communities "bear nearly the full burden of disproportionate black poverty." * * * [A]ffluent, predominately white suburbs in exclusive, high-growth jurisdictions are achieving the suburban ideal in part because only these communities are effectively walling themselves off from the service burdens associated with housing poor and moderate-income people. * * *

In the Washington, D.C. area, the affluent bastions of Prince George's County are outside the Beltway, to the south and east of the District. Not surprisingly, the fast growing high-tech corridors of Northern Virginia are located in the opposite direction due west of the District. Other metropolitan regions demonstrate the same pattern. In the Atlanta region, for example, the majority of the black middle-class is located far from the central city and is moving south while the best jobs, economic opportunities and schools are moving north. The "black middle-class is suburbanizing in one direction and the jobs and economic growth are suburbanizing in another. . . . This is true in the Washington, Atlanta, and Chicago regions, and really everywhere we have seen a significant black middle-class." This isolation from the high-growth economic sectors can negatively impact residents, increasing average commute times and limiting access to "New Economy" jobs.

One researcher, Myron Orfield, blames the real estate industry for the economic isolation of black middle-class suburbs. Orfield argues that the black middle class is constantly struggling to distance itself from the social distress of lower-income communities and in the process gets steered to the least controversial areas by a discriminatory real estate industry. When they reach a critical mass, he argues, whites flee and demand in the local housing market falls, causing poorer individuals to move in behind the middle-class blacks. Within a period as short as a decade, black middle-class migrants find themselves once again in close proximity to social distress and often move again, even farther away from centers of economic growth.

This pattern has clearly occurred in Prince George's County, which experienced a substantial decline in property values between 1994 and 1998 in northern parts of the county that attracted many low-and moderate-income persons from within the District. This decline in property values has been accompanied by a simultaneous increase in social distress indicators, including increased child poverty and crime. Simultaneously, affluent black Prince Georgians have been moving farther south, increasingly into neighboring Charles County, in search of a better quality of life.

In addition to this isolation from high-growth corridors, retailers have notoriously shunned Prince George's County, much to the chagrin of county leaders and residents. While much of the commercial sector's avoidance is likely based upon ignorance or discrimination, their underinvestment highlights a central weakness of racially segregated communities: a concentration of racial minorities can lead to a decline in access to and influence of dominant institutional actors that shape markets. * * *

The Prince George's County public schools have the second lowest test scores in the state of Maryland. "About 32 percent of all its third-, sixth-and eighth-grade students scored at a satisfactory level or better on the Maryland School Performance Assessment Program last year, well above Baltimore City's 16 percent score but well below top-ranked Howard County's 60 percent." * * *

In addition to funding problems, Prince George's County schools have a higher concentration of low-income students than do other suburban school systems in the region—another possible contributor to the county's low school performance. Given the performance and funding problems of Prince George's County schools, many affluent families are opting out of the public school system. "More than half of the system's students qualify for free or reduced-price lunches, which indicates that many prosperous families do not send their children to the public schools." Predominately middle-class African-American schools in the United States impoverish rapidly because majority-black communities tend to attract lower-income populations over time. Most middle-class parents with means and choices would not opt to send their children to a school with a sizeable and growing proportion of poor children.

This, perhaps, is one of the harshest realities for black communities. Many middle-class blacks who have opted to live in a "black sanctuary" are paying a premium for their classism in the form of private school tuition. Their white counterparts in affluent white suburbs have the option of relying on high-quality, well-funded public schools that typically have few poor children. At the same time, middle-class blacks can shun poor black children and the public schools they attend just as whites do. * * *

The crime rate in Prince George's County is higher than that of neighboring suburban, predominately white jurisdictions. During the 1990s, crime within the District of Columbia dropped significantly, while crime in Prince George's County rose slightly. Although the total increase in crime in Prince George's was only marginal, many of the County's inner-Beltway communities experienced a crime explosion that was disproportionate to their population growth. During the same period, the District of Columbia neighborhoods bordering these Prince George's communities experienced a rapid decrease both in crime and population, suggesting that the social distress formerly tied to the District's poorer neighborhoods is migrating to the county. * * *

Overall, poverty rates in Prince George's County have improved with the arrival of middle-class black residents. But the influx of poor people from the District of Columbia has had a mitigating impact. Despite the countywide decrease in poverty, including child poverty, child poverty still increased in fifty-four county communities between 1980 and 1990. Most of the largest increases were in communities located inside the Beltway in the western part of the county. Again, this increased poverty in the western parts of the county reflects a larger trend—the tendency of black communities to attract poorer migrants. Moreover, it appears that Prince George's County is attracting disproportionately more low-income people than other surrounding, majority-white suburban counties. Clearly concentrated poverty has a negative impact on the well-being of families relegated to high-poverty neighborhoods. Less well known is the potential impact that proximity to poverty and social distress has on the black middle class. Sociologist Mary Pattillo-McCoy, who has documented this impact in the Groveland community on the Southside of Chicago, concludes that the close proximity of the black middle class to poor neighborhoods renders the opportunity structure of black middle-class communities precarious. In short, children that grow up in middle-class white communities that typically are well-insulated from poverty, crime, and poor schools do not encounter the same risks that children living in black middle-class neighborhoods encounter on their passage to adulthood. * * *

RICHARD T. FORD, GEOGRAPHY AND SOVEREIGNTY: JURISDICTIONAL FORMATION AND RACIAL SEGREGATION
49 Stan. L. Rev. 1365, 1366–1371, 1373–1375, 1382–1386, 1399–1400 (1997).

Consider the following two racially identified jurisdictions:

District 12 * * * is * * * unusually shaped. It is approximately 160 miles long and, for much of its length, no wider than the I-85 corridor. It winds in snakelike fashion through tobacco country, financial centers, and manufacturing areas "until it gobbles in enough enclaves of black neighborhoods." Northbound and southbound drivers on I-85 sometimes find themselves in separate districts in one county, only to "trade" districts when they enter the next county * * *. One state legislator has remarked that "if you drove down the interstate with both car doors open, you'd kill most of the people in the district." The district even has inspired poetry: "Ask not for whom the line is drawn; it is drawn to avoid thee." [*Shaw v. Reno*, 509 U.S. 630, 635–36 (1993)]

Locals call the street the "Berlin Wall," or the "barrier," or the "Mason-Dixon Line." It divides the suburban Grosse Pointe communities, which are among the most genteel towns anywhere, from the East Side of Detroit, which is poor and mostly black. The Detroit side is studded with abandoned cars, graffiti-covered schools, and burned-out buildings. Two blocks away, within view, are neatly-clipped hedges and immaculate houses—a world of servants and charity balls, two-car garages and expensive clothes. On the one side, says John Kelly, a Democratic state senator whose district awkwardly straddles both neighborhoods, is "West Beirut;" on the other side, "Disneyland." [Kenneth T. Jackson, Crabgrass Frontier: The Suburbanization of the United States 278 (1985).]

Today, the former is a scandal and against the law, while the latter is the norm and enforced by law. The thesis of this article, in a nutshell, is that this is a stark and unacceptable contradiction. * * *

Legislative districting is often assumed to be the primary mechanism by which American democracy provides minority subgroups protection from potentially tyrannous majorities. But in fact, local government is a much more significant arbiter of subgroup relations because local governments are far more numerous than state and federal legislative districts and because, at the local level, subgroups have greater control over the composition of "their" jurisdictions. Local government is more potent because it actually provides regulatory and police power to subgroups, whereas districting simply provides an opportunity to elect a representative who alone has no police power, but who must instead negotiate with potentially hostile parties at a higher level of government. It is therefore surprising that the creation of local government receives so little attention in constitutional analysis and normative political theory. For all of the reasons that minority legislative districts are desirable, properly formed local governments are more desirable; and for all of the reasons that group-based districting is troubling, segregated local governments are even more so. * * *

[E]lectoral districts and local governments * * * are treated quite differently in American public law. This is so because law generally presents electoral districting as a process in which the state establishes a division as a convenience for the administration of the franchise (and is therefore responsible for the composition of the subdivision). Local government formation, on the other hand, is considered a process in which government merely recognizes or facilitates the desires of a preexisting, organic social group (and is therefore not implicated in the subdivision's demographic composition). This common conceptual split between the two types of jurisdictional subdivisions has the consequence of justifying strict judicial scrutiny for electoral districts that promote subgroup autonomy while leaving similarly homogenous local governments immune from constitutional attack.

But electoral districting and local government formation do not so easily correspond to these common descriptions: Districting is, in some sense, a recognition of demographic and geographic facts, whereas local government formation is a state policy, not a private right. In fact, public law oscillates between two competing rationales for any given subdivision, often invoking both in reference to the same controversy. So although local government is justified as the recognition of an independent group that desires an autonomous sphere, it is also justified as an administrative convenience of state government. And although electoral districting is formally defined as a convenience for the administration of the franchise, historically, it also served a less well-defined function of empowering geographically defined subgroups and, later, a more explicit function of empowering racial minorities under the Voting Rights Act.

Therefore, this article will highlight the similarities rather than the differences between electoral districting and local government formation: Both are the product of state action and a reflection of the affiliations of civil society. Because of these similarities, public law should abandon what is increasingly becoming a formal distinction between districting and local government, in which the former is considered to be state action and subject to strict constitutional scrutiny in all cases and the latter is considered to be mere recognition and therefore free from scrutiny in all but the most obvious cases of illegitimate state motivation. In both instances, the government acts to create formally empowered groups that would otherwise not exist. In both cases, the group is formally defined by residence and geography, but often informally defined by subgroup solidarity. * * *

[T]he Court has invalidated reapportionment plans that purposely provided for minority group representation by creating majority-minority electoral districts. In each of these cases, the Court has moved ever closer to the proposition that the Equal Protection Clause prohibits the state from using race as a factor in establishing electoral districts. The[se] * * * cases reflect and rely on a conception of race-conscious district reapportionment as "groupmaking" by the state. The Court has viewed the challenged majority-minority districts as exclusively the product of state action rather than as a recognition (however imperfect) of

voluntarily chosen and preexisting minority group political solidarity.
* * *

The[se] * * * cases recognize a novel type of constitutional wrong. None of the plaintiffs in the colorblind districting cases proves or even asserts having suffered vote dilution or infringement of the franchise due to the challenged reapportionments. Thus, although race-conscious reapportionment is often referred to as an "affirmative action gerrymander," these cases are not analogous to challenges to affirmative action by white plaintiffs: In those challenges, the plaintiffs were required to show that they were denied a benefit or injured because of their race. By contrast, the plaintiffs in these recent apportionment cases have neither alleged nor proved any racially specific harm whatsoever. Instead, their complaint has been that the state has taken race into account in creating electoral districts. These cases make explicit and direct analogies not to affirmative action cases, but to segregation cases: The claim is that the creation of racially identified subdivisions is, in and of itself, a violation of equal protection. * * * For example, in *Shaw v. Reno*, the Court expressed concern that "racial gerrymandering, even for remedial purposes, may balkanize us into competing racial factions" * * *.

The colorblind districting cases reflect and rely on the conception of electoral districting as the active *creation* of subdivisions by the state. In each of these recent cases, no objective quality defines the constitutionally problematic districts; instead, it is the action and intent of the state in creating racially defined subdivisions that is problematic. The colorblind districting cases evoke and rely on an active, motivated, single-minded state that purposefully employs racial categories. It is the subjective intent of the state that gives rise to the constitutional infirmity. * * * This conception of state creation of legislative districts in the colorblind districting cases is in stark opposition to the conception of the state's role in local government formation: There the courts go to pains to insist that the state does not create segregated local jurisdictions, but simply recognize the desires of the citizenry. But one could as easily argue that the states in the colorblind districting cases were also simply recognizing a salient racial group, one which has a shared history and status in American society, one which an Act of Congress requires states to recognize, and one which will certainly continue to be salient regardless of whether states recognize it. Conceived of in this manner, the constitutional objection to majority-minority districts vanishes: The state is not engaging in the active creation or maintenance of racial distinctions, but rather merely recognizing racial differences that preexisted the state districting body in question and that will continue regardless of what the state does. * * *

Just as electoral districts can easily be reconceived of as the recognition of groups that preexist state action, local governments can be seen as groupmaking by the state. Long-established constitutional doctrine affirms that local governments are subdivisions of the state and nothing more. The Constitution does not recognize local governments as independent political entities: As far as the Constitution is concerned, local governments, like special purpose districts, are merely state subdivisions. Although it is true that many local governments were proposed by groups of citizens and approved by the state in a mechanical fashion, many others are subject to review by state administrative boards. More importantly, whatever the formation process, it should not distract us from the fact that local governments are state subdivisions. The state cannot accomplish through its subdivisions what it cannot accomplish through its central legislative bodies. If subdivisions created with segregative intent are constitutionally impermissible, it should not matter whether the state legislature or the citizens of the subdivision acting with state authority have the illicit intent. It is the use of governmental authority, not any particular institutional framework, that triggers constitutional scrutiny.

When understood in this way, a segregated local government is at least as troubling as a segregated legislative district and probably more so. After all, a segregated district only allows a racial group representation at a higher level of government, where its representative must still compromise and engage with representatives of other communities in order to exercise state power. A segregated local government, by contrast, is a direct delegation of state power to a subgroup, which may then exercise that power without engaging with anyone outside the subgroup. * * *

Board of Education of Kiryas Joel Village School District v. Grumet [512 U.S. 687 (1994)] illustrates the use of local government as a means of subgroup empowerment and the related difficulties in distinguishing between subgroup creation and recognition. In *Kiryas Joel*, a village, and later a school district, were created for the explicit purpose of providing a religious minority with a sphere of autonomy. Here I wish to focus on the "background" of the case: the Court's treatment of the village rather than the school district, the focus of the litigation. The irony that I wish to explore is that the Court found the creation of the school district unconstitutional under the Establishment Clause, but found no infirmity in the creation of the village that preceded and made possible the creation of the school district. This seemingly inconsistent treatment of the village and school district was justified by the distinction between passive recognition and active creation. The Court argued, in essence, that the state merely recognized the Satmars in creating a village, but that it actively created a school district for them as a religious group. It must be noted that the recognition/creation distinction functioned to insulate the formation of a local government (and therefore the formation of local governments in general) from constitutional scrutiny. *Kiryas Joel* and its aftermath demonstrate the inadequacy of this distinction and suggest the need for a new metric for determining the proper role of the state in subgroup empowerment, an empowerment which necessarily alters (and thus recreates) the subgroup.

In *Kiryas Joel*, the Court found that the creation of a New York state school district controlled by one religious group, the Satmar Hasidim, violated the Establishment Clause. In 1977, the Village of Kiryas Joel incorporated under the laws of the state of New York. These laws make no reference to religion, and by all accounts, the power to create such subdivisions is delegated in a mechanical and nondiscretionary fashion to any group meeting the requisite criteria. However, in this case, the group seeking incorporation did so for the explicit purpose of creating a religiously homogenous community. After negotiations with non-Satmars who objected to being included in the village, the boundaries of the proposed village were altered to include only Satmars. The Village of Kiryas Joel includes only Satmars to this day.

In 1989, the New York state legislature passed a statute that provided that the Village of Kiryas Joel "is constituted as a separate school district . . . and shall have and enjoy all the powers and duties of a union free school district." The statute was challenged as a violation of the Establishment Clause. Writing for the majority, Justice Souter struck down the legislation, noting that it

> effectively identifies these recipients of governmental authority by reference to doctrinal adherence, even though it does not do so expressly . . . because of the way the boundary lines of the school district divide residents according to religious affiliation. . . . It is undisputed that those who negotiated the village boundaries when applying the general village incorporation statute drew them so as to exclude all but Satmars. . . . Carving out the village school district ran counter to customary districting practices in the State. . . . The origin of the district in a special Act of the legislature, rather than the State's general laws governing school district reorganization, is likewise anomalous.

It bears noting that Justice Souter treats synonymously the boundaries of the village and the boundaries of the school district. Of course, the boundaries of the school district and the village are geographically identical: The legislation established a school district coterminous with the village. But in the same breath, Souter goes to pains to establish that the segregated village that preceded and formed the basis of the school district was not constitutionally problematic. He notes that the formation of the school district "contrasts with the process by which the village . . . itself was created, involving, as it did, the application of a neutral state law designed to give almost any group of residents the right to incorporate."

To distinguish the unconstitutional school district from the constitutionally acceptable village, Justice Souter advances the distinction between recognition and creation: The state merely *recognized* the village of Kiryas Joel by delegating police power in a standardized and nondiscretionary manner, whereas the state actively *created* the school district of Kiryas Joel by departing from standard practices for the purpose of delegating public power to a group the state knew to be religiously homogenous. The irony is that Justice Souter's opinion itself blurs the distinction between village and district boundaries. That the village boundaries were drawn so as to exclude all but Satmars is evidence that the state employed religious criteria in creating . . . the school district?! It was the *village* that was actively drawn to exclude all but Satmars; that accomplished, the state merely created a school district coterminous with an existing subdivision at the request of its residents. More importantly, the distinction between the village and the school district is constitutionally irrelevant: If a subdivision created to isolate a religious group is unconstitutional, then both the village and the district are unconstitutional. The citizens of Kiryas Joel acted as an arm of the state and with state authority when they incorporated as a village, just as the legislature acted with state authority when it created the school district. * * *

[T]he Court's treatment of the Village of Kiryas Joel represents an emerging jurisprudence that allows government to sanction and facilitate segregation that appears to originate in voluntary association. This metric will almost always allow for the "recognition" of segregation in local governments, which are initially formed by citizens and later approved by state legislatures or administrative agencies. * * * [T]he Court has adopted a constitutional jurisprudence that distinguishes between those segregated jurisdictions in which segregation is a private choice that the state recognizes through the grant of jurisdictional autonomy and those that are the result of a state-created social condition. Although this distinction is intuitively plausible, it has proved to be problematic and malleable in precisely those cases in which it is advanced as part of a determinate equation for the resolution of public law disputes * * * [Moreover if the two types of jurisdictions were to be treated] functionally * * * one would expect the decisions to come out reversed. Majority black electoral districts represent a democratic compromise between citizens in an environment of racial polarization, and they provide political voice for a historically silenced minority group while maintaining a commitment to majoritarianism. On the other hand, segregated localities represent the legacy of de jure segregation for which the state is responsible, and they function to perpetuate racial divisions and inequality. Treated consequentially, one would again expect the reverse outcome: Majority-minority districts provide an insular group only with the power to send a representative to a broader and more inclusive institution where political power can be exercised only through compromise and persuasion. Local government, by contrast, provides an insular group with direct control over the police and regulatory power of the state, thereby facilitating policies that further entrench group divisions and social fragmentation. * * *

NOTE ON MILLIKEN V. BRADLEY

In *Milliken v. Bradley*, 418 U.S. 717, 94 S.Ct. 3112, 41 L.Ed.2d 1069 (1974) Chief Justice Burger writing for the Court defended a city's ability to limit admission to its schools to city residents (and thereby overturning a District Court's order encompassing 53 neighboring school districts in the effort to desegregate Detroit's school system). What do you think of his argument?

> * * * Here the District Court's approach to what constituted "actual desegregation" raises the fundamental question * * * as to the circumstances in which a federal court may order desegregation relief that embraces more than a single school district. The court's analytical starting point was its conclusion that school district lines are no more than arbitrary lines on a map drawn "for political convenience." Boundary lines may be bridged where there has been a constitutional violation calling for interdistrict relief, but the notion that school district lines may be casually ignored or treated as a mere administrative convenience is contrary to the history of public education in our country. No single tradition in public education is more deeply rooted than local control over the operation of schools; local autonomy has long been thought essential both to the maintenance of community concern and support for public schools and to quality of the educational process. Thus, in *San Antonio Independent School District v. Rodriguez*, 411 U.S. 1, 50, 93 S.Ct. 1278, 1305, 36 L.Ed.2d 16 (1973), we observed that local control over the educational process affords citizens an opportunity to participate in decision-making, permits the structuring of school programs to fit local needs, and encourages "experimentation, innovation, and a healthy competition for educational excellence."
>
> The Michigan educational structure involved in this case, in common with most States, provides for a large measure of local control, and a review of the scope and character of these local powers indicates the extent to which the interdistrict remedy approved by the two courts could disrupt and alter the structure of public education in Michigan. The metropolitan remedy would require, in effect, consolidation of 54 independent school districts historically administered as separate units into a vast new super

school district. Entirely apart from the logistical and other serious problems attending large-scale transportation of students, the consolidation would give rise to an array of other problems in financing and operating this new school system. Some of the more obvious questions would be: What would be the status and authority of the present popularly elected school boards? Would the children of Detroit be within the jurisdiction and operating control of a school board elected by the parents and residents of other districts? What board or boards would levy taxes for school operations in these 54 districts constituting the consolidated metropolitan area? What provisions could be made for assuring substantial equality in tax levies among the 54 districts, if this were deemed requisite? What provisions would be made for financing? Would the validity of long-term bonds be jeopardized unless approved by all of the component districts as well as the State? What body would determine that portion of the curricula now left to the discretion of local school boards? Who would establish attendance zones, purchase school equipment, locate and construct new schools, and indeed attend to all the myriad day-to-day decisions that are necessary to school operations affecting potentially more than three-quarters of a million pupils?

It may be suggested that all of these vital operational problems are yet to be resolved by the District Court, and that this is the purpose of the Court of Appeals' proposed remand. But it is obvious from the scope of the interdistrict remedy itself that absent a complete restructuring of the laws of Michigan relating to school districts the District Court will become first, a *de facto* "legislative authority" to resolve these complex questions, and then the "school superintendent" for the entire area. This is a task which few, if any, judges are qualified to perform and one which would deprive the people of control of schools through their elected representatives.
* * *

2. THE DISTRIBUTION AND REDISTRIBUTION OF LOCAL WEALTH

Local governments have an incentive to exclude low income persons from residence in part because non-residents are excluded not only from local housing opportunities but also from local public resources: the income generated by city taxation is typically used exclusively for the benefit of city residents. This section explores the limits on a city's ability to spend its tax-generated income exclusively on its own residents. It explores, in other words, the extent to which cities are required to redistribute locally-generated wealth to outsiders. Of course, the idea that those who are better off should be required to share (at least some of) their advantages with others is highly controversial. In local government law, the extent of the obligation to share financial resources has principally arisen in the context of financing local school systems.[24] Nearly every state has been through at least one round of school financing litigation, and a number of state courts (and some state legislatures) have sought to reduce the gap between the richest and poorest school districts.[25] It should be noted that, at least in the view of some experts, these efforts have so far made very little progress in

---

[24] For an analysis of the analogous problem of intra-group obligations to share resources, see Matthew Parlow, Equitable Fiscal Regionalism, 85 Temp. L. Rev. 49 (2012); Charles Haar and Daniel Fessler, The Wrong Side of the Tracks (1986).

[25] For a comprehensive listing of the relevant cases, see Meira Schulman Ferziger, Annotation, Validity of Public School Funding Systems, 110 A.L.R.5TH 293 (2003).

Cases that have declared school financing systems unconstitutional include: Kanawha County Public Library Board v. Board of Education of the County of Kanawha, 231 W.Va. 386 (2013); McCleary v. State, 173 Wash.2d 477 (2011); Montoy v. State, 279 Kan. 817, 112 P.3d 923 (2005); Columbia Falls Elementary School Dist. No. 6 v. State, 2005 MT 69, 326 Mont. 304, 109 P.3d 257 (2005); Hoke County Bd. of Educ. v. State, 358 N.C. 605, 599 S.E.2d 365 (2004); Idaho Schools For Equal Educational Opportunity v. State, 140 Idaho 586, 97 P.3d 453 (2004); Campaign for Fiscal Equity, Inc. v. State of New York, 100 N.Y.2d 893, 801 N.E.2d 326, 769 N.Y.S.2d 106 (2003); Claremont School Dist. v. Governor,147 N.H. 499, 794 A.2d 744 (2002); Tennessee Small School Systems v. McWherter, 91 S.W.3d 232 (Tenn.2002); Lake View School Dist. No. 25 of Phillips County v. Huckabee, 351 Ark. 31, 91 S.W.3d 472, 173 Ed. Law Rep. 248 (2002); State v. Campbell County School Dist., 2001 WY 90, 32 P.3d 325, 157 Ed. Law Rep. 366 (Wyo. 2001); Claremont School Dist. v. Governor, 144 N.H. 210, 744 A.2d 1107, 141 Ed. Law Rep. 862 (1999); Hull v. Albrecht, 192 Ariz. 34, 960 P.2d 634 (1998); DeRolph v. State, 78 Ohio St.3d 193, 677 N.E.2d 733 (1997); Carrollton-Farmers Branch Independent School Dist. v. Edgewood Independent School District, 826 S.W.2d 489 (Tex.1992); Abbott v. Burke, 119 N.J. 287, 575 A.2d 359 (1990); Rose v. Council for Better Educ., 790 S.W.2d 186 (Ky.1989); Helena Elementary School v. State, 236 Mont. 44, 769 P.2d 684 (1989); DuPree v. Alma School Dist., 279 Ark. 340, 651 S.W.2d 90 (1983); Washakie County School Dist. v. Herschler, 606 P.2d 310 (Wyo.1980), cert. denied, 449 U.S. 824, 101 S.Ct. 86, 66 L.Ed.2d 28; Pauley v. Kelly, 162 W.Va. 672, 255 S.E.2d 859 (1979); Seattle School Dist. v. State, 90 Wash.2d 476, 585 P.2d 71 (Wash. 1978); Horton v. Meskill, 172 Conn. 615, 376 A.2d 359 (1977); Serrano v. Priest, 5 Cal.3d 584, 96 Cal.Rptr. 601, 487 P.2d 1241 (1971). Those that have rejected constitutional challenges include: Lobato v. State of Colorado, 304 P.3d 1132 (2013); Committee for Educational Equality v. State, Supreme Court of Missouri, 294 S.W.3d 477 (2009); Bonner ex rel. Bonner v. Daniels, 907 N.E.2d 516 (Ind. 2009); Nebraska Coalition for Educational Equity and Adequacy v. Heineman, 273 Neb. 531, 731 N.W.2d 164 (2007); Roosevelt Elementary School Dist. No. 66 v. State, 205 Ariz. 584, 74 P.3d 258 (Ct.App.Div.1, 2003); Durant v. State, 251 Mich.App. 297, 650 N.W.2d 380 (2002), appeal denied, 467 Mich. 900, 654 N.W.2d 329 (2002), reconsideration denied, 467 Mich. 900, 658 N.W.2d 484 (2003); Stubaus v. Whitman, 339 N.J.Super. 38, 770 A.2d 1222 (App.Div.2001), certification denied, 171 N.J. 442, 794 A.2d 181 (2002); County of Sonoma v. Commission on State Mandates, 84 Cal.App.4th 1264, 101 Cal.Rptr.2d 784 (1st Dist.2000); Vincent v. Voight, 236 Wis.2d 588, 2000 WI 93, 614 N.W.2d 388 (2000); Lincoln County School Dist. No. One v. State, 985 P.2d 964 (Wyo.1999); Withers v. State, 163 Or.App. 298, 987 P.2d 1247 (1999); African American Legal Defense Fund, Inc. v. New York State Dept. of Educ., 8 F.Supp.2d 330 (S.D.N.Y.1998); Idaho Schools for Equal Educational Opportunity v. State, 132 Idaho 559, 976 P.2d 913 (1998); Leandro v. State, 346 N.C. 336, 488 S.E.2d 249 (1997); Matanuska-Susitna Borough School District v. State, 931 P.2d 391 (Alaska 1997); Kukor v. Grover, 148 Wis.2d 469, 436 N.W.2d 568 (1989); Fair School Finance Council v. State, 746 P.2d 1135 (Okl.1987); Hornbeck v. Somerset County Bd. of Educ., 295 Md. 597, 458 A.2d 758 (1983); Board of Educ., Levittown Union Free School Dist. v. Nyquist, 57 N.Y.2d 27, 453 N.Y.S.2d 643, 439 N.E.2d 359 (1982); Lujan v. Colorado State Bd. of Educ., 649 P.2d 1005 (Colo.1982); Board of Educ. v. Walter, 58 Ohio St.2d 368, 390 N.E.2d 813 (1979); Danson v. Casey, 484 Pa. 415, 399 A.2d 360 (1979); Olsen v. State, 276 Or. 9, 554 P.2d 139 (1976); Thompson v. Engelking, 96 Idaho 793, 537 P.2d 635 (1975); Shofstall v. Hollins, 110 Ariz. 88, 515 P.2d 590 (1973).

accomplishing their objective, although it appears that court-ordered reform has proved more successful then legislatively-initiated reform.[26]

Two judicial views of inter-city obligations concerning school financing are presented in the first two cases reproduced below. As with the cases on exclusionary zoning, alternative conceptions of inter-city relations and of the value of local sovereignty underlie the different opinions. The United States Supreme Court articulates one of these conceptions in San Antonio Independent School District v. Rodriguez, which relies on the concept of "local control."[27] Then, in Edgewood Independent School District v. Kirby, the Texas Supreme Court— reviewing a later challenge by the same school district involved in *Rodriguez*—suggests an alternative vision of local autonomy and inter-city obligations. What definition of "local control" does the *Kirby* opinion advance? Does either case suggest that rich school districts are entitled to spend money derived from their larger tax base only on themselves? Does either case suggest that poorer school districts are entitled to share in the resources of the richer districts? What relevance do the arguments about reallocation of wealth in these cases have to other services—such as health care or police protection?

The ideas debated in these cases reflect the influence of important scholarly writings[28] and the cases themselves have generated a large

---

[26] See Carlee Escue, William Thro, and R. Craig Wood, Some Perspectives on Recent School Finance Litigation, 268 Ed. Law Rep. 601 (2011); Michael Paris, Framing Equal Opportunity (2009); Note, A Right to Learn?: Improving Educational Outcomes through Substantive Due Process, 120 Harv. L. Rev. 1323 (2007); John Dayton and R. Craig Wood, School Funding Litigation: Scanning the Event Horizon, 224 Ed. Law Rep. 1 (2007); James Ryan and Thomas Saunders, Foreword to Symposium on School Finance Litigation: Emerging Trends or Dead Ends?, 22 Yale L. & Pol'y Rev. 463 (2004); William Evans et al., Schoolhouses, Courthouses, and Statehouses After Serrano, 16 J. Pol'y Analysis & Mgmt. 10 (1997); Note, Unfulfilled Promises: School Finance Remedies and State Courts, 104 Harv. L.Rev. 1072 (1991); "Efforts Are Failing to Close Gaps Separating Rich and Poor Schools", New York Times, February 19, 1985, page C1, col. 1.

[27] For analyses of the Supreme Court's recent invocation of the notion of local control, see Matthew Parlow, Equitable Fiscal Regionalism, 85 Temp. L. Rev. 49 (2012); David King, Formalizing Local Constitutional Standards of Review and the Implications for Federalism, 97 Va. L. Rev. 1685 (2011); David Barron, Fighting Federalism with Federalism: If It's Not Just a Battle Between Federalists and Nationalists, What is It?, 74 Fordham L. Rev. 2081 (2006); David Barron, A Localist Critique of the New Federalism, 51 Duke L.J. 377 (2001); David Barron, The Promise of Cooley's City: Traces of Local Constitutionalism, 147 U. Penn. L. Rev. 487 (1999); M. David Gelfand, The Constitutional Position of American Local Government: Retrospect for the Burger Court and Prospects for the Rehnquist Court, 19 Hastings Const. L.Q. 635 (1987); M. David Gelfand, Local Government in the American Federal System: The Bicentennial as a Time of Crisis and Opportunity, 19 The Urban Lawyer 568 (1987); Joan Williams, The Constitutional Vulnerability of American Local Government: The Politics of City Status in American Law, 1986 Wis. L. Rev. 83; M. David Gelfand, The Burger Court and the New Federalism: Preliminary Reflections on the Roles of Local Government Actors in the Political Drama of the 1980s, 21 B.C. L. Rev. 763 (1980).

[28] See, e.g., John Coons, William Clune & Stephen Sugarman, Private Wealth and Public Education (1970); Frank Michelman, Foreword: On Protecting the Poor Through the Fourteenth Amendment, 83 Harv. L. Rev. 7 (1968); Arthur Wise, Rich Schools, Poor Schools: The Promise of Equal Educational Opportunity (1968); Harold Horowitz and Diana Neitring, Equal Protection

literature.[29] One of the most influential ideas advanced in the school financing litigation was the concept of district power equalizing proposed by John Coons, William Clune and Stephen Sugarman; this concept was designed to assure "true local fiscal control" of school financing by cutting the tie between the amount of money that can be raised by a locality and the amount of district wealth. Under district power equalizing, school financing would depend on the tax rate of each district but it would not depend on the size of its tax base. The following excerpt[30] offers a brief articulation of the idea:

> The essence of district power equalizing is the simple elimination of wealth from the formula determining a school district's offering. Instead of offering being a function of both wealth and effort, it becomes a function of effort alone. The easiest way to perceive this is to suppose that the legislature has developed a table which specifies how much per pupil each district will be permitted to spend for each level of (locally chosen) tax effort against local wealth (preferably income, but, more realistically, property). Such a table might look like this:

Aspects of Inequalities in Public Education and Public Assistance Programs from Place to Place Within a State, 15 U.C.L.A. L. Rev. 787 (1968).

[29] See, e.g., Jeffrey S. Sutton, San Antonio Independent School District v. Rodriguez and Its Aftermath, 94 Va. L. Rev. 1963 (2008); Myron Orfield, The Region and Taxation: School Finance, Cities, and the Hope for Regional Reform, 55 Buff. L. Rev. 91 (2007); Laurie Reynolds, Uniformity of Taxation and The Preservation of Local Control in School Finance Reform, 40 U.C. Davis L. Rev. 1835 (2007); Matt Brooker, Riding the Third Wave of School Finance Litigation: Navigating Troubled Waters, 75 UMKC L. Rev. 183 (2006); James Ryan and Thomas Saunders, Foreword to Symposium on School Finance Litigation: Emerging Trends or Dead Ends?, 22 Yale L. & Pol'y Rev. 463 (2004); Emel Gokygit Wadhwani, Achieving Greater Inter-Local Equity in Financing Municipal Services: What We Can Learn from School Finance Litigation, 7 Tex. Forum on C.L. & C.R. 91 (2002); Charles Mahtesian, School Finance: Is Equity the Answer, 6 Governing 43 (1993); William Clune, New Answers to Hard Questions Posed by *Rodriguez*, 24 Conn. L. Rev. 721 (1992); Richard Briffault, The Role of Local Control in School Finance Reform, 24 Conn. L. Rev. 773 (1992); Symposium: Investing in Our Children's Future: School Finance Reform in the '90's, 28 Harv. J. Legis. 293 (1991); Richard Elmore and Milbrey McLaughlin, Reform and Retrenchment: The Politics of California's School Finance Reform (1982); Robert Inman and Daniel Rubinfeld, The Judicial Pursuit of Local Fiscal Equity, 92 Harv. L. Rev. 1662 (1979).

[30] From John Coons, William Clune and Stephen Sugarman, Educational Opportunity: A Workable Constitutional Test for State Financial Structures, 57 Calif. L. Rev. 303, 319–21 (1969).

	Local Tax Rate	Permissible Per Pupil Expenditure
10 mills	(minimum rate permitted)	$ 500
11 mills		550
12 mills		600
13 mills		650
14 mills		700
29 mills		1450
30 mills	(maximum rate permitted)	1500

Irrespective of the amount of the local collections the district would be permitted to spend that amount and only that amount per pupil fixed by law for the tax rate chosen. Rich districts and poor districts taxing at 12 mills would provide a $600 education. Poor districts and rich districts taxing at 30 mills would provide a $1500 education. Obviously this might require the redistribution of excess local collections from rich districts and the subvention of insufficient collections in poor districts. The magnitude of such effects would depend on the degree to which the state wishes to pay for the total cost of education; this in turn is related to the extent to which the state wishes to stimulate district effort. The formulas for controlling total cost and the respective state and local shares are infinitely variable and can incorporate many refinements. One that deserves mention would be an adjustment for municipal overburden in the case of large cities. Such fine tuning is easily handled under a power equalized system and could be employed to eliminate vestiges of wealth discrimination associated with certain economic and social differences among the districts other than differences in assessed wealth. Other examples of such differences are transportation costs and variations from area to area in cost of services such as salaries.

The effect, then, is to make all districts equal in their *power* to raise dollars for education. The variations from district to district in dollars per pupil spent upon education would thus be a function simply of local interest in public education. Power equalizing would not guarantee equal dollars per pupil—a goal we consider fatuous and counter-productive; it would merely make the money raising game a fair one and maximize the incentive for political effort at the local level. Its potential relevance to the movement for "community control" is obvious.
* * *

In reflecting on this passage, consider the view of inter-city relationships that underlies district power equalizing. Two aspects of the argument demand particular attention in this regard. First, the authors contend that it is just a matter of "fine-tuning" to ensure that each district will in fact have equal power under a district power equalizing scheme. Second, the authors implicitly assume that is possible to adjust funding formulas and thereby isolate a city's true "interest in education." Note, however, that a city's "interest in education" or relative power might be constructed by many factors other than wealth and that these factors are themselves a consequence of inter-city relationships that district-power equalizing would not affect. For example, communities with large populations of persons without school-age children might have a different "interest in education" than a neighboring locality even if each city had the same amount of funds to spend. Similarly, cities may not wish to increase local taxes for education because of the need to increase them to fund other social services that more affluent communities may not need to provide. Does it follow from these possibilities that state law should be structured to accommodate a city's seeming disinterest in education? Finally, you should be aware that district power equalizing may be impermissible under the law of some states, as Owens v. Colorado Congress of Parents, Teachers, and Students, infra, Chapter Four, suggests. (*Owens* is by no means unique. The Wisconsin Supreme Court struck down district power equalizing in Buse v. Smith, 74 Wis.2d 550, 247 N.W.2d 141 (1976), reasoning that the financing scheme violated the state constitutional requirement that "a tax must be spent at the level at which it is raised.") If district power equalizing is impermissible, does that leave federal or state control of local financing decisions as the only remaining alternative to permitting local school districts to base their financing on district wealth?

The two last cases in the section, Claremont School District v. Governor and Sheff v. O'Neill, address yet another approach to the issue of inter-local inequity in school funding. The New Hampshire Supreme Court in *Claremont* conceives of the locally-adopted property tax for education as a state tax. It proceeds from that premise to strike down the system of funding public education through local property taxes on the ground that such a system amounts to a non-uniform state education tax: poor cities must bear a bigger tax burden than wealthy ones. *Sheff* goes even further, finding that every aspect of public education—funding, the position of school district boundaries, the assignment of students to the district in which they reside—is the responsibility of state government.

Claremont and *Sheff* also introduce the right to an adequate public education. Rather than focussing solely on inter-local wealth inequities, *Claremont* and *Sheff* hold that there is a fundamental right under the state constitution to an adequate public education. The emphasis on adequacy marks an important new wave of challenges to state systems of funding public education. This emphasis has, in some respects, proved more successful than the earlier approaches.[31] Those approaches centered on either the federal Equal Protection Clause, as in *Rodriguez*, or state constitutional equality mandates, as in *Kirby*. The recognition of a right to an adequate public education may cast doubt on the lawfulness of funding public education through local property taxes. It also raises concerns about the lawfulness of other aspects of a state's system of public education. How does the emphasis on adequacy shift our understanding of the problem of inter-local inequity? How should a court go about identifying what constitutes an adequate public education? Can a court articulate such a standard independent of legislative guidance and local input?

The Connecticut Supreme Court faced these issues in a recent case expanding on its decision in *Sheff*. In Connecticut Coalition for Justice in Education Funding v. Bell, 990 A.2d 206 (Conn. 2010), a plurality opinion interpreted a relatively minimal state constitutional provision ("There shall always be free public elementary and secondary schools in the state") to require that the state provide its students with an adequate education. According to the plurality opinion, the state constitution:

> [e]ntitles Connecticut public school students to an education suitable to give them the opportunity to be responsible citizens able to participate fully in democratic institutions, such as jury service and voting. A constitutionally adequate education also will leave Connecticut's students prepared to progress to institutions of higher education, or to attain productive employment or otherwise contribute to the state's economy. To satisfy this standard, the state, through the local school districts, must provide students with an objectively "meaningful opportunity" to receive the benefit of this constitutional right. Moreover, we agree with the New York Court of Appeals' explication of the "essential" components requisite to this

---

[31] For discussions of this new wave of cases, see, e.g., Julia Simon-Kerr and Robynn Sturm, Justiciability and the Role of Courts in Adequacy Litigation: Preserving the Constitutional Right to Education, 6 Stan. J. Civ. Rts. & Civ. Liberties 83 (2010); Joseph P. Viteritti, The Inadequacy of Adequacy Guarantees: A Historical Commentary on State Constitutional Provisions That Are the Basis for School Finance Litigation, 7 U. Md. L.J. Race, Religion, Gender & Class 58 (2007); William S. Koski, When "Adequate" Isn't: The Retreat From Equity in Educational Law and Policy and Why it Matters, 56 Emory L.J. 545 (2006); Quentin Palfrey, The State Judiciary's Role in Fulfilling Brown's Promises, 8 Mich. J. Race & L 1, 13–25 (2002); Kelly Cochran, Comment, Beyond School Financing: Defining the Constitutional Right to an Adequate Education, 78 N.C. L. Rev. 349 (2000); Symposium: School Finance Reform, 14 J. L. & Pol. 411 (1998); Peter Enrich, Leaving Equality Behind: New Directions in School Finance Reform, 48 Vand. L. Rev. 101 (1995). For a discussion of how overcoming racial segregation, rather than funding inequities, should lie at the core of the next wave of cases, see Danielle Holley-Walker, A New Era for Desegregation, 28 Ga. St. U. L. Rev. 423 (2012); James Ryan, Schools, Race, and Money, 109 Yale L. J. 249 (1999); James Ryan, Sheff, Segregation, and School Finance Litigation, 74 N.Y.U. L. Rev. 529 (1999). For an emphasis on adjusting school district boundaries as way to address inequities, see Aaron Saiger, The School District Boundary Problem, 42 Urb. Law. 495 (2010).

> constitutionally adequate education, namely: (1) "minimally adequate physical facilities and classrooms which provide enough light, space, heat, and air to permit students to learn"; (2) "minimally adequate instrumentalities of learning such as desks, chairs, pencils, and reasonably current textbooks"; (3) "minimally adequate teaching of reasonably up-to-date basic curricula such as reading, writing, mathematics, science, and social studies;" and (4) "sufficient personnel adequately trained to teach those subjects."

The plurality opinion was signed by three members of the court; dissenting opinions also garnered three signatures. One dissenting opinion rejected the idea that the relevant constitutional provision required a suitable education; the other dissenting opinion considered the adequacy issue a political question properly left to the legislature. A seventh opinion, concurring in the judgment, called for deference to legislative and executive determinations of adequacy. In 2012, the Connecticut state legislature enacted a statute that sought to address the adequacy issue by making changes designed to reduce achievement gaps within the state, increase state funding, provide support for school choice, and improve teacher training, among other provisions. In light of the *Connecticut Coalition* opinions and the legislative reaction, what seems to be the right balance between judicial intervention and legislative decision making on educational adequacy? Did the plurality opinion go too far—or not far enough?

The *Connecticut Coaltion* case does not adopt the only possible standard for adequacy. A very different one was adopted in Kentucky by *Rose v. Council for Better Education,* 790 S.W.2d 186 (1989) and accepted more recently in *Gannon v. State of Kansas*, 319 P.3d 1196 (2014):

> [A]n efficient system of education must have as its goal to provide each and every child with at least the seven following capacities: (i) sufficient oral and written communication skills to enable students to function in a complex and rapidly changing civilization; (ii) sufficient knowledge of economic, social, and political systems to enable the student to make informed choices; (iii) sufficient understanding of governmental processes to enable the student to understand the issues that affect his or her community, state, and nation; (iv) sufficient self-knowledge and knowledge of his or her mental and physical wellness; (v) sufficient grounding in the arts to enable each student to appreciate his or her cultural and historical heritage; (vi) sufficient training or preparation for advanced training in either academic or vocational fields so as to enable each child to choose and pursue life work intelligently; and (vii) sufficient levels of academic or vocational skills to enable public school students to

compete favorably with their counterparts in surrounding states, in academics or in the job market.

Can a court mandate that that the necessary money be spent to achieve this standard? One dissenting opinion estimate that the cost of the *Connecticut Coalition* reforms would be $2 billion; the Kentucky/Kansas standard would likely cost more.

The final excerpt, by Richard Schragger, examines the arguments in favor of property-based financing of local services, including the schools, made in an important book by William Fischel. The Fischel-Schragger debate raises a fundamental question about all the materials that follow: is the attack on property-based financing wrong-headed?[32]

SAN ANTONIO INDEPENDENT SCHOOL DISTRICT V. RODRIGUEZ

Supreme Court of the United States, 1973.
411 U.S. 1, 93 S.Ct. 1278, 36 L.Ed.2d 16.

MR. JUSTICE POWELL delivered the opinion of the Court.

This suit attacking the Texas system of financing public education was initiated by Mexican-American parents whose children attend the elementary and secondary schools in the Edgewood Independent School District, an urban school district in San Antonio, Texas. They brought a class action on behalf of schoolchildren throughout the State who are members of minority groups or who are poor and reside in school districts having a low property tax base. Named as defendants were the State Board of Education, the Commissioner of Education, the State Attorney General, and the Bexar County (San Antonio) Board of Trustees. * * *

Until recent times, Texas was a predominantly rural State and its population and property wealth were spread relatively evenly across the State. Sizable differences in the value of assessable property between local school districts became increasingly evident as the State became more industrialized and as rural-to-urban population shifts became more pronounced. The location of commercial and industrial property began to play a significant role in determining the amount of tax resources available to each school district. These growing disparities in population and taxable property between districts were responsible in part for increasingly notable differences in levels of local expenditure for education. * * * Recognizing the need for increased state funding to help offset disparities in local spending and to meet Texas' changing educational requirements, the state legislature in the late 1940's undertook a thorough evaluation of public education with an eye toward

---

[32] For another analysis of Fischel's book, see Lee Anne Fennell, Homes Rule, 112 Yale L.J. 617 (2002).

major reform. * * * [These] efforts led to the passage of the * * * Texas Minimum Foundation School Program. Today, this Program accounts for approximately half of the total educational expenditures in Texas.

The Program calls for state and local contributions to a fund earmarked specifically for teacher salaries, operating expenses, and transportation costs. The State, supplying funds from its general revenues, finances approximately 80% of the Program, and the school districts are responsible—as a unit—for providing the remaining 20%. The districts' share, known as the Local Fund Assignment, is apportioned among the school districts under a formula designed to reflect each district's relative taxpaying ability. * * * Today every school district * * * [imposes] a property tax from which it derives locally expendable funds in excess of the amount necessary to satisfy its Local Fund Assignment under the Foundation Program. * * *

The school district in which appellees reside, the Edgewood Independent School District, has been compared throughout this litigation with the Alamo Heights Independent School District. This comparison between the least and most affluent districts in the San Antonio area serves to illustrate the manner in which the dual system of finance operates and to indicate the extent to which substantial disparities exist despite the State's impressive progress in recent years. Edgewood is one of seven public school districts in the metropolitan area. Approximately 22,000 students are enrolled in its 25 elementary and secondary schools. The district is situated in the core-city sector of San Antonio in a residential neighborhood that has little commercial or industrial property. The residents are predominantly of Mexican-American descent: approximately 90% of the student population is Mexican-American and over 6% is Negro. The average assessed property value per pupil is $5,960—the lowest in the metropolitan area—and the median family income ($4,686) is also the lowest. At an equalized tax rate of $1.05 per $100 of assessed property—the highest in the metropolitan area—the district contributed $26 to the education of each child for the 1967–1968 school year above its Local Fund Assignment for the Minimum Foundation Program. The Foundation Program contributed $222 per pupil for a state-local total of $248. Federal funds added another $108 for a total of $356 per pupil. * * *

Alamo Heights is the most affluent school district in San Antonio. Its six schools, housing approximately 5,000 students, are situated in a residential community quite unlike the Edgewood District. The school population is predominantly "Anglo," having only 18% Mexican-Americans and less than 1% Negroes. The assessed property value per pupil exceeds $49,000, and the median family income is $8,001. In 1967–1968 the local tax rate of $.85 per $100 of valuation yielded $333 per pupil over and above its contribution to the Foundation Program. Coupled with the $225 provided from that Program, the district was able to supply $558 per student. Supplemented by a $36 per-pupil grant from federal sources, Alamo Heights spent $594 per pupil. * * *

The case comes to us with no definitive description of the classifying facts or delineation of the disfavored class. Examination of the District Court's opinion and of appellees' complaint, briefs, and contentions at oral argument suggests, however, at least three ways in which the discrimination claimed here might be described. The Texas system of school financing might be regarded as discriminating (1) against "poor" persons whose incomes fall below some identifiable level of poverty or who might be characterized as functionally "indigent," or (2) against those who are relatively poorer than others, or (3) against all those who, irrespective of their personal incomes, happen to reside in relatively poorer school districts. Our task must be to ascertain whether, in fact, the Texas system has been shown to discriminate on any of these possible bases and, if so, whether the resulting classification may be regarded as suspect. * * *

Even a cursory examination * * * demonstrates that neither of the two distinguishing characteristics of wealth classifications can be found here. First, in support of their charge that the system discriminates against the "poor," appellees have made no effort to demonstrate that it operates to the peculiar disadvantage of any class fairly definable as indigent, or as composed of persons whose incomes are beneath any designated poverty level. Indeed, there is reason to believe that the poorest families are not necessarily clustered in the poorest property districts. * * *

Second, neither appellees nor the District Court addressed the fact that * * * lack of personal resources has not occasioned an absolute deprivation of the desired benefit. The argument here is not that the children in districts having relatively low assessable property values are receiving no public education; rather, it is that they are receiving a poorer quality education than that available to children in districts having more assessable wealth. Apart from the unsettled and disputed question whether the quality of education may be determined by the amount of money expended for it, a sufficient answer to appellees' argument is that, at least where wealth is involved, the Equal Protection Clause does not require absolute equality or precisely equal advantages. Nor indeed, in view of the infinite variables affecting the educational process, can any system assure equal quality of education except in the most relative sense. Texas asserts that the Minimum Foundation Program * * * assures "every child in every school district an adequate education." No proof was offered at trial persuasively discrediting or refuting the State's assertion.

For these two reasons—the absence of any evidence that the financing system discriminates against any definable category of "poor" people or that it results in the absolute deprivation of education—the disadvantaged class is not susceptible of identification in traditional terms. * * * However described, it is clear that appellees' suit asks this Court to extend its most exacting scrutiny to review a system that allegedly discriminates against a large, diverse, and amorphous class, unified only by the common factor of residence in districts that happen to have less taxable wealth than other districts. * * * We thus conclude that the Texas system does not operate to the peculiar disadvantage of any suspect class. * * *

Education, of course, is not among the rights afforded explicit protection under our Federal Constitution. Nor do we find any basis for saying it is implicitly so protected. As we have said, the undisputed importance of education will not alone cause this Court to depart from the usual standard for reviewing a State's social and economic legislation. * * * Even if it were conceded that some identifiable quantum of education is a constitutionally protected prerequisite to the meaningful exercise of either right, we have no indication that the present levels of educational expenditures in Texas provide an education that falls short. Whatever merit appellees' argument might have if a State's financing system occasioned an absolute denial of educational opportunities to any of its children, that argument provides no basis for finding an interference with fundamental rights where only relative differences in spending levels are involved and where—as is true in the present case— no charge fairly could be made that the system fails to provide each child with an opportunity to acquire the basic minimal skills necessary for the enjoyment of the rights of speech and of full participation in the political process. * * * Furthermore, the logical limitations on appellees' nexus theory are difficult to perceive. How, for instance, is education to be distinguished from the significant personal interests in the basics of decent food and shelter? * * *

This case represents far more than a challenge to the manner in which Texas provides for the education of its children. We have here nothing less than a direct attack on the way in which Texas has chosen to raise and disburse state and local tax revenues. We are asked to condemn the State's judgment in conferring on political subdivisions the power to tax local property to supply revenues for local interests. In so doing, appellees would have the Court intrude in an area in which it has traditionally deferred to state legislatures. * * * In addition to matters of fiscal policy, this case also involves the most persistent and difficult questions of educational policy, another area in which this Court's lack of specialized knowledge and experience counsels against premature interference with the informed judgments made at the state and local levels. * * *

It must be remembered, also, that every claim arising under the Equal Protection Clause has implications for the relationship between national and state power under our federal system. Questions of federalism are always inherent in the process of determining whether a State's laws are to be accorded the traditional presumption of constitutionality, or are to be subjected instead to rigorous judicial scrutiny. * * * In its reliance on state as well as local resources, the Texas system is comparable to the systems employed in virtually every other State. * * * The "foundation grant" theory * * * [was] devoted to establishing a means of guaranteeing a minimum statewide educational program without sacrificing the vital element of local participation. * * *

In an era that has witnessed a consistent trend toward centralization of the functions of government, local sharing of responsibility for public education has survived. * * * The persistence of attachment to government at the lowest level where education is concerned reflects the depth of commitment of its supporters. In part, local control means * * * the freedom to devote more money to the education of one's children. Equally important, however, is the opportunity it offers for participation in the decisionmaking process that determines how those local tax dollars will be spent. Each locality is free to tailor local programs to local needs. Pluralism also affords some opportunity for experimentation, innovation, and a healthy competition for educational excellence. An analogy to the Nation-State relationship in our federal system seems uniquely appropriate. Mr. Justice Brandeis identified as one of the peculiar strengths of our form of government each State's freedom to "serve as a laboratory; and try novel social and economic experiments." No area of social concern stands to profit more from a multiplicity of viewpoints and from a diversity of approaches than does public education.

Appellees do not question the propriety of Texas' dedication to local control of education. To the contrary, they attack the school-financing system precisely because, in their view, it does not provide the same level of local control and fiscal flexibility in all districts. Appellees suggest that local control could be preserved and promoted under other financing systems that resulted in more equality in educational expenditures. While it is no doubt true that reliance on local property taxation for school revenues provides less freedom of choice with respect to expenditures for some districts than for others, the existence of "some inequality" in the manner in which the State's rationale is achieved is not alone a sufficient basis for striking down the entire system. * * * It is also well to remember that even those districts that have reduced ability to make free decisions with respect to how much they spend on education still retain under the present system a large measure of authority as to how available funds will be allocated. They further enjoy the power to make numerous other decisions with respect to the operation of the schools. The people of Texas may be justified in believing that other systems of school financing, which place more of the financial responsibility in the hands of the State, will result in a comparable lessening of desired local autonomy. * * *

Appellees further urge that the Texas system is unconstitutionally arbitrary because it allows the availability of local taxable resources to turn on "happenstance." They see no justification for a system that allows, as they contend, the quality of education to fluctuate on the basis of the fortuitous positioning of the boundary lines of political subdivisions and the location of valuable commercial and industrial property. But any scheme of local taxation—indeed the very existence of identifiable local governmental units—requires the establishment of jurisdictional boundaries that are inevitably arbitrary. It is equally inevitable that some localities are going to be blessed with more taxable assets than others. Nor is local wealth a static quantity. Changes in the level of taxable wealth within any district may result from any number of events, some of which local residents can and do influence. For instance, commercial and industrial enterprises may be encouraged to locate within a district by various actions—public and private.

Moreover, if local taxation for local expenditures were an unconstitutional method of providing for education then it might be an equally impermissible means of providing other necessary services customarily financed largely from local property taxes, including local police and fire protection, public health and hospitals, and public utility facilities of various kinds. We perceive no justification for such a severe denigration of local property taxation and control as would follow from appellees' contentions. It has simply never been within the constitutional prerogative of this Court to nullify statewide measures for financing public services merely because the burdens or benefits thereof fall unevenly depending upon the relative wealth of the political subdivisions in which citizens live.

In sum, to the extent that the Texas system of school financing results in unequal expenditures between children who happen to reside in different districts, we cannot say that such disparities are the product of a system that is so irrational as to be invidiously discriminatory. * * *

MR. JUSTICE MARSHALL, with whom MR. JUSTICE DOUGLAS concurs, dissenting.

The Court today decides, in effect, that a State may constitutionally vary the quality of education which it offers its children in accordance with the amount of taxable wealth located in the school districts within which they reside. * * * The only justification offered by appellants to sustain the discrimination in educational opportunity caused by the Texas financing scheme is local educational control. * * * I do not question that local control of public education, as an abstract matter, constitutes a very substantial state interest. * * * The State's interest in local educational control—which certainly includes questions of educational funding—has deep roots in the inherent benefits of community support for public education. Consequently, true state dedication to local control would present, I think, a substantial justification to weigh against simply interdistrict variations in the treatment of a State's schoolchildren. But I need not now decide how I might ultimately strike the balance were we confronted with a situation where the State's sincere concern for local control inevitably produced educational inequality. For, on this record, it is apparent that the State's purported concern with local control is offered primarily as an excuse rather than as a justification for interdistrict inequality.

In Texas, statewide laws regulate in fact the most minute details of local public education. For example the State prescribes required courses. All textbooks must be submitted for state approval, and only approved textbooks may be used. The State has established the qualifications necessary for teaching in Texas public schools and the procedures for obtaining certification. The State has even legislated on the length of the school day. * * *

Moreover, even if we accept Texas' general dedication to local control in educational matters, it is difficult to find any evidence of such dedication with respect to fiscal matters. It ignores reality to suggest—as the Court does—that the local property tax element of the Texas financing scheme reflects a conscious legislative effort to provide school districts with local fiscal control. If Texas had a system truly dedicated to local fiscal control, one would expect the quality of the educational opportunity provided in each district to vary with the decision of the voters in that district as to the level of sacrifice they wish to make for public education. In fact, the Texas scheme produces precisely the opposite result. Local school districts cannot choose to have the best education in the State by imposing the highest tax rate. Instead, the quality of the educational opportunity offered by any particular district is largely determined by the amount of taxable property located in the district—a factor over which local voters can exercise no control. * * *

[I]t is essential to recognize that an end to the wide variations in taxable district property wealth inherent in the Texas financing scheme would entail none of the untoward consequences suggested by the Court or by the appellants. First, affirmance of the District Court's decisions would hardly sound the death knell for local control of education. It would mean neither centralized decisionmaking nor federal court intervention in the operation of public schools. Clearly, this suit has nothing to do with local decisionmaking with respect to educational policy or even educational spending. It involves only a narrow aspect of local control—namely, local control over the raising of educational funds. * * * [T]he District Court's decision [does not] even necessarily eliminate local control of educational funding. The District Court struck down nothing more than the continued interdistrict wealth discrimination inherent in the present property tax. Both centralized and decentralized plans for educational funding not involving such interdistrict discrimination have been put forward.[98] The choice among these or other alternatives would remain with the State, not with the federal courts. * * *

EDGEWOOD INDEPENDENT SCHOOL DISTRICT V. KIRBY

Supreme Court of Texas, 1989.
777 S.W.2d 391.

MAUZY, JUSTICE. * * *

There are approximately three million public school children in Texas. The legislature finances the education of these children through a combination of revenues supplied by the state itself and revenues supplied by local school districts which are governmental subdivisions of the state. Of total education costs, the state provides about forty-two percent, school districts provide about fifty percent, and the remainder comes from various other sources including federal funds. School districts derive revenues from local ad valorem property taxes, and the state raises

---

[98] Centralized educational financing is, to be sure, one alternative. On analysis, though, it is clear that even centralized financing would not deprive local school districts of what has been considered to be the essence of local educational control. Central financing would leave in local hands the entire gamut of local educational policymaking—teachers, curriculum, school sites, the whole process of allocating resources among alternative educational objectives.

A second possibility is the much-discussed theory of district power equalization put forth by Professors Coons, Clune, and Sugarman in their seminal work, Private Wealth and Public Education 201–242 (1970). Such a scheme would truly reflect a dedication to local fiscal control. Under their system, each school district would receive a fixed amount of revenue per pupil for any particular level of tax effort regardless of the level of local property tax base. Appellants criticize this scheme on the rather extraordinary ground that it would encourage poorer districts to overtax themselves in order to obtain substantial revenues for education. But under the present discriminatory scheme, it is the poor districts that are already taxing themselves at the highest rates, yet are receiving the lowest returns.

District wealth reapportionment is yet another alternative which would accomplish directly essentially what district power equalization would seek to do artificially. Appellants claim that the calculations concerning state property required by such a scheme would be impossible as a practical matter. Yet Texas is already making far more complex annual calculations involving not only local property values but also local income and other economic factors in conjunction with the Local Fund Assignment portion of the Minimum Foundation School Program.

A fourth possibility would be to remove commercial, industrial, and mineral property from local tax rolls, to tax this property on a statewide basis, and to return the resulting revenues to the local districts in a fashion that would compensate for remaining variations in the local tax bases.

None of these particular alternatives are necessarily constitutionally compelled; rather, they indicate the breadth of choice which would remain to the State if the present interdistrict disparities were eliminated.

funds from a variety of sources including the sales tax and various severance and excise taxes.

There are glaring disparities in the abilities of the various school districts to raise revenues from property taxes because taxable property wealth varies greatly from district to district. * * * The 300,000 students in the lowest-wealth schools have less than 3% of the state's property wealth to support their education while the 300,000 students in the highest-wealth schools have over 25% of the state's property wealth; thus the 300,000 students in the wealthiest districts have more than eight times the property value to support their education as the 300,000 students in the poorest districts. * * * Edgewood I.S.D. has $38,854 in property wealth per student; Alamo Heights I.S.D. in the same county, has $570,109 in property wealth per student.

The state has tried for many years to lessen the disparities through various efforts to supplement the poorer districts. Through the Foundation School Program, the state currently attempts to ensure that each district has sufficient funds to provide its students with at least a basic education. Under this program, state aid is distributed to the various districts according to a complex formula such that property-poor districts receive more state aid than do property-rich districts. However, the Foundation School Program does not cover even the cost of meeting the state-mandated minimum requirements. Most importantly, there are no Foundation School Program allotments for school facilities or for debt service. * * * Low-wealth districts use a significantly greater proportion of their local funds to pay the debt service on construction bonds while high-wealth districts are able to use their funds to pay for a wide array of enrichment programs.

Because of the disparities in district property wealth, spending per student varies widely, ranging from $2,112 to $19,333. Under the existing system, an average of $2,000 more per year is spent on each of the 150,000 students in the wealthiest districts than is spent on the 150,000 students in the poorest districts.

The lower expenditures in the property-poor districts are not the result of lack of tax effort. Generally, the property-rich districts can tax low and spend high while the property-poor districts must tax high merely to spend low. In 1985–86, local tax rates ranged from $.09 to $1.55 per $100 valuation. The 100 poorest districts had an average tax rate of 74.5 cents and spent an average of $2,978 per student. The 100 wealthiest districts had an average tax rate of 47 cents and spent an average of $7,233 per student. * * * Many districts have become tax havens. The existing funding system permits "budget balanced districts" which, at minimal tax rates, can still spend above the statewide average; if forced to tax at just average tax rates, these districts would generate additional revenues of more than $200,000,000 annually for public education.

Property-poor districts are trapped in a cycle of poverty from which there is no opportunity to free themselves. Because of their inadequate tax base, they must tax at significantly higher rates in order to meet minimum requirements for accreditation; yet their educational programs are typically inferior. The location of new industry and development is strongly influenced by tax rates and the quality of local schools. Thus, the property-poor districts with their high tax rates and inferior schools are unable to attract new industry or development and so have little opportunity to improve their tax base.

The amount of money spent on a student's education has a real and meaningful impact on the educational opportunity offered that student. High-wealth districts are able to provide for their students broader educational experiences including more extensive curricula, more up-to-date technological equipment, better libraries and library personnel, teacher aides, counseling services, lower student-teacher ratios, better facilities, parental involvement programs, and drop-out prevention programs. They are also better able to attract and retain experienced teachers and administrators.

The differences in the quality of educational programs offered are dramatic. For example, San Elizario I.S.D. offers no foreign language, no pre-kindergarten program, no chemistry, no physics, no calculus, and no college preparatory or honors program. It also offers virtually no extra-curricular activities such as band, debate, or football. At the time of trial, one-third of Texas school districts did not even meet the state-mandated standards for maximum class size. The great majority of these are low-wealth districts. In many instances, wealthy and poor districts are found contiguous to one another within the same county. * * *

Article VII, section 1 of the Texas Constitution provides:

A general diffusion of knowledge being essential to the preservation of the liberties and rights of the people, it shall be the duty of the Legislature of the State to establish and make suitable provision for the support and maintenance of an efficient system of public free schools. * * *

"Efficient" conveys the meaning of effective or productive of results and connotes the use of resources so as to produce results with little waste; this meaning does not appear to have changed over time. * * * Considering "the general spirit of the times and the prevailing sentiments of the people," it is apparent from the historical record that those who drafted and ratified article VII, section 1 never contemplated the possibility that such gross inequalities could exist within an "efficient" system. At the Constitutional Convention of 1875, delegates spoke at length on the importance of education for *all* the people of this state, rich and poor alike. * * *

The 1876 Constitution provided a structure whereby the burdens of school taxation fell equally and uniformly across the state, and each student in the state was entitled to exactly the same distribution of funds. The state's school fund was initially apportioned strictly on a per capita basis. Also, a poll tax of one dollar per voter was levied across the state for school purposes. These per capita methods of taxation and of revenue distribution seem simplistic compared to today's system; however they do indicate that the people were contemplating that the tax burden would be shared uniformly and that the state's resources would be distributed on an even, equitable basis.

If our state's population had grown at the same rate in each district and if the taxable wealth in each district had also grown at the same rate, efficiency could probably have been maintained within the structure of the present system. That did not happen. Wealth, in its many forms, has not appeared with geographic symmetry. The economic development of the state has not been uniform. Some cities have grown dramatically, while their sister communities have remained static or have shrunk. Formulas that once fit have been knocked askew. Although local conditions vary, the constitutionally imposed state responsibility for an efficient education system is the same for all citizens regardless of where they live.

We conclude that, in mandating "efficiency," the constitutional framers and ratifiers did not intend a system with such vast disparities as now exist. Instead, they stated clearly that the purpose of an efficient system was to provide for a "*general* diffusion of knowledge." (Emphasis added.) The present system, by contrast, provides not for a diffusion that is general, but for one that is limited and unbalanced. The resultant inequalities are thus directly contrary to the constitutional vision of efficiency. * * *

By statutory directives, the legislature has attempted through the years to reduce disparities and improve the system. * * * The legislature's recent efforts have focused primarily on increasing the state's contributions. More money allocated under the present system would reduce some of the existing disparities between districts but would at best only postpone the reform that is necessary to make the system efficient. A band-aid will not suffice; the system itself must be changed.

We hold that the state's school financing system is neither financially efficient nor efficient in the sense of providing for a "general diffusion of knowledge" statewide, and therefore that it violates article VII, section 1 of the Texas Constitution. Efficiency does not require a per capita distribution, but it also does not allow concentrations of resources in property-rich school districts that are taxing low when property-poor districts that are taxing high cannot generate sufficient revenues to meet even minimum standards. There must be a direct and close correlation between a district's tax effort and the educational resources available to it; in other words, districts must have substantially equal access to similar revenues per pupil at similar levels of tax effort. Children who live in poor districts and children who live in rich districts must be afforded a substantially equal opportunity to have access to educational funds. Certainly, this much is required if the state is to educate its populace efficiently and provide for a general diffusion of knowledge statewide.

Under article VII, section 1, the obligation is the legislature's to provide for an efficient system. In setting appropriations, the legislature must establish priorities according to constitutional mandate; equalizing educational opportunity cannot be relegated to an "if funds are left over" basis. We recognize that there are and always will be strong public interests competing for available state funds. However, the legislature's responsibility to support public education is different because it is constitutionally imposed. Whether the legislature acts directly or enlists local government to help meet its obligation, the end product must still be what the constitution commands—i.e. an efficient system of public free schools throughout the state. This does not mean that the state may not recognize differences in area costs or in costs associated with providing an equalized educational opportunity to atypical students or disadvantaged students. Nor does it mean that local communities would be precluded from supplementing an efficient system established by the legislature; however any local enrichment must derive solely from local tax effort.

Some have argued that reform in school finance will eliminate local control, but this argument has no merit. An efficient system does not preclude the ability of communities to exercise local control over the education of their children. It requires only that the funds available for education be distributed equitably and evenly. An efficient system will actually allow for more local control, not less. It will provide property-poor districts with economic alternatives that are not now available to them. Only if alternatives are indeed available can a community exercise the control of making choices. * * *

CLAREMONT SCHOOL DISTRICT V. GOVERNOR

Supreme Court of New Hampshire, 1997.
142 N.H. 462, 703 A.2d 1353.

BROCK, CHIEF JUSTICE.

In this appeal we hold that the present system of financing elementary and secondary public education in New Hampshire is unconstitutional. To hold otherwise would be to effectively conclude that it is reasonable, in discharging a State obligation, to tax property owners in one town or city as much as four times the amount taxed to others similarly situated in other towns or cities. This is precisely the kind of taxation and fiscal mischief from which the framers of our State Constitution took strong steps to protect our citizens. * * *

Funding for public education in New Hampshire comes from three sources. First, school districts are authorized to raise funds through real estate taxation. Locally raised real property taxes are the principal source of revenue for public schools, providing on average from seventy-four to eighty-nine percent of total school revenue. Second, funds are provided through direct legislative appropriations, primarily in the form of Foundation Aid, Building Aid, and Catastrophic Aid. Direct legislative appropriations account for an average of eight percent of the total dollars spent on public elementary and secondary education, ranking New Hampshire last in the United States in percentage of direct support to public education. Third, approximately three percent of support for the public schools is in the form of federal aid. * * *

The plaintiffs argue that the school tax is a unique form of the property tax mandated by the State to pay for its duty to provide an adequate education and that the State controls the process and mechanism of taxation. * * * The question of whether property taxes for schools are local or State taxes is an issue of first impression. Part II, article 5 of the State Constitution provides that the legislature may "impose and levy proportional and reasonable assessments, rates, and taxes, upon all the inhabitants of, and residents within, the said state." This article requires that "all taxes be proportionate and reasonable— that is, equal in valuation and uniform in rate." * * * Determining the character of a tax as local or State requires an initial inquiry into its purpose.

> In order . . . that the tax should be proportional . . . it is required that the rate shall be the same throughout the taxing district;— that is, if the tax is for the general purposes of the state, the rate should be the same throughout the state; if for the county, it should be uniform throughout the county;—and the requisite of proportion, or equality and justice, can be answered in no other way.

State v. U.S. & C. Express Co., 60 N.H. 219, 243 (1880) (Stanley, J.). We find the purpose of the school tax to be overwhelmingly a State purpose and dispositive of the issue of the character of the tax.

"[T]he local school district, an entity created by the legislature almost two centuries ago, exists for the public's benefit, to carry out the mandates of the State's education laws." Opinion of the Attorney General,

No. 82–100–I (Sept. 8, 1982). "Indeed, school district monies, a public trust, can only be spent in furtherance of these educational mandates, and to promote the values set forth in the 'Encouragement of Literature' clause, N.H. Const., pt. 2, Art. 83." * * * Providing an adequate education is thus a duty of State government expressly created by the State's highest governing document, the State Constitution. In addition, public education differs from all other services of the State. No other governmental service plays such a seminal role in developing and maintaining a citizenry capable of furthering the economic, political, and social viability of the State. Only in part II, article 83 is it declared a duty of the legislature to "cherish" a service mandated by the State Constitution. Furthermore, education is a State governmental service that is compulsory. That the State, through a complex statutory framework, has shifted most of the responsibility for supporting public schools to local school districts does not diminish the State purpose of the school tax. Although the taxes levied by local school districts are local in the sense that they are levied upon property within the district, the taxes are in fact State taxes that have been authorized by the legislature to fulfill the requirements of the New Hampshire Constitution. * * *

The question then is whether the school tax as presently structured is proportional and reasonable throughout the State in accordance with the requirements of part II, article 5. Evidence introduced at trial established that the equalized tax rate for the 1994–1995 school year in Pittsfield was $25.26 per thousand while the rate in Moultonborough was $5.56 per thousand. The tax rate in Pittsfield, therefore, was more than four times, or over 400 percent, higher than in Moultonborough. Likewise, the equalized tax rate for the 1994–1995 school year in Allenstown was $26.47 per thousand while the rate in Rye was $6.86 per thousand—a difference in tax rates of almost 400 percent. We need look no further to hold that the school tax is disproportionate in violation of our State Constitution. Indeed, the trial court acknowledged that the plaintiffs "presented evidence that the school tax may be disproportionate if it is a state tax." * * *

There is nothing fair or just about taxing a home or other real estate in one town at four times the rate that similar property is taxed in another town to fulfill the same purpose of meeting the State's educational duty. Compelling taxpayers from property-poor districts to pay higher tax rates and thereby contribute disproportionate sums to fund education is unreasonable. Children who live in poor and rich districts have the same right to a constitutionally adequate public education. Regardless of whether existing State educational standards meet the test for constitutional adequacy, the record demonstrates that a number of plaintiff communities are unable to meet existing standards despite assessing disproportionate and unreasonable taxes. * * * We hold, therefore, that the varying property tax rates across the State violate part II, article 5 of the State Constitution in that such taxes, which support the public purpose of education, are unreasonable and disproportionate. To the extent that the property tax is used in the future to fund the provision of an adequate education, the tax must be administered in a manner that is equal in valuation and uniform in rate throughout the State. * * *

We hold that in this State a constitutionally adequate public education is a fundamental right. * * * We emphasize that the fundamental right at issue is the right to a State funded constitutionally adequate public education. It is not the right to horizontal resource replication from school to school and district to district. The substance of the right may be achieved in different schools possessing, for example, differing library resources, teacher-student ratios, computer software, as well as the myriad tools and techniques that may be employed by those in on-site control of the State's public elementary and secondary school systems. But when an individual school or school district offers something less than educational adequacy, the governmental action or lack of action that is the root cause of the disparity will be examined by a standard of strict judicial scrutiny. * * *

Our decision does not prevent the legislature from authorizing local school districts to dedicate additional resources to their schools or to develop educational programs beyond those required for a constitutionally adequate public education. We recognize that local control plays a valuable role in public education; however, the State cannot use local control as a justification for allowing the existence of educational services below the level of constitutional adequacy. The responsibility for ensuring the provision of an adequate public education and an adequate level of resources for all students in New Hampshire lies with the State. * * *

HORTON, JUSTICE, dissenting: * * *

Many State duties have been delegated to its political subdivisions, and with this delegation has gone the responsibility to fund. Political subdivisions, at their own expense, carry out State duties on elections, fire and police protection, land use control and other exercises of the police power, provisions of highways, sanitation, and the structure and staffing of local government. For much of our history, the counties, towns, and cities provided, at their expense, the facilities, and some level of staffing, for our court system. The local school district, for some time, has financed the education for the children of the district. Under my determination of duty and delegation, I am driven to a holding that the constitutional education nut is properly delegated and the purpose, for taxation purposes, is demonstrably local. Funds raised by taxation are used for political purposes within the district, for the district's use, and expended by the district to achieve educational standards set by the State and the district, for the sole benefit of the district. Given the legislature's proper delegation, its clear designation of the taxing district, the discerned purpose of the tax, and its obvious proportionality within the taxing district, I would hold that the trial court was correct in deciding, in the context of this case, that the part II, article 5 tests of reasonability and proportionality have been met by the current tax system. * * *

SHEFF V. O'NEILL
Supreme Court of Connecticut, 1996.
238 Conn. 1, 678 A.2d 1267.

PETERS, C.J.

The public elementary and high school students in Hartford suffer daily from the devastating effects that racial and ethnic isolation, as well as poverty, have had on their education. Federal constitutional law provides no remedy for their plight. The principal issue in this appeal is whether, under the unique provisions of our state constitution, the state, which already plays an active role in managing public schools, must take further measures to relieve the severe handicaps that burden these children's education. The issue is as controversial as the stakes are high. We hold today that the needy schoolchildren of Hartford have waited long enough. The constitutional imperatives contained in article eighth, § 1,[1] and article first, §§ 1 and 20,[2] of our state constitution entitle the plaintiffs to relief. At the same time, the constitutional imperative of separation of powers persuades us to afford the legislature, with the assistance of the executive branch, the opportunity, in the first instance, to fashion the remedy that will most appropriately respond to the constitutional violations that we have identified. * * *

The stipulation of the parties and the trial court's findings establish the following relevant facts. Statewide, in the 1991–92 school year, children from minority groups constituted 25.7 percent of the public school population. In the Hartford public school system in that same period, 92.4 percent of the students were members of minority groups, including, predominantly, students who were either African-American or

---

[1] The constitution of Connecticut, article eighth, § 1, provides: "There shall always be free public elementary and secondary schools in the state. The general assembly shall implement this principle by appropriate legislation."

[2] The constitution of Connecticut, article first, § 1, provides: "All men when they form a social compact, are equal in rights; and no man or set of men are entitled to exclusive public emoluments or privileges from the community."

The constitution of Connecticut, article first, § 20, as amended by articles five and twenty-one of the amendments, provides: "No person shall be denied the equal protection of the law nor be subjected to segregation or discrimination in the exercise or enjoyment of his or her civil or political rights because of religion, race, color, ancestry, national origin, sex or physical or mental disability."

Latino. * * * Although enrollment of African-American students in the twenty-one surrounding suburban towns has increased by more than 60 percent from 1980 to 1992, only seven of these school districts had a minority student enrollment in excess of 10 percent in 1992. Because of the negative consequences of racial and ethnic isolation, a more integrated public school system would likely be beneficial to all schoolchildren.

A majority of the children who constitute the public school population in Hartford come from homes that are economically disadvantaged, that are headed by a single parent and in which a language other than English is spoken. The percentage of Hartford schoolchildren at the elementary level who return to the same school that they attended the previous year is the lowest such percentage in the state. Such socioeconomic factors impair a child's orientation toward and skill in learning and adversely affect a child's performance on standardized tests. The gap in the socioeconomic status between Hartford schoolchildren and schoolchildren from the surrounding twenty-one suburban towns has been increasing. The performance of Hartford schoolchildren on standardized tests falls significantly below that of schoolchildren from the twenty-one surrounding suburban towns.

Directly or indirectly, the state has always controlled public elementary and secondary education in Connecticut. The legislature directs many aspects of local school programs, including courses of study and curricula, standardized testing, bilingual education, graduation requirements and school attendance. Since 1941, as a result of a state statute, the public school district boundaries in Hartford have been coterminous with the boundaries of the city of Hartford. Since at least 1909, as a result of another state statute, schoolchildren have been assigned to the public school district in which they reside.

The legislature provides substantial support to communities throughout the state to finance public school operations. State financial aid is distributed so that the neediest school districts receive the most aid. Accordingly, in the 1990–91 and 1991–92 school years, overall per pupil state expenditures in Hartford exceeded the average amount spent per pupil in the twenty-one surrounding suburban towns. The state reimburses Hartford for its school renovation projects at a rate that is considerably higher than the reimbursement rate for the twenty-one surrounding suburban towns.

The state has not intentionally segregated racial and ethnic minorities in the Hartford public school system. Except for a brief period in 1868, no students in Connecticut have intentionally been assigned to a public school or to a public school district on the basis of race or ethnicity. * * * The state has nonetheless played a significant role in the present concentration of racial and ethnic minorities in the Hartford public school system. Although intended to improve the quality of education and not racially or ethnically motivated, the districting statute that the legislature enacted in 1909 is the single most important factor contributing to the present concentration of racial and ethnic minorities in the Hartford public school system. The districting statute and the resultant school district boundaries have remained virtually unchanged since 1909. The districting statute is of critical importance because it establishes town boundaries as the dividing line between all school districts in the state. * * * State law sets the borders of school districts to coincide with town boundaries, and requires all children to attend public school within the district in which they reside. The trial court expressly found that the enforcement of these statutes constitutes the "single most important factor" creating the present racial and ethnic imbalance in the Hartford public school system. The failure adequately to address the racial and ethnic disparities that exist among the state's public school districts is not different in kind from the legislature's failure adequately to address the "great disparity in the ability of local communities to finance local education" that made the statutory scheme at issue in *Horton [v. Meskill]*, 172 Conn. 615 [1977], unconstitutional in its application. * * *

[D]efendants urge us to follow federal precedents that concededly require, as a matter of federal constitutional law, that claimants seeking judicial relief for educational disparities pursuant to the equal protection clause of the fourteenth amendment to the United States constitution must prove intentional governmental discrimination against a suspect class. * * * For two reasons, we are not persuaded that we should adopt these precedents as a matter of state constitutional law. First and foremost, the federal cases start from the premise that there is no right to education under the United States constitution. *San Antonio Independent School District v. Rodriguez*, 411 U.S. 1, 35, 93 S. Ct. 1278, 36 L. Ed. 2d 16 (1973). Our Connecticut constitution, by contrast, contains a fundamental right to education and a corresponding affirmative state obligation to implement and maintain that right. Second, the federal cases are guided by principles of federalism as "a foremost consideration in interpreting any of the pertinent constitutional provisions under which [a court] examines state action." *San Antonio Independent School District v. Rodriguez*, supra, 44. * * * Principles of federalism, however, do not restrict our constitutional authority to enforce the constitutional mandates contained in article eighth, § 1, and article first, §§ 1 and 20. * * *

The issue presented by this case is whether the state has fully satisfied its affirmative constitutional obligation to provide a substantially equal educational opportunity if the state demonstrates that it has substantially equalized school funding and resources. The defendants urge us to adopt such a limited construction of our constitution. The plaintiffs, to the contrary, urge us to adopt a broader formulation. They argue that the combination of "racial segregation, the concentration of poor children in the schools, and disparities in educational resources . . . deprive [Hartford schoolchildren] of substantially equal educational opportunities." We agree with the plaintiffs in part. We need not decide, in this case, the extent to which substantial socioeconomic disparities or disparities in educational resources would themselves be sufficient to require the state to intervene in order to equalize educational opportunities. For the purposes of the present litigation, we decide only that the scope of the constitutional obligation expressly imposed on the state by article eighth, § 1, is informed by the constitutional prohibition against segregation contained in article first, § 20. Reading these constitutional provisions conjointly, we conclude that the existence of extreme racial and ethnic isolation in the public school system deprives schoolchildren of a substantially equal educational opportunity and requires the state to take further remedial measures. * * *

For Connecticut schoolchildren, the scope of the state's constitutional obligation to provide a substantially equal educational opportunity is informed and amplified by the highly unusual[3] provision in article first, § 20, that prohibits segregation not only indirectly, by forbidding discrimination, but directly, by the use of the term "segregation." * * * Linguistically, the term "segregation" in article first, § 20, which denotes "separation," is neutral about segregative intent. * * * Whatever this language may portend in other contexts, we are persuaded that, in the context of public education, in which the state has an affirmative obligation to monitor and to equalize educational opportunity, the state's awareness of existing and increasing severe racial and ethnic isolation imposes upon the state the responsibility to remedy "segregation . . . because of race [or] . . . ancestry. . . ." We therefore hold that, textually, article eighth, § 1, as informed by article first, § 20, requires the legislature to take affirmative responsibility to remedy segregation in our public schools, regardless of whether that segregation has occurred de jure or de facto.

The trial court's findings * * * demonstrate that Hartford's schoolchildren labor under a dual burden: their poverty and their racial and ethnic isolation. These findings regarding the causal relationship between the poverty suffered by Hartford schoolchildren and their poor academic performance cannot be read in isolation. They do not diminish the significance of the stipulations and undisputed findings that the

---

[3]   The only other constitutions that explicitly prohibit segregation are those of Hawaii and New Jersey. * * *

Hartford public school system suffers from severe and increasing racial and ethnic isolation, that such isolation is harmful to students of all races, and that the districting statute codified at § 10–240 is the single most important factor contributing to the concentration of racial and ethnic minorities in the Hartford public school system. The fact that, as pleaded, the plaintiffs' complaint does not provide them a constitutional remedy for one of their afflictions, namely, their poverty, is not a ground for depriving them of a remedy for the other. * * *

In light of the complexities of developing a legislative program that would respond to the constitutional deprivation that the plaintiffs had established, we conclude * * * that further judicial intervention should be stayed "to afford the General Assembly an opportunity to take appropriate legislative action." Prudence and sensitivity to the constitutional authority of coordinate branches of government counsel the same caution in this case. In staying our hand, we do not wish to be misunderstood about the urgency of finding an appropriate remedy for the plight of Hartford's public schoolchildren. Every passing day denies these children their constitutional right to a substantially equal educational opportunity. Every passing day shortchanges these children in their ability to learn to contribute to their own well-being and to that of this state and nation. We direct the legislature and the executive branch to put the search for appropriate remedial measures at the top of their respective agendas. We are confident that with energy and good will, appropriate remedies can be found and implemented in time to make a difference before another generation of children suffers the consequences of a segregated public school education. * * *

BERDON, J., concurring.

I join the Chief Justice in her well reasoned majority opinion that concludes that the racial and ethnic segregation that exists in our public school system deprives schoolchildren of their state constitutional right to a "substantially equal educational opportunity." * * * I write separately because, in my view and as the record reflects, a racially and ethnically segregated educational environment also deprives schoolchildren of an adequate education as required by the state constitution. * * * In order to provide an adequate or "proper" education, our children must be educated in a nonsegregated environment. The trial court found, "education in its fullest sense for both white and minority school children involves interracial and multiethnic exposure to each other and interaction between them, because racial and ethnic isolation [have] negative effects on both groups." * * * Children of every race and ethnic background suffer when an educational system is administered on a segregated basis. Education entails not only the teaching of reading, writing and arithmetic, but today, in our multicultural world, it also includes the development of social understanding and racial tolerance. If the mission of education is to prepare our children to survive and succeed in today's world, then they must be taught how to live together as one people. Anything less will surely result in a segregated society with one racial and ethnic community pitted against another. Instead of fostering social division, we must build an integrated society, commencing with educating our children in a nonsegregated environment. * * *

BORDEN, J., with whom CALLAHAN and PALMER, JJ., join, dissenting. * * *

I agree with the majority on the desirability—as a matter of public and educational policy—of eliminating from our public schools the type of racial and ethnic concentration demonstrated by this record. * * * The majority, however, has transformed a laudable educational philosophy into a constitutional mandate. * * * Under the facts found by the trial court, all of the adverse effects on the education of the plaintiffs result, not from their racial or ethnic isolation—either in whole or in part—but from their poverty. * * * The trial court also specifically found that "virtually all of the differences in performance between Hartford students and those in other towns, as well as differences in college attendance, can be explained by differences in socioeconomic status and the background factors that socioeconomic status represents." * * * The majority concludes, however, that the plaintiffs have been so deprived solely because of their racial and ethnic isolation. The majority reaches that conclusion, however, not only unconnected to but squarely contrary to those factual findings. * * *

The next substantive flaw in the majority opinion is the meaning that the majority attributes to the term "segregation" in article first, § 20. The majority somehow concludes that "segregation" means de facto, as well as de jure, segregation. * * * In attempting to divine the intent of the framers of article first, § 20, we are not faced with the difficult task of peering back through the mists of more than a century to a sparse historical record * * *. Among the delegates were former and future governors of this state, former and future United States Senators and Representatives, former and future state legislators, former members of this court, including two former chief justices, and many other delegates with distinguished pedigrees in government and politics. These men and women * * * knew * * * that throughout Connecticut there were local, intradistrict neighborhood school boundaries and schools that were, because of the housing patterns then prevalent, heavily concentrated by religion, race and ethnic background. * * * It is simply inconceivable that the convention delegates, with that knowledge, intended by the language they used in article first, § 20, to render unconstitutional or to call into serious constitutional question, every one of those school boundaries, schools and electoral districts. * * *

NOTE ON DEVELOPMENTS IN CONNECTICUT
AFTER SHEFF V. O'NEILL

In January, 2003, the plaintiffs and the State of Connecticut settled the *Sheff* case. Their settlement agreement was approved by the Connecticut General Assembly, by a vote of 87–60, in February, 2003. The agreement set a goal of providing, by 2007, at least 30% of Hartford students with an educational experience in a setting of reduced isolation through inter-district magnet schools, a voluntary inter-district transfer program, and similar mechanisms. The goals of this settlement, known as Phase I, were not met. On April 4, 2008, a new Phase II agreement was signed, this time with a final target date of June 30, 2013. The goal of Phase II was to meet 80% of the demand for a reduced-isolation setting for Hartford's minority students by the target date. Reduced isolation settings are defined either as magnet schools with no more than a 75% minority population or voluntary inter-district transfers that contribute to the reduction of racial or ethnic isolation. The agreement also provided that a failure to meet the 80% level would not be a material breach of the agreement if a minimum of 41% of Hartford-resident minority students were in a reduced isolation setting by 2013. To help implement the plan, the agreement provided for the establishment of a Comprehensive Management Plan, a Sheff Office within the State Department of Education, and a Regional School Choice Office. The agreement is replete with inter-year benchmarks for measuring progress and with plans for establishing more reduced isolation settings both in magnet schools and in suburban schools. The goals set for 2013, however, have not yet been achieved. Still, according to http://www.sheffmovement.org/, a website following these developments, some progress has been made. "Today," according to the website, "over 33% of Hartford Black and Latino children are attending integrated schools including 31 interdistrict magnet schools and over 30 participating suburban districts. * * * The main tools of integration have been inter-district magnet schools (run by both the Hartford Public Schools and CREC [the Capital Region Education Council]) and the Open Choice Program, which sends Hartford children to suburban schools. More than 1,600 Hartford students now take part in Open Choice, and over 5400 Hartford students and over 8000 suburban students attend 31 regional magnet schools, most within Hartford." No changes in school district boundaries, however, have been made.

RICHARD SCHRAGGER, CONSUMING GOVERNMENT
101 Mich. L. Rev. 1824, 1824, 1828–1834 (2003).

In his ambitious new book [The Homevoter Hypothesis: How Home Values Influence Local Government Taxation, School Finance, and Land Use Policies (2001)], William Fischel, a Professor of Economics at Dartmouth College, gives us a new political animal: "The Homevoter." The homevoter is simply a homeowner who votes. * * *

On Fischel's theory, home prices reflect the good and bad policies that local governments adopt—in economic terms, local taxing and spending decisions are "capitalized" into house values. This is a good thing, because it gives homevoters a strong incentive to monitor local behavior and invest in those amenities—like schools—that will maintain or contribute to higher property values. In the perfect homevoter world, if a local government raises property taxes to build a new high school, that tax increase should be offset by a corresponding increase in the homevoters' property values. But for capitalization to work, existing homeowners must own a scarce and desirable item that they can sell on the housing market—not just a home, but a home in a particular jurisdiction that has recently invested in a new high school.

Zoning, and the entire regime of land-use controls, is the mechanism for ensuring scarcity. Zoning restricts the development of new housing in the jurisdiction, thus ensuring that all the benefits of local investment accrue to existing homeowners in the form of increased property values. * * * This model functions, however, only by making a number of fairly heroic assumptions about the efficiency of the housing market and the behavior of homeowners and local government officials. * * *

Fischel's first claim—that local government decisions are reflected in house values—has intuitive appeal. Anyone who has ever purchased a home knows that the price of a particular house reflects a myriad of characteristics of the neighborhood, such as the quality of local schools or the availability of local amenities. Capitalization is not a foregone conclusion, however. * * *. As Fischel recognizes, even optimistic accounts of capitalization require that localities enforce rigid limits on new housing production. Without land use limitations, developers will respond to the increased demand for housing in the more desirable jurisdiction by building there, thus increasing supply and erasing any capitalization gains. Capitalization, in other words, may be more significant in non-developing, old-line suburbs, like those found in the Northeast, but much less so in the growth belts of the South and the West, where there is ample room for development. This means that as a descriptive matter we need to know something about local housing markets to know if home values are a good barometer of local behavior.

Fischel's second assumption is that local government officials have the fiscal ability and political power to respond to downward shifts in home values. As a matter of state law, this simply may not be the case: local governments are often constrained by state constitutional or statutory limitations in their ability to raise taxes, assume debt, or otherwise alter their mix of taxes and services. Moreover, for house prices to serve as a meaningful discipline on local government behavior, there must be a visible one-to-one relationship between the costs and benefits of a local decision. The decision to build a new performing arts center, invite a job-creating industry into the locality, or license a local landfill has to include all the decisions' costs and benefits. Yet in each of these cases, it is probable that the full costs and benefits of the local decision are not borne solely by the residents of the jurisdiction. Users of local amenities regularly cross borders to do so, and the costs of local siting decisions regularly fall on neighboring jurisdictions.

The existence of externalities means that the quality or availability of "local" amenities is often beyond the control of a specific local government or the homeowners who vote within it. Fischel tends to treat localities as isolated, autonomous actors: the hypothesis works because homevoters—like corporate shareholders—can trace the value of their housing investment directly back to the decisions made by the locality. But much of the value of one's housing investment—negative or positive—might very well turn on the specific decisions, activities, or fiscal health of neighboring jurisdictions.

Fischel has no place in his political economy for interlocal or regional effects. He seems to assume that the costs and benefits of local decisions stay within the jurisdiction, are captured by housing prices there, and thus can be rationally accounted for by home-owning residents when they and their elected representatives make local political decisions. Yet if regional or interlocal spillover effects dominate home values, then local governments may have little ability significantly to affect the primary determinants of shifting property values.

Fischel's shareholder analogy assumes not only that local office-holders are capable of responding to homevoter pressure to maintain or improve home values, but that they are also willing to do so. Once again analogizing local governments to corporate firms, Fischel argues that local office holders serve as "deliberate, value-maximizing agents" of their homeowning constituents. Fischel claims that in contrast to larger jurisdictions like big cities, where special interests are able to exercise significant political power, the majority tends to get what it wants in small-scale residential jurisdictions dominated by homeowners. The politics of local government, Fischel claims, is the politics of the "median voter," and the median voter in the suburbs is the homevoter. Local officials have learned that they neglect these constituents at their peril.
* * *

Though there is some evidence that small-scale jurisdictions follow a median voter model, Fischel is too quick to dismiss the influence of developers, commercial interests, and local elites on the politics of small places. * * * Indeed, Fischel's home-based, suburban politics sounds somewhat nostalgic in an America that is increasingly dominated by large, urbanized metropolitan regions. While Fischel's claim that most Americans live in municipalities with less than 100,000 residents may be formally true, the size of any particular municipality seems beside the point. In fact, the bulk of Americans live in large metropolitan areas with effective populations much greater than 100,000, are participants in regional political economies, and are subject to regional political pressures that have not respected formal jurisdictional boundaries for quite some time.

Homeowners are unlikely to be the dominant political force in these metropolitan regions. As commentators have pointed out, many formally "residential" locales now contain more office or retail space than nearby central cities. This emergent "post-suburban" metropolis—an interdependent mix of "business, retail, housing, and entertainment focal points scattered about the low-density cityscape"—requires a redefinition of "city" and "suburb" and a more nuanced portrait of local politics along the urban-suburban fringe than Fischel's model provides. * * *

The last critical assumption of the homevoter hypothesis is that homeowners prioritize wealth maximization in the form of higher property values above all else. * * * Certainly, property values are important to the suburban voter, but, as Fischel observes (with some puzzlement), many homeowners even object to property-value-enhancing local decisions. Fischel has to explain this "irrational" resistance as an example of risk aversion—homeowners simply cannot be certain whether a local policy decision will have adverse effects. Because their homes are their single largest assets, homeowners are going to err on the side of caution and reject most local government policy changes that have uncertain effects.

This explanation avoids other, perhaps more obvious, possibilities. Even a rational homeowner may be more sensitive to a significant short-term rise in property taxes that follows from increased property values than to underinvestment in long-term municipal services, like the school system. It is fairly common for local majorities to reject school bond issues even though an investment in schools should bring concomitant benefits in property values, perhaps because homeowners cannot calculate the value of the long-term investment, or simply do not want to pay higher taxes in the short term. More significantly, the homeowner may fail to treat her home as a commodity altogether, but choose instead to enhance its personal value at the expense of its market value. A homeowner may "rationally" reject a property-value-enhancing new development project because she prefers to retain the rural quality of her neighborhood, is sensitive to issues of sprawl, or is simply uncomfortable with the pace of change in her neighborhood. In short, the homevoter only exists to the extent that homeowners have the capacity and desire to act like ideal (profit-maximizing) corporate shareholders, that local officials have the capacity and desire to act like ideal corporate boards, and that both have a suitable mechanism in property values to judge the profitability of their collective enterprise. Local citizens and their officials are too imperfect—and most local communities are too complex and fluid—to be captured by this construct. * * *

3. SPRAWL AND EFFORTS TO CONTROL IT

A growing public dissatisfaction with what is known as urban sprawl underlies many of the recent efforts to find regional solutions to interlocal conflict. The concern over sprawl is not, however, entirely new. Writing more than 40 years ago, the urban theorist William H. Whyte wrote an article entitled "Urban Sprawl." He explained that "most Americans still assume there will be plenty of green space on the other side of the fence." He warned, however, that "this time there won't be" unless America significantly changed its pattern of urban development. In explaining why, Whyte wrote:

> The problem, of course, is not an absolute shortage of land. * * *
> The problem is the pattern of growth—or, rather, the lack of one.
> Because of the leapfrog nature of urban growth, even within the
> limits of most big cities there is to this day a surprising amount
> of empty land. But it is scattered; a vacant lot here, a dump
> there—no one parcel big enough to be of much use. And it is with
> this same kind of sprawl that we are ruining the whole
> metropolitan area for the future.

Whyte went on to explain that this sprawling development pattern was "bad aesthetics" and "bad economics." He explained, however, that it was not "too late to reserve open space while there is some left—land for parks, for landscaped industrial districts, and for just plain scenery and breathing space."[33]

Whyte's basic description of the problem—the ugliness and wastefulness of unplanned, sprawling development—still captures an essential aspect of the concern that motivates many of those working to stop sprawl. At the same time, those marching under the anti-sprawl banner by no means share a single understanding of why sprawl is a problem. For some, urban sprawl is problematic because it threatens to overrun nature by transforming agricultural and wilderness lands into suburban subdivisions. In a similar vein, many are moved to stop sprawl for environmental reasons; they believe, for example, that sprawl makes the automobile a necessity and thus clean air impossible. For others, urban sprawl is an affront to some idealized conception of urban form that is marked by a clearly visible downtown. Those of a less aesthetic bent object to urban sprawl on grounds reminiscent of Lewis Mumford's early concern with suburbanization: sprawling development engenders

---

[33] William Whyte, Urban Sprawl, in The Exploding Metropolis 133–134 (William Whyte ed. 1958).

anomie. Still others see sprawl as problematic because it entrenches the social inequities between communities along racial and class lines. Then there are those who emphasize the financial costs of sprawl, which they contend requires more expensive public infrastructure than does denser development. In this respect, urban sprawl has become a kind of catch-all term to describe a host of concerns about the direction of urban development.

After reviewing various critiques of sprawl, one recent commentator explained that "[s]prawl is not any form of suburban growth, but a particular form." He identified the following ten traits of the kind of suburban development that critics call sprawl:

> (1) unlimited outward extension, (2) low-density residential and commercial settlements, (3) leapfrog development, (4) fragmentation of powers over land use among many small localities, (5) dominance of transportation by private automotive vehicles, (6) no centralized planning or control of land-uses, (7) widespread strip commercial development, (8) great fiscal disparities among localities, (9) segregation of types of land uses in different zones, and (10) reliance mainly on the trickle-down or filtering process to provide housing to low-income households.[34]

At the same time, critics of sprawl are not without their own critics. Critics of the anti-sprawl movement see sprawl as an embodiment of the freedom that current law permits individuals and communities to exercise. They contend that concerns about sprawl are overblown, or worse yet, rooted in an elitist hostility to the preferences of middle-class residents. From this perspective, the cure to sprawl—limitations on property rights, the establishment of centralized bureaucracies—is likely to be worse than the disease.

The materials that follow provide an introduction to the growing debate over whether urban sprawl is in fact a problem, and, if it is, how it could best be solved.[35] The first three excerpts, by John Findlay, Langdon

---

[34] Anthony Downs, The Costs of Sprawl—And Alternative Forms of Growth, Speech at the Center for Transportation Studies Research (Minneapolis, May 19, 1998).

[35] There is a wealth of material on urban sprawl. See, e.g., Edward Sullivan and Jessica Yeh, Smart Growth: State Strategies in Managing Sprawl, 45 Urb. Law. 349 (2013); Thad Williamson, Sprawl, Justice, and Citizenship: The Civic Costs of the American Way of Life (2010); Michael Lewyn, Sprawl in Europe and America, 46 San Diego L. Rev. 85 (2009); Robert Brueggman, Sprawl: A Compact History (2006); David C. Soule (ed.), Urban Sprawl: A Comprehensive Reference Guide (2006); Peter Dreier, John Mollenkopf, and Todd Swanstrom, Place Matters: Metropolitics for the Twenty-first Century (2nd edition 2004); Dolores Hayden, A Field Guide to Sprawl (2004); Peter Calthorpe, The Regional City: Planning for the End of Sprawl (2001); Andres Duany et al., Suburban Nation: The Rise of Sprawl and the Decline of the American Dream (2000); James Kushner, Smart Growth, New Urbanism and Diversity: Progressive Planning Movements in America and Their Impact on Poor and Minority Ethnic Populations, 21 U.C.L.A. J. Envtl. L. & Pol'y 45 (2002); Clint Bolick, Subverting the American Dream: Government Dictated "Smart Growth" is Unwise and Unconstitutional, 148 U. Pa. L.

Winner, and Edward Soja, add texture to our understanding of just what is meant by urban sprawl. Interestingly, all three excerpts emphasize the degree to which sprawling development effaces the visible distinctions between central cities and suburbs. Nevertheless, Winner and Soja argue that sprawling development patterns entrench spatial boundaries along racial and class lines even as they obscure them. The fourth excerpt, by the journalist Joel Garreau, connects the concern over sprawl to a predominant theme in local government law: the public/private distinction. He argues that sprawling development has resulted in an increased privatization of the local realm.

The final three excerpts focus less on diagnosing the problem of sprawl than on devising solutions for stopping it. The first of these is from a legislative guidebook published by the American Planning Association, which sets forth the basic principles of the Smart Growth movement. This movement has mounted a concerted and influential effort to combat sprawl through a variety of institutional reform proposals.[36] The next two excerpts—one from a book by Gerrit Knaap and Arthur Nelson, and the other from an article by Carl Abbott—examine one of the most important of these reform proposals: the urban growth boundary. These excerpts focus specifically on land use policies adopted for Portland, Oregon. The final excerpt is a critique of the anti-sprawl movement by Gregg Easterbrook, who argues that opponents of sprawl are more interested in preserving their own way of life than in improving the lives of others.

In reading these materials, it is important to consider whether it makes sense to base regional solutions on an opposition to sprawl as opposed to some other societal ill—such as racial segregation or class inequity. In this regard it is useful to compare the excerpt on Smart Growth from the American Planning Association with the excerpt from Gregg Easterbrook. Does the Smart Growth movement's emphasis on consensus embody or discredit Easterbrook's concerns about the selfish premises of sprawl opponents? Alternatively, does Easterbrook's critique ignore the degree to which sprawl itself privileges the interest of some residents rather than others?

Rev. 859 (2000); William Buzbee, Urban Sprawl, Federalism, and the Problem of Institutional Complexity, 68 Fordham L. Rev. 57 (1999); Richard Moe and Carter Wilke, Changing Places: Rebuilding Community in the Age of Sprawl (1997); Real Estate Research Corporation, The Costs of Sprawl: Environmental and Economic Costs of Alternative Residential Development Patterns at the Urban Fringe (U.S. Gov't Printing Office 1974).

[36] For a description of other growth management techniques, see Arthur Nelson et al., Growth Management Principles and Practices (1995).

JOHN M. FINDLAY, MAGIC LANDS: WESTERN CITYSCAPES AND AMERICAN CULTURE AFTER 1940
Pp. 27–31, 33–36 (1992).

Rapid growth * * * made over the urban West through a continuing series of construction projects. Crucial to both the region's newly arrived residents and its newfound prosperity was the effort to house the swelling population. Each major city witnessed the rapid rise of outlying residential subdivisions where the homes were newer and the families younger and more affluent. Los Angeles led the way. Its recent arrivals tended to come from areas that favored single-family, unattached housing, as well as commuting to work by automobiles, and those preferences reinforced the tendency toward suburban settlement. Between 1946 and 1957 the county gained an average of almost 37,700 new subdivided lots each year. In large part because so much of the housing was relatively new, it tended to be of better quality in the West than in the remainder of the country. And the newer tracts for the most part consisted of owner-occupied, single-family, detached homes.

The proliferation of outlying housing tracts constituted not only a quantitative but also a qualitative change for the urban West. As suburbs grew they attracted commerce and industry, which made them less subordinate to central cities. Orange County provided a particularly clear example of the character and consequences of rapid growth in the postwar West. The area had long been peripheral to, and dependent upon, its neighbor Los Angeles, and as a result had seemed rather provincial. As late as 1950 it contained barely 200,000 residents. Much of its terrain consisted of orchards and cropland, and its largest city was the county seat of Santa Ana, with 45,000 people.

Thereafter Orange County began to grow at an "almost inconceivable" pace; by 1987 its population had reached 2.2 million. Both the extent and the form of the metropolitan area's growth helped to set it off from its neighbor. The bulk of Orange County's population was initially clustered in a series of bedroom communities located along the two freeway routes into Los Angeles, but after 1950 this northern tier of towns began to develop an independent economic base. The county also began to develop its own cultural attractions, including the Knotts Berry Farm amusement park in Buena Park, the Crystal Cathedral drive-in church in Garden Grove, and a number of popular shopping malls. Disneyland epitomized the new trend, helping to make Anaheim the leading city of the county. During the 1960s the Irvine Ranch, a rural stronghold that occupied about 20 percent of the county's land and impeded its urbanization, was developed into another nucleus for high-technology industry in southern California.

One of the fastest-growing and wealthiest counties in the country, Orange unofficially earned its independence from Los Angeles when the U.S. Census Bureau declared it a separate SMSA in 1963. At the same time, the state awarded the county its own branch campus of the University of California, at Irvine. Orange County had risen from the shadows of a greater metropolis to gain its own identity. Moreover, as Los Angeles seemed to be losing its value as a barometer of tomorrow, the "affluent technocracy" emerging in Orange County struck one observer as a more fitting "showplace of America's future." One appropriate measure of changes in Orange County was retail sales. While the old business districts of such cities as Santa Ana and Anaheim decayed, it seemed as though a shopping center sprang up at every freeway off-ramp, anchoring the retail segment of an economy that by the mid-1980s would have ranked forty-sixth among the nations of the world. One especially popular mall, South Coast Plaza, generated more sales annually than downtown San Francisco did. Developers attested its importance by building a new performing arts center nearby. By 1977 Orange County had acquired the highest density of settlement of any county in the state except San Francisco, yet it lacked a dominating central business district or any other traditionally shaped, central urban focus. Furthermore, even if the county had started out with some kind of conventional nucleus, the tide of new residents, new jobs, and new construction would probably have swept past it anyway.

Throughout the West, municipal boundaries raced outward to accommodate the growing numbers of inhabitants, and in the process many towns, like those in Orange County, lost their customary shapes and orientations. The figures tell a remarkable story. Between 1940 and 1970 the population of Phoenix multiplied nine times, but the area inside the city boundaries multiplied twenty-six times, so population density per square mile decreased threefold, from 6,814 to 2,347. The population of the city of San Jose increased more than four times between 1950 and 1970, while its area multiplied eight times and its density fell by almost half, from 5,605 to 3,190 per square mile. Quickly as the population of the metropolitan West increased, the extent of urbanized areas increased even faster.

The numerical and areal expansion of urban settlement significantly altered agrarian society, for much of the newly arrived population came from western hinterlands. Cities generally gained in importance at the expense of rural areas. In 1940 about one-third of the population of Arizona was urban; by 1970 the metropolis of Phoenix alone contained more than half of the state's residents—and, needless to say, most of its economic and political power. The growth of cities also compromised the often quite vital rural life that bordered urban areas. In Los Angeles, Orange, and Santa Clara counties in California, and in Washington's

King County and Arizona's Maricopa County, the new arrivals ultimately overwhelmed once vigorous farm economies. The newcomers' impact on citrus-growing, one southern Californian recalled, made it "readily apparent that agriculture and urbanization were not compatible."

As metropolitan regions of the West steadily became less rural and more suburban in appearance, their inhabitants commonly looked with favor upon the annexation of farmlands as another form of growth. And as the legal line between central city and suburb was repeatedly redrawn, the visual distinctions gradually disappeared. The low-rise, scattered look of the suburb became the prevailing image of entire cities, and central city districts blended into peripheral neighborhoods. The new look doubtless confused those accustomed to bold skylines, striking landmarks, and clear-cut divisions between central city and suburb. Daniel Boorstin, along with many others, identified Los Angeles as "one of the least 'legible' of the great settlements of the world." In San Jose during the early 1960s, annexation, new development, an absence of landmarks, and rapid population growth so conspired against an accurate sense of the city that many new residents often lost their way home. * * *

The older cities of northern California had first taken shape in the days of rail transportation, when a strong downtown and a high population density created a vertical urban form. They paid comparatively little attention to annexation, expecting to expand up rather than out. Western cities that experienced most of their growth in the twentieth century adopted different attitudes that mirrored their attachment to new means of transport. They anticipated extensive rather than intensive growth, and as a result they kept alert to opportunities for annexation. Their policies honored, not the old downtown, which too easily became congested with cars, but the many built and unbuilt subdivisions on the periphery, which promised a different kind of greatness.

The city of Seattle combined the old and the new urban forms. Its vital central business district and its natural barriers to outward sprawl helped to preserve its character as a high-density central city. Moreover, unlike San Francisco, Seattle did not face any serious challenge to its supremacy as a population center on Puget Sound. But its downtown leaders nonetheless felt threatened by outward expansion; the 1962 World's Fair was in part their response to suburban sprawl. Also unlike San Francisco, Seattle did have room to grow through annexation, and thus it could absorb some of the peripheral growth. When the population grew by 19.1 percent between 1950 and 1960, virtually all of the increase resulted from annexation of suburban tracts, rather than from natural increase or migration to the old central City. Seattle thus retained its vertical core, but at the same time it incorporated outlying districts within its borders.

Southwestern cities generally had less well-established downtowns, fewer natural restraints on sprawl, and more intense population growth. As a result, no balance between the old and the new seemed possible for them, and annexation played a critical role not only in cities' spatial growth but also in their demographic growth. In Phoenix, where annexation was seen by some as the central goal of postwar urban planning, 75 percent of the population in 1960 lived in neighborhoods that had been added to the central city since 1950. Between 1941 and 1954, towns in Los Angeles County annexed 458 separate parcels, and those in Orange County annexed 235 parcels. In every case, the reality or the prospect of annexation detracted from the power of the city center, lowered the density of settlement, increased the size of the population, and prevented municipal borders from becoming fixed and recognizable.
* * *

Rapid population growth and territorial expansion distorted the proper shape of the city, according to accepted wisdom. Conventional urban form, based upon the nineteenth-century American experience, might be pictured as a magnetic pole that kept particles in a tight orbit around a distinct nucleus. In the newer portions of the western metropolis during the mid-twentieth century, the particles increased in number too quickly to be held by the pull of the center. Rather than accumulating vertically, they escaped the magnetic field and formed orbits around new nuclei that competed against the attraction of the traditional center. Moreover, the particles increasingly became supercharged. They moved about the metropolis far more quickly and freely than before, and they adopted new paths that further weakened the coherence of the older form.

The heightened kinetic energy of life in the urban West derived from several sources. Most important was the steady arrival of newcomers, which gave the region a less rooted population. In Phoenix during the late 1950s, almost one-quarter of the population had arrived within the previous two years, and about another third had been there less than ten years. San Jose had fewer than seven out of every thousand residents of American metropolitan areas during the 1960s, but it attracted fifty-five out of every thousand net migrants to metropolitan areas during the same decade.

Moreover, throughout the region the newcomers tended to be youthful and, in the words of one demographer, "chronically mobile." They had scarcely settled down in one place before they moved on again. In Los Angeles, Carey McWilliams reported in 1949, "an address or telephone number is good, on an average, for only three or four months." A study of the California population found that those who had changed residences during the year 1965 were three times more likely than non-movers to do so again in 1966. In the Santa Clara Valley during the 1960s, there were twenty-one new arrivals and seventeen fresh departures *annually* for every hundred residents of the metropolitan area, and one-third of all recent arrivals stayed less than a year. The incessant movement of Mexicans back and forth across the international border added to the atmosphere of change.

Despite appearances, the perpetual motion between western cities was not altogether random. Some urban areas served primarily as way stations, others as destinations. Newcomers to California tended to move initially to San Francisco, Los Angeles, and San Diego on the coast. From these beachheads they went to such inland towns as San Jose, Sacramento, and Fresno, which received most of their newcomers from within the state.

Transiency prevailed at the intra-metropolitan level as well. It was fueled by the speculative inclination that had long characterized western land development. Westerners moved restlessly about their cities, exchanging one home for another almost as easily as they sold and bought cars. Between 1955 and 1960, about a third of the populations of Seattle and Los Angeles changed houses within their county of residence. Between 1965 and 1970, 40 percent of the population of the San Jose metropolitan area changed dwellings within county limits. Western cities offered little that was old or fixed; everything about them seemed to have arrived recently, and that included the family next door.

By dominating western transportation networks, automobiles heightened the impression of an atomistic society. Older cities depended heavily upon fixed routes of travel focusing on city centers; the newer cities offered more options, particularly to individuals in private autos who could ignore rail and bus routes as well as the downtowns through which such routes customarily passed. Although Los Angeles had long been seen as "the supreme automobile metropolis," other southwestern towns too now earned such titles as "Auto City" and "the automobile city *par excellence.*" * * *

LANGDON WINNER, SILICON VALLEY MYSTERY HOUSE

From M. Sorkin, Variations on a Theme Park:
The New American City and the End of Public Space.
Pp. 49–51, 55–56, 57–58 (1992).

It is an ingenious feature of capitalism to shift the social costs of production away from those reaping the profits. In Santa Clara County, this means that the heaviest burdens of social services—schools, police, fire departments, welfare agencies, and the like—fall upon the less affluent communities of the "south county," those with the greatest needs for public services and the smallest tax base. The average income of the thousands of production workers living in San Jose, Campbell, and

Milpitas is about one-fifth of the income earned by the professional managerial personnel of the "north county." Yet these municipalities are left to deal with problems of crime, drug use, illiteracy, and other social ills that afflict low-income and minority residents—to provide, in effect, the institutions of social repair that support the economic gains enjoyed elsewhere.

Drastic inequalities are apparent in the north as well. Just across Highway 101 from Frederick Terman's university-industrial complex, easily visible from atop Stanford's Hoover Tower, is East Palo Alto, a ghetto in which chronic poverty and unemployment among its black residents seem beyond remedy. East Palo Alto is a forgotten land, the neighborhood next door, territory excluded from and seldom acknowledged by "the community of technical scholars." The unprecedented concentration of wealth, talent, and problem-solving ability in the area has somehow left the problems of its poor and minority members unaddressed and unsolved. School children in East Palo Alto have test scores in the lowest tenth of the nation's youth, while children in Palo Alto routinely test in the top one percent. But for those in the white, self-actualizing utopia of Silicon Valley the poor and black are of little concern. Creative energy is reserved for integrating computer software, not integrating society.

The income gap between rich and poor in the region is growing steadily wider. For those at the lower end of the scale, the American Dream offers its traditional solace of upward mobility. Indeed, the minority communities of the south county show a certain cultural and economic vitality, filled with locally owned markets, ethnic restaurants, and shops catering to Hispanic and Asian residents. To all appearances, those doing well are the ones who have gathered enough resources to escape the assembly lines altogether and start businesses outside microelectronics. But the industry itself contains no ladder of upward movement for those on its bottom rungs. Even lower-level administrative jobs typically require an engineering bachelor's degree or better. The Yankee ideal that one can work hard, demonstrate talent, and thereby ascend through the ranks is simply not a tenable life strategy; the industry's rigidly stratified social structure contains no middle levels to which one can aspire. For technical professionals, rapid turnover in work opportunities usually means better pay and enhanced responsibility; for factory workers, however, it requires moving from one dead-end job to another in a never-ending cycle of sideward mobility.

Beyond this state of tedium and insecurity lies the prospect that the routine jobs upon which thousands depend will simply be eliminated. A common ideal shared by engineers and businessmen envisages totally automated factories—workplaces without workers. In computer-integrated manufacturing, or CIM, the goal is to coordinate the activities of design, testing, materials handling, fabrication, assembly, and inspection within completely computerized plants while keeping human presence to a minimum. Thus, developers of the Apple Macintosh factory prided themselves on having cut labor's share of production costs to less than two percent. As the hardware and programming techniques of the field become ever more sophisticated, the ancient dream of living with perfect automata seems within reach.

Although the valley's two primary social strata are separate in many respects, they do find common ground twice each day—on the roadways. Because thousands of production workers must travel front their homes in the south county to factories in the north, and because public transportation is woefully inadequate, the highways and side streets of the valley experience severe congestion in the morning, afternoon, and early evening. The industry's staggered work hours seem only to compound the problem. In Sunnyvale, the "evening" traffic jams on Highway 280 begins as early as 3:00 P.M. Thus, the handsome, speedy luxury cars owned by engineers and managers inch along bumper to bumper with the hordes of Old Chevies and Toyotas driven by the production workers. There is an ironic but uniformly unpleasant justice here.

Monumental congestion is merely one of the failings of Silicon Valley as an urban environment. Over the past decades the rapid growth in jobs has not been matched by adequate housing construction. Land-use policies strongly favored industrial expansion, creating a permanent job-housing imbalance throughout the region. When the influential Santa Clara County Manufacturing Group joined city and county planners in sounding the alarm, little was done to rezone the land for residential building. During the late 1970s the price of houses and rentals skyrocketed, making Silicon Valley one of the most expensive housing markets in the country. The continuing inflation in housing costs has become so severe that many companies now have difficulty attracting talented professionals to the area; on seeing how little house a handsome paycheck can buy, prospective employees think twice before moving.

The shortage of housing is matched by a paucity of public spaces. There is no civic center with the kind of theaters, museums, well-stocked libraries, or sports stadiums that up-and-coming cities usually boast. Neither are there parks or recreational areas of any significance. With the exception of the upscale Stanford Shopping Center, Eastridge, Valley Fair, and other malls that dot the landscape, the valley offers no public gathering places attractive to local residents or visitors. What Gertrude Stein once observed about Oakland could more aptly be said of Silicon Valley: " 'There is no there there.' " * * *

———

Looking for ways to enhance technical innovation while minimizing its costs, a number of firms have formed multinational consortia for research and development, sharing both facilities and staff. Production and personnel managers are easily transferred across national boundaries in order to improve worldwide operations. Some Silicon Valley spokesmen still worry about maintaining America's lead in microelectronics for "national security reasons," and they lobby for protectionist legislation to prevent foreign takeover of the microelectronics markets. But such talk is by now largely hollow. The leading corporations in the field are quickly becoming global combinations with no particular national allegiance.

The tendency to dissolve existing spatial boundaries is evident not only in production and finance but also in the very form of the organizations that rely upon computers and satellite communications. More and more, the space that matters is an electric space that requires no bodily human presence or physical movement. What are in effect whole rooms, buildings, streets, highways, and cities can be formed by computer programs linked by telecommunications signals. Conversations and meetings take place within the architecture of teleconferencing software. Complex decisions are made through the intersection of streams of computerized data. World-shaking events unfold through the confluence of digital messages. Silicon Valley, Route 128 in Massachusetts, and similar centers of high technology in the United States, Japan, and elsewhere are, in effect, launching pads which propel into orbit an expansive, powerful, but increasingly disembodied form of social organization.

A convenient metaphor for these digital electronic entities can be found in the representational signs used in office automation. The goal of such systems is to do away with such material encumbrances as rooms, desks, file cabinets, file folders, documents, and ultimately people, and to make the information formerly contained in such office paraphernalia available instantaneously on the screen. * * *

———

To enter the digital city one must first be granted access. Having "logged on," one's quality of participation is determined by the architecture of the network and its map of rules, roles, and relationships. Technical professionals are usually greeted by a computerized version of the social matrix, an organizational form in which there is at least superficial equality and ready access to information and one's coworkers. They experience computer networks as spheres of democratic or even anarchic activity. Especially for those ill at ease in the physical presence of others (a feeling not uncommon among male engineers), the phenomenon of disembodied space seems to offer comfort and fulfillment.

Here are new opportunities for self-expression, creativity and a sense of mastery! Some begin to feel they are most alive, most free when wandering through the networks; they often "disappear" into them for days on end.

Ordinary workers, on the other hand, typically face a much different set of possibilities. As they enter an electronic office or factory, they become the objects of top-down managerial control, required to take orders, complete finite tasks, and perform according to a set of standard productivity measures. Facing them is a structure that incorporates the authoritarianism of the industrial workplace and augments its power in ingenious ways. No longer are the Taylorite time-and-motion measurements limited by an awkward stopwatch carried from place to place by a wandering manager. Now workers' motions can be ubiquitously monitored in units calculable to the nearest microsecond. For telephone operators handling calls, insurance clerks processing claims, and keypunch operators doing data entry, rates of performance are recorded by a centralized computer and continuously compared to established norms. Failure to meet one's quota of phone calls, insurance claims, or keystrokes is grounds for managerial reprimand or, eventually, dismissal. A report issued by the Office of Technology Assessment revealed that by the late 1980s, four to six million American office workers were already subject to such forms of computer-based surveillance. Such systems do not, as utopian dreams of automation prophesied, "eliminate toil and liberate people for higher forms of work." While the old-fashioned secretary was expected to perform perhaps 30,000 keystrokes an hour, the norm for modern keypunch operators now is closer to 80,000.

For those who manage the systems of computerized work, the structures and processes offer a wonderfully effective means of control. Here is an electronic equivalent of Jeremy Bentham's Panopticon, the ingenious circular design that allowed the guardians of a prison, hospital, or school to observe every inmate while totally isolating the inmates from each other. For today's workers under panoptic scrutiny, the system is, of course totally opaque. They are allowed to see only what the program allows. Closely watched and clocked workers within the city of icons may find even fewer chances to express their individuality or participate in decisions than they did in the old-fashioned office or factory. When space is intangible, where do workers organize?

The ideologies that have arisen to describe and justify the new social patterns of the Information Age typically recognize only their positive aspects. "Information wants to be free," exclaims Stewart Brand, proponent of liberation through personal computing. "When a system runs on information, there is an endless supply for everyone," argues an otherwise solid study of the microelectronics industry. What such dewy-eyed conclusions overlook are the strong tools of institutional control made conveniently available to those who will shape the rules, roles, and relationships of the age of electronic information. To build an electronic space based upon democratic, egalitarian principles would require deliberate effort, not merely the cheerful assertion that liberation has already occurred. * * *

EDWARD SOJA, POSTMODERN GEOGRAPHIES: THE REASSERTION OF SPACE IN CRITICAL SOCIAL THEORY
Pp. 222, 224–225, 244–247 (1989).

What is this place? Even knowing where to focus, to find a starting point, is not easy, for, perhaps more than any other place, Los Angeles is everywhere. It is global in the fullest sense of the word. Nowhere is this more evident than in its cultural projection and ideological reach, its almost ubiquitous screening of itself as a rectangular dream machine for the world. * * *

As is true for so much of the patterning of twentieth century urbanization, Los Angeles both sets the historical pace and most vividly epitomizes the extremes of contemporary expression. Municipal boundary making and territorial incorporation, to take one illustrative example, has produced the most extraordinary crazy quilt of opportunism to be found in any metropolitan area. Tiny enclaves of county land and whole cities such as Beverly Hills, West Hollywood, Culver City, and Santa Monica pock-mark the "Westside" bulk of the incorporated City of Los Angeles, while thin slivers of city land reach out like tentacles to grab on to the key seaside outlets of the port at San Pedro and Los Angeles International Airport. Nearly half the population of the city, however, lives in the quintessentially suburban San Fernando Valley, one and a half million people who are statistically are counted as a part of the central city of the Los Angeles-Long Beach Standard Metropolitan Statistical Area. Few other places make such a definitive mockery of the standard classifications of urban, suburban, and exurban.

Over 130 other municipalities and scores of county administered areas adhere loosely around the irregular City of Los Angeles in a dazzling, sprawling patchwork mosaic. Some have names which are startlingly self-explanatory. Where else can there be a City of Industry and a City of Commerce, so flagrantly commemorating the fractions of capital which guaranteed their incorporation. In other places, names casually try to recapture a romanticized history (as in the many new communities called Rancho something-or-other) or to ensconce the memory of alternative geographies (as in Venice, Naples, Hawaiian Gardens, Ontario, Manhattan Beach, Westminster). In naming, as in so many other contemporary urban processes, time and space, the "once" and the "there", are being increasingly played with and packaged to serve the needs of the here and the now, making the lived experience of the urban increasingly vicarious, screened through *simulacra*, those exact copies for which the real originals have been lost.

A recent clipping from the Los Angeles Times tells of the 433 signs which bestow identity within the hyperspace of the City of Los Angeles, described as "A City Divided and Proud of It". Hollywood, Wilshire Boulevard's Miracle Mile, and the Central City were among the first to get these community signs as part of a "city identification program" organized by the Transportation Department. One of the newest signs, for what was proclaimed "the city's newest community", recognizes the formation of "Harbor Gateway" in the thin eight-mile long blue-collar area threading south to the harbour, the old Shoestring Strip where many of the 32,000 residents often forgot their ties to the city. One of the founders of the programme pondered its development: "At first, in the early 1960s, the Traffic Department took the position that all the communities were part of Los Angeles and we didn't want cities within cities . . . but we finally gave in. Philosophically it made sense. Los Angeles is huge. The city had to recognize that there were communities that needed identification. . . . What we tried to avoid was putting up signs at every intersection that had stores." Ultimately, the city signs are described as "A Reflection of Pride in the Suburbs". Where are we then in this nominal and noumenal fantasyland? * * *

Underneath this semiotic blanket there remains an economic order, an instrumental nodal structure, an essentially exploitative spatial division of labour, and this spatially organized urban system has for the past half century been more continuously productive than almost any other in the world. But it has also been increasingly obscured from view, imaginatively mystified in an environment more specialized in the production of encompassing mystifications than practically any other you can name. As has so often been the case in the United States, this conservative deconstruction is accompanied by a numbing depoliticization of fundamental class and gender relations and conflicts. When all that is seen is so fragmented and filled with whimsy and pastiche, the hard edges of the capitalist, racist and patriarchal landscape seem to disappear, melt into air.

With exquisite irony, contemporary Los Angeles has come to resemble more than ever before a gigantic agglomeration of theme parks, a lifespace comprised of Disneyworlds. It is a realm divided into show-cases of global village cultures and mimetic American landscapes, all-embracing shopping malls and crafty Main Streets, corporation-sponsored magic kingdoms, high-technology-based experimental prototype communities of tomorrow, attractively packaged places for rest and recreation all cleverly hiding the buzzing workstations and labour processes which help to keep it together. Like the original "Happiest

Place on Earth", the enclosed spaces are subtly but tightly controlled by invisible overseers despite the open appearance of fantastic freedoms of choice. The experience of living here can be extremely diverting and exceptionally enjoyable, especially for those who can afford to remain inside long enough to establish their own modes of transit and places to rest. And, of course, the enterprise has been enormously profitable over the years. After all, it was built on what began as relatively cheap land, has been sustained by a constantly replenishing army of even cheaper imported labour, is filled with the most modern technological gadgetry, enjoys extraordinary levels of protection and surveillance, and runs under the smooth aggression of the most efficient management systems, almost always capable of delivering what is promised just in time to be useful.
* * *

JOEL GARREAU, EDGE CITY: LIFE ON THE NEW FRONTIER
Pp. 184–185 (1991).

Sun City, Arizona, on the west side of metropolitan Phoenix, bills itself as the largest "adult" community in the world. It has ten shopping centers and forty-six thousand residents. It is a privately owned development that has fervently resisted incorporation into any municipality in order to avoid a new level of taxation. But, though private, it has taken on many trappings of a city. It runs everything from libraries to parks to swimming pools to an art museum to a crisis-counseling hotline to a fire department to a symphony orchestra. The squad cars of its legally franchised, armed, unpaid private posse routinely patrol the public streets. Its innocuously named Recreation Association, meanwhile, has the power to assess fees that are functionally indistinguishable from taxes. If a homeowner does not pay the fees, the association has the legal right—so far unexercised—to slap a lien on that person's house and sell it at auction.

Sun City is by no means an aberration. It represents several forms of private-enterprise governments—shadow governments, if you will—of which there are more than 150,000 in the United States. These shadow governments have become the most numerous, ubiquitous, and largest form of local government in America today, studies show. In their various guises shadow governments levy taxes, adjudicate disputes, provide police protection, run fire departments, provide health care, channel development, plan regionally, enforce esthetic standards, run buses, run railroads, run airports, build roads, fill potholes, publish newspapers, pump water, generate electricity, clean streets, landscape grounds, pick up garbage, cut grass, rake leaves, remove snow, offer recreation, and provide the hottest social service in the United States today: day care. They are central to the Edge City society we are building, in which office parks are in the childrearing business, parking-lot officials run police forces, private enterprise builds public freeways, and subdivisions have a say in who lives where.

These shadow governments have powers far beyond those ever granted rulers in this country before. Not only can they prohibit the organization of everything from a synagogue to a Boy Scout troop; they can regulate the color of a person's living room curtains. Nonetheless, the general public almost never gets the opportunity to vote its leaders out of office, and rarely is protected from them by the United States Constitution. * * *

AMERICAN PLANNING ASSOCIATION, GROWING SMART LEGISLATIVE GUIDEBOOK: MODEL STATUTES FOR PLANNING AND THE MANAGEMENT OF CHANGE, PHASES I AND II, 2002 EDITION, JANUARY 2002

Pp. xxv–xxvii, xxx–xxxi (2002).

Picture two metropolitan regions of the United States in the not-so-distant future. Each once had the same resources—water, air, land, and people—but a quick glance reveals that each took different paths in the latter part of the twentieth century.

In one region, the features that had once made it attractive are rapidly vanishing. The region's central city, which formerly prospered with an active downtown, strong manufacturing base, and vibrant neighborhood network, is now experiencing disinvestment. Its residents, at least those who remain, are disproportionately poorer and older, and their neighborhoods are not being renewed with younger families and new or rehabilitated housing. The aging suburbs that circle the city have also begun to experience similar patterns of disinvestment. However, the threat of blight and decline is even more ominous here since they have fewer financial resources than the central city due to a stagnant tax base and are unable to cope with changed demands for services and the need to maintain streets, parks, sewers, and the like.

The regions' outlying suburbs are located in what was once a rich and productive agricultural belt, with small independent towns of distinct and diverse qualities. But the agricultural land is quickly disappearing; the small towns have merged into a characterless blur on the region's landscape with homogenous strip shopping centers, fast food restaurants, and car dealerships. The region has reached a point where every place looks like every other place. The residents who had moved to these areas complain that the very attributes that had first drawn them to their communities are fading. Commuting delays grow longer and longer, and no matter how many fixes are made to the expressways, nothing helps to ease the congestion. Families and friends have less time to spend together, and citizens have limited opportunities to participate in community life.

Of course, a few communities in the outlying areas always seem to capture the prestigious office parks and shopping malls, and, consequently, they have low property taxes and very good public services. The rest, however, struggle to keep up with the demands of growth and financing shortfalls. Hoping to attract a large commercial or industrial development, they mortgage their future by offering tax incentives they cannot afford and zoning waivers that will destroy their landscape and community character. Service businesses in these outlying areas cannot entice employees because there is no affordable housing nearby and transportation from the central city and the inner-ring suburbs is infrequent, expensive, and inconvenient. School teachers and police officers in these communities complain that they cannot afford to live near where they work. They face long, time-consuming trips by automobile across the region to reach their jobs.

The natural environment is not much better. The air has taken on a biting, stinging quality. Development has been permitted in areas that periodically flood. Repeated damages from flooding threaten to drive out small businesses, creating an economic climate of apprehension and instability in a number of the region's communities. The wetlands and open spaces that had once been so prominent in the region and provided refuge for birds, fishes, and rare plant species are being filled and developed. Forested stream corridors are being denuded. There has been talk about purchasing these lands for a greenbelt system, but the elected officials in the region worry about the costs of acquisition and the loss of property taxes from denying development, so the idea is shelved.

In the second metropolitan region, it is a different story. The region's governments pride themselves on their willingness to cooperate with one another, plan for the general good, and offer their citizens opportunities to participate collaboratively in civic life. These characteristics give the region an international reputation and delegations from other states nationwide and even other countries regularly visit to learn from its successes. The planning for the region is animated by a strong set of commonly held values by the area's citizens and a vision of where the region wants to be in 20 years.

The central city and the inner-ring suburbs work together to prevent the area from slipping into decline. They continue to be vibrant communities, with bustling, diverse neighborhoods. They experience cycles of renewal and rebirth involving housing, retail business, and start-up companies. Because the region's leaders had agreed some years before to share tax revenue on a metropolitan basis, businesses have located where people can get to them easily, and no local government feels pressured to accept a business at a site that is not optimal or on terms that are not in the public interest, or to annex land only for tax ratables.

The federal government had given the region the opportunity to decide its own transportation destiny, to make decisions on where transportation dollars would be spent. As a consequence, the region's leaders had the foresight to opt for a transportation system that offers people many alternatives to automobiles, rather than just one or two. Mass transit, many believed, could be quicker, cheaper, and safer than automobiles, and an increasing number of people now leave their cars parked at home. The transportation system is now linked together, and it is possible to cross the region rapidly, moving from train to bus without significant delay. One environmental consequence of reduced auto travel is that the air has become cleaner and fresher.

The region's leaders also initiated a long-range plan to purchase, in advance of development, environmentally significant parcels containing wetlands, steep slopes, stream corridors, and natural habitats. This series of greenways form a continuous recreational and open space link within the region. Bike paths have been constructed through and alongside the greenway system, and as a result, the greenways double as transportation corridors. Because the region has taken steps to direct development away from flood-prone areas, its communities do not have to expend funds to clear up flood debris and repair public facilities. * * *

Growth has been carefully planned in the region to avoid prime agricultural lands, which benefit from a comprehensive farmland preservation program that relieves the pressure to develop them. The villages in the region's outskirts remain freestanding and retain their distinctive rural character.

The region's leaders have recognized an obligation to ensure that affordable housing is dispersed across the metropolitan area to provide opportunities for all and are taking active measures to guarantee that an adequate supply is built. In this way, teachers, police officers, bank and grocery clerks, waiters and waitresses, and people with other low-and moderate-wage jobs can live within reasonable distances of their employers. * * *

Many people sense that we are caught in a race against time. We must regain control over the impact of growth, decline, and change on our quality of life. We must give people new choices concerning housing, employment, transportation, and the environment. The stakes in this quest are high. * * * The future is closing in. * * * We must grow in a *smarter* way.

GERRIT KNAAP AND ARTHUR C. NELSON, THE
REGULATED LANDSCAPE: LESSONS ON STATE
LAND USE PLANNING FROM OREGON

Pp. 39–42, 51–53 (1992).

Urban growth boundaries (UGBs), which now encompass all urban areas in the state, represent a key component of urban-area comprehensive planning in Oregon. * * * Urban growth boundaries separate urban land from *rural land* and are the cornerstone of the Oregon land use program. * * * [T]he UGB is a line that delineates where urban development may take place in a metropolitan area; land within the UGB may be developed for urban use; land outside the UGB may not. * * * To achieve this goal, LCDC [the Land Conservation and Development Commission] requires that, "Urban growth boundaries shall be established to identify and separate *urbanizable land* from rural land" * * *.

From the beginning the UGB concept featured an intergovernmental approach to urban growth management. Today, with state participation in the delineation, implementation, and enforcement of all UGBs, intergovernmental participation remains a characteristic feature of the growth-boundary system. Under state land use goals and guidelines, local governments may, at their discretion, use tax incentives and disincentives, fee and less-than-fee acquisition, zoning, and urban service programming to guide urban development within UGBs; local governments may not, however, under the force of law, allow urban development outside an acknowledged UGB. Therefore, UGBs are enforced jointly by local governments and the state, while land use controls inside and outside UGBs are enforced only by local governments. This hierarchy of enforcement standardizes statewide the restrictions embodied in UGBs, while allowing variability in the management of growth within UGBs.

The primary function of UGBs was to help manage urban growth. Whereas other growth management instruments adopted in the early 1970s featured density zoning, development moratoria, and population caps, UGBs were intended, not to limit growth, but simply to manage the process and location of growth. * * * The objectives of UGBs, as specified by LCDC, include preservation of prime farmland; efficient provision of public facilities; reduction of air, water and land pollution; and creation of a distinctly urban ambience. When determining UGBs, local governments were required to make them large enough to meet the requirements for housing, industry and commerce, recreation, open space, and all other urban land uses until the year 2000. All land not contained within UGBs was subsequently designated for rural use until after 2000. Specifically, UGBs were to be established based on the following factors:

1. Demonstrated need to accommodate long-range urban population growth requirements consistent with LCDC goals

2. Need for housing, employment opportunities, and livability

3. Orderly and economic provision of public facilities and services

4. Maximum efficiency for land uses within, and on the fringe of, the existing urban area

5. Environmental, energy, economic, and social consequences

6. Retention of agricultural land as defined, with Class I being the highest priority for retention and Class VI the lowest priority, and

7. Compatibility of the proposed urban uses with nearby agricultural activities

Although they appeared relatively simple in concept, UGBs proved difficult to implement. Part of the difficulty stemmed from uncertainty over the rate of urban development, which made it problematic for planners to determine exactly how much land to include inside a UGB. Too little *urban land* could cause land price inflation; too much would not contain urban sprawl. Such concerns led many local governments to overestimate demands for urban land and err on the side of UGBs that would perhaps turn out to be too big.

Implementation of UGBs introduced political problems as well. Although boundary delineation was intended to be a cooperative affair, turf battles often arose between cities and their county governments, and, in larger metropolitan areas, among city governments. Later, conflicts often ensued between local governments and the Department of Land Conservation and Development (DLCD), the administrative arm of LCDC. According to LCDC, local governments frequently sought to include more land inside UGBs than was justified by demographic and economic trends. In most cases, LCDC forced local governments to reduce the sizes of their UGBs. Although it is difficult to generalize about the impact of this interaction, it appears that the LCDC's review of UGBs resulted in less land becoming eligible for urban development that would have been eligible under a purely local use program * * *.

The Portland metropolitan area encompassed nearly 30 units of government, but responsibility for delineating the metropolitan UGB belonged to the Columbia Region Association of Governments (CRAG). * * * CRAG included in the Portland metropolitan UGB 25 percent more land than they projected was necessary for urban development until the year 2000. LCDC, however, rejected CRAG's boundary, claiming it contained too much land. After removing only three square miles of land, CRAG was replaced by the Metropolitan Service District (Metro), a new and unique, elected, regional government with independent budgetary and land use authority. As one of its first official acts, while the UGB was still being reviewed by LCDC, Metro adopted CRAG's UGB.

Although LCDC still believed that the Metro UGB was too large, it was anxious to proceed with the acknowledgment process and reluctant to antagonize an elected government representing over half the population of the state, including the state's largest city. Thus Metro and LCDC struck a compromise. LCDC would acknowledge Metro's UGB, but Metro would place a ten-year moratorium on residential development in areas designated as prime agricultural land. This in effect created an intermediate growth boundary (IGB) within the urban growth boundary. Land within the IGB could be developed immediately; land within the UGB but outside the IGB could not be developed for ten years, and land outside the UGB could not be developed until the year 2000. * * * Although the UGB acknowledged by the LCDC was larger than necessary * * *, it was smaller than either CRAG or Metro would have adopted alone. The revised UGB contained a 15.3 percent *market factor* of excess vacant land; enough, according to Metro (1979) "that the market will not be affected for some years into the future." * * *

CARL ABBOTT, THE PORTLAND REGION: WHERE CITY AND SUBURBS TALK TO EACH OTHER—AND OFTEN AGREE
8 Housing Policy Debate 12–26, 28–44 (1997).

An informal poll of planning and design experts in 1988 rated Portland's efforts to deal with urban design issues among the best in the United States and the city makes regular appearances on lists of the nation's best-managed cities. * * * In a burst of institutional creativity in the 1970s, the Oregon legislature crafted a statewide system for mandated land use planning and the voters of the three core metropolitan counties created an elected regional government now known as Metro. The U.S. Department of Housing and Urban Development (HUD) recently credited region-wide cooperation for supporting a successful transition from traditional manufacturing to a knowledge-based economy. * * *

What Portland has accomplished centers on decisions about *urban design and the physical shape* of the central city and its related communities. * * * Portland is one of a limited number of U.S. metropolitan areas that measure favorably against the model of good urban form that increasingly dominates the contemporary literature of urban planning and design. * * * Metropolitan Portland is anchored by a strong and viable central core, as might be expected in a regional finance and business center. The downtown is walkable and attractive. * * * The central office core has increased its job total and upgraded average job quality over the past 20 years * * *. Downtown and adjacent districts claim nearly all the major metropolitan institutions and gathering places: museums (art, history, and science), arts center, several major hospitals, a public university, a medical school, a stadium, a convention center * * *. Downtown Portland has an unusually high share of office space within its region. * * * Portland lacks the "dead zone" of derelict industrial districts and abandoned neighborhoods that surrounds the high-rise core of many cities. * * *

Downtown Portland is bordered by viable residential neighborhoods at several economic scales, by neighborhoods in the making on waterfront industrial and rail-yard sites, and by strong industrial wholesaling districts. * * * Beyond the inner ring of apartment neighborhoods and industry lie Portland's streetcar suburbs, the residential districts that first developed between 1890 and 1940. In most cases, a third generation of families filled these neighborhoods in the 1970s, 1980s, and 1990s. These neighborhoods support an unusually prosperous set of neighborhood business districts and strong public schools. * * * [T]here is yet no evidence of middle-class exodus to private schools. * * * The conservation of older neighborhoods is most striking in the West Hills, a large crescent of upscale houses draped across the steep hills to the west of downtown. * * * Protected by elevation from the lower income residents and mixed uses of the downtown fringe, successful businessmen, ambitious professionals, and heirs of moneyed families have been able to maintain social status and leafy living without needing to flee to suburbia. * * *

Portland's suburbs have plenty of people * * * and large stretches of standard postwar cityscapes. Workers leave standard model subdivisions and apartment tracts to battle clogged suburban highways in order to reach jobs in commercial strips and office parks. Power retail stores compete with precast concrete manufacturing boxes and landscaped corporate headquarters for prime acreage. Mile by mile, much of Washington and Clackamas Counties looks like the suburbs of Seattle or Denver. In contrast to many other metropolitan areas, however, Portland's outer ring lacks metro-wide public facilities and concentrated employment centers that rival those of the historic downtown. There is no equivalent to Houston's Galleria-Post Oak district or the Tysons Corner complex in the Virginia suburbs of Washington, D.C. * * * Instead, the outer ring of the metropolitan area remains closely tied to the core through a radial highway system and a developing radial rail system. Indeed, the key structural reason that the Portland suburbs remain supplementary employment and consumption arenas is the lack of a suburban beltway. In the 1950s, highway engineers decided to bring the city's first limited-access freeways into the center of the city and connect them with a tight freeway loop that hugged the edges of the central business district. * * * The economic consequence was to maintain downtown Portland and its nearby neighborhoods as the most accessible parts of the metropolitan area after the demise of streetcars and inter-urban railways. * * *

Distant from both the rural South and Latin America, Portland in the 20th century has had small minority populations. Federally identified minorities (Asian, Native American, black, and Hispanic) constituted only 7.8 percent of the population in the three core counties of Multnomah, Washington, and Clackamas in 1980. By 1990, the figure had grown to 11.4 percent, largely as a result of large Asian and Hispanic migration. Portland is thus one of the "whitest" metropolitan areas in the nation. * * * Partly because of their small numbers, racial groups are relatively well integrated on the neighborhood scale. Portland in 1990 had only six census tracts that were more than 50 percent African American. Hispanics are scattered through lower-income city neighborhoods and live in large numbers on the rural fringe of the metropolitan area. Vietnamese are concentrated on the east side of Portland, while a substantial Korean population has settled in Washington County. * * *

Portland's new politics were informed by the urban renewal and freeway critics of the 1960s, who emphasized the value of small-scale and vernacular urban environments and the excitement of large cities. * * * Both quality-of-life liberals working in the growing information industries and members of minority communities reemphasized the values of place and sought to make neighborhoods effective instruments of resistance to large-scale changes in the urban fabric. Within this changing national discourse, Portland stood out not for the content of its vision but for the effectiveness of its leaders in transforming the common vision into a comprehensive set of public policies and for constructing powerful political coalitions around several planning goals. * * * The 1970s in Portland were marked by the construction of a powerful alliance between downtown business interests and residents of older neighborhoods. * * * In 1970 to 1972, an unusual alliance between city and state officials opened the opportunity to rethink downtown planning. * * * The younger generation of technically sophisticated citizen activists worked with city officials, downtown retailers, property owners, neighborhood groups, and civic organizations to treat previously isolated issues (parking, bus service, housing, retailing) as part of a single comprehensive package.

The resulting Downtown Plan of 1972 * * * offered integrated solutions to a long list of problems that Portlanders had approached piecemeal for two generations. The plan was technically sound because its proposals were based on improvements in access and transportation; it was politically viable because it prescribed tradeoffs among different interests as part of a coherent strategy. Specifics ranged from a waterfront park and pedestrian-oriented design to high-density retail and office corridors crossing in the center of downtown. The ideas found strong advocacy in the mayor's office and an institutional home in the form of a downtown design review process. * * *

A second piece of the strategy was to recycle older neighborhoods built from the 1880s through the 1930s. The city used housing and community development funds and leveraged private capital with tax-free borrowing for an extensive housing rehabilitation program. * * * A political bargain with neighborhood activists accompanied direct investment policy. After a series of confrontations between neighborhoods and city hall in the late 1960s, the * * * administration decided to legitimize and partially co-opt neighborhood activists by incorporating independent neighborhood associations as secondary participants in public decision making. * * *

The third element of the strategy was to shift investment from highways to public transit. A new Tri-County Metropolitan Transit District (Tri-Met) had absorbed the bankrupt bus system in 1969. One of the key features of the Downtown Plan was a transit mall that * * * increased the speed of bus service and facilitated transfers. The second major transit decision was the 1975 cancellation of the so-called Mount Hood Freeway, a five mile connector that would have devastated half a dozen lower middle-class neighborhoods in southeast Portland. Most of the federal money was transferred to build a successful 15-mile light-rail line from downtown to the eastern suburb of Gresham. At the start of the 1990s, Tri-Met's radial bus and rail system carried 43 percent of the workers who commuted into downtown Portland (compared with 20 percent in Phoenix, 17 percent in Salt Lake City, and 11 percent in Sacramento). * * *

Portland is a middle-class city of small business proprietors, skilled union members, managers, and professionals. * * * At the neighborhood and census tract level, Portland's social classes intermix at a relatively fine grain, with stable pockets of high-income housing adjacent to a variety of middle-and working-class districts. Recent comparative data on the segregation of the poor identify Portland as one of the most class-integrated metropolitan areas in the country. * * * The income gap between the central city and the suburbs is relatively small. * * * Within this homogeneous social landscape, even the highly volatile issue of low-income housing has been handled through consensus policies. Advocates for homeless persons and lower-income households have certainly had to battle for attention in city hall and downtown boardrooms. However, the Portland style is then to bring "well-behaved" advocacy groups into the conversation. Once on the team, such groups can trade acquiescence with long-term land development goals for substantial public commitments to low-income housing. In the 1980s, for example, agencies serving the homeless population of Portland's skid row * * * agreed to a cap on shelter beds in the district in return for a go-slow approach to redevelopment and an active program for relocating shelters and social services. * * *

A logical expansion of the * * * [political] coalition has been the definition of common agendas by the city of Portland and key suburban cities. The coalition developed in the 1980s around planning for a four-spoke light-rail system. With the exception of weakly organized suburban manufacturers who prefer cross-suburb road improvements, the Portland area's civic leadership now considers strong public transit to be one of the axioms of regional development. * * * Again, aspects of metropolitan social geography have facilitated a city-suburb alliance. The small size of Portland's racial minority populations and their dispersal through the metropolitan area have meant that city-suburban politics have not revolved around race and racial avoidance. Plans for intensified development in suburban communities do not carry an automatic implication of racial change. White Portlanders have still chosen suburban housing for a wide variety of reasons, but racial flight has not been prominent among them. * * *

The legal framework for Portland area planning, including the urban growth boundary (UGB), is set by Oregon's state system of land use planning. In 1973, the legislature established a mandatory planning program administered by the Land Conservation and Development Commission (LCDC). The legislation, which has survived numerous legal challenges and three statewide referenda, requires every Oregon city and county to prepare a comprehensive plan that responds to a set of statewide goals. The plans provide the legal support for zoning and other specific regulations, and LCDC can require local governments to revise unsatisfactory plans. Oregon thus operates with a system of strong local planning carried on within enforceable state guidelines that express a vision of the public interest. * * *

The UGB is coupled with * * * [an LCDC goal] which essentially mandates a "fair-share" housing policy by requiring that every jurisdiction within the UGB provide "appropriate types and amounts of land . . . necessary and suitable for housing that meets the housing needs of households of all income levels". In other words, suburbs are not allowed to use the techniques of exclusionary zoning to block apartment construction or to isolate themselves as islands of large-lot zoning. By limiting the speculative development of large, distant residential tracts, the LCDC system has tended to level the playing field for suburban development and discourage the emergence of suburban "super developers" with overwhelming political clout. In the Portland region, a housing rule adopted by LCDC now requires every jurisdiction to zone at least half its vacant residential land for apartments or for attached single-family housing. * * *

LCDC has also adopted a transportation rule that requires local jurisdictions to plan land uses and facilities to achieve a 20 percent reduction in vehicle miles traveled per capita over the next 20 years. The rule * * * requires a drastic rethinking of land use patterns and transportation investment to encourage mixed uses, higher densities, public transit, and pedestrians, thus reinforcing the light-rail strategy. It makes local land use planners and the Oregon Department of Transportation into allies while the federal Intermodal Surface Transportation Enhancement Act is forcing highway builders to rethink their jobs.

With the LCDC system as a framework, Portlanders through the 1990s have engaged in a prolonged and intelligent debate about metropolitan growth and form. Metro has been the lead agency for responding to expected population growth. Staff in 1988 realized that there was no established process for amending the Portland-area UGB, even though the state requires periodic review and anticipates incremental UGB expansion. The agency therefore designed a classic planning process to develop a "Region 2040" plan for up to a million more residents in the four core counties. The process was remarkable for the breadth of participation and included home builders, commercial real estate interests, and growth management advocates. It was also remarkable for actually changing ideas, starting as an effort to determine how much to expand the UGB and ending with a debate over how best to freeze or limit it. * * * A compact urban form benefits the undeveloped landscape and natural systems as well as the farms. * * * Environmental groups have therefore been strong supporters of a compact metropolis with its bias toward urban social and cultural values. * * * The majority of involved citizens in both Portland and the suburbs share a basic vision of a metropolis that above all else is "not Los Angeles" and "not Seattle." They agree that the best way to avoid the gridlock and endless subdivisions that characterize their West Coast neighbors is to support relatively compact land development within the constraints of the UGB. * * *

The compact city is not a perfect city. Portlanders in the 1990s have identified several real or potential costs of current growth strategies that need to be explicitly addressed. * * * The mid-1990s have brought a rising awareness within the city of Portland that increased density will consume existing local open space and vacant land. With thousands of new housing units inside the city limits, many residents fear that there will be no breathing space, no rest for the eye. * * * The buried issue is not so much the amount of open space as its accessibility by socioeconomic class. As their property taxes pay off Metro's bonds, Portlanders will be buying suburban parks and preserves. * * * Such spaces are great for hikers, mountain bikers, and weekend excursions. They are less useful for inner-neighborhood kids and summer youth programs. * * *

Portland has a serious shortage of affordable housing for new households and working-class families. * * * A tight housing market has also led to explosive price increases in previously undervalued neighborhoods. * * * The Metropolitan Home Builders Association and market advocates argue that the heart of the affordability problem is scarcity of housing as a product. A tight UGB is said to artificially constrict land supply and drive up the price of undeveloped land, with serious consequences for home prices. Support for their concern comes from comparative data for large metropolitan areas that show Portland with an extremely high rate of increase in median house price in the 1990s—higher even than Sunbelt cities such as Phoenix, Atlanta, and Miami, which have also grown substantially in the same period. Growth management advocates, and Metro in particular, think that the essential problem has been booming demand rather than limited supply. They point out that Portland has enjoyed flush times and what may be a one-time influx of capital from a wave of California in-migrants in the early 1990s. * * * They also note that Portland housing prices increased more slowly in the 1990s than in the region's previous boom of 1973 to 1979, before the UGB took effect. Believers in a compact Portland also assert that expanding the UGB would be a temporary fix at best, with most land freed by such an expansion being used for large-lot developments. Instead, they argue on the basis of national studies and modeling that a compact city promotes affordability by reducing infrastructure costs and encouraging small-lot development, infill, and accessory units. * * *

There is * * * little doubt that maintaining a tight UGB interrupts the classic trickle-down approach to affordable housing. Traditionally we have assumed that upper-income families in search of newer and bigger houses will walk away from perfectly good neighborhoods and hand them down the economic ladder. This process has made some affordable housing available, but it has also tended to devalue working-class neighborhoods except when aggregate demand is very high. Indeed, the trickle-down model has seriously undercut homeownership as a capital accumulation strategy for the working class. With a tight UGB, the Portland area will be less likely to hand down cheap housing for new households, but also less likely to undermine the investments of many working-class and middle-class families. * * *

A final issue is the generalizability of the Portland experience. What is there in the Portland story that other communities might want to imitate, and what problems or complications might they seek to avoid? * * * In looking for generalizable lessons in Portland's history of planning and policy making, it is useful to bear in mind that Portland in the aggregate is not a unique metropolitan area. Many aspects of its economic base, social geography, and demography certainly set it apart from the typical city of the South or Northeast. However, it is not sui generic, despite its "whiteness" and its muted class divisions. In particular, Portland bears many similarities to a number of "middle American" cities, including Indianapolis, Des Moines, Minneapolis-St. Paul, Omaha, Denver, Salt Lake City, Sacramento, and Seattle. * * *

Economic models of housing and land markets tend to project past consumer preferences into the future. We know from other consumption arenas, however, that tastes and behaviors change. * * * Portland in the 1990s shows that tastes for housing are similarly flexible and that suburban large-lot housing fails to satisfy a large segment of the market. Although standard suburban housing has remained plentiful, old neighborhoods with tightly packed houses have also become hot spots. New row houses, small-lot subdivisions, and upscale downtown condominiums jump off the market. * * *

The Portland experience offers several * * * suggestions about the use of UGBs. First is the reminder that growth boundaries are long-term commitments, not quick fixes. They work best when they are part of a planning implementation package that includes public transit investment, infill development, and affordable housing strategies. In Oregon, such coordination is formally mandated through a planning program in which growth containment operates in conjunction with efforts to achieve 13 other statewide planning goals. * * * UGBs need to be flexible enough to respond to changing circumstances. In Portland in the mid-1990s, the UGB has become a symbol as well as a tool. Many residents now regard it as a metaphor for the region's ability to control its own future in the face of global market forces. If the idea of a "frozen" UGB becomes a politically untouchable absolute, however, the region will lose adaptability and may invite future problems of congestion or housing affordability. * * *

Other cities might also think about the value of incremental approaches to growth management. It is common wisdom among community organizers that it is vital to start with small but winnable issues to build community confidence and political momentum before tackling the hard problems. The Portland experience suggests that an analogous approach may be relevant for citywide and regional planning and growth management. * * * Incremental policy making has allowed Portlanders to develop a habit of planning. Portland's civic community is comfortable and familiar with planning processes, issues, and terminologies. Planning issues are part of the civic discourse and a staple of local news reporting to an extent unusual in other cities. * * * The Portland experience suggests the importance of * * * conferences, meetings, and specialized publications sponsored by local institutions

* * * [such as] urban universities, government agencies, or nonprofit advocacy organizations * * *.

The central point of the preceding analysis is the importance of building stable political coalitions for moving a metropolitan regional agenda. Portlanders share a political culture that considers policy alliances and team building to be the normal way of doing public business. * * * At its worst, coalition politics ignores and isolates pockets of dissent in favor of a soft middle ground. At its best, it involves a search for a common public good that transcends the summation of individual and group interests. * * * An important result of Portland's city-level planning initiatives, for example, has been an ability to avoid viewing downtown and neighborhoods as rivals in a zero sum game. * * * The city-suburban coalition has a similar basis—a belief that there is enough growth for both city and suburbs to negotiate equitable cuts and to make such potentially explosive issues as fair-share housing politically palatable. * * * It is unlikely that the basis for coalition building will be the same in other metropolitan areas, where different issues may be foremost in the public mind. * * * Whatever the issue, the need for long-term commitments to a broad public interest argues strongly for networks of community support that outlast the short-term election cycle. Self-conscious coalitions built on shared visions of a community's future potentially have the necessary staying power. * * *

GREGG EASTERBROOK, COMMENT ON KAREN A.
DANIELSEN, ROBERT E. LANG, AND WILLIAM
FULTON'S "RETRACTING SUBURBIA: SMART
GROWTH AND THE FUTURE OF HOUSING"
10 Housing Policy Debate 541–547 (1999).

I hate traffic jams, parking hassles, and crowding. You hate traffic jams, parking hassles, and crowding. Everybody hates traffic jams, parking hassles, and crowding. "Citizens for More Traffic" is not on the lobbying radar, and there is no powerful "PIMBY" ("put it in my backyard") movement. Emerging voter dissatisfaction with traffic backups and overdevelopment * * * seems likely to put sprawl on the national political agenda * * *. Surely the arrival of sprawl as a political issue will help advance green space preservation and improve traffic engineering, two quality-of-life objectives that have long been underappreciated in urban and suburban planning. But will sprawl politics lead to fundamental changes in American growth policy? The answer to that question is less clear, and it is less clear, too, that fundamental changes would be a good idea.

Development should be as "smart" as possible, but the emerging national voter concern about development is in considerable danger of becoming a form of political selfishness. After all, when people complain to political leaders about traffic backups and parking shortages, what they mean is that they want government to get *everybody else* off the roads. They certainly do not mean they want policies that would put them out of their own cars or deprive them of parking. Similarly, when voters oppose construction of new housing subdivisions, what they mean is that *everybody else* should live in higher density circumstances. They certainly do not mean they are willing to have their own lots carved up to put in more housing per acre.

That is to say, as the issue is currently defined, when voters complain about sprawl, what they are really saying is that they want to *preserve* sprawl—at least their own version of it. So voters really do love sprawl after all! They just do not want other people horning in. * * * A high percentage of the people who are outraged about excessive growth live in single-family detached homes on large lots, drive down broad boulevards, commute by car, and park at work. * * * But history teaches that if you have something nice, other people will want in. Continuing increases in population and affluence have caused more and more Americans to want the lifestyle we call sprawl, and that spoils the fun for everybody already there.

Save Our Sprawl thinking already has reached its point of self satire, with the recent agreement between the chip maker Intel and the county government surrounding Portland, OR, that Intel will pay financial penalties if it creates too many new jobs. Portland is beautiful, livable, and desirable. Present residents want to keep it that way, which is fine up to a point. But Portland's chosen technique is to shut newcomers out, first by imposing growth boundaries, and now by adding job penalties. The result of such policies may maintain livability for the people already vested in Portland, but others will be denied the means to join them.

Portland's desire for a protected stasis might be more deserving of sympathy if it were not for the country's increasing population. Smart growth policies designed to preserve green space and improve traffic management are obviously desirable everywhere in the country, because population and automobile ownership are rising. Policies designed to restrict growth, on the other hand, may serve an elitist agenda, walling off desirable areas of first-generation sprawl for those who already have bought in, while shutting out new arrivals, prominently minorities and immigrants. Not coincidentally, anti-growth policies should drive up the value of existing nice communities and large-lot homes through supply and demand. Don't think the Save Our Sprawl lobby doesn't know this!

While Portland may or may not have a right to declare limits on its population growth, this is not an option for the country as a whole, unless Congress is to legislate fertility limits or severely restrict immigration.

Projections call for the U.S. population to peak at around 390 million people in about 2050, roughly a 50 percent increase over the current level. This means the country will have no choice but to construct roughly half again as much sprawl as now exists. Many, many new suburbs are going to be built in the decades to come, in the Sunbelt and elsewhere. These new suburbs should benefit from the lessons learned from existing expansion areas: The next wave of growth must be smarter. But there is going to be a next wave, and it not only will be sprawl, it *should* be sprawl, to grant minorities, immigrants, and others the chance to live in the same favored circumstances the current generation of suburban dwellers now enjoys.

Significant sprawl expansion is not a problem from a land-area standpoint. Despite the mythology of vanishing land, nationally the urban, suburban, and otherwise built-up area of the United States occupies only 3.4 percent of the country's surface. Another half century of continued sprawl at the current development rate (around 400,000 acres per year, in a country of about 2.2 billion acres, or 0.02 percent of the land area consumed per annum) would still leave only about 5 percent of the United States built up when the population peak occurs. Sprawl clearly can exist as a local problem, whenever the desirable land around desirable areas becomes stressed. From a national land-availability standpoint, however, sprawl is a nonissue.

Another nonoption for the country as a whole is to declare some sort of limit on the affluence being acquired in a growth economy. Not only are there more and more Americans every year, there are more and more with the financial means to acquire a detached home, a large-lot home, a second or third car (or, as is now regrettably the case, a second or third sport utility vehicle). Either we are going to tax away that affluence or restrain the economy so that income growth stops, or we are going face an ever-increasing number of families who can qualify for the mortgage on a handsome home. Creating so much affluence that dozens of millions can live in handsome homes is a fantastic social achievement, not a cause for hand wringing, as the Save Our Sprawl lobby suggests.

Could the needs of a growing population and the buying power of increasing affluence be met in an antisprawl context by intelligent use of higher density dwellings? * * * More efficient use of land for housing is an important policy goal, especially when it comes to preservation of green space. But * * * smart growth policies also could have a serious downside, including stifled economic growth. * * * [There are] tools to encourage developers to build—and purchasers to buy—"higher density" housing that consumes less land while being closer to stores and job sites. One idea * * * is the "location efficient" mortgage, which would favor those buying into higher density housing, on the theory that a buyer could have a better chance of qualifying for a home if there were no second car expense in the family budget, or if other efficiency conditions were met.

Location efficient mortgages sound like a tremendous idea for the right buyers. Generally, whatever gives people market incentives to decide on their own to embrace an efficient lifestyle should make for sound public policy. (I assume here that it is politically inconceivable that Congress would revoke the mortgage interest deduction, which would be by far the most effective way to shift market preferences toward smaller homes.) But would many people truly want such mortgages, or would they just end up as a subsidy program for people who cannot afford the suburbs?

Americans, including minority Americans, have emphatically voted with their feet in favor of the detached-home lifestyle. * * * The axial truth of this issue is that most Americans want a detached home with a lawn. Portland's experience, in which multifamily dwelling zones have become market favorites of upscale buyers, is likely to remain the exception; probably the main reason multifamily housing has become upscale in Portland is that growth boundaries have rendered high-density housing essentially the only new housing stock available, and lots of people are eager to buy into Portland by hook or by crook. Citizens may be well served if their detached homes are intelligently designed and sit in a region with green space and smart growth transportation. But programs such as location efficient mortgages could end up shunned by the middle class and the affluent, resulting in just another policy tool that groups the less well off and minorities in dense core-city areas.

To the extent lenders can work with developers to encourage new housing that is more efficient in its use of land, everybody will benefit. Most sprawl thinking, however, misses the fact that many developers already have become more efficient in their use of land. * * * [D]uring the very building binge phase during which, it is conventionally assumed, land has been wasted for willy-nilly sprawl indulgence, the density of American metropolitan and suburban life has been increasing. This is what would be expected, given that developers have financial incentives to become more efficient in their use of land. Talk to one of those odious shopping mall developers and you will hear more than you ever wanted to know about the art of space-efficiency calculation. Town house developers intensely study how to cram parking spaces into smaller and smaller areas and how to add square footage while shrinking footprints. Although American mall and supermarket developers have not yet started using roofs as parking areas, as the Europeans do, most obvious steps to reduce land waste are already common practice.

In that sense, sprawl is already in decline. The reason sprawl seems to be rising is because of the automobile, not the house. * * * As the

United States closes in on one car per person, every year affluence puts more vehicles on the road, with each one driven more miles. It is vehicle explosion, not construction trends, that creates the impression of unbridled sprawl.

Danielsen, Lang, and Fulton further laud the notion of designing communities to place homes, shopping, and employment close together. * * * Why couldn't the campus of a high-tech company be integrated with, or adjacent to, pleasant housing? Surely there will be instances in which this works. But as for the notion that lenders or government agencies can encourage density by planning combined housing/employment development packages, no thanks. Economic trends change too fast and too unpredictably; planning agencies would be lucky to bat .250 with such projects. * * *

Yes, it is infuriating to be stuck in traffic, but roads, cars, and trucks, for all their foibles, enable huge numbers of people to move relatively quickly and to make rapid adjustments in their destinations to meet changing employment and economic demands. These things tend to promote a successful economy. Nice houses with nice lawns do consume space and resources, but they are also the sort of rewards that encourage people to be highly productive. Malls may be stupefying, but they are furiously efficient distribution mechanisms for goods and services, as well as a reliable source of entry-level employment. Running throughout the sprawl debate is the notion that suburbs and traffic are not just exasperating (no doubt there) but actively bad, to be opposed by policy. There is a much greater likelihood that continuing American metropolitan expansion is a social good, correlated positively, not negatively, with the economy and with social progress. The period of postwar sprawl has coincided with unprecedented improvements in standards of living for almost all U.S. citizens, including most minority-group members; unprecedented reductions in institutional discrimination; unprecedented increases in education levels for almost everyone; a closing of the black/white wage gap; and other equally grand achievements. Has the growth of sprawled-out suburban life worked against these trends? More likely it has been a contributing influence. The real reason to Save Our Sprawl is that it is good for us.

C.   REGIONAL SOLUTIONS TO INTERLOCAL CONFLICT

The preceding section focused on the relationship between cities by examining the way that state and federal law creates, maintains, and responds to the distinction between central cities and suburbs. This focus may obscure the possibility that the central city and the suburbs jointly form an intermediate entity that is greater than any particular city but smaller than the state. That entity is the region.

There has been a dramatic resurgence of interest in recent years in regional government in particular and regionalism more generally.[37] The materials that follow address regional solutions to inter-local conflicts and consider a variety of institutional forms that regionalism might take. These forms range from interlocal agreements, at one extreme, to the establishment of full-fledged regional governments, at the other. All of these institutional innovations are designed to respond to the city/suburb divide considered thus far. In thinking about these materials on regional solutions, it is important to question whether the turn to the region does anything to resolve the basic conceptual difficulties that the materials on the city/suburb divide identify. Indeed, it is important to consider whether the emphasis on regionalism merely reproduces those same conceptual difficulties by shifting their locus.

One way to think about regionalism is as an effort to get the boundaries right in a way that our current city boundary lines do not. The region, however, may be just as legally constructed a concept as the city. If so, does it make sense to identify a particular class of problems as "regional" or to legally establish, and thus separate, some regions from others? Another way to think about regionalism is as an effort to re-think what the present boundaries that separate cities from one another can and should mean. The emphasis on the inter-connectedness of cities might spur efforts to rethink the legal significance now attached to inter-city boundaries. One might still wonder, however, whether the emphasis on the region might obscure our understanding of the legal significance attached to boundaries. What problems might arise from attempting to

---

[37] See, e.g., David Troutt, The Price of Paradise: The Costs of Inequality and a Vision for a More Equitable America (2013); Ashira Ostrow, Emerging Counties? Prospects for Regional Governance in the Wake of Municipal Dissolution, 122 Yale L.J. Online 187 (2013); Jae Hong Kim and Nathan Jurey, Local and Regional Governance Structures: Fiscal, Economic, Equity, and Environmental Outcomes, 28 J. Plan. Literature 2, 111–123 (2013); David Troutt, Katrina's Window: Localism, Resegregation, and Equitable Regionalism, 55 Buff. L. Rev. 1109 (2008); Laurie Reynolds, Local Governments and Regional Governance, 39 Urb. Law. 483 (2007); Alan Berube, Bruce Katz, and Robert Lang, Redefining Urban and Suburban America: Evidence from Census 2000 (2006); Peter Dreier, John Mollenkopf, and Todd Swanstrom, Place Matters: Metropolitics for the Twenty-first Century (2nd edition 2004); Myron Orfield, American Metropolitics: The New Suburban Reality (2002); Peter Calthorpe, The Regional City: Planning for the End of Sprawl (2001); Bruce Katz (ed.), Reflections on Regionalism (2000); David Rusk, Inside Game/Outside Game: Winning Strategies for Saving Urban America (1999); Myron Orfield, Metropolitics: A Regional Agenda for Community and Stability (1997); Anthony Downs, New Visions for Metropolitan America (1994); Peter Calthorpe, The Next American Metropolis: Ecology, Community, and the American Dream (1993); Neil Pierce, Citistates (1993). For discussions in the legal literature of the new interest in regionalism, see Laurie Reynolds, Intergovernmental Cooperation, Metropolitan Equity, and the New Regionalism, 78 Wash. L. Rev. 93 (2003); Sheryll Cashin, Localism, Self-Interest, and the Tyranny of the Favored Quarter: Addressing the Barriers to New Regionalism, 88 Geo. L. J. 1985 (2000); Richard Briffault, Localism and Regionalism, 48 Buff. L. Rev. 1 (2000).

distinguish between local problems, regional problems, and state problems?

Finally, in considering these materials, one should think about the relationship between regionalism and local control. Would regionalism mark a retreat from, or an embrace of, meaningful local self-government? What kind of regionalism do you have in mind in answering that question?

1. JOINT UNDERTAKINGS

The most obvious way to resolve interlocal conflicts, and thus to bring about a regional solution, is through interlocal agreement. The most obvious obstacle to such resolution would seem to be the lack of agreement between cities. The materials that follow focus on the forces that keep cities from reaching agreements with each other. The materials focus as well, however, on the concerns that arise even when cities want to engage in some cooperative activity.

Do interlocal agreements square with the conception of cities embodied in Dillon's Rule? Do longterm interlocal agreements threaten to undermine the democratic accountability of city governments to city voters? Do interlocal agreements—such as the Lakewood Plan mentioned in the excerpt from the report by the Advisory Commission on Intergovernmental Relations and discussed more fully by Gary Miller—promote or reduce fragmentation of America's metropolitan areas? In reflecting on these questions, keep in mind that interlocal agreements not only permit cities to contract into a cooperative arrangement but also permit cities to contract out of the legal framework that would apply in the absence of agreement. The legal regime that would apply in the event of "cooperation," therefore, must be compared to the one that would apply in the absence of agreement.[38]

In evaluating interlocal agreements, it is also important not to take for granted that the agreements are voluntary—that is, that they are entered into only if each contracting party considers the contract to be in its own, freely-chosen interest. It is important to ask how this concept of freely-chosen city self-interest is to be understood. To what extent are cities entitled to act as if they owe no obligations to neighboring cities? To

---

[38] For a general analysis of interlocal agreements, see, e.g. John Martinez, Local Government Law, Chapter 9 (2nd ed. 2012–13); David Roberts, Separate but Equal? Virginia's "Independent" Cities and the Purported Virtues of Voluntary Interlocal Agreements, 95 Va. L. Rev. 1551 (2009); Clayton P. Gillette, The Conditions of Interlocal Cooperation, 21 J.L. & Pol. 365 (2005); Laurie Reynolds, Intergovernmental Cooperation, Metropolitan Equity, and the New Regionalism, 78 Wash. L. Rev. 93 (2003); Clayton P. Gillette, Regionalization and Interlocal Bargains, 76 N.Y.U. L. Rev. 190 (2001); 1 Eugene McQuillin, Municipal Corporations, Chapter 3A (3d ed. 1987); Mark Hall and Jerry Wallack, Intergovernmental Cooperation and the Transfer of Powers, 1981 U. Ill. L. Rev. 775; Advisory Commission on Intergovernmental Relations, A Handbook for Interlocal Agreements and Contracts (1967).

what extent does state law necessarily define a city's possible understanding of its self-interest through numerous rules and doctrines that do not directly relate to the authority of cities to enter into interlocal agreements? These questions underlie the materials already considered on the city/suburb divide, and in particular the materials on exclusionary zoning and school financing. The materials in this section conclude with an excerpt by Gerald Frug that discusses the relevance of those cases to interlocal agreements. The materials are intended to widen the frame within which one evaluates the desirability of encouraging interlocal agreements. What is the right strategy for encouraging such agreements? What would be the impact on our current understanding of city-state and city-federal relations if interlocal agreements became more common and more ambitious?

INTERLOCAL AGREEMENTS

Advisory Commission on Intergovernmental Relations, Metropolitan America:
Challenge to Federalism, pp. 87–88 (1966).

Intergovernmental agreements are arrangements under which a local community conducts an activity jointly or cooperatively with one or more other governmental units, or contracts for its performance by another governmental unit. The agreements may be permanent or temporary; pursuant to special act or general law; effective with or without voter approval; and may be formal or informal in character. Intergovernmental agreements may be for the provision of direct services to citizens of two or more jurisdictions, such as water supply or police protection; or they may be for governmental housekeeping activities, such as joint purchasing or personnel administration activities.

Local governments in California make extensive use of this approach, with counties contracting to provide services to cities. This procedure has become known as the Lakewood plan, since Lakewood on becoming a city contracted to have practically all its governmental services provided by Los Angeles County. In March 1959, there were 887 contracts between cities and Los Angeles County, covering functions from assessing to dog control and street maintenance. Other types of intergovernmental agreements are also popular in California. Under the Joint Powers Act, two or more public agencies exercising common powers may agree that one of them should exercise power for all of them.

Elsewhere, a survey of intermunicipal contracts indicated that between 1950 and 1957, Cleveland had 30 contracts with 12 of its suburbs, and the 12 suburbs had 43 contracts with one another to provide services. And between 1950 and 1959, 81 of St. Louis County's 98 municipalities signed a total of 241 contracts for provision of municipal services by the county, including law enforcement, health and sanitation, and building regulation.

Intergovernmental agreements are useful in broadening the geographic base for planning and administering governmental services and controls. By enlarging the scale of administration, they make it possible to lower unit costs. Further, the boundaries are flexible and can be enlarged without difficulty when additional governments want to join an agreement. Where agreements are used to extend city services to developing fringe areas, they may be helpful in guiding orderly metropolitan growth.

A basic weakness of joint agreements is that they are practical only when the immediate local interest of each community receiving service is not in conflict with the interest responsible for providing it. Yet in providing areawide services such as public transportation or water supply, conflicts are likely to arise over the location of facilities or priorities for investment. Since agreements are voluntary, each community in effect has veto power within its own borders and can withdraw when its interests are affected adversely by decisions concerning areawide services. Intergovernmental agreements are thus not suited to effective decisionmaking on issues which transcend local interests; under a system of agreements such issues would require unanimity among the governments involved rather than decision by majority vote.

On issues that are more local in character, intergovernmental agreements may interfere with the citizens' ability to take part in making policy. Even though individual governments retain their freedom to pull out of an agreement, and thus retain ultimate control over their own policies, the weaving of a network of intergovernmental agreements tends to confuse the lines of actual responsibility to the point where effective local control may be seriously eroded. Further, the tendency is for each agreement to be made on an ad hoc basis for a particular need, so that the complete view is never brought into focus, making it more difficult to coordinate services and achieve a balance of needs and resources.

Intergovernmental contracts may be objectionable on other grounds where the seller municipality has a virtual monopoly on the service. If one community controls the water supply in an area, for example, only its own self-restraint protects the purchasing communities from being exploited on price and service. Where monopoly conditions exist, some outside authority is needed to protect the purchasers—a role performed in some States by utility regulatory bodies that review water contracts. * * *

GARY J. MILLER, THE POLITICAL ORIGINS
OF THE LAKEWOOD PLAN
[See Chapter 3, Section A–2, supra.]

GERALD FRUG, EMPOWERING CITIES IN A FEDERAL SYSTEM
19 The Urban Lawyer 553, 557–564, 565–566 (1987).

One way to see the importance of intercity cooperation is to look at the constitutional status of interstate cooperation. Some early federalists might have thought that there was no distinction between creating the federal government and ensuring cooperation among states—that action by the federal government was the same thing as action by the united states. But clearly others recognized, as we do, that these two concepts can be very different from each other; our current federal government represents only one possible form of interstate cooperation. Indeed, the only reference to interstate relationships in the Constitution treats cooperation among states as suspect: article I, section 10 provides: "No state shall, without the Consent of Congress, * * * enter into any Agreement or Compact with another State. * * *"

Why did the federalists who framed the Constitution want centralized control of interstate cooperation? Did they fear that interstate compacts could create a powerful counterforce to the national government? If Congress could not control the relationship among the states, would a very different form of federalism emerge?

I think it would, just as I think that the most effective way to strengthen cities' power is for cities to engage in joint activity and to learn to deal with intercity conflict on their own. The power that can be generated by collective action is widely recognized, as is the effort of centralized authorities to limit it. The ability of employees to increase their power by moving from individual employment contracts to unions—and the efforts of employers to prevent unionization—is one well-known example. The power that private corporations can create through agreements with each other—and the attempt by antitrust laws to limit these agreements—is another. Article I, section 10 of the Constitution, then, is not unusual in its attempt to empower centralized authorities to control collective activity. Efforts to create power through collective organization are generally threatened by countervailing efforts to restrain it. But these attempts to impose centralized control on collective action simply increase its importance; organizing strengthens the ability of individuals and groups to resist centralized power. The defense of local democracy can thus be enhanced if cities work together to advance their common interests.

In order to consider the chances of increasing intercity cooperation, we need to look more closely at the entitlements of individual cities considered separately. The prospects for any agreement depend on the powers that each potential party to the agreement can exercise on its own. This is a matter of basic contract and property law: there is no reason to negotiate over anything to which one is already entitled as a matter of law before the negotiation begins. How, then, should we understand the entitlements of one locality vis-à-vis those of another in the absence of agreement between them? Two different answers have been given to this question, answers that are based on very different ideas about the reason for and value of local democracy. I shall call these conceptions the "free choice" and "participation" theories of democracy.

The free choice theory of democracy is an individualist theory: it envisions the relationship among localities in the way people often imagine the relationship among self-interested individuals. Each locality is free to choose its own destiny, according to its own views of its own self-interest, unless and until it is regulated by law. Indeed, from this point of view, the very reason for establishing a local democracy is to allow the people within it to choose for themselves the kind of life they want to live. Thus advocates of free choice theory might defend exclusionary zoning—a city's decision to permit only certain kinds of housing within its border—as an example of local democratic decision making. They might argue as well that property-rich school districts—those who can support themselves with a low tax rate imposed on highly valued property—owe no obligations to property-poor school districts, even though the poor school districts could never achieve the same amount of income because they do not have adequate property to tax. If a locality cannot decide for itself the kind of community it is to have and cannot control the way it spends its own money on local education, a free choice advocate might argue, local democracy would have no meaning at all. From the free choice view, inter-local agreements are just another example of voluntary agreements between parties who meet each other at arm's length. When cities (like individuals) meet to contract, they can refuse to go along with any proposal they don't like; what each city agrees to will depend on what the people within it want.

The participation theory of democracy, by contrast, envisions local democracy not in terms of individual choice but in terms of a citizen's ability to participate as an equal in the decisions that affect her or his life. Participation theory rejects the relationship among individuals or groups—the sharp separation between self and others—that free choice theory espouses. Defenders of participation theory see such an "arm's-length" version of human relationships as incompatible with democratic existence. Every individual decision, they argue, produces external effects that need to be taken into account in decision making. Participation theory thus describes democracy in terms of a conversation designed to find a satisfactory resolution of differences; indeed, participation theory presents democracy not merely as a decision-making process but as a form of education, a way of creating a sense of self and an understanding of human relationships constructed through political conflict, negotiation, compromise, and disagreement.

Much of the attention of participation theory has focused on internal city organization. Participation theorists have argued that if democracy is to mean more in American life than simply choosing from time to time the individuals who will govern us—if democracy is to mean involvement by the members of a community themselves in the decision making that affects their lives—institutions need to be created that can foster citizen participation. In areas as large as American states and the nation as a whole, elections may be the only form democracy can take; if so, only in cities (and in large cities, only in neighborhoods) can people have the experience of engaging in democratic activity themselves. For participation theorists, the reason for having powerful local governments is to promote this kind of activity. * * *

This process of building democratic city institutions is critically important, but it should be clear that democracies cannot exist merely by perfecting their internal organization. Democratic institutions, like other entities, need to establish ways of living together. Indeed, any theory of democracy must confront the problem of establishing a relationship among individual democracies that is consistent with its democratic ideals. Advocates of participation theory, therefore, are likely to see the relationship among communities as similar to the relationship among people within any single community: both must be built on the recognition of connection and interdependence. Thus a participation theorist might treat the issue of exclusionary zoning as a problem of establishing a mechanism that will allow dialogue among the communities affected by the zoning action; both those excluded and those seeking to exclude must be allowed to participate in the process of resolving their interconnected housing problems. In such a dialogue there can be no automatic assumption that one community has a right to exclude the other's residents. Similarly, a defender of participation theory might deny that the question of school financing can be resolved by assuming that a property-rich school district has an entitlement to use "its own" resources on education without regard to the needs of others; instead, she or he might argue that both property-rich and property-poor school districts are entitled to no more than participation as an equal in working out how school funds are to be allocated. According to participation theory, when individuals or groups meet for the purposes of potential cooperation, they have to learn to understand themselves not as maximizers of their own self-interest but as people who are engaged as equals in the task of resolving their differences.

To be sure, it would be a mistake to overstate the contrast between the free choice and participation theories of democracy. If a local community did not have some degree of freedom of choice, it would not have many decisions to make; thus no one would want to participate in its affairs. Conversely, for a local community to make an informed and representative choice, some degree of popular participation in the decision-making process is indispensable. Thus there is no reason to believe that defenders of free choice necessarily oppose participation or that believers in participation reject the notion of choice. Nonetheless, as the exclusionary zoning and school financing examples are designed to illustrate, the two theories have very different points of emphasis. Indeed, the two theories suggest quite different strategies for promoting the kind of intercity cooperation that, I contend, is so essential to city empowerment.

To date, modern local government law has largely adopted a strategy based on free choice theory.[9] At first glance, this appears to be the right decision: free choice theory seems to provide a far more promising way to increase city power than does participation theory. In fact, participation theory hardly seems to permit any local power at all. According to the way I have presented the theory, a community can make virtually no decision about its own future by itself. Local decisions appear to be made only by some sort of romantic transcending of differences between cities— even the very stark differences between inner cities with black majorities and suburbs with white majorities. This process of transcending differences appears pretty vague and farfetched. By contrast, free choice theory seems understandable and in touch with what people are really like. If the object is to increase city power, then the idea of providing each city with some sort of autonomy to make choices—autonomy not only against the state and federal government but against other cities as well—seems the most sensible way to achieve the desired goal. Intercity cooperation would occur in the same way that cooperation occurs in other contexts—whenever the benefits of agreement to each contracting party outweigh the benefits of acting alone. The way to increase cooperation would be to encourage individual cities to see that their own self-interest will be advanced by it. If the benefits of cooperation actually exist, intercity agreements will be able to increase city power against state and federal governments.

The difficulty with the free choice strategy, however, lies in the power that it cedes to the state. If cities are understood, like self-interested individuals, to have entitlements against each other as well as

---

[9]   See, e.g., Village of Arlington Heights v. Metropolitan Housing Dev. Corp., 429 U.S. 252 (1977); Milliken v. Bradley, 418 U.S. 717 (1974); San Antonio Indep. School Dist. v. Rodriguez, 411 U.S. 1 (1973). But see, e.g., Serrano v. Priest, 557 P.2d 929 (Cal.Sup.Ct.1976); Southern Burlington County NAACP v. Township of Mount Laurel, 336 A.2d 713 (N.J.Sup.Ct.1975).

against the state, some entity other than the cities will have to have the authority both to decide what these entitlements are and to resolve the conflicts that they will generate. Traditionally, this authority has been exercised by the state legislature and state courts. But ceding authority to these state agencies in an effort to establish city power simultaneously gives them authority to limit it. The cities' effort to gain autonomy threatens that very autonomy by empowering a central government to decide what it is. The only solution free choice theory offers to this dilemma is the concept of federalism: federalist theory is supposed to specify the limits on centralized control of cities. As we have seen, however, no defensible limits have been found. On the contrary, as article I, section 10, of the Constitution suggests, federalist theory can be interpreted to permit a central government to restrict even cities' ability to cooperate with each other—and many states do.

Self-interested cooperation between cities is likely to be jeopardized by more than assertions of power by the states. Mutual suspicion can also undermine the possibility of intercity cooperative ventures. Because cities seek power from the state that can be used against one another, those that see themselves as well off may be unwilling to help others gain any power that might threaten what they see as "theirs." Cities might also think that they will gain more by trying to win power from the state than by trying to deal with their neighbors. This mutual suspicion can reduce cities' experience of dealing with intercity conflict—particularly the kind of conflict that requires one entity to sacrifice itself in the interest of others. When such a conflict arises, cities will routinely feel that their only real choice is to ask the state to resolve it rather than try to deal with it themselves. Thus a strategy based on free choice theory can lead to increasing state control not simply because of state aggrandizement but because of city abandonment of decision-making responsibility. To be sure, such a process is not inevitable. Cities might understand, and act to reverse, a trend toward city subservience to the state. To do so, however, will require a spirit of cooperation that a self-interested city might find rubs against the grain.

Perhaps, then, a better strategy to encourage more city cooperation and a strong city position against the state is suggested by participation theory. Rather than defining freedom in terms of the entitlements that separate one city from another, cities should recognize that protecting their freedom requires them to resolve their differences themselves. If they do not resolve their own differences, they have to ask some higher authority to do it for them, and every abandonment of their own role in the decision-making process is a gamble that the entity empowered to decide their fate will itself not threaten their interests. Every time a decision is made to defer decision-making responsibility to someone else, there is a loss of freedom—a loss of the ability to have a voice in determining one's own future. Since it is a fantasy to think that, in a world filled with others, a city can determine its future by itself, all it can reasonably expect is the ability to participate with others in the decision-making process. Indeed, whenever such joint decision making works, it strengthens the power of both parties, enabling them to live together in ways that they themselves create.

Of course, a joint decision will often require a city to sacrifice advantages it has over others. But reliance on these advantages is risky because they contain the seeds of their own destruction: they will continue to exist only as long as the state, from which they derive, permits them to. Cities, after *Hunter v. Pittsburgh,* have no constitutional protection from a state's reallocation of their entitlements to others. Advantages secured by using state power to perpetuate a city's privileged position are thus less secure than advantages won through mutual agreement: mutual agreement is likely to produce joint action designed to protect the agreed-upon result from invasion by the state, while advantages won by one city at the expense of another will remain in jeopardy as long as the loser has a chance to influence the state to reverse its decision. Paradoxically, then, compromise with others might lead to more city empowerment than assertions of autonomy and independence even for cities comparatively well off. If so, cities need to create mechanisms that enable them to engage in conflict resolution on their own. Few institutional forums now exist that permit cities to resolve mutual problems without resort to outside intervention. Creating institutions of this kind is a first priority for those who adopt a participation strategy.

A major problem people usually find with a strategy based on participation theory is that they do not believe it is realistic to expect individuals or groups to deal with each other in the way the theory proposes. Is not this a kind of compromise and mutual vulnerability against human nature? Defenders of participation theory respond to this kind of objection by emphasizing that the kind of intercity relationship envisioned by a participation strategy *is* unrealistic—and it will remain unrealistic unless cities are organized internally as participatory democracies. Only if people learn to relate to others within their own community in a democratic fashion—only if they learn how to deal with conflict in their daily lives—will they be able to treat relationships between cities in a similar fashion. Thus the nature of the internal organization of cities is an indispensable ingredient in creating a participatory intercity relationship. The participatory strategy for inter-governmental relations is a strategy for relations among *democracies,* not a strategy that can be adopted by anyone. According to participation theory, one should recall, democracy is not just a decision-making process but a form of education, a form of learning how to deal with others. Of course nonparticipatory institutions are unable to deal with each other democratically, advocates of participation theory might say; people who have never participated in joint decision-making cannot know what it means to engage in democratic self-governance.

Another problem people often find with a strategy based on participation theory stems from the homogenous nature of so many American cities. How can the citizens of modern suburbia find people sufficiently different from themselves to engage in the kind of intracity debate and compromise participation theory envisions? What intracity debate could possibly prepare them to confront the kind of dramatic differences that exist between cities—those, for example, between wealthy suburbs and impoverished inner cities? Defenders of participation theory respond to these questions by agreeing that adequate intracity experience is often unavailable. After all, many cities have been formed and continue to be operated in accordance with free choice theory; citizens of these cities cannot have an adequate democratic experience because they have defined their intercity boundaries antagonistically, excluding different kinds of people. For these cities, the possibility of any genuine democratic participation depends on establishing participatory intercity relationships. Opening oneself to people across city boundaries can thus be as indispensable to enabling a city to function democratically as building a democratic internal organization is to the creation of participatory intercity relationships. Indeed, since participatory intercity and participatory intracity relationships can both be seen as a prerequisite to each other, a major puzzle for theorists has been trying to figure out how a participatory democratic experience can possibly begin. The answer, it seems, is that there is no logical place: barriers to democratic self-governance must be confronted everywhere at once, whenever and however they can. * * *

Let us consider, as a concrete example, the issues of exclusionary zoning and school financing mentioned earlier. The present national strategy of dealing with these issues treats cities as self-interested entities, able to engage in whatever zoning or education decisions they want unless modified by legislative or judicial intervention. Since the federal courts have ruled against federal judicial intervention into these areas of decision-making (in order to honor state policies fostering local democracy), the entitlements of cities engaged in exclusionary zoning practices and property-rich school districts have been protected at the national level. In a number of states, however, judicial or legislative intervention has invalidated exclusionary zoning practices and ordered redistribution of revenues for education. In the case of school financing, this reallocation has been done in the name of local democracy, but this time the localities sought to be empowered are the property-poor school districts that are unable, given their property values, to raise the money for education that their citizens want. (Even restrictions on exclusionary zoning could be defended in the name of local democracy, although normally they are not discussed in these terms. Cities in which the people who are excluded by exclusionary zoning live have no voice in matters that powerfully affect their future.)

Although both federal and state decisions appeal to the virtues of local control, in neither case is the appeal very convincing. Under either the federal or state decisions, some cities have been stripped of their ability to participate in the decision making that vitally affects their interests, let alone of the ability to decide their future by themselves. Those protected by the federal courts might feel satisfied that their "autonomy" has been protected until state legislative or judicial decisions overturn their victory. When that happens, the losers in federal court can feel protected by the help they have won from the state, but only as long as the state continues to act in their interest. In fact, it should be clear that neither side actually has much to say about its own future; it is simply up to one court or another, one legislature or another, to decide what that future is. Given the absence of participatory democratic structures within most of these jurisdictions, little progress is likely to be made immediately by having cities work together to solve the problems of exclusionary zoning or school financing. Too much self-interest and mutual suspicion will distort the bargaining process. Yet there will never be a system of local power until localities attempt to work out these problems themselves. Even now, some form of intercity discussions can be helpful, if only to alleviate the effects of state intervention or federal nonintervention. * * *

2. PUBLIC AUTHORITIES AND SPECIAL DISTRICTS

One of the most common forms of local governmental organization is the "public authority" or "special district." (See, e.g., Municipal Authority v. Lowder and Ball v. James in Chapter One, Section C, supra.) These are entities created by the state to provide a service (or a combination of services) to a local community independent of city control. Indeed, housing authorities, highway authorities, port authorities, independent school boards, hospital corporations, redevelopment authorities, park districts, and similar governmental organizations often provide a substantial percentage (sometimes most) of local services.[39] The

---

[39] See generally, Nadav Shoked, Quasi-Cities, 93 B.U. L. Rev. 1971 (2013); Nicholas Bauroth, Pick Your Poison: The Exercise of Local Discretion on Special District Governance, 37 Pol. & Pol'y 1, 177–99 (2009); Jeffrey Baltruzak, The Core Plan or How I Learned to Stop Worrying and Love the Central City: Shifting Control of Regional Mass Transit to the Central City, 5 Pierce L. Rev. 271 (2007); Kathryn Foster, The Political Economy of Special-Purpose Government (1997); Nancy Burns, The Formation of American Local Governments: Private Values in Public Institutions (1994); Donald Axelrod, Shadow Government: The Hidden World of Public Authorities (1992); Jerry Mitchell (ed.), Public Authorities and Public Policy: The Business of Government (1992); 3A Antieau, Municipal Corporation Law, Chapters 30C–Q

jurisdictions of many public authorities and special districts extend across individual city boundaries. These entities therefore provide an alternative to interlocal agreements as vehicles for regional cooperation.

The independence of these public authorities and special districts from city government is often thought to take important public services out of politics, allowing them to be run in a more business-like manner. The following is a (relatively typical) defense of the creation of regional or multicounty authorities as a means of providing regional services:

> [T]he strengths of multicounty authorities lie in increased efficiency and flexibility of jurisdiction. Among the services that are best suited for administration by this kind of body are those that require accumulated expertise and technological sophistication in their management. Continuity of management, attraction of superior personnel, and corporate powers and decisionmaking will be most beneficial in such areas as transportation, water supply and sewerage, port direction, and pollution control. Services in which area-wide administration and planning would result in significant economies of scale and integration of separate facilities are also likely to benefit from administration by multicounty authorities. An area-wide policy is mandatory, for instance, if a transportation plan is effectively to coordinate bus, train, and subway services with auto travel on the roads, ferries, and bridges, and through tunnels.[40]

In the excerpt that follows, Professor Briffault contends that, far from enhancing regional cooperation, transferring city functions to a special district or public authority may have the perverse effect of further entrenching the legal separateness of cities. Does the next case, People ex. rel. Younger v. County of El Dorado, provide a convincing answer to Professor Briffault's concerns? After *Younger*, do California's cities have the power to address regional problems on their own, or are they relegated to addressing only problems that are solely of local concern?

The *Younger* case also implies a certain vision of democracy. To the extent state law permits special districts or public authorities to take on governmental roles formerly exercised by cities, it in effect permits public power to be exercised free from the state-imposed requirements, such as civil service rules for hiring personnel or competitive bidding rules for purchasing goods and services, that would apply if cities performed the identical task. At the same time, to the extent state law permits the exercise of power by special districts or public authorities, it channels regulatory authority from popularly elected general purpose governments

---

(1979); William Quirk and Leon Wein, A Short Constitutional History of Entities Commonly Known as Authorities, 56 Cornell L. Rev. 521 (1971).

[40] Comment, An Analysis of Authorities: Traditional and Multicounty, 71 Mich. L. Rev. 1376, 1429 (1973).

to specialized bureaucratic agencies. Does it make sense to give elected governments, like cities, less authority to address regional problems than appointed ones, like the Tahoe Regional Planning Agency? Is the concern about democratic accountability of regional authorities persuasively dealt with by Ball v. James, excerpted in Chapter One?

The Note on the Georgia Regional Transportation Authority, which concludes this subsection, demonstrates that public authorities, like special districts, continue to be established in response to the problems of metropolitan fragmentation.

RICHARD BRIFFAULT, OUR LOCALISM: PART II—LOCALISM AND LEGAL THEORY
90 Colum. L. Rev. 346, 375–378 (1990).

Since the turn of the century, state legislatures have invented a "baffling array" of "pseudo governments" to provide infrastructure services to the suburbs without disturbing suburban political autonomy. These entities—variously christened boards, districts, authorities and commissions—are authorized to construct, operate or finance physical infrastructure services, usually water supply services, sewers, parks or transportation, over an area including many general-purpose governments. These limited-purpose entities can pool the resources of a number of localities in an area, but solely to provide one or a handful of specified services.

Where the board's jurisdiction includes both the city and the suburbs and the city has already installed its own water supply or sewers out of its own funds, the board effectively redistributes city revenues to the installation and support of suburban services. Where the board or district includes only developing areas in need of the initial installation of new services, the creation of a single area-wide water or sewer system and the combination of revenues from numerous localities lead to substantial economies of scale, reducing the per capita cost of providing new infrastructure systems but undermining the competitive advantage of the central city and permitting suburbs to enjoy municipal services without submitting to annexation or consolidation.

The structure and design of these special-purpose units minimize the intrusion on suburban autonomy. First, they are limited-purpose governments. The metropolitan unit overlaps cities and suburbs but has no general governmental authority over the territory or residents within its jurisdiction. Cities and suburbs are not merged, and the city gains no lawmaking authority over the suburbs. Rather, different municipalities are linked only for a particular purpose, such as supplying water or removing wastes.

Second, these units provide services that facilitate separate suburban political existence without disrupting suburban class or ethnic homogeneity. In Oliver Williams's terminology, the metropolitan special districts perform "system-maintenance functions" without impinging on suburban "lifestyles." The physical infrastructure that metropolitan districts provide usually lacks broader implications for the economic or social demography of suburban communities. Special districts supply engineering solutions to technical problems; they do not directly engage in area-wide social or economic policymaking. Metropolitan districts do not zone or provide police, housing or schools on an area-wide city-suburb basis. Suburbs that have accepted regional provision of certain transportation facilities, like airports, have been able to reject other area-wide services, like metropolitan mass transit systems, because of the concern that the latter would increase the ability of central city residents to travel to the suburbs.

Third, special districts' financial and governance arrangements minimize their regional redistributive and political potential. The operation of these agencies is usually funded through service fees or user charges, with local service recipients paying a specified amount for each unit of service they receive. Local tax bases are generally not exposed to the public service needs of the region or of people residing outside local political boundaries.

The metropolitan boards generally lack regional popular political constituencies. Often their members are unelected, and are, instead, appointees or officials of the affected municipalities serving ex officio. The board members do not serve as representatives of a regional electorate, but either represent their home locality to the regional unit—where they vote on a "one government, one vote" and not a "one person, one vote" basis—or they are not locally representative at all. There are few political ties linking metropolitan districts directly to the residents of the metropolitan area, so that these districts do not significantly disturb the existing political alignment of cities and suburbs.

As metropolitan areas have grown, special districts have proliferated. There are now more than 28,000, and the special district is the most common form of local government. In most areas there are more special districts than municipalities. At one time, political scientists saw these metropolitan boards and districts as a bridge from local independence to regional government. They predicted that as local governments developed institutions for interlocal cooperation and saw the need for regional solutions to area-wide problems, metropolitan consolidation would follow. Instead, the opposite has occurred. State-authorized limited-purpose governments have provided suburbs with an alternative to annexation, consolidation to the central city or acceptance of full-fledged metropolitan governments. A suburb can maintain political independence, including control of its tax base, schools and lands, while still sharing in the economies of scale provided by infrastructure services organized and funded on a regional basis. * * *

PEOPLE EX REL. YOUNGER V. COUNTY OF EL DORADO
Supreme Court of California, 1971.
5 Cal.3d 480, 96 Cal.Rptr. 553, 487 P.2d 1193.

SULLIVAN, JUSTICE.

The Attorney General, on behalf of the People of the State of California, seeks a writ of mandate commanding the Counties of El Dorado and Placer to pay to the Tahoe Regional Planning Agency (Agency) the amounts of money respectively allotted to them by the Agency as being necessary to support its activities. * * * The issues thus presented to us are of great concern to California, to its neighbors and, indeed, to the entire country.

The controversy which we are required to review focuses upon the Lake Tahoe Basin—an area of unique and unsurpassed beauty situated high in the Sierras along the California-Nevada border. Mark Twain, an early visitor to the region, viewed the lake as "a noble sheet of blue water lifted six thousand three hundred feet above the level of the sea * * * with the shadows of the mountains brilliantly photographed upon its still surface * * * the fairest picture the whole earth affords." Year after year the lake and its surrounding mountains have attracted and captivated countless visitors from all over the world.

However, there is good reason to fear that the region's natural wealth contains the virus of its ultimate impoverishment. A staggering increase in population, a greater mobility of people, an affluent society and an incessant urge to invest, to develop, to acquire and merely to spend—all have combined to pose a severe threat to the Tahoe region. Only recently has the public become aware of the delicate balance of the ecology, and of the complex interrelated natural processes which keep the lake's waters clear and fresh, preserve the mountains from unsightly erosion, and maintain all forms of wildlife at appropriate levels. Today, and for the foreseeable future, the ecology of Lake Tahoe stands in grave danger before a mounting wave of population and development.

In an imaginative and commendable effort to avert this imminent threat, California and Nevada, with the approval of Congress, entered into the Tahoe Regional Planning Compact (Compact) the provisions of which are found in Government Code section 66801. The basic concept of the Compact is a simple one—to provide for the region as a whole the planning, conservation and resource development essential to accommodate a growing population within the region's relatively small area without destroying the environment.

To achieve this purpose, the Compact establishes the Tahoe Regional Planning Agency with jurisdiction over the entire region. The Agency has been given broad powers to make and enforce a regional plan of an unusually comprehensive scope. This plan, to be adopted on or before September 1, 1971, must include, as correlated elements, plans for land-use, transportation, conservation, recreation, and public services and facilities. The Compact emphasizes that in formulating and maintaining this regional plan, the Agency "shall take account of and shall seek to harmonize the needs of the region as a whole * * *."

The Agency is given the power to "adopt all necessary ordinances, rules, regulations and policies to effectuate the adopted regional * * *" plan. While ordinances so enacted establish minimum standards applicable throughout the region, local political subdivisions may enact and enforce equal or higher standards. "The regulations shall contain general, regional standards including but not limited to the following: water purity and clarity; subdivision; zoning; tree removal; solid waste disposal; sewage disposal; land fills, excavations, cuts and grading; piers, harbors, breakwaters, or channels and other shoreline developments; waste disposal in shoreline areas; waste disposal from boats; mobilehome parks; house relocation; outdoor advertising; flood plain protection; soil and sedimentation control; air pollution; and watershed protection. Whenever possible without diminishing the effectiveness of the * * * general plan, the ordinances, rules, regulations and policies shall be confined to matters which are general and regional in application, leaving to the jurisdiction of the respective states, counties and cities the enactment of specific and local ordinances, rules, regulations and policies which conform to the * * * general plan." The Compact also provides that "[v]iolation of any ordinance of the [A]gency is a misdemeanor." Finally, it states that "all public works projects shall be reviewed prior to construction and [except for certain state public works projects] approved by the [A]gency as to the project's compliance with the adopted regional general plan."

The governing body of the Agency is composed of ten members, five from California and five from Nevada. The Boards of Supervisors of El Dorado and Placer Counties and the City Council of the City of South Lake Tahoe each appoint one member; "[e]ach [such] member shall be a member of the city council or county board of supervisors which he represents and, in the case of a supervisor, shall be a resident of a county supervisorial district lying wholly or partly within the region." The Boards of County Commissioners of the Counties of Douglas, Ormsby and Washoe in the State of Nevada each select one member; each member must be a resident of the county from which he is appointed and may be, in the discretion of the board of county commissioners, but is not required to be, a member of the board which appoints him and a resident or owner of real property in the region. The Administrator of the California Resources Agency, or his designee, and the Director of the Nevada Department of Conservation and Natural Resources, or his designee, are *ex officio* members of the board. Finally, the Governors of California and Nevada each appoint one member, who "shall not be a resident of the region and shall represent the public at large."

The Compact permits the Agency to receive fees for its services, gifts, grants and other financial aids. It also provides for Agency financing as follows: "* * * [O]n or before December 30 of each calendar year the agency shall establish the amount of money necessary to support its activities for the next succeeding fiscal year commencing July 1 of the following year. The agency shall apportion not more than $150,000 of this amount among the counties within the region on the same ratio to the total sum required as the full cash valuation of taxable property within the region in each county bears to the total full cash valuation of taxable property within the region. Each county in California shall pay the sum allotted to it by the agency from any funds available therefor and may levy a tax on any taxable property within its boundaries sufficient to pay the amount so allocated to it. Each county in Nevada shall pay such sum from its general fund or from any other moneys available therefor." * * *

The positions of the parties before us may be summarized as follows: the Attorney General contends that the respondent counties have a clear duty, imposed by the Compact, to pay their share of the funds necessary to support the activities of the Agency and that we should compel the performance of this duty by a writ of mandate. The counties contend * * * that they are not required to make any payments to the Agency because the Compact is unconstitutional and void. * * *

The counties first contend that the Compact violates former sections 11, 12 and 13 of article XI of the California Constitution. * * * Generally speaking, these sections confer upon specified local governmental bodies broad powers over purely local affairs. But, as we shall point out, the Compact is unaffected by any of the above provisions since its subject matter is of regional, rather than local, concern. * * * [T]he purpose of the Compact is to conserve the natural resources and control the environment of the Tahoe Basin as a whole through area-wide planning. * * * Only an agency transcending local boundaries can devise, adopt and put into operation solutions for the problems besetting the region as a whole. Indeed, the fact that the Compact is the product of the cooperative efforts and mutual agreement of two states is impressive proof that its subject matter and objectives are of regional rather than local concern.

Respondent counties * * * contend that the Compact violates former section 11 of article XI of the California Constitution. That section provided: "Any county, city, town or township may make and enforce within its limits all such local, police, sanitary and other regulations as are not in conflict with general laws." The counties argue that the Compact gives the Agency power to adopt local, police and sanitary ordinances, rules and regulations, violations of which are declared misdemeanors by section 66801, article VI, subdivision (f). According to their argument, "[t]hese powers have been granted to respondent counties by the California Constitution and there is, therefore, a violation of Article XI, section 11, of the California Constitution in any attempt to grant these same powers to the Agency." In support of this contention, the counties cite *In re Werner* (1900) 129 Cal. 567, 574, 62 P. 97.

In *Werner,* this court struck down a state statute which purported inter alia to grant a sanitary district the power "[t]o make and enforce all necessary and proper regulations for suppressing disorderly and disreputable resorts and houses of ill fame within the district, and to determine the qualifications of persons authorized to sell liquors at retail * * *." This court * * * held that section 11 prohibited the Legislature from granting a sanitary district a power "which clearly falls within the police powers possessed by cities and other like corporations formed and organized for governmental purposes. * * *." Certain broad language in *Werner* * * * appears to support the proposition that no power to make regulations having a local effect may be conferred upon public corporate bodies not enumerated in section 11. However, *Werner* * * * involved only the power to enact penal ordinances, and they have consistently been interpreted as forbidding only the delegation of power to prescribe penalties for violations of ordinances. * * * The instant case is clearly distinguishable from *Werner* * * * since the Legislature has not delegated to the Agency the power of enacting penal legislation. It is the Legislature itself which has properly declared that: "Violation of any ordinance of the agency is a misdemeanor."

Nor has the Legislature, as it is claimed, granted to the Agency the same powers which have been granted to respondent counties by section 11. * * * It is sufficient to point out that the powers exercised by respondents are for local purposes, within the limits of the county. But, as we have explained, the broad powers conferred upon the Agency are not for *local* purposes, but solely to achieve the *regional* goal of preserving the Lake Tahoe Basin—a goal which local bodies have been unable to attain. Indeed, the Compact specifically reserves to local entities matters within their proper sphere of action: "Whenever possible without diminishing the effectiveness of the * * * general plan, the ordinances, rules, regulations and policies [of the Agency] shall be confined to matters which are general and regional in application, leaving to the jurisdiction of the respective states, counties and cities the enactment of specific and local ordinances, rules, regulations and policies which conform to the * * * general plan." * * *

The counties next contend that the Compact legislation unconstitutionally imposes a tax on them in violation of former section 12 of article XI (now § 37 of art. XIII). Former section 12 provided: "Except as otherwise provided in this Constitution, the Legislature shall have no power to impose taxes upon counties, cities, towns or other public or municipal corporations, or upon the inhabitants or property thereof, for county, city, town, or other municipal purposes, but may, by general laws, vest in the corporate authorities thereof the power to assess and collect taxes for such purposes." Pursuant to section 66801, article VII, subdivision (a), the counties must pay to the Agency the amounts of money allotted to them by the Agency to support its activities, which amounts the counties may raise by levying taxes on property within their jurisdiction. It is argued that contrary to the mandate of section 12, such taxes are imposed for "county * * * purposes," since the functions for which the Agency will spend the money "are those traditionally assumed by appropriate units of local government." The point of the argument is that the Legislature, although indirectly, is attempting "to impose taxes upon counties * * * for county * * * purposes." * * * Contrary to the above claim, we have held that "[t]he limitations of section 12 do not prevent the Legislature from authorizing a district to impose taxes for a state purpose, nor for a purpose that transcends the boundaries of the various municipalities that may be included within the limits of a larger district." * * *

Finally, we consider the claim that the Compact violates former section 13 of article XI. That section provided: "The Legislature shall not delegate to any special commission, private corporation, company, association or individual any power to make, control, appropriate, supervise or in any way interfere with any county, city, town or municipal improvement, money, property, or effects, whether held in trust or otherwise, or to levy taxes or assessments or perform any municipal function whatever * * *." The counties assert that the Agency is a "special commission" within the purview of the section and that the Legislature has unconstitutionally delegated to it the power to "interfere with" county improvements and to "perform" municipal functions. We find no merit in the contention. * * *

Although section 13 was intended primarily to prevent legislative interference with the financial affairs of municipalities, its prohibition extends to other forms of interference. However, our cases have recognized "that the section was intended to prohibit only legislation interfering with purely local matters. Special commissions have been upheld if they either fulfill a more than local purpose, under the 'larger municipality' doctrine, or promote a 'statewide purpose.'" * * * In the case at bench, the Compact was enacted to serve regional, not merely local, purposes. Indeed, here, one of the reasons for the establishment of the

Agency was the inability of the myriad of local entities to cope with the problem of preserving the Tahoe Basin. The Compact does not give the Agency power to build or maintain local parks or other improvements; it merely grants the Agency authority to assure that public works which are planned, built and maintained by appropriate local bodies do not interfere with the fulfillment of the regional plan. Any restriction upon local improvements is merely incidental to the execution of the Agency's regional duties. Consequently, the Compact does not violate former section 13 of article XI of the California Constitution. * * *

NOTE ON THE GEORGIA REGIONAL TRANSPORTATION AUTHORITY

As we have seen, there are a variety of ways that a state might respond to metropolitan fragmentation. One way to respond is to establish a kind of super-agency that is chiefly responsible for handling a particular interlocal problem. There is perhaps no better exemplar of this response than the recently established Georgia Regional Transportation Authority (GRTA).

In recent years, Atlanta has become a symbol of urban sprawl, earning the dubious moniker, "the new Los Angeles." Population in the Atlanta metropolitan statistical area has more than doubled since 1970, and suburban Gwinnett County, north of Atlanta, had the highest population growth of any county in the nation during the 1980s. Such growth has not been geographically compact. The Atlanta metropolitan area extends 110 miles across and consists of more than 6000 square miles. Increased traffic is but one of the many problematic consequences of the seemingly ceaseless outward suburban growth around Atlanta. There is little in the way of mass transit in the region, and a resident on average drives 35 miles a day, more than 15 miles more than a resident of the Los Angeles area. The resulting congestion on roads and highways has made transportation in and around Atlanta difficult, and it has resulted in dramatically increased air pollution.[41]

The decrease in the region's air quality set in motion a sequence of events that led to the establishment of the GRTA, one of the more significant reforms in urban governance in recent years. A federal statute served as the direct catalyst for the state reform effort. The Clean Air Act requires the Environmental Protection Agency to establish the National Ambient Air Quality Standards. States and localities must formulate plans to implement the standards, which the federal government then must certify in order for states and localities to be able to receive federal highway funds. The air pollution crisis in the Atlanta region continued to grow more severe throughout the 1990s, and the region's accompanying inability to formulate an implementation plan placed the state of Georgia at risk of losing nearly $1 billion in federal highway funds.

---

[41] See Orlyn Lockard, Note, Solving the "Tragedy": Transportation, Pollution and Regionalism in Atlanta, 19 Va. Envt'l. L. J. 161 (2000).

In 1999, after running a campaign focused on addressing problems of regional growth and transportation, Georgia Governor Roy Barnes proposed the GRTA as a dramatic response. The proposal became law less than two months after Governor Barnes took office. Prior to the formation of the GRTA, there was no central agency specifically charged with setting transportation policy for the Atlanta region. The Atlanta Regional Commission came closest to playing that role, but it possessed no legal authority to override the planning and land use decisions of localities within the region. The GRTA has far greater powers. See Georgia Regional Transportation Authority Act, S.B. 57, 145th Gen. Assem., Reg. Sess., 1999 Ga. Laws 112.

The GRTA has jurisdiction over those counties that are not now in compliance with national air quality standards. It is governed by a Board of Directors that consists of 15 members, but new seats are to be added if additional counties are brought under the authority's jurisdiction. The governor appoints each director for a multi-year term and each director is subject to removal by the governor for specified causes. There are no residency requirements for appointees, although appointees are to "reasonably reflect the characteristics of the general public within the jurisdiction or potential jurisdiction of the authority." Indeed, residency requirements were rejected in part to ensure that a "super-expert" would not be denied an appointment merely because of such a requirement.

The law gives the GRTA the power to build, operate and maintain (or to force localities to build, operate, and maintain) public transportation systems, other land transportation projects, and air quality control facilities. The GRTA has the authority to provide technical assistance to the state and to local governments; to coordinate and assist in planning among state, regional and local authorities for land transportation and air quality purposes; and to adopt regional plans based on such planning efforts. The Authority serves as the receiver of federal funds for purposes "related to the alleviation of air congestion and air pollution." The GRTA also has the power to control or limit access to any part of a state, county, or city road or highway, and the full power to review and approve, by a two-thirds vote of the directors, transportation plans and improvement programs.

Significantly, the new law provides that localities will be penalized for failing to comply with the GRTA's planning determinations.

> No local government which * * * fails or refuses to plan, coordinate, and implement local government services as provided for in this chapter and authorized pursuant to a resolution of the authority * * * shall be eligible for any state grant of any kind whatsoever except as such grants may be related directly to the physical, mental health, education, and police protection of its residents, nor shall any funds appropriated to or otherwise obtained by the Department of Transportation be utilized for designation, improvement, funding, or construction of any land public

transportation system or any part of the state highway system lying within the boundaries of such local government's jurisdiction * * * nor shall such local government be permitted to receive federal grants or funds for any such purpose.* * *

The precise scope of the GRTA's power over state and local land use development policy is not clear. One commentator has explained that it could potentially be very broad.

> The GRTA has two direct ways in which it can influence local land-use planning and development decision-making. First, it has the power to define "developments of regional impact" (DRIs), review them (presumably for consistency with air quality targets and standards as well as consistency with transportation lands) and, if local governments decide to allow their development, the GRTA can withhold the use of any state and federal transportation and other funds that may be spent on behalf of the project. * * * Depending on how the GRTA defines DRIs, however, this authority over local land use decision-making may be limited to a few large projects and still may not prevent those DRIs rejected by the GRTA from proceeding.

> A more direct way in which the GRTA may become involved in local land-use planning is through its ability to control or limit access to any road in the state highway system, county road system or municipal street system within its jurisdiction. * * * Although it has yet to describe how it may use these powers, one can imagine several possibilities. For example, it could simply deny access of DRIs to roads, thereby eliminating the potential for local governments to by-pass the GRTA's findings and decisions. * * * It could also limit the number of dwelling units that could take access from roads in rural or exurban areas, thereby minimizing the long-distance commuting and air pollution associated with such sprawl. * * * This power conceivably allows the GRTA to compel local governments to prepare land-use plans that preserve open spaces from development and concentrate development along transportation corridors and in nodes where transit stations may be located.[42]

The GRTA reflects a particular vision of politics in general and state/local political relations in particular. Notice that its members comprise a "Board of Directors" and that they are appointed rather than elected. Are there any federal constitutional constraints that might make it undesirable to choose board members by elections? Notice also that there are no residency requirements for a majority of the board members. Should there be residency requirements for all board members?

---

[42] Arthur Nelson, New Kid in Town: The Georgia Regional Transportation Authority and Its Role in Managing Growth in Metropolitan Georgia, 35 Wake Forest L. Rev. 625 (2000).

An additional point to consider concerns the authority's jurisdiction. Like most special authorities, the GRTA has responsibility for a particular issue: transportation. Notice in this regard that the law provides that the Authority serves as the receiver of federal funds for purposes "related to the alleviation of traffic congestion and air pollution." Given the range of issues that could be said to be related to the alleviation of traffic congestion and air pollution, from housing to labor standards to industrial policy, would it be appropriate to have the GRTA assume jurisdiction over all such issues? Suppose GRTA thought that the traffic congestion could not be solved unless federally-funded public housing was located in suburbs, or parts of central cities, that were reluctant to agree to such a siting. Should GRTA have the authority to use its enforcement mechanisms to overcome such resistance? If not, is it because the siting of public housing seems only tangentially related to the problems of traffic congestion and air quality?

Perhaps the problem inheres in the breadth of GRTA's power, rather than in its narrowness. Remember in *Younger* the California Supreme Court rejected the counties' home rule challenge to the Tahoe Regional Planning Agency; it concluded that the counties retained power over local matters, such as the opening of local parks. Does the GRTA effectively assume powers over all local land use decisions, at least with respect to those localities now within its jurisdiction?

In a related vein, the state created the GRTA in response to a particular problem: traffic congestion and the resulting air pollution. Some argue that the GRTA's speedy creation, coming into being only two months after first being proposed, provides evidence that the problems caused by metropolitan fragmentation can be addressed. One might argue in response, however, that the GRTA's swift creation shows only that metropolitan fragmentation privileges certain regional issues—those of particular concern to suburbanites—over other equally important regional issues. Is it conceivable, for example, that a similar authority could have been established with such swiftness to respond to a crisis in affordable housing, inner-city crime, public education, or even inequities in public transportation subsidies?

3. REGIONAL PLANNING

Land use planning is a key area in which reformers have sought regional solutions. The first excerpt briefly recounts the history of the relationship between regional planning and public land use regulation. The excerpt explains that zoning, the most important type of public land use regulation, became a local function only because of central intervention—first through federal prodding and then later through express state delegations. The excerpt explains as well that the initial vision of zoning embodied in the United States Department of Commerce Standard City Planning Enabling Act included an important regional component. In addition to setting forth the zoning powers of cities, the model act set forth the powers of a regional planning commission. Does the approach to regional planning adopted by the model act seem like a good one? Does the history of how cities came to exercise the zoning power affect your view of the proper answer to that question? The excerpt concludes with brief descriptions of the approach to regional planning that some states have adopted. They are intended to invite comparisons with the model act's proposed regional planning body as well as a legal regime that contemplates no regional planning at all. In evaluating these various planning approaches, consider whether it is a mistake to limit regional planning to the formulation of a plan for the "the physical development of the region."

To the extent that regional planning depends upon local input, it need not be understood simply as a supplement to local zoning or planning. What relationship is there between local and regional planning? To answer that question, one must consider whether cities should relate to each other over such matters in terms of the number of individuals in each city or simply as city entities. This is the question raised in the *Moore* case in terms of the Constitutional requirement of one person/one vote. The case concerns planning powers in particular, but it raises broader questions about regionalism as well. Which of the opinions in the case has the better argument about how councils of government have to be organized? Will large communities deal with small communities as equals only if each of them has equal representation? Alternatively, will communities deal with each other as equals only if representation is weighted according to population?

AMERICAN PLANNING ASSOCIATION, GROWING SMART LEGISLATIVE GUIDEBOOK: MODEL STATUTES FOR PLANNING AND THE MANAGEMENT OF CHANGE, PHASES I AND II, 2002 EDITION, JANUARY 2002
6–7—6–11, 6–15, 6–27 (2002).

The Standard City Planning Enabling Act (SCPEA), drafted by an advisory committee to the U.S. Department of Commerce and published in 1928, contained model legislation for regional planning. The SCPEA authorized the planning commission of any municipality or the county commissioners of any county to petition the governor to establish a planning region and create a planning commission for that region. The governor was to hold at least one public hearing before making a determination to grant the application, define the region, and appoint the regional planning commission.

Under the SCPEA model, the regional planning commission was composed of nine members, all of whom would be appointed and removed by the governor. The commission had the authority to prepare, adopt, and amend a "master regional plan for the physical development of the region." After adopting the plan, the regional planning commission was required to certify it to the governor, to the planning commission of each municipality in the region, to the council of each municipality that did not have a planning commission, to the county commissioners of each county located wholly or partially in the region, and to other organized taxing districts or political subdivisions wholly or partially included in the region.

Adoption of the regional plan by the municipal planning commission was optional; however, once the regional planning commission adopted it, the plan would have the same force and effect as a plan made and adopted locally. In addition, the municipal planning commission, "[b]efore adopting any amendment of the municipal plan which would constitute a violation of or departure from the regional plan certified to the municipal planning commission," was required to submit the amendment to the regional commission. The regional commission would then "certify to the municipal commission its approval, disapproval or other opinion concerning the proposed amendment."

Once the regional plan was adopted by the regional planning commission, no street, park, or other public way, ground, or open space; no public building or other public structure; and no public utility, whether publicly or privately owned or operated, could be constructed or authorized in unincorporated territory until the project was submitted to and approved by the regional planning commission. However, the planning commission's disapproval could be overruled by the body or officer having authority to determine the location, character, or extent of the improvement, provided that, in the case of a board, commission, or body, not less than two-thirds of its membership voted to do so and provided a statement of reasons for such overruling in the minutes of records of the body or officer. * * *

The federal government, through the National Planning Board (later the National Resources Committee) in the Department of the Interior, provided the major push for metropolitan, regional, state, and interstate planning. * * * By the end of the 1930s, according to a report of the U.S. Advisory Commission on Intergovernmental Relations, federal support had greatly expanded metropolitan and regional planning:

> In 1934, there were only 85 metropolitan and county planning bodies and 23 regional planning agencies in existence. By January 1937, there were 506 metropolitan multicounty and county planning agencies, of which at least 316 were official public bodies. Two years later, metropolitan planning agencies or regional planning boards, commissions, or associations were operating in at least 30 major cities. In addition to these metropolitan developments, by the close of the decade areawide

planning had also been extended to a number of small urban areas and several nonmetropolitan regions. * * *

In the 1950s, federal aid for comprehensive planning became available with the enactment of Section 701 of the Housing Act of 1954. This statute provided monies for local planning and planning for metropolitan areas by official regional or metropolitan planning agencies.

According to a study by the U.S. Advisory Commission on Intergovernmental Relations, at least 13 states passed regional planning enabling acts in the three years following the enactment of the 1954 Housing Act. This set the stage for a tremendous increase in the number of multijurisdictional planning organizations. During this period, according to the ACIR, the legislatures of at least nine of these states enacted legislation requiring or permitting the establishment of planning agencies for entire urbanized areas. The statutes usually authorized the agencies to apply for and receive federal grants. Some states adopted specific statutes that created planning commissions for certain metropolitan areas. By the beginning of the 1960s, some two-thirds of the nation's metropolitan areas were engaged in some type of areawide planning.

Complementing the "701" program was the Federal-Aid Highway Act of 1962. This statute required a "cooperative, comprehensive, and continuous" planning process as a prerequisite for federal financial assistance for interstate highway development in metropolitan areas. The act required regional transportation plans in urban areas with populations more than 50,000 as a condition to construction funds. In contrast to the "701" grants, which split cost evenly with local governments, the Highway Act provided matching grants of 70 percent of the cost of preparing the necessary studies.

In some parts of the U.S., metropolitan transportation planning was assigned to a special commission or entity. This was the case, and still is, in Boston, San Francisco, and Chicago. In others, the transportation planning function was assumed by a regional planning commission or metropolitan councils of government (COG), which were voluntary alliances of local governments formed to undertake planning or any type of joint governmental activity that its members could agree upon. * * * The expansion of COGs, prompted by the availability of federal funding, was dramatic. In 1961, for example, there were only 36 COGs, including 25 among the 212 metropolitan areas. By 1966, this number included 119 councils, of which 71 were metropolitan. By 1971, there were 247 metropolitan areas, and all of them had official regional planning, mostly under elected COGs. By 1978, there were 649 councils in the U.S. Of these, 292 were in metropolitan areas.

Four federal laws were responsible for this expansion, and they were all enacted in a watershed year of 1965. The Housing and Community Development Act of 1965 made regional councils eligible for planning funds. The Public Works and Economic Development Act of 1965 provided funding for multicounty economic development districts and authorized the establishment of federal multistate economic development commissions. The Appalachian Regional Development Act established the multistate Appalachian Regional Commission, which accomplished its work through multicounty development districts. Finally, the Water Resources Planning Act of 1965 authorized the establishment of federal multistate river basin commissions. Under Circular A–95, promulgated by the U.S. Office of Management and Budget, regional agencies received authority to review applications for federal assistance for compliance with regional and local plans. In addition, regional agencies began to prepare regional water-quality management plans under Section 208 of the federal Clean Water Act of 1972. * * *

In the 1980s, the federal government withdrew almost entirely from its support of regional planning. "Of the 39 programs designed and enacted during the preceding two decades to promote regional organization," wrote Bruce McDowell, "only one—metropolitan transportation planning—remained relatively unscathed by this sudden reversal of federal policy." In the multistate programs, which had created most river basin and economic development regions, the federal government withdrew funding and the organizations died. Only multistate agencies created by federal law or interstate compact survived. The federal economic development programs, through the Economic Development Administration, and the Appalachian programs managed to continue, but in greatly abbreviated form. * * *

An ongoing issue for some regional planning agencies is the matter of voting. Most regional agencies are structured and expected to function like a senate, with each member community having an equal vote. * * * [T]he U.S. Advisory Commission on Intergovernmental Relations proposed in the 1970s that regional agencies have the option of allowing proportionate-population weighted voting in certain issues, such as actions that would affect the finances and operations of constituent local governments. As regional agencies move into areas that are less advisory and more legislative, such as ranking transportation projects for a metropolitan area or approving policies that have distributional consequences, a weighted voting mechanism, either mandatory or optional, may be desirable. Indeed, a number of regional agencies * * * have various forms of weighted voting based on a jurisdiction's proportion to the total regional population. A 1994 ACIR analysis of 86 metropolitan planning organizations * * * that undertake regional transportation

planning found population-weighted voting in 18 MPOs in 10 states and the District of Columbia. * * *

EDUCATION/INSTRUCCION V. MOORE

United States Court of Appeals, Second Circuit, 1974.
503 F.2d 1187, cert. denied, 419 U.S. 1109, 95 S.Ct. 783, 42 L.Ed.2d 806 (1975).

Before LUMBARD, OAKES and TIMBERS, CIRCUIT JUDGES.

PER CURIAM: * * *

Plaintiffs are a non-profit Connecticut corporation organized for educational, charitable and cultural purposes, together with three individual citizens of Connecticut, two of whom reside in the City of Hartford and one in the Town of Windsor. Defendants are the Chairman of the Capitol Regional Planning Agency (CRPA), the Chairman of the Capitol Region Council of Governments (CRCOG), the Secretary of the United States Department of Housing and Urban Development (HUD), the Regional Director of that Department and twenty-nine individuals who are the chief elected officials of the twenty-nine towns which comprise the Capitol Region (i.e. the Hartford area). * * *

Plaintiffs challenge on equal protection grounds Public Act 821 which provides for the restructuring of the existing CRPA and CRCOG to create a new regional council of government if approved by at least 60% of the towns within the planning region—here, the Hartford area. Each member town of the new council is entitled to one representative on the council, such representative to be the chief elected official of that town.

The gravamen of plaintiffs' claim is that the Act's restructuring of the present regional bodies to create a new regional council in the Hartford area will result in under-representation of the City of Hartford on the new council. In the past Hartford has had five representatives on CRPA, or 8% of that body's membership. On the new council Hartford will have four representatives. A 1973 amendment gave Hartford four representatives on the council instead of the one initially provided, the three additional council members to be appointed by Hartford's city council. Hartford has a population of approximately 160,000, or about 24% of the regional population. Thus, plaintiffs argue, Hartford's vote will be greatly diluted, as compared for example with the Town of Andover, whose population is approximately 2,000, which will have one vote. Plaintiffs' claim in essence is that the legislature's failure to apportion the new regional council on a one man, one vote basis denies them the equal protection of the laws in violation of the Fourteenth Amendment. * * *

The critical question raised by defendants' motion to dismiss the complaint for failure to state a claim upon which relief can be granted is whether the proposed regional council of government for the Hartford

area is subject to the one man, one vote requirement. The district court held that it is not. We agree.

The statute in question does not provide for elective bodies.[3] The councils do not exercise general governmental powers, nor do they perform governmental functions, within the meaning of *Hadley v. Junior College District*, 397 U.S. 50 (1970), and *Avery v. Midland County*, 390 U.S. 474 (1968). Indeed, the councils do not have even the minimal governmental powers found insufficient to invoke the one man, one vote principle in the Supreme Court's most recent decisions in *Salyer Land Co. v. Tulare Water District*, 410 U.S. 719, 728 n. 7, 729 (1973), and *Associated Enterprises, Inc. v. Toltec District*, 410 U.S. 743 (1973).

The powers and functions of the councils are essentially to acquire information, to advise, to comment and to propose. As Judge Clarie aptly put it:

> "To the extent that the [council] is able to provide a forum for an interchange of ideas and an atmosphere conducive to the development of solutions to regional problems which know no geographic boundaries, its importance should not be minimized. But this does not bar recognition of the fact that it would be essentially advisory and non-governmental in both purpose and function, and the type of body which need not be apportioned on a strict numerical basis. As such, the [council] represents the kind of flexible experimentation which the Supreme Court has consistently recognized as being both desirable and constitutionally permissible."

We agree. * * *

OAKES, CIRCUIT JUDGE (dissenting): * * *

On the crucial question whether the new Council of Governments established in the Hartford area (COG) pursuant to the above state provisions exercises general governmental powers within the ambit of *Avery v. Midland County* and *Hadley v. Junior College District*, it seems to me that neither the COG nor its predecessor bodies, the Capitol Region Planning Agency (CRPA) and Capitol Region Council of Governments (CRCOG), can be considered solely in the light of the statutory authority delegated by the State of Connecticut, as the majority considers them. Rather, we must look to the overall role of the agency in question in the

---

[3]   The district court did not find it necessary to determine whether members of the council are elected or appointed, since the council clearly does not exercise general governmental powers nor does it perform governmental functions. We do note, however, that at least some members of the council do not automatically become council members by virtue of their election to office in their respective towns. The three additional members from Hartford, referred to above, are appointed by the city council under Special Act 73–79. And at least the members from West Hartford, Wethersfield and Glastonbury are selected by the respective town councils after the voters elect the councils themselves.

federal system as a whole. A regional planning body such as COG, though a creature of state law, is established with a view to its functions under federal law and the federal system. A regional planning agency cannot be looked at while wearing state-oriented blinders when one of its principal purposes is to play a substantial role in the decision-making process involved in the dispensation of federal funds affecting all the citizens of the affected area.

The test of performing governmental powers must be one based on economic reality, not the mechanical application of nineteenth century municipal law. For example, 42 U.S.C. § 3334 requires that any application for a federal loan or grant for the planning or construction of hospitals, libraries, sewers, water and sewage treatment facilities, highways, mass transit, airports or other transportation facilities, recreation, or open-space development must be submitted for review to an areawide agency, which in this case would be COG. COG may then comment and make its recommendations whether the application should be granted or not. Primary emphasis is given to whether the project would be consistent with comprehensive planning and whether the project contributes to the fulfillment of such planning. Supplementary grants, amounting to as much as any original grant, can be made, but only when there is a showing that the project will be "carried out in accord with areawide [comprehensive] planning and programming." In making the determination whether a project is in accord with an areawide plan, "the Secretary shall obtain, and give full consideration to, the comments of [the areawide planning bodies]." In other words, federal law provides a carrot and stick approach to insure that local governments comply with the area plan. Thus, while COG may have no statutory power under state law to affect local governments, being limited to planning functions, in light of the federal statutes COG's plans themselves can affect local government's abilities to receive federal funds and COG's comments on localities' applications may be altogether determinative.

Not only does the Connecticut COG have an ability to affect the approval of individual municipalities' applications for grants by the exercise of its planning function, but also the local municipalities are dependent upon the COG for establishment of a proper plan in the first instance. Thus, if COG does not do its job—failing to create an areawide plan or creating an areawide plan which does not meet federal requirements—even a non-member municipality's application for a grant for water and sewer facilities or an open space land program may be disapproved for failure to be part of a proper areawide plan.

This control of the purse strings for the building of such a large assortment of facilities is essentially "governmental" in nature in a day and age when municipalities are frequently financially incapable of total

self-reliance. In *Hadley,* the power to tax and spend was an important governmental power had by the district; in the year 1974 having a principal hand on the faucet of federal grants must be treated as at least as important as the local power to tax, especially where federal grants may pay up to 80 per cent of facilities' costs, especially since in so many cases the municipalities' powers to tax are often being exercised to their outer limits.

Beyond this, the COG has important powers under, *e.g.,* the Intergovernmental Cooperation Act, 42 U.S.C. § 4201 et seq., and NEPA, 42 U.S.C. § 4321 et seq. In this instance it also happens to operate a regional crime squad (with the help of LEAA money), engages in joint purchasing efforts and otherwise performs important functions that may properly be characterized as governmental in nature. * * *

None of this, of course, is to say that there must be the same precision in formulating a proper system of apportionment of representation on a regional planning agency as in a state legislature, just as state legislative reapportionment is not subject to the same strict standards as congressional reapportionment. Nor is it to fail to recognize the point underlying Mr. Justice Harlan's dissent in *Avery* that in a given case a regional planning agency may be of more concern to the rural members thereof than to the urban residents involved. These are considerations which could be taken into account, however, in establishing a formula which more equally protects or represents the people of Hartford than the one ultimately adopted, under the threat of this law suit, by the Connecticut Assembly by special act. Under the majority decision today, regional planning agencies for metropolitan areas may be weighted in representational makeup one-sidedly against the urban area in favor of the outlying suburbs and towns, and thus the central cities of states with a state legislature dominated by rural or suburban towns left behind the door when facilities or services requiring federal funding are established.

While the district court did not reach the question and the majority mentions it only in passing, a subsidiary question is whether, since there is no direct election of the members of the new COG as such, this case falls within the rule of *Sailors v. Board of Education,* 387 U.S. 105, 87 S.Ct. 1549, 18 L.Ed.2d 650 (1967), that makes the one-man one-vote doctrine of *Reynolds v. Sims* inapplicable to non-elected officials. The Connecticut statutes, however, make it very clear the COG will be basically composed of the "chief elected official" from each member town or city. Conn.Gen.Stat.Ann. § 4–124k. The "chief elected official" means "the highest ranking elected governmental official of any town, city or borough," and the term "elected official" means "any selectman, mayor, alderman or member of a common council or other similar legislative body * * *." While the case is one not precisely controlled by precedent in this

respect, it seems closest to *Bianchi v. Griffing*, 393 F.2d 457 (2d Cir.1968), where persons elected as town supervisors automatically became members of the county board of supervisors. Here as there the fact is that these officials are *elected*, they are not appointed, and the one office (that of "chief elected official") carries with it automatic membership on the regional council.

From all this it seems clear to me that there is a sufficiently substantial question of constitutionality as to require the convening of a three-judge court.

4. REGIONAL GOVERNMENT

The following excerpts by David Rusk and by Margaret Weir introduce a fourth institutional structure—beyond interlocal agreements, public authorities, and regional planning requirements—that might deal with problems in our metropolitan areas that cross local boundaries, namely, regional government.[43] Regional governments are less common in the United States than interlocal agreements, regional planning requirements, or public authorities. Nevertheless, versions of regional government do exist—for example, in Portland (Oregon), Indianapolis-Marion County (Indiana), Miami-Dade County (Florida), and Minneapolis-St. Paul (Minnesota)—and the materials that follow describe some of them in greater detail.

The Rusk excerpt is an advocacy piece. It is written by someone who wants to expand the current (relatively modest) forms of regional government into a major new type of local governmental organization. The excerpt therefore provides an opportunity to consider the arguments for creating strong regional governments in America. Does the author persuade you that regional governments are a good idea? If we created

---

[43] For additional reading on regional governments, see, e.g., Lisa Alexander, The Promise and Perils of "New Regionalist" Approaches to Sustainable Communities, 38 Fordham Urb. L.J. 629 (2011); Nestor Davidson, Fostering Regionalism: Comment on the Promise and Perils of "New Regionalist" Approaches to Sustainable Communities, 38 Fordham Urb. L.J. 675 (2011); Craig Bucki, Regionalism Revisted: The Effort to Streamline Governance in Buffalo and Erie County, New York, 71 Alb. L. Rev. 117 (2008); Laurie Reynolds, Local Governments and Regional Governance, 39 Urb. Law. 483 (2007); Janice C. Griffith, Regional Governance Reconsidered, 21 J.L. & Pol. 505 (2005); Myron Orfield, American Metropolitics: The New Suburban Reality (2002); Bruce Katz (ed.), Reflections on Regionalism (2000); Myron Orfield, Metropolitics: A Regional Agenda for Community and Stability (1997); H.V. Savitch & Ronald Vogel (eds.), Regional Politics: America in a Post-City Age (1996); Donald Rothblatt and Andrew Sancton (eds.), Metropolitan Governance: American-Canadian Intergovernmental Perspectives (1993); Kenneth Brunetti, Note, It's Time to Create a Bay Area Regional Government, 42 Hastings L. J. 1103 (1991); C. James Owen and York Willburn, Governing Metropolitan Indianapolis: The Politics of Unigov (1985); Richard Gustely, The Allocational and Distributional Impacts of Governmental Consolidation: The Dade County Experience, 14 Urb. Aff. Q. 349 (1977); Advisory Commission on Intergovernmental Relations, A Look to the North: Canadian Regional Experience, Substate Regionalism and the Federal System (1974); Robert Freilich et al., Home Rule for the Urban County: Observations on the New Jackson County Constitutional Charter, 39 UMKC L. Rev. 297 (1971); Note, The Urban County: A Study of New Approaches to Local Government in Metropolitan Areas, 73 Harv. L. Rev. 526 (1960).

strong regional governments in our metropolitan areas, would it be accurate to describe them as exercising "decentralized" or "local" power?

The Note on Regional Governments that follows the Rusk article identifies governmental forms that attempt to create a regional governance structure. These approaches establish regional governance without relying solely on inter-local cooperation, the establishment of limited-jurisdiction public authorities, an exclusive focus on land use planning, or the establishment of a full-fledged, consolidated regional government. Are the structures identified in the note consistent with Rusk's vision of regional government? Finally, Margaret Weir's article contrasts the political circumstances that led to the successful regional government in Oregon and Minnesota with those that undermined regional solutions in California and Illinois. Like Rusk, Weir clearly believes that regional solutions are desirable. Does her description of the alternatives in California and Illinois (what she characterizes as failures) convince you that regionalism is necessary? Could her sympathetic description of the politics that gave rise to regional government—grass roots political activism in Oregon and enlightened experts in Minnesota— be recast as special interest capture and metropolitan elitism? Consider the political impediments to regionalism in light of the earlier readings on exclusion and sprawl. Weir's article suggests that similar conditions promote both problems and that regionalism is a potential solution to both.

DAVID RUSK, CITIES WITHOUT SUBURBS
Pp. 85, 91–95, 122–124 (1993).

Reversing the fragmentation of urban areas is an essential step in ending severe racial and economic segregation. The "city" must be redefined to reunify city and suburb. Ideally, such reunification is achieved through metropolitan government. * * * Having a metropolitan government is much better than trying to get multiple local governments to act like a metropolitan government. The former is a more lasting and stable framework for sustained, long-term action. * * *

There are three different ways metropolitan governments can be created. In single-county metro areas, urban county governments can be fully empowered and municipal governments abolished; or county and municipal governments can be consolidated into new, unified governments. In multicounty metro areas, cities and existing counties can be combined into a single, regional government. Each of these three options will be discussed in turn.

Empowering urban counties. Except in New England, counties have been the basic framework of local government within which municipalities (a more intensive form of local government) come into being. Counties typically predate urban development. They are the creation of a state or territorial legislature, which initially partitioned the state or territory's land into large governing units. County jurisdictions are remarkably stable. There are today 3,042 counties in the United States; forty years ago there were 3,052 counties. (Such stability has given rise to the adage that "the legislature may create municipalities, but only God can create a county.")

County government has been the government of rural and small-town America. As urbanization occurs, municipalities are formed to control development through planning and zoning and to provide a more intensive level of local services. Generally, county government continues to be responsible countywide (including within municipalities) for certain services—the county courts (state criminal trials), county assessor (property tax assessment), county treasurer (property tax collection), county clerk (records and elections), and often a county hospital (indigent health care). In addition, counties provide public services (roads, parks, fire and police protection) to unincorporated areas of the county.

Over the decades, however, as areas have urbanized around older cities, counties have been empowered by legislatures to provide full municipal-type services to unincorporated areas. Urban county governments often rival or exceed major city governments in size and scope. Moreover, although county government is often more limited in the array of taxes it can levy, its tax base is much broader than that of municipal governments within its boundaries. (County government bond ratings are typically one full level above bond ratings of inelastic central cities located within them.)

County government, when developed to the greatest extent, becomes a major deliverer of urban services, such as the government of Los Angeles County. County government may become the dominant local unit of government, both providing services and controlling area development. Montgomery County, Maryland, is an outstanding example * * *.

The most direct—and probably most efficient—path to creating metropolitan government in the majority of metro areas is to empower urban county government, have it absorb the functions and responsibilities of all municipal governments within its boundaries, and abolish all municipalities. This is an action that is fully within the legal powers of most state legislatures even if at present such sweeping urban reorganization is beyond legislators' desires and political powers.

Consolidating cities and counties. Typically, movements to create area wide governmental units have focused on consolidating municipal governments with their surrounding county governments. In recent decades the most notable consolidations have merged the central city with single counties. Indianapolis-Marion County, Nashville-Davidson County, Jacksonville-Duval County are examples. * * *

Each city-county consolidation has been custom-made for its area. The ultimate structure represents a compromise with tradition and political realities. Traditional functions of county government may be absorbed into the new, unified government (Nashville-Davidson) or continued as independent functions while the new government assumes service-providing functions for all unincorporated areas (Indianapolis-Marion County). Bowing to political reality, certain municipal enclaves may remain (for example, the town of Speedway within Indianapolis), and rural residents may have to be reassured through creation of lower service, lower tax zones (Nashville).

Despite such compromises, city-county consolidations do initially achieve the key goals: unification of the tax base and centralization of planning and zoning authority. With the continued spread of suburbia and long-distance commuting, the long-term dilemma is that metro areas often grow beyond the consolidated boundaries of the consolidated governments. Indianapolis-Marion County, Nashville-Davidson County, and Jacksonville-Duval County were all highly successful consolidations of the 1960s. Today Indianapolis-Marion County is 59 percent of its ten-county metro area; Nashville-Davidson, 50 percent of its six-county area; and Jacksonville-Duval County, 70 percent of its five-county area. With the populations of outlying counties growing rapidly, their metropolitanization must be updated.

Combining counties into regional governments. The most significant multicounty combination is also the least remembered: the creation of New York City in 1898 * * *. Several independent local communities in what are now New York City's five boroughs were combined. For its first fifty years the consolidated result—New York City—functioned very well. Since the 1950s, however, the consequences of the White middle-class movement to the suburbs and the burgeoning low-income Black and Hispanic populations within the city have largely obscured New York City's earlier success as a consolidated, multicounty regional government. * * *

Conclusion and Recommendations

* * * Throughout history cities have been the arena of opportunity and upward mobility. In America the "city" has been redefined since World War II. The real city is now the whole urban area—city and suburb—the metropolitan area. Redeeming inner cities and the urban underclass requires reintegration of city and suburb.

This is the toughest political issue in American society. It goes right to the heart of Americans' fears about race and class. There will be no short-term, politically comfortable solutions.

The organization of metro areas into local governments has greatly affected the degree of racial and economic segregation. Within their expanding municipal boundaries, elastic cities have captured much of the growth of the suburbs. Elastic cities minimize city-suburb disparities, thereby lessening the separations between racial and economic groups.

Inelastic cities, in the battle over middle-class America, have lost to their suburbs. Some never even fought the good fight. Whatever the success of their downtown as regional employment centers, inelastic city neighborhoods have increasingly housed most of the metro area's poor Blacks and Hispanics.

How can responsibility for poor minorities be made a metropolitan-wide responsibility? How can all jurisdictions—city and suburb—assume a "fair share"?

Traditionally, the primary purpose of regional cooperation among local governments has been the delivery of public services. Regional arrangements usually avoid policies and programs that share the social burdens of inner-city residents. Yet this is the heart of the challenge. Areawide compacts on transportation planning, solid waste management, sewage treatment, and air quality management may be "good government," but they address the urban problem only if they attack racial and economic segregation.

For many small and medium-sized metro areas, the surest way to avoid or reverse patterns of racial and economic segregation is to create metro governments. This can be achieved by expanding the central city through aggressive annexation policies, by consolidating the city and county, or by fully empowering county government and abolishing or reducing the role of municipalities.

For larger, more complex metro areas, metro government may be neither politically feasible nor administratively desirable. Larger government is not necessarily more efficient government. At any scale, efficiency is largely a function of good management. Given the bureaucratic impulse of many large systems, metro government may be less efficient and less responsive as a deliverer of services than smaller governments.

It is not important that local residents have their garbage picked up by a metrowide garbage service or their parks managed by a metrowide parks and recreation department. It is important that all local governments pursue common policies that will diminish racial and economic segregation. The following four policies are essential:

1. "fair share" housing policies (supported by planning and zoning policies) that will encourage low-and moderate income housing in all jurisdictions;

2.   fair employment and fair housing policies to ensure full access by minorities to the job and housing markets;

3.   housing assistance policies to disperse low-income families to small-unit, scattered-site housing projects and to rent-subsidized private rental housing throughout a diversified metro housing market; and

4.   tax-sharing arrangements that will offset tax-base disparities between the central city and its suburbs.

In baldest terms, sustained success requires moving poor people from bad city neighborhoods to good suburban neighborhoods and moving dollars from relatively wealthy suburban governments to poorer city governments. The long-term payoff will be an overall reduction in poverty, dependency, and crime areawide, and "prosperous cities [which] are the key to vital regional economies and to safe and healthy suburbs."

State government must play the leading role. Local government is the creature of state government, which sets the ground rules for local initiative and can create new local governments and merge old ones. Furthermore, governors and state legislators can and do act as metrowide policymakers. State government also plays an increasingly important role in revenue sharing for local government. With the purse comes additional power (and responsibility) to make the organization of metro areas more rational and equitable.

State government must act. It must

1.   improve annexation laws to facilitate continuous central city expansion into urbanizing areas;

2.   enact laws to encourage city-county consolidation through local initiative or to reorganize local government by direct state statute;

3.   empower county governments with all municipal powers so that they can act as de facto metro governments, where appropriate;

4.   require all local governments in metro areas to have "fair share" affordable housing laws; and

5.   establish metro wide tax-sharing arrangements for local governments or utilize state aid as a revenue-equalizing mechanism.

As I stated earlier, reorganizing local government is primarily a task for initiative and hard work at the state and local levels. There are key roles, however, for the federal government. Since World War II the federal government's "urban policy" has been "suburban policy." It is past time for the federal government to deal with the consequences of its handiwork in terms of helping bridge the city-suburb gap. * * *

NOTE ON REGIONAL GOVERNMENTS

State law traditionally recognizes only two tiers of governmental authority: local governmental authority and state governmental authority. There are very few states that recognize anything resembling a distinct, intermediate, third tier of governmental authority—namely, regional governmental authority.

Even though state law does not traditionally recognize regional government as a distinct component of the state governmental structure, some governmental entities within states may have regional jurisdiction. For example, many states have established regional authorities like the Georgia Regional Transportation Authority. These regional authorities, however, are not regional governments. They are more akin to state administrative agencies. They are usually run by appointed rather than elected officials, and they usually have jurisdiction over only a limited set of issues that affect a given region. Such authorities are not general purpose governments akin to cities on the one hand or to states on the other.

In a related vein, there are cities or counties in some states of such geographic size that they in a sense govern a region. However, large counties or cities do not represent a distinct, third tier of regional government. Such cities or counties do not serve as governments for the region in the way that state governments serve as governments for the state. State governments serve as governments within a statewide legal system that also recognizes a distinct tier of local governmental authority, comprised of smaller-scale governmental entities such as cities and counties. By contrast, large city or county governments serve as the sole local governing entity within that region. The traditional two-tier governance structure can easily accommodate the possibility, in other words, that a given city or county might be large enough to encompass an entire region.

In those states that do recognize a distinct, regional tier of government, what does it look like? The two best examples (though there are others such as Unigov in Indianapolis and Miami-Dade in Florida) may be found in Minnesota and in Oregon.

In 1967, the Minnesota legislature created the Metropolitan Council for the Minneapolis-St. Paul region, an area comprised of numerous counties and more than 150 municipalities. The governor appoints the council members, and in this respect, the council follows the model of regional authorities rather than general purpose governments. On the other hand, the council's jurisdiction is broader than that of the typical limited-jurisdiction regional authority. In fact, the council initially served as the supervisory agency for several, limited-jurisdiction regional authorities, such as the Metropolitan Transit Commission, the Regional Transit Board, and the Metropolitan Waste Commission. In 1994, the state legislature abolished several of these special authorities and vested the council with direct operational control over these regional matters.[44]

In a similar vein, the legislation that created the council charged it with carrying out a regional land use policy planning function. Subsequent legislation has enhanced the council's regional planning authority, by allowing it to require each locality in the region to submit its land use plans to the council for approval. The metropolitan council has not, however, fully exercised its land use authority. As Myron Orfield, a member of the Minnesota House of Representatives and a central figure in the legislative reform efforts, explains:

> The Land Planning Act allows the council to require a local community to "modify a comprehensive plan or any part thereof which may have a substantial impact on or contain a substantial departure from metropolitan system plans." These terms are broad and open ended, but the Met Council has narrowly construed its authority. Under a system of self-imposed restraint, the council will require a plan amendment only when the local comprehensive plan imposes a burden on a metropolitan system that "threatens its capacity"—a fairly cataclysmic event. Consequently, the council has rarely used its authority to shape regional planning, and the Twin Cities region has continued to develop in an exceedingly, low-density, restrictive, fragmented way.

These important expansions of the council's authority—even though that authority has not always been used to its fullest—have made the council more akin to a distinct, regional tier of the state governmental structure than to a special authority that has jurisdiction over a particular regional matter. Indeed, as the scope of the council's authority over regional issues has grown, there has been increasing pressure to transform the council from an appointed to an elected body.

Regional government in the Minneapolis-St. Paul area also draws strength from the nation's most significant regional tax-sharing plan. The state fiscal disparities law, adopted by the Minnesota legislature in 1971, requires all taxing jurisdictions in the region—from villages to central cities to suburbs to school districts—to contribute 40 percent of the post-1971 increase in assessed value of commercial and industrial property into a regional fund. Distributions from this regional fund are then made to cities on the basis of their population and their tax capacity (measured by the per capita market value of commercial and industrial property within the jurisdiction). As of 1998, the fund totaled more than $400 million, with receiving cities outnumbering contributing cities nearly three to one. The common fund comprises about 20 percent of the region's total tax base. Interestingly, Minneapolis moved over time—and as a consequence of a downtown office boom—from being the largest net recipient to the largest net

---

[44] See David Rusk, Inside Game/Outside Game 222–248 (1999); Myron Orfield, Metropolitics: A Regional Agenda for Community and Stability 189–196 (1997).

contributor. Nevertheless, there remain enormous fiscal disparities within the region. In this regard, it is important to emphasize that the revenue-sharing system excludes all residential property from the common fund.

Interestingly, the nascent regional governmental structure that the state legislature created in the Minneapolis-St. Paul region more than three decades ago has been the target of significant reform efforts in the last several years. Prodded by a coalition comprised of constituents and representatives of central cities and constituents and representatives of inner-ring suburbs, the state legislature has passed several recent bills that would augment the council's authority, increase regional obligations in the area of housing, and expand regional tax-sharing. Many of these legislative efforts, however, have failed as a result of gubernatorial vetoes that have not been overridden.

Unlike Minnesota, Oregon's experiment in regional government involves the use of an elected regional governing entity. The Portland area's regional governance structure took effect following a 1979 referendum adopted by voters in a three-county region that surrounds Portland. The referendum authorized the creation of a metropolitan service district, known as Metro. The Metro helps to enforce the Urban Growth Boundary that directs development in the region. Metro has authority for a region inhabited by more than 1 million residents and made up of several counties and more than 20 cities.

Metro comes as close to a full-fledged, regional government as does any entity in the country. Significantly, Metro operates pursuant to its own home rule charter that voters in the region adopted in 1992. The home rule charter reflects the important degree of independent authority that Metro possesses to act as a governmental tier distinct from either the cities within its jurisdiction or the state, which possesses ultimate authority over it.

Metro is comprised of three governmental branches: a seven-member council, with each councilor elected from a district within the region; an Executive Officer, who is elected region-wide; and an Auditor, a certified public accountant who is also elected region-wide and who is responsible for conducting performance and management audits of Metro's operations and functions. Proposed amendments to the Metro home rule charter would consolidate the seven-member council and the Executive Officer and establish a Council president elected regionally.

The home rule charter gives Metro the power to ask for voter approval of a regional property tax, sales tax, or income tax. Metro also has the power to adopt limited "niche taxes" without voter approval. Thus far, Metro has used its taxing power very sparingly, adopting only modest niche taxes and a minimal property tax levy to fund the zoo.

The charter sets forth regional land-use planning as Metro's primary responsibility. Metro is also responsible for the operation of a regional solid waste disposal system; the operation of various regional facilities, ranging from the zoo to the state convention center; the administration of a regional parks and open space system; the development and marketing of data; and the planning of responses to natural disasters. By virtue of its home rule grant, the metro also has evolving power over issues of "metropolitan concern."

The Portland area's Metro stands, at least as a formal legal matter, as a paradigm example of a distinct, third tier of regional government within the overall state governance structure in Oregon. Like an independent city, Metro has home rule authority; that authority extends, however, over matters of "regional" rather than "local" interest. Metro does not exercise all of the powers of a local government, such as powers over law enforcement or fire protection. Nor is education within its ambit. It nonetheless possesses many more powers than the typical regional entity. Finally, Metro is comprised of officials who are elected region-wide.

A key question to consider in assessing the experiments in regional government underway in both Minnesota and Oregon is whether the three-tier model of state government—with local governments at the bottom, regional governments in the middle, and state governments at the top—is a wise one. After all, many of the problems of inter-local inequity thus far examined are arguably attributable to both the vertical separation between state and local affairs that the two-tier system fosters, and the horizontal separation between localities that the two-tier system encourages. Might not the three-tier system solve some problems of horizontal separation between localities within the region only by creating new lines of separation both horizontally between regions and vertically between the local, regional, and state tiers?

At the same time, it may be that the creation of a third-governmental tier may serve to empower localities within the region to consider a set of policy paths that would not have occurred to them in the absence of a shift away from the traditional two-tier governance structure. Of course, if the purpose behind regional government is to empower local governments to consider alternative policies that the current state law governance structure implicitly forecloses, it may be that regional governance is unnecessary. For example, to bring about regional land use planning and to control sprawling suburban growth, Maryland has reformed state law without turning to a three-tier governance model. Maryland, as Sheryll Cashin explains, "restricts all state spending to 'priority funding areas' that are designated by local governments but which must be served by existing infrastructure and which must meet state minimum density requirements."[45] Such state alteration of local incentives might be understood as a different means of accomplishing the same ends that the establishment of a full-fledged regional government like Metro is intended to bring about.

---

[45] See Sheryll Cashin, Localism, Self-Interest, and the Tyranny of the Favored Quarter: Addressing the Barriers to New Regionalism, 88 Geo. L. J. 1985, 2048 n. 292 (2000).

MARGARET WEIR, COALITION BUILDING FOR REGIONALISM
From Bruce Katz (Ed.), Reflections on Regionalism.
Pp. 127–129, 130–135, 140–146 (2000).

For over a century, urban planners and supporters of "good government" have argued in favor of metropolitanism. These advocates have criticized the growth of conflicting and overlapping local political and administrative jurisdictions on grounds of both efficiency and equity. In the postwar era, as suburbs grew and metropolitan political jurisdictions multiplied, a chorus of planners—many enjoying positions of influence within an expanding federal government—called for solutions ranging from outright government consolidations to voluntary cooperation among the maze of metropolitan governments. Despite the persistent complaints from urban experts about the irrationality and unfairness of metropolitan fragmentation, their ideas have had very limited practical impact on postwar American cities and suburbs. The wave of expert enthusiasm for metropolitan regionalism in the 1960s and 1970s left only a handful of city-county consolidations and a legacy of weak regional organizations with few resources and even less power. There were two important exceptions to this pattern of failure: Oregon adopted effective land-use regulation that provided a basis for strengthening metropolitanism in the coming decades; Minnesota created a Metropolitan Council for the Twin Cities area and passed fiscal disparities legislation that helped compensate for the financial consequences of metropolitan political fragmentation. It is revealing to compare the successes in Oregon and Minnesota with the failures to adopt comparable measures in Illinois and California, states that faced significant metropolitan fragmentation and suburban sprawl in the 1960s and 1970s. In the former two states, coalition building in state politics was the key to success. Studies of metropolitanism have focused on federal initiatives and on features of particular metropolitan areas, but the examples of Oregon and Minnesota illustrate the central role of states in enacting or blocking legislation needed to promote metropolitan regionalism.

The successful cases had three common elements: at least one politically powerful interest that saw metropolitan regionalism as a way to address its concerns, bipartisan coalition building, and relatively weak opposing groups. In Oregon, farmers, the environmental movement, and Portland city leaders, for different reasons, all supported the land-use legislation enacted in 1973. Oregon's Republican governor, Tom McCall, was pivotal to success. In Minnesota, Minneapolis city leaders pressed for legislation to create the Metropolitan Council and found support in a sympathetic governor. As in Oregon, moderate Republicans were critical to the victory. In both states the groups most likely to oppose metropolitan initiatives—developers and suburban interests—were unusually weak or quiescent.

The politics of Illinois and California looked much different on each of these dimensions. The availability of alternative goals and resources meant that environmental and urban interests in these states did not look to metropolitanism as a way to achieve their objectives. Thus even though a strong environmental movement existed in California and both states experienced significant sprawl and urban decline, those concerned with these problems sought other ways to address them. In addition, given the nature of political party divisions in these states, bipartisanship and gubernatorial support for metropolitanism were most unlikely. The election of Ronald Reagan as governor in 1966 effectively ruled out such an alliance in California; longstanding animosity and partisan division between city and suburb in the Chicago metropolitan region blocked the way in Illinois. Finally, opponents in these states were stronger. In California the political system magnified the power of developers, who staunchly opposed land-use regulation. In both Illinois and California, racial divisions between city and suburb promised that any serious efforts to promote metropolitan cooperation or to "open up the suburbs" could trigger venomous political fights that few politicians wanted to confront. * * *

In Oregon state regulation of land use provided the essential framework for metropolitan regionalism. The critical piece of legislation was a 1973 law that created a new Land Conservation and Development Commission (LCDC), appointed by the governor and charged with formulating goals for land use across the state. The law required counties and cities to draw up comprehensive plans that conformed to the LCDC goals. What put teeth in the act and distinguished Oregon land-use legislation is the LCDC power to reject local plans. In the year after its creation, the LCDC formulated goals that had important implications for the pattern of urban growth in Oregon. It required cities and counties to create urban growth boundaries, areas within which the cities could be expected to grow over the next twenty years and in which development would be encouraged. Outside these boundaries, land was zoned exclusively for farm use, making development much more difficult. The aim of the growth boundaries was to limit sprawl by making urban growth contiguous and stopping leapfrog patterns of development.

Bowing to political realities, the law did not create a new state agency responsible for drawing up plans but rather delegated planning responsibility to counties. The one exception was the Portland metropolitan area, which was designated as a special planning district ranging over three separate counties. Like many metropolitan regions, the Portland area in 1969 had established a council of local governments, the Columbia Region Association of Governments (CRAG), to meet federal requirements for a metropolitan planning district. As in other metropolitan areas, the organization operated on a voluntary basis and was composed of local governments, each of which had an equal vote. In 1973, however, the state legislature gave CRAG the legal authority to require the counties to comply with its land-use plans (including the urban growth boundary) and made membership mandatory for the three counties in the Portland metropolitan area. It also weighted voting within the association by population, thus giving the more densely populated city of Portland 40 percent of the votes. Local voters approved this delegation of power in a referendum. The strong city support for the agency and its dominant voice within the organization gave the city unusual leverage in metropolitan politics.

State-level initiatives for land-use planning were thus critical in supporting metropolitan planning efforts already under way in the Portland area. In 1969, with a local transportation system on the verge of bankruptcy, Portland had pressed the state legislature to establish a regional transportation agency that would allow it to tap into the suburban tax base. In return, the city agreed to the creation of a Metropolitan Services District, whose initial responsibilities included solid waste disposal and a financially precarious zoo. In 1978 the Metropolitan Service District (MSD) took over the responsibilities of CRAG, which was abolished, and in a departure from the usual organization of regional bodies across the county, the new MSD commissioners were to be directly elected, not appointed. Over time the responsibilities of the MSD grew to encompass authority over metropolitan land-use policies, including the urban growth boundary, as well as key metropolitan services and facilities ranging from garbage disposal to a major convention center. In 1992 the MSD was redesignated Metro and given even more authority with the status of a home rule government.

One of the most striking political features of these initiatives was the broad range of active support they generated. On the urban side, it was not just planners and good-government groups but politicians with substantial constituencies, such as Portland mayor Neil Goldschmidt, who strongly supported the land-use law and the other metropolitan initiatives associated with it. Likewise, environmentalists, an important new force in politics in the early 1970s, focused on the land-use regulation law as the central means of achieving their goals. This intertwining of urban and environmental interests and their support of a single legislative agenda was the only one of its kind across the nation. At the same time that Oregon was debating its land-use law, Congress was considering a land-use bill that provided incentives for states to engage in precisely the kind of planning Oregon was considering. In stark contrast to the political coalition that backed Oregon bill, the national legislation never attracted strong support from either environmental groups or urban interests, who did not see their agendas as intertwined. Perhaps most unusual, agricultural interests were key initiators of the 1973 Oregon legislation.

What facilitated this unusual political cooperation between urban, environmental, and agricultural groups? Part of the answer lies in Oregon distinctive geography. With nearly half of the state population concentrated in the Willamette Valley, which contains the state major cities as well as its richest agricultural land, the trade-offs between urbanization and the limited supply of rural land were much more starkly drawn in Oregon than in most states. In fact, the land-use legislation of 1973 only passed because of strong support from legislators in the Willamette Valley. Forty-nine of the sixty legislators from the valley backed it, whereas only nine of the thirty legislators from eastern and coastal regions supported it. This distinctive geography and the sharp trade-offs it posed accounted for the critical support of agricultural interests. In places where land is more plentiful, agricultural interests either have shown little interest in land-use regulation or have opposed it, fearing that it would strengthen state government at the expense of local decisionmaking. Moreover, in most places farmers have sought to preserve the right to dispose of their land as they wished including the right to benefit from the higher land prices that come with development. Such sentiments also existed in Oregon, especially from rural interests outside the Willamette Valley. However, the limited supply of land in the Willamette Valley altered the perspective of its farmers because of the obvious threat that urban sprawl posed to the entire agricultural industry there and the way of life it supported. * * *

In addition to these favorable political conditions, the interests that posed the greatest opposition to metropolitan regionalism elsewhere in the country were unusually weak in Oregon during the 1960s and 1970s. Suburban interests were particularly weak. Oregon's slow growth in the 1950s and 1960s meant that it had few full-service suburban governments and not much of a distinct suburban agenda when land-use regulation and metropolitan regionalism came under consideration. Oregon's racial homogeneity also played a role. In such racially homogenous metropolitan areas, the division between city and suburb is much less fraught with tension and conflict. For all of these reasons, suburban interests played little role in blocking state land-use legislation or in contesting the development of metropolitan government in Portland. The other major interests generally opposed to land-use regulation— developers and the housing industry—indeed did work against the 1973 legislation, but slow suburbanization left them weaker than in other states. Moreover, because other commercial interests with a stake in Portland supported metropolitan regionalism, business did not speak with a single voice on this issue. Together the broad support for land-use legislation, gubernatorial initiative, and bipartisan cooperation overwhelmed the weak opposition.

In Minnesota metropolitan regionalism took a different form and stemmed from distinct political impulses. Two key pieces of legislation in Minnesota created the Metropolitan Council in 1967 and the Fiscal Disparities Act of 1971. The immediate impetus for establishing the Metropolitan Council was a crisis over water and sewer lines in growing suburban areas, a problem that had become so severe that the federal government was threatening to withhold its home mortgage insurance from these areas. The legislature initially charged the new council with finding solutions to the sewage problems and later extended its purview to include a broad range of regional issues, including the sewers, solid waste disposal, and regional parks. Although early discussion had called for an elected board, the legislature ultimately decided that the governor would appoint board members. * * *

[T]he debate about metropolitanism in Minnesota was much more technocratic and elite oriented than in Oregon. One of the most important groups pushing for the creation of the council was the Citizens League, a nonpartisan civic organization that sponsored research on metropolitan policy concerns. With close ties to elites in business and politics, the Citizens League was a politically influential organization but not one that mobilized grass-roots support. * * * Most important in creating the Metropolitan Council was the state legislature, where one-person one-vote reapportionment finally broke the rural stranglehold on the legislature and gave the Twin Cities region nearly half the seats in 1967. The long tradition of progressive politics in Minnesota, the well organized civic elites of the Twin Cities, and the new dominance of the region in the legislature all made the creation of the Metropolitan Council a largely uncontroversial affair.

More sharply contested was the 1971 fiscal disparities bill. As passed, the act established regional tax-base sharing. Forty percent of the tax income from new commercial and industrial development would go into a common pool to be redistributed among political jurisdictions throughout the six-county metropolitan region on the basis of their commercial and industrial wealth. Drawing on ideas developed by the Citizens League, a Republican representative from a low-tax-capacity suburb led the effort to pass the bill. Driving him was the fear that the movement toward regional land-use planning and development would prevent districts such as his from developing more taxing capacity in the future. Representatives of affluent suburbs bitterly contested the bill, denouncing it as "communistic," "Robin Hood" legislation. These opponents nearly defeated the bill in the state senate. * * *

The ease with which the Metropolitan Council was created suggests that as in Oregon, cities and suburbs did not have the separate and conflictual identities characteristic of more racially divided metropolitan areas. The line between city and suburb was not perceived as a racial line, and this homogeneity allowed the legislature to treat the problems surrounding metropolitan service provision as practical or technical concerns that did not invoke highly charged political issues. Moreover, as in Oregon, the Twin Cities had no tradition of the machine politics that made suburbs in many other metropolitan areas suspicious of any forms of cooperation with the city. Racial homogeneity also made it easier for Republican representatives from lower-tax-capacity suburbs to join with Democratic representatives from the city in support of the fiscal disparities legislation. Common economic interests could not be overshadowed by racial divisions. * * *

Suburban development exploded in California in the decades after World War II and with it concerns about service delivery and the impact on cities. These problems usually were attacked with remedies that not only were ineffective in controlling sprawl, but also exacerbated fragmentation and exclusionary barriers in the suburbs. Two key examples are the 1954 Lakewood Plan, which was designed to address the suburban services problem, and the Local Agency Formation Committee (LAFCO), formed in 1963 to oversee incorporations and annexations.

The Lakewood Plan approached the problem of suburban services in Los Angeles County in a way that promoted political fragmentation, class stratification, and racial exclusion. * * * As Gary Miller's careful study shows, the Lakewood Plan created a sharp stratification by class among Los Angeles County municipalities, dividing the metropolitan area into jurisdictions of "service seekers" and "tax avoiders." These divisions followed racial lines as well. In the fifteen years after the Lakewood Plan went into effect, the county's black population became concentrated in just a few cities, and the number of nearly all-white jurisdictions grew. As Miller notes, "The Lakewood Plan cities were essentially white political movements." By allowing contracting, Los Angeles County had provided the means for separation and exit from broader political arenas rather than for building a common purpose throughout the metropolitan areas. Instead of linking the problems of the suburbs and the cities as Minnesota had sought to do, Los Angeles County widened the gulf.

Concern about metropolitan political fragmentation and unchecked growth in California lay behind the creation of LAFCO in 1963. In 1960 both the state legislature and Democratic governor Pat Brown launched studies of the proliferation of local governments and its impact on California's metropolitan areas. Prior to 1963, decisions about annexation and incorporation had to be approved by the counties alone, subject to electoral approval by the affected districts. One group in the state legislature, echoing the governor's commission, wanted to create a strong state agency that would have power over local boundaries. A second group, supported by the counties, wanted the power to reside with the counties. The compromise legislation called for county-level LAFCO boards composed of two representatives from cities, two county supervisors, and a fifth member to be chosen by the other four. In contrast to Oregon, California failed to create any new statewide or multicounty authority over local boundaries and growth. The highest level of decisionmaking was the county.

The new county-level LAFCOs did little to control the pace and direction of growth, nor did they stem jurisdictional fragmentation. Instead, the LAFCO process set off a power struggle among cities, counties, developers, and homeowners with the result that "rational analysis of issues like sprawl, efficient service provision, and fiscal equity has been no more apparent than in the days before LAFCO." With few resources for drawing up plans to guide growth and riven by political disputes, the LAFCOs have been reactive agencies with little independent impact on land-use patterns. * * *

[E]ven in the late 1960s and 1970s, California's environmentalists showed little interest in metropolitan regionalism. Instead, they focused their concern on wilderness and coastal areas. Moreover, as a new social movement that had grown by leaps and bounds, environmentalists were riven by factionalism and ideology. * * *

Although California failed to devise a regulatory process to manage metropolitan growth, the issues of land use, development, and housing did not disappear; instead, their politics played out in different arenas using different tools. Local political NIMBYism enacted through lawsuits and the initiative process became the central way that disputes over metropolitan land use were adjudicated. The impulse to manage development became intertwined with localism and exclusivism as slow-growth initiatives spread throughout California in the 1980s. The slow-growth movement proposed initiative after initiative, aiming to lodge growth controls at the most local levels of government. Many of the same impulses that led to coalition building and statewide legislation in Oregon were thus localized and much more narrowly cast in California. * * *

Most important was the central place of land-development interests in the California economy and in the political system. In much of the Southwest, land development and local boosterism provided the key to economic growth during the twentieth century. In contrast to Oregon, the power of land interests was well established long before the modern environmental movement appeared on the scene. And in contrast to Minnesota, most local elites were closely intertwined with development interests, who sharply opposed restrictions in the pattern of growth. The importance of money in California's political system magnified the power of development interests. In the 1960s the California legislature led the nation in the number of lobbyists and in the role of interest-group money in electoral campaigns. Land interests predominated in both. The power of land interests permeated both political parties, but their impact was especially significant for Republicans, because it effectively blocked the emergence of a moderate Republican leadership around metropolitan regionalism that was so important in Oregon and Minnesota. * * *

In Illinois, despite growing suburban sprawl and urban decline, metropolitan regionalism and land-use regulation did not draw the same kind of political attention they attracted in Oregon, Minnesota, or California. Broad regional organizations had existed in the Chicago area since the 1950s. * * * In the mid-1960s, a group of prestigious civic, business, financial, and educational leaders in the Chicago metropolitan area revived the call for metropolitan government. But the achievements of these organizations remained largely on paper, as they had little real authority to guide development. Instead, a maze of special districts with operational responsibilities carved up the region into functional areas for water, parks, and waste disposal. For the most part, the problems of growing suburbs were addressed through these ad hoc and functionally specific entities, among which there was little coordination and no overarching vision. * * *

Of critical importance was the power of the Chicago Democratic political organization. Although Chicago never commanded a majority in the state legislature, the tight organization of its delegation allowed the city to make legislative deals in its favor. * * * Chicago had little interest in regionalism, because it could generally get what it needed from the state and accordingly, saw no real threat to its dominance in the region. Moreover, through the Democratic organization, Chicago's mayor effectively controlled political arenas outside the city, including Cook County. Any new regional organizations would only dilute the city's power—and more important, that of the Democratic organization.

If the city was uninterested in regionalism, the suburbs abhorred the idea. In contrast to Minnesota, Chicago suburbs had a longstanding and deep animosity toward the city. With a tradition of reform that prided itself on efficient, honest government, suburban Chicago viewed the city as a pit of political corruption rife with dishonesty. Compounding this animosity were sharp partisan differences: most of the suburbs had long been dominated by Republicans. Any form of regional government threatened to disrupt the political balance in the metropolitan area.

Finally, proponents of metropolitan regionalism in Chicago ignored the way racial divisions affected their proposals. By the 1960s, as ethnic whites began to leave Chicago for the suburbs, race became a key factor dividing city from suburb, choking off suburban interest in any regional initiatives that might be linked with racial equity. Moreover, race cut two ways. Black leaders in Chicago had little interest in new forms of regional governance that would simply dilute black political power. * * *

These political realities left little room for the state legislature to consider measures promoting metropolitan regionalism. Although regional organizations continued to exist, they had no power. Instead, as George C. Hemmens notes in his study of the Chicago area, discussions with implications for the region occurred in two unconnected arenas: "Side by side, at the same time, with minimal interaction, there is a highly rational, civil, public process working on regional infrastructure decisions, and a highly political, combative, political process working on regional infrastructure decisions." The political process, driven by particularistic local interests as opposed to a broader regional vision, was the one that counted. * * *

5. BEYOND REGIONAL GOVERNMENT

Are there ways of organizing our metropolitan areas other than through interlocal agreements, public authorities, or regional government? The excerpt reproduced below argues that there are.[46] Is it possible to create a form of metropolitan organization that allows us to introduce regional thinking into local decisionmaking without abandoning the locality as the locus of decisionmaking? Does the proposal set forth in this excerpt accomplish this goal? Are there other ways of doing so?

GERALD FRUG, BEYOND REGIONAL GOVERNMENT
115 Harv. L. Rev. 1763, 1790–1803, 1811, 1831–1834 (2002).

Achieving * * * [a] confluence of local and regional interests will take effort. There is no solution to regional problems that will make everyone better off and no one worse off. Localities need to negotiate with each other to work out the kinds of changes in local authority— both increases and decreases—that will better protect collective interests while furthering, as much as possible, local self-determination. Doing so requires a new regional institution. But it does not require a regional government. What is needed instead is an institution that will permit the region's local governments to work together to advance regional interests. The fundamental issue presented by this alternative version of regionalism is not how to divide power between local and regional decision makers but how to turn regional decision making into a form of interlocal decision making. Clearly, important questions need to be

---

[46] For a further elaboration of the argument made in this section, see Gerald Frug and David Barron, City Bound: How States Stifle Urban Innovation (2008).

resolved about what such a regional entity would do. But the possible answers to these questions will vary depending on the level of citizens' confidence that the regional institution will advance local interests rather than simply override them. And this level of confidence will be affected by the structure of the regional institution. A structure that required the unanimous consent of all participating parties would inhibit the formation of any regional agenda. Nothing in America commands unanimous consent. Yet a structure that allowed local power to be overridden too easily would jeopardize the values provided by local decision making authority. The task of creating the right structure is therefore critical. * * *

[I propose] that state governments establish a specific kind of institution: * * * a regional legislature. Legislatures, after all, are the classic vehicles for enabling locally elected officials to gather together to hammer out a common agenda. A regional legislature * * * [can borrow] from two existing models—current state legislatures and regional planning agencies. Like a state legislature, a regional legislature could be relatively large, with members popularly elected from cities across the region. Unlike a state legislature, however, it would be organized to perform a single task: to serve as a vehicle for interlocal negotiations designed to forge a regional perspective on specific issues. State legislatures are not themselves an appropriate mechanism for undertaking this task. State legislators are elected from districts that disregard city lines. It is not plausible to expect people elected in this fashion (many from rural areas) to redesign their own institution to give a voice to cities. They could, however, create a regional legislature to do just that. * * *

To be effective, a regional legislature would have to have the power to ensure that its decisions, once made, will be followed by the region's local governments. It would thus have the power to control local policy, including the power to redefine what it means for local government institutions to pursue local interests. To be able to exercise this amount of power, the regional legislature should derive its authority from a delegation of power from the state legislature, not simply from a voluntary agreement between the region's cities. This source of power need not transform the regional legislature into a centralized regional government. The regional legislature should—and this is crucial—consist of democratically elected representatives of the local governments themselves. If it were so organized, it would be a mechanism for giving a voice to local governments. Local representatives would be in control of the agenda. Not only could they increase as well as decrease local power but, once a regionally oriented definition of local self-interest became internalized into local decision making, they could leave the formulation and implementation of policies in the hands of local governments.

Indeed, the more discussions within a regional legislature helped local officials understand the impact of their decisions on each other, the less the regional legislature would have to do. Still, a critical question remains. How can a regional legislature with this much power be organized without undermining the advantages gained by decentralizing power to local governments? * * *

[One source of ideas to address this question is] the European Union. The * * * [twenty-seven] nations that form the European Union have not abandoned their devotion to national sovereignty. They nevertheless have created a much more connected relationship with each other than have the cities that constitute America's metropolitan areas. Those of us interested in American regionalism can learn a good deal from this European experience, notwithstanding the stark differences between the two contexts. Some of these differences need to be emphasized. The European Union was formed as a response to two devastating world wars—a level of inter-jurisdictional conflict that has no parallel in metropolitan America. From the outset, the European focus has been on economic integration, an issue that is a matter for national policymaking in the United States. Trade barriers and a common currency—like many of the other issues that concern the European Union, such as defense and foreign policy—are not metropolitan issues in the United States. Moreover, unlike the member countries of the European Union, American cities are not sovereign nations. On the contrary, they are subject to the very kind of power exercisable by a higher sovereignty—state governments—that the members of the European Union are unwilling to cede to centralized control. American states have the power to merge cities with each other, even to eliminate them; a European Union with this kind of authority is not within anyone's contemplation. The fact that cities are not sovereign nations is also more than a reference to their lack of sovereign power. European countries have long been understood by many of their citizens in terms of their cultural, and not just their political, unity: a common language, a common history, even a common ancestry have often been thought to distinguish one nation from another. No one thinks of municipal boundaries as dividing one pre-political "people" from another. Finally, the European Union has established a wide variety of institutions that have no relevance in the American metropolitan context. Indeed, its complex institutional structure is not only unnecessary but cannot constitutionally be reproduced at the regional level in the United States.

Despite these differences, the European Union provides ways of thinking about separateness and togetherness that offer promise for the American metropolitan context. After all, many of the ways in which the European Union differs from American metropolitan areas might have made the formation of connections within Europe harder, not easier, to accomplish than regional cooperation in the United States. If European countries could overcome nationalist loyalties—not to mention the differences that led to two world wars—people who live in the same metropolitan area within the United States should be able to relate to each other at least as well. While it is true that American metropolitan areas are fragmented in very divisive ways—often along lines of race, ethnicity, and class—the European Union has also faced stark differences in wealth and ethnicity across the geographic area where inter-jurisdictional cooperation has been built. And Europe did not have a powerful government—like state governments—that could organize the necessary institutional structure to overcome these sources of conflict. The European Union's institutional structure had to be created by interlocal agreement—that is, by treaties. * * *

Still, it would be wrong to try to reproduce the structure of the European Union in American metropolitan areas. * * * I intend simply to rip from their European context specific institutional ideas that might help us reconceptualize the relationship between local separateness and regional togetherness in the United States. * * * What interests me about the institutional structure of the European Union lies in its attempt to build localism into the very fabric of European institutions, rather than simply to divide authority between a "centralized government" and "local control." Some elements of this model are familiar to American readers. Two of the governing institutions of the European Union are the European Parliament (elected roughly according to population) and the Council of the European Union (a body consisting of representatives of the member governments). The European Parliament's allocation of membership according to the population of the member nations, while assuring each country a minimum representation regardless of population, parallels the organization of the United States House of Representatives. The Council's allocation of equal membership to representatives of the constituent governments regardless of population parallels the organization of the United States Senate prior to the adoption of the Seventeenth Amendment (which retained equal membership but added democratic election of representatives). A problem with this aspect of the European (and federal) method of building local control into a larger union is that it offers an unconstitutional model for elected regional institutions in the United States. The United States Supreme Court has rejected "the federal analogy" for state and local governments because "[p]olitical subdivisions of States—counties, cities, or whatever—never were and never have been considered as sovereign entities." Thus, the familiar bicameral structure that allocates power in one of two governing bodies to political subdivisions as such is not an available option for metropolitan governance in the United States. Any regional institution has to be organized according to the one-person, one-vote principle. * * *

Today * * *, because a majority (often more than eighty percent) of the residents of metropolitan areas lives in the suburbs, the equality requirement puts the suburbs in control of any democratically elected metropolitan organization. The suburbs, however, are not a monolithic voting bloc. The current split between prosperous and declining suburbs renders uncertain the kind of alliance among political subdivisions that would control a regional legislature in most American metropolitan areas. This uncertainty presents its own problem: the requirement of one-person, one-vote would threaten every political subdivision within the regional legislature. Any local decision could be overruled by a coalition of other localities. Organizational ideas to deal with fear of loss of local control are therefore indispensable, given the emotional attachment to local decision making. Ideas about how to ensure that the desire for local control does not overwhelm the possibility of forging a regional agenda are also indispensable. * * * The structure of the European Union offers * * * [a useful suggestion] about how to achieve these conflicting objectives: qualified majority voting * * *.

The Council of the European Union (consisting of representatives of each of the twenty-seven member countries) first deals with its members' fear of loss of control by seeking to establish policy through consensus. But the formal decision making rules of the Council address the same fear. Different rules apply depending on the issue being decided: sometimes unanimity, sometimes a simple majority, and sometimes a qualified majority is required. The notion of a qualified majority is the most unfamiliar of these decision making methods to American readers. The European Union defines a qualified majority for Council decision making by allocating votes to individual members very roughly according to their population and, in addition, establishing a minimum number of votes (and sometimes a minimum number of members casting these votes) before a policy can be adopted. * * * The specifics of the ways in which these various ingredients have been set and reset for the Council are not of significance here. What is significant is the idea of organizing the Council in terms of qualified majority voting. A simple majority requirement demands too little regional consensus for policymaking to be widely acceptable, while a unanimity rule would make decision making impossible given the dozens of cities represented in a region (as opposed to the twenty-seven nations represented in the European Union). The ingredients of a qualified majority voting system, however, can protect individual jurisdictions by establishing the minimum level of agreement required for action, while at the same time giving greater weight to the views of the most populous cities in the region. * * *

A qualified majority voting mechanism would enable every locality in a region to be represented in a regional legislature and would simultaneously take into account population differences among the localities represented. Creating this kind of interlocal institution would be a major innovation in America: there is no institution in the country that allows a region's local governments to meet together and forge a common policy that is binding on all of them. The idea of giving a voice to every political subdivision would also be an innovation in the organization of population-based legislative bodies in the United States. Districts for state legislators and members of the House of Representatives routinely divide some cities while combining others; the effort to draw district lines for state and federal purposes concentrates on creating equally sized districts (and on tracking party membership and protecting incumbents) rather than on giving a voice to political subdivisions. This is one of the many ways in which the "local autonomy" that is so valued in the regionalism debate is completely disregarded in other contexts. On issues decided by the state and federal governments, cities are not decision makers at all. They are relegated, along with private corporations and interest groups, to being lobbyists. A regional legislature organized according to qualified majority voting, by contrast, would enable representatives of the cities themselves, acting collectively, to become the regional decision maker.

A principal reason why political subdivisions are not now represented in legislatures in the United States is the difficulty of squaring such a notion of representation with the constitutional requirement of one-person, one-vote. A qualified majority voting mechanism offers the best way to do so. It allows a legislature to be organized according to political subdivisions and to the size of local government populations simultaneously: every political subdivision would be represented in the legislature, but the number of representatives for each subdivision would vary with its population. At the same time, a qualified majority voting mechanism would prevent the domination of the legislature by a small number of the largest jurisdictions by establishing a specified minimum number of votes before a measure can be adopted. * * *

This is not to suggest that organizing a regional legislature with a qualified majority voting system would be easy. The minimum number of votes, the minimum number of jurisdictions supporting the measure, and the minimum regional population represented by the vote would have to be worked out (or eliminated from the formula). The process of enacting state legislation establishing these figures would engender a complex negotiation, with the results varying from region to region given the different populations—and number—of cities in each metropolitan area. Of course, once a regional legislature was established, the numbers could be revised over time as experience revealed the levels that were high enough to assuage the fear of loss of local control yet low enough to enable the pursuit of a regional agenda. * * * Yet virtually any agreed-upon figures are likely to be an improvement over the status quo. Currently, there is effectively a unanimity rule on some regional issues—those delegated to local decision making. Any jurisdiction can undermine a regional plan by refusing to cooperate with other cities. On other regional issues—those entrusted to the state or to neighboring localities—local jurisdictions need not even be consulted in the decision making process. Every metropolitan area in the country should be able to craft a qualified voting mechanism better than this oscillation between a local veto power and local irrelevance for regional decision making.

After working out the voting rules, a decision would also have to be made about how large a legislature to create. A regional legislature with a qualified majority voting system could be organized to give the least populous local government in the region one vote. The amount of representation given every other locality could then be built on this base, enabling each legislator to represent approximately equal numbers of people. Consider, for example, the Boston region. According to the most extensive definition of the region adopted by the 2000 census, there are 129 cities and towns in the region, ranging in population from 844 (South Hampton, New Hampshire) to 589,141 (Boston itself). The total regional population is 3,406,829. If each local government had a representative for every 844 people—thereby giving South Hampton one representative—it would mean a total of roughly 4000 representatives, with Boston having 698, Newton (a city of 83,829) having 99, and Newbury (a town of 6717) having 8. * * *

Those who think this legislature too large [most people, I assume] need not abandon the idea of creating a regional legislature with a qualified majority voting mechanism. They can simply reduce the number of representatives by giving each of them weighted votes. To ensure that every local government has a voice in the legislature, the minimum number of representatives would have to equal the number of cities. In the Boston area, the minimum number would be 129. With that number as a starting point, votes could then be allocated according to the local population. If each locality had only one representative, the Boston representative would get 698 votes and the South Hampton representative would get one. This kind of system already exists in some areas of the United States, and it * * * has been upheld as constitutional under the one-person, one-vote requirement. But there is no need for the number of representatives to be one per locality. Larger localities could have multiple representatives, and most smaller localities could have more than one, as long as the system allocated voting strength according to population.

In deciding how many representatives to have, it is important to recognize that the presence of people in the room—and not just their voting power—has an effect on the outcome. A one-representative-per-locality regional legislature would have many people in the room who, collectively, would have very few votes. Adding more people from the more populous towns would change the dynamic of the discussion. Besides, a one-vote-per-locality rule falsely suggests that local residents are not themselves divided on issues, while electing multiple representatives would allow local governments to have legislators who disagree with each other. * * * Whatever the number of legislators, the representative from small towns would be in the room with representatives from the largest city. And all of them collectively would be empowered to negotiate and vote on regional matters. * * *

Some advocates of local power will insist that any regional institutional structure is unacceptable. Instead, they might say, each local government should simply be empowered to make its own decisions for its residents. But local government law never has allowed—and could not conceivably allow—individual cities to decide an issue simply because their residents care deeply about it. The local governments located in the same metropolitan area are so closely connected to each other that virtually every local decision has extraterritorial impact, and local decisions often affect residents' rights in a manner inconsistent with state or federal law. That is why federal, state, and special purpose governments decide so many issues of importance to local residents. Neither local control nor centralized control accurately describes the status quo. The question is whether a better way to combine local and collective decision making can be designed. The judgment that it is better, of course, will depend not just on an analysis of its institutional structure but also on its ability to make progress on key regional issues.

Still, the question remains whether any regional institution, however cleverly constructed, is politically viable. Many people think that the answer to this question is "no." "The suburbs won't agree to the creation of a regional institution with real power," they say. In response, I want to point out that it is not the suburbs' decision. A state legislature could create the kind of institution I have been describing tomorrow if a majority of representatives from across the state agreed to do so. A majority vote by the state legislature, after all, is the way that special purpose governments are now created. Of course, suburban residents are represented in the state legislature. They will—and they should—have a voice in the decision making. But there are many different kinds of suburbs, people within the same suburb disagree with each other, there are other voices as well, and unanimous consent is not the way democratic societies operate. * * *

The relevant political issue raised by the prospects for regionalism, then, involves an inquiry into state legislative politics. Can a legislative majority be constructed that would approve some kind of regional institution? No one thinks that the task will be easy. But it is also not impossible. Farmers, environmentalists, and Portland city leaders, each with their own agendas, formed the coalition that brought metropolitan government to Portland. The support of the business community, the split between rural Republicans and Republicans representing affluent suburbs, and the influence of a sponsor from a low-tax-capacity suburb brought the Metropolitan Council and the Fiscal Disparities Act to Minneapolis-St. Paul. Myron Orfield's success in convincing the legislature (if not the Governor) to support further regional initiatives in Minneapolis-St. Paul came from representatives of low-tax-capacity suburbs, central cities, minorities, good-government groups, and church groups, among others. All of these efforts, it should be emphasized, focused on creating a different kind of institution than the one described above. The likelihood of building a political coalition, I have argued, will be affected by the organizational structure of the regional institution sought to be created. More support for regionalism can be gained if it is seen as building a new form of decentralized power rather than as simply one more example of centralization. To change the popular understanding of regionalism in this way, it is important to begin the effort to establish a regional legislature by focusing on an issue—such as transportation or smart growth—that undeniably affects people across the region and over which * * * [localities] have little control. * * * Once a regional legislature is established, detailed work can then be done— state by state—to determine how to add related, but much more contentious, issues to the initial agenda. * * *

Establishing an institution that furthers * * * [this] conception of regionalism requires * * * the state to decentralize more of its own power to localities. Some people claim that the state simply will not agree to do so. This position, however, fails to recognize how much influence a region could have over state policy if it could overcome * * * intraregional conflict * * *. More than half of Massachusetts's 6.3 million people live in the Massachusetts part of the Boston metropolitan area. Almost half of the population of California lives in the Los Angeles metropolitan region; adding only the San Francisco region brings the percentage to over two-thirds of the state. Metropolitan economies dominate not only state economies but the economy of the nation as a whole. The major hurdle impeding the decentralization of power is conflict within metropolitan regions, not between the metropolitan regions and the state. Local governments now rely on state-enacted legislation to gain power at the expense of their neighbors; they could instead rely on their neighbors to get the state to enact legislation in their common interest. * * *

D. THE CITY AND DEMOCRATIC THEORY: PART THREE

The materials in this chapter have focused attention on the significance of inter-group boundaries. Such boundaries could be understood either as barriers to inter-city cooperation or as necessary forms of protection from threatening outsiders. Indeed, city boundaries can easily be understood in both ways. Many of the cases in each section (such as the exclusionary zoning and school financing cases) illustrate both perspectives simultaneously. One explanation for the ambivalent nature of city boundaries is that they reproduce in the context of groups the familiar problem often raised about individuals: how do we establish a relationship with others if we need and desire their friendship yet fear that their power and influence can overwhelm our sense of self? The barriers that separate one person from another help define them as individuals, but they also isolate people from each other. A provocative reworking of the relationship between the self and others is the subject of the Calvino story reproduced below. Is his picture frightening or inspiring?

The excerpts that follow the Calvino story conclude our exploration of the nature and value of inter-group boundaries. Rosabeth Moss Kanter's analysis of nineteenth-century utopian communities and Philippe Aries' analysis of the relationship between the family and the city then present alternative conceptions of the history and significance of the boundaries between groups. Consider whether, according to these readings, group boundaries have been progressively strengthened or progressively weakened over the last two centuries. Which of these options do the authors seem to favor?

ITALO CALVINO, INVISIBLE CITIES
Pp. 64–65 (1974).

When he enters the territory of which Eutropia is the capital, the traveler sees not one city but many, of equal size and not unlike one another, scattered over a vast, rolling plateau. Eutropia is not one, but all these cities together; only one is inhabited at a time, the others are empty; and this process is carried out in rotation. Now I shall tell you how. On the day when Eutropia's inhabitants feel the grip of weariness and no one can bear any longer his job, his relatives, his house and his life, debts, the people he must greet or who greet him, then the whole citizenry decides to move to the next city, which is there waiting for them, empty and good as new; there each will take up a new job, a different wife, will see another landscape on opening his window, and will spend his time with different pastimes, friends, gossip. So their life is renewed from move to move, among cities whose exposure or declivity or streams or winds make each site somehow different from the others. Since their society is ordered without great distinctions of wealth or authority, the passage from one function to another takes place almost without jolts; variety is guaranteed by the multiple assignments, so that in the span of a lifetime a man rarely returns to a job that has already been his.

Thus the city repeats its life, identical, shifting up and down on its empty chessboard. The inhabitants repeat the same scenes, with the actors changed; they repeat the same speeches with variously combined accents; they open alternate mouths in identical yawns. Alone, among all the cities of the empire, Eutropia remains always the same. Mercury, god of the fickle, to whom the city is sacred, worked this ambiguous miracle.

ROSABETH MOSS KANTER, COMMITMENT AND COMMUNITY
Pp. 148–161, 169–175 (1972).

Two Pulls in Social Life

Utopian communities in the nineteenth century sought both to enhance meaningful interpersonal relationships and to provide political, economic, and other services for their members. They attempted both to express values and to implement practical concerns in a single social unit. If the term utopian has come to connote impractical and impossible, it may be owing to what many have felt to be an inherent contradiction between these two sets of aims of utopian communities. Criticisms have been leveled at utopian communities to the effect that social life cannot be both "human" and "efficient," that brotherhood and economics do not mix, that it is impossible both to satisfy individual needs and to work toward the collective good, and that value expression is incompatible with pragmatism. This theme of the incompatibility of two strains in social life is also central to sociological thought in the distinction between *Gemeinschaft* and *Gesellschaft*.

Gemeinschaft relations include the nonrational, affective, emotional, traditional, and expressive components of social action, as in a family; Gesellschaft relations comprise the rational, contractual, instrumental, and task-oriented actions, as in a business corporation. In Gemeinschaft relations, actors are said to interact as whole persons; in Gesellschaft relations, as specific parts of their personalities, interacting for specific and limited purposes. Three early social theorists, Ferdinand Toennies, Max Weber, and Emile Durkheim, were responsible for first formulating elements of this dichotomy.

Though Gemeinschaft and Gesellschaft refer to ideal types rather than actual social groups and are old-fashioned sociological terms, they are useful in describing the two pulls experienced by utopian communities. The Gemeinschaft aspects of a utopian community consist of those mutually expressive, supportive, value-oriented, emotion-laden, personally-directed, loving social relations often called "community." They include mutual recognition of the values, temperament, character, and human needs of group members. Their highest priority is maintenance of values and close relations, and they are based on commitment, the personal involvement of participating members. In contrast, the Gesellschaft elements in a utopian community consist of those relations that are functional for dealing with environments, whether physical, social, or supernatural; for "getting the job done"; for acquiring things the group needs from its environment; for maximizing feedback and exchange with other systems in the form of information, resources, or acceptance. They include any activity that is relevant to conducting environmental exchanges regardless of the specific people involved. Gesellschaft systems organize group relations around the demands of tasks. Since any group that forms a "community" must also produce something or manage exchanges with an environment, and since these aims may require different and possibly incompatible forms of organization, a tension is set up that can force the group to make a choice of emphasis. The predominant movement of many of the successful nineteenth-century groups was away from a heavy initial emphasis on community toward the predominance of Gesellschaft. This change meant the end of the community and its transformation into a specialized organization. Amana, for example, evolved from a highly value-oriented Gemeinschaft community, in which production was secondary and designed only to meet subsistence requirements of the group, to a business-oriented system, hoping nevertheless to maintain its now secondary spiritual and human concerns: "The new Amana [after its dissolution and reorganization] is something more than a modern business structure with emphasis on methods and efficiency and the earning power of the dollar. * * * There is a manifest desire to keep intact, as far as possible, the Community consciousness born of a precious heritage—a wealth of common aspirations and memories, and of spiritual assets that cannot be weighed, nor measured, nor tabulated, nor charted." The evolution of Oneida in a similar direction, ending in a joint-stock company carrying on a silverware-manufacturing business, is strikingly demonstrated by changes in the community's newspaper, *The Circular,* noted by Maren Lockwood. In 1851, three years after the founding of Oneida, almost all of *The Circular* was devoted to religion. By 1861, about half dealt with religion, and by 1870, less than a third. In 1876 *The Circular* was renamed *The American Socialist.*

This tension between the two pulls in social life was a factor in practically all of the nineteenth century communes studied, for the great majority of them were more than simple agricultural societies; they were to some extent concerned not only about production of enough goods and services for the community but also about their commercial and political relations with the larger society. Most of them had businesses of one kind or another, sometimes servicing the community primarily but also exchanging goods with the outside society. Zoar had both agriculture and industry, including woolen, linen, and flour mills, a timber planing business, and a wagon shop. Oneida in its early years engaged in farming and silk-jobbing besides running a flour mill, saw mill, and machine shop. It then began successful fruit-canning, bag-manufacturing, and animal trap businesses, and still later a successful silverware factory. Saint Nazianz sold cheese, beer, straw hats, shoes, and wheat. Among Harmony's items of commerce were hides, grains, furs, waxes, linen, tobacco, and cheese. The Shakers are still known for the furniture they manufactured.

The kinds of organization that are functional for production and business operations may often conflict with the commitment mechanisms that serve to maintain community feeling. This issue is being faced by communal groups today. As the Israeli kibbutzim, for example, industrialize and build modern factories on their grounds, they are coping with the issue of maintaining a value-oriented, communal society that at the same time permits efficient industrial production and remains fully a part of the modern world. So far they have avoided the several dilemmas arising from the two pulls in social life that contributed to the weakening of commitment and the dissolution of the successful nineteenth-century groups. These dilemmas involved pulls toward permeability, isomorphism, value indeterminism, and perpetuation strategies that undermined community.

Permeability refers to the degree to which community boundaries are open and permit penetration of movement across them, that is, the ease with which people can pass over the group's boundaries. Such easy passage is functional for economic and political tasks for several reasons. The necessity of dealing with external systems requires an organizational structure that is not totally encapsulated. For one thing, commercial enterprises need information about the state of the environmental systems with which they must deal—about market conditions, for example. Permeability facilitates the garnering of information and the attainment of feedback, for it is relatively easy for information and feedback-bearers to pass in and out of the organization. Similarly, organizations can exchange personnel if easy passage into the system is possible and can thereby learn about external systems. Furthermore, when boundaries between the organization and its environments are not well defined or rigid, the line between what constitutes the organization's and the environment's interests may appear to be erased, so that helping the organization meet its goals may at the same time fulfill more general public interests.

Permeability can further aid dealings with the environment through the creation of boundary roles for the organization—roles such as salesman, customer relations specialist, or ambassador—which must often operate both within and outside the organization simultaneously. Many nineteenth-century groups, for example, had salesmen. In order for these roles to be effective and to facilitate exchange with the external systems with which they deal, organization boundaries must be relatively permeable. In addition, organizations must perform jobs for their members, and to this end they require resources and personnel. If necessary, these must be quickly attainable and deployable without requiring a difficult passage through a rigid boundary. If labor is required to meet immediate needs, for example, it is not altogether functional to insist that manpower wait through a six-month probationary period or that it make financial contributions. If boundaries are relatively permeable, appropriate experts, resources, and staff can be more easily imported. The most production-oriented of the successful nineteenth-century groups (Amana, Oneida, Harmony, the Shakers, and Zoar) all opened their boundaries and waived their usual requirements in the hiring of outside labor at periods of peak demand. In Oneida in 1880 there were 200 hired workers at peak times in a community otherwise totaling only 288. Finally, permeable boundaries make it possible for the organization to co-opt threatening elements from the outside, since they may be more easily incorporated into the system.

Permeability, while it may aid exchange goals, nevertheless conflicts with many commitment mechanisms that help to maintain communal relations. For example, insulation from the outside is a major renunciation mechanism, but permeable boundaries are almost diametrically opposed to insulated boundaries. The community's distinctiveness and social isolation may be lost when boundaries are relatively permeable. Permeability means almost by definition that stringent entrance requirements, such as investment and ideological conversion, which serve as commitment mechanisms, can no longer exist. Furthermore, permeable boundaries interfere with the cross-boundary control that is functional for communal relations, since the social limits of an organization and its demarcation from the environment are somewhat vague. An organization with permeable boundaries tends to become more heterogeneous, because it more readily admits diverse elements to its ranks, whereas homogeneity is the attribute that facilitates communion in utopian communities. The provision of boundary roles further tends to create people who have at least two allegiances—inside and outside the system—but what is required by utopian communities to maintain their communality are strong exclusive loyalties. Since occupants of boundary roles are not encapsulated within the organization, they need not be totally committed to it. Finally, if it is easy to import relevant experts and personnel, if people can pass in and out of the system with relatively little difficulty, the organization will tend to become staffed by a corps of "professionals," personnel who are relatively disinterested in the purposes of the organization and have little personal stake in its success or failure. Nineteenth century groups had such personnel late in their lives in the form of hired labor. Yet the required characteristics for maintaining communal relations are just the opposite: a strong interest and involvement with the community qua community, as well as a sizable stake in its future.

Isomorphism refers to the structural similarity between the community and its environment. Such parallelism facilitates cross-boundary dealings and exchanges for several reasons. In the first place, social systems that attempt to conduct relations with one another should generally share language, symbols, and media of exchange, which isomorphism implies. Second, labor and experts imported from the outside are more easily deployable in organizations that are isomorphic with respect to the environment, since these personnel need not be resocialized in order to participate in the system; roles in such a system are familiar and can be adopted by new members with less elaborate preparation than in nonisomorphic systems. Similarly, resources and information can be imported without having to transmute them. To offer a simple example, if outsiders speak the same language, communication with them does not require translation. Structural isomorphism may also aid the attainment of exchange goals, since organizations find it easier to deal with each other if they are set up in a similar fashion. If there is point to point correspondence, through similar structures and roles, it will be easier to form a relationship: for example, there will be a purchasing agent to deal with salesmen. An organization may also find itself in a more competitive position if it imitates other organizations of similar type. Finally, a certain amount of similarity to external systems is necessary for an organization to have dealings with other social systems, for being different in a cultural sense poses a threat to other systems at the most, and at the least hampers outstanding and public relations.

Isomorphism for purposes of exchanging with environments interferes to an extent with organization for the attainment of communal goals, however. For utopian communities, the sharing of symbols and media of exchange often means accepting the terms of the larger society and thereby subverting their own ideals and values. Sometimes it forces them to give up a distinctive language and dress, or to end job rotation. It creates practical problems as well. One such problem arises when utopian communities that do not use money in their internal dealings and do not reimburse their own members for labor must pay outside labor in money, becoming in this respect isomorphic with other employing organizations. Internal conflicts and value conflicts may ensue when outsiders are paid in cash and members are not, as happened in Zoar. Isomorphism owing to the pressure for favorable public relations may be similarly detrimental to communal goals and commitment mechanisms. One of several pressures for the transformation of Oneida from a group-marriage commune into a joint-stock company resembling other production organizations was unfavorable publicity and the threat of legal action concerning its practice of free love. Isomorphism also obviates the need for resocialization, since the community already parallels the outside, but in so doing it eliminates the resocialization practices that have value as mortification and surrender mechanisms. While isomorphism may aid environmental and exchange goals, therefore, it may also interfere with the maintenance of communal systems, whose purpose in existing may be their expression of unique and different values.

Value indeterminism is a third functional characteristic of production and exchange systems, one which aids organizational flexibility, especially in light of the need to deal with environments that may be continually changing. In order to ensure the ability to meet the challenge of such change, production organizations may either divorce values from actions and decisions, or adopt values of such wide scope that they encompass a large number of alternative courses of action. In either event, the organization is left free, at least in terms of its values, to make decisions and take actions with respect to external systems. This value indeterminism of organizations is similar in concept to the indeterminism of the collective conscience in modern society described by Emile Durkheim. Communal systems, however, are supported by the opposite phenomenon, value determinism, characterized by elaborate ideologies, detailed specification of rules and procedures, and the basing of decisions on values and ideals. For utopian communities, then, the requirements of community versus those of outside relations provide a possible source of conflict. I am making no judgments about rationality or irrationality here, merely about the guiding and determining role of values.

Communes can take several paths to resolve this dilemma. One strategy is to make values highly determinate of the personal conduct of members but relatively indeterminate of organizational policies, that is, to make them specific with respect to the appropriate behavior of individual members but relatively vague with respect to appropriate organizational behavior. This solution tended to characterize the accommodation of the Shakers. Another solution is to have dual leadership: one set of leaders can interpret and protect the community's values, serving as ideological spokesmen and watchmen; the other set can take care of the day-to-day dealings of the community, free from any otherwise desirable ideological coercion. This arrangement was generally characteristic of Harmony, Zoar, Oneida, and Amana, all of which had business managers as well as spiritual leaders. Saint Nazianz also developed a dual leadership after its founder's death. In addition, however, all of the successful utopias toward the end of their lives (with the exception of Jerusalem, which dissolved much earlier) faced environments quite different in nature from those that existed when the utopias were founded. In order to deal with these changes, value indeterminism became increasingly prevalent in all of the communities. The fact that in Oneida the amount of space devoted to spiritual matters and ideology in community newspapers decreased over the years of the community's existence indicated that increasing attention was paid to practical matters. Even when rules proliferated, as with the Shakers, values tended to become obsolete. In fact, Joseph Eaton pointed out with respect to the Hutterites that a rule proliferation in itself represents an accommodation to a changing environment.

The use of perpetuation strategies represents another way in which social systems can be organized to facilitate cross-boundary exchanges. Provision for leadership succession and for recruitment are two such strategies. Not only do these mechanisms ensure adequate personnel and leadership for the Gesellschaft-type system to accomplish its ends in the external relationship, but they also make the organization appear to have a life extending into the indefinite future, which facilitates its entering into stable and relatively permanent contracts, obligations, and networks of ties with outside environments. Such organizations must make provision for the continual availability of leadership and personnel, as well as acceptance of them by current members. In contrast, communal relations in the abstract require no such provisions, for they need no personnel, accomplish no tasks, and need not outlive the community of the committed, since it was founded to satisfy the needs of a specific group of people. If a communal system expresses the symbolic outputs and emotional feelings of particular people, then as a group it need not continue when those people are no longer present. In fact, in one sense a communal relation is by definition a relationship among particular people who are committed not only to the system as such but also to each other as the system's participants. Commercial and political orders, however, are often required by their systemic nature to continue even when particular leaders and particular personnel are no longer available, for they have in a sense contracted with their members and with the outside world to continue to serve their needs with respect to the environment, and to continue to bring in the appropriate resources or feedback, regardless of which particular personnel cooperate to perform these tasks. In addition, such systems may have entered into contractual relations with the environmental sources of feedback and must continue to exist in order to carry out their contracts.

For nineteenth-century utopian communities, the problem of leadership succession was an acute one. Many, both successful and unsuccessful in terms of number of years of existence, fell apart when their founder and charismatic leader died. Those that provided for continuity of leadership, however, managed to outlive their founders. Charismatic leaders thus may facilitate commitment and sustain communal relations, but they are somewhat dysfunctional for the perpetuation of other kinds of organization, such as Gesellschaft systems.

Recruitment is another general means of ensuring perpetuation, but it too may interfere with communal relations. Member homogeneity and communion may be disturbed by the addition of new elements into the community. New recruits may not be moved by the same values as the original members, and elaborate selection and processing procedures may be required. Recruitment itself represents a relationship between an organization and an environmental system, in this case the utopia's "public," and by virtue of the decision to recruit, such communities may find themselves changing in order to be competitive in the personnel market. This phenomenon characterized many nineteenth-century utopias.

These are a few of the dilemmas faced by utopian communities of the past owing to the dual pulls in their social life between Gemeinschaft and Gesellschaft processes. Early in their histories the successful communes had concentrated on building community, on developing strong commitment, and gave only secondary importance to production and other goals with respect to their environment. As they grew, however, these secondary goals also grew in importance, and "conducting business" began to conflict with maintaining community feeling. By the end of their histories, many commitment mechanisms had disappeared, and commitment itself was eroding.

Prosperity and Decline

One indication of the increasing attention shown to practical matters in the successful nineteenth century groups is the fact that they tended, on the whole, to become financially prosperous. Whereas in their early years they had suffered through periods of struggle and hardship, by the time they dissolved they were often wealthy, or if they had many outstanding debts, these had followed a period of prosperity. For nineteenth century communities at least, financial prosperity may be associated with the decline of community—partly because it indicated the growth of efficient Gesellschaft organization and partly because of the social consequences of prosperity, such as emphasis on individual consumption. Prosperity may lead to bureaucracy and privatism. Richard Ely wrote in 1885 that whereas poverty can knit members into a compact whole, "prosperity can be fatal." Charles Gide stated: "Perhaps the gravest [peril] of all lies in the fact that these colonies are threatened as much by success as by failure * * * If they attain prosperity they attract a crowd of members who lack the enthusiasm and faith of the earlier ones and are attracted only by self-interest. Then there is a conflict between the older element and the new."

There is evidence that if financial prosperity is not associated with a utopian community's failure, then at least it is unrelated to its ability to continue in existence. A number of both successful and unsuccessful utopias weathered periods of hardship and suffered financial losses without dissolving, but then broke up at a time when they had accumulated great wealth and showed a profit. * * * [The] evidence suggests that at the very least one can agree with Ralph Albertson's conclusion that American utopias with few exceptions were successful in earning their living: "Few colonies, if any, failed because they could not make their living * * * They failed to like communal housekeeping. They failed to hold their young people. They failed to compete with growing industry and commerce in a new, unexploited country. But they did not fail to make an independent subsistence living—and pay off a lot of debts and help a lot of stranded people."

With prosperity came not only reinforcement of forms of organization that were often in tension with community but also other kinds of conflict that contributed to the death of successful nineteenth-century groups. In particular, competition between individuals and families increased, as did the desire for private rather than shared ownership. In 1895 in Zoar, a few years before its final dissolution, the newspaper, *Nugitna,* began agitating for the right to withdraw from the communal society and to acquire property. As forms of organization oriented toward production, commerce, and exchange superceded commitment mechanisms, the old zeal and devotion to communal ideals declined, the will to continue the community in its utopian, communal form decreased, and the end was in sight.

Prosperity is enough of an issue for communal groups even today that not only do many communes self-consciously choose austerity and poverty rather than affluence, but also some refuse to work at making any more money than will meet their immediate needs. The Bruderhof, for example, have a successful toy-manufacturing business and could sell as much as they produce; but they often stop production when they feel they have earned enough to meet their daily needs.

All of the factors described—environmental change, population aging, and a growing tendency away from community toward organizational efficiency—intertwined to erode the commitment that had held successful communes together in the nineteenth century. * * * The commitment that had enabled the successful nineteenth-century utopian communities to withstand threats to their existence early in their history, which had provided members with the determination to continue, which had developed relationships that could weather disagreement, dissatisfaction, or defections, and which had reinforced firm belief in the community's ideals and values, had declined by the time they dissolved. They faced a set of forces that grew in magnitude as the communities progressed, and which eventually proved too much for even the strongest. Some groups died slowly (like the Shakers), others dissolved formally, and still others reorganized to perform a specialized job. But whatever the issues, problems, and concerns that first brought these utopian communities together, the world they faced at their conclusion was very different from that existing at their beginning. In today's world, a new set of communes has arisen, growing out of the issues and concerns of today, but with much still to be learned about their problems and prospects by examining the lessons of the past. * * *

The major difference between establishing a new community in the nineteenth and twentieth centuries is the degree of difficulty a group encounters in constructing strong boundaries and creating a coherent group. Whereas it was relatively easy for groups to develop clearcut boundaries in the nineteenth century, it is relatively difficult today. Although the strength of a commune today is still contingent on the presence of commitment mechanisms, the problems of employing these mechanisms have been exaggerated by the difficulties of developing and maintaining boundaries in an urban era of mass communication, easy mobility, and rapid social change. Strong communities today can generate and maintain commitment because of their adaptive solutions to boundary problems, while weak communes succumb to the boundary-denying forces in the society and become limited communities of narrow scope.

Boundary Problems

Boundaries define a group, set it off from its environment, and give it a sharp focus, which facilitates commitment. Strong communities tend to have strong boundaries—physical, social, and behavioral. What goes on within the community is sharply differentiated from what goes on outside. As with the secret societies described by Georg Simmel, events inside the community may even be kept hidden from outsiders and reserved for members alone to know, witness, and perform. One kind of boundary may help to define another. Physical boundaries, as of location and territory, might define those people with whom a person may legitimately engage in a relationship. Social boundaries may define behavioral ones, as in a monogamous marriage, where the two people who have defined themselves through the relationship behave toward each other in ways that they do not exhibit toward others.

With strong boundaries, it is clear who belongs to the group and who does not. The outside may treat members as a unit for many purposes. Passing in and out of the community, both for new recruits and for old members, may be relatively difficult. The definition of a communal group as an expressive unit concerned with interchanges between its members, as a group of people interested in mutual support and a shared way of life, indicates in part the importance of boundaries, because of their value in preserving the uniqueness of interaction between the specific set of people comprising the community.

Many of the commitment mechanisms that differentiated successful from unsuccessful nineteenth-century communes revolved around erecting and maintaining strong affirmative boundaries, which distinguished the group from its environment, so that members created for themselves psychic boundaries that encompassed the community—no more and no less—as the object of commitment and fulfillment. The commitment-generating problems of some unsuccessful groups can even be pinpointed as boundary issues, such as the fact that New Harmony let anyone in, exercising no selectivity and no socialization, or the fact that members of Brook Farm practically commuted to Boston. Many of the difficulties that successful groups later encountered stemmed in part from a weakening of the boundaries: hiring outside workers, educating children on the outside, increasing numbers of visitors, adopting the fruits of outside social change, and most important, engaging in expanded commerce and trade or decreased internal production and consumption, which destroyed the kind of self-sufficiency that itself constitutes a boundary.

Communes are conscious and purposeful in their attempt to separate from the larger society and create a special group. In the nineteenth century, conditions were such that distinct boundaries could be erected with relative ease. Physical isolation was possible, as well as a relatively self-sufficient farm and light industry economy. Technological needs were low, and contact with the outside minimized, so that a group could become institutionally complete, a comprehensive community comprised of all social institutions. Communication was slow, so that it was possible for a group to remain hidden, developing and maintaining a distinctive culture. Travel was generally confined to small geographic areas. There were fewer options for life in the society—from choice of career to choice of life style—so that it was possible to find a homogeneous group of people who were willing to share beliefs, without the confusion and pressure of constant subjection to opposing views. Some commitment mechanisms even arose unintentionally: the distinctive language and dress style of such groups as Harmony and Amana were a function of the fact that they were immigrant groups with a transplanted culture, but could, in the nineteenth century, experience few pressures for assimilation.

Twentieth-century American society provides a very different kind of environment, one that is constantly intruding and penetrating the borders of groups, which contributes to the fact that the boundaries of most contemporary communes are weak and constantly shifting. Four characteristics of contemporary society are primarily responsible: urbanization, advanced technology, instant communication, and a white middle-class culture that is increasingly both national (fairly uniform across the country) and pluralistic and eclectic within the range of options provided nationally. More people live in cities and want to stay in cities, which has given rise to urban communes, a new phenomenon of this century, for evidence is lacking of any urban utopias in the last century. Advanced technology makes it less possible for any group to supply all or most of its needs by itself or for a small group easily to develop an economic base as a complete production unit. Thus, many communes today do not even attempt to constitute an economic unit, concentrating rather on being a family, which typifies the diminishment of scope characterizing a large proportion of the new communes. Institutional comprehensiveness is no longer as possible as it was in the nineteenth century. Instant communication means that new ideas and new stimuli can intrude constantly, increasing the difficulty of generating and maintaining a distinctive set of beliefs. Most communes today do not develop their own ideologies, and even when they do, they often borrow and incorporate bits and pieces from other people and other groups. The problems of ideological completeness, therefore—of any one group developing a unique, comprehensive ideology—are intensified.

These three factors—urbanization, technology, and mass communication—have supported the development of a national middle class culture that is increasingly both uniform across regions and pluralistic in terms of styles available. People are more mobile—particularly the young, who are the ripest recruits for the new communes. As they move, they carry with them across the nation the counterculture of which communes are one part. In addition, people and places are increasingly interchangeable. If strong utopian communities in fact resemble secret societies, then in the twentieth century most communes participate in a culture that has become too pervasive and widespread to develop such a secret, shared truth. Developing a distinctive culture, set off from that of the surrounding environment, is much more difficult today than in the nineteenth century; many contemporary communes choose not even to try, again retreating from their former scope. Rather than separating themselves from society, as did the communes of the last century, many become a link in a chain of the national counterculture, exchanging members with other communes. The fact that modern American culture is at the same time pluralistic and eclectic, surrounding the person with a much greater number of options than in the last century—with respect to careers, consumption, relationships—makes it harder for the individual both to make definitive choices (as of one group or one culture and life style within that group) and to find one set of people with whom he can share every aspect of his life, since everyone else has the same large number of options from which to extract a life style. The individual constructs his own social world out of the myriad choices confronting him, and the chance that many others will construct theirs in exactly the same way is much more limited than in the less diverse environment of the last century. Without a strong set of beliefs to indicate to the person why he should suspend his options, he generally continues to exercise them in the new communes. And most new communes, given the increased difficulty of placing limits on options, choose not to do so.

The boundary problems of today's communes are exacerbated by the fact that communes as a unique social arrangement lack definition and legitimacy in American society. For legal and official purposes, they must define themselves in terms of some other form such as a nonprofit corporation, a business, a church, an educational institution, or a family. Sunrise Hill set itself up as a trust fund; Synanon defined itself as a charitable foundation; the Fort Hill commune is organized into a holding corporation, "United Illuminating." Moreover, whereas the norms of the larger society indicate the ways in which legitimate social institutions are to be approached, there are not yet such established guidelines for communes. There are socially delimited ways of entering a family, for example—through marriage, birth, or legal adoption—but no similar guidelines for joining a commune. In America as a whole, strangers do not knock at the doors of residences asking for a place to sleep or inquiring whether they can become a member of that particular family, but they do approach communes with these requests. To some extent, communes are considered fair game for anyone, and their borders are easily penetrable.

Thus, it is more difficult today to develop strong boundaries than it was in the nineteenth century, and territorial or spatial limits no longer suffice to give a group coherence. Today's communes have had to develop other kinds of group-environment relations and other means of handling their boundary problems, for as Eric Berne pointed out, the existence of a group is in part dependent on being able to predict who will or will not be present and behaving in particular ways at specific events. That is, the very definition of a group is to some extent dependent on the existence of boundaries: "constitutional, psychological or spatial distinctions between members and non-members."

Boundaries transcend people, however; they also distinguish between events that occur within a group and those that do not. Boundary distinctions can be established on two principles, affirmative and negative. Affirmative principles define the group by what it accepts; negative, by what it rejects. Affirmative boundaries encompass only that which is accepted by the group; all events or people are excluded except those specifically included. A person is not "in" unless the group defines him as "in." Norms are positive, specifically defining appropriate behavior and events. Negative boundaries, in contrast, encompass everything but what the group specifically rejects; all events or people are included except those explicitly excluded. A person is not "out" unless the group defines him as "out." All behavior is permitted except that defined as inappropriate. Affirmative boundaries, then, are characteristic of secret societies in being exclusive and strict. Negative boundaries are characteristic of open societies in that they are inclusive and permissive. Affirmative boundaries are more conducive to building commitment than are negative boundaries.

Today's communes can be placed in two general categories, depending on the predominance of negative or affirmative boundaries. One set of communes, in line with today's diminishing scope and retreat themes, has primarily negative boundaries. I call these "retreat" communes. They tend to be small, anarchistic, and easily dissolved, predominantly rural and youth-oriented. Some urban communes also fall into this category, since they choose to specialize in domestic life rather than to develop a complete set of social institutions. They limit their goals to relationships, and like the rural retreat groups, they tend to be permissive, inclusive, and temporary. But the rural communes tend to be more purposeful and organized than the urban ones, and also to have some minimal shared economy, which urban houses generally lack. Thus, urban communes must be considered a different phenomenon, representing alternative forms of the family rather than new communities.

The other set of communes has affirmative boundaries. Rather than shrinking into a small family or avoiding the issue of boundaries altogether, these communes choose interaction with the wider society through service. Their mission gives them the focus around which to erect affirmative boundaries. They are either urban or rural, tend to have a strong core group holding the community together, and incorporate in their structure ways of coping with the mobility and turnover characteristic of today. They may also be larger and more enduring than retreat communes. More traditional utopias, such as the Bruderhof and Twin Oaks, and religious missionary communes are similar to the service communes in that they, too, have affirmative boundaries. In the twentieth century, however, affirmation alone may not be enough to give a group strength, and to the extent that a commune can define a special way in which it helps or transforms the larger social environment, it may gain added strength and ability to endure.

The distinction between retreat and service communes corresponds roughly to those made by other observers of the contemporary commune movement. Retreat groups tend to be what Bennett Berger called "noncreedal," in that they generally lack a shared ideology or creed; service communes more often are "creedal." Retreat communes tend to be solidarity-based and unintentional; service communes are generally ideology-based and intentional. Service communes are more similar to the utopias of the past, and many of the lessons of the past apply to them. Retreat communes, in contrast, are part of the new contemporary movement to regain Eden. * * *

[handwritten margin note: Retreat v. service communes]

PHILIPPE ARIES, THE FAMILY AND THE CITY IN THE OLD WORLD AND THE NEW

From V. Tufte and B. Myerhoff, Changing Images of the Family.
Pp. 29–41 (1979).

I should like to make some observations in this essay about the relationship between family history and urban history. My central theme will be that when the city (and earlier, the rural community) deteriorated and lost its vitality, the role of the family overexpanded like a hypertrophied cell. In an attempt to fill the gap created by the decline of the city and the urban forms of social intercourse it had once provided, the omnipotent, omnipresent family took upon itself the task of trying to satisfy all the emotional and social needs of its members. Today, it is clear that the family has failed in its attempts to accomplish that feat, either because the increased emphasis on privacy has stifled the need for social intercourse or because the family has been too completely alienated by public powers. People are demanding that the family do everything that the outside world in its indifference or hostility refuses to do. But we should now ask ourselves why people have come to expect the family to satisfy all their needs, as if it had some kind of all-encompassing power.

First, let us take a brief look at Western traditional societies from the Middle Ages to the eighteenth century, that is, before they had been affected by the Enlightenment and the Industrial Revolution. Each individual grew up in a community of relatives, neighbors, friends, enemies, and others with whom he or she had interdependent relationships. The community was more important in determining the individual's fate than was the family. When a young boy left his mother's apron strings, it was his responsibility to make a place for himself. Like an animal or a bird, he had to establish a domain, and he had to get the community to recognize it. It was up to him to determine the limits of his authority, to decide what he could do and how far he could go before encountering resistance from others—his parents, his wife, his neighbors. Securing his domain in this way depended more on the skillful use of natural talents than on knowledge or savoir-faire. It was a game in which the venturesome boy gifted in eloquence and with a dramatic flair had the advantage. All life was a stage: if a player went too far, he was put in his place; if he hesitated, he was relegated to an inferior role.

Since a man knew that his wife would be his most important and faithful collaborator in maintaining and expanding his role, he chose his bride with care. On her part, the woman accepted the domain she would have to protect, along with the man with whom she would live. Marriage strengthened the husband's position, as a result not only of his wife's work, but also of her personality, her presence of mind, her talents as player, actress, storyteller, her ability to seize opportunities and to assert herself.

The important concept, then, is that of *domain*. But this domain was neither private nor public, as these terms are understood today; rather, it was both simultaneously: private because it had to do with individual behavior, with one's personality, one's manner of being alone or in society, one's self-awareness and inner being; public because it fixed the individual's place within the community and established one's rights and obligations. Individual maneuvering was possible because the social space was not completely filled. The fabric was loose, and it behooved each person to adjust the seams to suit himself or herself within the limits set by the community. The community recognized the existence of the empty space surrounding people and things. It is worth remarking that the word *play* can mean both the act of playing and freedom of movement within a space. Perhaps, by the act of playing, the free space to play in was created and maintained. The state and society intervened in a person's life only infrequently and intermittently, bringing with them either terror and ruin or miraculous good fortune. But for the most part, individuals had to win their domains by coming to terms only with the men and women in their own small community.

The role of the family was to strengthen the authority of the head of the household, without threatening the stability of his relationship with the community. Married women would gather at the wash house, men at the cabaret. Each sex had its special place in church, in processions, in the public square, at celebrations, and even at the dance. But the family as such had no domain of its own; the only real domain was that each male won by his maneuvering, with the help of his wife, friends, and dependents.

In the course of the eighteenth century the situation began to change, influenced by three important trends. The first is the loss of "frontiers," to use American parlance; we might say that in earlier centuries the community had a frontier—or rather several frontiers—that could be pushed back by the audacious. Free areas were allowed to exist, and adventurous individuals were permitted to explore them. But in the eighteenth century, society—or more properly, the state—was loath to accept the fact that there were certain areas beyond its sphere of control and influence. Following upon the Enlightenment and industrialization, the state, with its sophisticated technology and organization, wiped out those frontiers: there was no longer an open area for the venturesome. Today the state's scrutiny and control extend, or are supposed to extend, into every sphere of activity. Today there is no free space for individuals to occupy and claim for themselves. To be sure, liberal societies allow individuals some initiative, but for the most part only in specific areas, such as school and work, where there is a preestablished order of promotion. This is a situation totally different from that in traditional society. In the new society, the concepts of play and free space are no longer accepted; society must be too well regulated.

The second phenomenon that produced this change is directly related to the first: this is the division of space into areas assigned to work and areas assigned to living. The worker is now required to leave what had been the domain in traditional society, the space where *all* activities had taken place, to go to work far away, sometimes very far away, in a very different environment. There the worker becomes subject to a system of rules and to a hierarchy of power. In this new world, the worker may, for all we know, be happier and more secure, involved in association with others, for example, through trade unions.

This specialized place devoted to work was invented by the new society in its abhorrence of uncontrolled space. To run industrial, commercial, and business enterprises successfully requires systems of tight control. Free-enterprise capitalism has demonstrated its ability to adapt, but this flexibility has nothing in common with the old concept of free space; rather it depends on the precise functioning of the unit as a whole. Although enterprises in a free-market economy may not be controlled by the state, they are no less controlled by society at large. One could reasonably argue that this displacement of workers was a form of "surveillance and punishment," as Foucault phrased it, similar to locking up children in school, the insane in asylums, and delinquents in prison. It was certainly, at the very least, a means of maintaining order and control.

The third and last important phenomenon that affected the transformations of the eighteenth and nineteenth centuries is different from the first two; it is psychological. But the chronological correlation with the other two is significant. The era witnessed not only an industrial revolution but an emotional revolution as well. Previously, feelings were diffuse, spread out over numerous natural and supernatural objects, including God, saints, parents, children, friends, horses, dogs, orchards, and gardens. Henceforth, they would be focused within the immediate family. The couple and their children became the objects of a passionate and exclusive love that transcended even death.

From that time on, a working man's life was polarized between job and family. But the people who did not go out to work (women, children, old men) were concerned exclusively with family life. Nor was the division between job and family either equal or symmetrical. Although there was no doubt some room for emotional involvement at work, the family was a more conducive setting; whereas the working world was subject to constant, strict surveillance, the family was a place of refuge, free from outside control. The family thus acquired some similarities to the individual domain in traditional society, but with an important distinction: the family is not a place for individualism. The individual must recede into the background for the sake of the family unit, and especially for the sake of the children. Furthermore, the family had become more removed from the community than in earlier times, and it tended to be rather hostile to the external world, to withdraw into itself. Thus, it became *the* private domain, the only place where a person could legitimately escape the inquisitive stare of industrial society. Even now, industrial society has not given up trying to fill the gaps created by the decline of traditional society; it does, nevertheless, show some respect for the new entity—the family—which has grown up in its midst as a place of refuge. Thus, the separation of space into work areas and living areas corresponds to the division of life into public sector and private sector. The family falls within the private sector.

These, then, were the main features of the new way of life. They evolved slowly in the industrialized West, and were not equally accepted in all places. Two important periods must be distinguished: the nineteenth century before the automobile conquered space, and the first half of the twentieth. The difference between the two lies in the degree of privacy that people enjoyed and in the nature of the public sector.

During the first period, roughly the whole of the nineteenth century, family life among the bourgeoisie and the peasantry was already much as it is today, that is, it was a private domain. But—and this distinction is very important—only women (including those who worked) were affected by the increased privacy; men were able to escape at times, and they no doubt considered it a male prerogative to do so. Women and children had virtually no life outside the family and the school; these comprised their entire universe. Men, on the other hand, had a lively meeting place outside their families and jobs—to wit, the city.

In peasant societies, age-old tradition and the innovations of the industrial era are so intertwined that it is difficult for the analyst to distinguish among them. Still, it should be noted that historians today agree that, thanks to the agricultural prosperity in Western Europe during the nineteenth century, a flourishing rural civilization developed there. This was no doubt true of the United States as well. Is it not said that in certain regions of the Midwest immigrants have maintained traditions that have long since disappeared in their original homelands? These flourishing subcultures testify to the enormous vitality of the rural communities at a time when privacy, the family, and the school were making great inroads upon them. The rural exodus had not yet destroyed peasant life; rather, it had made it easier. This was the era of the beautiful costumes and regional furniture we find displayed today in folk museums. It was a time when folk tales were easily collected. It was also, however, a time when, thanks to the schools, many peasants were trying desperately to force open the doors to government careers for their children (who by then had grown fewer in number). The elementary school teacher was an important person in nineteenth-century rural communities; this is not true today. But it is the urban, not the rural, development that I should now like to discuss.

The long nineteenth century marked a high point in the development of the city and its urban civilization. No doubt urban populations had already increased to frightening levels; the poor immigrants who descended en masse upon them from the villages appeared as a threat to the bourgeois property owners, who watched them encamp in their towns and viewed them as an army of criminals and rebels. But this image borne of fear need not deceive us today. To be sure, the large city was no longer what it had been in the seventeenth century, that is, a group of separate neighborhoods or streets, each constituting a community with a character of its own. In eighteenth-century Paris, the arrival of a transient population without a fixed place of residence upset this way of life. Traditional patterns of social intercourse based on neighborhoods and streets began to disappear. But new ones that maintained and developed the city's basic functions replaced them.

Central to these new patterns were the café and the restaurant, public meeting places where conversation flowed as abundantly as food and drink. The café was a place for discussion, an invention of the late eighteenth century. Previously there had been eating places, inns, and hostels, places to serve meals in the home or to provide food and lodging for transient guests. There were also taverns and cabarets where people went to drink, and often for the low life to be found there. But they were places of ill-repute, sometimes brothels. Cafés, on the other hand, were something completely new and different. They were strictly an urban phenomenon, unknown in rural areas. The cafés were meeting places in cities, which were growing very rapidly and where people did not know one another as they had before. In England the cafés were enclosed like cabarets, but the name *pub* describes their function well. In continental Europe, cafés opened onto the street and came to dominate them, thanks to their terraces. Cafés with their large terraces were in fact one of the most striking features of nineteenth-century cities. They were all but nonexistent in the medieval and Renaissance sections of the old cities, such as Rome, but they were very much in evidence in those same Italian cities around the large public squares that owe their existence to Cavour's vast urbanization and Italian unity. In Vienna, too, cafés were, and still are, the heart of the city. In Paris the opening of the cafés was probably the reason behind the shift to public life from closed places, like the famous gallery at the Palais Royal, to the linear, open space of the boulevard, the center of the city's night life.

Cafés no doubt originally served the aristocracy rather than the bourgeoisie. But they were quickly popularized and extended to all classes of society and to all neighborhoods. In nineteenth-century cities, there was not a neighborhood without at least one café, and more often several. In working-class neighborhoods, the small café played a vital role; it enabled communication that would otherwise have been impossible among the poorly housed residents who were often away at their jobs: the café served as message center. That is why the telephone became so immediately accessible after its advent. The café became the place where steady customers could make and receive telephone calls, leave and receive messages. It is easy to understand Maurice Aguilhon's surprise at the extraordinary number of small cafés in a city like Marseilles, each with its little network of neighbors and friends gathered around the counter and the telephone. The number and popularity of these cafés suggest that a new public sector had spontaneously developed in the nineteenth-century city.

Needless to say, the state's desire for control extended even to this new public sector. The state immediately understood the danger represented by the cafés and sought to limit it by establishing and enforcing codes and regulations. But it never completely succeeded. In addition self-righteous people, concerned with order and morality, were suspicious of the cafés, which they considered to be hotbeds of alcoholism, anarchy, laziness, vice, and political wrangling. In France even today urban planners relegate cafés to shopping districts in residential areas and at a good distance from any elementary or secondary schools. But the mistrust of the authorities and of the self-righteous has still failed to diminish the popularity of the cafés. In the nineteenth century, civilization was based on them.

Now let us compare the role played by the café in that era to that played by the family. The family was a private place, the café a public one. But they had one thing in common: they both managed to escape society's control. The family did so by right, the café in actual fact. These were the only two exceptions to the modern system of surveillance and order which came to include all social behavior. Thus, alongside the growing privacy of the family during the nineteenth and early twentieth centuries, a new and lively form of social intercourse developed in even the largest cities. This explains why the cities of the era were so full of life, and why the increased amount of privacy did not weaken the forms of social intercourse, at least among males.

Toward the middle of the twentieth century, these forms of social intercourse began to break down in Western industrialized societies. The social and socializing function of the city disappeared. The more the urban population grew, the more the city declined. I am reminded of the words of the comedian who suggested moving the cities to the countryside. That, in fact, was exactly what happened. Immense continuous urban areas developed in all countries, but especially in the United States, where they have replaced the city. There cities in the old sense have ceased to exist. This phenomenon, one of the most important in the history of our society, must be seen in the light of what we know about the family and the ways it has changed. I should like to show how the decay of the city and the loss of its socializing function have affected contemporary family life.

From the late nineteenth century, even before the advent of the automobile, rich city-dwellers began to regard the crowded cities as unwholesome and dangerous and to flee in search of purer air and more decent surroundings. En masse they began to settle in those neighborhoods on the outskirts of cities that were still sparsely populated, such as the sixteenth and seventeenth *arrondissements* in Paris, near the greenery of the Parc Monceau and the Bois de Boulogne. Later, thanks to the railroad, the streetcar, and, in time, the automobile, they pushed farther and farther out. This trend occurred in all Western industrialized societies, but it was in North America that it developed most fully and reached its most extreme proportions; so we shall examine it there.

Neighborhoods are segregated not only by social class but also by function. Thus, just as there are rich, bourgeois neighborhoods and poor, working-class ones, so, too, there are business districts and residential ones. Offices, businesses, factories, and shops are found in one location, houses and gardens in the other. The means of transportation most often used to get from one place to the other is the private car. In this scheme of things there is no longer room for the forum, the agora, the piazza, the corso. There is no room, either, for the café as meeting place. The only thing there is room for is the drive-in and the fast-food outlet. Eating establishments are to be found in both business and residential districts; depending on their location, they are busy at different times of the day. In business and industrial districts they are humming with activity at lunchtime; in residential neighborhoods they do most of their business at night. During the off-hours, in both places, they are empty and silent.

What is truly remarkable is that the social intercourse which used to be the city's main function has now entirely vanished. The city is either crowded with the traffic of people and cars in a hurry or it is empty.

Around noontime, office workers in business districts sometimes take an old-fashioned stroll when the weather is nice, and enjoy a piece of cake or an ice cream cone in the sun. But after five o'clock the streets are deserted. Nor do the streets in residential neighborhoods become correspondingly crowded, except around shopping centers and their parking lots. People return to their homes, as turtles withdraw into their shells. At home they enjoy the warmth of family life and, on occasion, the company of carefully chosen friends. The urban conglomerate has become a mass of small islands—houses, offices, and shopping centers—all separated from one another by a great void. The interstitial space has vanished.

This evolution was precipitated by the automobile and by television, but it was well underway before they had even appeared, thanks to the growth of the cult of privacy in the bourgeois and middle classes during the nineteenth century. To people born between 1890 and 1920 (now between sixty and ninety years old), the green suburb represented the ideal way of life, an escape from the bustle of the city to more rural, more natural surroundings. This shift to the suburbs, far from the noise and crowds of the city streets, was caused by the growing attraction of a warm private family life. In those areas where private family living was less developed, as in the working-class areas along the Mediterranean, societies dominated by obstinate males, community life fared better.

During the nineteenth and early twentieth centuries, the results of the increased privacy and the new family style of living were kept in check by the vitality of community life in both urban and rural areas. A balance was achieved between family life in the home and community life in the café, on the terrace, in the street. But this balance was destroyed and the family carried the day, thanks to the spread of suburbia that came with the new technology: the automobile and television. When that happened, the whole of social life was absorbed by private, family living.

Henceforth, the only function of the streets and cafés was to enable the physical movement between home and work or restaurant. For the most part, these ceased to be places of meeting, conversation, or recreation as the home, the couple, the family came to fulfill most of those functions. Today when a couple or a family leave the house to do something that cannot be done at home, they go in a mobile extension of the house, namely, the car. As the ark permitted Noah to survive the Flood, so the car permits its owners to pass through the hostile and dangerous world outside the front door.

Some of my American friends have suggested that in America the churches for a long time filled a public social function, somewhat as the café had done in Europe. Even today, many churches not only bring the faithful together to worship, but also organize suppers, banquets, and other get-togethers for various age groups, separate from religious services. This function, in my opinion, implies an identity between church and community: certainly it used to be that one went to the church of one's community or parents and did not change. The individual's church was not chosen but given by birth. We might, however, ask whether the socializing function of the church has diminished with the growth of religious mobility. Freedom of choice, the ability to change churches as one changes houses, jobs, or towns, may thus have transformed the church from a public space, or gathering place for the community, into a private club.

I believe I recognize in American society today a tendency to substitute, for public and anonymous socializing, a socializing in private clubs and special groups. The problem then is whether to regard this private socializing as an extension of the family or a substitute for it, and whether it is still providing, in the private sector, a festive function such as was formerly provided by the distractions of the street, the town square, the café, and places of accidental and unexpected meetings. One significant difference in the two sectors is that in the private sector everything is more or less predictable; in the public sector, as I have defined it, all events—even the most banal—have an unexpected and unplanned aspect.

Not long ago I found myself in Rome at midnight in the working-class neighborhood of Trastevere. There were still crowds of people in the streets, but there were no adults, only *ragazzi* of eighteen or twenty. They were mostly boys, because people there have not yet got into the habit, at least in working-class neighborhoods, of letting girls run around at night. Although children and adults are content to sit in front of the television set, adolescents are more interested in the life around them, in personal, spontaneous experiences. The young people of Trastevere were greeted by the marvelous Roman street, still the warm, picturesque setting of their daily life. But what about places where the setting no longer exists? Where do adolescents gather then? In the basements of houses, in underground garages, in the rooms of friends, usually enclosed. They may very well reject their families, but they still retain their tendency to seek seclusion. Today's frontier is this internal wall: it continues to exist even though it no longer has much to protect.

In the so-called postindustrial age of the mid-twentieth century, the public sector of the nineteenth century collapsed and people thought they could fill the void by extending the private, family sector. They thus demanded that the family see to all their needs. They demanded that it provide the passionate love of Tristan and Yseult and the tenderness of Philemon and Baucis; they saw the family as a place for raising children, but, at the same time, as a means of keeping them in a prolonged network of exclusive love. They considered the family a self-sufficient unit, though at times they were willing to enlarge the circle to include a few close friends. In the family, they hoped to recover the nostalgic world of the Jalna novels and to experience the pleasures of family warmth; from the private fortress of the family car they sought to discover the world outside. And they cherished the family as a place for all the childish things that continue even beyond childhood. These trends were intensified by the baby boom. Since then, the family has had a monopoly on emotions, on raising children, and on filling leisure time. This tendency to monopolize its members is the family's way of coping with the decline of the public sector. One can well imagine the uneasiness and intolerance that the situation has created.

Although people today often claim that the family is undergoing a crisis, this is not, properly speaking, an accurate description of what is happening. Rather, we are witnessing the inability of the family to fulfill all the many functions with which it has been invested, no doubt temporarily, during the past half-century. Moreover, if my analysis is correct, this overexpansion of the family role is a result of the decline of the city and of the urban forms of social intercourse that it provided. The twentieth-century postindustrial world has been unable, so far, either to sustain the forms of social intercourse of the nineteenth century or to offer something in its place. The family has had to take over in an impossible situation; the real roots of the present domestic crisis lie not in our families, but in our cities.

CHAPTER 4

THE RELATIONSHIP BETWEEN CITIES AND THEIR CITIZENS

■ ■ ■

The existence of federal and state power over cities, analyzed in Chapter Two, provides important background for the exploration in this chapter of the law governing the relationship between cities and their own citizens. Much of the law examined in this chapter is federal constitutional and statutory law designed to prevent city governments from invading citizens' rights. Indeed, fear of city restrictions on the freedom of its citizens—Madison's fear of the tyranny of the majority—pervades the cases reproduced below. This fear arises whenever cities try to control the character of city life, alter the nature of particular neighborhoods, reorganize local police services, or raise revenue. It also influences the rules that govern voting and popular participation in city decision making. A central question examined in this chapter, therefore, is the extent to which federal and state control of city government effectively protects citizens against the abusive exercise of city governmental power.

This chapter raises another basic issue as well. Some people argue that the value of decentralizing political power—if it has any value at all—must be found in the internal operation of city government. Local power is desirable, they contend, to the extent that it provides individuals with the ability to work together to control their own lives. This point of view can be found in this chapter in the efforts of communities (and neighborhoods) to control their own character, in their attempts to increase citizen influence and participation in forming city policy, and in their search for new ways to ensure cities' economic viability and deliver city services. This chapter's cases, therefore, can be read not only to determine whether federal and state law effectively protects minority rights against city power but also to investigate whether local government law encourages or inhibits the emergence of a vital form of local democracy. Many proponents of this perspective connect their arguments with Tocqueville's views of the decentralization of power presented in Chapter One, contrasting his position with the perspective described above which emphasizes the views articulated in that chapter by Madison. Madison's and Tocqueville's views thus provide an important theoretical background for understanding the materials that follow.

There is also a third way to read this chapter. Both of the understandings of the relationship between a city and its citizens just described can be interpreted as more concerned with protecting a private realm than with expanding a collectively generated notion of the public interest. The first perspective concentrates on defending the private rights of individuals against the exercise of governmental power. The second perspective, while emphasizing the importance of public life, imagines such a life as located solely within the confines of a city's boundaries. This second view could therefore generate an us vs. them attitude toward people across the city line—a self-interested parochialism advanced in the name of "local control." As the materials in Chapter Three suggest, however, there is an alternative understanding of democratic life, one that seeks to undermine the importance of city boundaries and build instead a public interest that benefits the region, indeed the nation, as a whole. From this perspective, there is no sharp break between the issues raised in Chapter Three and this chapter. Like the relationships among neighboring cities, the relationship between a city and its citizens can be organized to advance the public interest broadly defined—to advance, in other words, a less selfish definition of local control.

A. CITY CONTROL OF COMMUNITY CHARACTER

Many people treat a city's ability to control its own character as the fundamental ingredient of local self-government. For them, local self-governance means the ability of citizens to create for themselves the kind of city they want to live in.[1] As we have already seen, however, this

---

[1] For a general analysis of this version of the concept of local self-governance, see, e.g., David Troutt, The Price of Paradise: The Costs of Inequality and a Vision For a More Equitable America (2013); Lee Fennell, The Unbounded Home: Property Values Beyond Property Lines (2009). See also David Troutt, Localism and Segregation, 16–SUM J. Affordable Housing and Community Dev. L. 323 (2007); Richard Ford, Law's Territory (A History of Jurisdiction), 97 Mich. L. Rev. 843 (1999); Jennifer Nedelsky, Law, Boundaries, and the Bounded Self, 10 Representations 162 (1990); Gerald Neuman, Territorial Discrimination, Equal Protection and Self-Determination, 135 U. Pa. L. Rev. 261 (1987); William Marshall, Discrimination and the Right of Association, 81 Nw. U. L. Rev. 68 (1986). For an analysis of this idea in particular contexts, see, e.g., Daniel Mandelker, Housing Quotas for People with Disabilities, 43 Urb. Law. 915 (2011); Jamison E. Colburn, Localism's Ecology: Protecting and Restoring Habitat in the Suburban Nation, 33 Ecology L.Q. 945 (2006); Richard C. Schragger, The Limits of Localism, 100 Mich. L. Rev. 371 (2001); Sheryll Cashin, Localism, Self-Interest, and the Tyranny of the Favored Quarter: Addressing the Barriers to New Regionalism, 88 Geo. L. J. 1985 (2000); Katia Brener, Belle Terre and Single-Family Home Ordinances: Judicial Perceptions of Local Government and the Presumption of Validity, 74 N.Y.U. L. Rev. 447 (1999); Anna Georgiou, NIMBY's Legacy—A Challenge to Local Autonomy: Regulating the Siting of Group Homes in New York, 26 Fordham Urb. L. J. 209 (1999); Israel Colon and Brett Marston, Resistance to a Residential AIDS Home: an Empirical Test of NIMBY, 37 Journal of Homosexuality 135 (1999); David Hughes, When NIMBYs Attack: The Heights to which Communities will Climb to Prevent the Siting of Wireless Towers, 23 Iowa J. Corp. L. 469 (1998); Jeffrey Henig, To Know Them is to—? Proximity to Shelters and Support for the Homeless, 75 Social Science Quarterly 741 (1994); Ronald Stein, Regulation of Adult Businesses Through Zoning After Renton, 18 Pac. L. J. 351 (1987); Carol Rose, Preservation and Community: New Directions in the Law of Historic Preservation, 33 Stan. L. Rev. 473 (1981).

version of local self-governance is by no means unproblematic. In our examination of exclusionary zoning and school financing, for example, we saw that a city's attempt to control its own character had a negative impact on outsiders. Here, we examine how such an exercise of a city's power might be seen as a threat to its own citizens' constitutional rights. The following cases and materials examine the extent to which the Constitution restricts a city's ability either to regulate who can live in the city (Village of Belle Terre v. Boraas, City of Cleburne v. Cleburne Living Center) or to impose zoning restrictions on pornographic movie theaters and other "undesirable land uses" (City of Renton v. Playtime Theatres, Note on NIMBY). Why does the notion of community self-governance receive more attention in these cases than it did in some of the cases dealing with federal-city and state-city relations covered in Chapter Two? Is an ability to exclude "undesirables" or controversial land-uses a necessary or justifiable part of the notion of community self-governance? The excerpt from Michael Warner's book is a provocative defense of the concentration of pornography stores in specific neighborhoods; Warner's goal is not to quarantine pornography but rather to preserve a sort of community for people interested in sexually explicit communication. One issue that Warner raises in the pornography context can be generalized: who should be included in the word "community" when the ideal of community self-governance is advocated? The section concludes with an excerpt from Richard Ford that argues that cities must be able to enforce standards of behavior in order to establish an attractive community. Using the example of San Francisco's homelessness problem, Ford suggests that convincing taxpayers to support services for the homeless will require convincing the homeless to conform their behavior to "bourgeois" community norms.

VILLAGE OF BELLE TERRE V. BORAAS

Supreme Court of the United States, 1974.
416 U.S. 1, 94 S.Ct. 1536, 39 L.Ed.2d 797.

MR. JUSTICE DOUGLAS delivered the opinion of the Court.

Belle Terre is a village on Long Island's north shore of about 220 homes inhabited by 700 people. Its total land area is less than one square mile. It has restricted land use to one-family dwellings excluding lodging houses, boarding houses, fraternity houses, or multiple-dwelling houses. The word "family" as used in the ordinance means, "[o]ne or more persons related by blood, adoption, or marriage, living and cooking together as a single housekeeping unit, exclusive of household servants. A number of persons but not exceeding two (2) living and cooking together as a single housekeeping unit though not related by blood, adoption, or marriage shall be deemed to constitute a family."

Appellees, the Dickmans, are owners of a house in the village and leased it in December 1971 for a term of 18 months to Michael Truman. Later Bruce Boraas became a colessee. Then Anne Parish moved into the house along with three others. These six are students at nearby State University at Stony Brook and none is related to the other by blood, adoption, or marriage. When the village served the Dickmans with an "Order to Remedy Violations" of the ordinance, the owners plus three tenants thereupon brought this action under 42 U.S.C. § 1983 for an injunction and a judgment declaring the ordinance unconstitutional. * * *

This case brings to this Court a different phase of local zoning regulations from those we have previously reviewed. *Village of Euclid v. Ambler Realty Co.*, 272 U.S. 365, 47 S.Ct. 114, 71 L.Ed. 303, involved a zoning ordinance classifying land use in a given area into six categories. * * * The Court sustained the zoning ordinance under the police power of the State, saying that the line "which in this field separates the legitimate from the illegitimate assumption of power is not capable of precise delimitation. It varies with circumstances and conditions." And the Court added: "A nuisance may be merely a right thing in the wrong place, like a pig in the parlor instead of the barnyard. If the validity of the legislative classification for zoning purposes be fairly debatable, the legislative judgment must be allowed to control." * * * The main thrust of the case in the mind of the Court was in the exclusion of industries and apartments, and as respects that it commented on the desire to keep residential areas free of "disturbing noises"; "increased traffic"; the hazard of "moving and parked automobiles"; the "depriving children of the privilege of quiet and open spaces for play, enjoyed by those in more favored localities." The ordinance was sanctioned because the validity of the legislative classification was "fairly debatable" and therefore could not be said to be wholly arbitrary.

Our decision in *Berman v. Parker*, 348 U.S. 26, 75 S.Ct. 98, 99 L.Ed. 27, sustained a land use project in the District of Columbia against a landowner's claim that the taking violated the Due Process Clause and the Just Compensation Clause of the Fifth Amendment. The essence of the argument against the law was, while taking property for ridding an area of slums was permissible, taking it "merely to develop a better balanced, more attractive community" was not. We refused to limit the concept of public welfare that may be enhanced by zoning regulations. We said:

> "Miserable and disreputable housing conditions may do more than spread disease and crime and immorality. They may also suffocate the spirit by reducing the people who live there to the status of cattle. They may indeed make living an almost insufferable burden. They may also be an ugly sore, a blight on the community which robs it of charm, which makes it a place

from which men turn. The misery of housing may despoil a community as an open sewer may ruin a river.

"We do not sit to determine whether a particular housing project is or is not desirable. The concept of the public welfare is broad and inclusive. * * * The values it represents are spiritual as well as physical, aesthetic as well as monetary. It is within the power of the legislature to determine that the community should be beautiful as well as healthy, spacious as well as clean, well-balanced as well as carefully patrolled."

If the ordinance segregated one area only for one race, it would immediately be suspect under the reasoning of *Buchanan v. Warley*, 245 U.S. 60, 38 S.Ct. 16, 62 L.Ed. 149 where the Court invalidated a city ordinance barring a black from acquiring real property in a white residential area by reason of an 1866 Act of Congress, 14 Stat. 27, now 42 U.S.C. § 1982, and an 1870 Act, § 17, 16 Stat. 144, now 42 U.S.C. § 1981, both enforcing the Fourteenth Amendment. * * *

The present ordinance is challenged on several grounds: that it interferes with a person's right to travel; that it interferes with the right to migrate to and settle within a State; that it bars people who are uncongenial to the present residents; that it expresses the social preferences of the residents for groups that will be congenial to them; that social homogeneity is not a legitimate interest of government; that the restriction of those whom the neighbors do not like trenches on the newcomers' rights of privacy; that it is of no rightful concern to villagers whether the residents are married or unmarried; that the ordinance is antithetical to the Nation's experience, ideology, and self-perception as an open, egalitarian, and integrated society.

[handwritten margin note: student args]

We find none of these reasons in the record before us. It is not aimed at transients. Cf. *Shapiro v. Thompson*, 394 U.S. 618, 89 S.Ct. 1322, 22 L.Ed.2d 600. It involves no procedural disparity inflicted on some but not on others such as was presented by *Griffin v. Illinois*, 351 U.S. 12, 76 S.Ct. 585, 100 L.Ed. 891. It involves no "fundamental" right guaranteed by the Constitution, such as voting, *Harper v. Virginia State Board*, 383 U.S. 663, 86 S.Ct. 1079, 16 L.Ed.2d 169; the right of association, *NAACP v. Alabama ex rel. Patterson*, 357 U.S. 449, 78 S.Ct. 1163, 2 L.Ed.2d 1488; the right of access to the courts, *NAACP v. Button*, 371 U.S. 415, 83 S.Ct. 328, 9 L.Ed.2d 405; or any rights of privacy, cf. *Griswold v. Connecticut*, 381 U.S. 479, 85 S.Ct. 1678, 14 L.Ed.2d 510; *Eisenstadt v. Baird*, 405 U.S. 438, 453 454, 92 S.Ct. 1029, 1038–1039, 31 L.Ed.2d 349. We deal with economic and social legislation where legislatures have historically drawn lines which we respect against the charge of violation of the Equal Protection Clause if the law be " 'reasonable, not arbitrary' " and bears "a rational relationship to a [permissible] state objective." *Reed v. Reed*, 404 U.S. 71, 76, 92 S.Ct. 251, 254, 30 L.Ed.2d 225.

It is said, however, that if two unmarried people can constitute a "family," there is no reason why three or four may not. But every line drawn by a legislature leaves some out that might well have been included. That exercise of discretion, however, is a legislative, not a judicial, function.

It is said that the Belle Terre ordinance reeks with an animosity to unmarried couples who live together. There is no evidence to support it; and the provision of the ordinance bringing within the definition of a "family" two unmarried people belies the charge.

The ordinance places no ban on other forms of association, for a "family" may, so far as the ordinance is concerned, entertain whomever it likes.

The regimes of boarding houses, fraternity houses, and the like present urban problems. More people occupy a given space; more cars rather continuously pass by; more cars are parked; noise travels with crowds.

A quiet place where yards are wide, people few, and motor vehicles restricted are legitimate guidelines in a land-use project addressed to family needs. This goal is a permissible one within *Berman v. Parker*, *supra*. The police power is not confined to elimination of filth, stench, and unhealthy places. It is ample to lay out zones where family values, youth values, and the blessings of quiet seclusion and clean air make the area a sanctuary for people. * * *

MR. JUSTICE MARSHALL, dissenting. * * *

In my view, the disputed classification burdens the students' fundamental rights of association and privacy guaranteed by the First and Fourteenth Amendments. Because the application of strict equal protection scrutiny is therefore required, I am at odds with my Brethren's conclusion that the ordinance may be sustained on a showing that it bears a rational relationship to the accomplishment of legitimate governmental objectives.

I am in full agreement with the majority that zoning is a complex and important function of the State. It may indeed be the most essential function performed by local government, for it is one of the primary means by which we protect that sometimes difficult to define concept of quality of life. I therefore continue to adhere to the principle of *Village of Euclid v. Ambler Realty Co.*, 272 U.S. 365, 47 S.Ct. 114, 71 L.Ed. 303 (1926), that deference should be given to governmental judgments concerning proper land-use allocation. That deference is a principle which has served this Court well and which is necessary for the continued development of effective zoning and land-use control mechanisms. Had the owners alone brought this suit alleging that the restrictive ordinance deprived them of their property or was an irrational legislative classification, I would agree that the ordinance would have to be sustained. Our role is not and should not be to sit as a zoning board of appeals.

I would also agree with the majority that local zoning authorities may properly act in furtherance of the objectives asserted to be served by the ordinance at issue here: restricting uncontrolled growth, solving traffic problems, keeping rental costs at a reasonable level, and making the community attractive to families. The police power which provides the justification for zoning is not narrowly confined. See *Berman v. Parker*, 348 U.S. 26, 75 S.Ct. 98, 99 L.Ed. 27 (1954). And, it is appropriate that we afford zoning authorities considerable latitude in choosing the means by which to implement such purposes. But deference does not mean abdication. This Court has an obligation to ensure that zoning ordinances, even when adopted in furtherance of such legitimate aims, do not infringe upon fundamental constitutional rights. * * *

My disagreement with the Court today is based upon my view that the ordinance in this case unnecessarily burdens appellees' First Amendment freedom of association and their constitutionally guaranteed right to privacy. Our decisions establish that the First and Fourteenth Amendments protect the freedom to choose one's associates. Constitutional protection is extended, not only to modes of association that are political in the usual sense, but also to those that pertain to the social and economic benefit of the members. The selection of one's living companions involves similar choices as to the emotional, social, or economic benefits to be derived from alternative living arrangements.

The freedom of association is often inextricably entwined with the constitutionally guaranteed right of privacy. The right to "establish a home" is an essential part of the liberty guaranteed by the Fourteenth Amendment. *Meyer v. Nebraska*, 262 U.S. 390, 399, 43 S.Ct. 625, 626, 67 L.Ed. 1042 (1923); *Griswold v. Connecticut*, 381 U.S. 479, 495, 85 S.Ct. 1678, 1687, 14 L.Ed.2d 510 (1965) (Goldberg, J., concurring). And the Constitution secures to an individual a freedom "to satisfy his intellectual and emotional needs in the privacy of his own home." *Stanley v. Georgia*, 394 U.S. 557, 565, 89 S.Ct. 1243, 1248, 22 L.Ed.2d 542 (1969). Constitutionally protected privacy is, in Mr. Justice Brandeis' words, "as against the Government, the right to be let alone * * * the right most valued by civilized man." *Olmstead v. United States*, 277 U.S. 438, 478, 48 S.Ct. 564, 572, 72 L.Ed. 944 (1928) (dissenting opinion). The choice of household companions—of whether a person's "intellectual and emotional needs" are best met by living with family, friends, professional associates, or others—involves deeply personal considerations as to the kind and quality of intimate relationships within the home. That decision surely falls within the ambit of the right to privacy protected by the Constitution. * * *

The instant ordinance discriminates on the basis of just such a personal lifestyle choice as to household companions. It permits any number of persons related by blood or marriage, be it two or twenty, to live in a single household, but it limits to two the number of unrelated persons bound by profession, love, friendship, religious or political affiliation, or mere economics who can occupy a single home. Belle Terre imposes upon those who deviate from the community norm in their choice of living companions significantly greater restrictions than are applied to residential groups who are related by blood or marriage, and compose the established order within the community. The village has, in effect, acted to fence out those individuals whose choice of lifestyle differs from that of its current residents.

This is not a case where the Court is being asked to nullify a township's sincere efforts to maintain its residential character by preventing the operation of rooming houses, fraternity houses, or other commercial or high-density residential uses. Unquestionably, a town is free to restrict such uses. Moreover, as a general proposition, I see no constitutional infirmity in a town's limiting the density of use in residential areas by zoning regulations which do not discriminate on the basis of constitutionally suspect criteria. This ordinance, however, limits the density of occupancy of only those homes occupied by unrelated persons. It thus reaches beyond control of the use of land or the density of population, and undertakes to regulate the way people choose to associate with each other within the privacy of their own homes. * * *

Because I believe that this zoning ordinance creates a classification which impinges upon fundamental personal rights, it can withstand constitutional scrutiny only upon a clear showing that the burden imposed is necessary to protect a compelling and substantial governmental interest, *Shapiro v. Thompson*, 394 U.S. 618, 634, 89 S.Ct. 1322, 1331, 22 L.Ed.2d 600 (1969). * * * A variety of justifications have been proffered in support of the village's ordinance. It is claimed that the ordinance controls population density, prevents noise, traffic and parking problems, and preserves the rent structure of the community and its attractiveness to families. As I noted earlier, these are all legitimate and substantial interests of government. But I think it clear that the means chosen to accomplish these purposes are both overinclusive and underinclusive, and that the asserted goals could be as effectively achieved by means of an ordinance that did not discriminate on the basis of constitutionally protected choices of lifestyle. The ordinance imposes no restriction whatsoever on the number of persons who may live in a house, as long as they are related by marital or sanguinary bonds—presumably no matter how distant their relationship. Nor does the ordinance restrict the number of income earners who may contribute to rent in such a household, or the number of automobiles that may be maintained by its occupants. In that sense the ordinance is underinclusive. On the other hand, the statute restricts the number of unrelated persons who may live in a home to no more than two. It would therefore prevent three unrelated people from occupying a dwelling even if among them they had but one income and no vehicles. While an extended family of a dozen or more might live in a small bungalow, three elderly and retired persons could not occupy the large manor house next door. Thus the statute is also grossly overinclusive to accomplish its intended purposes.

There are some 220 residences in Belle Terre occupied by about 700 persons. The density is therefore just above three per household. The village is justifiably concerned with density of population and the related problems of noise, traffic, and the like. It could deal with those problems by limiting each household to a specified number of adults, two or three perhaps, without limitation on the number of dependent children. The burden of such an ordinance would fall equally upon all segments of the community. It would surely be better tailored to the goals asserted by the village than the ordinance before us today, for it would more realistically restrict population density and growth and their attendant environmental costs. Various other statutory mechanisms also suggest themselves as solutions to Belle Terre's problems—rent control, limits on the number of vehicles per household, and so forth, but, of course, such schemes are matters of legislative judgment and not for this Court. Appellants also refer to the necessity of maintaining the family character of the village. There is not a shred of evidence in the record indicating that if Belle Terre permitted a limited number of unrelated persons to live together, the residential, familial character of the community would be fundamentally affected.

By limiting unrelated households to two persons while placing no limitation on households of related individuals, the village has embarked upon its commendable course in a constitutionally faulty vessel. I would find the challenged ordinance unconstitutional. But I would not ask the village to abandon its goal of providing quiet streets, little traffic, and a pleasant and reasonably priced environment in which families might raise their children. Rather, I would commend the village to continue to pursue those purposes but by means of more carefully drawn and even-handed legislation.

CITY OF CLEBURNE, TEXAS V. CLEBURNE LIVING CENTER

Supreme Court of the United States, 1985.
473 U.S. 432, 105 S.Ct. 3249, 87 L.Ed.2d 313.

JUSTICE WHITE delivered the opinion of the Court. * * *

In July, 1980, respondent Jan Hannah purchased a building at 201 Featherston Street in the city of Cleburne, Texas, with the intention of leasing it to Cleburne Living Centers, Inc. (CLC), for the operation of a group home for the mentally retarded. It was anticipated that the home would house 13 retarded men and women, who would be under the constant supervision of CLC staff members. The house had four bedrooms and two baths, with a half bath to be added. * * * The city informed CLC that a special use permit would be required for the operation of a group home at the site, and CLC accordingly submitted a permit application. * * * After holding a public hearing on CLC's application, the city council voted three to one to deny a special use permit.

CLC then filed suit in Federal District Court against the city and a number of its officials, alleging, *inter alia*, that the zoning ordinance was invalid on its face and as applied because it discriminated against the mentally retarded in violation of the equal protection rights of CLC and its potential residents. * * *

[W]e conclude for several reasons that the Court of Appeals erred in holding mental retardation a quasi-suspect classification calling for a more exacting standard of judicial review than is normally accorded economic and social legislation. First, it is undeniable, and it is not argued otherwise here, that those who are mentally retarded have a reduced ability to cope with and function in the everyday world. * * * They are thus different, immutably so, in relevant respects, and the states' interest in dealing with and providing for them is plainly a legitimate one. How this large and diversified group is to be treated under the law is a difficult and often a technical matter, very much a task for legislators guided by qualified professionals and not by the perhaps ill-informed opinions of the judiciary. * * *

Second, the distinctive legislative response, both national and state, to the plight of those who are mentally retarded demonstrates not only that they have unique problems, but also that the lawmakers have been addressing their difficulties in a manner that belies a continuing antipathy or prejudice and a corresponding need for more intrusive oversight by the judiciary. Thus, the federal government has not only outlawed discrimination against the mentally retarded in federally funded programs, see § 504 of the Rehabilitation Act of 1973, 29 U.S.C. § 794, but it has also provided the retarded with the right to receive "appropriate treatment, services, and habilitation" in a setting that is "least restrictive of [their] personal liberty." Developmental Disabilities

Assistance and Bill of Rights Act, 42 U.S.C. §§ 6010(1), (2). * * * The State of Texas has similarly enacted legislation that acknowledges the special status of the mentally retarded by conferring certain rights upon them, such as "the right to live in the least restrictive setting appropriate to [their] individual needs and abilities," including "the right to live * * * in a group home." Mentally Retarded Persons Act of 1977, Tex.Rev.Civ.Stat.Ann., Art. 5547 300, § 7 (Vernon Supp.1985). * * * It may be, as CLC contends, that legislation designed to benefit, rather than disadvantage, the retarded would generally withstand examination under a test of heightened scrutiny. * * * Even assuming that many of these laws could be shown to be substantially related to an important governmental purpose, merely requiring the legislature to justify its efforts in these terms may lead it to refrain from acting at all. Much recent legislation intended to benefit the retarded also assumes the need for measures that might be perceived to disadvantage them. The Education of the Handicapped Act, for example, requires an "appropriate" education, not one that is equal in all respects to the education of non-retarded children; clearly, admission to a class that exceeded the abilities of a retarded child would not be appropriate. Similarly, the Developmental Disabilities Assistance Act and the Texas act give the retarded the right to live only in the "least restrictive setting" appropriate to their abilities, implicitly assuming the need for at least some restrictions that would not be imposed on others. Especially given the wide variation in the abilities and needs of the retarded themselves, governmental bodies must have a certain amount of flexibility and freedom from judicial oversight in shaping and limiting their remedial efforts.

Third, the legislative response, which could hardly have occurred and survived without public support, negates any claim that the mentally retarded are politically powerless in the sense that they have no ability to attract the attention of the lawmakers. Any minority can be said to be powerless to assert direct control over the legislature, but if that were a criterion for higher level scrutiny by the courts, much economic and social legislation would now be suspect.

Fourth, if the large and amorphous class of the mentally retarded were deemed quasi-suspect for the reasons given by the Court of Appeals, it would be difficult to find a principled way to distinguish a variety of other groups who have perhaps immutable disabilities setting them off from others, who cannot themselves mandate the desired legislative responses, and who can claim some degree of prejudice from at least part of the public at large. One need mention in this respect only the aging, the disabled, the mentally ill, and the infirm. We are reluctant to set out on that course, and we decline to do so.

Doubtless, there have been and there will continue to be instances of discrimination against the retarded that are in fact invidious, and that are properly subject to judicial correction under constitutional norms. But the appropriate method of reaching such instances is not to create a new quasi-suspect classification and subject all governmental action based on that classification to more searching evaluation. Rather, we should look to the likelihood that governmental action premised on a particular classification is valid as a general matter, not merely to the specifics of the case before us. Because mental retardation is a characteristic that the government may legitimately take into account in a wide range of decisions, and because both state and federal governments have recently committed themselves to assisting the retarded, we will not presume that any given legislative action, even one that disadvantages retarded individuals, is rooted in considerations that the Constitution will not tolerate.

Our refusal to recognize the retarded as a quasi-suspect class does not leave them entirely unprotected from invidious discrimination. To withstand equal protection review, legislation that distinguishes between the mentally retarded and others must be rationally related to a legitimate governmental purpose. This standard, we believe, affords government the latitude necessary both to pursue policies designed to assist the retarded in realizing their full potential, and to freely and efficiently engage in activities that burden the retarded in what is essentially an incidental manner. The State may not rely on a classification whose relationship to an asserted goal is so attenuated as to render the distinction arbitrary or irrational. See *United States Department of Agriculture v. Moreno*, 413 U.S. 528, 535, 93 S.Ct. 2821, 2826, 37 L.Ed.2d 782 (1973). Furthermore, some objectives—such as "a bare * * * desire to harm a politically unpopular group," *Moreno*, 413 U.S., at 534, 93 S.Ct., at 2826—are not legitimate state interests. Beyond that, the mentally retarded, like others, have and retain their substantive constitutional rights in addition to the right to be treated equally by the law.

We turn to the issue of the validity of the zoning ordinance insofar as it requires a special use permit for homes for the mentally retarded. We inquire first whether requiring a special use permit for the Featherston home in the circumstances here deprives respondents of the equal protection of the laws. If it does, there will be no occasion to decide whether the special use permit provision is facially invalid where the mentally retarded are involved, or to put it another way, whether the city may never insist on a special use permit for a home for the mentally retarded in an R–3 zone. This is the preferred course of adjudication since it enables courts to avoid making unnecessarily broad constitutional judgments.

The constitutional issue is clearly posed. The City does not require a special use permit in an R–3 zone for apartment houses, multiple dwellings, boarding and lodging houses, fraternity or sorority houses, dormitories, apartment hotels, hospitals, sanitariums, nursing homes for convalescents or the aged (other than for the insane or feeble-minded or alcoholics or drug addicts), private clubs or fraternal orders, and other specified uses. It does, however, insist on a special permit for the Featherston home, and it does so, as the District Court found, because it would be a facility for the mentally retarded. May the city require the permit for this facility when other care and multiple dwelling facilities are freely permitted?

It is true, as already pointed out, that the mentally retarded as a group are indeed different from others not sharing their misfortune, and in this respect they may be different from those who would occupy other facilities that would be permitted in an R–3 zone without a special permit. But this difference is largely irrelevant unless the Featherston home and those who would occupy it would threaten legitimate interests of the city in a way that other permitted uses such as boarding houses and hospitals would not. Because in our view the record does not reveal any rational basis for believing that the Featherston home would pose any special threat to the city's legitimate interests, we affirm the judgment below insofar as it holds the ordinance invalid as applied in this case.

The District Court found that the City Council's insistence on the permit rested on several factors. First, the Council was concerned with the negative attitude of the majority of property owners located within 200 feet of the Featherston facility, as well as with the fears of elderly residents of the neighborhood. But mere negative attitudes, or fear, unsubstantiated by factors which are properly cognizable in a zoning proceeding, are not permissible bases for treating a home for the mentally retarded differently from apartment houses, multiple dwellings, and the like. * * *

Second, the Council had two objections to the location of the facility. It was concerned that the facility was across the street from a junior high school, and it feared that the students might harass the occupants of the Featherston home. But the school itself is attended by about 30 mentally retarded students, and denying a permit based on such vague, undifferentiated fears is again permitting some portion of the community to validate what would otherwise be an equal protection violation. The other objection to the home's location was that it was located on "a five hundred year flood plain." This concern with the possibility of a flood, however, can hardly be based on a distinction between the Featherston home and, for example, nursing homes, homes for convalescents or the aged, or sanitariums or hospitals, any of which could be located on the

Featherston site without obtaining a special use permit. The same may be said of another concern of the Council—doubts about the legal responsibility for actions which the mentally retarded might take. If there is no concern about legal responsibility with respect to other uses that would be permitted in the area, such as boarding and fraternity houses, it is difficult to believe that the groups of mildly or moderately mentally retarded individuals who would live at 201 Featherston would present any different or special hazard.

Fourth, the Council was concerned with the size of the home and the number of people that would occupy it. The District Court found, and the Court of Appeals repeated, that "[i]f the potential residents of the Featherston Street home were not mentally retarded, but the home was the same in all other respects, its use would be permitted under the city's zoning ordinance." Given this finding, there would be no restrictions on the number of people who could occupy this home as a boarding house, nursing home, family dwelling, fraternity house, or dormitory. The question is whether it is rational to treat the mentally retarded differently. It is true that they suffer disability not shared by others; but why this difference warrants a density regulation that others need not observe is not at all apparent. At least this record does not clarify how, in this connection, the characteristics of the intended occupants of the Featherston home rationally justify denying to those occupants what would be permitted to groups occupying the same site for different purposes. Those who would live in the Featherston home are the type of individuals who, with supporting staff, satisfy federal and state standards for group housing in the community; and there is no dispute that the home would meet the federal square-footage-per-resident requirement for facilities of this type. In the words of the Court of Appeals, "The City never justifies its apparent view that other people can live under such 'crowded' conditions when mentally retarded persons cannot."

In the courts below the city also urged that the ordinance is aimed at avoiding concentration of population and at lessening congestion of the streets. These concerns obviously fail to explain why apartment houses, fraternity and sorority houses, hospitals and the like, may freely locate in the area without a permit. So, too, the expressed worry about fire hazards, the serenity of the neighborhood, and the avoidance of danger to other residents fail rationally to justify singling out a home such as 201 Featherston for the special use permit, yet imposing no such restrictions on the many other uses freely permitted in the neighborhood.

The short of it is that requiring the permit in this case appears to us to rest on an irrational prejudice against the mentally retarded, including those who would occupy the Featherston facility and who would live under the closely supervised and highly regulated conditions expressly provided for by state and federal law.

The judgment of the Court of Appeals is affirmed insofar as it invalidates the zoning ordinance as applied to the Featherston home. The judgment is otherwise vacated. * * *

JUSTICE MARSHALL, with whom JUSTICE BRENNAN and JUSTICE BLACKMUN join, concurring in the judgment in part and dissenting in part. * * *

In my view, it is important to articulate, as the Court does not, the facts and principles that justify subjecting this zoning ordinance to the searching review—the heightened scrutiny—that actually leads to its invalidation. * * * [T]he interest of the retarded in establishing group homes is substantial. The right to "establish a home" has long been cherished as one of the fundamental liberties embraced by the Due Process Clause. See *Meyer v. Nebraska*, 262 U.S. 390, 399, 43 S.Ct. 625, 626, 67 L.Ed. 1042 (1923). For retarded adults, this right means living together in group homes, for as deinstitutionalization has progressed, group homes have become the primary means by which retarded adults can enter life in the community. * * * Excluding group homes deprives the retarded of much of what makes for human freedom and fulfillment—the ability to form bonds and take part in the life of a community.

Second, the mentally retarded have been subject to a "lengthy and tragic history" of segregation and discrimination that can only be called grotesque. During much of the nineteenth century, mental retardation was viewed as neither curable nor dangerous and the retarded were largely left to their own devices. By the latter part of the century and during the first decades of the new one, however, social views of the retarded underwent a radical transformation. Fueled by the rising tide of Social Darwinism, the "science" of eugenics, and the extreme xenophobia of those years, leading medical authorities and others began to portray the "feeble minded" as a "menace to society and civilization * * * responsible in a large degree for many, if not all, of our social problems." A regime of state-mandated segregation and degradation soon emerged that in its virulence and bigotry rivaled, and indeed paralleled, the worst excesses of Jim Crow. Massive custodial institutions were built to warehouse the retarded for life; the aim was to halt reproduction of the retarded and "nearly extinguish their race." Retarded children were categorically excluded from public schools, based on the false stereotype that all were ineducable and on the purported need to protect nonretarded children from them. State laws deemed the retarded "unfit for citizenship."

Segregation was accompanied by eugenic marriage and sterilization laws that extinguished for the retarded one of the "basic civil rights of man"—the right to marry and procreate. Marriages of the retarded were made, and in some states continue to be, not only voidable but also often a criminal offense. The purpose of such limitations, which frequently applied only to women of child bearing age, was unabashedly eugenic: to prevent the retarded from propagating. To assure this end, 29 states enacted compulsory eugenic sterilization laws between 1907 and 1931.

Prejudice, once let loose, is not easily cabined. As of 1979, most states still categorically disqualified "idiots" from voting, without regard to individual capacity and with discretion to exclude left in the hands of low-level election officials. Not until Congress enacted the Education of the Handicapped Act were "the door[s] of public education" opened wide to handicapped children. *Hendrick Hudson District Board of Education v. Rowley,* 458 U.S. 176, 192, 102 S.Ct. 3034, 3043, 73 L.Ed.2d 690 (1982). But most important, lengthy and continuing isolation of the retarded has perpetuated the ignorance, irrational fears, and stereotyping that long have plagued them.

In light of the importance of the interest at stake and the history of discrimination the retarded have suffered, the Equal Protection Clause requires us to do more than review the distinctions drawn by Cleburne's zoning ordinance as if they appeared in a taxing statute or in economic or commercial legislation. The searching scrutiny I would give to restrictions on the ability of the retarded to establish community group homes leads me to conclude that Cleburne's vague generalizations for classifying the "feebleminded" with drug addicts, alcoholics, and the insane, and excluding them where the elderly, the ill, the boarder, and the transient are allowed, are not substantial or important enough to overcome the suspicion that the ordinance rests on impermissible assumptions or out-moded and perhaps invidious stereotypes. * * *

NOTE ON *NIMBY*

The acronym NIMBY—for "Not in My Back Yard"—has become a common way to refer to widespread neighborhood opposition to the introduction of what are frequently called "undesirable land uses." Sometimes, however, it is the people involved, not the nature of the use, that are considered undesirable. In *Boraas* and *Cleburne,* for example, opposition to having groups of students and the mentally retarded living in the neighborhood, rather than to the buildings themselves, seems to have been the motivation for the local efforts to exclude. This kind of attempted exclusion is usually phrased, as it was in *Boraas,* in terms of a limit on the number of unrelated individuals allowed to live in a single family dwelling. Some state courts have followed *Boraas* and held these limits constitutional. In Dinan v. Board of Zoning Appeals, 220 Conn. 61, 74–75, 595 A.2d 864, 869 (1991), for example, the Connecticut Supreme Court upheld an exclusion of a five-person "rooming house":

> The municipal legislative body empowered to adopt zoning
> regulations in Stratford could reasonably have concluded that

roomers or such occupants as the plaintiffs' tenants are less likely to develop the kind of friendly relationships with neighbors that abound in residential districts occupied by traditional families. While the plaintiffs' tenants continue to reside on the property, they are not likely to have children who would become playmates of other children living in the area. Neighbors are not so likely to call upon them to borrow a cup of sugar, provide a ride to the store, mind the family pets, water the plants or perform any of the countless services that families, both traditional and nontraditional, provide to each other as a result of longtime acquaintance and mutual self-interest. The fact that both families and individuals differ with respect to their habits and conduct in relation to the community does not render invalid the legislative judgment that the probable effect of the kind of occupancy the plaintiffs seek to maintain would be detrimental in a neighborhood of single-family homes.

See also McMaster v. Columbia Board of Zoning Appeals, 395 S.C. 499, 719 S.E.2d 660 (2011) (not more than three unrelated individuals); State v. Champoux, 252 Neb. 769, 566 N.W.2d 763 (1997) (not more than two unrelated individuals); City of Brookings v. Winker, 554 N.W.2d 827 (Sup.Ct.S.D.1996) (same).

Other state courts, however, have invalidated these attempts to exclude unrelated adults who want to live together in a single family house. They have generally done so on the ground that the attempt to limit the number of unrelated individuals, but not of related individuals, is irrational. "Plainfield's ordinance," the Supreme Court of New Jersey declared, "would prohibit a group of five unrelated 'widows, widowers, older spinsters or bachelors—even of judges' from residing in a single unit within the municipality. On the other hand, a group consisting of 10 distant cousins could so reside without violating the ordinance." New Jersey v. Baker, 81 N.J. 99, 107, 405 A.2d 368, 371 (1979). See also McMinn v. Town of Oyster Bay, 66 N.Y.2d 544, 488 N.E.2d 1240, 498 N.Y.S.2d 128 (1985); Charter Township of Delta v. Dinolfo, 419 Mich. 253, 351 N.W.2d 831 (1984); City of Santa Barbara v. Adamson, 27 Cal.3d 123, 164 Cal.Rptr. 539, 610 P.2d 436 (1980).

As *Boraas* illustrates, students are one example of the kind of individuals some localities consider undesirable. In Kirsch v. Prince George's County, Maryland, 331 Md. 89, 626 A.2d 372 (1993), the Maryland Court of Appeals declared unconstitutional a "mini-dorm ordinance" that restricted the rental of residential property to three to five unrelated individuals "who are registered full-time or part-time students at an institution of higher learning." The Court distinguished *Boraas* in the following way:

Unlike the zoning ordinance analyzed in *Boraas*, the Prince George's County "mini-dorm" ordinance does not differentiate based on the nature of the use of the property, such as a fraternity house or a lodging house, but rather on the occupation of the persons who would dwell therein. Therefore, under the ordinance a landlord of a building originally constructed as a one, two or three family dwelling is permitted to rent the same for occupancy by three to five unrelated persons so long as they are not pursuing a higher education without incurring the burdens of complying with the arduous requirements of the ordinance. Such occupancy would equally add motor vehicles to a congested parking situation and pose the threat of increased noise and litter. Such a zoning classification of residential property is wholly unrelated to the stated purpose of the ordinance, and its impact upon persons who are registered as full-time or part-time students at an institution of higher learning denies those students equal protection of the laws under the Fourteenth Amendment to the United States Constitution and Article 24 of the Declaration of Rights.

These targeted exclusions have their defenders. In *Kirsch* itself, the dissent argued:

Several states of facts reasonably can be conceived that would justify the student/non-student classification. We can conceive that some students of the University of Maryland and Bowie State University might not like to live in the campus dormitories and would prefer to live off campus but close to their universities. We can conceive that as full or part-time students, they may only have limited funds and are therefore more willing to tolerate crowded, inferior living quarters. Real estate speculators, seizing upon this market, may buy small, inexpensive single-family residences close to these institutions of higher learning and rent formerly single-family homes to several students per house. Many of these students have cars which they might park on the street. As only nine-month tenants, the students may not be concerned about maintaining the property. Intolerant neighbors inconvenienced by the shortage of parking spaces and concerned about declining aesthetics of their neighborhoods may put their homes up for sale. Prospective buyers may not be eager to move into a neighborhood with neglected, crowded student group residences, so the speculators may be able to purchase more houses at deflated prices. The speculators, without doing anything more than is minimally necessary to rent the properties, can create more mini-dorms in close proximity to these two Universities. Soon there may be a real danger that many quiet college residential neighborhoods will be saturated with student mini-dorms. These assumed justifications are not irrational or arbitrary. It is also easy to conceive that there is no such problem with non-students or people with other occupations. These non-students are more likely to be employed full-time than are students, and with more money to spend on housing, they presumably may be less willing to tolerate crowded, inferior living conditions. Also, since they will live in the same residence all year long, rather than only for nine months of the year, the premises are less likely to be neglected. Non-student group residences are more likely to be disbursed throughout the county and not clustered around the two Universities.

Students and the mentally retarded are not the only kinds of people that stimulate neighborhood opposition. In Bannum v. City of St. Charles, 2 F.3d 267 (1993), the U.S. Court of Appeals for the Eighth Circuit upheld zoning restrictions on half-way houses for convicted criminals (non-violent criminals were to live in these half-way houses during the last stage of their sentence before their release). Bannum, a company in the business of operating half-way houses, relied on *Cleburne* in its attempt to invalidate the restrictions. "[N]egative attitudes and fear of offenders," it argued, "are not permissible bases for treating a * * * half-way house differently from apartment houses or other multiple person uses of property." But the Court disagreed:

> *Cleburne* is inapposite. The concerns the City of Cleburne relied on to require a permit would be irrational bases as applied to any home for the mentally retarded, and the Court concluded that the permit requirement was really based on irrational prejudice. Here, the classification in the amended ordinance is addressed to half-way houses which serve any prisoner, ex-prisoner, or juvenile offender. The City could rationally believe that some groups in this classification could pose a threat to the public welfare. Such concerns are not based on irrational prejudice, but rather on a realistic view that some members of these groups could pose a threat in some locations. It is not irrational for the City to believe that recidivism could be a problem with some persons served by half-way houses. This is a legitimate concern which can be addressed on a case-by-case basis through application for conditional permits.

Even the cases that have invalidated exclusions of unrelated individuals have indicated that limiting areas of the city to single family residences is constitutionally permissible. "Local governments are free to designate certain areas as residential," the Supreme Court of New Jersey declared in *Baker*, "and may act to preserve a family style of living. A municipality is validly concerned with maintaining the stability and permanence generally associated with single family occupancy and preventing uses resembling boarding houses or other institutional living arrangements." Similarly, the Supreme Court of Michigan said in *Dinolfo* that "preservation of traditional family values, maintenance of property values, and population and density control * * * are not only rational but laudable goals." *Cleburne* itself can be read to suggest that the local ordinance simply did not go far enough: if, the Court intimates, the city had banned all multi-family dwellings and health facilities, rather than concentrating solely on those limited to the mentally retarded, the ordinance would have been constitutional.

Multi-family housing is only the beginning of the kinds of uses that cities seek to exclude from "better" neighborhoods. The *Renton* case, which follows, deals with the attempt to exclude "adult motion picture theaters." These days even uses that are widely considered desirable additions to the community are excluded from residential neighborhoods. As *The New York Times* reports:

> NIMBY * * * once referred to disputes about garbage dumps and hazardous waste sites. In the 1980's, it came to symbolize a backlash against affordable (read: lower income) housing and social service sites like halfway houses and homeless shelters, virtually anything seen as a potential threat to property values. In many cases, it still refers to all of these. But in wealthy communities across the New York region, the pitched battles are now over ball fields and libraries, school buildings, churches and housing for the elderly—projects once seen as pillars of an upright community. Instead of pitting citizens against big developers or government, they often pit neighbor against neighbor in ugly feuds, dividing parts of the same town, for example, or homeowners and a local Little League. * * * Such heightened civic discord, marked by crowded zoning board hearings, petition drives, angry letters and bitter lawsuits, poses a thorny question: whether there are legitimate reasons for people to feel so beleaguered or the long bull market has spawned a comfort class of adults even more spoiled than their charge-card-carrying children.[2]

To be sure, not every attempt to exclude non-conforming uses is unjustifiable. Sometimes the opposition to a proposed use is grounded on legitimate notions of environmental protection—even environmental justice—or on understandable concern about having pornographic movie theaters, chain stores, or traffic congestion nearby. If it is proper to be skeptical only of some opposition to non-residential uses being placed in residential areas, how would one articulate when nimbyism is good and when it is bad?

CITY OF RENTON V. PLAYTIME THEATRES, INC.

Supreme Court of the United States, 1986.
475 U.S. 41, 106 S.Ct. 925, 89 L.Ed.2d 29.

JUSTICE REHNQUIST delivered the opinion of the Court. * * *

In May 1980, the Mayor of Renton, a city of approximately 32,000 people located just south of Seattle, suggested to the Renton City Council that it consider the advisability of enacting zoning legislation dealing with adult entertainment uses. No such uses existed in the city at that time. Upon the Mayor's suggestion, the City Council referred the matter to the city's Planning and Development Committee. * * * In April 1981, acting on the basis of the Planning and Development Committee's recommendation, the City Council enacted Ordinance No. 3526. The

---

[2]   David Herszenhorn, "Now It's 'Nothing in My Backyard': Just About Any Kind of Project Can Rile Homeowners," New York Times, April 16, 2000, Section 1, p. 35.

ordinance prohibited any "adult motion picture theater" from locating within 1,000 feet of any residential zone, single-or multiple-family dwelling, church, or park, and within one mile of any school. The term "adult motion picture theater" was defined as "[a]n enclosed building used for presenting motion picture films, video cassettes, cable television, or any other such visual media, distinguished or characteri[zed] by an emphasis on matter depicting, describing or relating to 'specified sexual activities' or 'specified anatomical areas' * * * for observation by patrons therein."

In early 1982, respondents acquired two existing theaters in downtown Renton, with the intention of using them to exhibit feature-length adult films. The theaters were located within the area proscribed by Ordinance No. 3526. At about the same time, respondents filed * * * [a] lawsuit challenging the ordinance on First and Fourteenth Amendment grounds, and seeking declaratory and injunctive relief. While the federal action was pending, the City Council amended the ordinance in several respects, adding a statement of reasons for its enactment and reducing the minimum distance from any school to 1,000 feet. * * *

In our view, the resolution of this case is largely dictated by our decision in *[Young v.] American Mini Theatres* [427 U.S. 50, 96 S.Ct. 2440, 49 L.Ed.2d 310 (1976)]. There, although five Members of the Court did not agree on a single rationale for the decision, we held that the city of Detroit's zoning ordinance, which prohibited locating an adult theater within 1,000 feet of any two other "regulated uses" or within 500 feet of any residential zone, did not violate the First and Fourteenth Amendments. 427 U.S., at 72–73, 96 S.Ct., at 2453 (plurality opinion of Stevens, J., joined by Burger, C.J., and White and Rehnquist, JJ.); *id.,* at 84, 96 S.Ct., at 2459 (Powell, J., concurring). The Renton ordinance, like the one in *American Mini Theatres,* does not ban adult theaters altogether, but merely provides that such theaters may not be located within 1,000 feet of any residential zone, single-or multiple-family dwelling, church, park, or school. The ordinance is therefore properly analyzed as a form of time, place, and manner regulation.

Describing the ordinance as a time, place, and manner regulation is, of course, only the first step in our inquiry. This Court has long held that regulations enacted for the purpose of restraining speech on the basis of its content presumptively violate the First Amendment. On the other hand, so-called "content-neutral" time, place, and manner regulations are acceptable so long as they are designed to serve a substantial governmental interest and do not unreasonably limit alternative avenues of communication.

At first glance, the Renton ordinance, like the ordinance in *American Mini Theatres,* does not appear to fit neatly into either the "content-based" or the "content-neutral" category. To be sure, the ordinance treats theaters that specialize in adult films differently from other kinds of theaters. Nevertheless, as the District Court concluded, the Renton ordinance is aimed not at the *content* of the films shown at "adult motion picture theatres," but rather at the *secondary effects* of such theaters on the surrounding community. The District Court found that the City Council's "*predominate* concerns" were with the secondary effects of adult theaters, and not with the content of adult films themselves. But the Court of Appeals, relying on its decision in *Tovar v. Billmeyer,* 721 F.2d 1260, 1266 (C.A.9 1983), held that this was not enough to sustain the ordinance. According to the Court of Appeals, if "*a motivating factor*" in enacting the ordinance was to restrict respondents' exercise of First Amendment rights the ordinance would be invalid, apparently no matter how small a part this motivating factor may have played in the City Council's decision. This view of the law was rejected in *United States v. O'Brien,* 391 U.S. 367, 382–386, 88 S.Ct. 1673, 1681–1684, 20 L.Ed.2d 672 (1968) * * *. The District Court's finding as to "predominate" intent, left undisturbed by the Court of Appeals, is more than adequate to establish that the city's pursuit of its zoning interests here was unrelated to the suppression of free expression. The ordinance by its terms is designed to prevent crime, protect the city's retail trade, maintain property values, and generally "protec[t] and preserv[e] the quality of [the city's] neighborhoods, commercial districts, and the quality of urban life," not to suppress the expression of unpopular views. As Justice Powell observed in *American Mini Theatres,* "[i]f [the city] had been concerned with restricting the message purveyed by adult theaters, it would have tried to close them or restrict their number rather than circumscribe their choice as to location."

In short, the Renton ordinance is completely consistent with our definition of "content-neutral" speech regulations as those that "are *justified* without reference to the content of the regulated speech." *Virginia Pharmacy Board v. Virginia Citizens Consumer Council, Inc.,* 425 U.S. 748, 771, 96 S.Ct. 1817, 1830, 48 L.Ed.2d 346 (1976) (emphasis added). The ordinance does not contravene the fundamental principle that underlies our concern about "content-based" speech regulations: that "government may not grant the use of a forum to people whose views it finds acceptable, but deny use to those wishing to express less favored or more controversial views." [*Police Dept. of Chicago v.*] *Mosley,* 408 U.S., at 95–96, 92 S.Ct., at 2289–2290.

It was with this understanding in mind that, in *American Mini Theatres,* a majority of this Court decided that, at least with respect to businesses that purvey sexually explicit materials, zoning ordinances designed to combat the undesirable secondary effects of such businesses are to be reviewed under the standards applicable to "content-neutral" time, place, and manner regulations. Justice Stevens, writing for the plurality, concluded that the city of Detroit was entitled to draw a distinction between adult theaters and other kinds of theaters "without violating the government's paramount obligation of neutrality in its regulation of protected communication," noting that "[i]t is th[e] secondary effect which these zoning ordinances attempt to avoid, not the dissemination of 'offensive' speech". Justice Powell, in concurrence, elaborated:

> "[The] dissent misconceives the issue in this case by insisting that it involves an impermissible time, place, and manner restriction based on the content of expression. It involves nothing of the kind. We have here merely a decision by the city to treat certain movie theaters differently because they have markedly different effects upon their surroundings * * *. Moreover, even if this were a case involving a special governmental response to the content of one type of movie, it is possible that the result would be supported by a line of cases recognizing that the government can tailor its reaction to different types of speech according to the degree to which its special and overriding interests are implicated."

The appropriate inquiry in this case, then, is whether the Renton ordinance is designed to serve a substantial governmental interest and allows for reasonable alternative avenues of communication. It is clear that the ordinance meets such a standard. As a majority of this Court recognized in *American Mini Theatres,* a city's "interest in attempting to preserve the quality of urban life is one that must be accorded high respect." 427 U.S., at 71, 96 S.Ct., at 2453 (plurality opinion); see *id.,* at 80, 96 S.Ct., at 2457 (Powell, J., concurring) ("Nor is there doubt that the interests furthered by this ordinance are both important and substantial"). Exactly the same vital governmental interests are at stake here.

The Court of Appeals ruled, however, that because the Renton ordinance was enacted without the benefit of studies specifically relating to "the particular problems or needs of Renton," the city's justifications for the ordinance were "conclusory and speculative." We think the Court of Appeals imposed on the city an unnecessarily rigid burden of proof. The record in this case reveals that Renton relied heavily on the experience of, and studies produced by, the city of Seattle. In Seattle, as in Renton, the adult theater zoning ordinance was aimed at preventing the secondary effects caused by the presence of even one such theater in a given neighborhood. See *Northend Cinema, Inc. v. Seattle,* 90 Wash.2d 709, 585 P.2d 1153 (1978). * * * We hold that Renton was entitled to rely on the experiences of Seattle and other cities, and in particular on the "detailed findings" summarized in the Washington Supreme Court's *Northend*

Cinema opinion, in enacting its adult theater zoning ordinance. The First Amendment does not require a city, before enacting such an ordinance, to conduct new studies or produce evidence independent of that already generated by other cities, so long as whatever evidence the city relies upon is reasonably believed to be relevant to the problem that the city addresses. That was the case here. Nor is our holding affected by the fact that Seattle ultimately chose a different method of adult theater zoning than that chosen by Renton, since Seattle's choice of a different remedy to combat the secondary effects of adult theaters does not call into question either Seattle's identification of those secondary effects or the relevance of Seattle's experience to Renton.

We also find no constitutional defect in the method chosen by Renton to further its substantial interests. Cities may regulate adult theaters by dispersing them, as in Detroit, or by effectively concentrating them, as in Renton. "It is not our function to appraise the wisdom of [the city's] decision to require adult theaters to be separated rather than concentrated in the same areas * * *. [T]he city must be allowed a reasonable opportunity to experiment with solutions to admittedly serious problems." *American Mini Theatres, supra,* 427 U.S., at 71, 96 S.Ct., at 2453 (plurality opinion). Moreover, the Renton ordinance is "narrowly tailored" to affect only that category of theaters shown to produce the unwanted secondary effects, thus avoiding the flaw that proved fatal to the regulations in *Schad v. Mount Ephraim,* 452 U.S. 61, 101 S.Ct. 2176, 68 L.Ed.2d 671 (1981), and *Erznoznik v. City of Jacksonville,* 422 U.S. 205, 95 S.Ct. 2268, 45 L.Ed.2d 125 (1975).

Respondents contend that the Renton ordinance is "under-inclusive," in that it fails to regulate other kinds of adult businesses that are likely to produce secondary effects similar to those produced by adult theaters. On this record the contention must fail. There is no evidence that, at the time the Renton ordinance was enacted, any other adult business was located in, or was contemplating moving into, Renton. In fact, Resolution No. 2368, enacted in October 1980, states that "the City of Renton does not, at the present time, have any business whose primary purpose is the sale, rental, or showing of sexually explicit materials." That Renton chose first to address the potential problems created by one particular kind of adult business in no way suggests that the city has "singled out" adult theaters for discriminatory treatment. We simply have no basis on this record for assuming that Renton will not, in the future, amend its ordinance to include other kinds of adult businesses that have been shown to produce the same kinds of secondary effects as adult theaters. See *Williamson v. Lee Optical Co.,* 348 U.S. 483, 488–489, 75 S.Ct. 461, 464–465, 99 L.Ed. 563 (1955).

Finally, turning to the question whether the Renton ordinance allows for reasonable alternative avenues of communication, we note that the ordinance leaves some 520 acres, or more than five percent of the entire land area of Renton, open to use as adult theater sites. The District Court found, and the Court of Appeals did not dispute the finding, that the 520 acres of land consists of "[a]mple, accessible real estate," including "acreage in all stages of development from raw land to developed, industrial, warehouse, office, and shopping space that is criss-crossed by freeways, highways, and roads."

Respondents argue, however, that some of the land in question is already occupied by existing businesses, that "practically none" of the undeveloped land is currently for sale or lease, and that in general there are no "commercially viable" adult theater sites within the 520 acres left open by the Renton ordinance. The Court of Appeals accepted these arguments, concluded that the 520 acres was not truly "available" land, and therefore held that the Renton ordinance "would result in a substantial restriction" on speech.

We disagree with both the reasoning and the conclusion of the Court of Appeals. That respondents must fend for themselves in the real estate market, on an equal footing with other prospective purchasers and lessees, does not give rise to a First Amendment violation. And although we have cautioned against the enactment of zoning regulations that have "the effect of suppressing, or greatly restricting access to, lawful speech," *American Mini Theatres,* 427 U.S., at 71, n. 35, 96 S.Ct., at 2453, n. 35 (plurality opinion), we have never suggested that the First Amendment compels the Government to ensure that adult theaters, or any other kinds of speech-related businesses for that matter, will be able to obtain sites at bargain prices. See *id.,* at 78, 96 S.Ct., at 2456 (Powell, J., concurring) ("The inquiry for First Amendment purposes is not concerned with economic impact"). In our view, the First Amendment requires only that Renton refrain from effectively denying respondents a reasonable opportunity to open and operate an adult theater within the city, and the ordinance before us easily meets this requirement.

In sum, we find that the Renton ordinance represents a valid governmental response to the "admittedly serious problems" created by adult theaters. See *id.,* at 71, 96 S.Ct., at 2453 (plurality opinion). Renton has not used "the power to zone as a pretext for suppressing expression," *id.,* at 84, 96 S.Ct., at 2459 (Powell, J., concurring), but rather has sought to make some areas available for adult theaters and their patrons, while at the same time preserving the quality of life in the community at large by preventing those theaters from locating in other areas. This, after all, is the essence of zoning. Here, as in *American Mini Theatres,* the city has enacted a zoning ordinance that meets these goals while also satisfying the dictates of the First Amendment. * * *

JUSTICE BRENNAN joined by JUSTICE MARSHALL, dissenting. * * *

The ordinance discriminates on its face against certain forms of speech based on content. Movie theaters specializing in "adult motion pictures" may not be located within 1,000 feet of any residential zone, single-or multiple-family dwelling, church, park, or school. Other motion picture theaters, and other forms of "adult entertainment," such as bars, massage parlors, and adult bookstores, are not subject to the same restrictions. This selective treatment strongly suggests that Renton was interested not in controlling the "secondary effects" associated with adult businesses, but in discriminating against adult theaters based on the content of the films they exhibit. * * * The ordinance's underinclusiveness is cogent evidence that it was aimed at the *content* of the films shown in adult movie theaters.

Shortly *after* this lawsuit commenced, the Renton City Council amended the ordinance, adding a provision explaining that its intention in adopting the ordinance had been "to promote the City of Renton's great interest in protecting and preserving the quality of its neighborhoods, commercial districts, and the quality of urban life through effective land use planning." The amended ordinance also lists certain conclusory "findings" concerning adult entertainment land uses that the Council purportedly relied upon in adopting the ordinance. The city points to these provisions as evidence that the ordinance was designed to control the secondary effects associated with adult movie theaters, rather than to suppress the content of the films they exhibit. However, the "legislative history" of the ordinance strongly suggests otherwise.

Prior to the amendment, there was no indication that the ordinance was designed to address any "secondary effects" a single adult theater might create. In addition to the suspiciously coincidental timing of the amendment, many of the City Council's "findings" do not relate to legitimate land use concerns. As the Court of Appeals observed, "[b]oth the magistrate and the district court recognized that many of the stated reasons for the ordinance were no more than expressions of dislike for the subject matter." That some residents may be offended by the *content* of the films shown at adult movie theaters cannot form the basis for state regulation of speech. * * * In sum, the circumstances here strongly suggest that the ordinance was designed to suppress expression, even that constitutionally protected, and thus was not to be analyzed as a content-neutral time, place, and manner restriction. The Court allows Renton to conceal its illicit motives, however, by reliance on the fact that other communities adopted similar restrictions. The Court's approach largely immunizes such measures from judicial scrutiny, since a municipality can readily find other municipal ordinances to rely upon, thus always retrospectively justifying special zoning regulations for adult theaters. Rather than speculate about Renton's motives for adopting such measures, our cases require that the ordinance, like any other content-based restriction on speech, is constitutional "only if the [city] can show that [it] is a precisely drawn means of serving a compelling [governmental] interest." *Consolidated Edison Co. v. Public Service Comm'n of N.Y.,* 447 U.S., at 540, 100 S.Ct., at 2334. Only this strict approach can insure that cities will not use their zoning powers as a pretext for suppressing constitutionally protected expression.

Applying this standard to the facts of this case, the ordinance is patently unconstitutional. Renton has not shown that locating adult movie theaters in proximity to its churches, schools, parks, and residences will necessarily result in undesirable "secondary effects," or that these problems could not be effectively addressed by less intrusive restrictions. * * * The Court finds that the ordinance was designed to further Renton's substantial interest in "preserv[ing] the quality of urban life." As explained above, the record here is simply insufficient to support this assertion. The city made no showing as to how uses "protected" by the ordinance would be affected by the presence of an adult movie theater. Thus, the Renton ordinance is clearly distinguishable from the Detroit zoning ordinance upheld in *Young v. American Mini Theatres, Inc.,* 427 U.S. 50, 96 S.Ct. 2440, 49 L.Ed.2d 310 (1976). The Detroit ordinance, which was designed to disperse adult theaters throughout the city, was supported by the testimony of urban planners and real estate experts regarding the adverse effects of locating several such businesses in the same neighborhood. *Id.,* at 55, 96 S.Ct., at 2445; see also *Northend Cinema Inc. v. Seattle,* 90 Wash.2d 709, 711, 585 P.2d 1153, 1154–1155 (1978), cert. denied, *sub nom. Apple Theatre, Inc. v. Seattle,* 441 U.S. 946, 99 S.Ct. 2166, 60 L.Ed.2d 1048 (1979) (Seattle zoning ordinance was the "culmination of a long period of study and discussion"). Here, the Renton Council was aware only that some residents had complained about adult movie theaters, and that other localities had adopted special zoning restrictions for such establishments. These are not "facts" sufficient to justify the burdens the ordinance imposed upon constitutionally protected expression.

Finally, the ordinance is invalid because it does not provide for reasonable alternative avenues of communication. The District Court found that the ordinance left 520 acres in Renton available for adult theater sites, an area comprising about five percent of the city. However, the Court of Appeals found that because much of this land was already occupied, "[l]imiting adult theater uses to these areas is a substantial restriction on speech." Many "available" sites are also largely unsuited for use by movie theaters. Again, these facts serve to distinguish this case from *American Mini Theatres,* where there was no indication that the Detroit zoning ordinance seriously limited the locations available for adult businesses. * * *

MICHAEL WARNER, THE TROUBLE WITH NORMAL
Pp. 149–150, 153, 157–159, 161–162, 172–173, 182–183, 186–190 (1999).

Along Christopher Street, you can tell immediately that something is wrong. In Harmony Video, for years one of the principal porn stores on New York's most legendary gay strip, they now display $3.95 videos of football teams, John Wayne movies, and music videos by the fundamentalist pop singer Amy Grant. Just up the block stands Christopher Street Books, the store that proudly bills itself as "New York's oldest gay establishment." In the front room it, too, sells bargain videos that seem to have been unloaded by a desperate wholesaler in Kansas: Bob Uecker's Wacky World of Sports, and Spanish-language children's cartoons. Whose idea of gay merchandise is this? In the back room where the peep show booths are, they are playing films of wrestling matches. A few customers still come in, mostly gay men over forty. They leave quickly.

These surreal scenes are among the effects of Mayor Rudy Giuliani's new zoning law limiting "adult establishments," which the city began to enforce in the summer of 1998 after a series of court stays and challenges. As this book goes to press, the court challenges are not over and won't be for a long time. The law has already allowed the city to padlock dozens of stores and clubs, including a gay bookstore. But the law's details contain many gray areas, and the resulting uncertainty and fear have a much wider, chilling effect than the closures. * * *

All over New York, in fact, a pall hangs over the public life of queers. Much more is at stake here than the replacement of one neighborhood by another, or the temporary crackdowns of a Republican mayor. As in other U.S. cities, sex publics in New York that have been built up over several decades—by the gay movement, by AIDS activism, and by countercultures of many different kinds—are now endangered by a new politics of privatization. This new political alignment has strong support among gays and lesbians, and the conflicts now flashing up illuminate the growing rift between identity-based lesbian and gay politics and its queerer counterparts. * * *

Mayor Giuliani's zoning amendment * * * can be boiled down to three forms of isolation:

- from concentration to dispersal (the five-hundred-feet rule keeps adult businesses from being close to one another);

- from conspicuousness to discretion (the signage regulations of the new bill are stricter than existing regulations); and

- from residential sites to remote ones.

All three impulses share the desire to make sex less noticeable in the course of everyday urban life and more difficult to find for those who want sexual materials. * * *

The zoning issue was clearly driven by real estate interests, even more than by the petitbourgeois moralism to which it gave such venomous expression. Consider that the *New York Times* editorialized seven times in favor of rezoning; the New York Times Corporation is a principal member of the Times Square Business Improvement District. It was the Times Square BID, even more than Mayor Giuliani's office, that spearheaded the rezoning effort. The Walt Disney Company insisted on eliminating the porn stores as a condition of its role in changing Times Square.

We are therefore confronted with a problem of political analysis. What lies behind this erosion of queer publics, since it seems local and uncoordinated and yet widespread and systematic? One common thread is the increasingly aggressive demand of market capital, which in the United States and elsewhere has seriously eroded the ancient ideal of an active public, a commonwealth. There is nothing new about that conflict, and commerce alone can hardly be said to threaten sex publics. It isn't just "the market" that is chilling New York's queer life. We might say, though, that the destruction of sex publics results from the new latitude given to market forces in the Clinton era and from the corporate populism that wants everything visibly normal. One of the hallmarks of 1990s politics is a tendency to see the state as responsible for ensuring the expansion of market capital, rather than for fostering a democratic public sphere. It is thought to be a servant of the market, rather than a check to the market. So we hear more about "public/private partnerships," and less about the rights of citizens who don't happen to be corporations. This understanding of the relations among state, market, and public has become, in the late 1990s at least, a new common sense, one that appears as common sense partly because it arises in so many contexts that it seems to transcend the particularities and interests of any single context. * * *

The politics of privatization, in my view, destroys real privacy even as it erodes public activity. To see how this could be so, it will be necessary to get over the common misconception that public and private are always opposites. There are so many competing definitions of public and private involved that it may be worth listing the main ones:

	Public	Private
1.	open to everyone	restricted to some
2.	accessible for money	closed even to those who could pay
3.	state related	nonstate, belonging to civil society
4.	official	nonofficial

5.	common	special or personal
6.	national or popular	group, class, or locale
7.	international or universal	particular or finite
8.	in physical view of others	concealed
9.	outside the home	domestic
10.	circulated in print or electronic media	circulated orally or in manuscript
11.	known widely	known to initiates
12.	acknowledged and explicit	tacit and implicit

13. "The world itself, in so far as it is common to all of us and distinguished from our privately owned place in it" (as Arendt puts it in *The Human Condition*).

Matters are further complicated by several senses of private that have no corresponding sense of public, including:

14. related to the individual, especially to inwardness, subjective experience, and the incommunicable;

15. discretely comported, in the sense of the French pudeur— expressible in English only through its opposite, impudence; and

16. genital or sexual.

None of these definitions are simple oppositions, or "binaries." Because the contexts overlap, most things are private in one sense and public in another. Books can be published privately; a public theater can be a private enterprise, a private life can be discussed publicly, and so on. So it requires no stretch of the imagination to see that pornography, "public sex," cruising, sex work, and other elements in a publicly accessible sexual culture are public in some ways, but still intensely private in others. "Public sex" is public in the sense that it takes place outside the home, but it usually takes place in areas that have been chosen for their seclusion, and like all sex involves extremely intimate and private associations. Sex work is public in being accessible for cash, but still private in many of the same ways, as well as being a private trade. When people speak of "public sex," the crudeness of the term misleads us about what is at stake. * * *

Interestingly, the Giuliani administration and other advocates of rezoning higher up in the political system did not speak the language of smut, filth, and shame. Giuliani did not condemn porn per se—at least not until his zoning plan received court approval. His arguments were limited to secondary effects and a rather vague but politically potent language about "quality of life." * * * [T]he rhetoric of "quality of life" tries to isolate porn from political culture by pretending that there are no differences of value or opinion in it, that it therefore does not belong in the public sphere of critical exchange and opinion formation. When Giuliani speaks of quality of life, he never acknowledges that different people might want different qualities in their lives, let alone that access to porn might be one of them.

The zoning bill seeks to privatize sex in part through this segregation of sexual matters from the public culture in which differences between people can be recognized. * * * By intervening to cut off discussion and elaboration of the qualities of life, the zoning bill actually contradicts one important theme in the conservative vision of the state: the zoning bill, ironically promoted by those who routinely denounce government intervention and celebrate the market economy known as the "private sector," authorizes not only a massive state restriction on commerce but also state support for a particular vision of the good life. The bill brings the resources of the state into play in order to cultivate one form of life—already normative—by making it easier of access and acknowledgment than rival forms of life, which are not less legal, only despised and made artificially difficult.

The assault on legitimate pornographic commerce is particularly ironic given the enormous changes in the porn trade since the last attempt at zoning it out of New York, in 1977. Since then, the VCR revolution has made videotapes the lion's share of the porn trade. Unlike peep shows and stripper clubs, of course, videotape rentals are commonly taken to another space: home. Much of the panic about porn is not about what happens on Times Square, but about what people are doing with their home entertainment centers, which are harder for conservatives to regulate. There is no political gain in attacking the home consumption of commercial video. But if the video can be identified with its urban circulation zone, then—with a large dose of hypocrisy and no small irony—regulating it can be presented as a way of protecting the home from urban squalor.

The intervention of the state to weaken public sexual culture probably would not be possible without this form of hypocrisy—an ideology of space that demonizes some of the essential functions of a city in order to idealize an impossibly purified privacy. What the Giuliani people hate most is the secondary effects of porn concentrated in a neighborhood. The first aim of the bill's five-hundred-feet rule is to disperse adult businesses. Few of the bill's opponents challenged this provision. * * * But for queers the concentration of adult businesses has been one of the best things about them. The gay bars on Christopher Street draw customers from people who come there because of its sex trade. The street is cruisier because of the sex shops. The boutiques that sell freedom rings and Don't Panic T-shirts do more business for the same reasons. Not all of the thousands who migrate or make pilgrimages to

Christopher Street use the porn shops, but all benefit from the fact that some do. After a certain point, a quantitative change is a qualitative change. A critical mass develops. The street becomes queer. It develops a dense, publicly accessible sexual culture. It therefore becomes a base for non-porn businesses like the Oscar Wilde Bookshop. And it becomes a political base from which to pressure politicians with a gay voting bloc. Lesbians and gay men continue to depend on this pattern in urban space, no matter how much the promise of private identity—secured through property, rights, and legitimate couplehood—might invite them to repudiate the world-making scene of sex.

Phone sex, the Internet, and sitcoms cannot take the place of this urban space and its often unrecognized practices of sexual citizenship. * * * That is what has been urged by columnists in gay lifestyle magazines, chiefly Michelangelo Signorile. In his *Life Outside*, a jeremiad driven by resentment toward the social network he ambiguously refers to both as "the party circuit" and as "gay culture," Signorile fuses that resentment with a common rhetoric of antiurbanism. Fortunately, he claims, two millennial trends can be identified: the "deghettoization" and "deurbanization" of gay life in America. These, of course, are pseudo-trends. Signorile offers no evidence to support his claim that either one is happening. He does quote a sociologist named Jerry Kramer to support his notion that gay life is moving to the suburbs; but even Kramer adds: "at least that's my perception. I would say it's hard to tell how much of it is actually a movement out, and how much of it is gays and lesbians who were living in the suburbs before and are just coming out now because they feel more protected." For the reasons I've given, however, the growth of a suburban or rural gay culture would not lessen the importance of an urban one. To make that argument plausible, Signorile must rely on the rhetorical force of the notion of a "gay ghetto." * * *

A neighborhood voluntarily created, freely entered and left, and constituted only by massive concentrations of capital and middle-class commerce can only be called a ghetto by those deaf to the echoes of history or blind to the rules of power. A district like Christopher Street, in fact, is neither a ghetto nor a neighborhood, in the usual sense of the terms. The local character of the neighborhood depends on the daily presence of thousands of nonresidents. Those who actually live in the West Village—at this point, increasingly straight—should not forget their debt to these mostly queer pilgrims. And we should not make the mistake of confusing the class of citizens with the class of property owners. Many of those who hang out on Christopher Street couldn't possibly afford to live there. Many are African American, gay, and young. Where are they being zoned off to?

One of the most disturbing fantasies in the zoning scheme is the idea that an urban locale is a community of shared interest based on residence and property. In *The Death and Life of Great American Cities* Jane Jacobs long ago noted that, "As a sentimental concept, 'neighborhood' is harmful to city planning." Yet the ideology of the neighborhood is politically unchallengeable in the current debate, which is dominated by a fantasy that people are sexual only at home, that the space relevant to sexual politics is the neighborhood. The zoning bill is an ideal instrument for protecting the heterosexual zone of privacy because its procedural politics * * * are set up to guarantee the dominance of the rhetoric of neighborhood at every step. The first requirement after the submission of the proposal was the meeting of every community board in the city, followed by the borough boards. Only then did the City Planning Commission hold public hearings at which non-neighborhood organizations could testify. But they were almost certainly given much less weight, and in the public media the assumption remained that people have a right to control their neighborhoods. * * *

The sexual culture of New York City serves people around the world, even if only as the distant reference point of queer kids growing up in North Carolina or Idaho, who know that somewhere things are different. Residents should not dictate the uses of the urban space around them to the exclusion of other users of the city. To do so is to fail to recognize what a city is. Urban space is always a host space. The right to the city extends to those who use the city. It is not limited to property owners. With the zoning scheme New York, perhaps the world's greatest metropolis, is pretending to be a suburb—though indeed one might want to ask whether a suburb is or should be in fact what it is in the NIMBY ideology: a geography of shame. * * *

RICHARD T. FORD, BOURGEOIS COMMUNITIES: A REVIEW OF GERALD FRUG'S CITY MAKING
56 Stan. L. Rev. 231, 241–247, 250–252 (2003).

[I]ncreasingly even the most liberal cities have cracked down on loitering, panhandling, and public urination; have closed parks at night or deliberately designed them to be unsuitable for sleeping; and have reduced or eliminated public services and benefits for the homeless. Santa Monica recently voted to prohibit sleeping on the beach and to require organizations that distribute free food to obtain permits. San Francisco's redesigned Union Square eliminated large shrubs for the express purpose of depriving the homeless of their use as beds, hiding places for possessions, and latrines. Frug is right that urbanities are resigned to and even enjoy a greater degree of deviance than suburbanites. But there are limits and every major city in America faces those limits. * * * I'll use the failure of left-liberals to face and make hard choices—specifically San Francisco's left-liberal government with respect to homelessness—as a vehicle for my sympathetic but critical reactions to [Frug's book] City

Making. San Francisco provides a useful foil to Frug's urbanism because in many ways the city is a liberal urbanist's wet dream: It boasts a politically progressive, well-educated, ethnically diverse population with a great deal of pride in, and commitment to, their city. * * *

San Francisco is an exemplary postmodern city, a welter of complexities and contradictions packed into its forty or so square miles of hilly landscapes. It is the gateway to the Pacific Rim, perched on the western edge of the nation, yet known as the most European of American cities. Its aesthetic style and social cadence are decidedly conservative when compared to, say New York's frantic avant garde or Miami's exuberant baroque. Yet it is also the most tolerant and progressive of American cities—the home of the counterculture of beatnik North Beach and hippie Haight Ashbury, ground zero for New Age alternative spirituality (Zen Buddhism in Marin County hot tubs, Wicca in Haight Ashbury flats, and Jim Jones' People's Temple), alternative medicine (from acupuncture to medicinal marijuana), and, of course, a celebration of human sexuality that makes Ellen DeGeneres look like Anita Bryant. San Francisco epitomizes a certain sybaritic California style—casual, friendly, unassuming, superficial (but as Oscar Wilde instructs, only shallow people don't care about appearances)—the home of homegrown hallucinogens, restaurants that rival Manhattan's and Paris' best, and, it is rumored, more bars, taverns, gin joints, and watering holes per capita than any other city on the North American continent.

It is common wisdom in the Golden State that a combination of volatile political correctness and complacent nostalgia made San Francisco a clear second runner to Los Angeles in terms of economic, political, and cultural significance. San Francisco—impractical, smug, and insular—looked to preserve its weathered pedigree, its delicate political sensibilities and precious lifestyle, while the cities of the future looked unapologetically to, well, the future. * * * All of this changed with the rise of the dot-com. Flush with found money the city became an economic center despite itself, an eerie deja vu of the nineteenth century gold rush. Long-term San Franciscans shared the streets with irascible Manhattan financiers and SUVs from Southern California dealerships. More change may accompany the end of the dot-com pipe dream and the corresponding hangover. After years of boomtown demand for offices, hotel rooms, and restaurant tables, San Francisco faces record vacancies as stock option prospectors clear out of town and head back home to the plow or in search of the next mother lode.

The city's traditional cash cow—tourism—has been hard hit by global economic malaise, fear of terrorism, and, according to many, the city's chronic homeless problem. The tourism industry and local businesses have long complained that panhandlers, vagrants, and the squalor that living on the streets inevitably generates were a large blemish on the pretty face the city needed to put forward to attract tourists and new businesses. It appears local residents agree: Last November liberal San Francisco's voters approved a proposal to eliminate or severely reduce cash general assistance payments to homeless adults, diverting the public funds saved to in-kind services and vouchers. The initiative, dubbed "Care Not Cash", was vehemently opposed by advocates for the homeless and some of the city's more leftish elected officials.

Care Not Cash, as its name suggests, was pitched to the city's overwhelmingly liberal electorate as a humane alternative to cash grants, which, according to the initiative's sponsors, often serve only to feed addictions. This is a colorable rationale for the initiative, but I suspect that the more potent motivation is one identified by the San Francisco Planning and Urban Research Association (SPUR) in its analysis of Care Not Cash: "Many people believe that . . . homeless people from other places come to San Francisco" in order to receive the generous cash grants. The fear that, through its generous cash assistance, the city has become a magnet for the homeless is doubtless mirrored by a corollary hope for Care Not Cash: that by reducing those benefits the city will encourage much of the current homeless population to go elsewhere. Care Not Cash may prove to be sound policy; it is without a doubt sound marketing. The proposal allows liberals torn between their ideologically driven compassion and their growing distaste for the city's entrenched and often belligerent homeless population a way to resolve their liberal crisis of conscience and still vote for a bourgeois quality of life.

The risk that generous benefits and liberal policies have made the city a magnet for the down and out, addicts, and just plain lazy bums is of course a classic instance of the collective action problem created by metropolitan fragmentation. Advocates for the homeless are right to fear a race to the bottom—what is Berkeley to do if its homeless population skyrockets after Care Not Cash is implemented? The idea that the city could be a magnet for homeless people from other places implies a fixed boundary that separates "our homeless" from homeless people from elsewhere. Formally, this distinction is problematic since local government law defines belonging through residence or domicile, a status that is at least ambiguous in the case of the homeless. And Frug's analysis would suggest a conceptual problem with the magnet hypothesis. Frug's decentered city does not allow for such a strong municipal boundary: The homeless, like other urbanites—perhaps even more so—may move between municipalities in the course of a year, a season, or even a day; a single homeless person potentially may "belong" to many cities. Why is only one responsible for providing the care or cash that he needs?

The common sense ethical intuition suggests that while a city is responsible for "its" homeless population, it is not responsible for homeless people who migrate to the city solely or primarily in order to collect general assistance. But it is difficult to distinguish public assistance-driven relocations from those driven by other factors such as the city's network of private nonprofit organizations that provide services for the homeless, or by the city's relatively tolerant population and relatively friendly public regulations, or even its relatively mild weather. And many people—not just the homeless—choose to locate in a particular jurisdiction for reasons that include public services. It would seem odd, even objectionable, if, for instance, residents of Palo Alto began to worry that the municipality was a "magnet" for parents with children who moved to the jurisdiction primarily in order to take advantage of the city's high quality public schools.

Still, there's something to the common sense concern that a city with generous benefits will become a magnet for the destitute. What distinguishes the weird idea of Palo Alto as a magnet for families with kids from the common sense idea of San Francisco as a magnet for the homeless is the perception that most families, even those who require more in services than they contribute in tax revenues, are contributing members of society, while the homeless are perceived * * * only as a drain on public resources. Most people, even those quite sympathetic to the homeless, see them as a social cost to be controlled, contained, and absorbed. We don't think of middle class families in these abstract and dehumanizing terms, even when, objectively speaking, they are just as "expensive."

Moreover, the homeless are "costly" in terms of more than objective social resources. The experience of San Francisco, Santa Cruz, Santa Monica, and other liberal cities demonstrates that the physical presence of an idle, vaguely menacing, often drug-addicted or mentally-ill street population constitutes a problem to be solved, not a lifestyle that can be accommodated by people of sufficient open mindedness. Although a diversity of people and experiences is one of the merits of city life, no one values a hostile encounter with a paranoid schizophrenic, a shakedown by a drug-addicted young adult in a public restroom, or the stench of urine in the streets.

This is more than a mere inconvenience for the bourgeoisie; it is a crisis for city making. If public restrooms become a hiring hall for prostitutes and a market for drug users, the taxpaying public will not use them and will not support them. If alleys and doorways are wet with urine or blocked by unconscious people, whether passed out from exhaustion, hunger, or intoxication, people will avoid walking, depriving the city of a vibrant street life and compounding traffic congestion. And notice how the problems reinforce one another: Prostitution and drug trafficking in public restrooms erodes public support for them, leaving the homeless (and anyone else out for the night) with nowhere to relieve themselves other than the streets. Ultimately a city is defined by its public spaces. Urbanites, weekend visitors, and tourists alike spend time in urban areas to enjoy the social life that occurs in parks, streets, squares, and promenades. When these are destroyed, so is urban social life, the imagined community of the city, and the civic commitment that inspires people to support social services for the less fortunate. * * *

A progressive bourgeois ambition for the homeless (as long as they remain homeless) has to include changing the widespread sense that they are public nuisances—embodied social costs to be minimized or borne—to a widespread embrace of the homeless as fellow citizens. But this requires more than consciousness raising: In order to change the perception of the homeless, the behavior of many of the homeless themselves will need to change. How can the city achieve such a change? Is it acceptable to require able-bodied homeless people to work in exchange for public benefits? If benefits are adequate, is the city justified in prohibiting panhandling? Can the city insist that addicts enter drug treatment programs and stay clean and sober? At what point, if any, is the city entitled to eliminate benefits for (and effectively expel) individuals who refuse to conform their behavior to expectations? These kinds of questions are of central importance to Frug's city making project. * * *

Let's be clear: Cities are the wrong level of government to deal with homelessness. The external economies, the pervasiveness of the problem, and the magnitude of the expense necessary to provide affordable housing and the social programs many homeless people need all suggest that state and federal level intervention is necessary. It's a tired liberal saw, but it's still true that this wealthiest of wealthy nations could house everyone adequately if it just dropped a few obsolete bomber programs that even the Pentagon doesn't want, or gave up the futile "war" on drugs that sends thousands of poor and desperate young men to prison and then closed a prison or two, or cut the bizarre agricultural subsidies that guarantee every American the right to bathe twice a day in high fructose corn syrup, or didn't exempt SUVs from the luxury automobile tax, or didn't eliminate inheritance or dividends taxes or. . . .

Oh, never mind. Cities can't afford to wait for the state or federal government to implement responsible public policy. The homeless are in San Francisco and, optimal or not, San Francisco will have to deal with them. The ability to deal with the manifestations of national and global phenomena at the local level with local resources is what distinguishes well-run livable cities from urban dystopias. And, misplaced state and federal priorities aside, it's not as if the city itself has no room to improve. * * * Let's * * * explore the way progressive bourgeois reformers might approach the tough choices that face our cities. What follows is hardly a policy white paper; instead it is a set of observations designed to be mildly provocative in the sense of stimulating new ideas and disrupting ideological pieties.

Let's begin with the observation that San Francisco's homeless—like its citizens generally—are a diverse group. The city's sky-high housing costs and sputtering economy will force many people into homelessness; homeless people live and work in the Bay Area but cannot afford even the most modest regular shelter the real estate market provides. At the same time, the city, with its famous tolerance and freewheeling bohemian lifestyle, attracts more than its fair share of people who simply want to "drop out" of mainstream society (to use an outdated but somehow appropriate bit of slang). There's nothing wrong with neohippies per se, but the city can't afford to accommodate as many people whose lifestyle choices don't include a steady income as those who'd like to come here. A reasonable goal for local homeless policy is to try to help the many homeless people who want nothing more than a job that will pay enough to cover the necessities of life while also discouraging people who prefer to live catch-as-catch-can from choosing San Francisco as their home base (bohofiles don't worry: We will get plenty of such free spirits regardless of public policy reform).

Public policy should seek to improve the lives of the many people who, through bad luck, lack of opportunities, victimization, or bad choices, find themselves homeless and want desperately to better their lives. It should also make the city attractive and hospitable to women walking alone at night, to families with kids, to racial minorities (regularly greeted with racial epithets by angry, stoned, or mentally ill street people), and, sure, to rich suburbanites too, whose company we scrappy city dwellers often enjoy and whose patronage and tax dollars we need.

That's the easy sell. Here's the hard one: It should do these good things at the expense of those people who prefer to remain strung out on the streets of San Francisco rather than housed and sober here or elsewhere (to be sure, addiction is addiction but sobriety, as any recovering addict will attest, requires a choice) or who consider life on the streets a lifestyle option preferable to gainful employment (contrary to a certain orthodoxy, there are such people, and they will tell you if you ask them). The sullen and belligerent able bodied people who spend their days on Haight Street and Market at 7th drinking, shooting up, hassling women, demanding handouts from passers-by, running scams, and vandalizing property, public and private alike, should face a stark choice: shape up or ship out.

And there's a harder sell yet: Even some of the people who are really trying to make a go of getting by in the city aren't going to make it. It's expensive to live in San Francisco and even many full time jobs don't support the cost of living. The city can try to accommodate some people through mechanisms like eviction control, rent control * * *, and various forms of housing assistance, but, given the largely state mandated limitations of the city budget, it won't be enough. It may be more humane for the city to encourage and help some of the people who slip into homelessness to relocate to places where it's less expensive to live than to lure and/or keep them here with generous but inadequate cash grants.

Local policies that have even the indirect effect of encouraging the out migration of the poor are often condemned: "The city is becoming a precious enclave of the rich, a yuppie playground. We shouldn't allow the city to become a market commodity, sold to the highest bidder." Agreed. But as long as housing is a market commodity, sold to the highest bidder, access to desirable localities will largely be a function of ability to pay. I have yet to hear a remotely feasible remedy to this state of affairs (other than some version of the liberal screed about misplaced federal and state governmental priorities I indulged in a few pages back). Affordable housing programs, social services, and eviction control for some, and a bus ticket to less expensive locales for others may be the best the city can do in the absence of a federal or statewide commitment to affordable housing. This is far from ideal, but no one really benefits from the current hodgepodge of underfunded and overtaxed * * * social programs, contradictory policies, and high-minded ideals honored in the breach that characterize the city's (and local homeless advocates') current approach to homelessness. It is time to consider ideas that may be anathema to a certain left-liberal sensibility in comparison to the *realistic* alternatives, rather than in comparison to an unrealized and fantastic ideal.

These very general ideas are not meant to do more than hint at the kinds of difficult but necessary decisions that I believe the goals and analysis of City Making ultimately entail. There are many approaches to the homelessness issue, many workable visions of the city. Admittedly my comments herein are animated by a "bourgeois morality" that not everyone shares. But any public ideal—any way of making cities into public places and political locations where a diverse group of strangers can be together—will fail to please everyone. We must reconsider our ends and commitments, as Frank Michelman admonishes, but then we must decide what to do, based on our tragically incompatible goals and ideals, flawed mortal knowledge, and best guesses, and within constraints beyond our control. We will never run out of uncertainties, perspectives we haven't internalized, complexities we haven't mastered, differences we can't accommodate. In an odd sense, the paralyzing anxiety that public norms require something close to unanimous assent or the imprimatur of objective Truth in order to be legitimate is shared by the new left and the new right: A vulgar cultural relativism can lead the left to attack any social norm or public project as exclusionary or hegemonic; similarly, the libertarian right insists that the subjectivity and incompatibility of individual values and goals makes the minimal, night watchman state the only legitimate form of government.

Unless we are to abandon the local public sphere to anomie, alienation, and the law of the concrete jungle, we will have to be satisfied with our best judgment, made in good faith, that our laws and norms offer everyone reasonable and humane options, even if they are not options everyone is happy to select from. This, at least from where I live, looks like the only way to achieve the important goal that I believe inspires City Making: to remake the city by making its residents, tourists, commuters, haute cuisine gourmands, nightclub revelers, and homeless alike into a community of strangers, a responsible and compassionate bourgeoisie. * * *

B. COMMUNITY SELF-DEFENSE AGAINST CHANGES IN CHARACTER

The preceding section examined the relationship between a city and its citizens; this section investigates the relationship between a city and its neighborhoods. If a neighborhood were a legal entity, its relationship to the city could be understood in the way that federal-city and state-city relationships were treated in Chapter Two.[3] But neighborhoods have no formal legal status, and the defense of neighborhood integrity against city power has relied not on notions of home rule but on the existence of individual Constitutional rights to property or on the assertion of political power by affected neighborhood residents.

There are many contexts in which fights between a city and its neighborhoods take place. We considered one in the previous section: the effort by the City of New York to "clean up" Christopher Street. Another classic city/neighborhood battle concerns economic development. How much power should a city have to dictate the means by which a neighborhood in economic distress should be "revitalized"? The first two readings—from Keith Aoki and Robert Caro—describe the battles engendered by the approach to redevelopment, known as urban renewal, that was ascendant from 1930–1970. The next two readings—by William Simon and Audrey McFarlane—present differing views of the newest innovation in urban redevelopment: the community economic development movement. How does community economic development differ from urban renewal? Is McFarlane's critique of community

---

[3] For an analysis of the potential for and value of neighborhood empowerment, see, e.g., Stephen Miller, Legal Neighborhoods, 37 Harv. Envtl. L. Rev. 105 (2013); Kenneth Stahl, Neighborhood Empowerment and The Future of the City, 161 U. Pa. L. Rev. 939 (2013). For an argument from an earlier generation, see, e.g., David Morris and Karl Hess, Neighborhood Power: The New Localism (1975).

economic development persuasive? If so, might urban renewal be preferable?

The final reading addresses a major legal restriction on a tool that cities often use to promote neighborhood redevelopment—namely eminent domain. In *Kelo*, the city took private property for private development. The question was whether the taking was for a "public use," as the United States Constitution requires.[4] From the perspective of the preservation of neighborhood character, does it matter whether a city promotes neighborhood redevelopment through a subsidy for business development rather than through takings of property as in *Kelo*? Is the problem the type of development the city is trying to promote or the process for determining what type of redevelopment should be pursued? Finally, to what extent does the obviousness of what is permanent and what is transitory in city life, the subject of the Italo Calvino story that begins the section, affect the possibility of neighborhood self-defense against city control?

ITALO CALVINO, INVISIBLE CITIES
P. 63 (1974).

The city of Sophronia is made up of two half-cities. In one there is the great roller coaster with its steep humps, the carousel with its chain spokes, the Ferris wheel of spinning cages, the death-ride with crouching motorcyclists, the big top with the clump of trapezes hanging in the middle. The other half-city is of stone and marble and cement, with the bank, the factories, the palaces, the slaughterhouse, the school, and all

---

[4] See Steven Eagle, Urban Revitalization and Eminent Domain: Misinterpreting Jane Jacobs, 4 Alb. Gov't L. Rev. 106 (2011); David Schwed, Pretextual Takings and Exclusionary Zoning: Different Means to the Same Parochial End, 2 Ariz. J. Envtl. L. & Pol'y 53 (2011); Robert Thomas, Recent Developments in Eminent Domain: Public Use, 44 Urb. Law. 705 (2011); Audrey G. McFarlane, Rebuilding the Public-Private City: Regulatory Taking's Anti-Subordination Insight for Eminent Domain and Redevelopment, 42 Ind. L. Rev. 97 (2009); Robin Paul Malloy, Private Property, Community Development, and Eminent Domain (2008); Richard Schragger, Cities, Economic Development, and the Free Trade Constitution, 94 Va. L. Rev. 1091 (2008); John Ryskamp, The Eminent Domain Revolt: Changing Perceptions in a New Constitutional Epoch (2007); Alberto B. Lopez, Weighing and Reweighing Eminent Domain's Political Philosophies Post-Kelo, 41 Wake Forest L. Rev. 237 (2006); Symposium, The Death of Poletown: The Future of Eminent Domain and Urban Development After County of Wayne v. Hathcock, 2004 Mich. St. L. Rev. 837 (2004); Nicole Stelle Garnett, The Public Use Question as a Takings Problem, 71 Geo. Wash. L. Rev. 934 (2003); Michael Heller and James Krier, Deterrence and Distribution in the Law of Takings, 112 Harv. L. Rev. 997 (1999); Carol Rose, Takings, Federalism, Norms, 105 Yale L. J. 1121 (1996); William Fischel, Regulatory Takings: Law, Economics, and Politics (1995); Glynn Lunney, A Critical Reexamination of Takings Jurisprudence, 90 Mich. L. Rev. 1892 (1992); Stephen Munzer, Compensation and Government Takings of Private Property, 33 Nomos 195 (1991); Jeremy Paul, The Hidden Structure of Takings Law, 64 S. Cal. L.Rev. 1393 (1991); Margaret Jane Radin, The Liberal Conception of Property: Cross Currents in the Jurisprudence of Takings, 88 Colum. L. Rev. 1667 (1988); Richard Epstein, Takings: Private Property and the Power of Eminent Domain (1985); Bruce Ackerman, Private Property and the Constitution (1977); Frank Michelman, Property, Utility and Fairness: Comments on the Ethical Foundations of the "Just Compensation" Law, 80 Harv. L. Rev. 1165 (1967); Joseph Sax, Takings and the Police Power, 74 Yale L. J. 36 (1964).

the rest. One of the half-cities is permanent, the other is temporary, and when the period of its sojourn is over, they uproot it, dismantle it, and take it off, transplanting it to the vacant lots of another half-city.

And so every year the day comes when the workmen remove the marble pediments, lower the stone walls, the cement pylons, take down the Ministry, the monument, the docks, the petroleum refinery, the hospital, load them on trailers, to follow from stand to stand their annual itinerary. Here remains the half-Sophronia of the shooting-galleries and the carousels, the shout suspended from the cart of the headlong roller coaster, and it begins to count the months, the days it must wait before the caravan returns and a complete life can begin again.

KEITH AOKI, RACE, SPACE, AND PLACE: THE RELATION BETWEEN ARCHITECTURAL MODERNISM, POST-MODERNISM, URBAN PLANNING, AND GENTRIFICATION
20 Fordham Urb. L. J. 699, 766–772 (1993).

Urban Renewal

During the 1950s, the real or imaginary horrors of urban existence * * * captured the attention of the public. Medical analogies proliferated, lingering as a vestige of an earlier generation's dread of urban disease and crime. Slums were seen as pathological malignancies that had to be removed by the scalpel of urban planning. Eventually, a relatively unified response to urban problems arose out of several factors: concerns about poor housing in the inner cities; fears about the economic costs of urban blight, such as loss of rich residents to the suburbs, loss of businesses and industries, and increasing social costs; pressures for office expansion; and major financial incentives from the federal government. The interaction of these factors were responsible for the genesis of the movement toward large-scale urban renewal projects. Coined in the late 1940s to replace the more accurate expression Slum Clearance, urban renewal was considered by its advocates as describing a type of radical surgery that would purge the city of unsafe, unsanitary, overcrowded buildings and replace them with a mixture of high-rise and walk-up apartments arranged geometrically in open blocks. Such projects would then generally operate under the administration of a municipal housing authority.

Urban renewal was widely supported in the nominally optimistic postwar era. Planners were considered to be working in the name of social and scientific progress, and even entrenched social problems might be solved through the intervention of enlightened modern design. * * * [U]rban renewal razed entire neighborhoods of nineteenth century tenements and row houses, which had been occupied by poor ethnic and minority communities. These structures were deemed unfit for habitation and were eliminated in the name of promoting public health, safety, and convenience. They were replaced by large geometric apartment blocks surrounded by asphalt and concrete—bleak embodiments of Le Corbusier's "tower in the park." These blocks were often bordered by major expressways that physically barred the new residents from entering the areas adjoining their new neighborhoods.

This inner city refurbishment was a manifestation of the planners' objective to once again make the central city attractive to those who could reconstruct its eroded tax base and infrastructure. The rapidly developing highway network, the expanding ring of suburban bedroom communities, and the flight of industry to the suburbs and other regions had brought about a decentralization of the metropolis and an erosion of its tax base. Revenue was needed to pay for expensive city services as well as to halt the city's imminent decline.

Accordingly, while officials and planners may have had certain altruistic motives in advancing urban renewal schemes, economic considerations were foremost in their minds. In their efforts to placate powerful interest groups, redevelopment planners allowed the predatory motives of developers and contractors to manipulate urban renewal plans to serve their own ends.

Sometimes, for example, powerful developers would persuade the government to demolish an area of the city and would then buy the land from the government at a low price. Another common strategy was for a developer to influence a municipality to preserve as "historic" the city land adjoining the developer's properties, greatly increasing the value of the developer's properties. Any low-or moderate-income housing located thereon would be promptly converted to luxury housing and expensive commercial leases. All such schemes resulted in both the displacement of poorer residents and a further decline in the city's affordable housing stock, all in the name of urban renewal.

Accordingly, the poor, who tended to be disproportionately racial and ethnic minorities, suffered in the brave new urban world built over their former homes. From 1949 to 1961, urban renewal displaced 85,000 families in 200 American cities, while federally funded renewal and highway programs displaced about 100,000 families and 15,000 businesses per year.

People who were displaced in this way quickly lost their ability to secure satisfactory replacement housing. Despite developers' promises to relocate them, many did not receive relocation services and were forced to bear the substantial costs of moving and living in more expensive apartment units. Such expenses could exhaust the savings of older residents. Resident purchasing power was also harmed by their forced withdrawal from neighborhood credit networks and business arrangements that had evolved over the years and which were often related to practices in the resident's country of origin. Such arrangements were often informal and thus not easily transferrable to new locations. In addition, re-establishing credit and a course of dealing in new surroundings could be an expensive hardship.

In disregard of such potential consequences, urban planners of this period placed much of their faith in the supposed deterministic power of the geometric modern environment. They appeared to assume, as had Le Corbusier in the 1920s, that the numerous problems of the slums stemmed from poor design and that a clean, new, modern environment would inevitably lead to a healthy new social order. Reminiscent of William Morris and other nineteenth century reformers who equated good morals with good design, the urban planners adopted the pleasing syllogism that poor housing quality demoralized its inhabitants and, therefore, better structures would introduce former slum dwellers to a better moral quality of life. Threaded through these rationales was a paternalistic hubris and confidence in the planners' own abilities to assist slum dwellers up from their dark, squalid nineteenth century life-styles into the bright, modern planned world of the mid-twentieth century.

Criticism of urban renewal projects escalated in the 1960s, when urban historian Jane Jacobs accused these schemes of destroying virtually all that was vital in urban life. Jacobs articulated an alternate vision of slum life in which the old neighborhoods supported a spontaneous, interactive, street-oriented communal lifestyle among the residents of these areas. Jacobs described how doors of row houses and brownstones opened directly onto the street, allowing interactions with passers-by and with the mixed use street and its stores and businesses. In this way, social relations developed in semipublic open spaces, and the entry of strangers was readily noticed. Jacobs claimed urban renewal uprooted and shattered such organic communities, scattering former neighbors into whatever substandard housing was available elsewhere, and helping to create a culture of disaffection and an environment of violence and vandalism.

The catastrophic failure of several large scale public housing projects gave critics such as Jacobs credibility and caused many observers to begin developing dim views of the validity of government intervention in housing markets. The Pruitt-Igoe housing project in St. Louis was one such failure, and it became a lightning rod for commentary on the fate of modern architecture and urban planning.

In the early 1950s, the inner city of St. Louis had contained extremely dilapidated slum housing, which in 1954, was demolished and replaced by the Pruitt-Igoe projects. Twelve thousand people were relocated into forty-three eleven-story high-rise structures covering fifty-seven acres. Initially racially integrated, the project's inhabitants rapidly became exclusively black. Eventually, the residents' fear of crime and the rapid deterioration of the physical plant brought about by poor maintenance resulted in almost complete resident abandonment of large areas of the Pruitt-Igoe projects, despite the availability of subsidized low rents. President Nixon's HUD Secretary, George Romney, presided at the project's demolition in 1972.

Pruitt-Igoe's failure was perhaps not so much a failure of the modernist architectural paradigm, but rather a situation of unstable equilibrium in which project managers virtually ignored early warning signs of problems. The misery of massive forced relocation combined with poor design and inadequate maintenance set off a downward vicious circle. Cheap materials, inadequate maintenance, and poor design contributed to building deterioration, provoking resident dissatisfaction. Elevators, for example, were frequently out of service and became easy targets for vandalism. Residents of upper floors, who had to use the elevators to reach their apartments, quickly abandoned them. When units became deserted, remaining residents scavenged them for working fixtures to replace those that had broken in their own apartments.

The project administrators, who were perhaps feeling overconfident about their new "machine for living," had not addressed such problems early enough. By the time they noticed that something was wrong, it was too late in the downward vicious circle to correct the damage.

Such disasters were products of a combination of hubris and inadvertence. The planners of projects like Pruitt-Igoe failed to understand and accommodate the drastically different culture and context of the 1950s slum neighborhood and its residents. An apartment super-block that minimized the amount of semi-private interior spaces in which social interactions between residents could occur, may have worked for white middle-class individuals without children, but was inadequate for extended families of relocatees from the slums. Slum dwellers, many of whom were connected with large families, were accustomed to a social and spatial environment that encouraged constant use of the streets, sidewalks, and corners as semiprivate meeting grounds or territories for interacting with one another. While architects initially praised Pruitt-Igoe for its absence of wasted space between dwelling units, it was precisely in such spaces that neighboring relations had developed in "normal" slums. This aspect of the culture of the development's inhabitants had been invisible to and went completely unaddressed by the planners.

The sudden loss of the community to which they were accustomed posed other problems for Pruitt-Igoe's residents. While parents liked the in-home conveniences, the inability to watch their children when the latter were outside the apartment was unsettling. Furthermore, the new setting lacked what Oscar Newman has called "defensible spaces": stairwells, elevators, and corridors that could be controlled or informally surveyed from within private spaces. Overall, the rapid transition from the strong, informal neighboring system of the slum to a quasi-institutional setting that spatially discouraged informal interactions between neighbors was traumatic. While dissatisfied with the slum's overcrowded conditions, physical danger from cold weather, poor wiring, bad plumbing, and fire, residents had become accustomed to and depended on its dense network of social relations.

In sum, the residents of Pruitt-Igoe felt justifiably alienated and dislocated by the poorly considered design decisions that had been imposed on them. Indeed, the planners had built structures that had nothing to do with the actual social context of the people who lived within them. Instead of allowing functions that occurred within the building to determine the nature of its structure, as prescribed by early modernist architectural theory, they simply crammed a predetermined geometric package full of fungible apartment units, pouring the largely involuntary residents in to complete the mix.

Somewhere in translation from early twentieth century Europe to mid-twentieth century United States, geometric form had been reified into a stock building prototype, which looked the same regardless of whether it housed a prison, hospital, apartments, corporate offices, or a school. To the growing number of critics of the modernist style its geometric forms and reductionist approach were seen as villains, responsible for dehumanizing and abstracting away human problems. However, it was the deviation from modernist functionalism, not modernist functionalism itself, that resulted in some of the worst embarrassments for which modern architecture has been held responsible. Housing projects built during the 1950s were riddled with problems: they were often energy gluttons, their flat roofs leaked, elevators broke down frequently, and interior isolated spaces were open invitations to muggings and violence. However, these horrors were due more to hack misapplications and distortions of the tenets of modernist architecture than to any a priori flaw at its theoretical core. After embarrassments like Pruitt-Igoe, the term urban renewal gradually slipped from the urban planner's vocabulary to be replaced by phrases like "urban revitalization" and "urban design."

In the rush to disclaim responsibility for widely-publicized fiascoes like Pruitt-Igoe as well as the growing tendency to villify modern architecture in general, many important social issues raised by the critics of urban renewal were left unaddressed. Given the relative powerlessness of inner city populations and their lack of a meaningful political input in urban planning decisions, the cultural and psychological problems of forced relocation were largely ignored and sidestepped by planners and other public officials. The public soon lost faith in the ability of urban planners to control the social consequences of publicly funded housing projects. Unfortunately, many valid insights about the important and vital interaction between structures and inhabitants that lie at the core of the modernist architectural paradigm disappeared as well. * * *

ROBERT CARO, THE POWER BROKER
Pp. 850–854, 859, 863–864, 868–869, 872–873, 875, 877–878 (1974).

One Mile

Robert Moses built 627 miles of roads in and around New York City. This is the story of one of those miles.

There is something strange about that mile. It is one of seven that make up the great highway known as the Cross-Bronx Expressway, but the other six, like most of the other miles of Moses' expressways, are—roughly—straight, on a road map a heavy red line slashing inexorably across the delicate crosshatch of streets in the borough's central expanse. There is logic—the ruthless, single-minded logic of the engineer, perhaps, but logic—in that line. When it curves, the curves are shallow, the road hastening to resume its former course. But during that one mile, the road swerves, bulging abruptly and substantially toward the north.

A closer look does not explain that bulge. It makes it not less puzzling but more. Detailed maps show the entire area blanketed with rectangles that represent city blocks—except for one open space, running east-west, parallel to the expressway, that represents an unusually wide avenue, and, directly adjacent to and below that open space, another, colored green, that represents a 148-acre park. And these empty spaces lie directly in the path that the expressway would have followed had it just continued on its former straight course. All it had to do to take advantage of that corridor—to utilize for right-of-way the avenue roadbed, together with a very narrow strip at the very top edge of the park—was to keep on the way it had been going.

If the location of that one mile of expressway was puzzling on maps when Moses first proposed it in 1946, it was more puzzling in reality. For while the maps showed rectangles, reality was what was on those rectangles: apartment houses lined up rank upon rank, a solid mile of apartment houses, fifty-four of them, fifty-four structures of brick and steel and mortar piled fifty, sixty and seventy feet high and each housing thirty or forty or fifty families. Walk through the area, the proposed route of the expressway and the blocks around it, and it was impossible not to see that keeping the road straight would hurt little. Only six small buildings—dilapidated brownstone tenements—would have to be torn down. Most of the right-of-way—the park and the avenue—was already in the city's possession. While turning the road to the north would destroy hundreds upon hundreds of homes, homes in which lived thousands of men, women and children. And it would cost millions upon millions of dollars—in condemnation costs for fifty-four apartment houses, in demolition costs for the tearing down of those buildings, in tax revenue that would otherwise be paid, year after year for generations, into city coffers by the buildings' owners.

If the bulge in the expressway was puzzling to anyone studying it, it was tragic to those who didn't have to study it, to the people who lived in or near that right-of-way. For to these people, the fifty-four apartment buildings that would have to be destroyed were not just buildings but homes. That mile of buildings was the very heart of the neighborhood in which they lived, a section of the Bronx known as "East Tremont."

The people of East Tremont did not have much. Refugees or the children of refugees from the little *shtetls* in the Pale of Settlement and from the ghettos of Eastern Europe, the Jews who at the turn of the century had fled the pogroms and the wrath of the Tsars, they had first settled in America on the Lower East Side. The Lower East Side had become a place to which they were tied by family and friends and language and religion and a sense of belonging—but from whose damp and squalid tenements they had ached to escape * * *. The Jews of East Tremont * * * were a long way from being rich, and their neighborhood proved it. There were no elevators in most of the five-and six-story buildings into which they began to flood (stopping at 182nd Street, southern border of an Italian neighborhood, as abruptly as if a fence had stood there) after the extension of the IRT elevated line just before World War I linked East Tremont to the downtown garment district. By the end of World War II, the buildings' galvanized iron pipes were corroding, causing leaks and drops in water pressure; a few still had bathtubs that sat up on legs. With some 60,000 persons living along its narrow streets, its "population density"—441 persons "per residential acre"—was considered "undesirable" by social scientists. "In moving through East Tremont one senses a feeling of crowdedness brought on by the lack of open space and close location of buildings," one wrote.

But the neighborhood provided its residents with things that were important to them. Transportation was important to the fathers who worked downtown, and the neighborhood had good transportation. * * * Jobs were important to the fathers who didn't work downtown, and the neighborhood had jobs available—good jobs * * * just ten minutes away. * * * Shopping was important to the mothers who stayed home and took care of the kids, and the neighborhood had good shopping. * * * Parks were important to the mothers, too. There were no playgrounds in the neighborhood—mothers' delegations had attempted in the past to talk to the Park Department about the situation but Moses' aides had never even deigned to grant them an appointment—but running down its length was

Southern Boulevard, whose broad center mall had grass plots plenty big enough for little children to play on, and surrounded by benches so mothers could keep their eyes on them to make sure they didn't run into the street. And the southwestern border of the neighborhood was Crotona Park. * * *

Thanks to Crotona Park, young adults as well as children didn't have to leave the neighborhood for recreation. "It was a *great* park. Twenty tennis courts right *there*. Where you could walk to them. Baseball diamonds, magnificent playgrounds with baskets—three-man games would be going on all weekend, you know. A big swimming pool that Moses had built during the Depression. Indian Lake. And kept really clean then, you know. * * * And thanks to Tremont Avenue, you didn't have to leave the neighborhood for entertainment. On the avenue's one mile in the neighborhood were seven movie houses. The Bronx Zoo—with its animals roaming behind moats instead of bars—was one stop away on the White Plains El, the New York Botanical Garden was three; you could *walk* with your children to those two perfect places to spend a Sunday with the kids.

The neighborhood provided the things that were important to its old people. * * * There was a place to play chess—or cards—or just sit and talk over a cup of coffee in cold weather, too. The "Y"—the East Tremont Young Men's Hebrew Association—listed more than four hundred "senior citizens" on its active membership roles. "There was no reason for an older person to be lonely in that neighborhood," says one who lived there. * * * "You knew where your kids were at night, too," says one mother. They were at the Y, which had 1,700 families as members. * * * Children who lived on Central Park West might be sent to expensive day camps and, when they got older, to sleep-away camps in the Adirondacks; the Y provided inexpensive day-camp and sleep-away programs—the largest run by any single institution in New York City—for children who lived on Crotona Park North.

Schools were terribly important to the people of East Tremont * * *, and East Tremont had good schools. They were old—PS 44, at 176th and Prospect, the neighborhood's junior high school, had been built in 1901, and the city said there was simply no money to replace it but there were no double sessions and standards were high. PS 67, off Southern Boulevard, was the first elementary school in New York to offer lessons— and supply instruments—for any child who wanted to learn to play the violin. And all the schools were close, close enough for kids to walk to.

To the people of East Tremont, East Tremont was family. In its bricks were generations. * * * East Tremont was friends—real friends, not just acquaintances you happened to meet because they took their children to the same playground to which you took your children, or because they belonged to the same PTA as you, but friends whom you had grown up with and were going to grow old with, boys and girls—turned men and women—who knew and understood you and whom you knew and understood. * * * East Tremont was a feeling of being known—in the streets and in the stores * * *. East Tremont was a sense of continuity, of warmth, of the security that comes—and only comes—with a sense of belonging. * * * No one would have called East Tremont a *united* community. It possessed, one study observed, a "myriad of social systems covering religious *Landsmannschaft* groups, fraternal, educational, political and fund-raising groups" engaged in "a constant and shrill competition for loyalty," a competition which was not even resolved in the two areas where East Tremont might have been expected to be solid: politics and religion. FDR's hold was absolute—but only so far as FDR was concerned; in nonpresidential elections, men who once, long ago, had preached from soapboxes were loyal to an older faith: Socialist, Communist, American Labor and Progressive parties could all count on substantial votes in East Tremont. "In East Tremont," the study noted, "the Yiddishist and Hebraist each had his following with a supporting system of cultural clubs, bookstores, debating societies, etc." The neighborhood's seven synagogues were constantly competing for members and prestige. East Tremont may have been a loud community, a shrill community, a materialistic, money-conscious community. But it was a community. * * *

The letters came on December 4, 1952.

For years, East Tremont had been vaguely aware that one of Robert Moses' highways was going to run through the neighborhood, that part of it was already under construction over in the East Bronx somewhere. But there had been no hard facts available, and, as Mrs. Lillian Edelstein says, "it had gone on so long, and you keep hearing and hearing and nothing happens, and after a while it doesn't mean anything to you." When they thought about it—if they thought about it—they were sure it would run along the edge of Crotona Park; "I mean, it was so obvious you just figured it was going to go there," Mrs. Edelstein says. "It was in the wind for a long time that he was going to come through the apartment houses. But we just didn't believe it."

But on December 4, a Tuesday, the letters were there in hundreds of mailboxes, letters signed by "Robert Moses, City Construction Coordinator," informing each recipient that the building in which he or she lived was in the right-of-way of the Cross-Bronx Expressway, that it would be condemned by the city and torn down—and that they had ninety days to move. * * *

But East Tremont's panic was soon replaced by hope.

The hope was based on faith in Robert Moses, or, more accurately, in the Moses mystique. East Tremont's pious Jews still held the campaign of 1934 against him—"I hated him since the time he said he wasn't Jewish," one says—but they still believed in his image as a man above politics and bureaucrats. Believing in that image, the people of East Tremont were sure that if they could only present Moses with an alternate route through their neighborhood that was truly better than the route he had chosen, he would accept it. And it did not take them very long to find out that such a route was indeed available.

Bronx Borough President James J. Lyons; Lyons' chief engineer, Moses' old Planning Commission ally Arthur V. Sheridan; and Sheridan's veteran aides had all been in on the laying out of the route Moses had chosen. But when the East Tremont committee asked for an appointment with Lyons, Lyons aide Charles F. Rodriguez recalls, "Lyons fobbed them off to Sheridan, and Sheridan fobbed them off to someone else"—and the someone else happened to be a recent addition to the staff named Edward J. Flanagan * * *. [W]hen the housewives mentioned the possibility of an alternate route, Flanagan, without letting them finish, said of course there was, took out a pen, said, "There's no reason the route couldn't go this way," and sketched on a map before him the route through Crotona Park that was precisely what they had had in mind. Flanagan was silenced—no one from East Tremont ever got an appointment with him again—but he had given the housewives conviction that the alternate route was feasible. The Bronx County Chapter of the New York State Society of Professional Engineers agreed to make a formal study of it.

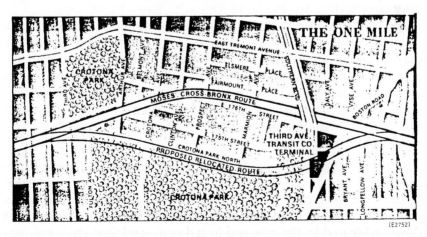

And one member of the society had enough experience with large-scale highway construction to do so—experience garnered working, indirectly, for Robert Moses. Bernard Weiner, a refugee with a heavy accent, was the brilliant engineer who, after working during the 1920's on the

Westchester parkway system, had gone to work for Madigan Hyland and designed, among other Moses projects, all the concrete bridges on the Circumferential Parkway—although he could not pronounce "Circumferential"—and the revolutionary three-span skew frame interchange that carries the Whitestone Expressway and Grand Central Parkway across each other in Queens. Then his independent outlook—he kept insisting that if Moses did not increase the grades on the Circumferential, it was going to flood in heavy rains—got him dropped from the team. Weiner, who had found it impossible, despite his experience and acknowledged brilliance, to get a good job since, had learned the price of opposing Moses, and he was not willing to pay it in full any more, but he was willing to pay part of it. When the Bronx Chapter asked him to do studies of the alternate route, he agreed only "on condition that I would be anonymous" (another engineer's name was signed to them), but he did do them—with his usual thoroughness, drawing up not just a sketch but a complete engineering study that demonstrated that the route through the park was not only feasible but met every federal and state standard for expressway design.

The arguments in favor of the park route were clear. By making only a gentle alteration in the road's route—swinging it just two blocks (one block in some places) to the south, 1,530 apartments would be saved at no cost to anyone: the road would not be made longer, its curves would not be made sharper—its efficiency as a traffic-moving device would not be harmed in the least. "We were happy then," recalls Lillian Edelstein. "We had been worried, but when we found there was a feasible alternate route, we figured we were in business."

The arguments in favor of the alternate route were so clear. Believing in the myth of Moses, the housewives of East Tremont were sure he would accept them. And it wasn't until they tried to present them to him that panic set in again. For neither he nor any of his aides would even listen to those arguments. There would be no point in any meeting, Moses' office told Mrs. Edelstein when she telephoned after letters and telegrams had gone unanswered. The Coordinator had already decided on the route. It would not be changed. * * *

Mrs. Edelstein had been informed at the very beginning of her fight that there were ample grounds for a full-scale legal, court battle, a battle which would, even if not successful in changing the expressway route, force the city to give tenants comparable new apartments. But, she was also informed, the legal fees could run to ten thousand dollars. * * * Ten thousand dollars? Lillian Edelstein had difficulty raising amounts far smaller than that. "The feeling among people was, what's the use," explains Arthur Katz. "You can't lick City Hall. And even if you could, you certainly can't lick Robert Moses. We were told by the politicians we saw that when Robert Moses wanted his way, that was it. For a while at the start—with Lyons, when he promised—they had hope. But now * * *." "You'd think people would fight for their homes," says Saul Janowitz. But Mrs. Edelstein had to beg and plead to persuade families to chip in a dollar bill at a time, and each time the dollar bills were harder to come by.

Nonetheless, a small band fought. Most of its members were businessmen who knew the mass evictions of their customers would destroy their businesses * * *. But mostly, it was Lillian Edelstein who fought.

Finding engineers willing to defy Moses, the housewife put them to work drawing maps detailed enough to prove from every engineering standpoint that their route was technically feasible. Then she put them to work obtaining hard figures: exactly how much more Moses' mile would cost than theirs. When they came up with those figures—Moses' route would require the demolition of fifty-four apartment houses, ninety one-or two-family homes and fifteen one-story "taxpayers" housing sixty stores, for a total of 159 separate buildings; condemning and demolishing them would cost more than $10,000,000 more than would be required if the road ran where they wanted it to, even without the cost of relocating 1,530 families and the loss of the real estate taxes (close to $200,000 per year at current rates) from the demolished buildings, income the city would be losing year after year forever she undertook the harder fight of bringing those maps and figures to the attention of the public and of public officials. * * *

The City Planning Commission gave the tenants the type of public hearing that might have been expected from a body controlled by a man who, if given his way, would have abolished public hearings. A large delegation had taken the day to ask the commission not to approve the Moses route—a long day. Commission chairman John J. Bennett, at that moment secretly negotiating a Title I transaction for which he needed that man's approval, refused to let even one tenant speak, saying that no public hearing was required. But there was a whole series of hearings before the Board of Estimate. Sometimes Moses was present himself. "He always looked surprisingly young and vigorous," Katz recalls. "He was very cool and detached. He didn't say anything. He had his assistants to do the talking for him. He sat and listened. He made some notes. My greatest anger at him was that he didn't seem to be affected by all this— people were getting up and telling these stories of hardship." But, despite Moses' presence, the Board kept postponing a final vote on his request to have the city authorize condemnation proceedings. After an emotional meeting with the ETNA group and several Bronx councilmen in Wagner's office at which the Mayor was visibly moved (and at which he said, "Every member of the Board will want to know the difficulties facing each family in the path of the expressway"), the Mayor interrupted one Board session—at which Moses had confidently expected the issue to be resolved—to order McCullough, who had done a "study" of the tenants' alternate route for Impellitteri in a matter of minutes, to give it a little more consideration. The engineer returned a month later with a report stating that while the alternate route would spare the protesters' homes, it would require the condemnation of almost as many homes belonging to other people. You see, Moses told the Board, it was just as he was always trying to explain to them: changing a route would just "trade in" one group of protesters for another; no matter where you tried to build a highway in the city, there would be protests, so the only way to handle them was to ignore them. ETNA's leaders, who had been certain that not a single home would have to be touched for the alternate route they had proposed, were shocked by McCullough's findings until they realized the trick that the engineer had played. He had studied an alternate route, all right, but not *their* alternate route. Instead, he had selected a route that would require large-scale condemnation and studied that instead. Epstein explained this to Wagner. Over Hodgkiss' violent objections, the Mayor ordered McCullough to study the right alternate route this time, to let Epstein oversee the study to make sure it was fair, and to complete the study before the Board's next meeting when a final decision would be made.

"A defeat for Moses," the *Post* reported. The tenants felt it was. "We felt we had won," Lillian Edelstein recalls. Epstein, trying to reassure her, had told her, in her words, "It's like a jury trial. If they stay out long enough, they won't convict you. Because it was dragging so—month after month, I figured something is happening to hold him and his crew."

On the day of the final hearing before McCullough, assembled in his office in the Municipal Building was a full panoply of Moses Men: Arthur S. Hodgkiss, assistant general manager of the Triborough Bridge and Tunnel Authority; Stuart Constable, acting executive officer of the New York City Department of Parks; W. Earle Andrews and Ernest J. Clark of Andrews, Clark and Buckley, consulting engineers; Milton Goul, district engineer, State Department of Public Works District Number 10, designated to represent the State Department of Public Works by Bertram Tallamy, Superintendent; Arthur B. Williams, liaison engineer, New York State Department of Public Works—and, representing Lyons, Edward J. Flanagan, who, during the entire proceedings, would utter not one word. These engineers and a dozen assistants had been assembled for the occasion on the orders of Robert Moses. * * * Lyons moved the question, saying, "This is an engineer's problem, not a layman's problem, and all the engineers unanimously support this route." One by one the Board members voted—in the affirmative. The last man to vote was Robert F. Wagner, Jr. He voted in the affirmative, too.

"It was so fast," Lillian Edelstein would recall years later. "I was positive at that last hearing that we would win. Because of Wagner. He had said so straight out that he would never let them do it. He had *promised*." Lillian Edelstein wanted to ask the Mayor what care had been taken for the families, what the relocation plans were. But she couldn't. She was crying. Katz asked instead. Lyons tried to stop him from speaking, but he went ahead anyway. Quoting Wagner's words that he would not vote for acquisition until he had been satisfied as to the relocation plans, he asked the Mayor what those plans were. The Mayor said he did not know. * * *

Why *wouldn't* Moses shift the route of the Cross-Bronx Expressway slightly, thereby saving 1,530 apartments, millions in state and city money, months of aggravation and delay—and making his expressway straighter as well?

"I asked George Spargo that," says Joseph Ingraham, the *Times* reporter who was occasionally on Moses' payroll and who spent so much time socializing with the Moses team that he sometimes seemed to be one of its members. "On the day of the ribbon cutting they were opening a whole bunch of sections of different expressways, and it was raining, really pouring. George said, 'Let's sit this out, and we'll catch up to them at the next stop.' We went into a small bar in the Bronx and I asked him there. He said, 'Oh, one of Jimmy Lyons' relatives owns a piece of property up there and we would have had to take it if we used that other route, and Jimmy didn't want it taken, and RM had promised him we wouldn't.' At the time, George even told me the piece of property involved, but I've forgotten."

The people of East Tremont also wondered why Moses wouldn't shift the route. "I mean, we heard lots of rumors about the bus terminal," Lillian Edelstein recalls. "The politicians were always trying to tell us that was the reason. But we could never find out anything about it. And, I mean, I never believed that. I could never believe that even Robert Moses would take fifteen hundred homes just to save a bus terminal."

Spargo's statement may have been untrue. So may the rumors. If any relative of Bronx Borough President James J. Lyons owned property along either the alternate or actual expressway route, the author was unable to find evidence of that fact—although, since, in the Bronx, politicians' ownership of property was habitually concealed through a many-layered network of intermediaries and bag men, a network baffling even to contemporary investigators and all but impenetrable twenty years later, his failure is not conclusive. Moses' refusal to alter the route—unexplainable on the basis of his given reasons, all of which are demonstrably false—may have had nothing to do with the fact that the "bus terminal" of which Lillian Edelstein speaks—actually the "Tremont

Depot" of the Third Avenue Transit Company, at the northeast corner of Crotona Park—lies in the path of the alternate route and would have had to be condemned if that route was adopted. It is possible that Moses' selection of the original route—it was he, not any engineer, who selected it—was based on no more than whim, and that his subsequent refusal to alter it was due to nothing more than stubbornness, although if so it was a whim quite inconsistent with Moses' customary whims: almost invariably over a period of forty years, whenever he had a choice of routes, he selected the one that would keep his road straight, not the one that would make the road curve.

However, in attempting to find an explanation for Moses' refusal to change the route, the Third Avenue Transit depot stands out. With the exception of six old, small, dilapidated brownstone tenements, housing a total of nineteen families, it was the only structure of any type that would have had to be condemned if the alternate route was used. In effect, for whatever reason, Robert Moses elected to tear down 159 buildings housing 1,530 families instead of tearing down six buildings housing nineteen families—and the terminal. It is a fact that the Third Avenue Transit Company secretly told Moses it was very anxious not to have the terminal condemned, for its location was strategic for its buses. And it is also a fact that for twenty years it was considered an open secret in Bronx political circles that key borough politicians held large but carefully hidden interests in Third Avenue Transit. And it is also a fact that, in Bronx politics of the period, what Third Avenue Transit wanted, Third Avenue Transit got.

But the unfortunate element in searching for the explanation of Moses' refusal is that in the perspective of the history of New York City it is unimportant. Whether Moses refused to change the route for a personal or political reason, the point is that his reason was the only one that counted. Neighborhood feelings, urban planning considerations, cost, aesthetics, common humanity, common sense—none of these mattered in laying out the routes of New York's great roads. The only consideration that mattered was Robert Moses' will. He had the power to impose it on New York. * * *

WILLIAM H. SIMON, THE COMMUNITY ECONOMIC DEVELOPMENT MOVEMENT

2002 Wisc. L. Rev. 377, 377–378, 380–382, 386–387, 411–412, 416–418, 419–420.

Within a five-minute walk of the Stony Brook subway stop in the Jamaica Plain section of Boston, you can encounter the following:

- A renovated industrial site of about five acres and sixteen buildings that serves as a business incubator for small firms that receive technical assistance from the Jamaica Plain

Neighborhood Development Corporation (JPNDC), a nonprofit community development corporation, which is also housed there. Known as the Brewery after its former proprietor, a beer-maker, the complex is owned by a nonprofit subsidiary of JPNDC.

- A 44,000-foot "Stop & Shop" supermarket. The market opened in 1991 after years in which the community had been without a major grocery store. It lies next to a recently renovated Community Health Center and a large high-rise public housing project. The land on which the market and health center sit was developed and is owned by a limited partnership that includes, in addition to a commercial investor, JPNDC and the Tenant Management Corporation of the housing project. Some of the income from the market and health center leases goes into a Community Benefits Trust Fund that supports job training and business development activities.

- A cluster of small, attractive multi-unit residential buildings containing a total of forty-one homes. These units were built with support from the Federal Low Income Housing Tax Credit, and they are occupied by low and moderate income families at rents limited to thirty percent of family income. The buildings are owned by a limited partnership in which the general partners are a subsidiary of JPNDC and a resident cooperative; the limited partners include five conventional business corporations and a nonprofit corporation with a board composed of prominent government and business figures that promotes housing development throughout the state.

- Two recently renovated apartment buildings—one with eleven units and one with forty-five units—designed with common areas and facilities for medical support for elderly residents. The project benefits from large federal grants. It is owned by JPNDC; the units are rented to the tenants at rents that cannot exceed thirty percent of their income.

- A wood-frame building containing three apartments recently renovated by JPNDC with support from various public programs. JPNDC then sold it at a price well below market value to an individual, who, as a condition of ownership set out in the deed, must live in one of the units and rent the others only to people who meet specified income eligibility conditions at specified rents.

These institutions are products of the Community Economic Development (CED) Movement. * * * Such projects figure prominently in the most optimistic and innovative approaches to urban poverty on both the left and the right. They exemplify a kind of social entrepreneurialism that is flourishing across the country. * * * Looming over the current CED Movement are memories of two earlier experiments in community development, "urban renewal" or Redevelopment (a word I capitalize to indicate that it is a term of art referring to a special legal process), and the Community Action Program. Both are widely regarded as discredited, and to some extent, the current Movement has been shaped in reaction to their failures. * * *

The Redevelopment process was created by the states under the impetus of the National Housing Act of 1949, which provided grants and other support for local efforts to revitalize "blighted" areas. The federal grant program came to be called "urban renewal." The state process it supported begins with the designation of an area as "blighted." A municipal agency then collaborates with private investors to formulate a plan of public and private investments to improve the area. The agency can draw on municipal powers of spending, eminent domain, land use regulation, and public finance with streamlined procedures. The plan often provides for public provision of structural improvements, as well as the condemnation and delivery to private developers of large tracts of land, perhaps at a substantial "write down" (below-cost price). The private developers undertake various improvements on their own account and perhaps build community facilities, such as parks, meeting places, or low income housing. The plans, and ensuing contracts, often limit or designate special uses for state and local taxes for the improvements. * * *

Redevelopment has been harshly criticized for decades. The critics have shown that, over and over, the development facilitated by the process has come at the expense of the initial residents of the communities being developed. In the worst case scenario, which has been often enacted, it takes the form of "Negro removal"—displacing low income, minority people by destroying rental housing or commercial buildings they used or occupied and replacing them with upper income housing or business facilities serving the affluent. The West End in Boston and the Western Addition in San Francisco are two famous examples.

The Redevelopment process encouraged such injustice by weakening democratic constraints on governmental aid to development, by creating various fiscal incentives for localities to undertake the development, and by subsidizing the private participants through sweetheart land deals, cheap financing, tax breaks, and publicly provided infrastructure tailored to their investments. There is substantial evidence that the returns in economic growth to public Redevelopment investments have been small or negative and that the distributive effects of the program have been, on balance, regressive.

In 1974, the federal government ended specific support for Redevelopment and folded these funds into the Community Development Block Grant (CDBG) program. * * * Nevertheless, Redevelopment did not die, surviving as a state law process. In some states, its use expanded in the 1980s and 1990s under the impetus of property tax limitation efforts, such as California's Proposition 13. By limiting revenues from the existing tax base, these measures prompted local governments to seek new taxable development. The consequence in California has been called "the fiscalization of land use"; municipalities exercise their regulatory power over land use with a view to enhancing their tax revenues. * * * The process continues to attract critics, who call it a wasteful public subsidy and arbitrary in its effects on taxation. * * *

The Community Action Program emerged from the Economic Opportunity Act of 1964, the controversial centerpiece of the Kennedy and Johnson Administrations' War on Poverty. A central provision of this act contemplated the delivery of a range of social services through "Community Action Programs" (CAPs). The Act provided for certification and support by the federal government of a single "community action" agency for low income urban neighborhoods. Both public and private nonprofit agencies could apply, but in either case, they were obliged to demonstrate "maximum feasible participation of the residents" of the geographic areas in which they were focused. The agencies were expected to administer a range of services, most notably, educational enrichment and job training programs, but also including "community economic development."

The CAP program was an attempt to force decentralization of urban government. One premise was simply that municipalities were often too centralized and bureaucratic to effectively design and deliver services to poor neighborhoods. Another was that many municipalities were dominated by white political coalitions insensitive to racial minorities. The program responded to the first problem by inducing the formation of neighborhood institutions and giving them responsibilities for social service administration. It responded to the second by setting up relations between these local agencies and the federal government that were substantially independent of local power structures.

These programs disappointed the expectations of their designers in two distinct ways. For the most part, the citizen participation goals were never realized. Turnout in elections tended to be tiny, and ongoing involvement in the CAPs was limited. The programs tended to be dominated by their staffs, or in some cases, unaccountable boards. At best, the organizations were competent service providers; at worst, they were inefficient and patronage-ridden. Some CAPs appear to have been more effective in mobilizing constituents, but they were no more successful as organizations in the long run. These programs tended to engage in confrontation with established municipal power structures to demand more resources and attention to their communities. Although such confrontation was exactly what some of the program's designers hoped for, the protests from established local Democratic figures came as a surprise to Lyndon Johnson, who had no taste for inner city mobilization that threatened the Party's core constituents. The federal government failed to support the activist CAPs and came to regard them as liabilities. Unlike Redevelopment, the Community Action Program did not survive in name (though many CAPs continue as local social service providers), and its activities withered in the 1970s. * * *

CED institutions have three salient functional characteristics. The first is relational density and synergy. CED efforts are designed to multiply the contexts and roles in which people confront each other. As the political process links political activity to residence, so CED links economic development to residence. By striving to internalize control over economic processes within the community, CED increases the number of linked roles that residents potentially play. People who might otherwise encounter each other only as neighbors now meet as employers and employees, sellers and consumers, property owners and property occupiers, planners and citizens, administrators and service recipients.

The second is geographic focus. At the most mundane level, the physical community is a focal point, a convenient space to bring people together for multiple, varied encounters. More ambitiously, a residential community can give physical expression to a sense of distinctive common culture. The new social policy now emphasizes the call of modern urbanism with space for "detail, identity, and a sense of place," as opposed to, for example, "the anonymity of much public housing that is divorced from its surroundings."

The third characteristic is face-to-face encounters. CED efforts tend to replace remote impersonal relations, for example, between absentee owners and tenants or customers, or distant bureaucrats and their charges, with face-to-face relations. In doing so, they extend to economic development generally a basic principle of land use planning—the physical structure of the urban environment should be configured so that there will be more face-to-face interactions among neighbors. For example, Jane Jacobs's four principles of land use planning—mixed use, short blocks, buildings of varying age, and density—are all designed to increase the number and variety of face-to-face encounters. * * *

CED programs arise in part from dissatisfaction with bureaucracy. The principal economic complaint about bureaucracy is that bureaucrats have poor incentives and poor information. * * * The economist's stock alternative to bureaucracy is the market. But economists acknowledge that markets have incentive and information problems too, and they are more likely than bureaucratic organizations to be thwarted by difficulties that can be called coordination problems. * * * So the turn to CED also reflects a sense of the limits of conventionally understood markets. * * *

As an example of a CED institution * * *, consider the South Shore Bank, founded in 1972 in what was then a seriously distressed neighborhood of Chicago. A group of social activists was able to raise $3.2 million in philanthropic support to buy an existing commercial bank. They then proceeded to re-orient the bank's practices to support a CED strategy. * * *. The bank's lending strategy has four especially interesting features. First, in "concentrated lending," the bank focuses its commercial real estate lending on a specific community, and within the community on specific areas targeted for development. Second, in "leverage," the bank tries to focus commercial lending in a way that complements its affiliates' subsidized housing development. It makes commercial loans to private, preferably small and local developers to build or rehabilitate housing near the subsidized projects its affiliates are developing. Development activities occur in mutually reinforcing "concentric rings" of private and NGO-led effort.

Third, in addition to being geographically targeted, some of the bank's private lending is conditional. The bank initially limited its purchase-money lending for rental properties to borrowers planning to live on the premises. It eventually relaxed this requirement, but it has continued to insist that the borrower commit to rehabilitate the property. It will not lend to landlords who simply want to hold the property for speculative purposes or to "milk" it to maximize short-term return while permitting it to deteriorate. Finally, the bank's affiliates provide technical assistance to its local landlord borrowers on such matters as construction, maintenance, regulatory compliance, and accounting. Many of these borrowers are new landlords entering their first business venture. Experience in the training programs has developed face-to-face, mutually supportive relations among them. Two ethnically-based networks of small landlords—one African-American, the other recent Croatian immigrants—have developed; they maintain and continue to invest in small-scale, moderate-rental property. The bank's founder insists that these people could not have been identified through conventional business methods: "[H]ad we conducted a market survey in 1973 to get a sense of how many potential entrepreneurs we had in the community . . . the answer would have been 'none'. . . . [These people were] invisible, and now they're an industry—the core of the South Shore's recovery." * * *

We have noted that the geographic focus of CED strategies creates a focal point for collaborative effort and gives physical expression to a sense of common interest and identity. The face-to-face theme in CED is sometimes associated with a Romantic celebration of the intrinsic superiority of personal over impersonal relations. More often, we see face-to-face relations valued as conducive to social capital. Part of the idea is that one is likely to be more understanding of and respectful toward the interests of people of whom one is personally aware. Another part is the suggestion that the sense of being observed creates a potentially healthy pressure to conform to local norms. This is the basis of Jane Jacobs' notion of "eyes on the street," the primary goal of her planning precepts. Safe and attractive neighborhoods are neighborhoods in which people are actually or potentially watching each other. The sense of safety comes in part from the probability that others will give assistance in the event of crisis. But it also rests on the belief that the experience of being watched itself inhibits deviance. CED strategies apply this principle to economic relations. They assume that one will be more scrupulous in fulfilling duties that are associated with face-to-face relations and they try to induce such relations. * * * It is no accident that "faith-based" organizations are among the most prominent CED activists. They are associated with Islamic, Catholic, and Protestant institutions. Moral themes associated with the Protestant Ethic have influenced secular CED practitioners as well. These themes are discipline, surveillance, personal formality, and the valorization of wealth. * * *

AUDREY G. MCFARLANE, WHEN INCLUSION LEADS TO EXCLUSION: THE UNCHARTED TERRAIN OF COMMUNITY PARTICIPATION IN ECONOMIC DEVELOPMENT
66 Brook. L. Rev. 861, 923–925 (2001).

* * * [M]uch urban activity has been channeled into neighborhood-specific, community development corporations that have taken on a major role as the actors at the local level that seek to fill the gaps in affordable housing and retail services. Studies have shown that while these self-help organizations are radical in one sense (because they are willing to take on problems in neighborhoods that are understood in the popular urban imagination to be beyond hope and barren of resources), they are mainly conservative in that they channel their activity into existing federal and foundation programs. This fact supports Manuel Castells' observation that urban social movements fail over the long term because once the fight is over, their energies are turned to administrative and managerial struggles of trying to balance the books and deliver services efficiently.

The other limitation of the citizen power claim is its "geographical situatedness"—it locates the source of a citizen's interest and power within the confines of his or her community. In fact, the poor black neighborhood is viewed as an autonomous, self-sustaining unit capable of articulating and protecting the interests of its residents. It equates community control of decisions with community control of conditions within neighborhoods. Therefore it treats the problems as internally, rather than externally, driven and ignores what has happened to these neighborhoods in the ensuing thirty-odd years. Indeed, continued globalization has relocated manufacturing to the southern United States and the Third World; decentralization of the metropolitan area has taken jobs and retail services from central cities, and last but not least, middle class and affluent people have moved the peripheries of the metropolitan area such that there are now new urban areas called exurbs and other urban areas called edge cities. This approach might have had a glimmer of hope when segregation locked all classes together, but not today.

The idea of the inner-city neighborhood as a politically autonomous entity also has implications for the rest of the city. For instance, should all neighborhoods have political control of development and other financial decisions with respect to their neighborhoods? Will not the more affluent neighborhoods do better under these schemes if they are able to retain their resources for their own needs? This has already started to take place, to a certain extent, with the rise of home ownership associations as a form of neighborhood organization and the proliferation of special benefits districts that provide enhanced services to city neighborhoods. The neighborhoods that are being left behind in these new subunits of local government are, more often than not, the poor black neighborhoods. Therefore, empowerment of these communities as economically flourishing or politically powerful units does not seem to be a viable endeavor. * * *

eminent domain (5 A).

KELO V. CITY OF NEW LONDON
Supreme Court of the United States, 2005.
545 U.S. 469, 125 S.Ct. 2655, 162 L.Ed.2d 439.

JUSTICE STEVENS delivered the opinion of the Court.

In 2000, the city of New London approved a development plan that, in the words of the Supreme Court of Connecticut, was "projected to create in excess of 1,000 jobs, to increase tax and other revenues, and to revitalize an economically distressed city, including its downtown and waterfront areas." 268 Conn. 1, 5, 843 A.2d 500, 507 (2004). In assembling the land needed for this project, the city's development agent has purchased property from willing sellers and proposes to use the power of eminent domain to acquire the remainder of the property from unwilling owners in exchange for just compensation. The question presented is whether the city's proposed disposition of this property qualifies as a "public use" within the meaning of the Takings Clause of the Fifth Amendment to the Constitution.[1] * * *

The city of New London (hereinafter City) sits at the junction of the Thames River and the Long Island Sound in southeastern Connecticut. Decades of economic decline led a state agency in 1990 to designate the City a "distressed municipality." In 1996, the Federal Government closed the Naval Undersea Warfare Center, which had been located in the Fort Trumbull area of the City and had employed over 1,500 people. In 1998, the City's unemployment rate was nearly double that of the State, and its population of just under 24,000 residents was at its lowest since 1920.

These conditions prompted state and local officials to target New London, and particularly its Fort Trumbull area, for economic revitalization. To this end, respondent New London Development Corporation (NLDC), a private nonprofit entity established some years earlier to assist the City in planning economic development, was reactivated. In January 1998, the State authorized * * * a $10 million bond issue toward the creation of a Fort Trumbull State Park. In February, the pharmaceutical company Pfizer Inc. announced that it would build a $300 million research facility on a site immediately adjacent to Fort Trumbull; local planners hoped that Pfizer would draw new business to the area, thereby serving as a catalyst to the area's rejuvenation. After receiving initial approval from the city council, the NLDC continued its planning activities and held a series of neighborhood meetings to educate the public about the process. In May, the city council authorized the NLDC to formally submit its plans to the relevant state agencies for review. Upon obtaining state-level approval, the NLDC finalized an integrated development plan focused on 90 acres of the Fort Trumbull area.

The Fort Trumbull area is situated on a peninsula that juts into the Thames River. The area comprises approximately 115 privately owned properties, as well as the 32 acres of land formerly occupied by the naval facility (Trumbull State Park now occupies 18 of those 32 acres). The development plan encompasses seven parcels. Parcel 1 is designated for a waterfront conference hotel at the center of a "small urban village" that will include restaurants and shopping. This parcel will also have marinas for both recreational and commercial uses. A pedestrian "riverwalk" will originate here and continue down the coast, connecting the waterfront areas of the development. Parcel 2 will be the site of approximately 80 new residences organized into an urban neighborhood and linked by public walkway to the remainder of the development, including the state park. This parcel also includes space reserved for a new U.S. Coast Guard Museum. Parcel 3, which is located immediately north of the Pfizer

---

[1] "[N]or shall private property be taken for public use, without just compensation." U.S. Const., Amdt. 5. That Clause is made applicable to the States by the Fourteenth Amendment.

facility, will contain at least 90,000 square feet of research and development office space. Parcel 4A is a 2.4-acre site that will be used either to support the adjacent state park, by providing parking or retail services for visitors, or to support the nearby marina. Parcel 4B will include a renovated marina, as well as the final stretch of the riverwalk. Parcels 5, 6, and 7 will provide land for office and retail space, parking, and water-dependent commercial uses. * * *

The city council approved the plan in January 2000, and designated the NLDC as its development agent in charge of implementation. The city council also authorized the NLDC to purchase property or to acquire property by exercising eminent domain in the City's name. The NLDC successfully negotiated the purchase of most of the real estate in the 90-acre area, but its negotiations with petitioners failed. As a consequence, in November 2000, the NLDC initiated the condemnation proceedings that gave rise to this case. * * * Petitioner Susette Kelo has lived in the Fort Trumbull area since 1997. She has made extensive improvements to her house, which she prizes for its water view. * * * In all, the nine petitioners own 15 properties in Fort Trumbull—4 in parcel 3 of the development plan and 11 in parcel 4A. Ten of the parcels are occupied by the owner or a family member; the other five are held as investment properties. There is no allegation that any of these properties is blighted or otherwise in poor condition; rather, they were condemned only because they happen to be located in the development area. * * *

The disposition of this case * * * turns on the question whether the City's development plan serves a "public purpose." Without exception, our cases have defined that concept broadly, reflecting our longstanding policy of deference to legislative judgments in this field. * * * Viewed as a whole, our jurisprudence has recognized that the needs of society have varied between different parts of the Nation, just as they have evolved over time in response to changed circumstances. Our earliest cases in particular embodied a strong theme of federalism, emphasizing the "great respect" that we owe to state legislatures and state courts in discerning local public needs. * * * Given the comprehensive character of the plan, the thorough deliberation that preceded its adoption, and the limited scope of our review, it is appropriate for us * * * to resolve the challenges of the individual owners, not on a piecemeal basis, but rather in light of the entire plan. Because that plan unquestionably serves a public purpose, the takings challenged here satisfy the public use requirement of the Fifth Amendment.

To avoid this result, petitioners urge us to adopt a new bright-line rule that economic development does not qualify as a public use. * * * [N]either precedent nor logic supports petitioners' proposal. Promoting economic development is a traditional and long accepted function of government. There is, moreover, no principled way of distinguishing economic development from the other public purposes that we have recognized. In our cases upholding takings that facilitated agriculture and mining, for example, we emphasized the importance of those industries to the welfare of the States in question * * *; in *Berman [v. Parker*, 348 U.S. 26, 75 S.Ct. 98, 99 L.Ed. 27 (1954),] we endorsed the purpose of transforming a blighted area into a "well-balanced" community through redevelopment * * *. It would be incongruous to hold that the City's interest in the economic benefits to be derived from the development of the Fort Trumbull area has less of a public character than any of those other interests. Clearly, there is no basis for exempting economic development from our traditionally broad understanding of public purpose.

Petitioners contend that using eminent domain for economic development impermissibly blurs the boundary between public and private takings. Again, our cases foreclose this objection. Quite simply, the government's pursuit of a public purpose will often benefit individual private parties. * * * The owner of the department store in *Berman* objected to "taking from one businessman for the benefit of another businessman," referring to the fact that under the redevelopment plan land would be leased or sold to private developers for redevelopment. Our rejection of that contention has particular relevance to the instant case: "The public end may be as well or better served through an agency of private enterprise than through a department of government—or so the Congress might conclude. We cannot say that public ownership is the sole method of promoting the public purposes of community redevelopment projects."

It is further argued that without a bright-line rule nothing would stop a city from transferring citizen A's property to citizen B for the sole reason that citizen B will put the property to a more productive use and thus pay more taxes. Such a one-to-one transfer of property, executed outside the confines of an integrated development plan, is not presented in this case. While such an unusual exercise of government power would certainly raise a suspicion that a private purpose was afoot,[17] the hypothetical cases posited by petitioners can be confronted if and when they arise. They do not warrant the crafting of an artificial restriction on the concept of public use. * * *

In affirming the City's authority to take petitioners' properties, we do not minimize the hardship that condemnations may entail, notwithstanding the payment of just compensation. We emphasize that

---

[17] Courts have viewed such aberrations with a skeptical eye. See, e.g., 99 Cents Only Stores v. Lancaster Redevelopment Agency, 237 F.Supp.2d 1123 (C.D.Cal.2001); cf. Cincinnati v. Vester, 281 U.S. 439, 448, 50 S.Ct. 360, 74 L.Ed. 950 (1930) (taking invalid under state eminent domain statute for lack of a reasoned explanation). These types of takings may also implicate other constitutional guarantees. See Village of Willowbrook v. Olech, 528 U.S. 562, 120 S.Ct. 1073, 145 L.Ed.2d 1060 (2000) (per curiam).

nothing in our opinion precludes any State from placing further restrictions on its exercise of the takings power. Indeed, many States already impose "public use" requirements that are stricter than the federal baseline. Some of these requirements have been established as a matter of state constitutional law, while others are expressed in state eminent domain statutes that carefully limit the grounds upon which takings may be exercised. As the submissions of the parties and their amici make clear, the necessity and wisdom of using eminent domain to promote economic development are certainly matters of legitimate public debate. This Court's authority, however, extends only to determining whether the City's proposed condemnations are for a "public use" within the meaning of the Fifth Amendment to the Federal Constitution. Because over a century of our case law interpreting that provision dictates an affirmative answer to that question, we may not grant petitioners the relief that they seek. * * *

JUSTICE O'CONNOR, with whom THE CHIEF JUSTICE, JUSTICE SCALIA, and JUSTICE THOMAS join, dissenting. * * *

This case * * * presents an issue of first impression: Are economic development takings constitutional? I would hold that they are not. * * * The Court's holding[ ] in *Berman* * * * [was] true to the principle underlying the Public Use Clause. * * * [T]he extraordinary, precondemnation use of the targeted property inflicted affirmative harm on society * * * through blight resulting from extreme poverty * * *. [T]he relevant legislative body had found that eliminating the existing property use was necessary to remedy the harm. Thus a public purpose was realized when the harmful use was eliminated. * * * Here, in contrast, New London does not claim that Susette Kelo's and Wilhelmina Dery's well-maintained homes are the source of any social harm. Indeed, it could not so claim without adopting the absurd argument that any single-family home that might be razed to make way for an apartment building, or any church that might be replaced with a retail store, or any small business that might be more lucrative if it were instead part of a national franchise, is inherently harmful to society and thus within the government's power to condemn.

In moving away from our decisions sanctioning the condemnation of harmful property use, the Court today significantly expands the meaning of public use. It holds that the sovereign may take private property currently put to ordinary private use, and give it over for new, ordinary private use, so long as the new use is predicted to generate some secondary benefit for the public—such as increased tax revenue, more jobs, maybe even aesthetic pleasure. But nearly any lawful use of real private property can be said to generate some incidental benefit to the public. Thus, if predicted (or even guaranteed) positive side-effects are enough to render transfer from one private party to another constitutional, then the words "for public use" do not realistically exclude any takings, and thus do not exert any constraint on the eminent domain power. * * *

The Court protests that it does not sanction the bare transfer from A to B for B's benefit. * * * First, it maintains a role for courts in ferreting out takings whose sole purpose is to bestow a benefit on the private transferee—without detailing how courts are to conduct that complicated inquiry. * * * The trouble with economic development takings is that private benefit and incidental public benefit are, by definition, merged and mutually reinforcing. In this case, for example, any boon for Pfizer or the plan's developer is difficult to disaggregate from the promised public gains in taxes and jobs. * * *

A second proposed limitation is implicit in the Court's opinion. The logic of today's decision is that eminent domain may only be used to upgrade—not downgrade—property. * * * [W]ho among us can say she already makes the most productive or attractive possible use of her property? The specter of condemnation hangs over all property. Nothing is to prevent the State from replacing any Motel 6 with a Ritz-Carlton, any home with a shopping mall, or any farm with a factory. * * * It was possible after *Berman* * * * to imagine unconstitutional transfers from A to B. * * * [The decision] endorsed government intervention when private property use had veered to such an extreme that the public was suffering as a consequence. Today nearly all real property is susceptible to condemnation on the Court's theory. * * * Any property may now be taken for the benefit of another private party, but the fallout from this decision will not be random. The beneficiaries are likely to be those citizens with disproportionate influence and power in the political process, including large corporations and development firms. As for the victims, the government now has license to transfer property from those with fewer resources to those with more. * * *

JUSTICE THOMAS, dissenting. * * *

The consequences of today's decision are not difficult to predict, and promise to be harmful. So-called "urban renewal" programs provide some compensation for the properties they take, but no compensation is possible for the subjective value of these lands to the individuals displaced and the indignity inflicted by uprooting them from their homes. Allowing the government to take property solely for public purposes is bad enough, but extending the concept of public purpose to encompass any economically beneficial goal guarantees that these losses will fall disproportionately on poor communities. * * * In the 1950's, no doubt emboldened in part by the expansive understanding of "public use" this Court adopted in *Berman,* cities "rushed to draw plans" for downtown development. B. Frieden & L. Sagalayn, Downtown, Inc. How America

Rebuilds Cities 17 (1989). "Of all the families displaced by urban renewal from 1949 through 1963, 63 percent of those whose race was known were nonwhite, and of these families, 56 percent of nonwhites and 38 percent of whites had incomes low enough to qualify for public housing, which, however, was seldom available to them." Public works projects in the 1950's and 1960's destroyed predominantly minority communities in St. Paul, Minnesota, and Baltimore, Maryland. In 1981, urban planners in Detroit, Michigan, uprooted the largely "lower-income and elderly" Poletown neighborhood for the benefit of the General Motors Corporation. J. Wylie, Poletown: Community Betrayed 58 (1989). Urban renewal projects have long been associated with the displacement of blacks; "[i]n cities across the country, urban renewal came to be known as 'Negro removal.'" Pritchett, The "Public Menace" of Blight: Urban Renewal and the Private Uses of Eminent Domain, 21 Yale L. & Pol'y Rev. 1, 47 (2003). Over 97 percent of the individuals forcibly removed from their homes by the "slum-clearance" project upheld by this Court in *Berman* were black. Regrettably, the predictable consequence of the Court's decision will be to exacerbate these effects. * * *

C. PAYING THE CITY'S EXPENSES

The manner in which a city exercises its power to raise and spend revenue affects the internal life of cities just as crucially as its regulation of city activity or its condemnation of city property. The topic of city taxation and finance, however, is so vast and complex that it can easily fill an entire casebook.[5] In order to avoid a truncated (and therefore inadequate) treatment of the problems raised by local taxation, borrowing, and expenditures, this section will focus solely on a number of innovative methods cities are now employing in the effort to solve their fiscal problems.

Chapter Two of this casebook explored the degree of control that states may exercise over their cities. The state's exercise of this control is one of the reasons cities have fiscal problems; states often impose significant limitations on cities' ability to generate revenue. States not only control the nature and extent of city taxation[6] but also commonly restrict cities' authority to borrow money.[7] The exercise of this state

---

[5] See, e.g., Richard Pomp, State and Local Taxation (7th ed. 2011); Walter Hellerstein, Kirk J. Stark, John Swain, and Joan M. Youngman, State and Local Taxation, Cases and Materials on State and Local Taxation (9th ed. 2009).

[6] See generally, John Martinez, Local Government Law, Chapter 25 (2nd ed. 2012–13); Daniel Mullins, Tax and Expenditure Limits on Local Governments (1995); Rubin Cohn, Municipal Revenue Powers in the Context of Constitutional Home Rule, 51 Nw. U. L. Rev. 27 (1956).

[7] See, e.g., Municipal Building Authority v. Lowder, in Chapter One. See generally, John Martinez, Local Government Law, Chapter 25 (2nd ed. 2012–13); M. David Gelfand (ed.), State and Local Government Debt Financing (2008); Bettie Mann, State Constitutional Restrictions on Local Borrowing and Property Taxing Powers (1964).

power to decide how much revenue cities can raise contributes to many cities' chronic lack of funds. Moreover, as we have seen, state mandates of city expenditures[8] and state-imposed reallocation of city-generated funds to neighboring jurisdictions[9] add to this pervasive strain on city budgets.

State-imposed controls on city income and expenditures, however, constitute only one of the reasons that many cities have begun to seek innovative ways to raise revenue. Another impetus derives from the problem of relying on taxation as a principal source of funds. The defects in the property tax—the traditional (and still the most important) source of local income—have become the subject of an enormous literature. The National Commission on Urban Problems, for example, criticized the property tax for imposing a disproportionately heavy burden on housing (residential property makes up roughly half of the tax base), for deterring housing maintenance (taxes increase as the value of the property increases), for imposing an unfair burden on the poor (the poor spend a larger percentage of their income on housing than do the rich), and for being unfairly administered (the task of assessing property values is fraught with complexity and the risk of unequal treatment).[10] To be sure, the validity of the complaints against the property tax are hotly debated in the economics literature.[11] Nevertheless it seems clear that the widespread popular resentment against local property taxes has fueled a considerable reaction against them.

The first subsection below examines an important set of state and federal limitations on the authority of cities to generate revenue through the imposition of taxes or other types of payment obligations. These limitations require cities to abide by a norm of equality in generating revenue. The subsection begins with an examination of the successful effort, organized by initiative, to limit cities' ability to raise property taxes. As the support for Proposition 13 illustrates, reliance on the property tax not only has declined over the last forty-five years but is likely to continue to do so in the future.[12] But the traditional alternatives to the property tax—the sales and income taxes—have generated considerable problems of their own. Local sales taxes have risen sharply

---

[8] See generally, Advisory Commission on Intergovernmental Relations, Mandates: Cases in State-Local Relations (1990).

[9] See, e.g., Edgewood Independent School District v. Kirby in Chapter Three.

[10] National Commission on Urban Problems, Building the American City 358–59 (1969).

[11] See, e.g., Michael Bell, David Brunori and Joan Youngman, The Property Tax and Local Autonomy (2010); Walter Hellerstein, Kirk J. Stark, John Swain, and Joan M. Youngman, State and Local Taxation, Cases and Materials on State and Local Taxation (9th ed. 2009); Richard Musgrave and Peggy Musgrave, Public Finance in Theory and Practice (5th ed. 1989); J. Richard Aronson and John Hilley, Financing State and Local Governments (4th ed. 1986).

[12] Advisory Commission on Intergovernmental Relations, Significant Features of Fiscal Federalism 1995 Edition, Volume 2, Table 33.

in recent years.[13] But many experts argue that local sales taxes cause a decline in the amount of retail business activity in the city levying the tax and that the sales tax (like the property tax) imposes a disproportionate burden on the poor.[14] (Other problems with local reliance on the sales tax are explored in Jonathan Schwartz's article, excerpted below.) Similar criticisms have been expressed about the efforts of an increasing number of cities to impose local income taxes (particularly if only city residents are taxed).[15] Given these many alternative places to shop or to live in regional areas, these critics argue, imposition of local sales or income taxes can easily be counterproductive: they can lead not to city prosperity but to city decline.

Although reliance on city taxes obviously cannot be eliminated in the foreseeable future, many cities have begun to explore alternatives. In the 1960s and 1970s, the most popular alternative consisted of obtaining grants-in-aid from the federal government; since 1980, however, the percentage of local budgets supported by these federal grants has declined.[16] Another alternative—borrowing money to pay for essential city services—is clearly not a viable option, although New York City had to learn this lesson the hard way.[17] Counting on transfer payments from other governments or on borrowing money just to keep even leaves cities in a vulnerable position. Cities have to find ways of obtaining their own funds—preferably, without raising taxes. The cases and materials reproduced below explore a variety of ways that cities have employed to find additional revenue—or to cut expenses because of lack of revenue.

---

[13] Advisory Commission on Intergovernmental Relations, Significant Features of Fiscal Federalism 1995 Edition, Volume 2, Table 33.

[14] For a discussion of the economic consequences of the tax, see, e.g., Richard Pomp, State and Local Taxation (7th ed. 2011); Walter Hellerstein, Kirk J. Stark, John Swain, and Joan M. Youngman, State and Local Taxation, Cases and Materials on State and Local Taxation (9th ed. 2009); Richard Musgrave and Peggy Musgrave, Public Finance in Theory and Practice (5th ed. 1989); Jerome Hellerstein, Significant Sales and Use Tax Developments During the Past Half Century, 39 Vand. L. Rev. 961 (1986).

[15] Walter Hellerstein, Kirk J. Stark, John Swain, and Joan M. Youngman, State and Local Taxation, Cases and Materials on State and Local Taxation (9th ed. 2009). See also, Clayton Gillette, Who Should Authorize a Commuter Tax?, 77 U. Chi. L. Rev. 223 (2010); William Fox, The Personal Income Tax as a Component of State Tax Structure, 39 Vand. L. Rev. 1081, 1089 (1986); David Munhnick, A Municipal Income Tax for Boston: Discourse in Possibilities, 5 Suffolk U. L. Rev. 1 (1970). For statistical data concerning local income taxes, see Advisory Commission on Intergovernmental Relations, Significant Features of Fiscal Federalism 1995 Edition, Volume 1, Tables 20–21 and Volume 2, Table 33.

[16] Advisory Commission on Intergovernmental Relations, Significant Features of Fiscal Federalism 1995 Edition, Volume 2, Tables 10 and 33; Marcus Pohlmann, Governing the Postindustrial City 114 (1993). For an analysis of the legal issues raised by federal grants-in-aid, see Frank Michelman and Terrance Sandalow, Materials on Government in Urban Areas: Cases, Comments, Questions 970–1212 (1970); Richard Cappalli, Restoring Federalism Values in the Federal Grant System, 19 The Urban Lawyer 493 (1987). See also Lawrence County v. Lead-Deadwood School District in Chapter Two.

[17] See generally, M. David Gelfand, Seeking Local Government Financial Integrity Through Debt Ceilings, Tax Limitations, and Expenditures Limits: The New York City Fiscal Crisis, the Taxpayers' Revolt, and Beyond, 63 Minn. L. Rev. 545 (1979).

1. TAXES AND FEES

The following cases and materials explore local revenue sources and the impact of constitutional protections on cities' ability to raise revenue. These constitutional protections derive, for example, from state constitutional tax caps, such as California's Proposition 13, requirements for tax uniformity, equal protection clauses at the state and federal level, and state constitutional prohibitions against special legislation.

Nordlinger v. Hahn, Jonathan Schwartz's article "Prisoners of Proposition 13" and the California Legislative Analysts report all analyze the inequality generated by California's Proposition 13. In *Nordlinger*, the United States Supreme Court applied a deferential standard to Proposition 13's limit on local property taxes: it upheld the initiative notwithstanding plaintiffs' allegations that it had generated inequality between cities' long-time residents and newcomers. What view of inter-city relationships does the *Nordlinger* court adopt in upholding the impact of Proposition 13? How are these understandings of inter-city relationships affected by Jonathan Schwartz's analysis of the shift to a reliance on sales taxes after the enactment of Proposition 13? The third reading, from the California Legislative Analyst's Office, emphasizes another, often overlooked, consequence of Proposition 13. The allocation system required in order to implement Proposition 13's tax cap is staggeringly complex and highly centralized. The state legislature decides how to allocate tax revenues and only the state legislature can change that allocation.

The readings that follow the examination of Proposition 13 explore selectively imposed revenue raising devices—fees, dues, and special assessments—that are designed to avoid imposing general taxes on city residents or property owners.[18] In considering whether these devices are legitimate, it is important to see that the issue is not only a legal one. The reading by Laurie Reynolds suggests that the choice between taxes and "dues" is one between two very different visions of what a city is. Do you agree with Reynolds that there is a problem with the shift from general taxation to what she calls a "dues mentality"? If so, should the solution be to impose legal limits on the power of cities to rely on dues instead of taxes? The second reading, by Gerald Frug and David Barron, focuses on the different treatment, as a legal matter, of the tax/fee distinction in Massachusetts and California. In both of the cases discussed in the reading, the question was whether it was more appropriate to charge only some people for local services or to spread the costs more widely. Which of the two approaches offers the better way to determine whether a city can

---

[18] For a general survey of the law governing special assessments, see John Martinez, Local Government Law, Chapter 24 (2nd ed. 2012–13).

obtain additional revenue from some of its citizens or property owners but not others?

The final article, by Eric Montarti, explores another approach to local revenue: tax increment financing. Tax increment financing is used in many American cities to finance redevelopment of economically depressed, underdeveloped or lighted areas. In theory it allows a local authority to fund redevelopment by capturing the increase in property tax revenue that results from the redevelopment. But it might also deprive the local government as a whole of general tax revenue it would otherwise have enjoyed. With federal redevelopment funding on the decline and local revenues increasingly capped or limited, tax increment financing is often the only way to fund redevelopment projects. On the other hand, if the redevelopment would have occurred in any event, tax increment financing may unduly subsidize private construction and allocate tax revenues to bondholders that otherwise could have been used to fund general city services. Is tax increment financing ultimately robbing Peter to pay Paul?

NORDLINGER V. HAHN

Supreme Court of the United States, 1992.
505 U.S. 1, 112 S.Ct. 2326, 120 L.Ed.2d 1.

JUSTICE BLACKMUN delivered the opinion of the Court.

In 1978, California voters staged what has been described as a property tax revolt by approving a statewide ballot initiative known as Proposition 13. The adoption of Proposition 13 served to amend the California Constitution to impose strict limits on the rate at which real property is taxed and on the rate at which real property assessments are increased from year to year. In this litigation, we consider a challenge under the Equal Protection Clause of the Fourteenth Amendment to the manner in which real property now is assessed under the California Constitution.

Proposition 13 followed many years of rapidly rising real property taxes in California. * * * By 1978, property tax relief had emerged as a major political issue in California. In only one month's time, tax relief advocates collected over 1.2 million signatures to qualify Proposition 13 for the June 1978 ballot. On election day, Proposition 13 received a favorable vote of 64.8% and carried 55 of the State's 58 counties. California thus had a novel constitutional amendment that led to a property tax cut of approximately $7 billion in the first year. A California homeowner with a $50,000 home enjoyed an immediate reduction of about $750 per year in property taxes.

As enacted by Proposition 13, Article XIIIA of the California Constitution caps real property taxes at 1% of a property's "full cash value." "Full cash value" is defined as the assessed valuation as of the 1975–1976 tax year or, "thereafter, the appraised value of real property when purchased, newly constructed, or a change in ownership has occurred after the 1975 assessment." The assessment "may reflect from year to year the inflationary rate not to exceed 2 percent for any given year." Article XIIIA also contains several exemptions from this reassessment provision. One exemption authorizes the legislature to allow homeowners over the age of 55 who sell their principal residences to carry their previous base-year assessments with them to replacement residences of equal or lesser value. A second exemption applies to transfers of a principal residence (and up to $1 million of other real property) between parents and children.

In short, Article XIIIA combines a 1% ceiling on the property tax rate with a 2% cap on annual increases in assessed valuations. The assessment limitation, however, is subject to the exception that new construction or a change of ownership triggers a reassessment up to current appraised value. Thus, the assessment provisions of Article XIIIA essentially embody an "acquisition value" system of taxation rather than the more commonplace "current value" taxation. Real property is assessed at values related to the value of the property at the time it is acquired by the taxpayer rather than to the value it has in the current real estate market.

Over time, this acquisition-value system has created dramatic disparities in the taxes paid by persons owning similar pieces of property. Property values in California have inflated far in excess of the allowed 2% cap on increases in assessments for property that is not newly constructed or that has not changed hands. As a result, longer term property owners pay lower property taxes reflecting historic property values, while newer owners pay higher property taxes reflecting more recent values. For that reason, Proposition 13 has been labeled by some as a "welcome stranger" system—the newcomer to an established community is "welcome" in anticipation that he will contribute a larger percentage of support for local government than his settled neighbor who owns a comparable home. Indeed, in dollar terms, the differences in tax burdens are staggering. * * * According to her amended complaint, petitioner Stephanie Nordlinger in November 1988 purchased a house in the Baldwin Hills neighborhood of Los Angeles County for $170,000. The prior owners bought the home just two years before for $121,500. * * * In early 1989, petitioner received a notice from the Los Angeles County Tax Assessor, who is a respondent here, informing her that her home had been reassessed upward to $170,100 on account of its change in ownership. * * * Petitioner later discovered she was paying about five times more in taxes than some of her neighbors who owned comparable homes since 1975 within the same residential development. * * *

[P]etitioner brought suit against respondents in Los Angeles County Superior Court. She sought a tax refund and a declaration that her tax was unconstitutional. * * *

The Equal Protection Clause of the Fourteenth Amendment, § 1, commands that no State shall "deny to any person within its jurisdiction the equal protection of the laws." * * * This Court's cases are clear that, unless a classification warrants some form of heightened review because it jeopardizes exercise of a fundamental right or categorizes on the basis of an inherently suspect characteristic, the Equal Protection Clause requires only that the classification rationally further a legitimate state interest. See, e.g., *Cleburne v. Cleburne Living Center, Inc.*, 473 U.S. 432, 439–441, 105 S.Ct. 3249, 3254–3255, 87 L.Ed.2d 313 (1985) * * *. We have no difficulty in ascertaining at least two rational or reasonable considerations of difference or policy that justify denying petitioner the benefits of her neighbors' lower assessments. First, the State has a legitimate interest in local neighborhood preservation, continuity, and stability. *Village of Euclid v. Ambler Realty Co.*, 272 U.S. 365, 47 S.Ct. 114, 71 L.Ed. 303 (1926). The State therefore legitimately can decide to structure its tax system to discourage rapid turnover in ownership of homes and businesses, for example, in order to inhibit displacement of lower income families by the forces of gentrification or of established, "mom-and-pop" businesses by newer chain operations. By permitting older owners to pay progressively less in taxes than new owners of comparable property, the Article XIIIA assessment scheme rationally furthers this interest.

Second, the State legitimately can conclude that a new owner at the time of acquiring his property does not have the same reliance interest warranting protection against higher taxes as does an existing owner. The State may deny a new owner at the point of purchase the right to "lock in" to the same assessed value as is enjoyed by an existing owner of comparable property, because an existing owner rationally may be thought to have vested expectations in his property or home that are more deserving of protection than the anticipatory expectations of a new owner at the point of purchase. A new owner has full information about the scope of future tax liability before acquiring the property, and if he thinks the future tax burden is too demanding, he can decide not to complete the purchase at all. By contrast, the existing owner, already saddled with his purchase, does not have the option of deciding not to buy his home if taxes become prohibitively high. To meet his tax obligations, he might be forced to sell his home or to divert his income away from the purchase of food, clothing, and other necessities. In short, the State may decide that it is worse to have owned and lost, than never to have owned at all. * * *

The two exemptions at issue here rationally further legitimate purposes. * * * Article XIIIA is not palpably arbitrary, and we must decline petitioner's request to upset the will of the people of California. * * *

JUSTICE STEVENS, dissenting. * * *

Although the State may have a valid interest in preserving some neighborhoods, Proposition 13 not only "inhibit[s the] displacement" of settled families, it also inhibits the transfer of unimproved land, abandoned buildings, and substandard uses. Thus, contrary to the Court's suggestion, Proposition 13 is not like a zoning system. A zoning system functions by recognizing different uses of property and treating those different uses differently. Proposition 13 treats all property alike, giving all owners tax breaks, and discouraging the transfer or improvement of all property—the developed and the dilapidated, the neighborly and the nuisance. * * * I cannot agree that a tax windfall for all persons who purchased property before 1978 rationally furthers * * * [the interest of neighborhood preservation]. To my mind, Proposition 13 is too blunt a tool to accomplish such a specialized goal. * * *

The second state interest identified by the Court is the "reliance interests" of the earlier purchasers. Here I find the Court's reasoning difficult to follow. Although the protection of reasonable reliance interests is a legitimate governmental purpose, this case does not implicate such interests. A reliance interest is created when an individual justifiably acts under the assumption that an existing legal condition will persist; thus reliance interests are most often implicated when the government provides some benefit and then acts to eliminate the benefit. In this case, those who purchased property before Proposition 13 was enacted received no assurances that assessments would only increase at a limited rate; indeed, to the contrary, many purchased property in the hope that property values (and assessments) would appreciate substantially and quickly. It cannot be said, therefore, that the earlier purchasers of property somehow have a reliance interest in limited tax increases. * * * Proposition 13 provides a benefit for earlier purchasers and imposes a burden on later purchasers. To say that the later purchasers know what they are getting into does not answer the critical question: Is it reasonable and constitutional to tax early purchasers less than late purchasers when at the time of taxation their properties are comparable? * * *

JONATHAN SCHWARTZ, PRISONERS OF PROPOSITION
13: SALES TAXES, PROPERTY TAXES, AND THE
FISCALIZATION OF MUNICIPAL LAND USE DECISIONS
71 S. Cal. L. Rev. 183, 184–186, 197–205 (1997).

After nearly twenty years, Proposition 13 has fundamentally altered the manner in which state and local levels of government interact with each other and the citizens of California. Indeed, one commentator maintains that "[c]ounty, city and town government, traditionally financed by property taxes, is more or less a thing of the past in California—Proposition 13 has ended such democratic notions and frills as town hall meetings and local control of schools." While supporters of Proposition 13 intended to limit the scope and power of government, the initiative has actually empowered the state to act in areas traditionally left to local politicians.

As some predicted, local governments have reacted to this changing fiscal reality by maintaining a level of freedom in areas of government, like planning, that are still amenable to local control. While Proposition 13 has had severe and dramatic consequences for land use, "[s]uch details were of little concern to the angry voters who followed self-styled populists Howard Jarvis and Paul Gann to the polls to vote for [Proposition 13]." Instead, the initiative's supporters merely wanted to cut their property tax bills. * * * Proposition 13 was, at least partially, a response to the fiscal realities of 1978 * * *: "[B]oth local property taxes and the overall state and local tax burden were far above the national average. Moreover, property taxes were escalating rapidly; had Proposition 13 failed, the homeowners' property tax bill would have almost doubled between 1974 and 1978." * * *

With ever-increasing limits placed on the powers of local governments to raise taxes and the concurrent demands for public services, public officials have turned to funding sources with lower cognitive profiles. Chief among these revenue streams has been the sales tax. While the current California sales tax rate is six percent, cities generally receive an additional one percent of the sales tax and counties receive one-quarter percent on transactions occurring within the local government's boundaries. To this 7.25% minimum tax, voters added another half cent for public safety programs in 1993. Many counties have added assorted other sales taxes for a variety of purposes that have brought the rate to as high as 8.5% in some areas.

Given the voter-imposed limits on other revenue sources, the local portion of the sales tax has become ever more significant, growing from 15.54% of city general fund revenues in the ten years before Proposition 13 to 26.85% subsequently. * * * This shift in favor of the sales tax "has had a major effect on the dynamics of local government, spurring local officials to elevate sales tax-producing projects such as shopping centers and auto malls over other land uses—a syndrome known as 'fiscalization of land use.' " This fiscalization of land use has altered the ways in which local officials view planning and development. In the words of one observer, "the vision of a model city is a monster mall surrounded by car dealers." * * *

While cities have reacted to the increasing importance of sales taxes in a number of different ways, some basic lessons can be drawn from the experiences of communities throughout California. Cities now target increased sales taxes as a way to generate needed revenue: " 'All of the cities are after the same thing. . . . Since Proposition 13, probably the only way that cities can attract revenue, other than what's given to us, is the sales tax. It's kind of a dog-eat-dog situation.' " As a result, cities have attempted to maximize the amount of sales taxes generated within their borders through a variety of tactics, including the use of eminent domain to make way for a shopping center's expansion, fee waivers, sales tax rebates, lease guarantees, bond payments, cash, and shop-at-home campaigns.

When these tactics work, they can bring added tax revenues to cities without forcing local officials to seek voter approval to increase tax rates. As an added political benefit, actions taken by local officials to bring sales-tax-generating businesses to the community can often be couched in terms that focus on both the added construction and retail jobs created by the development and the convenience and civic pride that come with such businesses. When such redevelopment schemes fail, cities may be forced to cover the costs of bond payments to avoid defaulting on commitments to developers and bond holders.

As a general proposition, California's tax limitations have "brought an overreliance on sales tax . . . causing in some cases cities to approve land uses because of what returns to them, instead of what is necessarily best for the city and the area." In one instance, the city of Indio sacrificed a historic neighborhood through the use of its powers of eminent domain so that a mall developer could triple the size of the local shopping center. Similarly, a planned Home Depot in Santa Rosa threatens to replace a mobile home park.

In Huntington Beach, automobile dealers in the city's "Boulevard of Cars" persuaded the city to spend $361,000 to erect an eighty-five foot tall sign that violates the city's own sign ordinance by arguing that the sign will pay for itself with additional sales tax revenue. Local governments have long sought automobile dealers because of the enormous amounts of sales taxes they generate. In fact, California's redevelopment law was amended in 1993 to prevent local redevelopment agencies from abusing programs originally designed to alleviate problems associated with urban blight by instead providing incentives to automobile dealers. Before that, however, many cities developed auto malls like the one in Huntington Beach to generate sales taxes. Even now, cities use similar, though non-redevelopment related, tactics to provide business incentives to automobile dealers and other retailers. * * *

In the rush to generate increased sales taxes by bringing shopping centers and large discount retailers to town, cities threaten to take customers away from established businesses. As one concerned citizen put it, " 'I'm concerned about all these shopping malls. . . . What they're doing is trading our heritage and our cities on the hope that these shopping malls will lure more money. But, in fact, they lure it away from existing business and change the nature of our cities.' " Importantly, new retail development does not dramatically increase the level of commerce in a given area. Instead, because in a certain sense it is a zero-sum proposition, such new development only shifts sales from one business or city to another. Additionally, because many existing businesses are located in downtown areas of cities, efforts to locate shopping malls and discount retailers in undeveloped areas has, in some instances, led to urban decay: " 'This whole thing is destroying the hearts of communities and their downtowns, as sales taxes are drawn from there into these big box retail developments like Wal-Mart.' " * * *

In addition to the unintended consequences that relate to existing businesses and downtowns, sales tax dependence has created a system of local government finance that minimizes the value of new housing and manufacturing development. Specifically, because housing and manufacturing generate property rather than sales taxes, such developments no longer provide the same level of financial rewards to cities. As such, the system encourages land use decisions that create lower paying retail and service jobs instead of higher paying manufacturing positions; in the words of one official, " 'All we're doing is sitting on a tax system the last few years that creates $5-an-hour jobs and not $15-an-hour jobs.' "

Similarly, the decreased share of property taxes allocated to cities and the resulting importance of sales taxes has disfavored housing. Prior to Proposition 13, a local government's share of the property tax was better able to provide a sufficient level of revenue for cities to fund the expenses associated with a new house. Now, many developments, particularly those that require significant investment in infrastructure like roads and sewers, fail to pay for themselves, at least in the eyes of local governments. As a result, financially strapped cities question the wisdom of accepting housing developments that require expenditures of city funds * * *.

Perhaps even more unfortunate than the consequences associated with the fiscalization of land use, sales tax dependence has encouraged cities to compete with one another to attract sales-tax-generating businesses. Given that cities with a shortage of open space for new development or less attractive demographics may find it difficult to attract large retailers and compete with cities that actively court such businesses, this competition forces local governments to provide ever larger incentives to lure and keep businesses. These incentives, combined with the system of city financing created by Proposition 13, encourage local officials to enter into costly and risky agreements with retailers. These agreements threaten to undermine the fiscal health of local governments while also decreasing the benefits of any bargain reached with a coveted business. * * *

CALIFORNIA LEGISLATIVE ANALYST'S OFFICE,
RECONSIDERING AB 8: EXPLORING ALTERNATIVE
WAYS TO ALLOCATE PROPERTY TAXES
February 3, 2000.

* * * California's property owners pay over $20 billion of property taxes each year. These tax revenues—the third largest source of tax revenues in California—are then allocated among several thousand local governments, pursuant to a complex state statute. While significant legislation pertaining to the property tax allocation system has been enacted over the years, the allocation system is still commonly referred to as "AB 8," after the bill which first implemented the system. * * * Over the years, the Legislature, local governments, the business community, and the public have become increasingly critical of the state's property tax allocation system because (1) it does not allocate revenues in a way that reflects modern needs and preferences of local communities and (2) it centralizes authority over local revenues in Sacramento. * * *

Prior to the passage of Proposition 13 by the California voters in 1978, each governmental entity (city, county, special district, and school district) would set a property tax rate annually. This rate would be combined with other local governments' tax rates to form a property owner's property tax bill. The taxpayer's total property tax owed would be determined by summing together the various rates and applying the total to the property's assessed value. Because the rates were connected to a specific government entity and set annually, taxpayers could see what percentage of their property taxes was going to each local government.

To implement Proposition 13, the Legislature enacted the AB 8 property tax allocation system. A single countywide rate of 1 percent replaced the numerous individual government tax rates. Although taxpayers gained the assurance that their rate could not increase from year-to-year, they lost the ability to see which entities receive revenues from their payments. * * *

[Under AB8] the allocation of revenues to any local government:

- Is based largely on the level of property taxes that it received in the mid-1970s, relative to other local governments in the same county.

- Generally cannot be changed, except by state legislation.

- Varies significantly across taxpayers in the same county— and in comparison with taxpayers in other parts of the state. * * *

AB 8 system reduces government accountability. The link between the level of government allocating the tax (the state) and the entity that spends the tax revenues (cities, counties, special districts, and schools) has been severed. * * * The same forces that diminish taxpayers' ability to hold their governments accountable also reduce local governments' ability to control their own finances. * * * Local officials have no power to raise or lower their property tax share on an annual basis to reflect the changing needs of their communities. * * *

The state has left the distribution of property tax revenues among local entities largely unchanged since the 1970s. Counties receive a similar proportion of property tax revenues despite many changes to their program responsibilities. Water districts that received property taxes 25 years ago continue to do so, despite a general trend for these and other resource-related services to be funded by user charges rather than general taxes. Local citizens and their elected representatives lack effective fiscal authority to change the allocation of property taxes to reflect their community's current priorities. This problem is especially acute for cities and counties that provide many of their municipal services through independent special districts. If these special districts levied a property tax rate in the 1970s, they typically continue to receive a share of the property tax today.

Finally, if residents desire an enhanced level of a particular service, there is no local forum or mechanism to allow property taxes to be reallocated among local governments to finance this improvement. For example, Orange County currently receives a very low share of property taxes collected within its borders—typically only 4 percent to 7 percent. If Orange County residents and business owners wished to expand county services, they have no practical way to redirect the approximately 3 percent to 4 percent of property taxes currently allocated to water and sanitation districts to pay for this program enhancement. Instead, if residents wish to increase overall county services, they would need to finance this improvement through a mechanism such as an assessment or special tax. In this way, the overall level of government taxation and expenditures can be higher than it would be if communities had greater local control. * * *

LAURIE REYNOLDS, TAXES, FEES, ASSESSMENTS, DUES, AND THE "GET WHAT YOU PAY FOR" MODEL OF LOCAL GOVERNMENT

56 Fla. L. Rev. 373, 379–381, 385, 392–396, 431, 440 (2004).

* * * Local taxes, like taxes levied at the state and federal level, are general charges to raise revenue for the operational costs of government; they are assessed against all who are within the scope of the government's taxing authority. Though they differ widely with regard to the way in which the tax rate is set and the extent to which a particular tax may be regressive or progressive, taxes are levied without consideration of whether the individual taxpayer will benefit from the services to be funded by the tax. Thus, taxes collectivize the cost of service and spread it across the taxpaying population, either at a flat rate or prorated on the basis of ability to pay or other indicia of wealth. Moreover, according to urban economists, taxation promotes communal responsibility for the provision of government services and ensures that services compete against each other in the local political process for a share of the general tax revenue pie. * * *

In fundamental contrast to taxes, local government dues crucially depend on the relationship between the payer and the purpose for which the revenue raised will be spent. That is, by calculating the charge with a computation of the benefit received by the payer or to offset the cost imposed on the general population by the payer's activity, dues treat government activities just like any other market transaction in a consumer economy. As a result, dues have a privatizing effect on government services. In addition, if they are levied on all users equally, dues may be more regressive in their impact than taxes.

Local governments have a wide range of dues techniques at their disposal. These include: fees to use government-owned facilities, like a public transit system; assessments levied against property owners to pay for a locale-specific capital improvement, like sidewalks or street lights; regulatory fees designed to offset the negative impact of private sector activity, like a fee imposed on paint producers to counteract the effects of lead poisoning; or charges based on consumption of a government-provided service, like garbage collection or local utility service. Though they employ a wide variety of implementation techniques and computation formulae, and though their validity depends on a number of device-specific legal tests, the underlying premise is the same for all dues techniques: dues can be levied so long as the person or property being charged stands in direct and substantial relationship to the reason for which the charge has been assessed. * * *

Though local government funding decisions undoubtedly rest on a variety of case-specific considerations, some generalizations are possible. * * * Prior to 1970, * * * local governments typically used a mixture of dues and taxes, but resorted to dues relatively infrequently. Beyond the application of whatever legal restrictions were imposed on the use of dues, their popularity appears to have been limited by a broad community consensus that the cost of many government services should be borne equally by all taxpayers.

Over the past thirty years, however, that attitude has changed and a number of additional considerations now factor into the government's choice between dues and taxes. * * * What is noteworthy or unusual * * * is not that the range of important considerations has increased over the past three decades, but rather how the more recent factors so completely weigh in on the side of dues. Thus, in the early years of the twenty-first century, it is no surprise that dues are becoming the financing mechanism of choice for local governments. * * *

Since the 1970s, and originating in California with Proposition 13, a fairly large number of states have imposed stringent limits on their local governments' ability to raise revenue. The restrictions are expressed in a number of ways: in some states, government taxing powers are limited to a particular dollar amount or percentage; and in others, no new taxes can be imposed without a super-majority vote of the legislature or vote of the taxpayers themselves. Despite the wide variation in the actual technique employed, the common underlying motivation of these taxpayer "revolts" is the rejection of the argument that limits in government spending should be achieved during legislative budgeting sessions. * * * Governments could have used general tax revenues to replace lost federal funds or to fulfill mandates from higher levels of government. When coupled with the growing prevalence of tax limits, however, the increasingly dramatic need for more revenues (coming from the local, state, and federal level) further pushes local governments to adopt more and more dues to fund new infrastructure. * * *

Before 1970, growth, development, and increased population were generally seen as a stimulus to economic improvement and an enhancement of overall local prosperity. * * * Starting with the 1970s, however, community attitudes shifted markedly; growth came to be seen as a deterrent, rather than a contributor, to a community's high quality of life. If growth imposes a cost on the community, the reasoning goes, it is only fair to assess the source of the growth with the costs it imposes. * * *

Though much of the responsibility for the enormous increase in dues techniques must be placed at the doorstep of the local governments themselves, the state judiciary has often been willing to facilitate this profound shift in local government finance. In numerous judicial opinions, the courts have bent, stretched, or ignored the traditional delineations between taxation and dues. * * *

Because the starting point for the local government's initial choice between dues and taxes has been seriously skewed in favor of dues, the government's allocation of revenue between the two devices is likely to reflect that imbalance. In other words, as a result of the current preponderance of anti-tax incentives, local governments turn to dues, not only when a reasoned policy judgment indicates that dues would most properly reflect the community's consensus about fairness in the provision of local government services, but as the only realistic way to raise revenue in the face of substantial barriers to tax financing. * * * Second, the essential dues characteristic that revenues be segregated has the additional effect of removing dues-funded projects from the general revenue budgeting process. Because they are not deposited into the municipality's general revenues fund, but rather isolated and pledged to the project for which they are levied, dues are not involved in what urban economists call "full line forcing": the give and take of the budget debate that sets spending priorities for local revenues. As a result, in today's typical city council chambers, there is usually no debate on whether the municipality should spend its revenues to build a new sewer or, in the alternative, to provide more housing opportunities for the poor. Because of the difference in funding techniques, that debate will not take place, and no elected official will be forced to choose between them. The sewers, if they are built, are likely to involve strictly segregated charges and a pledged revenue stream, untouchable and beyond the reach of local government officials. What remains for the general revenue debate are disputes over spending between, on the one hand, public goods like police and fire services and, on the other hand, social services. * * *

Evidence of the ways this dues mentality has been translated into anti-tax sentiment was brought home to me most recently in a local bond election to fund the renovation and expansion of the Champaign County Nursing Home. Many of the project's passionate supporters urged voter approval by appealing to our dues mentality. They argued that citizens should vote for the bond because some day the voter or someone dear to the voter will need the facility; they encouraged the "what's in it for me" mentality that has been reinforced by decades of dues. Largely missing from the discussion was a debate about whether the community, as an amalgam of many different individuals of different ages and with different health needs, has a responsibility to care for the elderly who need it, irrespective of whether any individual voter ever sets foot inside the doors of the nursing home. Thus, the local debate is no longer about the totality of the package—the nursing home for you, the community college for me—but rather an item-by-item dissection of cost and benefit to determine whether a majority of the community concludes that each service it is being asked to fund would further its own self interest. The redistributive function of taxes seems to have taken a back seat to the consumer attitude that seeks a benefit in every government expense. Though this phenomenon undoubtedly has a variety of sources and causes, the rapid increase in the use of dues techniques contributes to the sentiment by conditioning citizens to examine the relationship between cost and benefit on which every dues technique is premised. * * *

GERALD FRUG AND DAVID BARRON, CITY BOUND: HOW STATES STIFLE URBAN INNOVATION
Pp. 87–89 (2008).

Taxes are not the only way that cities obtain revenue. Locally-imposed fees—ranging from charges imposed for issuing licenses to requirements that commercial developers provide, or pay for, affordable housing—are another source of cash. Cities that have made extensive use of fees have generated a considerable source of income. Like taxes, the imposition of user fees influences local politics. In California, where fees have played a large role for years, an increased reliance on fees has generated a fee-for-service mentality, and it, in turn, has transformed what a city government is—what it provides, and whom it exists to serve. In the place of a general service government providing public goods to all residents, local governments increasingly function as a retailer of services purchased and consumed by individual users. Here again, the source of revenue affects the nature of the city that receives it.

Fees are potentially an important form of local power for Boston. Although the Massachusetts Home Rule Amendment denies Boston the power to levy taxes without state authorization, Boston can assess and collect fees on its own. The state's authorizing legislation is quite broad, and the procedure for obtaining fees is simply passing a local ordinance (approval by the city council and Mayor). Because the legal treatment of fees and taxes is so different, there often is a legal battle in Massachusetts over whether a specific assessment is a fee or a tax. If it is interpreted as a fee, the assessment is typically upheld as within the municipality's power. If it is read as a tax, it is struck down because the Home Rule Amendment requires a specific delegation of power from the state legislature. Court decisions in Massachusetts have tended to follow the second option, thereby limiting the ability that Boston would otherwise have had to generate revenue from fees.

The Massachusetts Supreme Judicial Court articulated the test for determining whether an assessment is a fee or a tax in *Emerson College v. City of Boston.* As the court explained, fees differ from taxes in three ways. A fee is

> charged in exchange for a particular governmental service which benefits the party paying the fee in a manner not shared by other members of society; paid by choice, in that the party paying the fee has the option of not utilizing the governmental service and thereby avoiding the charge; and the charges are collected not to raise revenues but to compensate the governmental entity providing the service for its expense.[9]

The *Emerson* decision addressed an "augmented fire services availability" fee assessed upon buildings in Boston that required significantly more personnel and resources for fire protection than more conventional buildings. Although the ordinance imposing the fee was established pursuant to specific state authorizing legislation, the court struck down the fee as a tax. The court noted that the benefits arising from the payment of the fee affected neighboring buildings as well as the individuals within the buildings being charged. It found that the fees were compelled, despite the fact that they could be reduced if the building owners installed fire safety equipment. Finally, it found that the proceeds of the fee were not targeted to support the augmented fire services but supported fire and police services generally, a fact that was consistent with the revenue-generating purpose of a tax rather than the compensatory purpose of a fee.

In other cities, differences in legal language and judicial interpretations have facilitated more reliance on fees. This is particularly the case in California, where, on average, fees constituted 25% of city budgets in the late 1970s and 41% in the mid-1990s. California cities turned to user fees primarily because of the legal constraints on taxation imposed by Proposition 13, and judicial decisions have facilitated the transition. The legal issue in California courts is different from the tax/fee controversy in Massachusetts. Proposition 13 in California, in addition to imposing strict limits on property taxes, required that any "special taxes" passed by a local government receive a two-thirds majority. California courts have read this restriction narrowly. Many assessments have been categorized not as special taxes but as fees. The California Supreme Court justified its narrow reading by criticizing the initiative procedure that led to Proposition 13's restriction, calling it "inherently undemocratic" because a state-wide majority of voters sought to prohibit a majority of local voters from providing services that would benefit local residents.

Many charges that would fall squarely in the tax category in Massachusetts are considered fees in California. San Francisco, for

---

    9   Emerson College v. City of Boston, 462 N.E.2d 1098 (Mass. 1984).

example, passed a transit fee that imposed a $5 per square foot charge on new developments downtown to "provide revenue for the San Francisco Municipal Railway system to offset the anticipated increased costs to accommodate the new riders during peak commute hours generated by the construction of new office space in the downtown area." The benefit of this fee was not exclusive to the owner of the building (in fact, very little benefit can be said to be attributable to the developer). It ultimately benefited the commuters of San Francisco. But a California appellate court looked directly to the "impact" that the developer was causing to justify the fee. The court explained that the fee imposed was a good estimate of the increased costs caused by the construction. Furthermore, the court noted, "[d]evelopers have been required to pay for streets, sewers, parks and lights as a condition for the privilege of developing a particular parcel" even though they ultimately benefited the public as a whole.[11] Massachusetts' insistence on there being a particularized benefit to the person paying the fee is strikingly absent here. California's leniency towards impact fees appears to stem from its willingness to interpret fees as a negative imposition (like a "fine" for imposing a cost) as opposed to a purchase of special benefits. * * *

ERIC MONTARTI, A BRIEF LESSON IN TAX INCREMENT FINANCING

http://heartland.org/policy-documents/brief-lesson-tax-increment-financing

The gradual decline of federal involvement in urban redevelopment has led local governments to search for methods of funding commercial and residential projects with sources other than block grants or general revenue sharing. One such method that has become increasingly popular is tax increment financing (TIF).

TIF is often dubbed a "public-private partnership" because it relies on public action to stimulate private investment. The private investment then assists in retiring the public expenditure. Sound complicated? Although the financing of redevelopment often seems like a labyrinth of players, procedures, and payments, TIF is a rather simple financial tool to understand.

How Does TIF Work?

Tax increment financing funds projects through the issuance of bonds that pay for acquisition, demolition, and infrastructure costs associated with redevelopment. In theory, the process is straightforward. A municipal development authority sees a blighted area in which development could occur given enough preparation, such as sewage or sidewalk upgrades, or construction of a parking garage. The local

---

[11] Russ Building Partnership v. City & County of San Francisco, 234 Cal. Rptr. 1 (Cal. Ct. App. 1987).

government bodies that draw taxes from the blighted area agree to the development, a TIF district is drawn around the area, and its property tax base is frozen. The taxes on this frozen base continue to go to the local governments covering the district for a specified time.

The authority then sells bonds to fund the improvements. A private developer, enticed by the improved infrastructure, builds an office building or other commercial or residential structures. The property tax revenues on the blighted land that were flat or declining now increase. This rise, or tax increment, is captured by the municipal development authority and set aside to retire the bonds that funded the improvements. Once the bonds are retired, the higher taxes revert to the city, county, school board, and any other taxing body that covers the district.

TIF began as a match for federal redevelopment funds in California in 1951. As the federal government's role in funding urban renewal projects shrank, TIF became an attractive option for paying for redevelopment. Today, all states except Arizona, Delaware, North Carolina, and West Virginia, have authorized TIF through legislation.

The Costs and Benefits of TIF

TIF helps local governments pay for part of a project without state or federal funds and without payments out of their general budget. Thus, it is referred to as a "self-financing tool" that supposedly distributes new benefits without imposing any costs. However, TIF projects create a situation in which participants are both winners and losers.

Local governments benefit from higher property tax revenues once the bonds are retired and may receive more wage taxes if the development project results in a creation of new jobs. However, the local authorities will have to wait until the TIF bonds are retired and the taxes are returned to the coffers (often twenty years) to pay for any increased service needs within the district. In addition, they will have to cover any shortfall if the projected tax increment fails to materialize.

Taxpayers benefit because a blighted area is improved by the development, and they may see lower taxes in the long run because of the project. On the other hand, taxpayers are the ones underwriting a development project deemed too risky by private investors, and they will have to cover any increased service needs of the TIF district until the debt is retired.

What Makes a Good TIF?

A seemingly neutral development tool, TIF can be bent to the will of its proponents. In Pittsburgh, for example, TIF has largely been used to build retail developments and commercial establishments not in blighted areas, but on some of the most valuable real estate in the region. The most notorious use of TIF was for the construction of a new downtown department store and refurbishment of the company's former store into office space. The price tag for this development was $130 million, not including relocation costs and lost tax revenues. The increased value of the buildings? Only $38 million. At this rate, Pittsburgh will experience rapidly diminishing returns from the overuse of TIF. * * *

2. LAND USE AND "LINKAGE"

This subsection considers the limitations on a city's power to impose costs on selected activities in order to generate revenue. The first excerpt below, taken from an article by Fred Bosselman and Nancy Stroud, analyzes the attempts of San Francisco and Boston to require office building developers to build (or pay for) additional city housing as a condition to allowing them to proceed with their commercial ventures.[19] Is the "rational nexus" test that the authors discuss the same as the test required by Koontz v. St. Johns River Management District, the case that follows the excerpt? Can the kinds of exactions that Bosselman and Stroud describe be defended after Koontz? What impact does Koontz have on the ability of cities to require developers to provide a public benefit— providing public space, improving infrastructure, supporting community services—as a condition of being permitted to build? Underlying Koontz is a concern about the exercise of governmental power against developers. A note following the case raises the opposite concern: the exercise of the power of developers over government decision making.

---

[19] For an analysis of exactions of this kind, see e.g., Timothy Mulvaney, Exactions for the Future, 64 Baylor L. Rev. 511 (2012); David Callies, Mandatory Set-Asides as Development Conditions, 42/43 Urb. Law. 307 (2011); Michael Nadler, The Constitutionality of Community Benefits Agreements: Addressing the Exactions Problem, 43 Urb. Law. 587 (2011); Michelle DaRosa, When are Affordable Housing Exactions an Unconstitutional Taking?, 43 Willamette L. Rev. 453 (2007); Mark Fenster, Regulating Land Use in a Constitutional Shadow: The Institutional Contexts of Exactions, 58 Hastings L.J. 729 (2007); Carlos A. Ball and Laurie Reynolds, Exactions and Burden Distribution in Takings Law, 47 Wm. & Mary L. Rev. 1513 (2006); Mark Fenster, Takings Formalism and Regulatory Formulas: Exactions and the Consequences of Clarity, 92 Cal. L. Rev. 609 (2004); David L. Callies, Unconstitutional Land Development Conditions and the Development Agreement Solution: Bargaining for Public Facilities after Nollan and Dolan, 51 Case W. Res. L. Rev. 663 (2001); Shelley Ross Saxer, Planning Gain, Exactions, and Impact Fees: A Comparative Study of Planning Law in England, Wales, and the United States, 32 Urb. Law. 21 (2000); Molly McUsic, Looking Inside Out: Institutional Analysis and the Problem of Takings, 92 N.W. Univ. L. Rev. 591 (1998); Dan Coenen, Business Subsidies and the Dormant Commerce Clause, 107 Yale L. J. 965 (1998); Nancy Stroud and Susan Trevarthen, Defensible Exactions after Nollan v. California Coastal Commission and Dolan v. City Of Tigard, 25 Stetson L. Rev. 719 (1996); Andrew G. Dietderich, An Egalitarian's Market: The Economics of Inclusionary Zoning Reclaimed, 24 Fordham Urb. L. J. 23 (1996); Douglas Kendall and James Ryan, "Paying" For The Change: Using Eminent Domain to Secure Exactions and Sidestep Nollan and Dolan, 81 Va. L. Rev. 1801 (1995); Alan Altshuler and Jose Gomez-Ibanez, Regulation for Revenue: The Political Economy of Land Use Exactions (1993); Stewart Sterk, Competition Among Municipalities as a Constraint on Land Use Exactions, 45 Vand. L. Rev. 831 (1992); Constraint on Land Use Exactions: Rethinking the Unconstitutional Conditions Doctrine, 91 Colum. L. Rev. 473 (1991); James Frank and Robert Rhodes (eds.), Development Exactions (1987); Robert Ellickson, The Irony of "Inclusionary Zoning," 54 S. Cal. L. Rev. 1167 (1981).

Of course, a fundamental question still remains: is it a good idea for cities to seek to improve their financial condition by imposing charges on selected business activity? Are these kinds of impositions on the private sector counter-productive? Would cities better improve their own (and their citizens') financial status if they adopted the opposite policy—giving businesses inducements to move to town rather than exacting money from them if they do?

FRED BOSSELMAN AND NANCY STROUD, MANDATORY TITHES: THE LEGALITY OF LAND DEVELOPMENT LINKAGE

9 Nova L. J. 383, 390–392, 396–398, 404, 407–411 (1985).

In 1980 the City of San Francisco began implementing a linkage program to encourage office developers to build housing. Specifically, under the Office Housing Production Program developers of office buildings containing more than 50,000 square feet are required to build or finance the amount of new housing in the City that will be needed to house the office workers generated by the development. The requirement is based on the following assumptions: office use generates one employee per two hundred and fifty square feet; forty percent of all office employees in San Francisco reside in San Francisco; and 1.8 working adults occupy each residential unit. This generates a requirement of approximately nine new dwelling units per 10,000 square feet of office space.

The new housing can be for people of any income level, but the developers are given incentives to produce modestly priced housing by allowing them to provide fewer units if the units are for moderate income people. There are no restrictions on the location in San Francisco in which the housing must be built. As alternative to building housing, the developer may contribute to a municipal housing trust—known as the Shared Appreciation Mortgage Pool. The amount of contribution is 6,000 dollars for each housing unit required. The trust funds are used to reduce mortgage payments of low and middle income house buyers. As of April 1984, the City of San Francisco states that its program has generated almost 3000 units of housing, a majority of which were for low and moderate income families. In addition, the trust fund has accrued approximately five million dollars. Despite its success, critics have continued to argue that San Francisco's program ought to be oriented exclusively toward moderately priced housing, and studies are currently underway that may lead to revision of the program.

Boston has now adopted a linkage program based on a somewhat similar analysis. The Boston program applies to developers of office, retail, hotel and institutional facilities and to developers of any use which will reduce the amount of existing low and moderate income housing. The threshold for application of the program is 100,000 square feet of floor area. Each such developer must pay a fee of forty-two dollars per square foot of floor area at the time the certificate of occupancy is issued, and must contract to pay a similar fee in each of the subsequent eleven years. The fee is to be turned over to a neighborhood housing trust to be used for the development of low and moderate income housing. The fee amounts to five dollars per square foot spread out over a twelve-year period in equal payments. The first major project to which the fee is being applied is a 326 million dollar International Place office complex built by the Chiofaro Company in downtown Boston. * * *

In a field such as land use law, where the courts of different states take widely varying positions, it is risky to generalize on the prospects of a new regulatory technique. Nevertheless, there do seem to be some common trends in the analysis of development exactions by the courts of a number of prominent states. An examination of these trends may yield some useful speculation on the way that state courts will determine the validity of linkage programs. * * * Over the past twenty years the courts of virtually all of the states have come to use the term "rational nexus" to describe the test used to measure the validity of development exactions. The early court decisions adopting the rational nexus formulation were viewed by most commentators as a liberation of local governments from the strictures of earlier rules. The scholars who first proposed the test saw it as a "cost-accounting approach" that would make it "possible to determine the costs generated by new residents and thus to avoid charging the newcomers more than a proportionate share." The succeeding years witnessed a number of opinions, particularly in California, that applied the rational nexus test to uphold exactions using the loosest possible type of nexus. This led some commentators to treat the rational nexus test much like the rational basis test for equal protection—as a test the government always passes. At other times the court decisions incorporating the rational nexus test seemed to use it in such a widely varying manner that the term seems to represent nothing more than a loosening of the more restrictive standards used to evaluate the financing of local improvements through special assessments. More recently, however, courts have begun to put more meat on the rational nexus bones so that it becomes the basis for fairly rigorous analysis, in the manner that its original proponents intended, rather than a slogan used to justify any currently popular municipal policy.

The more rigorous version of the rational nexus test, as currently applied, requires a two-part analysis. First, it requires some real showing that the particular development will create a "need" and that the amount of the exaction bears some roughly proportional relationship to the share of the overall need that is contributed by this particular development. The second part of the test requires that the funds or property exacted from the developer be earmarked to be used in a way that provides some degree of "benefit" to the development from which the exaction was received. When the exaction relates to traditional public services and facilities usually provided to new residential development, the courts have generally accepted the proposition that the new development causes some need for new facilities such as streets, sewers, water, parks, and schools. * * *

How will linkage programs fare under the more rigorous analysis required by the evolving test of rational nexus? * * * The extent to which exactions may be imposed for housing-related linkage programs should depend on the local government's ability to show (1) that there is a need for housing, (2) that the need is caused by new development, (3) that the exaction is proportional to the need caused, (4) that the exaction will be used to remedy the need, and (5) that the remedy will benefit the occupants of the new development.

Both Boston and San Francisco experience a high demand for housing, and few would argue that these cities meet any objective test for housing need. Other cities, however, may have a difficult time meeting such a test, particularly if they are experiencing a net outflow of population. Assuming that a need for housing exists, what is its cause? Proof of causation in the development process is no simple matter and can be the source of endless debate. The key issue is the determination of what causes a need for new housing. San Francisco and Boston both believe that the need for housing is stimulated by the new employment that results from the construction of new office buildings. This argument has been challenged at both tiers of its logic. Does the construction of office buildings create jobs? Do jobs create a need for housing? * * *

If the argument that development creates new jobs is accepted, one reaches the issue of whether the new jobs create a need for new housing. The answer is not as simple as it appears. Jobs come and go in a never-ending stream as businesses open and close, expand and contract. The peculiar value of cities may stem from the very flexibility with which their job market can respond to constant change. In such an environment, the addition of any new job does not necessarily mean that the net number of jobs is increased because the job may have been transferred from another location in the community. If the business is moving to promote efficiency in operation, on balance more jobs may have been lost than gained, which would suggest that future out-migration might cause a decline in housing demand.

Even if the total number of jobs does increase, the demand for housing does not necessarily increase along with it. A city's population is constantly changing through in-migration and out-migration, birth and death. Recent years have seen dramatic decreases in average household size, which has to some extent been accompanied by the splitting up of larger dwelling units. The existing housing stock is constantly changing as people build additions or convert housing to non-residential use or vice versa. New housing units are built while others are demolished. Few large cities have trustworthy statistical measures that keep tract of such small-scale changes in the housing supply as conversions and abandonments. The complexity of the housing market does not mean that a relationship between jobs and housing cannot be shown, but it does mean that a fairly sophisticated analysis will be needed * * *. Whether the office-housing linkage in cities like San Francisco or Boston would be able to pass the causation element of a modern rational nexus test will depend on whether the documentation by the planning department of the relationship between office development and the need for housing can survive the scrutiny of litigation.

The causal connection needed to justify inclusionary zoning programs—that new housing creates a need for new low-income housing—is even less clear. Its proponents argue that if developers can be required to provide streets, sewers and other facilities needed to service their development they should also be required to provide housing for the workers who would be needed to operate these facilities and services. If a state accepts even the loosest causal connection as a basis for development exactions this argument may be satisfactory, so it is not surprising to find that California is the site of many inclusionary zoning programs. Other states might find it harder to accept the argument that new housing causes a need for jobs for lower income people.

If a causal relation between the development and the need for housing is established, the next step is to measure the proportional share of the need attributed to the particular development. Would the linkage programs in Boston and San Francisco meet a test of proportionality? Neither program explicitly credits the new development with any of the property tax or other revenue it will generate toward potential housing programs. On the other hand, the city may be able to argue that the exaction is so small in relation to the need that even with such credits the fee is not disproportionately high. * * *

KOONTZ v. ST. JOHNS RIVER WATER MANAGEMENT DISTRICT

Supreme Court of the United States, 2013.
568 U.S. ___, 133 S.Ct. 2586.

JUSTICE ALITO delivered the opinion of the Court.

Our decisions in *Nollan v. California Coastal Comm'n*, 483 U.S. 825 (1987), and *Dolan v. City of Tigard*, 512 U.S. 374 (1994), provide important protection against the misuse of the power of land-use regulation. In those cases, we held that a unit of government may not condition the approval of a land-use permit on the owner's relinquishment of a portion of his property unless there is a "nexus" and "rough proportionality" between the government's demand and the effects of the proposed land use. In this case, the St. Johns River Water Management District believes that it circumvented *Nollan* and *Dolan* because of the way in which it structured its handling of a permit application submitted by Coy Koontz, Sr. * * *

In 1972, petitioner purchased an undeveloped 14.9-acre tract of land on the south side of Florida State Road 50, a divided four-lane highway east of Orlando. * * * Although largely classified as wetlands by the State, the northern section drains well * * *. The same year that petitioner purchased his property, Florida enacted the Water Resources Act * * *. Under the Act, a landowner wishing to undertake * * * construction must obtain from the relevant district a Management and Storage of Surface Water (MSSW) permit, which may impose "such reasonable conditions" on the permit as are "necessary to assure" that construction will "not be harmful to the water resources of the district." In 1984, in an effort to protect the State's rapidly diminishing wetlands, the Florida Legislature passed the Warren S. Henderson Wetlands Protection Act, which made it illegal for anyone to "dredge or fill in, on, or over surface waters" without a Wetlands Resource Management (WRM) permit. Under the Henderson Act, permit applicants are required to provide "reasonable assurance" that proposed construction on wetlands is "not contrary to the public interest," as defined by an enumerated list of criteria. Consistent with the Henderson Act, the St. Johns River Water Management District, the district with jurisdiction over petitioner's land, requires that permit applicants wishing to build on wetlands offset the resulting environmental damage by creating, enhancing, or preserving wetlands elsewhere.

Petitioner decided to develop the 3.7-acre northern section of his property, and in 1994 he applied to the District for MSSW and WRM permits. Under his proposal, petitioner would have raised the elevation of the northernmost section of his land to make it suitable for a building * * *. To mitigate the environmental effects of his proposal, petitioner offered to foreclose any possible future development of the approximately 11-acre southern section of his land by deeding to the District a conservation easement on that portion of his property. The District considered the 11-acre conservation easement to be inadequate, and it informed petitioner that it would approve construction only if he agreed to one of two concessions. First, the District proposed that petitioner reduce the size of his development to 1 acre and deed to the District a conservation easement on the remaining 13.9 acres. * * * In the alternative, the District told petitioner that he could proceed with the development as proposed, building on 3.7 acres and deeding a conservation easement to the government on the remainder of the property, if he also agreed to hire contractors to make improvements to District-owned land several miles away. * * * [T]hose projects would have enhanced approximately 50 acres of District-owned wetlands. When the District asks permit applicants to fund offsite mitigation work, its policy is never to require any particular offsite project, and it did not do so here. Instead, the District said that it "would also favorably consider" alternatives to its suggested offsite mitigation projects if petitioner proposed something "equivalent." Believing the District's demands for mitigation to be excessive in light of the environmental effects that his building proposal would have caused, petitioner filed suit * * *.

We have said in a variety of contexts that "the government may not deny a benefit to a person because he exercises a constitutional right." *Regan v. Taxation With Representation of Wash.*, 461 U.S. 540, 545 (1983). * * * *Nollan* and *Dolan* "involve a special application" of this doctrine that protects the Fifth Amendment right to just compensation for property the government takes when owners apply for land-use permits. Our decisions in those cases reflect two realities of the permitting process. The first is that land-use permit applicants are especially vulnerable to the type of coercion that the unconstitutional conditions doctrine prohibits because the government often has broad discretion to deny a permit that is worth far more than property it would like to take. By conditioning a building permit on the owner's deeding over a public right-of-way, for example, the government can pressure an owner into voluntarily giving up property for which the Fifth Amendment would otherwise require just compensation. So long as the building permit is more valuable than any just compensation the owner could hope to receive for the right-of-way, the owner is likely to accede to the government's demand, no matter how unreasonable. Extortionate demands of this sort frustrate the Fifth Amendment right to just compensation, and the unconstitutional conditions doctrine prohibits them.

A second reality of the permitting process is that many proposed land uses threaten to impose costs on the public that dedications of property can offset. Where a building proposal would substantially increase traffic congestion, for example, officials might condition permit approval on the owner's agreement to deed over the land needed to widen a public road. Respondent argues that a similar rationale justifies the exaction at issue here: petitioner's proposed construction project, it submits, would destroy wetlands on his property, and in order to compensate for this loss, respondent demands that he enhance wetlands elsewhere. Insisting that landowners internalize the negative externalities of their conduct is a hallmark of responsible land-use policy, and we have long sustained such regulations against constitutional attack. See *Village of Euclid v. Ambler Realty Co.*, 272 U.S. 365 (1926).

Nollan and *Dolan* accommodate both realities * * *. Our precedents thus enable permitting authorities to insist that applicants bear the full costs of their proposals while still forbidding the government from engaging in "out-and-out . . . extortion" that would thwart the Fifth Amendment right to just compensation. * * * The principles that undergird our decisions in *Nollan* and *Dolan* do not change depending on whether the government approves a permit on the condition that the applicant turn over property or denies a permit because the applicant refuses to do so. * * * [T]he impermissible denial of a governmental benefit is a constitutionally cognizable injury. Nor does it make a difference, as respondent suggests, that the government might have been able to deny petitioner's application outright without giving him the option of securing a permit by agreeing to spend money to improve public lands. See *Penn Central Transp. Co. v. New York City*, 438 U.S. 104 (1978). * * * Even if respondent would have been entirely within its rights in denying the permit for some other reason, that greater authority does not imply a lesser power to condition permit approval on petitioner's forfeiture of his constitutional rights. * * *

We turn to the Florida Supreme Court's * * * holding that petitioner's claim fails because respondent asked him to spend money rather than give up an easement on his land. * * * We note as an initial matter that if we accepted this argument it would be very easy for land-use permitting officials to evade the limitations of *Nollan* and *Dolan*. Because the government need only provide a permit applicant with one alternative that satisfies the nexus and rough proportionality standards, a permitting authority wishing to exact an easement could simply give the owner a choice of either surrendering an easement or making a payment equal to the easement's value. Such so-called "in lieu of" fees are utterly commonplace, and they are functionally equivalent to other types of land use exactions. For that reason and those that follow, we reject respondent's argument and hold that so-called "monetary exactions" must satisfy the nexus and rough proportionality requirements of *Nollan* and *Dolan*. * * *

The fulcrum this case turns on is the direct link between the government's demand and a specific parcel of real property. Because of that direct link, this case implicates the central concern of *Nollan* and *Dolan*: the risk that the government may use its substantial power and discretion in land-use permitting to pursue governmental ends that lack an essential nexus and rough proportionality to the effects of the proposed new use of the specific property at issue, thereby diminishing without justification the value of the property. * * * [W]hen the government commands the relinquishment of funds linked to a specific, identifiable property interest such as a bank account or parcel of real property, a "per se [takings] approach" is the proper mode of analysis under the Court's precedent. * * *

Respondent and the dissent argue that if monetary exactions are made subject to scrutiny under *Nollan* and *Dolan*, then there will be no principled way of distinguishing impermissible land-use exactions from property taxes. * * * It is beyond dispute that "[t]axes and user fees . . . are not 'takings.' " * * * [T]he need to distinguish taxes from takings is not a creature of our holding today that monetary exactions are subject to scrutiny under *Nollan* and *Dolan*. Rather, the problem is inherent in this Court's long-settled view that property the government could constitutionally demand through its taxing power can also be taken by eminent domain. * * * For present purposes, it suffices to say that despite having long recognized that "the power of taxation should not be confused with the power of eminent domain," *Houck v. Little River Drainage Dist.*, 239 U.S. 254, 264 (1915), we have had little trouble distinguishing between the two.

Finally, we disagree with the dissent's forecast that our decision will work a revolution in land use law by depriving local governments of the ability to charge reasonable permitting fees. Numerous courts—including courts in many of our Nation's most populous States—have confronted constitutional challenges to monetary exactions over the last two decades and applied the standard from *Nollan* and *Dolan* or something like it. Yet the "significant practical harm" the dissent predicts has not come to pass. * * * [T]he dissent's argument that land use permit applicants need no further protection when the government demands money is really an argument for overruling *Nollan* and *Dolan*. * * * We hold that the government's demand for property from a land-use permit applicant must satisfy the requirements of *Nollan* and *Dolan* even when the government denies the permit and even when its demand is for money. The Court expresses no view on the merits of petitioner's claim that respondent's actions here failed to comply with the principles set forth in this opinion and those two cases. * * *

JUSTICE KAGAN, with whom JUSTICE GINSBURG, JUSTICE BREYER, and JUSTICE SOTOMAYOR join, dissenting. * * *

Nollan and *Dolan* * * * serve * * * to stop the government from imposing an "unconstitutional condition"—a requirement that a person give up his constitutional right to receive just compensation "in exchange for a discretionary benefit" having "little or no relationship" to the property taken. Accordingly, the *Nollan-Dolan* test applies only when the property the government demands during the permitting process is the kind it otherwise would have to pay for—or, put differently, when the appropriation of that property, outside the permitting process, would constitute a taking. * * * The key question then is: Independent of the permitting process, does requiring a person to pay money to the government, or spend money on its behalf, constitute a taking requiring just compensation? Only if the answer is yes does the *Nollan-Dolan* test apply.

But we have already answered that question no. *Eastern Enterprises v. Apfel*, 524 U.S. 498 (1998) * * * involved a federal statute requiring a former mining company to pay a large sum of money for the health benefits of retired employees. Five Members of the Court determined that the law did not effect a taking, distinguishing between the appropriation of a specific property interest and the imposition of an order to pay money. * * * [A] requirement that a person pay money to repair public wetlands is not a taking. Such an order does not affect a "specific and identified propert[y] or property right[ ]"; it simply "imposes an obligation to perform an act" (the improvement of wetlands) that costs money. To be sure, when a person spends money on the government's behalf, or pays money directly to the government, it "will reduce [his] net worth"—but that "can be said of any law which has an adverse economic effect" on someone. Because the government is merely imposing a "general liability" to pay money—and therefore is "indifferent as to how the regulated entity elects to comply or the property it uses to do so"—the order to repair wetlands, viewed independent of the permitting process, does not constitute a taking. And that means the order does not trigger the *Nollan-Dolan* test, because it does not force Koontz to relinquish a constitutional right. * * * The majority thus falls back on the sole way the District's alleged demand related to a property interest: The demand arose out of the permitting process for Koontz's land. But under the analytic framework that *Nollan* and *Dolan* established, that connection alone is insufficient to trigger heightened scrutiny. * * * *Nollan* and *Dolan* apply only if the demand at issue would have violated the Constitution independent of that proposed exchange. Or put otherwise, those cases apply only if the demand would have constituted a taking when executed outside the permitting process. And here, under *Apfel*, it would not.

The majority's approach, on top of its analytic flaws, threatens significant practical harm. By applying *Nollan* and *Dolan* to permit conditions requiring monetary payments—with no express limitation except as to taxes—the majority extends the Takings Clause, with its notoriously "difficult" and "perplexing" standards, into the very heart of local land-use regulation and service delivery. Cities and towns across the nation impose many kinds of permitting fees every day. Some enable a government to mitigate a new development's impact on the community, like increased traffic or pollution—or destruction of wetlands. Others cover the direct costs of providing services like sewage or water to the development. Still others are meant to limit the number of landowners who engage in a certain activity, as fees for liquor licenses do. All now must meet *Nollan* and *Dolan*'s nexus and proportionality tests. The Federal Constitution thus will decide whether one town is overcharging for sewage, or another is setting the price to sell liquor too high. And the flexibility of state and local governments to take the most routine actions to enhance their communities will diminish accordingly. * * *

At bottom, the majority's analysis seems to grow out of a yen for a prophylactic rule: Unless *Nollan* and *Dolan* apply to monetary demands, the majority worries, "land-use permitting officials" could easily "evade the limitations" on exaction of real property interests that those decisions impose. But that is a prophylaxis in search of a problem. No one has presented evidence that in the many States declining to apply heightened scrutiny to permitting fees, local officials routinely short-circuit *Nollan* and *Dolan* to extort the surrender of real property interests having no relation to a development's costs. And if officials were to impose a fee as a contrivance to take an easement (or other real property right), then a court could indeed apply *Nollan* and *Dolan*. * * *

I also would affirm the judgment below for * * * [an] independent reason[ ], * * * even assuming that a demand for money can trigger *Nollan* and *Dolan*. * * * [T]he District never demanded that Koontz give up anything (including money) as a condition for granting him a permit. * * * Rather than reject the applications * * * the District suggested to Koontz ways he could modify them to meet legal requirements. * * * The District never made any particular demand respecting an off-site project (or anything else); as Koontz testified at trial, that possibility was presented only in broad strokes, "[n]ot in any great detail." * * * Instead, the District suggested to Koontz several non-exclusive ways to make his applications conform to state law. * * * [T]his case well illustrates the danger of extending *Nollan* and *Dolan* beyond their proper compass. Consider the matter from the standpoint of the District's lawyer. The District, she learns, has found that Koontz's permit applications do not satisfy legal requirements. It can deny the permits on that basis; or it can suggest ways for Koontz to bring his applications into compliance. If every suggestion could become the subject of a lawsuit under *Nollan* and *Dolan*, the lawyer can give but one recommendation: Deny the permits, without giving Koontz any advice—even if he asks for guidance. * * * Nothing in the Takings Clause requires that folly. * * *

NOTE ON THE ALLOCATION OF POWER

The Court in *Koontz* was concerned about the excessive pressure that the government can exercise over private individuals by imposing conditions on its granting of permits. One might also be concerned about the excessive pressure that private individuals might exert over the government by imposing conditions on an offer of money to support government projects. Consider, for example, the situation presented to the Supreme Judicial Court of Massachusetts in Durand v. IDC Bellingham, 440 Mass. 45, 793 N.E.2d 359 (2003). IDC owned a power plant in the town of Bellingham, and it began discussions with town officials about opening a second one. The possibility of IDC offering possible financial inducements to the town with regard to its proposed expansion was raised. Town officials mentioned that the town needed a new high school but was facing an $8 million dollar shortfall in its plans to construct one. Shortly thereafter, IDC's president publicly announced it would make a gift of $8 million dollars to the town if it decided to build the second plant, the plant received the necessary financing and approvals, and the plant operated successfully for a year. The offer was discussed in an open town meeting, and IDC made clear that, although the high school had been mentioned, the promised gift could be used by the town for any municipal purpose. After preliminary work on the plant, IDC applied to the town's zoning board of appeals for five special permits required to build the second plant; IDC's application was approved. Landowners then filed suit, claiming that the zoning approvals were illegal because the "extraneous consideration" of the gift was an impermissible ingredient in the towns' zoning decision. The Massachusetts Supreme Judicial Court rejected the landowners' argument and upheld the zoning approval. The court found that the zoning approval was a valid legislative act—that it was not arbitrary or unreasonable under state law. "We * * * find no persuasive authority," the court said, "for the proposition that an otherwise valid zoning enactment is invalid if it is in any way prompted or encouraged by a public benefit voluntarily offered."

Does the *Durand* decision seem right? It is not uncommon for private individuals to offer cities money to support public services, such as a public school or public park. One does not have to be cynical: sometimes these gifts can come without strings attached. But sometimes the gift-giver has an agenda. Is there—should there be—a limit on the ability of cities to receive private gifts? Is there—should there be—a limit on the kind of conditions that the gift-giver can impose? In *Durand*, there was no contract exchanging zoning approval for the gift. The gift was dependent on the plant being built, but it was a voluntary gift. The reason the city welcomes these kinds of gifts, one should recognize, is the same as the reason it seeks exactions: the legal and political limits on taxation (see above) make private support for public benefits very attractive.

3. CITY PROPERTY OWNERSHIP

In this subsection, we examine the possibility of advancing city welfare by increasing the economic power of cities rather than (as in the previous sections) having cities depend on income derived from taxing (or imposing charges on) the economic power of others.[20] One way to increase

---

[20] For a classic argument for such an approach, see Frederic Howe, The City: The Hope of Democracy (1905).

city influence and income is through a greater use of the entitlements that cities have as property owners.

The first excerpt below is a summary of Hendrik Hartog's important book, Public Property and Private Power: The Corporation of the City of New York in American Law, 1730–1870 (1983). Professor Hartog emphasizes the historic importance of city property ownership as a vehicle for the exercise of power by the City of New York.[21] An excerpt from a book by David Osborne and Ted Gaebler then suggests that the idea that cities can derive income from property ownership rather than from taxes is not simply a matter of history. Osborne and Gaebler list a multitude of current profit-making ventures by American cities. One question one might ask about the kinds of city activity that these two excerpts describe is whether "public" competition with "private" business is desirable. Should cities be allowed to engage in business—in *any* kind of business? A second line of inquiry addresses the legal rules that currently govern city business activity. The cases that follow the Osborne and Gaebler excerpt explore two types of city businesses: selling electrical services in competition with a private utility company and operating a city garbage collection service in a manner that threatens to drive a private competitor out of business. Do the cases adequately deal with the complexities involved in city business activity? What rules *should* govern city competition with private business?

GERALD FRUG, PROPERTY AND POWER: HARTOG ON THE LEGAL HISTORY OF NEW YORK CITY
1984 Am.Bar Foundation Research J. 673, 673–678.

Public Property and Private Power

Hendrik Hartog's *Public Property and Private Power* describes the "conceptual transformation" that radically altered the legal status and powers of the city of New York in the eighteenth and nineteenth centuries. According to this interesting and well-written account, the legal doctrines that affected New York City changed over a 140-year period in two significant ways. First, the legal system fractured the originally close connection between the city's property ownership and its power. Although in the eighteenth century the city was a corporation whose "property and governmental rights were blurred and mixed," in the nineteenth century it was stripped of its ability to use its ownership of property as a tool of governance. Second, the eighteenth-century conception of the city as neither a public nor a private entity was replaced with an understanding of it as a "public" corporation whose powers were

---

[21] For an analysis of Professor Hartog's argument, see, e.g., Joan Williams, Review: The Development of the Public/Private Distinction in American Law, 64 Tex. L. Rev. 225 (1985); Carol Rose, Public Property, Old and New, 79 Nw. U. L. Rev. 216 (1984).

significantly different from those of "private" business corporations. Thus Professor Hartog describes the transformation of the city's legal status in terms of two pairs of legal concepts: property and power, and public and private.

Professor Hartog organizes his account of the changing legal status of the city into three periods: the eighteenth century, the early nineteenth century, and the mid-nineteenth century In the eighteenth century, he tells us, the City of New York was not characterized as a "public" as distinguished from a "private" corporation because no such general conceptual categories of corporations existed. Instead, every corporation, including the city, was viewed as a unique institution whose powers were understandable only in terms of the specific charter granted it by the state. The most important of New York City's charters, the one granted by Governor John Montgomerie in 1730, allowed the city to pass regulations for the public good, run jails and courthouses, maintain an exclusive franchise to operate ferries between Manhattan and Long Island, and own and manage a vast amount of real estate—including most of Manhattan Island north of Canal Street, the underwater land that surrounded Manhattan, and the waterfront of Brooklyn. All of these powers were understood together as the city's property. Accordingly, the city had the autonomy allowed any other property owner to shape its own identity independent of state control; its status as a property owner gave the city its power. This was true even though the city's authority to act as a property owner was based on a delegation of governmental power; such a delegation was the source of the authority exercised by every corporate property owner.

Of all the city's grants of power from the state, the most important was its ability to own real property. In the eighteenth century, city officials, like the officials of other corporations, did not concentrate their attention on providing services to the public; instead, "[t]he proper business of the [city] corporation was the management, care, and disposal of the real estate it owned." In part, this emphasis stemmed from the fact that real estate was the source of the city's revenue; until the 1760s, the city rarely resorted to direct taxation to provide city income. But the more important reason for the city's concentration on the management of its real property, according to Professor Hartog, was that the city used its property rights as a major vehicle for performing its functions of planning and governance. In the eighteenth century, there was no distinction between a corporation's property ownership and its governmental power, between property and sovereignty. Far from being divided into separate components—a private sphere of property management and a public sphere of government—the city used its property as a way of making governmental policy.

Professor Hartog's most original contribution to the study of the eighteenth-century city is his discussion of how New York City used its disposal of waterlots in lower Manhattan as a vehicle for effectuating public policy. In the deeds conveying waterlots to wealthy and favored citizens, the city imposed conditions requiring the purchasers to engage in construction—of streets and docks, for example—timed to coincide with the city's development plans. In this way, the city shifted the burden of expensive capital projects on to private individuals and relieved the government both of the cost of the projects and the need to build a bureaucracy to implement them. Moreover, it redistributed wealth from the rich to the larger community without transgressing the political ideology demanding limits on the role of government in society.

> Waterlot grants offered the possibility of achieving positive governmental goals—paving the streets, developing the harbor—at a time when there was no theory of direct government action. How do you get something done if you do not know how, or rather, if you cannot conceive of doing it yourself? You get someone else to do it for you * * * a chartered city with a substantial estate could use its wealth to achieve goals, to induce change * * *. The promised reward of the waterlot (and its profits) gave the city the power to coerce grantees to do things that they were not obliged as citizens to do.

By the early nineteenth century, this vision of the city as a legitimate property owner capable of wielding power through the exercise of its property rights had virtually disappeared. Instead of its property being the source of city power, the city became divided into separate spheres: its "public" nature allowed it to exercise "power," while its separate "private" sphere allowed it to exercise "property rights." Indeed, property ownership, rather than enhancing the city's governmental powers, became an anomaly: property ownership seemed to make the corporation both a public and a private institution simultaneously. Accordingly, the corporation's exercise of property rights became more narrowly construed, and arguments were advanced to take the city out of the landowning business altogether. The use of city property was limited to its generation of revenue, and waterlot grants were awarded without conditions. "The corporation of the city of New York had become a public institution, financed largely by public taxation and devoting its energy to distinctively public concerns."

Even the source of the city's ability to exercise power had changed. The city began to seek the enactment of specific state legislation to authorize its actions even when authority for its actions might have been found in the Montgomerie charter.

By the early nineteenth century, some city leaders had already concluded that "it would be altogether unsafe and erroneous to resort to the charter solely, upon any question of power, or its mode of exercise." As a government, its only "charter" was the accumulated relevant statutes of the New York legislature. The Montgomerie Charter still protected the city from legislative intervention into its property; but it was only the starting point for an evolving city government.

For the first third of the nineteenth century, these state legislative acts were "invariably drafted by city employees" and were passed only with the consent of the city. Thus no state infringement of city autonomy seemed to result from the practice of petitioning the state to authorize city activity. Indeed, reliance on state authorization seemed a more secure basis for city power than its corporate status, given the widespread antagonism of the time to the monopolistic power of corporate enterprise. Moreover, reliance on state legislative authorization allowed the city to avoid its previously excessive dependence on wealthy private citizens for effectuation of city policy. By creating a "public" sphere separate from that of the private interests of its citizens, the city could avoid being corrupted by private interests and ensure that it did not favor some of its citizens over others. It could instead become "an autonomous planner creating a stable context for private decision making."

For Professor Hartog, this early nineteenth-century vision of the city's "public" role is symbolized by its decision to obtain legislative authorization to lay out the streets of Manhattan according to a uniform rectangular grid. The city's imposition of a uniform plan for Manhattan, regardless of private boundaries, topographical differences, or potential uses of the land, was a bold assertion of public power. Such an exercise of "public" authority was sharply distinguishable from the kind of "private" authority property owners had to make decisions about their own property. Only the city could create the proper structure for land development; only property owners could make choices about the nature of that development. "The formal design of the city was public; but that design remained only a context for private decision making." Indeed the rhetoric used to defend the city's plan was

> a model for the justification of republican public authority: deferential toward private initiative, concerned to remain within the limits of proper public authority, yet insistent on the legitimacy of public control of a public sphere. The commissioners left largely unstated their own preferences as to the most proper, appropriate, or attractive development of city streets, for those were all areas of private choice. But they made it absolutely clear that private landowners had no right to expect

the map to incorporate their particular plans or streets, for that was an area of public choice.

Not only was the city corporation divided into its public (governmental) and private (property owning) spheres, but all social decision making was organized around the same public/private distinction: some kinds of decisions were appropriate for government while others were appropriate for property owners, and the two kinds of decisions constantly had to be distinguished from each other.

Yet in the early nineteenth century one important aspect of the public/private distinction had still not been developed: there were still no separate bodies of law regulating "municipal corporations" and business corporations. Both kinds of corporations remained part of an "undifferentiated 'law' of corporations." As a result, the Corporation of the City of New York retained a number of the advantages and disadvantages generally attributed to corporations. All corporations retained areas of autonomy immune from state control, and all corporations were limited to those powers specifically delegated to them by the state, whether through legislation or the award of a charter. Indeed, legal theorists contrasted the Corporation of the City of New York not with other kinds of corporations but with unincorporated cities and towns. These entities, unlike corporations, were subject to unrestricted legislative power; moreover, unlike corporations, their authority was not limited to carrying out specific delegations from the state. It was not until the 1820s that the distinction between incorporated cities and unincorporated towns disappeared. Even then, important legal questions remained unresolved: Would the new general category of local governments be subject to unlimited state power (like unincorporated towns) or have rights against the state (like corporations)? Would local governments be able to exercise the full range of governmental power (like the state) or be limited to narrowly construed delegations (like corporations)?

The answers to these questions were not settled until the mid-nineteenth century when the courts began to develop a uniform system of local government law. In the final part of his book, Professor Hartog describes this development, one that made yet another dramatic change in the legal conception of city power. The courts held that the state had an unlimited amount of control over cities (making cities, unlike private corporations, merely creatures of the state) and that cities could not exercise the full range of governmental powers (making cities more like private corporations than the state).

> In place of local autonomy and political decentralization, the new law of municipal corporations posed the absolute centrality of state power and the insignificance of local publics in the political order. In place of the distinctive chartered rights of cities and the

particular customs of local communities—both of which earlier served to frustrate the designs of central authorities—the new "law" held localities to explicit delegations of legislative power.

Moreover, rather than following the tradition of judicial deference to legislative decision making, the courts began to scrutinize delegations of power to local governments, construing narrowly the powers of municipal corporations (just as they did the powers of business corporations). The courts interposed themselves between the legislature and the cities, interpreting local power in terms of uniform judicial standards rather than particular legislative intent.

One method the courts used to regulate the cities was to redefine the ways cities were simultaneously public and private. Rather than seeing the private sphere as based on a local government's ownership of private property, the courts divided city governance functions into "proprietary" and "governmental" functions. If a function was defined as proprietary, the courts could treat a city like a private corporation; conversely, if a function was defined as governmental, the courts could treat a city as being just like the state. Courts even treated certain functions—such as the building of an aqueduct for New York City's water supply—as proprietary for some purposes and as governmental for others. By asserting that the city was acting as a proprietor in building the aqueduct, the courts denied the city the defense of sovereign immunity when it was sued in tort; by labeling the operation of the aqueduct a governmental function, the courts could ensure control over how the city operated the aqueduct.

This new form of applying the public/private distinction to the city put a double constraint on city power. In refusing to allow the city to protect its power under sovereign immunity by labeling activities "proprietary," the courts assumed that only in its public capacity was the city exercising independent power: "[They] identified a municipal corporation as a public entity for purposes of liability when it exercised judgment and discretion and characterized it as a 'private' entity whenever it was bound strictly by the dictates of legislation. As an autonomous decision maker, it was public; as a dependent agency it was private."

But when dealing with the question of state authority over city activities, it became clear that the "public" nature of the city's power also required control. For example, Professor Hartog describes how New York City's franchise to operate ferries to Brooklyn, considered by Chancellor Kent in 1836 to be " 'an absolute grant of vested property, or an estate in fee, which could not lawfully be questioned or disturbed, except by due process of law,' " became understood later in the century to be part of the public sphere of the corporation, subject to legislative repeal and intervention. "By 1865," he writes, "the corporation of the city of New York had become legally indistinguishable from propertyless institutions of derivative public administration * * *. [E]ven its corporate capacity to own property existed only as a function of its representation of the interests of the state." During the same time that the courts were tightening their restrictions on local authority, the state legislature stopped seeking the city's consent before enacting legislation affecting local interests and, in 1857, declared that it was free to intervene at will in the city's affairs. "From then on, 'domination over the affairs of New York City went merrily and perniciously on from session to session of the legislature.'"

In summary, then, Professor Hartog describes a dramatic transformation of the legal status of the City of New York during the years 1730 to 1870:

> The eighteenth-century corporation had regarded property as essential to an autonomous government. The corporation of the early nineteenth century had worked to separate corporate property from dependent republican government, leaving that property in a residual sphere of private, corporate autonomy. But (by the mid-nineteenth century) * * * the private sphere of the corporation (as distinguished from the "proprietary" sphere of the municipal corporation) no longer existed.

New York City changed from being considered a corporation exercising the rights of a property owner to being considered a governmental entity threatening to the rights of property owners, one that required strict legislative and judicial supervision. In its status as a "creature of the state," the city could still sometimes act in a proprietary capacity and thus be seen as more a private corporation than a government. But even this private aspect of its nature no longer gave the city substantial protection from state control. * * *

DAVID OSBORNE AND TED GAEBLER, ENTERPRISING GOVERNMENT: EARNING RATHER THAN SPENDING

From David Osborne and Ted Gaebler, Reinventing Government.
Pp. 196–197, 200–202, 214–216 (1992).

Pressed hard by the tax revolts of the 1970s and 1980s and the fiscal crisis of the early 1990s, entrepreneurial governments are increasingly * * * searching for nontax revenues. They are measuring their return on investment. They are recycling their money, finding the 15 or 20 percent that can be redirected. Some are even running for-profit enterprises.

> The Milwaukee Metropolitan Sewerage District transforms 60,000 tons of sewage sludge into fertilizer every year and sells it—generating $7.5 million in revenue.

Phoenix earns $750,000 a year by siphoning off the methane gas generated by a large wastewater treatment plant and selling it to the city of Mesa, for home heating and cooking.

Chicago turned a $2 million annual cost into a $2 million source of revenue by contracting with a private company to tow away abandoned cars. The city once spent $24 per car to tow cars; now a private company pays $25 a car for the privilege.

The St. Louis County Police developed a system that allows officers to call in their reports, rather than write them up. The department then licensed the software to a private company—earning $25,000 every time it sells to another police department.

The Washington State ferry system generated $1 million a year in new revenues during the early 1980s by rebidding its food service contract; more than $150,000 a year by bidding out a contract to sell advertising in the terminal building; and another $150,000 a year by letting a contract to operate duty-free shops on its two international boats.

Paulding County, Georgia, built a 244-bed prison, when it needed only 60 extra beds, so it could charge other jurisdictions $35 a night to handle their overflow. In the jail's first year of business, it brought in $1.4 million, $200,000 more than its operating costs.

Enterprising police departments in California are earning money by renting out motel rooms as weekend jails. The courts often let those convicted of drunk driving serve their time on weekends. So some police departments reserve blocks of cheap motel rooms, pay someone to sit outside and make sure everyone stays in their room, and rent the rooms to convicted drivers as jail cells at $75 a night. * * *

Fairfield [California] * * * [was] the city that invented the mission-driven budget * * *. In 1976, a developer approached then city manager Gale Wilson for permission to develop a small shopping center. Wilson and his staff believed that Fairfield—which sits astride Highway 80, halfway between San Francisco and Sacramento—would grow into a perfect location for a large regional mall (Fairfield had 51,700 people in 1976; today it has 80,000.) So they created a Redevelopment Authority, which bought 90 acres of land for $3.6 million, sold 48 to the developer for a $2 million profit, and built a new highway interchange. The developer put in a "super regional mall" with more than a million square feet and five large department stores. As part of the agreement, Fairfield negotiated a piece of the action: 10 to 17 percent of net cash flow for 65 years. When Proposition 13 limited the city's take from property taxes, Wilson negotiated a 55-cent-per-acre assessment for off-site improvements—roads, sewers, and the like—for 25 years. It now brings in between $400,000 and $500,000 a year and covers the cost of the bonds floated to pay for the improvements.

After the mall opened, in 1985, the city began leasing and selling off its other parcels. Overall, according to Fairfield's calculations, its investment of $8 million in land purchases and relocation costs had generated, by mid-1991, $6.4 million in sales, $9.4 million in increased property taxes, and $15.4 million in sales taxes. The profit-sharing agreement is generating $120,000 a year, and ground leases from the second major parcel developed, the Gateway Plaza, will kick in soon. The city still owns about 35 acres, which it intends to sell or lease as the market can absorb them.

Fairfield has since taken a similar approach to its other development projects. When a developer tried to build a large residential development just outside city limits, for instance, the city backed a county proposition that made it difficult to develop land outside a city, then proposed a deal that convinced the developer to build in Fairfield. The city built a public golf course around which the developer could build, then allowed him to increase the number of homes in the project from 800 to 1,200. The only catch: the developer had to donate land for the golf course and a public school, build a public road into the project, and put in the storm drainage system.

The city used revenue from the course and clubhouse to pay off the $7 million it borrowed to build the course. The result: The developer got higher value building lots, because they surrounded a golf course, and the city built its first public golf course with no subsidy from the taxpayers.

The project worked so well, in fact, that the city then negotiated a similar deal with another developer—in which the developer not only donated land but built a reservoir. As we write, Fairfield is studying the option of selling the first course and investing the profit of $20 to $25 million in some other amenity, such as a sports complex. "We intervened in the market by creating more value," explains City Manager Charlie Long. "The golf course created higher home prices because it created more value, and we then take that increment of profit and put it in the public sector to pay for more amenities."

Lest you think this kind of entrepreneurship can happen only in California, Cincinnati earns 17 percent of the profits from a hotel and office complex in the city center, for which the city assembled the land and arranged the financing; San Antonio is a partner in several real estate projects, including a Sheraton hotel; and the Metropolitan Area Transit Authority in Washington, D.C., has developed lucrative real estate above and around some of its subway stations. Orlando, Florida, even struck a deal in which a developer built a new city hall.

Orlando Mayor Bill Frederick, first elected in 1980 in the wake of a nationwide tax revolt, understood that his citizens wanted lower taxes. (He pushed property taxes down by 29 percent over the next decade.) He knew that if he wanted to accomplish anything, he would have "to look to new solutions—especially when it comes to finances."

"If Orlando had taken 5 percent of its General Fund revenue in 1980 and used it to finance a 30-year series of bonds," he explains, "we could have built only $30 million worth of capital projects." Instead Orlando used a series of profit-making authorities and funds to build nearly $2.5 billion worth of facilities—an expanded airport, a new basketball arena, wastewater treatment plants, a performing arts center—with virtually no subsidy from local taxpayers.

The crowning achievement was city hall. To avoid dipping into general revenues, the city used seven acres around the old city hall as a lure—asking developers to compete for the right to develop the land. The winner, Lincoln Property Company, agreed to build a $32.5 million, 246,000-square-foot, state-of-the-art city hall, complete with its own closed-circuit television system. In exchange, it got the right to build two office towers adjacent to city hall. Ground rents from the towers will pay off the city's construction bonds.

In addition, the city will receive 20 percent of the net proceeds from office and retail rents over a set income level, plus 20 percent of the proceeds from any sale or refinancing. (If Lincoln fails to build city hall to the city's satisfaction, or fails to begin paying ground rents on the first office tower in 1992 and the second in 1996, it will forfeit a $750,000 deposit.) The city expects the project's revenues to pay off its 30-year bonds in 10 to 12 years. * * *

The San Francisco suburb of San Bruno owns its cable television system * * *. David Thomas, who runs it, is a typical entrepreneur. He has pride of ownership. He is mission-driven. He plans ahead. He strives to please his customers. He is aware of his competitors—and he beats the pants off them. In 1991, San Bruno charged its 11,200 subscribers $12.55 for a 31-channel package.

Private cable companies in the county charged an average of $19.57 for the comparable package. Yet even at San Bruno's low price, the system generated enough money to upgrade all its hardware—cables, boxes, everything—every 10 years, without borrowing a dime. (This is after it returns 5 percent of gross revenues to the city.) "We don't use the word *profit*," Thomas smiles, "but we do use the term retained earnings."

We saw the same mind-set in Santa Clara. Like San Bruno's cable company, Santa Clara's publicly owned electric utility returns 5 percent of gross revenues to the city, but still charges 30 to 40 percent less than its private competitor does in surrounding communities. Thirty years ago, it spearheaded a group of other municipal utilities to form the Northern California Power Agency, which then built a large, 200-megawatt geothermal energy project, as well as the last major dam in California. When tax credits favored wind energy, the utility bought 2,600 acres and leased them out to private companies to build windmills.

Santa Clara's Water and Sewer Utility created a solar division—in effect, the nation's first solar utility. It provides hot water units for apartment buildings and swimming pools. The utility buys, installs, and maintains the equipment, charging the customer a monthly fee for six months of the year to cover the costs.

When the city's housing market became extremely tight, Santa Clara's Redevelopment Agency leased the existing city golf course to developers, who are putting in 2,000 apartment units; used the lease revenues to pay for a new golf and tennis club built over the city's old landfill; and put in wells to tap the natural gas generated by the buried garbage. The new course anchors the Santa Clara Trade and Convention Center (built next to Great America), which includes a 240,000-square-foot convention center, a 502-room hotel, and an office building. "One of our major goals was to create a long-term revenue stream for the city," says City Manager Jennifer Sparacino, "and it is definitely accomplishing that." Despite problems filling up the office building, the entire deal is already generating a positive return.

The private sector often complains about public enterprise, arguing that government should not compete with business. And many public leaders buy the argument. Lewis V. Pond, city manager of San Bruno, wants to sell the cable system. "We can't make money," he told us, "because we're a government." But where is it written that government should handle only lemons, while business gets all the profit centers? As Don Von Raesfeld said during the Great America debate, "It's been awfully interesting to me in my career as a city manager here that the people are always willing to push on to government losers in this country. The winners are always to be preserved to the private enterprise system."

In reality, there are several good reasons why government *should* sometimes compete with the private sector Some services are natural monopolies. It is inefficient to string two or three sets of electrical lines and or bury two or three sets of gas lines in a city, for example. In such cases, governments can grant a private monopoly and regulate its prices, or they can create a public monopoly. The latter option often delivers a better deal to the public. For 100 years, publicly owned utilities have sold electricity at lower prices than their private counterparts. Today, publicly owned cable television systems do the same.

In other areas, where there is insufficient private competition, public enterprise can act as a competitive yardstick, forcing private firms to lower their prices and pursue greater efficiency. The Phoenix Department of Public Works does this by competing in garbage collection.

Finally, there are some occasions on which the private sector chooses to abandon a profitable business. Marriott sold Great America even though it was profitable, because industrial development would have been *more* profitable. (Being private, Marriott could ignore the public costs, which would have been enormous.) The Mets dropped a minor league franchise they owned in Visalia not because it was unprofitable, but because they decided to limit their farm system to the eastern United States. When no private buyers turned up, Visalia did just what Santa Clara did. It took over the franchise, proved it could make money for six years, and sold it to local owners for a profit. * * *

TOLEDO EDISON COMPANY V. CITY OF BRYAN

Supreme Court of Ohio, 2000.
90 Ohio St.3d 288, 737 N.E.2d 529.

Toledo Edison Company is a public utility that generates, transmits, distributes, and sells electric power to customers in northwest Ohio, including Williams County * * *. Appellees Bryan, Pioneer, Montpelier, and Edgerton ("municipalities") are all municipal corporations located in Williams County * * * that own and operate their own utilities that produce electricity for their inhabitants. * * * Chase Brass & Copper Company ("Chase Brass") is a corporation engaged in smelting and is located in Williams County, but outside of all the municipalities' geographic limits. * * * The municipalities * * * constructed an electric power transmission line in Williams County that runs from one of Bryan's municipal electrical substations directly to Chase Brass. In July 1995, all the municipalities adopted ordinances authorizing them to sell electricity to Chase Brass via the Chase Brass transmission line. On October 17, 1995, Chase Brass terminated its thirty-three-year history of purchasing electricity from Toledo Edison and began purchasing electricity from the municipalities. The municipalities had to purchase electricity in order to fulfill their obligation to provide Chase Brass with electricity. * * * On February 23, 1996, Toledo Edison filed a complaint for injunctive and declaratory relief in the Williams County Court of Common Pleas, seeking a declaration that the municipalities' sale of electricity to Chase Brass was illegal and unconstitutional. * * *

LUNDBERG STRATTON, J. * * *

Many of Ohio's inhabitants are provided electrical service by public utilities. The Ohio Public Utilities Commission has divided Ohio into territories pursuant to the Certified Territories Act. Under the CTA, each electricity-producing public utility is assigned a territory under which it has the exclusive right to sell electricity to the inhabitants of that territory. However, a public utility's exclusive right to provide electricity within its territory is subject to an exception. The Ohio Constitution provides that municipalities may acquire or produce utility services or products for the municipality and its inhabitants and sell surplus product or service. The question is whether a municipality can use this constitutional authority to purchase electricity solely for the purpose of reselling it to an entity outside the municipality's geographic boundaries.

The Ohio Constitution addresses a municipality's authority to produce and acquire a public utility product or service in Section 4, Article XVIII:

"Any municipality may acquire, construct, own, lease and operate within or without its corporate limits, any public utility the product or service of which is or is to be supplied to the municipality or its inhabitants, and may contract with others for any such product or service."

Section 4 authorizes a municipality to establish, maintain, and operate a power plant to produce electricity. * * * However, a municipality's authority to produce or purchase electricity is limited "primarily to the furnishing of services to their own inhabitants." *State ex rel. Wilson v. Hance* (1959), 169 Ohio St. 457, 461, 8 O.O.2d 471, 473, 159 N.E.2d 741, 744.

Section 6, Article XVIII of the Ohio Constitution provides the criteria pursuant to which a municipality may sell electricity:

"Any municipality, owning or operating a public utility for the purpose of supplying the service or product thereof to the municipality or its inhabitants, may also sell and deliver to others any transportation service of such utility and the surplus product of any other utility in an amount not exceeding in either case fifty per cent of the total service or product supplied by such utility within the municipality * * *."

Section 6 allows a municipality that owns or operates a utility for the purpose of generating its own electricity to sell surplus electricity. Critical to our analysis of Section 6 is the meaning of the word "surplus." * * *

Read in pari materia, Sections 4 and 6 only allow a municipality to purchase electricity primarily for the purpose of supplying its residents and reselling only surplus electricity from that purchase to entities outside the municipality. This interpretation necessarily precludes a municipality from purchasing electricity solely for the purpose of reselling the entire amount of the purchased electricity to an entity outside the municipality's geographic limits.

This holding comports with this court's determination that the framers "intended to * * * prevent * * * municipalities from entering into the general public-utility business outside their boundaries in competition with private enterprise." *Hance,* 169 Ohio St. at 461, 8 O.O.2d at 473, 159 N.E.2d at 744. Public utilities that provide electricity, such as Toledo Edison, are subject to substantial regulatory controls by the Public Utilities Commission of Ohio, including regulation of rates. Each electric utility is given a territory by the Public Utilities Commission within which it has the exclusive right to sell its electricity. In contrast a municipality's production or purchase of electricity is not regulated by the PUCO. To allow municipalities the unfettered authority to purchase and then resell electricity to entities outside their boundaries could create unfair competition for the heavily regulated public utilities. Thus, we hold that * * * a municipality is prohibited from in effect engaging in the business of brokering electricity to entities outside the municipality in direct competition with public utilities. * * *

HADLEY, J., dissenting. * * *

In *Travelers Ins. Co. v. Wadsworth* (1924), 109 Ohio St. 440, 142 N.E. 900, * * * this court held that in the absence of specific prohibition, the city acting in a proprietary capacity may exercise its powers as would an individual or private corporation." * * * Specifically referring to electrical utilities, in *State ex rel. McCann v. Defiance* (1958), 167 Ohio St. 313, 4 O.O.2d 369, 148 N.E.2d 221, * * * the court ruled, "The General Assembly has no power to * * * [limit] the * * * authority of a municipality * * * to sell and deliver to others the portion of the surplus product of such utility that it is authorized by Sections 4 and 6 of Article XVIII of the Constitution to sell and deliver to such others." * * * Thus a municipality has full and complete power to enter into whatever arrangement it deems necessary for the ownership, operation, and control of public utilities by itself or in conjunction with other municipalities, subject to the fifty-percent limitation.

The majority concludes without authority that since municipalities are not regulated by the Public Utility Commission, "[t]o allow municipalities the unfettered authority to purchase and then resell electricity to entities outside their boundaries could create unfair competition for the heavily regulated public utilities." Examining the limitation provision, I find that Section 6, Article XVIII does not provide an "unfettered authority" * * *. The debates and proceedings of the constitutional convention clearly indicate that the framers considered whether municipalities would be competitive with private corporations for utilities and concluded that the fifty-percent provision would be the only necessary limitation and that the implementation of that limitation should be left to the courts. * * *

BAGFORD V. EPHRAIM CITY

Supreme Court of Utah, 1995.
904 P.2d 1095.

STEWART, ASSOCIATE CHIEF JUSTICE:

Plaintiffs John M. Bagford and Fae H. Bagford * * * own and operate Sanpete Valley Disposal and Landfill, a garbage collection and disposal business located in Sanpete County, Utah. From 1984 until August or September 1989, the Bagfords provided garbage collection services to residential and commercial customers in Ephraim City and other municipalities and unincorporated areas in Sanpete County. * * * The Bagfords used informal, oral agreements with customers pursuant to which the Bagfords provided their garbage collection services. They offered garbage collection to their customers on a weekly basis, fifty-two weeks each year, and charged their customers for each pickup the customers actually required. * * * Whenever the residents put the garbage out, the Bagfords picked it up.

In 1989, Ephraim City decided to develop a municipal garbage collection system to bring the city into compliance with federal and state health and safety regulations. Ephraim City formed a citizens ad hoc committee to study the issue and eventually accepted the committee's recommendation to contract with a private company to provide regular garbage collection services for residents within the city. In May and June 1989, Ephraim City accepted bids for garbage collection services and subsequently awarded a residential service contract to the successful bidder. The Bagfords were among several competitors that bid unsuccessfully for the contract. In October 1989, Ephraim City adopted Ordinance 10–412, which provides:

> All residences * * * charged residential electrical service rates
> will have garbage collection as arranged by Ephraim City.

At the time the ordinance was enacted, the Bagfords provided garbage collection services to 176 residential customers in Ephraim City and to a number of commercial enterprises. The latter were not affected by Ephraim's change in policy.

Ephraim City also adopted monthly garbage collection charges to be assessed against each residence. The charges are included on the monthly billing for municipal electrical services sent to each residence and must be paid even if the resident does not use the garbage collection services provided by the city. As a result, the Bagfords' 176 residential customers terminated their agreements with the Bagfords and began using the garbage collection services provided by Ephraim City to avoid having to pay double for garbage collection. The Bagfords continue to provide weekly garbage collection services to approximately thirty-two commercial customers.

The Bagfords then brought this action for inverse condemnation against Ephraim City, alleging that the enactment and implementation of the ordinance resulted in a taking of property within the meaning of article I, section 22 of the Utah Constitution and asserting that they were entitled to damages for that taking. * * * Article I, section 22 of the Utah Constitution provides, "Private property shall not be taken or damaged for public use without just compensation." * * * [T]o create a protectable property interest, a contract must establish rights more substantial in nature than a mere unilateral expectation of continued rights or benefits. Absent an exclusive franchise or the equivalent thereof, no vested, legally enforceable interest arises, and consequently, there is no property that can provide the basis for compensation in an inverse condemnation proceeding. * * * Thus, a contract that is terminable at the will of either party does not by itself give rise to a protectable property interest because the mere expectation of benefits under such a contract does not give the promisor a legally enforceable right against a promisee to provide future service and therefore does not by itself provide a basis for compensation for loss of future business.

The Bagfords contend that their oral agreements with their customers were protectable property interests within the meaning of article I, section 22. However, the Bagfords' agreements with their customers were simply offers to collect garbage that the customers could accept or reject each week. Because the agreements were terminable at will by either the Bagfords or their customers, the Bagfords possessed no enforceable, legally binding rights until they had collected garbage from their customers, and then the only enforceable right the Bagfords possessed was the right to compensation for the services already rendered. The Bagfords had no legal right to perform garbage collection services indefinitely. The expectation that they could continue to collect their customers' garbage was not a contract right cognizable under article I, section 22.

We recognize that the Bagfords no doubt invested capital to acquire the necessary equipment to carry on their garbage collection business for Ephraim City residents and suffered revenue losses caused by Ephraim City's change of policy. Nevertheless, the Takings Clause does not insure businesses against all losses caused by competition or by the effect of governmental regulations. * * * The city has not granted the Bagfords a franchise that establishes either an exclusive or even a nonexclusive right to collect garbage from the residents of the city. The Bagfords possess no certificate of public convenience and necessity and no contract with, or license from, Ephraim City granting them a right to collect residential garbage within the city. Their business in Ephraim City was based only on the expectation of being able to continue doing business there, not on a legal right to do so. It follows that their investment of money in the expectation that they would be able to continue their business in Ephraim City indefinitely is not a protectable property interest.

Even if it could be said that the Bagfords had a franchise of some sort, they clearly did not have an exclusive franchise. A nonexclusive franchise does not protect a franchise holder from losses caused by competition. * * * [C]ompetition by a governmental agency that causes a private business financial losses is not a "taking" of property. Thus, although a private company may possess a franchise to provide garbage collection services within a service area, no taking occurs if the government operates a competing service within that service area. "It is generally accepted that a governmental agency is not precluded from competing with its franchisee despite the fact that the franchise is diminished or destroyed by such competition." *Stillings v. City of Winston-Salem*, 311 N.C. 689, 319 S.E.2d 233, 238 (N.C.1984). If the governmental agency does not prohibit the private company from continuing to offer its services, there is no compensable taking. * * *

The Bagfords contend that the effect of the ordinance was to prohibit them from engaging in their business in Ephraim City since the residents would not pay twice for the same service. * * * It is clearly correct that the Bagfords were put at a severe, if not fatal, competitive disadvantage by the ordinance. A private business's competitive disadvantage in competing with a municipality does not, however, result in a taking of the private business property. * * *

4. CUTTING COSTS THROUGH PRIVATIZATION

In the preceding subsection, we focused on the desirability of cities taking over functions that have traditionally been performed by the private sector; in this subsection, we examine the opposite idea—the notion that the private sector might assume functions that have been traditionally performed by cities.[22] Of course, the call for "privatization" of governmental functions is by no means limited to city services; on the contrary, privatization is an idea that has been widely debated not only throughout the United States but around the world.

In theory at least, any governmental service can be delivered by a private business under a government contract. Garbage collection,

---

[22] See e.g., Mildred Warner, Privatization and Urban Governance: The Continuing Challenges of Efficiency, Voice, and Integration, 29 Cities 2, 38–43 (2012); Pascale Joassart-Marcelli and Juliet Musso. Municipal Service Provision Choices Within a Metropolitan Area. 40 Urb. Affairs Rev. 492–519 (2005); Jeffrey Brudney, Sergio Fernandez, Jay Eungha Ryu, and Deil S. Wright, Exploring and Explaining Contracting Out: Patterns among the American States, 15 J. of Public Administration Research and Theory 393–414 (2005); Ellen Dannin, Red Tape or Accountability: Privatization, Public-ization, and Public Values, 15 Cornell J.L. & Pol'y 111 (2005). For an analysis of privatization more generally, see, e.g., Jon Michaels, Privatization's Progeny, 101 Geo. L. J. 1023 (2013); Alex Kozinski and Andrew Bentz, Privatization and Its Discontents, 63 Emory L.J. 263 (2013).

ambulance services and health care are familiar candidates for privatization, but there is no reason to stop there. Public schools could be replaced by private schools as long as students are given government-subsidized vouchers to pay for them. Police departments could be replaced by private security guards, judges could be replaced by professional arbitrators, and fire departments could be replaced by private emergency businesses. Once you begin to take the idea of privatization seriously, you can quickly come to the view that government could be reduced to the performance of three tasks: the collection of revenue by taxation, the choice of services this revenue should buy, and the negotiation and drafting (and, perhaps, the monitoring) of contracts with private businesses for the delivery of the chosen services. In fact, some of these jobs could be contracted out too. For example, government could hire a collection agency to enforce its laws, a private management consultant to determine what services to provide, and private lawyers to negotiate and draft its contracts. Taken to its limits, then, privatization could transform government simply into a revenue-generating mechanism run by a few people whose job would be to begin the process of contracting out, choosing the consultants and lawyers who, in turn, would continue the cycle of contracting and recontracting. As a means of employment and delivery of services, the state really could wither away.

Such an extreme form of privatization is not just hypothetical. Sandy Springs, Georgia, a suburb of Atlanta with a population of 94,000, has contracted out virtually its entire government to private companies. (It retains a public police and fire department.) It has a total of 7 public employees, and it rents space for its "city hall," staffed by private employees, in a one story industrial park. Interviewed by the *New York Times*, its city manager, John McDonough, said: "The privatized approach saves money * * * because corporations hire superior workers and give them better training. * * * It's all about the caliber of the employee and the customer focus that comes out of the private sector."[23]

To explore a specific example of privatization, the subsection begins with James Ramsey's provocative argument that the New York City subway system be sold to the private sector. Following Ramsey's argument, a Note examines a radically different approach to public transportation issues: the possibility of cities (or private employers) offering public transportation services for free. What conceptions of city services generate these opposite approaches to the same issue? Like many other advocates, Ramsey locates the benefit of privatization in the greater efficiency of private business management. What are its costs? The case that concludes this section, Richardson v. McKnight, explores one possible cost. In the process of determining whether prison guards employed by a

---

[23] David Segal, A Georgia Town Takes the People's Business Private, New York Times, June 23, 2012.

private company are entitled to immunity against constitutional tort actions, the Supreme Court, in a 5–4 decision, engages in a full-scale debate about the difference between private prisons and public prisons. Of course, the case can properly be understood simply by focusing on the doctrine of immunity. The reason to read the *Richardson* case here, however, is different: it provides an opening for a discussion of the role of constitutional protections in the performance of government functions when privately delivered.[24] What is the impact of privatization on other values—such as the democratic control of public policymaking?

One additional question should also be kept in mind while reading this subsection. It is not obvious that the issue of privatization should be posed simply in terms of whether a city or a private entity should provide a particular service. Even when services are contracted out to a private company, a public role in these services is still often thought essential, as the Note on Free Public Transportation suggests. Is it better, therefore, to see the choice not in terms of a stark public vs. private alternative but in terms of the need to design a mixed public-private form of service delivery? If so, how does one envision what the "public" and the "private" roles are? In the next section we examine a related issue: there we consider whether services delivered by the city government can be understood as privatized if they are treated simply as consumer goods— treated, in other words, as no different in principle from the kinds of goods offered by the private sector.

JAMES RAMSEY, SELLING THE NEW YORK CITY SUBWAY: WILD-EYED RADICALISM OR THE ONLY FEASIBLE SOLUTION?

From S. Hanke, Prospects for Privatization 95–103 (1987).

Analysis of the Problem

The financial reason for the subways' difficulty is easy to state: labor costs per passenger mile have risen faster than the sum of revenues and subsidies per passenger mile. The difficult question is why. The near impossible question is what to do about it. Moreover, the problem has a puzzling aspect when one examines the situation in more detail. As labor costs rose relative to other costs, capital equipment was not substituted for labor, as would be the case in any normal profit-maximizing industry. The reason, of course, is political; the degree of pressure that a municipal union can bring to bear on a city government and the arrangements that the government can make because of its rule-making ability inevitably

---

[24] A more recent case dealing with private prisons, Minneci v. Pollard, 132 S.Ct. 617 (2012), can similarly be understood simply in terms of the Court's finding that adequate state tort remedies exist for prisoners denied medical attention, thus making the available of a constitutional tort suit unnecessary. But that case also raises the question of whether the requirement of providing medical care in private prisons is the same as that required of public prisons.

force bodies like the Transit Authority into trying to pay for wage increases that projected revenues do not justify by reducing maintenance and repair of capital equipment—in short, by disinvesting in capital.

A private firm's response to a higher wage rate is to substitute capital and technology for labor. Thus the full impact of the wage increment is muted through the more extensive use of capital and relatively less use of high-priced labor. In even more difficult circumstances, the private firm will reduce output, sell off nonprofitable portions of the firm, or in extremis declare bankruptcy. For purely political reasons, municipal transit authorities are not allowed these options. The ultimate response that mitigates excessive union demands—unemployment and the closing of the firm—is not available to them; worse, before the ultimate collapse of the system, labor productivity falls as the existing capital stock is depreciated so that the problem is compounded at each round of labor negotiations. Unfortunately, despite what municipal authorities seem to think, deferred maintenance is not an interest-free loan; the real interest rate of such loans is very high.

Between 1968 and 1979 total full-time [Transit Authority] employees fell from 34,649 to 34,007, a reduction of less than 2 percent. But labor costs per passenger rose from 20 cents to 63 cents over the same period. * * * Looking at increases in wages and other benefits is only one side of the coin; the other is the productivity of the labor force. Thus, if productivity grew at a faster rate than the rate of increase in wages, labor costs per unit of output could fall. An initial view of the situation is provided by the observation that in the 1960s the number of passengers per employee was between 170 and 180, but by the beginning of the 1970s that figure had fallen to 128. An optimistic estimate of the national average transit-productivity gain as a percent per year is positive, but it is as likely to be negative. Perhaps the best guess is that the national average transit-productivity gains are zero. It is reasonable to surmise that the MTA's contribution to the national average is negative. Further, while the ratio of capital to labor for the United States domestic economy has been growing at about 2.5 percent a year since 1948 and that for transit has grown at only 0.52 percent a year, and this figure does not adequately allow for the long-term deterioration of capital equipment through neglected maintenance. On balance, the change in the capital-labor ratio for the New York City Transit Authority (NYCTA) is probably negative. * * *

The initial explanation for this dismal record is the power of the unions. Federal, state, and local legislation provides transportation unions with strong powers, both economic and political. In New York City and its suburbs the Transport Worker's Union (TWU) is a monopoly whose degree of control is unmatched by any firm or even trio of firms in any industry in the country. Local 100 of the TWU bargains for eight out of ten private labor contracts and covers 93 percent of the buses and 95 percent of the bus operators. Of course, the subways are completely unionized. This gives the union enormous economic power—whether or not it has the "legal right to strike"; indeed, the legal prohibition does not seem to be much of a barrier to strikes and has been no barrier to higher wage agreements.

If the economic power of the union is combined with political leverage, the union's ability to tax the rest of society is impeded only by political reluctance to raise fares and the length of debates on tax increases. Once a municipality has taken on direct responsibility for providing a service, even through the device of an "authority," the pressure to politicize most issues is overwhelming. An ostensible strike against the TA on economic issues becomes a political battle involving the political gains and losses to the incumbent politician. In this situation, well-organized blocs of voters, like those provided by the TWU, provide a degree of political influence matched by few other groups. Better still from the union's viewpoint, settlements now have direct access to the public purse; settlements that would immediately bankrupt a private firm can be financed indefinitely by taxing the general public. While the public purse is not unlimited, a politically influential group's ability to extract large sums at the expense of anonymous taxpayers is high and is obviously in the self-interest of the politician supported by a well-organized union cadre.

One important lesson not lost on the subway riders is that the fare is only a small part of the actual cost of riding the subway. In truth, the fare has become even more irrelevant; the real total cost is already high and rising rapidly. * * * The real cost is measured in lack of safety, uncertainty as to the time of travel, filthy surroundings, overcrowding, and often some disturbing riders. One dollar is a very small part of the cost, and each time people experiment with alternative modes of getting to work, for example, during a subway strike, they discover that the real costs of the subway are greater than the use of a private car or a charter bus. In fact, ridership on the express buses is rising rapidly as commuters leave the subways—a clear indication that the riding public is willing to pay more, far more, for a quality ride. The main lesson from this discussion is that if the fare were raised and the quality of the service significantly improved, one could easily generate an increase in ridership resulting from an overall reduction in the total price to the rider. The mere substitution of clean, well-lit stations and clean, quiet trains would greatly improve the desirability of subway travel.

No mention has yet been made of management's role in the half-century decline of the subway system. Ironically, especially within the last few years, senior management has been notable for its drive, knowledge, and concern to create a useful public service. Traditionally, the first group to be blamed for poor performance is management, and in a private firm that view is quite correct. But in an organization that is highly subject to political influence, the charge is not necessarily true. By and large the senior management knows what must be done to improve the system, but for political reasons it cannot do it.

The political power of the unions has already been mentioned. But pressures for inefficiency come from the riders as well. Political pressure keeps the fare down, and when there is an allowed increase the amount is too little and too late. Subway lines and stations that economically should be closed or have their service reduced because of lack of ridership are kept open through political intervention at an enormous cost.

The reader may imagine the difficulties to be faced if he or she had to cope with a work force that cannot be effectively disciplined (MTA workers' lack of commitment to their jobs is notorious), service that cannot be changed to meet changing demands, capital projects that are a political battle, the exhausting prospect that even routine decisions face potential political intervention, and, finally, revenues that are held down until a crisis is precipitated.

Political control of a firm leads to gross economic inefficiency. The differences between alternative situations lie in how the inefficiencies are manifested. For some operations—for example, the Washington, D.C., system—the plant and equipment are modern and clean, but the subsidies are enormous. In New York, the subsidies are relatively modest by public-transportation standards, but the employee-pension burden is so egregious (it is possible to retire at nearly full pay after only twenty years of service) and work-force discipline is so negligible that the outcome is a decaying system. As the subsidies for other transportation systems decline, they will also begin to depreciate capital in order to pay for intemperate wage and pension increments.

The Only Feasible Solution

There should be one simple but outstandingly clear lesson from the above discussion. The current system is not viable; there is no sum of money, no subsidy so great, that cannot be eaten up by union demands and political intervention. Indeed, the more the system is subsidized and the more management and the unions recognize that fact, the more inefficient the entire system will become and the higher the costs will be. Some device is needed that will limit union demands to the bounds of reason and concentrate the minds of management on trying to generate an efficient system that serves the public. The following suggestion, which is politically feasible, could produce this necessary miracle.

The proposal is to sell off the subway system line by line over a period of about five years. The fundamental elements of the scheme are that there are to be no price controls, no entry barriers to new subway firms other than those dictated by safety, and no political intervention in behalf of the unions, and the city is to share in the profits of the system. The last element is crucial to the political feasibility of the proposal.

A team of evaluators chosen in part by the city and in part by the potential bidders for the subway will evaluate the net "market value" of the current capital stock of that part of the system to be sold. This capital price must be paid in order for the bidding firm to acquire the right to provide subway service in the city. The choice of which firm is to rebuild and run the subway will be by competitive bids on net profit share to the city; that is, the highest bid share of gross profits (net of all capital costs) to be paid to the city wins the right to provide subway service on the line or lines bought. But it must be expressly agreed that no price controls and no mandated service requirements will be imposed. In a California oil lease sale where this bidding scheme was tried, the net profit share was 94.77 percent.

The city can use its profit share in any way it chooses—for example, to finance subway rides for the poor by giving them an income subsidy paid from the profit shares. Alternatively, it can pay for the provision of uneconomical service. One objective of the scheme is to separate the need for an efficient transportation system from the politically understandable wish to subsidize certain segments of the electorate.

By moving to a privately funded and operated system wherein any gains or losses are the direct responsibility of the owners, the minds of management will be concentrated on providing the service demanded by the public. Only when managers' jobs depend on their efforts and efficiency will there be a serious effort to control costs. The objective of the firm is now simply stated and easily understood—to make money. But what the general public does not understand is that this seemingly crass dictum in practice would help solve numerous complex problems and provide the rider better service at a lower cost.

The management of privately owned firms is far more efficient than that of publicly owned or controlled firms, simply because of the difference in the pressures that managers face in the two situations. In publicly owned or controlled firms, not only are there fewer and smaller personal incentives to be efficient; political control adds a further and, in the end, disastrous thrust to fiscal myopia, to the acceptance of the expedient response, and an effort to solve today's difficulty at a greater cost tomorrow. This is in part because the period for the payoff from political decisions is short, often less than a year and seldom greater than two years. It is therefore no great surprise to view the political reluctance for the long-range solutions that inevitably incur short-run difficulties. It is expedient for the politician to curry favor now and leave the problems to the next election, the next administration, or the next generation of users. It is easier to take a popular stance on low fares today than to recommend the investment needed for a viable system tomorrow. Unfortunately, the outcome of this political exchange is worse for both riders and taxpayers.

While it is well recognized that private firms face greater pressures to respond to consumer wishes and to moderate costs, it is not so well recognized that private firms can withstand union pressures more easily. This is not to say that a powerful union cannot force inefficiencies and raise wage rates above competitive levels but to say that with any degree of union power the deleterious effects will be reduced. When a public authority like the NYCTA runs the subways, the unions recognize that they have access to the public treasury and general tax revenues; any deficits created by their own demands can always be filled through public monies.

Critics will say that while the above comments are well and good, experience has shown that no private company can run a transit system unsubsidized and that no private firm can raise the funds needed to rebuild the system. The answer is that experience has shown that when transit fares are held below economic levels by government fiat, incumbent firms go broke, and no one else will be interested in the economic equivalent of self-flagellation.

What is clear to even the most skeptical of critics is that there is an enormous reservoir of demand for relatively efficient transportation. The use of a car for a typical commuter is about one hour's drive plus about $30.00 a day. A commuter bus costs $6 to $10 a day, and it is inconvenient because of the necessity of sticking to a fixed and limited schedule. This is the currently allowed competition for the subway. If there were no price constraints, the city would be flooded with proposals for providing public transportation in innovative ways. If the lack of price constraints results in a profitable situation, one need not worry about the ability to raise the necessary capital funds.

The issue of financial viability has now been reduced to one with purely emotional content. Only the "rich" will be able to afford to ride the subway; so long as the subway is a monopoly the public will be gouged unmercifully. Much colorful language can be employed in the argument, but the true situation is far more prosaic. As usual in such debates, there is a subtle propensity for those enamored of municipal control and tax-based subsidies to argue both ways simultaneously—privately run systems are not financially viable because no one will use them at the profitable price (there is strong competition) and the subway is a monopoly and people must pay any price charged (there is no competition at all).

The truth of the matter is that subways face considerable competition, although for some trips subways would clearly be the preferred mode. Insofar as the subways are sold line by line and bus lines are sold separately, subways and buses provide competition for some trips as well as opportunities for cooperative service for others; for example, crosstown bus service linked to uptown-downtown subway service. Even from the outlying boroughs, express buses, car pooling, jitney cabs (if allowed), shared limousines, nonmedallion cabs, private cars, and motorcycles provide alternative modes of transportation.

Some idea of a market-clearing price can be inferred from several items of information. The Regional Plan Association estimated in 1980 that it would take a 45-cent fare increase (plus increases on the Long Island Rail Road) to raise $1 billion a year for rebuilding the system. After eliminating all subsidies and before realizing the existing and known potential for efficiency gains, an "average fare" of about $1.20 emerged, certainly less than $1.50. But even in 1986, fares within Manhattan could be 75 to 90 cents and only fares to the ends of the outer boroughs might reach $3.00

If express buses can operate profitably in 1986 at $3.00 to $5.00 a ride as simple commuter operations, the subway could provide far better service for much less. Consequently, from this perspective, a maximum profitable price in 1986 from the outer boroughs is less than, say, $3.00 on average; short trips should be less than the current $1.

So far this discussion has ignored technological innovations, lowering the total cost of labor by substituting relatively cheaper capital equipment, and simple efficiency gains from work-rate changes. It has been estimated that relatively minor changes of this type can lower costs by 20 percent or more. Another example would be the elimination of token clerks, about 4,000 high-paid jobs, and another 3,000 "conductors." New rail lines seem to manage with only one driver.

A counterargument that can be raised at this point is that the price increases recommended will so lower demand that costs must rise even more. This argument is invalid on two counts. First, even accurate measures of the relative price responsiveness of demand would not be of much relevance in this situation, because what is at issue is the demand for a vastly improved system, not a higher price for the existing network. What is needed to calculate the effect on ridership is to evaluate the responsiveness of demand to increases in quality; it is the net effect of quality and price that will determine the gain in the ridership.

Second, the notion that cents per rider must rise if ridership falls can only be true for a system locked into overmanning. For most firms, if demand falls permanently, the firm shrinks to accommodate. It is usually only when demand falls to very low levels that one begins to experience

serious increases in average cost to a fall in demand. The subways are by
no means close to such a point.

Another argument made by those in favor of tax-supported systems is
that if the subways were to charge the full economic cost, firms would
relocate and New York City would lose jobs. The argument is false. First,
it is true that transportation is a key issue in the decisions of firms
whether to remain in the city or relocate, but it is *not* whether the fare is
60 cents or 75 cents or even $2.00 but the fact that employees are
continually late, rushing off early to get a train, unwilling to work late,
tired, irritable, and exhausted from inhuman conditions on the subway—
in short, the abysmal level of services, or lack of them, is the problem.

Second, whatever the true costs of transportation in the city, the firm
and its employees still pay the full costs no matter how low the nominal
fare, because the shortfall must be made up in taxes. A viable New York
City requires a viable transit system, and that requires a city government
committed to open entry into the transit business, receptivity to
innovative ideas, and above all the courage *not* to set price ceilings.
Ironically, while this is the only strategy that can achieve a useful
transportation network, it is the only one not yet tried by the city.

The most emotional issue of all concerns the poor. The nonworking
poor seldom need transportation; attention here will therefore be focused
on the working poor. Grant for a moment that these people would rather
not work at all or would rather work locally than pay a higher subway
fare. Employers would soon see their labor forces shrinking and would
have to raise wages to get their workers back. In this case, then, the
system is self-correcting. Further, fares based on distance traveled could
lower fares for the working poor, since many work within their own
neighborhoods and do not commute to Manhattan from the outer
boroughs.

What can be done for the nonworking poor? The answer is not to keep
fares artificially low for 95 percent of the population who can pay but to
give an extra income subsidy to the nonworking poor and let them spend
it how they will. Such a subsidy can be financed directly from the profits
of the system paid to the city. But what if there are no profits paid in?
This phenomenon can only be temporary, and there are two answers.
First, since the firm is not making profits, everyone using the system is
already being subsidized at the expense of the equity owners. Second, the
city can finance the poor immediately in anticipation of future profit
revenues.

For political reasons the city may wish to provide subway service to
areas where alternative transportation is so cheap and efficient that the
privately run subway system cannot compete. Under the existing scheme

the city could use its profit share or any other revenue to purchase the extra service from the privately run system.

The final issue, and the most crucial one, is whether the proposed scheme is politically feasible. The opposition is powerful, but the answer can be yes. The TWU definitely does not want to see its members' pay reduced to that earned by their colleagues in private industry. All those who still believe others can be taxed to pay for their subway will be against the idea of paying their own way, no matter how inefficient and wasteful such a procedure is. There is a sizable body of people who firmly believe that only municipally provided services are desirable and that all such services should be paid for by taxing the "rich." Such people will only grudgingly compromise to accept some nonzero fare.

On the other side is the grim reality that the above proponents have reduced a once-great system to a shambles. Further, a number of people recognize that the only viable and affordable solution is to institute a private system of intracity transit like the intercity system. In any event, both New York City and the state can no longer afford to subsidize transportation at ever-increasing amounts because of the pressure of alternative and desperately needed capital expenditures on items less amenable to privatization, such as road repair, sewage plants, and street cleaning. Leadership, full discussion of the issues, and a clear recognition of the self-interest involved in many of the arguments may be the only way to escape from the transit morass.

NOTE ON FREE PUBLIC TRANSPORTATION

Supporters of public transportation have long sought to encourage ridership and promote equality by making fares affordable. Some have suggested accomplishing these goals by having no fares at all. Opinions about whether free public transportation would be worth the public subsidy it would require are influenced by the analogies people offer for public transportation. Those who consider running buses, streetcars, and subways like running any other business—like, say, operating United Air Lines— think that those who use a form of transportation should pay the full cost of supporting it. Others, however, have analogized public transportation to public streets: if streets are free to drivers, why shouldn't buses, streetcars, and trains be free to passengers? Other analogies have also been suggested. "It's not inconceivable," Delos Wilcox wrote in 1915, "that the time may come when public utility services will be furnished free, as elevator service is."[25]

In 1998, Jeff Johnson, the Green Party's candidate for lieutenant governor in Rhode Island, argued that the state should offer free public transportation to all citizens, paid for by increased gasoline taxes. Free buses, he contended, would encourage people to get out of their cars, which would

---

[25] Delos Wilcox, Fundamental Planks in a Public Utility Program, 57 Annals of the American Academy of Political and Social Science 8, 14 (Jan. 1915).

mean less pollution and fewer repair expenses "I believe we should tax what we don't want, and not tax what we do want," he said.[26]

Free public transportation is not just an idea. Commerce, California and Amherst, Massachusetts offer it, as does the Aubagne, a city in France. Tallinn, Estonia is the largest municipality offering free public transportation, albeit only to city residents and not outsiders. Still, there are cities that once offered free public transportation but have discontinued it, including Portland, Oregon (which had it from 1975 to 2012).[27] A more limited version of the idea has taken hold in Seattle, Washington. In the early 1990s, the University of Washington expanded by 10 per cent, while reducing the number of parking spaces, by offering employees sharply discounted transit passes. Other employers in the area then adopted the idea, which led on average to a 90 per cent increase in transit usage. Indeed, David Luberoff reports, "the free employer-provided passes and other transportation benefits are so ubiquitous and popular that most of the region's high-tech firms can't hire new employees without offering similar perks." Federal law has been changed to support these efforts:

> Until a few years ago, free parking provided by employers was a non-taxable benefit. A free transit pass, however, was taxable. Now, in federal legislation passed at the urging of retiring U.S. Senator Daniel Patrick Moynihan, the playing field has been largely leveled, leading many transit agencies to make a stronger push for employer-provided transit pass programs.[28]

RICHARDSON V. McKNIGHT
Supreme Court of the United States, 1997.
521 U.S. 399, 117 S. Ct. 2100, 138 L.Ed.2d 540.

JUSTICE BREYER delivered the opinion of the Court. * * *

Ronnie Lee McKnight, a prisoner at Tennessee's South Central Correctional Center (SCCC), brought this federal constitutional tort action against two prison guards, Darryl Richardson and John Walker. He says the guards injured him by placing upon him extremely tight physical restraints, thereby unlawfully "subject[ing]" him "to the deprivation of" a right "secured by the Constitution" of the United States. Rev. Stat. § 1979, 42 U.S.C. § 1983. Richardson and Walker asserted a qualified immunity from § 1983 lawsuits, see *Harlow v. Fitzgerald*, 457 U.S. 800, 807, 102 S.Ct. 2727, 73 L.Ed.2d 396 (1982), and moved to dismiss the action. * * * Tennessee had "privatized" the management of a number of its correctional facilities * * *. [C]onsequently a private firm, not the state government, employed the guards. * * *

---

[26] Campaign Journal, The Providence Journal-Bulletin, October 2, 1998 Pg. 4B.

[27] http://portlandafoot.org/2012/09/rip-free-public-transit-in-portland-11275-9112/.

[28] David Luberoff, Right on the Money, Governing Magazine (September 2000).

We take the Court's recent case, *Wyatt v. Cole*, 504 U.S. 158, 112 S.Ct. 1827, 118 L.Ed.2d 504 (1992), as pertinent authority. The Court there considered whether private defendants, charged with § 1983 liability for "invoking state replevin, garnishment, and attachment statutes" later declared unconstitutional were "entitled to qualified immunity from suit." It held that they were not. * * * *Wyatt*, consistent with earlier precedent, described the [immunity] doctrine's purposes as protecting "government's ability to perform its traditional functions" by providing immunity where "necessary to preserve" the ability of government officials "to serve the public good or to ensure that talented candidates were not deterred by the threat of damages suits from entering public service." Earlier precedent described immunity as protecting the public from unwarranted timidity on the part of public officials by, for example, "encouraging the vigorous exercise of official authority," *Butz v. Economou*, 438 U.S. 478, 506, 98 S.Ct. 2894, 57 L.Ed.2d 895 (1978), by contributing to "'principled and fearless decision-making,'" *Wood v. Strickland*, 420 U.S. 308, 319, 95 S.Ct. 992, 43 L.Ed.2d 214 (1975), and by responding to the concern that threatened liability would, in Judge Hand's words, "'dampen the ardour of all but the most resolute, or the most irresponsible'" public officials. *Harlow*, 457 U.S., at 814.

The guards argue that those purposes support immunity whether their employer is private or public. Since private prison guards perform the same work as state prison guards, they say, they must require immunity to a similar degree. To say this, however, is to misread this Court's precedents. The Court has sometimes applied a functional approach in immunity cases, but only to decide which type of immunity—absolute or qualified—a public officer should receive. And it never has held that the mere performance of a governmental function could make the difference between unlimited § 1983 liability and qualified immunity, especially for a private person who performs a job without government supervision or direction. Indeed a purely functional approach bristles with difficulty, particularly since, in many areas, government and private industry may engage in fundamentally similar activities, ranging from electricity production, to waste disposal, to even mail delivery.

Petitioners' argument also overlook certain important differences that, from an immunity perspective, are critical. First, the most important special government immunity-producing concern—unwarranted timidity—is less likely present, or at least is not special, when a private company subject to competitive market pressures operates a prison. Competitive pressures mean not only that a firm whose guards are too aggressive will face damages that raise costs, thereby threatening its replacement, but also that a firm whose guards are too timid will face threats of replacement by other firms with records that demonstrate their ability to do both a safer and a more effective job.

These ordinary marketplace pressures are present here. The private prison guards before us work for a large, multistate private prison management firm. The firm is systematically organized to perform a major administrative task for profit. It performs that task independently, with relatively less ongoing direct state supervision. It must buy insurance sufficient to compensate victims of civil rights torts. And, since the firm's first contract expires after three years, its performance is disciplined, not only by state review, but also by pressure from potentially competing firms who can try to take its place.

In other words, marketplace pressures provide the private firm with strong incentives to avoid overly timid, insufficiently vigorous, unduly fearful, or "non-arduous" employee job performance. And the contract's provisions—including those that might permit employee indemnification and avoid many civil-service restrictions—grant this private firm freedom to respond to those market pressures through rewards and penalties that operate directly upon its employees. To this extent, the employees before us resemble those of other private firms and differ from government employees.

This is not to say that government employees, in their efforts to act within constitutional limits, will always, or often, sacrifice the otherwise effective performance of their duties. Rather, it is to say that government employees typically act within a different system. They work within a system that is responsible through elected officials to voters who, when they vote, rarely consider the performance of individual subdepartments or civil servants specifically and in detail. And that system is often characterized by multidepartment civil service rules that, while providing employee security, may limit the incentives or the ability of individual departments or supervisors flexibly to reward, or to punish, individual employees. Hence a judicial determination that "effectiveness" concerns warrant special immunity-type protection in respect to this latter (governmental) system does not prove its need in respect to the former. Consequently, we can find no special immunity-related need to encourage vigorous performance.

Second, "privatization" helps to meet the immunity-related need "to ensure that talented candidates" are "not deterred by the threat of damages suits from entering public service." *Wyatt*, 504 U.S., at 167. It does so in part because of the comprehensive insurance-coverage requirements just mentioned. The insurance increases the likelihood of employee indemnification and to that extent reduces the employment-discouraging fear of unwarranted liability potential applicants face. Because privatization law also frees the private prison-management firm from many civil service law restraints, it permits the private firm, unlike a government department, to offset any increased employee liability risk with higher pay or extra benefits. In respect to this second government-immunity-related purpose then, it is difficult to find a special need for immunity, for the guards' employer can operate like other private firms; it need not operate like a typical government department.

Third, * * * [o]ur qualified immunity cases do not contemplate the complete elimination of lawsuit-based distractions. And it is significant that, here, Tennessee law reserves certain important discretionary tasks—those related to prison discipline, to parole, and to good time—for state officials. Given a continual and conceded need for deterring constitutional violations and our sense that the firm's tasks are not enormously different in respect to their importance from various other publicly important tasks carried out by private firms, we are not persuaded that the threat of distracting workers from their duties is enough virtually by itself to justify providing an immunity. Moreover, Tennessee, which has itself decided not to extend sovereign immunity to private prison operators (and arguably appreciated that this decision would increase contract prices to some degree), can be understood to have anticipated a certain amount of distraction. * * *

We close with three caveats. First, we have focused only on questions of § 1983 immunity and have not addressed whether the defendants are liable under § 1983 even though they are employed by a private firm. Because the Court of Appeals assumed, but did not decide, § 1983 liability, it is for the District Court to determine whether, under this Court's decision in *Lugar v. Edmondson Oil Co.*, 457 U.S. 922, 102 S.Ct. 2744, 73 L.Ed.2d 482 (1982), defendants actually acted "under color of state law."

Second, we have answered the immunity question narrowly, in the context in which it arose. That context is one in which a private firm, systematically organized to assume a major lengthy administrative task (managing an institution) with limited direct supervision by the government, undertakes that task for profit and potentially in competition with other firms. The case does not involve a private individual briefly associated with a government body, serving as an adjunct to government in an essential governmental activity, or acting under close official supervision.

Third, *Wyatt* explicitly stated that it did not decide whether or not the private defendants before it might assert, not immunity, but a special "good faith" defense. * * * Like the Court in *Wyatt*, and the Court of Appeals in this case, we do not express a view on this last-mentioned question. * * *

JUSTICE SCALIA, with whom THE CHIEF JUSTICE, JUSTICE KENNEDY and JUSTICE THOMAS join, dissenting.

In *Procunier v. Navarette*, 434 U.S. 555, 98 S.Ct. 855, 55 L.Ed.2d 24 (1978), we held that state prison officials, including both supervisory and subordinate officers, are entitled to qualified immunity in a suit brought under 42 U.S.C. § 1983. Today the Court declares that this immunity is unavailable to employees of private prison management firms, who perform the same duties as state-employed correctional officials, who exercise the most palpable form of state police power, and who may be sued for acting "under color of state law." * * *

"[O]ur cases clearly indicate that immunity analysis rests on functional categories, not on the status of the defendant." *Briscoe v. LaHue*, 460 U.S. 325, 342, 103 S.Ct. 1108, 75 L.Ed.2d 96 (1983). * * * Private individuals have regularly been accorded immunity when they perform a governmental function that qualifies. We have long recognized the absolute immunity of grand jurors, noting that like prosecutors and judges they must "exercise a discretionary judgment on the basis of evidence presented to them." *Imbler [v. Pachtman]*, 424 U.S. 409, at 423, n.20 [1976]. "It is the functional comparability of [grand jurors'] judgments to those of the judge that has resulted in [their] being termed 'quasi-judicial' officers, and their immunities being termed 'quasi-judicial' as well." * * * I think it highly unlikely that we would deny prosecutorial immunity to those private attorneys increasingly employed by various jurisdictions in this country to conduct high-visibility criminal prosecutions. * * * There is no more reason for treating private prison guards differently. * * *

The Court suggests two differences between civil-service prison guards and those employed by private prison firms which preclude any "special" need to give the latter immunity. First, the Court says that "unwarranted timidity" on the part of private guards is less likely to be a concern, since their companies are subject to market pressures that encourage them to be effective in the performance of their duties. If a private firm does not maintain a proper level of order, the Court reasons, it will be replaced by another one—so there is no need for qualified immunity to facilitate the maintenance of order.

This is wrong for several reasons. First of all, it is fanciful to speak of the consequences of "market" pressures in a regime where public officials are the only purchaser, and other people's money the medium of payment. Ultimately, one prison-management firm will be selected to replace another prison-management firm only if a decision is made by some political official not to renew the contract. This is a government decision, not a market choice. If state officers turn out to be more strict in reviewing the cost and performance of privately managed prisons than of publically managed ones, it will only be because they have chosen to be so. The process can come to resemble a market choice only to the extent that political actors will such resemblance—that is, to the extent that political actors (1) are willing to pay attention to the issue of prison services, among the many issues vying for their attention, and (2) are willing to place considerations of cost and quality of service ahead of such political considerations as personal friendship, political alliances, in-state ownership of the contractor, etc. Secondly and more importantly, however, if one assumes a political regime that is bent on emulating the market in its purchase of prison services, it is almost certainly the case that, short of mismanagement so severe as to provoke a prison riot, price (not discipline) will be the predominating factor in such a regime's selection of a contractor. A contractor's price must depend upon its costs; lawsuits increase costs; and "fearless" maintenance of discipline increases lawsuits. The incentive to down-play discipline will exist, moreover, even in those states where the politicians' zeal for market-emulation and budget-cutting has waned, and where prison-management contract renewal is virtually automatic: the more cautious the prison guards, the fewer the lawsuits, the higher the profits. In sum, it seems that "market-competitive" private prison managers have even greater need than civil-service prison managers for immunity as an incentive to discipline.

The Court's second distinction between state and private prisons is that privatization "helps to meet the immunity-related need to ensure that talented candidates are not deterred by the threat of damages suits from entering public service" as prison guards. This is so because privatization brings with it (or at least has brought with it in the case before us) (1) a statutory requirement for insurance coverage against civil-rights claims, which assertedly "increases the likelihood of employee indemnification," and (2) a liberation "from many civil service law restraints" which prevent increased employee risk from being "offset . . . with higher pay or extra benefits." As for the former (civil-rights liability insurance): surely it is the availability of that protection, rather than its actual presence in the case at hand, which decreases (if it does decrease, which I doubt) the need for immunity protection. (Otherwise, the Court would have to say that a private prison-management firm that is not required to purchase insurance, and does not do so, is more entitled to immunity; and that a government-run prison system that does purchase insurance is less entitled to immunity.) And of course civil-rights liability insurance is no less available to public entities than to private employers. But the second factor—liberation from civil-service limitations—is the more interesting one. First of all, simply as a philosophical matter it is fascinating to learn that one of the prime justifications for § 1983 immunity should be a phenomenon (civil-service laws) that did not even exist when § 1983 was enacted and the immunity created. Also as a philosophical matter, it is poetic justice (or poetic revenge) that the Court should use one of the principal economic benefits of "prison out-sourcing"—namely, the avoidance of civil-service salary and tenure encrustations—as the justification for a legal rule rendering out-sourcing more expensive. Of course the savings attributable to out-sourcing will not be wholly lost as a result of today's holding; they will be transferred in part from the public to prisoner-plaintiffs and to lawyers. It is a result that only the American Bar Association and the American Federation of Government Employees could love. But apart from philosophical fascination, this second factor is subject to the same objection as the first: governments need not have civil-service salary encrustations (or can exempt prisons from them); and hence governments, no more than private prison employers, have any need for § 1983 immunity.

There is one more possible rationale for denying immunity to private prison guards worth discussing, albeit briefly. It is a theory so implausible that the Court avoids mentioning it, even though it was the primary reason given in the Court of Appeals decision that the Court affirms. It is that officers of private prisons are more likely than officers of state prisons to violate prisoners' constitutional rights because they work for a profit motive, and hence an added degree of deterrence is needed to keep these officers in line. The Court of Appeals offered no evidence to support its bald assertion that private prison guards operate with different incentives than state prison guards, and gave no hint as to how prison guards might possibly increase their employers' profits by violating constitutional rights. One would think that private prison managers, whose § 1983 damages come out of their own pockets, as compared with public prison managers, whose § 1983 damages come out of the public purse, would, if anything, be more careful in training their employees to avoid constitutional infractions. And in fact, States having experimented with prison privatization commonly report that the overall caliber of the services provided to prisoners has actually improved in scope and quality.

In concluding, I must observe that since there is no apparent reason, neither in history nor in policy, for making immunity hinge upon the Court's distinction between public and private guards, the precise nature of that distinction must also remain obscure. Is it privity of contract that separates the two categories—so that guards paid directly by the State are "public" prison guards and immune, but those paid by a prison-management company "private" prison guards and not immune? Or is it rather "employee" versus "independent contractor" status—so that even guards whose compensation is paid directly by the State are not immune if they are not also supervised by a state official? Or is perhaps state supervision alone (without direct payment) enough to confer immunity? Or is it * * * the formal designation of the guards, or perhaps of the guards' employer, as a "state instrumentality" that makes the difference? Since, as I say, I see no sense in the public-private distinction, neither do I see what precisely it consists of.

Today's decision says that two sets of prison guards who are indistinguishable in the ultimate source of their authority over prisoners, indistinguishable in the powers that they possess over prisoners, and indistinguishable in the duties that they owe towards prisoners, are to be treated quite differently in the matter of their financial liability. The only sure effect of today's decision—and the only purpose, as far as I can tell— is that it will artificially raise the cost of privatizing prisons. Whether this will cause privatization to be prohibitively expensive, or instead simply divert state funds that could have been saved or spent on additional prison services, it is likely that taxpayers and prisoners will suffer as a consequence. Neither our precedent, nor the historical foundations of § 1983, nor the policies underlying § 1983, support this result. * * *

D. STATE RECEIVERSHIP AND MUNICIPAL BANKRUPTCY

If a city's expenses exceed its revenue, it has little choice: unless it can increase tax rates or persuade the state to allow it to tap new revenue sources, it has to cut expenses. States do not allow deficit financing at the municipal level. Moreover, for cities in distress, raising taxes is likely to be counter-productive, particularly if, at the same time, the city is also forced to cut expenses. If taxes are on the rise and services are in decline, the city will fall into a vicious cycle. The more it taxes and cuts services, the more people who can afford to do so will flee to neighboring jurisdictions. And the more that happens, the more the city will become populated by poor people who cannot afford to flee. Yet not enough money can be raised by taxing the poor to support the services that they need. Cuts, therefore, would have to go deeper. These cuts would have to focus on the kind of services—like schools, police, fire, sanitation, and street lighting—that are most essential to the quality of life and, when cut, accelerate the city's decline. The reason these services have to be targeted is that some expenses—such as pension costs and debt service—can't be cut because they are legally enforceable obligations. New costs, such as for demolition of abandoned buildings, also arise. Demolition is necessary not only to prevent their use as crime sites. Abandoned buildings affect the surrounding neighborhood, reducing both property values and the resulting property taxes, thereby further exacerbating the revenue gap. Given these demands on the city budget and the difficulty of raising revenue, cities in distress are forced to cut essential city services.

When the crisis gets bad enough, the legal system offers three possible paths to follow. The first is subjecting the city to a state receivership; the second is municipal bankruptcy; the third is the pursuit of traditional common law remedies in court.[29] This section investigates the first two options. Their impact is not the same. Emergency managers appointed under a state receivership can reduce city expenses, but they cannot, unlike a bankruptcy court exercising power under Chapter 9 of the U.S. Bankruptcy Code, relieve the city of its contractual obligations. Section 903 of the Bankruptcy Code specifically provides that "a State law prescribing a method of composition of indebtedness * * * may not bind any creditor that does not consent to such composition."

"It would be sensible," Michelle Anderson has written, "if the choice among Chapter 9, a state insolvency program, and a judicial receivership depended on the nature of the city's fiscal distress. But this is not the case * * * because states rarely offer more than one of the three systems to manage insolvency."[30] Twenty-three states, she has found, have some form of state takeover laws, but the power given to the state under these laws varies widely, ranging from oversight programs to placing the state in control of the city altogether. The bankruptcy option is available only if the state has authorized cities to pursue it; twenty-seven have done so. Most of these states impose strict pre-conditions and approval requirements before bankruptcy is permitted. In short, in any given situation, the choice of paths depends on state law, with cities, here as elsewhere, allowed only the choices that the state permits. Sometimes—most famously, in 2014, in Detroit—a city has been simultaneously subjected to a receivership and bankruptcy proceedings.

This section begins with two readings on state receiverships: an excerpt from Michelle Anderson's article Democratic Dissolution and a case, Powers v. Secretary of Administration. These readings explore the power of the state over cities in crisis, but they also illustrate the limited focus of the state's attention. As Michelle Anderson puts it, the basic conception is that it is "only local government management that stands in the way of solvency." Basic structural issues that led to the crisis are not addressed, and existing contracts (as noted above) cannot be altered. Thus the emergency manager has a limited menu of options—privatization being very much one of them—to pursue. Some

---

[29] For an analysis of these three options, see Michael McConnell and Randal Picker, When Cities Go Broke: A Conceptual Introduction to Municipal Bankruptcy, 60 U. Chi. L. Rev. 425 (1993). See also Richard Schragger, Democracy and Debt, 121 Yale L. J. 860 (2012); Clayton Gillette, Bondholders and Financially Stressed Municipalities, 39 Fordham Urb. L.J. 639 (2012); Lyle Kossis, Examining the Conflict Between Financial Receivership and Local Autonomy, 98 Va. L. Rev. 1109 (2012); Heather Forrest, State Court Receivership Alternatives to Chapter 9, 29 Am. Bankr. Inst. J. 12 (2010); Omer Kimhi, Legal Remedies to Municipal Financial Crises, 88 B.U. L. Rev. 633 (2008). For an analysis of the possibility of a bankruptcy process for states, see Daniel Skeel, Is Bankruptcy The Answer for Troubled Cities and States, 50 Hous. L. Rev. 1063 (2013). For an analysis of alternative strategies for revitalizing cities in decline, see, e.g., John Gallagher, Revolution Detroit: Strategies for Urban Reinvention (2013); Margaret Dewar and June Thomas (eds.), The City After Abandonment (2012).

[30] Michelle Wilde Anderson, The New Minimal Cities, 123 Yale L.J. 1118, 1155 (2014).

commentators have suggested that the states are in a better position to address the fundamental issues facing cities in distress than a federal bankruptcy court and that they should be empowered to do so.[31] Such a shift from the federal courts to the states would require a radical rethinking of bankruptcy law, as well as an interpretation of the Contracts Clause of the United States Constitution that would permit states to provide debt relief for municipalities in trouble. Is the problem with state receivership that the state exercises too much power over cities or too little?

The final two readings explore municipal bankruptcy. A case, In re Stockton, California, analyzes both the role of the Contracts Clause in bankruptcy and, more importantly, the provision of the Bankruptcy Code denying a federal bankruptcy court the power to interfere with either a municipality's governmental power or its property and revenues. As the case suggests, this provision was motivated, at least in part, by the concerns about federal-state relationship explored in Chapter Two of the casebook. What is the impact of Printz v. United States on a bankruptcy court's ability to alter city decision making? Is the fact that the bankruptcy proceedings are voluntary—that is, that they are initiated by the municipality—sufficient to overcome the concerns about coercion expressed in NFIB v. Sibelius?

Some commentators have been critical of the limitation on the power of bankruptcy courts over city power and revenues, arguing that it enables debtor municipalities unfairly to protect city residents at the expense of bondholders and city employees relying on pensions.[32] To be sure, as they point out, this deference to local decision making is not unlimited. The Bankruptcy Code also requires the municipality to engage in good faith negotiation with creditors. This requirement can be interpreted to protect creditors against excessive favoritism to residents. Still, under current law, a city is granted considerable discretion concerning its policies and revenues.

The final reading below, an excerpt from another article by Michelle Anderson, expresses an opposite concern: bankruptcy law might disadvantage city residents rather than favor them. She argues that a bankruptcy proceeding should not only ensure that a city's debts are reduced but that the city's ability to provide neighborhood safety and habitability is protected. The same concern was voiced by the bankruptcy court in In re City of Detroit, Michigan, 504 B.R. 97 (2013). The court

---

[31] Michael McConnell and Randal Picker, When Cities Go Broke: A Conceptual Introduction to Municipal Bankruptcy, 60 U. Chi. L. Rev. 425 (1993).

[32] See, e.g., Clayton Gillette, Fiscal Federalism, Political Will, and the Strategic Use of Municipal Bankruptcy, 79 U. Chi. L. Rev. 281 (2012); Michael McConnell and Randal Picker, When Cities Go Broke: A Conceptual Introduction to Municipal Bankruptcy, 60 U. Chi. L. Rev. 425 (1993).

stressed that a focus on the residents of Detroit was "of paramount importance":

> The City's debt and cash flow insolvency is causing its nearly 700,000 residents to suffer hardship. * * * Its services do not function properly due to inadequate funding. The City has an extraordinarily high crime rate; too many street lights do not function; EMS does not timely respond; the City's parks are neglected and disappearing; and the equipment for police, EMS and fire services are outdated and inadequate. Over 38% of the City's revenues were consumed by servicing debt in 2012, and that figure is projected to increase to nearly 65% of the budget by 2017 if the debt is not restructured. Without revitalization, revenues will continue to plummet as residents leave Detroit for municipalities with lower tax rates and acceptable services. Without the protection of chapter 9, the City will be forced to continue on the path that it was on until it filed this case. In order to free up cash for day-to-day operations, the City would continue to borrow money, defer capital investments, and shrink its workforce. This solution has proven unworkable. It is also dangerous for its residents. If the City were to continue to default on its financial obligations, as it would outside of bankruptcy, creditor lawsuits would further deplete the City's resources. On the other hand, in seeking chapter 9 relief, the City not only reorganizes its debt and enhances City services, but it also creates an opportunity for investments in its revitalization efforts for the good of the residents of Detroit.

How much can a state receivership or a bankruptcy process help in this effort toward revitalization? What else is needed—and who has the power to accomplish whatever that is?

MICHELLE WILDE ANDERSON, DEMOCRATIC DISSOLUTION: RADICAL EXPERIMENTATION IN STATE TAKEOVERS OF LOCAL GOVERNMENTS

39 Fordham Urban L.J. 577, 579–586, 602, 605, 618–619, 621 (2012).

Fiscal crisis is generally described in numbers. Here are a few from the city of Benton Harbor, Michigan. More than 48% of its residents live below the poverty line, compared to just 7% in St. Joseph, Benton Harbor's sister city across the river. Formerly a thriving industrial hub for the region, Benton Harbor saw the rapid flight of thousands of white families and jobs from the 1960s to the 1980s. Today, the city is 91% black. St. Joseph is 88% white. At least five decades of bitter race relations separate the cities sometimes known to each other as "Benton Harlem" and "St. Johannesburg." * * * A March 2011 audit estimated

Benton Harbor's debt at $6 million—quite a figure for a city of just over 10,000 people. Deepening the fiscal crisis, appliance maker Whirlpool Corporation announced layoffs in 2011 of 5,000 employees, many of whom worked at the company's world headquarters in Benton Harbor. * * *

As a result of a law passed in 2011, the [Benton Harbor] City Council is now limited to three powers: calling council meetings to order, adjourning meetings, and approving council minutes. The authority, substance, and process in between—setting the meeting, proposing agenda items, determining policy, and managing operations—all lie in the hands of the city's "emergency manager," a state appointee. Under the 2011 law, when the state places a city in receivership because of fiscal distress, the emergency manager assumes the responsibilities of all elected officials for the city. In addition to functionally firing elected officials, the 2011 law gives emergency managers significant new powers. Most notably, they can now break existing collective bargaining agreements and other contracts, negotiate and approve any future agreements on the city's behalf, and ban the city's entry into new collective bargaining agreements for up to five years. They can also privatize the city for the long-term, if not permanently, by contracting out for services, selling public assets, and cancelling local programs.

Michigan's law is similar in key respects to a new state receivership law passed in Rhode Island in 2010. The new laws in Michigan and Rhode Island represent a major change from older models of state receiverships, in which states generally granted emergency bailout funding in exchange for local consent to the appointment of state receivers, and these receivers then guided financial recovery planning alongside local officials. Breaking with these models in the name of fiscal exigency, Michigan and Rhode Island now permit a state takeover without bailout funding or local consent, and they dramatically increase the powers granted to emergency managers.

The new laws suspend a city's charter and its sitting government, imposing the authority of the state through an appointee of the governor. A legislative sponsor of the Michigan bill thus referred to the legislation as "financial martial law." A more precise description of the new statutes is, in my view, "democratic dissolution"—that is, changes that suspend local democracy, even though the city remains a legal entity. For an unbounded period of time, a city's corporate status is held in place while its charter and system of government are replaced by a single official acting with unprecedented authority, discretion, and autonomy. This unusual combination means that the receiverships dissolve democratic self-rule for the city, but not in a way that changes the taxable land base of the city or the service needs of its population. In other words, local power is absorbed by the state but the local budget is not—the struggling city must continue to sustain the costs of an independent municipal government (including the emergency manager's salary, staffing costs, and administrative expenses) through revenues collected locally. Whereas a true dissolution removes a locality's borders and thus merges its land base and people with a larger county or township government, a democratic dissolution preserves the municipal corporation but suspends its government. * * *

The clear message of these laws—that it is only local government management that stands in the way of solvency—is a gross oversimplification of the causes of fiscal decline. Centralization of power by the state on these terms does not ameliorate structural causes of financial distress, like concentrated poverty, the loss of middle-class jobs across a region, or local borders that fragment a single metropolitan area into socioeconomically segregated cities. Indeed, local democratic dissolution may only exacerbate fiscal malaise over the longer term by facilitating changes (like the abrupt sale of public assets) that produce quick returns at the cost of permanent sustainability. Along the way, radical state takeovers can enflame antagonism between state and local actors, further disempower a beleaguered local electorate, and dramatically undermine the transparency and accountability of local governance. * * *

Laws permitting state intervention in the finances of struggling municipalities have been on the books in most states since the Great Depression. Dozens of cities, both large and small, have come under state supervision since the 1970s. * * * Municipal insolvency legislation generally establishes triggering conditions for intervention, such as specific economic criteria. It empowers a state financial board or state-appointed receiver to gather information about the city's financial condition, to manage its debt (usually by providing guarantees to creditors for the city's loans, thereby enabling the city to access credit markets), and to manage the city's finances through approval of a rehabilitation plan with revenue and spending changes. State interventions have ranged from "oversight" systems with weak intervention authority to "control" systems with strong intervention authority. Central to the differences among these approaches is the status of local officials during the period of intervention, as well as the power of the receiver to raise taxes and user fees, reduce expenditures, eliminate services, issue new service contracts, liquidate municipal assets, and engage in negotiations over collective bargaining agreements.

Receivership laws reflect differing theories about why local governments fail. Some theories emphasize internal causes, such as the incompetence and untrustworthiness of municipal officials, or defects in the local political economy, particularly the dominance of a narrow band of special interests in local politics. Other explanations stress external factors, such as socioeconomic decline, regional change, and racial discrimination. If causal theories vary, so too do the legislative purposes of state intervention. Receiverships can serve any or all of four constituencies and their interests. First is the people of the city, who depend on the faltering local government to ensure public safety, provide services, protect property values, and the like. Second is other municipalities in the state, which may suffer a contagion effect of the local crisis if municipal bond markets deem all cities in the state to be a less secure investment because the state allowed one of its cities to default on debt obligations. The third main constituency of municipal insolvency laws is bondholders or creditors, who have a strong interest in avoiding the restructuring of debt permitted in municipal bankruptcy. Lastly, receiverships affect local public employees and retirees, who depend on and have relied upon contracts with the local government for their household financial security. Like bondholders, these current and former employees have a vested interest in avoiding bankruptcy and its potential rupture of collective bargaining agreements. A state legislature's theory of the causes of fiscal distress and its purposes for intervention shape its legal intervention to ameliorate the crisis.

Traditionally, state receiverships were coupled with increased financial support from the state. * * * Given the current degree of state fiscal stress and falling levels of state aid for local governments, however, states are loathe to send bailout funding to even the most troubled local governments. States are thus looking for cheaper solutions to local problems—i.e., reforms that address local fiscal stress and its potential contagion impacts on the creditworthiness of other municipalities in the state without providing state financial support, whether offered as grants, loans, or loan guarantees. Michigan and Rhode Island are thus conducting an experiment of great interest to states with troubled municipalities. Can a state slash funding for local governments while using an unprecedentedly strong state receivership as a backstop to fiscal distress? * * * The dissolutions enacted in Michigan and Rhode Island * * * do not seek, and cannot achieve, a major fiscal restructuring that relieves a struggling area of the costs of sustaining an independent municipal government through existing revenues. * * * The core problem with the statutes in Michigan and Rhode Island is that legislators fell prey to the illusion that by entirely sacrificing * * * local democracy, they could ameliorate local fiscal crisis. They also set one public policy value above all others: the management of negative externalities, i.e., the preservation of municipal creditworthiness and bond markets in the state. In elevating this objective—even though, paradoxically, that objective lies farthest beyond a receiver's control—they explicitly eliminated local democracy and effectively demoted or endangered all of the other values. * * *

A state receiver's authority in time of crisis should be held in check by * * * narrowly defined triggering conditions, a locally inclusive selection process [of the state receiver], structural reform efforts, stronger state oversight, and clear sunset provisions. * * * [E]lected officials for the city, including both the mayor and city council, should retain their general governing authority. Most critically, they should continue to control city land use law and policy, arguably the most powerful dimension of local authority when it comes to shaping a city and its revenues over the long term. Essentially, this reform would limit the emergency manager to fiscal authority, including all control of revenues and spending. Such authority should be defined by statute to include the power to operate, manage, and curtail services for the locale—critical tools for controlling spending locally. * * * This fiscal authority, however, should be specifically defined to exclude the power to sell public land assets * * *, [which are] among the most valuable and non-fungible assets for economic development and land use planning in a city, even in a down market. * * *

The state should also use the lever of financial coercion to support formation of a regional council to facilitate structural changes that promote financial sustainability. The council should be composed of officials from the state, the municipality (including both the emergency manager and an elected official), neighboring municipalities, and the township or county government. The council would be charged with considering long-term structural reform at the regional level, particularly service sharing, consolidation, merger, dissolution, and revenue-sharing. Any resulting deals developed within this body could be rewarded with front-end subsidization by the state as an incentive for cooperation. Such coordination would support the goal of local defragmentation, which has become critical in Michigan and other states, and it would permit long-term thinking about the way that a city's existing borders may impede recovery. * * *

POWERS V. SECRETARY OF ADMINISTRATION

Supreme Judicial Court of Massachusetts, 1992.
412 Mass. 119, 587 N.E.2d 744.

LIACOS, CHIEF JUSTICE.

On September 11, 1991, in response to a recommendation from the Governor, the Senate and the House of Representatives each passed * * * "An Act establishing a receivership for the city of Chelsea" (Receivership Act). The Receivership Act provided, inter alia, that: (1) a "fiscal crisis" existed in Chelsea; (2) a receivership must be established and a receiver appointed by the Governor to an initial one year term "[i]n order to institute a comprehensive long-term solution to [Chelsea's] financial problems"; (3) "[the] receiver shall be the chief executive officer of

[Chelsea] and shall be responsible for the overall operation and administration of [Chelsea]"; (4) the office of the mayor of Chelsea shall be vacated and shall remain vacant during the term of the receivership; (5) the Chelsea "board of aldermen shall be vested only with the power to advise [the] receiver concerning matters previously within its jurisdiction under the [Chelsea] charter"; (6) the receiver shall be vested with all powers previously vested in the office of the mayor, as well as additional enumerated powers; and (7) the receiver shall report to the Secretary of Administration (Secretary), who "shall have authority to reappoint the receiver for additional one-year terms * * * [and] may also terminate the receiver for cause at any time." On September 12, 1991, the Governor signed the Receivership Act, the provisions of which became effective upon passage, and appointed a receiver for Chelsea.

On September 17, 1991, the plaintiffs, citizens of and homeowners in Chelsea, filed a complaint with the Supreme Judicial Court for the county of Suffolk alleging that * * * the Receivership Act was passed in violation of art. 89 of the Amendments to the Constitution of the Commonwealth, more commonly known as the Home Rule Amendment. * * * As this court previously has noted, § 8 of the Home Rule Amendment, which limits the circumstances under which the Legislature can pass "special laws" which apply to only one particular city or town, "clearly evidenc[es] a concern that no city or town be singled out for special treatment." *Doris v. Police Comm'r of Boston*, 374 Mass. 443, 446, 373 N.E.2d 944 (1978). Accordingly, § 8 provides that, in the absence of explicitly defined special circumstances, the Legislature has the authority to "act in relation to cities and towns * * * only by general laws which apply alike to all cities or to all towns, or to all cities and towns, or to a class of not fewer than two." To the extent that the Legislature wants to pass a "special law," § 8 provides four separate procedures * * *. The parties do not dispute that the only § 8 procedure in issue before us is that procedure which provides the Legislature may pass a special law "by a two-thirds vote of each branch of the general court following a recommendation by the governor." * * * [T]he parties stipulate that "[e]ach branch of the Legislature passed the Act by a two-thirds vote." * * * The plaintiffs, however, point to the * * * [fact that the] Act was passed on a "voice vote" * * *. [W]e reject the plaintiffs' contention that a voice vote does not meet the requirements of § 8. * * *

The plaintiffs also claim that the Receivership Act violates § 1 of the Home Rule Amendment [which grants cities and towns "the right of self-government in local matters."] * * * To the extent that the plaintiffs intend to argue that the Receivership Act violates the underlying purpose of the Home Rule Amendment because the act removed from the city's elected officials the authority to address Chelsea's fiscal crisis and vested it in an appointed receiver, this argument is without merit. This court has recognized in previous decisions that the Home Rule Amendment grants the Legislature extensive authority over municipal government. * * * Section 1 prevents a municipality from exercising powers in a manner that is inconsistent with "such standards and requirements as the general court may establish by law in accordance with the provisions of [the Home Rule Amendment.]" * * * Therefore, to the extent that there was a conflict between exercise of the authority granted to the receiver and the authority held by Chelsea's elected government, § 1 required that the elected government give way. The Receivership Act does not conflict with § 1 of the Home Rule Amendment. * * *

The plaintiffs argue that the appointment of a receiver violates the "one person, one vote" rule of the equal protection clause of the Fourteenth Amendment to the United States Constitution because their "constitutional right" to elect their municipal officials has been ignored. This argument is without merit. The plaintiffs have not referred us to any State or Federal constitutional provision to support their claim that they have a constitutional right to elective municipal officials, nor can we find one. As this court previously has held, the Home Rule Amendment recognizes the Legislature's broad authority over municipalities. This authority includes the power to choose to provide an appointive, rather than elective, form of municipal government. *Opinion of the Justices*, 368 Mass. 849, 854, 332 N.E.2d 896 (1975). * * * With regard to Federal constitutional impediments to an appointive municipal government, the United States Supreme Court has stated that "[w]e see nothing in the [Federal] Constitution to prevent experimentation. At least as respects nonlegislative officers, a State can appoint local officials or elect them or combine the elective and appointive systems." *Sailors v. Board of Educ. of the County of Kent*, 387 U.S. 105, 111, 87 S.Ct. 1549, 1553, 18 L.Ed.2d 650 (1967). Because the plaintiffs do not have a constitutional right to an elective form of municipal government, and because the Legislature has chosen to provide Chelsea with an appointed receiver, the "one person, one vote" rule is inapplicable to the present case. * * *

IN RE CITY OF STOCKTON, CALIFORNIA

United States Bankruptcy Court, E.D. California, 2012.
478 B.R. 8.

CHRISTOPHER M. KLEIN, BANKRUPTCY JUDGE.

The retired employees of the City of Stockton want this court to order the City to keep paying for their health benefits during this chapter 9 case. The difficulty is that 11 U.S.C. § 904 forbids the court from using any of its powers to "interfere with" property or revenues of a chapter 9 debtor. Accordingly, although the City's unilateral interim reduction of retiree health benefit payments may lead to tragic hardships for individuals in the interval before their claims are redressed in a chapter 9 plan of adjustment, the motion for injunctive relief must be denied. * * *

The City of Stockton filed this chapter 9 case on June 28, 2012. * * * The Stockton City Council adopted a budget for the Fiscal Year commencing July 1, 2012, that, by state law, must be balanced. The required balance was achieved by cutting costs, including unilaterally reducing retiree health benefits. This adversary proceeding seeks: an injunction prohibiting the City from implementing the retiree health benefit reduction; a declaration that the changes are unlawful; and an order compelling the City to pay for the retiree health benefit for all retirees entitled to it as of July 1, 2012; and attorney fees. For purposes of the present analysis (but without deciding the question), the retiree health benefits are regarded as bargained-for and vested contractual rights. * * *

This adversary proceeding is premised at bottom on the Contracts Clause of the United States Constitution: "No State shall . . . pass any . . . Law impairing the Obligation of Contracts." Art. I, § 10, cl. 1. * * * The first cause of action * * * alleges that in "unilaterally changing the terms of the Retiree Health Benefit, the City impaired contractual obligations, in violation of Article I section [10] of the United States Constitution and 42 U.S.C. § 1983." * * * While the Contracts Clause is a key navigational star in the firmament of our Constitution and economic universe, it is subject to being eclipsed by the Bankruptcy Clause: "The Congress shall have Power to . . . establish . . . uniform Laws on the subject of Bankruptcies throughout the United States." Art. I, § 8, cl. 4. Significantly, the Contracts Clause bans a state from making a law impairing the obligation of contract; it does not ban Congress from making a law impairing the obligation of contract. This asymmetry is no accident. The Bankruptcy Clause necessarily authorizes Congress to make laws that would impair contracts. * * * The goal of the Bankruptcy Code is adjusting the debtor-creditor relationship. Every discharge impairs contracts. * * * It follows, then, that contracts may be impaired in this chapter 9 case without offending the Constitution. * * * The federal bankruptcy power also, by operation of the Supremacy Clause, trumps the similar contracts clause in the California state constitution. * * *

A delicate state-federal relationship of mutual sovereigns in which the Tenth Amendment looms large provides the framework for municipal bankruptcy and gives context to this dispute. A pair of chapter 9 provisions honors state-federal balance by reserving certain state powers and by correlatively limiting the powers of the federal court: 11 U.S.C. §§ 903 and 904. Section 903 reserves to the state the power to control political and governmental powers, as well as expenditures:

§ 903. Reservation of State power to control municipalities

This chapter does not limit or impair the power of a State to control, by legislation or otherwise, a municipality of or in such State in the exercise of the political or governmental powers of such municipality, including expenditures for such exercise, but—

(1) a State law prescribing a method of composition of indebtedness of such municipality may not bind any creditor that does not consent to such composition; and

(2) a judgment entered under such a law may not bind a creditor that does not consent to such composition. * * *

Section 904 complements § 903. In view of the inability of a state to control or condition chapter 9 proceedings after the municipal case is filed with the state's permission, § 904 imposes limits on the federal court to assure that powers reserved to the states are honored:

§ 904. Limitation on jurisdiction and powers of court

Notwithstanding any power of the court, unless the debtor consents or the plan so provides, the court may not, by any stay, order, or decree, in the case or otherwise, interfere with—

(1) any of the political or governmental powers of the debtor;

(2) any of the property or revenues of the debtor; or

(3) the debtor's use or enjoyment of any income-producing property.

As the construction of § 904 is central to the instant matter, its history is important. The statutory limit on the authority of the court that is now § 904 has been enacted four times. Each revision has reduced the latitude within which the court can act. The limit has come to be described as "absolute." The overall goal is a balance that does not offend the Tenth Amendment: "The powers not delegated to the United States by the Constitution, nor prohibited by it to the States, are reserved to the States, or to the people."

The evolution of the limit on court authority in what is now § 904—from 1934 to its current version—is instructive. * * * The first enactment of the limit on court authority was in the first municipal bankruptcy law in 1934:

The judge ... (11) shall not, by any order or decree, in the proceeding or otherwise, interfere with (a) any of the political or governmental powers of the taxing district, or (b) any of the property or revenues of the taxing district necessary *in the opinion of the judge* for essential governmental purposes, or (c) any income-producing property, unless the plan of readjustment so provides. (emphasis supplied).

The Supreme Court disapproved the 1934 statute as an unconstitutional interference with the sovereignty of a state on two theories. First, structurally, municipal bankruptcy was an impossible contradiction of federalism. Second, the particular statutory terms might enable the federal government to impose its will on an unwilling sovereign state. *Ashton v. Cameron Cnty. Water Improvement Dist. No. 1*, 298 U.S. 513, 532 (1936). * * *

Congress reacted to *Ashton* in 1937 by reenacting the municipal bankruptcy provisions with revisions designed to reduce the opportunity for excessive federal control over state sovereignty. One significant change was deletion of the phrase "in the opinion of the judge" so as to make the concept of "property or revenues necessary for essential services" less dependant on the subjective view of a federal judge. * * * The Supreme Court validated the 1937 municipal bankruptcy statute in *United States v. Bekins*, 304 U.S. 27 (1938), reasoning that it was a cooperative enterprise by state and federal sovereigns that was carefully drawn so as not to infringe state sovereignty. It emphasized that a state "retains control of its fiscal affairs" and that "no control or jurisdiction over that property and those revenues of the petitioning agency necessary for essential governmental purposes is conferred" on the federal court.

The third version of the statutory limit on court authority was part of a modernization of former Bankruptcy Act chapter IX in 1976. * * * [T]he qualification "necessary for essential government services" was deleted from the ban on interference with property or revenues of the debtor. * * * The deletion of the phrase "necessary for essential government services" from § 82(c)(2) aimed to broaden the limitation. The words "necessary" and "essential" invited unnecessary litigation. The "governmental services" language reflected an obsolete distinction between governmental and proprietary functions that the Supreme Court abolished in 1946. The phrase overlapped and confused the related ban on judicial interference with income-producing property.

The 1976 version was reenacted in 1978 as 11 U.S.C. § 904 with the addition of the preambular phrase "Notwithstanding any power of the court." This additional limiting language forbids resort to a federal court's inherent or equitable powers. It reflects reinvigorated sensitivity in 1978 by Congress to the need to avoid unnecessary intrusions of state sovereignty in order to obviate the risk of invalidation by the Supreme Court. That heightened concern stemmed, in part, from the Supreme Court's then-recent invocation of the Tenth Amendment to invalidate part of a labor statute. *Nat'l League of Cities v. Usery*, 426 U.S. 833 (1976), overruled, *Garcia v. San Antonio Metro. Transit Auth.*, 469 U.S. 528 (1985). * * *

The message derived from this history regarding the power of this court to interfere with the City's actions regarding retiree health benefits compels the conclusion that § 904 prevents any federal court from doing what the plaintiffs request, regardless of whether the City's action is fair or unfair. The concern has constitutional proportions. Chapter 9 passed constitutional muster on the basis that the federal bankruptcy power be exercised at the request of, but not at the expense of, the sovereign state in an exercise of cooperation among sovereigns. * * * The entire structure of chapter 9 has been influenced by this pervasive concern to preserve the niceties of the state-federal relationship. The foundation involves multiple levels of consent. No chapter 9 case can be filed other than a voluntary case filed by the municipality with the consent of the state. 11 U.S.C. § 109(c)(2). The municipality consents by filing the voluntary case. 11 U.S.C. § 301, incorporated by § 901(a). Consent is implicit in the restriction that only the municipality can propose a plan of adjustment. 11 U.S.C. § 941. Another consent is the express consent recognized in § 904 that the City has declined to give in this proceeding. 11 U.S.C. § 904. * * * In short, the § 904 limitation on the court's authority is absolute, with only the two exceptions stated in § 904: consent; and provision in a plan of adjustment (which can only be proposed by the municipality). * * * It is impossible to envision how granting the plaintiffs' prayer for an "order compelling the City to maintain the Retiree Health Benefit * * *" would not require the payment of money from the City's property or revenues. * * * It follows that the relief sought is barred by § 904(2) as an interference with the City's "property or revenues." * * *

The real remedy for the plaintiffs lies in participating in the process of formulating a plan of adjustment. As this court has previously explained, the lessons of recent chapter 9 cases teach that successful plans of adjustment are most likely to be achieved by the parties in interest all coming to the table and participating in bona fide negotiations. Every issue that is resolved by agreement will enhance the prospects for a successful plan of adjustment. To that end, the court has appointed a judge as standing mediator for this case to facilitate a negotiated solution. * * *

MICHELLE WILDE ANDERSON, THE NEW MINIMAL CITIES
123 Yale L.J. 1118, 1120, 1122–1124, 1193–1195, 1197–1204, 1210–1211, 1214–1218 (2014).

Unable to meet obligations to creditors while also keeping government services in operation, the City of Detroit entered a state receivership on March 14, 2013 and filed for bankruptcy on July 18. That makes Detroit the twenty-eighth city to declare municipal bankruptcy or to enter a receivership for fiscal crisis since late 2008, a window of time that has seen five of the six largest municipal bankruptcies in American history. In a long-term transformation of local finance that has accelerated in the recent recession, these cities and others are engaging in slash-and-burn budgeting to address falling revenues, rising expenses, and mounting debt. In San Bernardino, the third California city to declare bankruptcy in the recent recession, the City Attorney followed another round of deep cuts to the police department with solemn advice to residents: "Lock your doors and load your guns." * * *

Local government is shrinking in these and other struggling cities. Years, if not decades, of budget cuts and asset sales have left little beyond a stripped-down version of core service functions like irregular police and fire protection, rudimentary sanitation, and water supply. * * * How low can these cuts go? While laws provide an entitlement to a public education, and we have long struggled to interpret what constitutes a legally adequate education, there is little to nothing to indicate what other services the local public sector must provide. Beyond education, is there some minimum level of public services and public space needed to achieve neighborhood safety and habitability?

This is a humanitarian question, but it is also a doctrinal challenge. * * * Decisionmakers must evaluate, in essence, whether a city could cut still more deeply into spending on current residents to pay off creditors, or whether it is creditors, rather than residents, who have to bear the next round of cuts. Standards for local public services must necessarily inform this balancing of interests between creditors and current residents. Creditors such as bondholders, retired public employees, contractors, and tort plaintiffs have contracts and legal judgments that quantify a city's obligations to them. Residents, by contrast, have no such legal instruments with which to monetize their share of a city's revenues. * * * Municipal bankruptcy and receivership laws articulate a duty to protect "basic public safety" and minimum services "consistent with public health and safety," but these laws lack guidance as to what those broad concepts mean as a practical matter. * * * Where to set the floor under public service cuts is a critical legal issue in public insolvencies * * *.

My goal is not to assert that residents' interests are the only ones urgently at stake in a bankruptcy. "Creditors" is a monolithic word that stands in for thousands of individuals as well as institutions. Among them are retirees who worked for decades in insolvent cities plagued by poverty, crime, and, in some cases, demoralizing working conditions. From the point of view of individual retirees, most pension commitments are not extravagant: the average annual police pension in Detroit, for example, is $30,000 a year, and general city workers (like librarians or sanitation workers) receive about $18,000 a year. If these payments fall through, there may be nothing except poverty programs to fall back on, because many of these retirees, including most former fire and law enforcement employees, are excluded by law from Social Security. * * * The word "creditor" also stands for investors who lent these cities money in good faith, believing loans to municipalities to be one of the most stable, predictable assets available in American financial markets. When a city defaults on its obligations to bondholders, it creates risk in municipal bond markets that may drive up borrowing costs for other cities in the future. * * * I thus stand on the foundation that creditor perspectives on municipal insolvency are compelling from both a humanistic perspective and a policy one. I leave the full articulation of those perspectives, however, to other work * * *. Instead, I focus here on residents' position in the struggle toward the "least bad" compromise that is the nature of insolvency. * * *

[In a] prospective recovery plan, * * * a Chapter 9 court * * * [must] "evaluate whether it is probable that the debtor can both pay pre-petition debt and provide future public services at the level necessary to its viability as a municipality." What service levels do cities need to meet that standard? * * * I find it surprising to report that neither Chapter 9 case law nor state law regulations or guidelines define legally adequate service levels—things like the advisable number of firefighters needed for a given unit of population or a given incident rate. It would seem that city officials, bankruptcy courts, and state receivers are completely on their own in trying to apply these terms. * * *

[W]hen a city enters insolvency, both state and federal law assume that city residents are entitled to some degree of basic services provided by the government. Past cases assume that residents—not as individuals, but as a class—are entitled to have a 911 emergency system that dispatches police officers and firefighters, along with solid waste pick up, wastewater treatment, and other basics. * * * At its heart, citywide spending in pursuit of meaningful health, safety, and welfare amounts to a commitment to habitability. It is a rubric that sounds in human rights, moral duties, social contract theory, and social justice, and it stands for the idea that some urban conditions are intolerable. Habitability invites reflection about the just city, not simply the solvent one. While the anti-tenement movement of the early twentieth century wrote building codes, and the anti-poverty movement of the 1960s and '70s established a warranty of habitability to protect tenants, we have never had a collective public conversation about habitability at larger neighborhood scales. * * * [U]rban-scale habitability is a question of collective conditions, such as crime rates, fire risk, emergency response times, access to clean water, access to wastewater disposal systems, and street lighting. * * *

Land-use controls on new construction provide a first useful source of minimum standards for the built environment in a neighborhood. A subdivision, i.e., a neighborhood constructed from scratch, is subject to a city's planning and subdivision codes. These are regulatory mechanisms that require landowners to satisfy certain conditions prior to receiving a permit to build. For instance, developers of large-scale subdivisions might be required to install street lighting, construct sewerage infrastructure, build roads, and provide some amount of dedicated open space (like a park) for their residents. * * * [B]ecause they constitute the local view of what the private sector should provide as a basis for livable communities, subdivision codes say a great deal about that city's norms for safe, stable, and comfortable neighborhoods. * * * A baseline like the subdivision code numbers gives the public and decisionmakers a way to discuss relative investments from one neighborhood to the next.

A city's building codes are the backbone of habitability analysis for individual buildings, but so too are they important for neighborhood-scale analysis. Buildings and their blocks are synergistic: blight drags down the property values and quality of life for persons nearby. * * * [C]ities can condemn buildings that create safety hazards. * * * The city can declare such a structure unfit for occupancy or a safety risk (i.e., by posing an attractive nuisance to children, or harboring criminal activity), and issue a notice (along with fines) to the landowner that the structure constitutes a public safety hazard and the condition must be corrected or the building demolished within a statutorily-defined time period. If the necessary stabilization or demolition is not corrected, the city can abate the hazard itself (including through demolition) and attach a lien to the property to assign those costs to landowners. These procedures require public investments up front * * *. Such investments are nonetheless wise both in terms of residential habitability and the city's long-term property tax revenues.

Environmental regulations provide habitability standards applicable to water and sanitation systems. In old neighborhoods, water and sewerage infrastructure may be outdated and inadequate, risking the contamination of soil, waterways, or drinking water. * * * Like building code enforcement against low-income dwellings, this is a story of regulation without funding attached, in which safety standards are applied adversarially against an agent * * * who will have to locate substantial funds for abatement. Before, during, and after an insolvency, a city must both provide safe and functional infrastructure and comply with environmental regulation, thus making this part of the on-going cost of doing business for a city and one more source of standards for assessing residents' public safety needs.

In the context of collective bargaining, unions often advocate for minimum staffing requirements—i.e., the number of firefighters who must be dispatched for a major blaze. These provisions represent the union's own interests, of course, in keeping members safe and enlarging the workforce covered by the agreement, but they also represent one view of how many staff people it takes for a local service provider to protect the safety of workers and residents, and do so efficiently. * * * In addition to benchmarks for staffing levels within any given service, city planners need to determine appropriate service outputs as well as the prioritization among services competing for city funds. Specific metrics might include: average emergency response times across a state or region, per capita police and fire department staffing levels, or the benefits of public spending in terms of reduced private costs.

Habitability should be about more than urban containment and damage control; it should be about urban betterment. Dating back to at least the 1960s, researchers, public officials, policy advisors, think tanks, and others have been considering best practices for cities that house neighborhoods of concentrated poverty. Broad consensus exists across these sources that to combat crime and stabilize communities, cities cannot simply hire more police. From community policing efforts to afterschool programs for teenagers, from job training to economic development efforts, cities have a role in providing, or at least facilitating, long-term investments that improve individuals' economic stability and flourishing. * * *

Deliberation about equitable, adequate levels of public investment has long been underway in the context of education, and there is a great deal to be learned from that history. After decades of reform efforts focused on reducing the fiscal inequality among school districts, education advocates in the late 1980s began turning from equity to adequacy, arguing that the state need not eliminate disparities, but instead should serve as a guarantor of "an acceptable basic level of educational services." * * * [T]hey began to argue for substantive minimum standards defined by district characteristics such as class sizes, teacher qualifications, and materials. They emphasized adequacy of inputs as well as performance outputs, but the inputs were substantive (such as guaranteed access to textbooks or maximum class size limits) rather than per capita funding rules. These efforts relied primarily on constitutional and statutory language regarding the right to a public education, but also on a wider moral platform that some levels of investment in education were simply too low to vindicate the values underlying a free public education. * * * Adequacy theories in education have faced challenges * * *. Nonetheless, by struggling through that debate, education has pushed past a vague commitment to provide public schools and toward a set of specific regulations subjected to public scrutiny and input. * * *

For more than a decade, creative academic and policy work under the banner of the "shrinking cities movement" in the United States, Germany, and other nations has focused on the land-use challenges faced by post-industrial cities that have lost dramatic shares of their population in recent decades. * * * Shrinking cities land-use planners * * * advise a set of withdrawals from the desperate competition for large-scale growth and development that has chronically generated a poor return on public subsidies—the packages of tax incentives and infrastructure investments to induce major land uses like automalls and aquariums, cineplexes and science parks, museums and stadiums. Instead of chasing growth, shrinking cities theories focus on the more modest task of "enhanc[ing] the quality of life of residents without adding jobs, people, or even increasing income levels." The "just city," imagines Susan Fainstein, is one that focuses on the needs and well-being of current city residents, rather than some population remembered from the past or courted for the future. * * *

[S]ome cities' descent into municipal insolvency involved fiscal mismanagement, if not corruption. But even in these few cities—and certainly in all the others—mismanagement can be a scapegoat explanation for insolvency that distracts from other systemic challenges, including concentrated poverty, the overhang of costs created by population loss, public subsidization of new cities at the expense of old ones, and so forth. Insolvent cities need a safety net, not punishment. Their creditors may well deserve the same. * * * [H]igher level governments bear some responsibility for fostering the legal, political, and economic conditions for decline, and there is no reason to shy away from calling them to the table for in-kind and monetary assistance. * * * The consequences of a bare bones public sector in high-poverty areas are not a mystery. * * * [U]ninhabitable conditions in a poor community do not correct on their own. * * * [W]ithout intervening public investment in basic infrastructure and public safety, such communities simply deteriorate and depreciate over time. * * *

E. DELIVERING CITY SERVICES

This section returns to a question first raised at the outset of this chapter: what is the purpose of city government? Why do we have cities at all, rather than simply allow the states to govern local areas through branch offices? Sections A and B suggested one possible answer: the purpose of city government is to enable people to control the character of their own community, whether defined as the city as a whole or as a neighborhood within the city. In this section, we explore another answer: cities are valuable because they provide city services to local residents. (Yet other answers to the question are offered in sections F and G, below. There it is suggested that the objective of city government should be to generate economic development or to foster democratic participation in governmental decision making.)

Since the mid-nineteenth century, the delivery of public services has become an important—perhaps the most important—city function. This section explores the current controversy over this familiar city activity. As

Guido Martinotti argues in a provocative article, this "first generation" conception of cities—one that conceives of cities as having a relationship principally with its own residents—has been supplemented, if not replaced, by alternative understandings of city functions.[33] A second conception, Martinotti contends, focuses city attention not on its residents but on its users: tourists, students, and suburban residents seeking entertainment and diversion. A third conception directs city attention principally to business people: city governments, in this view, should concentrate on connecting business executives in large cities across the planet rather than on providing amenities to city residents or even to the people who live in the same metropolitan area. These alternative objectives for city government activity are explored in the next section.

This section opens with Gerald Frug's analysis of two competing models of city services. The first model conceives of city services as consumer goods and, therefore, as comparable to services provided by the private sector.[34] The second model suggests that city services have a different purpose, one that he describes as "community building." To explore how these two models work out in practice, the subsection concentrates on two local services: policing and schools.

David Sklansky's article, The Private Police, analyzes the fast-growing business of offering private security guards. How are city police services the same as, and how are they different from, private police services? Debra Livingston then explores a very different—but also rapidly growing—innovation in the delivery of police services: community policing. Does the conception of police that she describes suggest a role for "public" police that "private" police cannot perform?[35]

The same kinds of questions arise with many traditional city services that are now the target of reform efforts along consumerist lines. The Note on School Choice that concludes this section addresses another

---

[33] Guido Martinotti, A City for Whom? Transients and Public Life in the Second-Generation Metropolis, in Robert Beauregard and Sophie Body-Gendrot (eds.), The Urban Moment: Cosmopolitan Essays on the Late-20th-Century City (1999).

[34] See generally, Lee Anne Fennell, Beyond Exit and Voice: User Participation in the Production of Local Public Goods, 80 Tex. L. Rev. 1 (2001).

[35] For further reading on community policing, see, e.g., Linda Miller, Karen Hess, and Christine Orthmann, Community Policing: Partnerships for Problem Solving (2013); Matthew Parlow, The Great Recession and Its Implications for Community Policing, 28 Ga. St. U. L. Rev. 1193 (2012); Fritz Umbach, The Last Neighborhood Cops: The Rise and Fall of Community Policing in New York Public Housing (2010); Jeremy M. Wilson, Community Policing in America (2006); Wesley G. Skogan, Police and Community in Chicago: A Tale of Three Cities (2006); Mike Brogden and Preeti Nijhar, Community Policing: National and International Models and Approaches (2005); Linda Miller and Karen Hess, The Police in the Community: Strategies for the 21st Century (1998); David Bayley, Police for the Future (1994); Herman Goldstein, Problem-Oriented Policing (1990); Malcolm Sparrow, Mark Moore and David Kennedy, Beyond 911: A New Era for Policing (1990); Jerome Skolnick and David Bayley, The New Blue Line (1986). For a more general analysis of the role of land use and policing in fostering order and disorder, see Nicole Stelle Garnett, Ordering the City: Land Use, Policing, and the Restoration of Urban America (2009).

important context for considering these efforts. The case that follows, *Owens v. Colorado Congress of Parents, Teachers, and Students,* considers the legal framework within which choices about privatizing city schools, through a vouchers system, must be made. *Owens* holds that a school vouchers program violates the state constitutional requirement of local control over education by siphoning off local school property taxes for the use of private institutions. *Owens* reaches that conclusion on the basis of precedent that also prohibits the state from requiring wealthy school districts to contribute some of "their" school property taxes to less prosperous communities. Would you describe the *Owens* position—which prohibits both school vouchers and interlocal property tax sharing—as embracing a consumerist or community building conception of city services? Or, does *Owens* suggest yet a third conception?

GERALD FRUG, CITY MAKING: BUILDING COMMUNITIES WITHOUT BUILDING WALLS
Pp. 167–169, 171–177 (1999).

Local government law now organizes the provision of public services, like decisions about land use, in a way that fosters metropolitan fragmentation. It does so by allowing each individual city to generate its own revenue, provide its own services, and limit the availability of its services to city residents. Because of this method of allocating city services, moving across a city line has become a mechanism for effectuating a dramatic change in one's quality of life. City services are better in some jurisdictions than others, and the taxes one has to pay for them could well be lower. One problem that many people experience with this way of organizing city services is that the housing prices in the most favored jurisdictions are high. Thus the kind of services one can receive tends to be tied to the amount of money one has. But the divisive effect of this structure is not limited to the fact that it generates inequality, although that itself is important. It also promotes a consumer-oriented understanding of city services and, as a result, undermines the public nature of public services. These days, the difference between public and private services usually refers to nothing more than the fact that the government, rather than a non-profit organization or private corporation, provides them. Even if it does, one still evaluates them, in the manner one adopts when shopping for a pair of socks, by determining where one can get the most bang for the buck. * * * [I]t is important to specify the problems with this what's-in-it-for-me model of city services, not only its popular version but its academic counterpart, commonly called the theory of public goods. * * *

The current academic literature predominately discusses city services in the language of economics: whether a city should provide any particular service is thought to turn on analysis of the concept of "public goods." Public goods, according to the standard definition, are either the kind of goods that one person can consume without diminishing anyone else's ability to do so (they are "nonrival") or the kind that cannot easily be allocated solely to those who pay for them (they are "nonexcludable"). The examples of public goods regularly referred to in the literature are national defense and lighthouses. People can benefit from services such as these no matter how many other people are also doing so. Moreover, it would be unreasonably expensive to try to stop anyone from taking advantage of them. Thus they are services that the market cannot properly apportion and, consequently, that government can legitimately offer. As the proponents of the theory of public goods recognize, however, American cities do not protect the national defense or build lighthouses. Instead, they provide services—like police, fire, sanitation, and education—that not only can be allocated to some people at the expense of others but often are. As a result, the theory of public goods, when applied to local governments, largely consists of arguments about whether, and to what extent, it is efficient for cities to supply these kinds of "mixed" or "impure" public goods.

Those engaged in this argument usually take Charles Tiebout's influential article, "A Pure Theory of Local Expenditures," as a starting point. Tiebout sought to let the market determine the kinds of services cities should offer. He therefore set himself the task of imagining how an efficient market for city services could be created: is there a mechanism comparable to conventional market competition for private goods, he asked, that could allocate local public goods efficiently? The mechanism he identified was mobility. Metropolitan residents, he contended, decide to live in a particular city because it provides the mix of public goods that they are looking for, and cities compete for residents by offering packages of public goods that they think will be attractive. Tiebout's picture of people choosing cities by voting with their feet had immediate intuitive appeal. His article was written in 1956—a time when the suburbanization of America was intensifying—and the idea of mobility fit comfortably with a widespread belief in freedom of choice ("I have a right to live wherever I want"). * * *

I do not rely on the theory of public goods in this book * * *. The literature * * * is based on two assumptions which I reject—one about the nature of city services and one about the nature of cities. The first is the assumption that city services can be understood simply as objects of consumption. Tiebout portrays people shopping for a city in which to live just like they shop for any other consumer good: they choose a city by determining whether the package of services it provides is worth the price charged for it in taxes. The only difference from private market transactions that Tiebout allows is that consumers make their choice not by handing over a credit card but by moving to the location where they get the best deal. Along with others who work within the public goods tradition, Tiebout also assumes that a city is similar to a voluntary association, such as a political organization, church, or chat group. People are seen as choosing a city in which to live in the way they choose a country club: what attracts them is the fact that they share interests in common with others making the same choice. This homogeneity is even said to promote efficiency: since the rich and poor tend to want different levels of services, both groups are thought to be better off if they move to homogeneous cities. By picturing cities as locations where people share interests or values in common, public goods theorists thus embrace a suburban image of what cities are like. * * *

This consumer-oriented vision of city services has significant undesirable consequences. First of all—by definition—it abandons for public services the notion of equality traditionally associated with the public sector, replacing the one-person, one-vote principle associated with democracy with the one-dollar, one-vote rule of the marketplace. It thus has a built-in bias in favor of the rich. Everyone knows that those with more money not only can afford more consumer goods than those with less money but are considered entitled to them. It is because of this inherent bias that market-based allocations are commonly rejected for the public sphere. It is considered unacceptable, for example, to treat voting rights, jury duty, and military service as commodities available for sale, just as it is considered unfair to allocate many city services, such as admission to public schools or public parks, according to the ability to pay. Indeed, it is a crime to pay a police officer to protect oneself rather than someone too poor to make such a payment.

The consumer-oriented vision of city services, again by definition, also equates the concept of freedom of choice with that of freedom of consumer choice. By doing so, it perpetuates a pervasive, but false, justification for the radical differences that now exist between the quality of city services available in different parts of America's metropolitan regions. The public goods literature is filled with rhetoric about how public services in America are allocated in accordance with differences in people's "preferences" or "tastes." And many suburbanites say that they moved to their particular suburb because they (unlike others?) cared about the quality of education for their children. Yet it seems odd to suggest that the division of America's metropolitan areas into areas with good schools and safe neighborhoods and areas with deteriorating schools and high crime rates is explicable in terms of people's differing "tastes." People who live in unsafe neighborhoods or send their children to inadequate schools don't do so because they have a taste for them. They do so because they feel they have no other choice. If they had a choice (and I am not using the word to mean "consumer choice"), they would prefer better schools and less crime.

These two defects can be understood simply as illustrations of a third, more fundamental, problem with the consumer-oriented vision of city services. Once again by definition, it radically limits the aspect of the self considered relevant in the design and implementation of public services. Consumption is an individual activity: spurred by their own economic interest, people buy consumer goods one by one (or family by family) with little concern about the impact of their purchase on those living nearby. As a result, values commonly associated with democracy— notions of equality, of the importance of collective deliberation and compromise, of the existence of a public interest not reducible to personal economic concerns—are of secondary concern, or no concern at all, to consumers. Yet it is widely recognized, in political theory as well as daily life, that reducing human experience to the act of consumption falsifies it. It is commonly said, for example, that human beings see themselves not simply as consumers but also as citizens—and that they think differently in these two different roles. As Mark Sagoff puts it,

> Last year, I fixed a couple of tickets and was happy to do so since I saved fifty dollars. Yet, at election time, I helped to vote the corrupt judge out of office. I speed on the highway; yet I want the police to enforce laws against speeding . . . I love my car; I hate the bus. Yet I vote for candidates who promise to tax gasoline to pay for public transportation.

The consumer-oriented understanding of city services makes this distinction disappear by collapsing citizens into what Tiebout calls "consumer-voters." The impact of this disappearance is not simply on the outcome of government decisionmaking, important as that is. It affects the evolution of American society itself and, thereby, the forces which shape and nurture consumer preferences. The consumer-oriented vision of public services strengthens the consumptive aspect of the self over alternatives: consumer preferences help generate a social world that, in turn, shape consumer preferences. By doing so, it narrows the aspects of human nature that city services have the potential of fostering. * * *

In this book, I offer community building as a substitute for the public goods conception of city services. * * * [N]o one thinks of America's central cities as being like country clubs, political action committees, or other voluntary associations. They are characterized not by the similarities among the people who live in them but by the wide variety of different kinds of people they include: gay and straight, cosmopolitan and streetwise, elderly and college grad, Latino and Anglo, office employee and service worker. Rather than being like a voluntary association, they thus are an example of what I shall call a fortuitous association—a group of people in which individuals simply find themselves, one that demands an ability to get along with the other members of the group no matter how different they are. In this chapter, I embrace this fortuitous association version of cities rather than the voluntary association model assumed by public goods theorists. * * * No doubt voluntary associations make an important contribution to * * * [human freedom and growth]. But there are a multitude of entities that foster the benefits offered by voluntary associations: political parties, interest groups, organized religion, clubs of all kinds. The advantage of fortuitous associations as diverse as heterogeneous cities, by contrast, is much harder to come by. Clearly, these advantages come at a cost—ranging from the annoyance that unfamiliar people often generate to the stark fear that they sometimes cause. Costs such as these are imposed by every form of association, including the most important fortuitous association in American life—the family. One does not choose who one's parents or children (or in-laws or siblings) are, but they have an ability to provoke both joy and pain in a way quite different from a voluntary association with chosen friends. Of course, the disparate strangers that constitute a big city are nothing like one's family. But that is the point. Heterogeneous cities offer a form of human association, other than the family and voluntary associations, that can help shape who we are. They offer an opportunity to expand our capacity to cope with, and, hopefully, learn to appreciate, the variety of people who live in America's metropolitan areas.

Like the benefits provided by voluntary associations, the benefits offered by fortuitous associations can be obtained only with conscious effort and nurturing. That is the reason that cities need to engage in community building. The consumer-oriented vision not only inhibits such an effort but strengthens the opposite phenomenon: the separation and division of the people who live in America's metropolitan areas into unequal, even antagonistic, groups. * * * But the reason to transform city services into vehicles for community building is not just to reverse this negative impact. Community building requires the widespread support of metropolitan residents, and these days this support is unlikely to be generated simply by an evangelical appeal to the values of diversity and tolerance. Its chances of success are better if community building is seen as a mechanism for solving the kinds of problems that metropolitan residents have in common. And many of these problems involve city services. Concerns about the quality of public schools and violent crime cross city boundary lines throughout America's metropolitan regions, as do concerns about commuting and the environmental damage caused by suburban growth. These concerns have the potential of uniting different kinds of people rather than dividing them if metropolitan residents come to realize that the ever-increasing centrifugal dynamic that now affects metropolitan regions throughout the country aggravates urban problems for a majority of Americans, not just the residents of central cities. This does not mean that cities have to abandon totally the consumer-oriented focus adopted by public goods theorists. But it does mean that the conception of city services that stresses self-protection and fragmentation has to be replaced with one that builds on the notion that the ability to live in a diverse society is inextricably dependent on the welfare of others.

Such a basis for city services is not a new idea. As I envision it, community building is a contemporary version of the reason that city services were organized in the first place. It is important to consider for a moment the extraordinary idea, developed in America in the nineteenth century, that cities should provide a wide range of services. Until that time, there were (for example) no city police officers, no city fire departments, no public schools, no city parks, and no forms of public transportation in American cities. Why did nineteenth century thinkers and activists consider it a good idea to create these public services— thereby inventing what Eric Monkkonen calls the "service city?" The answer to this question is too complex to permit a neat summary here. But there is little in the historical account to suggest that city services were designed to fragment American cities into separate, homogenous components, each of which would supply consumer goods on a fee-for-service basis. On the contrary, one important reason for the creation of city services was the recognition by educated, enlightened elites that it was in their own self-interest to improve the circumstances of the immigrants and other poor people who were increasingly populating America's cities. This attitude is perhaps least surprising when one considers the creation of city police. Police historians emphasize that control of the "dangerous" classes—the imposition of a "middle-class sense of order on its citizens"—was an important objective in the creation of city-run police departments. Historians of American education have similarly found that the proponents of public education saw public schools as a way to instill moral values in, and impose order on, the children of the poor. Worried about crime, vice, poverty, disease, and class conflict, advocates considered public education "the most humane form of social control and the safest method of social renewal." Even city parks were seen, in Frederick Law Olmsted's words, as vehicles for elevating the poor "to [the] refinement and taste and the mental & moral capital of gentlemen." The intermingling of the different classes in the common space of parks, it was thought, would help cultivated people demonstrate to the rest of society the kinds of behavior necessary to life in a diverse city.

No doubt this nineteenth century vision of city services is based on a patrician condescension toward the poor and on a belief in assimilation to universal, middle-class values that are offensive to (at least many) modern readers. But if one strips it of its hierarchical overtones, it offers valuable lessons for the contemporary world. The founders' vision and community building share in common the idea that city services should be open to everyone and supported by everyone. Both agree that a consumer's understanding of "what's-in-it-for-me" fails to capture the ways in which city services can promote not just the public interest but individual self-interest as well. And, in both cases, the justification for these positions lies in the recognition that the behavior of different groups of people in our society have an impact on each other, whether one likes it or not. To be sure, a community building perspective replaces the founders' emphasis on assimilation and the imposition of a common set of values with one that stresses not merely the acceptance of cultural differences but the importance of increasing everyone's level of comfort when differences are encountered. Moreover, it now seems clear that those who live in prosperous suburbs have more to learn from the rest of society about how to live with different kinds of people than the other way around. Nevertheless, the central idea remains: like the nineteenth century thinkers who created America's public services, community building offers an alternative to the privatized conception of what city services are. * * *

DAVID A. SKLANSKY, THE PRIVATE POLICE
46 U.C.L.A. L. Rev. 1165, 1171–1193 (1999).

Private residential patrols * * * are growing in popularity throughout the country. Increasingly, moreover, private guards patrol not just the properties of individual customers but entire communities. Some of this is the result of the surge in walled-off, gated housing developments, which commonly use homeowner fees to pay for patrols by private security guards. As many as four million Americans may already live in these enclaves, and that number is growing rapidly; in Southern California, an estimated one-third of all new communities are gated. But even ungated communities are increasingly hiring private patrols, either with homeowner fees or with government-approved special assessments.

Residential security guards, moreover, are but one part—a relatively small but rapidly growing part—of the much larger workforce of private police personnel. That larger workforce has itself grown substantially faster over the past quarter century than both the population and the ranks of public law enforcement, effecting "a quiet revolution in policing." At this point, security guards in the United States actually outnumber law enforcement personnel; there are roughly three private guards for every two sworn officers. In California, the ratio is well over two to one. * * * Uniformed private officers guard and patrol office buildings, factories, warehouses, schools, sports facilities, concert halls, train stations, airports, shipyards, shopping centers, parks, government facilities—and, increasingly, residential neighborhoods. On any given day, many Americans are already far more likely to encounter a security guard than a police officer; in the words of one industry executive, "[t]he plain truth is that today much of the protection of our people, their property and their businesses, has been turned over to private security."

Nor is private policing limited to uniformed security guards. America has over 70,000 private investigators and over 26,000 store detectives; together these individuals outnumber FBI agents by almost ten to one. The ranks of private investigators, in particular, have swelled in recent years, growing by nearly 50% during the 1980s. Private detectives increasingly are hired not only to watch for shoplifters, but also to investigate, and not infrequently to spy on, everyone from insurance claimants and litigation opponents to employees, business partners, and even prospective neighbors.

In addition to these wholly private personnel, an estimated 150,000 police officers moonlight as private security guards, often in police uniform. This practice, too, appears to have escalated sharply; more than half of the officers in many metropolitan police departments now supplement their income with private security work. In a growing number of cases police departments themselves contract to supply their personnel to groups of merchants or residents, and then pay the officers out of the proceeds.

This public-to-private personnel leasing is the mirror image of the much larger practice of out-contracting, in which government agencies hire private security companies to perform work previously carried out by law enforcement officers. According to one estimate, the fraction of security work contracted out by federal, state, and local governments increased from 27% to 40% between 1987 and 1995. The trend seems likely to continue. Much out-contracted security work consists of parking enforcement, traffic direction, and other tasks unlikely to bring the private employees into contact with the criminal justice system. Increasingly, though, government agencies are hiring private security personnel to guard and patrol government buildings, housing projects, and public parks and facilities, and a small but growing number of local governments have begun to experiment with broader use of private police. A few municipalities have hired private security companies to provide general patrol services; more commonly, groups of residents or business owners in particular areas have received permission to tax themselves (and their dissenting neighbors) to pay for private patrols. * * *

About the actual activities of private security personnel there is little reliable information. Plainly, though, they often do a good deal more than observe and report. Generalizations beyond that are difficult, partly because the industry is secretive, and partly because security personnel do not all perform the same functions. Store detectives, for example, make frequent arrests; residential security guards typically do not. Even residential security guards, however, may carry out brief detentions with some frequency. And the security industry as a whole probably carries out significantly more stops, searches, and interrogations than is often imagined. More generally, despite the frequent claim by security firms that they are not "playing police," large numbers of private security personnel today appear chiefly engaged in what is, in essence, patrol work—work once understood as the principal function of public law enforcement. "[T]he modern . . . security guard's job, while different from that of modern public policemen, is very much like that of the traditional 'cop on the beat.'"

Not coincidentally, the traditional "cop on the beat" has been something of a vanishing species for much of the past half century; this much-bemoaned development plainly has had more than a little to do with the proliferation of private guards during the same period. The past few years, in fact, have seen increasing calls for a revival of traditional beat policing—calls, in other words, for police officers to act more like security guards. The response to these calls has been limited, in part, by the hard fact that police patrols are expensive. Even a greatly accelerated revival of beat policing, though, would be unlikely to reverse the massive growth of private security, because, as I discuss later, changing patterns of public policing have not been the only factor contributing to that growth.

Indeed, one of the most striking aspects of police privatization is its "pervasive, international character." The exponential growth of private security in the United States has been mirrored in Canada, the United Kingdom, Australia, New Zealand, and, to a lesser extent, the rest of the world. Private security is global in another sense as well: ownership and operation of the industry is increasingly multinational. * * *

The main legal limitations on the private police today are tort and criminal doctrines of assault, trespass, and false imprisonment—variants of the same doctrines that once defined the principal boundaries of permissible public policing. Unless the owner has given consent, a security guard's search of private property will generally constitute a trespass. And arrests or detentions not authorized by state law generally will expose a security guard to civil and criminal liability for false imprisonment and, if force is involved, for assault.

Private security companies eager to appear unthreatening often stress that their personnel are limited to the search and arrest powers of ordinary citizens. It is a mistake, though, to make too much of this limitation. In the first place, it is not always true that security guards have only the powers of ordinary citizens. Many private guards, for example, are "deputized" or otherwise given full or partial police powers by state or local enactment, and most states have codified a "merchant's privilege" that allows store investigators, and in some instances other categories of private security personnel, to conduct brief investigatory detentions that would be tortious or criminal if carried out by ordinary citizens.

In the second place, the arrest powers of ordinary citizens in most states are not strikingly different, in some significant respects, from those of police officers. Officers can execute arrest warrants; private persons generally cannot. But the vast majority of arrests are made without a warrant, and the arrest powers of officers and civilians in that circumstance are relatively narrow. An officer, as a general matter, may arrest anyone he or she has probable cause to believe has committed a felony, and anyone who commits a misdemeanor in the officer's presence. A private citizen typically may also arrest for a misdemeanor committed in his or her presence, and for a felony he or she has probable cause to believe the arrestee has committed—as long as the felony has in fact been committed, by the arrestee or by someone else. * * *

None of this is to suggest that there are no significant legal distinctions between the powers of public and private police. The public police obviously have some well-defined powers that private security personnel lack. This is particularly true with regard to searches. Law enforcement officers but not private citizens can apply for and execute search warrants and electronic surveillance orders, and in many circumstances the Supreme Court has granted police officers, but not private citizens, broad powers to search without a warrant. In addition, police officers but not private citizens generally are empowered to command the assistance of bystanders. There are also differences in the consequences that attach to a failure to submit to arrest. Resisting even a lawful citizen's arrest typically is not a crime, although it frequently will be tortious. In contrast, most states now criminalize resisting an arrest by a law enforcement officer even when the arrest is illegal. * * *

Thinking about private policing unavoidably involves thinking about the public-private distinction more generally. This is partly because policing—peacekeeping, property protection, and law enforcement—touches on deep and contradictory intuitions regarding the proper allocations of responsibilities between the public and private spheres. On the one hand, peacekeeping, property protection, and law enforcement are often considered the clearest examples of functions that are essentially and necessarily public, and therefore essentially and necessarily the job of government. The idea here—loosely shared by John Locke and Max Weber, and latterly by Robert Nozick and Ronald Reagan—is that the very point of government is to monopolize the coercive use of force, in order to ensure public peace, personal security, and the use and enjoyment of property. (Hence the classic description of the libertarian ideal: "the night watchman state.") One reflection of this idea is the common notion that it is wrong to "take the law into your own hands." Another is the view, taken as self-evident by the Supreme Court, that "the most basic function of any government is to provide for the security of the individual and of his property."

On the other hand, private policing can easily be understood as the natural product of three paradigmatically private functions. The first is self-defense, widely viewed as an inherent right, particularly in America, just as "taking the law into your own hands" is seen as obviously wrong. The second is economic exchange, the "free market" that, as we will see, transformed the eighteenth-century constabulary from a civic duty to a specialized form of employment. The third is the use and enjoyment of property, generally thought to include the right of owners to place conditions on those invited onto their property.

Not surprisingly, therefore, the recent growth of private policing has elicited conflicting reactions, reflecting broader conflicts about government in general. The trend has been applauded on three different grounds. First, private policing has been welcomed as more flexible than traditional, public law enforcement. Private guard companies, unlike public police forces, are free from civil service rules, reporting requirements, and the range of other rules characteristically imposed on government agencies. In addition, private companies lack many of the bureaucratic traditions that may handicap the effectiveness of the public police, and they are often free from the constraints associated with a unionized workforce. These factors allow guard companies to act in ways in which government either cannot or will not.

Second, private policing has been celebrated as more accountable than its public counterpart. Unlike public police forces, private guard companies have to answer to the discipline of the market. In the words of one enthusiast, a privately employed police officer inevitably "recognizes the importance of establishing positive relationships with the consumers of the service and develops innovative approaches to community problems," whereas "the public police are paid through the compilation of public taxes and are, therefore, answerable to every business and citizen in the city but are not accountable to them." Private policing thus can be understood in part as a reaction against the excessive independence and insularity of modern police forces—an answer to the common complaint "that a police force should be responsive to those policed, while autonomous professionals . . . have a notorious tendency to believe that they know what is 'really' best for the clients, and therefore what the client 'ought' to want."

Third and finally, private policing has been thought beneficial because it empowers those it protects. Unlike the first two advantages of private policing, this third one does not have to do with the improved performance of those doing the policing, but rather from the effect on those who hire them. The argument here has two strands. The first is individualistic: it appeals to the notion that every citizen should take responsibility for his or her own protection, that it is ultimately enfeebling to depend on the government for protection. The second is communitarian: the idea here is that arranging for private policing generally entails a more or less voluntary association of residents or business owners that, in the process of providing joint security, also builds social capital—which itself can help reduce crime. The first strand of the empowerment argument thus envisions private security as the natural outgrowth of individual self-defense; the second strand sees it as a commercial variant on citizen patrols.

Each of these claimed advantages of private policing, of course, has a flip side. For example, the greater flexibility of private guard companies stems from their freedom from regulations and traditions that have developed largely because they were thought necessary to control the uniformed, armed, quasi-military forces patrolling our streets. Where some see the greater flexibility of private policing, others see the threat of policing that is uncontrolled. Indeed, the most persistent complaint about private guard companies—a complaint that, we will see, has deep roots in the nineteenth century, and that today serves as a perennial focus of television exposes—is that they are insufficiently regulated.

The frequency with which this complaint is raised serves as a reminder that the supposed accountability of private policing has a troubling side as well. Private companies are thought more accountable than government because they answer to their particular customers instead of to the general public. But this is not clearly to everyone's advantage. In particular, those who come into contact with private guards but do not help to pay for them may not welcome the fact that such guards are accountable exclusively to their customers. And even some of the customers, when they venture outside their own territory, may wish that the various uniformed patrol personnel they encounter were less proprietary, more answerable to the general public.

More broadly, there are grounds for doubting that market forces will deliver optimum levels of police protection. In the lingo of economics, policing gives rise to three sorts of externalities. First, there is the free-rider problem: if my neighbors pay for a private patrol car to drive by their homes periodically, burglars may be scared away from my house, too. Because there is no practical way to limit all the benefits of patrol service to those who pay for it, markets might be expected to supply a suboptimal level of patrolling. Second, there is the problem of displacement. The patrol car in my neighborhood may push burglars into surrounding neighborhoods, increasing crime there while decreasing it where I live. Indeed, some industry executives boast that private patrols, once established in an area, create further marketing opportunities by moving crime to adjacent, underpatrolled areas. Alarm systems, advertised by lawn placards and window decals, may have a similar effect within neighborhoods. Third, there is the problem mentioned above: policing protects some people by interfering with other people, and there is no obvious way to require those who are protected to pay for the burdens imposed on those they are protected from. All these externalities can be anticipated to warp private expenditures for police protection away from what economists would consider socially efficient. One might expect the private sector to overfund crime control strategies with large negative externalities, and to underfund strategies with large positive externalities: more money for home alarms than for private patrols, and more for private patrols than for antipoverty foundations.

Nor, finally, are the broad effects of private policing on its employers unambiguously positive. Public law enforcement has been celebrated as "socializing" the coercive use of force. To the extent that private policing is seen as an extension of self-defense, it can be—and has been—deplored as a retreat from that process. On the other hand, to the extent that private policing is seen as a commercial variant on citizen patrols, the commercial aspect may be thought to eliminate much of the civic value. And not everyone is enthusiastic about citizen patrols even in their pure form; American history gives ample cause for disquiet about amateur law enforcement. * * *

DEBRA LIVINGSTON, POLICE DISCRETION AND THE
QUALITY OF LIFE IN PUBLIC PLACES: COURTS,
COMMUNITIES, AND THE NEW POLICING
97 Colum. L. Rev. 551, 565, 568, 573–578, 652, 655–656, 658–661, 663–665 (1997).

George Kelling and Mark Moore have provided a useful categorization of police history that portrays the emergence of community policing as a result of perceived inadequacies in the ideas associated with what they term the "reform era" in American policing—a period that they posit to have extended roughly from shortly after the turn of the century into the 1970s. * * * [T]he broad outline of this account—the rise of police professionalism in this century, the transition to principles of scientific management with centralized command and military-style discipline, the reconceptualization of the police officer as law enforcement agent focusing on serious crimes, and the movement of patrol officers into automobiles and to rapid dispatch—has become part of the textbook story of the modern American police. It has also become common wisdom that many of the central assumptions of this story (assumptions about how the police can best do their job and, indeed, about what that job is) have been drawn dramatically into question in the current era. * * *

[R]eform era police relied upon neutral enforcement of the criminal law and detached professionalism as the bases for their authority * * *. [C]ommunity police place renewed emphasis on community or political support: "Certainly, law continues to be a major source of justification, but it is not sufficient to authorize police actions to maintain order, negotiate conflicts, and solve problems. Neighborhood or community support and involvement are required to accomplish those tasks." Next, partly because the police in a community policing regime are open to community-nominated problems, the definition of the police role is broader, more dynamic, and more proactive than before—involving not simply crime control through rapid response, random patrol by automobile, and reactive investigation, but also a renewed focus on order maintenance, crime prevention, and * * * problem-solving. In theory, community policing is a "preventive, penetrating, consensual," as opposed to "reactive, restricted, procedural due process model" of policing. By focusing on order maintenance and prevention, advocating a more visible presence in policed areas, and basing its legitimacy on the consent of policed populations, community policing emulates police services that private security firms now offer the well-to-do in the protection of their private property.

The police organization itself, and its tactics, are also different in a community policing department. Since operational and tactical decisions come from local assessment of problems and require neighborhood input, community policing necessitates decentralized decisionmaking within the large, urban department. Reform era police chiefs sought to centralize command and control and to formulate elaborate rules and policies to limit the discretion of lower ranking officers. Community policing implies the opposite: "Consulting with community groups, problem solving, maintaining order, and other such activities are antithetical to the reform ideal of eliminating officer discretion through routinization and standardization of police activities." Participative management that involves line officers and sergeants in the development of police initiatives (effected through use of temporary task forces, matrix-like units, and other organizational innovations borrowed from the private sector) is part of the concept. So, too, are many police tactics, like foot patrol and community organizing, that bring officers into a more intimate relationship with the community.

Today, hundreds of police departments across the country (not to mention local prosecutors in places like Washington, D.C., Philadelphia, and Indianapolis) are experimenting with both community and problem-oriented policing. Though largely sympathetic to this experimentation, academics have warned that the concept of "community" in community policing is imprecise at best, and even idealized. They have observed that a bewildering and sometimes inappropriate variety of police initiatives could well be implemented in community policing's name. Old concerns about the proliferation of police corruption within decentralized departments have resurfaced, and new worries have emerged about whether police time will be properly allocated when police are free to work with other city agencies and with community residents. Even proponents of the new strategies attest to the value of central ideas within the reform era paradigm. They caution that community policing, by rejecting the predominantly reactive posture of reform era police in favor of proactive, community-based crime prevention, presents heightened risks of discriminatory law enforcement and inappropriate police involvement in community life and private affairs. Nevertheless, community and problem-oriented policing—perhaps the first movements in American policing, despite all the cautions of academics, that have been based upon a realistic assessment of policing's complexities—are the orienting philosophies structuring change in policing today. * * *

[I]n the community policing era, the accountability of police both to the communities they serve and to the rule of law is best assured by recognizing explicitly the inevitability—and even, properly managed, the desirability—of police discretion. * * * [I]t is discretion that permits local police departments to respond to a neighborhood's quality-of-life concerns and to its preferences about the character of police intervention. Discretion is part of the solution to the tension that has existed between police and many communities; it can be a strength. * * *

It is easy to discount the role that local politics and neighborhood reciprocity can play in managing the discretion that police inevitably employ in dealing with quality-of-life concerns. Neighborhoods are not homogenous and problems of disorder sometimes emerge by virtue of "racial, cultural, and economic tensions that arise among those who legitimately live, work, and recreate in a given area." With whom, then, do the police consult in determining that the young men who loiter outside a convenience store, often violating an ordinance against public drinking, pose a problem? Communities never speak with a single voice and police can do great harm in places in which there are significant tensions by even inadvertently contributing to the perception that they have taken sides.

At the same time, neighborhoods do exist. Their public spaces are characterized by patterns of interactions among those going to school, or work, those playing in parks, and those bantering on public streets. [Wesley] Skogan's work, moreover, provides important empirical support that residents within a community, regardless of ethnicity, class, and age, often agree on the character of its disorder problems. Police consultation with elected representatives and with neighborhood residents can thus help in the identification of problems that are of broad concern. And if there are complexities in identifying the community with whom police are to consult, it is also true that police-community consultation makes a difference in the allocation of police resources. Without such consultation, "police suffer from a biased view of community concerns."

Accountability, then, may emerge at least to some degree from the policing problem itself and as part of the effort to resolve it. When police and citizens together "nominate the problems with which [they] will deal, the tactics that each will use to address those problems, and the outcomes that are desired," the agreement that flows out of this exchange is itself a standard by which to evaluate the police department's performance. The formal mechanisms through which police departments have historically promoted community-police reciprocity—like advisory councils or regular community meetings held in local precincts—may also be rendered more vital by the "problem" focus in community and problem-oriented policing reforms. "Before any major action is undertaken, whether a shift in resources or implementation of a new problem-solving approach, the community-oriented police department discusses that change with the appropriate neighborhood." * * *

[Still,] there are inherent limits to the role that political controls and informal neighborhood involvement should play in promoting police accountability. Just as community and problem-oriented policing reforms cannot signal retreat to a legal regime in which police are delegated authority to maintain order as they deem appropriate, the advent of these new policing philosophies cannot mean a return to the corrupt political control of policing that the reform era successfully—perhaps too successfully—transformed. "[P]ublic police must be distributed fairly across cities on the basis of neighborhood need, not neighborhood political clout." Police, in addition, "must be free to enforce the law without fear that the person or class of offenders against whom they take action has the power to retaliate against the enforcing officers" through the political process. Most important, police must resist rather than respond to community mandates that would violate the constitutional rights of others or require police to act beyond their lawful authority.

In practice, then, police must stand at some remove from politics and from communities while at the same time remaining open to neighborhood concerns and to neighborhood preferences about the character of police intervention. In fact, an important part of their role in quality-of-life policing is likely to involve educating citizens about limits— imposed by law and by the finite resources of police departments—on what police can be expected to accomplish. Both the law and the professional autonomy conferred on police by the reforms of this century will continue to play an important role in maintaining a necessary distance between police and local communities. The challenge in community policing—critical to police helping to enhance the quality of neighborhood life—is to identify those contexts that can promote the accountability of police to local communities while preserving an important measure of police autonomy. * * *

The most ardent advocates of the new policing reforms are not dismissive of the dangers of police corruption, discrimination, and even brutality that a closer connection between police and communities may present. Professor Goldstein has cautioned that in police departments where "police corruption or misuse of police authority is already common, it may simply not be feasible to experiment with community policing." Even in police departments with relatively good records for the control of police misconduct, there is a heightened need for monitoring mechanisms in a community and problem-oriented policing regime. "No matter how good the training, how instrumental management has been in shaping the culture, and how positive supervision has been, the circumstances of police work will continue to allow for corruption, malfeasance, and incompetence." Monitoring mechanisms aim at minimizing these problems by ensuring that needed information is obtained from the community about the activities of police officers on the street and the response of community residents * * *

There is also a need for external monitoring mechanisms, both because such mechanisms help ensure the integrity and ongoing character of the monitoring function and because in many communities they enhance the legitimacy of evaluations that are performed. * * * Today, a majority of big cities have at least a hybrid complaint system in which police may investigate complaints, "but civilians sit on the board that recommends discipline." To date, most such boards have focused narrowly on the performance of individual police officers rather than on broader questions about the quality of police services or the overall acceptability of particular policing practices within local neighborhoods. Police scholars, moreover, have expressed reservation about at least some civilian review mechanisms, noting that it is important that such mechanisms work to strengthen rather than undercut "the traditional system for controlling police conduct—the process whereby the chief supervises his personnel and is held accountable for their performance." The principle that citizens should participate in reviewing complaints brought against police officers, however, is widely accepted today and is viewed by many as a means by which citizens can have input into "the acceptable limits of police practices in enforcing laws and maintaining order." * * *

NOTE ON SCHOOL CHOICE

There is arguably no more important service provided locally in the United States than education. Nevertheless, dissatisfaction with the public schools in many central cities (and some suburbs), as well as more ideological objections to a government-run educational system, have led to increasingly vocal calls for reform. Reformers do not usually seek to abolish public education. They seek instead to find ways to put "choice" into a system that is said to be an inefficient, government-run monopoly. Parents should not be forced to send their children to the school to which their local government assigns them, reformers contend. They should be able, with government assistance, to exercise their own judgment in selecting the right school for their children.

Very different plans for re-organizing public education have been offered under the rubric of "school choice." Some plans offer publicly-supported vouchers to parents to pay for schools while others do not; some allow schools to set admission fees higher than the face amount of the voucher and others forbid any extra charge; some allow students to attend only public schools and others include private schools as well. All of these distinctions are important, but even plans that are on the same side of these issues differ from each other.

Consider, for example, the plan offered by John Chubb and Terry Moe in their influential book, Politics, Markets, and America's Schools (1990). Chubb and Moe reject vouchers, prohibit admission fees over the publicly-provided support for education, and limit their plan to public schools. Within these parameters, they propose a market-based system of school choice. Although they reject vouchers, they build their system on publicly-supported "scholarships" paid directly to the school. They have the state set a minimum amount for these scholarships. But they allow local school systems to use tax revenue to supplement the scholarships offered the district's children. Thus, although they reject admission fees, "children from different districts may have different-sized scholarships." Finally, while they limit their plan to public schools, they have what they call a "minimal" requirement to be a public school—"roughly corresponding to the criteria many states now employ in accrediting private schools." Existing private schools would therefore be eligible to become public schools. "Our guiding principle in the design of a choice system," they say, "is this: public authority must be put to use in creating a system that is almost beyond the reach of public authority."

Having organized school finance and the supply of schools in this manner, they then outline what they mean by choice among schools:

— Each student will be free to attend any public school in the state, regardless of district, with the relevant scholarship—consisting of federal, state, and local contributions—flowing to the school of choice. In practice, of course, most students will probably choose schools in reasonable proximity to their homes. But districts will have no claim on their own residents.

— To the extent that tax revenues allow, every effort will be made to provide transportation for students that need it. This is important in helping to open up as many alternatives as possible to all students, especially the poor and those located in rural areas.

— To assist parents and students in choosing among schools, the state will provide a Parent Information Center within its local

Choice Office. This Center will collect comprehensive information on each school in the district, and its parent liaisons will meet personally with parents in helping them judge which schools best meet their children's needs. The emphasis here will be on personal contact and involvement. Parents will be required to visit the center at least once, and encouraged to do so often. Meetings will be arranged at all schools so that parents can see first-hand what their choices are.

— The applications process will be handled in simple fashion by the Parent Information Center. Once parents and students decide which schools they prefer, they will fill out applications to each, with parent liaisons available to give advice and assistance (including filling out the applications themselves, if necessary). All applications will be submitted to the Center, which in turn will send them out to the schools.

— Schools will make their own admissions decisions, subject only to nondiscrimination requirements. This is absolutely crucial. Schools must be able to define their own missions and build their own programs in their own ways, and they cannot do this if their student population is thrust on them by outsiders. They must be free to admit as many or as few students as they want, based on whatever criteria they think relevant—intelligence, interest, motivation, behavior, special needs—and they must be free to exercise their own, informal judgments about individual applicants.

— Schools will set their own "tuitions." They may choose to do this explicitly—say, by publicly announcing the minimum scholarship they are willing to accept They may also do it implicitly by allowing anyone to apply for admission and simply making selections, knowing in advance what each applicant's scholarship amount is. In either case, schools are free to admit students with different-sized scholarships, and they are free to keep the entire scholarship that accompanies each student they have admitted. This gives all schools incentives to attract students with special needs, since these children will have the largest scholarships. It also gives schools incentives to attract students from districts with high base-level scholarships. But no school need restrict itself to students with special needs, nor to students from a single district.

— The applications process must take place within a framework that guarantees each student a school, as well as a fair shot at getting into the school he or she most wants. It is important, however, that such a framework impose only the most minimal restrictions on the schools. We suggest something like the following. The Parent Information Center will have the responsibility for seeing that parents and students are informed, that they have visited the schools that interest them, and that all applications are submitted by a given date. Schools will then be required to make their admissions decisions within a set time, and students who are accepted into one or more schools will be required to select one as their final choice. Students who are not accepted anywhere, as well as schools that have yet to attract as many students as they want, will participate in a second round of applications, which will work the same way. After this second round, some students may remain without schools (although, judging from the East Harlem experience, probably very few). At this point, parent liaisons will take informal action to try to match up these students with appropriate schools. If any students still remain, a special safety net procedure will be invoked to ensure that each is assigned to a specific school.

— Schools must also be free to expel students or deny them readmission when, based on their own experience and standards, they believe the situation warrants it (as long as they are not "arbitrary and capricious"). This is essential if schools are to define and control their own organizations, and it gives students a strong incentive to live up to their side of the educational "contract."[36]

Gerald Frug also rejects vouchers and extra admission fees, and he too limits his school choice proposal to public schools (a term he defines as schools run by cities or school districts). But he sees his plan not as a market system but as consistent with community building:

Consider a system * * * in which parents could choose to send their child to any public school in their metropolitan area as long as diversity, and not segregation, was promoted by their choice. To ensure that such a plan would produce the greatest possible heterogeneity, admission to every school in the region would be equally open to all metropolitan residents. In other words, no admission preference would be offered to students who lived within a school district's boundaries. Such an open admissions policy would resolve the conflict often asserted between self-interest and the allocation of school funding—why would anyone agree to allocate money to a diverse school rather than the one their own children attended?—by giving every child an equal chance of attending the best funded school. It would also alter the structure of a number of current school choice programs, commonly called "controlled choice" plans, in order to make students' chances of being "insiders" and "outsiders" more equal. Under many current plans, such as the one adopted in Cambridge, Massachusetts, parents can choose to send their children to any public school as long their choice promotes diversity. But they are largely limited to sending their children to schools within the school district in which they live because they can send them to another district's school only if there is "room" for

---

[36] John Chubb and Terry Moe, Politics, Markets, and America's Schools 221–223 (1990).

them—that is, only if seats remain after all students who live in the district have been admitted—and only if the school district agrees to participate in the admission of outsiders. As a result, only a few "outsiders" are added to a student body predominantly entitled to admission as a matter of right.

A decision to give an admission preference to district residents honors the school choice of some parents over that of others through the adoption of a state policy favoring neighborhood schools. It does not follow, however, that a region-wide school choice plan would establish the opposite policy, destabilizing neighborhood schools by bringing in a flood of outsiders. Its actual effect would depend on the outcome of regional negotiations over school funding because it would bring to the surface the conflict * * * between support for neighborhood schools and school choice. If it turned out that most people in the metropolitan area preferred neighborhood schools, the regional negotiation process would likely focus on making schools comparable enough so that most parents would choose to send their children to neighborhood schools. After all, a school choice program that offered no admission preference to neighborhood residents would undermine neighborhood schools (assuming most people preferred them) only if they substantially varied in quality. If, on the other hand, most people preferred to send their children to the best school in the region wherever it is located, the negotiations might focus instead on the dynamic that now makes residents of poor neighborhoods as reluctant to apply to out-of-district schools as residents of the more prosperous districts are to receive them.

Chances are, some elements of both of these agendas would be addressed. Many schools would become more integrated because children would no longer be disqualified from attending a school solely on the grounds that their parents cannot afford to buy a house nearby. Some parents would send their children to out-of-district schools either because they thought they were better or because (when a parent worked in the area, for example) they were more convenient. On the other hand, a region-wide school choice program—even if combined with a regional allocation of educational resources—is unlikely to generate many transfers from suburban schools to those of poor African American and Latino neighborhoods. And many residents of these neighborhoods might continue to send their children to neighborhood schools, rather than to a suburban school, because of fear of racial antagonism, loss of identification with African American or Hispanic culture, or the undermining of ties to neighborhood institutions. * * * The community building plan that I've just described is not, therefore, the equivalent of a metropolitan plan for integrating the region's schools. Rather than trying to desegregate the schools overnight, it * * * concentrates * * * on revising local government law. The proposal rejects the current legal rules that rely on school boundary lines to divide the region into unequally-funded school districts populated by students readily identifiable in terms of racial and class categories. And it installs in their place a system that makes both educational resources and students the responsibility of the region as a whole. These changes will increase the diversity of many metropolitan schools, but they clearly are only one ingredient in the task of doing so. * * *

Altering the rules that govern school funding and admissions requirement [in the way just proposed] would transform the reference to "our" property and "our" children into a gesture toward a heterogeneous group, and it would assign to an equally heterogenous group the task of deciding how to strengthen the school system. The process of regional negotiations would itself contribute to the task of community building by focusing everyone in the region on the job of educating all of the region's children rather than on the fortifying the barriers that separate them from each other. This region-wide focus is essential. A major ingredient in the powerful, sometimes violent, opposition to integration in the 1960s and 1970s was the fact that suburbanization allowed privileged whites not to participate in the transformation of the public schools. The greatest opposition to integration occurred when, with suburban neighborhoods exempted, integration efforts focused only on white neighborhoods experienced by their residents, because of their proximity to black neighborhoods, as transitional and easily vulnerable to change. The vast majority of people who live in America's metropolitan areas would benefit from eliminating the legally-created suburban escape hatch. School funding would become more fairly allocated. All residents of the metropolitan area—not just the most mobile—would have a choice about the best school for their children. The concentration of poor children into a limited number of schools would be reduced. All public schools would, once again, be open to everyone regardless of income. And, above all, parents and children from all income, racial, and ethnic categories would be able to develop more of a relationship with the variety of people who live in their metropolitan area and thus benefit from the decrease in tension and increase in opportunities for learning that fortuitous associations offer. Once school systems became organized as fortuitous associations rather than as a series of separate voluntary associations, educational funding and innovation might even increase (thereby demonstrating the truth in the slogan "green follows white").[37]

No doubt those who prefer the Chubb and Moe proposal would argue that Frug's proposal gives parents too limited a choice: no one is entitled to

---

[37] Gerald Frug, City Making: Building Communities Without Building Walls 186–190 (1999).

send a child to a formerly private school or even to an out-of-district public school if their child's admission makes the school more homogeneous. Why not, they might ask, give parents an absolutely free choice of schools that their children can attend? One way to answer this question is to suggest that no school choice proposal gives parents an absolutely free choice of schools. All of them offer only a "controlled choice," even though the label is now usually applied simply to a subset of school choice plans. The plans are distinguishable from each other only in terms of who exercises control, that is, whether admissions officers or government officials are given power to decide whether the child "fits in" to the school. School choice proponents who seek to limit the government's role in education insist that, while children can apply to any school they like, wherever it is located, they should not get in unless the school officials decide to admit them. Of course, admissions officers, as well as local governments, can incorporate diversity rather than homogeneity into their definition of the kind of students they think will fit into their school. Still, the critical distinction among school choice plans is that advocates who favor allocating power to admissions officers justify doing so on the grounds that it allows individual schools to design their own student population. That way, the argument runs, different kinds of schools, made up of different kinds of students, can compete with each other for customers.

By envisioning each school as a product offered in the market by those who run it, does a consumer-oriented version of school choice adopts a privatized vision of educational services whether or not it relies on vouchers and whether or not the proposal includes private schools among those eligible to participate in government funding? Does such a system encourage a competition for exclusivity and, thereby, destabilize diverse schools throughout the metropolitan area? If so, why does it have these consequences?

OWENS v. COLORADO CONGRESS OF PARENTS, TEACHERS AND STUDENTS

Supreme Court of Colorado, 2004.
92 P.3d 933.

JUSTICE BENDER delivered the Opinion of the Court. * * *

The Colorado Opportunity Contract Pilot Program is designed to meet the "educational needs of high-poverty, low-achieving children in [Colorado's] highest-poverty public schools." Participation in the program is mandatory for any school district that, "for the 2001–02 school year, had at least eight schools that received an academic performance rating of 'low' or 'unsatisfactory' * * * and which . . . continues to operate said schools in the 2003–04 school year." Other school districts may voluntarily participate in the program.

The program is available to low-income, low-achieving children who attend public school in a participating school district. Only those children who are eligible to receive free or low-cost lunch under the National School Lunch Act may participate. Academic criteria vary according to the child's age. * * * If a child is eligible to participate in the program and has been accepted by a qualified nonpublic school, the child's parents may enter into a contract with the school district in which the child is enrolled. The school district is then required to make four assistance payments to the parents, who in turn must endorse the check "for the sole use of the participating nonpublic school." The school district is required to pay the lesser of "the participating nonpublic school's actual educational cost per pupil," or a percentage of the school district's per pupil operating revenues.

As the program is currently enacted, enrollment is subject to statutory caps. During the 2004–05 school year, enrollment is limited to one percent of a participating school district's total student population. That percentage increases to two percent during the 2005–06 school year, four percent during the 2006–07 school year, and finally to six percent from the 2007–08 school year onward. The plaintiffs challenged the program on several grounds, including that the program * * * violates the local control provisions of article IX, section 15 of the Colorado Constitution. * * * Because we see no way to reconcile the requirements of section 15 with the Pilot Program as it is currently enacted, we hold that the program is unconstitutional beyond a reasonable doubt.

The principle of local control has deep roots in Colorado's constitutional history. The Colorado Constitution was adopted in 1876 in an atmosphere of deep distrust of centralized authority. * * * The provisions governing education reflect the delegates' ambivalence about legislative power. Article IX, section 2 empowers the General Assembly to create and maintain a public school system:

> The general assembly shall, as soon as practicable, provide for the establishment and maintenance of a thorough and uniform system of free public schools throughout the state, wherein all residents of the state, between the ages of six and twenty-one years, may be educated gratuitously.

Article IX, section 15 then provides that control over instruction in the public schools shall devolve to local school boards, whose members are elected by the residents of the school districts:

> The general assembly shall, by law, provide for organization of school districts of convenient size, in each of which shall be established a board of education, to consist of three or more directors to be elected by the qualified electors of the district.

Said directors shall have control of instruction in the public schools of their respective districts. * * *

With the adoption of article IX, Colorado became one of only six states with an express constitutional local control requirement. * * * And since its adoption, this Court has consistently emphasized the importance of local control to the state's educational system. * * * [B]eginning with *Belier v. Wilson*, 59 Colo. 96, 147 P. 355 (1915), this Court has had numerous occasions to define the contours of the local control requirement of section 15, and in each case we have held that control over locally-raised funds is essential to effectuating the constitutional requirement of local control over instruction.

In *Belier*, we held that taxes raised in one school district could not be used to fund a public high school in another district. The legislation at issue in *Belier* allowed contiguous school districts to establish a union high school, which students who resided in either district could attend. Tax revenues raised in both districts were to be used to fund the union high school, while control over instruction would fall to the board of the district in which the union high school was located. We concluded that such a scheme violated the "letter and spirit" of article IX, section 15, because the electors in the paying district had no "voice in the selection of those who manage and control the school" in the receiving district.

That same year, in *School District No. 16 v. Union High School No. 1*, we considered the constitutionality of a statute that allowed a student who resided in a district without a high school to attend a high school in a neighboring district at the expense of the student's district of residence. 60 Colo. 292, 152 P. 1149 (1915). As in *Belier*, we held that funds raised in one district could not be used to pay for public school in another district, and explained that imposing such a requirement on a local school district "clearly interfered with the control of instruction" in the paying district. Essential to this holding was the idea that local control requires a school district to have discretion over any instruction paid for with locally-raised funds.

Finally, in *Craig v. People ex rel. Hazzard*, we held that the General Assembly may accomplish inter-district funding without running afoul of article IX, section 15 only by drawing funds exclusively from the state-controlled public school income fund. 89 Colo. 139, 299 P. 1064 (1931). In that case, we rejected a challenge to a statute that permitted a high school student to attend a public school in a neighboring district in certain circumstances. Under the statute, in the event that a student attended a neighboring district's school, the superintendent of the state public school fund was authorized to withhold from the student's district an amount sufficient to pay the student's tuition and transfer that amount to the neighboring district We held that this scheme comports with article IX, section 15 because it "only involves the apportionment of the public school fund by the superintendent of public instruction, and does not concern the apportionment, distribution, or expenditure of county or school funds raised by taxation."

In the *Belier* era, we scrupulously honored the framers' preference, as expressed in article IX, section 15, for local over state control of instruction, even in the face of legislative efforts to address serious shortcomings on the part of local school districts. These cases confirmed the constitutional status of the local control requirement by stressing the importance of district control of locally-raised funds over and above the legislature's power to guide and implement educational policy.

The defendants frankly acknowledge that from a funding point of view, the General Assembly would have the authority to enact the Pilot Program but for the *Belier* line of cases, and accordingly they urge us to overturn them. The defendants argue that these cases should be understood as "limited to [their] facts" because they were decided at a time where state involvement in the management and funding of the public schools was far more limited than it is today. Thus, the defendants contend that these cases are simply inapplicable to today's cases involving modern school finance.

We cannot accept this proposition. The *Belier* line of cases is not, as the defendants argue, relevant only to an archaic system of public school management. We have reaffirmed the vitality of our interpretation of article IX in those cases many times since *Belier* and its progeny were decided, most recently to reject a constitutional attack posed to our state-wide system of public finance. See *Lujan v. Colorado State Board of Education*[, 649 P.2d [1005], at 1021–22, 1023 [1982]. If we were to abandon *Belier* now and uphold the Pilot Program, we would also, as we explain below, abandon the rationale of our public school finance system as we understood it in *Lujan*.

In *Lujan* we held that the local control provision of section 15 protects school districts against legislative efforts to require them to spend locally-raised funds on instruction that the district does not control, and preserves the districts' democratic framework. In that case, we considered whether the Public School Finance Act violates the equal protection provisions of the Colorado Constitution or the mandate of article IX, section 2 that the state provide a "thorough and uniform" system of public schools. Under the Finance Act, the public schools derive a significant percentage of their operating income from local property tax revenues. Because assessed property values vary from district to district, property-rich school districts are able to generate substantially more income from property tax revenues than property-poor school districts, which results in a disparity among the income the districts receive. Thus, for example, at the time *Lujan* was decided the Frisco School District was able to raise $386.52 per student, while the South Conejos School District raised only $23.60 per student. Applying rational basis review, we held that this disparity among districts in the amounts raised and spent per pupil does not violate the equal protection guarantees of our state constitution because the financing scheme achieves the important governmental purpose of fostering local control of education, as is required by article IX, section 15.

Our interpretation of article IX, section 15 in *Belier* was essential to this holding. * * * Allowing a district to raise and disburse its own funds enables the district to determine its own educational policy, free from restrictions imposed by the state or any other entity:

> The use of local taxes affords a school district the freedom to devote more money toward educating its children than is otherwise available in the state-guaranteed minimum amount. It also enables the local citizenry greater influence and participation in the decision making process as to how these local tax dollars are spent. Some communities might place heavy emphasis on schools, while others may desire greater police or fire protection, or improved streets or public transportation. Finally, local control provides each district with the opportunity for experimentation, innovation, and a healthy competition for educational excellence.

In *Lujan* we made clear that control over instruction is inextricably linked to control over locally-raised funds. The representative structure created in article IX, section 15 functions by entrusting locally-elected district board members with the discretion to disburse locally-raised tax revenues on education. In this way, district residents are able to tailor educational policy to meet the needs of the individual districts, without state interference.

Given our analysis in *Lujan*, which relies and builds upon *Belier*, if we were now to hold that the constitutional local control requirement does not require control over locally-raised funds, we would undermine the rationale of our state-wide system of public school finance. Such a conclusion would force a reexamination of our public school finance policy and could result in a disruption of the present system.

The defendants contend that, notwithstanding the cases discussed above, our decision in this case should be controlled by our analysis in [*Board of Education v.] Booth* [984 P.2d 639 (Colo.1999)]. In that case, we considered the constitutionality of the Charter Schools Act's second-appeal provision. Specifically, we considered whether the General Assembly had the power to authorize the state board of education to approve a charter school application that a district board had twice rejected. We held that this scheme was constitutional because it struck an appropriate balance between state and local power in an area that invoked both the State's general supervisory powers under article IX, section 2 and the local districts' control of instruction under article IX, section 15.

In considering whether our analysis in *Booth* is applicable to this case, it is important to recognize the limited effect of the state board's second-appeal approval power in that case. The state board's decision did not direct the opening of the proposed charter school over the local board's objections. Rather, state approval of the second-appeal application simply required the local board to negotiate in good faith with the proponents of the charter school to resolve the objections that the local board had identified in its orders denying the charter application. Through such negotiations, the local district and the proponents would arrive at a binding contract that would allow the charter school to open and operate on terms acceptable to the local district. The charter school statute met constitutional requirements because it closely circumscribed the state board's authority in the appeals process while simultaneously preserving the local board's control of instruction given in the charter school. The very limited nature of the state board's role is illustrated by the fact that we rejected as ultra vires the state board's attempt to order the local board to provide status reports on its future contract negotiations with the proponents.

In this case, we are not asked to assess whether the state's constitutional authority to supervise education infringes on the local boards' constitutional authority to control instruction. Rather, under the Pilot Program, the local boards do not retain any authority to determine which schools or which students are eligible to participate in the program, the amount of district funds to be devoted to the program, or the character of instruction paid for by those funds. The Pilot Program deprives the school districts of all local control of instruction. Thus, there are no constitutional powers to balance in this case, and therefore *Booth* does not apply. * * *

Local authority over locally-raised funds preserves the representative body created by section 15 and gives substance to the constitutional requirement that local boards "shall have control of instruction in the public schools of their respective districts." The Pilot Program violates these principles by requiring the school districts to pay funds—including those derived from locally-raised tax revenues—to parents, who in turn are required to pay those funds to nonpublic schools. By denying local districts discretion to allocate their locally-raised funds, the program not only violates the clear mandates of our cases construing article IX, section 15, but also undermines the basic rationale of our state-wide school finance system: effectuating local control over public schools. Thus, in accordance with *Lujan*, we hold that control over locally-raised funds is essential to effectuating local control of instruction, and the Pilot Program violates this requirement by stripping local districts of any discretion over the character of instruction participating students will receive at district expense.

The defendants also argue that school finance and "school choice" have evolved significantly since *Belier* was decided, and thus "[a]pplying the *Belier* rule is incongruous with today's school finance policy and would limit the General Assembly's authority over educational policy." As evidence, they point to the fact that currently, local tax revenues account for approximately forty percent of public school funds, whereas when the *Belier* line of cases were decided, nearly ninety-five percent of school funds were derived from local tax revenues. Implicit in this argument is that with greater state funding comes greater state control over educational policy. This Court has long recognized, however, that the constitutional division of power between the state and local boards is not measured by funding. * * * [T]he amount of funding derived from local tax revenues as compared to state contributions is immaterial to our analysis of the level of discretion the Colorado Constitution confers on local school boards today.

At base, the defendants argue that the public schools have failed, and the General Assembly should have the power to address that failure through programs such as the Pilot Program. Thus, the defendants contend, the General Assembly has reasonably chosen to confer power over instruction directly upon the parents of public school children and allow them to choose to send their children to private school. Our task is not to pass judgment on the wisdom of the General Assembly's policy choices. Rather, it is solely to determine whether those policy choices comport with constitutional requirements. Our analysis of article IX, section 15 reveals that the framers sought to empower the electors in each school district, including the parents of public school students, with control over instruction through the creation of local school boards which would represent the will of their electorate. If the General Assembly wants to change this fundamental structure, it must either seek to amend the constitution or enact legislation that satisfies the mandates of the Colorado Constitution.

We hold that the Pilot Program as enacted by the General Assembly conflicts clearly and irreconcilably with the Colorado Constitution, and the plaintiffs have met their burden of proving the program is unconstitutional beyond a reasonable doubt. * * *

JUSTICE KOURLIS dissenting: * * *

The Colorado Opportunity Contract Pilot Program takes state and local education dollars, assigns them to a particular student who qualifies, and allows that student to expend the dollars on education at identified nonpublic institutions. The question before the court, simply stated, is whether that program violates article IX, section 15 of the Colorado Constitution, which gives school districts in this state control over the instruction that students receive in the public schools of their respective districts. Because the school district loses no control whatsoever over the education provided in its public schools, but merely loses some revenue that it would otherwise have, I do not view the program as unconstitutional. * * *

F. ECONOMIC DEVELOPMENT

In recent years, a vast urban studies literature has explored cities' role in economic development.[38] In their book City Bound, Gerald Frug and David Barron analyze four current ideas about what city economic development might mean.[39] They describe these ideas in terms of four possible city futures: a global city, a tourist city, a middle class city, and a regional city. A global city concentrates on developing connections to the global economy—through technology, finance, and innovative research—as the city's primary strategy for growth. A tourist city seeks to attract visitors from around the world as its major emphasis—concentrating on cultural and sports facilities, convention centers, festival marketplaces, hotels, and restaurants. A middle class city treats providing services for residents, above all public education, as its most important function. A regional city focuses on surrounding cities and towns in the metropolitan area, and thus is more concerned with the city's relationship to development in its suburbs than to its relationship with Shanghai.

These four futures are not mutually exclusive. An effort to become a middle-class city by improving public education might also strengthen efforts to become a global one. A city focused on tourism might invest in neighborhood preservation in order to create an authentic urban feel for visitors, and, thereby, improve the fortunes of middle-class neighborhoods. But these four urban futures are also not necessarily mutually reinforcing. A city that is focused on its connection to the global

---

[38] See, e.g., Bruce Katz and Jennifer Bradley, The Metropolitan Revolution: How Cities and Metros Are Fixing Our Broken Politics and Fragile Economy (2013); Sammis White and Zenia Kotval (eds.), Financing Economic Development in the 21st Century (2d. ed. 2013); Edward Glaeser, Triumph of the City: How Our Greatest Invention Makes Us Richer, Smarter, Greener, Healthier and Happier (2011); David Schleicher, The City as a Law and Economics Subject, 2010 U. Ill. L. Rev. 1507 (2010); Richard Schragger, Decentralization and Development, 96 Va. L. Rev. 1837 (2010); Klaus Segbers, The Making of Global City Regions: Johannesburg, Mumbai/Bombay, Sao Paulo, and Shanghai (2007); Audrey McFarlane, Putting the "Public" Back into Public-Private Partnerships for Urban Development, 30 W. N. Eng. L. Rev. 39 (2007); Saskia Sassen, Global Networks, Linked Cities (2002); Peter Marcuse and Ronald van Kempen, Globalizing Cities: A New Spatial Order (2000); Paul Knox and Peter Taylor, World Cities in a World System (1995).

[39] Gerald E. Frug and David J. Barron, City Bound: How States Stifle Urban Innovation (2008).

economy may pursue policies that make it inhospitable to middle-class families with small children. It might, for example, concentrate on the development of high-end housing for part-time residents who have no kids at all. A city that is dedicated to tourism might make building tourist attractions in the downtown area a high priority at the expense of investment in neighborhoods far from the city center. A city concerned primarily with its relationship to the region might adopt transportation policies designed to serve suburban commuters rather than those directed at renovating its airport, even though the airport might do more to make the city appealing to visitors and investment from abroad.

This section concentrates on three of the four city futures explored in City Bound: the global city, the tourist city, and the middle class city. (The regional city has already been the focus of Chapter Three.) It then turns to a city future not discussed in the book: the immigrant city. The immigrant city concentrates its development strategy on attracting, and improving the lives of, new city residents from countries outside the United States. While reading these materials, consider whether local government law equally permits the pursuit all of these futures or, on the contrary, channels city decision making to favor some choices over others. Answering this question requires rethinking the previous sections of this casebook. How do state and federal law promote or inhibit each of these possible city futures (Chapter Two)? How does the metropolitan setting of city life affect city efforts to promote these different definitions of development (Chapter Three)? What impact do other local government rules—above all, rules about city finance—have on these alternative city policies (earlier parts of Chapter Four)?

It is important to keep in mind that the city futures examined below are simply illustrations. There are many other ideas, two of which seem worth mentioning here. The first is Richard Florida's argument, advanced in his book The Rise of the Creative Class, suggesting that an economic development strategy should focus on attracting the right kind of people to the city rather than on attracting businesses by giving them tax breaks. Businesses move to locations where their employees and potential employees want to live. Creating the right city ambience will bring these people to town, stimulate business investment, and, at the same time, promote city vitality. "[C]ities need a *people* climate," he says, "even more than they need a business climate." The people he has in mind are what he calls the creative class. The core of this group "include people in science and engineering, architecture and design, education, arts, music and entertainment, whose economic function is to create new ideas, new technology and/or new creative content." Around this core are creative professionals in business, law, health care and similar fields. These people will be joined by others like them, and, together, they will help promote not just business investment but the kind of street life, amenities (restaurants, entertainment, lifestyle) and values (openness, tolerance, diversity) that generate city development. Florida's idea includes ingredients of the global city (the competition for the creative class is world-wide), the tourist city (the amenities will attract tourists), the middle class city (many of these people are not rich), and the immigrant city (a source of the creative class). But it has its own distinctiveness.[40] How does the legal system promote or inhibit a city's effort to embrace this idea? What problems are generated if a city organizes itself to pursue it?

Another idea requires a super-rich investor being willing to buy a large section of a city and to transform it into a center for businesses and residents. Detroit and Las Vegas provide two examples of this strategy. In Detroit, Don Gilbert—the founder and chairman of Rock Ventures, an entity that includes Quicken Loans and other businesses, and a person with a net worth of more than $3 billion—has invested more than a billion dollars in downtown Detroit. He controls 40 properties there, has moved Quicken Loans to the area, and has attracted more than 80 other small companies to join it. He plans to make money on his investments— the properties were cheap—but he has a grander vision too: revitalizing downtown Detroit as an innovative business center and a place to live (he offers subsidies to those willing to live in the area). In Las Vegas, Tony Hsieh, the founder of Zappos.com, has invested $350 million in the city's downtown—that is, in the city itself, an area of concentrated poverty, a mile north of the Strip. (The Strip is located outside of town.) According to the plan's website, The Downtown Project, Hsieh's idea is to bring together "communities of passion" filled with small businesses, activities, cafes, public spaces, fashion, music, art, and ten thousand new residents. By doing so, he seeks to enable the kind of connectedness that allows people to inspire each other while pursuing their own passions. And, by locating this development in the heart of the city, the project will bring a depressed community back to life.[41]

Gilbert's and Hsieh's plans are not the same—Gilbert focuses more on attracting small business, while Hsieh wants to create "the most community-focused large city in the world." But they share in common the reliance on a single private investor. Their plans also have some

---

[40] Richard Florida, The Rise of the Creative Class And How It's Transforming Work, Leisure, Community, and Everyday Life 283, 8 (2002). Later books focus on the global dimension of the idea (Richard Florida, The Flight of the Creative Class: the New Global Competition for Talent (2005)) and on individual decision making about where to live (Richard Florida, What's Your City? How the Creative Economy is Making Where Your Live The Most Important Decision of Your Life (2008)).

[41] Tim Alberta, Is Dan Gilbert Detroit's New Superhero? The National Journal, February 27, 2014; David Segal, A Missionary's Quest to Remake Motor City, The New York Times, April 14, 2013; downtownproject.com; John Glionna, Las Vegas Plan Steps on Some Toes, Los Angeles Times, February 28, 2014; Sarah Corbett, How Zappo's Founder Turned Las Vegas into a Start-Up Fantasyland, Wired, January 21, 2014; Timothy Pratt, What Happens When Brooklyn Moves to Vegas, New York Times Magazine, October 19, 2012.

similarities with Richard Florida's argument, but Florida sees the development of the creative class as an organic process arising out of a changing economic environment, not the work of an investor. What is the theory of economic development that the Detroit and Las Vegas projects embrace? How would other neighborhoods in the city be affected by their success? What are the advantages and disadvantages of having a private investor play such a critical role in the undertaking? Perhaps the most fundamental question for these ideas, like for Richard Florida's and those in the materials that follow, is: when we speak of economic development, what kind of development do we have in mind?

1. THE GLOBAL CITY

Over the last few decades, an increasing number of urban scholars have explored what John Friedmann called, in his seminal article, "The World Cities Hypothesis." In advancing his hypothesis, Friedmann rejected the widely held view that key features of the globalization of the world economy—the dramatically enhanced mobility of capital, sharp reductions in travel time, unprecedented advances in communications technology, and large-scale domestic and international migration—have deprived cities of their historic economic advantage. On the contrary, he argued, cities have become even more important because the changing nature of the world economy requires the centralization of key functions in particular cities, even if other aspects of the production processes are dispersed. Business leaders move their companies to world cities to ensure proximity to other corporate headquarters or to a variety of specialized services (such as public relations firms, legal offices, and financial institutions) that have become indispensable to effective participation in the global marketplace. Immigrants—domestic and international, rich and poor—move to the same cities to provide the support services that the ever-more-concentrated business sector needs. There is, in short, a worldwide demand for specific locations, a demand that has organized the world's cities into a hierarchy ranked in terms of their relationship with the global economy.

What constitutes a world city is a matter of considerable dispute. This subsection concentrates on one ingredient that everyone seems to acknowledge: the city's role in international finance. In her book The Global City, from which the first excerpt that follows is taken, Saskia Sassen concentrates on this ingredient. Global cities, she says,

> now function in four new ways: first, as highly concentrated command points in the organization of the world economy; second, as key locations for finance and for specialized service firms, which have replaced manufacturing as the leading economic sectors; third, as sites of production, including the

production of innovations, in these leading industries; and fourth, as markets for the products and innovations produced.

As this description suggests, not every city in the world can be a global city. At any given time, only a small number of major cities perform the role described above, and a major topic in the literature concerns which cities qualify. True global cities—above all, London, New York and Tokyo—function as international economic actors on a world scale. Other cities, however, can be somewhere on the hierarchical list, at least as a secondary actor. And every city can seek to raise its place on the list of competitors for a more important role.

Three cases follow the excerpt from The Global City. They explore some of the legal issues raised by the pursuit of outside investment as an economic development strategy. The first, Maready v. The City of Winston Salem, upholds the legality of state and city financial support for this kind of investment. This kind of government support has generated intense inter-jurisdictional competition designed to attract businesses to one's own city in a metropolitan area (and the country) rather than another.[42] The second, Kelo v. City of New London (from Section B, above), examines the constitutionality of eminent domain undertaken for the same objective. The final case, Matter of Kaur v. New York State Urban Development Corporation, is an example of the use of one of these development powers—eminent domain—to pursue another definition of a global city: becoming a global center of higher education and research. Kaur illustrates how cities are using education and health care—"eds and meds," as they are called—as triggers for economic development. Are Maready, Kelo, and Kaur examples of cities' embrace of the global city goal? If not, what is the vision of the city's future that the cities are seeking to foster?

---

[42] For an argument that the Commerce Clause poses a restraint on inter-jurisdictional competition to attract businesses, see Peter Enrich, Saving the States from Themselves: Commerce Clause Constraints on State Tax Incentives for Business, 110 Harv. L. Rev. 377 (1996); see also Philip Frickey, The Congressional Process and the Constitutionality of Federal Legislation to End the Economic War among the States, The Region, June 1996, at 58; Walter Hellerstein and Dan Coenen, Commerce Clause Restraints on State Business Development Incentives, 81 Cornell L. Rev. 789 (1996). For a critique of Enrich's argument, see Clayton Gillette, Business Incentives, Interstate Competition, and the Commerce Clause, 82 Minn. L. Rev. 447 (1997). For a general analysis of the strategy of offering incentives to businesses on a local scale, see Richard Schragger, Rethinking the Theory and Practice of Local Economic Development, 77 U. Chi. L. Rev. 311 (2010); Peter D. Enrich, Business Tax Incentives: A Status Report, 34 Urb. Law. 415 (2002); Scott Ziance, Making Economic Development Incentives More Efficient, 30 Urb. Law. 33 (1998); for an analysis on a global scale, see Jane Jacobs, Cities and the Wealth of Nations (1984).

SASKIA SASSEN, THE GLOBAL CITY: NEW YORK, LONDON, TOKYO
Pp. 3–5, 7–10, 334–336 (1991).

The point of departure for the present study is that the combination of spatial dispersal and global integration has created a new strategic role for major cities. * * * [T]he changes in the functioning of cities have had a massive impact upon both international economic activity and urban form: Cities concentrate control over vast resources, while finance and specialized service industries have restructured the urban social and economic order. Thus a new type of city has appeared. It is the global city. Leading examples now are New York, London, and Tokyo. These three cities are the focus of this book. * * *

How does the position of these cities in the world economy today differ from that which they have historically held as centers of banking and trade? When Max Weber analyzed the medieval cities woven together in the Hanseatic League, he conceived their trade as the exchange of surplus production; it was his view that a medieval city could withdraw from external trade and continue to support itself, albeit on a reduced scale. The modern molecule of global cities is nothing like the trade among self-sufficient places in the Hanseatic League, as Weber understood it. The first thesis advanced in this book is that the territorial dispersal of current economic activity creates a need for expanded central control and management. In other words, while in principle the territorial decentralization of economic activity in recent years could have been accompanied by a corresponding decentralization in ownership and hence in the appropriation of profits, there has been little movement in that direction. Though large firms have increased their subcontracting to smaller firms, and many national firms in the newly industrializing countries have grown rapidly, this form of growth is ultimately part of a chain. Even industrial homeworkers in remote rural areas are now part of that chain. The transnational corporations continue to control much of the end product and to reap the profits associated with selling in the world market. The internationalization and expansion of the financial industry has brought growth to a large number of smaller financial markets, a growth which has fed the expansion of the global industry. But top-level control and management of the industry has become concentrated in a few leading financial centers, notably New York, London, and Tokyo. These account for a disproportionate share of all financial transactions and one that has grown rapidly since the early 1980s. The fundamental dynamic posited here is that the more globalized the economy becomes, the higher the agglomeration of central functions in a relatively few sites, that is, the global cities. * * *

A second major theme of this book concerns the impact of this type of economic growth on the economic order within these cities. It is necessary to go beyond the Weberian notion of coordination and [Daniel] Bell's notion of the postindustrial society to understand this new urban order. Bell, like Weber, assumes that the further society evolves from nineteenth-century industrial capitalism, the more the apex of the social order is involved in pure managerial process, with the content of what is to be managed becoming of secondary importance. Global cities are, however, not only nodal points for the coordination of processes; they are also particular sites of production. They are sites for (1) the production of specialized services needed by complex organizations for running a spatially dispersed network of factories, offices, and service outlets; and (2) the production of financial innovations and the making of markets, both central to the internationalization and expansion of the financial industry. To understand the structure of a global city, we have to understand it as a place where certain kinds of work can get done, which is to say that we have to get beyond the dichotomy between manufacturing and services. The "things" a global city makes are services and financial goods. * * *

A third major theme explored in this book concerns the consequences of these developments for the national urban system in each of these countries and for the relationship of the global city to its nation-state. While a few major cities are the sites of production for the new global control capability, a large number of other major cities have lost their role as leading export centers for industrial manufacturing, as a result of the decentralization of this form of production. Cities such as Detroit, Liverpool, Manchester, and now increasingly Nagoya and Osaka have been affected by the decentralization of their key industries at the domestic and international levels. According to the first hypothesis presented above, this same process has contributed to the growth of service industries that produce the specialized inputs to run global production processes and global markets for inputs and outputs. These industries—international legal and accounting services, management consulting, financial services—are heavily concentrated in cities such as New York, London, and Tokyo. We need to know how this growth alters the relations between the global cities and what were once the leading industrial centers in their nations. Does globalization bring about a triangulation so that New York, for example, now plays a role in the fortunes of Detroit that it did not play when that city was home to one of the leading industries, auto manufacturing? Or, in the case of Japan, we need to ask, for example, if there is a connection between the increasing shift of production out of Toyota City (Nagoya) to offshore locations (Thailand, South Korea, and the United States) and the development for the first time of a new headquarters for Toyota in Tokyo. * * *

The fourth and final theme in the book concerns the impact of these new forms of and conditions for growth on the social order of the global city. * * * I will examine to what extent the new structure of economic activity has brought about changes in the organization of work, reflected in a shift in the job supply and polarization in the income distribution and occupational distribution of workers. Major growth industries show a greater incidence of jobs at the high-and low-paying ends of the scale than do the older industries now in decline. Almost half the jobs in the producer services are lower-income jobs, and half are in the two highest earnings classes. In contrast, a large share of manufacturing workers were in the middle-earnings jobs during the postwar period of high growth in these industries in the United States and United Kingdom.

Two other developments in global cities have also contributed to economic polarization. One is the vast supply of low-wage jobs required by high-income gentrification in both its residential and commercial settings. The increase in the numbers of expensive restaurants, luxury housing, luxury hotels, gourmet shops, boutiques, French hand laundries, and special cleaners that ornament the new urban landscape illustrates this trend. Furthermore, there is a continuing need for low-wage industrial services, even in such sectors as finance and specialized services. A second development that has reached significant proportions is what I call the downgrading of the manufacturing sector, a process in which the share of unionized shops declines and wages deteriorate while sweatshops and industrial homework proliferate. This process includes the downgrading of jobs within existing industries and the job supply patterns of some of the new industries, notably electronics assembly. It is worth noting that the growth of a downgraded manufacturing sector has been strongest in cities such as New York and London.

The expansion of low-wage jobs as a function of growth trends implies a reorganization of the capital-labor relation. To see this, it is important to distinguish the characteristics of jobs from their sectoral location, since highly dynamic, technologically advanced growth sectors may well contain low-wage dead-end jobs. Furthermore, the distinction between sectoral characteristics and sectoral growth patterns is crucial: Backward sectors, such as downgraded manufacturing or low-wage service occupations, can be part of major growth trends in a highly developed economy. It is often assumed that backward sectors express decline trends. Similarly, there is a tendency to assume that advanced sectors, such as finance, have mostly good, white-collar jobs. In fact, they contain a good number of low-paying jobs, from cleaner to stock clerk. * * *

There is clearly one class of workers who benefited from this new industrial complex. They are the new professionals, managers, brokers of all types, whose numbers increased dramatically in these three cities, and to some extent in all cities. How do they fit into the economic and political system of the city? The evidence in this book suggests that it is important to distinguish this new class of high-income workers from the wealthy, also a significant presence in leading cities. This is definitely a class of high-income workers, who, unlike top-level executives and managers, have no significant control or ownership in the large corporations and investment banks for which they work. They are not really part of C. Wright Mills's power elite. They are ultimately a stratum of extremely hard-working people whose alliance to the system leads them to produce far more profit than they get back in their admittedly very high salaries and bonuses. In some ways it could be argued that they engage in self-exploitation insofar as they work extremely hard, put in very long hours and ultimately make significantly less money than the stratum of top level managers and executives, who earn ten to twenty times as much. The recent crisis in the stock market, which eventually led to the dismissal of significant numbers of these workers, especially in New York, has laid bare the extent to which they have no claim on the system or their employers, unlike top-level managers who, when displaced by mergers, can claim large sums of compensation or "golden parachutes." This book also suggests that high-income gentrification and the type of conspicuous consumption associated with it serves a strong ideological function of securing the alliance of these workers to a system for which they produce immense profits in exchange for relatively low returns and few claims.

The new high-income workers are the carriers of a consumption capacity and consumption choices that distinguish them from the traditional middle class of the 1950s and 1960s. While their earned income is too little to be investment capital, it is too much for the basically thrifty, savings-oriented middle class. These new high-income earners emerge as primary candidates for new types of intermediate investments: arts, antiques, and luxury consumption. The conjunction of excess earnings and the new cosmopolitan work culture creates a compelling space for new lifestyles and new kinds of economic activities. It is against this background that we need to examine the expansion of the art market and of luxury consumption on a scale that has made them qualitatively different from what they were even fifteen years ago—a privilege of elites. The growth of a stratum of very high income workers has produced not only a physical upgrading of expanding portions of global cities, but also a reorganization of the consumption structure.

The high income of the new workers is not sufficient to explain the transformation. Less tangible factors are considerable. The new work culture is a cosmopolitan one, for the objective conditions of work are world oriented, being embedded in a context of growing internationalization in the economies of these cities. The growing number of young professional women has further contributed to an urbanization of the professional class rather than the suburbanization typical of an earlier period. Concomitantly, we see what amounts to a new social aesthetic in everyday living, where previously the functional criteria of the middle class ruled. An examination of this transformation reveals a dynamic whereby an economic potential—the consumption capacity represented by high disposable income—is realized through the emergence of a new vision of the good life. Hence the importance not just of food but of cuisine, not just of clothes but of designer labels, not just of decoration but of authentic objets d'art. This transformation is captured in the rise of the ever more abundant boutique and art gallery. Similarly, the ideal residence is no longer a "home" in suburbia, but a converted former warehouse in ultraurban downtown. Consequent to this new social aesthetic is, of course, a whole line of profitmaking possibilities, from "nouveaux" restaurants to a thriving art market. What is notable is the extent to which a numerically small class of workers imposed such a visible transformation—of the nature of commerce and consumption—on strategic areas of these extremely large cities. This is, I argue, connected to questions of the social reproduction of a strategic but powerless class of workers.

Immigrants in New York and London, in turn, have produced a low-cost equivalent of gentrification. Areas of New York once filled with shut-up storefronts and abandoned buildings are now thriving commercial and residential neighborhoods. On a smaller scale, the same process has occurred in London. The growing size and complexity of immigrant communities has generated a demand and supply for a wide range of goods, services, and workers. In both cities, the residential and social separateness of the immigrant community becomes a vehicle to maximize the potential it contains. Small investments of money and direct labor in homes and shops by individuals become neighborhood upgrading because of the residential concentration of immigrants. This upgrading does not fit the conventional notions of upgrading, notions rooted in the middle-class experience. Its shapes, colors, and sounds are novel. They, like the cosmopolitan work culture of the new professionals, are yet another form of the internationalization of global cities. * * *

MAREADY V. THE CITY OF WINSTON-SALEM

Supreme Court of North Carolina, 1996.
342 N.C. 708, 467 S.E.2d 615.

WHICHARD, JUSTICE.

Plaintiff-appellant, William F. Maready, instituted this action against the City of Winston-Salem [and] Forsyth County, * * * [contending] that N.C.G.S. § 158–7.1, which authorizes local governments to make economic development incentive grants to private corporations, is unconstitutional because it violates the public purpose clause of the North Carolina Constitution * * *. This action challenges twenty-four economic development incentive projects entered into * * * pursuant to N.C.G.S. § 158–7.1. The projected investment * * * in these projects totals approximately $13,200,000. The primary source of these funds has been taxes levied * * * on property owners in Winston-Salem and Forsyth County. City and County officials estimate an increase in the local tax base of $238,593,000 and a projected creation of over 5,500 new jobs as a result of these economic development incentive programs. They expect to recoup the full amount of their investment within three to seven years. The source of the return will be revenues generated by the additional property taxes paid by participating corporations. To date, all but one project has met or exceeded its goal. * * * The expenditures are in the form of reimbursement to the recipient for purposes such as on-the-job training, site preparation, facility upgrading, and parking.

Article V, Section 2(1) of the North Carolina Constitution provides that "the power of taxation shall be exercised in a just and equitable manner, for public purposes only." In *Mitchell v. North Carolina Indus. Dev. Fin. Auth.*, 273 N.C. 137, 159 S.E.2d 745 (1968), Justice (later Chief Justice) Sharp, writing for a majority of this Court, stated:

> The power to appropriate money from the public treasury is no greater than the power to levy the tax which put the money in the treasury. Both powers are subject to the constitutional proscription that tax revenues may not be used for private individuals or corporations, no matter how benevolent. * * *

Plaintiff * * * argues, and the trial court apparently agreed, that this question falls squarely within the purview of *Mitchell*. There we held unconstitutional the Industrial Facilities Financing Act, a statute that authorized issuance of industrial revenue bonds to finance the construction and equipping of facilities for private corporations. The suit was filed as a test case, before any bonds were issued, to enjoin the appropriation of $37,000 from the State Contingency and Emergency Fund for the purpose of enabling the Authority to organize and begin operations. We find *Mitchell* distinguishable.

One of the bases for the *Mitchell* decision was that the General Assembly had unenthusiastically passed the enacting legislation, declaring it to be bad policy. The opinion stated:

> At the time the General Assembly passed the Act, it declared in Resolution No. 52 that it considered the Act bad public policy. It explained that it felt compelled to authorize industrial revenue bonds in order to compete for industry with neighboring states which use them. As proof of its reluctance to join the industry-subsidizing group of states, the General Assembly requested the President and the other forty-nine states to petition Congress to

make the interest on all such bonds thereafter issued subject to all applicable income-tax laws.

The resolution recited that the General Assembly passed the act reluctantly, with reservations, and as a defensive measure. The Assembly's obvious apprehension over using public funds to benefit private entities in this manner clearly served to undermine the Court's confidence in the constitutionality of the legislation. The converse is true here in that the Assembly has unequivocally embraced expenditures of public funds for the promotion of local economic development as advancing a public purpose.

Further, and more importantly, the holding in *Mitchell* clearly indicates that the Court considered private industry to be the primary benefactor of the legislation and considered any benefit to the public purely incidental. Notwithstanding its recognition that any lawful business in a community promotes the public good, the Court held that the "Authority's primary function, to acquire sites and to construct and equip facilities for private industry, is not for a public use or purpose." The Court rightly concluded that direct state aid to a private enterprise, with only limited benefit accruing to the public, contravenes fundamental constitutional precepts. In reiterating that it is not the function of the government to engage in private business, the opinion quoted with approval the following language from the Supreme Court of Idaho:

> "An exemption which arbitrarily prefers one private enterprise operating by means of facilities provided by a municipality, over another engaged, or desiring to engage, in the same business in the same locality, is neither necessary nor just. . . . It is obvious that private enterprise, not so favored, could not compete with industries operating thereunder. If the state-favored industries were successfully managed, private enterprise would of necessity be forced out, and the state, through its municipalities, would increasingly become involved in promoting, sponsoring, regulating and controlling private business, and our free private enterprise economy would be replaced by socialism. The constitutions of both state and nation were founded upon a capitalistic private enterprise economy and were designed to protect and foster private property and private initiative."

Thus, the Court implicitly rejected the act because its primary object was private gain and its nature and purpose did not tend to yield public benefit. * * *

Significantly, the direct holdings of * * * [*Mitchell* and subsequent] cases—that industrial revenue bond financing is unconstitutional—were overturned by a specific constitutional amendment. In 1973 the North Carolina Constitution was amended to add Article V, Section 9, which allows counties to create authorities to issue revenue bonds for industrial and pollution control facilities. While this amendment was narrowly tailored to address a specific situation, it nonetheless diminishes the significance of *Mitchell* * * *. Moreover, the Court's focal concern in *Mitchell* * * *, the means used to achieve economic growth, has also been removed by constitutional amendment. In 1973 Article V, Section 2(7) was added to the North Carolina Constitution, specifically allowing direct appropriation to private entities for public purposes. This section provides:

> The General Assembly may enact laws whereby the State, any county, city or town, and any other public corporation may contract with and appropriate money to any person, association, or corporation for the accomplishment of public purposes only.

N.C. Const. art. V, § 2(7). "Under subsection (7) direct disbursement of public funds to private entities is a constitutionally permissible means of accomplishing a public purpose provided there is statutory authority to make such appropriation." *Hughey v. Cloninger*, 297 N.C. 86, 95, 253 S.E.2d 898, 904 (1979). Hence, the constitutional problem under the public purpose doctrine that the Court perceived in *Mitchell* * * * no longer exists.

While *Mitchell* and its progeny remain pivotal in the development of the doctrine, they do not purport to establish a permanent test for determining the existence of a public purpose. The majority in *Mitchell* posed the question: "Is it today a proper function of government for the State to provide a site and equip a plant for private industrial enterprise?" This explicit recognition of the importance of contemporary circumstances in assessing the public purpose of governmental endeavors highlights the essential fluidity of the concept. While the *Mitchell* majority answered the question in the negative, the passage of time and accompanying societal changes now suggest a positive response. * * *

This Court most recently addressed the public purpose question in *Madison Cablevision v. City of Morganton*, 325 N.C. 634, 386 S.E.2d 200, where it unanimously held that N.C.G.S. § 160A, art. 16, part 1, which authorizes cities to finance, acquire, construct, own, and operate cablevision systems, does not violate the public purpose clause of Article V, Section 2(1). The Court stated that "two guiding principles have been established for determining that a particular undertaking by a municipality is for a public purpose: (1) it involves a reasonable connection with the convenience and necessity of the particular municipality; and (2) the activity benefits the public generally, as opposed to special interests or persons." Application of these principles here mandates the conclusion that N.C.G.S. § 158–7.1 furthers a public purpose and hence is constitutional.

As to the first prong, whether an activity is within the appropriate scope of governmental involvement and is reasonably related to communal needs may be evaluated by determining how similar the activity is to others which this Court has held to be within the permissible realm of governmental action. We conclude that the activities N.C.G.S. § 158–7.1 authorizes are in keeping with those accepted as within the scope of permissible governmental action. * * * Economic development has long been recognized as a proper governmental function. * * * Urban redevelopment commissions have power to acquire property, clear slums, and sell the property to private developers. In that instance, as here, a private party ultimately acquires the property and conducts activities which, while providing incidental private benefit, serve a primary public goal.

As to the second prong of the *Madison Cablevision* inquiry, under the expanded understanding of public purpose, even the most innovative activities N.C.G.S. § 158–7.1 permits are constitutional so long as they primarily benefit the public and not a private party. * * * Moreover, an expenditure does not lose its public purpose merely because it involves a private actor. Generally, if an act will promote the welfare of a state or a local government and its citizens, it is for a public purpose.

Viewed in this light, section 158–7.1 clearly serves a public purpose. Its self-proclaimed end is to "increase the population, taxable property, agricultural industries and business prospects of any city or county." N.C.G.S. § 158–7.1(a). However, it is the natural consequences flowing therefrom that ensure a net public benefit. The expenditures this statute authorizes should create a more stable local economy by providing displaced workers with continuing employment opportunities, attracting better paying and more highly skilled jobs, enlarging the tax base, and diversifying the economy. Careful planning pursuant to the statute should enable optimization of natural resources while concurrently preserving the local infrastructure. The strict procedural requirements the statute imposes provide safeguards that should suffice to prevent abuse.

The public advantages are not indirect, remote, or incidental; rather, they are directly aimed at furthering the general economic welfare of the people of the communities affected. While private actors will necessarily benefit from the expenditures authorized, such benefit is merely incidental. It results from the local government's efforts to better serve the interests of its people. Each community has a distinct ambience, unique assets, and special needs best ascertained at the local level. Section 158–7.1 enables each to formulate its own definition of economic success and to draft a developmental plan leading to that goal. This aim is no less legitimate and no less for a public purpose than projects this Court has approved in the past.

Finally, while this Court does not pass upon the wisdom or propriety of legislation in determining the primary motivation behind a statute, it may consider the circumstances surrounding its enactment. * * * To date, courts in forty-six states have upheld the constitutionality of governmental expenditures and related assistance for economic development incentives. Only California and Idaho lack reported decisions on this issue, though they too have statutes authorizing such expenditures. * * * Thus, by virtue of the trial court's ruling, North Carolina currently stands alone * * *. Considered in this light, it would be unrealistic to assume that the State will not suffer economically in the future if the incentive programs created pursuant to N.C.G.S. § 158–7.1 are discontinued. * * * The General Assembly thus could determine that legislation such as N.C.G.S. § 158–7.1, which is intended to alleviate conditions of unemployment and fiscal distress and to increase the local tax base, serves the public interest. New and expanded industries in communities within North Carolina provide work and economic opportunity for those who otherwise might not have it. This, in turn, creates a broader tax base from which the State and its local governments can draw funding for other programs that benefit the general health, safety, and welfare of their citizens. The potential impetus to economic development, which might otherwise be lost to other states, likewise serves the public interest. We therefore hold that N.C.G.S. § 158–7.1, which permits the expenditure of public moneys for economic development incentive programs, does not violate the public purpose clause of the North Carolina Constitution. * * *

JUSTICE ORR dissenting. * * *

The logic upon which the majority opinion rests its conclusion that the expenditure of these funds was for a public purpose can be stated as follows: The creation of new jobs and an increase in the tax base ipso facto benefits the general public. Therefore, local government expenditure of tax dollars to a private business for its private benefit in order to induce the business to either expand or locate in the community is for a public purpose if it creates new jobs and increases the tax base. The fallacy of this reasoning begins with the assumption that new jobs and a higher tax base automatically result in significant benefit to the public. The trial court's finding of fact number 9 addresses the factual and evidentiary failings of this assumption:

> No evidence was presented that incentives paid or committed by
> the City and County improved the unemployment rate or that
> they otherwise resulted in meaningful economic enhancement.
> No evidence was presented that the incentive grants made by
> the City and County reduced the net cost of government or
> resulted in a reduction in the amount or rate of property taxes

paid by, or the level of services rendered to, the citizens of
Winston-Salem and/or Forsyth County.

The argument presented by the defendants relies on the evidence of a
projected total from the twenty-four projects of 5,532 new jobs and a
projected tax base increase of $238,593,000. As impressive as those
numbers appear, they must be viewed in the proper context. Based on
January 1995 estimates, the work force in Forsyth County totalled
152,030, with an estimated 145,840 employed. Therefore, even if all of the
projected 5,532 new jobs came to fruition, it still represents less than four
percent of the employed work force in the county. In addition, an
estimated eighty-five percent of those new jobs went to individuals
already in Forsyth County, many of whom were presumably employed
with other businesses. With respect to the increased tax base, the
County's 1995 property tax base was valued at $15,633,231,770. The
increase in the property tax base projected by defendants from the
projects is $238,593,000, or slightly more than one and one-half percent of
the overall tax base. Therefore, the conclusion that there is anything
more than limited benefit accruing to the public in this case cannot be
supported by the existing evidence. * * *

The majority * * * relies on a "changing times" theory to ignore the
law as set forth in *Mitchell* * * *. While economic times have changed and
will continue to change, the philosophy that constitutional interpretation
and application are subject to the whims of "everybody's doing it" cannot
be sustained. * * * Advocates for these business incentives contend that
without them, North Carolina will be at a significant competitive
disadvantage in keeping and recruiting private industry. They further
contend that the economic well-being of our state and its citizens is
dependent on the continued utilization of this practice. These arguments
are compelling, and even plaintiff admits that a public purpose is served
by general economic development and recruitment of industry. However,
plaintiff and those supporting his point of view argue that direct grants to
specific, selected businesses go beyond the acceptable bounds of public
purpose expenditures for economic development. Instead, they say that
this is selected corporate welfare to some of the largest and most
prosperous companies in our State and in the country. Moreover, these
opponents contend that the grants are not equitably applied because they
generally favor the larger companies and projects and, in this case, under
the County's Economic Incentives Program Guidelines, completely
eliminate retail operations from being considered. In challenging the
actual public benefit, a question also is raised about the economic loss and
devastation to smaller North Carolina communities that lose valued
industry to larger, wealthier areas. * * *

Also troubling is the question of limits under the majority's theory. If
it is an acceptable public purpose to spend tax dollars specifically for

relocation expenses to benefit the spouses of corporate executives moving to the community in finding new jobs or for parking decks that benefit only the employees of the favored company, then what can a government not do if the end result will entice a company to produce new jobs and raise the tax base? If a potential corporate entity is considering a move to Winston-Salem but will only come if country club memberships are provided for its executives, do we sanction the use of tax revenue to facilitate the move? I would hope not, but under the holding of the majority opinion, I see no grounds for challenging such an expenditure provided that, as a result of such a grant, the company promises to create new jobs, and an increased tax base is projected. * * *

KELO V. CITY OF NEW LONDON
[See Chapter 4, Section B, supra.]

MATTER OF KAUR V. NEW YORK STATE URBAN DEV. CORP.
Court of Appeals of New York, 2010.
15 N.Y.3d 235.

CIPARICK, J.

In this appeal, we are called upon to determine whether respondent's exercise of its power of eminent domain to acquire petitioners' property for the development of a new Columbia University campus was supported by a sufficient public use, benefit or purpose (see NY Const, art I, § 7 [a]; EDPL 207 [C] [4]). We answer this question in the affirmative and conclude, pursuant to our recent holding in *Matter of Goldstein v. New York State Urban Dev. Corp.*, 13 NY3d 511 [2009]), that the Empire State Development Corporation's (ESDC) findings of blight and determination that the condemnation of petitioners' property qualified as a "land use improvement project" were rationally based and entitled to deference. We also conclude that the alternative finding of "civic purpose," likewise, had a rational basis.

Petitioners in this proceeding are the owners of different commercial establishments located in the West Harlem neighborhood of Manhattan. * * * On December 18, 2008, respondent ESDC issued a determination * * * concluding that it should use its power of condemnation to purchase 17 acres of privately owned property, including petitioners', in connection with the Columbia University Educational Mixed Use Development Land Use Improvement and Civic Project (the Project). Located in the Manhattanville section of West Harlem, the Project site will extend from the south side of West 125th Street to the north side of West 133rd Street and will be bounded by Broadway and Old Broadway on the east and 12th Avenue on the west. The majority of the buildings located within the proposed Project site are commercial * * *. The Project contemplates the construction of a new urban campus that would consist of 16 new state-of-the-art buildings, the adaptive reuse of an existing building and a multi-level below-grade support space. Approximating 6.8 million gross square feet in size, the Project provides for the creation of about two acres of publicly accessible open space, a retail market along 12th Avenue and widened, tree-lined sidewalks. The new buildings will house, among other things, teaching facilities, academic research centers, graduate student and faculty housing as well as an area devoted to services for the local community. Columbia University, a not-for-profit educational corporation, will exclusively underwrite the cost of this Project and not seek financial assistance from the government.

The origins of the Project trace back to 2001 when Columbia first approached the New York City Economic Development Corporation (EDC) to redevelop the West Harlem area. Following Columbia's interest in revitalizing the neighborhood and expanding its campus, EDC commenced a general economic study of the neighborhood. * * * In 2003, EDC hired Urbitran Associates (Urbitran), an engineering, architecture and planning firm, to conduct a separate study, examining the neighborhood conditions of West Harlem. * * * [T]he study revealed that several of the buildings throughout West Harlem were dilapidated. * * * Meanwhile, * * * Columbia began to purchase property located within the Project site. ESDC met with Columbia and EDC for the first time in March 2004 to discuss the proposed condemnation of petitioners' land. On July 30, 2004, ESDC and Columbia entered into an agreement, which provided that Columbia would pay ESDC's costs associated with the Project. In September 2006 * * * ESDC retained Allee King Rosen & Fleming (AKRF) to perform a neighborhood conditions report of the Project site on its behalf. * * * [O]n November 1, 2007, AKRF issued its Manhattanville Neighborhood Conditions Study. This study concluded that the Project site was "substantially unsafe, unsanitary, substandard, and deteriorated" or, in short, blighted.

As ESDC prepared to issue its "blight study" of the Project site, Columbia moved towards obtaining the necessary agency approval to realize its expansion plan. Indeed, the public process for this Project was extensive and formally began when the New York City Planning Commission (CPC) first considered whether to authorize the rezoning of about 35 acres of West Harlem, including the 17-acre Project site. The rezoning of this area, recommended in EDC's West Harlem Master Plan, triggered a thorough review according to New York City's Uniform Land Use Review Procedure (ULURP). * * * In its findings, CPC noted that Columbia "is of significant importance to the City and State as a center of educational excellence and a source of economic growth, and the Academic Mixed Use Development Plan is intended to fulfill these public purposes." Thus, CPC approved the rezoning that would allow Columbia

to construct "a new urban campus * * * and a new open space network
* * *." CPC further recognized that the proposed Project may require the
use of eminent domain, which, if necessary, "would serve a public purpose
insofar as it would allow for realization of the public benefits of the
Columbia proposal."

Following CPC's approval of the rezoning in West Harlem, the City
Council held a public hearing on this matter and on December 19, 2007, it
approved the 35-acre rezoning of West Harlem. * * * With the "blight
studies" * * * in hand and with the knowledge that the City Council had
approved the Project site for rezoning, on July 17, 2008, ESDC adopted a
General Project Plan (GPP) that would enable Columbia to move forward
with its plan to build an urban campus in West Harlem. * * * ESDC
solicited public comment on the GPP, holding a duly noticed hearing on
September 2 and 4, 2008. This hearing, which lasted over 13 hours, was
attended by 98 members of the community, including petitioners and
their counsel. * * * Taking into consideration the questions raised by the
petitioners during the hearing and their substantial written submissions
that followed, on December 18, 2008, ESDC adopted a modified GPP * * *.
ESDC sponsored the Project both as a "land use improvement project"
pursuant to the New York State Urban Development Corporation Act
(UDC Act) and as a "civic project" pursuant to a different paragraph of
the same Act.

In so sponsoring this Project, ESDC specified the public uses,
benefits and purposes of the Project * * *. It found, for example, that the
Project would address the city and statewide "need for educational,
community, recreational, cultural and other civic facilities" and would
enable New York City and the State to maintain their positions as "global
center[s] for higher education and academic research." ESDC further
determined that Manhattanville "suffer[ed] from long-term poor
maintenance [and] lack of development and disinvestment" and the
Project would help curb the "current bleak conditions [that] are and have
been inhibiting growth and preventing the site's integration into the
surrounding community." * * * ESDC noted that the Project would create
* * * jobs during the construction of the new campus as well as * * *
permanent jobs following the Project's completion. ESDC found that the
Project would generate substantial revenue, estimating that "tax revenue
derived from construction expenditures and total personal income during
this period" at $122 million for the State and $87 million for New York
City. Moreover, ESDC indicated that another purpose of the Project was
the creation of much needed public space. * * * In addition * * *, ESDC
highlighted that the Project made provision for infrastructure
improvements—most notably to the 125th Street subway station—as well
as substantial financial commitment by Columbia to the maintenance of
West Harlem Piers Park. ESDC further acknowledged that Columbia

would open its facilities—including its libraries and computer centers—to students attending a new public school that Columbia is supplying the land to rent-free for 49 years. Columbia would also open its new swimming facilities to the public. * * *

Petitioners' main argument on this appeal is that the Project approved by ESDC is unconstitutional because the condemnation is not for the purpose of putting properties to "public use" within the meaning of article I, § 7 (a) of the NY Constitution, which provides that "[p]rivate property shall not be taken for public use without just compensation." * * * In *Matter of Goldstein*, we reaffirmed the long-standing doctrine that the role of the Judiciary is limited in reviewing findings of blight in eminent domain proceedings. Because the determinations of blight and public purpose are the province of the Legislature, and are entitled to deference by the Judiciary, we stated * * *[:] "It is only where there is no room for reasonable difference of opinion as to whether an area is blighted, that judges may substitute their views as to the adequacy with which the public purpose of blight removal has been made out for that of the legislatively designated agencies." Indeed, we observed that "[t]he Constitution accords government broad power to take and clear substandard and insanitary areas for redevelopment. In so doing, it commensurately deprives the Judiciary of grounds to interfere with the exercise." * * * [I]t cannot be said that ESDC's finding of blight was irrational or baseless. Indeed, ESDC considered a wide range of factors including the physical, economic, engineering and environmental conditions at the Project site. * * * Accordingly, * * * there is record support—"extensively documented photographically and otherwise on a lot-by-lot basis"—for ESDC's determination that the Project site was blighted * * *.

In addition to attacking the neighborhood blight studies and ESDC's determination based on those studies, petitioners also challenge the constitutionality of the statutory term "substandard or insanitary area." They argue that we should find this term void for vagueness. This contention is * * * unpersuasive. * * * Not only this Court, but the Supreme Court has consistently held that blight is an elastic concept that does not call for an inflexible, one-size-fits-all definition (*see Berman v. Parker*, 348 US 26, 33–34 [1954]). Rather, blight or "substandard or insanitary areas," as we held in *Matter of Goldstein*, must be viewed on a case-by-case basis. Accordingly, because the UDC Act provides adequate meaning to the term "substandard or insanitary area," we reject petitioners' argument that the statute is unconstitutionally vague on its face. * * *

We also conclude that ESDC properly qualified this Project, in the alternative, as a "civic project" within the meaning of the UDC Act. Of course, ESDC is statutorily empowered to exercise eminent domain in furtherance of a civic project regardless of whether a project site suffers from blight. A civic project is defined as "[a] project or that portion of a multi-purpose project designed and intended for the purpose of providing facilities for educational, cultural, recreational, community, municipal, public service or other civic purposes" (UDC Act § 3 (6) (d)). * * * [C]onsonant with the policy articulated in the UDC Act, ESDC has a history of participation in civic projects involving private entities. The most recent example of a civic project is the Atlantic Yards project, which authorized a private entity to construct and operate an arena for the Nets professional basketball franchise (see *Matter of Develop Don't Destroy (Brooklyn) v. Urban Dev. Corp.*, 59 AD3d 312 [1st Dept 2009], lv denied 13 NY3d 713 [2009]). The petitioners in that case argued that the project did not qualify as a "civic project" because the arena would be used by a professional basketball team and operated by a private profit-making entity. In rejecting that argument, the Appellate Division explained "that a sports arena, even one privately operated for profit, may serve a public purpose." * * * [T]he court observed that "the proposed arena will serve a public purpose by providing a needed recreational venue in the area of the project."

The proposed Project here is at least as compelling in its civic dimension as the private development in *Matter of Develop Don't Destroy (Brooklyn)*. Unlike the Nets basketball franchise, Columbia University, though private, operates as a nonprofit educational corporation. Thus, the concern that a private enterprise will be profiting through eminent domain is not present. Rather, the purpose of the Project is unquestionably to promote education and academic research while providing public benefits to the local community. Indeed, the advancement of higher education is the quintessential example of a "civic purpose." It is fundamental that education and the expansion of knowledge are pivotal government interests. The indisputably public purpose of education is particularly vital for New York City and the State to maintain their respective statuses as global centers of higher education and academic research. To that end, the Project plan includes the construction of facilities dedicated to research and the expansion of laboratories, libraries and student housing.

In addition to these new educational facilities, the Project will bestow numerous other significant civic benefits to the public. For example, the Project calls for the development of approximately two acres of gateless, publicly accessible park-like and landscaped space as well as an open-air market zone along 12th Avenue. Other civic benefits include upgrades in transit infrastructure and a financial commitment to West Harlem Piers Park. Moreover, this Project is projected to stimulate job growth in the local area. In addition to hiring 14,000 people for construction at the Project site, Columbia estimates that it will accommodate 6,000 permanent employees once the Project is completed. In sum, there can be no doubt that the Project approved by ESDC—which provides for the expansion of Columbia's educational facilities and countless public benefits to the surrounding neighborhood, including cultural, recreational and job development benefits—qualifies as a "civic project" under the UDC Act. * * *

2. THE TOURIST CITY

In their influential book The Tourist City, Dennis Judd and Susan Fainstein describe the transition of major cities into vehicles for attracting tourists.[43] Tourist cities shift their focus from the needs of city residents to the desires of people living elsewhere. They therefore sell themselves as a place to visit to people in nearby suburbs, across the country, and around the world. In part, they do so by advertising in a manner similar to businesses marketing a consumer product, highlighting the value of their heritage, vitality, and unique attractions. But they also construct their infrastructure and provide amenities to ensure that the tourists will have something to do, and will be able to get around, when they are in the city.

It is not hard to understand why the tourist city has proved to be so appealing. It has been especially attractive in the post-industrial era because it does not require a city to convince people to move to the city to live. A city simply has to entice temporary visitors, and they can be directed to those parts of the city in which the evidence of the post-war urban crisis can largely be kept from view. From this perspective, the emergence of the tourist city is symptomatic of urban decline and a reflection of disparate political influence within the city. But the tourist city is influential in prosperous cities as well. Along with the embrace of the global city, it provides a familiar way to promote and sustain the local economy. Tourists come for a short time, and they spend significant amounts of money during their stay. They do not demand the social services that residents need, and they can spread the word about the city's appeal to others. In this way, visitors can help the city sell itself as an attractive place to live and work. The tourist city thus overlaps with the entertainment-focused approach to becoming a global city.

There are a variety of definitions of a tourist city that a city might embrace. The first is to make the city as a whole—or, more accurately, the neighborhoods within the city that outsiders identify as being the whole city—a place that tourists want to visit. This might be called a "tourist-friendly city." The second is to create specific areas within the city—areas that John Hannigan calls the "fantasy city" and Dennis Judd calls the "tourist bubble"—that attract pleasure seekers: locations

---

[43] Dennis Judd and Susan Fainstein (eds.), The Tourist City (1999). See also Melanie K. Smith (ed.), Tourism, Culture and Regeneration (2007).

ranging from shopping environments to sports stadiums to gambling casinos to convention centers to theme parks.[44] The final idea is to focus on a single dramatic event that will "put the city on the map": the Olympics, the World Cup, or a World Expo. These ideas can and do overlap, but each of them raises its own problems under the existing legal structure.

The three articles and books excerpted below focus on the fantasy city or tourist bubble. These developments not only reflect city governmental efforts to attract people who live outside the city but are an attempt to emphasize the connection between cities and pleasure rather than between cities and work or between cities and the provision of necessary services. Perhaps it's not surprising, therefore, that two of the three excerpts below refer to Disneyland. M. Christine Boyer and Michael Sorkin address the relationship between central city entertainment destinations—places like Quincy Market in Boston, the Inner Harbor in Baltimore, South Street Seaport in New York City, Watertower Place in Chicago, the Skyways in Minneapolis, Ghiradelli Square in San Francisco—and Disneyland. What is the meaning of these spaces for civic life? In what way is their reliance on fantasy designed to paper over the realities faced by (unseen) city residents? Peter Eisinger's article, unlike the others, does not mention Disneyland. But, like the others, his discussion of city funding of sports stadiums focuses not on the usual problem critics address—is the funding of these stadiums a waste of money?[45]—but on the sense of priorities that they reflect. How much money, he asks, should a city spend on these kinds of facilities rather than on the traditional city services offered city residents—police, fire, sanitation, schools? One final question is implicit in these readings but not discussed: how does local government law promote or inhibit the creation of these tourist bubbles?

---

[44] Dennis Judd, Constructing the Tourist Bubble, in Dennis Judd and Susan Fainstein (eds.), The Tourist City (1999); John Hannigan, Fantasy City: Pleasure and Profit in the Postmodern Metropolis (1998).

[45] See. e.g., Jack Williams, Jessica O'Quin, and Joshua Stein, Public Financing of Green Cathedrals, 5 Alb. Gov't L. Rev. 123 (2012); Garrett Johnson, The Economic Impact of New Stadiums and Arenas on Cities, 2011 Den. U. Sports & Ent. L.J. 1 (2011); Marc Edelman, Sports and the City: How to Curb Professional Sports Teams' Demands for Free Public Stadiums, 6 Rutgers J. L. & Pub. Pol'y 35 (2008); Frank A. Mayer III, Stadium Financing: Where We Are, How We Got Here, and Where We Are Going, 12 Vill. Sports & Ent. L.J. 195 (2005); Mathew Parlow, Publicly Financed Sports Facilities: Are They Economically Justifiable? A Case Study of the Los Angeles Staples Center, 10 U. Miami Bus. L. Rev. 483 (2002); Symposium: Sports Facilities and Development, 10 Marq. Sports L.J. 173 (2000); Mark Rosentraub, Are Public Policies Needed to Level the Playing Field Between Cities and Teams?, 21 J. Urb. Aff. 377 (1999); Mark Rosentraub, Major League Losers: The Real Cost of Sports and Who's Paying for It (1997). See also Meir Gross, Legal Gambling as a Strategy for Economic Development, 12 Econ. Develop. Q. 203 (1998).

M. CHRISTINE BOYER, CITIES FOR SALE: MERCHANDISING HISTORY AT SOUTH STREET SEAPORT

From Michael Sorkin (ed.), Variations on a Theme Park.
181–184, 200–201, 204 (1992).

Tucked beneath the Brooklyn Bridge and an elevated highway, the South Street Seaport looks as if it had been snipped from an old city map and carelessly set down beside the superdeveloped financial district of lower Manhattan. Once considered a leftover space of derelict structures, narrow streets, and abandoned piers, it is today an upscale marketplace catering to employees from the Wall Street area, curious tourists, and urban explorers. An evocation of the city's maritime history and the sights and adventures of its mercantile days, South Street Seaport resembles Quincy Market in Boston, Harbor Place in Baltimore, Fisherman's Wharf in San Francisco, the Riverwalk in New Orleans, and other such waterfront districts that were restructured in the 1970s and 1980s to become leisure-time zones combining shopping and entertainment with office and residential development.

South Street Seaport is a historic tableau with Fulton Street at its center. Crossing a wide roadway, the spectator leaves the modern city of corporate skyscrapers and enters a historic architectural promenade. On the south is Schermerhorn Row, a block of merchants' countinghouses built in the early nineteenth century, now rehabilitated for boutiques, restaurants, and museum spaces. Across from these red-brick landmarks, a reconstructed cast-iron warehouse and a fancifully recreated Fulton "Festival" Market replace the market sheds that had occupied that spot since 1822. On Water Street toward the western margins of this eleven-block officially designated historic district stands the South Street Seaport Museum with its art gallery, library, reception center, and shops selling stationery, books, and charts. Under the elevated East River Drive, which runs above South Street, a boardwalk opens onto the waterfront berths of renovated ships and a brand-new exhibition pavilion with still more shops and restaurants.

In reality however, the Seaport's imaginary historical museum is everywhere, surrounding the spectator with an artfully composed historic ambience. The rough-and-tumble Fulton Fish Market sheds—the last reminders that South Street Seaport was once a working waterfront—are carefully blocked from view. And, lest the spectator wander too far upriver from this historic tableau and ruminate upon the melancholy ruins and haunting memories of the original waterfront, Richard Haas's enormous trompe l'oeil mural replicating the images of Schermerhorn Row and the Brooklyn Bridge quickly turns attention back toward the tableau.

A tour along the waterfront of Manhattan reveals several such isolated, self-enclosed patches of development, and more are to come: the (proposed) Riverwalk development, a minicity on a platform jutting into the East River; South Street Seaport and the adjacent development of East River Landing; the gigantic skyscraper complex proposed for South Ferry; the miraculous ninety-two-acre landfill of Battery Park City; another platform in the river across from the Jacob Javits Convention Center called Hudson River Center; and finally the reduced but still gargantuan Trump project at Penn Yards, intended to reclaim acres of abandoned waterfront, underused railroad yards, and factories a mile further up the Hudson. Certainly no unified image of the city emerges from this series of disparate scenic views. Nor does a visionary masterplan establish a logical and orderly arrangement of the scenery. New York is no longer a city concerned with such high-Modernist aspirations as providing a broad range of housing, efficient public transportation, or leisure and work spaces for the masses. Indeed, most of the contemporary enclaves along New York's once-forgotten waterfront are postindustrial service centers planned to attract the young urban professionals and double-income childless couples increasingly populating the city. These developments are premixed design packages that reproduce preexisting urban forms: office and residential towers, townhouses and hotels, stores and restaurants, health clubs, performing-arts centers, museums, esplanades, marinas, parks, and squares.

And, crucially, these city scenes do not mean to decontextualize architecture by eradicating all ties to the city's historical past as do Modernist sites such as the United Nations on the East River and Lincoln Center for the Performing Arts on the Upper West Side. On the contrary, these newer sites are laden with historical allusions to the traditional vision of the city: a coherent place of intimate streets, lined with small-scale facades and shopping arcades, ornamented with signs, punctuated by open spaces, trees, lampposts, and benches. The aim is theatrical: to represent certain visual images of the city, to create perspectival views shown through imaginary prosceniums in order to conjure up emotionally satisfying images of bygone times. Architecture and the theater use similar means to design places of pleasure and spectacle, manipulating scenery, ornament, and facades, to underscore the sentiment of their play.

However they may be fused or confused, there is of course always a distinction between the represented image of the city and its reality. In fact, New York's developed pockets are divided by swaths of neglect. But rather than arousing condemnation, this chaotic arrangement and disconnected juxtaposition of city segments is accepted and indeed celebrated as the result of rampant but healthy development. Because each fragment is well composed, it absorbs the spectator's attention, upstaging the neglected in-between spaces. For those who travel along this imaginary architectural promenade, centers of spectacle efface the distinctions between the real cityscape and the show. * * *

In their desire to solidify the traces of the past into a unified image, to restore an intactness that never was, developers of historicized open-air bazaars and storehouses of heterogeneity like South Street Seaport, where consumers can buy anything from anywhere, have so conflated geographical space and historical time that the actual uniqueness of place and context have been completely erased. These illusionary environments of simulation provide the decor for our acts of consumption. In contemporary times, commodities are no longer marketed for their utility and efficiency alone, but as part of a system of values that gives them added meaning. The further away the commodity seems from the functional, the useful, and the necessary, the more appealing it appears. When the commodity is placed within a system of signs symbolizing entire life-styles and supporting environments, the system itself seeks to increase consumption by suggesting that a particular lifestyle requires the acquisition of not one but an entire series of goods. Consequently, simulated landscapes of exotic and imaginary terrains, cleverly combining the fantastic with the real, become the ideal background props for our contemporary acts of consumption, set-ups that intensify the commodity's power of seduction.

The cleverly formulated landscapes of Disneyland—meticulously designed to encourage consumption—might be called the original historic-marketplace tableau. Visitors to this fantastical space become the narrators of a story that deceptively harmonizes contradictory elements. In the landscapes of Frontierland, Adventureland, Tomorrowland, even Fantasyland, they compose the stories of how Americans achieved victory over Indians, exotic countries, outer space—in short, over historical memory. At Disneyland, the American way of life is displayed as a universal sign of progress. Symbolically, whatever path the traveler may take, the voyage begins and ends at Main Street USA, where the tourist shops lie. Hence Main Street becomes the center of Disneyland's story, a shrewd commercial tale that tells of consumption American style. By presenting the facades of Main Street, and all its "lands" for that matter, as miniature versions of a fantastic past, Disneyland sparks the visitor's imagination and willingness to buy. Yet it is not the environment that is falsified, for everything in Disneyland is absolutely fantastical, but the fact that Disneyland is quintessentially a landscape for consumption, not for leisure. * * *

The contemporary spectator in quest of public urban spaces increasingly must stroll through recycled and revalued territories like South Street Seaport, city tableaux that have been turned into gentrified, historicized, commodified, and privatized places. These areas once existed outside of the marketplace but now their survival depends on advertising and on the production of an entertaining environment that sells. "Just looking" at these city spaces remains a pleasurable public experience but an experience that increasingly comes down to that moment of association when private desires become linked to future promises offered by items for sale. On one level, then, South Street Seaport bears witness to the instrumental and rational production of a public marketspace where communal celebrations and festivals still occur, albeit in truncated and modified form. On another level, however, by targeting the spectator with narrative style-of-life advertising, the Seaport and other such compositions speak directly to private fantasies colluding in the privatization of public space. These shifts of public and private spheres are turning the streets and spaces of our cities inside-out. Public ways and communal spaces are being designed by the private sector as interior shopping streets within large corporate skyscrapers or festival markets where public admittance is carefully controlled. The private sphere of nostalgic desires and imagination is increasingly manipulated by stage sets and city tableaux set up to stimulate our acts of consumption, by the spectacle of history made false.

PETER EISINGER, THE POLITICS OF BREAD AND CIRCUSES
35 Urban Affairs Review 316, 316–318, 321, 323, 328–331 (2000).

During the period of rapid urbanization in the late nineteenth century, the great task of American municipal governments was to manage the politics of city building for a burgeoning populace by providing the public services essential to health, safety, and civic education. A century later, city governments are consumed by a very different task. City regimes now devote enormous energies and resources not simply to the basic and traditional municipal functions but also to the task of making cities, in the words of Judd and Fainstein, "places to play." This undertaking entails the construction of expensive entertainment amenities, often in partnership with private investors, designed to appeal primarily to out-of-town visitors, including the suburban middle classes. This is true even in the nation's poorest, most decrepit cities, such as Detroit and Newark. Putting the best face on this urban obsession, Sharon Zukin noted that "culture is more and more the business of cities." But another way to view this development is to say that increasingly, the urban civic arena is preoccupied by a politics of bread and circuses.

Building a city as an entertainment venue is a very different undertaking than building a city to accommodate residential interests.

Although the former objective is often justified as a means to generate the resources to accomplish the latter aim, the two are not easily reconciled. For example, one feature that distinguished the development of municipal services in the late nineteenth century was their fundamental democratic nature. These were not just for the well-to-do but also for the common people. Indeed, as Jon Teaford pointed out, American city dwellers of all classes had greater access to clean water, free schools, public libraries, parks, and public health facilities than did even the comfortable urban middle classes in the great cities of Europe. Today, however, the city as a place to play is manifestly built for the middle classes, who can afford to attend professional sporting events, eat in the new outdoor cafes, attend trade and professional conventions, shop in the festival malls, and patronize the high-and middlebrow arts. Many, if not most, of these are visitors to the city, and in the view of local leaders, they must be shielded from the city's residents. The city is no longer regarded as the great melting pot, the meeting place of diverse classes and races. Thus, for example, the proposal for a "Yankee Village" surrounding Yankee Stadium in the Bronx would involve increasing parking capacity and constructing a new mass-transit station within the confines of the stadium to ensure that no matter how they travel to the ballgame, "fans will not come into contact with Bronx locals".

It is not surprising that political and civic leaders increasingly are intent on spending their political and fiscal resources to support such entertainment facilities. Such amenities not only offer literally monumental evidence of mayoral achievement, but more important, local leaders believe that they hold out the prospect of economic revival by bringing the middle class back into the cities from which it fled long ago, not as resident taxpayers but at least as free-spending visitors. Thus city leaders make entertainment projects a keystone of their urban economic development strategy, hoping that they will generate ancillary investment, high employment multipliers in the hospitality and retail sectors, and local tax revenues.

A substantial literature, however, suggests that such expectations are generally misplaced. The economic effects of stadium investments, casino projects, convention centers, and other entertainment amenities generally show up on the negative side of the balance sheet, and in the few cases when they do not, their effects are highly localized. Cost overruns in the construction phase, high public subsidies for operating expenses and debt service, sweetheart deals for professional sports team owners, overoptimistic job creation projections, the unlikelihood of stimulating ancillary development beyond the immediate neighborhood, and the absence of evidence that new entertainment venues actually increase total regional entertainment spending mean that such projects almost never pay for themselves.

Although a great deal of attention has been paid to the issue of economic impacts of entertainment amenities, little effort has been made to consider the broader consequences for cities of pursuing a politics of bread and circuses. What does it mean for cities to spend their money and their political capital in pursuit of the discretionary entertainment spending of visitors rather than the tax payments of a resident middle class? Does courting the middle class as visitors mean the creation of a different sort of city than one designed either to bring the middle class back as residents or to serve the diverse and often poorer resident population? * * * In the nineteenth century, urban recreational facilities were designed for the urban populace. Although the great city parks built after the Civil War were often far from the immigrant quarters and thus beyond the easy reach of slum dwellers too poor to pay the carfare, for "middle-class urbanites and their working-class cousins ... the great parks were accessible refuges from the drabness of the city, and thousands flooded the municipal preserves each weekend". * * * In contrast, today's entertainment facilities, marketed vigorously by tourism promoters, are designed to bring visitors to the city. Tourism is a way of importing spending and exporting the tax burden. * * * An estimated 80% to 95% of convention-goers stay overnight in the host city, paying hefty room taxes in the process. They represent a highly desirable type of visitor because they tend to spend considerably more per day than ordinary tourists or attendees at cultural performances or sporting matches. These latter events are aimed at * * * out-of-town visitors * * * from suburban counties * * *.

In seeking to build publicly subsidized entertainment projects to attract visiting spenders, local elites risk deepening distrust of government, creating deep polarities, and breeding cynicism among residents in the city. Consider first the democratic challenges of public financing of huge capital projects for entertainment purposes. Because these efforts are both so costly and so important to local elites, the preference is to shield the funding decision from the uncertain outcome of a public vote. Sometimes a bond or tax referendum is unavoidable if the project requires a levy on local taxpayers, however. This is a minor risk for local elites because more than half the time, voters refuse to pass such referenda. However, a negative outcome is rarely a permanent obstacle to the eventual commitment of public subsidies. It simply delays the project as leaders search for ways to detour around voter disapproval. In such cases, if resorting to means other than a public vote to use public funds does not stoke the fires of voter frustration, then other factors associated with large capital expenditures for entertainment amenities are likely to do so. These include the high opportunity costs associated with making such large investments, the potential for driving up the cost of public borrowing for other projects, and the diminution of local fiscal flexibility. * * *

When local elites build big entertainment projects with public help, they run the risk not only of breeding cynicism but also of polarizing their community. The issue lends itself to stark, if oversimplified, contrasts—stadiums for millionaires or schoolrooms for poor children. When sports facilities are concerned, it holds out the potential for driving a wedge between the young and the old and between men and women. When the issue is a convention or performing arts center, the wedge is likely to divide social classes and perhaps the races. When local elites push to support casino gambling, the cleavage falls along religious lines No other type of major capital expenditure—not for roads, schools, wastewater treatment facilities, public buildings, jails, or sewers—has the potential to generate such intense divisions in local politics. * * *

Big entertainment projects may be regarded as spongelike in character: They often have a tendency to absorb a disproportionate share of resources that might go to other projects or other places in the city. When Houston Mayor Bob Lanier refused to accede to the demands by the Oiler football team for a new city-financed stadium, he framed the issue in either-or terms for a U.S. Senate subcommittee: "Sure, sports are important to a city's image, but in my judgment it's more important to have parks, police, water, and youth programs". All politics is about making choices, of course, but the allocation of such great amounts of money, energy, and attention to entertainment amenities carries with it a special harsh irony in poor big cities with competing needs. Mayor Lanier claimed to be speaking for "working-class taxpayers" who would never be able to afford to sit in the luxury boxes their tax dollars would help to finance. In reality, the deepest line of cleavage created by the pursuit of entertainment projects is often that between downtown interests and residential neighborhoods, a conflict that subsumes a whole set of mutually reinforcing racial, class, big business—small business, and even city-suburban divisions. As a critic of the New Jersey Performing Arts Center (NJPAC) in Newark complained, "It is being built by nonresidents for nonresidents. They will come and get dumped off at the front, see the show, and then leave without having any impact on the community". * * *

Few people would argue with the proposition that facilities that bring high or even mass culture, sports, and recreational opportunities to a city may enhance the quality of urban life. Stadiums and performing arts centers and festival malls help to transform places that would otherwise simply be markets or dormitories or, to remember George Sternlieb's phrase, "sandboxes" into destinations. Thus a case can be made that at some level, public encouragement and facilitation of these entertainment amenities are a legitimate governmental function in a generally affluent society.

The issue, then, is not whether to spend public money; rather, the issue is a matter of balance or proportionality. When the public costs of building a stadium, convention center, or festival mall compromise the basic services provided to residents of the city, exhaust the municipality's fiscal flexibility, or consume its political energies, then priorities have become unbalanced. The principle might be reduced to the simple, though rarely observed, injunction that entertainment amenities should be subsidized by the public only in those places that can afford it. In judging how much of a city's resources to commit to entertainment amenities, at least two rules of thumb should be kept in mind. One is that most entertainment projects are highly profitable to their investors, at least eventually, and many could be—indeed, would be—built without much public support at all. A second is that most of these projects provide quite low economic returns to the city in the way of jobs and tax revenues.

The problem, of course, is that few cities are bold enough to call the bluff of a team owner seeking a new stadium or the hotel industry seeking a new convention center. And then to justify their accession to the demands of these developers, city officials exaggerate the returns to the city. Thus it is all too common for a city to use its scarce resources not to build infrastructure, fund youth recreation programs, subsidize homeless shelters, or enrich the schools but to help wealthy investors construct entertainment facilities for well-off visitors who produce few payoffs for residents. When local leaders fail to calibrate public expenditures to public returns and speak instead of creating a "big-league" image or a "world-class" city as a way of justifying expenditures on entertainment amenities, then it is fair to conclude that they are offering their constituents not the best basic services that have long been core municipal responsibilities but rather the thin sustenance of bread and circuses.

MICHAEL SORKIN, SEE YOU IN DISNEYLAND
From M. Sorkin (ed.), Variations on a Theme Park 217–218, 227, 231–232 (1992).

Whatever else it represents, Disneyland is also a model of Los Angeles. Fantasyland, Frontierland, Tomorrowland—these are the historic themes of the city's own self-description, its main cultural tropes. The genius of the city, however, resides not simply in dispersal but in juxtaposition, the invention of the possibility of the Loirish Bungalow sitting chockablock with the Tudoroid. The view through the framing window of the passing car animates the townscape, cinematizing the city. This consumption of the city as spectacle, by means of mechanical movement through it, recapitulates the more global possibilities of both the multinational corridor created by air travel and the simultaneous electronic everywhere of television. Disneyland offers a space in which narrative depends on motion, and in which one is placed in a position of spectatorship of one's own spectatorship.

While the car may be LA's generator, it's also its "problem," motor of democracy and alienation both, repressor of pedestrianism and its happy random encounters. There's a school (popular along the learnedly kitsch axis of early architectural postmodernism) that exalts Disneyland as a solution to the dissipation of the public realm engendered by cars. This is achieved by relegating cars to a parking periphery, creating an auto-free zone at its center, and using efficient, technologized transport (that charismatic monorail) to mediate. But this is only half of the story. In fact, Disneyland less redeems LA than inverts it. The reason one circulates on foot in Disneyland is precisely to be able to ride. However, the central experience, by anyone's empirical calculation, is neither walking nor riding but waiting in line. Most of a typical Disney day is thus spent in the very traffic jam one has putatively escaped, simply without benefit of car. Indeed, what's perfect, most ultimately viable, at Disneyland is riding. After hours of snaking through the sun with one's conscientiously well-behaved fellow citizens comes the kinetic payoff: brief, thrilling, and utterly controlled, a traffic engineer's wet dream. * * *

––––––

As a utopia, Disneyland's innovation lies not in its fantasy of regulation but in the elision of its place-making. Disneyland is the Holy See of creative geography, the place where the ephemeral reality of the cinema is concretized into the stuff of the city. It should come as no surprise that the most succinct manifestation to date of this crossover is the "Disney-MGM Studios" theme park, recently opened at Disney World. Here, the agenda of dislocated authenticity is carried back to its point of origin. The attraction (much indebted to its precursor Universal Studios Tour back in Los Angeles, now also in Orlando) is explicitly about movies, both the space of their realization (the "studio") and about the particular narrative spaces of particular movies.

Although the attraction is in Florida, at Disney World, and although its recreational agenda is precisely to purvey "creative geography," Disney-MGM is at pains to locate itself in a particularly referential space: Hollywood, the locus classicus of movie-making. Main Street's axial introduction is accomplished with an imaginative recasting of Hollywood Boulevard, heavy on the deco. Visitors enter through a gateway borrowed from the now-incinerated Pan-Pacific Auditorium, past a replica of the famous Crossroads of the World tower, a reincarnate Brown Derby, and a welter of familiar Los Angeles architecture, here scaled down and aggregated with an urbanity unknown at the unedited source. * * *

––––––

Jeffrey Katzenberg, head of Disney's movie division, suggests that we "think of Disney World as a medium-sized city with a crime rate of zero."

Although the claim is hyperbole (petty larceny mainly leads to expulsion from the kingdom, more serious infractions to the summoning of adjoining police forces), the perception is not: the environment is virtually self-policing. Disney World is clearly a version of a town ("Imagine a Disneyland as big as the city of San Francisco," goes a recent ad). And it's based on a particular urbanism, a crisp acceleration of trends everywhere visible but nowhere so acutely elaborated. The problems addressed by Disneyzone are quintessentially modern: crime, transportation, waste, the relationship of work and leisure, the transience of populations, the growing hegemony of the simulacrum.

But finally, Disneyzone isn't urban at all. Like the patent medicine-plugging actor who advertises his bona fides as "I'm not a doctor but I play one on TV," Disney invokes an urbanism without producing a city. Rather, it produces a kind of aura-stripped hypercity, a city with billions of citizens (all who would consume) but no residents. Physicalized yet conceptual, it's the utopia of transience, a place where everyone is just passing through. This is its message for the city to be, a place everywhere and nowhere, assembled only through constant motion. Visitors to Disneyzone are reduced to the status of cartoon characters. (Indeed, one of the features of the studio tour is the opportunity for visitors to cinematically interpolate themselves into *Who Framed Roger Rabbit?*) This is a common failing in utopian subjectivity, the predication on a homogenized, underdimensioned citizenship. However, it's also true that there's probably no more acquiescent subject than the postindustrial tourist. And there's surely no question that a holiday-maker wants a version of life pared of its sting, that vacationing finds its fulfillment in escape. The Disney visitor seeks and delights in the relationship between what he or she finds and its obverse back home, terrain of crime, litter, and surliness.

In the Disney utopia, we all become involuntary flaneurs and flaneuses, global drifters, holding high our lamps as we look everywhere for an honest image. The search will get tougher and tougher for the fanned-out millions as the recombinant landscape crops up around the globe. One of the latest nodes appears about to be sprung at Surajkund, near New Delhi, where India's first theme park gleams in the eye of the local tourism department. "We have a whole integrated concept of a fun center," as the New York Times quotes S. K. Sharma, state secretary for tourism. "Like all big cities, Delhi is getting polluted. It is getting choked with people. People need amusement and clear air." * * *

3. THE MIDDLE CLASS CITY

For most city residents, the most familiar conception of their city—and of its future—is being a middle class city. This is a city focused on its residents not on outsiders, on its city services not on its marketing ability or financial sector, and on its ability to be the home not simply of the rich and poor but of those in between. The difficulties facing a middle class city are well known. Barry Bluestone and Mary Huff Stevenson describe these difficulties in terms of a "triple revolution" in American society: a demographic change caused by new immigration and the doubling of the minority population; an industrial revolution that led to the loss of traditional blue-collar jobs and the rise of an information-based economy; and the spatial revolution caused by suburbanization. A Brookings Institution study found that middle class neighborhoods in many major cities have shrunk significantly since 1970.[46]

Some argue that the decline of the middle class city is not a cause for concern. The new wave of gentrification in major American cities, they say, has simply triggered a natural process of spatial sorting, with middle class families moving to the suburbs as prices in the central city have risen. Others argue that central cities could not stop this middle class exodus even if they wanted to. The industries that once created middle class urban jobs no longer do, and the market forces underlying gentrification are too powerful to be countered by individual cities. At best, cities can hope that their pursuit of tourism and global finance will benefit the middle class families still living in town. If that doesn't work, it would simply prove that cities are no longer hospitable to the middle class.

Whether or not these arguments seem persuasive, no successful city could actually embrace them wholeheartedly. City leaders worry that, unless they adopt policies specifically targeted at increasing their share of the middle class, their cities will become a home for the rich and the very poor. A city starkly divided in this way is not a desirable goal. Around the world, polarized cities generate insecurity for both the rich and the poor—insecurity that can take form of violence, economic desperation, and the decline of public space and public life. Besides, there is no reason to think local residents—that is, city voters—want their city's economic development strategy to focus primarily on attracting wealthy outsiders who can price them out of their own neighborhoods. At the same time, cities without a middle class can make it difficult for the poor to improve their lives. The Brookings Institution study describes the basis for this concern:

> If rising economic inequality has contributed to rising economic segregation, the ability of lower-income individuals to choose and access middle-income neighborhoods may have declined. This, in turn, may limit their access to associated amenities like jobs,

---

[46] Barry Bluestone and May Huff Stevenson, The Boston Renaissance: Race, Space, and Economic Change in an American Metropolis (2000); Jason Booza, Jackie Cutsinger, and George Galster, Brookings Institution Metropolitan Policy Program, Where Did They Go? The Decline of Middle-Income Neighborhoods in Metropolitan America (2006).

decent health care, safe neighborhoods, and adequate political representation. A lack of middle-income neighborhoods may also limit opportunities for low and moderate-income homeowners to "move up" the property ladder, if the house-price differential between lower- and higher-income neighborhoods is too high.

No city looks forward to a future in which a large segment of its population will be locked in poverty.

The readings below explore some of the possible ingredients in fostering a middle class city. The first excerpt, by Richard Schragger, contrasts two competing views of a city's role in economic development. The first treats the city as a product to be marketed to interested outsiders—to investors or tourists, for example. The second describes the city as a process—as a complex organism largely outside of the city's control, with the city's government's role envisioned as localized efforts to promote middle class values and middle class economic prosperity. The first of these alternatives has been explored in the previous sub-sections; this sub-section explores the second.[47] One kind of city intervention, as Professor Schragger suggests, is to promote small business rather than large-scale national and international enterprise. The second reading below, an excerpt from Gerald Frug and David Barron's book City Bound, suggests possible ways to pursue such a strategy. The third reading, again by Richard Schragger, addresses a possible concern: do cities have the capacity to limit the power of mobile capital over the city's future? The final reading, Hernandez v. City of Hanford, deals with cities' legal power to curb chain stores—or, at the minimum, to locate them in some parts of the city rather than others. The reason to do so, it is often said, is to promote small business and middle class jobs. The current symbol of the anti-chain store movement focuses on Wal-Mart, but it has a long history dating to the 1920s and 1930s.[48] The Hernandez case raises a fundamental question: Do chain stores promote or inhibit the fostering of a middle class city? Does it turn on whether you think of city residents as consumers or producers? One overall question should be kept in mind when reading this sub-section: Is it harder for a city to adopt policies to promote a middle class city than to adopt policies to promote a global or tourist city? If so, why should that be?

---

[47] See also Mobilizing Local Government Law for Low Wage Workers, 1 U. Chi. Legal F. 187 (2009).

[48] See Richard Schragger, The Anti-Chain Store Movement, Localist Ideology, and the Remnants of the Progressive Constitution, 1920–1940, 90 Iowa L. Rev. 1011 (2005).

RICHARD SCHRAGGER, RETHINKING THE THEORY AND
PRACTICE OF LOCAL ECONOMIC DEVELOPMENT
77 U. Chi. L. Rev. 311, 314, 317–321, 323–328, 332–338 (2010).

* * * [T]he idea that cities "compete" with one another to attract persons, goods, and capital * * * has been most fully embraced by law and economics scholars who start with Charles Tiebout's construct of a market in local government. Tieboutian governments compete to provide services to residents. This competition must be for something; if the demand for city space (and for a particular city's space) was outside the control of any particular city, then the language of competition would make little sense. Competition implies some level of agency, an ability to improve the product being offered. So we arrive at the notion that cities compete to provide amenities to firms and residents, that this competition disciplines local governments so that they provide efficient public services, and that this competition further encourages salutary innovation. * * *

A different way to look at the city is as a process. Consider Jane Jacobs's famous *The Death and Life of Great American Cities.* Jacobs approached the urban environment—the city, the neighborhood, the street—ecologically. She showed us how a safe street emerges from tiny interactions among hundreds of independent and noncoordinated actors, how an urban economy emerges from small-scale production and invention, and how small changes at the street or neighborhood level can cause catastrophic changes in the urban landscape. In short, *Death and Life* shows us how order arises out of the seeming disorder of urban life. It is a caution to those who would attempt to create a pre-packaged and attractive urban landscape—a product—out of a process.

Similarly, the "new economic geography"—for which Paul Krugman recently won a Nobel Prize—approaches cities as "self-organizing" systems: "systems that, even when they start from an almost homogeneous or almost random state, spontaneously form large-scale patterns." The new economic geography holds that given particular parameters, urban systems will exhibit certain spatial regularities— seemingly natural development patterns that emerge from a set of basic assumptions. A growing city, on this account, is more "like a developing embryo" than it is like a widget that is produced and sold in the marketplace. * * *

A key insight in * * * [this model] is that small differences in initial conditions or small perturbations in an otherwise stable equilibrium can lead to dramatically different outcomes; that once growth or decline starts, it does so explosively or catastrophically; and that the spatial order that emerges may have little to do with individuals' or firms' preferences understood in isolation. There was nothing particularly unique about the geographical place that became Silicon Valley—given slightly different initial conditions, such an agglomeration of high-tech firms could have arisen elsewhere. * * * Does * * * this mean that cities cannot do anything about their economic development * * *? Not necessarily. City self-organization grants a large role both to historical accident and the self-reinforcing effects of economic development. Luck matters because small random events (David Packard and William Hewlett begin their business in Silicon Valley) can produce large consequences (once HP is there, other firms want to be there). Thus, cities might be able to intervene in the local economy in such a way as to nudge the process forward. * * *

So why are people and firms flocking to particular places? * * * Consider a number of explanations. One possibility is that certain cities became more efficient in their provision of essential public services. If we saw significant improvements in urban schools or a notable reduction in city taxes with no noticeable decrease in city services, we might conclude that resurgent cities were simply performing better. But we do not see dramatic improvements along those lines, and certainly not consistently across cities. Though it is commonly asserted that cities can only attract and keep the middle class if they improve their education systems, education gains do not seem to have preceded the urban boom in places like New York, Chicago, and Boston. And dramatic improvements in education or increases in education spending do not seem to explain the boom in Las Vegas or other Sunbelt cities. Dramatic improvements in city provision of other kinds of services—trash pick-up, social services, infrastructure—also do not seem to be forerunners of an urban resurgence, though perhaps they have accompanied it. * * *

If cities have not gotten better at providing goods and services, then something else might explain the urban resurgence. For some theorists, the preferred theory is that firms have chosen to congregate in cities because of the economic gains of agglomeration. * * * This story is a popular one, and it helps explain why cities continue to exist, but it does not tell us why certain cities become the hosts of certain agglomerations. Why did financial services agglomerations end up in London and New York? * * * One possibility as to why particular cities are thriving is that firms go where the labor is and that labor likes certain amenities. This explanation for the urban resurgence argues that rising cities have been able to attract skilled labor or individuals with high levels of human capital. Certainly, cities with higher growth seem to have higher numbers of college-educated residents. Attracting such residents, famously labeled the "creative class" by Richard Florida, seems an obviously smart strategy. Thus, much effort has been made to create the kinds of amenities that highly skilled people favor. Those amenities might include particular kinds of shops, cultural offerings, a vibrant urban street life, or a generally "bohemian, tolerant atmosphere." The more young, college-educated people there are in a city, the more likely it will be successful. The idea is that if you build it, they will come, and the jobs will follow them. * * *

The problem with this claim is that it is not at all clear whether these high human capital individuals are migrating to Boston and Las Vegas because of the amenities or whether the amenities are there because of the high human capital individuals. Indeed, the amenity story might have the causation exactly backwards. As Michael Storper and Michael Manville point out, this is certainly true of places like Silicon Valley, which had no preexisting amenities to offer before it became a technological center; Las Vegas, which was similarly devoid of the kinds of urban amenities that serve a growing permanent population; and Hollywood, which developed its amenities simultaneously with the development of the motion picture industry. Places like Atlanta and Charlotte have all seen their consumer amenities grow with the influx of a more skilled population. * * *

How should we evaluate * * * [different] approaches to economic development? * * * [One] policy—location subsidies to large employers— has been and continues to be a standard tool of city economic development offices. Their efficacy, however, has been strongly disputed. Cities appear not to gain back what they put in, either in the short term or the long term, and there is some evidence that subsidies do not ultimately alter the location decisions of firms. And even if location subsidies do enhance local welfare, they do not improve overall welfare— one city loses what another city gains. This is especially true if the firm relocates in the same economic region, as Goldman Sachs would have had it moved to New Jersey. * * *

[An alternative] focus on small startups might be better over the long term. By investing in human capital, the city keeps and improves its labor force, which may be the key determinant for attracting new firms. And by backing small, entrepreneurial ventures the city reduces its vulnerability to one employer or industry, which could leave or decline. Moreover, smaller ventures have the capacity to grow and may be more attached and committed to their original locations. Indeed, by encouraging small-scale innovation, the city might help seed a home-grown agglomeration at low cost. Growing your own is better than stealing from others or preventing others from stealing from you. It enlarges the economic pie rather than just shifting it around.

At least that might be the theory. Jane Jacobs, for one, argued that a growing city needs to generate new ideas, processes, and services—to "add[ ] new work to old." She favored a small business strategy, arguing that the city should encourage entrepreneurial firms and the learning that goes on in those firms. In an unavoidably volatile economy, the city's most important "skill" is its ability to reset its product life cycle by generating new startup firms (Jacobs called them "breakaways"). In her estimation, large, vertically integrated multinationals have less ability to drive such a process; a more fluid and open local economy does better than one dependent on large firms. * * *

So should cities be in the business of subsidizing existing firms or growing new ones? How one answers this question implicates a long-running debate in urban economic development concerning the degree to which cities should look outward or inward for economic growth. The outward argument is economic base theory, which holds that cities can only grow economically by increasing exports to other places. Fewer exports means less money for local spending and less growth overall. This means that economic development strategy is unlikely to favor small businesses that service the local community, or businesses that are intended to substitute locally made goods for those that the city formerly imported. The export-based theory of local economic development tends to favor large transnational corporations or those corporations that can exploit local resources for cross-border sale. And it favors specialization— for example, producing goods and services that cannot be imported.

Economic base theory has been the dominant approach to local economic development for some time, but it has not been uncritically adopted. In the 1950s, Charles Tiebout questioned whether exports were the only mechanism of city growth. Tiebout claimed that as a local economy grows "its market becomes large enough to efficiently produce some goods and services that it had previously imported." Jacobs also argued, even more strongly, that import substitution could drive city growth, as locals make for themselves what others had formerly made for them. A city can grow by providing more goods and services for itself, and by preventing money and resources from flowing outside the local economy. The implication is that self-sufficiency and leakage prevention should be a large part of economic development efforts.

Current-day import-substitution advocates do not argue that making your own is sufficient—as Jacobs and Tiebout recognized, export growth is still needed. But current advocates do point to trends in the latter half of the twentieth century to support their argument that economies are becoming more local and that those economies are also growing. As US manufacturing declined during the second half of the twentieth century, the portion of the metropolitan-area economy that was produced and consumed locally rose. This increasing localness has been attributed to the rise of the service sector economy in general. In larger cities, localness has increased as a bigger share of the local economy moved towards professional services. Producers of accounting, legal, marketing, and management consulting services tend to locate near their clients, within the same city or metropolitan area. It is this clustering that appears to account for the dramatic economic growth of particular "global cities," like New York, London, or Tokyo. * * *

There is a significant shift in emphasis * * * reflected in the decision either to support a large-scale multinational investment bank or to fund local startups. Local economic development strategies can seek to enhance "global competitiveness"—an oft-used phrase in city development circles. Or, a local economic development strategy might focus on supporting those firms and industries that mainly provide goods and services to locals. * * * As a practical matter, any economic development strategy that shifts money from taxpayers to private firms has to be measured against some other use of taxpayer money—say, building better schools, providing more policing, or producing better health care. And this gets us back to the question of what makes a city do better or worse economically. Providing good municipal services and creating healthy, smart people is something that any city should aspire to. But doing so does not ensure economic success. There are lots of reasons for this: any given city policy will be mismatched to the metropolitan-wide scale of economic development; much is driven by chance or path dependency; larger economic and technological events will over-shadow local interventions. Some of these problems can be overcome. But the biggest problem is that we do not really know enough about what works and what does not.

All of which may be beside the point. One might argue that government should provide services to make people smarter, healthier, and safer anyway—whether those policies attract and retain economy-producing residents and firms or not. Indeed, there are lots of good reasons to enact policies that reduce inequality, foster participation, or limit urban sprawl, even if we are unsure what effects those policies will have on economic growth. Certainly, much of reformist local government scholarship is driven by this view. If one adopts a competitive paradigm of city growth, however—the assumption that a city's economic development is really a competition for mobile taxpayers—then the city cannot (and should not) engage in policies that attend solely to the well-being of current residents. Those policies will fail, undermining local welfare by inhibiting economic growth. Cities must compete, and one way to do so is to reduce taxes to the point of subsidizing highly mobile residents and highly mobile industry. * * * [H]ow policymakers address urban problems—and centrally the problem of economic development—turns importantly on how we conceive of the city and the metaphors we use to describe it. * * *

GERALD FRUG AND DAVID BARRON, CITY BOUND: HOW
STATES STIFLE URBAN INNOVATION
Pp. 200–204 (2008).

Cities have a significant amount of discretion in promoting small business development. They can modify the impact of local permitting requirements—at least to the extent that state law allows—that many critics see as a barrier to establishing a new business. This criticism applies especially to new small businesses. They can use their zoning powers so that parts of town might be particularly attractive to manufacturing or small retailers. And they can encourage these businesses to locate in the city through incentives such as tax breaks or infrastructure development just as they do for global and tourist businesses.

In developing such a strategy, cities have several options. One is to promote industrial jobs. It's wrong to think of this option as a return to the dark, satanic mill. These days, small industrial enterprises fit into areas of the city in ways that often cannot even be noticed, and they engage in small-scale manufacturing, in a small amount of space, that supports the rest of the economy. Some of the controversy over global and tourist development focuses on the elimination of just these kinds of small-scale industries in favor of high-rise residential development and office buildings. One objection to the Queens West Development project— a 74-acre project on the waterfront facing mid-town Manhattan, controlled by a subdivision of New York state's Empire Development Corporation—is that it will eliminate a number of small industrial workplaces that provide middle class employment. * * * [I]ndustrial jobs are often at stake when the city plans to redo a neighborhood for tourist purposes as well.

Although New York City is promoting developments that threaten industrial jobs, it has also recognized the need to protect and promote industrial development within the city's boundaries. The city lost hundreds of thousands of industrial jobs after 1950, but more than 500,000 of these jobs remain. Most of the industrial enterprises still in the city have fewer than 20 employees, and the city is seeking to develop this sector of its economy in a number of ways. It is creating industrial business zones within the city, providing incentives to businesses to locate within them, guaranteeing not to rezone these areas to allow residential housing, seeking to restrict illegal conversions of other industrial sites to residential uses, setting aside city-owned land for industrial use, and taking steps to reduce the bureaucratic obstacles for new industrial businesses. Most of these initiatives are within the city's power to adopt on its own, although not all (for example, it needs legislative approval to extend the current real estate tax reduction provided to commercial businesses to these small-scale industrial businesses). The question remains, however, whether all of these efforts—and more like them—will even begin to counter-balance the city's simultaneous efforts to promote the global and tourist alternatives.

Boston's Back Streets Initiative is similar to New York's strategy, although it is focused on protecting the city's small and medium-sized commercial as well as industrial businesses. When the program was launched in 2001, the Mayor noted that roughly 20 percent of the city's jobs came from these businesses, and he set a goal of ensuring no net decline in these kinds of jobs. A primary focus of the Bank Streets Initiative is land use development for industrial purposes. Boston's legal powers—in particular, the combined development and planning powers of the Boston Redevelopment Authority, which administers the Back Streets Initiative—enable the city to preserve existing industrial areas. The Redevelopment Authority can also assure industrial users that the areas will not be rezoned for new luxury residential development and can help assemble parcels for businesses in need of more space. But other aspects of the state's legal structure raise problems for this effort. Because many of Boston's industrial sites are located on the city's harbor, they occupy city land that is subject to state land use controls. Boston Marine Industrial Park, one major site, has been deemed a "designated port area" by the state office dealing with coastal zone management. As a result, the state has imposed limits on the kinds of uses permitted in the area.

Perhaps even more important than these industry-focused initiatives is an attempt to promote small-scale enterprises more generally. More than 97% of the 26 million firms in the United States have fewer than 20 employees, and over the last decade these firms generated 60–80% of new jobs nationwide. The organization of employment is similar in major cities in the United States. In New York City, there are more than 200,000 small businesses (96% with fewer than 50 employees), and they provide two-thirds of the city's private sector jobs. An economic development strategy that focused on these kinds of enterprises might stimulate economic development for the middle class, and, at the same time, enable these small businesses to generate more attractive, thriving neighborhoods. This kind of development characterizes a multitude of city neighborhoods not on the tourist or global circuit. Paul Grogan and Tony Proscio [in their book, *Comeback Cities: A Blueprint for Urban Neighborhood Revival* (2000)] describe one example of this kind of neighborhood revival in the South Bronx in New York City. Of course, there are problems too: advancement opportunities in these small businesses are often less developed than in large firms. Nevertheless, the space needs are small, the job locations are spread throughout the city, and the effort to match local residents with local jobs can have a positive impact on other city problems, such as the transportation system.

One way to organize this effort is to focus specifically on employment opportunities in immigrant neighborhoods. A 2007 report issued by the Center for an Urban Future does just that. * * * [I]t begins with the observation that small-scale enterprises in immigrant neighborhoods are growing rapidly in New York City and other major cities, even as other kinds of jobs in the city are stabilizing or declining. And the jobs varied enormously: food manufacturing (fortune cookies, pita bread, empanadas, jerk chicken), child care, transportation (91% of New York City's cab drivers are immigrants), publishing, service businesses (insurance, medical, immigration, accounting), travel agencies, restaurants. According to the report, "despite the increasing significance of immigrant-run businesses, city economic development officials have hardly begun to incorporate them into the overall economic development strategy." The report concludes by making a number of recommendations—ranging from regulatory reform to offering loans to changing parking rules—that would re-direct the city's economic development strategy towards these kinds of businesses.

Another focus for such an economic development effort can be on the city's poorest neighborhoods. Michael Porter has become a well-known advocate of this emphasis, and, in 1994, he founded a not-for-profit organization, the Initiative for a Competitive Inner City, to promote it. The focus is on high-poverty neighborhoods—areas that include census tracks with 20% or greater poverty rate or 50% unemployment or half the city's median income. The goal, in other words, is to help the poor gain access to middle class jobs. A study published by the Initiative found that there were 814,000 private businesses in these neighborhoods in the 100 largest cities in the nation. Newly created jobs were predominately in the service sector and, given their location, proximity to the high-end global business neighborhood can be a major asset. Many of the initiatives suggested above for the immigrant city could be helpful in these neighborhoods too.

There are other ideas as well. San Francisco has a Department of Economic and Workforce Development within the Mayor's Office, and its recent program, CityBuild, organized in conjunction with community organizations and the transportation department, is designed to create a one-stop location for finding construction jobs and to provide training for these jobs. Denver offers loans to businesses operating within designated to parts of the city to supplement private financing of new businesses. New York City has issued tax-exempt bonds to help rebuild lower Manhattan after 9/11, and the beneficiaries include small businesses. And there's no reason to limit oneself to ideas already underway. * * * New York City issued bonds for the new Yankee stadium, bonds that the Yankees themselves will pay off. If this can be done for the Yankees, could bonds be issued to provide loans to small businesses in immigrant neighborhoods and the inner city? If not, we'd need to investigate what the legal restraints are that would permit the Yankee loan but not these kinds of loans.

Many of the efforts just described are within the city's current legal power as defined by state law. Even so, the existing legal structure limits the possible impact of all of them. First of all, the constraints * * * concerning other ingredients of developing a middle class city—education, housing, transportation, and the like—prevent the city from organizing a comprehensive approach to attracting the middle class. Without such an integrated effort, a focus on economic development might well not succeed. It may be hard to attract the residents needed to expand the city's small business sector if middle class housing options are few and the public schools are failing. Equally significantly, much of the city's current development strategy is not in the city's hands. * * * [I]ndependent public authorities and public/private partnerships have become the major way development decisions are made. Given who the decision makers are and the kinds of investment calculations they are likely to make, these kinds of institutions can easily overlook or devalue the efforts to promote middle class businesses. Their isolation from local democratic control may explain their tendency to focus on the global city and tourist city. As a result, the city's overall economic strategy can threaten the ability of the middle class to live in the city more than enable it.

There also is the problem of financing small business development. Economic development for the global city and the tourist city is currently financed principally through tax increment financing. This mechanism is not well designed to promote the kind of interstitial efforts to create small businesses throughout the city that we have been discussing. The economic development strategy for middle class business requires the city's financial support and its willingness to provide tax exemptions. To be sure, this kind of assistance is provided for global and tourist business to an even greater extent. But, in those cases, the city government (or the public authority) makes a financial calculation that the increased property values will generate tax revenue to reimburse the city's costs. This kind of calculation is less plausible when a small business strategy is the focus, if only because of its incremental nature.

There is another major problem as well—a problem that applies not only to the middle class city but to the global city and tourist city. All of these strategies have to be understood in a regional context, because the suburbs, in their own way, are organized to attract global business, tourism, and the middle class. Nowhere have the suburbs been more successful than in attracting the middle class. Given the power of the suburbs to do so, it may be that no central city economic development strategy focused on middle class jobs can succeed. No American city can pursue a vision of its future as if it were isolated from the region in which it is located. Its plans for the future—above all, its plans to nurture a middle class city—require it to confront the legally-created difficulties of being a regional city.

RICHARD SCHRAGGER, MOBILE CAPITAL, LOCAL ECONOMIC REGULATION, AND THE DEMOCRATIC CITY

123 Harv. L. Rev. 483, 483–484, 508–513, 519, 521–526, 537–538 (2009).

This Article examines municipal efforts to control, regulate, and redistribute mobile capital. The conventional economic story is that it is quite difficult (and counter-productive) for sub-national governments to attempt to control capital flows or engage in redistribution. Local governments are said to be particularly disabled because they are relatively small and cannot easily control migration across their borders. Because of inter-jurisdictional competition, local governments have a relatively limited set of policy choices. Mobile capital will flee aggressive efforts to regulate it. Thus, urban politics must invariably be biased in favor of mobile capital—cities must be "business friendly"—while robust economic regulation must necessarily take place at a higher level of government. More importantly, territorially-limited local jurisdictions can only weakly counter large-scale processes like deindustrialization, suburbanization, and globalization. Plant closings, the movement of manufacturing to the south or overseas, the movement of persons out of old, cold cities to new, warm ones, or out of cities into suburbs, while potentially painful, are unavoidable consequences of relatively open economic markets.

Cities nonetheless have long sought to entice mobile capital; they have also attempted to constrain or redistribute capital once it was in place. The latter is my focus here, as cities have recently engaged in a flurry of efforts to redistribute, place conditions on, or limit the entry of, capital. * * * These initiatives and movements are small but notable because they tend to cut against the conventional economic and political wisdom. Indeed, despite the standard view that economic regulation cannot take place at the local level, cities—not principally states or the national government—are the main innovators here. This new "regulatory localism" indicates that cities might be able to pursue policies that are less biased toward mobile capital. This is encouraging, for it suggests that locals may be able to adopt policies that are responsive to values other than economic growth, that cities may be able to regulate capital so as to reduce their vulnerability to economic booms and busts, and that those citizens who are normally marginalized by a politics of capital attraction can still assert influence over economic policy, even in an increasingly globalized economic environment. * * *

The movement to place conditions on mobile capital is a by-product of inter-local competition. Despite evidence that government incentives do not significantly affect corporate location decisions, municipalities have found it increasingly difficult to avoid providing ever more generous corporate subsidies to attract new business. The effort to assert controls over subsidized capital after it arrives has led to the development of accountability mechanisms in the form of clawback provisions or community benefits agreements.

The former are not a new concept. * * * The first of the modern American clawback provisions was adopted by New Haven over twenty years ago. Now twenty states and over 100 cities have clawback provisions. These provisions vary in their scope, triggers, and penalties, but generally require subsidized firms to provide a specified public benefit. Often the primary requirement is that the firm remain in the community for a particular period of time or forfeit the subsidy. Clawback provisions are cousins to plant closing statutes. Those statutes require certain businesses to provide notice to local communities before ceasing operations and, in some cases, require businesses to make specified payments to affected employees or into a community assistance fund.

Community benefits agreements are of a more recent vintage—the first full-fledged CBA appeared in 2001. CBAs are agreements negotiated between prospective developers and community groups over the terms of specific development projects. In exchange for community political support, the developer commits to limit displacement of current residents and provide resettlement support or specified units of low-income housing. CBAs can also involve agreements for developers to provide certain neighborhood services such as parks, recreation, or child-care facilities, and they often involve developer commitments to pay a living wage, adopt local-favoring hiring preferences, or provide for environmentally-friendly or sustainable building or development practices. There is no requirement that a CBA be connected to a project receiving public subsidies, but that has usually been the case. Community bargaining leverage is at its strongest when developers are seeking government subsidies or project approvals. Communities can create roadblocks in the zoning process to cause costly delays for developers.

Clawbacks and CBAs are efforts to ensure that public investments in private enterprise generate a concomitant public benefit, and that the costs of the project do not unduly burden particular neighborhoods. * * * [A]s the growth rate in a number of major cities has turned from negative to positive, developers are seeing new opportunities in formerly undesirable neighborhoods. * * * The CBA process is in part a function of both a new urban political leverage and developer confidence that the costs of compliance can be passed on to future residents or commercial tenants. Moreover, because it is a site-specific, private agreement, the

CBA can bypass municipal officials or traditional federal grant-receiving housing or redevelopment agencies. * * * [T]he private nature of the agreement insulates the bargain from constitutional takings or equal protection challenges. Developer concessions to a private group do not constitute exactions subject to federal constitutional limitations. CBA groups are not state actors; they do not wield any formal authority over the development process. They can merely threaten political pressure. * * *

This role raises some obvious concerns. The most important issues are the representativeness of the CBA bargaining groups, their relative insulation from or susceptibility to political capture, and the redistributive effects of particular deals as between poverty, labor, and resident groups, as between neighborhoods within the city, and as between current residents and future residents. Private-side deal-making in the shadow of political mobilization can easily take on the character of extortion or a payoff, whether initiated by community groups, local public officials, or by the developers. Developers have an interest in tamping down opposition to a project as early as possible and may use the CBA process to do so. * * *

Nevertheless, the older clawbacks and the newer CBA movement are a response to past promises made and not kept—private-side development that did not deliver economic benefits or that distributed economic burdens and benefits unfairly. That those promises were not kept might have been a product of a lack of foresight by government officials or a function of their outright collusion with mobile capital—both are in evidence in the history of urban renewal. The effort by non-profit and community-based organizations to assert a more defined role in that process reveals a skepticism of both the public and the private sector. It also reflects the legal and political limitations inherent in that relationship. On the legal side are procedural and substantive limits on the ability of local government to demand concessions from developers, even those it is subsidizing. On the political side are the twin pathologies of giveaways and exploitation, both of which are at their height in the urban redevelopment game. * * *

Many of the same groups seeking to impose conditions on capital entering the city through CBAs have also encouraged municipalities to adopt local minimum wage ordinances, and a significant number of municipalities have done so. The vast majority of these ordinances are "living wage" laws, which regulate the wages of those businesses that contract with the city or the wages of city employees themselves. A handful of cities have adopted ordinances that apply to all businesses within the municipality, exempting small businesses; a few cities have adopted ordinances that only apply to big box stores. The first local living wage campaign began in Baltimore in 1994; 122 cities have now adopted some version of a living wage or local minimum wage ordinance.

These wage laws are components of a more comprehensive campaign to redefine the relationship between labor and capital at the municipal level. * * * Community-labor coalitions have used local contracting and land use law to promote labor-friendly urban policy agendas. Those groups have also sought to align with progressive mayors to adopt other local legislation favorable to employees, such as health care mandates in San Francisco, or labor neutrality legislation in Milwaukee. * * * [L]abor's effort to unionize and support low-wage service workers aligns with the city's interests. The working poor overwhelmingly reside in the city. The services they provide in retail, hospitality, domestic service, cleaning, and security, however, are heavily consumed by non-residents—visitors who use the city's hotels, restaurants, hospitals, universities, and other locally-based and dependent amenities; highly-paid office workers who commute into the city; and suburbanites, who often purchase services from low-wage workers who reside in the city. Cities shoulder the burden of the large numbers of working poor who service the regional economy; cities can assist them by shifting costs onto their employers, and in part, onto non-residents. * * *

As with all the regulatory deals made between the city and business, the city's ability to extract wage concessions without hurting local consumers, taxpayers, or local job seekers turns on the city's relative economic power and/or its ability to shift costs onto non-residents. (The latter is a variant of the former to the extent that outsiders will only continue paying so long as they desire access to the city.) If tourists or business travelers continue to find Los Angeles attractive or if Wal-Mart wants access to Chicago's economically robust consumer base, they will have to play by the cities' economic rules. Until recently, cities have not appeared to have much ability to dictate terms or shift costs to non-residents. Indeed, * * * there continue to be significant economic constraints on the city—namely the ability for firms like Wal-Mart to locate right across the border in neighboring jurisdictions. There are also the political constraints that follow from the city's overall dependence on in-coming capital.

In addition, legal doctrines may prevent cities from capitalizing on their new-found economic muscle. Local wage and labor laws have been challenged as falling outside of the authority of home rule jurisdictions. * * * Even if they lose their preemption arguments based on existing law, employers can ask state or federal legislatures to adopt newly preemptive legislation. The influence of labor-community groups at the local level and their efficacy depends not only on local political processes, but also on how immune local law-making is from contrary state or federal intervention. In most cases, state legislatures can easily override local laws if there is the political desire. * * *

A third way to assert local control over mobile capital is to exclude certain forms of capital from the jurisdiction altogether. We see these efforts with local anti-chain or anti-big box store ordinances. Numerous cities have adopted such ordinances, which may limit the square footage of particular retail outlets, may impose specific conditions on large stores * * *, or may exclude chain stores from particular areas of the city altogether. Some local jurisdictions have required that in-coming big box developers apply for a conditional use permit or engage in a market impact study before proceeding. * * * Thus far, courts have been almost uniformly deferential to chain store bans and other local barriers to the entry of capital or persons (as they are to zoning generally), despite their often protectionist motivations or effects. * * *

If localities are redistributing, why are they able to do so? * * * [A] central point to emphasize is that industries are differently mobile. It is no surprise that local minimum wage and labor organizing movements have targeted relatively place-dependent service industries. Hospitals, hotels, universities, nursing homes, and government offices are relatively location-bound. Organizing local labor markets is an advisable strategy because it can take advantage of spatial dependence, particularly in large metropolitan areas. Service-based economies are heavily local and increasingly dominant; a steadily rising share of the urban workforce produces goods and services that are sold and consumed within the same metropolitan area. Those geographically-dependent goods and services cannot easily flee. Moreover, the larger shift from an industrial economy to a service—and knowledge-based economy has, in some cases, made location more salient rather than less. * * * Knowledge workers need other knowledge workers—those agglomeration effects are strongest in cities. Certain cities may therefore have advantages in particular labor markets.

An additional reason for the potential localization of industrial policy is that labor (particularly laborers in information and knowledge industries) is often mobile as well. Firm location depends a great deal on where the people are, and where the people are turns on their quality of life, their relative educational attainments, and their desire for specific amenities or an architectural aesthetic. * * * Place-specific characteristics can thus influence location decisions and thereafter hold particular firms, either because a specific location generates value for the firm, because labor is attracted to that place and the firm follows, or because the work and services are inherently local. * * *

Any potential limits on capital mobility only provide leverage if locals can translate that leverage into policy through a municipal politics often dominated by business interests. * * * As a matter of strategy, there is little doubt that cities are currently dependent upon large-scale, transnational capital to survive. How can cities become counterweights to private economic power if they are dependent upon it? A decentralist regulatory order offers one possibility. But it applies only to those cities that have the economic and political wherewithal to make choices about the form and timing of local investment. For the declining cities of the rust belt and elsewhere, the ability to dictate terms is fairly limited. Without a great deal of inter-governmental support, those cities are generally confined to market-based attraction strategies; they have few alternatives. * * *

Cities therefore need at the least to strike better deals with mobile capital. * * * Another approach would be to adjust the relationship between relatively mobile, large-scale capital and relatively immobile, small-scale capital by privileging the latter over the former. We cannot return to the small-scale political economy that characterized the producerist economic order. Nevertheless, local policy-makers can focus their efforts on promoting small-scale enterprise, even in a global economy. * * * This strategy is arguably more consistent with the city's long-run economic stability. Cities do not currently have an effective response to the boom and bust cycle. The problem is that mobile capital once attracted can then leave, generating substantial negative effects given that many residents and the city itself are fixed in place. It thus makes sense for a city to try to reduce the volatility of capital flows, even if that means that its residents experience a lower level of economic well-being in the short term. Local government reformers would do well to consider a legal and political structure that is more responsive to long-term, immobile capital rather than one that incentivizes the chase for highly mobile capital.

Of course, there is always the question of ends. What should be the goal of local economic development efforts? If it is to help cities and their residents "productively fit[ ] into the global economy" one might adopt a particular set of strategies: redistribution at the national level to even out the dislocations caused by large-scale economic restructuring, job training, assistance in internal migration, regionalism, encouraging urban entrepreneurialism, and market-based economic development. But the goal might be larger. Recall that the rejection of the corporatist medieval and early colonial city represented the end of monopoly, mercantilism, and autocracy in favor of open markets, democracy, and individual economic freedom. One may wish to reassert these same goals in the face of the power and authority of large, hierarchical corporate entities. The goal of the city would be to become less a passive recipient of global capital than a shaper of local capital in a direction more conducive to freedom. * * *

HERNANDEZ V. CITY OF HANFORD

Supreme Court of California, 2007.
41 Cal. 4th 279, 59 Cal.Rptr.3d 442, 159 P.3d 33.

GEORGE, C.J. * * *

In 1989, the City of Hanford amended its general plan to provide for a new commercial district in the vicinity of 12th Avenue and Lacey Boulevard. This new district originally was designated the "Regional Commercial" district but later was renamed the Planned Commercial or PC district. The district encompassed several hundred acres of land and was intended to accommodate the location of malls, large "big box" stores, and other retail uses. * * * [W]hen the city was considering the creation of the new district in 1989, it was concerned that the extent of anticipated commercial development in the proposed district might well have a negative effect on the city's downtown commercial district. * * * [T]he 1989 ordinance included department stores and the sale of home furnishings within the list of permitted uses within the new district, but did not include furniture stores or the sale of furniture as a permitted use. * * *

On March 4, 2003, * * * the city council held a "study session" * * *. Plaintiffs, as well as representatives of the downtown furniture stores and representatives of the PC district department stores, attended and participated in the study session. * * * At the conclusion of the session, the council instructed the city staff to draft a proposed revision of the ordinance * * *. Ultimately, on July 15, 2003, the city council adopted the amendment to the city zoning provisions relating to the sale of furniture in the PC district that is challenged in this case, Hanford Ordinance 03–03 (Ordinance No. 03–03). * * * Section 2 of Ordinance No. 03–03 adds as permissible uses within the PC district: "Department Stores" as defined in the ordinance, "Home Furnishing Accessories" as defined in the ordinance, and "Stores, which sell mattresses and metal bed frames with basic headboards and footboards that do not include shelves, drawers or sitting areas." Finally, section 3 of the ordinance adds a paragraph to the PC zoning provisions that specifically states: "The sale of furniture is prohibited in the PC zone district except by Department Stores in accordance with the definition of Department Stores" as set forth in the ordinance. * * *

Before reaching the equal protection issue upon which the Court of Appeal based its decision, we turn first to the more general (and more sweeping) contention that plaintiffs raised below and upon which they continue to rely in this court—that the zoning ordinance at issue is invalid because the "primary purpose" of the ordinance's general prohibition of the sale of furniture in the PC district assertedly was to "regulat[e] economic competition." * * * [P]laintiffs' claim that the city exceeded its authority under the police power by enacting a zoning ordinance that regulates or restricts economic competition * * *. The * * * recent case of *Wal-Mart Stores, Inc. v. City of Turlock* (2006) 138 Cal.App.4th 273 (*Wal-Mart*) provides * * * [an apt response]. In *Wal-Mart*, the City of Turlock enacted a zoning ordinance that, while permitting the operation of traditional "big box" discount stores in a designated district, prohibited the development, anywhere in the city, of so-called discount superstores—defined generally as large discount stores that include a full-service grocery department. * * * Wal-Mart filed an action challenging the validity of the ordinance on a variety of grounds, including the contention that the ordinance exceeded the city's police powers because it was "designed to suppress economic competition, and is not reasonably related to the public welfare." In rejecting this argument, the Court of Appeal in *Wal-Mart* stated: "With respect to Wal-Mart's claim of anticompetitive purpose, we agree with the trial court that, while the Ordinance likely will have an anticompetitive effect on the grocery business in [the City of Turlock], that incidental effect does not render arbitrary an Ordinance that was enacted for a valid purpose. While zoning ordinances may not legitimately be used to control economic competition, they may be used to address the urban/suburban decay that can be its effect. The appellate court in *Wal-Mart* concluded: "In summary, the police power empowers cities to control and organize development within their boundaries as a means of serving the general welfare. [The City of Turlock] legitimately chose to organize the development within its boundaries using neighborhood shopping centers dispersed throughout the city. The Ordinance is reasonably related to protecting that development choice." * * *

Our court has not previously had occasion to address the question whether a municipality, in order to protect or preserve the economic viability of its downtown business district or neighborhood shopping areas, may enact a zoning ordinance that regulates or controls competition by placing limits on potentially competing commercial activities or development in other areas of the municipality. More than a half-century ago, however, this court explained that "[i]t is well settled that a municipality may divide land into districts and prescribe regulations governing the uses permitted therein, and that zoning ordinances, when reasonable in object and not arbitrary in operation, constitute a justifiable exercise of police power." (*Lockard v. City of Los Angeles* (1949) 33 Cal.2d 453, 460). As the circumstances underlying *Wal-Mart* demonstrate, even when the regulation of economic competition reasonably can be viewed as a direct and intended effect of a zoning ordinance or action, so long as the primary purpose of the ordinance or action—that is, its principal and ultimate objective—is not the impermissible *private* anticompetitive goal of protecting or disadvantaging a particular favored or disfavored business or individual, but instead is the advancement of a legitimate *public* purpose—such as the preservation of a municipality's downtown business district for the benefit of the municipality as a whole—the ordinance reasonably relates to the general welfare of the municipality and constitutes a legitimate exercise of the municipality's police power.[10] * * *

In the present case, it is clear that the zoning ordinance's general prohibition on the sale of furniture in the PC district—although concededly intended, at least in part, to regulate competition—was adopted to promote the legitimate public purpose of preserving the economic viability of the Hanford downtown business district, rather than to serve any impermissible private anticompetitive purpose. Furthermore, * * * here the zoning ordinance's restrictions are aimed at regulating "*where*, within the city" a particular type of business generally may be located, a very traditional zoning objective. Under these circumstances, we agree with the lower court's conclusion that the zoning ordinance cannot be found invalid as an improper limitation on competition. * * *

[A]lthough the Court of Appeal agreed that the challenged zoning ordinance's general prohibition on the sale of furniture in the PC district is permissible, that court concluded the ordinance in question violates the equal protection clause by limiting the exception created by the ordinance to only the sale of furniture by large department stores, and not making the exception available to other retail stores wishing to sell furniture within the same amount of square footage permitted for furniture sales by large department stores. * * * In evaluating the Court of Appeal's resolution of this issue, we begin with the question of the appropriate equal protection standard applicable in this case. * * * The zoning ordinance at issue in the present case does not involve suspect classifications or touch upon fundamental interests and thus, as the Court of Appeal recognized and as all parties agree, the applicable standard under which plaintiffs' equal protection challenge properly must be evaluated is the rational relationship or rational basis standard. * * * Because the city viewed large department stores as particularly

---

[10] Numerous cases in other jurisdictions have upheld zoning ordinances that limit some or all commercial development in outlying locations in order to protect or strengthen the economic viability of a municipality's central business district. (See, e.g., Jacobs, Visconsi & Jacobs v. City of Lawrence (10th Cir. 1991) 927 F.2d 1111, 1119 ["[T]he district court correctly concluded that retaining the vitality of the downtown area was a legitimate interest of the city commission. Declining to rezone property in a manner that would threaten the vitality of the downtown retail area is rationally related to that purpose"]; E & G Enterprises v. City of Mount Vernon (Iowa Ct.App. 1985) 373 N.W.2d 693, 694 ["Mount Vernon's effort to preserve its downtown business area is a valid exercise of police power. . . . [P]reservation of that area promotes the public welfare, including the maintenance of property values"]; Forte v. The Borough of Tenafly (App.Div. 1969) 106 N.J. Super. 346 ["May a municipality which wishes to preserve, rehabilitate and improve an established business area devoted chiefly to retail stores, zone the rest of the municipality against retail sales? We hold that it may"]; Chevron Oil Company v. Beaver County (1969) 22 Utah 2d 143 [county's refusal to rezone land in outlying area to permit "highway services" development was justified "on the ground that any tourist business which would go to the isolated junction area would be a loss to the established businesses of Beaver City"].)

significant elements of the PC district, and because the management of those stores had made clear the importance to them of retaining their ability to offer furniture sales that typically were offered by their sister stores in other locations, it was rational for the city to decide to provide an exception from the general prohibition on furniture sales in the PC district for such large department stores and only such stores. The circumstance that the city also decided to limit the exemption afforded to department stores by placing a square-foot limit on the area within each store in which furniture could be displayed does not in any manner detract from the rationality of limiting the exception to large department stores.

Accordingly, contrary to the Court of Appeal's determination, we conclude that the ordinance's differential treatment of large department stores and other retail stores is rationally related to one of the legitimate legislative purposes of the ordinance—the purpose of attracting and retaining large department stores within the PC district. * * *

4. THE IMMIGRANT CITY

Immigration has long been thought of as primarily a federal issue. Moreover, the local dimension of immigration has frequently focused mostly on a few large immigrant-receiving places, such as New York, Los Angeles, Chicago, Houston, and Miami. A Brookings study has demonstrated, however, that this picture is no longer valid, if indeed it ever was.[49] Immigrants now constitute 13% of the population of the United States, and, in the 1990s alone, the number of immigrants increased by 57%. The immigrant population continued to rise steadily through the first decade of this century, and there are now more than 40 million immigrants in the country.[50] Not only is immigration now a facet of life for central cities across the country, but more immigrants now live in the suburbs than in the central cities. The age of the immigrant city in the United States, in short, has arrived.

The following article by Rick Su is part of a growing focus on the local role for immigration issues.[51] That focus raises significant legal questions

[49] Audrey Singer, Brookings Center on Urban and Metropolitan Policy, The Rise of New Immigrant Gateways (2004).

[50] Fred Dews, What Percentage of the U.S. Population is Foreign Born? http://www. brookings.edu/blogs/brookings-now/posts/2013/09/what-percentage-us-population-foreign-born.

[51] Alex Triantaphyllis, Proposing A Locally Driven Entrepreneur Visa, 126 Harv. L. Rev. 2403 (2013); Stella Burch Elias, The New Immigration Federalism, 74 Ohio St. L.J. 703 (2013); Rick Su, Urban Politics and the Assimilation of Immigrant Voters, 21 Wm. & Mary Bill Rts. J. 653 (2012); Rick Su, A Localist Reading of Local Immigration Regulations, 86 N.C. L. Rev. 1619 (2010); Rick Su, Immigration as Urban Policy, 38 Fordham Urb. L. J. 363 (2010); Peter Spiro, Formalizing Local Citizenship, 37 Fordham Urb. L.J. 559 (2010); Christina Rodriguez, The Significance of the Local in Immigration Regulation, 106 Mich. L. Rev. 567 (2008); Matthew Parlow, A Localist's Case for Decentralizing Immigration Policy, 85 Denver U. L. Rev. 4 (2007); Peter Schuck, Taking Immigration Federalism Seriously, 2007 U. Chi. Legal F. 57 (2007); Gerald Neuman, Strangers to the Constitution: Immigrants, Borders, and Fundamental Law (1996).

with respect to a local government's power under state and federal law to address immigration either directly or indirectly. The article examines both efforts by cities to limit their role in enforcement of federal immigration policy and city-imposed restrictions on immigrants, particularly undocumented immigrants. The two cases that follow—Garcia v. Dicterow and Lozano v. City of Hazleton—explore the legality of specific ingredients of these contradictory policies. Like the Su article, the cases raise in the context of immigration a pervasive theme of the casebook as a whole: If neither local autonomy nor city powerless is an acceptable role for cities on a particular issue, how should city power be structured as a legal matter? The final excerpt, also by Rick Su, frames the immigration issue in terms of this overarching question—more specifically, in terms of the relationship between city power as a general matter and the current incentives that lead cities either to welcome or to target new immigrants.

RICK SU, A LOCALIST READING OF LOCAL IMMIGRATION REGULATIONS

86 N.C. L. Rev. 1619, 1633–1636, 1640–1652 (2008).

From a legal perspective, a locality's role in our nation's immigration enforcement regime has long been a controversial subject. On the one hand, a vigorous debate rages over whether local police officials even have the power to enforce federal immigration laws, with some asserting that such powers should be reserved exclusively for federal officials by nature of federal preemption. On the other hand, among those who assume local enforcement is permitted, there is disagreement over whether federal immigration laws require local officials to cooperate with the federal government, or whether cooperation is solely at the discretion of the local community. These conflicts are not isolated to the legal academic literature. Indeed, the federal government's own positions on these questions have been inconsistent.

Congress skirted many of these issues in 1996 when it passed a series of measures to enable and encourage more local participation in federal enforcement efforts. The most prominent of these is section 287(g) of the Immigration and Naturalization Act ("INA"), which specifically established a procedure by which state or local governments can enter into a "memorandum of understanding" ("MOU") with the Department of Homeland Security that sets forth the scope of their intent to assist in federal immigration efforts and the conditions that they must follow in order to receive this federal delegation of power. It may be too quick for us to assume that a "delegation" of federal immigration enforcement powers in this manner is constitutional. At the same time, its growing popularity is worth noting. Although section 287(g) was almost entirely ignored in the years after its passage, after the State of Florida reached an agreement in 2002, more than forty states and localities have entered into a MOU with the federal government.

Besides enabling cooperative arrangements, Congress also imposed a series of restrictions on the ability of state and local governments to expressly forbid any other government, agency, or official from cooperating with the federal immigration enforcement authorities. The clear target of these provisions were nonenforcement efforts at the local level: so-called "sanctuary" provisions that limited when police or other government employees could inquire about, or act upon, legal immigrant status while serving in their capacity as a municipal employee. Unlike section 287(g), Congress's anti-sanctuary measures faced a constitutional challenge almost immediately after they were enacted, which the Second Circuit heard and dismissed in City of New York v. United States. The court held that the provisions in question did not compel state or local governments to enact or administer any federal regulatory programs in violation of the Tenth Amendment or any other constitutional provision; they simply prohibited them from "restricting the voluntary exchange of immigration information with" federal immigration officials. In the court's eyes, to hold otherwise would be to allow state and local governments to "engage in passive resistance that frustrates federal programs." * * *

[C]ounter-intuitively, for communities concerned about the detrimental effects of immigration enforcement on their community, entering into enforcement MOUs with the federal government pursuant to section 287(g) may be a more effective tool than sanctuary provisions. This is because MOUs offer cities and towns a seat at a table that usually excludes their presence. The fact is that, irrespective of whether a locality voluntarily participates in federal enforcement activity or aggressively resists cooperation, the local field offices of the federal government's enforcement apparatus will continue to carry out its assigned task—possibly in a manner that raises local concerns. To some, this supports the argument that sanctuary and other local noncooperation efforts should not be struck down for frustrating federal enforcement objectives. But it also suggests that, rather than disengagement, direct participation through cooperative arrangements—or even assuming primary immigration enforcement responsibilities altogether—might actually be a more effective tool for balancing the needs of the community and the enforcement interests of the federal government. * * *

[L]ocal involvement in immigration regulations is not always solely or even primarily concerned about immigration per se, but in an attempt to circumvent or negotiate obligations and constraints that have been imposed by state law. Thus, instead of being a sign of local power with regard to immigration, local immigration regulations may simply be a consequence of local powerlessness in another context. For example, many of the localities that have assumed federal immigration powers through section 287(g) have not done so with a desire to efface the federal-local line by enlisting with federal enforcement efforts. Rather, the intention is often to further reinforce the federal-local divide by trying to distinguish federal from local responsibilities in an attempt to save on local costs over which local governments have little control. In this way, they have much in common with local sanctuary provisions. More than symbolic resistance to federal immigration policy, most local non-enforcement provisions are simply calculated attempts to avoid spending local funds on immigration enforcement, especially in a way that would make provision of other local services as required by state law less effective or efficient in the process. Indeed, it is interesting to note that, notwithstanding the fact that these two local responses are portrayed as polar extremes, most local immigration policies exhibit features of both responses—cooperation and noncooperation—simultaneously. * * *

[L]ocalities are also beginning to employ regulatory schemes that employ statuses defined by federal immigration laws but do not directly intersect with federal enforcement efforts. I refer to these as indirect regulations of immigration. Indirect regulations rely on federal immigration laws to mark out the targeted group, but operate by redefining the immigrant's relationship with the local community. This could involve delineating the ways in which residents and other private actors are permitted to interact with certain groups of immigrants in the community; or it might entail adjusting who is entitled to certain local government services and how those services are provided. In both cases, indirect regulations almost always invoke powers that are traditionally allocated to localities although they rely, at least facially, on classifications designated by federal law.

Though by no means the first, a pair of ordinances adopted by the Town of Hazleton in Eastern Pennsylvania is by far the most well-known indirect regulation effort at the local level. Not only have these ordinances received tremendous attention since they were passed in 2006, but they have also served as a prototype for communities across the country. Hazleton's ordinances involved two major components. First, Hazleton made it illegal for any landlord to rent to illegal immigrants by requiring landlords to verify that all tenants possessed a municipal occupancy permit, which could only be obtained by showing evidence of legal residency or citizenship. Second, Hazleton adopted an ordinance that allowed the town to suspend or revoke the license of any business that hired illegal immigrants—in essence attaching additional penalties to conduct that was already prohibited by federal law. Legal challenges were instituted against Hazleton and other copycat communities on federal preemption and other legal grounds immediately after they were enacted. Thus far, the district courts that have ruled on these claims have split on the results.

Indirect regulations do not give localities the type of immediate control (or sense of control) that direct enforcements offer. Nevertheless, they proffer certain advantages that make them popular options. First, they allow localities a means to enforce immigration laws "on the cheap." Instead of working to expel illegal immigrants directly, indirect regulations promote self-removal by depriving access to valuable or necessary resources in the community. Moreover, front-line screening responsibilities are often delegated to private parties. Second, indirect regulations allow localities to tailor their regulatory controls such that, instead of excluding solely on the basis of federal immigration grounds, they can take additional local concerns into consideration. This means that they can exclude only those immigrants considered undesirable to the community, such as renters or common employees. This is particularly useful when local measures of desirability do not correspond perfectly with federal immigration statutes. In addition, instead of relying on federal deportation, a relatively inconvenient tool and one outside of their immediate control, local communities can address the perceived costs by targeting them directly. In short, through indirect regulations, a local community need not treat all illegal immigrants in the same way even if the federal government recognizes no distinctions—it can effectively set its own admissions criteria, even (or especially) if they differ from federal standards. * * *

The rationale that Hazleton articulated—financial burden on local services, diminishing quality of life, and nuisance—are not only concerns that are intimately local, but also ones that are not necessarily or immediately related to illegal or even foreign immigrants per se. Furthermore, although the court challenge against Hazleton revolved around a legal question, it is worth noting that much of the trial was dedicated to determining whether recent demographic changes led to higher crime rates, "subject[ed] . . . hospitals to fiscal hardship and legal residents to substandard quality of care, [or] contribute[d] to other burdens on public services" such as education. As the district judge seemed to acknowledge, this case was as much about foreign immigration as it was about the transition of the old Hazleton of roughly 23,000 residents into the new Hazleton, fifty percent larger and composed of large numbers of "Latino families [that] moved from New York and New Jersey to Hazleton seeking a better life, employment and affordable housing."

The problem that Hazleton poses for proponents of immigration federalism interested in local experimentation lies not in the fact that communities like Hazleton will seek to reject immigrants on the basis of community or local concerns as opposed to federal immigration-related considerations. Indeed, the purpose of promoting local experimentation is precisely so that local concerns can be quickly factored into the broader immigration discourse, and the consequences of their diverse actions (i.e., steps to exclude and steps to embrace) can be effectively assessed. The problem lies in the fact that communities like Hazleton are not isolated entities, and both their responses and the consequences of their responses are tied to broader structural arrangements that make certain actions more effective than others. Thus, certain communities may benefit from taking specific actions, and be incentivized to do so because of the particular significance that the current local legal structure places upon residency and municipal boundaries. Those that look like they are benefiting from their actions under the current local legal regime, however, may fare quite differently if particular background rules are changed—for example if local public goods like education, or local receipts through property or sales taxes, were not allocated according to municipal boundary lines. In light of this, what local activity or local "experimentalism" may tell us about immigration policy as a whole may be very limited. Indeed, at the most fundamental level, they will likely be simple reflections of the legal and incentive structure of localism and the horizontal relationship between neighboring communities. * * *

[O]ne of the most common local responses to immigration does not invoke federal immigration laws at all. I refer to these as neutral regulations of immigration. In contrast to other local immigration regulations, the connection between neutral regulations and immigration is often not clear at first blush. This is because neutral regulations ordinarily involve exercises of power that are traditionally associated with local governments, such as land-use zoning, quality of life ordinances, or the allocation of local resources. Thus, on their face, neutral regulations generally do not differ much from any number of local ordinances or policymaking activities that localities undertake in furtherance of conventional local interests. What distinguishes neutral regulations, however, is that they tend to have a disproportionate effect on immigrants, and are often enacted and enforced precisely for this reason. Indeed, even though they do not invoke immigration or immigration laws directly, there is usually little doubt among the parties involved with neutral regulations that immigration and immigrant status play a significant role. In practice, neutral regulations share much in terms of motivations and consequences with more conventional local immigration regulations.

Notwithstanding the roundabout nature of neutral regulations, they represent some of the earliest attempts to address immigration at the local level. The particular way in which the City of San Francisco sought to enforce its laundry licensing requirements in *Yick Wo v. Hopkins* against Chinese immigrants at the end of the nineteenth century is one example. Another is the widespread use of public health and safety regulations to either "quarantine" immigrants within specific neighborhoods, or prevent their landing altogether. Similar uses of neutral regulations are afoot today. Local governments all across the country have turned to housing and zoning code provisions governing residential overcrowding to address influxes of low-income, predominantly Hispanic immigrants who are more likely to share housing with extended family members. Anti-loitering and other quality of life measures have been used to remove congregations of immigrant day-laborers in public spaces. And although mostly symbolic, English-only ordinances have been used to further broadcast local resistance to immigrants. None of these specifically target immigrants or rely on federal immigration laws. But at the same time it is clear that these regulations concern immigration in a very real way.

In addition, immigration is factoring into policymaking at the local level, which constitutes another aspect of neutral regulations. Localities are responsible for making a number of decisions that affect the provision of services in that community. Although these decisions are ordinarily mundane in substance and narrow in scope, there are hints that more and more of them are being made with an eye toward their effect on immigrant newcomers. For example, there are accounts that communities have rejected bond issues to build new schools in part because residents perceived the benefits of new schools as going primarily to the immigrant children who represent a larger percentage of the school-age population than the general population. There are also concerns that certain services are being underfunded, or eliminated altogether, because the perception is that they are disproportionately used by "foreigners."

Again, neutral regulations offer certain advantages. Like direct regulations, neutral regulations rely primarily on municipal action, and thus give local communities substantial control over when and how they are used. Like indirect regulations, they can be tailored to target activities and conduct that are not necessarily considered relevant under federal immigration laws. Because neutral regulations do not rely on federal immigration laws at all, however, they can go further than regulations that target individuals purely on the basis of their immigration status. Moreover, because they are based on neutral criteria, many of these measures are difficult to distinguish from local regulations that are within the purview of local governments to adopt.

Not unlike their direct and indirect counterparts, neutral regulations of immigration implicate both the vertical and horizontal aspects of localism. Even though neutral regulations tend to rely on more traditional local powers, questions about delegations of state power and state preemption are involved, and many neutral regulations have been struck down on these grounds. Horizontal concerns are implicated as well. To the extent that neutral regulations are even more difficult to distinguish from more traditional efforts at communal self-definition or self-determination than indirect regulations, it is often the case that they tend to be more concerned about the local spatial residency of immigrants in their jurisdiction than their presence in the United States as a whole. * * *

GARCIA V. DICTEROW
Court of Appeal of California, 2008.
2008 WL 5050358.

IKOLA, J.

In an action against the City of Laguna Beach and other defendants (collectively the City), plaintiffs Eileen Garcia and George Riviere sought (1) a "declaration that the City['s] expenditure of taxpayer funds and taxpayer-financed resources for the operation of [a day labor site] is unlawful, void, and a waste of taxpayer funds," and (2) "injunctive relief restraining and preventing the City . . . from expending any further taxpayer funds or taxpayer-financed resources for the operation of the [day labor site]." * * *

In March 1993, "the City amended its Municipal Code to prohibit the solicitation of employment on any street, highway, public area, or non-residential parking area within the City, other than in an area specifically designated by resolution of the City Council for solicitation of employment." The City also "adopted a resolution formally designating an area on . . . Laguna Canyon Road as the City's day labor hiring area." The City thereby tried "to eliminate 'nuisances' associated with day laborer solicitation and locate it, in the City Manager's opinion, 'in a place that would be least offensive to people in the community.' In the City Manager's opinion, the nuisances included trespassing on private property, littering, vandalism, disruption of businesses and residences, and interference with street traffic." After the establishment of the day hiring center, "[a]ccording to the City Manager, . . . the nuisances associated with the solicitation of employment City-wide . . . decreased substantially." The center became "known as the Laguna Beach Day Worker Center" (the Center).

The Center is located on land owned by the California Department of Transportation (CalTrans) and the Orange County Parks Department. In June 2006, after CalTrans demanded the removal of the Center, "the City agreed to . . . indemnify CalTrans for any losses or damages arising out of the City use of the property and entered into a lease with CalTrans for the property" at a rental rate of $420 per month. "Since 1993, the City has expended taxpayer funds and taxpayer-financed resources on the [Center], including but not limited to adding a driveway, fencing, landscaping, benches, a waterline, and drinking fountain as well as installing portable toilets and paying for trash pick up."

In a March 1999 memorandum, the City's director of community services summarized a meeting "requested by some of the day workers to resolve on-going problems at the Center." Four workers attended the meeting (as spokespersons for the day laborers) and recommended "that workers should be banned from the hiring area if they violate the safety rules [by] running across the street, standing outside of the hiring area, or rushing the cars," and "hoped the city would help with enforcement by supplying staff at the area."

Thereafter, "[b]eginning in approximately August 1999, the City of Laguna Beach has provided taxpayer funds, usually in the form of annual Community Assistance Grants, to the South County Cross Cultural Council ('South County'), a private non-profit, tax exempt organization which has used the funds to operate and manage the [Center]." Since 1999, the City has provided approximately $206,500 to South County. * * *

South County does not, and is not required by the City to, "verify that day laborers who use the Center to obtain employment are eligible to work in the United States." The City has taken no "steps to determine whether day laborers using the Center are legally present in the United States and legally eligible for employment in the United States." The "President and Executive Director of South County, is aware that some of the day laborers who utilize the Center to obtain employment may be undocumented aliens." The City's city manager "testified that at the time the Center was established in 1993 the City and the day laborers had an 'unspoken arrangement that we would not be calling in the INS [Immigration and Naturalization Service, workers are] cooperating by going to a location that's less of a problem, and we're cooperating by not calling INS.'" "As early as 1991, some City officials indicated that they did not want federal immigration officials called in to try to address the City's day laborer issues, and in 1999, the City's Chief of Police assured day laborers who use the Center that the City would not call in federal immigration officials." "According to a joint study published in January 2006 by the University of California at Los Angeles, the University of Illinois at Chicago, and the New School University, seventy-five percent (75%) of the day laborer work force consists of undocumented workers. The City was provided a copy of this study . . . before Plaintiffs filed this lawsuit." In 2006, plaintiff Garcia provided city "council members with copies of a report by the Center for the Study of Urban Poverty indicating that eighty-five percent (85%) of those persons seeking employment at day laborer sites are undocumented aliens." "The City also has received citizen complaints that the Center fosters illegal immigration." The City's police department has posted and distributed program guidelines and handouts at the Center "stating, in both English and Spanish: 'The Laguna Beach Police Department wants to help you find work. We need your assistance and cooperation in helping us to keep this area [a] safe place to be hired by contractors, homeowners and others. . . . The City of Laguna Beach wants you and your family and friends to be a part of the community and to enjoy a healthy quality of life. . . . We want to help you find work so that you can stay here or send money to your loved ones back home." * * *

Plaintiffs allege "the City's use of taxpayer resources to operate the Center" is an illegal expenditure that violates three federal statutes "proscribing the employment of undocumented aliens"—title 8 of the United States Code sections 1324a, 1324, and/or 1621. * * * Under section 1324a, a person or entity is prohibited from referring "for a fee, for employment in the United States an alien knowing the alien is an unauthorized alien." (§ 1324a(a)(1)(A).) The statute prescribes civil and/or misdemeanor criminal penalties. (§ 1324a(e)(4) [cease and desist order with civil money penalty] and (f) [criminal penalties and injunctions for pattern or practice violations, including imprisonment of not more than six months].) * * *

Without citing any legal authority to support their contention, plaintiffs assert South County is the City's agent for purposes of operating the Center. * * * But plaintiffs provide no evidence the City has any legal right to control South County. Although the City does fund South County with an annual grant, there is no evidence in South County's grant application for the fiscal year 2007 through 2008, or anywhere else in the stipulated facts and exhibits, of any "strings" attached to the grant. * * * Because plaintiffs have not proved South County is the City's agent, they correspondingly have not shown the City acts indirectly to illegally refer unauthorized aliens for employment for a fee. * * *

Under section 1324(a)(1)(A)(iv), any "person" who "encourages . . . an alien to come to . . . or reside in the United States, knowing or in reckless disregard of the fact that such coming to . . . or residence is or will be in violation of law" is subject to criminal penalties. * * * Plaintiffs argue the City, by "operating and underwriting a marketplace where undocumented aliens can offer their unlawful labor to employers," encourages such aliens to illegally reside in the United States. They stress "that employment is the magnet that attracts illegal aliens to come to and reside in this country." They contend "the City has sought to assist day laborers to find employment at the Center despite actual or constructive knowledge that they were likely to be undocumented aliens." They point, for example, to the guidelines and handouts posted and distributed at the Center by the City's police department * * *.

[T]he City, although it promises not to summon the INS to the Center, cannot and does not promise aliens it can shield them from deportation. (Indeed, by requiring workers to congregate in a single location, the City has arguably created a more attractive target for the INS.) Nor has the City, by creating the Center and requiring workers to use it, necessarily enhanced their chances of obtaining employment. The single location may have increased competition among the congregated workers, resulting, for example, in laborers "rushing the cars." Without the Center, smaller clusters of workers would undoubtedly gather in various places known to prospective employers. We conclude the City's creation and funding of the Center does not rise to the level of "encouraging" prohibited by the statute.

Two more factors reinforce our conclusion. First, plaintiffs identify no named illegal aliens or even a specific number of particular unnamed but known illegal aliens who have obtained employment through the Center. Yet the statute prescribes punishment "for each alien in respect to whom such a violation occurs," thus contemplating the involvement of a particular known alien or aliens. * * * Secondly, * * * the City's conduct does not constitute referral for employment for a fee prohibited under section 1324a. * * * In sum, the City does not encourage illegal aliens to reside within the United States in contravention of section 1324(a)(1)(A)(iv) or 1324(a)(1) (A) (v)(II). * * *

Under section 1621, illegal aliens are generally ineligible to receive any "local public benefit." Such benefits are defined generally in section 1621(c) to include any grant provided by a local government or "any retirement, welfare, health, disability, public or assisted housing, postsecondary education, food assistance, unemployment benefit, or any other similar benefit for which payments or assistance are provided to an individual, household, or family eligibility unit by an agency of a . . . local government."

Plaintiffs argue the City violates section 1621 because South County provides benefits to undocumented aliens, *and* South County is the City's agent. As discussed above, plaintiffs have not met their burden of proof to show South County is the City's agent and therefore their section 1621 contention fails. * * *

Plaintiffs argue that under "the well-established federal preemption doctrine, a locality is prohibited from taking actions which . . . undermine or frustrate federal law." Plaintiffs overstate the preemption doctrine, which does not apply to all actions of a state or locality but only to its laws and regulations: "As to preemption generally, the law is as follows." [S]tate law that conflicts with federal law is "without effect." (*Smiley v. Citibank* (1995) 11 Cal.4th 138, 147.) Because plaintiffs argue the City's *conduct,* i.e. its support of the Center, is preempted by federal law, as

opposed to any specific ordinance, they fail to state a preemption claim.
* * *

LOZANO V. CITY OF HAZLETON

United States Court of Appeals for the Third Circuit, 2012.
724 F.3d. 297.

McKEE, CHIEF JUDGE.

[The City of Hazleton, Pennsylvania enacted two ordinances that, in combination, restrict rental housing for immigrants lacking lawful immigration status. The two ordinances were the Illegal Immigration Relief Act Ordinance ("IIRAO") and the Rental Registration Ordinance ("RO"). After the District Court permanently enjoined enforcement of the ordinances, the Court of Appeals affirmed on the ground that the housing restrictions "impermissibly 'regulate immigration' and are both field and conflict pre-empted by federal immigration law." *Lozano v. City of Hazleton*, 620 F.3d 170 (3d Cir 2010) ("*Lozano II*"). The Supreme Court then granted the City's petition for a writ of certiorari, and vacated and remanded for reconsideration in light of two subsequently decided Supreme Court decisions concerning state regulation of immigration. *Chamber of Commerce v. Whiting*, 131 S. Ct. 1968 (2011) and *Arizona v. United States*, 132 S. Ct. 2492 (2012).]

* * * The Court upheld Arizona's efforts to regulate the employment of unauthorized aliens through a business licensing law in *Whiting*, but largely rejected Arizona's efforts to enact its own immigration policies, both within and outside of the employment context, in *Arizona*. With those cases as our compass, we now reconsider our prior ruling upholding the District Court's permanent injunction. * * *

The RO sets up a rental registration scheme that operates in conjunction with anti-harboring provisions in the IIRAO to prohibit unauthorized aliens from residing in any rental housing within the City. The RO requires any prospective occupant of rental housing over the age of eighteen to apply for and receive an occupancy permit. To receive the permit, the prospective occupant must pay a ten-dollar fee and submit certain basic information and "[p]roper identification showing proof of legal citizenship and/or residency" to the * * * [Hazelton Code Enforcement Office]. Landlords must inform all prospective occupants of this requirement, and landlords are prohibited from allowing anyone over the age of eighteen to rent or occupy a rental unit without registering with the City and receiving a permit. A landlord found guilty of violating these requirements must pay an initial fine of $1000 per unauthorized occupant. That landlord is also subject to an additional fine of $100 per day, per unauthorized occupant, until the violation is corrected.

Authorized occupants of rental housing who allow anyone without an occupancy permit to reside with them are subject to the same fines. * * *

[T]he anti-harboring provisions in the IIRAO make legal immigration status a condition precedent to entering into a valid lease. A tenant lacking lawful status "who enters into such a contract shall be deemed to have breached a condition of the lease." The IIRAO makes it "unlawful for any person or business entity that owns a dwelling unit in the City to harbor an illegal alien in the dwelling unit, knowing or in reckless disregard of the fact that an alien has come to, entered, or remains in the United States in violation of law." "Harboring" is broadly defined to include "let[ting], leas[ing], or rent[ing] a dwelling unit to an illegal alien." An "illegal alien" is defined as "an alien who is not lawfully present in the United States, according to the terms of United States Code Title 8, section 1101 et seq." * * *

[T]he Supreme Court was careful in *Arizona* to stress the important national interests that are implicated when local governments attempt to regulate immigration and the concomitant need to leave such regulations in the hands of the federal government. "The federal power to determine immigration policy is well settled. Immigration policy can affect trade, investment, tourism, and diplomatic relations for the entire Nation, as well as the perceptions and expectations of aliens in this country who seek the full protection of its laws." In finding three of the four challenged provisions in *Arizona* pre-empted, the Court reiterated the primacy of the federal government's concern for the treatment and regulation of aliens in this country.

In *Lozano II*, we held that the housing provisions impermissibly "regulate immigration" in contravention of the Supreme Court's pronouncement that a state or locality may not determine "who should or should not be admitted into the country, and the conditions under which a legal entrant may remain." In concluding that the housing provisions constituted impermissible regulation of immigration, we recognized that "the fact that aliens are the subject of a state statute does not render it a regulation of immigration." We did not hold that the housing provisions were a regulation of immigration simply because "aliens are the subject of" those provisions. Rather, we determined that "[t]hrough its housing provisions, Hazleton attempts to regulate residence based *solely* on immigration status." *Lozano II*, 620 F.3d at 220 (emphasis added). Thus, we concluded that enforcement of the housing provisions must be enjoined because "[d]eciding which aliens may live in the United States has always been the prerogative of the federal government." The housing provisions of Hazleton's ordinances are nothing more than a thinly veiled attempt to regulate residency under the guise of a regulation of rental housing. By barring aliens lacking lawful immigration status from rental housing in Hazleton, the housing provisions go to the core of an alien's residency. States and localities have no power to regulate residency based on immigration status.

For these same reasons, we also concluded that the housing provisions are field pre-empted by the * * * [Immigration and Naturalization Act ("INA")]. That statute is centrally concerned with "the terms and conditions of admission to the country and the subsequent treatment of aliens lawfully admitted." The INA's comprehensive scheme "plainly precludes state efforts, whether harmonious or conflicting, to regulate residence in this country based on immigration status." We noted that although Hazleton's housing provisions do not control actual physical entry into, or expulsion from, Hazleton or the United States, "in essence, that is precisely what they attempt to do." * * * [W]e see nothing in the Supreme Court's decisions in *Whiting* or *Arizona* that undermines these conclusions. * * *

The City argues that, by authorizing state and local officials to arrest individuals guilty of harboring, see 8 U.S.C. § 1324(c), Congress [in the INA] specifically invited state and local governments into this field. According to the City, this "invitation"—along with the requirement in 8 U.S.C. § 1373 that federal agencies respond to inquiries from states and localities regarding any alien's immigration status—forecloses any argument that the housing provisions are field pre-empted. However, while § 1324(c) allows state officials to arrest for violations of crimes enumerated in that section, the federal statute does not authorize states to prosecute those crimes. Instead, under federal law, the prosecution of such violations must take place in federal court and is at the sole discretion of federal officials. See 8 U.S.C. § 1329. * * *

In *Arizona*, the Court emphasized that "[a] principle feature of the [INA's] removal system is the broad discretion exercised by immigration officials." "Federal officials . . . must decide whether it makes sense to pursue removal at all [and,] [i]f removal proceedings are commenced, [whether] aliens may seek . . . discretionary relief allowing them to remain in the country or at least to leave without formal removal." Yet, by prohibiting the only realistic housing option many aliens have, Hazleton is clearly trying to prohibit unauthorized aliens from living within the City. As we explained in *Lozano II*, the housing provisions, in effect, constitute an attempt to remove persons from the City based entirely on a snapshot of their current immigration status. Accordingly, the housing provisions interfere with the federal government's discretion in deciding whether and when to initiate removal proceedings. See *Lozano II*, 620 F.3d at 221–22.[26]

---

[26] In *Keller v. City of Fremont*, 719 F.3d 931 (8th Cir. 2013), a divided panel of the Court of Appeals for the Eighth Circuit has recently concluded that a local ordinance, almost identical to the housing provisions in the RO and IIRAO, does not interfere with federal removal discretion. The majority reasoned that the "rental provisions would only indirectly effect 'removal' of any

Indeed, interference with the federal removal process and the discretion entrusted to the Executive Branch are key reasons for the Supreme Court's conclusions that § 6 and § 3 of Arizona's S.B. 1070 law are conflict pre-empted. The Court reached that conclusion even though neither provision purports to physically remove any aliens from Arizona or the United States. In affirming an injunction against § 6, which would have given Arizona police authority to arrest an individual based on probable cause to believe the individual has committed a removable offense, the Court determined that the provision "would allow the State to achieve its own immigration policy," which could result in "unnecessary harassment of some aliens . . . whom federal officials determine should not be removed." The Court also found that "[b]y authorizing state officers to decide whether an alien should be detained for being removable, § 6 violates the principles that the removal process is entrusted to the discretion of the Federal Government." Similarly, in invalidating § 3, which criminalized failure to carry an alien registration document in violation of federal law, the Court noted that, in addition to intruding on a field occupied by Congress, the provision also conflicts with federal law because it would give Arizona the power to act "even in circumstances where federal officials . . . determine that prosecution would frustrate federal policies."

The same infirmities are evident here. Like the preempted provisions in *Arizona*, the housing provisions constitute an attempt to unilaterally attach additional consequences to a person's immigration status with no regard for the federal scheme, federal enforcement priorities, or the discretion Congress vested in the Attorney General. Congress has not banned persons who lack lawful status or proper documentation from obtaining rental or any other type of housing in the United States. Hazleton's decision to impose this "distinct, unusual and extraordinary burden[ ] . . . upon aliens" impermissibly intrudes into the realm of federal authority. *Hines [v. Davidowitz]*, 312 U.S. [52] at 65–66 [(1941)]. Through the housing provisions, Hazleton is seeking to achieve "its own immigration policy," one which will certainly result in "unnecessary harassment of some aliens . . . whom federal officials determine should not be removed." *Arizona*, 132 S. Ct. at 2506. Hazleton may not unilaterally prohibit those lacking lawful status from living within its boundaries, without regard for the Executive Branch's enforcement and policy priorities. "If every other state enacted similar legislation to

---

alien from the City," in a manner comparable to how "denying aliens employment inevitably has the effect of 'removing' some of them from the State." We disagree. Restricting housing touches directly on residency and federal removal discretion. As we explained in *Lozano II*, "[i]t is difficult to conceive of a more effective method of ensuring that persons do not enter or remain in a locality than by precluding their ability to live in it." The Eighth Circuit also concluded that the rental restrictions do not determine who should or should not be admitted into the country and do not conflict with federal anti-harboring law. For the reasons explained above, we disagree with these conclusions as well.

overburden the lives of aliens, the immigration scheme would be turned on its head." *United States v. Alabama*, 691 F.3d at 1295 n.21. Accordingly, the housing provisions conflict with federal law.

In addition to undermining the comprehensive procedures under which federal officials determine whether an alien may remain in this country, Hazleton's housing provisions would create significant foreign policy and humanitarian concerns. As the Court in *Arizona* emphasized, federal decisions in this arena "touch on foreign relations and must be made with one voice." "One of the most important and delicate of all international relationships . . . has to do with the protection of the just rights of a country's own nationals when those nationals are in another country." "It is fundamental that foreign countries concerned about the status, safety, and security of their nationals in the United States must be able to confer and communicate on this subject with one national sovereign, not the 50 separate states." * * *

Despite the obvious trespass into matters that must be left to the national sovereign, the City continues to insist there is no conflict preemption because it is merely engaging in "concurrent enforcement" of federal immigration laws. Under that theory, virtually any local jurisdiction could prohibit activity that is also prohibited by federal law as long as the local prohibition is not expressly pre-empted and the locality is not acting in a field that is occupied by federal law. * * * [T]he City's argument simply cannot be reconciled with the Supreme Court's holding in *Arizona*. There, the Court reasoned that "[a]lthough § 5(C) attempts to achieve one of the same goals as federal law—the deterrence of unlawful employment—it involves a conflict in the method of enforcement." The Court went on to explain that it had previously "recognized that a [c]onflict in technique can be fully as disruptive to the system Congress enacted as conflict in overt policy." Thus, the Court found § 5(C) preempted even though the provision imposed sanctions only on conduct already prohibited under federal law.

Furthermore, it must be remembered that the housing provisions are not "concurrent" with federal law, despite Hazleton's argument to the contrary. * * * Although the Supreme Court has yet to define "harboring" as that term is used in 8 U.S.C. § 1324(a)(1)(A)(iii), we have found that culpability requires some act of concealment from authorities. * * * Renting an apartment in the normal course of business is not, without more, conduct that prevents the government from detecting an alien's unlawful presence. Thus, it is highly unlikely that renting an apartment to an unauthorized alien would be sufficient to constitute harboring in violation of the INA. * * *

As we have explained, the RO requires those seeking to occupy rental housing to register with the City and obtain an occupancy permit. To obtain an occupancy permit, the applicant need only pay the requisite registration fee and submit the name and address of the prospective occupant, the name of the landlord, the address of the rental unit, and "proof of legal citizenship and/or residency." As the City itself points out, under the terms of the RO alone, all applicants are issued an occupancy permit upon providing the required information and the requisite fee— even if the applicant indicates that she lacks legal status. Those who occupy rental housing without complying with this registration scheme are subject to fines of $100 to $300, or imprisonment for up to 90 days in default of payment. Thus, the rental registration scheme of the RO standing alone operates as a requirement that a subset of Hazleton's population—those residing in rental housing—register their immigration status with the City.

It is beyond dispute that states and localities may not intrude in the field of alien registration. Thus, in *Arizona*, the Supreme Court found pre-empted § 3 of Arizona's S.B. 1070 law, which forbade "willful failure to complete or carry an alien registration document" in violation of federal law. Hazleton's rental registration scheme similarly intrudes into the field of alien registration. One of the rental registration scheme's primary functions is to require rental housing occupants to report their immigration status to the City of Hazleton and penalize the failure to register and obtain an occupancy permit pursuant to that requirement. This attempt to create a local alien registration requirement is field pre-empted.

In arguing that the RO is nothing like an alien registration system, the City claims "the most notable difference" is that the RO applies equally to citizens and aliens alike while the federal Alien Registration Act applies only to noncitizens. We are not persuaded. It is highly unlikely that the local registration laws invalidated on field pre-emption grounds in *Hines* or *Arizona* would have been upheld if they applied to citizens and aliens alike. The RO's registration scheme cannot avoid pre-emption merely because it requires both citizens and noncitizens to declare their immigration status. * * *

Rick Su, Local Fragmentation as Immigration Regulation
47 Houston L. Rev. 367 (2010).

[B]oundary and membership controls at the national and local level are essentially joined. They are joined not simply because immigration and local government law occasionally intersect in operation or effect. Rather, the connection also lies in the fact that they can be understood as interdependent counterparts in the same regulatory scheme. * * * [T]he legal structure responsible for the fragmentation of our lived environment into segregated neighborhoods and differentiated communities can be understood as a second-order immigration regulation. It is a mechanism that allows for finer regulatory controls than those that can be implemented with the crude tools of boundary and membership controls at the national level. It also serves as a means by which, in the absence of a national consensus, the competing interests surrounding immigration can still be negotiated and reconciled on the ground. * * *

[I]t is not difficult to see how local spatial controls like zoning parallel our national immigration regime. Both rely on geographic jurisdictions and physical boundaries, and both act as organizational tools that create and maintain social and physical geography. To be sure * * * the manner in which local spatial controls operate is limited; they act mainly with regards to certain kinds of movement (those associated with residency) and against certain types of individuals (primarily on the basis of class, though in ways that are inextricably intertwined with race and ethnicity). But despite the multitude of accounts about the hardening of our national borders, it is important to note that, under even our most restrictive immigration regimes, they too operated in much the same way. While strict prohibitions limit the transnational movement of some, broad concessions are provided to accommodate the mobility of others. Moreover, the individuals who tend to be restricted at our national borders also tend to be ones most likely to face barriers and obstacles at the local and neighborhood level. In this respect, the two systems complement and map onto one another. * * *

It is noteworthy then, as Seymour Toll observed in his extensive history of municipal zoning in America, that "[t]he immigrant is in the fiber of zoning." Indeed, some of the earliest land-use restrictions to be employed at the local level were those enacted "to keep the Chinese out of 'American' neighborhoods." The facts behind cases like *Yick Wo v. Hopkins* and *Soon Hing v. Crowley* demonstrate how early municipal licensing and labor requirements for laundries were often imposed for the "purpose of compelling the subjects of China to quit and abandon their business and residence in the city and county and state." Other efforts, however, were more direct. Because Chinese launderers often lived in or above their shops, concern about laundries was often inseparable from alarm over Chinese residents. It is with this in mind that Los Angeles passed ordinances that regulated or outright prohibited the operation of laundries in certain districts, while Modesto, also in California, quite literally relegated them to the 'wrong' side of the track. Foregoing proxies altogether, the regulatory escalation peaked in San Francisco with the passage of the Bingham Ordinance, which specifically forbade any Chinese resident from locating, residing, or carrying on a business anywhere outside of a designated district.

Despite the persistence of municipal officials, few of these early restrictions survived judicial review; overt animus and explicit targeting made them vulnerable under the emerging equal protection jurisprudence. But the confluence of immigration and the development of local spatial controls did not end with these efforts. More recognizable forms of land use zoning—with their emphasis on land-and development-oriented restrictions—which initially sprouted in the West began to truly blossomed in the urban centers of the eastern seaboard and the burgeoning Midwest. Moreover, concerns about foreign immigration continued to be an important motivation.

Take, for example, the ordinance that is most often identified as the first comprehensive municipal zoning regime: a 1916 zoning plan passed by New York City that divided the city into several districts and imposed various height and use restrictions in each. Although concerns about the availability of sunlight for pedestrians and skylight for office buildings played a role, it was motivated in large part by alarm over the presence of immigrant factory workers in "native" districts. In other words, intimately tied to the concerns about skyscrapers was an "even more explosive land-use battle" between the retail merchants and their supplier on Fifth Avenue, where the "garment trades" newest manufacturing buildings arose close enough to the department stores to threaten retail property value and offend the stores' carriage-trade clientele, especially at the noon hour, when immigrant workers flooded the shopping district. Thus, for the Fifth Avenue Association that formed to lobby for comprehensive zoning in New York, concerns about factories and specific types of land-use were never far from their concerns that their sidewalks were "becoming increasingly jammed with immigrant, lower-class, foreign-speaking workers."

Similar concerns can also be seen in the rise of the suburbs, and the subsequent inter-municipal fragmentation that became the basis of the modern metropolitan form. By the turn of the twentieth century, immigrants were already disproportionately concentrated in the central city. And notwithstanding the promise of zoning in dividing neighborhoods, it was clear that "as American cities swelled with a new immigrant population, the single-class elite residential district" that many natives sought were increasingly "incompatible with the urban core." As a consequence, not long after zoning was first introduced with the endorsement of the National League of Cities and the federal government, local spatial controls like zoning were not only embraced for its ability to parse an existing community into separate districts with the hopes of buffering "native" neighborhoods from immigrants. When applied broadly and uniformly across an entire community, it could serve to stifle inter-municipal migration as well. * * *

[T]he City of New York's effort to zone out immigrant laborers working on Fifth Avenue at the turn of the twentieth century was not intended as an effort to stop immigration, and thus never translated into a broader campaign for immigration restrictions. Indeed, notwithstanding the tension between the Fifth Avenue store owners and the immigrant garment workers they sought to exclude, they also shared a unique relationship: the livelihood of the former depended on the labor and goods supplied by the latter. Thus, unlike the broad stroke of federal immigration reform, municipal zoning offered Fifth Avenue storeowners a finer brush with which to balance their need for immigrant labor and aversion to their presence. And there are signs that a similar negotiation is at work in today. The controversy over immigrant residency in suburban enclaves can be seen as an attempt to utilize local boundaries to navigate their ambivalent relationship with immigrants as neighbors and immigrants as workers: that fact that "the new immigrants challenge[ ] the suburban image while their labor helps to preserve and enhance it."
* * *

One of the earliest cases to deal with the issue of contemporary illegal immigration, the Supreme Court in *Plyler [v. Doe]* was asked to decide whether the Equal Protection Clause prevents the State of Texas from denying illegal immigrants the right to obtain a free public education in its local schools. In rejecting the plaintiff's call for strict scrutiny, the Court refused to recognize access to free public education as a fundamental right and declined to accept illegal status as a suspect classification. Nevertheless, in a divided 5–4 opinion, the Court still struck down this provision of the Texas Educational Code as unconstitutional. Noting the relative innocence of the undocumented children involved in this case who, unlike their parents, had no direct control over their presence in this country, and the importance of education in ensuring that no permanent under-caste develops in our egalitarian constitutional order, the court applied heightened scrutiny and found the state's justifications for its prohibition lacking.

The *Plyler* decision is traditionally seen as an attempt to negotiate the confusion that dominates the judicial and political debates over the issue of illegal immigration. On the one hand, in refusing to treat undocumented immigrants as a suspect class, it reinforces the importance of legal statuses in a nation governed by the rule of law. On the other hand, the Court was well aware of the fact that undocumented immigrants are embedded in the social and economic fabric of our society, and will likely remain a part indefinitely. As a result, the Court's decision was both pragmatic and idealistic—it employed traditional doctrinal standards, but did so in a controversial manner to realize broader constitutional norms: "The Equal Protection Clause was intended to work nothing less than the abolition of all caste-based and invidious class-based legislation. . . . The existence of . . . an underclass presents most difficult problems for a Nation that prides itself on adherence to principles of equality under law." Thus, in rejecting the State's effort to preserve "the state's limited resources for the education of its lawful residents," *Plyler* stands as an affirmation of the membership of illegal immigrants in our overarching community, and the responsibility that we all have to ensure an educational opportunity of all our children.

But how extensive is this obligation? And, more importantly, how extensive is the "we"? Standing alone, *Plyler* seems to signify a high watermark for both immigrant protections and the anti-caste principles of the Equal Protection Clause. Yet *Plyler* was not the first time that the Court addressed a constitutional challenge to provisions of the Texas Educational Code. Eight years earlier in *San Antonio School District v. Rodriuguez*, the Court denied an Equal Protection challenge against the state's education funding scheme, which contributed to dramatically uneven funding outcomes for schools located in different geographic districts. Nor was *Plyler* the last. Just one year later, the Court in *Bynum v. Martinez* denied a challenge to a provision of Texas's education code that denied free public education to children whose parents did not have residency in the local school district and whose presence in the district was for the primary purpose of attending school. Seen alongside *Rodriguez* and *Bynum*, *Plyler* appears neither as promising as many of its advocates celebrated, nor as costly as its critics contended. Indeed, what these cases illustrate is that even while the Court was willing to undermine the symbolic sanctity of the national polity by extending its scope to include those who have been purposefully excluded, it was only willing to do so after preserving the divisions across local communities.

Consider first how the holding of *Rodriguez* complicates both the promise and the principles of *Plyler*. In *Rodriguez*, Mexican-American parents initiated a class action on behalf of poor students residing in communities with low property tax base. * * * Rejecting plaintiffs attempt to portray the case as one about discrimination against the "poor" or an identifiable suspect class, and holding that access to education is not a fundament right, the Court dismissed the Equal Protection challenge in a divided 5 to 4 decision that found the state's funding scheme to be rationally related to a compelling state interest. * * * If the holding of *Plyler* secured the right of alien children to receive free public education irrespective of their status, *Rodriguez* ensured that they had no claim upon any community outside of the local political jurisdiction which they resided. Similarly, if an underlying message of *Plyler* was that the importance of education to our republic obligated us as a polity to collectively provide such a service as a public good, even to those who do not have formal membership in such a polity, *Rodriguez* affirms the practice of avoiding such obligations by defining oneself as being a part of a separate community, albeit on the local level. * * *

Of course, *Rodriguez* is only one of *Plyler*'s bookends. The other, decided one term after *Plyler*, was *Martinez v. Bynum*. * * * At one level, *Bynum* echoes *Rodriguez* in affirming the degree to which local communities are not only allowed, but expected to prefer its residents over the claims of outsiders. As the *Bynum* Court held, a "bona fide residence requirement, appropriately defined and uniformly applied, furthers the substantial state interest in assuring that services provided by residents are enjoyed only by residents." In the Court's view, to ignore or reject this interest not only impinges on state and local autonomy, but "there can be little doubt that the proper planning and operation of the schools would suffer significantly." At another level, however, the Court's ruling on local residency in *Bynum* is directly tied to issues at the heart of *Plyler*. Because of Morales's unique situation, the Court's decision was not simply about the integrity of the boundaries around the McAllen school district, or even that of the State of Texas. At issue was also the effect that this local residency requirement has on transnational migration and the rights and privileges of national citizenship. Indeed, the challenged provision in *Bynum* was a part of immigration stemming efforts at issue in *Plyler*. As the district court found, "[a]t least one of the legislative purposes behind § 21.031(d) was to inhibit the migration of persons residing in Mexico to attend schools in the United States"; and the Supreme Court specifically quoted the district court's finding that the adverse impacts of invalidating § 21.031(d) would not only be "overcrowded classrooms and related facilities," but also because it would require the "expansion of bilingual programs."

Read alongside *Plyler*, the result in *Bynum* appears surprising. Under *Plyler*, an undocumented child with no legal right to reside in the court and subject to removal cannot be denied free access to a public school in the jurisdiction where he and his parents reside. Under *Bynum*, however, an American citizen child can be foreclosed from attending any public school in the United States because his parents are unable to secure residency in a local community. Indeed, the import of *Bynum* can be seen as going even further than just the deprivation of educational opportunities; because of the vital role that education plays in American society and the almost universal adoption of similar residency requirements in localities across the nation, this deprivation could be seen as constituting a de facto exclusion of an American citizen from residing in the United States altogether.

But if we begin, as we did here, with *Rodriguez*, the result of *Bynum* is not so much an affront to the commitments of *Plyler* or the guarantees of citizenship, but rather an important clarification of their limits. * * * The Court specifically rejected Texas's argument in *Plyler* that it can deny free public education to undocumented students in order to save limited state resources for "its" residents. At the same time, the ability of localities to favor residents over outsiders was embraced as one of the primary reasons why McAllen school district's denial. In short, *Plyler* alone tells only one part of the overall story. It reveals only a small slice of how local government laws were structured to target immigrants and regulate immigration, and it provides only a small window of the overall immigration regime at work. When *Plyler* is seen alongside *Rodriguez* and *Bynum*, however, the reach and consequence of the Court's decision put into proper context. The important point is that, in the end, all three cases were essentially about the same thing: controlling cross-border and cross-community flows. To be sure, some of the efforts were directed at the national border while others were directed at local boundaries, and consequently the Court employed different adjudicatory tools in their analysis. Nevertheless, seen in the context presented above, it is not entirely clear that one is as conceptually or legally different from the others as is commonly assumed. * * *

By positing local fragmentation as a component of our immigration regime, we have come to a more expansive vision of how different tiers of regulatory controls interact in the context of immigration. But this fragmentation describes a particular form of spatial, communal, and institutional organization. * * * There are * * * consequences to using fragmentation in this manner, and we would do well to recognize some of these in considering the role of fragmentation in immigration policies going forward. Indeed, for all that it pays off by enabling short-term compromises, it also extracts in long-term costs. * * *

First, it is important to recognize that opposition to immigration is often as much a distributional issue as it is one of prejudice or cultural anxiety. What I mean is that alongside the native-immigrant conflict, or even the national-local divide, there is also an inter-local dimension centered on how the relative benefits and burdens of immigration are allocated among communities, many of which view each other as both neighbors and competitors. It is no wonder then that tensions most often arise in inner-city neighborhoods or poor rural towns, many of which feel that they have the most to lose and the least options to accommodate or withstand change relative to what they perceive to be their peers. Indeed, even when opposition coalesces in more affluent suburban communities, it often arises from feelings that their community is being asked to absorb the impact of immigration to a degree that is disproportionate from what is being asked of even more exclusive neighbors in the region. Some of the most forceful arguments against immigration have been in the name of protecting what many perceive to be the most vulnerable communities. Yet this inequitable distribution of benefits and burdens is not only the very basis upon which our immigration regime may have been set up, it is also a direct consequence of how local fragmentation has been orchestrated through the use of legal and social mechanisms of control. In this respect, to the extent that fragmentation stifles opposition to immigration in certain respects, it is also responsible for exacerbating inter-local tensions that in turn produces other grounds for opposition that are directly tied to the differentiation that fragmentation employs.

Second, local fragmentation has implications for how we assess the promise of assimilation. At the most basic level, it is because the exclusion and insularity that fragmentation breeds stifles the interpersonal interactions and institutional exposure that is often associated with the assimilation process. But it also because local fragmentation itself sets up an internal tension in the very idea of assimilation itself that is hard to unravel. Assimilation, however defined, requires a model—a particular target toward which assimilation is directed. The fact that this model is malleable and varies over *time* has led many to see assimilation as a historical process involving not only changes among immigrant groups, but also concurrent shifts in how the dominant "culture" is defined. But the "target" of assimilation also varies across *space*; certain communities as opposed to others are often considered to be more exemplary, more mainstream, more "American." And that privilege is maintained not only by the characteristics of that community itself or of those who reside there, but also how that community holds itself in opposition to neighboring localities or even alternatives that have yet to be realized. Thus if fragmentation stifles assimilation by drawing dividing lines, those lines also define the parameters of what we consider to be successful assimilation— parameters in which the end-goal of assimilation in the spatial context may necessarily be that which is defined by exclusion and thus cannot legitimately be reached. This is not to say that immigrants do not assimilate, or that the American mainstream has not been subject to revisions. But it does illustrate one reason why even if assimilation appears to be fluid and inevitable from a historical perspective, the process always appears to be on the brink of collapse at any given time; whereas space is effaced through the luxury of hindsight, its destabilizing role is brought into stark focus when we assess the state of the process looking forward.

Third, the effect of local fragmentation on local decision-making has direct consequences for how national decisions over immigration are reached. Of the many controversial arguments that Peter Brimelow makes in Alien Nation, his now famous exhortation of American immigration policy, the one he emphasizes the most is his claim that our current system is undemocratic. On this general point, I agree. Where we diverge is that while Brimelow takes it as a given from simplistic polling data that the vast majority of Americans simply want less immigration, I believe the actual sentiment on the ground is a lot more diverse and fractured. Another problem with fragmentation then is that although it allows for a certain degree of negotiating these competing interests, as an institutional structure it is ill-suited to foster the type of broad-ranging discourse that immigration, in all its layered complexity, requires. It is not that participatory democracy is not viable or useful in small-scale settings of fractured communities. Rather, it is that the manner in which we've structured the relationship between these communities, especially the emphasis that we've placed on boundaries and membership, foster a defensive posture centered on avoidance and non-confrontation rather than genuine engagement, however cautious or reluctant that may be. Stated in the language of Albert Hirschman's seminal study of organizations, the type of fragmentation that now typifies American society is structured around "exit" rather than "voice." And as a pivotal basis of our nation's overall response to immigration, it is not surprising that the effect of this manner of organizing our lived environment is also reflected in how we define the imaginary community of the nation-state through our immigration policies.

In short, just as ignoring or denying the relevance of the local leads to an incomplete picture of our immigration regime, broadly denouncing or wholly accepting the role of fragmentation is also too cursory an approach. How it influences immigration is multifaceted and complex, and thus the manner in which we address fragmentation as an immigration issue should be equally aware and refined. Fragmentation of some sort may prove too valuable or useful an organizing tool to jettison wholesale. But we need not accept the particular form of fragmentation that has arisen either. Just as it is the case with our formal admission criteria and removal standards, any approach to our fragmentation policy will ultimately lie in the details: how we address the exclusionary consequences of fragmentation while enabling communities of distinction and self-determination, how we balance desires for efficiency and proficiency with a genuine commitment to participatory democracy, how we ensure a measure of distributive justice while giving effect to individual choice. The fact that a great deal of possibilities lies in how we define the significance of space and membership, and the institutional consequences of dividing lines, provides much room for innovative proposals. From a solely local outlook, reforms ranging from regional councils and inter-local proportional voting aimed at transforming individual perception and affiliation on the one hand, to large-scale county consolidation and neighborhood-level decentralization targeting distributional inequalities and institutional responsiveness on the other have been proposed. If, as suggested here, neither the role of the local nor, more particularly, the purpose of fragmentation lends itself to easy characterization, then we would do well to incorporate similar efforts in the broader discourse on the slow and continuous process of immigration reform as well. * * *

G. CITIZENS' ABILITY TO INFLUENCE CITY POLICY THROUGH VOTING

We have thus far considered the relationship between cities and their residents by examining the various purposes for which cities are organized—to protect a community's character, to deliver necessary services, or to provide fun and pleasure to residents. We now consider the law that governs how citizens may influence the policy choices that cities may make with respect to these matters.

There are a number of informal ways that citizens might be understood to affect city policy choices. As the excerpts in Chapter One from Charles Tiebout and James Buchanan contend, one way might be the choice to live in a city or to leave it. Another might be through decisions concerning where to work or to spend one's money: will it be in a business in the city or outside of it and, if it is in the city, in what neighborhood? Citizens might influence city policy as well through their decisions concerning city services. Will they send their children to a public school or a private one and, if private, will it be within the city's boundaries or outside of them? If there is a city park or library, will residents use it or permit it to fall into disrepair? If there is a public transportation system, will residents choose to drive less as a consequence? Citizens might also attempt to influence policy by protesting city decisions, or they might choose not to oppose city decisions that others might find objectionable. Political organization would not necessarily have to take the form of a campaign that would lead to votes being cast for city officials or on referendum questions. It might instead take the form of lobbying, demonstrations, or resistance on the streets. In fact, cities have long been the locus for some of the most dramatic instances of civil unrest.

In the subsections that follow, we address only the most familiar, formal way in which citizens may attempt to influence city policy: through the exercise of their right to vote. Voting is a very important means of influencing a city's governing decisions, and the way that the law defines and limits the ability of people to vote has powerful consequences for the kinds of policy choices that cities make. The first subsection investigates the extent of citizens' ability to control governmental policy by exercising their power to vote for city officials; in the next subsection, we examine their power to formulate city policy through an initiative or a referendum. A key question to keep in mind in readings these materials concerns who should decide the voting rules that apply to cities. Are cities themselves well-suited to decide such matters or does it make sense for a higher level of government to make the choice? If so, are states or the federal government better positioned to decide voting rules for cities?

1. VOTING EQUALITY

Our inquiry into the subject of voting begins with Avery v. Midland County, the case that extended to local governments the principle of one person/one vote originally announced for state legislatures in Reynolds v. Sims, 377 U.S. 533, 84 S.Ct. 1362, 12 L.Ed.2d 506 (1964). As Justice Harlan's dissent in *Avery* and subsequent cases suggest, applying the one person/one vote principle to local governments achieves "voter equality" only if one understands citizens simply as individuals rather than in terms of their identities as members of different groups. Yet voters often experience city politics—and their own voting—in terms of a division along racial, political or neighborhood lines (and, in county elections, along city/suburban lines as well). Although every individual has an equal vote under the one person/one vote formula, people can nevertheless think that even under this formula they and people like them (Blacks or Republicans or small town residents) will never have the voting strength to influence governmental policy. The following cases and materials concentrate on this question of group disenfranchisement.[52] The Supreme Court has dealt with the issue of group disenfranchisement in a variety of contexts: the minority group has been understood in geographical, political, and racial terms.[53] As the Note on Groups and Voting Equality describes, a key dispute in formulating local voting rules concerns whether each official of the city's legislative body should be elected at-large, and thus by the electorate as a whole, or district-by-district, and thus only by residents of their discrete neighborhood. The article on District Elections in San Francisco describes the potential advantages and disadvantages of the two approaches. It emphasizes the differences between the two systems in terms of the political results, but, as the Note describes, there can be a differences in terms of race as well. After the

---

[52] See, e.g., Kenneth Stahl, Local Government, "One Person, One Vote," and the Jewish Question, 49 Harv. C.R.-C.L. L. Rev. 1 (2014); Daryl Levinson, Rights and Votes, 121 Yale L.J. 1286 (2012); Anthony Thompson, Unlocking Democracy: Examining the Collateral Consequences of Mass Incarceration on Black Political Power, 54 How. L.J. 587 (2011); Adam Cox and Richard Holden, Reconsidering Racial and Partisan Gerrymandering, 78 U. Chi. L. Rev. 553 (2011); Sheryll D. Cashin, Democracy, Race, and Multiculturalism in the Twenty-First Century: Will the Voting Rights Act Ever be Obsolete? 22 Wash. U. J.L. & Pol'y 71 (2006); Pamela Karlan, Exit Strategies in Constitutional Law: Lessons for Getting the Least Dangerous Branch Out of the Political Thicket, 82 B.U. L. Rev. 667 (2002); David Cannon, Race, Redistricting, and Representation: The Unintended Consequences of Black Majority Districts (1999); David Lublin, The Paradox of Representation: Racial Gerrymandering and Minority Interests in Congress (1997); Pamela Karlan and Daryl Levinson, Why Voting Is Different, 84 Calif. L. Rev. 1201 (1996).

[53] See, e.g., Board of Estimate v. Morris, 489 U.S. 688, 109 S.Ct. 1433, 103 L.Ed.2d 717 (1989) (geography); Vieth v. Jubelirer, 541 U.S. 267, 124 S.Ct. 1769, 158 L.Ed.2d 546 (2004) (politics); Bush v. Vera, 517 U.S. 952, 116 S.Ct. 1941, 135 L.Ed.2d 248 (1996) (race).

Note, an article by Lani Guinier, which emphasizes the racial impact, describes an alternative to both at-large and district representation: proportional representation.

"[T]he spectre of proportional representation," as Professor Sanford Levinson has argued, haunts the discussion of the issue of group representation in political life.[54] The term "proportional representation" is often invoked (pejoratively) to mean the claim that every group should have a right to elect representatives in proportion to the group's percentage of the city's population. Defenders of proportional representation, however, do not define the concept in this way. As a matter of democratic theory, proportional representation simply means an electoral system characterized by elections in which seats are allocated in proportion to the number of votes received by those running for office. One form of proportional representation, for example, allows each voter to cast as many votes as there are positions to be filled in the city council. Because those who receive the largest number of votes win the available positions, members of minority groups are able to give all their votes to "their" candidate and thereby help ensure his or her election. Lani Guinier's article offers an argument for this version of proportional representation. An alternative version, adopted for city elections in Cambridge, Massachusetts, allows each voter to vote for as many candidates as s/he chooses as long as s/he lists them in order of preference; a minority candidate can win an election if s/he receives a sufficient number of "Number 1" votes. In both of these schemes, the "minority" group one chooses to identify oneself with is selected in the process of voting. Would one of these voting plans (or some similar scheme) better protect "minority" voices than the Constitutional tests announced in cases decided to date by the Supreme Court? Or would such a plan lead to an undesirable splintering of city politics?[55]

---

[54] Sanford Levinson, Commentary: Gerrymandering and the Brooding Omnipresence of Proportional Representation: Why Won't It Go Away? 33 U.C.L.A. L. Rev. 257 (1985).

[55] For discussions of these and related issues, see, e.g., Nicholas Stephanopoulos, Our Electoral Exceptionalism, 80 U. Chi. L. Rev. 769 (2013); Richard Engstrom, Cumulative and Limited Voting: Minority Electoral Opportunities and More, 30 St. Louis U. Pub. L. Rev. 97 (2010); Developments in the Law, Voting and Democracy, 119 Harv. L. Rev. 1127 (2006); Heather K. Gerken, Second-Order Diversity, 118 Harv. L. Rev. 1099 (2005); Richard Pildes, The Constitutionalization of Democratic Politics, 118 Harv. L. Rev. 28 (2004); Samuel Issacharoff, Pamela Karlan, and Richard Pildes, The Law of Democracy: Legal Structure of the Political Process 713–784 (1998); Paul McKaskle, Of Wasted Votes and No Influence: An Essay on Voting Systems in The United States, 35 Hous. L. Rev. 1119 (1998); David Farrell, Comparing Electoral Systems (1997); Pamela Karlan, Maps and Misreadings: The Role of Geographic Compactness in Racial Vote Dilution Litigation, 24 Harv. C.R.-C.L. L. Rev. 173 (1989); Peter Schuck, The Thickest Thicket: Partisan Gerrymandering and Judicial Regulation of Politics, 87 Colum. L. Rev. 1325, 1361–77 (1987); Arend Lijphart and Bernard Grofman (eds.), Choosing an Electoral System: Issues and Alternatives (1984); John Low-Beer, The Constitutional Imperative of Proportional Representation, 94 Yale L.J. 163 (1984); Akhil Amar, Choosing Representatives by Lottery Voting, 93 Yale L.J. 1283 (1984); Vernon Bogdanor and David Butler (eds.), Democracy and Elections: Electoral Systems and Their Political Consequences (1983).

This subsection concludes with an excerpt from an article by Jamin Raskin. Raskin reminds us that, no matter which voting scheme is adopted, some city residents remain disenfranchised in almost every city in America. He presents an argument for enfranchising one such group: residents aliens. Should aliens be entitled to vote in city elections? Is alien suffrage more appropriate for city elections than for state or federal elections?

AVERY V. MIDLAND COUNTY
Supreme Court of the United States, 1968.
390 U.S. 474, 88 S.Ct. 1114, 20 L.Ed.2d 45.

MR. JUSTICE WHITE delivered the opinion of the Court.

Petitioner, a taxpayer and voter in Midland County, Texas, sought a determination by this Court that the Texas Supreme Court erred in concluding that selection of the Midland County Commissioners Court from single-member districts of substantially unequal population did not necessarily violate the Fourteenth Amendment. We granted review because application of the one man, one vote principle of Reynolds v. Sims, 377 U.S. 533, 84 S.Ct. 1362, 12 L.Ed.2d 506 (1964), to units of local government is of broad public importance. We hold that petitioner, as a resident of Midland County, has a right to a vote for the Commissioners Court of substantially equal weight to the vote of every other resident. * * *

Although the forms and functions of local government and the relationships among the various units are matters of state concern, it is now beyond question that a State's political subdivisions must comply with the Fourteenth Amendment. The actions of local government are the actions of the State. A city, town, or county may no more deny the equal protection of the laws than it may abridge freedom of speech, establish an official religion, arrest without probable cause, or deny due process of law.

When the State apportions its legislature, it must have due regard for the Equal Protection Clause. Similarly, when the State delegates lawmaking power to local government and provides for the election of local officials from districts specified by statute, ordinance, or local charter, it must ensure that those qualified to vote have the right to an equally effective voice in the election process. If voters residing in oversize districts are denied their constitutional right to participate in the election of state legislators, precisely the same kind of deprivation occurs when the members of a city council, school board, or county governing board are elected from districts of substantially unequal population. If the five senators representing a city in the state legislature may not be elected from districts ranging in size from 50,000 to 500,000, neither is it permissible to elect the members of the city council from those same districts. In either case, the votes of some residents have greater weight than those of others; in both cases the equal protection of the laws has been denied.

That the state legislature may itself be properly apportioned does not exempt subdivisions from the Fourteenth Amendment. While state legislatures exercise extensive power over their constituents and over the various units of local government, the States universally leave much policy and decisionmaking to their governmental subdivisions. Legislators enact many laws but do not attempt to reach those countless matters of local concern necessarily left wholly or partly to those who govern at the local level. What is more, in providing for the governments of their cities, counties, towns, and districts, the States characteristically provide for representative government—for decisionmaking at the local level by representatives elected by the people. And, not infrequently, the delegation of power to local units is contained in constitutional provisions for local home rule which are immune from legislative interference. In a word, institutions of local government have always been a major aspect of our system, and their responsible and responsive operation is today of increasing importance to the quality of life of more and more of our citizens. We therefore see little difference, in terms of the application of the Equal Protection Clause and of the principles of Reynolds v. Sims, between the exercise of state power through legislatures and its exercise by elected officials in the cities, towns, and counties. * * *

MR. JUSTICE HARLAN, dissenting.

I could not disagree more with this decision. * * * There are convincing functional reasons why the Reynolds rule should not apply to local governmental units at all. The effect of Reynolds was to read a long debated political theory—that the only permissible basis for the selection of state legislators is election by majority vote within areas which are themselves equal in population—into the United States Constitution, thereby foreclosing the States from experimenting with legislatures rationally formed in other ways. Even assuming that this result could be justified on the state level, because of the substantial identity in form and function of the state legislatures, and because of the asserted practical necessities for federal judicial interference referred to above, the "one man, one vote" theory is surely a hazardous generalization on the local level. As has been noted previously, no "practical necessity" has been asserted to justify application of the rule to local governments. More important, the greater and more varied range of functions performed by local governmental units implies that flexibility in the form of their structure is even more important than at the state level, and that by depriving local governments of this needed adaptability the Court's holding may indeed defeat the very goals of Reynolds.

The present case affords one example of why the "one man, one vote" rule is especially inappropriate for local governmental units. The Texas Supreme Court held as a matter of Texas law:

> "Theoretically, the commissioners court is the governing body of the county and the commissioners represent all the residents, both urban and rural, of the county. But developments during the years have greatly narrowed the scope of the functions of the commissioners court and limited its major responsibilities to the nonurban areas of the county. It has come to pass that the city government * * * is the major concern of the city dwellers and the administration of the affairs of the county is the major concern of the rural dwellers."

Despite the specialized role of the commissioners court, the majority has undertaken to bring it within the ambit of Reynolds simply by classifying it as "a unit of local government with general responsibility and power for local affairs." Although this approach is intended to afford "equal protection" to all voters in Midland County, it would seem that it in fact discriminates against the county's rural inhabitants. The commissioners court, as found by the Texas Supreme Court, performs more functions in the area of the county outside Midland City than it does within the city limits. Therefore, each rural resident has a greater interest in its activities than each city dweller. Yet under the majority's formula the urban residents are to have a dominant voice in the county government, precisely proportional to their numbers, and little or no allowance may be made for the greater stake of the rural inhabitants in the county government.

This problem is not a trivial one and is not confined to Midland County. It stems from the fact that local governments, unlike state governments, are often specialized in function. Application of the Reynolds rule to such local governments prevents the adoption of apportionments which take into account the effect of this specialization, and therefore may result in a denial of equal treatment to those upon whom the exercise of the special powers has unequal impact. Under today's decision, the only apparent alternative is to classify the governmental unit as other than "general" in power and responsibility, thereby, presumably, avoiding application of the Reynolds rule. Neither outcome satisfies Reynolds' avowed purpose: to assure "equality" to all voters. The result also deprives localities of the desirable option of establishing slightly specialized, elective units of government, such as Texas' county commissioners court, and varying the size of the constituencies so as rationally to favor those whom the government affects most. * * *

Despite the majority's declaration that it is not imposing a "straitjacket" on local governmental units, its solution is likely to have other undesirable "freezing" effects on local government. One readily foreseeable example is in the crucial field of metropolitan government. A common pattern of development in the Nation's urban areas has been for the less affluent citizens to migrate to or remain within the central city, while the more wealthy move to the suburbs and come into the city only to work. The result has been to impose a relatively heavier tax burden upon city taxpayers and to fragmentize governmental services in the metropolitan area. An oft-proposed solution to these problems has been the institution of an integrated government encompassing the entire metropolitan area. In many instances, the suburbs may be included in such a metropolitan unit only by majority vote of the voters in each suburb. As a practical matter, the suburbanites often will be reluctant to join the metropolitan government unless they receive a share in the government proportional to the benefits they bring with them and not merely to their numbers. The city dwellers may be ready to concede this much, in return for the ability to tax the suburbs. Under the majority's pronouncements, however, this rational compromise would be forbidden: the metropolitan government must be apportioned solely on the basis of population if it is a "general" government.

These functional considerations reinforce my belief that the "one man, one vote" rule, which possesses the simplistic defects inherent in any judicially imposed solution of a complex social problem, is entirely inappropriate for determining the form of the country's local governments. * * *

NOTE ON GROUPS AND VOTING EQUALITY

A simple idea of democracy is reflected in the slogan "majority rule." But most democracies are not content to submit all questions to a simple majority vote. And for good reasons. Formal equality in a strictly majoritarian system can result in systematic unfairness: a durable faction of 50% plus one person could control all political contests, excluding almost half the population from any meaningful voice in public policy. Such a system would result in a tyranny of the majority in which minority groups with important concerns are systematically denied a meaningful opportunity to influence the political process.

Such concerns are not new: James Madison's description of the mischief of political factions is a critique of the potential tyranny of a local majority. The minority group Madison wanted to protect was property owners (hence his cautionary examples: the rage for paper money and abolition of debts) while today we might focus on racial minorities. But both concerns highlight the need for a political structure that advances popular sovereignty while protecting the interests of minorities, one that is democratic but not demagogic.

Many democracies have developed political systems that explicitly incorporate representation for minority political groups as groups—in effect providing members of those groups a significantly greater say in politics than they would receive in a strict "winner take all" majoritarian system. Indeed, the bicameral structure of the United States Congress is an example of such a system. Each state receives two votes in the upper house regardless of its population. This system allows each voting resident of a less populous state to exert more influence than each voter in a more populous state.

Even if we were not interested in protecting minority groups, formal equality of the vote is an ambiguous mandate in practice. The definition of meaningful equality in voting becomes especially difficult when one considers multi-member legislative bodies such as city councils, county boards of supervisors, state legislatures, and Congress. For example, a city council could elect its members in at least four ways, each consistent with the constitutional mandate of formal equality of the vote. A city could:

1.   Elect all councilors in city-wide elections in which all voting residents vote once for each open seat and the winner for each seat is selected by a simple majority or plurality vote.

2.   Divide the city into as many geographical districts of equal population as there are councilors and allow the residents of each district to elect "their" own councilor by simple majority or plurality vote.

3.   Elect all councilors in city-wide elections in which all voting residents rank the candidates and the most popular candidates fill the vacancies. This system requires a method of "weighing" the rankings—any such method will be potentially controversial.

4.   Elect all councilors in city-wide elections in which all voting residents may vote for each open seat in the following manner: Each voter "holds" a number of votes equal to the number of open seats. Each voter can then vote once in each race or may pool her votes in fewer races, voting multiple times for one candidate.

All four of these systems provide formal equality of the vote. Yet these four systems could produce radically different results in the same election. Consider a city with group polarized voting dynamics, an insular minority group that comprises 40% of the population and an equally insular 60% majority. The first system would guarantee a sweep for the majority group. The second system could insure some minority representation depending on the residential patterns of the two groups and the position of the district boundaries (it could also guarantee a sweep for the majority if the district boundaries were gerrymandered so as to split the minority vote). The third and fourth systems could provide for significant minority representation, depending on how the minority group members collectively ranked or pooled their votes. The question, then, is whether and to what extent the members of various groups are entitled to a political structure that maximizes their opportunity to influence the political process.

Several Supreme Court cases are relevant to a consideration of this question. In Board of Estimate v. Morris, 489 U.S. 688, 109 S.Ct. 1433, 103 L.Ed.2d 717 (1989), the Court addressed quantitative vote dilution—the requirement of mathematical equality of the vote. At issue was the method by which New York City elected members of one of its primary legislative bodies, the Board of Estimate. The Board of Estimate consisted of eight members: three elected city-wide plus the presidents of each of the city's five boroughs (who were elected by the residents of the boroughs). Because the boroughs had widely disparate populations yet had equal representation on the Board, a federal appeals court held that the structure was inconsistent with the Equal Protection Clause of the Fourteenth Amendment. The Supreme Court affirmed. The Court rejected New York's arguments that the Board as presently structured was essential to the government of a regional entity— the City of New York—and that it reflected natural and political boundaries between the boroughs. These interests, the Court held, could not justify a deviation from the principle of one person-one vote. The Court also declined the city's invitation to consider, not the mathematical equality of citizen votes, but the degree of influence any given citizen would have over the local political process as a whole. The Court noted that under Reynolds v. Sims the relevant inquiry is " 'whether the vote of any citizen is approximately equal to that of any other citizen.' "

The most vexed area of voting equality jurisprudence has involved racial minority groups who have causes of action for vote dilution under the Fourteenth and Fifteenth Amendments to the Constitution and the Voting Rights Act of 1965. In City of Mobile v. Bolden, 446 U.S. 55, 100 S.Ct. 1490, 64 L.Ed.2d 47 (1980), black voters from the City of Mobile, Alabama challenged an at-large electoral system for the selection of the city's multi-member governing body. The Mobile City Commission consisted of three members. Although blacks constituted 35.4% of the population of the city, no black had ever been elected to the Commission. The district court and court of appeals found Mobile's electoral system unconstitutional, noting that "[c]riticism [of multi member districts] is rooted in their winner-take-all aspects, their tendency to submerge minorities." The Supreme Court reversed, holding that multi-member districts violate the Constitution and the Voting Rights Act only if their purpose is to invidiously minimize or cancel out the voting potential of racial or ethnic minorities. "It is not enough to show that the group allegedly discriminated against has not elected representatives in proportion to their numbers. A plaintiff must prove that the disputed plan 'was conceived or operated as a purposeful device to further racial discrimination.' "

Responding to City of Mobile v. Bolden, Congress amended Section 2 of the Voting Rights Act in 1982. "Congress substantially revised Section 2," the Court said in Thornburg v. Gingles, 478 U.S. 30, 106 S.Ct. 2752, 92 L.Ed.2d

25 (1986), "to make clear that a violation [of Section 2] could be proven by showing discriminatory effect alone and to establish as the relevant legal standard the 'results test.'" In *Thornburg*, the Court held that a minority group must prove three elements to establish that the creation of a multimember district had a discriminatory effect and thus violated Section 2: that the minority group is large enough to constitute a majority in a single-member district; that it is politically cohesive; and that the white majority votes sufficiently as a bloc to enable it usually to defeat the minority's preferred candidate. Not until Holder v. Hall, 512 U.S. 874, 114 S.Ct. 2581, 129 L.Ed.2d 687 (1994), did the Court return to the issue it faced in City of Mobile v. Bolden: the use of an at-large electoral system, rather than single-district voting, to choose the members of a governing commission of a city or other local governmental entity.

In *Holder*, black voters from Bleckley County, Georgia, challenged under Section 2 the County's system of selecting all five members of its governing commission through an at-large election. Although blacks constituted 20% of the population of the county, no black person had ever run for or been elected to the office of Bleckley County Commissioner. The district judge, who himself had run for public office, declared that he "wouldn't run if [he] were black in Bleckley County." In a 5–4 decision, the Court held that plaintiffs could not maintain a Section 2 challenge to the at-large method of choosing the County Commission. Justices Kennedy and O'Connor and Chief Justice Rehnquist, in two separate opinions, grounded this result on statutory interpretation. Section 2, they said, was inapplicable to a dispute over what they called the "size of a governmental body"—that is, to the choice between county-wide at-large elections and single-member districting. A wide variety of single-member districting schemes could conceivably be adopted in Bleckley County, they said, and Section 2 provided no benchmark for determining which of them should be used as a comparison with an at-large election. Because there was no benchmark that would provide a basis for deciding the extent of minority vote dilution, they reasoned, the size of a government body, unlike legislative districting, was not subject to a vote dilution challenge under Section 2. The final two votes for the majority position were provided in a separate opinion by Justice Thomas, in which Justice Scalia concurred. Justice Thomas interpreted Section 2 much more narrowly than the plurality, reading it as limited solely to issues involving citizens' access to the ballot (such as voting qualifications). If accepted, Justice Thomas' interpretation would thus overrule all previous cases, such as *Thornburg*, that had interpreted Section 2 to permit a challenge of legislative districting on the grounds of minority vote dilution. In his opinion, Justice Thomas made the following argument against the Court's vote dilution jurisprudence:

> It should be clear that the assumptions that have guided the Court reflect only one possible understanding of effective exercise of the franchise, an understanding based on the view that voters are "represented" only when they choose a delegate who will mirror

their views in the legislative halls. But it is certainly possible to construct a theory of effective political participation that would accord greater importance to voters' ability to influence, rather than control, elections. And especially in a two-party system such as ours, the influence of a potential "swing" group of voters composing 10%–20% of the electorate in a given district can be considerable. * * * [T]here are undoubtedly an infinite number of theories of effective suffrage, representation, and the proper apportionment of political power in a representative democracy * * *. The matters the Court has set out to resolve in vote dilution cases are questions of political philosophy, not questions of law. As such, they are not readily subjected to any judicially manageable standards that can guide courts in attempting to select between competing theories.

But the political choices the Court has had to make do not end with the determination that the primary purpose of the "effective" vote is controlling seats or with the selection of single-member districting as the mechanism for providing that control. * * * Once one accepts the proposition that the effectiveness of votes is measured in terms of the control of seats, the core of any vote dilution claim is an assertion that the group in question is unable to control the "proper" number of seats—that is, the number of seats that the minority's percentage of the population would enable it to control in the benchmark "fair" system. The claim is inherently based on ratios between the numbers of the minority in the population and the numbers of seats controlled. * * * The ratio for which this Court has opted, and thus the mathematical principle driving the results in our cases, is undoubtedly direct proportionality. * * *

[T]he Court * * * accept[s] the one underlying premise that must inform every minority vote dilution claim: the assumption that the group asserting dilution is not merely a racial or ethnic group, but a group having distinct political interests as well. Of necessity, in resolving vote dilution actions we have given credence to the view that race defines political interest. We have acted on the implicit assumption that members of racial and ethnic groups must all think alike on important matters of public policy and must have their own "minority preferred" representatives holding seats in elected bodies if they are to be considered represented at all. * * * We have involved the federal courts, and indeed the Nation, in the enterprise of systematically dividing the country into electoral districts along racial lines—an enterprise of segregating the races into political homelands that amounts, in truth, to nothing short of a system of "political apartheid." * * * The assumptions upon which our vote dilution cases have been based should be repugnant to any nation that strives for the ideal of a color-blind Constitution. * * *

As a practical political matter, our drive to segregate political districts by race can only serve to deepen racial divisions by destroying any need for voters or candidates to build bridges between racial groups or to form voting coalitions. * * * In my view, our current practice should not continue. Not for another Term, not until the next case, not for another day. The disastrous implications of the policies we have adopted under the Act are too grave.* * * I can see no reasonable alternative to abandoning our current unfortunate understanding of the Act. * * *

Justices Stevens, Blackmun, Souter and Ginsburg dissented. They interpreted Section 2 to apply to the size of a local government body as well as to legislative districting. Since Congress had determined such a scope for Section 2, Justice Stevens declared, it would be "inappropriate" to comment on the portion of Justice Thomas' argument quoted above. The argument, according to Justice Stevens, is "best described as an argument that the statute be repealed or amended in important respects."

In reaction to the difficulties of vote dilution jurisprudence, the District Court for the District of Maryland turned away from geographic districting and imposed instead a voting plan based on cumulative voting. The district court preferred cumulative voting to race conscious districting as a remedy for a Section 2 violation because the former "is less likely to increase polarization between different interests," but at the same time "will allow the voters, by the way they exercise their votes, to 'district' themselves," potentially mimicking race conscious reapportionment if and when voters indeed have racially distinctive political interests. Cane v. Worcester County, 847 F.Supp. 369, 373 (D.Md.1994). The district court's imposition of cumulative voting was reversed on appeal. The Fourth Circuit Court of Appeals held that the district court had abused its discretion, not because cumulative voting was inherently improper but because "even when the legislative body fails to offer a remedy or its proposed remedy is legally unacceptable, the court, in exercising its discretion to fashion a remedy that complies with § 2, must to the greatest extent possible give effect to the legislative policy judgment underlying the current electoral scheme * * *." Cane v. Worcester County, 35 F.3d 921 (4th Cir.1994).

WADE CROWFOOT WITH DAVID BINDER, DISTRICT ELECTIONS IN SAN FRANCISCO
February, 2000 SPUR Newsletter.

This coming November, San Francisco politics will undergo dramatic transformation. The city will no longer elect members of the Board of Supervisors from citywide, at-large elections, but rather from district elections, in which voters choose one supervisor to represent their geographical district. District elections promise to redraw the political landscape of San Francisco. They will change the way that candidates run for the Board, the role that local organizations play in these elections, and ultimately how decisions are made in City Hall. * * *

The change to the district election system is actually a reintroduction of a system that was used to elect supervisors more than 20 years ago. The concept was first advocated in 1972 by a group of neighborhood associations, labor unions, and public leaders who contended that district elections would result in a more inclusive Board. As a result of this growing movement, voters passed a measure in 1976 to create a system of district elections. The first district elections were held in November 1977. These first district elections did in fact increase the diversity of the Board. San Francisco elected its first female African American supervisor, Ella Hill Hutch, its first Asian American supervisor, Gordon Lau, and its first openly gay supervisor, Harvey Milk. However, in that same election, Dan White became a supervisor. As many remember, after a political falling out, Supervisor White assassinated then-Mayor George Moscone and Supervisor Milk in November 1978.

District elections * * * were repealed by the voters in 1980. While other factors surely impacted the repeal of district elections, the tragic assassinations severely damaged the image of the district electoral system. More recently, in 1994, a citywide decision was made to reconsider the way that the Board of Supervisors is elected. By approving Proposition L in November of 1994, voters created an Elections Task Force that explored potential alternatives to electing the Board. This task force presented recommended alternatives to the Board of Supervisors, two of which the Board selected to put on the ballot in November 1996 for consideration by the voters. These two alternatives were district voting and "preference voting"—a complex system of ranking and reallocation of votes for each candidate.

In that 1996 election, San Francisco voters approved Proposition G, which reinstated district elections, and rejected Proposition H, which would have introduced the preference voting system. District elections, to be implemented in the year 2000, became city law. * * * Proposition G laid out a fairly straightforward process for electing members to the Board of Supervisors. The basic tenets of the new system include:

- District Boundaries: San Francisco is segmented into eleven districts. All districts had similar overall populations in the 1990 Census (between 60,000 and 65,000 people) as mandated by state and federal election law. District boundaries were drawn to keep neighborhoods united as much as possible.

- Run-offs: If no candidate receives a majority of the votes cast within a district, the two top vote-getters qualify for a run-off election. Run-offs will be held on the second Tuesday of December of that year.

- Terms of Office: Supervisors will generally serve four-year terms. However, in order to establish a staggered rotation of supervisors (five or six supervisors elected every two years), some district supervisors elected in 2000 will serve two-year terms, while others will serve four-year terms. The clerk of the Board will determine "by lot" whether supervisors representing even numbered districts or those representing odd numbered districts must run again in 2002.

- Term Limits: District supervisors will be limited to serving two four-year terms. The two-year term from 2000 to 2002 that some supervisors will serve does not count toward term limits.

- Board President: Supervisors shall by majority vote elect one board member as president for a two-year term. This is a significant change from the current system, in which the supervisor who received the highest number of votes in the last election serves as board president. * * *

Understanding the impact of district elections on local politics first requires a sense of electoral demographics in San Francisco. Most importantly, it is necessary to recognize the distinction between the city's overall residents, its registered voters, and its likely voters. Fewer than one-third of San Francisco residents actually voted in the most recent general election (in November 1999)—about 250,000 voters of almost 800,000 total residents. Residents who did not vote were either ineligible (under 18 or non-citizens), unregistered, or registered voters who simply did not participate in the election. Significant differences exist between the demographics of San Francisco's overall population and the demographics of citywide registered and likely voters. In short, San Francisco's likely voters tend to be older and more white than the overall population of the city. In other words, older residents and white residents are more likely to vote than younger residents and people of color living in San Francisco.

The significant differences that exist between the composition of the city's overall residents and actual voters suggests that political conclusions cannot necessarily be drawn about the city's districts based on the demographics of its overall population. In order to get a true sense of the composition of the electorate in the district, one must study the composition of the district's voters. * * * The liberal/progressive core in San Francisco consists of Districts 5, 6, 8, and 9. These districts are located in the geographic heart of the city and include large neighborhoods such as the Haight, Castro, Mission, Noe Valley and Bernal Heights. Although neighborhoods within these districts show varying support on specific issues and candidates, each of these districts can be considered solidly liberal/ progressive. These four districts are considered the core of the city's political left due to * * * their support for local and statewide measures considered liberal/progressive: pro-tenant, pro-taxation, pro-labor, and pro-environment. In contrast, these districts exhibit weak support for conservative or moderate candidates, as well as measures considered conservative/ moderate: tough-on-crime measures and those measures restricting homeless behavior. * * *

The moderate/conservative base in San Francisco consists of Districts 2, 4, and 7. These districts include the northernmost portion of the city (District 2) and the southwest region of the city (Districts 4 and 7). Well-recognized neighborhoods in these districts include the Marina, Pacific Heights, Sunset, West Portal, and Lakeshore/ St. Francis Wood. These three districts have exhibited relatively high support for conservative and moderate candidates (including Republicans) in the 1990s, and have exhibited support for measures considered moderate/conservative, including crime measures. In contrast, these districts exhibit weak support for measures considered liberal/progressive. * * *

Four districts in San Francisco can be considered "swing districts" due to their varying support for liberal/progressive or moderate/ conservative viewpoints depending on specific issues or candidates. These swing districts include 1, 3, 10 and 11. Well-recognized areas within these districts include northeast neighborhoods such as North Beach and Chinatown, and southern neighborhoods such as Excelsior, Visitacion Valley and Bayview Hunters Point, as well as the Richmond. Interestingly, many neighborhoods in these swing districts contain high proportions of ethnic minorities. This includes a high Asian population in Districts 1 and 3, as well as growing Asian and Latino populations in District 11, and an established African American population in District 10. * * *

After 20 years of at-large elections to select San Francisco's supervisors, district elections will surely change the way politics are practiced in this city. What is not clear is who will emerge as the winners and losers in this district election system. In the mid-1970s, district elections ended the near exclusive leadership of straight white males in City Hall and ushered in a Board of Supervisors whose composition reflected the diversity of the city. Twenty years later, no such problem exists in city government. As we enter into district elections, only one of the Board's current members is a straight white male.

One group that has arguably been underrepresented in City Hall, ideological conservatives, may see their fortunes rise. District 7, in particular, has the potential to elect a Republican supervisor, a scenario considered nearly unthinkable under the at-large system. Minor parties such as the Greens, as well as Independents, may also benefit from district elections. District 9 in particular is comprised of a relatively high number of Green and Independent voters. Moreover, Independent candidates have the potential to run increasingly viable campaigns as the historic power of citywide groups such as the local Democratic Party weaken in the presence of very localized campaigns.

One possible result of the district election system is that it will usher in an era of renewed grassroots participation in supervisorial campaigns. Already, a collection of fresh faces to the local political scene have lined up to run in the city's various districts, buoyed by the promise of low-cost campaigns (with expenditure limits) dominated by old-fashioned "face-to-face" politicking. Some of these candidates report being inspired by Tom Ammiano's recent low-cost bid for mayor. On the other hand, this style of campaigning may run into a brick wall of well-funded "independent expenditure" campaigns that proved so effective in the recent mayoral election.

A wide range of outcomes on local governance has been predicted in the era of district elections. Supporters of district-based representation suggest that it will increase accountability of supervisors to their constituents and create a local government that is more accessible to the average San Franciscan. In contrast, critics of the district-based system suggest that it will shift focus from the diverse and complex issues facing San Francisco to more insulated and parochial neighborhood concerns. Whether district elections will result in an era of open, more responsive government or one of isolated fiefdoms is fodder for endless debate. What will surely evolve is a new and unprecedented political geography in San Francisco.

San Francisco's experiment in local democracy continues—no one can say with great confidence what will occur in the coming district elections. One thing is for sure: it will be an exhilarating ride for San Francisco's body politic. * * *

LANI GUINIER, NO TWO SEATS: THE ELUSIVE QUEST FOR POLITICAL EQUALITY
77 U. Va. L. Rev. 1413, 1458, 1461–1475, 1487–1493 (1991).

I argue that we should redefine the unit of analysis [for claims of vote dilution] from fixed territorial constituencies to voluntary interest constituencies. * * * The term "interest" refers to self-identified interests, meaning those high salience needs, wants, and demands articulated by any politically cohesive group of voters. Interest representation emphasizes the importance of voter autonomy divorced from involuntary, fixed territorial constituencies. Using voting patterns, it measures as a politically cohesive group those voters who identify themselves with each other based on their own evaluation of their shared interests. As a statutory approach to vote dilution, interest representation measures the impact of electoral or voting rules on the legislative representation of self-identified minority voters' interests.

Interest representation attempts first to identify a violation of the right to a meaningful vote by locating politically cohesive minority interests that are submerged within winner-take-all voting structures. Interest representation identifies interest submergence by demonstrating the existence of alternative electoral systems that afford greater minority interest representation and satisfaction. Any such alternatives must recognize the intensity, as well as the existence, of minority voter preferences.

For example, in a 25% black jurisdiction with four at-large representatives, the current single-member districting model would assess the fairness of the election system against the potential representativeness of the alternative, a subdistricted system. The relative fairness of the at-large system would be challenged based on the assumption that black voters would be better represented if one majority-black district could be drawn. If blacks are numerous and concentrated enough to be a majority in one single-member district, the subdistricting strategy would use that district alternative to demonstrate the unfairness of the unmodified at-large system.

In contrast, an interest representation model would assess the fairness of the at-large system against the potential representativeness of an alternative voting system that allowed voters to cumulate their votes. I adopt a cumulative voting system because it permits recognition of both the existence and intensity of minority voter preference and allows strategic voting to enforce reciprocal coalitions. Cumulative voting modifies the at-large system to eliminate its winner-take-all characteristic.

In the modified at-large election, candidates would run jurisdiction-wide, but the threshold for election would be reduced from 51% to something less. In the case of a four person at-large council, the threshold for election would be 21%. Voters would each be given the same number of votes as open seats (four in this case) that they could distribute by their choice among the competing candidates. If black voters are a politically cohesive interest constituency, they might use all four of their votes on one candidate. In a 100 voter jurisdiction, where each black voter gave all four of her votes to one candidate, a 25% black minority could elect a representative. The intensity of their interests and their political cohesion would ensure black voters the ability to elect at least one representative.

When measured against the potential representativeness of an unmodified, winner-take-all at-large voting system at the election level, the cumulative voting system promises greater and more authentic black political representation. In addition, it offers the potential for greater black political power than the single-member districting model. The modified at-large system encourages black representation without disabling or diluting the votes of potential allies. By contrast, the single-member districting approach may require submerging Latino voters within majority-black districts or white Democratic voters within majority-white Republican districts.

Depending on strategic voting behavior, a modified at-large system could encourage coalitions of these voters to develop as a result of the choice of election system. Unlike the subdistricting model, the modified at-large system rewards cooperative, rather than competitive, behavior. Thus, interest representation offers black voters both the chance to elect candidates of their choice as well as the chance for their candidates to work in the legislature with potential legislative allies, trading votes to reflect the intensity of constituent preferences.

As an example, assume that in a jurisdiction with 1000 voters and 10 representatives, blacks are 25% of the population. A subdistrict plan provides roughly "proportionate representation" with 2 majority-black districts of 100 black voters each.

Although the subdistrict plan is a majoritarian approach, a bare majority of 51% in each district can elect a representative. The votes of 49 black voters in each district are unnecessary. In addition, of the 250 blacks in the jurisdiction, 50 of them are not "captured" in either majority-black district but are distributed randomly in the majority-white districts. They are potentially unrepresented in the governing body. Those blacks that are not geographically located in the two single-member districts are represented only "virtually," if at all.

Even more damaging, because only 51 blacks are needed to elect a representative, incumbent representatives may be able to control the electorate through political patronage, political contributions, and political control of the district lines. The black voters are not encouraged to participate actively in the political process because a low turnout still benefits the incumbent. Finally, the black voters in the two majority-black districts have no mechanism to encourage representatives from the majority-white districts virtually to represent their interests.

Whereas subdistricts reinforce authenticity and mobilization concerns by clearly removing black candidates from electoral competition with whites, as a matter of legitimacy a "winner-take-only-some," or interest representation, system actually ensures fewer disaffected voters than the subdistricted majority approach. It allows black voters and their representatives the opportunity to express the intensity of their preference for candidates and for legislative programs. Particular political transactions would depend not just on the number of supporters and opponents but on the relative intensity of preferences. This reflects the insight that if each electoral or legislative vote is insulated from every other, minority interests are consistently disadvantaged. Serial up or down voting permits "a cohesive, well financed majority community to reward itself with enhanced representation, if not outright monopoly" of representation.

In addition, the alternative, nonterritorial approach by its choice of voting arrangement encourages those minority voters or representatives whose votes are not needed to support a single candidate or a particular issue to join with sympathetic white voters to support progressive white candidates or to trade with them votes on issues of indifference. The necessity of strategic voting on salient issues may help identify and shape actual preferences, and coincidentally build cross-racial constituencies. Moreover, by disaggregating the majority, 51% of the people no longer control 100% of either the electoral or the legislative power. Thus, I would argue that the modified at-large, or interest representation, approach promises a more accountable and a more reciprocal voting system. * * *

Assuming for the moment that the approach taken by interest representation, if not better than single-member districts, at least effectively ensures black voter interest representation, the meaning of the term "interest" preference itself still requires further explication. My definition of interests refers to voluntary constituencies that self-identify their interests. Unlike a subdistricting system, interest submergence does not depend on a compulsory territorial constituency or on fixed interests. Rather, interest representation acknowledges the existence of intra-group differences as well as the importance of individual choice in choosing group affiliation. Interests, as expressed in group activity and identity, would be recognized in much the same way that geographic, territorial interests are traditionally thought to define distinct communities.

In other words, voluntary constituencies would be recognized to the extent they conceptually organize and attract sufficient numbers of like-minded voters. * * * [I]nterest representation, which requires strategic voting by a politically cohesive group, does not presume that all blacks will submerge their differences to present a monolithic front. Where voting patterns suggest overwhelming majority but not unanimous issue cohesion, interest representation would allow dissenting blacks to cast their votes as they chose. Interest representation is a phenomenon of choices, where the choices protected are the default positions of the black community: from advocacy by authentic representatives for distinctive group interests to advocacy by authentic representatives for the least well-off. Participation by all constituents would be encouraged. * * *

Although it is perhaps possible that interest representation could inadvertently moderate authentic representatives, alienate black voters by virtue of its complexity, or threaten black community autonomy, these fears are overstated. * * * [T]o the extent these concerns are substantial, they need to be balanced against the multiple advantages of interest representation.

First, interest representation attempts to produce citizens who are more committed to achieving political solutions to public policy problems. Because interest representation, unlike the districting strategy, depends on high voter turnout, incumbents will not be able to rely on low turnout to ensure their reelection. Instead, incumbents will find it necessary to mobilize voter interest and participation in an election, a task that will require incumbents to develop substantive programs and proposals. To counteract this, challengers will find it necessary to develop counterproposals, thereby heightening the differences between the candidates.

For their part, minorities may participate in election campaigns in greater numbers than they do in single-member districts, because elections will no longer be zero-sum solutions for minority interests. Minorities will finally have good prospects of winning some victories in the political process due to cumulative voting and the absence of territorial divisions of like-minded voters. This aggregate increase in the substantive content of campaigns will facilitate the self-identification of interest constituencies by heightening voter political awareness and participation as a result of the increased discussion and debate about policy issues. Voters who are energized in this way will actively monitor their issues agenda long after election day. Therefore, under interest representation voters may be more involved in the political process, at both the pre-and post-election stages, than are voters under a single-member district scheme.

Second, under an interest representation approach, incumbents are more accountable to constituents because the incumbents are more vulnerable to shifting alliances and regular removal. Because interest representation emphasizes issues, not the personalities of the candidates, incumbents are less likely to ignore the issues in favor of personal networking and campaigning. In addition, after the election, voter interest constituencies may be sufficiently mobilized to monitor the legislative activity of their elected representatives. Thus, interest representation does not simply reproduce the false consciousness or hierarchy of individual incumbents representing safe black districts; instead, incumbents will be constrained to reflect the policy preferences of their constituents—or else.

Third, interest representation generates incentives for community-based organizations to play a more active role in mobilizing the electorate and monitoring the legislature by both protecting and ratifying authentic representatives. In this sense, interest representation requires sustained organization in a campaign to educate, not merely turn out, voters. Representatives, chosen on the basis of shared interests rather than district proximity, would more likely affiliate with organizations or political parties to realize their goals. Strong minority political parties may then better represent minority voters, both substantively and organizationally.

Fourth, the interest representation approach avoids the resentment of race-conscious districting among groups that are not protected under the Voting Rights Act. Although majority-black single-member districts may elect some black representatives, they also submerge the interests of other groups that reside in the district, such as whites or religious minorities. Under the subdistricting strategy, winner-take-all majoritarianism precludes these voters from enjoying direct representation. This form of interest submergence does not occur under interest representation because the modified at-large system ensures representation to any politically cohesive group above the threshold of exclusion. Consequently, the resentment these voters might otherwise feel for their submergence in a single-member district will be ameliorated or eliminated altogether under interest representation.

Interest representation remedies, implemented pursuant to a voting rights claim, allow whites to form interest-based constituencies, too. Representation allows politically cohesive groups of voters, such as white women, to organize around their chosen issue agenda, without being limited for at least ten years (that is, until the next census is taken) by their own decisions about where to live or by others' arbitrary districting agendas. If geography fails to define completely the minority group interests, it also pigeonholes whites as well.

Fifth, interest representation promotes the value of consensus in group decisionmaking. As I use the term, consensus does not mean a uniform ideology. Rather, it means that participants who are satisfied a fair number of times are less likely to veto or actively fight decisions with which they may weakly disagree. In other words, because interest representation eliminates the winner-take-all feature of the single-district model, dissenters can expect some victories in the legislature or council. The modified at-large scheme will thus be viewed as fair by dissenters, who will, for that reason, be more likely to accept the majority's decision. Even if the minority loses a given vote, that vote will more likely be public-regarding because it will reflect the infusion of minority viewpoints. As a result, interest representation can produce a more informed consensus. * * *

Some may challenge interest representation as accelerating the momentum toward separatism. To its critics, interest representation, which reinforces minority group interests and creates a hospitable environment for minority political parties, arguably "thickens boundaries" between citizens, transforming elections from "occasions for seeking the broadest possible base of support by convincing divergent groups of their common interests" into events that "stress the cleavages separating their supporters from other segments of society."

These critics argue that interest representation inevitably leads to fringe parties, proliferates extremist viewpoints associated with some parliamentary or other proportionate party systems, or just results in stalemate. Critics claim all group-based remedies will promote intergroup conflict, balkanizing what instead should be a uniform, national identity built with stabilizing procedural rules. Critics say majority rule, for example, is necessary as a governing norm to finesse deep and long standing divisions. In this sense, winner-take-all majority rule is claimed to be both more stabilizing and more efficient than a proportionality principle that promotes deliberation or a "dispersed pluralism." * * *

[This argument] * * * suffers * * * from the false premise that interest representation destroys a preexisting general, common, uniform perspective or cultural understanding. For members of racial minority groups who have been, and continue to be, victimized as a result of their racial identity, a deep consensus that does not acknowledge the pervasiveness of the oppression that some, and the indignity that most, have suffered on account of race is impossible. Interest representation thus does not create conflict where none previously existed.

Moreover, a credible argument can be made that interest representation is, in fact, stabilizing. Although it makes present beneficiaries of electoral or voting rules, such as incumbents, perpetually vulnerable, such "cycling" is arguably desirable for four reasons associated with contemporary pluralist analysis. First, from the perspective of minority interests, interest representation is stabilizing when compared to existing political arrangements. For statutorily protected minorities, the stability ostensibly associated with winner-take-all majority rule is illusory, and its attendant efficiency comes at the cost of ignoring or marginalizing minority perspectives. In this sense, multiple, cross-cutting cleavages are more stabilizing than permanent, deep cleavages because the former better realize the majority rule assumption that shifting alliances are a check against the tyranny of the majority.

Indeed, recognizing the intensity of preferences need not lead to chaos because doing so will create incentives for groups presently alienated by their lack of meaningful political power to work within the political process. By giving such groups proportionate power, and consequently distributing preference satisfaction more widely, it helps compensate for their relative lack of power and legitimates the results of the political process. For example, interest representation may improve the collective decisionmaking process by promoting open discussion among a diverse set of participants and by encouraging strategies of negotiation and coalition-building with the possibility of present alliances as well as future victories. By thus giving minorities a fair share of the power, interest representation's proportionality principle surfaces antecedent racial conflict, which arguably delegitimates prejudice and limits its corrosive effect. In this way, interest representation arguably moderates political behavior.

Second, cycling helps reduce the tendency of politically entrenched interests to reproduce themselves or to emphasize the peculiarly transformative effects of their individual prestige and advancement. Such cycling arguably comports with a more participatory view of political power that potentially yields greater accountability or, at a minimum, affirms the importance of constantly renewing community-based ties. Third, interest representation may potentially reduce racial polarization by encouraging whites to identify or converge their interests with blacks. It avoids the polarizing debate about affirmative action, for example, because it does not create or impose external preferences for interests based on presumptions about group solidarity or injury. Interest preferences are voluntary, self-identified needs or wants that must be realized through organizational initiative and cooperation.

Even if a proportionality principle fails consistently to produce consensus, it may be stabilizing nonetheless if it is capable of generating less conflict than current empowerment strategies. Although there will probably still be some conflict, conflict is more likely to dissipate in an interest representation setting than in a subdistricting environment. For instance, because interest representation allows all groups to self-identify their interests with like-minded groups regardless of their location within the jurisdiction, whites are not directly disadvantaged through interest representation, as they may claim to be through majority-black districting remedies that construct districts in which some whites are district minorities who feel politically powerless.

Finally, the winner-take-some-but-not-all approach contemplates "strong democracy," meaning an invigorated electorate that participates (as opposed to spectates) throughout the political process. For example, interest representation could encourage the development of minority political organizations that would mobilize voters directly to articulate preferences and to monitor the legislative process and that would formalize bargains, or at least address issues of intense interest to the minority. Minority voters would thus be empowered to participate interactively through the organization and resources of an accountable, community-based, minority political party, which would have the effect of increasing the accountability of minority representatives.

One need not worry that the development of minority political parties or organizations will necessarily lead to stalemate because stalemate is less probable where, as in interest representation, participants experience continuous opportunities to cooperate and compromise. Indeed, studies of coalition systems do not conclude that stalemate is inevitable. For example, some scholars have concluded from the experience of foreign countries with systems resembling interest representation that long-term government stability can and in fact does exist as a function of the underlying social forces and structural features of such a political system. Furthermore, the argument that multiplication of parties leads to instability, a charge usually levelled against parliamentary systems of government, is less legitimate on a national scale where, as in the United States, the executive is independent of the legislature and certainly is not relevant at the level of local government, which I address here.

In sum, proponents of interest representation posit that changing electoral and collective voting procedures can improve the collective decisionmaking process by including and proportionately reflecting minority interests. Whatever the substantive results, the process can be legitimated and made more deliberative by choosing decisional rules that disaggregate the disproportionate power of the permanent, homogeneous majority. Similarly, conflict between interest groups may be inescapable but need not be unproductive or destabilizing. * * *

JAMIN RASKIN, LEGAL ALIENS, LOCAL CITIZENS: THE
HISTORICAL, CONSTITUTIONAL AND THEORETICAL
MEANINGS OF ALIEN SUFFRAGE
141 U. Pa. L. Rev. 1391, 1393–1394, 1460–1467 (1993).

As the franchise has expanded over the centuries to take in nearly all adult citizens, one group which voted and participated, at various points over a 150-year period, in at least twenty-two states and territories, lost its historic access to the ballot: inhabitants of individual states who are not citizens of the United States or, to use the reifying but inescapable idiom of immigration law, resident aliens. Today, with the extraordinary, though still largely unwritten, history of alien suffrage safely hidden from view, the U.S. citizenship voting qualification ropes off the franchise in every American state from participation by non-U.S. citizens. As a marker at the perimeter of the American body politic, the citizenship qualification carries the aura of inevitability that once attached to property, race, and gender qualifications. * * *

[T]he current blanket exclusion of noncitizens from the ballot is neither constitutionally required nor historically normal. Moreover, the disenfranchisement of aliens at the local level is vulnerable to deep theoretical objections since resident aliens—who are governed, taxed, and often drafted just like citizens—have a strong democratic claim to being considered members, indeed citizens, of their local communities. Although democratic theory cannot resolve the foundational political question of who belongs to "the people," the ideological traditions of both liberalism and republicanism make available compelling arguments for the inclusion of noncitizens as voters in local elections. The bedrock hostility of the liberal rights tradition to taxation and governance without representation makes noncitizen voting a logically unassailable, if not clearly mandatory, democratic practice. Republicanism presents a somewhat more complicated picture given its historic compatibility with exclusionary practices, but a progressive commitment to dialogic politics and the constitutive value of participation is arguably vindicated by defining universal suffrage without regard to nation-state citizenship. These arguments are deepened by evolving international norms of community-based democracy and human rights and strengthened by important instrumental considerations relating to the surge in immigration which the United States is currently experiencing. * * *

The United States is home to some ten million aliens who work in American businesses and government offices, serve in the armed forces, pay local, state, and federal taxes, and are subject to all of the obligations of citizenship, including military conscription. Since noncitizen voting is neither constitutionally obligatory nor taboo, states and municipalities may approach it as a matter of public policy. But aliens are not presently permitted to vote, or run for office, in any state election, and are therefore shut out from formal political participation at both the state and national level. There are, however, several important examples of noncitizen voting at the local level which can serve as models for interested localities. Since 1968, New York City has granted noncitizens who are the parents of school children the right to vote and run for community school board. The City of Chicago similarly gives noncitizens the right to vote in school board elections.

More expansively, a number of smaller localities in the State of Maryland—including Somerset, Barnesville, Chevy Chase Sections 3 and 5, and Martin's Additions—have for decades extended the franchise in all local elections to inhabitants who are not U.S. citizens. As more intimate communities whose alien populations are apparently composed, in substantial part, of World Bank and embassy personnel working in Washington, D.C., these Maryland jurisdictions rest their policies on both natural rights understandings and the early property-based conception of local voting rights. It is necessary to note that most of the inhabitants of these small communities tend to share a similar economic and social status which dilutes the threatening image many citizens have of aliens. They also share a physical proximity which permits them to have unrushed and disarming face-to-face encounters with one another.

But noncitizen voting in Maryland is not (simply, at least) a naive throwback to nineteenth-century small-town life. For on March 31, 1992, Takoma Park, Maryland, a well-integrated city bordering the District of Columbia with a population of 16,700, formally amended its municipal charter to give all residents, regardless of citizenship, the right to vote, and run for office, in local elections. The charter change followed several months of excited political debate and controversy which spilled over into the Washington, D.C. area as a whole. The issue first arose when the Takoma Park Elections Task Force completed its 1990 city council redistricting process. The Task Force found that its new wards had equal numbers of residents, as required by law, but that some wards had far more eligible voters than others because some contained a large alien population. This imbalance focused attention on two facts: the votes of citizens in wards with high citizen populations were worth much less than votes of citizens in wards with high numbers of aliens; and many city residents with all of the obligations of Takoma Park citizenship lacked the right to vote. The Task Force, by and large unaware of the rich history of alien suffrage in the United States, proposed to the City Council that it place on the November 5, 1991 ballot a referendum question on whether the citizens of Takoma Park favored extending local voting rights to noncitizens. * * *

The referendum debate unleashed its share of xenophobia and prejudice, but the discussion was generally remarkable for its sobriety. Advocates of the charter amendment mobilized democratic principles to argue for the change and emphasized the local nature of the proposal. The Share the Vote campaign worked to humanize the question by bringing to public attention a number of people, who had come to Takoma Park from all over the world and who would be enfranchised by the change. The Washington Post, for example, interviewed Colin Norman, a Washington correspondent for a British magazine and a citizen of the United Kingdom who came to Takoma Park in 1976.

> [Norman] says he may be more a part of the city than U.S. citizens who are newcomers to the area. "I have as much interest in the community as anyone he said * * * We're not asking for a voice at the national level or in foreign policy," Norman said. "But in local matters, we're no different than somebody who has moved to Takoma Park from California."

Supporters of the change also observed "an urgent practical side to this idea for those kept out of democracy's circle have other ways of making their grievances known * * *. It is better to confront social problems nonviolently in the halls of government than violently in the streets."

Opponents of the measure emphasized that illegal aliens would technically be able to vote along with permanent resident aliens. The former commissioner of the Immigration and Naturalization Service argued that alien suffrage "undermines the value of U.S. citizenship" and that five years "is not an unreasonable time to wait to be able to participate in our democracy." He also made a slippery slope argument that "if local voting by noncitizens is allowed, state and federal voting could be next. Either there is a policy basis for noncitizens to vote, or there is not. If we open the door, it cannot be closed halfway."

The November 5, 1991 noncitizen voting referendum passed by a vote of 1,199 to 1,107. Because the referendum was only advisory, debate continued. But on February 10, 1992, the Takoma Park City Council adopted, by a vote of five to one, a Charter Amendment removing the requirement that voters and candidates for public office in Takoma Park be U.S. citizens in order to participate in the city's biennial elections. In the meantime, Delegate John Morgan, who represents a district outside of Takoma Park, introduced a bill in the Maryland House of Delegates to prohibit noncitizen voting in local elections. On February 11, the House Committee on Constitutional and Administrative Law conducted a lengthy and impassioned hearing on the legislation. Bill proponents claimed that noncitizen voting would bring in a tide of unwanted immigrants, while Takoma Park and other noncitizen voting communities argued that this was a local question and home rule should not be invaded. On March 17, 1992, the bill was defeated by a vote of 11–6 and a final local effort to block implementation of the charter amendment fizzled. On March 31, 1992, Takoma Park became the largest and most recent municipality in the United States to adopt complete noncitizen voting. * * *

[T]he people who have joined us on our land are generally here to stay, and the question today is whether they will be democratically integrated and assimilated into our political culture or kept apart as a disenfranchised and increasingly disaffected population. A number of immigrant groups continue to live on the margins of American society. Recent cases of unrest, delinquency, and riot in immigrant communities, on both the east coast and the west coast, illustrate the dangers of excluding large numbers of people from political membership in their communities. But it is no answer to say that members of these excluded groups should simply apply for United States' citizenship; their very alienation renders improbable their participation in the citizenship naturalization process, which is more of an affirmation of a sense of social belonging than a first step towards achieving this goal. The virtue of extending the vote in local elections to noncitizens is that it invites noncitizens to participate in, and learn about, American political culture and practices without immediately requiring the greater psychic break of surrendering one's given nationality. Presumably the taste of democratic citizenship that some aliens get from local voting will make them hunger for a greater role in our politics. If so, the practice of alien suffrage, sometimes derided as a threat to the naturalization process, can become once again, as it was in the last two centuries, a pathway to naturalized citizenship. * * *

2. THE INITIATIVE AND THE REFERENDUM

The initiative and referendum are means by which voters can decide issues of city policy directly rather than by electing representatives to decide the issues for them. An initiative is a piece of legislation placed on the ballot by means of a petition signed by a (legally-defined) number of voters. Passing an initiative can thus be a means of enacting legislation that completely bypasses the representative process, although sometimes an initiative allows the legislature an opportunity to accept or reject the proposal. A referendum, by contrast, is an election called after a legislative body has already acted on a piece of legislation. Sometimes a referendum election is called by the legislature and sometimes by a petition signed by (the required number of) voters. A referendum thus enables voters to decide for themselves whether legislation passed by their representatives should be enacted.

The initiative and referendum have long been hailed as models of direct democracy, but they are not without their critics.[56] The following materials consider some of the advantages people find in, and some of the

---

[56] See, e.g., Shaun Bowler, When is it Okay to Limit Direct Democracy?, 97 Minn. L. Rev. 1780 (2013); Todd Donovan, Direct Democracy and Campaigns Against Minorities, 97 Minn. L. Rev. 1730 (2013); Maxwell Stearns, Direct (Anti-)Democracy, 80 Geo. Wash. L. Rev. 311 (2012); Kenneth Miller, Direct Democracy and the Courts (2009); Mark Baldassare and Cheryl Katz, The Coming of Age of Direct Democracy: California's Recall and Beyond (2008); Ethan J. Leib, Can Direct Democracy be Made Deliberative?, 54 Buff. L. Rev. 903 (2006); Elizabeth Garrett, Hybrid Democracy, 73 Geo. Wash. L. Rev. 1096 (2005); John Matsusaka, For the Many or the Few: The Initiative, Public Policy, and American Democracy (2004); Lynn Baker, Direct Democracy: Preferences, Priorities, and Plebiscites, 13 J. Contemp. Legal Issues 317 (2004); Elizabeth Garrett, Money, Agenda Setting, and Direct Democracy, 77 Tex. L. Rev. 1845 (1999); Samuel Issacharoff, Pamela Karlan, and Richard Pildes, The Law of Democracy: Legal Structure of the Political Process 665–712 (1998); Sherman Clark, A Populist Critique of Direct Democracy, 112 Harv. L. Rev. 434 (1998); Frank Michelman, "Protecting the People from Themselves," or How Direct can Democracy Be, 45 U.C.L.A. L. Rev. 1717 (1998); Keith Aoki, Direct Democracy, Racial Group Agency, Local Government Law, and Residential Racial Segregation: Some Reflections on Radical and Plural Democracy, 33 Cal. W. L. Rev. 185 (1997); David Magleby, Let the Voters Decide?: An Assessment of the Initiative and Referendum Process, 66 Colo. L. Rev. 13 (1995); Douglas Hsiao, Invisible Cities: The Constitutional Status of Direct Democracy in a Democratic Republic, 41 Duke L. J. 1267 (1992); Julian Eule, Judicial Review of Direct Democracy, 99 Yale L. J. 1503 (1990); Clayton Gillette, Plebiscites, Participation and Collective Action in Local Government Law, 86 Mich. L. Rev. 930 (1988); David Magleby, Direct Legislation: Voting on Ballot Propositions in the United States (1984).

problems critics raise about, these forms of direct democracy. City of Eastlake v. Forest City Enterprises raises the question whether aspects of the legislative—and administrative—processes that are absent when decision making is made by popular vote undermine the legitimacy of direct democratic decision making. Is there a way to organize popular decision making that might (at the minimum) approximate the amount of informed attention to the public interest that now takes place in administrative or legislative decision making? An article by Derrick Bell, and City of Cuyahoga Falls v. Buckeye Community Hope Foundation then shift the focus to other concerns: the role of money and of racism in influencing electoral results. Does Cuyahoga Falls offer support for Bell's preference for legislative rather than popular decision making? Finally, Richard DeLeon's analysis of municipal elections in San Francisco suggests that one's position about the role of direct democracy might vary with the context.

CITY OF EASTLAKE V. FOREST CITY ENTERPRISES, INC.

Supreme Court of the United States, 1976.
426 U.S. 668, 96 S.Ct. 2358, 49 L.Ed.2d 132.

MR. CHIEF JUSTICE BURGER delivered the opinion of the Court.

The question in this case is whether a city charter provision requiring proposed land use changes to be ratified by 55% of the votes cast violates the due process rights of a landowner who applies for a zoning change.

The city of Eastlake, Ohio, a suburb of Cleveland, has a comprehensive zoning plan codified in a municipal ordinance. Respondent, a real estate developer, acquired an eight-acre parcel of real estate in Eastlake zoned for "light industrial" uses at the time of purchase.

In May 1971, respondent applied to the City Planning Commission for a zoning change to permit construction of a multi-family, high-rise apartment building. The Planning Commission recommended the proposed change to the City Council, which under Eastlake's procedures could either accept or reject the Planning Commission's recommendation. Meanwhile, by popular vote, the voters of Eastlake amended the city charter to require that any changes in land use agreed to by the Council be approved by a 55% vote in a referendum. The City Council approved the Planning Commission's recommendation for reclassification of respondent's property to permit the proposed project. Respondent then applied to the Planning Commission for "parking and yard" approval for the proposed building. The Commission rejected the application, on the ground that the City Council's rezoning action had not yet been submitted to the voters for ratification.

Respondent then filed an action in state court, seeking a judgment declaring the charter provision invalid as an unconstitutional delegation of legislative power to the people. While the case was pending, the City Council's action was submitted to a referendum, but the proposed zoning change was not approved by the requisite 55% margin. Following the election, the Court of Common Pleas and the Ohio Court of Appeals sustained the charter provision.

The Ohio Supreme Court reversed. Concluding that enactment of zoning and rezoning provisions is a legislative function, the court held that a popular referendum requirement, lacking standards to guide the decision of the voters, permitted the police power to be exercised in a standardless, hence arbitrary and capricious manner. Relying on this Court's decisions in Washington ex rel. Seattle Title Trust Co. v. Roberge, 278 U.S. 116, 49 S.Ct. 50, 73 L.Ed. 210 (1928), Thomas Cusack Co. v. Chicago, 242 U.S. 526, 37 S.Ct. 190, 61 L.Ed. 472 (1917), and Eubank v. Richmond, 226 U.S. 137, 33 S.Ct. 76, 57 L.Ed. 156 (1912), but distinguishing James v. Valtierra, 402 U.S. 137, 91 S.Ct. 1331, 28 L.Ed.2d 678 (1971), the court concluded that the referendum provision constituted an unlawful delegation of legislative power. * * *

The conclusion that Eastlake's procedure violates federal constitutional guarantees rests upon the proposition that a zoning referendum involves a delegation of legislative power. A referendum cannot, however, be characterized as a delegation of power. Under our constitutional assumptions, all power derives from the people, who can delegate it to representative instruments which they create. See, e.g., The Federalist No. 39 (Madison). In establishing legislative bodies, the people can reserve to themselves power to deal directly with matters which might otherwise be assigned to the legislature. Hunter v. Erickson, 393 U.S. 385, 392, 89 S.Ct. 557, 561, 21 L.Ed.2d 616 (1969).

The reservation of such power is the basis for the town meeting, a tradition which continues to this day in some States as both a practical and symbolic part of our democratic processes. The referendum, similarly, is a means for direct political participation, allowing the people the final decision, amounting to a veto power, over enactments of representative bodies. The practice is designed to "give citizens a voice on questions of public policy." James v. Valtierra, supra, 402 U.S., at 141, 91 S.Ct., at 1333.

In framing a state constitution, the people of Ohio specifically reserved the power of referendum to the people of each municipality within the State.

"The initiative and referendum powers are hereby reserved to the people of each municipality on all questions which such municipalities may now or hereafter be authorized by law to control by legislative action * * *."

To be subject to Ohio's referendum procedure, the question must be one within the scope of legislative power. The Ohio Supreme Court expressly found that the City Council's action in rezoning respondent's eight acres from light industrial to high-density residential use was legislative in nature. Distinguishing between administrative and legislative acts, the court separated the power to zone or rezone, by passage or amendment of a zoning ordinance, from the power to grant relief from unnecessary hardship. The former function was found to be legislative in nature. * * *

The Ohio Supreme Court further concluded that the amendment to the city charter constituted a "delegation" of power violative of federal constitutional guarantees because the voters were given no standards to guide their decision. Under Eastlake's procedure, the Ohio Supreme Court reasoned, no mechanism existed, nor indeed could exist, to assure that the voters would act rationally in passing upon a proposed zoning change. This meant that "appropriate legislative action [would] be made dependent upon the potentially arbitrary and unreasonable whims of the voting public." The potential for arbitrariness in the process, the court concluded, violated due process.

Courts have frequently held in other contexts that a congressional delegation of power to a regulatory entity must be accompanied by discernible standards, so that the delegatee's action can be measured for its fidelity to the legislative will. Assuming, arguendo, their relevance to state governmental functions, these cases involved a delegation of power by the legislature to regulatory bodies, which are not directly responsible to the people; this doctrine is inapplicable where, as here, rather than dealing with a delegation of power, we deal with a power reserved by the people to themselves.[10]

In basing its claim on federal due process requirements, respondent also invokes Euclid v. Ambler Realty Co., 272 U.S. 365, 47 S.Ct. 114, 71 L.Ed. 303 (1926), but it does not rely on the direct teaching of that case. Under Euclid, a property owner can challenge a zoning restriction if the measure is "clearly arbitrary and

---

[10] The Ohio Supreme Court's analysis of the requirements for standards flowing from the Fourteenth Amendment also sweeps too broadly. Except as a legislative history informs an analysis of legislative action, there is no more advance assurance that a legislative body will act by conscientiously applying consistent standards than there is with respect to voters. For example, there is no certainty that the City Council in this case would act on the basis of "standards" explicit or otherwise in Eastlake's comprehensive zoning ordinance. Nor is there any assurance that townspeople assembling in a town meeting, as the people of Eastlake could do, Hunter v. Erickson, 393 U.S. 385, 392, 89 S.Ct. 557, 561, 21 L.Ed.2d 616 (1969), will act according to consistent standards. The critical constitutional inquiry, rather, is whether the zoning restriction produces arbitrary or capricious results.

unreasonable, having no substantial relation to the public health, safety, morals, or general welfare." If the substantive result of the referendum is arbitrary and capricious, bearing no relation to the police power, then the fact that the voters of Eastlake wish it so would not save the restriction. As this Court held in invalidating a charter amendment enacted by referendum:

> "The sovereignty of the people is itself subject to those constitutional limitations which have been duly adopted and remain unrepealed." Hunter v. Erickson, 393 U.S., at 392, 89 S.Ct., at 561.

But no challenge of the sort contemplated in Euclid v. Ambler Realty is before us. The Ohio Supreme Court did not hold, and respondent does not argue, that the present zoning classification under Eastlake's comprehensive ordinance violates the principles established in Euclid v. Ambler Realty If respondent considers the referendum result itself to be unreasonable, the zoning restriction is open to challenge in state court, where the scope of the state remedy available to respondent would be determined as a matter of state law, as well as under Fourteenth Amendment standards. That being so, nothing more is required by the Constitution.

Nothing in our cases is inconsistent with this conclusion. Two decisions of this Court were relied on by the Ohio Supreme Court in invalidating Eastlake's procedure. The thread common to both decisions is the delegation of legislative power, originally given by the people to a legislative body, and in turn delegated by the legislature to a narrow segment of the community, not to the people at large. In Eubank v. Richmond, 226 U.S. 137, 33 S.Ct. 76, 57 L.Ed. 156 (1912), the Court invalidated a city ordinance which conferred the power to establish building setback lines upon the owners of two-thirds of the property abutting any street. Similarly, in Washington ex rel. Seattle Title Trust Co. v. Roberge, 278 U.S. 116, 49 S.Ct. 50, 73 L.Ed. 210 (1928), the Court struck down an ordinance which permitted the establishment of philanthropic homes for the aged in residential areas, but only upon the written consent of the owners of two-third of the property within 400 feet of the proposed facility.

Neither Eubank nor Roberge involved a referendum procedure such as we have in this case; the standardless delegation of power to a limited group of property owners condemned by the Court in Eubank and Roberge is not to be equated with decisionmaking by the people through the referendum process. The Court of Appeals for the Ninth Circuit put it this way:

> "A referendum, however, is far more than an expression of ambiguously founded neighborhood preference. It is the city

itself legislating through its voters—an exercise by the voters of their traditional right through direct legislation to override the views of their elected representatives as to what serves the public interest."

Our decision in James v. Valtierra, upholding California's mandatory referendum requirement, confirms this view. Mr. Justice Black, speaking for the Court in that case, said:

"This procedure ensures that all the people of a community will have a voice in a decision which may lead to large expenditures of local governmental funds for increased public services * * *." (emphasis added).

Mr. Justice Black went on to say that a referendum procedure, such as the one at issue here, is a classic demonstration of "devotion to democracy * * *." As a basic instrument of democratic government, the referendum process does not, in itself, violate the Due Process Clause of the Fourteenth Amendment when applied to a rezoning ordinance. Since the rezoning decision in this case was properly reserved to the People of Eastlake under the Ohio Constitution, the Ohio Supreme Court erred in holding invalid, on federal constitutional grounds, the charter amendment permitting the voters to decide whether the zoned use of respondent's property could be altered. * * *

JUSTICE STEVENS, with whom MR. JUSTICE BRENNAN joins, dissenting * * *.

As the Justices of the Ohio Supreme Court recognized, we are concerned with the fairness of a provision for determining the right to make a particular use of a particular parcel of land. In such cases, the state courts have frequently described the capricious character of a decision supported by majority sentiment rather than reference to articulable standards. Moreover, they have limited statutory referendum procedures to apply only to approvals of comprehensive zoning ordinances as opposed to amendments affecting specific parcels. This conclusion has been supported by characterizing particular amendments as "administrative" and revision of an entire plan as "legislative."

In this case the Ohio Supreme Court characterized the Council's approval of respondent's proposal as "legislative." I think many state courts would have characterized it as "administrative." The courts thus may well differ in their selection of the label to apply to this action, but I find substantial agreement among state tribunals on the proposition that requiring a citywide referendum for approval of a particular proposal like this is manifestly unreasonable. Surely that is my view.

The essence of fair procedure is that the interested parties be given a reasonable opportunity to have their dispute resolved on the merits by reference to articulable rules. If a dispute involves only the conflicting rights of private litigants, it is elementary that the decision-maker must be impartial and qualified to understand and to apply the controlling rules.

I have no doubt about the validity of the initiative or the referendum as an appropriate method of deciding questions of community policy. I think it is equally clear that the popular vote is not an acceptable method of adjudicating the rights of individual litigants. The problem presented by this case is unique, because it may involve a three-sided controversy, in which there is at least potential conflict between the rights of the property owner and the rights of his neighbors, and also potential conflict with the public interest in preserving the city's basic zoning plan. If the latter aspect of the controversy were predominant, the referendum would be an acceptable procedure. On the other hand, when the record indicates without contradiction that there is no threat to the general public interest in preserving the city's plan as it does in this case, since respondent's proposal was approved by both the Planning Commission and the City Council and there has been no allegation that the use of this eight-acre parcel for apartments rather than light industry would adversely affect the community or raise any policy issue of citywide concern—I think the case should be treated as one in which it is essential that the private property owner be given a fair opportunity to have his claim determined on its merits.

As Justice Stern points out in his concurring opinion, it would be absurd to use a referendum to decide whether a gasoline station could be operated on a particular corner in the city of Cleveland. The case before us is not that clear because we are told that there are only 20,000 people in the city of Eastlake. Conceivably, an eight-acre development could be sufficiently dramatic to arouse the legitimate interest of the entire community; it is also conceivable that most of the voters would be indifferent and uninformed about the wisdom of building apartments rather than a warehouse or factory on these eight acres. The record is silent on which of these alternatives is the more probable. Since the ordinance places a manifestly unreasonable obstacle in the path of every property owner seeking any zoning change, since it provides no standards or procedures for exempting particular parcels or claims from the referendum requirement, and since the record contains no justification for the use of the procedure in this case, I am persuaded that we should respect the state judiciary's appraisal of the fundamental fairness of this decisionmaking process in this case.

DERRICK BELL, THE REFERENDUM: DEMOCRACY'S BARRIER TO RACIAL EQUALITY

54 Wash. L. Rev. 1, 1, 2–3, 6, 8, 9, 13–21, 24–26 (1978).

"Provisions for referendums demonstrate devotion to democracy, not to bias, discrimination, or prejudice."

JUSTICE HUGO BLACK

For most Americans, whether or not legally trained, Justice Black's statement is unexceptional, accepted as a truism in harmony with the principles of life in a free society. As proponents of referenda and initiatives never tire of asking, if voters are smart enough to elect representatives to make their laws, are they not just as able to make the laws themselves? At first glance, this seems logical. But blacks and other nonwhite groups in this society cannot afford the luxury of reliance on either truisms or the appearance of logic. Their status, success, and sometimes even survival may depend on an instant recognition of the real danger lurking behind what whites might consider "generally accepted principles." Experience is a far safer guide than rhetoric; and the experience of blacks with the referendum has proved ironically that the more direct democracy becomes, the more threatening it is. * * *

When Justice Black hailed referendum provisions as reflecting a devotion to democracy, and not proof of "bias, discrimination, or prejudice," his was not simply a rhetorical flourish. The statement embodied a central principle of his 1971 majority opinion in James v. Valtierra. In that case, black and Mexican-American indigents had challenged Article 34 of the California constitution, which required prior approval in a local referendum before a state public body could develop a federally financed low-rent housing project. They argued that Article 34 unreasonably discriminated, explicitly against the poor and implicitly against minority groups, because it mandated special voter approval for low-income housing. A three-judge federal court held that the provision imposed a special procedural burden on the legislative capacity to assist minorities, an action previously barred by the Supreme Court in Hunter v. Erickson. Consequently, the lower court ruled that Article 34 denied the plaintiffs equal protection. * * *

The Supreme Court, however, reversed. Justice Black, writing for a 5–3 majority, distinguished Hunter as involving a referendum that specifically burdened racial minorities. He perceived little evidence that the housing referendum required by Article 34 relied on "distinctions based on race." Noting that mandatory referenda were required by California law for other actions, albeit not connected with housing, Justice Black viewed the referendum as a legitimate vehicle for ensuring "that all the people of a community will have a voice in a decision which may lead to large expenditures of local governmental funds for increased public services and to lower tax revenues." * * *

Chief Justice Burger relied heavily on Justice Black's Valtierra opinion in City of Eastlake v. Forest City Enterprises, Inc. That decision upheld a charter provision of the suburban town of Eastlake, Ohio, which required approval of all zoning changes by a fifty-five percent referendum vote. The Ohio Supreme Court had found that the requirement frustrated a multifamily, high rise apartment project, in violation of the owner-developer's due process rights. Calling the referendum process "a basic instrument of democratic government," Chief Justice Burger adopted Justice Black's view that "[t]his procedure ensures that all the people of a community will have a voice in a decision which may lead to large expenditures of local governmental funds for increased public services." * * *

Referendum provisions simply repealing fair housing ordinances or laws and upsetting city council or zoning commission approval to build low-income housing have become a standard means of barring minorities from suburban, residential communities. * * * The question then is whether, in the practice of popular sovereignty, there are unacknowledged aspects of racial discrimination or some other basis, such as a serious danger to our legislative form of government, which entitle minority groups to special protection when their interests are disadvantaged by repeal of protective legislation through the use of initiative or referendum. * * *

Public officials, even those elected on more or less overtly racist campaigns, may prove responsive to minority pressures for civil rights measures once in office or, at least, be open to the negotiation and give-and-take that constitutes much of the political process. Thus, legislators may vote for, or executive officials may sign, a civil rights or social reform bill with full knowledge that a majority of their constituents oppose the measure. They are in the spotlight and do not wish publicly to advocate racism; they cannot openly attribute their opposition to "racist constituents." The more neutral reasons for opposition are often inadequate in the face of serious racial injustices, particularly those posing threats not confined to the minority community.

When the legislative process is turned back to the citizenry either to enact laws by initiative or to review existing laws through the referendum, few of the concerns that can transform the "conservative" politician into a "moderate" public official are likely to affect the individual voter's decision. No political factors counsel restraint on racial passions emanating from longheld and little considered beliefs and fears. Far from being the pure path to democracy that Justice Black proclaimed, direct democracy, carried out in the privacy of the voting booth, has diminished the ability of minority groups to participate in the democratic process. Ironically, because it enables the voters' racial beliefs and fears to be recorded and tabulated in their pure form, the referendum has been a most effective facilitator of that bias, discrimination, and prejudice which has marred American democracy from its earliest day.

Courts have been reluctant to grapple with or even acknowledge the plethora of racist influences and status and class concerns which come into play when the future of a fair housing law is to be decided at the voting booth, or when the electorate must approve, perhaps as in City of Eastlake by some super-majority, a legislative or administrative decision to construct a low-income housing project. Any serious consideration of the degree to which prejudice affects the outcome of race-related referenda must at the very least bring an end to the uncritical acceptance and repetition of the unproved assumptions that direct voting techniques are fair and faithful reflections of the country's highest democratic values.

Chief Justice Burger's majority opinion in City of Eastlake, for example, relied too heavily on the fiction that the referendum process is the exercise of a nondelegated legislative power which, for some unexplained reason, gains legitimacy and need not even be scrutinized to insure regularity, merely because it is exercised directly by the people. For support, the Chief Justice turned to history, comparing the referendum with the New England town meeting, which he deemed "both a practical and symbolic part of our democratic processes." But, as several historians have pointed out, the colonial town meeting's effectiveness was due largely to the cultural and political homogeneity of its participants. The town meeting was less a forum for conflicting opinions than a place for ratifying, usually by unanimous vote, prior understandings of the community. The meeting expressed the will of a homogenous electorate shaped by exclusionary controls on the admission of new residents. Such exclusionary controls were as tight as those now achieved by zoning referenda in modern suburbs.

Subtle social pressures in those small communities tended to minimize dissent, and even though the communities were small, they often lacked adequate information. James Madison, who preferred representative government because it fostered consideration and compromise of competing interests, believed that popular democracy was prone to majority dictatorship because there were few checks on the temptation to sacrifice minority interests or disadvantage unpopular individuals.

Madison's eighteenth-century fears became nineteenth-century reality when, for example, voters in the Oregon territory overwhelmingly approved an 1857 referendum law intended to exclude all free blacks. Despite its very small black population, residents of the territory had discussed barring blacks for several years, but neither the legislature nor constitutional conventions would approve such a measure because each political party feared that another would be able to exploit the issue. When the proposal was finally submitted to a popular vote, however, it received more support than an accompanying antislavery proposition. Voting on both issues reflected the whites' belief that they should not have to compete with slaves or free blacks for jobs, that blacks would bring crime and disease, and that Oregon should be preserved for the white race. The same motivation prompted the citizens of Kansas to adopt a similar restriction against blacks in 1855. Even earlier, Indiana and Illinois had voted by large majorities to include anti-black immigration provisions in their constitutions. Although anti-black immigration laws were seldom enforced, historian Leon Litwack regards them both as a constant reminder to Negroes of their inferior position in society and as a convenient excuse for whites to engage in mob violence and frequent harassment of the black population.

No court seems to have considered the potential of present-day barriers against low-income housing to convey the same message or similarly to encourage harassment of those minority families who manage to move into such areas. Certainly, the Court majorities in Valtierra and City of Eastlake failed to grasp the point, although Justice Stevens, dissenting in the Eastlake case, recognized the exclusionary impact of the referendum requirement.

A realistic assessment of referenda and initiatives must include an examination of how they have developed in practice as well as a description of their theoretical democratic virtues. Direct legislation, the creation of progressives of another era, today poses more danger to social progress than the problems of governmental unresponsiveness it was intended to cure. This is not to suggest that we ought to ignore the defects and disappointments of the representative system which today, as in the past, have spurred public recourse to direct legislation. All too often, both Congress and the President become targets and, one fears, the captives of powerful business interests. It is also undeniable that representatives may vote on bills which they do not understand or concerning which they have been improperly influenced.

Nevertheless, our distrust and dissatisfaction with the Congress, with state and local representatives, and with executive officials should not so quickly lead us to conclude that increased reliance on direct democracy will avoid those evils to which legislatures and Congress seem so vulnerable. Supporters of minority rights must be concerned that both the initiative and the referendum often serve those opposed to reform. It is clear, for example, that direct legislation is used effectively by residents of homogenous middle-class communities to prevent unwanted development—especially development that portends increased size or heterogeneity of population.

Today, direct democracy is used comparatively infrequently to curb abuses in government or otherwise to control elected officials. Rather, intense interest is generated when the issues are seemingly clear-cut and often emotional matters such as liquor, gun control, pollution, pornography, or race. Complicated taxation problems and matters of governmental structure, on the other hand, typically evoke little voter response.

The emotionally charged atmosphere often surrounding referenda and initiatives can easily reduce the care with which the voters consider the matters submitted to them. Tumultuous, media-oriented campaigns, such as the ones successfully used to repeal ordinances recognizing the rights of homosexuals in Dade County, Florida, St. Paul, Minnesota, and Eugene, Oregon, are not conducive to careful thinking and voting. A similar furor surrounded the innovative "anti-pornography" law enacted by initiative in the State of Washington but promptly declared unconstitutional in Spokane Arcades, Inc. v. Ray.

Appeals to prejudice, oversimplification of the issues, and exploitation of legitimate concerns by promising simplistic solutions to complex problems often characterize referendum and initiative campaigns. Of course, politicians, too, may offer quick cure-alls to gain electoral support and may spend millions on election campaigns that are as likely to obfuscate as to elucidate the issues. But we vote politicians into office, not into law. Once in office, they may become well-informed, responsible representatives; at the least, their excesses may be curtailed by the checks and balances of the political process.

The success or failure of ballot-box legislation, therefore, may depend less on the merits of the issue than on who is financing the campaign. One California public relations official boasted that he could put any issue on the California state ballot for $325,000. Even before the Supreme Court's rejection of spending regulations in First National Bank of Boston v. Bellotti, large corporations were investing huge sums in referenda campaigns. With so much at stake it is not surprising to find direct voting procedures criticized for phrasing proposals deceptively, for abusing the signature gathering process, especially by professional signature gathering organizations, and for political sloganeering intended to obscure and confuse public discussion.

The Court's failure to review more closely the many opportunities for misrepresentation, financial abuse, and outright fraud can only encourage campaigners to appeal to prejudice. The record of recent ballot legislation reflects all too accurately the conservative, even intolerant, attitudes citizens display when given the chance to vote their fears and prejudices, especially when exposed to expensive media campaigns. The security of minority rights and the value of racial equality which those rights affirm are endangered by the possibility of popular repeal. * * *

Unfortunately, the racial motivations and discriminatory impact of many modern referenda and initiatives cannot similarly be attacked directly because the measures are couched in racially neutral terms and may be viewed as serving some legitimate, nonracial public purpose. The current Court has refused to invalidate laws as invidiously discriminatory merely because they have discriminatory impact; the Court insists that a discriminatory purpose must be shown. Blacks and other minorities will encounter substantial difficulty when they challenge a referendum on race discrimination grounds because, as in Valtierra, they must show "that a law seemingly neutral on its face is in fact aimed at a racial minority."

However, the racially discriminatory impact of ballot legislation is not the only constitutional problem presented. The initiative and referendum are participatory political processes; they involve voting. Therefore, the cases protecting the right to vote and the equal power of every person's vote can be brought to bear, and the reasoning of those cases applied. Although the Court's dominant concern in the "one person, one vote" cases was to prevent the dilution of the individual citizen's vote, the Court was also concerned with the proper functioning of the republican form of government by insuring equally weighted votes. This concern for republicanism was articulated by Chief Justice Warren in Reynolds v. Sims: "The right to vote freely for the candidate of one's choice is of the essence of a democratic society, and any restrictions on that right strike at the heart of representative government."

This theme of protection of the republican system of government—and impliedly the protection of the society vouchsafed by that republican system—was announced more clearly in the cases involving at-large elections in multi-member districts. The Warren Court often expressed concern that at-large election schemes had long been used as a means of diluting the votes of minority groups or political parties. On more than one occasion, the Court warned that such legislative or local districts would be found unconstitutional where they were shown to operate "designedly or otherwise * * * under the circumstances of a particular case [to] minimize or cancel out the voting strength of racial or political elements of the voting population."

Referenda and initiatives are "at-large elections" on issues instead of candidates. Just as multi-member districts have the potential of minimizing or cancelling out the voting strength of racial or political groups in the election of officials, referenda and initiatives have a similar effect on direct legislation. In both cases the strength of the minority will be diluted.

The same danger to the republican process which was present in the multi-district cases is present here. The danger is twofold. First, in a particular referendum on a particular issue, a matter extremely harmful to minority interests but only moderately beneficial to non-minority interests may be passed; the ballot does not easily register intensity of interest as the legislative process does. Second, the initiative and referendum processes in general prevent meaningful participation by minority groups. As more legislation is passed through direct ballot, minorities are increasingly excluded from participating in decisions affecting the entire society. Of what value is it to protect an individual's right to vote for elected officials if the important decisions are made in referenda rather than in the legislature?

Thus, there is reason to scrutinize measures passed by initiative or referendum. In doing so the Court would be protecting participation in the political process and the integrity of the representational system, rather than directly remedying racial discrimination, with the belief that as long as the representational system is sound and minorities are effectively participating in the decisionmaking process, minorities can safeguard their own interests. Although in one sense any referendum or initiative operates counter to the representative system, the need for court protection of that system is strongest when the majority attempts through the direct ballot to take away something the minority obtained through the representative system. As a first step, Court scrutiny of ballot legislation might arguably be limited to such cases. * * *

CITY OF CUYAHOGA FALLS V. BUCKEYE COMMUNITY HOPE FOUNDATION

Supreme Court of the United States, 2003.
538 U.S. 188, 123 S.Ct. 1389, 155 L.Ed.2d 349.

JUSTICE O'CONNOR delivered the opinion of the Court. * * *

In June 1995, respondents Buckeye Community Hope Foundation, a nonprofit corporation dedicated to developing affordable housing through the use of low-income tax credits, and others (hereinafter Buckeye or respondents), purchased land zoned for apartments in Cuyahoga Falls, Ohio. In February 1996, Buckeye submitted a site plan for Pleasant Meadows, a multifamily, low-income housing complex, to the city planning commission. Residents of Cuyahoga Falls immediately expressed opposition to the proposal. After respondents agreed to various conditions, including that respondents build an earthen wall surrounded by a fence on one side of the complex, the commission unanimously approved the site plan and submitted it to the city council for final authorization.

As the final approval process unfolded, public opposition to the plan resurfaced and eventually coalesced into a referendum petition drive. At city council meetings and independent gatherings, some of which the mayor attended to express his personal opposition to the site plan, citizens of Cuyahoga Falls voiced various concerns: that the development would cause crime and drug activity to escalate, that families with children would move in, and that the complex would attract a population similar to the one on Prange Drive, the City's only African-American neighborhood. Nevertheless, because the plan met all municipal zoning requirements, the city council approved the project on April 1, 1996, through City Ordinance No. 48–1996.

On April 29, a group of citizens filed a formal petition with the City requesting that the ordinance be repealed or submitted to a popular vote. Pursuant to the charter, which provides that an ordinance challenged by a petition "shall [not] go into effect until approved by a majority" of voters, the filing stayed the implementation of the site plan. On April 30, respondents sought an injunction against the petition in state court, arguing that the Ohio Constitution does not authorize popular referendums on administrative matters. * * *

In November 1996, the voters of Cuyahoga Falls passed the referendum, thus repealing Ordinance No. 48–1996. In a joint stipulation, however, the parties agreed that the results of the election would not be certified until the litigation over the referendum was resolved. In July 1998, the Ohio Supreme Court, having initially concluded that the referendum was proper, reversed itself and declared the referendum unconstitutional. Buckeye Community Hope Foundation v. Cuyahoga Falls, 82 Ohio St.3d 539, 697 N.E.2d 181 (1998) (holding that the Ohio State Constitution authorizes referendums only in relation to legislative acts, not administrative acts, such as the site-plan ordinance). The City subsequently issued the building permits, and Buckeye commenced construction of Pleasant Meadows.

In July 1996, with the state-court litigation still pending, respondents filed suit in federal court against the City and several city officials, seeking an injunction ordering the City to issue the building permits, as well as declaratory and monetary relief. Buckeye alleged that "in allowing a site plan approval ordinance to be submitted to the electors of Cuyahoga Falls through a referendum and in rejecting [its] application for building permits," the City and its officials violated the Equal Protection and Due Process Clauses of the Fourteenth Amendment, as well as the Fair Housing Act, 42 U.S.C. § 3601. * * *

We have made clear that "[p]roof of racially discriminatory intent or purpose is required" to show a violation of the Equal Protection Clause. Arlington Heights v. Metropolitan Housing Development Corp., 429 U.S. 252, 265, 97 S.Ct. 555, 50 L.Ed.2d 450 (1977). * * * [I]n submitting the referendum petition to the voters, the City acted pursuant to the requirements of its charter, which sets out a facially neutral petitioning procedure. By placing the referendum on the ballot, the City did not enact the referendum and therefore cannot be said to have given effect to voters' allegedly discriminatory motives for supporting the petition. Similarly, the city engineer, in refusing to issue the building permits while the referendum was still pending, performed a nondiscretionary, ministerial act. He acted in response to the city law director's instruction that the building permits "could not . . . issue" because the charter prohibited a challenged site-plan ordinance from going into effect until "approved by a majority of those voting thereon". Respondents point to no evidence suggesting that these official acts were themselves motivated by racial animus. Respondents do not, for example, offer evidence that the City followed the obligations set forth in its charter because of the referendum's discriminatory purpose, or that city officials would have selectively refused to follow standard charter procedures in a different case.

Instead, to establish discriminatory intent, respondents * * * rely heavily on evidence of allegedly discriminatory voter sentiment. But statements made by private individuals in the course of a citizen-driven petition drive, while sometimes relevant to equal protection analysis, do not, in and of themselves, constitute state action for the purposes of the Fourteenth Amendment. * * * In fact, by adhering to charter procedures, city officials enabled public debate on the referendum to take place, thus advancing significant First Amendment interests. In assessing the referendum as a "basic instrument of democratic government," Eastlake v. Forest City Enterprises, Inc., 426 U.S. 668, 679, 96 S.Ct. 2358, 49 L.Ed.2d 132 (1976), we have observed that "[p]rovisions for referendums demonstrate devotion to democracy, not to bias, discrimination, or prejudice," James v. Valtierra, 402 U.S. 137, 141, 91 S.Ct. 1331, 28 L.Ed.2d 678 (1971). And our well established First Amendment admonition that "government may not prohibit the expression of an idea simply because society finds the idea itself offensive or disagreeable," Texas v. Johnson, 491 U.S. 397, 414, 109 S.Ct. 2533, 105 L.Ed.2d 342 (1989), dovetails with the notion that all citizens, regardless of the content of their ideas, have the right to petition their government. Again, statements made by decisionmakers or referendum sponsors during deliberation over a referendum may constitute relevant evidence of discriminatory intent in a challenge to an ultimately enacted initiative. See, e.g., Washington v. Seattle School Dist. No. 1, 458 U.S. 457, 471, 102 S.Ct. 3187, 73 L.Ed.2d 896 (1982) (considering statements of initiative sponsors in subjecting enacted referendum to equal protection scrutiny); Arlington Heights v. Metropolitan Housing Development Corp., 429 U.S., at 268, 97 S.Ct. 555. But respondents do not challenge an enacted referendum. * * *

Respondents fail to show that city officials exercised any power over voters' decisionmaking during the drive, much less the kind of "coercive power" either "overt or covert" that would render the voters' actions and statements, for all intents and purposes, state action. Nor, as noted above, do respondents show that the voters' sentiments can be attributed in any way to the state actors against which it has brought suit. * * * [I]n dismissing the claim against the mayor in his individual capacity, the District Court found no evidence that he orchestrated the referendum. Respondents thus fail to present an equal protection claim sufficient to survive summary judgment. * * *

RICHARD DELEON, LEFT COAST CITY: PROGRESSIVE POLITICS IN SAN FRANCISCO 1975–1991
Pp. 22–24 (1992).

As in most western cities, San Francisco's voters are endowed with the instruments of direct democracy: the initiative, referendum, and recall. These electoral tools, particularly the citizen initiative, have allowed progressive leaders to circumvent recalcitrant elected officials, to shape the city's political agenda, and to legislate policy directly. The slow-growth movement was organized almost entirely around initiative campaigns, and it is hard to imagine how that movement could have succeeded without them. The citizen ballot initiative is especially well suited to the city's growing population of highly educated middle-class professionals, who are inclined to be "elite directing" rather than "elite directed" even in the arcane policy spheres of land use and physical development. The frequent adoption of the citizen ballot initiative as a land-use planning tool is disturbing to many professional planners and business elites. Planning lawyers Daniel Curtin and M. Thomas Jacobsen, for example, contend that "the hallmarks of good land-use planning are that decisions are well-informed, that the planning process is flexible and responsive to changing circumstances and values, and that decisions reflect a comprehensive planning process and are accommodations of competing public interests. Arguably, each of these land-use goals is thwarted when land-use planning is done via the ballot box." Richard Morton, a former San Francisco Chamber of Commerce official, concurs with such criticisms, adding: "The city's lengthy battle over planning initiatives has contributed to political instability and a feeling of uncertainty among business people who need to plan for the long term."

The city's conservative groups also know how to employ the instruments of direct democracy. In 1989, for example, the Board of Supervisors unanimously passed and the mayor signed a "domestic partners" ordinance allowing city-employed unmarried couples who live together (including gay men and lesbians) to register their relationship at city hall. City workers who signed up under the law would receive many of the same rights, such as hospital visitation leaves, accorded to married couples. A week before the new measure was to take effect, a petition-gathering campaign organized by religious leaders and conservative groups succeeded in stopping implementation of the new law until it was put to the voters as a referendum on the November 1989 ballot. This citizen-initiated referendum measure, Proposition S, was fiercely contested and eventually lost by a slim margin. The pioneering ordinance was rendered null and void. A year later the progressives came back to the voters with an initiative, Proposition K, which was a slightly watered-down version of the referendum, Proposition S. Proposition K won by a significant margin, and the proposed domestic partners ordinance finally became law. * * *

H. THE CITY AND DEMOCRATIC THEORY: PART FOUR

The five readings that conclude this chapter present a conception of local democracy that differs from the one that has been emphasized in most of the chapter's cases and materials. The cases and materials have concentrated on protecting citizens from city governmental power or on mechanisms for citizen control of government, such as voting, that perpetuate a sharp distinction between those who govern and those who are governed. In the following readings, by contrast, the emphasis is on citizen participation as the basis for the relationship between a city and its citizens—or, more accurately, as the basis for the relationships among the citizens themselves. Benjamin Barber expands on the values of participation as a way of defining oneself and one's community; Archon Fung and Erik Olin Wright describe current efforts in the United States and elsewhere to institutionalize what the Barber excerpt calls "strong democracy"; John Gaventa presents an argument against the conventional reason advanced for lack of participation ("if they wanted to participate, they would"); and Hanna Pitkin and Sara Shumer sketch how the notion of participatory democracy might connect with current ideas about the necessity of bureaucratic organization, representative democracy, and technological expertise. What changes in the legal doctrine covered in the chapter would be necessary to promote the ideal these readings advance? Is the argument for participatory democracy simply a romantic fantasy or could it be put into practice in one's own community (or workplace or law school)? Even if it were put into practice, would it create a city of justice without its own defects? On this final question, Italo Calvino, appropriately enough, has the last word.

BENJAMIN BARBER, STRONG DEMOCRACY
Pp. 150–155, 173–193, 197–198 (1984).

Strong Democracy: Politics in the Participatory Mode

The future of democracy lies with strong democracy—with the revitalization of a form of community that is not collectivistic, a form of public reasoning that is not conformist, and a set of civic institutions that is compatible with modern society. Strong democracy is defined by politics in the participatory mode: literally, it is self-government by citizens rather than representative government in the name of citizens. Active citizens govern themselves directly here, not necessarily at every level and in every instance, but frequently enough and in particular when basic policies are being decided and when significant power is being deployed. Self-government is carried on through institutions designed to facilitate ongoing civic participation in agenda-setting, deliberation, legislation, and policy implementation (in the form of "common work"). Strong democracy does not place endless faith in the capacity of individuals to govern themselves, but it affirms with Machiavelli that the multitude will on the whole be as wise as or even wiser than princes and with Theodore Roosevelt that "the majority of the plain people will day in and day out make fewer mistakes in governing themselves than any smaller body of men will make in trying to govern them."

Considered as a response to the dilemmas of the political condition, strong democracy can be given the following formal definition: *strong democracy in the participatory mode resolves conflict in the absence of an independent ground through a participatory process of ongoing, proximate self-legislation and the creation of a political community capable of transforming dependent private individuals into free citizens and partial and private interests into public goods.*

The crucial terms in this strong formulation of democracy are *activity, process, self-legislation, creation,* and *transformation.* Where weak democracy eliminates conflict (the anarchist disposition), represses it (the realist disposition), or tolerates it (the minimalist disposition), strong democracy *transforms conflict.* It turns dissensus into an occasion for mutualism and private interest into an epistemological tool of public thinking.

Participatory politics deals with public disputes and conflicts of interest by subjecting them to a never-ending process of deliberation, decision, and action. Each step in the process is a flexible part of ongoing procedures that are embedded in concrete historical conditions and in social and economic actualities. In place of the search for a prepolitical independent ground or for an immutable rational plan, strong democracy relies on participation in an evolving problem-solving community that creates public ends where there were none before by means of its own activity and of its own existence as a focal point of the quest for mutual solutions. In such communities, public ends are neither extrapolated from absolutes nor "discovered" in a preexisting "hidden consensus." They are literally forged through the act of public participation, created through common deliberation and common action and the effect that deliberation and action have on interests, which change shape and direction when subjected to these participatory processes.

Strong democracy, then, seems potentially capable of transcending the limitations of representation and the reliance on surreptitious independent grounds without giving up such defining democratic values as liberty, equality, and social justice. Indeed, these values take on richer and fuller meanings than they can ever have in the instrumentalist setting of liberal democracy. For the strong democratic solution to the political condition issues out of a self-sustaining dialectic of participatory civic activity and continuous community-building in which freedom and equality are nourished and given political being. Community grows out of participation and at the same time makes participation possible; civic activity educates individuals how to think publicly as citizens even as citizenship informs civic activity with the required sense of publicness and justice. Politics becomes its own university, citizenship its own training ground, and participation its own tutor. Freedom is what comes out of this process, not what goes into it. Liberal and representative modes of democracy make politics an activity of specialists and experts whose only distinctive qualification, however, turns out to be simply that they engage in politics—that they encounter others in a setting that requires action and where they have to find a way to act in concert. Strong democracy is the politics of amateurs, where every man is compelled to encounter every other man without the intermediary of expertise.

This universality of participation—every citizen his own politician—is essential, because the "Other" is a construct that becomes real to an individual only when he encounters it directly in the political arena. He may confront it as an obstacle or approach it as an ally, but it is an inescapable reality in the way of and on the way to common decision and common action. *We* also remains an abstraction when individuals are represented either by politicians or as symbolic wholes. The term acquires a sense of concreteness and simple reality only when individuals redefine themselves as citizens and come together directly to resolve a conflict or achieve a purpose or implement a decision. Strong democracy creates the very citizens it depends upon *because* it depends upon them, because it permits the representation neither of *me* nor of *we,* because it mandates a permanent confrontation between the *me* as citizen and the "Other" as citizen, forcing *us* to think in common and act in common. The citizen is by definition a *we*-thinker, and to think of the *we* is always to transform how interests are perceived and goods defined. * * *

It has * * * become a habit of the shrewder defenders of representative democracy to chide participationists and communitarians with the argument that enlarged public participation in politics produces no great results Once empowered, the masses do little more than push private interests, pursue selfish ambitions, and bargain for personal gain, the liberal critics assert. Such participation is the work of prudent beasts and is often less efficient than the ministrations of representatives who have a better sense of the public's appetites than does the public itself. But such a course in truth merely gives the people all the insignia and none of the tools of citizenship and then convicts them of incompetence. Social scientists and political elites have all too often indulged themselves in this form of hypocrisy. They throw referenda at the people without providing adequate information, full debate, or prudent insulation from money and media pressures and then pillory them for their lack of judgment. They overwhelm the people with the least tractable problems of mass society—busing, inflation, tax structures, nuclear safety, right-to-work legislation, industrial waste disposal, environmental protection (all of which the representative elites themselves have utterly failed to deal with)—and then carp at their uncertainty or indecisiveness or the simple-mindedness with which they muddle through to a decision. But what general would shove rifles into the hands of civilians, hurry them off to battle, and then call them cowards when they are overrun by the enemy?

Strong democracy is not government by "the people" or government by "the masses," because a people are not yet a citizenry and masses are only nominal freemen who do not in fact govern themselves. Nor is participation to be understood as random activity by maverick cattle caught up in the same stampede or as minnow-school movement by clones who wiggle in unison. As with so many central political terms, the idea of participation has an intrinsically normative dimension a dimension that is circumscribed by citizenship. Masses make noise, citizens deliberate; masses behave, citizens act; masses collide and intersect, citizens engage, share, and contribute. At the moment when "masses" start deliberating, acting, sharing, and contributing, they cease to be masses and become citizens. Only then do they "participate."

Or, to come at it from the other direction, to be a citizen *is* to participate in a certain conscious fashion that presumes awareness of and engagement in activity with others. This consciousness alters attitudes and lends to participation that sense of the *we* I have associated with community. To participate *is* to create a community that governs itself, and to create a self-governing community *is* to participate. Indeed, from the perspective of strong democracy, the two terms *participation* and *community* are aspects of one single mode of social being: citizenship. Community without participation first breeds unreflected consensus and uniformity, then nourishes coercive conformity, and finally engenders unitary collectivism of a kind that stifles citizenship and the autonomy on which political activity depends. Participation without community breeds mindless enterprise and undirected, competitive interest-mongering. Community without participation merely rationalizes collectivism, giving it an aura of legitimacy. Participation without community merely rationalizes individualism, giving it the aura of democracy.

This is not to say that the dialectic between participation and community is easily institutionalized. Individual civic activity (participation) and the public association formed through civic activity (the community) call up two strikingly different worlds. The former is the world of autonomy, individualism, and agency; the latter is the world of sociability, community, and interaction. The world views of individualism and communalism remain at odds; and institutions that can facilitate the search for common ends without sabotaging the individuality of the searchers, and that can acknowledge pluralism and conflict as starting points of the political process without abdicating the quest for a world of common ends, may be much more difficult to come by than a pretty paragraph about the dialectical interplay between individual participation and community. Yet it is just this dialectical balance that strong democracy claims to strike. To justify this claim in detail is the task of the remaining part of this study. * * *

At the heart of strong democracy is talk. As we shall see, talk is not mere speech. It refers here to every human interaction that involves language or linguistic symbols. * * * Before embarking on a detailed discussion of the functions of talk in democracy, I want to make three general observations. First, strong democratic talk entails listening no less than speaking; second, it is affective as well as cognitive; and third, its intentionalism draws it out of the domain of pure reflection into the world of action.

In considering recent liberal theory and the idea of democracy as the politics of interest, one finds it easy enough to see how talk might be confused with speech and speech reduced to the articulation of interest by appropriate signs. Yet talk as communication obviously involves receiving as well as expressing, hearing as well as speaking, and empathizing as well as uttering. The liberal reduction of talk to speech has unfortunately inspired political institutions that foster the articulation of interests but that slight the difficult art of listening. It is far easier for representatives to speak for us than to listen for us (we do not send representatives to concerts or lectures), so that in a predominantly representative system the speaking function is enhanced while the listening function is diminished. The secret ballot allows the voter to express himself but not to be influenced by others or to have to account for his private choices in a public language. The Anglo American adversary system, expressed in legislative politics, in the judicial system, and even in the separation of powers into contending branches, also puts a premium on speaking and a penalty on listening. The aim in adversarial proceedings is to prevail—to score verbal points and to overcome one's interlocutors. In fact, speech in adversary systems is a form of aggression, simply one more variety of power. It is the war of all against all carried on by other means. * * *

Good listeners may turn out to be bad lawyers, but they make adept citizens and excellent neighbors. Liberal democrats tend to value speech, and are thus concerned with formal equality. Listeners, on the other hand, feel that an emphasis on speech enhances natural inequalities in individuals' abilities to speak with clarity, eloquence, logic, and rhetoric. Listening is a mutualistic art that by its very practice enhances equality. The empathetic listener becomes more like his interlocutor as the two bridge the differences between them by conversation and mutual understanding. Indeed, one measure of healthy political talk is the amount of *silence* it permits and encourages, for silence is the precious medium in which reflection is nurtured and empathy can grow Without it, there is only the babble of raucous interests and insistent rights vying for the deaf ears of impatient adversaries. The very idea of rights—the right to speak, the right to get on the record, the right to be heard—precludes silence. The Quaker meeting carries a message for democrats, but they are often too busy articulating their interests to hear it.

A second major requirement of talk in strong democracy is that it encompass the affective as well as the cognitive mode. Philosophers and legal theorists have been particularly guilty of overrationalizing talk in their futile quest for a perfectly rational world mediated by perfectly rational forms of speech. * * * Stripped of such artificial disciplines, however, talk appears as a mediator of affection and affiliation as well as of interest and identity, of patriotism as well as of individuality. It can build community as well as maintain rights and seek consensus as well as resolve conflict. It offers, along with meanings and significations, silences, rituals, symbols, myths, expressions and solicitations, and a hundred other quiet and noisy manifestations of our common humanity. Strong democracy seeks institutions that can give these things a voice—and an ear.

The third issue that liberal theorists have underappreciated is the complicity of talk in action. With talk we can invent alternative futures, create mutual purposes, and construct competing visions of community. Its potentialities thrust talk into the realm of intentions and consequences and render it simultaneously more provisional and more concrete than philosophers are wont to recognize. Their failure of

imagination stems in part from the passivity of thin democratic politics and in part from the impatience of speculative philosophy with contingency, which entails possibility as well as indeterminateness. But significant political effects and actions are possible only to the extent that politics is embedded in a world of fortune, uncertainty, and contingency.
* * *

The functions of talk in the democratic process fall into at least nine major categories. The first two are familiar to liberals and encompass most of what they understand as the functions of talk. The next six are muted and undervalued in liberal theory, in part because they are not well served by representative institutions and by the adversary system. The last summarizes the overall function of talk. The nine functions are:

1. The articulation of interests; bargaining and exchange

2. Persuasion

3. Agenda-setting

4. Exploring mutuality

5. Affiliation and affection

6. Maintaining autonomy

7. Witness and self-expression

8. Reformulation and reconceptualization

9. Community-building as the creation of public interests, common goods, and active citizens

1. The Articulation of Interests; Bargaining and Exchange. In most liberal polities, talk is understood as a primary medium of exchange among competing individuals who seek to maximize their self-interests through market interaction. Contracts are one good example. The model here is economic, and speech is little more than a system of mathematical signs—quantifications of competing expressions such as "I want" and "How much will you pay?"—that make possible the adjudication, aggregation, and exchange that is presumed to lie at the heart of politics. The term *interest* is crucial here, because it embodies the idea of the individual and his adversary social role * * * This narrow construction of talk certainly depicts one of the aspects it has in all democratic regimes. But this interpretation also raises problems. By reducing talk to the hedonistic speech of bargaining, it creates a climate hostile to the affective uses of talk and invulnerable to the subtle claims of mutualism. These limitations are most clearly evident in the "free-rider" problem, which continues to bedevil the shapers of public policy and of economic choice. Free-riders are self-interested individuals who do not care to comply with public policies and common decisions in the absence of careful policing and external coercion. Since they act exclusively out of self-interest and obey regulations only as the necessary price for winning the compliance of others, they are content to ride for nothing on the back of the "public" as long as they can get away with it. As we will see when we discuss the nature of public interests below, free-riders can exist only in a thin democracy where obligation is the provisional consequence of a bargain. Citizens do not and cannot ride for free, because they understand that their freedom is a consequence of their participation in the making and acting out of common decisions. To ride for free is to betray not others or an abstract promise but themselves.

2. *Persuasion.* Liberal democrats favor economic models of political interaction, but they are far too sophisticated to think that the shouting on the floor of the stock exchange and the bargains that such shouting seals exhaust the possibilities of political talk. They recognize persuasion and rhetoric as well, although they tend to regard these as tools to be used in convincing others of the legitimacy of one's own interests. Persuasion thus constitutes a second major function of talk in all democratic regimes. Among liberals, this function is conventionally associated with the idea of the "rationality of interests," a notion of talk that falls short of a truly public interest but that does envision a web of interest linking private to more general goods. * * * In this way, even the narrowest construction of persuasion moves the policy beyond talk as the expression of wholly private interests and becomes a link to stronger forms of democracy.

3. *Agenda-Setting.* In liberal democracies, agendas are typically regarded as the province of elites—of committees, or executive officers, or (even) pollsters. This is so not simply because representative systems delegate the agenda-setting function or because they slight citizen participation, but because they conceive of agendas as fixed and self-evident, almost natural, and in this sense incidental to such vital democratic processes as deliberation and decision-making.

Yet a people that does not set its own agenda, by means of talk and direct political exchange, not only relinquishes a vital power of government but also exposes its remaining powers of deliberation and decision to ongoing subversion. What counts as an "issue" or a "problem" and how such issues or problems are formulated may to a large extent predetermine what decisions are reached. * * *

For these reasons, strong democratic talk places its agenda at the center rather than at the beginning of its politics. It subjects every pressing issue to continuous examination and possible reformulation. Its agenda *is,* before anything else, its agenda. It thus scrutinizes what remains unspoken, looking into the crevices of silence for signs of an unarticulated problem, a speechless victim, or a mute protester. The agenda of a community tells a community where and what it is. It defines that community's mutualism and the limits of mutualism, and draws up plans for pasts to be institutionalized or overcome and for futures to be avoided or achieved. Far from being a mere preliminary of democracy, agenda-setting becomes one of its pervasive, defining functions.

4.   *Exploring Mutuality.* When talk is reduced to mere signing in a bargaining process, it can permit us at best only to explore our differences in the search for mutually beneficial exchanges. Rational-choice models such as the "prisoner's dilemma" translate even altruism into the language of interest. But because it permits us to treat our interlocutors as kin by virtue of our common language, rather than as adversaries by virtue of our divergent interests, strong democratic talk becomes a medium of mutual exploration. The functions of talk in deliberation (airing choices), bargaining (exchanging benefits), and decision-making (choosing goals) are complemented by the more complex, open-ended art of conversation. * * *

Fixing its own rules as it conducts itself, a conversation follows an informal dialectic in which talk is used not to chart distinctions in the typical analytic fashion but to explore and create commonalities. Analytic reason yields contradictions such as individual versus society, or freedom versus authority. Conversation gives life to a notion of "citizen" in which such antinomies are superseded. "The vagaries of me and you" (Peirce) dissolve in a form of talk possible only for "us." *Right* and *wrong* cease to be viable terms of judgment in an interchange that makes no claim to certainty or truth. Think of two neighbors talking for the first time over a fence, or two college freshmen talking over a first cup of coffee: there are no debates, no arguments, no challenges, no setting of priorities, no staking out of positions, no inventorying of interests, no distribution of goods, no awarding of prizes. There is only a "getting to know you" and thereby "getting to know *us*"—exploring the common context, traits, circumstances, or passions that make of two separate identities one single *we*. World leaders meeting at a summit will frequently devote an initial session to getting to know one another in very much this fashion, before they get down to the business of bargaining and exchange. And it is much more than protocol that motivates them; indeed, even protocol is a form of ritual in which civility is given its due, where there may be little more than civility to hold adversaries together. * * *

5.   *Affiliation and Affection.* Conversation enables us to know and even to understand one another, but we do not necessarily like what we know and understand. Thus it is useful to separate the exploratory from the affective uses of talk in democracy, even though these obviously overlap a good deal. For whereas in exploring mutuality, talk retains its cognitive structure (though it may stretch it for the sake of ambiguity), in serving affection and affiliation talk takes advantage of its potential for emotive expression, musical utterance, inflection, feeling, ritual, and

symbolism (or myth). We talk to infants, to animals, to lovers, to ourselves, and to God in sounds for which neither economists nor analytic philosophers would find much use. Yet the sound of music and the sound of poetry move and bind with a power that belongs to talk. Through words we convey information, articulate interests, and pursue arguments, but it is through tone, color, volume, and inflection that we feel, affect, and touch each other. We reassure, we frighten, we unsettle, we comfort, we intimidate, we soothe, we hate, and we love by manipulating the medium rather than the content of speech. Indeed, we can use the medium to contradict its message—as in Ring Lardner's whimsical line, " 'Shut up!' he explained"—or to create irony, that irksome tribute to the deeply layered texture (the deep structure) of all speech. And our talk is peppered with ritual speech: greetings and goodbyes, prayers and incantations, exclamations and expletives, all of which in their banality and conventionality express and reinforce the daily structures of common life.

In politics, noncognitive speech is less appreciated, perhaps once again because formal rationality and liberal democracy have forged so close a partnership. * * * Voting—which is already the least significant act of citizenship in a democracy—has in America been stripped of almost all pomp and ritual, largely in the name of the kind of efficiency symbolized by voting machines and the kind of privatism represented by the secret ballot. Voting should be an occasion for celebration as well as for choice, just as the exercise of freedom should be a rite as well as a right. In some localities, the Swiss still choose their representatives and vote on policies in day-long assemblies in which festive games, theater, drinking, and camaraderie accompany the formal voting process. Rousseau notes the invigorating effect that such celebrations have on the community's sense of identity as well as on individual citizens' autonomy and capacity for action. In contrast, our primary electoral act, voting, is rather like using a public toilet: we wait in line with a crowd in order to close ourselves up in a small compartment where we can relieve ourselves in solitude and in privacy of our burden, pull a lever, and then, yielding to the next in line, go silently home. Because our vote is secret—"private"— we do not need to explain or justify it to others (or, indeed, to ourselves) in a fashion that would require us to think publicly or politically. The public rites of voting can have an affiliating effect that is as valuable to democracy as the decision itself. In strong democracy, affect and effect are Siamese twins; neither can thrive without the other. After all, the right to choose belongs to citizens not to individuals, and citizens are defined by their membership in a community not by their capacity to vote, which follows only from membership. * * *

6. Maintaining Autonomy. Talk helps us overcome narrow self-interest, but it plays an equally significant role in buttressing the

autonomy of individual wills that is essential to democracy. * * * Talk is
the principal mechanism by which we can retest and thus repossess our
convictions, which means that a democracy that does not institutionalize
talk will soon be without autonomous citizens, though men and women
who call themselves citizens may from time to time deliberate, choose,
and vote. Talk immunizes values from ossification and protects the
political process from rigidity, orthodoxy, and the yoke of the dead past.

This, among all the functions of talk, is the least liable to
representation, since only the presence of our own wills working on a
value can endow that value with legitimacy and us with our autonomy.
Subjecting a value to the test of repossession is a measure of legitimacy as
well as of autonomy: forced knowingly to embrace their prejudices, many
men falter. Prejudice is best practiced in the dark by dint of habit or
passion. Mobs are expert executors of bigotry because they assimilate
individual wills into a group will and relieve individuals of any
responsibility for their actions. It is above all the imagination that dies
when will is subordinated to instinct, and as we have seen, it is the
imagination that fires empathy. * * * [I]n the social setting, it seems
evident that maxims that are continuously reevaluated and repossessed
are preferable to maxims that are embraced once and obeyed blindly
thereafter. At a minimum, convictions that are reexamined are more
likely to change, to adapt themselves to altered circumstances and to
evolve to meet the challenges offered by competing views. Political willing
is thus never a one-time or sometime thing (which is the great
misconception of the social-contract tradition), but an ongoing shaping
and reshaping of our common world that is as endless and exhausting as
our making and remaking of our personal lives. A moment's complacency
may mean the death of liberty; a break in political concentration may
spell the atrophy of an important value; a pleasant spell of privatism may
yield irreversible value ossification. Democratic politics is a demanding
business. * * *

7. *Witness and Self-Expression.* There is a second feature of talk
that undergirds the autonomous individual and secures his place in a
community of talk. The fact that an individual belongs to a political
community and assents to common decisions means ideally that he
reformulates his personal interests and beliefs in terms commensurable
with public interests and beliefs. But realistically, that fact may also
mean that the individual is outtalked or outvoted or even overruled by a
collective will that seems less likely to serve the public good than would
the individual's own will. A healthy democratic community will therefore
leave room for the expression of distrust, dissent, or just plain opposition,
even in lost causes where dissenters are obviously very much in the
minority. Here the function of talk is to allow people to vent their
grievances or frustration or opposition, not in hopes of moving others but

in order to give public status to their strongly held personal convictions. The cry "In spite of all, *I believe* * * * "is the hallmark of such usage, and conscientious objection to military service is an illuminating example.

This form of self-expression involves much more than merely letting off steam, though we would be foolish to undervalue the safety-valve function. It is a symbol of the community's heterogeneity and an acknowledgment that, though political decisions must be taken and common grounds for these decisions contrived in the absence of independent measures, the common will may comprise individuals whose compliance is reluctant. "I am part of the community, I participated in the talk and deliberation leading to the decision, and so I regard myself as bound; but let it be known that I do not think we have made the right decision," says the dissenter in a strong democracy. He means thus not to change the decision this time, for it has been taken, but to bear witness to another point of view (and thereby to keep the issue on the public agenda). * * *

8. *Reformulation and Reconceptualization.* As we have seen, the reformulation of terms and values insinuates itself into each of the other functions of talk. Agenda-setting as an ongoing function involves the persistent reconceptualization of public business, of the very idea of the public; the exploration of mutuality entails an enlargement of consciousness that brings with it new and broader understandings of common language; affiliation and affection depend on an empathy that changes how we view our interests and our separate identities; autonomy means rethinking our values and beliefs in a changing world; and witness suggests a challenge to common decisions commonly taken that may facilitate reevaluation. Only bargaining and persuasion (narrowly understood) are free of reformulation—which is, of course, exactly what is the matter with them. * * *

9. *Community-Building as the Creation of Public Interests, Common Goods, and Active Citizens.* All of the functions of talk discussed above converge toward a single, crucial end—the development of a citizenry capable of genuinely public thinking and political judgment and thus able to envision a common future in terms of genuinely common goods * * *. [T]alk is ultimately a force with which we can create a community capable of creating its own future and that talk is nourished by community even as it helps establish the conditions for community. * * *

ARCHON FUNG AND ERIK OLIN WRIGHT, DEEPENING
DEMOCRACY: INNOVATIONS IN EMPOWERED
PARTICIPATORY GOVERNANCE

29 Politics & Society 5 (2001).

* * * This article explores * * * real-world experiments in the redesign of democratic institutions, innovations that elicit the energy and influence of ordinary people, often drawn from the lowest strata of society in the solution of problems that plague them. In this article we will examine briefly five such experiments. * * * Although these five reforms differ dramatically in the details of their design, issue areas, and scope, they all aspire to deepen the ways in which ordinary people can effectively participate in and influence policies that directly affect their lives. From their common features, we call this reform family *Empowered Deliberative Democracy* (EDD). They have the potential to be radically democratic in their reliance on the participation and capacities of ordinary people, deliberative because they institute reason-based decision making, and empowered since they attempt to tie action to discussion. * * * These institutional reforms vary widely on many dimensions, and none perfectly realizes the democratic values of citizen' participation, deliberation, and empowerment. In its own way and quite imperfectly, however, each strives to advance these values and to an extent succeeds. * * *

1. * * * Chicago

Our first experiment concerns public education * * * in a city characterized by great poverty and inequality: Chicago, Illinois, whose 2.5 million residents make it the third largest city in the United States. In the late 1980s, the Chicago Public School system suffered attacks from all sides—parents, community members, and area businessmen charged that the centralized school bureaucracy was failing to educate the city's children on a massive scale. These individuals and groups formed a small but vocal social movement that managed to turn the top-heavy, hierarchical school system on its head. In 1988, the Illinois legislature passed a law that decentralized and opened the governance of Chicago schools to direct forms of neighborhood participation. The reform law shifted power and control from a centralized citywide headquarters to the individual schools themselves. For each of some 560 elementary (grades kindergarten through eighth) and high schools (grades nine through twelve), the law established a Local School Council. Each council is composed of six parents, two community members, two teachers, and the principal of the school, and its members (other than the principal) are elected every two years. The councils of high schools add to these eleven members one nonvoting student representative. These councils are empowered, and required by law, to select principals; write principal performance contracts that they monitor and review every three years; develop annual School Improvement Plans that address staff, program, infrastructure issues; monitor the implementation of those plans; and approve school budgets. These bodies typically meet monthly during the school year, and less frequently in the summer. This reform created the most formally direct democratic system of school governance by far in the United States. Every year, more than 5,000 parents, neighborhood residents, and schoolteachers are elected to run their schools. By a wide margin, the majority of elected Illinois public officials who are minorities serve on these councils.

The weaknesses of their decentralization soon became apparent. While many schools used their new powers to flourish, others foundered due to lack of capacity, knowledge, internal conflict, or bad luck. New regulations and departments within the Chicago Public Schools were refashioned to address these problems. For example, 1995 legislation requires each Local School Council member to undergo some twenty hours of training, provided by the central school administration, on topics such as budgeting, school improvement planning, principal selection, group process, and council responsibilities. The same law also created accountability provisions to identify the worst performing schools in the city. These schools receive additional management supervision, resources, and, in some cases, disciplinary punishment. * * *

2. * * * Milwaukee, Wisconsin

The next experiment moves away from the reconstruction of municipal government to new economic institutions that bring together workers and managers for the common cause of managing industrial labor markets. The * * * [Wisconsin Regional Training Partnership ("WRTP")] is a consortium of some forty firms employing more than 60,000 workers in the Milwaukee, Wisconsin area. WRTP, jointly governed by representatives from organized labor, managers of member firms, and public sector institutions such as area Technical Colleges and the Wisconsin State Department of Labor, aims to improve the health of area industry by joining labor and management to provide services that isolated firms would be unlikely to provide for themselves. Although the WRTP is also active in firm modernization and school-to-industrial work transitions, its most distinctive and developed efforts lie in the provision of incumbent and entry-level worker training.

Against a competitive background that has demanded continuous modernization of fixed and human capital since the late 1970s and 1980s, many Milwaukee area industrial firms responded to the failure of public and private training systems to keep pace with technological change by attempting to impose compensatory wage reductions or by moving productive facilities to areas of higher skill or lower labor cost. Beginning with an early prototype in 1988, the WRTP answered this deindustrialization by creating Worker Education Centers that attempted to improve area skill training. These centers are miniature schools located within firms that train workers in the most urgently needed basic or advanced skills. By early 1998, the WRTP had established more than forty education centers in the facilities of its member firms and others who requested technical assistance. Each center is jointly designed and operated by a labor-management committee that selects skill priorities, designs classes, markets those classes to the incumbent workforce, renegotiates labor contract terms that may be incompatible with such skill training (such as seniority rules, job classifications, and work rules), and administers the center. These centers sometimes receive their funding through public sources, but most often through firm-side contributions. They frequently employ instructors from area technical colleges to teach classes on-site.

The direct participation of workers in the design and management of these centers may enable them to succeed where previous attempts have failed. The centers take advantage of worker cooperation first by developing classes and training priorities-based, shop-floor experiences and perceptions of need. Neither technical college nor management-led training efforts can access this level of high-quality, frontline information about which skill areas deserve immediate investment and whether training routines are effectively imparting skills and knowledge to workers. The centers also use "peer networks" to market this training to other workers and thus build a degree of worker acceptance that management acting alone could not. Furthermore, the mutual confidence that comes from this cooperative effort gains management support in the form of resource investment in training and labor support that is manifest in less adversarial bargaining positions. These education centers embody the deliberative-democratic principles by shifting the power of design and implementation of incumbent-worker training from a state-centered technical college system to decentralized, firm-based learning centers. Finally, many of these centers brought together managers and workers accustomed to operating on opposite sides of a bargaining table in a deliberative effort to solve training problems.

3. * * * U.S. Endangered Species Act

For most the time since its establishment in 1973, the U.S. Endangered Species Act has been the antithesis of deliberative action. Section 9 of that Act prohibits the "taking"—killing or injuring—of any wildlife listed as an endangered species through either direct means or indirect action such as modification of its habitat. In practice, this often imposed a strict bar on any development or resource extraction activities in or near the habitats of endangered species. This law had two main defects. First, it stopped productive development projects that may have had marginal impact on the ultimate viability of endangered species. Less obviously, the law protected only those species that are listed and receive administrative priority, and so created a listing process that frequently amounted to a high stakes political battle between developers and conservationists. As a result, too few species receive protection and some are nearly decimated by the time they do qualify.

In 1982, Congress created an option to escape these deep deadlocks called an "incidental take permit." Under this provision, an applicant can obtain a waiver from strict enforcement by producing a Habitat Conservation Plan (HCP) that allows human activity in the habitat of an endangered species so long as "take" occurs only incidentally, the plan includes measures to mitigate take, and the human activity does not impair the chances of the species' survival and recovery. Until recently, this relief option was little used because permitting procedures were unclear and plan production costs high. Only 14 HCPs were produced between 1982 and 1992. Since 1993, however, these plans and their associated permits have proliferated. By April 1999, 254 plans covering more than 11 million acres had been approved and 200 more were in various stages of development. This explosion in HCP activity grew out of an effort by Interior Secretary Bruce Babbitt and several associates to use incidental take permit provision to avoid the lose-lose outcomes generated by strict application of the Endangered Species Act's section 9. Under the process, developers, environmentalists, and other stakeholders could potentially work together to construct large-scale, eco-system conservation plans.

The most advanced HCPs have served this ambition by incorporating significant elements of the design of EDD. For example, large acreage, multispecies Conservation Plans in Southern California were developed by stakeholder committees that include officials from local and national environmental agencies, developers, environmental activists, and community organizations. Through deliberative processes, these stakeholders have developed sophisticated management plans that set out explicit numerical goals, measures to achieve those goals, monitoring regimes that assess plan effectiveness through time, and adaptive management provisions to incorporate new scientific information and respond to unforeseen events.

Beyond devolving responsibility and power for endangered species protection to local stakeholders, recent improvements to the national HCP regime proposed by the U.S. Fish and Wildlife Service attempt to create centralized learning and accountability devices to mitigate the defects of excessive localism. It has been widely recognized that high-quality HCPs possess common features such as quantitative biological goals, adaptive management plans, and careful monitoring regimes. Yet, a study of more than 200 plans revealed that less than half of all plans incorporate these basic features. In a proposed guidance, the Fish and Wildlife Service would instruct field agents to require these plan features in the development of HCPs and a condition of permit approval. To make HCP provisions and performance a matter of transparent public accountability and enable stakeholders of different HCPs to assess and learn from each other, this same Fish and Wildlife Service guidance will establish an HCP information infrastructure that tracks the details of HCP permits as well as plan performance.

4. * * * Porto Alegre, Brazil

Porto Alegre is the capital of the state of Rio Grande do Sul in Brazil and home to some 1.3 million inhabitants. Like many other local and national states in Latin America, a clientelistic government has ruled the city in recent decades through the time-tested machinery of political patronage. This system allocated public funds not according to public needs, but rather to mobilize support for political personages. As a result, "the budget becomes a fiction, shocking evidence of the discrepancy between the formal institutional framework and the actual state practices." Under similar arrangements elsewhere in Brazil, investigators revealed that the patronage-based "irregular allocation of social expenditures amounted to 64 percent of the total [budget]."

In 1988, a coalition of Left parties led by the Workers' Party, or Partido dos Trabalhadores (PT), gained control of the municipal government of Porto Alegre and went on to win successive elections in 1992 and 1996. Their most substantial reform measure, called "Participatory Budgeting" (PB), attempts to transform the clientelistic, vote-for-money budgeting reality into a fully accountable, bottom-up, deliberative system driven by the needs of city residents. This multi-tiered interest articulation and administrative arrangement begins with the sixteen administrative regions that compose the city. Within each region, a Regional Plenary Assembly meets twice per year to settle budgetary issues. City executives, administrators, representatives of community entities such as neighborhood associations, youth and health clubs, and any interested inhabitant of the city attends these assemblies, but only residents of the region can vote in them. They are jointly coordinated by members of municipal government and by community delegates.

At the first of these annual plenary meetings, held in March, a report reviewing and discussing the implementation of the prior year's budget is presented by representatives of the city government, and delegates are elected from those present at the assembly to participate in more or less weekly meetings over the following three months to work out the region's spending priorities for the following year. These delegate meetings are held in neighborhoods throughout the region and discuss a wide range of possible projects that the city might fund in the region, including issues such as transportation, sewage, land regulation, day care centers, and health care. At the end of three months, these delegates report back to the second regional plenary assembly with a set of regional budget proposals. At this second plenary, this proposal is voted on and two delegates and substitutes are elected to represent the region in a citywide body called the Participatory Budgeting Council, which meets over the following five months to formulate a citywide budget out of these regional agendas.

The city-level budget council is composed of two elected delegates from each of the regional assemblies, two elected delegates each from each of five "thematic plenaries" representing the city as a whole, a delegate from the municipal workers' union, one from the union of neighborhood associations, and two delegates from central municipal agencies. The group meets intensively, at least once per week from July to September, to discuss and establish a municipal budget that conforms to priorities established at the regional level while still coordinating spending for the city as a whole. Since citizen representatives are in most cases nonprofessionals, city agencies offer courses and seminars on budgeting for Council delegates as well as for interested participants from the regional assemblies. On 30 September of each year, the Council submits a proposed budget to the Mayor, who can either accept the budget or through veto remand it back to the Council for revision. The budget council responds by either amending the budget, or by overriding the veto through a supermajoritian vote of two-thirds. City officials estimate that some 100,000 people, or 8 percent of the adult population, participated in the 1996 round of Regional Assemblies and intermediate meetings.

5. * * * West Bengal * * *

Like the participatory budgeting reforms in Porto Alegre, Brazil, left-wing parties, revitalized substantive local governance in West Bengal * * *, India, as a central part of their political program. Although Indian states have enjoyed many formal arrangements for local self-government since independence, these institutions have been doubly constrained. Externally, larger state bureaucracies enjoyed the lion's share of financing and formal authority over most areas of administration and development over this period. Internally, traditional elites used social and economic power to dominate formally democratic local structures. Until 1957, the franchise was restricted on status grounds. But even after universal suffrage, traditional leaders managed to control these bodies and their resources. Corruption was rampant, many locally administered services were simply not performed, and development resources squandered.

In a number of Indian states, significant reforms have attempted to solve these problems of local governance by deepening their democratic character. The earliest of these began in the late 1970s in the state of West Bengal. The Left Front Government, which took power there in 1977 and has enjoyed a growing base of support ever since, saw the Panchayat village governance system as an opportunity for popular mobilization and empowerment. In addition to instituting one of the most radical programs of land reform in India in order to break the hold of traditional power at the village level, the Left Front Government has, in several distinct stages from 1977 to the present, transformed the West Begali Panchayats in order to increase opportunities for members of disadvantaged classes to wield public power.

The first important step in Panchayat empowerment came in 1988, when the state government shifted responsibility for implementing many development programs from state ministries directly to Panchayats. Simultaneous with this expansion in function, their budgets more than doubled to approximately 2 million rupees per Panchayat. Then, in 1993, a series of Constitutional and state statutory amendments dramatically enhanced the potential for further expansion of Panchayat democracy. Three changes were particularly important. First, these reforms increased the financing capacity of the lowest level Panchayat authorities—the Gram Panchayats—by imposing a revenue-sharing scheme with the Districts and gave the Gram Panchayats their own taxing power. Second, these measures stipulated that one-third of the seats in Panchayat assemblies and leadership positions would be occupied by women and that lower caste— Scheduled Caste and Scheduled Tribe (SC/ST)—persons would occupy leadership positions in all of these bodies in proportion to their population in the District. Finally, and most important for our purposes, the 1993 reforms established two kinds of directly deliberative bodies, called Gram Sabhas, to increase the popular accountability of Gram Panchayat representatives. The Gram Sabha consists of all of the persons within a Gram Panchayat area (typically around 10,000) and meets once per year in the month of December. At this meeting, elected Gram Panchayat representatives review the proposed budget for the following year and review the accomplishment (or lack thereof) of the previous year's budget and action items. Similar meetings occur twice a year at an even more disaggregated level of Panchayat governance. * * *

JOHN GAVENTA, POWER AND POWERLESSNESS
Pp. 3–25 (1980).

Power and Participation

This is a study about quiescence and rebellion in a situation of glaring inequality. Why, in a social relationship involving the domination of a non-elite by an elite, does challenge to that domination not occur? What is there in certain situations of social deprivation that prevents issues from arising, grievances from being voiced, or interests from being recognized? Why, in an oppressed community where one might intuitively expect upheaval, does one instead find, or appear to find, quiescence? Under what conditions and against what obstacles does rebellion begin to emerge? * * *

[T]his study will explore * * * [one] explanation: in situations of inequality, the political response of the deprived group or class may be seen as a function of power relationships, such that power serves for the development and maintenance of the quiescence of the non-elite. The emergence of rebellion, as a corollary, may be understood as the process by which the relationships of power are altered.

The argument itself immediately introduces a further set of questions to be explored: what is the nature of power? How do power and powerlessness affect the political actions and conceptions of a non-elite?

In his recent book, *Power: A Radical View,* Lukes has summarized what has been an extended debate since C. Wright Mills, especially in American political science, about the concept and appropriate methods for its study.[4] Power, he suggests, may be understood as having three dimensions, the first of which is based upon the traditional pluralists' approach, the second of which is essentially that put forward by Bachrach and Baratz in their consideration of power's second face,[5] and the third of which Lukes develops. In this chapter, I shall examine the dimensions briefly, arguing that each carries with it, implicitly or explicitly, differing assumptions about the nature and roots of participation and non-participation. I shall argue further that together the dimensions of power (and powerlessness) may be developed into a tentative model for more usefully understanding the generation of quiescence, as well as the process by which challenge may emerge. * * *

The Nature of Power and Roots of Quiescence

The One-Dimensional Approach. The one-dimensional approach to power is essentially that of the pluralists, developed in American political

---

[4]   Steven Lukes, Power: A Radical View (Macmillan, London, 1974).

[5]   Peter Bachrach and Morton S. Baratz, "The Two Faces of Power", American Political Science Review, 56 (1962), 947–52; and Bachrach and Baratz, Power and Poverty: Theory and Practice (Oxford University Press, New York, 1970).

science most particularly by Robert Dahl and Nelson Polsby. "My intuitive idea of power", Dahl wrote in an early essay, "is something like this: A has power over B to the extent that he can get B to do something that B would not otherwise do." In the politics of a community, Polsby later added, power may be studied by examining "who participates, who gains and loses, and who prevails in decision-making".

The key to the definition is a focus on behaviour—doing, participating—about which several assumptions are made * * *. First, grievances are assumed to be recognized and acted upon. * * * Secondly, participation is assumed to occur within decision-making arenas, which are in turn assumed to be open to virtually any organized group. * * * Thirdly, because of the openness of the decision-making process, leaders may be studied, not as elites, but as representative spokesmen for a mass. * * *

Within the one-dimensional approach, because a) people act upon recognized grievances, b) in an open system, c) for themselves or through leaders, then *non-participation* or *inaction* is not a political problem. * * * The biases of these assumptions might appear all the more readily were this approach strictly applied to the quiescence of obviously deprived groups. Political silence, or inaction, would have to be taken to reflect "consensus", despite the extent of the deprivation. Yet, rarely is the methodology thus applied, even by the pluralists themselves. To make plausible inaction among those for whom the status quo is not comfortable, other explanations are provided for what appears "irrational" or "inefficient" behaviour. And, because the study of non-participation in this approach is sequestered by definition from the study of power, the explanations must generally be placed within the circumstance or culture of the non-participants themselves. The empirical relationship of low socio-economic status to low participation gets explained away as the apathy, political inefficacy, cynicism or alienation of the impoverished. * * *

Even within its own assumptions, of course, this understanding of the political behaviour of deprived groups is inadequate. What is there inherent in low income, education or status, or in rural or traditional cultures that itself explains quiescence? If these are sufficient components of explanation, how are variations in behaviour amongst such groups to be explained? Why, for instance, do welfare action groups spring up in some cities but not in others? * * * If most blacks are of a relatively low socio-economic status, why did a highly organized civil rights movement develop, and itself alter patterns of political participation? * * *

The Two-Dimensional Approach. "It is profoundly characteristic", wrote Schattschneider, that "responsibility for widespread nonparticipation is attributed wholly to the ignorance, indifference and shiftlessness of the people." But, he continued:

> There is a better explanation: absenteeism reflects the suppression of the options and alternatives that reflect the needs of the nonparticipants. It is not necessarily true that people with the greatest needs participate in politics most actively—whoever decides what the game is about also decides who gets in the game.

In so writing, Schattschneider introduced a concept later to be developed by Bachrach and Baratz as power's "second face", by which power is exercised not just upon participants within the decision-making process but also towards the exclusion of certain participants and issues altogether. Political organizations, like all organizations, develop a "mobilization of bias * * * in favour of the exploitation of certain kinds of conflict and the suppression of others. * * * Some issues are organized into politics while others are organized out." And, if issues are prevented from arising, so too may actors be prevented from acting. The study of politics must focus "both on who gets what, when and how and who gets left out and how"—and how the two are interrelated. * * *

In this view, then, apparent inaction within the political process by deprived groups may be related to power, which in turn is revealed in participation and non-participation, upon issues and non-issues, which arise or are prevented from arising in decision-making arenas. But though the second view goes beyond the first, it still leaves much undone. * * * While Bachrach and Baratz insist that the study of power must include consideration of the barriers to action upon grievances, they equally maintain that it does not go so far as to include how power may affect conceptions of grievances themselves. If "the observer can uncover no grievances", if "in other words, there appears to be universal acquiescence in the status quo", then, they argue, it is not "possible, in such circumstances, to determine empirically whether the consensus is genuine or instead has been enforced". * * *

But, if the power of the "defenders of the *status quo*" serves to affect their awareness that they are being challenged, why cannot the powerlessness of potential challengers similarly serve to affect their awareness of interests and conflict within a power situation? That is, just as the dominant may become so "secure" with their position as to become "oblivious", so, too, may such things as routines, internalization of roles or false consensus lead to acceptance of the *status quo* by the dominated. In short, I shall agree with Lukes that the emphasis of this approach upon observable conflict may lead it to neglect what may be the "crucial point": "the most effective and insidious use of power is to prevent such conflict from arising in the first place".

The Three-Dimensional Approach. In putting forward a further conception of power, Lukes argues that "A exercises power over B when A affects B in a manner contrary to B's interests." The means by which A may do so go significantly beyond those allowed within the first two approaches.

First, "A may exercise power over B by getting him to do what he does not want to do, but *he also exercises power over him by influencing, shaping or determining his very wants.*" Not only might A exercise power over B by prevailing in the resolution of key issues or by preventing B from effectively raising those issues, but also through affecting B's conceptions of the issues altogether. Secondly, "this may happen in the absence of observable conflict, which may have been successfully averted", though there must be latent conflict, which consists, Lukes argues, "in a contradiction between the interests of those exercising power and the *real interests* of those they exclude". Thirdly, the analysis of power must avoid the individualistic, behavioral confines of the one- and to some extent the two-dimensional approaches. It must allow "for consideration of the many ways in which *potential issues* are kept out of politics, whether through the operation of social forces and institutional practices or through individuals' decisions". In so extending the concept of power, Lukes suggests, "the three-dimensional view * * * offers the prospect of a serious sociological and not merely personalized explanation of how political systems prevent demands from becoming political issues or even from being made". * * *

Perhaps more significant * * * are the implications of this three-dimensional approach for an understanding of how power shapes participation patterns of the relatively powerless. In a sense, the separation by the pluralists of the notion of power from the phenomenon of quiescence has indicated the need for such a theory, while in the second and third approaches are its beginnings. In the two-dimensional approach is the suggestion of barriers that prevent issues from emerging into political arenas—i.e. that constrain conflict. In the three-dimensional approach is the suggestion of the use of power to pre-empt manifest conflict at all, through the shaping of patterns or conceptions of non-conflict. Yet, the two-dimensional approach may still need development and the three-dimensional prospect has yet to be put to empirical test.

This book therefore will pick up the challenge of attempting to relate the three dimensions of power to an understanding of quiescence and rebellion of a relatively powerless group in a social situation of high inequality. Through the empirical application further refinements of the notion of power may develop, but, of equal importance, more insights may be gleaned as to why non-elites in such situations act and believe as they do. * * *

Power and Powerlessness: Quiescence and Rebellion—
A Tentative Relationship

Power, it has been suggested, involves the capacity of A to prevail over B both in resolution of manifest conflict and through affecting B's actions and conceptions about conflict or potential conflict. Intuitively, if the interests of A and B are contrary, and if A (individual, group, class) exercises power for the protection of its interests, then it will also be to A's advantage if the power can be used to generate and maintain quiescence of B (individual, group, class) upon B's interests. In that process, the dimensions of power and powerlessness may be viewed as interrelated and accumulative in nature, such that each dimension serves to re-enforce the strength of the other. The relationships may be schematized * * * as follows:

As A develops power, A prevails over B in decision-making arenas in the allocation of resources and values within the political system. If A prevails consistently, then A may accumulate surplus resources and values which may be allocated towards the construction of barriers around the decision-making arenas—i.e. towards the development of a mobilization of bias, as in the second dimension of power. The consistent prevalence of A in the decision-making arenas plus the thwarting of challenges to that prevalence may allow A further power to invest in the development of dominant images, legitimations, or beliefs about A's power through control, for instance, of the media or other socialization institutions. The power of A to prevail in the first dimension increases the power to affect B's actions in the second dimension, and increases the power to affect B's conceptions in the third.

The power of A is also strengthened by the fact that the powerlessness of B is similarly accumulative, and that power and powerlessness may each re-enforce the other towards the generation of B's quiescence. In the decision-making arena, B suffers continual defeat at the hands of A. Over time, B may cease to challenge A owing to the anticipation that A will prevail. But B's non-challenge allows A more opportunity to devote power to creating barriers to exclude participation in the future. The inaction of B in the second-dimensional sense becomes a sum of the anticipation by B of defeat and the barriers maintained by A over B's entering the decision-making arena anyway, and the re-enforcing effect of one upon the other.

In turn, the second-dimensional relationship may re-enforce the sense of powerlessness, the maintained non-participation, the ambiguous consciousness, or other factors which comprise the indirect mechanisms of power's third dimension. Further withdrawal of B though, in turn, allows more security for A to develop further legitimations or ideologies which may be used indirectly to affect the conceptions of B. And, as has been seen, the powerlessness of B may also increase the susceptibility of B to introjection of A's values. In the third-dimensional sense, then, B's response becomes understood as the sum of B's powerlessness and A's power, and the re-enforcing effects of the one upon the other.

Once such power relationships are developed, their maintenance is self-propelled and attempts at their alteration are inevitably difficult. In order to remedy the inequalities, B must act, but to do so B must overcome A's power, and the accumulating effects of B's powerlessness. In order to benefit from the inequalities, A need not act, or if acting, may devote energies to strengthening the power relationships. Indeed, to the extent that A can maintain conflict within the second-or third-dimensional arenas, then A will continue to prevail simply through the inertia of the situation. * * * In such a situation, power relationships can be understood only with reference to their prior development and their impact comprehended only in the light of their own momentum.

Challenge, or rebellion, may develop if there is a shift in the power relationships—either owing to loss in the power of A or gain in the power of B. (The two need not be the same owing to the possibility of intervention by other actors, technological changes, external structural factors, etc.) But even as challenge emerges, several steps in overcoming powerlessness by B must occur before the conflict is on competitive ground. B must go through a process of *issue and action formulation* by which B develops consciousness of the needs, possibilities, and strategies of challenge. That is, B must counter both the direct and indirect effects of power's third dimension. And, B must carry out the process of *mobilization of action upon issues* to overcome the mobilization of bias of A against B's actions. B must develop its own resources—real and symbolic—to wage the conflict. Only as the obstacles to challenge by B in the second and third dimensions are overcome can the conflict which emerges in the first dimension be said to reflect B's genuine participation—i.e. self-determined action with others similarly affected upon clearly conceived and articulated grievances.

This formulation of the steps in the emergence of effective challenge provides further understanding of the means by which A may prevail over the outcome of any latent or manifest conflict. In the first instance, A may simply remain aloof from B, for to intervene in a situation of potential conflict may be to introduce the notion of conflict itself. But, if conceptions or actions of challenge do arise on the part of B, A may respond at any point along the process of issue-emergence. That is, the powerless may face barriers to effective challenge in the processes of the formulation of issues, of the mobilization of action upon issues, or in the decision-making about issues—any or all of which may affect the outcome of the conflict. What are for B barriers to change are for A options for the maintenance of the status quo.

But, by the same token, as the barriers are overcome, so, too, do A's options for control lessen. And, just as the dimensions of power are accumulative and re-enforcing for the maintenance of quiescence, so, too, does the emergence of challenge in one area of a power relationship weaken the power of the total to withstand further challenges by more than the loss of a single component. For example, the development of consciousness of an issue re-enforces the likelihood of attempted action upon it, in turn re-enforcing consciousness.

A single victory helps to alter inaction owing to the anticipation of defeat, leading to more action, and so on. Once patterns of quiescence are broken upon one set of grievances, the accumulating resources of challenge—e.g. organization, momentum, consciousness—may become transferable to other issues and other targets.

For this reason, the development and maintenance of a generalized pattern of quiescence of B by A in situations of latent conflict will always be in A's interests. A will act to thwart challenges by B regardless of whether they appear, in the immediate sense, to be directed against A; for once the patterns are broken, the likelihood of further action by B increases and the options for control wielded by A decrease. For this reason, too, A will support A' on matters of common interest *vis—vis* the behaviour and conceptions of B; and B must ally with B' for the emergence of effective challenge against A—giving rise over time to social grouping and social classes of the relatively powerful and the relatively powerless. * * *

HANNA PITKIN AND SARA SHUMER, ON PARTICIPATION
2 democracy 43, 50–54 (1982).

When people say that democracy is "obviously" not suitable for a large population, they fall captive to an abstract notion of assembling more and more people in one place: "no room can hold them all." But that is not how democratic movements grow, nor how real democratic polities function. Consider the American Tocqueville discovered in the 1830s, a people deeply engaged in democratic self-government: their "most important business" and their greatest pleasure. Take away politics from the American, Tocqueville said, and you rob him of half his existence, leaving a "vast void in his life" and making him "incredibly unhappy." Yet Tocqueville's America was no city-state, nor could its citizens assemble in one place. If size was no bar then to so lively a democratic engagement, it need not be now.

Face-to-face citizen assemblies are indeed essential to democracy, but one single assembly of all is not. Representation, delegation, cooperation, coordination, federation, and other kinds of devolution are entirely compatible with democracy, though they do not constitute and cannot guarantee it. Disillusioned democrats from Robert Michels to Frances Fox Piven and Richard A. Cloward have argued that any large organization and any differentiated leadership necessarily must take the life out of democracy, rigidifying into bureaucratic hierarchy. But formless, spontaneous mobs in the streets disrupting an established order cannot by themselves be a source of enduring change or even enduring challenge. Even if ossification were ultimately inevitable for any democratic engagement, surely the democrat's task would still be to prolong and revitalize the early, militant stage of popular involvement. The point is not to eschew all organization and all differentiated leadership, confining democracy to the local and spontaneous, but to develop those organizational forms and those styles of authority that sustain rather than suppress member initiative and autonomy. From historical examples we know that such forms and styles exist; it has sometimes been done.

Democrats need to think hard—both historically and theoretically—about the circumstances and the institutions by which large-scale collective power can be kept responsible to its participatory foundations. In the new American states, for example, after the disruption of British rule, radicals insisted on unicameral legislatures, weak or collective executives, frequent elections, rotation in office to prevent formation of a class of professional politicians. Most important, representatives were elected by participatory town or country meetings, thus by political bodies with an identity and some experience in collective action, rather than by isolated voters. Consequently, dialogue between representatives and their constituencies was frequent and vigorous; representatives were often instructed and sometimes recalled. But there are many possibilities for vital and fruitful interaction between the local and the national community. Recent resolutions on nuclear disarmament passed by New England town meetings are a promising experiment. All such devices, however, depend ultimately on the character of the citizenry, their love of and skill in exercising freedom; and these, in turn, rest mainly on the direct experience of meaningful local self-government.

Tocqueville argued that what made the American nation democratic was the vitality of direct participation in small and local associations. Face-to-face democracy was the foundation—not a substitute—for representative institutions, federalism, and national democracy. In direct personal participation, Tocqueville observed, people both learn the skills of citizenship and develop a taste for freedom; thereafter they form an active rather than deferential, apathetic, or privatized constituency for state and national representation, an engaged public for national issues. Size is not an insurmountable problem. On the basis of local, face-to-face politics, all sorts of higher and more distant structures of representation and collective power can be erected without destroying democracy—

indeed, they can enhance it. Lacking such a basis, no institutional structures or programs of indoctrination can produce democracy.

From the question of size, turn next to that of technology. Has the technological complexity of modern society, requiring specialized expertise, rendered democracy obsolete? Here it is useful to remember that while the technological society may be new, the claims for expertise against democracy are very old, at least as old as Plato's *Republic*. The idea that ordinary people are incompetent to deal intelligently with the issues affecting their lives rests now, as it always has, on an overly narrow idea of what constitutes politically relevant knowledge, and a confusion between knowledge and decision.

First off, stupidity knows no class. Maybe most people are foolish, but foolishness is found in all social strata. Education removes some kinds of ignorance, but may entrench or instill others. The cure is not to exclude some but to include as diverse a range of perspectives and experience as possible in political deliberation. Second, expertise cannot solve political problems. Contemporary politics is indeed full of technically complex topics, about which even the educated feel horribly ignorant. But on every politically significant issue of this kind, the "experts" are divided; that is part of what makes the issues political. Though we may also feel at a loss to choose between them, leaving it to the experts is no solution at all.

Finally, while various kinds of knowledge can be profoundly useful in political decisions, knowledge alone is never enough. The political question is what we are to *do;* knowledge can only tell us how things are, how they work, while a political resolution always depends on what we, as a community, want and think right. And those questions have no technical answer; they require collective deliberation and decision. The experts must become a part of, not an alternative to, the democratic political process.

Technology as such is not the problem for democracy; the problems here are popular deference to experts, and the belief in technology as an irresistible force, an "imperative" beyond human control. Since such deference and fatalism originate in people's experience, which is rooted in social conditions, they may be fought wherever they arise; and that is reason for hope and perseverance. The apathetic oppressed constitute an enormous pool of potential democratic energy. And as the historical examples remind us, even the most oppressed people sometimes rediscover within themselves the capacity to act. Democrats today must seek out and foster every opportunity for people to experience their own effective agency: at work, at school, in family and personal relations, in the community. Democratic citizenship is facilitated by democratic social relations and an autonomous character structure; dependency and apathy must be attacked wherever people's experience centers. Yet such attacks remain incomplete unless they relate personal concerns to public issues, extend individual initiative into shared political action. A sense of personal autonomy, dignity, and efficacy may be requisite for, but must not be confused with, citizenship.

And so we return to the need for direct, personal political participation. As Tocqueville already made clear, not just any kind of small or local group can provide the democratic experience: the point is not gregariousness but politicization. To support democracy, face-to-face groups must themselves be internally democratic in ways already discussed, must deal with issues that really matter in their members' lives, and must have genuine power to affect the outcomes of those issues. One can experience freedom or learn citizenship no better in a "Mickey Mouse" group where nothing of importance is at stake than in a hierarchical organization.

Tocqueville's America was already big, but many important matters could still be addressed and resolved on the small scale. Confronting the realities of large-scale private power and social problems today requires national and even international organization. Such organization can be democratic, we have argued, if it rests on an active, engaged citizenry. Technology, too, can be democratically handled by such a citizenry. But such a citizenry emerges only from *meaningful* small-scale participation. Is that still a realistic possibility in a society such as ours?

To answer that crucial question, one must distinguish between short- and long-run requirements. In the long run, if we truly want full democracy, there is no doubt that we shall have to change our society and economy in fundamental ways. But in the short run, the right means toward that goal are participatory democratic movements. That such movements can still occur was shown in the 1960s; nothing fundamental has changed since then. Today's democrat must hope that in the brief experience of active participation that follows a flaring up of the democratic impulse, ordinary people, discovering the connections between local problems and national structures, coming up against the repressive power of established privilege, will themselves discover the need for more fundamental changes. We must be prepared to use the impulses toward and the experience of democracy, where they occur and while they last, to produce the social and economic changes that will further facilitate democracy. Each time it is, one might say, a race between the radicalizing and liberating potential of political action, and the dispiriting and paralyzing effects of the repression and political defeat likely to follow.

Confronting this most central and difficult problem, we need to recall not only Tocqueville and Revolutionary America, but also the movements of the 1960s, to build on their achievements and learn from their mistakes. On the whole, these movements did not see themselves as building participatory alternatives, nor as engaged in a long-term transformation of consciousness and social conditions to make possible a more democratic America. They looked for immediate changes on specific issues, mobilized people for short-term successes, and saw their own internal organization largely in instrumental terms. Even the Students for a Democratic Society, which did begin with a larger vision and did value internal democracy, eventually became absorbed in ending the Vietnam War. Neglecting democratic organization for immediate policy changes, the 1960s movements failed in what Goodwyn has called "democratic patience," the capacity to sustain democratic momentum for the long haul. Yet they left behind a changed America, and many less conspicuous yet active neighborhood groups, and radical opposition groups in unions, the professions, and among consumers.

A democratic movement for the 1980s must come out of such groups, out of local organizing around the grievances and aspirations people now feel. It must encourage local autonomy, ways of doing for ourselves and doing without, so as to cut loose from the system. Yet it must also encourage a widening perspective on the issues, their connections with the larger social structures of private power; it must foster alliances and debate among such groups. People must organize in ways that constantly enlarge rather than suppress movement members' active engagement, independent judgment, and preparedness for continued struggle.

Such local and ad hoc beginnings by no means preclude a commitment to radical systemic social and economic change. In the long run, democracy's full realization might well entail abolishing the joint-stock limited-liability corporation; or abolishing private ownership of the means of production; or even abandoning the Faustian dream of mastering and exploiting nature to gain infinitely expanding wealth.

But that is to get ahead of ourselves. For surely the privileged elites of corporate power will not permit such radical changes today or tomorrow, nor are our fellow citizens ready to fight on such grounds. We must not postpone the practice of participatory democracy until after such changes are achieved, nor expect it to emerge automatically from them. Democracy is our best means for achieving social change and must remain our conscious goal. Then the vicious circle of social process, in which democracy seems to presuppose the conditions that only democracy can bring about, can become grounds for hope: wherever we do cut into the circle, we thereby transform all the rest of its course. We can begin where we are.

ITALO CALVINO, INVISIBLE CITIES
Pp. 161–163 (1974).

I should not tell you of Berenice, the unjust city, which crowns with triglyphs, abaci, metopes the gears of its meat-grinding machines (the men assigned to polishing, when they raise their chins over the balustrades and contemplate the atria, stairways, porticos, feel even more imprisoned and short of stature). Instead, I should tell you of the hidden Berenice, the city of the just, handling makeshift materials in the shadowy rooms behind the shops and beneath the stairs, linking a network of wires and pipes and pulleys and pistons and counterweights that infiltrates like a climbing plant among the great cogged wheels (when they jam, a subdued ticking gives warning that a new precision mechanism is governing the city). Instead of describing to you the perfumed pools of the baths where the unjust of Berenice recline and weave their intrigues with rotund eloquence and observe with a proprietary eye the rotund flesh of the bathing odalisques, I should say to you how the just, always cautious to evade the spying sycophants and the Janizaries' mass arrests, recognize one another by their way of speaking, especially their pronunciation of commas and parentheses; from their habits which remain austere and innocent, avoiding complicated and nervous moods; from their sober but tasty cuisine, which evokes an ancient golden age: rice and celery soup, boiled beans, fried squash flowers.

From these data it is possible to deduce an image of the future Berenice, which will bring you closer to knowing the truth than any other information about the city as it is seen today. You must nevertheless bear in mind what I am about to say to you: in the seed of the city of the just, a malignant seed is hidden, in its turn: the certainty and pride of being in the right—and of being more just than many others who call themselves more just than the just. This seed ferments in bitterness, rivalry, resentment; and the natural desire of revenge on the unjust is colored by a yearning to be in their place and to act as they do. Another unjust city, though different from the first, is digging out its space within the double sheath of the unjust and just Berenices.

Having said this, I do not wish your eyes to catch a distorted image, so I must draw your attention to an intrinsic quality of this unjust city germinating secretly inside the secret just city: and this is the possible awakening—as if in an excited opening of windows—of a later love for justice, not yet subjected to rules, capable of reassembling a city still more just than it was before it became the vessel of injustice. But if you peer deeper into this new germ of justice you can discern a tiny spot that is spreading like the mounting tendency to impose what is just through what is unjust, and perhaps this is the germ of an immense metropolis.
* * *

From my words you will have reached the conclusion that the real Berenice is a temporal succession of different cities, alternately just and unjust. But what I wanted to warn you about is something else: all the future Berenices are already present in this instant, wrapped one within the other, confined, crammed, inextricable.

INDEX

References are to Pages

959